Alan L.

OREGON

EVIDENCE

THIRD EDITION

BY

LAIRD C. KIRKPATRICK

HERSHNER PROFESSOR OF JURISPRUDENCE
UNIVERSITY OF OREGON SCHOOL OF LAW

MICHIE
PARKER PUBLICATIONS DIVISION
Carlsbad, California

8227111

To My Fellow Members of the Oregon State Bar

CONTENTS

ARTICLE I
GENERAL PROVISIONS

Contents

ARTICLE II
JUDICIAL NOTICE

ARTICLE III
BURDEN OF PERSUASION; BURDEN OF
PRODUCING EVIDENCE; PRESUMPTIONS

ARTICLE IV
RELEVANCY

Contents

RULE 404

Contents

ARTICLE V PRIVILEGES

Contents

Contents

Contents

ARTICLE VI
WITNESSES

Contents

ARTICLE VII
OPINIONS AND EXPERT TESTIMONY

Contents

ARTICLE
VIII HEARSAY

Contents

Contents

Contents

ARTICLE IX
AUTHENTICATION AND IDENTIFICATION

ARTICLE X
CONTENTS OF WRITINGS, RECORDINGS, AND PHOTOGRAPHS

PREFACE

The positive response of Oregon lawyers and judges to the first two editions of *Oregon Evidence* has been the impetus for the preparation of this Third Edition. In the seven years since publication of the Second Edition, there have been a number of significant developments in Oregon evidence law. The Oregon Legislature has enacted new evidence rules and made important amendments to existing rules. The appellate caselaw interpreting the Oregon Evidence Code has been greatly expanded. Finally, the United States Supreme Court has announced a number of constitutional decisions affecting the admissibility of evidence that are binding in state courts.

As in previous editions, the Third Edition attempts to organize and present the material in a manner of greatest use to busy trial lawyers and judges. At the beginning, the book sets forth the entire Evidence Code (without Legislative Commentary) in order to provide quick accessibility to the rules. Then, each rule is restated individually with its accompanying Legislative Commentary, followed by a textual discussion of the rule that includes relevant caselaw and other authority. It should be noted that the Commentary was not officially adopted by the Legislative Assembly and was not enacted as part of the legislation. Nonetheless, it is of considerable value to judges and lawyers in interpreting these rules.

The Oregon Supreme Court and the Court of Appeals deserve commendation for numerous thoughtful and well-reasoned opinions that clarify ambiguities, resolve inconsistencies, and provide guidance for application of the Oregon Rules of Evidence. A statutory code cannot be expected to resolve all evidentiary issues that arise in the courtroom, and the decisions of the Oregon appellate courts flesh out the framework of Oregon evidence law that is provided by the Code.

The Code was adopted by the 1981 Legislature and is substantially based upon the Federal Rules of Evidence (although there are also some important areas of difference). There are now thirty-six other states that have adopted evidence codes based on the Federal Rules. Judicial interpretations given to identical rules in these jurisdictions can be cited as persuasive authority in interpreting the Oregon Evidence Code. The other states adopting counterparts of the Federal Rules are: Alaska, Arizona, Arkansas, Colorado, Delaware, Florida, Hawaii, Idaho, Indiana, Iowa, Kentucky, Louisiana, Maine, Maryland, Michigan, Minnesota, Mississippi, Montana, Nebraska, Nevada, New Hampshire, New Mexico, North Carolina, North Dakota, Ohio, Oklahoma, Rhode Island, South Dakota, Tennessee, Texas, Utah, Vermont, Washington, West Virginia, Wisconsin, and Wyoming.

Federal authorities are also useful in construing Oregon rules that are based upon the Federal Rules of Evidence. Federal case authority can be found in the following treatises on the Federal Rules of Evidence: M. Graham, Handbook of Federal Evidence (West); G. Weissenberger, Federal Evidence (Anderson); S.

Preface

Saltzburg, M. Martin & D. Capra, Federal Rules of Evidence Manual (Michie); C. Wright & K. Graham, Federal Practice and Procedure (West); J. Weinstein & M. Berger, Weinstein's Evidence (Matthew Bender); C. Mueller & L. Kirkpatrick, Federal Evidence 2d (Lawyers Cooperative); and C. Mueller & L. Kirkpatrick, Modern Evidence (Little, Brown & Co.).

As always, I am grateful to my wife, Carole, and my sons, Duncan, Ryan, and Morgan for their support and understanding of the time demands of this project and for their partnership in all other aspects of life.

Laird C. Kirkpatrick
Hershner Professor of Jurisprudence
University of Oregon Law School

ACKNOWLEDGMENTS
(FIRST EDITION)

I would like to acknowledge the capable research assistance provided by Michael Weirich, Greg McGillivary, and Seri Wilpone. Mr. Weirich and Ms. Wilpone are 1982 graduates of the University of Oregon Law School, and Mr. McGillivary is a member of the Class of 1983.

I am deeply grateful to Maxine Lee for her extraordinary dedication and competence in typing the final manuscript. The assistance of Marilyn Martin, Mary Jo Guy, Dina Jian, Carrie Blain, Ronnie Baty, and Denise Medlock in typing earlier research that led to this book is also very much appreciated.

I am particularly indebted to Judge Richard L. Unis, who played a major role in the development of the Oregon Evidence Code, for taking the time to read the entire manuscript prior to publication. Drawing upon his vast knowledge of Oregon evidence law, Judge Unis provided numerous helpful comments and suggested additional citations that have been incorporated into this book.

Recognition should also be given to Judge Robert E. Jones, the other members of the Advisory Committee on Evidence Law Revision, the legislators and staff members who worked on the code, and countless other Oregon lawyers and judges who contributed to the advancement of Oregon evidence law by helping make the new evidence code a reality.

ACKNOWLEDGMENTS
(SECOND EDITION)

The author expresses appreciation to Lore Rutz, a 1989 graduate of the University of Oregon Law School, for her outstanding research assistance in the preparation of this Second Edition. The assistance of Brian Berkenmeier, Class of 1990, and Gregory Hazarabedian, Class of 1991, in checking legal citations is also gratefully acknowledged. My secretary, Maxine Lee, provided her usual highly competent support to the project. The author is grateful to the editorial staff at Butterworth Legal Publishers, particularly Deborah Willow and Ray Krontz, for their excellent production work with respect to both editions.

ACKNOWLEDGMENTS
(THIRD EDITION)

I would like to acknowledge the capable research assistance of Eric Dewey, a 1996 graduate of the University of Oregon Law School, Tamara Brickman, Class of 1998, and Dan Gunter and Andrea Powers, Class of 1997. My secretary, Sue Heim, provided invaluable help in the final stages of this project. I would also like to thank Pamela Whiting of Michie for her careful editing and production assistance.

FOREWORD TO THE FIRST EDITION

Oregon Evidence is the first complete guide to the new Oregon Rules of Evidence. It not only contains the complete text of the Oregon Evidence Code enacted by the 1981 Oregon Legislative Assembly and the Commentary, which is the official statement of legislative intent, but also provides an in-depth discussion of each rule and its interrelationship with other provisions of the code.

The author, Professor Laird C. Kirkpatrick, with remarkable clarity and compactness, provides insight into evidentiary issues and pinpoints aspects of the rules which are not readily apparent, citing numerous cases as concrete illustration of important points.

Where the Oregon Evidence Code has specifically followed, relied upon, or even adopted a particular rule of the Federal Rules of Evidence, which has often been the case, that fact is noted and recent federal decisions interpreting the particular rule are generously cited and discussed. Prior Oregon cases are cited when they influenced the drafters of the code or continue to have precedential value. This book emphasizes what the Oregon law of evidence is, not what it once was, or might have been.

This book has been especially designed so that it can be easily read and studied in the library or office, yet may be used quickly and expeditiously during the course of trials to provide lawyers and judges with answers to evidentiary problems. A complete, easily-referenced and comprehensive index has been specifically designed for this purpose.

Oregon lawyers, judges, and students of the law will find this single-volume text a most useful, practical, everyday working tool for research in the office or library as well as an indispensable trial aid.

Richard L. Unis
Circuit Court Judge, Multnomah County
[Justice, Oregon Supreme Court, 1990–1996]

OREGON EVIDENCE CODE
TABLE OF RULES

ARTICLE V. PRIVILEGES

ARTICLE VI. WITNESSES

ARTICLE X.
CONTENTS OF WRITINGS, RECORDINGS AND PHOTOGRAPHS

OREGON EVIDENCE CODE

ARTICLE I.   GENERAL PROVISIONS

Rule 100. ORS 40.010. **Short Title**. Rules 100 to 1008 (ORS 40.010 to 40.585 and 41.415) shall be known and may be cited as the Oregon Evidence Code.

Rule 101. ORS 40.015. **Applicability of Oregon Evidence Code.**
(1) **Courts.** The Oregon Evidence Code applies to all courts in this state except for:
   (a) The small claims division of the Oregon Tax Court as provided by ORS 305.545;
   (b) The small claims department of a district court as provided by ORS 46.415; and
   (c) The small claims department of a justice court as provided by ORS 55.080.
(2) **Proceedings generally.** The Oregon Evidence Code applies generally to civil actions, suits and proceedings, criminal actions and proceedings and to contempt proceedings except those in which the court may act summarily.
(3) **Rules of privilege.** Rules 503 to 514 (ORS 40.225 to 40.295) relating to privileges apply at all stages of all actions, suits and proceedings.
(4) **Rules inapplicable.** Rules 100 to 412 (ORS 40.010 to 40.210) and Rules 601 to 1008 (ORS 40.310 to 40.585 do not apply in the following situations:
   (a) The determination of questions of fact preliminary to admissibility of evidence when the issue is to be determined by the court under Rule 104 (ORS 40.030).
   (b) Proceedings before grand juries, except as required by ORS 132.320.
   (c) Proceedings for extradition, except as required by ORS 133.743 to 133.857.
   (d) Sentencing proceedings, except proceedings under ORS 163.150 or as required by ORS 137.090.
   (e) Proceedings to revoke probation, except as required by ORS 137.090.
   (f) Issuance of warrants of arrest, bench warrants or search warrants.
   (g) Proceedings under ORS chapter 135 relating to conditional release, security release, release on personal recognizance, or preliminary hearings, subject to ORS 135.173.
   (h) Proceedings to determine proper disposition of a child in accordance with ORS 419B.325(2) and 419C.400(3).
   (i) Proceedings under ORS 813.210 to 813.230, 813.250 and 813.255 to determine whether a driving while under the influence of intoxicants diversion agreement should be allowed or terminated.

Rule 102. ORS 40.020. **Purpose and construction.** The Oregon Evidence Code shall be construed to secure fairness in administration, elimination of unjustifiable expense and delay, and promotion of growth and development of the law of evidence to the end that the truth may be ascertained and proceedings justly determined.

Rule 103. ORS 40.025. **Rulings on evidence.**

(1) **Effect of erroneous ruling.** Evidential error is not presumed to be prejudicial. Error may not be predicated upon a ruling which admits or excludes evidence unless a substantial right of the party is affected, and:

  (a) **Objection.** In case the ruling is one admitting evidence, a timely objection or motion to strike appears of record, stating the specific ground of objection, if the specific ground was not apparent from the context; or

  (b) **Offer of proof.** In case the ruling is one excluding evidence, the substance of the evidence was made known to the court by offer or was apparent from the context within which questions were asked.

(2) **Record of offer and ruling.** The court may add any other or further statement which shows the character of the evidence, the form in which it was offered, the objection made and the ruling thereon. It may direct the making of an offer in question and answer form.

(3) **Hearing of jury.** In jury cases, proceedings shall be conducted, to the extent practicable, so as to prevent inadmissible evidence from being suggested to the jury by any means, such as making statements or offers of proof or asking questions in the hearing of the jury.

(4) **Plain error.** Nothing in this rule precludes taking notice of plain errors affecting substantial rights although they were not brought to the attention of the court.

Rule 104. ORS 40.030. **Preliminary questions.**

(1) **Questions of admissibility generally.** Preliminary questions concerning the qualification of a person to be a witness, the existence of a privilege or the admissibility of evidence shall be determined by the court, subject to the provisions of subsection (2) of this section. In making its determination the court is not bound by the rules of evidence except those with respect to privileges.

(2) **Relevancy conditioned on fact.** When the relevancy of evidence depends upon the fulfillment of a condition of fact, the court shall admit it upon, or subject to, the introduction of evidence sufficient to support a finding of the fulfillment of the condition.

(3) **Hearing of jury.** Hearings on the admissibility of confessions shall in all cases be conducted out of the hearing of the jury. Hearings on other preliminary matters shall be so conducted when the interests of justice require or, when an accused is a witness, if the accused so requests.

(4) **Testimony by accused.** The accused does not, by testifying upon a pre-liminary matter, become subject to cross-examination as to other issues in the case.

(5) **Weight and credibility.** This section does not limit the right of a party to introduce before the jury evidence relevant to weight or credibility.

Rule 105. ORS 40.035. **Limited admissibility.** When evidence which is admissible as to one party or for one purpose but not admissible as to another party or for another purpose is admitted, the court, upon request, shall restrict the evidence to its proper scope and instruct the jury accordingly.

Rule 106. ORS 40.040. **When part of transaction proved, whole admissible.** When part of an act, declaration, conversation or writing is given in evidence by one party, the whole on the same subject, where otherwise admissible, may at that time be inquired into by the other; when a letter is read, the answer may at that time be given; and when a detached act, declaration, conversation or writing is given in evidence, any other act, declaration, conversation or writing which is necessary to make it understood may at that time also be given in evidence.

ARTICLE II.   JUDICIAL NOTICE

Rule 201(a). ORS 40.060. **Scope.** Rule 201 (ORS 40.060 to 40.085) governs judicial notice of adjudicative facts. Rule 202 (ORS 40.090) governs judicial notice of law.

Rule 201(b). ORS 40.065. **Kinds of facts.** A judicially noticed fact must be one not subject to reasonable dispute in that it is either:
(1) Generally known within the territorial jurisdiction of the trial court; or
(2) Capable of accurate and ready determination by resort to sources whose accuracy cannot reasonably be questioned.

Rules 201 (c) and 201(d). ORS 40.070. **When mandatory or discretionary.**
(1) A court may take judicial notice, whether requested or not.
(2) A court shall take judicial notice if requested by a party and supplied with the necessary information.

Rule 201(e). ORS 40.075. **Opportunity to be heard.** A party is entitled upon timely request to an opportunity to be heard as to the propriety of taking judicial notice and the tenor of the matter noticed. In the absence of prior notification, the request may be made after judicial notice has been taken.

Rule 201(f). ORS 40.080. **Time of taking notice.** Judicial notice may be taken at any stage of the proceeding.

Rule 201 (g). ORS 40.085. **Instructing the jury.**
(1) In a civil action or proceeding, the court shall instruct the jury to accept as conclusive any fact or law judicially noticed.
(2) In a criminal case, the court shall instruct the jury that it may, but is not required to, accept as conclusive any fact judicially noticed in favor of the prosecution.

Rule 202. ORS 40.090. **Kinds of law.** Law judicially noticed is defined as:
(1) The decisional, constitutional and public statutory law of Oregon, the United States and any state, territory or other jurisdiction of the United States.
(2) Public and private official acts of the legislative, executive and judicial departments of this state, the United States, and any other state, territory or other jurisdiction of the United States.
(3) Rules of professional conduct for members of the Oregon State Bar.
(4) Regulations, ordinances and similar legislative enactments issued by or under the authority of the United States or any state, territory or possession of the United States.
(5) Rules of court of any court of this state or any court of record of the United States or of any state, territory or other jurisdiction of the United States.
(6) The law of an organization of nations and of foreign nations and public entities in foreign nations.
(7) An ordinance, comprehensive plan or enactment of any county or incorporated city in this state, or a right derived therefrom. As used in this subsection, "comprehensive plan" has the meaning given that term by ORS 197.015.

ARTICLE III.   BURDEN OF PERSUASION; BURDEN OF PRODUCING EVIDENCE; PRESUMPTIONS

Rule 305. ORS 40.105. **Allocation of the burden of persuasion.** A party has the burden of persuasion as to each fact the existence or nonexistence of which the law declares essential to the claim for relief or defense the party is asserting.

Rule 306. ORS 40.110. **Instructions on the burden of persuasion.** The court shall instruct the jury as to which party bears the applicable burden of persuasion on each issue only after all of the evidence in the case has been received.

Rule 307. ORS 40.115. **Allocation of the burden of producing evidence.**
(1) The burden of producing evidence as to a particular issue is on the party against whom a finding on the issue would be required in the absence of further evidence.
(2) The burden of producing evidence as to a particular issue is initially on the party with the burden of persuasion as to that issue.

1

Rule 308. ORS 40.120. **Presumptions in civil proceedings.** In civil actions and proceedings, a presumption imposes on the party against whom it is directed the burden of proving that the nonexistence of the presumed fact is more probable than its existence.

Rule 309. ORS 40.125. **Presumptions in criminal proceedings.**
(1) The judge is not authorized to direct the jury to find a presumed fact against the accused.
(2) When the presumed fact establishes guilt or is an element of the offense or negates a defense, the judge may submit the question of guilt or the existence of the presumed fact to the jury only if:
  (a) A reasonable juror on the evidence as a whole could find that the facts giving rise to the presumed fact have been established beyond a reasonable doubt; and
  (b) The presumed fact follows more likely than not from the facts giving rise to the presumed fact.

Rule 310. ORS 40.130. **Conflicting presumptions.** If presumptions are conflicting, the presumption applies that is founded upon weightier considerations of policy and logic. If considerations of policy and logic are of equal weight, neither presumption applies.

Rule 311. ORS 40.135. **Presumptions.**
(1) The following are presumptions:
  (a) A person intends the ordinary consequences of a voluntary act.
  (b) A person takes ordinary care of the person's own concerns.
  (c) Evidence willfully suppressed would be adverse to the party suppressing it.
  (d) Money paid by one to another was due to the latter.
  (e) A thing delivered by one to another belonged to the latter.
  (f) An obligation delivered to the debtor has been paid.
  (g) A person is the owner of property from exercising acts of ownership over it or from common reputation of the ownership of the person.
  (h) A person in possession of an order on that person, for the payment of money or the delivery of a thing, has paid the money or delivered the thing accordingly.
  (i) A person acting in a public office was regularly appointed to it.
  (j) Official duty has been regularly performed.
  (k) A court, or judge acting as such, whether in this state or any other state or country, was acting in the lawful exercise of the jurisdiction of the court.
  (l) Private transactions have been fair and regular.
  (m) The ordinary course of business has been followed.
  (n) A promissory note or bill of exchange was given or indorsed for a sufficient consideration.

(o) An indorsement of a negotiable promissory note, or bill of exchange, was made at the time and place of making the note or bill.

(p) A writing is truly dated.

(q) A letter duly directed and mailed was received in the regular course of the mail.

(r) A person is the same person if the name is identical.

(s) A person not heard from in seven years is dead.

(t) Persons acting as copartners have entered into a contract of copartnership.

(u) A man and woman deporting themselves as husband and wife have entered into a lawful contract of marriage.

(v) A child born in lawful wedlock is legitimate.

(w) A thing once proved to exist continues as long as is usual with things of that nature.

(x) The law has been obeyed.

(y) An uninterrupted adverse possession of real property for 20 years or more has been held pursuant to a written conveyance.

(z) A trustee or other person whose duty it was to convey real property to a particular person has actually conveyed it to the person, when such presumption is necessary to perfect the title of the person or the person's successor in interest.

(2) A statute providing that a fact or a group of facts is prima facie evidence of another fact establishes a presumption within the meaning of this section.

ARTICLE IV.   RELEVANCY

Rule 401. ORS 40.150. **Definition of "relevant evidence."** "Relevant evidence" means evidence having any tendency to make the existence of any fact that is of consequence to the determination of the action more probable or less probable than it would be without the evidence.

Rule 402. ORS 40.155. **Relevant evidence generally admissible.** All relevant evidence is admissible, except as otherwise provided by the Oregon Evidence Code, by the Constitutions of the United States and Oregon, or by Oregon statutory and decisional law. Evidence which is not relevant is not admissible.

Rule 403. ORS 40.160. **Exclusion of relevant evidence on grounds of prejudice, confusion or undue delay.** Although relevant, evidence may be excluded if its probative value is substantially outweighed by the danger of unfair prejudice, confusion of the issues, or misleading the jury, or by considerations of undue delay or needless presentation of cumulative evidence.

Rule 404. ORS 40.170. **Character evidence; admissibility.**

(1) **Admissibility generally.** Evidence of a person's character or trait of character is admissible when it is an essential element of a charge, claim or defense.

(2) **Admissibility for certain purpose prohibited; exceptions.** Evidence of a person's character is not admissible for the purpose of proving that the person acted in conformity therewith on a particular occasion, except:

    (a) **Character of accused.** Evidence of a pertinent trait of character offered by an accused, or by the prosecution to rebut the same;

    (b) **Character of victim.** Evidence of a pertinent trait of character of the victim of the crime offered by an accused, or by the prosecution to rebut the same or evidence of a character trait of peacefulness of the victim offered by the prosecution to rebut evidence that the victim was the first aggressor;

    (c) **Character of witness.** Evidence of the character of a witness, as provided in Rules 607 to 609 (ORS 40.345 to 40.355); or

    (d) **Character for violent behavior.** Evidence of the character of a party for violent behavior offered in a civil assault and battery case when self-defense is pleaded and there is evidence to support such defense.

(3) **Other crimes, wrongs or acts.** Evidence of other crimes, wrongs or acts is not admissible to prove the character of a person in order to show that the person acted in conformity therewith. It may, however, be admissible for other purposes, such as proof of motive, opportunity, intent, preparation, plan, knowledge, identity, or absence of mistake or accident.

Rule 405. ORS 40.175. **Methods of proving character.**

(1) **Reputation or opinion.** In all cases in which evidence of character or a trait of character of a person is admissible, proof may be made by testimony as to reputation or by testimony in the form of an opinion. On cross-examination, inquiry is allowable into relevant specific instances of conduct.

(2) **Specific instances of conduct.**

    (a) In cases in which character or a trait of character of a person is admissible under subsection (1) of Rule 404 (ORS 40.170(1)), proof may also be made of specific instances of the conduct of the person.

    (b) When evidence is admissible under subsection (3) of Rule 404 (ORS 40.170(3)), proof may be made of specific instances of the conduct of the person.

Rule 406. ORS 40.180. **Habit; routine practice.**

(1) Evidence of the habit of a person or of the routine practice of an organization, whether corroborated or not and regardless of the presence of eyewitnesses, is relevant to prove that the conduct of the person or organization on a particular occasion was in conformity with the habit or routine practice.

(2) As used in this section, "habit" means a person's regular practice of meeting a particular kind of situation with a specific, distinctive type of conduct.

Rule 407. ORS 40.185. **Subsequent remedial measures.** When, after an event, measures are taken which, if taken previously, would have made the event less likely to occur, evidence of the subsequent measures is not admissible to prove negligence or culpable conduct in connection with the event. This section does not require the exclusion of evidence of subsequent measures when offered for another purpose, such as proving ownership, control, or feasibility of precautionary measures, if controverted, or impeachment.

Rule 408. ORS 40.190. **Compromise and offers to compromise.**
(1) (a) Evidence of furnishing or offering or promising to furnish, or accepting or offering or promising to accept, a valuable consideration in compromising or attempting to compromise a claim which was disputed as to either validity or amount, is not admissible to prove liability for or invalidity of the claim or its amount.
(b) Evidence of conduct or statements made in compromise negotiations is likewise not admissible.
(2) (a) Subsection (1) of this section does not require the exclusion of any evidence otherwise discoverable merely because it is presented in the course of compromise negotiations.
(b) Subsection (1) of this section also does not require exclusion when the evidence is offered for another purpose, such as proving bias or prejudice of a witness, negating a contention of undue delay, or proving an effort to obstruct a criminal investigation or prosecution.

Rule 409. ORS 40.195. **Payment of medical and similar expenses.** Evidence of furnishing or offering or promising to pay medical, hospital or similar expenses occasioned by an injury is not admissible to prove liability for the injury. Evidence of payment for damages arising from injury or destruction of property is not admissible to prove liability for the injury or destruction.

Rule 410. ORS 40.200. **Withdrawn plea or statement not admissible.**
(1) A plea of guilty or no contest which is not accepted or has been withdrawn shall not be received against the defendant in any criminal proceeding.
(2) No statement or admission made by a defendant or a defendant's attorney during any proceeding relating to a plea of guilty or no contest which is not accepted or has been withdrawn shall be received against the defendant in any criminal proceeding.

Rule 411. ORS 40.205. **Liability insurance.**
(1) Except where lack of liability insurance is an element of an offense, evidence that a person was or was not insured against liability is not admissible upon the issue whether the person acted negligently or otherwise wrongfully.

(2) Subsection (1) of this section does not require the exclusion of evidence of insurance against liability when offered for another purpose, such as proving agency, ownership or control, or bias, prejudice or motive of a witness.

Rule 412. ORS 40.210. **Sex offense cases; relevance of victim's past behavior.**

(1) Notwithstanding any other provision of law, in a prosecution for a crime described in ORS 163.355 to 163.427, or in a prosecution for an attempt to commit such a crime, reputation or opinion evidence of the past sexual behavior of an alleged victim of such crime is not admissible.

(2) Notwithstanding any other provision of law, in a prosecution for a crime described in ORS 163.355 to 163.427, or in a prosecution for an attempt to commit such a crime, evidence of a victim's past sexual behavior other than reputation or opinion evidence is also not admissible, unless such evidence other than reputation or opinion evidence is:

(a) Admitted in accordance with subsection (3) (a) and (b) of this section; and

(b) Is evidence that:

   (A) Relates to the motive or bias of the alleged victim; or

   (B) Is necessary to rebut or explain scientific or medical evidence offered by the state; or

   (C) Is otherwise constitutionally required to be admitted.

(3) (a) If the person accused of committing rape, sodomy or sexual abuse or attempted rape, sodomy or sexual abuse intends to offer under subsection (2) of this section evidence of specific instances of the alleged victim's past sexual behavior, the accused shall make a written motion to offer such evidence not later than 15 days before the date on which the trial in which such evidence is to be offered is scheduled to begin, except that the court may allow the motion to be made at a later date, including during trial, if the court determines either that the evidence is newly discovered and could not have been obtained earlier through the exercise of due diligence or that the issue to which such evidence relates has newly arisen in the case. Any motion made under this paragraph shall be served on all other parties, and on the alleged victim through the office of the prosecutor.

(b) The motion described in paragraph (a) of this subsection shall be accompanied by a written offer of proof. If the court determines that the offer of proof contains evidence described in subsection (2) of this section, the court shall order a hearing in camera to determine if such evidence is admissible. At such hearing the parties may call witnesses, including the alleged victim, and offer relevant evidence. Notwithstanding subsection (2) of Rule 104 (ORS 40.030(2)), if the relevancy of the evidence which the accused seeks to offer in the trial depends upon the fulfillment of a condition of fact, the court, at the hearing in camera or at a subsequent hearing in camera scheduled for such purpose, shall accept evidence on the issue of whether such condition of fact is fulfilled and shall determine such issue.

(c) If the court determines on the basis of the hearing described in paragraph (b) of this subsection that the evidence which the accused seeks to offer is relevant and that the probative value of such evidence outweighs the danger of unfair prejudice, such evidence shall be admissible in the trial to the extent an order made by the court specifies evidence which may be offered and areas with respect to which the alleged victim may be examined or cross-examined. An order admitting evidence under this subsection may be appealed by the government before trial.

(4) For purposes of this section:

(a) "In camera" means out of the presence of the public and the jury; and

(b) "Past sexual behavior" means sexual behavior other than the sexual behavior with respect to which rape, sodomy or sexual abuse or attempted rape, sodomy or sexual abuse is alleged.

ARTICLE V.   PRIVILEGES

Rule 503. ORS 40.225. **Lawyer-client privilege.**

(1) **Definitions.** As used in this section, unless the context requires otherwise:

(a) "Client" means a person, public officer, corporation, association or other organization or entity, either public or private, who is rendered professional legal services by a lawyer, or who consults a lawyer with a view to obtaining professional legal services from the lawyer.

(b) "Confidential communication" means a communication not intended to be disclosed to third persons other than those to whom disclosure is in furtherance of the rendition of professional legal services to the client or those reasonably necessary for the transmission of the communication.

(c) "Lawyer" means a person authorized, or reasonably believed by the client to be authorized, to practice law in any state or nation.

(d) "Representative of the client" means a principal, an employee, an officer or a director of the client:

(A) Who provides the client's lawyer with information that was acquired during the course of, or as a result of, such person's relationship with the client as principal, employee, officer or director, and is provided to the lawyer for the purpose of obtaining for the client the legal advice or other legal services of the lawyer; or

(B) Who, as part of such person's relationship with the client as principal employee, officer or director, seeks, receives or applies legal advice from the client's lawyer.

(e) "Representative of the lawyer" means one employed to assist the lawyer in the rendition of professional legal services, but does not include a physician making a physical or mental examination under ORCP 44.

(2) **General rule of privilege.** A client has a privilege to refuse to disclose and to prevent any other person from disclosing confidential communications made for the purpose of facilitating the rendition of professional legal services to the client:

    (a) Between the client or the client's representative and the client's lawyer or a representative of the lawyer;

    (b) Between the client's lawyer and the lawyer's representative;

    (c) By the client or the client's lawyer to a lawyer representing another in a matter of common interest;

    (d) Between representatives of the client or between the client and a representative of the client; or

    (e) Between lawyers representing the client.

(3) **Who may claim the privilege.** The privilege created by this section may be claimed by the client, a guardian or conservator of the client, the personal representative of a deceased client, or the successor, trustee, or similar representative of a corporation, association, or other organization, whether or not in existence. The person who was the lawyer or the lawyer's representative at the time of the communication is presumed to have authority to claim the privilege but only on behalf of the client.

(4) **Exceptions.** There is no privilege under this section:

    (a) If the services of the lawyer were sought or obtained to enable or aid anyone to commit or plan to commit what the client knew or reasonably should have known to be a crime or fraud;

    (b) As to a communication relevant to an issue between parties who claim through the same deceased client, regardless of whether the claims are by testate or intestate succession or by inter vivos transaction;

    (c) As to a communication relevant to an issue of breach of duty by the lawyer to the client or by the client to the lawyer;

    (d) As to a communication relevant to an issue concerning an attested document to which the lawyer is an attesting witness; or

    (e) As to a communication relevant to a matter of common interest between two or more clients if the communication was made by any of them to a lawyer retained or consulted in common, when offered in an action between any of the clients.

Rule 504. ORS 40.230. **Psychotherapist-patient privilege.**

(1) **Definitions.** As used in this section, unless the context requires otherwise:

    (a) "Confidential communication" means a communication not intended to be disclosed to third persons except:

        (A) Persons present to further the interest of the patient in the consultation, examination or interview;

        (B) Persons reasonably necessary for the transmission of the communication; or

        (C) Persons who are participating in the diagnosis and treatment under the direction of the psychotherapist, including members of the patient's family.

    (b) "Patient" means a person who consults or is examined or interviewed by a psychotherapist.

    (c) "Psychotherapist" means a person who is:

        (A) Licensed, registered, certified or otherwise authorized under the laws of any state to engage in the diagnosis or treatment of a mental or emotional condition; or

        (B) Reasonably believed by the patient so to be, while so engaged.

(2) **General rule of privilege.** A patient has a privilege to refuse to disclose and to prevent any other person from disclosing confidential communications made for the purposes of diagnosis or treatment of the patient's mental or emotional condition among the patient, the patient's psychotherapist or persons who are participating in the diagnosis or treatment under the direction of the psychotherapist, including members of the patient's family.

(3) **Who may claim the privilege.** The privilege created by this section may be claimed by:

    (a) The patient.

    (b) A guardian or conservator of the patient.

    (c) The personal representative of a deceased patient.

    (d) The person who was the psychotherapist, but only on behalf of the patient. The psychotherapist's authority so to do is presumed in the absence of evidence to the contrary.

(4) **General exceptions.** The following is a nonexclusive list of limits on the privilege granted by this section:

    (a) If the judge orders an examination of the mental, physical or emotional condition of the patient, communications made in the course thereof are not privileged under this section with respect to the particular purpose for which the examination is ordered unless the judge orders otherwise.

    (b) There is no privilege under this rule as to communications relevant to an issue of the mental or emotional condition of the patient:

        (A) In any proceeding in which the patient relies upon the condition as an element of the patient's claim or defense; or

        (B) After the patient's death, in any proceeding in which any party relies upon the condition as an element of the party's claim or defense.

    (c) Except as provided in ORCP 44, there is no privilege under this section for communications made in the course of mental examination performed under ORCP 44.

    (d) There is no privilege under this section with regard to any confidential communication or record of such confidential communication that would otherwise be privileged under this section when the use of the communication or record is allowed specifically under ORS 426.070, 426.074, 426.075, 426.095, 426.120 or 426.307. This paragraph only applies to the use of the communication or record to the extent and for the purposes set forth in the described statute sections.

Rule 504-1. ORS 40.235. **Physician-patient privilege.**
(1) **Definitions.** As used in this section, unless the context requires otherwise:
  (a) "Confidential communication" means a communication not intended to be disclosed to third persons except:
    (A) Persons present to further the interest of the patient in the consultation, examination or interview;
    (B) Persons reasonably necessary for the transmission of the communication; or
    (C) Persons who are participating in the diagnosis and treatment under the direction of the physician, including members of the patient's family.
  (b) "Patient" means a person who consults or is examined or interviewed by a physician.
  (c) "Physician" means a person authorized and licensed or certified to practice medicine in any state or nation, or reasonably believed by the patient so to be, while engaged in the diagnosis or treatment of a physical condition. "Physician" includes licensed or certified naturopathic and chiropractic physicians.
(2) **General rule of privilege.** A patient has a privilege to refuse to disclose and to prevent any other person from disclosing confidential communications in a civil action, suit or proceeding, made for the purposes of diagnosis or treatment of the patient's physical condition, among the patient, the patient's physician or persons who are participating in the diagnosis or treatment under the direction of the physician, including members of the patient's family.
(3) **Who may claim the privilege.** The privilege created by this section may be claimed by.
  (a) The patient;
  (b) A guardian or conservator of the patient;
  (c) The personal representative of a deceased patient; or
  (d) The person who was the physician, but only on behalf of the patient. Such person's authority so to do is presumed in the absence of evidence to the contrary.
(4) **General exceptions.** The following is a nonexclusive list of limits on the privilege granted by this section:
  (a) If the judge orders an examination of the physical condition of the patient, communications made in the course thereof are not privileged under this section with respect to the particular purpose for which the examination is ordered unless the judge orders otherwise.
  (b) Except as provided in ORCP 44, there is no privilege under this section for communications made in the course of a physical examination performed under ORCP 44.
  (c) There is no privilege under this section with regard to any confidential communication or record of such confidential communication that would otherwise be privileged under this section when the use of the communication or record is specifically allowed under ORS 426.070,

426.074, 426.075, 426.095, 426.120 or 426.307. This paragraph only applies to the use of the communication or record to the extent and for the purposes set forth in the described statute sections.

Rule 504-2. ORS 40.240. **Nurse-patient privilege.** A licensed professional nurse shall not, without the consent of a patient who was cared for by such nurse, be examined in a civil action or proceeding, as to any information acquired in caring for the patient, which was necessary to enable the nurse to care for the patient.

Rule 504-3. ORS 40.245. **School employee-student privilege.**
(1) A certificated staff member of an elementary or secondary school shall not be examined in any civil action or proceeding, as to any conversation between the certificated staff member and a student which relates to the personal affairs of the student or family of the student, and which if disclosed would tend to damage or incriminate the student or family. Any violation of the privilege provided by this subsection may result in the suspension of certification of the professional staff member as provided in ORS 342.175, 342.177 and 342.180.
(2) A certificated school counselor regularly employed and designated in such capacity by a public school shall not, without the consent of the student, be examined as to any communication made by the student to the counselor in the official capacity of the counselor in any civil action or proceeding or a criminal action or proceeding in which such student is a party concerning the past use, abuse or sale of drugs, controlled substances or alcoholic liquor. Any violation of the privilege provided by this subsection may result in the suspension of certification of the professional school counselor as provided in ORS 342.175, 342.177 and 342.180. However, in the event that the student's condition presents a clear and imminent danger to the student or to others, the counselor shall report this fact to an appropriate responsible authority or take such other emergency measures as the situation demands.

Rule 504-4. ORS 40.250. **Clinical social worker-client privilege**. A clinical social worker licensed by the State Board of Clinical Social Workers shall not be examined in a civil or criminal court proceeding as to any communication given the clinical social worker by a client in the course of noninvestigatory professional activity when such communication was given to enable the licensed clinical social worker to aid the client, except:
(1) When the client or those persons legally responsible for the client's affairs give consent to the disclosure;
(2) When the client initiates legal action or makes a complaint against the licensed clinical social worker to the board;
(3) When the communication reveals a clear intent to commit a crime which reasonably is expected to result in physical injury to a person;
(4) When the information reveals that a minor was the victim of a crime, abuse or neglect; or

(5)   When the licensed clinical social worker is a public employee and the public employer has determined that examination in a civil or criminal court proceeding is necessary in the performance of the duty of the social worker as a public employee.

Rule 505. ORS 40.255. **Husband-wife privilege.**
(1)   **Definitions.** As used in this section, unless the context requires otherwise:
    (a)   "Confidential communication" means a communication by a spouse to the other spouse and not intended to be disclosed to any other person.
    (b)   "Marriage" means a marital relationship between husband and wife, legally recognized under the laws of this state.
(2)   **Privilege as to confidential communications.** In any civil or criminal action, a spouse has a privilege to refuse to disclose and to prevent the other spouse from disclosing any confidential communication made by one spouse to the other during the marriage. The privilege created by this subsection may be claimed by either spouse. The authority of the spouse to claim the privilege and the claiming of the privilege is presumed in the absence of evidence to the contrary.
(3)   **Privilege as to testimony.** In any criminal proceeding, neither spouse, during the marriage, shall be examined adversely against the other as to any other matter occurring during the marriage unless the spouse called as a witness consents to testify.
(4)   **Exceptions.** There is no privilege under this section:
    (a)   In all criminal actions in which one spouse is charged with bigamy or with an offense or attempted offense against the person or property of the other spouse or of a child of either, or with an offense against the person or property of a third person committed in the course of committing or attempting to commit an offense against the other spouse;
    (b)   As to matters occurring prior to the marriage; or
    (c)   In any civil action where the spouses are adverse parties.

Rule 506. ORS 40.260. **Member of clergy-penitent privilege.**
(1)   **Definitions.** As used in this section, unless the context requires otherwise:
    (a)   "Confidential communication" means a communication made privately and not intended for further disclosure except to other persons present in furtherance of the purpose of the communication.
    (b)   "Member of the clergy" means a minister of any church, religious denomination or organization or accredited Christian Science practitioner who in the course of the discipline or practice of that church, denomination or organization is authorized or accustomed to hearing confidential communications and, under the discipline or tenets of that church, denomination or organization, has a duty to keep such communications secret.

(2) **General rule of privilege**. A member of the clergy shall not, without the consent of the person making the communication, be examined as to any confidential communication made to the member of the clergy in the member's professional character.

Rule 507. ORS 40.262. **Counselor-client privilege.** A professional counselor or a marriage and family therapist licensed by the Oregon Board of Licensed Professional Counselors and Therapists under ORS 675.715 shall not be examined in a civil or criminal court proceeding as to any communication given the counselor or therapist by a client in the course of a noninvestigatory professional activity when such communication was given to enable the counselor or the therapist to aid the client, except:

(1) When the client or those persons legally responsible for the affairs of the client give consent to the disclosure. If both parties to a marriage have obtained marital and family therapy by a licensed marital and family therapist or a licensed counselor, the therapist or counselor shall not be competent to testify in a domestic relations action other than child custody action concerning information acquired in the course of the therapeutic relationship unless both parties consent;

(2) When the client initiates legal action or makes a complaint against the licensed professional counselor or licensed marriage and family therapist to the board;

(3) When the communication reveals the intent to commit a crime or harmful act; or

(4) When the communication reveals that a minor is or is suspected to be the victim of crime, abuse or neglect.

Rule 508a. ORS 40.265. **Stenographer-employer privilege.** A stenographer shall not, without the consent of the stenographer's employer, be examined as to any communication or dictation made by the employer to the stenographer in the course of professional employment.

Rule 509. ORS 40.270. **Public officer privilege.** A public officer shall not be examined as to public records determined to be exempt from disclosure under ORS 192.501 to 192.505.

Rule 509-1. ORS 40.272. **Disabled person-sign language interpreter privilege.**

(1) As used in this section:

(a) "Disabled person" means a person who cannot readily understand or communicate the spoken English language, or cannot understand proceedings in which the person is involved, because of deafness or because of a physical hearing impairment or cannot communicate in the proceedings because of a physical speaking impairment.

(b) "Sign language interpreter" or "interpreter" means a person who translates conversations or other communications for a disabled person or translates the statements of a disabled person.

(2) A disabled person has a privilege to refuse to disclose and to prevent a sign language interpreter from disclosing any communications to which the disabled person was a party that were made while the interpreter was providing interpretation services for the disabled person. The privilege created by this section extends only to those communications between a disabled person and another, and translated by the interpreter, that would otherwise be privileged under Rule 503 to 514 (ORS 40.225 to 40.295).

Rule 509-2. ORS 40.273. **Non-English speaking person-interpreter privilege.**
(1) As used in this section:
  (a) "Interpreter" means a person who translates conversations or other communications for a non-English speaking person or translates the statements of a non-English speaking person.
  (b) "Non-English speaking person" means a person who, by reason of place of birth or culture, speaks a language other than English and does not speak English with adequate ability to communicate in the proceedings.

(2) A non-English speaking person has a privilege to refuse to disclose and to prevent an interpreter from disclosing any communications to which the non-English speaking person was a party that were made while the interpreter was providing interpretation services for the non-English speaking person. The privilege created by this section extends only to those communications between a non-English speaking person and another, and translated by the interpreter, that would otherwise be privileged under Rule 503 to 514 (ORS 40.225 to 40.295).

Rule 510. ORS 40.275. **Identity of informer.**
(1) As used in this section, "unit of government" means the Federal Government or any state or political subdivision thereof.
(2) A unit of government has a privilege to refuse to disclose the identity of a person who has furnished information relating to or assisting in an investigation of a possible violation of law to a law enforcement officer or member of a legislative committee or its staff conducting an investigation.
(3) The privilege created by this section may be claimed by an appropriate representative of the unit of government if the information was furnished to an officer thereof.
(4) No privilege exists under this section:
  (a) If the identity of the informer or the informer's interest in the subject matter of the communication has been disclosed to those who would have cause to resent the communication by a holder of the privilege or by the informer's own action, or if the informer appears as a witness for the unit of government.

(b) If it appears from the evidence in the case or from other showing by a party that an informer may be able to give testimony necessary to a fair determination of the issue of guilt or innocence in a criminal case or of a material issue on the merits in a civil case to which the unit of government is a party, and the unit of government invokes the privilege, and the judge gives the unit of government an opportunity to show in camera facts relevant to determining whether the informer can, in fact, supply that testimony. The showing will ordinarily be in the form of affidavits, but the judge may direct that testimony be taken if the judge finds that the matter cannot be resolved satisfactorily upon affidavit. If the judge finds that there is a reasonable probability that the informer can give the testimony, and the unit of government elects not to disclose identity of the informer, the judge on motion of the defendant in a criminal case shall dismiss the charges to which the testimony would relate, and the judge may do so on the judge's own motion. In civil cases, the judge may make any order that justice requires. Evidence submitted to the judge shall be sealed and preserved to be made available to the appellate court in the event of an appeal and the contents shall not otherwise be revealed without consent of the unit of government. All counsel and parties shall be permitted to be present at every stage of proceedings under this paragraph except a showing in camera, at which no counsel or party shall be permitted to be present.

(c) If information from an informer is relied upon to establish the legality of the means by which evidence was obtained and the judge is not satisfied that the information was received from an informer reasonably believed to be reliable or credible. The judge may require the identity of the informer to be disclosed. The judge shall, on request of the unit of government, direct that the disclosure be made in camera. All counsel and parties concerned with the issue of legality shall be permitted to be present at every stage of proceedings under this paragraph except a disclosure in camera, at which no counsel or party shall be permitted to be present. If disclosure of the identity of the informer is made in camera, the record thereof shall be sealed and preserved to be made available to the appellate court in the event of an appeal, and the contents shall not otherwise be revealed without consent of the unit of government.

Rule 511. ORS 40.280. **Waiver of privilege by voluntary disclosure.** A person upon whom Rules 503 to 514 (ORS 40.225 to 40.295) confer a privilege against disclosure of the confidential matter or communication waives the privilege if the person or the person's predecessor while holder of the privilege voluntarily discloses or consents to disclosure of any significant part of the matter or communication. This section does not apply if the disclosure is itself a privileged communication. Voluntary disclosure does not occur with the mere commencement of litigation or, in the case of a deposition taken for the purpose of perpetuating testimony, until the offering of the deposition as evidence. Voluntary disclosure does occur, as to psychotherapists in the case of a mental or emotional condition and physicians in the case of a physical condition upon the holder's offering of any person as a witness who testifies as to the condition.

Rule 512. ORS 40.285. **Privileged matter disclosed under compulsion or without opportunity to claim privilege.** Evidence of a statement or other disclosure of privileged matter is not admissible against the holder of the privilege if the disclosure was:
(1) Compelled erroneously; or
(2) Made without opportunity to claim the privilege.

Rule 513. ORS 40.290. **Comment upon or inference from claim of privilege.**
(1) The claim of a privilege, whether in the present proceeding or upon a prior occasion, is not a proper subject of comment by judge or counsel. No inference may be drawn from a claim of privilege.
(2) In jury cases, proceedings shall be conducted, to the extent practicable, so as to facilitate the making of claims of privilege without the knowledge of the jury.
(3) Upon request, any party against whom the jury might draw an adverse inference from a claim of privilege is entitled to an instruction that no inference may be drawn therefrom.

Rule 514. ORS 40.295. **Effect on existing privileges.** Unless expressly repealed by section 98, chapter 892, Oregon Laws 1981, all existing privileges either created under the Constitution or statutes of the State of Oregon or developed by the courts of Oregon are recognized and shall continue to exist until changed or repealed according to law.

ARTICLE VI.   WITNESSES

Rule 601. ORS 40.310. **General rule of competency.** Except as provided in Rules 601 to 606 (ORS 40.310 to 40.335), any person who, having organs of sense can perceive, and perceiving can make known the perception to others, may be a witness.

Rule 602. ORS 40.315. **Lack of personal knowledge.** Subject to the provisions of Rule 703 (ORS 40.415), a witness may not testify to a matter unless evidence is introduced sufficient to support a finding that the witness has personal knowledge of the matter. Evidence to prove personal knowledge may, but need not, consist of the testimony of the witness.

Rule 603. ORS 40.320. **Oath or affirmation.**

(1) Before testifying, every witness shall be required to declare that the witness will testify truthfully, by oath or affirmation administered in a form calculated to awaken the conscience of the witness and impress the mind of the witness with the duty to do so.

(2) An oath may be administered as follows: The person who swears holds up one hand while the person administering the oath asks: "Under penalty of perjury, do you solemnly swear that the evidence you shall give in the issue (or matter) now pending between _____ and _____ shall be the truth, the whole truth and nothing but the truth, so help you God?" If the oath is administered to any other than a witness, the same form and manner may be used. The person swearing must answer in an affirmative manner.

(3) An affirmation may be administered as follows: The person who affirms holds up one hand while the person administering the affirmation asks: "Under penalty of perjury, do you promise that the evidence you shall give in the issue (or matter) now pending between _____ and _____ shall be the truth, the whole truth and nothing but the truth?" If the affirmation is administered to any other than a witness, the same form and manner may be used. The person affirming must answer in an affirmative manner.

Rule 604. ORS 40.325. **Interpreters.** An interpreter is subject to the provisions of the Oregon Evidence Code relating to qualification as an expert and the administration of an oath or affirmation that the interpreter win make a true translation.

Rule 605. ORS 40.330. **Competency of judge as witness.** The judge presiding at the trial may not testify in that trial as a witness. No objection need be made in order to preserve the point.

Rule 606. ORS 40.335. **Competency of juror as witness.** A member of the jury may not testify as a witness before that jury in the trial of the case in which the member has been sworn to sit as a juror. If the juror is called so to testify, the opposing party shall be afforded an opportunity to object out of the presence of the jury.

Rule 607. ORS 40.345. **Who may impeach.** The credibility of a witness may be attacked by any party, including the party calling the witness.

Rule 608. ORS 40.350. **Evidence of character and conduct of witness.**

(1) The credibility of a witness may be attacked or supported by evidence in the form of opinion or reputation, but:

   (a) The evidence may refer only to character for truthfulness or untruthfulness; and

   (b) Evidence of truthful character is admissible only after the character of the witness for truthfulness has been attacked by opinion or reputation evidence or otherwise.

(2) Specific instances of the conduct of a witness, for the purpose of attacking or supporting the credibility of the witness, other than conviction of crime as provided in Rule 609 (ORS 40.355), may not be proved by extrinsic evidence. Further, such specific instances of conduct may not, even if probative of truthfulness or untruthfulness, be inquired into on cross-examination of the witness.

Rule 609. ORS 40.355. **Impeachment by evidence of conviction of crime; exceptions.**

(1) For the purpose of attacking the credibility of a witness, evidence that the witness has been convicted of a crime shall be admitted if elicited from the witness or established by public record, but only if the crime
 (a) was punishable by death or imprisonment in excess of one year under the law under which the witness was convicted, or
 (b) involved false statement or dishonesty.
(2) Evidence of a conviction under this section is not admissible if:
 (a) A period of more than 15 years has elapsed since the date of the conviction or of the release of the witness from the confinement imposed for that conviction, whichever is the later date; or
 (b) The conviction has been expunged by pardon, reversed, set aside or otherwise rendered nugatory.
(3) When the credibility of a witness is attacked by evidence that the witness has been convicted of a crime, the witness shall be allowed to explain briefly the circumstances of the crime or former conviction; once the witness explains the circumstances, the opposing side shall have the opportunity to rebut the explanation.
(4) The pendency of an appeal therefrom does not render evidence of a conviction inadmissible. Evidence of the pendency of an appeal is admissible.
(5) An adjudication by a juvenile court that a child is within its jurisdiction is not a conviction of a crime.
(6) A conviction before, on or after November 4, 1993, of any of the statutory counterparts of offenses designated as violations as defined in ORS 161.565, may not be used to impeach the character of a witness in any criminal or civil action or proceeding.

Rule 609-1. ORS 40.360. **Impeachment for bias or interest.**
(1) The credibility of a witness may be attacked by evidence that the witness engaged in conduct or made statements showing bias or interest. However, before this can be done, the statements must be related to the witness and the conduct described, with the circumstances of times, places and persons present, and the witness shall be asked whether the witness made the statements or engaged in such conduct, and, if so, allowed to explain. If the statements are in writing, they shall be shown to the witness.
(2) If a witness fully admits the facts claimed to show the bias or interest of the witness, additional evidence of that bias or interest shall not be admitted. If the witness denies or does not fully admit the facts claimed to show bias or

interest, the party attacking the credibility of the witness may then offer evidence to prove those facts.

(3) Evidence to support or rehabilitate a witness whose credibility has been attacked by evidence of bias or interest shall be limited to evidence showing a lack of bias or interest.

Rule 610. ORS 40.365. Religious beliefs or opinions. Evidence of the beliefs or opinions of a witness on matters of religion is not admissible for the purpose of showing that by reason of their nature the credibility of the witness is impaired or enhanced.

Rule 611. ORS 40.370. Mode and order of interrogation and presentation.

(1) **Control by court.** The court shall exercise reasonable control over the mode and order of interrogating witnesses and presenting evidence so as to make the interrogation and presentation effective for the ascertainment of the truth, avoid needless consumption of time and protect witnesses from harassment or undue embarrassment.

(2) **Scope of cross-examination.** Cross-examination should be limited to the subject matter of the direct examination and matters affecting the credibility of the witness. The court may, in the exercise of discretion, permit inquiry into additional matters as if on direct examination.

(3) **Leading questions.** Leading questions should not be used on the direct examination of a witness except as may be necessary to develop the witness' testimony. Ordinarily leading questions should be permitted on cross-examination. When a party calls a hostile witness, an adverse party, or a witness identified with an adverse party, interrogation may be by leading questions.

Rule 612. ORS 40.375. Writing used to refresh memory. If a witness uses a writing to refresh memory for the purpose of testifying, either while testifying or before testifying if the court in its discretion determines it is necessary in the interests of justice, an adverse party is entitled to have the writing produced at the hearing, to inspect it, to cross-examine the witness thereon, and to introduce into evidence those portions which relate to the testimony of the witness. If it is claimed that the writing contains matters not related to the subject matter of the testimony, the court shall examine the writing in camera, excise any portions not so related, and order delivery of the remainder to the party entitled thereto. Any portion withheld over objections shall be preserved and made available to the appellate court in the event of an appeal. If a writing is not produced or delivered pursuant to order under this section, the court shall make any order justice requires, except that in criminal cases when the prosecution elects not to comply the order shall be one striking the testimony or, if the court in its discretion determines that the interests of justice so require, declaring a mistrial.

Rule 613. ORS 403.380. **Prior statements of witnesses.**

(1) **Examining witness concerning prior statement.** In examining a witness concerning a prior statement made by the witness, whether written or not, the statement need not be shown nor its contents disclosed to the witness at that time, but on request the same shall be shown or disclosed to opposing counsel.

(2) **Extrinsic evidence of prior inconsistent statement of witness.** Extrinsic evidence of a prior inconsistent statement by a witness is not admissible unless the witness is afforded an opportunity to explain or deny the same and the opposite party is afforded an opportunity to interrogate the witness thereon, or the interests of justice otherwise require. This provision does not apply to admissions of a party-opponent as defined in Rule 801 (ORS 40.450).

Rule 615. ORS 40.385. **Exclusion of witnesses.** At the request of a party the court may order witnesses excluded until the time of final argument, and it may make the order of its own motion. This rule does not authorize exclusion of

(1) a party who is a natural person, or

(2) an officer or employee of a party which is not a natural person designated as its representative by its attorney, or

(3) a person whose presence is shown by a party to be essential to the presentation of the party's cause, or

(4) the victim in a criminal case.

ARTICLE VII. OPINIONS AND EXPERT TESTIMONY

Rule 701. ORS 40.405. **Opinion testimony by lay witnesses.** If the witness is not testifying as an expert, testimony of the witness in the form of opinions or inferences is limited to those opinions or inferences which are:

(1) Rationally based on the perception of the witness; and

(2) Helpful to a clear understanding of testimony of the witness or the determination of a fact in issue.

Rule 702. ORS 40.410. **Testimony by experts.** If scientific, technical or other special knowledge will assist the trier of fact to understand the evidence or to determine a fact in issue, a witness qualified as an expert by knowledge, skill, experience, training or education may testify thereto in the form of an opinion or otherwise.

Rule 703. ORS 40.415. **Bases of opinion testimony by experts.** The facts or data in the particular case upon which an expert bases an opinion or inference may be those perceived by or made known to the expert at or before the hearing. If of a type reasonably relied upon by experts in the particular field in forming opinions or inferences upon the subject, the facts or data need not be admissible in evidence.

Rule 704. ORS 40.420. **Opinion on ultimate issue.** Testimony in the form of an opinion or inference otherwise admissible is not objectionable because it embraces an ultimate issue to be decided by the trier of fact.

Rule 705. ORS 40.425. **Disclosure of fact or data underlying expert opinion.** An expert may testify in terms of opinion or inference and give reasons therefor without prior disclosure of the underlying facts or data, unless the court requires otherwise. The expert may in any event be required to disclose the underlying facts or data on cross-examination.

ARTICLE VIII. HEARSAY

Rule 801. ORS 40.450. **Definitions.** As used in Rules 801 to 806 (ORS 40.450 to 40.475), unless the context requires otherwise:

(1) **Statement.** A "statement" is:
   (a) An oral or written assertion; or
   (b) Nonverbal conduct of a person, if intended as an assertion.
(2) **Declarant.** A "declarant" is a person who makes a statement.
(3) **Hearsay.** "Hearsay" is a statement, other than one made by the declarant while testifying at the trial or hearing, offered in evidence to prove the truth of the matter asserted.
(4) **Statements which are not hearsay.** A statement is not hearsay if:
   (a) **Prior statement by witness.** The declarant testifies at the trial or hearing and is subject to cross-examination concerning the statement, and the statement is:
      (A) Inconsistent with the testimony of the witness and was given under oath subject to the penalty of perjury at a trial hearing or other proceeding, or in a deposition;
      (B) Consistent with the testimony of the witness and is offered to rebut an inconsistent statement or an express or implied charge against the witness of recent fabrication or improper influence or motive; or
      (C) One of identification of a person made after perceiving the person.
   (b) **Admission by party-opponent.** The statement is offered against a party and is:
      (A) That party's own statement, in either an individual or a representative capacity,
      (B) A statement of which the party has manifested the party's adoption or belief in its truth;
      (C) A statement by a person authorized by the party to make a statement concerning the subject;

    (D) A statement by the party's agent or servant concerning a matter within the scope of the agency or employment, made during the existence of the relationship; or

    (E) A statement by a coconspirator of a party during the course and in furtherance of the conspiracy.

  (c) The statement is made in a deposition taken in the same proceeding pursuant to ORCP 39 I.

Rule 802. ORS 40.455. **Hearsay rule.** Hearsay is not admissible except as provided in Rules 801 to 806 (ORS 40.450 to 40.475) or as otherwise provided by law.

Rule 803. ORS 40.460. **Hearsay exception; availability of declarant immaterial.** The following are not excluded by Rule 802 (ORS 40.455), even though the declarant is available as a witness:

(1) [Reserved.]

(2) **Excited utterance.** A statement relating to a startling event or condition made while the declarant was under the stress of excitement caused by the event or condition.

(3) **Then existing mental, emotional or physical condition.** A statement of the declarant's then existing state of mind, emotion, sensation or physical condition, such as intent, plan, motive, design, mental feeling, pain or bodily health, but not including a statement of memory or belief to prove the fact remembered or believed unless it relates to the execution, revocation, identification, or terms of the declarant's will.

(4) **Statements for purposes of medical diagnosis or treatment.** Statements made for purposes of medical diagnosis or treatment and describing medical history, or past or present symptoms, pain or sensations, or the inception or general character of the cause of external source thereof insofar as reasonably pertinent to diagnosis or treatment.

(5) **Recorded recollection.** A memorandum or record concerning a matter about which a witness once had knowledge but now has insufficient recollection to enable the witness to testify fully and accurately, shown to have been made or adopted by the witness when the matter was fresh in the memory of the witness and to reflect that knowledge correctly. If admitted, the memorandum or record may be read into evidence but may not itself be received as an exhibit unless offered by an adverse party.

(6) **Records of regularly conducted activity.** A memorandum, report, record, or data compilation, in any form, of acts, events, conditions, opinions, or diagnoses, made at or near the time by, or from information transmitted by, a person with knowledge, if kept in the course of a regularly conducted business activity, and if it was the regular practice of that business activity to make the memorandum, report, record, or data compilation, all as shown by the testimony of the custodian or other qualified witness, unless the source of information or the method of circumstances of preparation indicate lack of trustworthiness. The term "business" as used in this subsection

includes business, institution, association, profession, occupation, and calling of every kind, whether or not conducted for profit.

(7) **Absence of entry in records kept in accordance with the provisions of subsection (6) of this section.** Evidence that a matter is not included in the memoranda, reports, records, or data compilations, and in any form, kept in accordance with the provisions of subsection (6) of this section, to prove the nonoccurrence or nonexistence of the matter, if the matter was of a kind of which a memorandum, report, record, or data compilation was regularly made and preserved, unless the sources of information or other circumstances indicate lack of trustworthiness.

(8) **Public records and reports.** Records, reports, statements, or data compilations, in any form, of public offices or agencies, setting forth:

(a) The activities of the office or agency;

(b) Matters observed pursuant to duty imposed by law as to which matters there was a duty to report, excluding however, in criminal cases matters observed by police officers and other law enforcement personnel; or

(c) In civil actions and proceedings and against the government in criminal cases, factual findings, resulting from an investigation made pursuant to authority granted by law, unless the sources of information or other circumstances indicate lack of trustworthiness.

(9) **Records of vital statistics.** Records or data compilations, in any form, of births, fetal deaths, deaths or marriages, if the report thereof was made to a public office pursuant to requirements of law.

(10) **Absence of public record or entry.** To prove the absence of a record, report, statement, or data compilation, in any form, or the nonoccurrence or nonexistence of a matter of which a record, report, statement, or data compilation, in any form, was regularly made and preserved by a public office or agency, evidence in the form of a certification in accordance with Rule 902 (ORS 40.510), or testimony, that diligent search failed to disclose the record, report, statement, or data compilation, or entry.

(11) **Records of religious organizations.** Statements of births, marriages, divorces, deaths, legitimacy, ancestry, relationship by blood or marriage, or other similar facts of personal family history, contained in a regularly kept record of a religious organization.

(12) **Marriage, baptismal and similar certificates.** A statement of fact contained in a certificate that the maker performed a marriage or other ceremony or administered a sacrament, made by a clergyman, public official, or other person authorized by the rules or practices of a religious organization or by law to perform the act certified, and purporting to have been issued at the time of the act or within a reasonable time thereafter.

(13) **Family records.** Statements of facts concerning personal or family history contained in family bibles, genealogies, charts, engravings on rings, inscriptions on family portraits, engravings on urns, crypts, or tombstones, or the like.

(14) **Records of documents affecting an interest in property.** The record of a document purporting to establish or affect an interest in property, as proof of content of the original recorded document and its execution and delivery by each person by whom it purports to have been executed, if the record is a record of a public office and an applicable statute authorizes the recording of documents of that kind in that office.

(15) **Statements in documents affecting an interest in property.** A statement contained in a document purporting to establish or affect an interest in property if the matter stated was relevant to the purpose of the document, unless dealings with the property since the document was made have been inconsistent with the truth of the statement or the purport of the document.

(16) **Statements in ancient documents.** Statements in a document in existence 20 years or more the authenticity of which is established.

(17) **Market reports and commercial publications.** Market quotations, tabulations, lists, directories, or other published compilations, generally used and relied upon by the public or by persons in particular occupations.

(18) [Reserved.]

(18a) **Complaint of sexual misconduct.**

(a) A complaint of sexual misconduct or complaint of abuse as defined in ORS 419B.005 made by the witness after the commission of the alleged misconduct or abuse at issue. Except as provided in paragraph (b) of this subsection, such evidence must be confined to the fact that the complaint was made.

(b) A statement made by a child victim or person with developmental disabilities as described in paragraph (d) of this subsection, which statement concerns an act of abuse, as defined in ORS 419B.005, or sexual conduct performed with or on the child or person with developmental disabilities by another, is not excluded by ORS 40.455 if the child or person with developmental disabilities either testifies at the proceedings and is subject to cross-examination or is chronologically or mentally under 12 years of age and is unavailable as a witness. However, when a witness under 12 years of age or a person with developmental disabilities is unavailable as a witness, the statement may be admitted in evidence only if the proponent establishes that the time, content and circumstances of the statement provide indicia of reliability, and in a criminal trial that there is corroborative evidence of the act of abuse or sexual conduct and of the alleged perpetrator's opportunity to participate in the conduct and that the statement possesses indicia of reliability as is constitutionally required to be admitted. No statement may be admitted under this paragraph unless the proponent of the statement makes known to the adverse party the proponent's intention to offer the statement and the particulars of the statement no later than 15 days before trial, except for good cause shown. For purposes of this paragraph, in addition to those situations described in ORS 40.465(1), the child or person with developmental disabilities shall be considered "unavailable" if the child or person with developmental disabilities has a substantial lack of memory of the subject matter of the statement, is presently incompetent to testify, is unable to communicate about the abuse or sexual conduct because of fear or other similar reason or is substantially likely, as established by expert testimony, to suffer lasting severe emotional trauma from testifying. Unless otherwise agreed by the parties, the court shall examine the child or person with developmental disabilities in chambers and on the record or outside the presence of the jury and on the record. The examination shall be conducted immediately prior to the commencement of the trial in the presence of the attorney and the legal guardian or other suitable adult as designated by the court. If the child or person with developmental disabilities is found to be unavailable, the court shall then determine the admissibility of the evidence. The determinations shall be appealable under ORS 138.060(3). The purpose of the examination shall be to aid the court in making its findings regarding the availability of the child or person with developmental disabilities as a witness and the reliability of the statement of the child or person with developmental disabilities. In determining whether a statement possesses indicia of reliability under this paragraph, the court may consider, but is not limited to, the following factors:

    (A) The personal knowledge of the child or person with developmental disabilities of the event;

    (B) The age and maturity of the child or extent of disability of the person with developmental disabilities;

    (C) Certainty that the statement was made, including the credibility of the person testifying about the statement and any motive the person may have to falsify or distort the statement;

    (D) Any apparent motive the child or person with developmental disabilities may have to falsify or distort the event, including bias, corruption or coercion;

    (E) The timing of the statement of the child or person with developmental disabilities;

    (F) Whether more than one person heard the statement;

    (G) Whether the child or person with developmental disabilities was suffering pain or distress when making the statement;

    (H) Whether the child's young age makes it unlikely that the child fabricated a statement that represents a graphic, detailed account beyond the child's knowledge and experience;

    (I) Whether the statement has internal consistency or coherence and uses terminology appropriate to the child's age or to the extent of the disability of the person with developmental disabilities;

    (J) Whether the statement is spontaneous or directly responsive to questions; and

    (K) Whether the statement was elicited by leading questions.

  (c) This subsection applies to all civil, criminal and juvenile proceedings.

  (d) For the purposes of this subsection, "developmental disabilities" means any disability attributable to mental retardation, autism, cerebral palsy, epilepsy or other disabling neurological condition that requires training or support similar to that required by persons with mental retardation, if either of the following apply:

    (A) The disability originates before the person attains 22 years of age, or if the disability is attributable to mental retardation the condition is manifested before the person attains 18 years of age, the disability can be expected to continue indefinitely, and the disability constitutes a substantial handicap to the ability of the person to function in society.

    (B) The disability results in a significant subaverage general intellectual functioning with concurrent deficits in adaptive behavior that are manifested during the developmental period.

(19) **Reputation concerning personal or family history.** Reputation among members of a person's family by blood, adoption or marriage, or among a person's associates, or in the community, concerning a person's birth, adoption, marriage, divorce, death, legitimacy, relationship by blood or adoption or marriage, ancestry, or other similar fact of a person's personal or family history.

(20) **Reputation concerning boundaries or general history.** Reputation in a community, arising before the controversy, as to boundaries of or customs affecting lands in the community, and reputation as to events of general history important to the community or state or nation in which located.

(21) **Reputation as to character.** Reputation of a person's character among associates of the person or in the community.

(22) **Judgment of previous conviction.** Evidence of a final judgment, entered after a trial or upon a plea of guilty, but not upon a plea of no contest, adjudging a person guilty of a crime other than a traffic offense, to prove any fact essential to sustain the judgment, but not including, when offered by the government in a criminal prosecution for purposes other than impeachment, judgments against persons other than the accused. The pendency of an appeal may be shown but does not affect admissibility.

(23) **Judgment as to personal, family or general history, or boundaries.** Judgments as proof of matters of personal, family, or general history, or boundaries, essential to the judgment, if the same would be provable by evidence of reputation.

(24) **Testimony of child victim or witness of sexual abuse.** Notwithstanding the limits contained in subsection (18a) of this section, in any proceeding in which a child under 12 years of age at the time of trial, or a person with developmental disabilities as described in subsection (18)(d) of this section, may be called as a witness to testify concerning as act of abuse, as defined in ORS 419B.005, or sexual conduct performed with or on the child or person with developmental disabilities by another, the testimony of the child or person with developmental disabilities taken by contemporaneous examination and cross-examination in another place under the supervision of the trial judge and communicated to the courtroom by closed circuit television or other audiovisual means. Testimony will be allowed as provided in this subsection only if the court finds that there is a substantial likelihood,

established by expert testimony, that the child or person with developmental disabilities will suffer severe emotional or psychological harm if required to testify in open court. If the court makes such a finding, the court, on motion of a party, the child, the person with developmental disabilities or the court in a civil proceeding, or on motion of the district attorney, the child or the person with developmental disabilities in a criminal or juvenile proceedings, may order that the testimony of the child or the person with developmental disabilities be taken as described in this subsection. Only the judge, the attorneys for the parties, the parties, individuals necessary to operate the equipment and any individual the court finds would contribute to the welfare and well-being of the child or person with developmental disabilities may be present during the testimony of the child or person with developmental disabilities.

(25) Any document containing data prepared or recorded by the Oregon State Police pursuant to ORS 813.160(1)(b)(C) or (E), or pursuant to ORS 475.235(3), if the document is produced by data retrieval from the Law Enforcement Data System or other computer system maintained and operated by the Oregon State Police, and the person retrieving the data attests that the information was retrieved directly from the system and that the document accurately reflects the data retrieved.

(26) **Other exceptions.**

    (a) A statement not specifically covered by any of the foregoing exceptions but having equivalent circumstantial guarantees of trustworthiness, if the court determines that:

        (A) The statement is relevant;

        (B) The statement is more probative on the point for which it is offered than any other evidence which the proponent can procure through reasonable efforts; and

        (C) The general purposes of the Oregon Evidence Code and the interests of justice will best be served by admission of the statement into evidence.

    (b) A statement may not be admitted under this subsection unless the proponent of it makes known to the adverse party the intention to offer the statement and the particulars of it, including the name and address of the declarant, sufficiently in advance of the trial or hearing, or as soon as practicable after it becomes apparent that such statement is probative of the issues at hand, to provide the adverse party with a fair opportunity to prepare to meet it.

Rule 804. ORS 40.465. **Hearsay exceptions where the declarant is unavailable.**

(1) **Definition of unavailability.** "Unavailability as a witness" includes situations in which the declarant:

    (a) Is exempted by ruling of the court on the ground of privilege from testifying concerning the subject matter of a statement;

(b) Persists in refusing to testify concerning the subject matter of a statement despite an order of the court to do so;

(c) Testifies to a lack of memory of the subject matter of a statement;

(d) Is unable to be present or to testify at the hearing because of death or then existing physical or mental illness or infirmity, or

(e) Is absent from the hearing and the proponent of the declarant's statement has been unable to procure the declarant's attendance (or in the case of an exception under subsection (3)(b), (c) or (d) of this section, the declarant's attendance or testimony) by process or other reasonable means.

(2) **Exception to unavailability.** A declarant is not unavailable as a witness if the declarant's exemption, refusal, claim of lack of memory, inability, or absence is due to the procurement or wrongdoing of the proponent of the declarant's statement for the purpose of preventing the witness from attending or testifying.

(3) **Hearsay exceptions.** The following are not excluded by Rule 802 (ORS 40.455) if the declarant is unavailable as a witness:

(a) **Former testimony.** Testimony given as a witness at another hearing of the same or a different proceeding, or in a deposition taken in compliance with law in the course of the same or another proceeding, if the party against whom the testimony is now offered, or, in a civil action or proceeding a predecessor in interest, had an opportunity and similar motive to develop the testimony by direct, cross, or redirect examination.

(b) **Statement under belief of impending death.** A statement made by a declarant while believing that death was imminent, concerning the cause or circumstances of what the declarant believed to be impending death.

(c) **Statement against interest.** A statement which was at the time of its making so far contrary to the declarant's pecuniary or proprietary interest, or so far tended to subject the declarant to civil or criminal liability, or to render invalid a claim by the declarant against another, that a reasonable person in the declarant's position would not have made the statement unless the person believed it to be true. A statement tending to expose the declarant to criminal liability and offered to exculpate the accused is not admissible unless corroborating circumstances clearly indicate the trustworthiness of the statement.

(d) **Statement of personal or family history.**

(A) A statement concerning the declarant's own birth, adoption, marriage, divorce, legitimacy, relationship by blood or adoption or marriage, ancestry, or other similar fact of personal or family history, even though the declarant had no means of acquiring personal knowledge of the matter stated; or

(B) A statement concerning the foregoing matters, and death also, of another person, if the declarant was related to the other by blood, adoption, or marriage or was so intimately associated with the other's family as to be likely to have accurate information concerning the matter declared.

(e) **Statement made in professional capacity.** A statement made at or near the time of the transaction by a person in a position to know the facts stated therein, acting in the person's professional capacity and in the ordinary course of professional conduct.

(f) **Other exceptions.** A statement not specifically covered by any of the foregoing exceptions but having equivalent circumstantial guarantees of trustworthiness, if the court determines that

(A) the statement is offered as evidence of a material fact;

(B) the statement is more probative on the point for which it is offered than any other evidence which the proponent can procure through reasonable efforts; and

(C) the general purposes of the Oregon Evidence Code and the interests of justice will best be served by admission of the statement into evidence. However, a statement may not be admitted under this paragraph unless the proponent of it makes known to the adverse party the intention to offer the statement and the particulars of it, including the name and address of the declarant, sufficiently in advance of the trial or hearing, or as soon as practicable after it becomes apparent that the statement is probative of the issues at hand, to provide the adverse party with a fair opportunity to prepare to meet it.

Rule 805. ORS 40.470. **Hearsay within hearsay.** Hearsay included within hearsay is not excluded under Rule 802 (ORS 40.455) if each part of the combined statements conforms with an exception set forth in Rule 803 or 804 (ORS 40.460 or ORS 40.465).

Rule 806. ORS 40.475. **Attacking and supporting credibility of declarant.** When a hearsay statement, or a statement defined in Rule 801(4)(b) (C), (D) or (E) (ORS 40.450(4)(b)(C), (D) or (E)), has been admitted in evidence, the credibility of the declarant may be attacked, and if attacked may be supported, by any evidence which would be admissible for those purposes if the declarant had testified as a witness. Evidence of a statement or conduct by the declarant at any time, inconsistent with the hearsay statement of the declarant, is not subject to any requirement under Rule 613 (ORS 40.380) relating to impeachment by evidence of inconsistent statements. If the party against whom a hearsay statement has been admitted calls the declarant as a witness, the party is entitled to examine the declarant on the statement as if under cross-examination.

ARTICLE IX. AUTHENTICATION AND IDENTIFICATION

Rule 901. ORS 40.505. Requirement of authentication or identification.

(1) **General provision.** The requirement of authentication or identification as a condition precedent to admissibility is satisfied by evidence sufficient to support a finding that the matter in question is what its proponent claims.

(2) **Illustrations.** By way of illustration only, and not by way of limitation, the following are examples of authentication or identification conforming with the requirements of subsection (1) of this section:

   (a) **Testimony of witness with knowledge.** Testimony by a witness with knowledge that a matter is what it is claimed to be.

   (b) **Nonexpert opinion on handwriting.** Nonexpert opinion as to the genuineness of handwriting, based upon familiarity not acquired for purposes of the litigation.

   (c) **Comparison by trier or expert witness.** Comparison by the trier of fact or by expert witnesses with specimens which have been authenticated.

   (d) **Distinctive characteristics and the like.** Appearance, contents, substance, internal patterns or other distinctive characteristics, taken in conjunction with circumstances.

   (e) **Voice identification.** Identification of a voice, whether heard firsthand or through mechanical or electronic transmission or recording, by opinion based upon hearing the voice at any time under circumstances connecting it with the alleged speaker.

   (f) **Telephone conversation.** Telephone conversations, by evidence that a call was made to the number assigned at the time by the telephone company to a particular person or business, if:

      (A) In the case of a person, circumstances, including self-identification, show the person answering to be the one called; or

      (B) In the case of a business, the call was made to a place of business and the conversation related to business reasonably transacted over the telephone.

   (g) **Public records or reports.** Evidence that a writing authorized by law to be recorded or filed and in fact recorded or filed in a public office, or a purported public record, report, statement, or data compilation, in any form, is from the public office where items of this nature are kept.

   (h) **Ancient documents or data compilation.** Evidence that a document or data compilation, in any form:

      (A) Is in such condition as to create no suspicion concerning its authenticity;

      (B) Was in a place where it, if authentic, would likely be; and

      (C) Has been in existence 20 years or more at the time it is offered.

   (i) **Process or system.** Evidence describing a process or system used to produce a result and showing that the process or system produces an accurate result.

(j) **Methods provided by statute or rule.** Any method of authentication or identification otherwise provided by law or by other rules prescribed by the Supreme Court.

Rule 902. ORS 40.510. **Self-authentication.** Extrinsic evidence of authenticity as a condition precedent to admissibility is not required with respect to the following:

(1) **Domestic public documents under seal.** A document bearing a seal purporting to be that of the United States, or of any state, district, commonwealth, territory, or insular possession thereof, or the Panama Canal Zone, or the Trust Territory of the Pacific Islands, or of a political subdivision, department, officer, or agency thereof, and a signature purporting to be an attestation or execution.

(2) **Domestic public documents not under seal.** A document purporting to bear the signature, in an official capacity, of an officer or employee of any entity included in subsection (1) of this section, having no seal, if a public officer having a seal and having official duties in the district or political subdivision of the officer or employee certifies under seal that the signer has the official capacity and that the signature is genuine.

(3) **Foreign public documents.** A document purporting to be executed or attested in an official capacity by a person authorized by the laws of a foreign country to make the execution or attestation, and accompanied by a final certification as to the genuineness of the signature and official position of (A) the executing or attesting person, or (B) any foreign official whose certificate of genuineness of signature and official position relates to the execution or attestation or is in a chain of certificates of genuineness of signature and official position relating to the execution or attestation. A final certification may be made by a secretary of embassy or legation, consul general, consul, vice consul, or consular agent of the United States, or a diplomatic or consular official of the foreign country assigned or accredited to the United States. If reasonable opportunity has been given to all parties to investigate the authenticity and accuracy of official documents, the court may, for good cause shown, order that they be treated as presumptively authentic without final certification or permit them to be evidenced by an attested summary with or without final certification.

(4) **Certified copies of public records.** A copy of an official record or report or entry therein, or of a document authorized by law to be recorded or filed and actually recorded or filed in a public office, including data compilations in any form, certified as correct by the custodian or other person authorized to make the certification, by certificate complying with subsection (1), (2) or (3) of this section or otherwise complying with any law or rule prescribed by the Supreme Court.

(5) **Official publications.** Books, pamphlets or other publications purporting to be issued by public authority.

(6) **Newspapers and periodicals.** Printed materials purporting to be newspapers or periodicals.

(7) **Trade inscriptions and the like.** Inscriptions, signs, tags or labels purporting to have been affixed in the course of business and indicating ownership, control or origin.

(8) **Acknowledged documents.** Documents accompanied by a certificate of acknowledgment executed in the manner provided by law by a notary public or other officer authorized by law to take acknowledgments.

(9) **Commercial paper and related documents.** Commercial paper, signatures thereon and documents relating thereto to the extent provided by ORS chapters 71 to 83.

(10) **Presumptions under law.** Any signature, documents or other matter declared by law to be presumptively or prima facie genuine or authentic.

(11) **Document bearing seal of tribal government**
  (a) A document bearing a seal purporting to be that of a federally recognized Indian tribal government or of a political subdivision, department, officer, or agency thereof, and a signature purporting to be an attestation or execution.
  (b) A document purporting to bear the signature, in an official capacity, of an officer or employee of any entity included in paragraph (a) of this subsection, having no seal, if a public officer having a seal and having official duties in the district or political subdivision or the officer or employee certifies under seal that the signer has the official capacity and that the signature is genuine.

(12) **State police data.** Any document containing data prepared or recorded by the Oregon State Police pursuant to ORS 813.160(1)(b)(C) or (E), or pursuant to ORS 475.235(3), if the document is produced by data retrieval from the Law Enforcement Data System or other computer system maintained and operated by the Oregon State Police, and the person retrieving the data attests that the information was retrieved directly from the system and that the document accurately reflects the data retrieved.

Rule 903. ORS 40.515. **Subscribing witness' testimony unnecessary.** The testimony of a subscribing witness is not necessary to authenticate a writing unless required by the laws of the jurisdiction whose laws govern the validity of the writing.

ARTICLE X.   CONTENTS OF WRITINGS, RECORDINGS AND PHOTOGRAPHS

Rule 1001. ORS 40.550. **Definitions for ORS 40.550 to 40.585.** As used in Rules 1001 to 1008 (ORS 40.550 to 40.585), unless the context requires otherwise:

(1) **Duplicate.** "Duplicate" means a counterpart produced by the same impression as the original, or from the same matrix, or by means of photography, including enlargements and miniatures, by mechanical or electronic

re-recording, by chemical reproduction, by optical imaging, or by other equivalent techniques that accurately reproduce the original, including reproduction by facsimile machines if the reproduction is identified as a facsimile and printed on nonthermal paper.

(2) **Original.** "Original" of a writing or recording is the writing or recording itself or any counterpart intended to have the same effect by a person executing or issuing it. An "original" of a photograph includes the negative or any print therefrom. If data are stored in a computer or similar device, any printout or other output readable by sight, shown to reflect the data accurately, is an "original."

(3) **Photographs.** "Photographs" includes still photographs, X-ray films, video tapes and motion pictures.

(4) **Writings and recordings.** "Writings" and "recordings" mean letters, words or numbers, or their equivalent, set down by handwriting, typewriting, printing, photostating, photographing, magnetic impulse, optical imaging, mechanical or electronic recording or other form of data compilation.

Rule 1002. ORS 40.555. **Requirement of original.** To prove the content of a writing, recording or photograph, the original writing, recording or photograph is required, except as otherwise provided in Rules 1001 to 1008 (ORS 40.550 to 40.585) or other law.

Rule 1003. ORS 40.560. **Admissibility of duplicates.** A duplicate is admissible to the same extent as an original unless:
(1) A genuine question is raised as to the authenticity of the original; or
(2) In the circumstances it would be unfair to admit the duplicate in lieu of the original.

Rule 1003-1. ORS 40.562. **Admissibility of reproduction.**
(1) If any business, institution or member of a profession or calling, in the regular course of business or activity, has kept or recorded any memorandum, writing, entry, print, representation or a combination thereof, of any act, transaction, occurrence or event, and in the regular course of business has caused any or all of the same to be recorded, copied or reproduced by any photographic, photostatic, microfilm, micro-card, miniature photographic, optical imaging or other process that accurately reproduces or forms a durable medium for so reproducing the original, the original may be destroyed in the regular course of business unless held in a custodial or fiduciary capacity and the principal or true owner has not authorized destruction or unless its preservation is required by law. Such reproduction, when satisfactorily identified, is as admissible in evidence as the original itself in any judicial or administrative proceeding whether the original is in existence or not and an enlargement or facsimile of such reproduction is likewise admissible in evidence if the original reproduction is in existence and available for inspection under direction of the court. The introduction

of a reproduced record, enlargement or facsimile does not preclude admission of the original.

(2) If any department or agency of government, in the regular course of business or activity, has kept or recorded any memorandum, writing, entry, print, representation or combination thereof, of any act, transaction, occurrence or event, and in the regular course of business, and in accordance with ORS 192.040 to 192.060 and 192.105, has caused any or all of the same to be recorded, copied or reproduced by any photographic, photostatic, microfilm, micro-card, miniature photographic, optical imaging or other process that accurately reproduces or forms a durable medium for so reproducing the original, the original may be destroyed in the regular course of business unless held in a custodial or fiduciary capacity and the principal or true owner has not authorized destruction or unless its preservation is required by law. Such reproduction, when satisfactorily identified, is as admissible in evidence as the original itself in any judicial or administrative proceeding whether the original is in existence or not and an enlargement or facsimile of such reproduction is likewise admissible in evidence if the original reproduction is in existence and available for inspection under direction of the court. The introduction of a reproduced record, enlargement or facsimile does not preclude admission of the original.

Rule 1004. ORS 40.565. **Admissibility of other evidence of contents.** The original is not required, and other evidence of the contents of a writing, recording or photograph is admissible when:

(1) **Originals lost or destroyed.** All originals are lost or have been destroyed, unless the proponent lost or destroyed them in bad faith;

(2) **Original not obtainable.** An original cannot be obtained by any available judicial process or procedure;

(3) **Original in possession of opponent.** At a time when an original was under the control of the party against whom offered, that party was put on notice, by the pleadings or otherwise, that the contents would be a subject of proof at the hearing, and the party does not produce the original at the hearing; or

(4) **Collateral matters.** The writing, recording or photograph is not closely related to a controlling issue.

Rule 1005. ORS 40.570. **Public records.** The contents of an official record or of a document authorized to be recorded or filed and actually recorded or filed, including data compilations in any form, if otherwise admissible, may be proved by copy, certified as correct in accordance with Rule 902 (ORS 40.510) or testified to be correct by a witness who has compared it with the original. If such a copy cannot be obtained by the exercise of reasonable diligence, then other evidence of the contents may be given.

Rule 1006. ORS 40.575. **Summaries.** The contents of voluminous writings, recordings or photographs which cannot conveniently be examined in court may be presented in the form of a chart, summary or calculation. The originals, or duplicates, shall be made available for examination or copying, or both, by other parties at a reasonable time and place. The court may order that they be produced in court.

Rule 1007. ORS 40.580. **Testimony or written admission of party.** Contents of writings, recordings or photographs may be proved by the testimony or deposition of the party against whom offered or by the party's written admission, without accounting for the nonproduction of the original.

Rule 1008. ORS 40.585. **Functions of court and jury.** When the admissibility of other evidence of contents of writings, recordings or photographs under Rules 1001 to 1008 (ORS 40.550 to 40.585) depends upon the fulfillment of a condition of fact, the question whether the condition has been fulfilled is ordinarily for the court to determine in accordance with Rule 104 (ORS 40.030). However, the issue is for the trier of fact to determine as in the case of other issues of fact when the issue raised is:

(1)   Whether the asserted writing ever existed;
(2)   Whether another writing, recording or photograph produced at the trial is the original; or
(3)   Whether the other evidence of contents correctly reflects the contents.

ARTICLE I

GENERAL PROVISIONS

RULE 100.* ORS 40.010. SHORT TITLE

Rules 100 to 1008 (ORS 40.010 to 40.585 and 41.415) shall be known and may be cited as the Oregon Evidence Code.

LEGISLATIVE COMMENTARY

Oregon Rule of Evidence 100 gives the title of this evidence code. It is based on Rule 1103 of the Federal Rules of Evidence.

TEXT

Rules 100 to 1008 are officially designated as the Oregon Evidence Code. They do not, however, constitute a complete codification of all Oregon law relating to evidence. It will still be necessary to refer to Oregon statutes, case law, the Oregon Rules of Civil Procedure, the federal and state constitutions, and the Code of Professional Responsibility.

The Code took effect January 1, 1982, and applies to all actions, cases, and proceedings then pending "except to the extent that application would not be feasible or would work injustice, in which event former evidential principles shall apply." 1981 Or. Laws ch 892 § 101.

---

*Section 100, Ch 892, 1981 Or Sess Laws provides: "Captions and headings. The article and section headings or captions included in this Act [the Oregon Evidence Code] are used only for convenience in locating or explaining provisions of this Act and are not intended to be part of the statutory law of the State of Oregon." However, the captions and headings are included in this text for the convenience of the reader.

RULE 101.   ORS 40.015. APPLICABILITY OF OREGON EVIDENCE CODE

(1) [Courts.] The Oregon Evidence Code applies to all courts in this state except for:
  (a) The small claims division of the Oregon Tax Court as provided by ORS 305.545;
  (b) The small claims department of a district court as provided by ORS 46.415; and
  (c) The small claims department of a justice's court as provided by ORS 55.080.
(2) [Proceedings generally.] The Oregon Evidence Code applies generally to civil actions, suits and proceedings, criminal actions and proceedings and to contempt proceedings except those in which the court may act summarily.
(3) [Rules of privilege.] Rules 503 to 514 (ORS 40.225 to 40.295) relating to privileges apply at all stages of all actions, suits and proceedings.
(4) [Rules inapplicable.] Rules 100 to 412 (ORS 40.010 to 40.210) and Rules 601 to 1008 (ORS 40.310 to 40.585) do not apply in the following situations:
  (a) The determination of questions of fact preliminary to admissibility of evidence when the issue is to be determined by the court under Rule 104 (ORS 40.030).
  (b) Proceedings before grand juries, except as required by ORS 132.320.
  (c) Proceedings for extradition, except as required by ORS 133.743 to 133.857.
  (d) Sentencing proceedings, except proceedings under ORS 163.150 or as required by ORS 137.090.
  (e) Proceedings to revoke probation, except as required by ORS 137.090.
  (f) Issuance of warrants of arrest, bench warrants or search warrants.
  (g) Proceedings under ORS chapter 135 relating to conditional release, security release, release on personal recognizance, or preliminary hearings, subject to ORS 135.173.
  (h) Proceedings to determine proper disposition of a child in accordance with ORS 419B.325(2) and 419C.400(3).
  (i) Proceedings under ORS 813.210 to 813.230, 813.250 and 813.255 to determine whether a driving while under the influence of intoxicants diversion agreement should be allowed or terminated.

LEGISLATIVE COMMENTARY

Oregon Rule of Evidence 101 describes the courts and types of proceedings to which the Oregon Evidence Code applies. Subsection (1) is based on Rule 101 of the Federal Rules of Evidence, which declares that the federal rules apply in federal courts and before federal magistrates. Subsections (2) through (4) are based on Rule 1101 of the Federal Rules of Evidence, which creates certain exceptions to the scope of the federal rules. As the exceptions to the application of the Oregon Evidence Code are less complex, they have been combined in this rule for clearer organization.

Subsection (1). This subsection indicates that the Oregon Evidence Code generally applies to all courts of Oregon. Put differently: any court over which the Supreme Court has general administrative and supervisory authority under ORS 1.002 is a court to which the rules of evidence apply. However, the Legislative Assembly does not intend to repeal or limit the effect of statutes which provide for certain divisions or departments of courts to conduct proceedings without regard to the technical rules of evidence. Appropriate exception is therefore made for the small claims division of a district court under ORS 46.415, the small claims division of the Tax Court under ORS 305.545, and the small claims department of a justice court under ORS 55.050. These may continue to conduct informal hearings and dispositions of actions as provided for in those statutes.

Currently, the rules of evidence except those of privilege do not apply to administrative agencies in contested cases. ORS 183.450. Nothing in ORE 101 should be construed to alter present Oregon practice under the administrative procedures statutes.

Subsection (2). This subsection states the general principle that, except as otherwise provided, the rules of evidence apply to all actions, suits and proceedings conducted in a court of justice. Contempt is punishable summarily when it is committed in the immediate view and presence of the court. ORS 33.030. The circumstances that suspend application of the rules of evidence in this situation are not present, however, in other cases of criminal contempt. Subsection (2) is subject to the qualifications expressed in the succeeding subsections.

While the Oregon Evidence Code applies to all proceedings, it is not a compendium of all the rules of evidence that apply to proceedings. A number of evidential issues are not addressed, and many others are treated in a general fashion. These are left for judicial lawmaking.

Subsection (3). This subsection is made necessary by the limited applicability of the remaining rules of the Evidence Code. The privilege rules themselves, of course, contain internal exceptions and recognize other exceptions under other statutes. The Legislative Assembly recognizes that a particular privilege may, therefore, not apply in a given proceeding.

Subsection (4). Subsection (4) indicates particular proceedings in which the non-privilege rules of evidence do *not* apply. The Legislative Assembly does not intend this subsection as an expression of when due process or other constitutional considerations require an evidential hearing.

Paragraph (a). This paragraph restates the provisions of the second sentence of Rule 104(1), relating to preliminary questions. It is inserted here for convenience.

Paragraph (b). This paragraph is intended to deal with what evidence can be admitted in grand jury proceedings, not with what amount of admitted evidence is necessary to support an indictment. ORS 132.320 states that a grand jury may receive only evidence that would be admissible at trial except for certain experts' reports and affidavits from unavailable witnesses. The Oregon Supreme Court has held that the statute is admonitory only, and the fact that a grand jury may have been prejudiced by hearsay evidence not allowed under the statute is not grounds for dismissing or quashing an indictment. *State v. McDonald,* 231 Or 24, 361 P2d 1001 (1961). The Legislative Assembly disapproves this case law. It intends that the statute means what it says.

It should be noted that ORS 132.320 does not say that the Oregon Evidence Code applies in its entirety to grand jury proceedings. The Legislative Assembly specifically rejected an amendment to this effect. Thus, only the substantive rules of admissibility of evidence apply. Other rules of evidence do not.

Paragraph (c). Extradition proceedings are covered in detail by statute. ORS 133.743 to 133.857. As they are essentially administrative in character, and as the question of the guilt or innocence of the accused is not an issue, application of the formal rules of evidence would be inappropriate and impracticable.

Paragraph (d). This paragraph exempts sentencing from the rules of evidence and directs attention instead to the statute that specifically governs sentencing procedure. ORS 137.090. Early case law based upon the statute would imply that the state can prove any aggravating circumstance by unsworn statements. *Coffman v. Gladden,* 229 Or 99, 366 P2d 171 (1961). This case was decided before the institution of presentence reports. Since then, ORS 137.090 has been interpreted as requiring the sentencing court to take the testimony of witnesses when considering any aggravating information that is not contained in the presentence report, if the defendant requests. *State v. Collins,* 43 Or App 265 (1979); *State v. Brown,* 44 Or App 597 (1980). A remaining issue is whether witnesses who are sworn are restricted to giving testimony subject to the rules of evidence. *State v. McKinney,* 7 Or App 248, 489 P2d 976 (1971). As an investigator can put hearsay evidence in a presentence report, *State v. Scott,* 237 Or 390, 390 P2d 328 (1964), it seems pointless to prevent a witness under oath from saying the same thing. However, it can be argued that a trained probation officer is able to eliminate untrustworthy hearsay and bring to the court's attention only hearsay that is reliable and valuable for its legitimate use. The Legislative Assembly considers judges capable of determining the reliability of hearsay evidence, and agrees that it is pointless to assign different values to the same hearsay depending upon the manner in which it is presented to the court.

Paragraph (e). A probation revocation proceeding consists of an adjudicatory and a dispositional phase. This paragraph does not mandate the application of the Oregon Evidence Code to either, although the Legislative Assembly recognizes that due process may require the application of certain rules in the adjudicatory phase. *Gagnon v. Scarpelli,* 441 US 778, 782 n5, 786, 93 SCt 1756, 36 LEd2d 656 (1973) (use of hearsay to sustain finding of violation impermissible in certain circumstances); *United States v. Segal,* 549 F2d 1293 (9th Cir), cert. denied 431 US 919, 97 SCt 2187, 53 LEd 2d 231 (1977). The dispositional phase of a revocation proceeding is conceptually no different from sentencing with respect to the presentation of aggravating or mitigating circumstances. Therefore, the limitations of ORS 137.090 should apply here. See Rule 101(4)(d), supra.

Paragraph (f). Warrants of arrest and search warrants are issued upon complaint or affidavit showing probable cause. ORS 133.110, 133.545 and 133.555. The nature of the proceedings makes application of the rules of evidence inappropriate and impracticable.

Paragraph (g). Proceedings under ORS chapter 135 relating to conditional release, security release or release on personal recognizance do not call for application of the rules of evidence.

Federal Rule 1101(d)(3) exempts preliminary examinations from the rules of evidence, as do the majority of state evidence codes patterned after the federal rules. Oregon follows suit in principle, but its practice will be much stricter. The Legislative Assembly exempted preliminary hearings from the Oregon Evidence Code "subject to § 88b of this Act." This new statute, which follows the American Law Institute's Model Code of Pre-Arraignment Procedure (Tent. Draft No. 5, April 25, 1972), in effect restores all of the Evidence Code with the exception of the rule against hearsay, and even that only upon showing of good cause. The result is considerably stricter than the federal practice. Although the preliminary hearing is not a criminal prosecution of the accused, but only a judicial inquiry to determine whether there is probable cause to believe that a crime has been committed and that the defendant committed it, it is a formal proceeding that must be held in accordance with procedures established by law. ORS 135.070 to 135.225 now grant the accused an array of protections, including the right to counsel, the right to subpoena witnesses, the right to cross-examine witnesses and the right to make or waive the making of a statement. A general application of the rules of evidence is consistent with the spirit and intent of those statutes. The Legislative Assembly also understands that evidential rules are already applied in most preliminary hearings in Oregon, and wishes the practice to continue.

Paragraph (h). The Legislative Assembly deleted the Advisory Committee's blanket exemption of juvenile departments from courts to which the Oregon Evidence Code applies. Rule 101(1). The Legislative Assembly believes that the Code should apply in the adjudicatory phase of a juvenile court proceeding, whether for delinquency or dependency. However, it added paragraph (h) to subsection (4) of Rule 101 to clarify that during the dispositional phase of a juvenile court proceeding, evidence may be admitted in accordance with ORS 419.500(2). This statute allows the receipt of materials relating to the child's mental, physical and social history and prognosis without regard to their competency or relevancy under the rules of evidence.

TEXT

Rule 101(1) provides that the code applies to all courts in this state with the exception of specified departments or divisions authorized to hear small claims proceedings. The code applies to appellate courts as well as trial courts, and certain rules are of particular importance upon appeal. See Rule 103(1) and Rule 201(f). Justice courts are covered subject to the exception stated in Rule 101(l)(c).

Rule 101 does not make the code applicable to administrative proceedings, although ORS 183.450 adopts the rules of privilege and establishes other minimum evidentiary standards for contested case administrative hearings. In *Zurita v. Canby Nursery*, 115 Or App 330, 334, 838 P2d 625 (1992), rev denied 315 Or 443, 847 P2d 410 (1993), the court held that under ORS 656.283(7) workers' compensation hearings are not governed by the rules of evidence.

Rule 101(2) makes clear that the code applies to all types of court proceedings, except summary contempt hearings and the proceedings listed in Rule 101(4). No general distinctions are drawn between civil and criminal cases, although certain rules have applicability to only one type of proceeding (see, e.g., Rules 308, 309 and 412), and other rules create differing procedural consequences depending on whether the case is civil or criminal (see, e.g., Rule 201 (g)).

Rule 101(3) establishes that the privilege rules contained in Article V have broader applicability than the other rules in the code. They are not subject to the exceptions of Rule 101(4). They apply in pretrial and posttrial proceedings, including depositions and grand jury proceedings.

Preliminary Questions Regarding the Admissibility of Evidence

Rule 101(4) exempts certain proceedings from the rules of evidence with the exception of the rules of privilege. Rule 101(4)(a) exempts any hearing by a judge to determine the qualifications of a person to be a witness, the existence of a privilege or any other issue affecting the admissibility of evidence. This exemption is restated in Rule 104(1). Thus suppression hearings are exempt from the rules of evidence except rules of privilege. *State v. Wright*, 315 Or 124, 129, 843 P2d 436 (1992). See Marsh, *Does Evidence Law Matter in Criminal Suppression Hearings?*, 25 Loy L A L Rev 987 (1992).

In *United States v. Boyce*, 797 F2d 691 (8th Cir 1986), the court, relying upon *United States v. Raddatz*, 447 US 667, 100 SCt 2406, 65 LEd2d 424 (1980), reaffirmed traditional doctrine that the Confrontation Clause is not violated when the government relies upon hearsay evidence at suppression hearings, because the right to confront witnesses does not apply to the same extent as at trial.

Grand Jury Proceedings

Rule 101(4)(b) provides that the rules of evidence are not applicable to grand jury proceedings except to the extent required by ORS 132.320. This statute provides in relevant part:

(1) Except as provided in subsections (2) and (3) of this section, in the investigation of a charge for the purpose of indictment, the grand jury shall receive no other evidence than such as might be given on the trial of the person charged with the crime in question.

(2) A report or a copy of a report made by a physicist, chemist, medical examiner, physician, firearms identification expert, examiner of questioned

documents, fingerprint technician, or an expert or technician in some comparable scientific or professional field, concerning the results of an examination, comparison or test performed by such person in connection with the case which is the subject of a grand jury proceeding, shall, when certified by such person as a report made by such person or as a true copy thereof, be received in evidence in the grand jury proceeding.

(3) An affidavit of a witness who is unable to appear before the grand jury shall be received in evidence in the grand jury proceeding if, upon application by the district attorney, the presiding judge of the circuit court of the county in which the grand jury is sitting authorizes such receipt after good cause has been shown for the witness' inability to appear. ...

In *State v. McDonald,* 231 Or 24, 34, 361 P2d 1001, 1006 (1961), cert. denied 370 US 903 (1962), the Oregon Supreme Court held that this statute is "admonitory in character only, not mandatory, advising the grand jury to disregard incompetent evidence in returning an indictment and to consider evidence only of such character that it may be used in the trial to support a conviction of the accused." The Commentary to Rule 101(4)(b) states: "The Legislative Assembly disapproves this case law. It intends that the statute means what it says."

It is unclear what effect this remark in the Commentary should have considering that: the Commentary was not adopted by the entire legislature, ORS 132.320 has never been amended to overrule *State v. MacDonald,* and the evidence code otherwise exempts grand jury proceedings from the rules of evidence. Perhaps the most significant question is not whether ORS 132.320 is *admonitory* or *mandatory,* but whether the receipt of inadmissible evidence by a grand jury would constitute a sufficient basis for dismissing an indictment or reversing a conviction.

Rule 103(1) provides that error may not be predicated upon a ruling that admits or excludes evidence unless a substantial right of the party is affected. It would be difficult to conclude that the legislature intended every instance of inadmissible evidence received by a grand jury—but not by a trial jury—to be reversible error. Arguably, if the rules of evidence are to be applied to grand jury proceedings, the standard of Rule 103(1) should also be applied. Nothing in the language of ORS 132.320, in its legislative history or in the Commentary to Rule 101(4)(b), suggests that this statute was intended to overturn the principle that evidentiary error must be shown to be prejudicial before it will be grounds for reversal or dismissal.

The Supreme Court addressed this issue in *State v. Stout,* 305 Or 34, 747 P2d 1174 (1988), where the court held that an indictment need not be quashed even if it was based in part on inadmissible hearsay evidence. The court noted that ORS 135.510 specifies the grounds for setting aside a grand jury indictment. The court has consistently held that the grounds listed in this statute are exclusive, and they do not include the admission of hearsay evidence. Therefore, the court held there is no statutory basis for setting aside a grand jury indictment based on the admission of hearsay evidence. The court also noted that an indictment cannot be set aside on the ground of insufficient evidence. The court suggested that there might be some "irregularities" sufficient to justify setting aside an indictment, even though they are not listed in the statute, but that admission of hearsay evidence is not among them.

In *State v. Dike,* 91 Or App 542, 756 P2d 657 (1988), the Court of Appeals held that an indictment could not be set aside on the ground that the prosecutor improperly asked the defendant about his "sexual preference." See generally Westling, *Use of Hearsay Testimony Before Oregon Grand Juries,* 62 Or L Rev 505 (1983); Note, *The Prosecutory Unnecessary Use of Hearsay Evidence Before the Grand Jury,* 61 Wash U L Q 191 (1983).

See generally ANNOT., *Grand Jury: Admission of Hearsay Evidence Incompetent at Trial as Affecting, in Absence of Statutory Regulation, Validity of Indictment or Conviction,* 37 ALR3d 612 (1971); ANNOT., *Validity of Indictment Where Grand Jury Heard Incompetent Witness,* 39 ALR3d 1064 (1971).

Sentencing Hearings—Generally

Rule 101(4)(b) establishes that sentencing hearings are not subject to the rules of evidence. However, ORS 137.090 provides:

(1) In determining aggravation or mitigation, the court shall consider:
    (a) Any evidence received during the proceeding;
    (b) The presentence report, where one is available; and
    (c) Any other evidence relevant to aggravation or mitigation that the court finds trustworthy and reliable.
(2) When a witness is so sick or infirm as to be unable to attend, the deposition of the witness may be taken out of court at such time and place, and upon such notice to the adverse party, and before such person authorized to take depositions, as the court directs.

In *State v. Deck,* 84 Or App 725, 735 P2d 637 (1987), a majority of the Court of Appeals held that the hearsay bar applies to testimony of witnesses in a sentencing hearing about circumstances that are put forward to justify aggravation of punishment, where the testimony implicates the defendant in criminal activity for which he has never been charged or tried. In this case, the victim of sexual abuse by the defendant testified in aggravation at the sentencing hearing that defendant's daughter told her that she (the daughter) had also been abused by the defendant. The sentence was vacated and the case remanded for resentencing. *Deck* implicitly rejects the suggestion in the Legislative Commentary that hearsay is admissible when related under oath by a witness at the sentencing hearing.

In a specially concurring opinion in *Deck,* four judges expressed the view that the hearsay rules do not apply to bar all hearsay testimony in sentencing proceedings. However, the concurring judges found the hearsay testimony in this case to violate defendant's right of confrontation under the state and federal constitutions.

Other courts have also indicated that constitutional restrictions may apply to evidence offered by the prosecution at sentencing hearings. See *United States v. Fatico,* 441 F Supp 1285, 1289 (EDNY 1977), rev'd on other grounds 579 F2d 707

(2nd Cir 1978): "[A]lthough the Rules of Evidence may be ignored in sentencing proceedings, the Constitution may not be." In a subsequent decision, the same court held that if the prosecutor intends to have the court consider at sentencing facts that may substantially enhance the sentence, such facts must be proven by "clear, unequivocal and convincing evidence." *United States v. Fatico (Fatico II)*, 458 F Supp 388, 408 (EDNY 1978), aff'd 603 F2d 1053 (2nd Cir 1979), cert denied 444 US 1073 (1980). See also *United States v. Weston*, 448 F2d 626, 634 (9th Cir 1971); *State v. Brown*, 44 Or App 597, 602 n4, 606 P2d 678 (1980) ("we have reservations about the propriety of allowing a prosecutor in a summary sentencing proceeding to put on a case implicating a defendant in serious criminal activity for which the defendant has never been charged or tried").

In *State v. Swartzendruber*, 120 Or App 552, 558, 853 P2d 842 (1993), the court held that evidence that has been illegally seized under Article I, section 9 may not be considered in a sentencing hearing.

Capital Sentencing Hearings

Rule 101(4)(d) was amended by the 1995 Legislature to make the Evidence Code generally applicable to capital sentencing hearings under ORS 163.150.

The Supreme Court had previously applied the relevance standard of OEC 401 to capital sentencing hearings. See *State v. Stevens*, 319 Or 573, 580, 879 P2d 162, 165 (1994).

For a discussion of the cases applying the relevancy standard in capital sentencing hearings, see Text after Rule 401, infra.

See generally Silverstein, *Confrontation at Capital Sentencing Hearings: Illinois Violates the Federal Constitution by Permitting Juries to Sentence Defendants to Death on the Basis of Ordinarily Inadmissible Hearsay*, 22 Loy U Chi L J 65 (1991).

Preliminary Hearings

Rule 101(4)(g) purports to exempt preliminary hearings from the evidentiary requirements of the code, just as FRE 1101 exempts preliminary hearings from the Federal Rules of Evidence. However, ORS 135.173 provides as follows:

> The Oregon Evidence Code shall apply in any preliminary hearing under this chapter, except that hearsay may be admitted if the court determines that it would impose an unreasonable hardship on one of the parties or on a witness to require that the primary source of the evidence be produced at the hearing, and if the witness furnishes information bearing on the informant's reliability and, as far as possible, the means by which the information was obtained.

This statute raises serious problems of interpretation. It is unclear what type of hardship on a party or a witness is contemplated by the statute. The reference to "informant" is ambiguous. Presumably, it means the declarant who made the hearsay statement regardless of whether or not that person is a regular police informant. The statute does not expressly allow exemption from the rules of evidence other than the hearsay rule, even though other evidentiary requirements could impose an unreasonable hardship upon the prosecutor in some cases.

The 1981 Oregon Legislature also amended ORS 135.185 to add the following additional sentence:

> When hearsay evidence was admitted at the preliminary hearing, the magistrate, in determining the existence of probable cause, shall consider (a) the extent to which the hearsay quality of the evidence affects the weight it should be given, and (b) the likelihood of evidence other than hearsay being available at trial to provide the information furnished by hearsay at the preliminary hearing.

This provision should be contrasted with Federal Rule of Criminal Procedure 5.1(a), which declares: "The finding of probable cause may be based upon hearsay evidence in whole or in part."

Miscellaneous Proceedings

Proceedings for extradition, issuance of warrants of arrest, bench warrants or search warrants, proceedings relating to conditional release, security release, or release on personal recognizance are all excluded from the rules of evidence by Rule 101(4). These proceedings are regulated in detail by statute.

In *State v. Fink,* 79 Or App 590, 720 P2d 372, rev denied 302 Or 36, 726 P2d 935 (1986), the court held that the results of a polygraph examination could be considered in evaluating the credibility of an informant, noting that the Evidence Code does not apply to the issuance of search warrants.

The adjudicatory phase of a probation revocation hearing is also excluded from the rules of evidence by Rule 101(4)(e). As the Commentary notes, the Constitution may require that more than hearsay evidence be offered. *Gagnon v. Scarpelli,* 411 US 778, 93 SCt 1756, 36 LEd2d 656 (1973). The dispositional phase of a probation revocation proceeding is comparable to a sentencing hearing and is governed by ORS 137.090. See generally ANNOT., *Admissibility of Hearsay Evidence in Probation Revocation Hearings,* 11 ALR4th 999 (1982).

The adjudicatory phase of a juvenile proceeding under ORS Chapter 419 is subject to the rules of evidence (see Rule 101(1) and (2)), although the dispositional phase is exempted by Rule 101(4)(h) and ORS 419B.325(2).

In *State v. Hovies,* 320 Or 414, 418, 887 P2d 347, 349 (1994), the court held (1) that the Oregon Evidence Code applies to the trial of traffic infractions and (2) that it was error to refuse to allow the defendant the right of cross-examination.

In *State ex rel Juvenile Dept v. Beasley,* 314 Or 444, 449, 840 P2d 78 (1992), the court reaffirmed that the Oregon Evidence Code applies to a proceeding to terminate parental rights.

RULE 102.   ORS 40.020. PURPOSE AND CONSTRUCTION

The Oregon Evidence Code shall be construed to secure fairness in administration, elimination of unjustifiable expense and delay, and promotion of growth and development of the law of evidence to the end that the truth may be ascertained and proceedings justly determined.

LEGISLATIVE COMMENTARY

Oregon Rule of Evidence 102 declares the purpose and proper approach to the construction of the Oregon Evidence Code. It is based on Rule 102 of the Federal Rules of Evidence. ORE 102 replaces ORS 41.020, a more general description of the law of evidence.

TEXT

Rule 102 sets forth a rule of construction to guide the courts in interpreting the code. It represents a legislative mandate that the rules be interpreted in a manner that will (1) secure fairness in administration, (2) eliminate unjustifiable expense and delay, and (3) promote growth and development of evidence law in a manner that will facilitate the ascertainment of truth and the just determination of proceedings.

The rule is virtually identical to FRE 102. According to Professor Edward Cleary, the reporter to the Federal Rules Advisory Committee, Federal Rule 102 is intended to allow "expansion by analogy to cover new or unanticipated situations." *Proposed Rules of Evidence: Hearings Before the Subcommittee on Criminal Justice of the House Committee on the Judiciary,* 93d Cong, 1st Sess 4 (Supp 1973).

Rule 102 is intended to deter an overly rigid or technical construction of the rules and encourage an interpretation that keeps pace with technological advances and changing times. Rule 102 should be considered in applying rules where broad discretion is vested in the trial judge, such as Rules 403, 404(3), 601, 609, 701, 702, 803(26), 804(3)(f), 901, and 1003. The discretion of trial judges is significantly expanded by the new code. Rule 102 is intended to guide the exercise of that discretion. See *State v. Douglas,* 292 Or 516, 542 n42, 641 P2d 561 (1982) (Rule 102 cited in dissenting opinion).

RULE 103.   ORS 40.025. RULINGS ON EVIDENCE

(1) **[Effect of erroneous ruling.] Evidential error is not presumed to be prejudicial. Error may not be predicated upon a ruling which admits or excludes evidence unless a substantial right of the party is affected, and:**

(a) [Objection.] In case the ruling is one admitting evidence, a timely objection or motion to strike appears of record, stating the specific ground of objection, if the specific ground was not apparent from the context; or

(b) [Offer of proof.] In case the ruling is one excluding evidence, the substance of the evidence was made known to the court by offer or was apparent from the context within which questions were asked.

(2) [Record of offer and ruling.] The court may add any other or further statement which shows the character of the evidence, the form in which it was offered, the objection made and the ruling thereon. It may direct the making of an offer in question and answer form.

(3) [Hearing of jury.] In jury cases, proceedings shall be conducted, to the extent practicable, so as to prevent inadmissible evidence from being suggested to the jury by any means, such as making statements or offers of proof or asking questions in the hearing of the jury.

(4) [Plain error.] Nothing in this rule precludes taking notice of plain errors affecting substantial rights although they were not brought to the attention of the court.

LEGISLATIVE COMMENTARY

Oregon Rule of Evidence 103 is identical to Rule 103 of the Federal Rules of Evidence. By enacting this rule the Legislative Assembly does not intend to change current Oregon practice with regard to rulings on evidence, with one exception.

Subsection (1). Under subsection (1), rulings on evidence cannot be assigned as error unless a substantial right is affected, and the nature of the error was called to the attention of the trial judge to alert the court to the proper course of action and enable opposing counsel to take proper corrective measures. The objection and the offer of proof are the techniques for accomplishing these ends.

Subsection (1) abolishes the rule established by the Oregon Supreme Court in civil cases, and suggested for criminal cases, that erroneously admitted evidence is deemed prejudicial unless the contrary is affirmatively shown. *Meyer v. Harvey Aluminum,* 263 Or 487, 495, 501 P2d 795 (1972); *Elam v. Soares,* 282 Or 93, 102–103, 577 P2d 1336 (1978); see *State v. McLean,* 255 Or 464, 473–480, 468 P2d 521 (1970). The Legislative Assembly intends that no presumption regarding evidential error operate in favor of either party in the appeal of a civil case. The Legislative Assembly approves the suggestion in *Elam v. Soares,* supra, that the concepts of "presumptions" and "burdens" as used in the trial of cases are not appropriate for application in the appellate process. 282 Or at 103.

Subsection (1) does not otherwise change the law in Oregon with respect to harmless error. Section 3 of Article VII (Amended) of the Oregon Constitution requires the appellate courts of this state to affirm, notwithstanding any evidential error committed by the trial court, if there is (1) substantial and convincing evidence of guilt, in a criminal case, and (2) little if any likelihood that the error affected the verdict. *State v. Naylor,* 291 Or 191, 629 P2d 1308 (1981); *State v. Van Hooser,* 266 Or 19, 511 P2d 359 (1972). Subsection (1) of the rule is also in accord with current ORS 19.125, 131.035, and 138.230. Under these statutes, a ruling of a trial court must be not only erroneous but prejudicial to warrant reversal. *Edwards, Guardian v. Hovet,* 185 Or 284, 200 P2d 955 (1949); *Kuffel v. Reiser,* 268 Or 152, 519 P2d 365 (1974).

Paragraph (a). This paragraph restates the Oregon rule that if counsel wishes to raise an error of the trial court on appeal the court must be so advised by offer, objection, motion or other appropriate action so it may avoid the error. *Frangos v. Edmunds,* 179 Or 577, 173 P2d 596 (1946).

Paragraph (b). Paragraph (b) is consistent with the present requirement that in making an offer of proof, counsel should be distinct and clear. An offer of proof should embody the pertinent facts in such terms as to be understood and ruled upon in the intended sense by the trial judge, and examined and applied in the proper light by any reviewing court. *Downey v. Traveler's Inn,* 243 Or 206, 412 P2d 359 (1966).

Subsection (2). Under subsection (2), a true and complete record of what occurred in the trial court must be reproduced for the appellate court. The second sentence of this subsection is meant to resolve doubts about what testimony a witness would have given, and in nonjury cases, to provide the appellate court with material for possible final disposition of the case in the event it reverses a ruling that excluded evidence. The subsection is couched in discretionary language because of the practical impossibility of stating a satisfactory rule in mandatory terms.

Subsection (3). To the extent practicable, evidence that is excluded must be prevented from coming to the attention of the jury. For example, questions on which an offer of proof is based should not be asked in the presence of the jury. This subsection is consistent with the holding in *State v. Jordan,* 146 Or 504, 26 P2d 558 (1933), affirmed 146 Or 504, 30 P2d 751, that doubtful questions of evidence or procedure should not be proposed or discussed in the jury's presence, and that the court should exclude the jury while hearing preliminary testimony on the question of admissibility of evidence.

Subsection (4). In this subsection the Legislative Assembly reaffirms the plain error principle, which allows the courts to act when the adversary system breaks down. Subsection (4) qualifies subsection (1) of this rule, particularly with regard to a ruling admitting evidence when no timely objection or motion to strike appears in the record. Subsection (4) does not change the Oregon rule that a question not raised and preserved in the trial court will not be considered upon appeal unless, upon examination of the entire record, the reviewing court finds that the error is manifest and that the ends of justice will not otherwise be satisfied. *State v. Hickmann,* 21 Or App 303, 540 P2d 1406 (1975).

TEXT

RULE 103(1)
Error Affecting "Substantial Right"

Rule 103(1) establishes that not all evidentiary error is prejudicial error. In order to be grounds for reversal, the error must (1) affect a substantial right of a party and (2) be properly preserved in the record. Evidentiary error that does not affect a substantial right of a party is usually referred to as harmless error.

The standard for prejudicial error stated in Rule 103(1) is similar to that already recognized under Oregon law:

> No judgment shall be reversed or modified except for error substantially affecting the rights of a party. (ORS 19.125(2))

> No departure from the form or mode prescribed by law, error or mistake in any criminal pleading, action or proceeding renders it invalid, unless it has prejudiced the defendant in respect to a substantial right. (ORS 131.035)

> The court shall, in every stage of an action, disregard any error or defect in the pleadings or proceedings which does not affect the substantial rights of the adverse party. (ORCP 12B)

> After hearing the appeal, the court shall give judgment, without regard to the decision of questions which were in the discretion of the court below or to technical errors, defects or exceptions which do not affect the substantial rights of the parties. (ORS 138.230)

In determining whether the substantial rights of a party have been violated, the courts have traditionally focused upon the probable effect of the error upon the verdict reached. See *State v. Cahill,* 208 Or 538, 293 P2d 169, aff'd per curiam 298 P2d 214, cert denied 352 US 895 (1956); *State v. McCready,* 31 Or App 591, 571 P2d 160 (1977). But see *State v. Wederski,* 230 Or 57, 62, 368 P2d 393, 395 (1962): "If the only way defendants can be assured fair trials is for appellate courts to reverse an occasional judgment in the face of what well may be overwhelming evidence of guilt, then that is the course we must take."

An outcome-oriented focus may be required by section 3 of amended Article 11 of the Oregon Constitution, which provides: "If the supreme court shall be of opinion, after consideration of all the matters thus submitted, that the judgment of the court appealed from was such as should have been rendered in the case, such judgment shall be affirmed notwithstanding any error committed during the trial ...." See Lusk, *Forty-Five Years of Article VII, § 3, Constitution of Oregon,* 35 Or L Rev 1 (1955).

It is arguable that a substantial right could be violated under Rule 103(1) without affecting the outcome of the trial, at least if the error undermined the fundamental fairness of the proceeding. However, one commentator states that the legislative history of the federal rule, upon which the Oregon rule is based, suggests that such an interpretation was not contemplated. See 1 J. Weinstein &

M. Berger, WEINSTEIN'S EVIDENCE, (1988) § 103[06] (hereinafter cited as *Weinstein's Evidence*).

On the question of defining harmless error, see generally Berger, *When, If Ever, Does Evidentiary Error Constitute Reversible Error?*, 25 Loy L A L Rev 893 (1992); Leonard, *Appellate Review of Evidentiary Rulings*, 70 N C L Rev 1155 (1992); Saltzburg, *The Harm of Harmless Error*, 59 Va L Rev 988 (1973); R. Traynor, *The Riddle of Harmless Error* (1970); Teitelbaum, Sutton-Barbere & Johnson, *Evaluating the Prejudicial Effect of Evidence: Can Judges Identify the Impact of Improper Evidence on Juries?*, 1983 Wis L Rev 1147; Note, *What's the Harm in Harmless Error*, 81 Ky L J 257 (1992–3); ANNOT., *Error in Evidentiary Ruling in Federal Civil Case as Harmless or Prejudicial under Rule 103(a), Federal Rules of Evidence*, 84 ALR Fed 28 (1987).

Evidentiary Error Not to Be Presumed

The rule provides that evidentiary error is not presumed to be prejudicial, contrary to prior appellate decisions. See *Meyer v. Harvey Aluminum,* 263 Or 487, 495, 501 P2d 795, 798–9 (1972). The legislature adopted the view of the concurring opinion in *Elam v. Soares,* 282 Or 93, 106, 577 P2d 1336 (1978) (Howell, J., concurring), which stated:

> I acknowledge that this court on several occasions has stated that error occurring during the trial is "presumed" or "deemed" to be prejudicial upon appeal. I believe that such error should not be presumed to be either prejudicial or harmless. Our function should be to determine (1) whether error was committed and (2) if so, does the error require reversal. That decision should be made without any presumptions.

For cases applying the rule that evidential error is not presumed to be prejudicial, see *Van Gordon v. Portland General Electric Co.,* 294 Or 761, 662 P2d 714 (1983); *Credit Alliance v. Amhoist Credit,* 74 Or App 257, 268, 702 P2d 1121 (1985).

An appellant should be careful to designate the relevant portions of the trial record that demonstrate not only the evidentiary error but why it was prejudicial. A respondent claiming that any prejudice resulting from evidentiary error was cured by other developments in the trial must designate the relevant portions of the record to support such a contention. *King City Realty, Inc. v. Sunpace Corp.,* 291 Or 573, 583, 633 P2d 784, 790 (1981).

The effect of Rule 103(1) in criminal cases is made less certain by the fact that the Commentary provides that "[t]he Legislative Assembly intends that no presumption regarding evidential error operate in favor of either party in the appeal of a *civil* case." (Emphasis added.) Precode cases followed a different rule in criminal cases. See *State v. Evans,* 290 Or 707, 716, 625 P2d 1300, 1304 (1981) ("It may be that all errors in criminal cases are presumed to be prejudicial, with the result that error cannot be said to be 'harmless' unless any such presumption is overcome."); *State v. Bishop,* 7 Or App 558, 492 P2d 509 (1972). However, the language of the rule applies to criminal cases as well as civil, and it is doubtful that a different standard was intended for criminal cases involving merely evidentiary error. Constitutional error sometimes gives rise to a presumption of prejudice. See *State v. Halford*, 101 Or App 660, 663, 792 P2d 467 (1990) (evidence that a defendant has refused to testify has a "presumably harmful effect," quoting *State v. Wederski*, 230 Or 57, 60, 368 P2d 393 (1962)); *State v. Gefre*, 137 Or App 77, 84, 903 P2d 386 (1995).

Constitutional Error

A distinction must be drawn between constitutional error and nonconstitutional evidentiary error. In a criminal case, if the error is a violation of the Federal Constitution, it must be shown to be harmless beyond a reasonable doubt before a conviction may be affirmed. *Chapman v. California*, 386 US 18, 87 SCt 824, 17 LEd2d 705 (1967); *State v. Stilling*, 285 Or 293, 590 P2d 1223, cert denied 444 US 880 (1979). The Oregon Supreme Court has stated that other errors in criminal cases will be found harmless if there is "(1) substantial and convincing evidence of guilt ... and (2) little if any likelihood that the error affected the verdict." *State v. Carr*, 302 Or 20, 725 P2d 1287 (1986). See also *State v. Langley*, 314 Or 247, 839 P2d 692 (1992), decision adhered to on reconsideration 314 Or 511, 840 P2d 691 (1993); *State v. Mains*, 295 Or 640, 663, 669 P2d 1112, 1126 (1983), quoting *State v. Van Hooser*, 266 Or 19, 25–6, 511 P2d 359, 363 (1973).

Court Trials

Although the rules of evidence apply to the same extent in court trials as in jury trials, appellate courts are much less likely to find evidentiary error to violate the "substantial right" of a party or to be grounds for reversal in a court trial. See *Ruble Forest Products, Inc. v. Lancer Mobile Homes of Oregon, Inc.*, 269 Or 315, 524 P2d 1204 (1974). It will generally be presumed that the trial court disregarded inadmissible evidence and relied only on competent evidence unless it reasonably appears from the record that incompetent evidence influenced the trial court in its decision. *Thomas v. Howser*, 262 Or 351, 497 P2d 1163 (1972). But see *Hurt v. Cupp*, 5 Or App 89, 92, 482 P2d 759, 761 (1971) ("[C]ontrary presumption when a judge obtains prejudicial information by his affirmative extrajudicial action taken in the absence and without the knowledge of the parties").

In *State v. Collins*, 68 Or App 101, 680 P2d 713, rev denied 297 Or 458, 683 P2d 1372 (1984), the trial court admitted evidence that defendant had committed a previous sexual assault on a child. The appellate court refused to find reversible error, even assuming the evidence should not have been received, because the case was tried to the court and it did not appear from the record that the incompetent evidence had influenced the trial court in its decision.

Examples of Harmless Error

Evidentiary error may be found to be harmless in a variety of circumstances. In *Bremner v. Charles*, 123 Or App 95, 104, 859 P2d 1148, 1154–5

(1993), rev denied 318 Or 381, 870 P2d 221 (1994), the court stated that as a general rule, the exclusion of evidence will not constitute reversible error if the jury has been given substantially the same information as was contained in the offer of proof. However, prejudice may be found in cases such as this one where the testimony of an easily impeachable witness is allowed while the substantially similar testimony of a less assailable witness is excluded.

In *State v. Walton*, 311 Or 223, 231, 809 P2d 81 (1991), the court held that any error in admitting defendant's pre-*Miranda* statements was harmless beyond a reasonable doubt, satisfying the federal constitutional standard. Any error was also harmless under OEC 103(1) and the Oregon Constitution, Article VII, section 3, because there was convincing evidence of defendant's guilt in the record as a whole, and little, if any, likelihood that this error affected the jury's verdict.

In *Travis v. Unruh,* 66 Or App 562, 674 P2d 1192, rev denied 297 Or 82, 679 P2d 1367 (1984), the court found the error of allowing an expert to summarize a study in a medical journal to be harmless. Even though hearsay, the evidence was cumulative of other testimony.

In *Wohlers v. Ruegger,* 58 Or App 537, 649 P2d 602 (1982), the court held that allowing the plaintiff's witness to be improperly impeached by a prior complaint not written by that witness could not have "materially affected the substantial rights" of the plaintiff. The prior complaint was a complaint in negligence against both the plaintiff and defendant in the present action. The allegations could have prejudiced the plaintiff only if the jury had found the plaintiff to be contributorily negligent, which it had not on the verdict form.

In *Angus v. Joseph,* 60 Or App 546, 655 P2d 208 (1982), rev denied 294 Or 569, 660 P2d 683 (1983), the court refused to find prejudicial error in the admission of certain documents because "there was substantial evidence to uphold the trial judge's findings of fact even without consideration of the evidence objected to ...."

Exclusion of evidence on an inappropriate ground will generally be considered harmless error if it should have been excluded on some other ground. In *Ledbetter v. Complete Abrasive Blasting Systems,* 76 Or App 10, 13–4, 707 P2d 1292, 1294 (1985), the court stated: "We will not ordinarily reverse a trial court for sustaining an objection if there was any ground on which that objection could have been sustained."

Similarly, an appellate court generally will not reverse a trial court when it makes a "correct ruling admitting evidence but articulates an erroneous reason for it." *State v. Nielsen,* 316 Or 611, 629, 853 P2d 256 (1993). See also *Carlson v. Piper Aircraft Corp.,* 57 Or App 695, 705 n12, 646 P2d 43, 49, rev denied 293 Or 801, 653 P2d 999 (1982) ("When it appears from the record that the trial court arrived at a correct result but on grounds different from those which, in our opinion, are more correct, the judgment of the trial court will be affirmed.").

However, there are exceptions where admitting evidence on an incorrect theory can be reversible error. For example, in *State v. Taylor,* 137 Or App 286, 290, 904 P2d 191 (1995), an out-of-court statement was erroneously held admissible under OEC 404. Therefore, there was no basis on which the defendant could ask for a limiting instruction. Even though the evidence might have been admissible on another theory, "the state's nonhearsay argument does not remedy the practical effects of the trial court's error, which allowed the jury to consider the evidence for all purposes."

Examples of Prejudicial Error

Sometimes evidentiary error can be cured at the trial level by an order striking the testimony and instructing the jury to disregard it. However, sometimes such an instruction is insufficient and a mistrial is required. In *State ex rel Adult and Family Services v. McCollam,* 58 Or App 433, 648 P2d 1331 (1982), quoting *State v. Jones,* 279 Or 55, 566 P2d 867 (1977), the court stated: "There may, however, be cases in which the testimony which the jury is instructed to 'disregard' is so prejudicial that, as a practical matter, 'the bell once rung, cannot be unrung' by such admonishment."

In *State v. Hubbard,* 297 Or 789, 800, 688 P2d 1311, 1319 (1984), the court stated: "We ... hold that a decision to exclude evidence relevant to bias or interest which is error, is reversible if it denies the jury an adequate opportunity to assess the credibility of a witness whose credibility is important to the outcome of the trial."

In *State v. Isom,* 306 Or 587, 761 P2d 524 (1988), the defendant in an aggravated murder prosecution was impeached with statements he made to police after having been given *Miranda* warnings and after he told the officers he did not wish to talk to them and that he wanted a lawyer. The court held this error affected a substantial right of the defendant.

Form of Objection

Rule 103(1) requires that before a ruling admitting evidence can be challenged, a specific and timely objection of record must have been made. Generally, neither the mere statement of an objection without specification of grounds nor general objections, such as "incompetent, irrelevant and immaterial," will satisfy the requirements of Rule 103(1). See *Simpson v. Sisters of Charity of Providence,* 284 Or 547, 566, 588 P2d 4 (1978).

In the absence of exceptional circumstances, appellate courts will refuse to hear arguments for exclusion of evidence that were not made to the trial court. *State v. Cole,* 244 Or 455, 458, 418 P2d 844 (1966). Thus, a party normally will not be allowed to challenge on appeal a trial court ruling admitting evidence if an incorrect ground of objection was stated, even though the evidence should have been excluded on some other ground. See *United States v. Fox,* 613 F2d 99 (5th Cir 1980) (objection as to relevancy inadequate to preserve objection on ground of hearsay).

In *Koberstein v. Sierra Glass Co.,* 65 Or App 409, 411, 671 P2d 1190, 1192 (1983), modified 66 Or App 883, 675 P2d 1126, rev denied 297 Or 83, 679 P2d 1367 (1984), the court stated:

Plaintiffs objection did not apprise the court of the grounds for the objection. "The prevailing rule is that an objection, general in terms, if overruled, cannot avail the objector on appeal." *Smith v. Oregon Agricultural Trucking Ass'n*, 272 Or 156, 159–60, 535 P2d 1371 (1975). Although there are exceptions to this rule, none applies here.

The objection should be made only to the portion of the evidence that is inadmissible. In *State v. Madison*, 290 Or 573, 580, 624 P2d 599 (1981), the court held that an "objection to evidence as a whole is insufficient when any part of the evidence objected to is admissible." In *Brown v. J.C. Penney Co.*, 297 Or 695, 688 P2d 811 (1984), the court stated: "One who objects to an exhibit on the ground that it is not to be received because it contains irrelevant matter must object to those specific parts, and an objection to the entire exhibit, if it contains relevant matter, will 'avail nothing on appeal.'" Accord *State v. Sims*, 105 Or App 318, 320, 804 P2d 1205, rev denied 311 Or 433, 812 P2d 828 (1991).

In *State v. Keller*, 315 Or 273, 283, 844 P2d 195 (1993), the court held that an objection is "timely" if it is made as soon as its applicability to the offered evidence is known to the objecting party. However, an objection need not necessarily be made to the first question in a series of foundation questions, because in such case the court may have no basis properly to assess admissibility.

A party is generally allowed to make a "continuing" objection to a category of evidence rather than repeating the objection each time additional evidence of the same type is offered. If the initial objection was overruled erroneously, the error is preserved with respect to all the evidence of the same category that was erroneously admitted. *Noteboom v. Savin*, 213 Or 583, 589, 322 P2d 916 (1958). However, if the initial objection was correctly overruled, and the subsequent evidence is of a different type or there is a different basis for objecting to the subsequent evidence, the claim of error will normally not be considered in the absence of subsequent objection.

It is not essential to cite **authority** in support of an objection in order to preserve the issue for appeal, as long as the nature of the objection is sufficiently specific and clear. See *State v. Hitz*, 307 Or 183, 188, 766 P2d 373 (1988) ("raising an issue at trial ordinarily is essential; identifying a source for a claimed position is less so; making a particular argument is even less so").

Motions In Limine

Neither the Oregon Evidence Code nor the Federal Rules of Evidence address the question of whether an objection can be made to evidence in advance of trial by means of a motion in limine. Such motions are routinely made and were allowed in Oregon under precode case law (see, e.g., *State v. Madison*, 290 Or 573, 624 P2d 599 (1981)). They are expressly permitted in criminal cases under ORS 133.673 in challenging evidence of the prosecution by a motion to suppress. See generally, ANNOT., *Modern Status of Rules As to Use of Motions in Limine or Similar Preliminary Motion to Secure Exclusion of Prejudicial Evidence or Reference to Prejudicial Matters*, 63 ALR3d 311 (1975); COMMENT, *The Use of Motion In Limine in Civil Litigation*, 1977 Ariz St L J 443. Federal courts have been receptive to motions in limine. See, e.g., *United States v. Cook,* 608 F2d 1175, 1186 (9th Cir 1979), cert denied 444 US 1034 (1980):

> There is no need in this case to decide when, during the pretrial proceedings or the trial, a motion in limine should be made, or when it should be ruled upon. The matter should be left to the discretion of the trial court with a reminder that advance planning helps both parties and the court. Trial by ambush may produce good anecdotes for lawyers to exchange at bar conventions, but tends to be counter-productive in terms of judicial economy. Other courts considering the problem have recommended a provisional ruling in advance of proposed testimony, with the judge free to meet any deception by modifying the ruling. (*Reyes v. Missouri Pacific R.R. Co.,* 589 F2d 791 (5th Cir 1979); *Werner v. Upjohn Co.,* 628 F2d 848 (4th Cir 1980), *cert denied* 449 US 1080 (1981).

In *State v. Foster,* 296 Or 174, 674 P2d 587 (1983), the Supreme Court took a receptive view towards motions in limine, at least in cases where they resolve evidentiary issues that might cause prejudice if they were raised at trial. In *Foster,* the prosecution's principal witness was the defendant's accomplice, who had been required to take a polygraph examination as a condition of his plea agreement with the state. Both before trial and during the witness' testimony, the defendant sought trial court rulings that, if the witness were cross-examined about the plea agreement, no testimony about the polygraph examination could be given or elicited on redirect examination. The trial court indicated it was inclined to admit evidence of the polygraph, and therefore the defense attorney did not mention the plea agreement in cross-examination. The Court of Appeals refused to consider the claimed error, commenting that the trial judge "was never actually called upon to make a ruling," because the plea agreement was not mentioned by the defendant. The Supreme Court reversed, finding that the defendant had adequately protected the record. The court stated: "The court's ruling at that point was definite and defense counsel was required to do no more. ... [T]he judge could change his or her mind ... but unless that is done counsel should be entitled to rely on the court's ruling." See also *State v. McClure,* 298 Or 336, 692 P2d 579 (1984) (defendant may challenge a pretrial ruling of the trial court admitting a prior conviction to impeach the defendant if he testifies, even though the defendant does not take the stand at trial).

The Court of Appeals has noted the difficulties that can arise in connection with pretrial motions and rulings on evidentiary matters. In *State v. Browder,* 69 Or App 564, 567, 687 P2d 168 (1984), the court stated:

> A pre-trial ruling on the admissibility of evidence is necessarily more difficult for the trial court, because it lacks a full context on which to base its decision. Although the parties often make elaborate offers of proof, sometimes to the point of essentially presenting their whole case, that remains, in many cases, an awkward and inefficient way to create a context to enable a trial judge to rule on the matter. In most cases, only proffered evidence which carries an *unusual* potential for prejudice should be ruled on before trial. Preferably evidence should be presented and ruled on in the normal course of the

trial rather than within the permissive ambit of an omnibus hearing under ORS 135.037(3).

The pretrial ruling must be sufficiently definite in order to preserve the claim of error on appeal. In *State v. Jackson,* 68 Or App 506, 683 P2d 120, rev denied 297 Or 546, 685 P2d 997, cert denied 469 US 983, 105 SCt 389, 83 LEd2d 323 (1984), the court found that the defendant had not properly preserved for appeal his request to exclude evidence, when the request had been raised in a pretrial hearing and the trial court had not made a definitive ruling, but only given a tentative indication of how it was likely to rule.

When a definitive pretrial ruling is made on the record with respect to a motion to exclude or allow evidence, it should not be necessary for a party to raise the issue again at trial in order to preserve the issue for appeal. However, given the uncertainty in existing appellate case law, the safest course of action would be to renew the motion at trial at least in cases where the issue is likely to be an important assignment of error on appeal.

The federal cases are divided on whether assertion of an objection by pretrial motion alone is sufficient to preserve the issue under Federal Rule 103. Compare *Sheehy v. Southern Pacific Transp. Co.,* 631 F2d 649 (9th Cir 1980) (holding error preserved), with *Collins v. Wayne Corp.,* 621 F2d 777 (5th Cir 1980) (holding error waived). See ANNOT., *Sufficiency in Federal Court of Motion in Limine to Preserve or Appeal Objection to Evidence Absent Contemporary Objection at Trial,* 76 ALR Fed 619 (1986).

Offer of Proof

If the objection is sustained and the proffered evidence is excluded, Rule 103(1) imposes the general requirement that the proponent of the evidence make an offer of proof in order to preserve the claim of error on appeal, except in those cases where the nature of the evidence is apparent from the context.

The purpose of the offer of proof is to allow the appellate court to determine both whether the exclusion of evidence was error and, if so, whether the error affected a substantial right of the appellant. Offers of proof are usually needed only for testimonial evidence because exhibits should be part of the trial court record, even when they are not received into evidence. It can be error to refuse to allow a party to make an offer of proof. *State v. Rodriguez,* 115 Or App 281, 287, 840 P2d 711 (1992).

In numerous cases, the appellate courts have refused to consider assignments of error based upon exclusion of evidence because no offer of proof was made. See, e.g., *State v. Smith,* 319 Or 37, 43, 872 P2d 966 (1994); *State v. Adams,* 296 Or 185, 674 P2d 593 (1983); *State v. Luther,* 296 Or 1, 672 P2d 691 (1983).

In *State v. Busby,* 315 Or 292, 298, 844 P2d 897 (1993), the court refused to consider a constitutional challenge to OEC 609 by a defendant who claimed that the availability of prior conviction impeachment prevented him from taking the stand and presenting his version of the facts. The court refused to consider the challenge because the defendant had not made a proper offer of proof regarding the nature of the testimony he would have presented. Thus the court was unable to determine whether any error was likely to have affected the result of the case.

In *State v. Clowes*, 310 Or 686, 692, 801 P2d 789 (1990), the court held that the trial judge acted within his discretion in requiring defendants to present evidence of their choice-of-evils defense in a pretrial offer of proof. Such an offer of proof allowed the trial judge to determine the relevancy of such evidence.

In *State v. Olmstead*, 310 Or 455, 459–61, 800 P2d 277 (1990), the court held that when the trial court excludes an entire class of evidence by declaring, in advance, that it is inadmissible as a matter of law, no offer of proof is necessary in order to raise the issue on appeal. An offer of proof provides no additional information that bears on the legal question underlying the trial court's ruling.

Offer of Proof on Cross-Examination

In *State v. Affeld*, 307 Or 125, 764 P2d 220 (1988), the Supreme Court, overruling a prior line of cases, held that an offer of proof is required on cross-examination as well as direct examination. The court stated:

> Article VII (Amended), § 3 of the Oregon Constitution requires this court to affirm judgments of lower courts if, in the opinion of this court, the judgment achieved the correct result, even if error was committed. That constitutional provision makes it incumbent on lower courts and the parties appearing in lower courts to ensure that the record reviewed by this court is adequate for this court to make a reasoned decision. A record can be adequate in situations in which the scope of testimony is restricted by the trial court only if an offer of proof is made. There is no reason not to require an offer of proof on cross-examination. The only situations in which an offer of proof is not required are those situations in which an offer of proof is impossible because of a trial court's refusal to allow the offer to be made.

307 Or at 128–129, 764 P2d at 222 (1988).

But in *Schacher v. Dunne*, 109 Or App 607, 610 n1, 820 P2d 865, 867 n1 (1991), rev denied 313 Or 74, 828 P2d 457 (1992), the court held that it is not necessary to make an offer of proof on cross-examination when the substance of the evidence is apparent from the context within which questions were asked.

Form of Offer of Proof

The trial court has discretion to determine the form of an offer of proof. The court may allow counsel to summarize the witness' anticipated testimony or to offer an affidavit or deposition if one is available. *State v. Philips*, 314 Or 460, 466, 840 P2d 666 (1992) (proper to make an offer of proof in question and answer form and also for a party's counsel to state what the proposed evidence is expected to be).

Rule 103(2) provides that the court may require the offer of proof to be made in question and answer form. Rule 103(3) requires that offers of proof generally be made outside the presence of the jury.

The trial court ruling excluding the evidence is likely to be sustained on appeal unless the entire offer is found to be admissible. *Smith v. White,* 231 Or 425, 372 P2d 483 (1962). Therefore, evidence of more questionable admissibility should be omitted or segregated into a separate offer of proof. In *Fazzolari v. Portland School District No. 1J,* 78 Or App 608, 717 P2d 1210 (1986), aff'd 303 Or 1, 734 P2d 1326 (1987), the court held that the plaintiff failed to preserve a claimed error of the trial court's refusal to admit a summary of police reports of criminal activity. The court stated: "[P]laintiff attacks the exclusion of an exhibit which concededly contains some irrelevant material. In this circumstance, plaintiff had the burden of excising the irrelevant portions of the exhibit to preserve the claimed error."

Some cases have required that the grounds for admissibility be stated to the trial court before they will be considered on appeal, even though such a requirement goes beyond the language of the rule. In *Simpson v. Simpson,* 83 Or App 86, 730 P2d 592 (1986), rev denied 303 Or 454, 737 P2d 1248 (1987), the court held: "When a court excludes evidence as irrelevant for the reason asserted by the objecting party, the proponent of the evidence may not complain on appeal, unless he has informed the trial court of its relevance." See also *Huff v. White Motor Corp.,* 609 F2d 286, 290 n2 (7th Cir 1979).

RULE 103(2)
Court's Assistance in Making Record

Rule 103(2) imposes a general obligation upon trial courts to participate in making a full record for purposes of appeal. It is obviously of considerable assistance to appellate courts when trial courts (1) indicate any additional factors not immediately apparent from the record concerning the character or form of the evidence that might bear on its admissibility; (2) make clear the particular objection upon which they are ruling; (3) state the precise nature and scope of their ruling; (4) ensure that any offer of proof is in a form that will enable the reviewing court to determine whether a substantial right of the appellant was affected. If these procedures are followed, it should enable the reviewing court in a non-jury case to make a final disposition of the matter without the necessity of a remand.

RULE 103(3)
Avoiding Exposing Jury to Inadmissible Evidence

Rule 103(3) requires that inadmissible evidence should not be suggested to the jury by any means. The policy adopted in this rule is of sufficient importance that it is also addressed in two other rules. See Rules 104(3) and 513(2).

Inadmissible evidence may be suggested to the jury by a wide variety of means, including offers of proof, questions to prospective jurors and witnesses that reveal the existence of improper evidence, placing of exhibits where they can be seen by jurors prior to their admission, making arguments to the court regarding the admissibility of evidence, or by comments of attorneys in their opening statements or closing arguments. Also, witnesses may sometimes blurt out inadmissible evidence that is not responsive to the question posed.

Ethical prohibitions against bringing inadmissible evidence to the attention of the jury are contained in the Code of Professional Responsibility. Disciplinary Rule 7-106(C) provides:

> In appearing in his professional capacity before a tribunal, a lawyer shall not:
>
> 1. State or allude to any matter that he has no reasonable basis to believe is relevant to the case or that will not be supported by admissible evidence.
>
> 2. Ask any question that he has no reasonable basis to believe is relevant to the case and that is intended to degrade a witness or other person.
>
> 3. Assert his personal knowledge of the facts in issue, except when testifying as a witness.
>
> 4. Assert his personal opinion as to the justness of a cause, as to the credibility of a witness, as to the culpability of a civil litigant, or as to the guilt or innocence of an accused. ...
>
> ...
>
> 7. Intentionally or habitually violate any established rule of procedure or of evidence.

RULE 103(4)
Plain Error Doctrine

Rule 103(4) incorporates the plain error doctrine, which in exceptional circumstances allows evidentiary error to be considered as a basis for a new trial or reversal on appeal despite the absence of objection at trial. Under this doctrine, unpreserved error may be considered when the appellate court "upon examination of the entire record, can say that the error is manifest and that the ends of justice will not otherwise be satisfied." *State v. Avent,* 209 Or 181, 183, 302 P2d 549 (1956). See also *State v. Abel,* 241 Or 465, 406 P2d 902 (1965); *State v. Kessler,* 289 Or 359, 371 n17, 614 P2d 94 (1980).

The plain error doctrine is recognized primarily in criminal cases. It is more likely to be applied to the erroneous admission of evidence than to an erroneous exclusion, because of the likely absence of a sufficient record to review the latter type of error. See generally Campbell, *Extent to Which Courts of Review Will Consider Questions Not Properly Raised and Preserved—Part 1,* 7 Wis L Rev 91 (1932); Vestal, *Sua Sponte Consideration in Appellate Review,* 27 Fordham L Rev 477 (1958–9); Note, *Raising New Issues on Appeal,* 64 Harv L Rev 652 (1951).

In *State v. Woodfield,* 62 Or App 69, 659 P2d 1006, rev denied 295 Or 259, 668 P2d 381 (1983), the court held that it was not plain error for the trial court to fail to give, sua sponte, an instruction on the unreliability of eyewitness identification. In *State v. Berry,* 76 Or App 1, 707 P2d 638 (1985), the court rejected the defendant's contention that an evidentiary ruling by the trial court was plain error under this rule.

However, in *State v. Jenkins,* 63 Or App 858, 666 P2d 869 (1983), the court found plain error where the prosecutor attempted to impeach the unrepresented defendant with prior convictions that clearly were not admissible under Rule 609. Even though the defendant had not moved for a mistrial, the court held that the trial court should have granted a mistrial on its own motion. In *State v. Mains,* 295 Or 640, 669 P2d 1112 (1983), the court found plain error in comments made by the trial judge in the questioning of a witness, although the error was held to be harmless on the facts of this case.

Invited Error

If the error was invited by the conduct of the appellant, it is unlikely to be a sufficient basis for reversal. See *Hall v. Banta,* 283 Or 387, 583 P2d 1139 (1978) (answer "solicited" by complaining party); *United States v. Lerma,* 657 F2d 786 (5th Cir 1981) (error invited by cross-examination). A party cannot introduce evidence in the trial court and then on appeal claim error in the admission of such evidence. *Kentner v. Gulf Insurance Co.,* 298 Or 69, 73, 689 P2d 955 (1984); *City of Salem v. Cannon,* 235 Or 463, 385 P2d 740 (1963). Also a party cannot claim error on appeal with respect to evidence introduced by an opponent when the party later offers the same evidence himself for an independent reason. *State v. Brown,* 299 Or 143, 699 P2d 1122 (1985).

RULE 104.   ORS 40.030. PRELIMINARY QUESTIONS

(1) **[Questions of admissibility generally.] Preliminary questions concerning the qualification of a person to be a witness, the existence of a privilege or the admissibility of evidence shall be determined by the court, subject to the provisions of subsection (2) of this section. In making its determination the court is not bound by the rules of evidence except those with respect to privileges.**

(2) **[Relevancy conditioned on fact.] When the relevancy of evidence depends upon the fulfillment of a condition of fact, the court shall admit it upon, or subject to, the introduction of evidence sufficient to support a finding of the fulfillment of the condition.**

(3) **[Hearing of jury.] Hearings on the admissibility of confessions shall in all cases be conducted out of the hearing of the jury. Hearings on other preliminary matters shall be so conducted when the interests of justice require or, when an accused is a witness, if the accused so requests.**

(4) **[Testimony by accused.] The accused does not, by testifying upon a preliminary matter, become subject to cross-examination as to other issues in the case.**

(5) **[Weight and credibility.] This section does not limit the right of a party to introduce before the jury evidence relevant to weight or credibility.**

LEGISLATIVE COMMENTARY

Oregon Rule of Evidence 104 outlines the respective roles of court and jury in deciding preliminary questions. The rule tracks the language of Rule 104 of the Federal Rules of Evidence. The Legislative Assembly intends that its adoption not change prevailing Oregon law on preliminary questions of admissibility.

Subsection (1). This subsection assigns to the trial judge the responsibility for making certain preliminary determinations regarding qualifications, privilege and admissibility. Is the alleged expert a qualified physician? Was a stranger present during a conversation between attorney and client? Is a witness whose former testimony is offered unavailable? In each instance, the admissibility of evidence will turn on the answer to the question.

To the extent that these preliminary inquiries are factual, the judge will necessarily receive evidence and act as a trier of fact. The subsection provides that in doing so the judge is not bound by the rules of evidence, except those relating to privilege. Preliminary questions may also call for an evaluation of evidence in terms of a legal standard. When a hearsay statement is offered as a declaration against interest, for example, a decision must be made whether it possesses the required against-interest characteristics. The judge is to make these decisions as well.

Subsection (1) is consistent with ORCP 59B and ORS 136.310, which provide that the court shall decide "all questions of law, including the admissibility of testimony, [and] the facts preliminary to such admission. ..." The subsection has general application, but must be read as subject to subsections (2) and (3) of this rule.

Subsection (2). Subsection (2) recognizes that in some situations the relevance of an item of evidence depends upon the existence of a particular preliminary fact. Thus, when an oral statement is relied upon to prove notice to X, it is without probative value unless X heard it. If a letter purporting to be from Y is relied upon to establish an admission by Y, it has no probative value unless Y wrote or authorized it. Relevancy in this sense has been labeled "conditional relevancy." Morgan, *Basic Problems of Evidence* 45–46 (1962). Problems arising in connection with it are to be distinguished from problems of logical relevancy treated under Rule 401.

If preliminary questions of conditional relevancy were determined solely by the judge, as provided in subsection (1), the functioning of the jury as a trier of fact would be greatly restricted and in some cases virtually destroyed. These are appropriate questions for juries. The accepted treatment, provided in the rule, is the treatment generally given to questions of fact. The judge makes a preliminary determination whether the foundation evidence is sufficient to support a finding of fulfillment of the condition. If so, the item is admitted. If, after all the evidence on the issue is in, the jury could not reasonably conclude that fulfillment of the condition is established, the judge withdraws the matter from the jury's consideration.

Subsection (2) is consistent with the holding of *Menefee v. Blitz,* 181 Or 100, 179 P2d 550 (1947), which indicates that when the relevance of an item of evidence depends upon the submission of preliminary proof in the form of a foundation, or condition precedent, the party offering the dependent testimony must submit the preliminary proof or establish the condition precedent before the dependent fact can be deemed admissible.

Subsection (3). Under subsection (3), preliminary hearings on the admissibility of confessions must be conducted outside the hearing of the jury. This is in accord with *State v. Jordan,* 145 Or 504, 26 P2d 558 (1933) and *State v. Brewton,* 238 Or 590, 395 P2d 874 (1964). Whether other preliminary matters should be so heard must be left to the discretion of the trial judge, to act as the interests of justice require. Frequently, evidence which is relevant to the fulfillment of a condition precedent to admissibility is also relevant to weight or credibility, and time is saved by taking foundation proof in the presence of the jury. Much evidence on preliminary questions, although not relevant to jury issues, may be heard by the jury with no adverse effect.

When an accused is a witness as to a preliminary matter, the accused has the right to be heard outside the jury's presence upon the accused's request. Regard for the right of an accused not to testify generally in a case dictates that the accused be given this option.

Subsection (4). Subsection (4) imposes a limit on cross-examination to encourage an accused to participate in the determination of preliminary matters. The accused may testify in such matters without exposure to cross-examination generally. The limitation is necessary because of the scope of cross-examination permitted under ORE 611. The subsection does not address the question of subsequent use of testimony given by an accused at a hearing on a preliminary matter.

Subsection (5). Subsection (5) declares that nothing contained in the first four subsections of this rule should be construed to limit the right of a party to introduce before the jury evidence relevant to weight or credibility. This is consistent with § 6 of Article I of the Oregon Constitution, with ORS 41.900(16) and with the holding in *State v. Estabrook,* 162 Or 476, 91 P2d 838 (1939). Although the Legislative Assembly repeals ORS 41.900, it retains the substantive legal principles of that section in the several rules of the Oregon Evidence Code.

TEXT

RULE 104(1)
Preliminary Questions

Rule 104(1) generally allocates the determination of preliminary questions affecting the admissibility of evidence to the court, subject to Rule 104(2), which allocates the ultimate determination of certain questions to the jury. Questions of law are exclusively for the court. Most preliminary questions of fact affecting the admissibility of evidence are also determined by the court under Rule 104(1), generally by a preponderance of the evidence standard. See *State v. Pinnell,* 311 Or 98, 114, 806 P2d 110, 120 (1991) (preponderance standard applies in determining unavailability of a hearsay declarant).

Examples of preliminary questions that are determined by the court include whether a witness qualifies as an expert, see OEC 702; whether an original writing is unavailable so that secondary evidence may be admitted, see OEC

1004; whether hearsay fits an exception, see OEC 803; whether a hearsay declarant is unavailable, see OEC 804(1); the applicability of a privilege, see *State v. Langley*, 314 Or 247, 263–4, 839 P2d 692 (1992); and whether a statement is an adoptive admission, see *State v. Carlson*, 311 Or 201, 211, 808 P2d 1002 (1991).

Suppression hearings or hearings on motions in limine are additional examples of proceedings under OEC 104(1) where a preliminary question, such as the legality of a search, determines the admissibility of evidence.

Evidence Rules Generally Inapplicable

In making its determination of a preliminary question affecting the admissibility of evidence, the court may receive evidence from both the proponent and opponent. OEC 104(1) provides that the court is not bound by the rules of evidence, except the rules of privilege, in making its determination. Of necessity, the court often must consider the evidence itself in determining the preliminary question affecting its admissibility. As the Advisory Committee's note to FRE 104(a) states:

> This view is reinforced by practical necessity in certain situations. An item, offered and objected to, may itself be considered in ruling on admissibility, though not yet admitted in evidence. Thus the content of an asserted declaration against interest must be considered in ruling whether it is against interest. Again, common practice calls for considering the testimony of a witness, particularly a child, in determining competency.

Suppression hearings fall within OEC 104(1) and are exempt from the rules of evidence other than the privilege rules. *State v. Wright*, 315 Or 124, 129, 843 P2d 436 (1992). However, courts may apply the rules of evidence by analogy. See Marsh, *Does Evidence Law Matter in Criminal Suppression Hearings?*, 25 Loy L A L Rev 987 (1992). Cases interpreting the identical language of FRE 104 have held that federal suppression hearings are not subject to the Federal Rules of Evidence. *United States v. Killebrew*, 594 F2d 1103 (6th Cir), cert denied 442 US 933 (1979); *United States v. Barnes*, 604 F2d 121 (2nd Cir 1979), cert denied 446 US 907 (1980).

See generally, Bridge, *Burdens Within Burdens at a Trial Within a Trial*, 23 B C L Rev 927 (1982); Imwinkelried, *Judge Versus Jury: Who Should Decide Questions Of Preliminary Facts Conditioning the Admissibility of Scientific Evidence?* 25 Wm & Mary L Rev 577 (1984); ANNOT., *Admissibility of Hearsay Evidence for Court's Determination, Under Rule 104(a) of the Federal Rules of Evidence, of Preliminary Question of Fact*, 39 ALR Fed 720 (1978).

RULE 104(2)
Conditional Relevancy

Rule 104(2) recognizes that the jury plays a role in determining questions of conditional relevancy. Conditional relevancy means a situation where evidence is relevant only if another fact is proven. For example, the relevance of a letter purportedly written by a party will depend upon a finding that the letter was actually written by that party. The relevance of a contract signed by a purported agent will depend upon a finding that that person was in fact an agent. Under Rule 104(2), the ultimate determination of authenticity and agency in the above examples is made by the jury. The court's role is limited to determining whether there is sufficient evidence to support a finding by the jury that the condition of fact has been fulfilled. If sufficient evidence is offered to support a jury finding of authenticity or agency, the letter or contract would be admissible, whether or not the trial judge is personally persuaded by the proof of authenticity or agency.

If the court concludes that a reasonable jury could not find that the condition of fact has been proven, e.g., agency or authenticity, the court should exclude the evidence. In all other cases, except where fulfillment of the condition is proven as a matter of law, the court should instruct the jury to decide whether the preliminary fact has been established and to disregard the evidence if the jury finds the preliminary fact has not been proven. See *Preliminary Draft of Proposed Federal Rules of Evidence for United States Courts and Magistrates,* 46 FRD 161, 186–7 (March 1969).

The rationale underlying Rule 104(2) is that the judge should not be allowed to invade the jury's role as ultimate fact finder by the process of ruling on the admissibility of evidence. If a particular piece of evidence were kept from the jury because the judge was not persuaded that it was authentic, even though there was sufficient evidence to support a jury finding of authenticity, the right to a jury trial would be infringed.

Advance proof of fulfillment of a condition of fact is not necessarily a prerequisite for the introduction of conditionally relevant evidence. Rule 104(2) expressly provides that such evidence may be received subject to later introduction of evidence sufficient to support a finding of fulfillment of the condition. For example, a court may admit a contract purportedly signed by an agent subject to later proof that the person was in fact an agent. Courts may require the proponent of the evidence to provide a good faith assurance that the necessary evidence exists and will be offered later in the trial. Courts may then admit such evidence conditionally subject to being connected up later in the trial. If proof of fulfillment of the condition is not subsequently offered, the opponent should move to strike the evidence.

Rule 104(2) should be considered in conjunction with several other rules that address the same issue in specific contexts. Rule 602 provides that before a witness may testify, a court must find only sufficient evidence to support a finding that the witness has personal knowledge, leaving the ultimate determination of the witness' knowledge up to the jury. Rule 901 provides that a proponent of evidence must offer only sufficient proof to support a jury finding of authenticity, with the ultimate determination of authenticity being left to the jury. Rule 1008 provides that while most questions involving the fulfillment of a condition of fact arising under Article X are for the court, the following issues are expressly reserved for the trier of fact: "(1) Whether the asserted writing ever existed; (2) Whether another writing, recording or photograph produced at the trial is the original; or (3) Whether the other evidence of contents correctly reflects the contents."

See generally Nance, *Conditional Relevancy Reinterpreted*, 70 BU L Rev 447 (1990); Allen, *Myth of Conditional Relevancy*, 25 Loy L A L Rev 871 (1992).

RULE 104(3)
Hearing Outside Jury's Presence

Rule 104(3) provides that hearings on preliminary matters must be conducted outside the presence of the jury in three situations: (1) When they involve the admissibility of a confession; (2) When the accused will be a witness and requests that the jury be excluded; and (3) When the interests of justice so require. In all other cases the matter is discretionary with the court, subject to the general guidelines of Rule 103(3) and the specific requirements of Rule 513(2) that an opportunity should generally be provided to make claims of privilege outside the presence of the jury. Except perhaps where the admissibility of a confession is involved, failure of a party to make a request that the jury be excluded will normally waive the objection.

The report of the House Committee on the Judiciary regarding Federal Rule 104(c), which is identical to Rule 104(3), states: "The Committee construes the second sentence of subdivision (c) as applying to civil actions and proceedings as well as to criminal cases, and on this assumption has left the sentence unamended." H R Rep No 650, 93d Cong, 1st Sess 6 (1973). This provision of the Oregon rule should also be construed to apply to civil proceedings.

RULE 104(4)
Testimony by Accused

Rule 104(4) provides that testimony by an accused upon a preliminary matter does not subject him to cross-examination as to other issues in the case. This rule might seem unnecessary for two reasons. First, merely because the defendant has testified regarding a preliminary matter does not necessarily mean that he or she has waived the fifth amendment privilege against self-incrimination as to other matters. See McCormick, McCORMICK'S HANDBOOK OF THE LAW OF EVIDENCE (J. Strong, ed. 4th ed 1992) § 134 (hereinafter McCormick, *Evidence*). Second, Rule 611(2), which controls the scope of cross-examination, generally limits cross-examination to the scope of direct examination. However, Rule 611(2) provides the trial court with discretion to permit cross-examination concerning new matters. Rule 104(4) makes clear that such discretion cannot be exercised against an accused testifying on a preliminary matter.

Rule 104(4) does not restrict the use at trial or other subsequent proceedings of testimony taken at a hearing on a preliminary matter. But see ORS 135.037(4), governing omnibus hearings in criminal cases that provides:

... Except in a prosecution of the defendant for perjury or false swearing, or impeachment of the defendant, no admissions made by the defendant or his attorney at the hearing shall be used against the defendant unless the admissions are reduced to writing and signed by the defendant and his attorney.

See generally *United States v. Salvucci,* 448 US 83, 100 SCt 2547, 65 LEd2d 619 (1980) (whether a criminal defendant's testimony given at a suppression hearing is admissible at trial for impeachment purposes is an open question); *Simmons v. United States,* 390 US 377, 88 SCt 967, 19 LEd2d 1247 (1968); *Harris v. New York,* 401 US 222, 91 SCt 643, 28 LEd2d 1 (1971).

The report of the Senate Committee on the Judiciary regarding FRE 104(d), which is identical to Rule 104(4), states:

This rule is not, however, intended to immunize the accused from cross-examination where, in testifying about a preliminary issue, he injects other issues into the hearing. If he could not be cross-examined about any issues gratuitously raised by him beyond the scope of the preliminary matters, injustice might result. Accordingly, in order to prevent any such unjust result, the committee intends the rule to be construed to provide that the accused may subject himself to cross-examination as to issues raised by his own testimony upon a preliminary matter before a jury.

RULE 104(5)
Weight and Credibility

Rule 104(5) states what is probably implicit. It makes clear that even though a court has ruled evidence to be admissible this in no way restricts an opponent from attacking the credibility of the witness or evidence or attempting to persuade the trier of fact to give little or no weight to the evidence.

Other restrictions may apply, however. The Commentary states that this rule is intended to be consistent with Article I, section 6 of the Oregon Constitution and the holding of *State v. Estabrook,* 162 Or 476, 91 P2d 838 (1939). Article I section 6 provides that "[n]o ... witness ... [shall] be questioned in any Court of Justice touching his religious [sic] belief to affect the weight of his testimony."

State v. Estabrook found reversible error in the cross-examination of a character witness regarding the religious beliefs of that witness. See also Rule 610 (barring impeachment on the basis of religious belief).

RULE 105.   ORS 40.035. LIMITED ADMISSIBILITY

When evidence which is admissible as to one party or for one purpose but not admissible as to another party or for another purpose is admitted, the court, upon request, shall restrict the evidence to its proper scope and instruct the jury accordingly.

LEGISLATIVE COMMENTARY

Oregon Rule of Evidence 105 is identical to Rule 105 of the Federal Rules of Evidence. It permits the admission of evidence for a limited purpose and the instruction of the jury accordingly. The availability and effectiveness of this practice must be taken into consideration in deciding whether to exclude evidence for unfair prejudice under Rule 403. The Legislative Assembly does not intend to imply that limiting or curative instructions are sufficient in all situations, or that Rule 105 limits the authority of a court to order a severance in a multi-defendant case.

This rule is consistent with current Oregon practice. See *State v. Moore,* 180 Or 502, 176 P2d 631 (1947); *Brooks v. Bergholm,* 265 Or 1, 470 P2d 154 (1970); *Cramer v. Mengerhausen,* 275 Or 223, 550 P2d 740 (1976).

TEXT

Limiting Instructions

Rule 105 addresses a recurring dilemma in the law of evidence. When evidence is admissible for one purpose, but not another, to admit the evidence may seriously prejudice the opponent if the jury considers it for the prohibited purpose. Conversely, to exclude the evidence may seriously prejudice the proponent who would be denied the use of the evidence even for the permissible purpose.

In such a situation, a court usually has only three options:

1. Sever the trial of multiple charges, claims or parties. See *State v. Bray,* 55 Or App 694, 639 P2d 702, rev denied 292 Or 825, 648 P2d 849 (1982).
2. Exclude the evidence entirely under Rule 403, if the prejudicial effect of the evidence substantially outweighs its probative value.
3. Allow the evidence to be received subject to a limiting instruction under Rule 105. See *State v. Stevens,* 311 Or 119, 806 P2d 92 (1991) (approving limiting instruction that evidence admissible for one purpose but not another).

A limiting instruction is appropriate in a wide variety of circumstances. There are a number of rules in the code that expressly allow evidence for a limited purpose even though it would not be admissible generally or for another purpose. See, e.g., Rule 404(3) (allowing evidence of prior crimes to show motive, opportunity, intent, etc., but not to show propensity toward criminal conduct); Rule 407 (allowing evidence of subsequent remedial measures to prove ownership, control feasibility of precautionary measures or impeachment, but not to prove negligence or culpable conduct); Rule 411 (allowing evidence of insurance to prove agency, ownership, control or bias or prejudice of a witness, but not to prove negligence or wrongful conduct); Rules 608 and 609 (allowing evidence of bad character for veracity or evidence of prior convictions to impeach a witness' credibility but not to prove a propensity toward criminal conduct); Rule 801(3) (defining out-of-court statements as nonhearsay if offered for purposes other than to prove the truth of the matter asserted).

In deciding whether to admit evidence subject to a limiting instruction under Rule 105 or exclude it entirely under Rule 403, a court should consider the effectiveness of a limiting instruction under the circumstances, the availability of other evidence, the importance of the issue to be proved, the probative value of the evidence, the degree of prejudice to the opponent, the good faith of the proponent, and the importance of the evidentiary policies that could be undermined by allowing the evidence to be received. See 21 C. Wright & K. Graham, FEDERAL PRACTICE AND PROCEDURE (1977) § 5063 at 312–4. See generally, Tanford and Cox, *The Effects of Impeachment Evidence and Limiting Instructions on Individual and Group Decisionmaking,* 12 Law & Human Behavior 477 (1988); Blinka, *Delusion or Despair: The Concept of Limited Admissibility in the Law of Evidence,* 13 Am J Trial Advoc 781 (1989).

Rule 105 requires that counsel specifically request a limiting instruction; failure to do so will generally waive the right to claim error on appeal. Upon receiving an appropriate request, the court is required to give the instruction. The trial court retains the right to give a limiting instruction sua sponte and should do so in appropriate cases, such as where it is necessary to prevent a finding of plain error on appeal. However, courts should be certain that the failure to request a limiting instruction is not a deliberate choice of trial counsel. The attorney may wish to avoid emphasizing the evidence or alerting the jury to its possible prohibited use. The instruction is usually given at the time the evidence is received but may also be given at the conclusion of the trial.

Counsel would be wise to do more than simply request a limiting instruction; its form should be specified. When possible, the limiting instruction should be submitted to the court in writing. If any party objects to the form of the instruction given, a timely and specific exception must be made to preserve the issue for appeal. See ORCP 59H.

A limiting instruction is constitutionally inadequate in at least one circumstance. In *Bruton v. United States,* 391 US 123, 88 SCt 1620, 20 LEd2d 476 (1968), the United States Supreme Court held that a codefendant's confession implicating the defendant could not be introduced in a joint trial, despite a limiting instruction that the confession was to be considered only against the codefendant. If the codefendant does not take the stand and subject himself or herself to cross-examination, the defendant's Sixth Amendment right of confrontation is violated. See generally Gaskins, *Evidentiary Problems in Multiple Defendant Cases: How to Plan For and Deal With Them,* 13 N C Central L J 62 (1981).

RULE 106. ORS 40.040. WHEN PART OF TRANSACTION PROVED, WHOLE ADMISSIBLE

When part of an act, declaration, conversation or writing is given in evidence by one party, the whole on the same subject, where otherwise admissible, may at that time be inquired into by the other; when a letter is read, the answer may at that time be given; and when a detached act, declaration, conversation or writing is given in evidence, any other act, declaration, conversation or writing which is necessary to make it understood may at that time also be given in evidence.

LEGISLATIVE COMMENTARY

Oregon Rule of Evidence 106 states the rule on admissibility of the whole where part of a transaction is proved. It replaces ORS 41.880, which is repealed, with language intended to reflect the actual case-law interpretation of that statute. The text of ORS 41.880 is amended (1) to allow contemporaneous as well as later introduction of the remainder of a writing or event, (2) but only, in either event, if the remaining evidence is otherwise admissible. See *Black v. Nelson,* 246 Or 161, 424 P2d 251 (1967) (remainder excluded as irrelevant), and *Myers v. Cessna Aircraft Corp., et al.,* 275 Or 501, 553 P2d 355 (1976) (remainder excluded as hearsay).

The Legislative Assembly considered but did not adopt Federal Rule of Evidence 106. The federal rule applies only to a "writing or recorded statement." It would exclude the possibility of admitting the remainder of any contemporaneous act, declaration or conversation. This limitation is inconsistent with the broad purpose of the rule, which is one of fairness.

TEXT

Rule of Completeness

Rule 106 is designed to ensure that evidence regarding an act, declaration, conversation, or writing is not presented to the jury out of context. It authorizes the opponent to inquire into the remainder thereof or to offer additional evidence necessary to make the original evidence understood. It is broader than FRE 106 because it covers oral statements and acts as well as writings.

Rule 106 is an amended form of former ORS 41.880 (repealed 1981), which provided:

> When part of an act, declaration, conversation or writing is given in evidence by one party, the whole, on the same subject, may be inquired into by the other; when a letter is read, the answer may be given; and when a detached act, declaration, conversation or writing is given in evidence, any other act, declaration, conversation, or writing which is necessary to make it understood may also be given in evidence.

The most significant change between the rule and the earlier statute is that the rule authorizes the supplementary evidence to be offered contemporaneously. Under the statute, an opponent could offer the supplementary evidence only on cross-examination, as part of his or her own case-in-chief or in rebuttal. Contemporaneous introduction can prevent a misleading impression, which might be difficult to erase, from being created in the minds of the jury.

The rule appears to authorize the supplementary evidence only when offered contemporaneously. However, the Commentary makes clear the intent of the legislature to allow both contemporaneous and later introduction of the supplementary evidence.

The rule modifies the former statute by limiting the supplementary evidence to evidence that is otherwise admissible. Although the requirement that the supplementary evidence be "otherwise admissible" appears to apply only to the first of the three phrases in the rule, the Commentary indicates that the legislature intended this restriction to apply to the entire rule. This qualification means that use of part of a writing to impeach a witness on cross-examination does not automatically make the entire writing admissible on behalf of the party calling the witness. *Black v. Nelson,* 246 Or 161, 164–5, 424 P2d 251 (1967).

In *State v. Middleton,* 295 Or 485, 668 P2d 371 (1983), the defendant offered evidence of a portion of a plea agreement entered into by a prosecution witness. The court held that this did not allow the prosecutor to offer evidence of another portion of the agreement—that the witness was required to take and pass a polygraph examination—because such evidence is generally inadmissible. See also *State v. Charboneau,* 323 Or 38, 49, 913 P2d 308 (1996) (same); *State v. Batty,* 109 Or App 62, 70, 819 P2d 732, 736–7 (1991), rev denied 312 Or 588, 824 P2d 417 (1992) (for supplementary evidence about an act, conversation, or writing to be admissible under Rule 106 there must be an independent basis for admission).

It would seem that the "otherwise admissible" requirement should not apply to evidence offered under Rule 106 to counteract inadmissible evidence introduced by an opponent. See discussion of curative admissibility under Rule 402, infra. Other situations may arise where strict application of the "otherwise admissible" requirement could thwart the purpose of the Rule.

Cross-Examination or Extrinsic Evidence

Rule 106 has two distinct aspects. The first governs situations where an opponent seeks to bring out additional evidence through cross-examination of a witness. If part of an act, declaration, conversation, or writing is discussed in the witness' direct testimony, the rule allows cross-examination upon the whole of the same subject. Rule 106 presumably eliminates any possible argument under Rule 611 that such cross-examination is beyond the scope of direct. An ambiguity is created by the phrase "at that time be inquired into." Did the legislature intend to allow cross-examination on the issue in question prior to the completion of direct examination? The Commentary does not address this issue. In the absence of unusual circumstances that could cause the jury to be misled, cross-examination after direct examination is concluded will be sufficiently contemporaneous to achieve the objective of the rule.

The second aspect of Rule 106 applies when the opponent attempts to offer supplementary evidence by means other than cross-examination. The rule provides: "when a detached act, declaration, conversation or writing is given in evidence, any other act, declaration, conversation or writing which is necessary to make it understood may at that time also be given in evidence." This section of the rule significantly alters the normal order of proof by allowing one party to offer evidence during the presentation of the other party's case. Such a procedure could disrupt the orderly presentation of evidence. In applying this rule, courts are likely to be more receptive to a contemporaneous offer of evidence that consists only of the remainder of a writing or an additional writing than to a proposal by an opponent immediately to call ten witnesses to supplement testimony of a witness regarding a particular conversation.

The key language in this section is the phrase "necessary to make it understood." In many cases it will not be "necessary" for the supplementary evidence to be offered contemporaneously for the jury to understand the original evidence. If there is a significant danger that the jury would be misled by hearing evidence of a writing, act, declaration, or conversation taken out of context the rule authorizes the supplementary evidence to be admitted contemporaneously.

Letters do not appear to be subject to the "necessary to make it understood" qualification of the rule. The rule provides without stated limitation that "when a letter is read, the answer may at that time be given."

Although the rule is directed toward allowing the opponent of the evidence to offer the supplementary evidence necessary for completeness, presumably a court would have discretion, in an appropriate case, to require the proponent to offer a complete version of a writing to avoid the need for contemporaneous supplementary evidence by the opponent. This is the approach taken by FRE 106.

The policy of Rule 106 was previously adopted with respect to depositions by ORS 45.260, which provides:

> If only part of a deposition is offered in evidence by a party, an adverse party may require him to introduce all of it which is relevant to the part introduced and any party may introduce any other parts, so far as admissible under the rules of evidence. When any portion of a deposition is excluded from a case, so much of the adverse examination as relates thereto is excluded also.

This statute was not repealed by the new evidence code and continues to regulate the admission of depositions.

See generally ANNOT., *Requirement Under Rule 106 of Federal Rules of Evidence, That When Writing or Recorded Statement or Part Thereof is Introduced in Evidence, Another Part or Another Writing or Recorded Statement Must Also be Introduced in Evidence*, 75 ALR Fed 892 (1985); COMMENT, *Federal Rule of Evidence 106: A Proposal to Return to the Common Law Doctrine of Completeness*, 62 Notre Dame L Rev 382 (1987).

ARTICLE II
JUDICIAL NOTICE

RULE 201(a). ORS 40.060. SCOPE

Rule 201 (ORS 40.060 to 40.085) governs judicial notice of adjudicative facts. Rule 202 (ORS 40.090) governs judicial notice of law.

LEGISLATIVE COMMENTARY

Oregon Rule of Evidence 201(a) is similar to Rule 201(a) of the Federal Rules of Evidence. However, Federal Rule 201(a) declares that Federal Rule 201 governs only judicial notice of adjudicative facts, while this rule makes it clear that Article II governs both judicial notice of adjudicative facts and judicial notice of law. In addition, the subdivisions of Federal Rule 201 have been separated into several sections to provide for easier understanding and clearer organization.

ORE 201(a), by itself, works no change in Oregon law. Oregon statutes provided for both judicial notice of facts, ORS 41.410, and judicial notice of law, ORS 41.420 to 41.480 and ORS 221.710.

Judicial notice may be taken of all types of law. The only facts that may be noticed under Article II, however, are adjudicative. No rule deals with judicial notice of legislative facts. This limitation is in conformity with Federal Rule 201(a). The reasons for the limitation are found in the commentary following the federal rule, which the Legislative Assembly adopts:

> "The omission of any treatment of legislative facts results from fundamental differences between adjudicative facts and legislative facts. Adjudicative facts are simply the facts of the particular case. Legislative facts, on the other hand, are those which have relevance to legal reasoning and the lawmaking process, whether in the formulation of a legal principle or ruling by a judge or court or in the enactment of a legislative body. The terminology was coined by Professor Kenneth Davis in his article 'An Approach to Problems of

Evidence in the Administrative Process,' in 55 Harv L Rev 364, 404–407 (1942). The following discussion draws extensively upon his writings. In addition, see the same author's 'Judicial Notice,' in 55 Colum L Rev 945 (1955); *Administrative Law Treatise* ch 15 (1958); 'A System of Judicial Notice Based on Fairness and Convenience,' in *Perspective of Law* 69 (1964).

"The usual method of establishing adjudicative facts is through the introduction of evidence, ordinarily consisting of the testimony of witnesses. If particular facts are outside the area of reasonable controversy, this process is dispensed with as unnecessary. A high degree of indisputability is the essential prerequisite.

"Legislative facts are quite different. As Professor Davis says:

"'My opinion is that judge-made law would stop growing if judges, in thinking about questions of law and policy, were forbidden to take into account the facts they believe, as distinguished from facts which are "clearly ... within the domain of the indisputable." Facts most needed in thinking about difficult problems of law and policy have a way of being outside the domain of the clearly indisputable' 'A System of Judicial Notice,' supra at 82.

"An illustration is *Hawkins v. United States*, 358 US 74, 79 SCt 136, 3 LEd 2d 125 (1958), in which the Court refused to discard the common law rule that one spouse could not testify against the other, saying, 'Adverse testimony given in criminal proceedings would, we think, be likely to destroy almost any marriage.' This conclusion has a large intermixture of fact, but the factual aspect is scarcely 'indisputable.' See Hutchins and Slesinger, 'Some Observations on the Law of Evidence—Family Relations,' in 13 Minn L Rev 675 (1929). If the destructive effect of the giving of adverse testimony by a spouse is not indisputable, should the Court have refrained from considering it in the absence of supporting evidence?

"'If the Model Code or the Uniform Rules had been applicable, the Court would have been barred from thinking about the essential factual ingredient of the problems before it, and such a result would be obviously intolerable. What the law needs at its growing points is more, not less, judicial thinking about the factual ingredients of problems of what the law ought to be, and the needed facts are seldom "clearly" indisputable.' 'A System of Judicial Notice,' supra at 83.

"Professor Morgan gave the following description of the methodology of determining domestic law:

"'In determining the content or applicability of a rule of domestic law, the judge is unrestricted in his investigation and conclusion. He may reject the propositions of either party or of both parties. He may consult the sources of pertinent data to which they refer, or he may refuse to do so. He may make an independent search for persuasive data or rest content with what he has or what the parties present ... [T]he parties do no more than to assist; they control no part of the process.' Morgan, 'Judicial Notice,' in 57 Harv L Rev 269, 270–271 (1944).

"This is the view which should govern judicial access to legislative facts. It renders inappropriate any limitation in the form of indisputability, any formal requirements of notice other than those already inherent in affording opportunity to hear and be heard and exchanging briefs, and any requirement of formal findings at any level. It should, however, leave open the possibility of introducing evidence, through regular channels in appropriate situations. See *Borden's Farm Products Co. v. Baldwin*, 293 US 194, 55 SCt 187, 79 LEd 281 (1934), where the cause was remanded for the taking of evidence as to the economic conditions and trade practices underlying the New York Milk Control Law.

"Similar considerations govern the judicial use of nonadjudicative facts in ways other than formulating laws and rules. Thayer described them as a part of the judicial reasoning process.

"'In conducting a process of judicial reasoning, as of other reasoning, not a step can be taken without assuming something which has not been proved; and the capacity to do this with competent judgment and efficiency, is imputed to judges and juries as part of their necessary mental outfit.' Thayer, *Preliminary Treatise on Evidence* 279–280 (1898).

"As Professor Davis points out, 'A System of Judicial Notice,' supra at 73, every case involves the use of hundreds or thousands of non-evidence facts. When a witness in an automobile accident case says 'car,' everyone, judge and jury included, furnishes, from nonevidence sources within himself, the supplementing information that the 'car' is an automobile, not a railroad car, that it is self-propelled, probably by an internal combustion engine, that it may be assumed to have four wheels with pneumatic rubber tires, and so on. The judicial process cannot construct every case from scratch, like Descartes creating a world based on the postulate *Cogito, ergo sum*. These items could not possibly be introduced into evidence, and no one suggests that they be. Nor are they appropriate subjects for any formalized treatment of judicial notice of facts. See Levin and Levy, 'Persuading the Jury with Facts Not in Evidence: The Fiction-Science Spectrum,' in 105 U Pa L Rev 139 (1956).

"Another aspect of what Thayer had in mind is the use of nonevidence facts to appraise or assess the adjudicative facts of the case. Pairs of cases from two jurisdictions illustrate this use and also the difference between non-evidence facts thus used and adjudicative facts. In *People v. Strook*, 347 Ill 460, 179 NE 821 (1932), venue in Cook County had been held not established by testimony that a crime occurred at 7956 South Chicago Avenue, since judicial notice would not be taken that the address was in Chicago. However, the same court subsequently ruled that venue in Cook County was established by testimony that a crime occurred at 8900 South Anthony Avenue, since notice would be taken of the common practice of omitting the name of the city when speaking of local addresses, and the witness was testifying in Chicago. *People v. Pride*, 16 Ill 2d 82, 156 NE 2d 551 (1951). And in *Hughes v. Vestal*, 264 NC 500, 142 SE 2d 361 (1965), the Supreme Court of North Carolina disapproved the trial judge's admission in evidence of a state-published table of automobile stopping distances on the basis of judicial notice, though the court itself had referred to the same table in an earlier case in a 'rhetorical and illustrative' way in determining that the defendant could not have stopped her car in time to avoid striking a child who suddenly appeared in the highway and that a nonsuit was properly granted. *Ennis v. Dupree*, 262 NC 224, 136 SE 2d 702 (1964). See also *Brown v. Hale*, 263 NC 176, 139 SE 2d 210 (1964);

Clayton v. Rimmer, 262 NC 302, 136 SE 2d 562 (1964). It is apparent that this use of non-evidence facts in evaluating the adjudicative facts of the case is not an appropriate subject for a formalized judicial notice treatment.

"In view of these considerations, the regulation of judicial notice of facts by the present rule extends only to adjudicative facts.

"What, then, are 'adjudicative' facts? Davis refers to them as those 'which relate to the parties,' or more fully:

"'When a court or an agency finds facts concerning the immediate parties—who did what, where, when, how, and with what motive or intent—the court or agency is performing an adjudicative function, and the facts are conveniently called adjudicative facts. ...

"'Stated in other terms, the adjudicative facts are those to which the law is applied in the process of adjudication. They are the facts that normally go to the jury in a jury case. They relate to the parties, their activities, their properties, their businesses.' 2 *Administrative Law Treatise* 353."

TEXT

Scope

Rule 201(a) defines the scope of judicial notice under the Oregon Evidence Code. The code governs only judicial notice of adjudicative facts and law. It does not cover judicial notice of legislative facts or nonevidence facts. The fact that the code does not cover these latter two categories does not mean that such facts cannot be noticed, but merely that they are not subject to the limitations and procedures of Rule 201. It is clear that Rule 201 covers "only a small fraction of material usually subsumed under the concept of 'judicial notice.'" 1 *Weinstein's Evidence,* § 201[01] (1988).

To determine the applicability of Rules 201 and 202, it is necessary to distinguish the four concepts included within judicial notice: adjudicative facts, law, legislative facts, and nonevidence facts. These terms are not defined in the code, although descriptions and definitions are contained in the Commentary.

Adjudicative Facts

Adjudicative facts are those facts that would need to be proven by evidence if judicial notice were not taken. As the Commentary states (quoting Professor Davis), legislative facts are "the facts that normally go to the jury in a jury case" and are those facts "to which the law is applied in the process of adjudication."

Professor Davis goes on to describe adjudicative facts as facts that "relate to the parties, their activities, their properties, their businesses." This part of his description is less accurate and potentially misleading. Courts routinely notice facts as "adjudicative" even though they have no unique or special relationship to either the litigants or the dispute. For example, dates, tide tables, phases of the moon, geographical boundaries, and world history are frequent subjects of judicial notice, but can hardly be said to relate to the immediate litigants more than to anyone else.

When judicial notice is taken, the jury is instructed to find the fact and proof need not be offered.

Judicial notice of adjudicative facts can be taken not only by the jury but also by the court, and not only at trial, but also in a pretrial or posttrial proceeding or upon appeal (see Rule 201(f)).

Judicial Notice of Law

If a rule of law rather than a fact is noticed, Rule 202 controls. Judicial notice of the law occurs when the court finds the law applicable to the case in order to instruct the jury or make a ruling. For a discussion of judicial notice of law, see Text after Rule 202, infra.

Legislative Facts

In the course of litigation, at both the trial and appellate levels, it is often necessary for courts to interpret constitutions, statutes, or regulations or to create or modify rules of common law. In order to discharge this most basic judicial function, courts often must consider facts other than the adjudicative facts proved at trial. The facts considered by courts in the course of making legal interpretations and rulings are known as **legislative facts**.

Legislative facts are excluded from Rule 201 because its requirements are too stringent. Many of the facts courts need to consider in developing case law would not meet the indisputability requirement of Rule 201(b). As Professor Davis says:

> My opinion is that judge-made law would stop growing if judges, in thinking about questions of law and policy, were forbidden to take into account the facts they believe, as distinguished from facts which are "clearly ... within the domain of the indisputable." Facts most needed in thinking about difficult problems of law and policy have a way of being outside the domain of the clearly indisputable [citation in Commentary].

See *Ecumenical Ministries of Oregon v. Oregon State Lottery Commission*, 318 Or 551, 558, 871 P2d 106, 110 (1994) (judicial notice of legislative facts is not subject to the Oregon Evidence Code and parties are not entitled as a matter of right to present evidence to demonstrate such facts). Accord *State v. Clowes*, 310 Or 686, 692 n7, 801 P2d 789 (1990).

Judicial notice taken in the opinions of appellate courts is most commonly judicial notice of legislative facts rather than adjudicative facts, although rarely does the court designate the type of notice being taken. See *State v. Brown*, 297 Or 404, 420 n7, 687 P2d 751 (1984) (notice of legislative facts expressly stated). In *Chartrand v. Coos Bay Tavern*, 298 Or 689, 694, 696 P2d 513, 517 (1985), the court cautioned:

In determining the appropriateness of a court's action in taking judicial notice, it must constantly be borne in mind that judicial notice may be employed for a wide variety of purposes. A failure to distinguish between the purposes for which courts take judicial notice of fact creates the danger that someone will assume that once an appellate court has at one time or another taken judicial notice of a fact for one purpose it is a proper subject for notice for a completely different purpose.

Nonevidence Facts

Nonevidence facts are those that are not normally established by proof at trial, because they are reasonably assumed to be known by the trier of fact. Thus the process of a jury considering nonevidence facts is often referred to a "jury notice." Nonevidence facts include the meaning of ordinary words and basic scientific principles, such as the law of gravity. It would be difficult to try a case if lawyers could not assume a basic level of knowledge and experience on the part of jurors to allow them to comprehend and evaluate the evidence formally adduced in the case.

A jury is also expected to be able to draw reasonable inferences from evidence that has been introduced. See *State v. Cervantes*, 319 Or 121, 873 P2d 316 (1994) (even though there was no direct evidence to establish that the charged crime was committed in Coos County, a fact essential to venue, a reasonable jury could draw this inference based on the testimony in the case, including the fact that the case was investigated by the Coos Bay police and the Coos County Crime Victim's Assistance office had contact with the victim in an official capacity).

Usually no instruction is given to the jury to notice nonevidence facts, but a general instruction to draw upon their common experience is sometimes given. See *Rostad v. Portland Ry. Light & Power Co.*, 101 Or 569, 201 P 184 (1921) (instruction that jurors use their experience as people and knowledge of affairs to weigh and analyze the evidence held proper).

See generally Keeton, *Legislative Facts and Similar Things: Deciding Disputed Premise Facts*, 73 Minn L Rev 1 (1988); Fraher, *Adjudicative Facts, Non-Evidence Facts, and Permissible Jury Background Information*, 62 Ind L J 333 (1987); Roberts, *Judicial Notice: An Essay Concerning Human Misunderstanding*, 61 Wash L Rev 1435 (1986); Turner, *Judicial Notice and Federal Rule of Evidence 201—A Rule Ready for Change*, 45 U Pitt L Rev 181 (1983); ANNOT., *What Constitutes "Adjudicative Facts" Within Meaning of Rule 201 of Federal Rules of Evidence, Concerning Judicial Notice of Adjudicative Facts*, 35 ALR Fed 440 (1977).

RULE 201(b). ORS 40.065. KINDS OF FACTS

A judicially noticed fact must be one not subject to reasonable dispute in that it is either:

(1) Generally known within the territorial jurisdiction of the trial court; or

(2) Capable of accurate and ready determination by resort to sources whose accuracy cannot reasonably be questioned.

LEGISLATIVE COMMENTARY

Oregon Rule of Evidence 201(b), based on Rule 201(b) of the Federal Rules of Evidence, provides that a court may only take judicial notice of facts that are not subject to reasonable dispute. The Legislative Assembly adopted a standard of indisputability because judicial proceedings are adversary in nature. Traditional methods of proof, including rebuttal evidence, cross-examination and argument, should only be dispensed with in clear cases.

As Professor Davis says:

"The reason we use trial-type procedure, I think, is that we make the practical judgment on the basis of experience, that taking evidence, subject to cross-examination and rebuttal, is the best way to resolve controversies involving disputes of adjudicative facts, that is, facts pertaining to the parties. The reason we require a determination on the record is that we think fair procedure in resolving disputes of adjudicative facts calls for giving each party a chance to meet in the appropriate fashion for meeting disputed adjudicative facts, including rebuttal evidence, cross-examination, usually confrontation, and argument (either written or oral or both). The key to a fair trial is opportunity to use the appropriate weapons (rebuttal evidence, cross-examination, and argument) to meet adverse materials that come to the tribunal's attention." "A System of Judicial Notice Based on Fairness and Convenience," in *Perspectives of Law* 69, 93 (1964).

Rule 201(b) is consistent with Uniform Rule 9(1) and (2), which limits judicial notice of facts to those "so universally known that they cannot reasonably be the subject of dispute," those "so generally known or of such common notoriety within the territorial jurisdiction of the court, that they cannot be the subject of dispute," and those "capable of immediate and accurate determination by resort to easily accessible sources of indisputable accuracy." The early textbooks mentioned these general categories and then treated in detail such specific topics as facts relating to court personnel and court records and other governmental facts. See, e.g., McCormick, *Evidence* §§ 324–328 (1st ed 1954). The California draftsmen, with a background of detailed statutory regulation of judicial notice, followed a similar pattern. California Evidence Code §§ 451, 452. The Uniform Rules were drafted on the theory that these particular matters are included within the general categories, and therefore need no specific mention. The present rule follows the last approach.

The phrase "propositions of generalized knowledge," found in Uniform Rule 9(1) and (2), does not appear in the present rule. The phrase came from the original Model Code, where, it is believed, it was intended to give some minimum recognition to the right of a judge in the judge's legislative capacity (not acting as trier of fact) to take judicial notice of very limited categories of knowledge. The resulting limitations, however, were unworkable and contrary to existing practice. What was left to be noticed judicially was a "proposition of generalized knowledge" that was also an "adjudicative fact." The concept lacks practical significance. While judges take judicial notice of "propositions of generalized knowledge" in a variety of situations—for example, when they determine the validity and meaning of statutes, or formulate common law rules, or decide whether evidence should be admitted, or assess the sufficiency and effect of evidence—these operations are all essentially nonadjudicative in nature. When judicial notice is seen as a significant vehicle for progress in the law, these are the areas involved, particularly in developing fields of specialized knowledge. See McCormick § 331 at 712. The Legislative Assembly does not believe that judges now instruct juries as to "propositions of generalized knowledge" derived from encyclopedias or other sources, or that they are likely to do so, or, indeed, that it is desirable that they do so. There is a vast difference between ruling on the basis of judicial notice that radar evidence of speed is admissible, and explaining to the jury its principles and degree of accuracy; or between using a table of stopping distances of automobiles at various speeds in a judicial evaluation of testimony, and telling the jury its precise application in the case.

Rule 201(b) differs from Oregon's former statutory scheme in attempting to provide broad guidelines for judicial notice of facts, rather than enumerating specific categories of facts subject to judicial notice, as in ORS 41.410. Because Oregon courts did not bind themselves in the past to noticing only those matters set out in ORS 41.410, the new guidelines, although broad, do not change Oregon law. See, e.g., *Oregon v. Miles,* 8 Or App 189, 492 P2d 497 (1972); *Smith v. Portland Traction Co.,* 226 Or 221, 359 P2d 899 (1961); *Croft v. Lambert,* 228 Or 76, 357 P2d 513 (1961); *Brown v. Gessler,* 191 Or 503, 230 P2d 541 (1951).

TEXT

Facts Not Subject to Reasonable Dispute

Rule 201(b) states the requirements for an adjudicative fact to be judicially noticed. Notice is allowed only if the fact is "not subject to reasonable dispute." The reason for such indisputability may be either that the fact is "generally known within the territorial jurisdiction of the trial court" or that it is "capable of accurate and ready determination by resort to sources whose accuracy cannot reasonably be questioned."

The standard for judicial notice is strict. One court has commented that judicial notice should apply only to "self-evident truths that no reasonable person could question, truisms that approach platitudes or banalities." *Hardy v. Johns-Manville Sales Corp.,* 681 F2d 334, 347 (5th Cir 1982).

In adopting general guidelines for determining what adjudicative facts may be noticed, Rule 201(b) takes a different approach than the former Oregon statute, which specified particular categories of facts that might be noticed. ORS 41.410 (repealed 1981) provided:

FACTS JUDICIALLY NOTICED. There are certain facts of such general notoriety that they are assumed to be already known to the court and evidence of them need not be produced. The following facts are assumed to be thus known but the court may resort for its aid to appropriate books or documents of reference:

(1) The true significance of all English words and phrases, and all legal expressions.

(2) Whatever is established by law.

(3) Public and private official acts of the legislative, executive, and judicial departments of this state, and of the United States.

(4) The seals of all the courts of this state, and of the United States.

(5) The accession to office, and the official signatures and seals of office of the principal officers in the legislative, executive, and judicial departments of this state, and of the United States.

(6) The existence, title, national flag, and seal of every state or sovereign recognized by the executive power of the United States.

(7) The seals of courts of admiralty and maritime jurisdiction, and of notaries public.

(8) The seal of any of the executive departments of the United States and of any corporation, all of the stock of which is beneficially owned by the United States.

(9) The laws of nature, the measure of time, and the geographical divisions and political history of the world.

Despite the limited authorization of the statute to notice only facts in the above categories, the Oregon Supreme Court interpreted the authority of courts to notice facts more broadly and did not limit it to the categories specified in the statute. In *Meier v. Bray,* 256 Or 613, 620, 475 P2d 587 (1970), the Supreme Court stated that courts could take judicial notice of facts that are of common knowledge or general notoriety, including matters which, although not known by the court, are capable of verification. Therefore, the difference between the approach of Rule 201(b) and prior law is not as great as would appear from examination of the former statute alone.

According to the Commentary, authorization for judicial notice of "propositions of generalized knowledge" was intentionally omitted from the rule. Propositions of generalized knowledge are less likely to be indisputable than are specific facts. Courts are unlikely to notice generalized discussions in medical or other treatises, but may notice specific, indisputable facts contained in such reference works.

Personal knowledge by the judge of a specific fact does not satisfy the requirements of Rule 201(b). See *Gov't Of Virgin Islands v. Gereau,* 523 F2d 140 (3rd Cir 1975) (construing FRE 201(b)). Such a basis for judicial notice also was not recognized under prior law. In *State ex rel Juvenile Department v. Martin,* 271 Or 603, 533 P2d 780 (1975), the court held that a judge may not properly take judicial notice on the basis of personal information he or she has acquired.

Under Rule 201(b), it may sometimes be necessary for a court to consult other sources to determine whether a source relied upon to support judicial notice is one whose "accuracy cannot reasonably be questioned." In accordance with the policy of Rule 104(1), the court should not be bound by the rules of evidence in making its determination of the reliability of the source. The information used in making this determination should be stated in the record.

Courts will generally notice the principles underlying scientific instruments, tests and processes and may consider the relevant literature in determining whether the instrument, test or process has sufficient reliability and acceptance in the scientific community to justify admission into evidence. *United States v. Foster,* 580 F2d 388 (10th Cir 1978). Courts, however, generally will not take judicial notice of the manner in which the test or process was conducted, the qualifications of the persons conducting the test, the reliability of the particular instrument used, or any other facts that may relate to whether the test or process was properly conducted or produced an accurate result on a specific occasion. See *State v. Hanson,* 85 Wis 2d 233, 270 NW 212 (1978); *State v. Gerdes,* 291 Minn 353, 191 NW2d 428 (1971); McCormick, *Evidence,* §§ 204, 330 (3rd ed 1984).

In addition to Rule 201, which provides general authorization for judicial notice of adjudicative facts, there are a few particularized statutes outside the evidence code authorizing judicial notice. See, e.g., ORS 545.070(2) (organization and boundaries of irrigation districts).

Court Records

Under precode Oregon law, it was held that judicial notice could generally not be taken of court records in previous cases or in other courts. See *State v. Hynes,* 27 Or App 37, 554 P2d 1030 (1976); *State v. English,* 28 Or App 957, 554 P2d 201 (1976); *State ex rel Juvenile Department v. Martin,* 271 Or 603, 533 P2d 780 (1975). This restriction has been modified by the new code.

The Commentary to Rule 202(5) states that the legislature rejected a proposal to extend judicial notice to all "records" of courts. The Commentary, however, states that "any evidence concerning court records that can properly be noticed will be noticed as a verifiable fact under Rule 201(b)." Thus, the legislature appeared to contemplate that judicial notice under Rule 201(b) could extend to court records.

In *State v. Farber,* 56 Or App 351, 642 P2d 668 (1982), aff'd 295 Or 199, 666 P2d 821, appeal dismissed 464 US 987, 104 SCt 475, 78 LEd2d 675 (1983), the appellate court took judicial notice of circuit court records in a related case. In *State ex rel Juvenile Department v. Williams,* 55 Or App 951, 958, 640 P2d 675 (1982), the court held that a juvenile court properly took notice of its prior commitment order to establish that a juvenile had been committed to the facility from which she was charged with running away.

OEC 201(b) should be interpreted to allow the records of any court to be noticed under the rule, provided that a "ready" determination can be made from sources whose accuracy cannot reasonably be questioned.

Under FRE 201, courts have held that judicial notice may be taken not only of the court's own records in earlier cases, *United States v. Fatico,* 441 F Supp 1285 (EDNY 1977), rev'd on other grounds 579 F2d 707 (2nd Cir 1978), cert denied 444 US 1073 (1980); *Kinnett Dairies, Inc. v. Farrow,* 580 F2d 1260 (5th Cir 1978), but of records of other courts as well. See *St. Louis Baptist Temple, Inc. v. Federal Deposit Insurance Corp.,* 605 F2d 1169 (10th Cir 1979); *Green v. Warden,* 699 F.2d 364, 369 (7th Cir 1983) (federal courts may take notice of proceedings in other courts "both within and outside the federal judicial system").

A distinction must be drawn between noticing the existence of court records or information in court records and noticing the truth of that information. The fact that certain records or entries exist or certain statements were made may be indisputable. However, the truth of these statements may be disputable, and hence will not be subject to judicial notice. See 21 C. Wright & K. Graham, FEDERAL PRACTICE & PROCEDURE (1977) § 5104; C. Mueller & L. Kirkpatrick, MODERN EVIDENCE (1995) § 2.4.

Cases Taking Judicial Notice

State v. Clark, 98 Or App 478, 779 P2d 215 (1989): The court took judicial notice of the conviction of a codefendant.

State v. Kennedy, 95 Or App 663, 667, 771 P2d 281 (1989): The court held that it was error for the trial court to refuse to take judicial notice that the drug "Eskalith" is administered in 300 mg capsules. The court stated: "We agree that this was a fact that the court could properly have judicially noticed. It is capable of accurate and ready determination [from the Physician's Desk Reference]."

Cleveland v. Goin, 299 Or 435, 703 P2d 204 (1985): The court took judicial notice that Clatsop County is not adjoining Linn County.

Simpson v. Simpson, 73 Or App 1, 697 P2d 570 (1985), reversed on other grounds 299 Or 578, 704 P2d 509 (1985): The court took judicial notice of the Lane County Circuit Court register of actions.

State v. Tooley, 297 Or 602, 687 P2d 1068 (1984): The court took judicial notice of the usual contents of hearing notices pertaining to the revocation of drivers' licenses.

Barrett v. Coast Range Plywood, 294 Or 641, 661 P2d 926, 928 n1 (1983): The court took judicial notice of the dictionary definition of "functional overlay."

State v. Wagner, 63 Or App 204, 662 P2d 799 (1983): The court held that the trial judge did not err in taking judicial notice that the drug "Darvocet-N-100" was a controlled substance under Oregon law.

State v. Clark, 286 Or 33, 593 P2d 123 (1979): In this case decided prior to the effective date of the Oregon Evidence Code, the Court of Appeals held that a trial judge can properly take judicial notice of the fact that observable symptoms or "signs" of alcohol intoxication include the following: (1) Odor of the breath; (2) Flushed appearance; (3) Lack of muscular coordination; (4) Speech difficulties; (5) Disorderly or unusual conduct; (6) Mental disturbance; (7) Visual disorders; (8) Sleepiness; (9) Muscular tremors; (10) Dizziness; (12) Nausea.

Examples of cases taking judicial notice under FRE 201(b) include the following: *United States v. Southard,* 700 F2d 1 (1st Cir), cert denied 464 US 823, 104 SCt 89, 78 LEd2d 97 (1983) (that it is more than 15 minutes driving time from New Haven to Rhode Island border); *United States v. Piggie,* 622 F2d 486

(10th Cir), cert denied 499 US 863 (1980) (federal prison is within the territorial jurisdiction of the United States); *Government of Canal Zone v. Burjan,* 596 F2d 690 (5th Cir 1979) (governmental boundaries); *United States v. Blunt,* 558 F2d 1245 (6th Cir 1977) (a particular federal correctional institution was located on federal land); *Government of Virgin Islands v. Testamark,* 528 F2d 742 (3rd Cir 1976) (prior conviction of defendant); *Equal Employment Opportunity Commission v. Delta Air Lines, Inc.,* 485 F Supp 1004 (ND Ga 1980) (only females become pregnant); *Caulfield v. Board of Education,* aff'd 632 F2d 999 (2nd Cir 1980), cert denied 450 US 1030 (1981) (a large percentage of the teaching force in New York City, particularly in the lower levels, is composed of women); *Record Museum v. Lawrence Township,* 481 F Supp 768 (DNJ 1979) ("the phenomenon known as the Counterculture of the Seventies wherein untraditional attire such as spoons and handcrafted pipes adorn both home and person"); *United Klans of America v. McGovern,* 453 F Supp 836 (ND Ala 1978), aff'd 621 F2d 152 (5th Cir 1980) (that Klan is a white hate group); *Besse v. Burlington Northern, Inc.,* 79 FRD 623 (D Minn 1978) (present value discount table); *State Bank of Fargo v. Merchants National Bank and Trust Co.,* 451 F Supp 775 (DND 1978), aff'd 593 F2d 341 (8th Cir 1979) (federal credit unions operate in North Dakota); *Mainline Investment Corp. v. Gaines,* 407 F Supp 423 (ND Tex 1976) (the existence of the Arab oil embargo and related historical facts).

Cases Refusing Judicial Notice

State v. Farrar, 309 Or 132, 179, 786 P2d 161, 191, cert denied 498 US 879 (1990): The court affirmed the trial court's refusal to give an instruction that violence lessens with age and is situational, finding no basis for judicial notice of such facts.

Thompson v. Telephone & Data Systems, Inc., 132 Or App 103, 888 P2d 16 (1994): The court held that in ruling on a motion for judgment on the pleadings it is improper to notice adjudicative facts outside the pleadings. Thus, the court refused to notice a document that was allegedly appended to a pleading filed in a different proceeding in a different jurisdiction.

State v. Proctor, 94 Or App 720, 724, 767 P2d 453 (1989), rev denied 308 Or 33, 774 P2d 1108: The court found that a courtroom demonstration by the prosecutor during closing argument regarding how a stray fingerprint could be left on tape "went far beyond any matter capable of judicial notice, involving as it did matters of forensic fingerprint analysis properly addressed only by experts." The court found both the demonstration and the closing argument based upon it to be improper. The court adopted and applied the following rule: "Any fact of which the court can take judicial notice, although evidence of it has not been formally introduced, constitutes a proper subject for comment by counsel, provided the argument is relevant to some issue in the case. ..." Id. (quoting *Kuehl v. Hamilton,* 136 Or 240, 244, 297 P 1043 (1931)).

State v. Kennedy, 95 Or App 663, 667–8, 771 P2d 281 (1989): The court affirmed the refusal of the trial judge to take judicial notice from the Physician's Desk Reference [PDR] of the symptoms of manic depression and of the behavioral effects of lithium. The state objected on the ground that the PDR could not establish the extent to which such symptoms related to the defendant. The court held: "We agree that the PDR is not a resource that is beyond question regarding generalizations pertaining to the symptoms of manic depression or the behavioral effects produced by the toxicity of serum lithium levels for particular individuals.... Those matters involve issues that require expert testimony."

State ex rel La Manufacture Francaise Des Pneumatiques Michelin v. Wells, 294 Or 296, 657 P2d 207, 210 (1982): The court held that it could not take judicial notice of the "scope of Michelin U.S.A.'s or Sears Roebuck & Company's distribution of Michelin products in the United States."

Bylund v. Department of Revenue, 292 Or 582, 641 P2d 577 (1982): The court held that it would be inappropriate to take judicial notice of the methods of accounting or evaluation of property, unless these are prescribed by law or regulation.

A-1 Sandblasting & Steamcleaning Co. v. Baiden, 293 Or 17, 643 P2d 1260, 1264 (1982): The court stated that it had been presented with nothing "within the reach of judicial notice to show that liability insurance would have a greater 'evil tendency' to promote tortious or otherwise unlawful operations when it covers only expected, though undesired, negligently caused injuries."

John Henry Company v. MacDonald, 92 Or App 659, 759 P2d 1126, rev denied 307 Or 77, 763 P2d 731 (1988): The trial judge refused to take judicial notice of the corporate status of the plaintiffs. The appellate court did not decide whether this refusal was error, holding that if it was error it was harmless.

Examples of cases where judicial notice was refused under FRE 201(b) include the following: *Eain v. Wilkes,* 641 F2d 504 (7th Cir), cert denied 454 US 894 (1981) (that Israel routinely tortures prisoners); *United States v. Baker,* 641 F2d 1311 (9th Cir 1981) (that all commercial fishermen in the area had knowledge of a court injunction against salmon fishing in certain waters); *Melong v. Micronesian Claims Commission,* 643 F2d 10 (D C Cir 1980) (the authenticity of 172 pages of Commission minutes and correspondence); *United States v. Bourque,* 541 F2d 290 (1st Cir 1976) (whether or not the Internal Revenue Service ever loses tax returns); *United States v. Southard,* 700 F2d 1 (1st Cir), cert denied 464 US 823, 104 SCt 89, 78 LEd2d 97 (1983) (that defendant *knew* there was more than 15 minutes driving time between New Haven and Rhode Island State Line. "Although we hesitate to lay down a hard and fast rule, we are hard put to think of a situation in which a judicially-noticed fact could be used as the basis for proving knowledge of that fact by the defendant." 700 F2d at 25–6).

Other Authorities

Annotations on the subject of judicial notice include: ANNOT., *Judicial Notice as to Location of Street Address Within Particular Political Subdivision,* 86 ALR3d 484 (1978); ANNOT., *What Constitutes "Adjudicative Facts" Within Meaning of Rule 201 of Federal Rules of Evidence, Concerning Judicial Notice of Adjudicative Facts,* 35 ALR Fed 440 (1977); ANNOT., *Propriety of Taking Judicial Notice of Geographic Facts for Purposes of Proof of Venue in Federal Criminal Prosecution,* 15

ALR Fed 715 (1973); ANNOT., *Judicial Notice as to Assessed Valuations*, 42 ALR3d 1439 (1972); ANNOT., *Admissibility in Evidence, Automobile Negligence Action, of Charts Showing Braking Distance, Reaction Times, Etc.*, 9 ALR3d 976 (1976); ANNOT., *Judicial Notice of Drivers' Reaction Time and of Stopping Distance of Motor Vehicles Traveling at Various Speeds*, 84 ALR2d 979 (1962); ANNOT., *Judicial Notice of Intoxicating Quality, and the Like, of a Liquor or Particular Liquid, From its Name*, 49 ALR2d 764 (1956).

RULE 201(c), (d). ORS 40.070. WHEN MANDATORY OR DISCRETIONARY

(1) A court may take judicial notice, whether requested or not.
(2) A court shall take judicial notice if requested by a party and supplied with the necessary information.

LEGISLATIVE COMMENTARY

Oregon Rules of Evidence 201(c) and 201(d) are identical to Rules 201(c) and 201(d) of the Federal Rules of Evidence.

Under ORE 201(c), the judge has discretionary authority to take judicial notice of matters whether or not the judge has been requested to do so. Judicial notice is mandatory, under ORE 201(d), only when a party requests it and supplies the necessary information. The drafters of the Federal Rules of Evidence recommended this scheme because it is simple, workable and avoids troublesome distinctions in the many situations in which the process of taking judicial notice is not recognized as such.

The benefits of providing for mandatory taking of judicial notice are apparent. First, a party intending to use judicial notice as a substitute for proof on a matter can better plan its case, assured that notice will be taken when it is requested and the necessary information is supplied. Second, the mandatory provision affords a basis for appeal if the two prerequisites are met and the court fails to take judicial notice of a matter.

Although Oregon statutes did not state any procedural requirements for the taking of judicial notice, case law had established that it is the duty of counsel requesting notice to bring the knowledge of the established fact before the court. Unless this is done, a court may refuse to take judicial notice of a fact. *Stites v. Morgan*, 229 Or 116, 366 P2d 324 (1961). ORE 201(d) expands on this requirement by providing that judicial notice is mandatory only if a party requests that notice be taken and supplies the necessary information to the court; the notice is otherwise discretionary.

TEXT

RULE 201(c)
Court Taking Judicial Notice Sua Sponte

Rule 201(c) gives the trial judge discretion to take judicial notice whether requested to do so or not. Courts are unlikely to take judicial notice in favor of a party when that party objects and indicates a preference for offering proof on the point. If the court intends to take judicial notice on its own, it should generally give advance notice to the parties so that they will have an opportunity to exercise their right to request a hearing under Rule 201(e).

RULE 201(d)
When Judicial Notice Mandatory

Rule 201(d) makes judicial notice mandatory when requested by a party and when the court is supplied with the necessary information. This enables parties to plan their trial strategy knowing what proof will be required. If judicial notice were not mandatory, parties would always need to be prepared to prove the fact in case the court was unwilling to take judicial notice.

The request for judicial notice should be in writing, when possible, advising the court of the specific adjudicative fact for which notice is requested and stating whether notice is requested because the fact is commonly known or because it is subject to verification by a source whose accuracy cannot reasonably be questioned. In the latter case, the source should be cited for the court and made available for examination. Unless the fact is obvious, the court should also be supplied with evidence to indicate that the source is in fact one whose accuracy cannot reasonably be disputed. A copy of any written request should, of course, be furnished to opposing counsel.

Although the rule does not expressly require a timely request for judicial notice, such a requirement is likely to be implied. A timely request is particularly important in cases where the propriety of taking judicial notice may be contested. The opponent may need time to obtain information to challenge the propriety of taking judicial notice.

In *Creasy v. Hogan,* 292 Or 154, 637 P2d 114, 124 (1981), the court stated: "Normally, such a request [for judicial notice] is made during the presentation of evidence and at all events prior to the commencement of jury deliberations, so that the court can, when appropriate to do so, instruct the jury that the facts are as judicially noticed by the court."

A request to admit under ORCP 45 should always be considered as a preliminary or alternative procedure to a request for judicial notice. ORCP 45 allows the fact to be established in advance of trial and is not limited to facts that are "not subject to reasonable dispute."

RULE 201(e). ORS 40.075. OPPORTUNITY TO BE HEARD

A party is entitled upon timely request to an opportunity to be heard as to the propriety of taking judicial notice and the tenor of the matter noticed. In the absence of prior notification, the request may be made after judicial notice has been taken.

LEGISLATIVE COMMENTARY

Oregon Rule of Evidence 201(e) grants an opportunity to be heard as to the propriety of taking judicial notice, upon timely request. The rule is identical to Rule 201(e) of the Federal Rules of Evidence. It provides no formal scheme for giving notice.

Oregon has had no comparable rule, statutory or judicial. The Legislative Assembly agrees with the Advisory Committee on the Federal Rules of Evidence, however, that:

> Basic considerations of procedural fairness demand an opportunity to be heard on the propriety of taking judicial notice and the tenor of the matter noticed ... An adversely affected party may learn in advance that judicial notice is in contemplation, either by virtue of being served with a copy of a request by another party under [ORE 201(d)] that judicial notice be taken, or through an advance indication by the judge. Or [the party] may have no advance notice at all. The likelihood of the latter is enhanced by the frequent failure to recognize judicial notice as such. And in the absence of advance notice, a request made after the fact could not in fairness be considered untimely.

TEXT

Opportunity to Be Heard

Rule 201(e) provides that upon timely request, parties are entitled to an opportunity to be heard concerning the propriety of taking judicial notice and the tenor of the matter noticed. A right to such a hearing may be constitutionally mandated. See *Garner v. Louisiana*, 368 US 157, 82 SCt 248, 7 LEd2d 207 (1961); *Ohio Bell Telephone Co. v. Public Utilities Commission*, 301 US 292, 57 SCt 724, 81 LEd 1093 (1937).

The rule does not require the court to give advance notice to the parties of its intention to take judicial notice. However, courts should provide such advance notice in absence of exceptional circumstances. If advance notice is not given, a party must still be given an opportunity to be heard after judicial notice has been taken. If the party persuades the court that taking judicial notice was an error, the instruction to the jury will have to be withdrawn, and in some cases a mistrial may be necessary.

The rule does not define what constitutes a timely request. Presumably the request must be filed within a reasonable time after the court has notified the parties of its intent to take judicial notice or after a request for judicial notice has been made by an opponent. If a party anticipates that the court may be considering taking judicial notice of a particular fact, and the party wishes to challenge the propriety of doing so, the party would be wise to file an advance request to be heard on the issue.

RULE 201(f).   ORS 40.080. TIME OF TAKING NOTICE

Judicial notice may be taken at any stage of the proceeding.

LEGISLATIVE COMMENTARY

Oregon Rule of Evidence 201(f) provides that judicial notice may be taken at any stage of a proceeding, whether in the trial court or on appeal. The rule is identical to Rule 201(f) of the Federal Rules of Evidence and accords with Uniform Rule 12 and California Evidence Code § 459. It clarifies Oregon case law, which is in conflict on whether an appellate court may assume the existence of a fact not brought to the attention of the trial court. See *State v. Jacobs,* 11 Or App 218, 501 P2d 353 (1972); *Kepl v. Manzanita Corp.,* 246 Or 170, 424 P2d 674 (1967); *State v. Jones,* 240 Or 129, 400 P2d 524 (1965); *Stites v. Morgan,* 229 Or 116, 366 P2d 324 (1961); *Board of Medical Examiners v. Buck,* 192 Or 66, 232 P2d 791 (1951); *Webb v. Clatsop County School District No. 3,* 188 Or 324, 215 P2d 368 (1950).

Adoption of ORE 201(f) does not mean that a court can deprive a criminal defendant, entitled to a jury determination of a factual issue, of that right by notice of a necessary fact after the opportunity for jury determination has passed. The Legislative Assembly agrees with the holding in *United States v. Jones,* 580 F2d 219 (6th Cir 1978), a case which involved illegal interception of telephone conversations. The evidence at trial showed that the tapped telephone was furnished by South Central Bell Telephone Company. It did not show that the telephone company was a "person engaged as a common carrier" within the federal criminal statute. On appeal, the court refused to take judicial notice that the company was a common carrier. Federal Rule 201(g), it reasoned, "plainly contemplates that the jury in a criminal case shall pass upon facts which are judicially noticed. This it could not do if this notice were taken for the first time after it had been discharged and the case was on appeal. We, therefore, hold that Rule 201(f), authorizing judicial notice at the appellate level, must yield in the face of the express congressional intent manifested in [Rule] 201(g) for criminal jury trials." 580 F2d at 221.

TEXT

Time of Taking Notice

Under Rule 201(f), the instruction to the jury to take judicial notice of a particular adjudicative fact may be given at the beginning of a trial, during the trial or at its conclusion prior to jury deliberations. See *Creasy v. Hogan,* 292 Or 154, 637 P2d 114 (1981) (error for trial court to instruct jury regarding definition of word after jury had begun its deliberations). Rule 201(f) also authorizes a court to take judicial notice at a pretrial or posttrial hearing or upon appeal. Judicial notice is sometimes utilized in hearings on motions for summary judgment. See, e.g., *Haye v. United States,* 461 F Supp 1168 (CD Cal 1978); *United Klans of America v. McGovern,* 453 F Supp 836 (ND Ala 1978), aff'd 621 F2d 152 (5th Cir 1980).

The Commentary, in approving *United States v. Jones,* 580 F2d 219 (6th Cir 1978), indicates that to avoid depriving the defendant of the right to a jury determination of the issue, posttrial judicial notice of an adjudicative fact should not be taken in a criminal case in favor of the prosecution. This rule can cause problems when the prosecution fails to establish venue during its case-in-chief and then seeks to remedy the omission by having judicial notice of venue taken after a verdict has been rendered. The court almost faced this issue in *State v. Cervantes,* 319 Or 121, 873 P2d 316 (1994), where the prosecutor failed to put on direct evidence that the crime had been committed in Coos County, a fact essential to venue. The court avoided the need to reverse the verdict by finding that there was sufficient evidence introduced for a reasonable jury to draw the inference that the crime was committed in Coos Bay, which the jury could be expected to know was in Coos County. The evidence included the fact that the case was investigated by the Coos Bay police and the Coos County Crime Victim's Assistance office had contact with the victim in an official capacity.

The limitation against taking judicial notice on appeal in a criminal case has been held not to apply in a trial where the jury was waived. *Gov't of Canal Zone v. Burjan,* 596 F2d 690 (5th Cir 1979). See generally ANNOT., *Effect of Rule 201(g) of the Federal Rules of Evidence, Providing for Instruction in Criminal Case that Jury Need Not Accept as Conclusive Fact Judicially Noticed, on Propriety of Taking Judicial Notice on Appeal Under Rule 201(f),* 409 ALR Fed 911 (1980).

In most cases, the type of judicial notice taken by an appellate court will be of legislative facts rather than adjudicative facts, and the restrictions and requirements of Rule 201 will not apply. See discussion under Rule 201(a). However, occasionally judicial notice will be taken of an adjudicative fact on appeal. Cf. *In re Morten,* 67 Or App 235, 239 n1, 677 P2d 735, 737, rev denied 297 Or 83, 679 P2d 1368 (1984) (contested custody proceeding; court noted that it had authority under Rule 201(f) to take judicial notice of the fact that the mother's marriage to another person had been dissolved during the pendency of the appeal).

When an appellate court does take judicial notice of an adjudicative fact, advance notice should generally be given to the parties so that they will have an opportunity to exercise their right under Rule 201(e) to request a hearing regarding the propriety of judicial notice.

Rule 201(b), which makes judicial notice mandatory when the court is presented with a timely request and the necessary information, is arguably applicable upon appeal. Appellate courts may, however, be able to avoid the mandatory effect of this rule by holding that a request for judicial notice made for the first time upon appeal is not timely.

RULE 201(g). ORS 40.085. INSTRUCTING THE JURY

(1) In a civil action or proceeding, the court shall instruct the jury to accept as conclusive any fact or law judicially noticed.

(2) In a criminal case, the court shall instruct the jury that it may, but is not required to, accept as conclusive any fact judicially noticed in favor of the prosecution.

LEGISLATIVE COMMENTARY

Oregon Rule of Evidence 201(g) is based on Rule 201(g) of the Federal Rules of Evidence. The language of the federal rule has been changed for clarity only.

Subsection (1). Subsection (1) provides that in civil cases the judge shall instruct the jury to regard judicially noticed facts and laws as established; there is to be no contradictory evidence before the jury. In this respect, Rule 201(g) is consistent with the standard of indisputability required by Rule 201(b). To allow the jury to hear evidence contradicting a judicially noticed fact would defeat the function of judicial notice as a means of expediting proof of certain matters. Ample procedural protection is afforded by the opportunity to be heard upon request under Rule 201(e). Subsection (1) expresses current Oregon law, which is stated in ORS 17.425 and ORCP 59B.

Subsection (2). Subsection (2) addresses the question of judicial notice in criminal cases. Here the judge may properly instruct the jury to find a fact judicially noticed in favor of the defense. In the reverse situation, however, constitutional considerations outweigh the need to expedite proof of certain matters. A mandatory instruction on a fact judicially noticed effectively removes the issue from the jury's consideration. Judicial notice of an element of the prosecution's prima facie case would thus be contrary to the defendant's Sixth Amendment right to a jury trial. For this reason, the jury should be permitted to hear evidence in disproof of any fact judicially noticed in favor of the prosecution. *State v. Lawrence,* 120 Utah 323, 234 P2d 600 (1951) (reversing conviction based on judicial notice that automobile stolen by defendant was worth in excess of amount required for larceny, on ground that defendant was denied jury consideration of value of stolen car). An example would be a prosecution for violation of Sunday closing laws where the defendant has conceded every element of the crime including the date on which the business was open. In such a case, the court may judicially notice that the date fell on a Sunday, but it may not require the jury so to find and thus direct a verdict against the accused.

The view that a judicially noticed fact is indisputable in a criminal case appears to have been adopted by statute in Oregon. ORS 136.310, applicable to criminal proceedings, provides that "whenever the knowledge of the court is by statute made evidence of a fact, the court shall declare such knowledge to the jury, which is bound to accept it as conclusive." See also ORCP 59B, made applicable to criminal proceedings by ORS 136.330. However, the Oregon courts have never clearly addressed the constitutional problem when ORS 136.310 is applied in favor of the prosecution. In *State v. Kincaid,* 133 Or 95, 103–104, 285 P2d 1015 (1930), a prosecution for operation of a dance hall in a town of less than 500 people, the Supreme Court did not allow the trial judge to notice the population of the town, a missing element of the prosecution's case. Recognizing that as a general rule judicial notice could be taken of the population of a town as indicated in the latest census, the Supreme Court nevertheless declared that when the alleged offense occurred nine years after the census, a conviction could not be based upon judicial notice of the census figures. The state was required to prove the population of the town at the time of the alleged offense.

This subsection removes any ambiguity in Oregon law regarding judicial notice in criminal cases, by providing that a jury is not required to accept facts that are judicially noticed in favor of the prosecution. A similar policy underlies the rule regarding use of presumptions in criminal cases. ORE 309.

TEXT

Instructing the Jury

Rule 201(g) draws a distinction between civil and criminal cases with regard to the effect of judicial notice. In a civil case judicial notice is binding on the jury, and evidence contradicting the judicially noticed fact may not be received. In a criminal case, judicial notice taken in favor of the prosecution is not binding on the jury. According to the Commentary, evidence contradicting the judicially noticed fact may be received. When judicial notice is taken in favor of the prosecution, the jury should be instructed that it "may, but is not required to" find the judicially noticed fact. Judicial notice in favor of the prosecution in a criminal case is thus similar to an inference under Rule 309.

The rule does not directly address the effect of judicial notice in favor of a defendant in a criminal case. The Commentary states that such notice should be conclusive. Conclusive judicial notice against the prosecution, unlike conclusive judicial notice against a defendant, does not raise Sixth Amendment concerns.

See *State v. Kennedy,* 95 Or App 663, 668, 771 P2d 281 (1989) ("We need not decide, however, whether OEC 201(g) requires that a jury be instructed that facts judicially noticed in favor of the defense are conclusive because, even assuming that such an instruction was required, any error in failing to give the instruction was harmless.")

The application of Rule 201(g)(2) in a court trial was addressed in *State v. Willard,* 96 Or App 219, 772 P2d 948 (1989). In a trial to the court, the judge took judicial notice that the place of arrest (Nyberg Road exit from I-5, Washington County) was located in the State of Oregon. On appeal, defendant challenged this taking of judicial notice on the ground that it relieved the prosecution of proving an element of the offense. Furthermore, the defendant argued that the effect of a court taking judicial notice in a court trial was to make judicial notice mandatory, in violation of Rule 201(g)(2). The appellate court agreed that "a trial judge, sitting as a trier of fact, is no more entitled to treat a judicially noticed fact as conclusively proven in a criminal case than would be a jury." 96 Or App at 221. However, the court stated that a trial judge "is entitled, as is a jury, to treat judicially noticed facts as evidence. Nothing in the record of this case compels a conclusion that the trial judge did anything more." Id.

RULE 202.   ORS 40.090. KINDS OF LAW

Law judicially noticed is defined as:
(1) **The decisional, constitutional and public statutory law of Oregon, the United States and any state, territory or other jurisdiction of the United States.**
(2) **Public and private official acts of the legislative, executive and judicial departments of this state, the United States, and any other state, territory or other jurisdiction of the United States.**
(3) **Rules of professional conduct for members of the Oregon State Bar.**
(4) **Regulations, ordinances and similar legislative enactments issued by or under the authority of the United States or any state, territory or possession of the United States.**
(5) **Rules of court of any court of this state or any court of record of the United States or of any state, territory or other jurisdiction of the United States.**
(6) **The law of an organization of nations and of foreign nations and public entities in foreign nations.**
(7) **An ordinance, comprehensive plan or enactment of any county or incorporated city in this state, or a right derived therefrom. As used in this subsection, "comprehensive plan" has the meaning given that term by ORS 197.015.**

LEGISLATIVE COMMENTARY

Oregon Rule of Evidence 202 was adopted because the Federal Rules of Evidence do not address judicial notice of law, and the Oregon statutes on the subject have limited judicial notice of law to a few areas. The Legislative Assembly believes that a broader approach is more in keeping with the goal of judicial notice: to expedite the administration of justice. It therefore adopts Rule 202, which greatly expands the scope of judicial notice of law in this state.

Subsection (1). Under subsection (1) the decisional, constitutional and public statutory law of Oregon, the United States and any state, territory or other jurisdiction of the United States may be noticed. In addition, relevant decisions of all sister-state courts, including those at the intermediate-appellate level, may be noticed. This subsection is based on § 452 of the California Evidence Code. As the Comment to that section notes, courts of sister states can be considered to be as responsive to the need for properly determining the law as equivalent courts in this state.

Oregon has enacted the Uniform Judicial Notice of Foreign Law Act, ORS 41.420 to 41.480, which enables Oregon courts to take judicial notice of the constitutions, common law, civil law and statutes of every other jurisdiction of the United States. Oregon courts may continue to do so under subsection (1). This subsection, therefore, does not change Oregon law.

Subsection (2). Subsection (2) provides for judicial notice of all official acts of the legislative, executive and judicial departments of this state, the United States and any other state, territory or other jurisdiction of the United States. It is based upon former ORS 41.410(3), but is broader, in that it provides for judicial notice of official acts of the branches of government of *other* states and of territories and possessions of the United States. To this extent this subsection changes Oregon law.

The expanded scope of judicial notice under subsection (2) is best illustrated by considering the types of acts of Oregon governmental agencies a court has already been able to notice under ORS 41.410(3). These include civil service commission rules, *Beistel v. Public Employee Relations Board,* 6 Or App 115, 486 P2d 1305 (1971); regulations and official acts of the Department of Higher Education, *Vandever v. State Bd. of Higher Education,* 8 Or App 50, 491 P2d 1198 (1971); statutes and regulations of the State Board of Forestry, *Eugene Stud and Veneer, Inc. v. State Bd. of Forestry,* 3 Or App 20, 469 P2d 635 (1970); the statutory authority of the Superintendent and the rules and regulations of the Board of Control of the Oregon Fairview Home as to release of inmates, *Jarrett v. Wells,* 235 Or 51, 53, 383 P2d 995 (1963); and rules of a state agency filed with the Secretary of State for compilation and publication, such as rules of the Public Utility Commission, *Fulton Insurance Company v. White Motor Company,* 261 Or 206, 222–223, 493 P2d 138, 146 (1972). Under the similar California provision, California courts have taken judicial notice of a wide variety of administrative and executive acts, including proceedings and reports of Congressional committees, records of the California State Board of Education and the records of a county planning commission.

Subsection (3). Subsection (3) provides for judicial notice of the Rules of Professional Conduct of the Oregon State Bar. These rules are rules of the Supreme Court, in effect, because they must be adopted by that court under ORS 9.490. A court may therefore take judicial notice of them to the same extent it takes notice of other rules of the Supreme Court.

It is unclear whether subsection (3) of ORS 41.410 extended to the Rules of Professional Conduct for members of the Oregon State Bar. Subsection (3) may therefore represent a change in Oregon law.

Subsection (4). Subsection (4) provides for judicial notice of regulations and legislative enactments adopted by or under the authority of the United States or any state, territory, or possession of the United States, including public entities therein. Consonant with the Comment to § 452 of the California Evidence Code, the phrase "regulations and legislative enactments" includes ordinances and other similar legislative enactments, as not all public entities legislate by ordinance. This subsection also provides for judicial notice of documents published in the *Federal Register.* These include presidential proclamations and executive orders having general applicability and legal effect, as well as orders, regulations, rules, certificates, codes of fair competition, licenses, notices and similar instruments having general applicability and legal effect that are issued, prescribed or promulgated by federal agencies.

The subsection clarifies existing Oregon Rules. Although not bound by 44 USC 1507, which declares that "the contents of the *Federal Register* shall be judicially noticed," Oregon courts have indicated a willingness to notice material published in the *Federal Register* if properly brought to a court's attention. *Mogul Transportation Co. v. Larison,* 181 Or 252, 181 P2d 139 (1947).

Subsection (5). Subsection (5) provides that judicial notice may be taken of the rules of court of (1) any court in this state, (2) any court of record in the United States, or (3) any state, territory or possession of the United States. Oregon apparently did not allow judicial notice of local court rules. *Stivers v. Byrkett,* 56 Or 565, 108 P 1014, 109 P 386 (1910). This area should be included in order to cover judicial notice of law adequately. There is little reason for not doing so, as the Supreme Court is promulgating rules of court and local court rules are available in any county courthouse.

The Legislative Assembly rejected the proposal that it extend judicial notice in blanket fashion to the "records" of courts. Any evidence concerning court records that can properly be noticed will be noticed as a verifiable fact under Rule 201(b). Many of the statements within court records are excludable as hearsay. *State ex rel Juvenile Dept. v. Martin,* 271 Or 603, 533 P2d 780 (1975); *Hood v. Hatfield,* 235 Or 38, 383 P2d 1021 (1963).

Subsection (6). Subsection (6) provides for judicial notice of the law of an organization of nations, foreign nations and public entities in foreign nations. It changes current Oregon law by making all foreign law subject to judicial notice. Under former ORS 41.460, the laws of foreign countries had to be proved. The court determined the foreign law, which was not subject to the provisions concerning judicial notice. See also *Oregon v. Moy Looke,* 7 Or 54 (1879).

Subsection (7). Subsection (7) is based on ORS 16.510(2) and ORCP 20D(2). However, it dispenses with the current rule that judicial notice of an ordinance, comprehensive plan or enactment of a county or city, or of a right derived therefrom, may only be taken when the pleadings refer to the document by title and date of enactment or approval, if approval is necessary to render it effective. The pleading requirement is a survivor of the common law rule that municipal ordinances cannot be noticed and must be pleaded and proved as facts. As municipal ordinances no longer have to be proved, the pleading requirement has outlived its usefulness.

TEXT

Judicial Notice of Law

Rule 202 significantly expands the types of law that may be judicially noticed. No comparable provision is contained in the Federal Rules of Evidence, which are limited to judicial notice of adjudicative facts.

Judicial notice of law should be sharply distinguished from other types of judicial notice. It is a traditional responsibility of courts to determine the law and to instruct the jury thereon. Because certain law, such as foreign law, was not always easily accessible, the courts at common law viewed its determination as a question of fact. Like other issues of fact, the law had to be pleaded, and the question was assigned to the jury.

The trend has been steadily away from requiring law to be pleaded and proven to the jury as an issue of fact. Judicial notice of law is the term used to indicate that these requirements will not be imposed. Thus, the primary significance of Rule 202 is to eliminate for the laws listed therein any requirement of pleading or proof to the jury. The determination of the listed laws is exclusively for the court.

The rule presumably requires the court to take judicial notice in all cases where the court is furnished by counsel with sufficient reliable information to do so. Such an interpretation would be consistent with Rule 201(d), governing judicial notice of adjudicative facts, which provides: "A court shall take judicial notice if requested by a party and supplied with the necessary information." The court is not limited by the rules of evidence in determining the applicable law. See Rule 101(4)(a); Rule 104(1).

In *Warm Springs Forest Products Industries v. Employee Benefits Insurance Co.*, 300 Or 617, 621, 716 P2d 740 (1986), the court held that "A party cannot demand that a court take judicial notice of undocumented law when the party does not supply the court with the necessary information." Therefore, the court in this case refused to take judicial notice of tribal law, custom, or usage of the Warm Springs Indian Reservation when the parties had failed to provide a basis for such notice.

Although the listing in the rule is comprehensive, it does not cover all laws that might be relevant to litigation in Oregon courts. Rule 202 should be interpreted as listing only those laws for which judicial notice is mandatory if the court is furnished with the necessary information. Because of the difficulty of proving law to a jury, the court in an appropriate case should take judicial notice of other laws as well.

> [T]he tendency is toward permitting the judges to do what perhaps they should have done in the beginning, that is, to rely on the diligence of counsel to provide the necessary materials, and accordingly to take judicial notice of all law. This seems to be the goal toward which the practice is marching. McCormick, *Evidence* § 335 at 776 (2d ed 1972).

In addition to Rule 202, several statutes provide for judicial notice of law. Judicial notice is expressly authorized for city charters (ORS 221.710(1)); county home rule charters (ORS 203.770(1)); rules and executive orders filed with the Secretary of State (ORS 183.360(4)); and the laws of other jurisdictions in workers' compensation proceedings (ORS 656.126(4)). But see *Byrnes v. City of Hillsboro*, 104 Or App 95, 798 P2d 1119 (1990) (refusing to notice local legislative history).

Judicial notice of law was held to be proper in the following cases: *Feinstein v. Milsner*, 131 Or App 248, 252, 884 P2d 583, 585 (1994) (notice of relevant statutes); *Shahtout v. Emco Garbage Co.*, 298 Or 598, 695 P2d 897 (1985) (governmental safety regulations); *State v. Self*, 75 Or App 230, 240, 706 P2d 975 (1985) (law of another state); *Fujimoto v. City of Happy Valley*, 55 Or App 905, 640 P2d 656, 659 n5 (1982) (LCDC acknowledgment order); *Elliott v. Oregon International Mining Co.*, 60 Or App 474, 654 P2d 663, 666 (1982) (statutes, although "plaintiffs must allege sufficient facts in their complaint to bring themselves within the purview of the statute.").

When a party claims attorney fees, the statutory basis for the claim must be sufficiently alleged. The court will not rely on Rule 202 to notice a statute allowing attorney fees, when there is nothing in the pleading indicating that the statute would be applicable. *Parkhurst v. Faessler*, 62 Or App 539, 661 P2d 571 (1983).

ARTICLE III

BURDEN OF PERSUASION; BURDEN OF PRODUCING EVIDENCE; PRESUMPTIONS

RULE 305.   ORS 40.105. ALLOCATION OF THE BURDEN OF PERSUASION

A party has the burden of persuasion as to each fact the existence or non-existence of which the law declares essential to the claim for relief or defense the party is asserting.

LEGISLATIVE COMMENTARY

Oregon Rule of Evidence 305 allocates the burden of persuasion. The rule is closely modeled on California Evidence Code § 500. There is no comparable federal rule. Article III begins with this rule number to avoid parallel numbering to the Federal Rules of Evidence which might mislead.

As used in the rule, "burden of persuasion" means the obligation of a party to produce a particular conviction in the mind of the trier of fact as to the existence or nonexistence of a fact. If the requisite degree of conviction is not achieved, the trier of fact must assume that the fact does not exist. Morgan, *Basic Problems of Evidence* 19 (1957); 9 Wigmore, *Evidence* § 2485 (3d ed 1940); California Evidence Code § 500, Comment at 1079 (West 1965).

The degree of conviction required by the burden of persuasion (sometimes called the "standard of proof") varies according to the matter. In civil cases, the trier of fact usually must be convinced that the existence of a particular fact is more probable than its nonexistence. This is described as proof by a "preponderance of the evidence." However, in some instances a party is required to produce a substantially greater degree of belief. In actions that allege fraud or gift, for example, the trier of fact must be persuaded by "clear and convincing evidence," which means that the truth of the facts asserted must be highly probable. *Cook v. Michael,* 214 Or 513, 330 P2d 1026 (1958). Finally, in criminal cases, the prosecution must persuade the trier of fact of the existence of the essential facts "beyond a reasonable doubt."

Rule 305 indicates that the burden of persuasion as to a particular fact rests on the party to whose case the fact is essential. It should be noted that the rule does *not* attempt to indicate what facts are essential to any particular claim for relief or defense. The elements of a prima facie case or defense are determined by substantive law, not by the law of evidence.

Where the substantive law does not dictate which party has the burden of persuasion on an issue, the court should consider the following factors in making the allocation; (1) access to the evidence; (2) fairness to the litigants; (3) special policy considerations, such as those disfavoring certain defenses; and (4) probability of the existence or nonexistence of the fact. 9 Wigmore § 2486 at 275; McCormick, *Evidence* § 337 at 785–788 (2d ed 1972).

In allocating the burden of persuasion to the party to whose case a fact is essential, Rule 305 departs from ORS 41.120 and 41.240. These statutes—which are repealed—allocate the burden of persuasion according to whether the allegations in the pleadings are in affirmative or negative form. This approach has been criticized as establishing a meaningless standard:

> That the burden is on the party having the affirmative (or) that a party is not required to prove a negative ... is no more than a play on words since practically any proposition may be stated in either affirmative or negative form. Thus, a plaintiff's exercise of ordinary care equals absence of contributory negligence in the minority of jurisdictions which place this element in plaintiff's case. In any event, the proposition seems simply not to be so. Cleary, "Presuming and Pleading: An Essay on Juristic Immaturity," in 12 Stan L Rev 5, 11 (1959).

ORS 41.210 has been literally applied on occasion. See *First Nat'l Bank v. Malady,* 242 Or 353, 408 P2d 724 (1966) (insurance company bringing declaratory judgment action to test coverage held to have burden of proof, although insured would have burden in action on policy). At other times, Oregon courts have refused to follow the strict language of the statute and have allocated the burden of persuasion on the basis of access to proof, probabilities and policy considerations. See *Secretary of State v. Hanover Ins. Co.,* 242 Or 541, 411 P2d 89 (1966); *Carpenter v. Carpenter,* 153 Or 584, 57 P2d 1098 (1936); *Hanns v. Hanns,* 246 Or 282, 423 P2d 499 (1967). To the latter extent, Rule 305 does not depart substantially from existing law.

The burden of persuasion is but one of two "burdens of proof" found in the law of evidence. The other is the burden of producing evidence discussed in Rule 307. A party that has the burden of persuasion must persuade the trier of fact that an alleged fact is true. Logically prior to this, however, the same party has the burden of producing sufficient evidence for the court to find that the trier of fact would be reasonable in so finding. To carry the burden of persuasion, a party must have already satisfied the burden of producing evidence; the converse proposition is not true.

TEXT

Allocation of the Burden of Persuasion

In Article III, the legislature makes no reference to the "burden of proof." Because it has two distinct meanings, "burden of proof" is a frequently confused concept. It may refer to the party's burden of producing evidence, or it may refer to a party's obligation to persuade the trier of fact regarding the existence or nonexistence of a fact. In Article III, these two meanings of burden of proof are clearly separated. Rule 305 allocates the burden of persuasion. Rule 307 allocates the burden of producing evidence. Reference to the "burden of proof" should therefore be avoided in litigation subject to the Oregon Evidence Code.

According to the Commentary, the purpose of Rule 305 is to allocate the burden of persuasion on different issues based on whether they are defined as elements of a claim or defense under the substantive law. Former law allocated the burden of persuasion according to the allegations in the pleadings. The new approach may in fact not be significantly different, because the allegations required to be stated in the pleadings usually are the elements of a claim or defense as defined by the substantive law. Making the question an issue of substantive law rather than an issue of pleading will not solve all problems in determining which party has the burden of persuasion.

In some cases, the substantive law will clearly specify whether an issue is an element of a claim or defense, and the burden of persuasion can easily be assigned in accordance with Rule 305. In other cases, there may be no statutory or appellate law on the issue, and the trial court will have to make the allocation. The Commentary states that in making such allocation, the court should consider the following factors: "(1) access to the evidence; (2) fairness to the litigants; (3) special policy considerations, such as those disfavoring certain defenses; and (4) probability of the existence or nonexistence of the fact."

In a recent case, the Oregon Supreme Court listed factors to be considered in allocating the "burden of proof":

> (1) Precedent; (2) Whether the facts are within the peculiar knowledge of a party; (3) Whether the party has the burden of pleading the affirmative allegation; (4) Upon whose case is the existence of the fact essential; (5) Probability. The extent to which a party's contention departs from conduct which would be expected in the light of ordinary human experience; (6) Whether disfavored contentions (fraud, contributory negligence, statute of limitations, truth in defamation) should be handicapped; (7) In case of a statute, whether the application of the statute is essential to a party's right to recover; (8) In case of a statute, the policy which the statute aims to effect; (9) Timing. Whether matters

occurring after the accrual of a cause of action should be treated as affirmative defenses; (10) Whether the burden should be imposed upon the one who pleads the facts; (11) Whether the burden should be imposed on the one who invokes the judicial remedy. (*Nelson v. Hughes,* 290 Or 653, 658–659, 625 P2d 643, 645–646 (1981) (footnotes omitted))

These considerations would appear to apply to the allocation of the burden of persuasion as well as to the burden of production. See Rule 307(2).

An illustrative case decided under Rule 305 is *Lindland v. United Business Investments,* 298 Or 318, 693 P2d 20 (1984). In this case, the court found reversible error in an instruction that the defendant had the burden of proving that it fully performed its duty of full, fair, and frank disclosure. After an examination of the substantive law, the court concluded that the burden of proving breach should be on the plaintiff.

Rule 305 would seem to be qualified in criminal cases by ORS 161.055. While Rule 305 generally places the burden of persuasion with regard to defenses upon a defendant, ORS 161.055 provides that the prosecution has the burden of disproving beyond a reasonable doubt defenses raised by a criminal defendant, other than affirmative defenses. Nothing in the Commentary suggests an intent to modify this statute. See also ORS 136.430, which provides: "The law of evidence in civil actions is also the law of evidence in criminal actions and proceedings, except as otherwise specifically provided in the statutes relating to crimes and criminal procedure." See generally COMMENT, Mullaney and Patterson: *Due Process Protections and the Defendant's Burden of Proving Affirmative Defenses,* 15 Will L Rev 85 (1978).

Rule 305 is also qualified by Rule 308. If fact A is an element of a civil claim under the substantive law, Rule 305 will initially assign the burden of persuasion regarding that issue to the plaintiff. However, if a presumption is applicable and the plaintiff proves the facts giving rise to the presumption that A exists, under Rule 308 the burden of persuasion will shift to the defendant to establish A's nonexistence.

The Commentary suggests that Rule 305 may change current Oregon law regarding the allocation of the burden of persuasion in a declaratory judgment proceeding. See *First National Bank v. Malady,* 242 Or 353, 358, 408 P2d 724 (1965) (generally, in a declaratory judgment action, plaintiff who initiates action and makes affirmative allegations must bear the burden of persuasion as to those allegations). For a more specific statement of the view of the Advisory Committee, see the Advisory Committee's commentary to Rule 305, contained in *Proposed Oregon Evidence Code: Report of the Legislative Interim Committee on the Judiciary* (1980). Whether the new rule will have such an effect is uncertain. The court could find proof of the plaintiff's allegations to be "essential to the claim for relief," and therefore continue to allocate the burden of persuasion to the plaintiff. In *State Farm Fire & Casualty Co. v. Reuter,* 299 Or 155, 166 n9, 700 P2d 236 (1985), the court, without citing the code, applied the traditional rule that the insurer in a declaratory judgment action has the burden of proving noncoverage.

Under California Evidence Code section 500 (West 1966), which was the model for Rule 305, the insured has the burden of persuasion on the issue of coverage in a declaratory judgment action brought by the insurer. See *State Farm Mutual Automobile Insurance Co. v. Spann,* 31 Cal App 3d 97, 106 Cal Rptr 923 (1973). However, this was also the rule in California prior to the adoption of section 500. See *American Home Assurance Co. v. Essy,* 179 Cal App 2d 19, 3 Cal Rptr 586 (1960). See generally ANNOT., *Burden of Proof in Actions Under General Declaratory Judgment Acts,* 23 ALR2d 1243 (1952).

The standard of evidence required to satisfy the burden of persuasion is not specified by the rule, and instead is controlled by statute, case law, or the federal and state constitutions. In criminal cases, the proof necessary for a conviction must be beyond a reasonable doubt. In most civil cases, a preponderance of the evidence standard controls. See ORS 10.095(5). However, in some civil cases, proof by clear and convincing evidence is required.

In *Riley Hill General Contractor v. Tandy Corp.,* 303 Or 390, 408, 737 P2d 595 (1987), the court held:

> [I]n a common law deceit action the trial judge, when referring to the basic elements of the claim, should tell the jury that proof by clear and convincing evidence is required, which means that the truth of the facts is highly probable. However, when considering the issue of damages, be they general or punitive, the judge should instruct the jury that the proponent need only prove those damages by preponderance, or greater weight of the evidence.

Other civil cases requiring a clear and convincing proof standard include *Zockert v. Fanning,* 310 Or 514, 800 P2d 773, 781 (1990) (contested adoption proceedings); *Paulson v. Paulson,* 241 Or 88, 91, 404 P2d 199 (1965) (oral contract to make a will); *Albino v. Albino,* 279 Or 537, 550, 568 P2d 1344 (1977) (constructive trust); *In re Lathen,* 294 Or 157, 159, 654 P2d 1110 (1982) (bar disciplinary proceeding); *Thornton v. Johnson,* 253 Or 342, 453 P2d 178, 454 P2d 647 (1969) (violation of Corrupt Practices Act).

Examples of cases requiring a preponderance standard include the following: *Mutual of Enumclaw Insurance Co. v. McBride,* 295 Or 398, 667 P2d 494 (1983) (action to void fire insurance policy for fraud or false swearing); *Bernard v. Vatheuer,* 303 Or 410, 737 P2d 128 (1987) (proof of oral joint venture agreement). See generally Orloff & Stedinger, *A Framework for Evaluating the Preponderance-of-the-Evidence Standard,* 131 U Pa L Rev 1159 (1983).

RULE 306.   ORS 40.110. INSTRUCTIONS ON THE BURDEN OF PERSUASION

The court shall instruct the jury as to which party bears the applicable burden of persuasion on each issue only after all of the evidence in the case has been received.

LEGISLATIVE COMMENTARY

Oregon Rule of Evidence 306 is original. It is a corollary of the Morgan approach to presumptions adopted in Rule 308.

The rule recognizes that the burden of persuasion is not immutably fixed at the commencement of an action. In most cases the burden will remain on the party to whose claim for relief or defense a fact is essential. In some cases, however, the operation of a presumption may shift the burden of persuasion to the opposing party.

Because the basic facts giving rise to a presumption must be established by the evidence in the case, the burden of persuasion should not be finally assigned until the case is ready to go to the jury. McCormick, *Evidence* § 345 at 827 (2d ed 1972). This accords with present practice.

Rule 306 is not intended to prevent attorneys from commenting on the burden of persuasion during voir dire or their opening or closing remarks, nor is it meant to preclude trial judges from making preliminary statements as to the burden of persuasion.

After the burden of persuasion is assigned, the court shall instruct the jury as to the degree of conviction necessary to satisfy the burden: proof by preponderance of the evidence, proof by clear and convincing evidence, or proof beyond a reasonable doubt. See *Cook v. Michael,* 214 Or 513, 330 P2d 1026 (1958).

TEXT

Instructions on the Burden of Persuasion

The purpose of Rule 306 is to emphasize that because of Rule 308 the burden of persuasion is not fixed regarding all issues at the commencement of trial. Under Rule 308, a presumption in a civil case may shift not only the burden of producing evidence but also the burden of persuasion.

As the Commentary suggests, the rule should not be construed to preclude judges from making preliminary comments as to the burden of persuasion, or attorneys from referring to the burden of persuasion during voir dire or their opening or closing remarks.

Rule 306 would seem generally inapplicable to criminal cases. In criminal cases, Rule 309, rather than Rule 308, controls the effect of presumptions and does not shift the burden of persuasion to the defendant. See *Sandstrom v. Montana,* 442 US 510, 99 SCt 2450, 61 LEd2d 39 (1979) (holding that the burden of persuasion regarding an element of the offense cannot constitutionally be shifted to the defendant).

Although the rule states that "[t]he court shall instruct the jury as to which party bears the applicable burden of persuasion," the issue will often not be as simple as the phrasing of the rule suggests. Whether the burden of persuasion regarding the nonexistence of the presumed fact has shifted to the opponent under Rule 308 will depend on whether the facts giving rise to the presumption are established. In cases where such facts are contested, the court will often be unable to determine whether these facts have been established; that will be an issue for the jury. Therefore, the instruction by the court contemplated by Rule 306 will often not be a fixed assignment of the burden of persuasion, but a conditional assignment. The instruction may have to include the preliminary qualification that if the jury finds the facts giving rise to the presumption to be established, then the burden of persuasion to prove the nonexistence of the presumed fact is assigned to the opponent of the presumption.

RULE 307. ORS 40.115. ALLOCATION OF THE BURDEN OF PRODUCING EVIDENCE

(1) **The burden of producing evidence as to a particular issue is on the party against whom a finding on the issue would be required in the absence of further evidence.**

(2) **The burden of producing evidence as to a particular issue is initially on the party with the burden of persuasion as to that issue.**

LEGISLATIVE COMMENTARY

Oregon Rule of Evidence 307 defines and allocates the burden of producing evidence. The rule is a slightly modified version of California Evidence Code § 550.

The "burden of producing evidence" on an issue means the liability to an adverse ruling if further evidence on the issue is not produced. The adverse ruling may be a finding or a directed verdict. It is always by the court. In a jury trial, the burden of producing evidence empowers the judge to decide the case without jury consideration. A party is subject to an adverse decision on a question of fact if a reasonable person could not find in its favor on the question. Once it has produced that quantum of favorable evidence, the burden of producing evidence is satisfied, and the party will survive a motion for a nonsuit or directed verdict. See McCormick, *Evidence* § 338 at 789–791 (2d ed 1972); California Evidence Code § 550, Comment at 1083 (West 1965).

At the outset of a case, the burden of producing evidence is on the party with the burden of persuasion. Upon that party's discharge of the burden of producing evidence the burden will lift from it. The burden of producing evidence will shift to the adverse party if, and only if, the initial party has produced such favorable evidence on the issue that it would be entitled to a finding as a matter of law. See McCormick § 338 at 791–793.

Rule 307 is in accord with existing Oregon law. ORS 41.210 provides that the "burden of proof" lies on the party who would be defeated if no evidence were given on either side. Similarly, Oregon courts have held that the party having the burden of producing evidence must produce substantial evidence to avoid a nonsuit or directed verdict. *Larson v. Hansen,* 223 Or 533, 355 P2d 235 (1960); *Fish v. Southern Pacific Co.,* 173 Or 294, 143 P2d 917 (1943).

TEXT

Allocation of the Burden of Production

Rule 307 clearly distinguishes the burden of producing evidence from the burden of persuasion covered by Rule 305. The burden of producing evidence is applicable at the commencement of trial and dictates which party must produce sufficient evidence on a particular issue to avoid an adverse finding, a directed verdict, a judgment of dismissal, or a judgment of acquittal. The burden of persuasion usually does not come into play until after all the evidence is produced and the case is submitted to the finder of fact for determination.

The burden of producing evidence can be satisfied by producing circumstantial evidence as well as direct evidence, and also by presumptions, inferences, and in some cases judicial notice. The burden of producing evidence may shift back and forth between the parties during the course of the trial depending upon the evidence offered by each side.

If a presumption is established, it will not only satisfy the burden of production with respect to the presumed fact, but will shift the burden to the opposing party to provide rebutting evidence. Under Rule 308, a presumption in a civil case will also shift the burden of persuasion to the opposing party. However, an inference can only satisfy the burden of production. It does not shift either the burden of production or the burden of persuasion to the opponent.

There can be both official and unofficial shifting of the burden of producing evidence in trials. Rule 307 addresses only the question of when the burden is officially shifted. Under Rule 307(1), the burden will shift when the producing party has introduced such favorable evidence on the issue that it would be entitled to a finding or directed verdict on that issue as a matter of law. In many cases, the party will not be entitled to a favorable ruling as a matter of law, although the evidence will be sufficient to go to the jury. In such cases, it might be viewed that there is an unofficial shifting of the burden of production, because if the opponent does not produce contrary evidence, the jury is likely to find against the opponent on the issue. Nonetheless, Rule 307 does not place the burden of producing evidence upon the opponent in this situation, because the opponent can take the chance that the jury will disbelieve the proponent's evidence and decide in the opponent's favor. See *Nelson v. Hughes,* 290 Or 653, 666 n17, 625 P2d 643 (1981).

The Commentary does not discuss the applicability of Rule 307 in criminal cases. Rule 307(1) refers to instances where the court would be required to direct a finding against a party in the absence of further evidence. In criminal cases, however, a court may not direct a verdict or finding on an element of the offense against a criminal defendant. See *Sandstrom v. Montana,* 442 US 510, 516 n5, 99 SCt 2450, 61 LEd2d 39 (1979). See also Rules 309(1) and 201(g). Therefore, the burden of producing evidence to rebut an element of the prosecution's case cannot shift to the defendant.

In criminal cases, ORS 161.055 provides that the defendant has the burden of raising certain defenses, but that the prosecution has the burden of disproving those defenses, other than affirmative defenses, beyond a reasonable doubt. To the extent that this allocation might be viewed as inconsistent with Rule 307(2), the statute should prevail. Nothing in the Commentary indicates a legislative intent to modify ORS 161.055.

RULE 308.   ORS 40.120. PRESUMPTIONS IN CIVIL PROCEEDINGS

In civil actions and proceedings, a presumption imposes on the party against whom it is directed the burden of proving that the nonexistence of the presumed fact is more probable than its existence.

LEGISLATIVE COMMENTARY

Oregon Rule of Evidence 308 outlines the effect of a presumption in a civil action. The rule is based upon Federal Rule 301 as prescribed by the United States Supreme Court in October 1972. It represents a major change in Oregon law.

Under ORE 308, once a party invoking a presumption establishes the basic facts giving rise to it, the burden of establishing the nonexistence of the presumed fact shifts to the opposing party. Morgan, *Basic Problems of Evidence* (1962). Plaintiff, for example, may raise the presumption that a letter duly addressed and mailed was received in the regular course of the mail. See Rule 311(1)(h). The judge in such a case would determine whether the evidence is sufficient to support a finding of the existence of the basic facts: that the letter was properly addressed, that it was mailed, and that it was not returned. If so, the judge would instruct the jury that if they find the basic facts to be true, then the burden is on defendant to prove by a preponderance of the evidence that the letter was *not* received. The jury should never hear the word "presumption" during this instruction.

The constitutionality of imposing the burden of persuasion on the party against whom a presumption operates was settled in *Dick v. New York Life Ins. Co.,* 359 US 437, 79 SCt 921, 3 LEd 2d 935 (1959). In that case, an action under an accidental death clause, the Supreme Court ruled without reservation that the North Dakota presumption of accidental death imposes on a defendant insurer the burden of proving that the death of an insured was due to suicide.

The Legislative Assembly rejected the so-called "bursting bubble" theory under which a presumption vanishes on the introduction of evidence contrary to the presumed fact, even though the evidence may not be credible. Thayer, *Preliminary Treatise on Evidence* (1898). This approach gives presumptions too slight and evanescent an effect. Morgan and Maguire, "Looking Backward and Forward at Evidence," in 50 Harv L Rev 909 (1937).

The Legislative Assembly also rejected a middle approach to presumptions represented by current Oregon Practice. Under Oregon law, a presumption does not disappear from the case when contradictory evidence is introduced, nor does it shift the burden of persuasion to the adversary. Rather, the jury is instructed that a presumption is like any other evidential fact, and its existence does not endow the facts upon which it is based with any special value for evidential purposes. The jury is further instructed to weigh the evidence as a whole, including the presumption, and if its mind is equally divided on the issue, to decide against the party upon whom the burden of persuasion rests. *U.S. National Bank v. Underwriters at Lloyds,* 239 Or 298, 396 P2d 765 (1964).

The Legislative Assembly decided to change Oregon practice on presumptions for several reasons. First, it is extremely difficult to phrase a jury instruction without conveying the impression that the presumption itself is evidence. That proposition has long been discredited. *See,* e.g., McCormick § 345 at 825 n 60; *Wyckoff v. Mut. Life Ins. Co.,* 173 Or 592, 147 P2d 227 (1944). Second, under the current approach to presumptions, the jury must weigh the force of the legal conclusion mandated by the presumption against the testimony of witnesses and other direct evidence. That is a difficult or impossible task. Finally, the considerations of fairness, policy and probability, which underlie the creation of presumptions, are not satisfied by giving them any lesser effect. Cleary, "Presuming and Pleading: An Essay on Juristic Immaturity," in 12 Stan L Rev 4 (1959).

The approach set forth in this rule is simple and workable, and gives due consideration to the policies behind the creation of presumptions. All presumptions, whether legislatively or judicially created, must be treated in the manner prescribed by this section.

TEXT

Presumptions in Civil Proceedings

Rule 308 changes prior Oregon law by providing that a presumption shifts the burden of persuasion to the opponent to establish the nonexistence of the presumed fact. Rule 308 is limited to civil actions and proceedings. Criminal cases are governed by Rule 309.

Rule 308 gives presumptions much greater force than they had under prior Oregon law. Under former law a presumption did not shift the burden of persuasion but could be considered as an evidential fact to help the party having the affirmative of the issue carry the burden of persuasion. *U.S. National Bank v. Underwriters at Lloyds,* 239 Or 298, 396 P2d 765 (1964).

Rule 308 allows a presumption to shift the burden of persuasion regarding a presumed fact from the allocation that would otherwise be assigned by the substantive law pursuant to Rule 305. It will no longer be possible to determine at the commencement of a civil trial which party has the burden of persuasion regarding which issues. For this reason, Rule 306 provides that instructions regarding which party bears the applicable burden of persuasion should be given only after all the evidence has been received.

This rule applies only to presumptions, not to inferences. A presumption is a rule of law requiring that once a basic fact is established the jury must find a certain presumed fact, unless there is evidence rebutting that presumed fact. An inference merely permits a jury to find an inferred fact from a basic fact, but does not require the jury to do so. For further discussion of the distinction between these two concepts, see the textual discussion under Rule 311.

Rule 308 adopts what is often described as the Morgan view of presumptions, named after Professor Edmund Morgan of Harvard Law School. See Morgan, *Instructing the Jury Upon Presumptions and Burden of Proof,* 47 Harv L Rev 59 (1933); Morgan, *Further Observations on Presumptions,* 16 S Cal L Rev 245 (1943). The Morgan view is adopted by Rule 301 of the Uniform Rules of Evidence (1974). The approach of Rule 308 differs from the majority view at common law, which provides that a presumption disappears, or at least is reduced to an inference, in the face of legally sufficient rebutting evidence. See McCormick, *Evidence,* (3d ed 1984) § 345. For a perceptive critique of the approach adopted by Rule 308, see Lansing, *Enough is Enough: A Critique of the Morgan View of Rebuttable Presumptions in Civil Cases,* 62 Or L Rev 485 (1983).

Rule 308 also differs from FRE 301, which provides as follows:

> In all civil actions and proceedings not otherwise provided for by Act of Congress or by these rules, a presumption imposes on the party against whom it is directed the burden of going forward with evidence to rebut or meet the presumption, but does not shift to such party the burden of proof in the sense of the risk of nonpersuasion, which remains throughout the trial upon the party on whom it was originally cast.

Federal authority will therefore not be useful in interpreting Rule 308. However, the following states have adopted rules substantially identical to Rule 308, and decisions from these jurisdictions may provide useful interpretative authority: Arkansas, Delaware, Maine, Montana, Nebraska, Nevada, New Mexico, North Dakota, Utah, Wisconsin, and Wyoming. See 1 *Weinstein's Evidence* (1988) § 301[05].

Rule 308 will require a change in instructions given to juries regarding presumptions. The Commentary indicates that the word *presumption* should no longer be used. The jury should be instructed in terms of which party has the burden of persuasion with regard to a particular issue without mentioning the word *presumption.* In *Riley Hill General Contractor v. Tandy Corp.,* 303 Or 390, 408 n9, 737 P2d 595 (1987), the court commented that "In a properly tried civil case, the term 'presumption' should not be heard by the jury."

The type of instruction given will depend on the quantum of evidence offered in support of the fact giving rise to the presumption which is usually referred to as the basic fact. If insufficient evidence is offered to support a jury finding that the basic fact exists, the presumption will not be triggered and no instruction will be given. In some cases, the evidence offered of the basic fact will be so overwhelming as to justify a finding as a matter of law, or the basic fact may be established by stipulation of the parties. In such cases, the court would instruct the jury to find the presumed fact, unless the opponent carries the burden of persuasion to establish its nonexistence. In most cases, the evidence offered in support of the basic fact is likely to be sufficient but not conclusive as a matter of law. In such cases, both the basic fact and the presumed fact should be submitted to the jury. The jury should be instructed that if it finds the basic fact, then it must find the presumed fact, unless the opponent of the presumption carries the burden of persuasion to establish the nonexistence of the presumed fact. See Mueller, *Instructing the Jury Upon Presumptions in Civil Cases: Comparing Federal Rule 301 with Uniform Rule 301,* 12 Land & Water L Rev 219 (1977).

☞ **CAVEAT:**

The Commentary states that the legislature intends Rule 308 to apply to "[a]ll presumptions, whether legislatively or judicially created." The Commentary does not discuss the conflict between Rule 308 and ORS 71.2010(31), which controls the effect of presumptions under the Uniform Commercial Code. This statute adopts the view that a presumption does not shift the burden of persuasion. ORS 71.2010(31) states: "'Presumption' or 'presumed' means that the trier of fact must find the existence of the fact presumed unless and until evidence is introduced which would support a finding of its nonexistence." Because the UCC provision is more specific and is important to the consistent interpretation of the Uniform Commercial Code, it should prevail over Rule 308.

With respect to presumptions, see generally Seidl & Harwood, *Article III: Burdens of Proof and the Morgan Approach to Presumptions,* 19 Will L Rev 361 (1983); Broun, *The Unfulfillable Promise of One Rule for All Presumptions,* 62 N C L Rev 697 (1984); McCauliff, *Burdens of Proof: Degrees of Belief, Quanta of Evidence, or Constitutional Guarantees?,* 35 Vand L Rev 1293 (1982).

RULE 309.   ORS 40.125. PRESUMPTIONS IN CRIMINAL PROCEEDINGS

(1) **The judge is not authorized to direct the jury to find a presumed fact against the accused.**

(2) **When the presumed fact establishes guilt or is an element of the offense or negates a defense, the judge may submit the question of guilt or the existence of the presumed fact to the jury only if:**

   (a) **A reasonable juror on the evidence as a whole could find that the facts giving rise to the presumed fact have been established beyond a reasonable doubt; and**

   (b) **The presumed fact follows more likely than not from the facts giving rise to the presumed fact.**

LEGISLATIVE COMMENTARY

Oregon Rule of Evidence 309 states the effect of presumptions in criminal proceedings. The rule is a modification of Federal Rule 303, which was recommended by the United States Supreme Court in 1972 but deleted by the Congress in enacting the Federal Rules of Evidence. Federal Rule 303 was based upon A.L.I. Model Penal Code § 1.12(5)P.U.D.(1962) and *United States v. Gainey*, 380 US 63, 85 SCt 754, 13 LEd 2d 658 (1965).

Rule 309 indicates that a presumption may not be used against an accused to remove any matter in a criminal proceeding from final determination by the jury. Such an action would violate the axiom that a verdict cannot be directed against the accused, 9 Wigmore, *Evidence* § 2495 at 312 (3d ed 1940), or its corollary that a judge is without authority to direct a finding against the accused as to any element of a crime, A.L.I. Model Penal Code, § 1.12(1) P.U.D. (1962). Were it not for the rule, the existence of an adverse presumption might compel a defendant to introduce rebuttal evidence, including the defendant's testimony, and thus force a waiver of the constitutional right to remain silent. McCormick, *Evidence* § 344 at 819 (2d ed 1972).

The net effect of this rule is to reduce presumptions in criminal cases to nothing more than permissible inferences when they are used against the accused. For example, the prosecution in a controlled substances case may wish to use the presumption of knowledge of illegal importation from the fact of possession of heroin. The judge, in this circumstance, must determine as a matter of law that guilty knowledge follows from possession more likely than not. If so, the judge may allow the prosecution to argue the inference, and may consider the inference in passing on any motion testing the sufficiency of evidence. Normally, however, the inference would not be the subject of judicial comment. See *State v. Vance*, 285 Or 383, 398–399, 591 P2d 355 (1979) (Linde, J., concurring).

Rule 309 modifies the evidential effect of a presumption only when it is used against an accused. When used on behalf of a criminal defendant, a presumption continues to impose on the prosecution the burden of proving that the nonexistence of the presumed fact is more probable than its existence.

Because the operation of presumptions may infringe upon the rights of the accused, the United States Supreme Court has carefully limited their effect through a series of criminal decisions. In *Tot v. United States*, 319 US 463, 63 SCt 1241, 87 LEd 1519 (1943), the court held that a statutory presumption cannot be sustained if there is no rational connection between the fact proved and the fact to be presumed. Compare *United States v. Gainey*, supra (rational connection exists between proved fact of unexplained presence at still site and presumed fact of carrying on illegal distilling business), with *United States v. Romano*, 382 US 136, 86 SCt 279, 15 LEd 2d 210 (1965) (unexplained presence does not, however, support reasonable inference about defendant's specific function in connection with distilling operation).

In *Leary v. United States*, 395 US 6, 89 SCt 1532, 23 LEd 2d 57 (1969), the Supreme Court revealed that a stricter test than mere "rational connection" must be met. The court held that a presumption establishing an element of an offense is constitutional only if the presumed fact is more likely than not to flow from the basic facts. The court struck down, on this ground, a rule that possession of marijuana presumes guilty knowledge of its illegal importation. Although most marijuana is imported, the court concluded that it would be pure speculation to say that a majority of possessors know the source of their marijuana. See also *Turner v. United States,* 396 US 398, 90 SCt 642, 24 LEd 2d 610, rehearing denied, 397 US 958, 90 SCt 929, 25 LEd 2d 144 (1970), involving the same presumption but different drugs. After an extensive review of the evidence, the *Turner* court upheld the presumption as to heroin because all heroin consumed in the United States is illegally imported; it struck down the presumption as to cocaine, because a reasonable possibility exists that the purchase has been legal.

In *Barnes v. United States,* 412 US 837, 93 SCt 2357, 37 LEd 2d 380 (1973), the Supreme Court indicated that a presumption that follows from basic facts beyond a reasonable doubt is sufficient to pass the test of due process. This decision exposed the final question, whether such a connection is also constitutionally necessary. In *Ulster County Court v. Allen,* 442 US 140, 99 SCt 2213, 60 LEd 2d 777 (1979), the Supreme Court ruled that it is not, except in one circumstance: "As long as it is clear that the presumption is not the sole and sufficient basis for a finding of guilt, it need only satisfy the [more-probable-than-not] test described in Leary." 442 US at 167.

The Legislative Assembly sought to avoid any conflict with the defendant's constitutional rights, but not unnecessarily to hinder the prosecution of criminal cases, e.g., first degree robbery, in which the fact that the gun was loaded very often must be inferred from the facts of its display. See *State v. Vance,* supra. Therefore, Rule 309 provides that the presumed fact must follow more likely than not from the basic facts. It also provides that the judge may not submit the existence of the presumed fact to the jury unless a reasonable juror on the evidence as a whole could find that the basic facts have been established beyond a reasonable doubt.

Perhaps because of the delay in articulating federal constitutional principles governing the effect of presumptions in criminal cases, Oregon law on point is in a formative state. Following the reasoning in *Tot v. United States,* supra, the Oregon Court of Appeals impliedly ruled that a jury may infer an element establishing a prima facie case if there is rational connection between the presumption and the facts upon which it is based. *State v. Offord,* 14 Or App 195, 512 P2d 1375 (1973). Although the court cited *Leary v. United States* and *Turner v. United States,* supra, it did not apply either the "more likely than not" or the "reasonable doubt" standard. See also *State v. Bartolon,* 8 Or App 538, 495 P2d 772 (1972). ORE 309 is intended to culminate developments at both the state and federal levels.

TEXT

Presumptions in Criminal Proceedings

In criminal cases, the Federal Constitution imposes two significant constraints on the use of presumptions or inferences against a criminal defendant. First, the Constitution prohibits the court from directing the jury to find a fact that is an element of the prosecution's case against the defendant, even in the absence of rebutting evidence. *Sandstrom v. Montana,* 442 US 510, 516 n5, 99 SCt 2450, 61 LEd2d 39 (1979). The effect of this restriction is generally to require presumptions in criminal cases to be submitted to the jury as inferences, i.e., the jury is told that it *may* find the inferred fact, not that it *must* do so. Second, even an inference generally may not be submitted unless the inferred fact follows "more likely than not" from the facts giving rise to the inference. *Ulster County Court v. Allen,* 442 US 140, 99 SCt 2213, 60 LEd2d 777 (1979). Finally, as a matter of state law, inference instructions generally cannot be given against the defendant on an element of the crime because they violate the rule against judicial comment on the evidence. *State v. Rainey,* 98 Or 459, 693 P2d 635 (1985).

First Constraint: Inference, Not Presumption

Rule 309 recognizes and incorporates both of these constitutional limitations. Rule 309(1) provides: "The judge is not authorized to direct the jury to find a presumed fact against the accused." This rule is similar to Rule 201(g), which provides that in a criminal case a jury may not be required to accept as conclusive any fact judicially noticed in favor of the prosecution. Under Rule 309(1), the jury cannot be told to find a presumed fact against a criminal defendant, even if the defendant offers no rebutting evidence. The jury can be told only that it may, but is not required to, find the fact. Thus, when a prosecutor attempts to use a statutory or judicially created presumption in a criminal case, it is necessary to convert the presumption into an inference.

It would have been clearer if the legislature had used *inference* instead of *presumption* and *inferred fact* instead of *presumed fact* throughout Rule 309. The fact that possibly misleading terminology was used should not be allowed to obscure the effect of the rule, which as the Commentary acknowledges, is "to reduce presumptions in criminal cases to nothing more than permissible inferences when they are used against the accused."

Second Constraint: Inference Follows More Likely than Not

The second constitutional limitation on the use of presumptions or inferences in criminal cases is incorporated into Rule 309(2). This subsection allows an inference to be submitted that "establishes guilt or is an element of the offense or negates a defense" only when two requirements are satisfied: (1) sufficient evidence has been offered of the existence of the facts giving rise to that inference to support a jury finding beyond a reasonable doubt; and (2) the inferred fact follows more likely than not from the facts giving rise to the inference.

When a prosecutor considers using a statutory or judicially created presumption in a criminal case, it is necessary to ensure that it meets the requirements of Rule 309(2). A presumption may be permissible in civil cases that would not be permissible (even as an inference) in criminal cases, because it does not meet the "more likely than not" standard of Rule 309(2).

The mere fact that a presumption has been adopted by the legislature does not establish that it satisfies the requirements of Rule 309(2). The Commentary to Rule 311 states that with respect to the presumptions listed in Rule 311, "the Legislative Assembly has made no determination that the presumed facts flow from the basic facts beyond a reasonable doubt." Nothing indicates that the legislature has made a determination that they satisfy the more-likely-than-not standard of Rule 309(2) either. Individual analysis will be necessary in each case.

For an example of an inference found to satisfy the standard of Rule 309(2) on the evidence in the case, see *State v. Lindoff*, 56 Or App 742, 642 P2d 1214, rev denied 293 Or 394, 650 P2d 927 (1982) (identity of person from identity of name). For examples of inferences found not to satisfy the standard of Rule 309(2), see *State v. Short*, 88 Or App 567, 746 P2d 742 (1987) (no rational connection between failure to pay check within 10 days after it has been refused and knowledge at time check was written that it would be dishonored); *State v. Rainey*, 60 Or App 302, 653 P2d 584 (1982), affirmed on other grounds 298 Or 459, 693 P2d 635 (1985) (no rational connection between delivery of a controlled substance and knowledge of its character).

☞ CAVEAT:

Rule 309(2) is constitutionally inadequate in one relatively narrow circumstance. *Ulster County Court v. Allen*, 442 US 140, 99 SCt 2213, 60 LEd2d 777 (1979) requires that when the inference is the sole basis establishing an element of the offense or the guilt of the defendant, the inferred fact must follow from the facts giving rise to the inference "beyond a reasonable doubt." When such a situation arises, the constitutionally required standard should, of course, be applied rather than the more-likely-than-not standard of Rule 309(2).

Rule 309 applies only to presumptions in favor of the prosecution. The code is silent regarding the effect to be given to presumptions in favor of a criminal defendant. According to the commentary, "[w]hen used on behalf of a criminal defendant, a presumption continues to impose on the prosecution the burden of proving that the non-existence of the presumed fact is more probable than its existence." This suggestion to apply Rule 308 to presumptions against the prosecution, while appropriate, will require courts to overlook the fact that Rule 308 by its terms covers only civil actions and proceedings.

Jury Instructions

When an instruction is given under Rule 309, several guidelines should be followed. The word *presumption* should not be used in the instruction. The Oregon Supreme Court has already cautioned against such usage. In *State v. Stilling*, 285 Or 293, 297, 590 P2d 1223, 1226, cert denied 444 US 880 (1979), the court stated: "We hold that usage of the words 'disputable presumption' or 'presumption' in a jury instruction on the intent element of a crime to be impermissible when the presumption runs contrary to the burden of proof in the case." In *Sandstrom v. Montana*, 442 US 510, 519, 99 SCt 2450, 61 LEd2d 39 (1979), the Supreme Court held that an instruction that "the law presumes that a person intends the ordinary consequences of his voluntary acts" was constitutionally defective because the jury might have interpreted the word *presume* to mean either that the presumption was conclusive or that it shifted the burden of persuasion to the defendant on the element of intent.

Even if the word "inference" rather than "presumption" is used in the instruction, error may still be found if any additional instruction is given indicating that the jury is *required* to find a particular fact against the defendant. For example, in *State v. Short,* 88 Or App 567, 746 P2d 742 (1987), the judge's inference instruction was found to be erroneous in part because it was followed by this statement: "You are not required to draw this inference unless you find all the above facts [giving rise to the inference] have been proved to you beyond a reasonable doubt." This additional language suggested that the jury *was* required to draw the inference if the basic facts were established, and they were admitted by the defendant in this case. Thus the "inference" was really a presumption.

In a Rule 309 instruction, the jury should generally be told that it must find the facts giving rise to the inference beyond a reasonable doubt before it may find the inferred fact. The jury should be specifically informed that they are not required to find the inferred fact.

No Judicial Comment on Evidence

The potential availability of even an inference instruction under Rule 309 has been significantly narrowed by *State v. Rainey,* 298 Or 459, 693 P2d 635 (1985). In *Rainey* the court stated:

> [W]hen used against a defendant with reference to an element of the crime, an instruction on an inference ought not to be used. ... It is the task of the advocate, not the judge, to comment on inferences. ... Inferences when used against the defendant should be left to argument without any instruction.

298 Or at 466–7, 693 P2d at 640.

The court justified its holding on the ground that an inference might be so general or abstract that it would be of little help to the jury. Also the court noted that an inference instruction by the trial judge is likely to have the same effect as judicial comment on the evidence, which is generally prohibited. ORCP 59E provides: "The judge shall not instruct with respect to matters of fact nor comment thereon." ORCP 59E applies to criminal actions as well as civil actions. See ORS 136.330.

Although the *Rainey* opinion could be viewed as discouraging all inference instructions on behalf of the prosecution, the holding of the case is limited to inferences against a defendant "with reference to an element of the crime." It is possible that other types of inferences will continue to be allowed on behalf of the prosecutor in appropriate circumstances.

Certainly inferences can be used to support a conclusion that there is sufficient evidence to send a case to the jury or to support a conviction. For example, in *State v. Lindoff,* 56 Or App 742, 642 P2d 1214, rev denied 293 Or 394, 650 P2d 927 (1982), the arresting officer was unable at trial to identify the defendant as the person to whom he issued the citation for driving while his license was suspended. The court held that the statutory inference of identity of person from identity of name was sufficient to make a prima facie case when there was a "perfect correlation between the name of the defendant and the identification given the arresting officer."

Inferences can also be used by the trial judge when the court is serving as finder of fact. In *State v. Wigget*, 75 Or App 474, 707 P2d 101 (1985), the defendant assigned as error the trial court's failure to grant his motion for acquittal on the ground that he was too intoxicated to form the intent to commit the offense. The court affirmed, citing Rules 309 and 311(1)(a) and stating: "His conduct is in itself evidence from which the trial court, as trier of fact, could reasonably have concluded that he intended to do what he did." 75 Or App at 479, 707 P2d at 103.

Rainey also does not bar an instruction to jurors that they may draw their own inferences from the evidence. See *State v. Hines*, 84 Or App 681, 735 P2d 618, rev denied 303 Or 590, 739 P2d 570 (1987) (approving Uniform Criminal Jury Instruction No. 1005, which provides: "In deciding this case you may draw inferences and reach conclusions from the evidence, provided that your inferences and conclusions are reasonable and are based upon your common sense and experience.").

Rainey does not prevent the jury from being instructed on a rule of substantive law. In *State v. Caldwell*, 98 Or App 708, 710, 780 P2d 789 (1989), a prosecution for kidnapping, rape, and robbery, the court held that the following instruction was proper because it stated a rule of law rather than an inference: "One who has the purpose of forcibly raping another has the purpose of causing physical injury."

If a defendant has offered substantial evidence disputing the existence of the inferred fact, courts are particularly likely to refuse to instruct the jury regarding the inference. If the facts giving rise to the inference are not sufficiently established to support a jury finding beyond a reasonable doubt, Rule 309(2)(A) provides that the instruction should not be given.

There are several ambiguities in Rule 309. Does Rule 309(2) really mean "the judge may submit the question of guilt … to the jury only if" the requested inference satisfies subsections (a) and (b)? Surely not, because even if the inference is invalid, there may be sufficient evidence apart from the inference to support a finding of guilt.

✍ QUERY:

Does Rule 309 apply to all inferences in favor of the prosecution, or are there inferences that do not tend to establish guilt or constitute an element of the offense or negate a defense, to which the rule is not applicable? If so, what limitations apply to such inferences? Neither the rule nor the Commentary addresses these questions. See proposed but rejected Federal Rule 303, discussed in C. Mueller & L. Kirkpatrick, MODERN EVIDENCE (1995) § 3.15.

Recent Cases

In numerous recent criminal cases, error has been found in jury instructions regarding presumptions or inferences. In *State v. Campbell*, 100 Or App 153, 155, 785 P2d 370, rev denied 310 Or 71, 792 P2d 104 (1990), the court held that giving the following inference instruction was reversible error: "If you find that a firearm was pointed at another within firing range, then you are permitted but you are not required to infer that the firearm was loaded." This instruction was held to violate the no comment rule of *State v. Rainey*, supra.

In *State v. Allen*, 104 Or App 622, 802 P2d 690, rev denied 311 Or 426, 812 P2d 826 (1990), the court rejected the argument that use of breathalyzer test results created an unconstitutional presumption with respect to the defendant's blood alcohol level.

It has been held to be error for a trial court to instruct that intent to steal can be inferred from the defendant's presence in a dwelling under circumstances showing unlawful entry. *State v. Johnson*, 55 Or App 98, 103–4, 637 P2d 211, 214, rev denied 292 Or 722, 644 P2d 1131 (1981); *State v. Carden*, 58 Or App 655, 662, 650 P2d 97, 101, rev denied 293 Or 653, 653 P2d 998 (1982) (although not reversible error if defendant failed to object).

In *State v. Flack*, 58 Or App 330, 648 P2d 857 (1982), the court found error in a jury instruction that "it is presumed that an unlawful act was done with unlawful intent." The court stated: "We disapprove of the challenged instruction and urge that it never be given. ..." 58 Or App at 336, 648 P2d at 860.

In *State v. Rainey*, 298 Or 459, 693 P2d 635 (1985), the court held that giving of an instruction that proof of unlawful delivery of a controlled substance is prima facie evidence of knowledge of its character was reversible error. This instruction, combined with another instruction that "prima facie means evidence ... sufficient to establish a given fact and which if not rebutted or contradicted will remain sufficient," was deemed likely to be interpreted as a presumption, which is not permissible against a defendant in a criminal case.

In *State v. Nossaman*, 63 Or App 789, 797, 666 P2d 1351, 1356 (1983), the court held it was error to give an instruction in a criminal case that certain evidence was "sufficient evidence unless equaled or outweighed by other evidence." The court stated:

> We disapprove the instruction, because it does not make clear to the jury that finding the presumed fact is merely an inference that it is permitted to draw. Instead, it could give the jury the impression that, in the absence of evidence from the defendant, an element of the charge is to be presumed from proof of different facts, a violation of OEC 309(1).

In *State v. Woodfield*, 62 Or App 69, 659 P2d 1006, rev denied 295 Or 259, 668 P2d 381 (1983), an instruction that every witness is presumed to speak the truth was challenged by the defendant in a case where there were 37 state's witnesses and only six witnesses for the defendant. The court refused to rule upon the question, holding that defendant had not made a proper objection to the instruction in the trial court.

In *State v. Conway,* 75 Or App 430, 707 P2d 618, rev denied 300 Or 451, 712 P2d 110 (1985), the court found the giving of an inference instruction to be an improper comment on the evidence, but harmless error.

See generally NOTE, *The Improper Use of Presumptions in Recent Criminal Law Adjudication,* 38 Stan L Rev 423 (1986); Hoffman & Schroeder, *Burdens of Proof,* 38 Ala L Rev 31 (1986).

RULE 310.   ORS 40.130. CONFLICTING PRESUMPTIONS

If presumptions are conflicting, the presumption applies that is founded upon weightier considerations of policy and logic. If considerations of policy and logic are of equal weight, neither presumption applies.

LEGISLATIVE COMMENTARY

Oregon Rule of Evidence 310 is patterned after Uniform Rule 301(b) (Final Draft, August 1974). It sets forth the rule to be followed when one issue in a case generates two or more presumptions that conflict with each other.

Thayer's solution to the problem would be to disregard conflicting presumptions and give them no effect. The facts upon which the presumptions are based would be considered as evidence, along with all other relevant facts. This is a practical solution when all presumptions are based upon probability, or upon procedural convenience. However, a presumption may also rest on logic or social policy. McCormick, *Evidence,* § 345 at 823 (2d ed 1972). Under Thayer, when one presumption is based on procedural convenience and a conflicting presumption is based on social policy, both must be disregarded. Doing this eliminates the procedural convenience of one presumption and denies expression to the social policy behind the other. "A weighing of the reasons underlying the particular presumptions in question will lead to a rational solution of any conflict; an inflexible rule that every presumption vanishes upon the introduction of evidence of a fixed kind and quantity will often produce an irrational solution." Morgan, "Some Observations Concerning Presumption," in 44 Harv L Rev 906, 932 n 41 (1931).

The effect of conflicting presumptions under Oregon law is not altogether clear. Early cases held that conflicting presumptions balance and cancel each other. *State ex rel v. Olcott,* 67 Or 214, 135 P 95 (1913); *McVay v. Byars,* 171 Or 449, 138 P2d 210 (1943). However, there was also support for the rule that the judge should apply the presumption resting in weightier considerations of policy and logic. *State v. Wakefield,* 11 Or 615, 218 P 115 (1924); *Smith v. Smith,* 169 Or 650, 131 P2d 447 (1942). More recently, the Oregon Supreme Court considered a conflict between two presumptions based on probabilities. *Dicillo v. Osborn,* 204 Or 171, 282 P2d 611 (1955). Noting that probability-based presumptions are not concerned with social policy, unlike presumptions of marriage and legitimacy, the court held as a matter of law that there is no way to tell which presumption is stronger. Application of ORE 310 would have yielded the same result.

TEXT

Conflicting Presumptions

Rule 310 adopts the sensible view that in those unusual cases where there are conflicting presumptions, both should not automatically disappear. The judge is given authority to choose one presumption over the other if the judge is persuaded that presumption is founded upon weightier considerations of policy and logic.

The rule is undoubtedly easier to state than to apply. If both presumptions are based on social policy rather than probabilities, it may be difficult to determine which is the stronger social policy. If one presumption is based on social policy and the conflicting presumption is based on high probability, it also may be difficult for the court to resolve this conflict.

In *Smith v. Smith,* 169 Or 650, 652, 131 P2d 447 (1942), the Oregon Supreme Court stated that the presumption of validity of a subsequent marriage "is one of the strongest disputable presumptions known in law." In *Steinberg v. Steinberg,* 34 Or App 293, 297, 578 P2d 487, 490 (1978), the court held that "[t]he presumption that the subsequent marriage is valid prevails over the presumption that the prior spouse continued to live."

The presumption that "[a] child born in lawful wedlock is legitimate," (see Rule 311(v)) has generally been viewed by courts as a strong presumption that will prevail over many other presumptions. See ANNOT., *Presumption of Legitimacy of Child Born After Annulment, Divorce, or Separation,* 46 ALR 3d 158 (1972). On the other hand, the presumption of identity of person from identity of name (see Rule 311(r)) has generally been viewed as a relatively weak presumption. See 29 AM JUR 2d *Evidence,* § 167 (2d ed 1967).

RULE 311. ORS 40.135. PRESUMPTIONS

(1) The following are presumptions:
    (a) A person intends the ordinary consequences of a voluntary act.
    (b) A person takes ordinary care of the person's own concerns.
    (c) Evidence willfully suppressed would be adverse to the party suppressing it.
    (d) Money paid by one to another was due to the latter.
    (e) A thing delivered by one to another belonged to the latter.
    (f) An obligation delivered to the debtor has been paid.
    (g) A person is the owner of property from exercising acts of ownership over it or from common reputation of the ownership of the person.

(h) A person in possession of an order on that person, for the payment of money or the delivery of a thing, has paid the money or delivered the thing accordingly.

(i) A person acting in a public office was regularly appointed to it.

(j) Official duty has been regularly performed.

(k) A court, or judge acting as such, whether in this state or any other state or country, was acting in the lawful exercise of the jurisdiction of the court.

(L) Private transactions have been fair and regular.

(m) The ordinary course of business has been followed.

(n) A promissory note or bill of exchange was given or indorsed for a sufficient consideration.

(o) An indorsement of a negotiable promissory note, or bill of exchange, was made at the time and place of making the note or bill.

(p) A writing is truly dated.

(q) A letter duly directed and mailed was received in the regular course of the mail.

(r) A person is the same person if the name is identical.

(s) A person not heard from in seven years is dead.

(t) Persons acting as copartners have entered into a contract of copartnership.

(u) A man and woman deporting themselves as husband and wife have entered into a lawful contract of marriage.

(v) A child born in lawful wedlock is legitimate.

(w) A thing once proved to exist continues as long as is usual with things of that nature.

(x) The law has been obeyed.

(y) An uninterrupted adverse possession of real property for 20 years or more has been held pursuant to a written conveyance.

(z) A trustee or other person whose duty it was to convey real property to a particular person has actually conveyed it to the person, when such presumption is necessary to perfect the title of the person or the person's successor in interest.

(2) A statute providing that a fact or a group of facts is prima facie evidence of another fact establishes a presumption within the meaning of this section.

LEGISLATIVE COMMENTARY

Oregon Rule of Evidence 311 contains a partial list of statutory presumptions. The rule has no federal analogue. It is based on ORS 41.360, which is repealed, and incorporates the majority of presumptions codified under that section. The presumptions repealed and recodified and the reasons therefor are listed below.

The effect of the presumptions listed in this rule will be different in civil and criminal cases. See ORE 308 and 309. Their inclusion is not meant to suggest that any will necessarily pass constitutional muster in a criminal case if used as the sole evidence on a question of fact, i.e., the Legislative Assembly has made no determination that the presumed facts flow from the basic facts beyond a reasonable doubt. See *Ulster County Court v. Allen*, 442 US 140, 99 SCt 2213, 60 LEd2d 777 (1981).

The enumeration of presumptions in this rule does not impair the integrity of judicially created presumptions; nor does it affect the power of the courts to create new presumptions in the future.

Subsection (1). The presumptions in this subsection replace two sets of propositions that were listed as "presumptions" under prior statutes. ORS 41.350, 41.360.

Conclusive presumptions. Subsection (1) does not preserve any of the "conclusive presumptions" found in ORS 41.350. These are not true presumptions. When the basic fact giving rise to a conclusive presumption is established, the presumed fact must be taken as true and the adversary is not allowed to dispute the presumed fact. As McCormick points out, "… the courts are not stating a presumption at all, but are simply expressing a rule of law…" McCormick, *Evidence* § 342 at 802 (2d ed 1972). ORS 41.350 is repealed. Only a few of its provisions are recodified.

Under ORS 41.350(1), intent to murder was conclusively presumed from the deliberate use of a deadly weapon which causes death within a year. ORS 41.350(2) created a conclusive presumption of malicious and guilty intent from the deliberate commission of an unlawful act for the purpose of injuring another. Both rules were repealed as the Oregon Supreme Court has held that they cannot be constitutionally applied against a defendant in a criminal case. *State v. Elliott*, 234 Or 522, 383 P2d 382 (1963).

ORS 41.350(3) was recodified under ORS chapter 42, relating to execution, formalities and interpretation of writings.

ORS 41.350(4) stated that whenever a party has, by declaration, act or omission, intentionally and deliberately led another to believe a particular thing true and to act upon such belief, the party shall not, in any litigation arising out of such declaration, act or omission, be permitted to falsify it. This was repealed because it merely repeats the judicially established principle of estoppel in pais, or equitable estoppel. *Second Northwestern Finance Corp. v. Mansfield*, 121 Or 236, 252 P 400 (1927). By its repeal, the Legislative Assembly does not intend to affect the law of estoppel as expressed in *Earls v. Clarke*, 223 Or 527, 355 P2d 213 (1960) and *Bennett v. City of Salem*, 192 Or 531, 235 P2d 772 (1951).

ORS 41.350(5) was recodified under ORS chapter 91, relating to landlord and tenant.

Under ORS 41.350(6), the issue of a wife cohabiting with her husband who was not impotent or sterile at the time of conception of the child was conclusively presumed to be legitimate. This rule duplicated ORS 109.070(1) and therefore was repealed.

ORS 41.350(7) conclusively presumed the judgment, decree or order of a court when statute declared the same to be conclusive. It provided further that the judgment, decree or order shall be pleaded if there is an opportunity to do so, but if there is no such opportunity then it may be used as evidence with like effect. The first thought is a truism, while the second is addressed in ORCP 20B and ORS 43.110 through 43.220. The subsection was therefore repealed.

ORS 41.350(8) conclusively presumed any other presumption which by statute was expressly made conclusive. This was repealed as a tautology.

Permissive presumptions. Rule 311 retains all of the "permissive presumptions" in ORS 41.360 with the exception of those created by subsections (1), (2), (6), (10), (11), (17), (18), (27), (28), (34), (36) and (39) of that section.

ORS 41.360(1), the presumption of innocence, is not a true rebuttable presumption because there is no presumed fact following from a basic fact. This "presumption" is merely a way of emphasizing to the jury the prosecutor's burden of persuasion. While an instruction on the innocence of the defendant should certainly be given, it has no place in a list of rebuttable presumptions. The provision was recodified in ORS 17.250, which lists instructions that are to be given by the court "on all proper occasions."

The presumption that an unlawful act is done with unlawful intent, ORS 41.360(2), was deleted as it was held to be unconstitutional as applied against a defendant in a criminal case. *State v. Bartolon,* 8 Or App 538, 495 P2d 772 (1972). The Legislative Assembly believes that it also should not be applied in civil cases. A party should not be able to shift the burden of persuasion to the opposing party on the issue of intent, merely by establishing that an unlawful act has occurred. See ORE 308.

ORS 41.360(6) seated the presumption that higher evidence would be adverse from the fact that inferior evidence has been produced. This provision is unnecessary in view of ORS 17.250(7), and was therefore deleted.

ORS 41.360(10), creating the presumption that "former rent or installments of a debt have been paid when a receipt for latter is produced," was deleted for several reasons. First, it is nearly unintelligible. Second, it can be misinterpreted to mean that all *prior* payments are presumed to have been made. Third, any person who holds a receipt for payment of rent or an instalment of a debt has no need for the presumption.

Under ORS 41.360(11), it was presumed that things in the possession of a person are owned by that person. This presumption was deleted because the inference of ownership based on possession is not strong enough to warrant treatment as a presumption. In addition, the burden of persuasion usually is already allocated to the party disputing the claim that the person possessing things owns them.

ORS 41.360(17) was deleted as a potentially inaccurate statement of existing law, particularly in criminal cases. This subsection created the presumption that a judicial record, when not conclusive, still correctly determines or sets forth the rights of the parties.

Also deleted was ORS 41.360(18), the presumption that all matters within an issue were submitted to the jury and passed upon by them. This is an unnecessary provision: res judicata and collateral estoppel operate to establish conclusively the issues on which a judgment rests.

The Legislative Assembly agrees with the revisers of the California Evidence Code in repealing the presumption that acquiescence follows from a belief that the thing acquiesced in is conformable to the right or fact. ORS 41.360(27). "Although it may be appropriate under some circumstances to infer from the lack of protest that a person believes in the truth of a statement made in his presence, it is undesirable to require such a conclusion. The surrounding circumstances may vary greatly from case to case, and the trier of fact should be free to decide whether acquiescence resulted from belief or some other cause." 6 *California Law Revision Commission, Reports, Recommendations and Studies,* Tentative Recommendation and a Study Relating to the Uniform Rules of Evidence, at 1042–43 (June 1964).

Finally, ORS 41.360(28) was deleted because it was over-broad and might be misapplied. It created the presumption that things happen according to the ordinary course of nature and the ordinary habits of life. Any benefit derived from relying on this presumption may be obtained by requesting the court judicially to notice facts that describe the ordinary course of nature or the ordinary habits of life, when these are matters of common knowledge.

Subsections (34), (35) and (36) of ORS 41.360 have been recodified in Article IX of Oregon Evidence Code, relating to authentication and identification.

ORS 41.360(39) created a presumption of intent to defraud creditors from a failure to deliver personal property capable of delivery immediately upon sale. The Legislative Assembly repealed this provision in view of its many exceptions and limited scope. It leaves to the courts the development of the law regarding the evidential effect of "badges of fraud." See *Evans v. Trude and Champlin,* 193 Or 648, 240 P2d 940 (1952); *Blackabee v. Seaweard,* 112 Or 675, 231 P 146 (1924).

Notwithstanding the above, subsection (1) of Rule 311 does include four statements carried over from ORS 41.360 which are not presumptions in the technical sense of the word. These "presumptions" are found in paragraphs (a), (b), (L) and (w). The Legislative Assembly believes these are sufficiently important to include in the Oregon Evidence Code although they indicate no basic facts giving rise to the presumed fact.

Subsection (2). A number of other statutes provide that certain facts give rise to a "disputable presumption," or are "prima facie" or "primary" evidence of other facts. See, e.g., ORS 30.910 (product not unreasonably dangerous for its intended use), ORS 73.3070 (signature on negotiable instrument genuine), ORS 377.635 (junk near junkyard placed there by owner or operator), and ORS 656.802 (respiratory ailment of fireman employed for 5 or more years result of employment). Subsection (2) makes it clear that these provisions also create rebuttable presumptions within the meaning of the rule, and are therefore subject to Article III of the Oregon Evidence Code.

TEXT

Available Presumptions

Rule 311 contains most of the presumptions listed in former ORS 41.360 (repealed 1981), except that a number of presumptions were eliminated as being ill-advised or contrary to policy. All conclusive presumptions were removed from the evidence code, because they are, in effect, rules of substantive law rather than rules of evidence.

Any statute creating a conclusive presumption is not subject to the Oregon Evidence Code provisions concerning presumptions. See *Hodge v. Hodge,* 301 Or 433, 722 P2d 1235 (1986) (holding ORS 109.070(1), which provides that a child of a wife cohabiting with her husband who is not sterile or impotent at the time of the child's conception "shall be conclusively presumed to be the child of the husband," not to be a presumption under the code; also, because facts giving rise to the conclusive presumption were not proven, statute was inapplicable). See also *State ex rel Juvenile Department v. Merritt,* 83 Or App 378, 732 P2d 46 (1987) (conclusive presumption is a rule of substantive law not subject to Oregon Evidence Code).

Neither Rule 311 nor any other rule defines a presumption. A presumption is a rule of law requiring that once a basic fact is established the jury must find a certain presumed fact, in absence of evidence rebutting that presumed fact. Compare former ORS 41.340 (repealed 1981) (defining a presumption as "a deduction which the law expressly directs to be made from particular facts."). Under the generally accepted definition set forth above, a "true" presumption requires a basic fact giving rise to the presumed fact, e.g., if A, then B. A presumption is distinguished from an inference by its mandatory nature. The jury is required to find a presumed fact in absence of evidence disproving that presumed fact. In the case of an inference, the jury is allowed but not mandated to find the inferred fact.

As the Commentary acknowledges, not all of the subparts of Rule 311 constitute presumptions "in the technical sense of the word" because they do not have a "basic fact giving rise to a presumed fact." The Commentary cites as examples subparts (a), (b), (L), and (w). See also subparts (m) and (x). They were included in Rule 311, perhaps unwisely, because they were deemed "sufficiently important." Some statutory "presumptions" also are not true presumptions. See, e.g., ORS 44.370 (witness presumed to speak truth). It may be difficult and often inappropriate to apply Rules 308, 309, and 310 to any maxim, assumption, or statement of law that does not constitute a true presumption.

Rule 309 requires that a presumption in a criminal case generally be submitted to the jury in the form of an inference. Moreover, even an inference may not be submitted unless it meets the requirements of Rule 309(2) and applicable constitutional standards. Each presumption listed under Rule 311 must be analyzed to assure that it meets these standards before an instruction based on the presumption is given in a criminal case. See also ORCP 59E; ORS 136.330 (prohibiting judicial comment on the evidence).

Other Statutory Presumptions

Rule 311 does not represent a complete listing of all statutory presumptions. See, e.g., ORS 30.910 (in a products liability action, a product as manufactured and sold or leased is presumed not to be unreasonably dangerous for its intended use); ORS 41.930 (matters stated in affidavit of custodian of hospital records are presumed to be true); ORS 43.140 (a judicial order, other than a final order, judgment, or decree, creates a disputable presumption concerning the matter directly determined between the same parties, representatives, or successors in interest); ORS 44.370 (witness presumed to speak the truth); ORS 98.450(2) (if goods with value over $20 are deliberately and intentionally mailed or sent to an individual without first receiving an order, they are presumed to be gifts); ORS 107.105(1)(e) (both spouses have contributed equally to the acquisition of properties during the marriage, whether such property is jointly or separately held); ORS 109.070(2) (child born in wedlock, there being no decree of separation, is presumed to be child of mother's husband); ORS 112.725 (property acquired during marriage by a spouse of that marriage while domiciled in a community property state is presumed to be community property; real property situated in this state and personal property wherever situated acquired by a married person while domiciled in a noncommunity property state is presumed not to be community property); ORS 412.035(3) (under specified circumstances, minor presumed to reside in state for purposes of aid to blind program); ORS 609.157 (presumption that dog has been engaged in killing or injuring livestock under certain circumstances); ORS 656.310(1) (presumption that sufficient notice of workers' compensation injury was given and timely filed and that injury was not occasioned by the wilful intention of injured worker to injure or kill self); ORS 656.802 (presumption that certain diseases resulted from firefighter's employment); ORS 657.155(2) (presumption that individual who leaves the normal labor market area for major portion of any week is unavailable for work for purposes of unemployment compensation).

Other Judicially Created Presumptions

In addition, there are a number of judicially created "presumptions" in Oregon case law. See, e.g., *Brien v. Belsma*, 108 Or App 500, 505, 816 P2d 655, 668 (1991) (presumption of undue influence with respect to the transfer of property where party asserting undue influence establishes that a confidential relationship existed between a grantor and a grantee, the grantee has a position of dominance over the grantor and that suspicious circumstances exist); *Briscoe v. Schneider*, 97 Or App 352, 775 P2d 925, rev denied 308 Or 405, 781 P2d 855 (1989) (presumption that a will, last known to be in the decedent's control, which cannot be found after the time of death, was destroyed with the intention of revoking it); *First Interstate Bank v. Henson-Hammer*, 98 Or App 189, 779 P2d 167 (1989) (preceding presumption is only as strong as the decedent's control over the original will, taking into consideration the interests of anyone else with access to the will); *Cloud v. United States National Bank of Oregon*, 280 Or 83, 90, 570 P2d 350, 355 (1977) (presumption of competency); *Hood River County v. Dabney*, 246 Or 14, 28, 423 P2d 954, 961 (1966) (citizen presumed to know land taxable); *Kruse v. Coos Head Timber Co.*, 248 Or 294, 306, 432 P2d 1009, 1015 (1967) (presumption that a person has capacity to contract); *Dahl v. Clackamas County*, 243 Or 152, 154, 412 P2d 364, 365 (1966) (state is presumed to continue in ownership of all riverbeds below high water mark of all navigable streams until state is shown to have parted with title); *Hobgood v. Sylvester*, 242 Or 162, 166, 408 P2d 925, 927 (1965) (presumption that people ordinarily keep track of their property); *United States National Bank v. Underwriters at Lloyd's*, 239 Or 298, 318–21, 382 P2d 851 (1964) (presumption against suicide); *Kankkonen v. Hendrickson*, 232 Or 49, 55–6, 374 P2d 393, 396 (1962) (presumption that a decedent left heirs or next of kin capable of inheriting property; presumption of death where the age of a person, were he alive, would be beyond human expectation or experience); *Eckleberry v. Kaiser Foundation Northern Hospitals*, 226 Or 616, 625, 359 P2d 1090, 1094 (1961) (presumption that physicians have necessary medical knowledge to practice their profession); *Dungey v. Fairview Farms, Inc.*, 205 Or 615, 621, 290 P2d 181, 183 (1955) (every operator of a motor vehicle is presumed to know the rules of the road and their application); *Multnomah County v. Dant & Russell, Inc*, 158 Or 350, 356, 75 P2d 986, 988 (1938) (persons are presumed to intend to carry out their oral and written contracts); *Broad v. Kelly's Olympian Co.*, 156 Or 216, 229, 66 P2d 485, 490 (1937) (a person is presumed to be familiar with the contents of any document that bears his signature); *Cousineau v. Cousineau*, 155 Or 184, 190–1, 63 P2d 897, 900 (1936) (presumption that the law of another state is the same as the law of Oregon); *De La Montanya v. De La Montanya*, 131 Or 23, 26, 278 P 580 (1929) (presumption that a woman contracting marriage is sane); *Richter v. Richter*, 117 Or 621, 633, 223 P 543 (1924) (the law presumes chastity and virtue, not lust and concubinage); *Gantenbein v. Bowles*, 103 Or 277, 288, 203 P 614, 618 (1922) (directors of a corporation are presumed to know its financial condition); *In re Lathen*, 294 Or 157, 654 P2d 1110 (1982) (presumption of innocence applies in bar disciplinary proceedings); *State v. Stroup*, 290 Or 185, 620 P2d 1359 (1980) (crimes having their origin in common law must have a mens rea element).

The judiciary has continuing authority to create new presumptions. See *Bonner v. Arnold*, 296 Or 259, 265–6, 676 P2d 290, 293 (1984) (Lent, J., specially concurring).

Inferences

There are also some judicially created inferences that allow but do not require the jury to find an inferred fact from the existence of a basic fact. See, e.g., *State v. Vance*, 285 Or 383, 591 P2d 355 (1979) (inference that if a firearm is pointed at another person within firing range, the weapon is loaded); *Thorp v. Corwin*, 260 Or 23, 488 P2d 413 (1971) (res ipsa loquitur). The requirements for the res ipsa loquitur doctrine are:

> 1) The accident must be of a kind that ordinarily does not occur in the absence of someone's negligence;
> 2) The accident must have been caused by an agency or instrumentality within the defendant's exclusive control; and
> 3) The accident must not have been due to any voluntary action or contribution on plaintiff's part.

Mayor v. Dowsett, 240 Or 196, 220, 400 P2d 234 (1965).

When an inference is applicable, the jury is instructed that it may find the inferred fact, not that it must do so. Unlike presumptions, inferences are not subject to Rule 308 and do not shift the burden of persuasion to the opponent in a civil case. See *Watzig v. Tobin,* 292 Or 645, 655, 642 P2d 651 (1982) (res ipsa loquitur does not shift burden of persuasion or production).

The line between an inference and a presumption is not always clearly drawn. Under current Oregon law, it is uncertain whether there is a presumption or an inference of negligence by a bailee when property is returned in a damaged condition. See *Roberts v. Mitchell Bros. Truck Lines,* 43 Or App 161, 602 P2d 343 (1979) (Court of Appeals uses the term inference), aff'd 289 Or 119, 611 P2d 297 (1980) (Oregon Supreme Court uses the term disputable presumption). Although it used presumption terminology, the Supreme Court stated that this was not an appropriate case to resolve the question of whether the rule was an inference or a presumption. 289 Or at 126 n2, 611 P2d at 301 n2. Because the Supreme Court does not appear to intend that this "presumption" shift the burden of persuasion, the court is likely to redefine it as an inference under the new evidence code to avoid the effect of Rule 308.

Prima Facie Evidence

Under Rule 311(2), a statute providing that a fact or group of facts is prima facie evidence of another fact establishes a presumption within the meaning of this rule. For examples of such statutes, see ORS 646.638(4) (permanent injunction or final judgment obtained by state under Unlawful Trade Practices Act is prima facie evidence in private action that defendant engaged in the unlawful practice); ORS 659.415(1) ("A certificate by a duly licensed physician that the physician approves the worker's return to the worker's regular employment shall be prima facie evidence that the worker is able to perform such duties").

It should be noted that presumptions or statutes providing that a certain fact is prima facie evidence of another fact are often used for purposes other than submission to the jury under Rule 308 or 309. They may be used by the court for various procedural purposes, such as determining the admissibility of evidence under Rule 104, 901, or 902(10), or in evaluating the sufficiency of evidence against a motion to dismiss or for a directed verdict.

Recent Cases Applying Rule 311

Rule 311(1)(a): In *State v. Wigget,* 75 Or App 474, 479, 707 P2d 101, 103 (1985), the defendant assigned as error the trial court's failure to grant his motion for acquittal on the ground that he was too intoxicated to form the intent to commit the offense. The court affirmed, citing Rules 309 and 311(1)(a), and stating: "His conduct is in itself evidence from which the trial court, as trier of fact, could reasonably have concluded that he intended to do what he did."

Rule 311(1)(c): See *Stephens v. Bohlman,* 138 Or App 381, 386, 909 P2d 208 (1996) (evidence that an alleged tortfeasor attempted to conceal true cause of injury permits a jury to draw an adverse inference); *Austin v. Consolidated*

Freightways, 74 Or App 680, 683, 704 P2d 525, 527, rev denied 300 Or 332, 710 P2d 147 (1985).

Rule 311(1)(L) & (m): See *SAIF v. Barkman,* 101 Or App 20, 26, 789 P2d 8 (1990) ("[W]e do not think that the presumptions cited by AOL are relevant to the substantive question of 'good faith' under ORS 18.455. That discrete fact, which the statute makes a condition to discharge from liability for contribution, requires more direct proof than the abstract presumptions of obedience to law, fairness and regularity and adherence to the ordinary course of business can supply.").

Rule 311(1)(q): See *State v. Liefke,* 101 Or App 208, 211, 789 P2d 700 (1990); *Van Dyke v. Varsity Club Inc.,* 103 Or App 99, 101, 796 P2d 382, rev denied 310 Or 476, 799 P2d 647 (1990).

Rule 311(1)(r): In *State v. Lindoff,* 56 Or App 742, 642 P2d 1214, rev denied 293 Or 394, 650 P2d 927 (1982), the court found that the presumption of identity of person from identity of name met the requirements of *Ulster County Court v. Allen,* 442 US 140, 99 SCt 2213, 60 LEd2d 777 (1979), that there be "a rational connection between the fact proved and the ultimate fact presumed" and that the ultimate fact is "more likely than not to flow from the former."

Rule 311(1)(s): In *State v. Lerch,* 63 Or App 707, 719–20, 666 P2d 840 (1983), aff'd 296 Or 377, 677 P2d 678 (1983), the court held that it was not error for the trial judge to refuse to give an instruction that "A person must be missing for seven years before he will be presumed to be dead."

Rule 311(1)(v): In *Milburn and Milburn,* 98 Or App 668, 780 P2d 775 (1989), a dissolution proceeding where the husband was awarded custody, the court held that OEC 311(1)(v) put the burden on the wife to prove that the husband was not the father. Although the wife attempted to do so by offering evidence of nonaccess at the time of conception, the court found the evidence inconclusive and insufficient to overcome the presumption. The court held that OEC 311(1)(v) and ORS 109.070(2) had the same effect for purposes of this case. In *Department of Human Resources v. Mock,* 83 Or App 1, 730 P2d 553 (1986), rev denied 302 Or 615, 733 P2d 450 (1987), the court held that this presumption was inapplicable in a case where the child was born after the dissolution of the marriage.

Rule 311(1)(w): In *State v. Spencer,* 82 Or App 358, 728 P2d 566 (1986), reversed on other grounds 305 Or 59, 750 P2d 147 (1988), a DUI prosecution, defendant argued that there was an improper showing that the officer performing the test had a valid permit. The certification on the permit indicated that it was valid in 1984, but defendant argued that this did not establish that the officer was still qualified when he administered the breath test in 1985. The state sought to rely on the presumption created by this rule. The court held that it was unnecessary to rely on this presumption, because, by statute, the permit has continuing validity unless it is revoked or terminated by the Department of State Police.

Rule 311(1)(x): In *Koberstein v. Sierra Glass Co.,* 65 Or App 409, 412, 671 P2d 1190, 1192 (1983), modified 66 Or App 883, 675 P2d 1126, rev denied 297 Or 83, 679 P2d 1367 (1984), the trial court instructed the jury that "Defendants are presumed to obey the law." Although the court reversed on another ground, it held that this instruction was one-sided and that upon retrial the court should give only the instruction that all parties are presumed to obey the law.

Rule 311(2): See *Foxe v. M. T. Container Transit, Inc.,* 299 Or 523, 703 P2d 975 (1985); *State v. Rainey,* 298 Or 459, 693 P2d 635 (1985).

ARTICLE IV

RELEVANCY

RULE 401.   ORS 40.150. DEFINITION OF "RELEVANT EVIDENCE"

"Relevant evidence" means evidence having any tendency to make the existence of any fact that is of consequence to the determination of the action more probable or less probable than it would be without the evidence.

LEGISLATIVE COMMENTARY

Oregon Rule of Evidence 401 defines "relevant evidence." The rule is identical to Rule 401 of the Federal Rules of Evidence. In adopting it, the Legislative Assembly also approves the following commentary to the federal rule:

"Problems of relevancy call for an answer to the question whether an item of evidence, when tested by the processes of legal reasoning, possesses sufficient probative value to justify receiving it in evidence. Thus, assessment of the probative value of evidence that a person purchased a revolver shortly prior to a fatal shooting with which [the person] is charged is a matter of analysis and reasoning.

"The variety of relevancy problems is coextensive with the ingenuity of counsel in using circumstantial evidence as a means of proof. An enormous number of cases fall into no set pattern, and this section is designed as a guide for handling them. On the other hand, some situations recur with sufficient frequency to create patterns susceptible of treatment by specific rules. Rule 404 and those following it are of that variety; they also serve as illustrations of the applications of the present rule as limited by the exclusionary principles of Rule 403.

"Passing mention should be made of so-called 'conditional' relevancy. Morgan, *Basic Problems of Evidence* 45–46 (1962). In this situation, probative value depends not only upon satisfying the basic requirements of relevancy as described above but also upon the existence of some matter of fact. For example, if evidence of a spoken statement is relied upon to prove notice, probative value is lacking unless the person sought to be charged heard the statement. The problem is one of fact, and the only rules needed are for the purpose of determining the respective functions of judge and jury. See [ORE 104(2)] and 901. The discussion which follows under this section is concerned with relevancy generally, not with any particular problem of conditional relevancy.

"Relevancy is not an inherent characteristic of any item of evidence but exists only as a relation between an item of evidence and a matter properly provable in the case. Does the item of evidence tend to prove the matter sought to be proved? Whether the relationship exists depends upon principles evolved by experience or science, applied logically to the situation at hand. James, 'Relevancy, Probability and the Law,' 20 Cal L Rev 689, 696 n 15 (1941), in *Selected Writings on Evidence and Trial* 610, 615 n 15 (Fryer ed 1957). [For example, in appraising the probative worth of offered evidence, courts consider the distance in time between the facts offered and the matter sought to be proved. This factor is often termed 'remoteness.' McCormick, *Evidence* § 185 at 439 n 30 (2d ed 1972).] The rule summarizes this relationship between an item of evidence and a matter properly provable in a case as a 'tendency to make the existence' of the fact to be proved 'more probable or less probable.' Compare Uniform Rule 1 (2) which states the crux of relevancy as a 'tendency in reason,' thus perhaps emphasizing unduly the logical process and ignoring the need to draw upon experience or science to validate the general principle upon which relevancy in a particular situation depends.

"The standard of probability under the rule is 'more ... probable than it would be without the evidence.' Any more stringent requirement is unworkable and unrealistic. As McCormick § 185 at 436 says, 'A brick is not a wall,' or as Falknor, 'Extrinsic Policies Affecting Admissibility,' in 10 Rutgers L Rev 574, 576 (1956), quotes Professor McBaine, '... [I]t is not to be supposed that every witness can make a home run.' Dealing with probability in the language of the rule has the added virtue of avoiding confusion between questions of admissibility and questions of the sufficiency of the evidence. [See *State v. Sack*, 210 Or 552, 300 P2d 427 (1956).]

"The rule uses the phrase 'fact that is of consequence to the determination of the action' to describe the kind of fact to which proof may properly be directed. The language is that of California

Evidence Code § 210; it has the advantage of avoiding the loosely used and ambiguous word 'material.' Tentative Recommendation and Study Relating to the Uniform Rules of Evidence (Art. I, General Provisions), Cal Law Rev Comm Rep, Rec & Studies 10–11 (1964). The fact to be proved may be ultimate, intermediate or evidentiary; it matters not, so long as it is of consequence in the determination of the action. Cf. Uniform Rule 1 (2) which requires that the evidence relate to a 'material' fact.

"The fact to which the evidence is directed need not be in dispute. While situations will arise which call for the exclusion of evidence offered to prove a point conceded by the opponent, the ruling should be made on the basis of ... considerations [set forth in] Rule 403 rather than under any general requirement that evidence is admissible only if directed to matters in dispute. Evidence which is essentially background in nature can scarcely be said to involve disputed matter, yet it is universally offered and admitted as an aid to understanding. Charts, photographs, views of real estate, murder weapons and many other items of evidence fall in this category. A rule limiting admissibility to evidence directed to a controversial point would invite the exclusion of this helpful evidence, or at least the raising of endless questions over its admission. Cf. California Evidence Code § 210, defining relevant evidence in terms of tendency to prove a disputed fact."

Rule 401 changes Oregon law only to the extent that it eliminates the distinction currently maintained in this state between materiality and relevancy. The Legislative Assembly believes that the elimination of the distinction will have little, if any, practical effect.

While relevancy concerns the relation between the facts in evidence and the conclusions to be drawn from them, materiality concerns the "relation between the proposition for which the evidence is offered and the issues in the case." McCormick § 185 at 434. ORS 41.220 and 41.230 have maintained the distinction between these concepts by providing respectively that only material allegations need be proved, and that evidence at trial must "correspond with" the substance of the material allegations.

Rule 401 merges the concepts of materiality and relevancy in the definition of "relevant evidence." It incorporates the concept of "materiality," while avoiding the use of that ambiguous word, by requiring that evidence involve a fact that "is of consequence to the determination of the action." This maintains the current requirement that evidence at trial must relate to issues that have been pleaded or that are dictated by the substantive law on which the pleadings are based. *Mills v. Dunn Bros, Inc.,* 264 Or 156, 503 P2d 1250 (1972); *Arrien v. Levanger,* 263 Or 363, 502 P2d 573 (1972).

Likewise, Rule 401 incorporates the limited notion of relevancy by requiring that evidence must tend to make a fact more probable or less probable than it would be without the evidence. This restates Oregon law to the effect that "any evidence which tends to render the fact probable or improbable is relevant." *Klingback v. Mendiola,* 138 Or 234, 239, 6 P2d 237 (1931). In this state, if a fact "will advance the search for truth" or "throws some light upon the issue," it is relevant. *Trook v. Sagert,* 171 Or 680, 688, 690, 138 P2d 900 (1943). Similarly, evidence is relevant and is admitted if it "logically tends to prove the essential fact." *Tanner v. Farmer,* 243 Or 431, 436, 414 P2d 340 (1966).

A recent Oregon case, *Byrd v. Lord Brothers Contractors, Inc.,* 256 Or 421, 473 P2d 1018 (1970), illustrates the standard of probability set forth in the definition of "relevant evidence." The case involved an action to recover damages for personal injuries suffered when the plaintiff was hit by a piece of concrete as he drove beneath an overpass under construction. The defendant sought to introduce evidence that boys were seen running away from the overpass at about the time of the accident, and six blocks away from the site of the accident. The evidence was allowed on the following reasoning:

> "Admittedly, the boys could have come from numerous other places than the overpass and could have been running for any one of the various reasons that boys run. The relation between the boys and the overpass is an attenuated one, but we believe that, after the introduction of the evidence in question, there was a greater possibility that the concrete was thrown from the overpass than would have so appeared in the absence of such evidence." 256 Or at 424–425.

TEXT

Definition of Relevant Evidence

Rule 401 adopts a broad definition of *relevant evidence,* defining it as evidence "having any tendency to make the existence of any fact that is of consequence to the determination of the action more probable or less probable than it would be without the evidence." Evidence having only the slightest probative value would meet the requirements of Rule 401. However, evidence having only the slightest probative value is more likely to be excluded under Rule 403.

The view of relevancy taken under Rule 401 is that of Thayer, who stated: "The law furnishes no test of relevancy. For this, it tacitly refers to logic and general experience, assuming that the principles of reasoning are known to its judges and ministers, just as a vast multitude of other things are assumed as already sufficiently known to them." J. Thayer, A PRELIMINARY TREATISE ON EVIDENCE (1898) 265.

The determination of relevance thus allows the trial court to draw upon its own experience, knowledge, and common sense in determining whether a logical relationship exists between offered evidence and the fact to be proven. In some cases, it will be appropriate for counsel to provide the court with additional information that will assist in determining whether evidence has probative value. Scientific research has disproven many linkages commonly thought to exist and has identified other connections and correlations that are not generally known. Evidence offered for the purpose of assisting a court to make a determination on a question of admissibility is not subject to the rules of evidence. See Rule 101(4)(a).

Relevancy is a relational concept that carries meaning only in context. *State v. Guzek*, 322 Or 245, 251, 906 P2d 272 (1995) (whether a fact is relevant and provable "is determined not by the rules of evidence, but by the pleadings, the other evidence introduced in the case, and the applicable substantive law").

Relevance depends on the allegations at issue in a particular case. For example, in *Blankenship v. Union Pacific Railroad Co.*, 87 Or App 410, 742 P2d 680 (1987), rev denied 305 Or 21, 749 P2d 136 (1988), the court held that a sound recording of noise from defendant's railroad yard that allegedly caused plaintiff's hearing loss and tinnitus was irrelevant, because defendant had stipulated that the yard noise had caused plaintiff's injuries. However, in *Rea v. Union Pacific Railroad Co.*, 87 Or App 405, 742 P2d 678 (1987), rev denied 304 Or 680, 748 P2d 142 (1988), the court held that such a sound recording was relevant and admissible in a case involving similar injuries where defendant had not stipulated to causation.

The purpose for which evidence is claimed to be relevant generally must be explained to the trial judge in order to preserve for appeal any error in the exclusion of such evidence. In *Simpson v. Simpson*, 83 Or App 86, 730 P2d 592 (1986), rev denied 303 Or 454, 737 P2d 1248 (1987), the court held: "When a court excludes evidence as irrelevant for the reasons asserted by the objecting party, the proponent of the evidence may not complain on appeal, unless he has informed the trial court of its relevance."

Otherwise irrelevant evidence may become relevant and admissible to respond to evidence offered by an opponent. See discussion of curative admissibility under Rule 402.

Roles of Judge and Jury

In most cases, the judge makes the sole determination of whether evidence is relevant. However, in some cases, where the relevance of one fact is conditional upon proof of another fact, the jury will make the ultimate determination of relevancy under Rule 104(2). In such cases, the court will make an initial determination of relevancy but will instruct the jury to disregard the evidence if the fact upon which relevancy depends is not proven. See discussion of Rule 104(2).

Impeachment Evidence Is Relevant

Evidence offered solely for the purpose of impeachment meets the definition of relevancy in this rule, because the credibility of any witness is deemed to be a fact that is of consequence to the determination of the action. In *State v. Hubbard*, 297 Or 789, 796, 688 P2d 1311 (1984), the court held that "it is always permissible to show the interest or bias of an adverse witness" and that "matters which would otherwise be irrelevant may be offered to show the bias or interest of a witness," citing *Clevenger v. Schallhorn*, 205 Or 209, 215, 286 P2d 651 (1955); *Smith v. Pacific Truck Express*, 164 Or 318, 329, 100 P2d 474 (1940); *State v. Dowell*, 274 Or 547, 550, 547 P2d 619 (1976); *O'Harra v. Pundt*, 210 Or 533, 543, 310 P2d 1110 (1957).

Nonetheless, the court in *Hubbard* held that the trial judge has discretion to limit the extent of inquiry into bias or interest.

> The discretion to limit only obtains once sufficient facts have been established from which the jury may infer that bias or interest. Typically, this would require wide latitude be given to the cross-examiner to ask and receive answers to questions sufficient to demonstrate to the jury the nature of the bias or interest ... [except in those cases where the bias or interest has been made apparent by the circumstances or by the direct examination of the witness.]

297 Or at 798.

Materiality

Rule 401 merges the concepts of relevancy and materiality. Under prior law, relevance referred to the tendency of evidence to establish a particular fact and materiality referred to whether the proposition to be proven was an issue in the case. See, e.g., *Thompson v. Rathbun,* 18 Or 202, 22 P 837 (1889) (promissory note different from one alleged in complaint is immaterial evidence). Under the new rule, the concept of materiality is encompassed by the requirement that the fact to be proven should be "of consequence" to the action. Immateriality is no longer an independent ground for an objection. An objection under Rule 401 that evidence is irrelevant will be sufficient to raise an immateriality objection.

On the admissibility of evidence that is relevant, but subject to exclusion by virtue of another rule, statute, or constitutional provision, see discussion under Rule 402.

Evidence Found Relevant

Precedents are of limited value in applying Rule 401 because the determination of relevancy depends upon the facts and issues in dispute in each case. The slightest factual variation may result in a different assessment of relevancy. Nonetheless, the following are examples of recent cases finding evidence to be relevant under Rule 401.

State v. Gefre, 137 Or App 77, 81, 903 P2d 386 (1995): Refusal to take a breath test is relevant to whether defendant was intoxicated at time of his arrest.

Fugate v. Safeway Stores, 135 Or App 168, 171–4, 897 P2d 328 (1995): In personal injury action, it was error to exclude evidence that after accident plaintiff suffered physical abuse from husband that was relevant to damages claimed for neck injury.

State v. Williams, 313 Or 19, 31, 828 P2d 1006, 1014, cert denied *Williams v. Oregon,* 113 SCt 171 (1992): The court held that photographs of defendant's tire tracks and the tire tracks at the murder scene were admissible, even though the prosecution's expert could not say "conclusively" that the tire tracks at the scene matched defendant's tires. The court held that it was not necessary for evidence to meet such a high standard of persuasiveness to satisfy the definition of relevance in Rule 401.

State v. Thompson, 131 Or App 230, 233–6, 884 P2d 574, 576–8 (1994): In this kidnapping and rape prosecution, the defendant contended that the complainant consented and was claiming rape because she had used drugs with the defendant and was fearful her boyfriend would beat her for her drug use. The court held that it was error to exclude evidence that the complainant's boyfriend had beaten her on previous occasions when he had caught her using drugs because such evidence directly supported defendant's theory.

State v. Millar, 127 Or App 76, 81, 871 P2d 482, 485 (1994): In this sex abuse prosecution, defendant admitted placing his hand down the front of victim's pants but claimed he was merely attempting to retrieve a toy that the victim had placed in her pants. Under such circumstances, it was not error to introduce a pornographic magazine entitled "Tender Shavers," which was found under the couch where defendant regularly slept. Defendant's apparent interest in the genitalia of teenage girls was relevant to rebut his explanation of his intent when he placed his hand down the victim's pants.

State v. Trinh, 126 Or App 324, 327, 868 P2d 774, 781, rev denied 318 Or 661, 873 P2d 322 (1994): The court approved the admission of a shotgun taken from defendant's possession about seven months before the crime was committed. The shotgun was of a unique type, and even though the prosecutor did not claim it was the weapon used in the murder, it was relevant to prove that "defendant had a proclivity for possessing unique guns of the kind found at the scene of the crime."

State v. Bayse, 122 Or App 608, 614, 859 P2d 542, 545 (1993): In this prosecution of a grandmother for custodial interference, the court held that it was error to exclude defense evidence concerning abuse of the children by the parents. Such evidence was relevant to rebut the state's claim that defendant fled with the children because she knew she had no legal right to custody, an element of the offense. Evidence of the prior abuse provided an alternate explanation for her flight.

State v. Rood, 118 Or App 480, 485, 848 P2d 128, rev denied 317 Or 272, 858 P2d 1314 (1993): The court held that evidence that the defendant had purchased X-rated videos was relevant to corroborate testimony of the alleged sex abuse victims that X-rated videos were played when they were abused. Because such evidence was offered to corroborate the victims' description of the circumstances and events surrounding the crimes, the court held that it did not violate the rule of *State v. Vanderham,* 78 Or App 589, 717 P2d 647 (1986), which held it was reversible error to admit evidence that the defendant possessed a pornographic magazine two years earlier to prove his propensity to commit a sex crime.

Huffman & Wright Logging Co. v. Wade, 109 Or App 37, 44–5, 817 P2d 1334, 1338–9 (1991), aff'd 317 Or 445, 857 P2d 101 (1993): Members of the "Earth First!" environmental group were sued for compensatory and punitive damages for trespass. At trial, plaintiff offered evidence that the environmental group believed in activities such as tree spiking and vandalizing industrial equipment in support of its claim for punitive damages. The appellate court found no abuse of discretion in admitting such evidence on the issue of defendants' likelihood to repeat their unlawful behavior.

State v. Carrillo, 108 Or App 442, 445–6, 816 P2d 654, 655–6, rev denied 312 Or 527, 822 P2d 1196 (1991): Defendant was charged with burglary and attempted rape. Evidence of the victim's awareness that the defendant had previously killed his girlfriend was held relevant on the issue of whether the victim would have invited defendant into her apartment. The court refused to address whether the evidence should have been excluded under Rule 403, holding that an objection on the basis of mere relevance does not preserve an error under Rule 403 or 404(3).

State v. Robinson, 104 Or App 613, 802 P2d 688 (1990): In this DUII prosecution, the court held that it was error to exclude medical records showing the defendant had a limp, which may have rebutted prosecution evidence that defendant was staggering at the time of arrest.

Pfeifer v. DME Liquidating, Inc., 101 Or App 106, 110, 789 P2d 266 (1990): The court held that "evidence of how the parties acted after the purported rescission is probative of whether they intended to rescind."

Department of Transportation v. Lundberg, 100 Or App 601, 603, 788 P2d 456 (1990), aff'd 312 Or 568, 825 P2d 641, cert denied 113 SCt 467 (1992): In this eminent domain proceeding involving a strip of the defendant's land that bordered the street, the court held that a Portland city ordinance requiring landowners to dedicate a ten-foot strip of land adjacent to the street as a right-of-way was properly admitted on the question of value. The court stated that "any competent evidence tending to prove an effect on market value that would be considered by a prospective buyer is relevant to the issue of value in an eminent domain case."

State v. Brinager, 96 Or App 160, 162, 771 P2d 658 (1989): Defendant was convicted of criminally negligent homicide. The court held evidence relevant that witnesses had seen defendant driving erratically for a ten- to fifteen-minute interval that ended approximately five minutes before, and two and a half miles from, the collision. The court applied the rule that "there must be other evidence from which the jury could find that the party's conduct some time and distance before the accident continued up to at least shortly before the accident," quoting *Cox v. Jacks,* 268 Or 180, 184, 519 P2d 1041 (1974). The court held that multiple observations by the witnesses during the interval they observed defendant satisfied this requirement.

State v. Sanger, 89 Or App 493, 749 P2d 1202 (1988): Defendant was convicted of burglary and theft. Some of the stolen items were found in the apartment of an accomplice named Furtado. To connect defendant with the items, the prosecution offered evidence that parole papers belonging to the defendant were also found at the apartment and that defendant was not residing at another apartment where he told his parole officer he was living. The appellate court held that the evidence was relevant to show defendant's connection with the stolen property. The court refused to consider the issue of whether evidence of defendant's parole status violated Rule 404(3), because this objection was not raised in the trial court.

State v. Goff, 297 Or 635, 686 P2d 1023 (1984): The defendant mother was convicted of child neglect, based upon evidence that she had left her young children alone for approximately five hours. The court held the following evidence to be relevant and admissible: (1) that the mother was at a Halloween party drinking beer; (2) during her absence, the house caught fire and the children burned to death; and (3) matches were available in the house. The court found that the whereabouts of the mother was relevant on the question of whether the risk to the children was "unjustifiable." The evidence of the fire and the availability of matches that caused the fire was relevant on the question of whether the risk was "substantial."

State v. Lerch, 296 Or 377, 677 P2d 678 (1984): The court held that hair-comparison was relevant under Rule 401, even when it was not conclusively shown that the hair being matched with hair found in the defendant's apartment came from the murder victim.

State v. Smith, 66 Or App 374, 675 P2d 1060, rev denied 297 Or 339, 683 P2d 1370 (1984): The court held that it was not error to admit a jacket the defendant had purchased two months after the assault, when the jacket was similar in appearance to the jacket worn by the assailant and there was evidence that the defendant customarily wore that type of coat. The court found the evidence relevant to show "defendant's proclivity for wearing clothing similar to that worn by the victim's assailant." 66 Or App at 380, 675 P2d at 1065.

State v. Brown, 64 Or App 747, 669 P2d 1190 (1983), aff'd 297 Or 404, 687 P2d 751 (1984): In a rape prosecution, the prosecution offered evidence that defendant had blood type A—the same type found in the semen taken from a vaginal swab from the rape victim. Defendant argued this evidence was irrelevant, because approximately 32 percent of the population has blood type A. The court affirmed, stating: "The fact that the blood-type test only limits responsibility to 32 percent of the population affects the weight of the testimony, but does not render it irrelevant." 64 Or App at 749, 669 P2d at 1191.

Carlson v. Piper Aircraft Corp., 57 Or App 695, 646 P2d 43, rev denied 293 Or 801, 653 P2d 999 (1982): The court held that the trial court did not abuse its discretion in admitting evidence relating to possible spatial disorientation by the pilot in connection with an aircraft accident. The court found such evidence to be relevant in light of the defendant's theory of causation and the question of whether the probative value of the evidence was outweighed by prejudice, possible confusion, or time consumption was a question for the trial judge.

Evidence Found Irrelevant

State v. Guzek, 322 Or 245, 251, 906 P2d 272 (1995): Victim impact evidence found irrelevant in capital sentencing hearing.

[Author's Note: This holding is overturned by a 1995 amendment to ORS 163.150 allowing victim impact evidence in capital sentencing hearings.]

State v. Hillier, 132 Or App 40, 42–3, 887 P2d 846–7 (1994): It was held error for the state to introduce an exhibit containing certified copies of Administrative Rules pertaining to breathalyzers, along with memoranda, letters, and other documents pertaining to such equipment. The appended documentation was ruled to be inadmissible hearsay, irrelevant, and prejudicial, and misleading under OEC 403.

State v. Hite, 131 Or App 59, 61–2, 883 P2d 890, 892 (1994): In this rape and sodomy prosecution, the court found no error in the exclusion of defense evidence that a child sexual abuse victim allegedly used drugs. The court also held that it was improper to admit evidence of nude photographs of other women found in the defendant's possession, since they were irrelevant to the charged crime.

Paragano v. Gray, 126 Or App 670, 680, 870 P2d 837, 843 (1994): The court found no error in the trial judge limiting evidence about plaintiffs' backgrounds and life stories.

State v. Presley, 108 Or App 149, 152, 814 P2d 550, 552 (1991): The court held that evidence of a child's statements made while she was asleep—"Daddy, get off me. Daddy, stop, leave me alone."—was inadmissible on grounds of relevancy. The court found an insufficient foundation to establish a nexus between the child's statements while sleeping and her father's actual conduct. The court held that the evidence "could not support the factual inferences that the jury was permitted to make."

State v. Stone, 104 Or App 534, 538–9, 802 P2d 668 (1990): The court held that evidence of gang-related activity involving the defendant was irrelevant to prove that the defendant knew the car in which he was riding was stolen.

State v. Troen, 100 Or App 442, 447, 786 P2d 751 (1990), rev denied 310 Or 791, 801 P2d 841 (1991): The court found no error in the exclusion of evidence of motive offered by the defendant. The court stated: "Defendant's motive, that is, why he did what he did, is immaterial to the allegations that he acted with a conscious objective to commit burglary or with an awareness that his conduct constituted burglary or theft .... The issue was whether defendant acted with a particular state of mind, not why he had that mental state."

McPike v. Enciso's Cocina Mejicana, Inc., 93 Or App 269, 762 P2d 315 (1988): Plaintiff's decedent was a 10-year-old girl who died from a sulphite reaction after eating at defendant's restaurant. The court affirmed the ruling of the trial judge excluding evidence that subsequent to the child's death: (1) various government agencies had taken action to ban or restrict the use of sulphites; (2) one defendant food distributor stopped distributing sulphites and the other added warnings to its sulphite containers; and (3) the restaurant owner discontinued use of sulphites.

State v. Baker, 87 Or App 285, 742 P2d 633, rev denied 304 Or 405, 745 P2d 1225 (1987): The court upheld exclusion by the trial judge of two photographs of a traffic sign located on the road defendant was traveling immediately before the accident. The photographs were found to be irrelevant, because there was no evidence that the photographs were taken from where defendant was traveling on the road.

State ex rel State of Washington v. Dilworth, 85 Or App 169, 735 P2d 1281 (1987): In a filiation proceeding, the court held the following evidence offered by respondent to be irrelevant that: (1) mother was married to another person at the time of the alleged intercourse; (2) mother had a relationship with a third party, when there was no evidence of sexual involvement with that third party; (3) mother had sexual activity with other men at a time significantly earlier than the time of conception.

State v. Peacock, 75 Or App 217, 706 P2d 982 (1985): The court found the prosecutor's inquiry into the issue of whether the defendant's attorney filed a notice of intent to rely on a mental disease or defect defense prior to trial to be irrelevant and prejudicial.

State v. Parks, 71 Or App 630, 693 P2d 657 (1985): The defendant was convicted of assault. He testified that the shooting was an accident, he did not intend to injure the victim, and he would never shoot anybody. In rebuttal, the state offered testimony that 20 years before the defendant had chased another person around a service station swinging a hammer and yelling threats. The court found this evidence irrelevant and its admission to be prejudicial error.

State v. Eby, 296 Or 63, 673 P2d 522 (1983): The court held that evidence that a prosecution witness had agreed to testify truthfully as a condition of a plea agreement was an improper attempt to bolster the credibility of the witness. The evidence of this condition in the plea agreement was held to be inadmissible and irrelevant.

Prior Conduct or Events to Prove Negligence

Evidence of similar prior conduct, events, accidents, or negligence is generally held not admissible to prove negligence or lack of negligence in the case being litigated. *Warner v. Maus,* 209 Or 529, 304 P2d 423 (1956) (questioning driver about 10 prior accidents held improper and irrelevant); *Southern Pacific Co. v. Consolidated Freightways, Inc.,* 203 Or 657, 281 P2d 693 (1955) (numerous prior collisions at same intersection not admissible); *Blue v. City of Union,* 159 Or 5, 75 P2d 977 (1938) (prior acts of similar negligence by defendant inadmissible); *Peters v. Consolidated Freight Lines, Inc.,* 157 Or 605, 73 P2d 713 (1937) (prior negligent acts of trucking company inadmissible); *Rayburn v. Day,* 126 Or 135, 268 P 1002 (1928) (prior negligence by doctor in leaving surgical sponge inside a different patient on another occasion inadmissible).

However, evidence of prior similar conduct or events is often held admissible to prove causation, danger, knowledge or intent, or the existence of a particular defect. See *Oberg v. Honda Motor Co.,* 316 Or 263, 267–8, 851 P2d 1084 (1993), rev'd on other grounds 114 SCt 2331 (1994) (documents generated by the Consumer Product Safety Commission relating to the safety of all terrain vehicles were admissible on the issue of notice to defendant of the vehicles' dangerousness); *Downey v. Traveler's Inn,* 243 Or 206, 412 P2d 359 (1966) (evidence that other employees using the same cleaning solution under similar circumstances also suffered skin irritations similar to those suffered by plaintiffs admissible to prove causation); *Clary v. Polk County,* 231 Or 148, 372 P2d 524 (1962) (evidence of prior accidents at same location admissible to show the dangerous defects in a county road); *Saunders v. A.M. Williams & Co.,* 155 Or 1, 62 P2d 260

(1936) (fall subsequent to the fall injuring plaintiff admissible to show the dangerousness of defendant's oily floor); *Gynther v. Brown & McCabe,* 67 Or 310, 134 P 1186 (1913) (evidence of similarly misunderstood signals by a hatch tender on prior occasions admissible to show a dangerously defective signaling system); *Rader v. Gibbons and Reed Co.,* 261 Or 354, 494 P2d 412 (1972) (evidence of prior incidents of rocks falling on the highway admissible to show notice to the defendant); *Krause v. Southern Pacific Co.,* 135 Or 310, 295 P 966 (1931) (evidence of prior collisions with a low bridge was admissible to show defendant's knowledge of the danger); *Adams v. Dunn,* 283 Or 33, 581 P2d 939, vacated on other grounds 284 Or 513, 587 P2d 466 (1978) (similar failure to diagnose appendicitis on earlier occasion admissible to show notice); *Croft v. Gulf & Western Industries, Inc.,* 12 Or App 507, 506 P2d 541 (1973) (prior malfunctioning of traffic lights admissible on issue of knowledge). Cf. ANNOT., *Products Liability: Admissibility of Evidence of Other Accidents to Prove Hazardous Nature of Product,* 42 ALR3d 780 (1972).

On the admissibility of evidence of prior acts, see generally the discussion under Rule 404(3).

Absence of prior similar incidents or occurrences is generally not admissible to prove absence of negligence. However, such evidence may be admitted to show that a particular condition was not dangerous, that the defendant was unaware of the danger, or that the condition would not likely cause the injury. *Smith v. Portland Traction Co.,* 220 Or 215, 349 P2d 286 (1960) (evidence of no other falls from the door of a bus was relevant to show the defendant did not know of any danger in this method of discharging passengers); *Robertson v. Coca Cola Bottling Co.,* 195 Or 668, 247 P2d 217 (1952) (evidence of no prior claims of bottle explosions admissible to show lack of knowledge by the defendant); *Tucker v. Unit Crane & Shovel Corp.,* 256 Or 318, 473 P2d 862 (1970) (evidence that crane had been used for nine years without an accident allowed on issue of whether product was unsafe for its intended use); *Quigley v. School Dist. No. 45J3,* 251 Or 452, 446 P2d 177 (1968) (prior safe use of school gym by other children allowed to show absence of knowledge of dangerous condition); *Baker v. Lane County,* 37 Or App 87, 586 P2d 114 (1978) (lack of knowledge of prior accidents admitted to prove absence of dangerous condition); *Reiger v. Toby Enterprises,* 45 Or App 679, 609 P2d 402 (1980) (products liability action; evidence of prior safe use of product admitted on question of whether it was dangerously defective); *Wilk v. Georges,* 267 Or 19, 514 P2d 877 (1973) (slip and fall case; lack of prior falls admissible on issue of owner's knowledge of dangerous condition).

See generally ANNOT., *Admissibility of Evidence of Absence of Other Accidents or Injuries at Place Where Injury or Damage Occurred,* 10 ALR5th 371 (1993); ANNOT., *Products Liability: Admissibility of Evidence of Absence of Other Accidents,* 51 ALR4th 1186 (1987); ANNOT., *Modern Status as to Admissibility of Evidence of Prior Accidents or Injuries at Same Place,* 21 ALR4th 472 (1983).

Prior Similar Frauds

Evidence of prior similar frauds may be admissible to prove that the defendant intended to deceive or had knowledge of the falsity of the statements, or to prove a scheme or plan to defraud. *Karsun v. Kelley,* 258 Or 155, 482 P2d 533 (1971) (prior misrepresentation by stockbroker admissible to show scheme to defraud); *Carpenter v. Kraninger,* 225 Or 594, 358 P2d 263 (1960); *Green v. Uncle Don's Mobile City,* 279 Or 425, 568 P2d 1375 (1977); *Castor v. Erlandson,* 277 Or 147, 560 P2d 267 (1977). See Rule 404(3).

Settlements with Others

In *Holger v. Irish,* 113 Or App 290, 298, 834 P2d 1028 (1992), aff'd 316 Or 402, 851 P2d 1122 (1993), where plaintiff sued his surgeon, it was held error for the trial judge to inform the jury of the plaintiff's pretrial settlement with the co-defendant hospital. The trial court should not have informed the jury about the settlement, "because the jury might have inferred that [the plaintiff] had already been fully compensated."

On the general inadmissibility of settlements to prove liability for or invalidity of the claim or its amount, see Rule 408, infra.

Prior Litigation

In *Gibson v. Tzantarmas,* 108 Or App 270, 276, 815 P2d 221, 224 (1991), the court held that evidence that the plaintiff had been involved in other lawsuits was irrelevant "and could only serve to suggest that defendant is litigious or a person of bad character."

In *McWilliams v. Szymanski,* 101 Or App 617, 620–1, 792 P2d 457, rev denied 310 Or 281, 796 P2d 1206 (1990), the court held there was no error in the admission of complaints filed by plaintiffs against another party for the same injuries. The plaintiffs claimed that they were pleading in the alternative and that introduction of the other complaints constituted unfair prejudice, but the court found no OEC 403 violation in the circumstances of the case.

See generally Mansfield, *Evidential Use of Litigation Activity of the Parties,* 43 Syracuse L Rev 695 (1992).

Conviction of Codefendants

In *State v. Clark,* 98 Or App 478, 481, 779 P2d 215 (1989), the court stated: "A codefendant's conviction resulting from the same transaction generally may not be introduced as substantive evidence of a defendant's guilt." However, the court here approved admission of the evidence to contradict a fact asserted by defendant.

Similar Contracts

Evidence of similar contracts is generally not admissible to prove the terms or making of the contract in issue. *Seabrook v. Foley Box Factory,* 122 Or 511, 259 P 890 (1927); *Hepler v. Santerno,* 244 Or 246, 417 P2d 390 (1966). However, evidence of other contracts may be admissible to explain a contract term by showing a prior course of dealing or to show the authority of an agent. See McCormick, *Evidence* (3d ed 1984) § 469. Cf. *Second Northwestern Finance Corp. v. Mansfield,* 121 Or 236, 252 P 400 (1927).

Prices Previously or Subsequently Paid as Evidence of Value

Prices previously or subsequently paid for real or personal property may be relevant to establishing the value of the property at any particular point in time. *Moore Mill & Lumber Co. v. Foster,* 216 Or 204, 336 P2d 39 (1959) (price paid for land six years before held admissible); *State Highway Commission v. Oregon-Washington Lumber Co.,* 24 Or App 187, 544 P2d 1058 (1976) (same); *Mattechek v. Pugh,* 153 Or 1, 55 P2d 730 (1936) (price paid for household goods three years before held admissible). But see *City of Portland v. Nudelman,* 45 Or App 425, 436, 608 P2d 1190 (1980) (no abuse of discretion by trial court in excluding evidence of price paid by present owner; "[I]t is within the sound discretion of the trial court to admit or exclude testimony as to the purchase price of property paid by the owner of property taken in a condemnation proceeding.").

Evidence of a party's own statements of valuation may also be relevant. See *Grover v. Sturgeon,* 255 Or 578, 469 P2d 617 (1970) (prior admission of party regarding the value of shares held admissible). Such statements are receivable against the party as an admission but may not be received in favor of the party unless they fit within a hearsay exception.

Similar Property as Evidence of Value

Prices paid for other property may be relevant to establish the value of property in dispute, provided the other property is sufficiently similar, is located in a comparable location, was sold reasonably near in time to the property in question, and was sold voluntarily under normal and fair market conditions. *Annett v. Post,* 45 Or App 121, 607 P2d 785 (1980); *Hall v. Banta,* 283 Or 387, 583 P2d 1139 (1978). In *State Highway Commission v. Blaue,* 231 Or 216, 371 P2d 972 (1962), the court held that evidence of the sale price of similar property near the condemned property four years earlier was not too remote and hence was admissible.

The evidence must involve actual sales rather than mere offers to sell or purchase that were not accepted. *State Highway Commission v. Morehouse Holding Co.,* 225 Or 62, 357 P2d 266 (1960).

Usage

ORS 41.270(2) provides: "Evidence may be given of usage to explain the true character of an act, contract, or instrument when such true character is not otherwise plain, but usage is never admissible except as a means of interpretation."

ORS 41.270(1) states: "Usage shall be proved by the testimony of at least two witnesses."

In cases arising under the Uniform Commercial Code, usage is defined by ORS 71.2050(2) as: "[A]ny practice or method of dealing having such regularity of observance in a place, vocation, or trade as to justify an expectation that it will be observed with respect to the transaction in question." ORS 71.2050(6) requires advance notice by a party before offering evidence of usage under ORS 71.2050(2).

Business Practices

Evidence of business practices may be admissible in negligence cases, not to establish the standard of care, but to assist the trier of fact in determining whether due care was exercised. *Adkins v. Barrett,* 196 Or 597, 250 P2d 387 (1952) (common practice in truck repair business to use a certain size spindle in an axle); *Silver Falls Timber Co. v. Eastern & Western Lumber Co.,* 149 Or 126, 40 P2d 703 (1935) (practice of other companies to suspend logging operations during extreme fire hazard). Cf. *Zimmerman v. West Coast Trans-Oceanic S.S. Lines,* 199 Or 78, 258 P2d 1003 (1953) (usual method for raising hatch cover with block and tackle).

In *Anderson v. Malloy,* 700 F2d 1208, 1211–2 (8th Cir 1983), a case alleging negligence on the part of defendant motel for failing to provide proper security, the court held that evidence of security measures taken by other motels in the area was properly admissible under FRE 401. The court held that the trier of fact may properly consider the defendant's deviation from accepted custom or practice followed by other motels in substantially similar circumstances.

Evidence of practice is not admissible if it is in conflict with the statutory duty or where an absolute standard of care is fixed by law. *Frame v. Arrow Towing Service,* 155 Or 522, 530, 64 P2d 1312 (1937).

Company Rules, Industry Standards, Safety Codes, and Construction Contracts

Company rules, industry standards, safety codes, and construction contracts, although not establishing an absolute standard of care, may be admissible on the question of whether the applicable standard of care was violated. See *Hansen v. Abrasive Engineering and Manufacturing, Inc.,* 317 Or 378, 385–7, 856 P2d 625, 629–30 (1993) (approving admission of ANSI advisory standards and OOSHC and OSHA rules on the issue of whether defendant failed to meet the standard of care that defendant owed to plaintiff); *Greist v. Phillips,* 322 Or 281, 287, 906

P2d 789 (1995) (proper to allow jury to consider specifications of negligence based on federal regulations requiring truck to have operative speedometer and prohibiting driver from being on duty for more than seventy hours in eight consecutive days).

See also *Hecker v. Oregon R. Co.*, 40 Or 6, 66 P 270 (1901) (violation of a company rule that train bell be rung for a quarter of a mile where approaching road crossing relevant to the determination of negligence); *Cole v. Multnomah County*, 39 Or App 211, 592 P2d 221 (1979) (county jail procedures manual admitted); *Waterway Terminals Co. v. P.S. Lord Mechanical Contractors*, 242 Or 1, 406 P2d 556 (1965) (terms of construction contract for protection of property from fire admissible); *Archer v. Rogers Construction, Inc.*, 252 Or 165, 447 P2d 380 (1968) (highway construction contract incorporating provisions of "American Association of State Highway Officials Manual" admissible to determine the existence of negligence in the display of warning signs). But see *Jones v. Montgomery Ward*, 49 Or App 231, 619 P2d 907 (1980) (error to admit defendant's rules instructing its employees on how to deal with shoplifters; the guidelines were more stringent than the law required and would tend to confuse the jury about the applicable standard for legal liability); *Jones v. Mitchell Bros. Truck Lines*, 266 Or 513, 511 P2d 347 (1973) (safety manual excluded).

In *Shahtout v. Emco Garbage Co.*, 298 Or 598, 695 P2d 897 (1985), the court held that in common-law tort actions it may be appropriate to instruct the jury regarding standards established by governmental safety regulations, even though the safety regulations were not designed to protect the plaintiff and hence do not provide the basis for a negligence per se claim. The regulations do not establish a legal duty, but may assist the jury in determining whether a common-law duty was breached. See also *Golden "B" Products, Inc. v. Clark Equipment Co.*, 58 Or App 555, 649 P2d 813, modified on other grounds 60 Or App 39, 652 P2d 832 (1982) (evidence of code and safety standard violations held admissible).

See generally, Tompkins, *Admissibility of Reports, OSHA Regs., Standards and Publications*, 57 Defense Counsel J 446 (1990); ANNOT., *Admissibility in Evidence, On Issue of Negligence, of Codes or Standards of Safety Issued or Sponsored by Governmental Body or by Voluntary Association*, 58 ALR 3d 148 (1974); ANNOT., *Admissibility in Evidence of Rules of Defendant in Action for Negligence*, 50 ALR 2d 16 (1956).

Similar Objects

Sometimes a question arises as to whether a duplicate or similar object is sufficiently relevant to be received into evidence when the actual object at issue in the case is unavailable. Courts are receptive to such exhibits, provided there are no material differences between the substitute and the original and the original would be admissible if available. See *Rich v. Cooper*, 234 Or 300, 380 P2d 613 (1963) ("leaden sap" similar to one used by defendant admitted); *Lane v. Hatfield*, 173 Or 79, 143 P2d 230 (1943) (pair of bloomers of identical color to dress worn by decedent child admitted to show visibility of the child); *Murray v.*

Firemen's Ins. Co., 121 Or 165, 254 P 817 (1927) (lace cover and tablecloth identical to those destroyed in fire admitted to help jury determine their value). See also *Carnine v. Tibbetts,* 158 Or 21, 74 P2d 974 (1937) (exhibition of a skeleton allowed in the discretion of the trial court where it would help jury understand injuries suffered by plaintiff). See ANNOT., *Admissibility in Evidence of Sample or Samples of Article or Substance of which the Quality, Condition or the Like is Involved in Litigation,* 95 ALR 2d 681 (1964).

Exhibitions or Demonstrations of Injuries

In a personal injury case, exhibition by the plaintiff of wounds or injuries is generally deemed relevant and allowed. *Pooschke v. Union Pac. R.R. Co.,* 246 Or 633, 426 P2d 866 (1967) (injured leg wrapped in bandage); *Hendricks v. Sanford,* 216 Or 149, 337 P2d 974 (1959) (healed wound on back); *Bowerman v. Columbia Gorge Motor Coach System, Inc.,* 132 Or 106, 284 P 579 (1930) (removal of glass eye).

However, in *Lampa v. Hakola,* 152 Or 626, 55 P2d 13 (1936), it was held to be error to allow a plaintiff to demonstrate subjective symptoms of injury to his back in front of the jury, where the demonstration was accompanied by expressions of pain. See also *Peters v. Hockley,* 152 Or 434, 53 P2d 1059 (1936) (reversible error to permit a demonstration where physician raised plaintiff's arm in front of the jury, causing her to cry out in pain).

Photograph of Homicide Victim

A photograph of a homicide victim is made relevant and admissible as a matter of statutory law. ORS 41.415 provides: "In a prosecution for any criminal homicide, a photograph of the victim while alive shall be admissible evidence when offered by the district attorney to show the general appearance and condition of the victim while alive."

In *State v. Williams,* 313 Or 19, 27–31, 828 P2d 1006, 1012–4, cert denied 113 SCt 171 (1992), the court upheld the constitutionality of this statute and on the facts of the case found the photographs to be relevant under Rule 401 and not unduly prejudicial under Rule 403.

Other Courtroom Demonstrations

The trial judge has wide discretion in regulating courtroom demonstrations. See Rule 611(1). If counsel uses a demonstration during argument to the jury, it is subject to the general rule limiting argument to evidence in the record or matters of which the court can take judicial notice. In *State v. Proctor,* 94 Or App 720, 767 P2d 453 (1989), the prosecutor during closing argument demonstrated how a stray fingerprint could be left on tape by applying a piece of masking tape to a beverage case on which a graphite fingerprint had earlier been deposited, lifting off the fingerprint and displaying it to the jury. Neither the masking tape nor the beverage case had been presented in evidence. The court held:

The demonstration in closing argument here went far beyond any matter capable of judicial notice, involving as it did matters of forensic fingerprint analysis properly addressed only by experts. The science of fingerprint analysis, and in particular the unique properties of graphite as a mode of fingerprint transfer, are not matters within the common knowledge or experience of the jury. It was improper for the prosecuting attorney to introduce that material in closing argument when the defendant had no opportunity to challenge it through cross-examination or presentation of opposing evidence.

94 Or App at 724, 767 P2d at 455 (1989).

Tests or Experiments

Tests or experiments may be relevant evidence. However, to be relevant they must be conducted under the same or substantially similar conditions as the circumstances being litigated. *Myers v. Cessna Aircraft Corp.*, 275 Or 501, 553 P2d 355 (1976); *Foster v. Agri-Chem Inc.*, 235 Or 570, 385 P2d 184 (1963). The trial court has broad discretion in determining the admissibility of such evidence. *Tuite v. Union Pacific Stages, Inc.*, 204 Or 565, 284 P2d 333 (1955). The court must balance the relevance of the evidence against the dangers of unfair prejudice or misleading the jury. See *American National Watermattress Corp. v. Manville*, 642 P2d 1330, 1337–9 (Alaska 1982).

If the foundation laid for the experiment does not show sufficient similarity, the evidence may be excluded. *Dyer v. R.E. Christiansen Trucking, Inc.*, 318 Or 391, 868 P2d 1325–31 (1994) (affirming exclusion by trial judge of a videotape demonstrating a tractor-trailer/pup-trailer combination traveling a right-hand curve on wet pavement and sweeping into the oncoming lane part way through the curve; court found the circumstances of the demonstration and the actual case to be sufficiently dissimilar to justify exclusion of the videotape); *Hall v. Brown*, 102 Or 389, 202 P 719 (1921). The circumstances need not be identical, however, and the test is whether the difference in conditions is sufficiently great to risk misleading or confusing the jury. *Loibl v. Niemi*, 214 Or 172, 327 P2d 786 (1958). If the experiment is intended to be a "re-enactment" of the event in question, courts require a more nearly identical set of conditions than is required for other types of experimental evidence. See *Randall v. Warnaco, Inc., Hirsch-Weiss Div.*, 677 F2d 1226, 1233–4 (8th Cir 1982).

Courts are sometimes more receptive to experiments and tests where the results are merely described and no opinion is given based upon the test results. *State v. Gill*, 3 Or App 488, 474 P2d 23 (1970). Courts may also be more receptive to tests that were not conducted in preparation for the lawsuit. *Foster v. Agri-Chem Inc.*, 235 Or 570, 385 P2d 184 (1963).

See generally ANNOT., *Admissibility, as Against Hearsay Objection, of Report of Tests or Experiments Carried Out by Independent Third Party*, 19 ALR3d 1008 (1968); ANNOT., *Admissibility of Experimental Evidence, Skidding Tests, or the Like, Relating to Speed or Control of Motor Vehicle*, 78 ALR2d 218 (1961); ANNOT., *Admissibility of Experimental Evidence to Show Visibility or Line of Vision*, 78 ALR2d 152 (1961); ANNOT., *Admissibility of Experimental Evidence as to Explo-*

sion, 76 ALR2d 402 (1961); ANNOT., *Admissibility of Experimental Evidence to Determine Chemical or Physical Qualities or Character of Material or Substance,* 76 ALR2d 354 (1961); ANNOT., *Admissibility in Evidence, in Civil Action, of Tachograph or Similar Paper or Tape Recording of Speed of Motor Vehicle, Railroad Locomotive, or the Like,* 73 ALR2d 1025 (1960); ANNOT., *Admissibility in Evidence, in Automobile Negligence Action, of Charts Showing Braking Distance, Reaction Times, etc.,* 9 ALR3d 976 (1966); ANNOT., *Testing Qualifications of Expert Witness, Other Than Handwriting Expert, by Objective Tests or Experiments,* 78 ALR2d 1281 (1961).

Statistical Evidence

Statistical evidence is generally admissible, provided a proper foundation is established, the rules governing expert testimony are satisfied, and the probative value of the evidence is not outweighed by the considerations specified in Rule 403. See generally Goodman, *Jurors' Comprehension and Assessment of Probabilistic Evidence,* 16 Am J Trial Advoc 573 (1992); COMMENT, *When the Blue Bus Crashes into the Gate: The Problem with People v. Collins in the Probabilistic Evidence Debate,* 46 U Miami L Rev 975 (1992); Barnes, *A Common Sense Approach to Understanding Statistical Evidence,* 21 San Diego L Rev 809 (1984); Kaye, *Is Proof of Statistical Significance Relevant?,* 61 Wash L Rev 1333 (1986); Brook, *The Use of Statistical Evidence of Identification in Civil Litigation: Well-Worn Hypotheticals, Real Cases, and Controversy,* 29 St Louis U L J 293 (1985).

Jury Views

The Oregon rule, contrary to the rule in many other jurisdictions, is that a jury view is not evidence. It is merely a device to enable the jury to better understand the testimony offered at the trial. Whether to allow a jury view is within the sound discretion of the trial court and the appellate court will not reverse except for abuse of discretion. *Southern Oregon Orchards Co. v. Bakke,* 106 Or 20, 210 P 858 (1922); *Taylor v. Baughman,* 38 Or App 179, 589 P2d 1160 (1979).

No rule in the code directly addresses views by the jury. Instead, they are regulated by statute. ORS 10.100 provides:

> Whenever, in the opinion of the court, it is proper that the jury should have a view of real property which is the subject of the litigation, or of the place in which any material fact occurred, it may order the jury to be conducted in a body, in the custody of a proper officer, to the place, which shall be shown to them by the judge or by a person appointed by the court for that purpose. While the jury are thus absent, no person, other than the judge or person so appointed, shall speak to them on any subject connected with the trial.

Evidence Indicating Consciousness of Guilt

Evidence tending to show consciousness of guilt is admissible against the defendant in a criminal case. Such evidence may include escape, see *State v.*

McIntire, 2 Or App 429, 468 P2d 536 (1970); concealment, see *State v. Stookey,* 253 Or 367, 454 P2d 267 (1969), *State v. Brown,* 231 Or 297, 372 P2d 779 (1962); making of false exculpatory statements, see *State v. Carroll,* 251 Or 197, 444 P2d 1006 (1968), *State v. Maple,* 23 Or App 626, 544 P2d 183 (1975); use of an alias after the crime, see *United States v. Boyle,* 675 F2d 430, 432 (1st Cir 1982); giving false identification, see *United States v. Kalish,* 690 F2d 1144, 1155 (5th Cir 1982), cert denied 459 US 1108, 103 SCt 735, 74 LEd2d 958 (1983); and procuring of false alibi testimony, see *Kellensworth v. State,* 633 SW2d 21, 23–4 (Ark 1982).

Evidence of flight is often admitted to show consciousness of guilt. See *State v. Barr,* 62 Or App 46, 51, 660 P2d 169 (1983) (defendant fled after being released on bail); *State v. Eaton,* 31 Or App 653, 571 P2d 173 (1977). However, the court must be satisfied that the evidence of the defendant's departure or relocation constitutes flight before the evidence will be relevant on consciousness of guilt. See *United States v. Beahm,* 664 F2d 414, 419–20 (4th Cir 1981) (error to allow jury to draw inference of guilt from fact that defendant went to another state after receiving a note asking him to contact an FBI agent).

The refusal of a person arrested for driving under the influence of intoxicants to take a breathalyzer test is generally admissible against that person in subsequent civil or criminal litigation. See ORS 487.805(4). The use of the defendant's refusal as evidence against him has been held not to violate the defendant's due process rights or federal privilege against self-incrimination. *South Dakota v. Neville,* 459 US 553, 103 SCt 916, 74 LEd2d 748 (1983). But see *State v. Green,* 68 Or App 518, 684 P2d 575, rev denied 297 Or 601, 687 P2d 795 (1984) (evidence that defendant refused to take field sobriety tests inadmissible).

Evidence showing consciousness of fault is also admissible in civil cases. See *Stephens v. Bohlman,* 138 Or App 381, 386, 909 P2d 208 (1996) (in medical malpractice action, evidence that defendant doctor participated in covering up cause of patient's death is admissible as "circumstantial evidence of his belief that he acted negligently").

See also ANNOT., *Admissibility of Evidence Relating to Accused's Attempt to Commit Suicide,* 22 ALR3d 840 (1968); ANNOT., *Admissibility and Effect, on Issue of Party's Credibility or Merits of His Case, of Evidence of Attempts to Intimidate or Influence Witness in Civil Action,* 4 ALR4th 829 (1981). Cf. ANNOT., *Impeachment of Defendant in Criminal Case by Showing Defendant's Prearrest Silence—State Cases,* 35 ALR4th 731 (1985).

Sentencing Hearings

Although sentencing hearings are generally not subject to the rules of evidence, an exception is made for capital sentencing hearings under ORS 163.150. See Rule 101(4)(d). ORS 163.150 also contains an independent relevance requirement, which has been construed to have the same meaning as Rule 401. The statute also expressly excludes repetitive evidence that has previously been received during the trial on the issue of guilt.

In *State v. Stevens,* 319 Or 573, 580, 879 P2d 162, 165 (1994), the court held that the standard of relevance set forth in OEC 401 applies in penalty phase proceedings of criminal trials. The court held that it was error to exclude testimony by the defendant's former wife about how his "daughter may feel about him and what might be best for her in terms of his punishment." The court held that such evidence was relevant to the defendant's character or background because "a rational juror could infer that there are positive aspects about defendant's relationship with his daughter that demonstrate that defendant has the capacity to be of emotional value to others."

However, in *State v. Wright*, 323 Or 8, 13–5, 913 P2d 321 (1996), the court held that defendant was not entitled to call witnesses to testify simply that they did not believe defendant should receive the death penalty, because such opinion testimony does not satisfy the "helpfulness" requirement of Rule 701 that "subsumes" a relevancy analysis.

ORS 163.150 provides that in capital sentencing hearings the court may admit "victim impact evidence relating to the personal characteristics of the victim or the impact of the crime on the victim's family." This statute overrules *State v. Guzek*, 322 Or 245, 906 P2d 272 (1995), which held that victim impact evidence was irrelevant in the penalty phase of an aggravated murder trial.

Evidence of the defendant's commission of other crimes or acts of violence is generally admissible in capital sentencing hearings on the issue of future dangerousness. See *State v. Montez*, 309 Or 564, 611–2, 789 P2d 1352 (1990) (defendant's uncorroborated admission of killing someone); *State v. Moen*, 309 Or 45, 65–76, 786 P2d 111 (1990) (prior convictions for negligent homicide and forgery and an incident where defendant allegedly discharged a gun during an argument); *State v. Williams*, 322 Or 620, 632–3, 912 P2d 364 (1996) (fight with other inmate even though prison disciplinary charges dismissed).

Similarly, a defendant's statements about his plans to commit future crimes may be admissible. See *State v. Williams*, 313 Or 19, 43, 828 P2d 1006, 1021, cert denied *Williams v. Oregon*, 113 SCt 171 (1992) (evidence that defendant told a witness that he would like to rape a girl was relevant in the sentencing phase of a homicide prosecution on the issue of future dangerousness and its probative value was not outweighed by the danger of unfair prejudice).

In *Dawson v. Delaware*, 112 SCt 1093 (1992), the Supreme Court held that the First and Fourteenth amendments prohibit the introduction in a capital sentencing proceeding of the fact that the defendant was a member of the Aryan Brotherhood where such evidence had no relevance to the issues being decided in the proceeding.

RULE 402.   ORS 40.155. RELEVANT EVIDENCE GENERALLY ADMISSIBLE

All relevant evidence is admissible, except as otherwise provided by the Oregon Evidence Code, by the Constitutions of the United States and Oregon, or by Oregon statutory and decisional law. Evidence which is not relevant is not admissible.

LEGISLATIVE COMMENTARY

Oregon Rule of Evidence 402 states the rule, followed in Oregon, that all relevant facts are admissible unless they violate specific exclusionary rules. *Trook v. Sagert,* 171 Or 680, 688, 138 P2d 900 (1943); ORS 41.230.

The language of the rule is based on Rule 402 of the Federal Rules of Evidence, which declares that all relevant evidence is admissible in federal courts except as otherwise provided by the Constitution of the United States, by Act of Congress, by the Federal Rules of Evidence or by other rules prescribed by the Supreme Court pursuant to statutory authority. Federal Rule 402 is modified to provide that the exceptions to admissibility are set forth in the Oregon Evidence Code, the Constitutions of the United States and Oregon and in Oregon's statutory and decision law.

The principle that all relevant evidence may be admitted, except where the law otherwise provides, is "a presupposition involved in the very conception of a rational system of evidence." Thayer, *Preliminary Treatise on Evidence* 264 (1898). It is the foundation upon which the structure of admission and exclusion rests. For similar provisions see California Evidence Code §§ 350, 351. Provision that all relevant evidence is admissible is also found in Uniform Rule 7(f), Kansas Code of Civil Procedure § 60-407(f), and New Jersey Evidence Rule 7(f), but these texts only exclude evidence that is not relevant by implication.

Not all relevant evidence is admissible. It may be excluded by these rules, by Oregon statutory and decisional law consistent with these rules, or by constitutional considerations.

Succeeding rules in Article IV, in response to the demands of particular policies, require the exclusion of evidence even though the evidence is relevant. In addition, Article V recognizes a number of privileges that protect relevant information; Article VI imposes limitations upon witnesses and the manner of dealing with them; Article VII specifies requirements with respect to opinions and expert testimony; Article VIII excludes hearsay not falling within an exception; Article IX spells out the handling of authentication and identification; and Article X restricts the manner of proving the contents of writings and recordings.

Other rules outside the evidence code also require the exclusion of relevant evidence. ORS 45.250, for example, places limits on the use of relevant depositions by imposing requirements of notice and unavailability of the deponent. Similarly, ORS 133.683 excludes evidence of the fruits of unlawful searches or seizures, and ORS 133.703 excludes the testimony of an unidentified informant under certain circumstances.

Rule 402 recognizes but makes no attempt to spell out the constitutional considerations which impose basic limitations upon the admissibility of relevant evidence. Examples are evidence obtained by unlawful search and seizure, *Weeks v. United States,* 232 US 383, 34 SCt 341, 58 LEd 652 (1914); *Katz v. United States,* 389 US 347, 88 SCt 507, 19 LEd 2d 576 (1967), and incriminating statements elicited from an accused in violation of the right to counsel, *Massiah v. United States,* 377 US 201, 84 SCt 1199, 12 LEd 2d 246 (1964).

TEXT

Relevant Evidence Generally Admissible

Rule 402 establishes relevance as the primary criterion of admissibility by (1) declaring all irrelevant evidence to be inadmissible; and (2) providing that all relevant evidence is admissible, except as otherwise provided by the Oregon Evidence Code, the constitutions of the United States and Oregon, and by Oregon statutory and decisional law.

Exclusion Under Case Law

Unlike FRE 402, Rule 402 provides that evidence may be excluded by prior decisional law as well as by statutes and constitutional provisions. Such a qualification was presumably deemed necessary in order to continue certain rules of exclusion outside the evidence code that are recognized by prior case law. See, e.g., *State ex rel Heath v. Kraft,* 20 Or 28, 23 P 663 (1890) (vote at public election is privileged).

In *State ex rel Juvenile Dept. v. Beasley,* 314 Or 444, 454–5, 840 P2d 78 (1992), the court held that under OEC 402 case law outside the evidence code can be used as a ground for excluding evidence. The decision affirmed the ruling of the trial court in a termination of parental rights proceeding refusing to allow the six-year-old child to be called as a witness. The court adopted the rule of *Chandler v. State,* 230 Or 452, 370 P2d 626 (1962), which allows the trial judge to balance the probative value of the testimony against the risk of severe emotional or psychological harm to the child from testifying.

The court held that the *Chandler* rule survives the adoption of the Oregon Evidence Code.

Exclusion Under Electronic Eavesdropping Statutes

There are a number of statutes requiring exclusion of evidence obtained by wiretaps or electronic eavesdropping. See, e.g., ORS 133.735(1) (suppression of intercepted communications); ORS 41.910 (suppression of illegally intercepted communications); ORS 165.540(1) (interception of telecommunication or radio communication).

In *State v. Carston,* 323 Or 75, 913 P2d 709 (1996), the court held that a search warrant could not be based on conversations intercepted from a cordless phone by an informant using a scanner. Thus, the court suppressed the evidence obtained pursuant to ORS 165.540(1). The court held that a cordless telephone convesation did not fit the exemption in ORS 165.540(4) for a "radio broadcast transmitted for the use of the general public."

In *State v. Tucker,* 307 Or 386, 768 P2d 397 (1989), the court held that improperly obtained wiretap evidence was also inadmissible for purposes of impeachment under ORS 41.910 and 133.735.

Exclusion Under Other Statutes

There are a considerable number of statutes outside the evidence code providing for the exclusion of evidence. See, e.g., ORS 133.683 (suppression of fruits of prior unlawful search); ORS 41.905(1) (conviction or acquittal of traffic offense not admissible in subsequent civil litigation arising out of same facts); ORS 44.520 (privilege for media persons). See also the statutes creating a privilege or restricting the disclosure of records discussed under Rule 514.

Parol Evidence Rule

One of the most important statutory rules of exclusion outside the evidence code is the parol evidence rule. ORS 41.740 provides:

> When the terms of an agreement have been reduced to writing by the parties, it is to be considered as containing all those terms, and therefore there can be, between the parties and their representatives or successors in interest, no evidence of the terms of the agreement, other than the contents of the writing, except where a mistake or imperfection of the writing is put in issue by the pleadings or where the validity of the agreement is the fact in dispute. However, this section does not exclude other evidence of the circumstances under which the agreement was made, or to which it relates, as defined in ORS 42.220, or to explain an ambiguity, intrinsic or extrinsic, or to establish illegality or fraud. The term "agreement" includes deeds and wills as well as contracts between parties.

In cases governed by the Uniform Commercial Code, parol evidence is restricted by ORS 72.2020 as follows:

> Terms with respect to which the confirmatory memoranda of the parties agree or which are otherwise set forth in a writing intended by the parties as a final expression of their agreement with respect to such terms as are included therein may not be contradicted by evidence of any prior agreement or of a contemporaneous oral agreement but may be explained or supplemented: (1) By course of dealing or usage of trade as provided in ORS 71.2050 or by course of performance as provided in ORS 72.2080; and (2) By evidence of consistent additional terms unless the court finds the writing to have been intended also as a complete and exclusive statement of the terms of the agreement.

The parol evidence doctrine is viewed as a rule of the substantive law governing contracts rather than as an evidence rule.

Curative Admissibility

The prohibition against irrelevant evidence stated in Rule 402 may be qualified to some extent by the doctrine of "curative admissibility." This doctrine, which is sometimes referred to as "opening the door," has been explained by the Oregon Supreme Court as follows: "[W]here one party offers inadmissible evidence, which is received, the opponent may then offer similar facts whose only claim to admission is that they negative or explain or counterbalance the prior inadmissible evidence, presumably upon the same fact, subject matter or issue." *Wynn v. Sundquist,* 259 Or 125, 136, 485 P2d 1085, 1090 (1971) (references omitted). Although this doctrine can apply where evidence is inadmissible for a reason other than irrelevancy, most frequently the issue arises in connection with irrelevant evidence.

The courts have tended to allow subsequent inadmissible evidence only in situations where it is truly necessary to prevent unfairness or misleading of the jury on a significant issue. See *Lang v. Oregon Nurses Ass'n,* 53 Or App 422, 427–8, 632 P2d 472, rev denied 291 Or 771, 642 P2d 308 (1981). A narrow scope to the doctrine is particularly appropriate in cases where the party now seeking to offer inadmissible evidence failed to object to the earlier inadmissible evidence offered by his or her opponent.

In *United States v. Winston,* 447 F2d 1236, 1240 (DC Cir 1971) (citations omitted), the court stated:

> The doctrine of curative admissibility is one dangerously prone to overuse. The doctrine is to prevent prejudice and is not to be subverted into a rule for injection of prejudice. Introduction of otherwise inadmissible evidence under shield of this doctrine is permitted "only to the extent necessary to remove any unfair prejudice which might otherwise have ensued from the original evidence."

In *State v. Renly,* 111 Or App 453, 458, 827 P2d 1345, 1348 (1992), a sex abuse prosecution, the court held that a question by defense counsel regarding whether a CSD worker interviewed any other children who witnessed the alleged sexual abuse did not "open the door" to prosecution evidence proving specific acts of abuse involving other children.

RULE 403. ORS 40.160. EXCLUSION OF RELEVANT EVIDENCE ON GROUNDS OF PREJUDICE, CONFUSION, OR UNDUE DELAY

Although relevant, evidence may be excluded if its probative value is substantially outweighed by the danger of unfair prejudice, confusion of the issues, or misleading the jury, or by considerations of undue delay or needless presentation of cumulative evidence.

LEGISLATIVE COMMENTARY

Oregon Rule of Evidence 403 recognizes that certain circumstances call for the exclusion of evidence that is of unquestioned relevance. These circumstances entail risks that range all the way from inducing decision on a purely emotional basis, at one extreme, to nothing more harmful than delaying decision by repetition of evidence, at the other. These situations call for balancing the probative value of and need for evidence against the harm likely to result from its admission. Slough, "Relevancy Unraveled," in 5 Kan L Rev 1, 12–15 (1956); Trautmann, "Logical or Legal Relevancy—A Conflict in Theory," in 5 Vand L Rev 385, 392 (1952); McCormick, *Evidence* § 185 at 438–441 (2d ed 1972). The remaining rules in this article are concrete applications that have evolved in particular situations. However, they reflect the policies underlying the present rule, which is designed as a guide for handling situations for which no specific rules have been formulated.

Rule 403 is based on Rule 403 of the Federal Rules of Evidence and is generally consistent with Oregon law. It differs slightly from both, however.

Federal Rule 403 includes "waste of time" as a reason for excluding relevant evidence. The Legislative Assembly deleted this language in the belief that relevant evidence is never a "waste of time" unless it is cumulative. Rule 403 provides for exclusion on the ground of "needless presentation of cumulative evidence."

Oregon case law had adopted "surprise" as an independent basis for excluding relevant evidence. *Carter v. Moberly*, 263 Or 193, 501 P2d 1276 (1972); *Krause v. Eugene Dodge, Inc.*, 265 Or 486, 509 P2d 1199 (1973). Rule 403 does not assign surprise this status, because surprise is usually coupled with the danger of prejudice and confusion of the issues. Cf. McCormick § 185 at 440 n. 34. Rather than exclude evidence solely on the basis of unfair surprise, a court should consider granting the more appropriate remedy of a continuance. While Uniform Rule 45 incorporates "surprise" as a ground for excluding relevant evidence, and is followed in Kansas Code of Civil Procedure § 60-445, surprise is not included in California Evidence Code § 352, or New Jersey Rule 4, although the latter otherwise substantially embody Uniform Rule 45.

"Unfair prejudice," in the context of ORE 403, means an undue tendency to suggest decisions on an improper basis, commonly although not always an emotional one. In deciding whether to exclude on grounds of unfair prejudice the court should consider the probable effectiveness of a limiting instruction. It should also bear in mind the availability of other means of proof, and of other evidence under Rule 106.

The exclusion of relevant evidence for risk of unfair prejudice, confusion of issues, misleading the jury or cumulation of evidence finds ample support in Oregon decisional law. See *State v. Joseph*, 10 Or App 367, 499 P2d 30 (1972); *State v. Freeman*, 232 Or 267, 374 P2d 453 (1963); *State v. Flett*, 134 Or 300, 380 P2d 643 (1963) (unfair prejudice); *Juckeland v. Miles and Sons Trucking Service*, 254 Or 514, 462 P2d 668 (1973), *Carter v. Moberly*, 263 Or 193, 501 P2d 1276 (1972), *State v. Harns*, 241 Or 224, 405 P2d 492 (1965), *Loibl v. Nienie*, 214 Or 172, 327 P2d 786 (1958) (confusion of issues and misleading the jury); *Krause v. Eugene Dodge, Inc.*, 265 Or 486, 409 P2d 1199 (1973) (cumulative evidence).

Prejudice is not cognizable in any case of impeachment by evidence of prior conviction of a crime of false statement. ORE 609(1)(b); see also *Smith v. Durant*, 271 Or 643, 646–649, 534 P2d 955 (1975). It is to be considered, however, in the case of impeachment by evidence of a felony conviction. ORE 609(1)(a).

TEXT

Exclusion on Grounds of Prejudice, Confusion, Delay

Rule 403 states five factors that are to be balanced against the probative value of evidence in determining its admissibility. Three of the factors are described as "dangers" and two of the factors are described as "considerations." The three dangers are: (1) unfair prejudice; (2) confusion of the issues; and (3) misleading the jury. The two considerations are: (1) undue delay and (2) needless presentation of cumulative evidence.

The Commentary also suggests that the court should consider three other factors: (1) the probable effectiveness of a limiting instruction under Rule 105; (2) the availability of other means of proof; and (3) the likelihood of supplementation with other evidence under Rule 106.

As the Commentary notes, a third consideration included in FRE 403—"waste of time"—was omitted because of its overlap with the restriction against needlessly cumulative evidence. "Surprise," a ground for exclusion recognized under prior Oregon law, was omitted because granting a continuance, rather than excluding the evidence, was viewed as a more appropriate remedy. Even though surprise is not listed as an independent ground for excluding evidence, surprise may be a factor in finding that evidence will result in undue delay, unfair prejudice, and confusion of the issues. See *Lease America Corp. v. Insurance Co. of North America,* 88 Wis2d 395, 276 NW2d 767 (1979).

There are two additional grounds for excluding evidence recognized under prior Oregon law that are not expressly incorporated into Rule 403. They are "remoteness," see *Carter v. Moberly,* 263 Or 193, 501 P2d 1276 (1972) (negligent conduct ten miles from the scene of the collision too remote), *Marshall v. Martinson,* 268 Or 46, 518 P2d 1312 (1974); and "vagueness," see *Phillips v. Creighton,* 211 Or 645, 316 P2d 302 (1957) (excluding references to a speeding car that the witness could not identify as that of the defendant). However, the same result would probably be reached in these cases applying the five factors in Rule 403 and the definition of relevant evidence contained in Rule 401.

It is important for a party to make a separate objection under Rule 403, because a general relevancy objection under Rule 401 does not preserve an error under Rule 403. *State v. Carrillo,* 108 Or App 442, 445–6, 816 P2d 654, 655–6, rev denied 312 Or 527, 822 P2d 1196 (1994).

Rule 403 requires that the probative value of evidence be *substantially* outweighed by the factors listed in Rule 403 before exclusion is justified. The rule thus adopts a policy favoring the admissibility of evidence in close cases.

Although the rule does not expressly so require, appellate courts interpreting FRE 403 have strongly encouraged trial courts to make a record of the factors considered in making the determination to exclude or admit evidence. See, e.g., *United States v. Long,* 574 F2d 761, 766 (3rd Cir), cert denied 439 US 985 (1978); *United States v. Dwyer,* 539 F2d 924, 928 (2nd Cir 1976). Such a record will often need to be made outside the presence of the jury.

Trial courts have broad discretion in balancing the factors specified in Rule 403. On appeal, the trial court's decision will generally be reviewed only for abuse of discretion. *Carlson v. Piper Aircraft Corp.*, 57 Or App 695, 646 P2d 43, 46–7, rev denied 293 Or 801, 653 P2d 999 (1982); *Page v. Cushing*, 80 Or App 690, 724 P2d 323, rev denied 302 Or 159, 727 P2d 129 (1986). Cf. *State v. Hubbard*, 297 Or 789, 797, 688 P2d 1311 (1984) (withholding judgment on "[w]hether discretionary rulings can be considered error.").

However, occasionally evidence is made admissible by statute and is not subject to exclusion under Rule 403. See, e.g., ORS 41.415 ("In a prosecution for any criminal homicide, a photograph of the victim while alive shall be admissible evidence when offered by the district attorney to show the general appearance and condition of the victim while alive."). See also *State v. Williams*, 313 Or 19, 27–31, 828 P2d 1006, 1012–4, cert denied 113 SCt 171 (1992) (upholding constitutionality of this statute).

In some situations, a party may offer to stipulate to certain facts in order to avoid the prejudicial effect of evidence being introduced to prove such matters. Where there has been an adequate stipulation to a fact, evidence to prove that fact may be excluded under Rule 403. In *State v. McKendall*, 36 Or App 187, 198, 584 P2d 316, 322–3 (1978), the court stated: "[Where] a defendant offers to stipulate to a fact, proof of the fact would be prejudicial to the defendant, and the evidence offered in proof is not probative of any issue other than that which the stipulation addresses, the evidence is inadmissible." However, if the stipulation does not cover all purposes for which the evidence is admissible, the stipulation will not necessarily preclude introduction of the evidence. See, e.g., *State v. Smith*, 58 Or App 458, 462, 648 P2d 1294, 1296 (1982) (defendant stipulated to identity and location of murder victim's body; photographs of body nonetheless held admissible to prove intent to kill).

Sometimes a motion for a separate trial is more appropriate than a motion to exclude the evidence under Rule 403. In *State v. Armenta*, 74 Or App 219, 702 P2d 1113 (1985), the court held that where evidence is admissible as to one charge and inadmissible as to another, the proper remedy is a motion for a separate trial, not premature exclusion of the evidence under Rule 403.

In *State v. Parker*, 119 Or App 105, 109, 849 P2d 105, rev denied 317 Or 584, 859 P2d 541 (1993), the court held that OEC 403 was not applicable to motions for separate trials, even though prejudice is an appropriate factor to be considered when a severance motion is made. The court stated that the most compelling argument against requiring an OEC 403 balancing process is that "to require a trial court to make such a determination at the pretrial stage deprives the court of the opportunity to consider the effect of the evidence in the context of the trial evidentiary record."

The concept of undue prejudice would appear to encompass two analytically distinct forms of prejudice. The first is the injection of emotionalism into the proceeding, resulting in undue hostility, sympathy, or anger on the part of the jury. The second aspect of unfair prejudice is the likelihood that the jury will misuse the evidence in some way or place undue emphasis upon it, even though the evidence does not necessarily appeal to the emotions.

Recent Cases

Precedents will be of limited value in applying Rule 403, because the balancing required by the rule depends upon the unique facts of each case. However, the following are examples of recent cases decided under Rule 403:

Evidence Held Admissible Under Rule 403

State v. Hart, 309 Or 646, 652–3, 791 P2d 125 (1990): The court held that under OEC 403, a defendant is not entitled to have statements he made to a police officer in a prepolygraph test interview suppressed, even though the defendant argued that the state's use of such statements could force him to offer an explanation that would make the jury aware of the polygraph test.

State v. Nefstad, 309 Or 523, 554–6, 789 P2d 1326 (1990): A witness's identification of the defendant accompanied by the statement that he looked "sleazy" and had a "wild look" was "not character evidence under OEC 404(1) or (2), nor was it uncharged misconduct evidence under OEC 404(3)." The court held that under OEC 403 the probative value of the identification outweighed the unfair prejudice of the accompanying adjectives. The court also approved admission of a photograph of the murder victim.

State v. Harberts, 109 Or App 533, 538, 820 P2d 1366, 1368 (1991), aff'd as modified 315 Or 408, 848 P2d 1187 (1993): Voluntary statements made by defendant during the course of a polygraph examination should not have been excluded under Rule 403. The trial court had concluded that the statements would be misleading without an explanation that they were taken in the context of a polygraph examination. The court held that the statements could be properly sanitized and that the decision whether to bring out the circumstances in which they were obtained belonged to the defendant.

Persad v. Kaiser Foundation Hospital, Inc., 106 Or App 615, 619, 809 P2d 706, rev denied 312 Or 80, 816 P2d 610 (1991): A hearsay statement was found prejudicial "only in the sense that it was highly probative," and this is "not the kind of prejudice that OEC 403 contemplates." The court found the evidence had "no tendency to persuade the jury to decide the case adversely for reasons unrelated to the issue at hand."

State v. Shearer, 101 Or App 543, 547–8, 792 P2d 1215, rev denied 310 Or 205, 795 P2d 555 (1990): In this sex abuse prosecution, the defendant called an expert who testified that defendant did not match the profile of a pedophile. The court found no OEC 403 violation in the fact that the state impeached defendant's expert by showing that in another unrelated sex abuse prosecution the expert had testified that the person charged did not fit the psychological profile of a sex abuser and yet the person later admitted the acts.

State v. Hubbard, 297 Or 789, 688 P2d 1311 (1984): The Supreme Court found reversible error in the refusal of the trial judge to allow cross-examination of the arresting officer regarding his knowledge of internal police department procedures and sanctions against officers who use unnecessary force. On the facts of this case, the court found this issue relevant on the potential bias and interest of the witness in the outcome of the case because it might tend to show that his version of the events was slanted in order to avoid departmental discipline. The discretion of the trial judge to exclude evidence relevant to bias or interest only obtains once sufficient facts have been established from which the jury may infer that bias or interest.

State v. Martin, 95 Or App 170, 769 P2d 203 (1989): Defendant challenged admission of tape recordings of telephone conversations, alleging they were of poor quality and that the mere presence of his voice on the tapes triggered a conclusion of culpability. The appellate court found no abuse of discretion in admitting the tapes.

State v. Smith, 86 Or App 239, 739 P2d 577 (1987): The defendant was convicted for driving on September 25 while his operator's license was suspended. He called his son as a witness, who testified that the father did not drive on September 25 and that the defendant's car had not moved from the side of the house since that date. In rebuttal, the prosecutor called the arresting officer who testified that he saw the defendant driving the car on September 26. The court found this testimony to be proper impeachment.

Martinez v. Democrat-Herald Publishing Co., 64 Or App 690, 669 P2d 818, rev denied 296 Or 120, 672 P2d 1193 (1983): In this action against defendant for allegedly portraying plaintiff in a "false light" through publication of a photograph showing her to be involved in an apparent drug transaction, the court found no error in the admission of evidence of prior marijuana use by the plaintiff.

State v. Huffman, 65 Or App 594, 672 P2d 1351 (1983): The court held that there was no violation of Rule 403 in admitting evidence of threats against a prosecution witness made subsequent to the trial where the defendant allegedly committed perjury. The evidence was deemed relevant in showing a continuing conspiracy to avoid being convicted of the charge brought at the first trial, and the relevance was found to outweigh any prejudicial effect.

Evidence Held Not Admissible Under Rule 403

Lutz v. State of Oregon, 130 Or App 278, 283–4, 881 P2d 171 (1994): A father sued the state for the death of his son. The state sought to introduce evidence that the father took the boy's body from the funeral home in Newport and transported it in his car to Oregon City for cremation to save $125 in funeral expenses. This evidence was offered to controvert the father's claim that he suffered damage from the loss of his son's society and companionship. The court affirmed the exclusion of such evidence as unfairly prejudicial under OEC 403.

James v. General Motors of Canada, Ltd., 101 Or App 138, 145, 790 P2d 8, rev denied, 310 Or 243, 796 P2d 360 (1990): Court affirms trial judge's exercise of discretion in excluding expert testimony regarding prior incidents the expert was familiar with involving persons being ejected from a vehicle. The court stated that "their causes and their similarity to the incident in question was sketchy and speculative, and each incident could have become the subject of a prolonged and confusing diversion of the trial."

State v. Meyers, 132 Or App 585, 889 P2d 374 (1995): The court affirmed the exclusion under OEC of a taped telephone conversation between the defendant and his former wife, whom he was accused of raping and assaulting. The court reaffirmed the deference given to OEC 403 rulings by trial courts, provided that "findings are made on the record to back up this discretionary call." The court found sufficient indication in the record that the trial judge had undertaken an appropriate balancing of probative value versus unfair prejudice.

State v. Lyon, 304 Or 221, 744 P2d 231 (1987): The Supreme Court held that polygraph test results are inadmissible as evidence in the courts of Oregon, even when admissibility has been stipulated by the parties. The court based its ruling primarily on Rule 403.

State v. Pigg, 87 Or App 625, 743 P2d 770 (1987): Defendant was convicted of sexual abuse. At trial, the state offered evidence that defendant had been contacted by a police officer regarding the allegation of sexual abuse, had denied the allegation, told the officer that he was busy with college final exams and would call the officer in four or five days to discuss the matter further, but never did so. The prosecutor offered this evidence of defendant's prearrest "silence" for the purpose of demonstrating his consciousness of guilt. The Court of Appeals reversed under Rule 403, finding that the probative value of the evidence was outweighed by the danger that it would unfairly prejudice the jury. The court found that the evidence had little probative value, because there "were many possible explanations for defendant's failure to call the officer, including, as defendant testified was the case, that he had been acting on the advice of counsel."

Mission Insurance Company v. Wallace Security Agency, Inc., 84 Or App 525, 734 P2d 405 (1987): Plaintiff alleged that defendant's employee started a fire, for which the plaintiff was required to pay a substantial sum to its insured. Plaintiff assigned as error the exclusion of a psychiatrist's testimony concerning the personality traits of sociopaths and fire setters, arguing that the testimony was relevant to the issue of whether defendant's employee was fit to be a security guard and whether he might have set the fire himself. The court held that any possible relevance was outweighed by the danger of undue prejudice and the potentially misleading introduction of collateral evidence.

ABCD ... Vision, Inc. v. Fireman's Fund Insurance Companies, 84 Or App 645, 651, 734 P2d 1376 (1987): The court held that the trial judge did not abuse his discretion in refusing to admit testimony concerning an insurance policy that the parties did not execute, because "[t]he testimony's potential for prejudice and confusion substantially outweighed its probative value."

State v. Moore, 72 Or App 454, 695 P2d 985, rev denied 299 Or 154, 700 P2d 251 (1985): Defendant was convicted of assault for shooting her husband. The appellate court held that the trial judge acted within the scope of his discretion in excluding the testimony of a witness from a local women's crisis center regarding phone calls received from the defendant, which occurred many months prior to the incident that was the basis of the criminal charges. The last contact the defendant had with the crisis center was approximately seven months before the shooting. The court held that such evidence would have been cumulative of defendant's testimony and that other considerations reflected in Rule 403 justified exclusion as well.

State v. Dolan, 74 Or App 16, 701 P2d 478 (1985): In this burglary prosecution, the court held that it was prejudicial to admit evidence that the defendant had used an alias in an otherwise innocent, unconnected incident two months prior to the burglary.

State v. Peacock, 75 Or App 217, 706 P2d 982 (1985): The court held that a prosecutor's inquiry into whether the defendant's attorney filed a notice of intent to rely on a mental disease or defect defense was irrelevant and prejudicial.

State v. Hickam, 71 Or App 471, 692 P2d 672 (1984): The court reversed the conviction of defendant, finding that evidence of the defendant's notice of intent to rely on lack of responsibility and lack of intent, his notice of withdrawal of those defenses, and the intervening court order requiring psychiatric evaluation of defendant should have been excluded under Rule 403. The court found that any relevancy of such evidence was outweighed by the danger of unfair prejudice.

State v. Holterman, 69 Or App 509, 687 P2d 1097, rev denied 298 Or 172, 691 P2d 481 (1984): The court held that the trial judge did not abuse his discretion in excluding evidence offered by the defendant that defendant claimed tended to show that another person committed the crime. The appellate court agreed that the evidence was speculative and that its probative value was far outweighed by its potential to mislead the jury.

Photographs, Videotapes

With respect to exclusion of photographs, Rule 403 is qualified to some extent by a statute adopted as part of the Victim's Right Initiative in 1986. ORS 41.415 provides:

> In a prosecution for any criminal homicide, a photograph of the victim while alive shall be admissible evidence when offered by the condition of district attorney to show the general appearance and condition of the victim while alive.

Arnold v. Burlington Northern Railroad, 89 Or App 245, 249, 748 P2d 174, rev denied 305 Or 576, 753 P2d 1382 (1988): The court held that the trial court did not abuse its discretion in admitting a videotape by the plaintiff that demonstrated a day in the plaintiff's life. The appellate court agreed that "the probative value of the film—its ability to illustrate graphically the impact of the plaintiff's injuries on his life—outweighed its prejudicial value—the danger of eliciting undue sympathy for the plaintiff."

State v. Eby, 63 Or App 35, 39, 663 P2d 778, 780, rev'd on other grounds 296 Or 63, 673 P2d 522 (1983): The court approved admission of photographs of the victim's corpse over a Rule 403 objection, stating: "The photographs were relevant to show such matters as how and where the victim died, the location of the wound on the victim's body and the bullet's trajectory .... Defendant's stipulations did not admit these matters."

State v. Lerch, 63 Or App 707, 666 P2d 840 (1983), aff'd 296 Or 377, 677 P2d 678 (1984): Defendant claimed reversible error in the admission of a photograph of the defendant nude from the waist up, for the purpose of showing that the defendant had sufficient strength to strangle the murder victim in the manner he had previously described to the police. The defendant argued that his strength could have been shown in other, less prejudicial ways. The court affirmed, stating that "the state has the burden of establishing guilt beyond a reasonable doubt and thus has the right to prove every essential element of the crime in the most convincing manner." 63 Or App at 716, 666 P2d at 847.

State v. Smith, 58 Or App 458, 462, 648 P2d 1294, 1296 (1982): The court held that gory photographs of the murder victim were admissible to prove intent to kill the victim, even though the defendant had offered to stipulate to the identity of the victim and the position of her body in the house. Under the circumstances of the case, the court found that the probative value of the photographs to prove intent outweighed the danger of unfair prejudice.

For illustrative pre-Code Oregon cases, see *Pooschke v. Union Pac. R.R. Co.,* 246 Or 633, 426 P2d 866 (1967) (admission of color photograph of plaintiff's injured leg not error); *Wilson v. Piper Aircraft Corp.,* 282 Or 61, 577 P2d 1322, rehearing denied 282 Or 411, 579 P2d 1287 (1978) (excluding motion picture showing dummies lying "dead" by airplane covered with fake blood).

Federal Cases

Illustrative federal cases interpreting FRE 403 include the following:

Unfair Prejudice

Grimes v. Employers Mutual Liability Ins. Co., 73 FRD 607 (D Alaska (1977)) (overruling in part and sustaining in part objections, on ground of unfair prejudice, to film of paralyzed plaintiff performing daily activities); *Allen v. Seacoast Products, Inc.,* 623 F2d 355 (5th Cir 1980) (no unfair prejudice in allowing plaintiff to demonstrate procedure for removing and replacing artificial eye); *United States v. McRae,* 593 F2d 700 (5th Cir), cert denied 444 US 862 (1979) (admission of color photograph of woman who was shot in eye not abuse of trial court's discretion).

Confusion of the Issues

United States v. Harris, 542 F2d 1283 (7th Cir 1976) (refusal to allow evidence that defendant could not post bond, to rebut evidence that defendant in past had received large amounts of money); *United States v. Steffen,* 641 F2d 591 (8th Cir), cert denied 452 US 943 (1981) (excluding evidence offered by defendant that other persons alleged to be involved were not prosecuted); *United States v. Johnson,* 585 F2d 119 (5th Cir 1978) (similar); *Bob Maxfield, Inc. v. American Motors Corp.,* 637 F2d 1033 (5th Cir), cert denied 454 US 860 (1981) (evidence of alleged similar conduct by defendant against two other former dealers excluded); *United States v. Briscoe,* 574 F2d 406 (8th Cir), cert denied 439 US 858 (1978) (excluding evidence that heroin was also found in an apartment next door to defendant's apartment).

Misleading the Jury

In re Air Crash Disaster at J.F.K. Int'l Airport, 635 F2d 67 (2nd Cir 1980) (excluding evidence that the United States had previously consented to liability); *United States v. Massey,* 594 F2d 676 (8th Cir 1979) (misleading use of mathematical probabilities); *United States v. Hathaway,* 534 F2d 386 (1st Cir), cert denied 429 US 819 (1976) (excluding evidence of cancelled checks offered by defendant that were of marginal relevance to issues in case); *E.I. du Pont de Nemours & Co. v. Berkley and Co.,* 620 F2d 1247 (8th Cir 1980) (excluding uncertain, nonprobative deposition of plaintiff's attorney).

Undue Delay

United States v. Hearst, 563 F2d 1331 (9th Cir 1977), cert denied 435 US 1000 (1978) (court refused to allow playing of one hour and forty-five-minute tape of psychiatric interview of defendant; tape also found to be needlessly cumulative); *United States v. Gleason,* 616 F2d 2 (2nd Cir 1979), cert denied 444 US 1082 (1980) (limiting evidence to two out of eight examples of defendant's alleged cohort acting unlawfully on his own); *United States v. Williams,* 613 F2d 560 (5th Cir 1980) (narcotics prosecution; no error to exclude offer of defendant's tax return to show legitimate business income).

Needless Presentation of Cumulative Evidence

United States v. Haynes, 554 F2d 231 (5th Cir 1977) (upholding trial court's limitation on number of impeachment witnesses); *United States v. Lomax,* 598 F2d 582 (10th Cir 1979) (refusal to receive stolen check as an exhibit to impeach prosecution witness when the witness admitted stealing the check); *United States v. Diecidue,* 603 F2d 535 (5th Cir 1979), cert denied 445 US 946, 446 US 912 (1980) (cumulative impeachment evidence).

Other Authorities

See generally ANNOT., *Evidence Offered by Defendant at Federal Criminal Trial as Inadmissible, Under Rule 403 of Federal Rules of Evidence, on Ground that Probative Value is Substantially Outweighed by Danger of Unfair Prejudice, Confusion of Issues, or Misleading Jury,* 76 ALR Fed 700 (1986); ANNOT., *Propriety Under Rule 403 of the Federal Rules of Evidence, Permitting Exclusion of Relevant Evidence on Grounds of Prejudice, Confusion, or Waste of Time, of Attack on Credibility of Witness for Party,* 48 ALR Fed 390 (1980); Imwinkelried, *The Meaning of Probative Value and Prejudice in Federal Rule of Evidence 403: Can Rule 403 Be Used to Resurrect the Common Law of Evidence?,* 41 Vand L Rev 879

(1988); Gold, *Limiting Judicial Discretion to Exclude Prejudicial Evidence*, 18 UCD L Rev 59 (1984); Teitelbaum, Sutton-Barbere & Johnson, *Evaluating the Prejudicial Effect of Evidence: Can Judges Identify the Impact of Improper Evidence on Juries?*, 1983 Wis L Rev 1147; Gold, *Federal Rule of Evidence 403: Observations on the Nature of Unfairly Prejudicial Evidence*, 58 Wash L Rev 497 (1983); ANNOT., *Admissibility and Prejudicial Effect of Evidence, in Criminal Prosecution, of Defendant's Involvement with Witchcraft, Satanism, or the Like*, 18 ALR5th 804 (1994).

RULE 404.   ORS 40.170. CHARACTER EVIDENCE; ADMISSIBILITY

(1) **[Admissibility generally.]** Evidence of a person's character or trait of character is admissible when it is an essential element of a charge, claim or defense.

(2) **[Admissibility for certain purpose prohibited; exceptions.]** Evidence of a person's character is not admissible for the purpose of proving that the person acted in conformity therewith on a particular occasion, except:

   (a) **[Character of accused.]** Evidence of a pertinent trait of character offered by an accused, or by the prosecution to rebut the same;

   (b) **[Character of victim.]** Evidence of a pertinent trait of character of the victim of the crime offered by an accused, or by the prosecution to rebut the same or evidence of a character trait of peacefulness of the victim offered by the prosecution to rebut evidence that the victim was the first aggressor;

   (c) **[Character of witness.]** Evidence of the character of a witness, as provided in Rules 607 to 609 (ORS 40.345 to 40.355); or

   (d) **[Character for violent behavior.]** Evidence of the character of a party for violent behavior offered in a civil assault and battery case when self-defense is pleaded and there is evidence to support such defense.

(3) **[Other crimes, wrongs or acts.]** Evidence of other crimes, wrongs or acts is not admissible to prove the character of a person in order to show that the person acted in conformity therewith. It may, however, be admissible for other purposes, such as proof of motive, opportunity, intent, preparation, plan, knowledge, identity, or absence of mistake or accident.

LEGISLATIVE COMMENTARY

Oregon Rule of Evidence 404 describes the conditions under which evidence of a person's character may be considered by the trier of fact in a civil or criminal case. The rule is based on Rule 404 of the Federal Rules of

Evidence. However, the federal rule was modified and reorganized to reflect the legislative intent more clearly. Thus, subsection (1) does not appear in Federal Rule 404, but was added so that a single rule will codify all situations where evidence of character is admissible; it is derived from Federal Rule 405(b). Paragraph (2)(b) rejects the federal restriction on admission of evidence of a victim's character trait of peacefulness to homicide cases. Paragraph (2)(d) also does not appear in Federal Rule 404, but was added to codify present Oregon law regarding character evidence of the pugnaciousness of parties to a civil action.

Oregon Rule 404 is otherwise identical to Federal Rule 404.

Subsection (1). Questions concerning a person's character may arise in fundamentally different ways. One is when character itself is an element of a crime, claim or defense. Here the nature of the actions puts "character in issue." If a person's possession of a character trait determines the legal rights and liabilities of the parties, and if that trait has been put in issue by the pleadings, then the fact of character must be open to proof. McCormick, *Evidence* § 187 (2d ed 1972); *Guedon v. Rooney,* 160 Or 261, 87 P2d 209 (1939). Examples of "character in issue" are the competency of the driver in an action for negligent entrustment and the character of the plaintiff in an action for defamation. It is quite clear, in these situations, that character evidence is generally relevant and that the only problem relates to allowable methods of proof. Subsection (1) allows the admission of character evidence in such situations. For allowable methods of proof, see Rule 405.

Subsection (2). Unlike situations involving "character in issue," the use of character evidence to prove conduct raises questions of relevancy. Subsection (2) addresses the basic issue whether such circumstantial character evidence should be admitted. If the evidence is admissible under this subsection, Rule 405 will generally determine the appropriate method of proof. If the character evidence relates to a witness, however, Rules 608 and 609 determine the method of proof.

Subsection (2) states the rule in most jurisdictions, including Oregon. It rejects the use of circumstantial character evidence generally but recognizes several important exceptions. McCormick §§ 188–194; *Rich v. Cooper,* 234 Or 300, 380 P2d 613 (1963).

Paragraph (a). Under this paragraph, an accused in a criminal trial may introduce evidence of a pertinent trait of the accused's own character (often misleadingly described as "putting character in issue"), which the prosecution may then rebut with contradictory evidence. This is current Oregon law. *State v. Miles,* 8 Or App 189, 492 P2d 497 (1972); *State v. Rowley,* 6 Or App 13, 485 P2d 1120 (1971).

Paragraph (b). Under this paragraph, an accused in a criminal trial may introduce evidence of a pertinent trait of character of the victim, to support, for example, a claim of self-defense when charged with homicide or assault. The prosecution may then rebut with contradictory evidence.

Also under this paragraph, the prosecution may introduce evidence of a victim's character trait of peacefulness to rebut evidence that the victim was the first aggressor. In this case, the prosecution need not wait until the defense produces evidence of the victim's reputation for violence or aggressiveness. The rule is well settled in Oregon. *State v. Holbrook,* 98 Or 43, 188 P 947 (1920); *State v. Wilkins,* 72 Or 77, 142 P 589 (1914); *State v.*

Thompson, 49 Or 46, 88 P 583 (1907). It rests on a determination that the character trait of the victim for peace or violence has a revealing significance that may well outweigh the possibility of prejudice. See McCormick § 193.

Paragraph (b) changes existing Oregon practice, and differs from Federal Rule 404 and the rule in most jurisdictions, in that it does not limit the introduction of evidence of a victim's character trait of peacefulness to homicide cases, but allows such evidence in any criminal trial where the accused produces evidence that the victim was the first aggressor. The Legislative Assembly finds that the reasons for adopting this exception in homicide cases have equal force in other criminal cases, e.g., assaults. Similarly, there is no reason to believe that prejudice, distraction from issues and consumption of time will be any greater dangers when such evidence is introduced in nonhomicide criminal cases. Indeed, the appeal to pity and vengeance implicit in praise of the character of the victim may be less effective when the victim still lives.

It should be noted that in a prosecution for rape, sodomy or sexual abuse, reputation or opinion evidence of the past sexual behavior of the victim is governed by Rule 412. That rule, based on the Privacy Protection for Rape Victims Act of 1978, PL 95-540 (92 Stat 2046), supersedes paragraph (2)(b) of ORE 404 to prevent admission of evidence of the character of the victim, otherwise admissible under this paragraph, to support a claim of consent.

Paragraph (c). This paragraph allows admission of evidence concerning the character of a witness for truthfulness or untruthfulness, for the purpose of supporting or attacking the credibility of the witness. See Rules 607 through 609. It agrees with Oregon case law holding that a witness may be impeached by evidence that the witness' reputation for truthfulness is bad. *Lucas v. Kaylor,* 136 Or 541, 299 P2d 197 (1931); *McIntosh v. McNair,* 53 Or 87, 99 P 74 (1909).

Paragraph (d). This paragraph allows admission of evidence of the character for violent behavior of either party in a civil action for assault or battery, when one of the issues is who committed the first act of aggression. This paragraph was added expressly to retain existing Oregon law. *Brooks v. Bergholm,* 256 Or 1, 470 P2d 154 (1970); *Linkhart v. Savely,* 190 Or 484, 227 P2d 187 (1950).

Although the exceptions set forth in subsection (2) have their reason for existence more in history than in logic, an underlying justification can fairly be found in the relative presence and absence of prejudice in the various situations. Faulknor, "Extrinsic Policies Affecting Admissibility," in 10 Rutgers L Rev 574, 584 (1956); McCormick § 190. In any event, the criminal exceptions under paragraphs (a) and (b) are so deeply imbedded in our jurisprudence as to assume almost constitutional proportions and override doubts as to the basic relevancy of the evidence.

It should be stressed that the exceptions to inadmissibility set forth in subsection (2) involve specific character traits, not character generally. Thus, paragraphs (a) and (b) allow admission of evidence relating to a "pertinent trait of character" and the "character trait of peacefulness." Paragraph (c) refers to Rule 608, which limits character evidence about witnesses to evidence bearing upon their "character for truthfulness or untruthfulness." Finally, paragraph (d) is limited to evidence of "reputation for violent behavior." This limitation to pertinent traits of character, rather than character generally, is in accord with the prevailing view in the United States and present Oregon law. McCormick § 191; *State v. Selby,* 73 Or 378, 144 P 657 (1914). The argument is made that circumstantial use of character ought to be allowed in civil cases to the same extent that it is in criminal cases, i.e., evidence of good character should be admissible in the first instance, subject to rebuttal by evidence of bad character. Faulknor, supra at 581–583 (1956); Tentative Recommendation and a Study Relating to the Uniform Rules of Evidence, (Art. V, Extrinsic Policies Affecting Admissibility), Cal Law Rev Comm Rep, Rec & Studies 657–658 (1964). The difficulty with expanding the use of character evidence in civil cases is set forth by the California Law Revision Commission in its ultimate rejection of Uniform Rule 47:

> "Character evidence is of slight probative value and may be very prejudicial. It tends to distract the trier of fact from the main question of what actually happened on the particular occasion. It subtly permits the trier of fact to reward the good [person] and to punish the bad [person] because of their respective characters despite what the evidence in the case shows actually happened." *Id.* at 615.

The above considerations persuaded the Legislative Assembly not to expand the use of circumstantial character evidence in civil cases. Paragraphs (c) and (d) merely retain the uses of such evidence sanctioned under existing law. Subsection (2) should not be construed to allow admission of character evidence in circumstances where it would not be currently admitted, such as character evidence with respect to care, carelessness or "accident proneness" in negligence cases.

Subsection (3). Subsection (3) deals with a specialized but important application of the general rule excluding circumstantial use of character evidence. Consistent with that rule, evidence of other crimes, wrongs or acts is not admissible to prove character for the purpose of suggesting that conduct on a particular occasion was in conformity therewith. However, such evidence may be offered for purposes that do not fall within the prohibition. See *State v. Brown,* 231 Or 297, 372 P2d 779 (1962) (evidence of stealing cars admitted to show intent to avoid punishment for present crime); *State v. Long,* 195 Or 81, 244 P2d 1033 (1952) (evidence of murder of truck owner admitted to establish motive: defendant shortly afterward used truck to commit a robbery). This rule holds true in both civil and criminal cases. *Karsun v. Kelley,* 258 Or 155, 482 P2d 533 (1971). The list of purposes set forth in subsection (3) for which evidence of other crimes, wrongs or acts may be admitted is not meant to be exclusive.

When evidence of other crimes, wrongs or acts is sought to be admitted under subsection (3), the court is not required to admit the evidence. The court must determine whether the danger of undue prejudice outweighs the probative value of the evidence, taking into account the availability of other means of proof and other factors appropriate for making decisions of this kind under Rule 403. Slough and Knightly, "Other Vices, Other Crimes," in 41 Iowa L Rev 325 (1956). No mechanical solution to the problem is offered or is desirable.

TEXT

Character Evidence—Generally

Rule 404(1) provides that evidence of a person's character may be received in those relatively rare instances where character is an essential element of a charge, claim, or defense. Subject to several exceptions, Rule 404(2) prohibits evidence of a person's character for purposes of showing that the person acted in accordance with that character on a particular occasion. The exceptions are: (1) evidence of a pertinent character trait when offered by a criminal defendant, or by the prosecution to rebut the same; (2) evidence of a pertinent character trait of a crime victim under certain circumstances; (3) evidence of character of a witness for truthfulness or untruthfulness in either civil or criminal cases; (4) evidence of character for violent behavior of a party to a civil assault and battery case when self-defense is pleaded and there is evidence to support such a defense. When evidence is admissible under the exceptions to Rule 404(2), it must be in the form of reputation or opinion evidence. See Rule 405 and the textual discussion thereunder.

Rule 404(3) provides for the admissibility of certain character evidence, specifically evidence of other crimes, wrongs, or acts, when offered for some purpose other than to prove action in accordance with that character on a particular occasion. The listed examples of permissible purposes are motive, opportunity, intent, preparation, plan, knowledge, identity, or absence of mistake or accident.

Neither the rule nor the Commentary defines what is meant by character evidence. "Character" for purposes of evidence law means a person's disposition or propensity to engage or not to engage in certain types of behavior. Peaceableness, truthfulness, and recklessness would all be examples of traits of character. See *State v. Johns*, 301 Or 535, 548, 725 P2d 312 (1986) (defining "character" for purposes of Rule 404(3) as "disposition or propensity to commit certain crimes, wrongs or acts.") Cf. *State v. Nefstad*, 309 Or 523, 554–6, 789 P2d 1326 (1990) (statement that defendant looked "sleazy" and had a "wild look" was not character evidence).

The rationale for generally excluding evidence of character is that it may tend to divert the attention of the jury from what a person did on a specific occasion to what that person has done in the past. Although evidence regarding a person's propensities may have probative value in determining conduct on a particular occasion, it is deemed to be outweighed by the danger of misleading the jury and unfairly prejudicing a party.

RULE 404(1)
Character as an Element of a Charge, Claim, or Defense

The cases where character evidence may be admitted under Rule 404(1) as an element of a "charge, claim or defense" are relatively rare. What is usually in issue is not a person's character but what a person did on a particular occasion.

The Commentary lists negligent entrustment (where the character of an employee is in issue) and defamation as examples of claims where character is in issue and hence evidence of character may be allowed under this subsection.

Additional examples of those very few situations where character could be considered to be an element of a claim are child custody disputes where the character of the parent for parenting is in issue, and wrongful death cases where the character of the decedent bears upon the question of damages. See also *State v. Montez*, 309 Or 564, 611–2, 789 P2d 1352 (1990) (in capital sentencing hearing defendant's character is in issue on question of future dangerousness).

In *Shirley v. Freunscht*, 303 Or 234, 735 P2d 600 (1987), the court disagreed with the statement in the Commentary that defamation cases are necessarily a proper example of cases where the plaintiff's character constitutes an element of the claim. The court held that a plaintiff in a defamation case puts his reputation in issue, but not his character generally. Therefore, evidence regarding specific instances of conduct that may bear on his character but have not affected his reputation are irrelevant to the plaintiff's claim. However, the plaintiff's character may be an element of a *defense,* in cases where the alleged defamation involves the character of the plaintiff and the defendant asserts truth as a defense. Specific instances of conduct offered to support the defense of truth will be admissible only if they are relevant to the specific character trait at issue.

In *State v. Lunow*, 131 Or App 429, 885 P2d 731 (1994), an assault prosecution, the court held that the defendant was entitled to introduce prior specific instances of violent behavior by the victim that were known to the defendant to support his claim of self-defense. The court held that "reasonable belief" in the need to defend oneself is an element of self-defense under OEC 404(1), and therefore evidence of the victim's character in any form—reputation, opinion, or specific instances—is admissible under OEC 405(2)(a) to prove it. The court appears to have reached the right result for the wrong reasons. It seems erroneous to view a victim's **character** as an **element** of a self-defense claim under Rule 404(1). A better approach would be to find that prior acts of violence by the victim (known to the defendant) are not excluded by OEC 404(2) if they are not being offered for the forbidden purpose of proving conduct on a particular occasion but instead are being offered only to prove reasonable fear by the defendant. OEC 404(3) expressly authorizes proof of other crimes, wrongs, or acts when offered for a relevant purpose other than proving conduct in accordance with character on a particular occasion. Proving the effect on the defendant (causing a belief in the need to use self-defense) has long been held to be a permissible purpose. See *State v. Bishop*, 49 Or App 1023, 1032, 621 P2d 1196 (1980), rev denied 290 Or 727 (1981). See Mueller & Kirkpatrick, MODERN EVIDENCE (1995) 4.23.

There are several other situations where an individual's reputation, as distinguished from his character, may be relevant, and those cases are beyond this rule. For example, in a false arrest action, plaintiff's reputation for the conduct for which he was arrested may be relevant on the issue of defendant's good faith belief in making the arrest. See *O'Brien v. Eugene Chemical Exports, Inc.,* 63 Or

App 284, 664 P2d 1106 (1983) (reputation must be for same type of conduct for which plaintiff was arrested).

RULE 404(2)
Character to Prove Conduct on Particular Occasion

Rule 404(2) states the general prohibition against the use of character evidence to prove conduct in accordance with that character on a specific occasion and sets forth exceptions to this rule. The methods by which character may be proved when these exceptions are applicable is controlled by Rule 405 (allowing only reputation or opinon evidence, not specific instances of conduct).

RULE 404(2)(a)
Character Trait of Criminal Defendant

Under Rule 404(2)(a), every criminal defendant may offer evidence of a pertinent trait of character as a defense to the charge. What constitutes a pertinent trait depends upon the crime charged. A reputation for honesty would be irrelevant to a crime of violence, and a reputation for nonviolence would be irrelevant to a crime of larceny. See generally ANNOT., *Admissibility of Evidence of Pertinent Trait Under Rule 404(a) of the Uniform Rules of Evidence,* 56 ALR 4th 402 (1987); ANNOT., *When is Evidence of Trait of Accused's Character "Pertinent" for Purposes of Admissibility Under Rule 404(a)(1) of the Federal Rules of Evidence,* 49 ALR Fed 478 (1980).

Reputation or opinion evidence that the defendant was "law abiding" has been held to be admissible as a pertinent trait of character regardless of the nature of the charge. *United States v. Hewitt,* 634 F2d 277 (5th Cir 1981). In a narcotics prosecution, evidence of a defendant's reputation for "truth and veracity" was held to be properly excluded as not a pertinent trait. *United States v. Jackson,* 588 F2d 1046 (5th Cir), cert denied 442 US 941 (1979).

Despite the decision in *State v. Bailey,* 87 Or App 664, 667, 743 P2d 1123 (1987), a reputation for honesty should generally be considered a pertinent character trait in a prosecution for theft. In *Bailey,* the court stated: "[D]efendant can introduce evidence of her character trait for honesty *only if* it relates to her propensity to commit theft." The court was concerned that evidence regarding the defendant's honesty not be received on the issue of the defendant's credibility as a witness. However, this concern is more appropriately addressed by a limiting instruction than by having the character witness go into detail regarding what type of honesty is encompassed by the opinion or reputation evidence. To require such elucidation would be an invitation to the character witness to testify to impermissible specific acts evidence.

Character evidence offered by a criminal defendant must be in the form of reputation or opinion evidence, not specific instances of conduct. See *State v. Reeder,* 137 Or App 421, 423–5, 904 P2d 644 (1995) (only reputation and opinion evidence is admissible; evidence of specific instances of conduct, including

absence of sexual abuse complaints in prior contacts with children, is not admissible).

If the defendant testifies and the defendant's credibility is attacked by the prosecutor, evidence of his or her character for "truth and veracity" may be admissible for purposes of rehabilitation, even though dishonesty is not an element of the crime charged. See Rule 608(1). Cf. *United States v. Lechoco,* 542 F2d 84 (DC Cir 1976) (insanity defense; suggestion by prosecutor that defendant lied to psychiatrist; defendant entitled to offer evidence of reputation for truthfulness and honesty).

In *State v. Zybach,* 93 Or App 218, 761 P2d 1334 (1988), rev'd on other grounds 308 Or 96, 775 P2d 318 (1989), the Court of Appeals held that earlier case law allowing evidence of other acts of sexual contact with the victim to show defendant's lustful disposition towards the victim was no longer valid under Rule 404(2). The court viewed proof of "lustful disposition toward the victim" as essentially proof that defendant acted in accordance with his disposition or propensities. Such use is barred by this rule unless an exception applies, and the court noted that Rule 404(2) contains no exception allowing such evidence when defendant has not placed his character in issue.

In *State v. Lawson,* 127 Or App 392, 872 P2d 986 (1994), rev denied 320 Or 110, 881 P2d 141 (1994), defendant daycare provider was charged with assault and criminal mistreatment of children in her care. In her defense, she offered testimony and reports from two psychologists that she lacked the character traits typically seen in child abusers. Although evidence of pertinent character traits of a criminal defendant is normally admissible under OEC 404(2)(a), the appellate court affirmed the exclusion of the evidence, because such "profile" evidence was a form of scientific evidence and there was not a sufficient foundation laid for it under the *Brown* standard. Taslitz, *Myself Alone: Individualizing Justice Through Psychological Character Evidence,* 52 Md L Rev 1 (1993).

Cross-Examination and Rebuttal

If a defendant chooses to offer evidence of a pertinent trait of his character pursuant to this rule, he takes a certain element of risk. By doing so, he opens the door to rebuttal evidence regarding his character that the prosecutor would not otherwise be able to offer. The contrary evidence may be brought out by (1) cross-examination of the defendant's character witnesses regarding specific instances of defendant's past conduct relevant to the character trait in issue; or (2) the prosecutor calling character witnesses to offer contrary reputation or opinion evidence with respect to that particular trait of defendant's character. See further discussion under Rule 405.

If a criminal defendant offers what is in essence character evidence by his own testimony, the state is entitled to rebut any false characterization. In *State v. Guritz,* 134 Or App 262, 266, 894 P2d 1235, 1237 (1995), a prosecution of the defendant for sodomy upon his young daughter, the defendant sought to portray himself as a "good father" who would not molest his daughter. He described his activities with his daughter, which included regularly taking her to places such as malls and the park. To rebut this evidence, the prosecutor offered evidence that the defendant purchased marijuana while at the park with his daughter. The court found that the defendant had placed his character "in issue" by this evidence, thereby justifying introduction of the marijuana evidence to rebut his "characterization" of himself as a good father.

Even though the prosecution can offer reputation or opinion evidence in rebuttal when the defendant offers character evidence under this rule, the fact that the defendant has offered character evidence regarding the *victim* does not open the door for the prosecution to offer character evidence regarding the defendant. In *State v. Peacock*, 75 Or App 217, 706 P2d 982 (1985), the court held that even though defendant offered evidence regarding the violent character of an assault victim, this did not justify the prosecution offering evidence of the violent character of the defendant, when the defendant had not placed his own character in issue.

RULE 404(2)(b)
Character Trait of Crime Victim

Rule 404(2)(b) allows evidence of a pertinent trait of character of a crime victim in three situations: (1) when offered by an accused to prove conduct of the victim on a particular occasion, except where such evidence must be excluded by Rule 412; (2) when offered by the prosecution to rebut character evidence offered by the accused regarding the victim; and (3) when offered by the prosecution on the peaceable character of the victim to rebut evidence that the victim was the first aggressor.

Evidence of a murder victim's peaceable character can be initiated by a prosecutor only if the defendant has offered evidence of the victim's character or evidence that the defendant acted in self-defense. Moreover, any evidence offered by the prosecution must be in the form of reputation or opinion evidence. Evidence that witnesses had never seen the victim become physically violent would violate the prohibition against proof by specific acts. See *State v. Hicks*, 133 Ariz 64, 649 P2d 267, 271–2 (1982).

In *State v. Marshall*, 312 Or 367, 373, 823 P2d 961 (1991), a robbery prosecution, defendant sought to offer evidence that the alleged crime victim had a "reputation" for giving property as collateral for a debt and claiming it was stolen. The Supreme Court held that evidence of reputation of such behavior actually amounted to specific act evidence and was not admissible under either Rule 404(2)(b) or Rule 405(1).

The fact that the defendant attacks the character of the victim does not open the door for the prosecutor to attack the character of the defendant. *State v. Peacock*, 75 Or App 217, 706 P2d 982 (1985), supra.

RULE 404(2)(c)
Character Trait of Witness

The broadest exception in Rule 404(2) pertains to the use of character evidence to impeach or rehabilitate witnesses. Under Rule 404(2)(c) and Rule 608(1), a witness testifying in either a civil or criminal case may be impeached by character evidence of untruthfulness or rehabilitated, under certain circumstances, by character evidence of truthfulness. For further discussion of this use of character evidence, see textual discussion of Rule 608.

RULE 404(2)(d)
Character for Violence in Civil Asssault and Battery Case

Rule 404(2)(d) allows evidence of the character of a party for violent behavior when offered in a civil assault and battery case where self-defense is pleaded and there is evidence to support such a defense. This exception is based on prior Oregon case law and is not included in FRE 404. See *Brooks v. Bergholm,* 256 Or 1, 470 P2d 154 (1970). This exception does not allow a plaintiff in a civil assault and battery action to present character evidence for peaceableness before the plaintiff's character has been attacked. *Sims v. Sowle,* 238 Or 329, 395 P2d 133 (1964).

RULE 404(3)
Prior Crimes, Wrongs, Acts to Prove Narrow Points

Rule 404(3) prohibits the use of evidence of other crimes, wrongs, or acts to prove character in order to show that a person acted in conformity with that character. To this extent, Rule 404(3) restates the prohibition in Rule 404(2). Rule 404(3) does allow, however, the use of such evidence for other purposes, such as to prove motive, opportunity, intent, preparation, plan, knowledge, identity, or absence of mistake or accident.

In *State v. Johns,* 301 Or 535, 725 P2d 312 (1986), the court emphasized that the rule is inclusionary rather than exclusionary and that the permissible uses of prior bad act evidence are not limited to those purposes listed in the rule. Evidence of other bad acts or crimes may be offered for any relevant purpose other than to show that a person acted in accordance with his character or propensity.

It is not always simple to determine when evidence is being offered for the prohibited purpose of proving conduct in accordance with one's propensities and when it is being offered for "other" permissible purposes. Using evidence of a defendant's prior bad acts for the permissible purpose of establishing his "intent" or "plan" on a particular occasion may be hard to distinguish from using such evidence for the prohibited purpose of proving that he had certain propensities and that he acted in accordance with those propensities on a particular occasion.

Rule 404(3) does not require that the prior acts be illegal. See *United States v. Evans,* 572 F2d 455 (5th Cir), cert denied 439 US 870 (1978). However, if the prior acts do not involve misconduct, courts sometimes view the rule as inapplicable. See *State v. Warren,* 81 Or App 463, 726 P2d 387, aff'd on other grounds 304 Or 428, 746 P2d 711 (1987) (Rule 404(3) inapplicable to defendant's statement, offered by mother of sex crime victim, that other mothers let defendant take baths with their children, because no misconduct was asserted).

Because evidence under Rule 404(3) is admitted only for a limited purpose, the party against whom the evidence is offered is entitled to a limiting instruction under Rule 105. *State v. Mayfield,* 302 Or 631, 647, 733 P2d 438 (1987). Failure to give such a limiting instruction when requested may constitute reversible error. *State v. Phelps,* 73 Or App 68, 698 P2d 43 (1985); *United States v. Yopp,* 577 F2d 362 (6th Cir 1978).

The proper interpretation and application of Rule 404(3) has been a frequent issue on appeal generating more appellate decisions than almost any other provision in the Evidence Code. In cases where evidence was erroneously received under this rule, appellate courts have often found the error to be grounds for reversal, because of the prejudicial impact that prior bad acts evidence can have on a jury.

In *State v. Johns,* 301 Or 535, 549, 725 P2d 312 (1986), the court's opinion by Justice Jones made the following observation:

> Perhaps litigation over the admissibility of "other crimes, wrongs or acts" evidence could be reduced if litigators and judges would follow the preachings of Coach Vince Lombardi to his players "to return to the basics." Trial Judges should return to the basic reasons for the inadmissibility of other crimes, wrongs, or acts, which are that: (1) such evidence is often irrelevant to prove the conduct in question; (2) the common law and its codification forbids the attempt to prove a defendant guilty by proving the defendant is a bad person or has bad character because of disposition or propensity for committing crimes, wrongs, or other bad acts; and (3) even if evidence that a defendant has committed other crimes has some legitimate probative value, the danger of unfair prejudice to the defendant may outweigh any such probative value.

Stipulations

In some cases, the opponent may be able to prevent receipt of prior bad acts evidence by stipulating to the fact the proponent is attempting to prove. See *United States v. Mohel,* 604 F2d 748 (2nd Cir 1979) (error to receive prior-crimes evidence to prove knowledge where defendant offered to stipulate to knowledge); *United States v. Coades,* 549 F2d 1303, 1306 (9th Cir 1977) (bank robbery prosecution; error to admit prior bank robbery conviction to prove intent when defendant offered to stipulate to intent; court remarked that this was "a deplorable example of prosecutorial over zealousness"). But see *United States v. Peltier,* 585 F2d 314 (8th Cir 1978), cert denied 440 US 945 (1979) (prosecution not required to accept stipulation when stipulation inadequate).

Exclusion Under Rule 403

Even if prior bad acts evidence qualifies for admission under Rule 404(3), it may nonetheless be excluded under Rule 403. Rule 404(3) does not require the court to admit evidence of other crimes, wrongs, or acts. It provides only that such evidence "may ... be admissible." If the probative value of evidence of prior crimes, wrongs, or acts is substantially outweighed by the danger of unfair prejudice, confusion of the issues, or misleading the jury, the evidence should be excluded under Rule 403.

In order for the Rule 403 issue to be properly raised, an attorney opposing introduction of prior bad acts evidence should object on both Rule 404(3) and Rule 403 grounds.

In *State v. Mayfield*, 302 Or 631, 733 P2d 438 (1987), the court stated with respect to this issue: "The judge errs if the judge fails to exercise discretion, refuses to exercise discretion or fails to make a record which reflects an exercise of discretion." 302 Or at 645. The court also commented: "In this state trial judges are granted broad discretion when findings are made on the record to back up this discretionary call." 302 Or at 647.

In *State v. Johns*, 301 Or 535, 557–8, 725 P2d 312 (1986), the Supreme Court adopted a five-part test for determining whether evidence admissible under Rule 404(3) should be excluded under Rule 403. The five factors to be considered by the trial judge are: (1) the need for the evidence; (2) the certainty that the other crime was committed and that the defendant was the actor; (3) the strength or weakness of the evidence; (4) its inflammatory effect on the jury; and (5) how time-consuming or distracting proof of the other crime or act will be. In making the determination whether the relevance of the evidence outweighs the danger of unfair prejudice or other dangers specified in Rule 403, the trial judge "must articulate reasons for that decision on the record." 301 Or at 550, 725 P2d at 321.

In *Johns,* the court affirmed the trial judge's conclusion, after balancing these factors, that the evidence of an earlier bad act—defendant's assault on his former wife—should be admissible in his prosecution for murdering his current wife. The evidence was needed, because the only witness to the shooting other than the defendant was the victim, and she was dead. The assault on the former wife was undisputed. It was strong evidence on the issue of intent—the key disputed issue in the case. There was nothing particularly inflammatory about the evidence. Finally, the trial court did not abuse its discretion in finding that the evidence was worth the time and effort and would not throw the presentation of the current murder prosecution out of balance.

The five factors articulated in *Johns* are generally consistent with pre-Code case law. In *State v. Sjogren,* 39 Or App 639, 643, 593 P2d 1188, 1190 (1979), the Court of Appeals had held that the admissibility of other crime evidence should be determined by:

> ... the actual need for the other-crimes evidence in the light of the issues and the other evidence available to the prosecution, the convincingness of the evidence that the other crimes were committed and that the accused was the actor, and the strength or weakness of the other-crimes evidence in supporting

the issue, ... the degree to which the jury will probably be roused by the evidence to overmastering hostility. (quoting McCormick, *Evidence*, § 157 at 332 (1954))

If the prior crime, wrong, or act is remote in time, a court is more likely to exclude it under Rule 403. *United States v. Corey*, 566 F2d 429 (2nd Cir 1977); *United States v. Gilliland*, 586 F2d 1384 (10th Cir 1978).

Certainty Required that Prior Bad Act Committed

Evidence of an alleged prior bad act by the defendant offered under Rule 404(3) is not admissible without a preliminary showing that the defendant committed such an act. The issue is for the court under Rule 104(1), and the applicable standard of proof is by a preponderance of evidence. *State v. Kim*, 111 Or App 1, 5, 824 P2d 1161, 1163, rev denied 314 Or 176, 836 P2d 1345 (1992). To admit evidence of alleged prior misconduct by the defendant without such a showing could be highly prejudicial.

Also, the certainty that the defendant committed the prior bad acts is a factor the court can consider in deciding whether to exclude the evidence under Rule 403. See *State v. Johns*, supra ("the certainty that the crime was committed and that defendant was the actor" is a factor the trial court must consider in deciding whether to admit or exclude the evidence).

Federal courts follow a lesser standard requiring only evidence sufficient to support a jury finding that defendant committed the prior acts. In *Huddleston v. United States*, 485 US 681, 108 SCt 1496, 99 LEd2d 771 (1988), the United States Supreme Court concluded that the issue is one of conditional relevancy for the jury under FRE 104(b) rather than an issue for the court under FRE 104(a) and that the evidence of prior acts may be admitted upon a showing of sufficient evidence to support a jury finding that the defendant engaged in the conduct alleged.

The *Huddleston* holding is not binding on the states. Many states with an evidentiary counterpart to FRE 404(b) have required a higher standard of proof than "sufficiency," and many have continued to do so even after the *Huddleston* decision.

In January 1989, the American Bar Association passed a resolution urging that the holding of *Huddleston* be overturned by amending FRE 404(b):

BE IT RESOLVED, That the American Bar Association urges that Rule 404(b) of the Federal Rules of Evidence, and similar state rules which govern the purposes for which extrinsic evidence of crimes, wrongs or acts may be admitted, be amended to provide that in criminal cases:

1. Questions of preliminary fact regarding the admissibility of evidence of the extrinsic act will be determined by the court; and

2. The existence of any preliminary fact required as a precondition to the admission of evidence of the extrinsic act must be demonstrated by the proponent by clear and convincing evidence.

3 BNA Criminal Practice Manual 75 (Feb. 22, 1989).

Evidence of Prior Crimes of Which Defendant Was Acquitted

Evidence of prior crimes of which the defendant has been acquitted is admissible, provided the defendant is allowed to offer evidence of the acquittal. *State v. Fears,* 69 Or App 606, 688 P2d 88, rev denied 298 Or 238, 691 P2d 482 (1984); *State v. Smith,* 271 Or 294, 532 P2d 9 (1975).

In *Dowling v. United States,* 493 US 342, 352–4 (1990), the United States Supreme Court held that neither the double jeopardy clause nor the due process clause bars the government from offering evidence in a later prosecution of a prior offense, of which the accused has been tried and acquitted.

In *State v. Cornell,* 109 Or App 396, 405, 820 P2d 11, 17 (1991), aff'd 314 Or 673, 842 P2d 394 (1992), the prosecution introduced evidence of a prior crime committed by defendant on the issue of identity. The defendant argued that he should have been entitled to offer evidence that he had not been charged with the prior crime. The court held that even though evidence that defendant was acquitted of a prior crime is admissible, evidence that a prior prosecution was not brought is not analogous, because there are a variety of reasons why a person may not have been prosecuted that are unrelated to the absence of guilt.

See generally ANNOT., *Admissibility of Evidence as to Other Offense as Affected by Defendant's Acquittal of that Offense,* 25 ALR4th 934 (1983); ANNOT., *Admissibility of Evidence As to Other Offense as Affected by Defendant's Acquittal of that Offense,* 86 ALR2d 1132 (1962); COMMENT, *Evidentiary Use of Prior Acquitted Crimes: The "Relative Burdens of Proof" Rationale,* 64 Wash U L Q 189 (1986).

Civil Cases

Although Rule 404(3) is likely to be used primarily in criminal proceedings, it is available in civil proceedings as well. In *Gibson v. Tzantarmas,* 108 Or App 270, 273–4, 815 P2d 221, 223 (1991), an action for trespass, the plaintiff was properly allowed to introduce evidence of similar acts of trespass and damage caused by defendant on another neighbor's property. The evidence was relevant to show intent or absence of accident or mistake.

See also *Miller v. Poretsky,* 595 F2d 780 (DC 1978) (prior acts of alleged racial discrimination); *Eaves v. Penn,* 587 F2d 453 (10th Cir 1978); *Harris v. Harvey,* 605 F2d 330 (7th Cir 1979). Such evidence has been allowed in civil cases under prior Oregon law. See *Brown v. Johnston,* 258 Or 284, 482 P2d 712 (1971); *Karsun v. Kelley,* 258 Or 155, 482 P2d 533 (1971). In *McCuller v. Gaudry,* 59 Or App 13, 650 P2d 148 (1982), the court held that a prior finding of racial discrimination by the Civil Rights Division of the Department of Labor was admissible in a civil action charging discrimination at defendant's tavern. Although Rule 404(3) was not cited, the case is an example of the admissibility of evidence of prior bad acts in a civil case.

For a discussion of the admissibility of prior bad acts to prove negligence or related matters, such as causation or the existence of a dangerous condition, see discussion under Rule 401, supra.

See generally ANNOT., *Admissibility of Evidence of Other Crimes, Wrongs, or Acts Under Rule 404(b) of Federal Rules of Evidence in Civil Cases,* 64 ALR Fed 648 (1983); ANNOT., *Admission in Civil Assault and Battery Actions of Similar Acts or Assaults Against Other Persons,* 66 ALR 2d 806; COMMENT, *Product Liability Litigation: Impact of Federal Rule of Evidence 404(b) Upon Admissibility Standards of Prior Accident Evidence,* 61 Wash U L Q 799 (1983).

Evidence of Subsequent Bad Acts

In some cases, evidence of crimes, wrongs, or acts *subsequent* to the charged offense may be admissible under Rule 404(3). See *State v. Smith,* 86 Or App 239, 739 P2d 577 (1987) (in prosecution for driving while suspended on September 25, defendant's son testified that father had not driven and car had not moved from side of house since that date; prosecution properly allowed to offer evidence that defendant drove on September 26 to impeach this testimony); *State v. Zybach,* 308 Or 96, 775 P2d 318 (1989) (subsequent incidents of sexual abuse admissible to show why victim had not reported the original sexual assault).

See also *United States v. Hearst,* 563 F2d 1331 (9th Cir 1977), cert denied 435 US 1000 (1978) (subsequent crimes by Patty Hearst admissible to rebut her defense that she was under duress when participating in the charged crime); *United States v. Terebecki,* 692 F2d 1345 (11th Cir 1982) (evidence of a similar act of fraud that occurred 15 months after the charged act held properly admitted under FRE 404(b)).

See generally ANNOT., *Admission of Evidence of Subsequent Criminal Offenses as Affected by Proximity as to Time and Place,* 92 ALR3d 545 (1979).

Pretrial Motions to Exclude Rule 404(3) Evidence

A pretrial motion to exclude or limit prior bad acts evidence is appropriate, although the judge may be unable to make a ruling until trial when it is established what issues are in dispute. See *State v. Lee,* 88 Or App 556, 746 P2d 242 (1987). See also discussion of motions in limine under Rule 609, infra, and Rule 103, supra.

Advance Notice of Rule 404(3) Evidence

Although Rule 404(3) does not require that the prosecutor give advance notice to a criminal defendant that prior crimes evidence will be offered, such notice is required by FRE 404(b) ("upon request by the accused, the prosecution in a criminal case shall provide reasonable notice in advance of trial, or during trial if the court excuses pretrial notice on good cause shown, of the general nature of any such evidence it intends to introduce at trial").

Even where a notice requirement is not contained in their state rule, some other state courts have indicated that advance notice should generally be given.

See *Burks v. Oklahoma,* 594 P2d 771 (Okla Crim App 1979); *State v. Billstrom,* 276 Minn 174, 149 NW2d 281 (1967).

Rule 404(3) Evidence Offered by Defendant

Evidence may be offered under Rule 404(3) by defendants as well as by plaintiffs or prosecutors. See *United States v. McClure,* 546 F2d 670 (5th Cir 1977); *United States v. Garvin,* 565 F2d 519 (8th Cir 1977).

In *United States v. Cohen,* 888 F2d 770, 776 (11th Cir 1989), the court held that it was error to exclude prior "bad act" evidence offered by a defendant where defendant claimed that a third person carried out the fraudulent scheme. Defendant offered evidence that the third person had previously engaged in a similar fraud. The appellate court noted that "the standard for admission is relaxed when the evidence is offered by defendant."

In *State v. Saavedra,* 103 NM 282, 705 P2d 1133 (1985), the court held that New Mexico Rule of Evidence 404(b), which is identical to OEC 404(3), may be used by criminal defendants. In this case, the defendant had argued that the actual perpetrator of the armed robbery and felony murder for which he was charged was a third person. Defendant offered evidence that the third person had been convicted of committing eight robberies under circumstances highly similar to the crime charged within the same two-month period. The New Mexico Supreme Court reversed defendant's conviction because the trial judge had excluded the prior crimes evidence.

In *State v. Bockorny,* 125 Or App 479, 487, 866 P2d 1230, 1235 (1993), rev denied 319 Or 150, 877 P2d 87 (1994), a husband and wife were both charged with the murder of a third person. Husband claimed wife committed the murder while he was passed out in another room. In support of his theory, defendant offered evidence of prior bad acts committed by wife, including prior assaults and use of weapons. Because the prior acts were dissimilar from the circumstances of the charged crime, they were not admissible to prove modus operandi or identity. Their only relevance was to prove that wife had a propensity to engage in violent conduct, a use that OEC 404(3) prohibits, even when the evidence pertains to a person other than the defendant.

In *State v. Bockorny,* 124 Or App 585, 589, 863 P2d 1296, 1298 (1993), rev denied 318 Or 351, 870 P2d 220 (1994), defendant wife attempted to assert a duress defense to the underlying felonies in an aggravated murder prosecution. She argued it was error to exclude evidence or prior violent acts by her husband known to her that would support her defense of duress. The court found no error, holding that the statute allowing a duress defense focuses not on past conduct but rather on whether defendant was forced to commit the crimes by a present threat of unlawful physical force on her so great that it overcame her earnest resistance. The court did not address whether past conduct by a threatening party may sometimes have a bearing on a defendant's reasonable perception of whether a current threat exists.

In *James v. General Motors of Canada, Ltd.,* 101 Or App 138, 790 P2d 8, rev denied 310 Or 243, 796 P2d 360 (1990), the plaintiff alleged that she fell out of a van because of a defective door handle. The defendant claimed that the plaintiff's husband shoved her out or caused her to jump. To support this theory, the defendant offered evidence of prior acts of violence by the plaintiff's husband. Because these acts did not involve domestic violence, nor bear sufficiently on the issues in the case, the court held it was error to receive evidence of them.

Evidence of prior bad acts of the victim was offered by the defendant in *State v. Cole*, 66 Or App 203, 673 P2d 587 (1983), rev denied 296 Or 486, 677 P2d 702 (1984). The court excluded the evidence on the ground that the prior events were not sufficiently similar to be relevant on the issue for which they were offered.

See generally COMMENT, *Of Propensity, Prejudice and Meaning: The Accused's Use of Exculpatory Specific Acts Evidence and the Need to Amend Rule 404(b)*, 87 Nw U L Rev 651 (1993).

Purposes Listed by Rule 404(3)

Illustrative cases under Rule 404(3) or FRE 404(b) where evidence of prior crimes, wrongs, or acts was offered for one of the purposes expressly listed in the rule:

Motive

In *State v. Westby*, 117 Or App 14, 17, 843 P2d 973 (1992), rev denied 318 Or 351, 870 P2d 220 (1994), a murder prosecution, the court approved admission of evidence that defendant previously stole a vehicle, because it reasonably could have been found to provide a motive for the charged crime. The state theorized the defendant stole money and a pickup from the victim because he wanted to leave Oregon to avoid prosecution on the theft crime and killed the victim to eliminate a witness.

In *State v. Hampton*, 317 Or 251, 257, 855 P2d 621, 624–5 (1993), a prosecution for assault on a police officer, the court held that evidence that the defendant was on parole at the time was relevant and admissible to explain defendant's motive for his assaultive behavior, i.e., to avoid apprehension and revocation of his parole. The court held that such motive is relevant to prove that defendant committed the assault charged and did so with the requisite mental state. The court further held under OEC 403 that the probative value of such evidence was not outweighed by the danger of prejudice.

In *State v. Rogers*, 313 Or 356, 385, 836 P2d 1308 (1992), cert denied 113 S Ct 1420 (1993), other crimes evidence showing infliction of pain on other prostitutes was admissible to prove the defendant had the same objective to intentionally cause intense pain to his murder victims by inflicting stabbing and cutting wounds to them before killing them.

In *State v. Brown*, 310 Or 347, 360–1, 800 P2d 259 (1990), the court held that evidence that the defendant was on probation, even if it suggested a prior crime, was admissible under Rule 404(3) because it tended to prove defendant's motive for the murder. The victim had provided evidence of criminal activity by defendant that was to be used at the probation hearing, thereby giving defendant a motive to kill her.

In *State v. Hopkins*, 127 Or App 1, 4, 870 P2d 849, 850 (1994), modified 127 Or App 622, 874 P2d 827, rev denied 319 Or 281, 879 P2d 1284, where defendant was prosecuted for attempting to run down police officers, it was found not to be error to introduce evidence that defendant possessed credit cards owned by others and cashed a forged check on the day of the charged crime. Such prior crimes were relevant in showing the motive of defendant to escape apprehension by the police and to rebut defendant's assertion that his conduct was not intentional.

In *State v. White*, 71 Or App 299, 692 P2d 167 (1984), rev denied 298 Or 705, 695 P2d 1372 (1985), an arson prosecution, the trial court granted defendant's motion in limine to exclude at trial evidence that the insurance claim submitted on the premises was fraudulent. The trial court found that the relevance of that evidence was outweighed by the prejudice to the defendant. The Court of Appeals reversed, holding that the evidence was admissible on the question of motive and common plan.

In *State v. Powell*, 82 Or App 13, 727 P2d 136 (1986), rev denied 302 Or 571, 731 P2d 1046 (1987), an unlawful racketeering prosecution, the trial court allowed evidence of numerous civil complaints and judgments against defendant's employer. The appellate court held that this evidence was properly received to establish not only motive, but opportunity, intent, preparation, plan, and knowledge.

See also *United States v. Seastrunk*, 580 F2d 800 (5th Cir 1978), cert denied 439 US 1080 (1979); *United States v. Dansker*, 537 F2d 40 (3rd Cir 1976), cert denied 429 US 1038 (1977); *State v. Guerrero*, 243 Or 616, 415 P2d 28 (1966) (defendant charged with attempted burglary of drugstore; paraphernalia common to drug users found upon defendant's person at the time of the arrest held properly admitted); *State v. Pruitt*, 34 Or App 957, 580 P2d 201 (1978) (evidence that the defendant used drugs seven months prior to robbery to show motive to steal drugs held erroneously admitted); *State v. Knutson*, 45 Or App 1051, 609 P2d 922 (1980) (defendant charged with conspiracy to manufacture drugs; evidence excluded that defendant had suffered large loss in a drug transaction one year previously offered to show motive based on financial need); *State v. Chase*, 47 Or App 175, 613 P2d 1104 (1980) (prosecution for unlawful delivery of controlled substance to a minor; court excluded evidence that defendant's motive was to encourage victim to engage in homosexual relations). See generally, ANNOT., *Admissibility of Evidence of Accused's Drug Addiction or Use to Show Motive for Theft of Property Other Than Drugs*, ALR4th 1298 (1980).

Opportunity

See *United States v. Stover*, 565 F2d 1010 (8th Cir 1977) (fact that defendant had escaped from prison admissible to establish his presence in vicinity where car stolen); *United States v. Green*, 648 F2d 587 (9th Cir 1981).

Intent

In *State v. Johns,* 301 Or 535, 555–6, 725 P2d 312 (1986), the court articulated six issues that should be considered by the trial judge in deciding whether to admit prior bad act evidence to prove intent:

(1) Does the present charged act require proof of intent?

(2) Did the prior act require intent?

(3) Was the victim in the prior act the same victim or in the same class as the victim in the present case?

(4) Was the type of prior act the same or similar to the acts involved in the charged crime?

(5) Were the physical elements of the prior act and the present act similar?

(6) If these criteria are met, is the probative value of the prior act evidence substantially outweighed by the danger of unfair prejudice, confusion of issues or misleading the jury, undue delay or presentation of cumulative evidence?

The sixth factor is of particular importance. The guidelines for determining whether evidence admissible under Rule 404(3) should nonetheless be excluded under Rule 403 are discussed above. Courts often evaluate how essential the prior bad act evidence is by considering it in connection with the other evidence available to the prosecutor to establish intent. A prosecutor is most likely to have prior bad acts evidence received at the end of the state's case-in-chief, when the need for such evidence can still be shown in the context of the entire case. In *United States v. Hadaway,* 681 F2d 214, 219 (4th Cir 1982), the court commented that if other crimes evidence is admitted in the middle of the prosecution's case-in-chief to prove intent, it may be followed by other proof beyond a reasonable doubt on intent, rendering the other crimes evidence unnecessary and prejudicial. In *Hadaway,* the court approved the admission of the other crimes evidence, in part because it was received at the conclusion of the prosecutor's case-in-chief when there was still uncertainty upon the proof admitted up to that point as to whether the defendant had the requisite mens rea.

The court in *Johns* refused to lay down categorical rules regarding: (1) whether one prior act is sufficient to prove intent; (2) the degree of similarity required between the past act and the current act when offered to prove intent (as distinguished from identity, which requires a higher standard of similarity); or (3) the permissible time lapse between the prior act and the current act. The court stated:

> Depending upon the circumstances of the case, sometimes one prior similar act will be sufficiently relevant for admissibility and sometimes not. A simple, unremarkable single instance of prior conduct probably will not qualify, but a complex act requiring several steps, particularly premeditated, may well qualify .... The more prior similar acts, the stronger the probative value; the fewer, the less probative value. The same is true of the similarity of the prior acts and of the time element. The prior acts need not be identical. The greater the degree of similarity of the prior acts, the greater the relevancy; the less similarity, the

less probative value. As to the time element, the closer in time of the prior act to the act charged, the greater the probative value; the more remote, the less probative value.

301 Or at 555, 725 P2d at 324.

There is an additional factor that is often of critical importance in determining the admissibility of prior bad acts evidence to prove intent—whether intent is a genuinely disputed issue in the case. A number of courts have held that prior bad acts are not admissible to prove intent merely because intent is an element of the crime. See *State v. Sicks*, 33 Or App 435, 438, 576 P2d 834 (1978) ("the better view is that evidence of similar acts with other persons will not be admitted [to show intent] ... simply because defendant has pled not guilty"); *United States v. Ring*, 513 F2d 1001, 1009 (6th Cir 1975) ("[I]ntent is not in issue when evidence of intent is inferable if the proscribed act is proven and defendant does not claim mistake or inadvertence."); *United States v. Gubelman*, 571 F2d 1252 (2nd Cir), cert denied 436 US 948 (1978) (issue for which other-crimes evidence is offered must be in dispute).

In *Johns*, supra, the defendant's intent was the central disputed issue in the case, and therefore this issue received little discussion. The defendant was charged with murdering his wife, and he claimed the shooting was accidental. Therefore, the court held it was proper to admit evidence of a similar assault on a former wife to prove intent.

Certainly prior bad acts evidence is much more likely to be admitted in cases where the defendant disputes the issue of intent. Sometimes the existence of a genuine dispute about intent, or a claim of mistake or accident, will be known from defendant's opening statement, in which case the door may be opened to admissible Rule 404(3) evidence during the prosecution's case-in-chief. In other cases, the issue may not surface until the defendant's case-in-chief, in which case the trial court may allow prior bad acts evidence to be admitted in rebuttal that the court would not have allowed during the prosecution's case-in-chief.

Intent is a disputed issue in sex crime cases where the defendant claims the victim consented. See *State v. Fears*, 69 Or App 606, 688 P2d 88, rev denied 298 Or 238, 691 P2d 482 (1984) (rape prosecution; defendant testified that the victim hitchhiker consented; the court held admissible to prove intent evidence that two nights previously the defendant had committed another rape of a girl to whom he had given a ride); *Youngblood v. Sullivan*, 52 Or App 173, 628 P2d 400, petition for review denied 291 Or 368, 634 P2d 1347 (1981) (when defendant in sex case claims consent, evidence of similar nonconsensual conduct with another admissible to rebut claim of consent; evidence tends to show unlawful intent); *State v. Smith*, 271 Or 294, 532 P2d 9 (1975); *State v. Seydell*, 252 Or 160, 446 P2d 678 (1968); *State v. Fleischman*, 10 Or App 22, 495 P2d 277 (1972).

Even when a defendant does not directly dispute the issue of intent, and perhaps offers no evidence at all, prior crime evidence may be admissible to prove intent in cases where the crime charged contains a particular mens rea requirement (such as specific intent), the other evidence in the case is insufficient to establish that mental element, and the prior crimes evidence is particularly probative with respect to that element.

For example, in *State v. Painter*, 113 Or App 337, 341–2, 833 P2d 303, rev denied 314 Or 392, 840 P2d 710 (1992), a prosecution for attempted rape and attempted kidnapping, the court approved admission of evidence of prior instances where defendant had picked up girls at the same parking lot and taken them to his apartment for sexual activity. The court concluded that the other incidents "were sufficiently similar to allow a jury to infer that defendant intended to attempt to kidnap and rape [the victim]."

In *State v. Walters*, 99 Or App 570, 783 P2d 531 (1989), rev'd on other grounds 311 Or 80, 804 P2d 1164, cert denied *Walters v. Oregon*, 111 SCt 2807 (1991), writ of habeas corpus granted 45 F3d 1355 (1995), the defendant was charged with attempted rape, attempted sodomy, and attempted kidnapping. The defendant had approached a thirteen-year-old girl, asked for help in finding a lost dog, and offered to pay her money if she would come with him to help look for it. At trial to prove intent, the prosecutor offered evidence that the defendant was convicted six years earlier of the rape of a thirteen-year-old that he had approached and asked for assistance in finding a lost dog. In neither case did the defendant actually own a dog. The court held this evidence was properly admitted on the issue of intent.

Recent Cases Admitting Prior Acts to Prove Intent

In *State v. Morgan,* 80 Or App 747, 751, 724 P2d 334, rev denied 302 Or 461, 730 P2d 1251 (1986), the defendant was convicted of attempted kidnapping and related offenses. While armed with a knife, he attempted to enter the car of a lone woman in a shopping mall. As part of its proof that defendant intended to take the victim from one place to another without her consent to cause her physical injury, the prosecution offered evidence of a prior rape conviction. In that incident, the defendant had also approached a woman who was alone in a shopping mall, pulled a gun, drove the car to an isolated location, and forced her to perform an oral sex act. The court held: "The prior crime in this case is similar to the crime charged, and evidence of that crime is relevant to show defendant's criminal intent."

In *State v. Lee,* 88 Or App 556, 746 P2d 242 (1987), the defendant was charged with manslaughter for causing the death of a child. The Court of Appeals held that evidence of prior mistreatment of the child by the defendant was admissible, noting that evidence offered to prove a defendant's assaultive disposition toward the same individual is relevant. The fact that the nature of the prior mistreatment was slightly different than the conduct that caused the death of the child was held not to be a reason for excluding the evidence. The court held that "[i]dentity of the prior acts and the present charged act is not required to prove intent or lack of mistake."

In *State v. Harris,* 81 Or App 574, 726 P2d 943 (1986), rev denied 302 Or 476, 731 P2d 442 (1987), the defendant was convicted of murder and attempted murder. The attempted murder charge was based upon the defendant firing a gun at the owner of a tavern while drunk. The court held that evidence of prior acts of violence with a gun by the defendant while drunk were properly admitted to prove intent.

See also *State v. Madison*, 290 Or 573, 624 P2d 599 (1981) (not abuse of discretion on facts of case to admit grounds for arrest in resisting arrest prosecution; relevant to show intent).

Recent Cases Excluding Prior Acts to Prove Intent

In *State v. Pratt*, 309 Or 205, 214, 785 P2d 350 (1990), cert denied 114 SCt 452 (1993), the aggravated murder conviction of the defendant was reversed on the ground that a prior bad act was improperly admitted on the issue of intent. The defendant was charged with murdering the victim in the course of attempting to rape her. The prosecutor introduced evidence of a prior rape by the defendant that had similarities to the present crime. However, the appellate court found admission of this evidence to be error as a matter of law because the differences in the circumstances of the prior act outweighed its similarities. The court stated that in applying OEC 404(3), the similarities of the prior act "cannot be considered in a vacuum." The trial judge also must "consider the differences between the physical elements of the two crimes," and the "dissimilarities must be as fully considered as the similarities."

Similarly, in *State v. Rinkin*, 141 Or App 355, 368–71, 917 P2d 1035 (1996), the court reversed a conviction for attempted sodomy upon a child, where the trial judge had admitted evidence of a past incident of attempted sodomy by the defendant where the physical elements of the prior act and the present act were found to have more dissimilarities than similarities.

See generally Teitelbaum & Hertz, *Evidence II: Evidence of Other Crimes as Proof of Intent*, 13 N M L Rev 423 (1983).

Plan

In *State v. Kim*, 111 Or App 1, 7–8, 824 P2d 1161, 1165, rev denied 314 Or 176, 836 P2d 1345 (1992), the court held that it was error for the trial judge to exclude evidence offered by the prosecution that defendant had previously murdered his wife and abused her while she was alive. Defendant was charged with killing the husband of a woman with whom he was romantically involved. Therefore, the evidence had relevance in showing a plan to kill both spouses so that defendant and the victim's wife could pursue their romantic interest.

See also *United States v. Barbieri*, 614 F2d 715 (10th Cir 1980) (evidence of prior prostitution scheme admissible); *United States v. Robbins*, 613 F2d 688 (8th Cir 1979) (defendant charged with impersonating an FBI agent; evidence of impersonation on prior occasions beyond those specified in indictment admissible); *State v. Zimmerlee*, 261 Or 49, 492 P2d 795 (1972); *Castor v. Erlandson*, 277 Or 147, 560 P2d 267 (1977); *State v. White*, 53 Or App 856, 632 P2d 1363 (1981).

See generally ANNOT., *Admissibility, Under Rule 404(b) of the Federal Rules of Evidence, of Evidence of Other Crimes, Wrongs, or Acts Similar to Offense*

Charged to Show Preparation or Plan, 47 ALR Fed 781 (1980); Imwinkelried, *Using a Contextual Construction to Resolve the Dispute Over the Meaning of the Term "Plan" in Federal Rule of Evidence 404(b),* 43 U Kan L Rev 1005 (1995).

Knowledge

Evidence of prior bad acts may be admissible to show knowledge, when knowledge is an issue in the current prosecution. In *State v. Allen,* 301 Or 569, 725 P2d 331 (1986), the defendant was convicted of arson. He hired an accomplice to commit the arson and gave him instructions on how to start the fire. The prosecutor offered evidence that defendant had once confessed to another similar arson seven years earlier, although he had never been charged or convicted of that arson. The prosecutor offered evidence regarding how the earlier offense had been committed and how the accomplice in the earlier incident had nearly been badly injured. Because the evidence showed that defendant provided safer instructions regarding how to start the fire in the current case, the evidence of the earlier incident was admissible to show that defendant acquired his more sophisticated knowledge as a result of that earlier incident.

See also *State v. Louis,* 296 Or 57, 672 P2d 708 (1983) (prosecution for indecent exposure; defendant argued he did not know he could be seen by neighbors when standing naked in front of living room window; evidence of prior incidents where police warned defendant about complaints from neighbors admitted to prove knowledge); *State v. Phelps,* 73 Or App 68, 698 P2d 43 (1985) (prosecution for unauthorized use of a motor vehicle; evidence that defendant possessed the key to another stolen car at time of arrest admissible on the issue of knowledge); *United States v. Moccia,* 681 F2d 61, 63 (1st Cir 1982) (prior possession of marijuana admissible on issue of knowledge, when defendant denied knowledge of marijuana in his freezer); *United States v. Witt,* 618 F2d 283 (5th Cir), cert denied 449 US 882 (1980) (defendant's prior statements showing involvement in other drug trafficking admissible in prosecution for distribution of heroin to show knowledge); *United States v. Witschner,* 624 F2d 840 (8th Cir), cert denied 449 US 994 (1980) (mail fraud prosecution; prior fraudulent claims admitted to show knowledge); *United States v. Herrera-Medina,* 609 F2d 376 (9th Cir 1979) (evidence of two prior incidents of defendant transporting illegal aliens admissible to show defendant's knowledge that passengers were illegal aliens); *Brown v. Johnston,* 258 Or 284, 482 P2d 712 (1971).

Identity

In *State v. Johns,* 301 Or 535, 551, 725 P2d 312 (1986), the court stated: "[T]his court and other courts have held that evidence of other crimes offered to prove identity is strictly limited to crimes committed 'by the use of a novel means or in a particular manner' so as to earmark the acts as the handiwork of the accused. In other words, to prove identity the prior acts must be a 'signature' crime."

In *State v. Johnson*, 313 Or 189, 197–201, 832 P2d 443 (1992), defendant was convicted of aggravated murder and rape. At his trial evidence was offered of a prior rape and murder allegedly committed by the defendant under similar circumstances offered to prove the identity of the defendant as the perpetrator of the charged crime. The Supreme Court reversed the conviction, holding that evidence of the prior crime was erroneously introduced under Rule 404(3). The court held that evidence offered to prove modus operandi must demonstrate (1) "*a very high degree of similarity* between the prior and charged misconduct" and (2) "*a distinctive nature of the methodology.*" Whether the prosecution has met its burden "requires a case-by-case determination." The court concluded "that the record does not support a finding that there is either a very high degree of similarity between the prior and charged misconduct or a methodology that is so distinctive as to earmark the crimes as the handiwork of one criminal."

Recent Cases Admitting Past Acts to Prove Identity

In *State v. Walton*, 311 Or 223, 234, 809 P2d 81 (1991), the court approved admission of evidence that defendant was involved in a previous robbery, because the use of a distinctive and unique sawed-off shotgun served to earmark both the prior robbery and the charged robbery as the "handiwork" of the same person.

In *State v. Pinnell*, 311 Or 98, 109–12, 806 P2d 110 (1991), aff'd 314 Or 673, 842 P2d 394 (1992), the court held that evidence of a prior robbery under very similar circumstances was admissible to prove modus operandi and identify the defendant as the perpetrator of the charged crime. For prior crime evidence to be admissible on the issue of identity, the prosecution must establish by a preponderance of evidence that "(1) there is a very high degree of similarity between the charged and uncharged crime; and (2) the methodology is attributable to only one criminal, that is, the methodology is distinctive so as to earmark the acts as the handiwork of the accused." The court concluded that those criteria were satisfied in this case.

In *State v. Cornell*, 109 Or App 396, 404, 820 P2d 11, 16 (1991), aff'd 314 Or 673, 842 P2d 394 (1992), the court held that there was no error in admitting evidence of prior robberies where defendant also hog-tied the victims to prove the identity of the defendant as the perpetrator of the instant crime.

In *State v. Bernson*, 93 Or App 115, 760 P2d 1362, rev denied 302 Or 246, 767 P2d 76 (1988), a murder prosecution, the court held that evidence of two prior crimes committed by the defendant, one a murder and one a sexual assault, were sufficiently similar to the charged offense to be admitted on the issue of identity.

In *State v. Wilson*, 69 Or App 569, 687 P2d 800 (1984), rev denied 298 Or 553, 695 P2d 49 (1985), the court held that the trial judge did not err in admitting testimony by two of the robbery victims that defendant had robbed them several months earlier. The court found that the challenged evidence was relevant, because defendant had tendered an alibi defense, which made identification of the perpetrator particularly important to the prosecution's case. The court stated: "The ability of the victims to observe defendant on that previous occasion could help the jury conclude that their present identifications of him were more likely to be accurate." 69 Or App at 573, 687 P2d at 803.

See also *State v. Browder*, 69 Or App 564, 687 P2d 168, rev denied 298 Or 172, 691 P2d 481 (1984) (prior crimes evidence offered to show modus operandi should not be excluded merely because the most relevant fact, a similar jacket worn by the defendant, could be proven in another manner).

Federal cases where prior crimes were admitted on the issue of identity include *United States v. Bailleaux*, 685 F2d 1105 (9th Cir 1982) (past and current crime both involved poisoning of food in a store and a demand for diamonds to forestall future poisonings); *United States v. Messersmith*, 692 F2d 1315 (1st Cir 1982) (prior crime involved same airline trip and same persons for purposes of illegally transporting Quaaludes); *United States v. Danzey*, 594 F2d 905 (2nd Cir), cert denied 441 US 951 (1979) (evidence of prior similar bank robberies admissible to show identity of defendant); *United States v. Park*, 525 F2d 1279, 1284 (5th Cir 1976) (citation omitted) ("[T]he identity exception is one of very limited scope. 'A prior or subsequent crime is not admissible for this purpose merely because it is similar, but only if it bears such a high degree of similarity as to mark it as the handiwork of the accused.'"); *United States v. Foutz*, 540 F2d 733 (4th Cir 1976) (insufficient similarity).

Recent Cases Excluding Past Acts to Prove Identity

In *State v. Langley*, 314 Or 511, 515, 840 P2d 691 (1992), adhered to 318 Or 28, 861 P2d 1012 (1993), the court held that there was insufficient similarity between a prior murder and the murder charged to support admission of the earlier murder on a modus operandi theory. The state relied on the allegedly distinctive manner of handling and burying the victims in the two crimes and the use of false stories to explain the victims' disappearance and to get their property. However, dissimilarities included the fact that one victim was suffocated and the other was bludgeoned. Although each victim was bound, different materials were used and they were bound in different positions.

In *State v. Westby*, 117 Or App 14, 17, 843 P2d 973 (1992), rev denied 318 Or 351, 870 P2d 220 (1994), a murder prosecution, the court held that it was error to admit evidence of three prior acts of misconduct involving theft. The court found the acts not admissible to show modus operandi, because they were too dissimilar to the facts of the charged offense where defendant allegedly stole the victim's property after the murder.

In *State v. Collins*, 73 Or App 216, 698 P2d 969 (1985), a murder prosecution, the court sustained the ruling of the trial judge excluding evidence of a murder by the defendant five years earlier under similar circumstances. The court agreed with the trial judge's finding that the circumstances were not sufficiently similar to qualify under the "signature" category of prior crimes evidence. The court held: "When evidence of a prior crime is offered to prove identity, the prior crime and the crime for which defendant is currently on trial must be so nearly identical in method as to earmark both as the handiwork of the defendant."

Absence of Mistake or Accident

Evidence of prior bad acts is sometimes offered to rebut a claim of mistake or accident. However, the issue of absence of mistake or accident often merges with the issue of defendant's intent at the time he committed the act. See *State v. Johns*, 301 Or 535, 550, 725 P2d 312 (1986) ("We agree with the Court of Appeals that intent and absence of mistake or accident are really the same issue here. Proof of intent eliminates mistake or accident.").

In *State v. Parker*, 119 Or App 105, 108, 849 P2d 1157, rev denied 317 Or 584, 859 P2d 541 (1993), the defendant argued that it was prejudicial error to deny his motion for separate trials of sex abuse charges involving three separate children. The appellate court held that even if the charges involving three victims had been separately tried, the evidence of his relationship and conduct with each child would be admissible in each of the separate trials, because the evidence was probative of intent and would make it more likely that the touching was not accidental.

See also *State v. Allen*, 301 Or 569, 725 P2d 331 (1986) (evidence of prior arson admissible to show fire not accidental); *State v. Lee*, 49 Or App 131, 619 P2d 292 (1980) (defendant charged with theft from store; possession of other goods in trunk stolen from other stores allowed to show possession not accidental); *State v. Mills*, 39 Or App 85, 591 P2d 396 (1979) (prior assaults on infant daughter admissible to show absence of accident or mistake); *State v. Seydell*, 252 Or 160, 446 P2d 678 (1968) (defendant charged with filing false insurance claim; defendant's earlier statements that he had burned a house for insurance money admissible).

Unlisted Purposes

The list of permissible purposes for other-crimes evidence that is set forth in Rule 404(3) is not exclusive. Other permissible purposes may include the following:

Element of Charged Crime

Prior crime evidence is admissible when a prior crime is an element of the offense charged. See Rule 404(1); *State v. Earp*, 69 Or App 365, 686 P2d 437, rev denied 298 Or 334, 691 P2d 483 (1984) (prior murder conviction admissible in aggravated murder prosecution, because such conviction is an element of the crime of aggravated murder under ORS 163.095(1)(c)); *State v. Hoover*, 248 Or 178, 433 P2d 244 (1967) (defendant charged with being a convicted felon in possession of a concealable firearm; judgment record of prior crime admissible to show status as a convicted felon).

Even if a prior crime is not an element, it may be inextricably intertwined with the charged crime. For example, the crime of selling an illegal drug generally requires proof of possession. Where the other crimes are **intrinsic** to the charged offense, they are admissible without a need to find an exception under Rule 404(3), which applies only to **extrinsic** offenses. See COMMENT, *Intrinsic or Extrinsic? The Confusing Distinction Between Inextricably Intertwined Evidence and Other Crimes Evidence Under Rule 404(b),* 88 Nw U L Rev 1582 (1994). See generally Mueller & Kirkpatrick, MODERN EVIDENCE § 4.20 (1995).

As an example of evidence that was closely enough connected with the charged offense to be admissible, see *State v. Carsner,* 117 Or App 406, 408, 844 P2d 257 (1992), rev denied 317 Or 163, 856 P2d 318 (1993) (prosecution for manufacture of a controlled substance; defendant argued it was error for the prosecution to introduce evidence of baggies and scales found at the scene to prove that the marijuana was grown for other than personal use claiming that this was evidence of "uncharged misconduct"; appellate court rejected this argument on the ground that the evidence was not about "uncharged" misconduct but was independently relevant to prove the charged crime of manufacture of a controlled substance).

To Show Factual Background

Prior bad act evidence may be admissible to show the factual background of closely connected crimes or the time sequence leading up to the commission of the crime charged. See *State v. Harmon,* 77 Or App 705, 714 P2d 271, rev denied 301 Or 240, 720 P2d 1279, cert denied 479 US 867 (1986) (admitting evidence of the defendant's drug use on the night of the crime "to complete the picture of the night's events. ...."; trial court did not err in finding probative value outweighed prejudicial impact on facts of case).

In *State v. Bartley,* 121 Or App 301, 854 P2d 996, rev denied 318 Or 25, 862 P2d 1305 (1993), where defendant was convicted of rape and other offenses, the court held that it was not error to admit evidence that defendant had been having intercourse with the victim on numerous occasions since she was 11 or 12. The evidence, although "inflammatory," had strong probative value in explaining "why the victim might act the way she did and yet still not consent to sexual intercourse with him."

In *State v. Hall,* 108 Or App 12, 17, 814 P2d 172, 174, rev denied 312 Or 151, 817 P2d 758 (1991), the defendant was charged with sexual abuse of his two granddaughters, who were living with defendant and his daughter. The court held that evidence of defendant's incestuous relationship with his daughter, the victims' mother, was admissible to show the factual background of the crime and the reasons for the children's delay in reporting the offenses.

However, in *State v. Brooks,* 57 Or App 98, 643 P2d 1324, rev denied 293 Or 373, 648 P2d 854 (1982), a murder prosecution, the prosecutor offered evidence of a series of credit card thefts and forgeries committed by the defendant, the victim and another party. The prosecutor argued that this evidence was admissible for its tendency to complete the story of the crime and to show a motive for the killing. The court found error in the admission of this evidence, holding that evidence of the prior crimes was not necessary to complete the picture of defendant's activities leading up to the commission of the crime.

See also *United States v. Gibson*, 625 F2d 887 (9th Cir 1980) (federal kidnapping prosecution; government allowed to show sexual assault against the victim to establish complete time sequence); *United States v. Masters*, 622 F2d 83 (4th Cir 1980) (prior-crimes evidence necessary for "full presentation" of offense); *State v. Sikes*, 247 Or 249, 427 P2d 756 (1967) (evidence allowed of sexual assault of victim prior to rape; "indivisible criminal transaction"); *State v. Hockings*, 29 Or App 139, 562 P2d 587 (1977), cert denied 434 US 1049 (1978) (evidence of use of marijuana by defendant prior to murder not error on facts of case).

To Rebut Entrapment Defense

Prior bad act evidence can be received to prove predisposition toward criminal conduct to rebut the defense of entrapment. See *United States v. Mack*, 643 F2d 1119, 1121–2 (5th Cir 1981) (other incidents of drug dealing by defendant admissible to rebut defense of entrapment by showing a specific propensity to deal in drugs); *United States v. Salisbury*, 662 F2d 738, 741 (11th Cir 1981), cert denied 457 US 1107, 102 SCt 2907, 73 LEd2d 1316 (1982); *United States v. Biggins*, 551 F2d 64 (5th Cir 1977); ANNOT., *Admission of Evidence of Other Offense in Rebuttal of Defense of Entrapment*, 61 ALR3d 292.

In *State v. Barr*, 62 Or App 46, 660 P2d 169 (1983), the court held that only other crimes similar to the crime for which the defendant is on trial are admissible to rebut a defense of entrapment. The court held it was error to admit evidence of a prior burglary to establish predisposition to commit the crime of theft for which defendant was being prosecuted.

Basis of Expert Testimony

Prior bad act evidence is sometimes admitted to show the history upon which an expert relies in making a diagnosis regarding the defendant's sanity. See *State v. Wall*, 78 Or App 81, 715 P2d 96, rev denied 301 Or 241, 720 P2d 1280 (1986) (evidence of prior crimes and bad acts admitted to show the history on which expert relied in making a diagnosis regarding defendant's sanity); *State v. Larsen*, 44 Or App 643, 649, 606 P2d 1159 (1980); *State v. Goss*, 33 Or App 507, 577 P2d 78 (1978). But see *State v. Olds*, 35 Or App 305, 581 P2d 118 (1978).

See also *United States v. Emery*, 682 F2d 493 (5th Cir), cert denied 459 US 1044, 103 SCt 465, 74 LEd2d 615 (1982) (prior crimes evidence admissible to support expert's opinion on sanity).

To Show Consciousness of Guilt

Prior bad acts are sometimes admitted to show the defendant's consciousness of guilt of the present offense. See *United States v. Posey,* 611 F2d 1389 (5th Cir 1980) (attempted bribe of law enforcement officer); *State v. Brown,* 231 Or 297, 372 P2d 779 (1962) (flight by defendant, including stealing of automobile); *State v. McIntire,* 2 Or App 429, 468 P2d 536 (1970) (escape). See ANNOT., *Admissibility of Evidence that Defendant Escaped or Attempted to Escape While Being Detained for Offense in Addition to That or Those Presently Being Prosecuted,* 3 ALR4th 1085 (1981). For a discussion of the admissibility of evidence of flight to avoid prosecution, see discussion under Rule 401.

To Show Reasonable Fear of Person

Prior acts of violence of a crime victim or a third party, if known to the defendant, may be admissible to prove that the defendant had a reasonable fear of that person. Such evidence bears on the defendant's state of mind and his right to use self-defense. See *State v. Bishop,* 49 Or App 1023, 1032, 621 P2d 1196 (1980), rev denied 290 Or 727 (1981) (admitting evidence of prior acts of violence by victim that were known to defendant to support self-defense claim). See Mueller & Kirkpatrick, MODERN EVIDENCE (1995) 4.23.

In *State v. Lunow,* 131 Or App 429, 885 P2d 731 (1994), an assault prosecution, the court held that the defendant was entitled to introduce prior specific instances of violent behavior by the victim that were known to the defendant to support his claim of self-defense. The court held that "reasonable belief" in the need to defend oneself is an element of self-defense under OEC 404(1), and therefore evidence of the victim's character in any form—reputation, opinion, or specific instances—is admissible under OEC 405(2)(a) to prove it. The court appears to have reached the right result for the wrong reasons. It seems erroneous to view a victim's **character** as an **element** of a self-defense claim under Rule 404(1). A better approach would be to find that prior acts of violence by the victim (known to the defendant) are not excluded by OEC 404(2) if they are not being offered for the forbidden purpose of proving conduct on a particular occasion but instead are being offered only to prove reasonable fear by the defendant.

In *State v. Bockorny,* 124 Or App 585, 589, 863 P2d 1296, 1298 (1993), rev denied 318 Or 351, 870 P2d 220 (1994), defendant attempted to assert a duress defense to the underlying felonies in an aggravated murder prosecution. She argued it was error to exclude evidence of prior violent acts by her husband known to her that would support her defense of duress. The court found no error, holding that the statute allowing a duress defense focuses not on past conduct but rather on whether defendant was forced to commit the crimes by a present threat of unlawful physical force on her so great that it overcame her earnest resistance. This decision seems questionable, because the past violent acts of the person accused of subjecting defendant to duress, provided they are known to defendant, bear directly on defendant's state of mind.

To Contradict Defendant's Testimony

Prior bad acts evidence may be allowed to correct an inaccurate statement or misleading inference or suggestion made by the defendant upon direct examination or volunteered upon cross-examination. *State v. Manrique,* 271 Or 201, 213, 531 P2d 239 (1975).

In *State v. Ferguson,* 84 Or App 565, 735 P2d 3 (1987), the defendant was convicted of assaulting a man. At trial, the court admitted as an excited utterance of an observer at the altercation the statement: "Jeff, don't kick the woman." Defendant argued that this statement should have been excluded, because it implied that he had assaulted someone else during the same incident. The court held that the statement was properly admitted to rebut defendant's testimony that he did not participate in the assault.

In *State v. Bovee,* 75 Or App 544, 706 P2d 1005 (1985), a sodomy prosecution, the defendant claimed that the charges were the result of a conspiracy by defendant's wife in order to obtain advantageous terms in a prospective marriage dissolution. Therefore, the court held it was proper to allow cross-examination of the defendant regarding his knowledge that other young boys had made similar allegations, but that inquiry should not be allowed into the details of the allegations.

However, in *State v. Mayfield,* 302 Or 631, 733 P2d 438 (1987), also a sodomy prosecution, the defendant asserted the theory that the eight-year-old victim, the daughter of his then fiancee, made the accusation falsely at a later date to prevent him from gaining custody or visitation rights with the newborn son of the defendant and the victim's mother. To rebut defendant's theory, the state offered evidence that defendant had also abused the three-year-old sister of the victim. The state claimed this rebutted defendant's theory in two ways. First, it supported the victim's testimony that the reason she made the accusation against defendant was, since he had abused both her and her younger sister, she also feared that he would abuse her newborn brother. Second, because there was independent evidence of abuse of the three-year-old sister, it was therefore unnecessary for the victim to fabricate her own charges of abuse by defendant, as defendant had suggested. The Supreme Court held that the admission of this evidence constituted reversible error. Even though it was relevant under Rule 401, it should have been excluded under Rule 403.

In *State v. Gardner,* 67 Or App 404, 679 P2d 306, rev denied 297 Or 339, 683 P2d 1370 (1984), the defendant was convicted of arson, in part upon the testimony of a prosecution witness named Bramwell, who testified that the defendant had discussed the arson with him. The trial court admitted evidence that Bramwell had manufactured an illegal drug in the defendant's kitchen while the defendant was present. The appellate court held that the trial court did not abuse its discretion in admitting such evidence, despite its prejudicial effect, because it helped to show the nature of defendant's relationship with Bramwell, which the defendant had attempted to minimize. The court noted that the evidence "made it more likely that defendant would confide in Bramwell about his arson plans and ask his advice, as Bramwell testified and defendant denied."

It is improper for a prosecutor to attempt to open the door for contradictory prior bad acts evidence by questions asked upon cross-examination. *State v. Johnson,* 277 Or 45, 559 P2d 496 (1977). Cf. *United States v. Cook,* 538 F2d 1000 (3rd Cir 1976). See further discussion of this issue under Rule 607.

To Prove Negligence

On the admissibility of evidence of prior acts or events to prove negligence or related factors such as causation or the existence of a dangerous condition, see discussion under Rule 401. See also ANNOT., *Modern Status of Rules as to Admissibility of Evidence of Prior Accidents or Injuries at Same Place,* 21 ALR4th 472.

Cross-Examination of a Character Witness

Prior bad act evidence is admissible to test upon cross-examination the credibility of a character witness who offers opinion or reputation evidence regarding a person's good character. See discussion under Rule 405(1); ANNOT., *Cross-examination of Character Witnesses for the Accused with Reference to Particular Acts or Crimes,* 13 ALR4th 796. See also *Michelson v. United States,* 335 US 469, 69 SCt 213, 93 LEd 168 (1948).

To Prove Future Dangerousness

In *State v. Wagner,* 305 Or 115, 752 P2d 1136 (1988), the defendant argued error in the admission of evidence of the defendant's previous bad acts and criminal conduct that did not result in convictions. The court found that such evidence was properly received to prove future dangerousness, thereby establishing a basis for capital punishment. See also *State v. Williams,* 313 Or 19, 43, 828 P2d 1006, 1021, cert denied *Williams v. Oregon,* 113 SCt 171 (1992).

In *State v. Montez,* 309 Or 564, 611, 612, 789 P2d 1352 (1990), the court held that evidence of prior bad acts, including the defendant's uncorroborated admission of killing someone, were admissible in the penalty phase of a capital trial. The court held that the OEC proscribes character evidence only when offered to prove past conduct, not when offered to predict future behavior. Moreover, such evidence was admissible under OEC 404(1) because the defendant's character was in issue with respect to the question of future dangerousness.

Doctrine of Chances

In *State v. Wieland,* 131 Or App 582, 584–9, 887 P2d 368 (1994), the defendant was charged with aggravated murder of his mother-in-law. The state claimed the motive for the murder was to conceal the fact that the defendant had committed three arson fires on his property in 1986. To prove that the 1986 fires were caused by arson, the state sought to introduce evidence of fires on the defendant's property in 1984 and 1991 to show the unlikelihood that so many fires would be caused by anything other than arson. The appellate court approved admission of the 1984 and 1991 fires under the "doctrine of chances," which suggests that multiple occurrences of an unusual event make it less likely that it occurred as a matter of chance. The court found the evidence relevant to show that the 1986 fires were caused by arson and OEC 403 did not compel its exclusion.

Other Purposes

In *State v. Zybach,* 308 Or 96, 775 P2d 318 (1989), the court held that evidence of other subsequent sexual assaults or overtures between defendant and a rape victim were admissible to show why the victim had not reported the original sexual assault. The court held that such evidence was "not admissible to show that defendant had a propensity to have sexual intercourse or similar contact with minor girls." 308 Or at 99–100. The court also stated:

> [W]e reject the Court of Appeal's statement that OEC 404(2) should be construed "narrowly in cases involving sex crimes." 92 Or App at 221. The rule excludes evidence of character, particularly evidence concerning propensity to commit a certain type of crime-be it murder, rape, robbery or otherwise. The rule is not "wide or narrow" depending on the crime.

308 Or at 99.

However, in *State v. McKay,* 309 Or 305, 308, 787 P2d 479 (1990), the court held that evidence of previous sexual contacts between the defendant and the victim was admissible "to demonstrate the sexual predisposition this defendant had for this particular victim, that is, to show the sexual inclination of defendant towards the victim, not that he had a character trait or propensity to engage in sexual misconduct generally."

In *State v. Harvey,* 82 Or App 595, 728 P2d 940 (1986), decision aff'd in part, reversed in part 303 Or 351, 736 P2d 191 (1987), the defendant was convicted of rape and sodomy for forcibly compelling his 14-year-old son and 11-year-old stepdaughter to engage in sexual acts with each other. The trial court admitted evidence of a prior bad act by the defendant, an incident in which he "hog-tied" his son as punishment. The court held that this evidence was properly admitted under Rule 404(3), because the state had to prove forcible compulsion and the evidence tended to prove that the son was subject to defendant's verbal commands because of the severe punishment he had received in the past.

Defendant Opening Door to Rule 404(3) Evidence

If the defendant introduces the prior bad acts evidence, or raises an issue that cannot fairly be considered without the evidence, an appellate court may hold that the defendant opened the door to the evidence and therefore cannot complain on appeal.

In *State v. Guritz*, 134 Or App 262, 266, 894 P2d 1235, 1237 (1995), a prosecution of the defendant for sodomy upon his young daughter, the defendant sought to portray himself as a "good father" who would not molest his daughter. He described his activities with his daughter, which included regularly taking her to places such as malls and the park. To rebut this evidence, the prosecutor offered evidence that the defendant purchased marijuana while at the park with his daughter. The court found that the defendant had placed his character "in issue" by this evidence, thereby justifying introduction of the marijuana evidence to rebut his "characterization" of himself as a good father.

In *State v. Hart,* 84 Or App 160, 733 P2d 469 (1987), defendant was prosecuted for a burglary where he was alleged to have stolen a large number of coins. He was found with numerous coins when arrested the next morning. Defendant called as a defense witness a cab driver who testified that he observed defendant with a large number of coins a year earlier, apparently to raise the inference that defendant might carry bags of coins for an innocent purpose. The trial court allowed the prosecutor on cross-examination to bring out that defendant had told the driver that the coins on the earlier occasion had been obtained in a robbery. The Court of Appeals stated: "Defendant had opened the door to the line of questioning and cannot now successfully argue that the evidence was unfairly prejudicial." 84 Or App at 164, 733 P2d at 471.

Recent Cases Excluding Evidence Offered Under Rule 404(3)

There have been a substantial number of cases where error was found in the admission of prior bad acts evidence under Rule 404(3). The following are examples:

State v. Middleton, 131 Or App 275, 278–80, 884 P2d 873 (1994): In a prosecution for carrying a concealed weapon, the trial court, to show motive, allowed in evidence that the defendant also had drug paraphernalia in his possession. The appellate court reversed, holding that such evidence was irrelevant and prejudicial.

State v. Hite, 131 Or App 59, 63–8, 883 P2d 890 (1994): In a rape and sodomy prosecution, the court held that it was improper to admit evidence of nude photographs of other women found in the defendant's possession, since they were irrelevant to the charged crime.

State v. Cearley, 133 Or App 333, 891 P2d 10 (1995): In this prosecution for animal neglect, the court held that evidence of a prior conviction of one of the defendants for animal neglect was improperly admitted. The court found that the evidence "was not independently relevant for a noncharacter purpose under OEC 404(3)."

State v. Mason, 100 Or App 240, 244–5, 785 P2d 378 (1990): In this sexual abuse prosecution, the court held that evidence that the defendant had also sexually abused the victim's mother under similar circumstances more than twenty years earlier should have been excluded under OEC 403 on the ground that the unfair prejudice of such evidence outweighed its probative value.

State v. Johns, 301 Or 535, 725 P2d 312 (1986): Defendant was convicted of the murder of his wife. He claimed the shooting was accidental and resulted as he attempted to take a revolver away from his wife in their bedroom. The prosecution offered evidence that seven months before the killing, defendant had demonstrated a handgun to two women who lived in the neighborhood. To demonstrate the importance of the safety on the revolver, he pointed the unloaded revolver towards one woman's face and fired. The court held that this evidence was not logically relevant to any issue in the case and should not have been received. However, the admission of this evidence was found not to constitute reversible error in light of the other evidence in the case.

State v. Gailey, 301 Or 563, 725 P2d 328 (1986): Defendant was convicted of a burglary which occurred on March 21. At trial, the prosecutor offered evidence that at the time of his arrest on March 21, defendant possessed property identified as being stolen from a burglary that occurred on March 20. Admission of the evidence under Rule 404(3) was found to be reversible error. The court held: "All this evidence proved was that defendant possessed stolen property from a burglary committed at a different time and place; this did not justify admitting such evidence on a theory that a person who possessed recently stolen property from the Place residence must have recently burglarized the Burke dwelling."

State v. Ollila, 82 Or App 491, 728 P2d 900 (1986): The prosecutor elicited testimony from the arresting officer that the defendant had admitted that he had a drinking problem and that he sometimes drank up to a 12-pack of beer a day. The officer was allowed to give this testimony over an objection by the defendant, but the court subsequently reconsidered its ruling and struck the testimony. The court instructed the jury to disregard the testimony but refused to grant the defendant's motion for a mistrial. The appellate court held that the evidence was sufficiently prejudicial that the motion for mistrial should have been granted.

State v. Vanderham, 78 Or App 589, 592, 717 P2d 647, 648 (1986): Defendant was convicted of raping a 12-year-old girl. The court held it was reversible error for the trial court to allow evidence that the defendant had possessed a pornographic magazine with a nude photograph of a young girl on the cover approximately two years prior to the criminal acts. The court stated: "Not only was the evidence remote in terms of time, but the length of time between possession of the magazine and the defendant's propensity to commit sexual offenses against children is tenuous, if not non-existent."

State v. McDonald, 77 Or App 267, 712 P2d 163 (1986): In this burglary prosecution, the court found reversible error in the admission of evidence of a prior burglary six months earlier that resulted in the conviction of the defendant. The court stated: "The six-month time lag is neither great enough to preclude relevancy ... nor short enough to ensure it .... The state had to show *some* factual similarity between the two burglaries. Because it failed to do so, the trial court erred in admitting the evidence."

State v. Bovee, 75 Or App 544, 547, 706 P2d 1005, 1006 (1985): Defendant was convicted of sodomy. The court found error in the admission of evidence of a prior act of sodomy by the defendant, stating that the evidence "is relevant, if at all, only to demonstrate defendant's propensity to commit the act alleged."

However, the court held that cross-examination of the defendant regarding his knowledge that other young boys made similar allegations was found to be proper in light of the fact that defendant claimed the present charges were merely the result of a conspiracy by defendant's wife in order to obtain advantageous terms in a prospective marriage dissolution. The court held that the trial judge was correct in restricting such cross-examination to knowledge of the allegations but not allowing inquiry into the details. The court stated: "Oregon courts have consistently recognized that, because evidence of previous sex crimes has a highly inflammatory effect on a jury, the general rule against admission of that kind of evidence should be strictly applied." 75 Or App at 548 n3, 706 P2d at 1007 n3.

Other Authorities

See generally Lewis, *Proof and Prejudice: A Constitutional Challenge to the Treatment of Prejudicial Evidence in Federal Criminal Cases,* 64 Wash L Rev 289 (1989); Myers, *Uncharged Misconduct Evidence in Child Abuse Litigation,* 1988 Utah L Rev 717; Roth, *Understanding Admissibility of Prior Bad Acts: A Diagrammatic Approach,* 9 Pepp L R 297 (1981); Krivosha, Lansworth & Pirsch, *Relevancy: The Necessary Element in Using Evidence of Other Crimes, Wrongs or Bad Acts to Convict,* 60 Neb L Rev 657 (1981); Uviller, *Evidence of Character to Prove Conduct: Illusion, Illogic and Injustice in the Courtroom,* 130 U Pa L Rev 845 (1982); Reed, *Admission of Other Criminal Act Evidence After Adoption of the Federal Rules of Evidence,* 53 U Cinn L Rev 113 (1984); Weissenberger, *Making Sense of Extrinsic Act Evidence: Federal Rule of Evidence 404(b),* 70 Iowa L Rev 579 (1985); Patterson, *Evidence of Prior Bad Acts: Admissibility Under the Federal Rules,* 38 Bay L Rev 331 (1986); Leonard, *The Use of Character to Prove Conduct: Rationality and Catharsis in the Law of Evidence,* 58 U Col L Rev 1 (1986); Gitchel, *Charting a Course Through Character Evidence,* 41 Ark L Rev 585 (1988); Crump, *How Should We Treat Character Evidence Offered to Prove Conduct?,* 58 U Col L Rev 279 (1988); Stuart, *Evidentiary Use of Other Crime Evidence: A Survey of Recent Trends in Criminal Procedure,* 20 Ind L Rev 183 (1987); Sharp, *Two-Step Balancing and the Admissibility of Other Crimes Evidence: A Sliding Scale of Proof,* 59 Notre Dame L Rev 556 (1984).

See also ANNOT., *Admissibility, Under Rule 404(b) of Federal Rules of Evidence, of Evidence of Other Crimes, Wrongs, or Acts Not Similar to Offense Charged,* 41 ALR Fed 497 (1979); ANNOT., *Admissibility in Federal Conspiracy Prosecution of Evidence of Defendant's Similar Prior Criminal Act,* 20 ALR Fed 125 (1974); ANNOT., *Admissibility, in Rape Case, of Evidence that Accused Raped or Attempted to Rape Person Other Than Prosecutrix,* 2 ALR 4th 330 (1980).

RULE 405.　ORS 40.175. METHODS OF PROVING CHARACTER

(1) [Reputation or opinion.] **In all cases in which evidence of character or a trait of character of a person is admissible, proof may be made by testimony as to reputation or by testimony in the form of an opinion. On cross-examination, inquiry is allowable into relevant specific instances of conduct.**

(2) [Specific instances of conduct.]

    (a) **In cases in which character or a trait of character of a person is admissible under subsection (1) of Rule 404 (ORS 40.170(1)), proof may also be made of specific instances of the conduct of the person.**

    (b) **When evidence is admissible under subsection (3) of Rule 404 (ORS 40.170(3)), proof may be made of specific instances of the conduct of the person.**

LEGISLATIVE COMMENTARY

Oregon Rule of Evidence 405 indicates the methods which may be used to prove character. It is closely linked with Rule 404. Rule 404 deals with the admissibility of character evidence and is the only rule under which character evidence may be admitted. Rule 405 specifies what form character evidence, when admissible, may take.

Rule 405 is based on Rule 405 of the Federal Rules of Evidence. Subsection (1) is identical to Federal Rule 405(a). Subsection (2) is a modified version of Federal Rule 405(b), in which the words "an essential element of a charge, claim, or defense" have been replaced with references to the situations where proof of specific instances of conduct may be used.

Subsection (1). Direct examination. This subsection represents a major change in Oregon evidence law. Until now, Oregon has followed the common law rules on use of character evidence on direct examination. Different types of character evidence have been admissible, depending on the type of character issue presented. All character issues fall into one of three categories.

Where character is an element of a claim or defense under the applicable substantive law—the situation described in ORE 404(1)—Oregon law has allowed proof of specific instances of conduct, but disallowed any evidence of opinion or reputation. *Guedon v. Rooney,* 160 Or 261, 87 P2d 209 (1939). Under the Evidence Code, not only are specific examples of conduct permitted, under subsection (2) of this rule, infra, but opinion and reputation evidence are also allowed under this subsection.

Where character is relevant as circumstantial evidence of some fact in issue—the situation described in ORE 404(2)(a) and (b) for criminal cases and ORE 404(2)(d) for civil—Oregon law has required proof by reputation evidence and disallowed evidence of either opinion or specific instances of conduct. *Rich v. Cooper,* 234 Or 300, 305–308, 380 P2d 613 (1963); *State v. Holbrook,* 98 Or 43, 192 P 640 (1920). Under the Evidence Code, reputation evidence remains admissible and opinion evidence may also be introduced, under this subsection. Specific instances of conduct still may not be shown.

Where character is relevant as circumstantial evidence of the veracity of a witness—the situation described in ORE 404(2)(c)—Oregon law has allowed proof by evidence of reputation and of conviction (a specific instance), but the law has not allowed opinion testimony or evidence of specific instances other than a criminal conviction. ORS 45.600. Under the Evidence Code, reputation and opinion evidence are both admissible on the issue of credibility, under this subsection and Rule 608(1), infra, while evidence of specific instances of conduct remains limited to (a more narrowly defined set of) convictions, under Rule 609(1), infra.

In recognizing opinion as a means of proving character in each of the situations above, when hitherto it was allowed in none, Rule 405 departs from usual contemporary practice in favor of that of an earlier day. See 7 Wigmore, *Evidence* § 1986 (3d ed 1940), pointing out that earlier practice permitted opinion and arguing strongly for evidence based on personal knowledge and belief instead of "the second-hand, irresponsible produce of multiplied guesses and gossip which we term 'reputation.'" It seems likely that evidence of reputation has in fact persisted because it is largely opinion in disguise. Moreover, while character has been regarded primarily in moral overtones susceptible of proof by reputation evidence (is the person chaste, peaceable, truthful?) an increasing number of legal issues turn on non-moral considerations (is the driver competent?). If character is defined as the kind of person one is, then account must be taken of the various ways to develop a picture of character. These may range from the opinion of the employer who has found the person honest to the opinion of the psychiatrist based upon examination and testing. No effective dividing line exists between character and mental capacity, and the latter traditionally has been provable by opinion.

Cross-examination. The final sentence of subsection (1) allows inquiry into relevant specific instances of conduct. This is consistent with current Oregon law. *State v. Shull,* 131 Or 224, 282 P 237 (1929).

Cross-examinations regarding instances of conduct should be consistent with the type of character evidence the witness has presented. Counsel should not cross-examine a reputation witness, for example, by inquiring whether the witness "knows" of a particular act. A reputation witness relates what others say about an individual, and therefore should be asked what the witness has "heard." By the same token, an opinion witness, who speaks from personal knowledge of an individual, should be asked whether the witness "knows" of instances of conduct. A majority of jurisdictions observe this distinction of form. *Michelson v. United States,* 355 US 469, 69 SCt 213, 93 LEd 168 (1948); Annot., 47 ALR 2d 1258. Although it has not always been honored in Oregon, see *State v. Shull,* supra, citing *State v. Ogden,* 39 Or 195, 65 P 449 (1901), the Legislative Assembly believes the practice is generally observed today and should be continued.

The second sentence of subsection (1) does not circumscribe inquiry into bases of opinion and reputation testimony other than specific instances of conduct.

Subsection 2. Of the three methods of proving character—reputation, opinion and specific instances of conduct—the last is the most convincing. At the same time, it possesses the greatest capacity to arouse prejudice, confuse, surprise and consume time. Consequently, ORE 405 confines the use of evidence of specific instances of conduct on direct examination to two situations: (1) to prove character when character is, in the strict sense, in issue and hence deserving of a searching inquiry, and (2) to prove motive, opportunity, intent or any other of the purposes covered by subsection (3) of Rule 404. Paragraphs (2)(a) and (2)(b) of Rule 405 deal with these situations respectively. They do not alter existing Oregon law. *Karsun v. Kelley,* 258 Or 155, 482 P2d 533 (1971); *State v. Brown,* 231 Or 297, 372 P2d 779 (1962); *State v. Pace,* 187 Or 498, 212 P2d 755 (1949).

Under Rule 405, evidence of specific instances of conduct is not permissible on direct examination of an ordinary opinion witness to prove character. This is also true of witnesses to the character of witnesses under subsection (2) of Rule 608. Opinion testimony on direct examination in these situations should be confined to the nature and extent of observations and acquaintance upon which the opinion is based.

TEXT

Methods of Proving Character

While Rule 404 specifies when character evidence is allowed, Rule 405 specifies the form in which such character evidence may be offered. There are generally thought to be three ways to prove a person's character: by reputation, by opinion, or by specific instances of conduct. When a party is offering evidence of a person's character as an essential element of a charge, claim, or defense under Rule 404(1), all of the above types of character evidence may be offered. When the evidence is offered pursuant to Rule 404(2), only reputation or opinion evidence may be used. When the evidence is offered pursuant to Rule 404(3), only evidence of specific instances of conduct may be used. Whenever character is proven by opinion or reputation evidence, inquiry is allowed on cross-examination into relevant specific instances of conduct.

Rule 405 should be considered in conjunction with not only Rule 404, but with Rules 608(1), 608(2), and 803(21) as well. Rule 608(1) authorizes the use of reputation or opinion evidence to attack or rehabilitate the character of another witness for truthfulness or untruthfulness. Rule 608(2) prohibits both (1) extrinsic evidence of specific instances of conduct and (2) cross-examination regarding specific instances of conduct of a witness for purpose of attacking or supporting the credibility of that witness. Rule 803(21) provides that evidence of reputation "of a person's character among associates of the person or in the community" is an exception to the hearsay rule.

A character witness, whether testifying as to reputation or opinion, will not be allowed to testify until a foundation has been laid showing that the witness has either sufficient acquaintance with the reputation of the person in the relevant community or sufficient personal contact with the individual to provide a basis for an opinion regarding that person's character. The contact must have been recent enough so that there will be a current basis for the testimony. 1 McCormick, *Evidence* (4th ed 1992) § 43 at 159 (footnotes omitted) states:

> [I]t is generally agreed that proof may be made not only of the reputation of the witness where he lives, but also of his repute, as long as it is "general" and established, in any substantial community of people among whom he is well known, such as the group with whom he works, does business, or goes to school.

See also *State v. Miller*, 52 Or App 335, 628 P2d 444 (1981). See generally ANNOT., *Admissibility of Testimony as to General Reputation at Place of Employment*, 82 ALR3d 525 (1978).

On the issue of the court's authority to limit the number of character witnesses called, see ANNOT., *Propriety and Prejudicial Effect of Trial Court's Limiting Number of Character or Reputation Witnesses*, 17 ALR3d 327 (1968).

It is not proper on direct examination to inquire into the basis of the opinion or the reasons for the reputation. If the witness were asked to testify to more than the opinion or reputation itself, the witness would probably describe specific instances of conduct, which is not a permitted form of proof on direct examination under Rule 405. See *State v. Parks*, 71 Or App 630, 693 P2d 657 (1985) (to rebut claim of defendant's nonviolence, prosecutor called witness who testified that 20 years earlier defendant had chased another person around a service station swinging a hammer; *held* improper; character evidence under Rule 404(2)(a) must be in form of opinion or reputation, not specific instances); *State v. Hicks*, 133 Ariz 64, 649 P2d 267 (1982) (error for character witness regarding character of victim to testify that he had never seen the victim become physically violent).

In *State v. Marshall*, 312 Or 367, 373, 823 P2d 961, 964 (1991), a robbery prosecution, defendant sought to offer evidence that the alleged crime victim had a "reputation" for giving property as collateral for a debt and claiming it was stolen. The Supreme Court held that evidence of "reputation" of such specific behavior actually amounted to specific act evidence and was not admissible under either Rule 404(2)(b) or Rule 405(1). See also *State v. Reeder*, 137 Or App 421, 423–5, 904 P2d 644 (1995) (in sex abuse prosecution, proper to exclude evidence of **absence** of sex abuse complaints arising out of defendant's prior contact with children, because proof may not be made by reference to specific instances of conduct).

The provision in Rule 405 authorizing opinion testimony about character is likely to cause courts to be more receptive to opinions of experts, such as psychiatrists and psychologists. Under FRE 404 and 405, it has been held to be reversible error to exclude testimony of a psychologist called by defendant to testify about a pertinent trait of defendant's character. *United States v. Staggs*, 553 F2d 1073 (7th Cir 1977). See also *State v. Christensen*, 129 Ariz 32, 628 P2d 580, 582–3 (1981); *People v. Jones*, 42 Cal2d 219, 266 P2d 38 (1954). But see *United States v. MacDonald*, 688 F2d 224, 227–8 (4th Cir 1982), cert denied 459 US 1103, 103 SCt 726, 74 LEd2d 951 (1983) (trial court did not abuse its discretion in excluding the opinion of a psychiatrist that defendant possessed a "personality configuration inconsistent with the outrageous and senseless murders of [his] family.") See generally ANNOT., *Opinion Evidence as to Character of Accused Under Rule 405(a) of Federal Rules of Evidence*, 64 ALR Fed 244 (1983). See further discussion of psychological syndrome evidence under Rule 702.

Cross-Examination of a Character Witness

Although inquiry into specific instances of conduct is generally prohibited during direct examination of a character witness, it is expressly allowed during cross-examination. For example, if a criminal defendant offers evidence of a pertinent trait of character under Rule 404(2)(a) as circumstantial evidence that he did not commit the crime charged, the prosecution may cross-examine the character witnesses called by the defendant regarding specific instances of the defendant's prior conduct bearing upon that trait. See ANNOT., *Cross-Examination of Character Witness for Accused with Reference to Particular Acts or Crimes*, 47 ALR2d 1258 (1956). As the United States Supreme Court stated in *Michelson v. United States*, 335 US 469, 479, 69 SCt 213, 93 LEd 168 (1948), "The price a defendant must pay for attempting to prove his good name is to throw open the entire subject which the law has kept closed for his benefit and to make himself vulnerable where the law otherwise shields him."

If a defendant chooses to offer evidence regarding a pertinent trait of character, ordinarily it will be in the form of reputation or opinion evidence offered by a character witness. However, there is authority that a defendant who testifies to personal history or specific instances of conduct to prove he possesses a particular character trait may be viewed as having put his character in issue, thereby opening the door to cross-examination or rebuttal testimony with respect to that trait. In *State v. Guritz*, 134 Or App 262, 266, 894 P2d 1235, 1237 (1995), a prosecution of the defendant for sodomy upon his young daughter, the defendant sought to portray himself as a "good father" who would not molest his daughter. He described his activities with his daughter, which included regularly taking her to places such as malls and the park. To rebut this evidence, the prosecutor offered evidence that the defendant purchased marijuana while at the park with his daughter. The court found that the defendant had placed his character "in issue" by this evidence, thereby justifying introduction of the marijuana evidence to rebut his "characterization" of himself as a good father. See also *United States v. Giese*, 597 F2d 1170, 1190 (9th Cir 1979) (allowing rebuttal evidence where a defendant cites "specific instances of conduct as proof that he possesses a relevant character trait such as peaceableness"); McCormick, *Evidence* (3d ed 1984) § 191, p. 568–9.

Upon cross-examination of a character witness, the witness may be asked not only about prior convictions of the person about whose character he is testifying, but also about prior arrests. See *United States v. Watson*, 587 F2d 365 (7th Cir 1978), cert denied 439 US 1132 (1979); *United States v. Edwards*, 549 F2d 362 (5th Cir), cert denied 434 US 828 (1977). Questions can also be asked regarding other prior conduct, even though not the subject of a conviction or offense, if it is relevant to the character trait about which the witness testified on direct examination. *United States v. Reese,* 568 F2d 1246 (6th Cir 1977).

It has been held improper to question the character witness on the effect that the charges at issue in the pending case will have on the defendant's reputation or on the witness' opinion of his or her character. *United States v. Williams,* 738 F2d 172 (7th Cir 1984) (such questions found objectionable because they "allowed the prosecution to foist its theory of the case repeatedly on the jury" and forced the character witnesses to speculate about a possible conviction); *United States v. Curtis,* 644 F2d 263 (3rd Cir 1981). It has also been held improper to cross-examine a character witness about character traits other than the trait about which the witness testified. *State v. Swensen,* 40 Or App 465, 595 P2d 518 (1979) (improper to cross-examine about defendant's reputation for peaceableness when the witness testified only to the defendant's reputation for truthfulness).

Courts have discretion under Rule 403 to restrict the scope of cross-examination where the questions may be unfairly prejudicial, or may confuse the issues or mislead the jury. Courts are likely to restrict questioning about specific instances that are too remote in time. *State v. Williams,* 44 Or App 387, 605 P2d 1361 (1980); 2 J. Weinstein and M. Berger, *Weinstein's Evidence* (1988) ¶ 405[2].

It is improper for an attorney to cross-examine a character witness regarding prior instances of conduct when the attorney does not have a reasonable basis for believing such conduct actually occurred. Because of the enormous danger of prejudice inherent in this type of cross-examination, trial courts may require an *in camera* showing of a basis for the questions before they are asked. McCormick states:

> The trial judge, it is believed, should be required, before permitting the prosecuting counsel to cross-examine the character witness on rumors of misconduct of the accused, or upon arrests, charges or convictions, to request the prosecutor to give his professional statement to the judge (in the absence of the jury) that he has reasonable ground to believe, and does believe, that the crimes or misconduct which are imputed by the rumors, or which are the subject of the arrests or charges, were actually committed by the accused, and that the judgments of conviction inquired about were actually pronounced. Reasonable grounds would require, it is suggested, that the prosecutor's assurance be based on the statements of witnesses, believed to be credible, who purport to have firsthand knowledge.

McCormick, *Evidence* (2d ed 1972) § 191 at 458.

Whenever prior specific instances of conduct are brought out upon cross-examination of a character witness, the proponent of the witness is entitled to a limiting instruction under Rule 105 that such inquiries are to be considered only as bearing on the credibility of the character witness, not as evidence that such conduct actually occurred.

According to the Commentary, if the character witness testifies as to a person's reputation, questions regarding specific instances of prior conduct asked upon cross-examination should be prefaced with "have you heard." The assumption is that if the witness has not heard of a significant, relevant instance of conduct, the witness' testimony as to the person's reputation is less credible. If the character witness testifies in the form of an opinion, the inquiry upon cross-examination should be prefaced with "do you know," because it is the witness' own knowledge and basis for the opinion that is being tested.

The cross-examiner is required to accept the witness' answer to a question regarding specific instances of conduct. Extrinsic evidence to impeach an answer given upon cross-examination is not allowed. *United States v. Ling,* 581 F2d 1118, 1121 (4th Cir 1978).

RULE 406.   ORS 40.180. HABIT; ROUTINE PRACTICE

(1) **Evidence of the habit of a person or of the routine practice of an organization, whether corroborated or not and regardless of the presence of eyewitnesses, is relevant to prove that the conduct of the person or organization on a particular occasion was in conformity with the habit or routine practice.**

(2) **As used in this section, "habit" means a person's regular practice of meeting a particular kind of situation with a specific, distinctive type of conduct.**

LEGISLATIVE COMMENTARY

Oregon Rule of Evidence 406 indicates the relevance of personal habit and organizational routine practice to prove conduct on a particular occasion. Subsection (1) is identical to Rule 406 of the Federal Rules of Evidence. Subsection (2) is a paraphrase of language in the Advisory Committee's Note to Federal Rule 406. McCormick effectively describes habit by contrasting it with character:

> "Character and habit are close akin. Character is a generalized description of one's disposition, or of one's disposition in respect to a general trait, such as honesty, temperance, or peacefulness. 'Habit,' in modern usage, both lay and psychological, is more specific. It describes one's regular response to a repeated specific situation." McCormick, *Evidence* § 195 at 462 (2d ed 1972).

Equivalent behavior on the part of a group is designated "routine practice of an organization," and has been admitted along with habit in Oregon to prove conduct on a particular occasion. *Krause v. Eugene Dodge, Inc.,* 265 Or 486, 509 P2d 1199 (1973); *Robbins v. Steve Wilson,* 255 Or 4, 463 P2d 585 (1970); *Start v. Shell Oil Co.,* 202 Or 99, 260 P2d 468 (1954); *Shaver Forwarding Co. v. Eagle Star Ins. Co.,* 172 Or 91, 139 P2d 769 (1943).

Agreement is general that habit evidence is highly persuasive as proof of conduct on a particular occasion. Again, quoting McCormick:

> "Character may be thought of as the sum of one's habits though doubtless it is more than this. But unquestionably the uniformity of

one's response to habit is far greater than the consistency with which one's conduct conforms to character or disposition. Even though character comes in only exceptionally as evidence of an act, surely any sensible man in investigating whether X did a particular act would be greatly helped in his inquiry by evidence as to whether he was in the habit of doing it." *Id.* § 195 at 463.

Subsection (1). Subsection (1) changes Oregon law by eliminating the requirement that there be no eyewitnesses to an event before evidence will be admitted to prove that the conduct on that occasion was in conformity with habit. *Fenton v. Aleshire,* 238 Or 24, 393 P2d 219 (1964). The Legislative Assembly rejected the "no eyewitness" rule as illogical and unfair. First, the presence or absence of eyewitnesses is a mere fortuity, and otherwise probative evidence should not be admitted or excluded on the basis of circumstance. Second, usually the eyewitness is the opposing party, who thus benefits not once, by having a favorable witness, but twice, by excluding evidence of habit that might rebut the testimony of that Witness. See Note, "Evidence—Habitual Conduct—Admissibility in a Civil Action," in 45 Or L Rev 65 (1965).

McCormick comments that courts have adopted the "no-eyewitness" limitation because they have failed to draw a clear line between character and habit. McCormick § 195 at 463, 464. He notes that this failure is aggravated by the custom of describing character in terms of "habit," such as "habit of care" or "habit of intemperance." He concludes that courts thus mistakenly apply, to evidence of true habit, restrictions developed for the far less probative and more prejudicial evidence of character. The Legislative Assembly does not contemplate a great influx of habit evidence as a result of the no-eyewitness rule, because it has adopted a very restrictive definition of habit in subsection (2).

With respect to the routine practice of an organization, the requirement that evidence of a practice be corroborated before its admission is similar to the no-eyewitness rule. A considerable body of authority now requires corroboration. McCormick § 195 at 464 n 18; Slough, "Relevancy Unraveled," in 5 Kan L Rev 404, 449 (1957). The Legislative Assembly rejected this requirement as well, however, on the ground that it relates to sufficiency of the evidence rather than admissibility. The corroboration requirement already has been rejected by implication in Oregon. *Start v. Shell Oil Co.,* 202 Or 99, 273 P2d 225 (1954). Its express rejection under this rule therefore does not change the law.

Section (2). The Legislative Assembly felt it desirable to include a definition of "habit" in Rule 406. The definition is intended to forestall the use, as habit evidence, of evidence of conduct which in fact shows a character trait.

There has been much confusion between the concepts of habit and trait of character. Much character evidence has been smuggled into court under the guise of habit. A character trait, such as character for care, is a person's tendency to act in a certain way in all the varying situations of life—in business, in family life, in handling an automobile, in walking across the street. A habit, on the other hand, is the person's regular practice of meeting a particular situation with a specific type of conduct which is *distinctive.* Conduct is "distinctive" if there is some aspect of the activity that would set it apart from the ordinary response to the same situation.

For example, an individual who always stops a motor vehicle at a particular stop sign cannot be said to be in the "habit" of stopping at that sign. The individual's behavior is not distinctive. It is a response that is required by law and that is typical of the same intersection. However, if the individual never stops at that particular sign, then that distinctive and specific conduct is "habit."

Other examples of habit or routine practice can be found in Oregon case law. *State v. Mims,* 36 Or 315, 61 P 888 (1900) (habit of deceased to arm himself whenever he became involved in quarrel); *McMillan v. Montgomery,* 121 Or 28, 253 P 879 (1927) (practice of bank to give notice of dishonor); *Start v. Shell Oil Co.,* supra (practice of employer to instruct stenographer to enclose materials with dictated letters, and of stenographer always to follow instructions); *Fenton v. Aleshire,* supra (habit of child to use particular cross-walk); *Krause v. Eugene Dodge,* supra ("inflexible rule, habit and custom" of auto dealer to require that all buyer's orders be completely filled out before being signed by buyer); cf. *Blue v. City of Union,* 159 Or 5, 75 P2d 977 (1938) (evidence of person repeatedly riding horse rapidly and carelessly about streets of city not habit evidence).

Another area of disagreement regarding habit is the extent to which instances of conduct must be multiplied, and consistency of behavior maintained, for conduct to rise to the status of habit. Lewan, "Rationale of Habit Evidence," in 16 Syracuse L Rev 39, 49 (1964). Adequacy of sampling and uniformity of response are key factors that must be considered. It is not possible in this general rule, however, to express more precise standards for measuring their sufficiency for evidential purposes.

TEXT

Habit Evidence

Unlike most of the rules in Article IV, Rule 406 is a rule of admission rather than exclusion. It authorizes admission of evidence of a person's habits to show that conduct on a particular occasion conformed to these habits, and evidence of an organization's routine practices to show that conduct on a particular occasion conformed to these practices.

Rule 406 must be contrasted with Rule 404. Rule 404 provides, subject to certain exceptions, that evidence of a person's character is not admissible for the purpose of proving that the person acted in conformity therewith on a particular occasion. If the behavior of the person is a habit, rather than a character trait, Rule 406 provides for its admissibility. It is therefore essential to distinguish between the concepts of character and habit.

To assist in making this determination, Rule 406, unlike its federal counterpart, defines *habit. Habit* is stated to be "a person's regular practice of meeting a particular kind of situation with a specific, distinctive type of conduct." While this definition will aid courts and practitioners, it will not eliminate all difficulties in drawing the line between inadmissible character evidence and admissible habit evidence. The distinction between the two concepts is more one of degree than of kind. Character is the broader concept, generally indicating a person's disposition or propensity towards certain behavior, such as honesty, safe driving, or peaceableness. *Habit* refers to a more specific trait of character, one that is repeated with sufficient regularity to give it high probative value.

Character evidence is generally inadmissible because its probative value is low in proving that a person acted in conformity with that character on a particular occasion, and because the danger of prejudice is great due to the moral overtones often associated with it. In the case of habit evidence, the equation changes: the probative value of habit evidence is likely to be higher in proving conduct on a particular occasion and the danger of prejudice is likely to be less.

There are three criteria for determining whether conduct qualifies as habit under Rule 406(b). (1) It must be the "regular practice" of the person in responding to a particular kind of situation; (2) it must be "specific"; and (3) it must be "distinctive."

The concept of "regular practice" contains two components: frequency and invariability. If the conduct takes place infrequently, the court is unlikely to find it to be a regular practice. For example, if a person has responded to a particular situation only twice, even if the response was the same both times, the court will probably not find the response to be a habit.

Frequency is not enough, however, to qualify a certain conduct as a "regular practice." Such conduct must also be practiced invariably, or at least consistently. If a person engages in a particular conduct, such as fastening a seat belt, only 51% of the time, this would probably not satisfy the "regular practice" requirement. The more consistently a particular response is made, the more likely the court will be to find it is a habit. An obvious line of cross-examination when conduct is claimed to be a "habit" is to explore the number of times the person has deviated from the pattern of behavior. How much deviation courts will allow and still find the conduct to be a habit remains to be determined. If a person has a particular response only slightly more often than another response, this evidence has marginal probative value in determining what the response was on any given occasion.

The second requirement is that the conduct be "specific." This criterion of specificity is a primary distinction between habit evidence and character evidence. A person's tendency to be accident-prone, or to be routinely careful is probably too general to satisfy the definition of habit. However, a driver's behavior in always using a hand signal in addition to a turn signal or in always traveling a particular route to the office may satisfy the specificity requirement.

The third requirement—that the conduct be "distinctive"—was apparently added to encourage a narrow construction of the rule. Although this requirement is emphasized by the Commentary, it presents the most difficulty of interpretation. Merely because conduct is unusual or distinctive does not establish that it is a habit. On the other hand, many behaviors that would seem clearly to be habits are not distinctive. Many of the cases cited with approval in the Commentary where habit evidence was admitted under prior Oregon law do not involve distinctive conduct.

In *Charmley v. Lewis,* 302 Or 324, 729 P2d 567 (1986), the court adopted a pragmatic definition of "distinctive" that eliminates many of the potential difficulties in applying the rule. The court stated:

> [W]e conclude that the use of "distinctive" does not so much require that a certain act be wholly unusual in the sense that no one else does it ... as that it at least be a semi-automatic and recurring response, beyond mere obedience to the law, by an actor confronted by a particular situation to which a variety of definable responses would be more or less equally reasonable.

302 Or at 334. In *Charmley,* the court approved admission of evidence of plaintiff's "habit" of using the crosswalk when crossing the street at a particular intersection.

Courts are generally much more receptive to evidence of the routine practice of an organization than to evidence of the habit of an individual. This is partly because there is not the danger of admitting prohibited character evidence under the guise of habit evidence, because organizations are usually not thought to have a "character." Also, routine practices of an organization, such as mailing out billings monthly, are more likely to be invariable than are many individual behaviors that might be claimed to be habits.

Neither the rule nor the Commentary addresses how habit is to be proven or how much proof is necessary to establish the existence of a habit. Courts are likely to be more receptive to testimony from one witness about ten instances of identical response to a particular situation than to testimony from ten witnesses about only one instance each. The rule does not address whether a habit can be proved by opinion testimony. Arguably such a method of proof is proper if the witness has a sufficient basis of knowledge. See Advisory Committee Note, FRE 406.

Federal Cases

Under FRE 406 or its state counterparts, the following are examples of conduct held to constitute habit: *Meyer v. United States,* 464 F Supp 317 (D Colo 1979), aff'd 638 F2d 155 (10th Cir 1980) (habit of dentist to inform his patients of the risks of a particular surgical procedure); *South v. Nat'l R.R. Passenger Corp. (Amtrak),* 290 NW2d 819 (ND 1980) (habit of engineer often not to blow whistle at a particular crossing); *Shelton v. United States,* 1 Fed Evid Rep 481 (4th Cir 1976) (habit of leaving car in neutral before being hooked to tow mechanism of car wash); *Keltner v. Ford Motor Co.,* 748 F2d 1265 (8th Cir 1984) (habit of drinking a six pack of beer four nights a week); *Loughan v. Firestone Tire & Rubber Co.,* 749 F2d 1519 (11th Cir 1985) (habit of keeping cooler of beer in truck and drinking on the job).

Under FRE 406 or its state counterparts, the following have been held not to constitute evidence of habit: *United States v. Sampol,* 636 F2d 621 (DC Cir 1980) (assassinating Chilean exiles); *Reyes v. Missouri Pacific R.R. Co.,* 589 F2d 791 (5th Cir 1979) (four convictions for drunkenness over a three-and-a-half year period does not establish a habit); *Wilson v. Volkswagen of America, Inc.,* 561

F2d 494 (4th Cir 1977), cert denied 434 US 1020 (1978) (three defaults for failure to comply with the discovery order entered against defendant out of 200 cases is not sufficient to establish a habit of willful noncompliance); *Utility Control Corp. v. Prince William Construction Co.,* 558 F2d 716 (4th Cir 1977) (signature by B as guarantor on prior contract does not establish habit of giving B authority to guarantee other contracts); *State v. Gardner,* 91 NM 302, 573 P2d 236 (NM Ct App), cert denied 91 NM 249, 572 P2d 1257 (1977) (defendant's conduct of beating former wife and former girlfriend does not establish a habit when offered to prove beating of current girlfriend).

Routine Practice

In *State v. Bailey,* 87 Or App 664, 743 P2d 1123 (1987), a prosecution of a grocery store employee for theft of food, the court held it was error to exclude evidence of store's routine practice of allowing employees to eat food from store and pay for it later.

Under FRE 406 or its state counterparts, the following have been held to constitute evidence of the routine practice of an organization: *Amoco Production Co. v. United States,* 619 F2d 1383 (10th Cir 1980) (routine practice of reserving mineral interests in deeds admissible to establish that such reservation was likely in a deed, the original of which was unavailable); *United States v. Callahan,* 551 F2d 733 (6th Cir 1977) (routine practice of making payments to other union locals); *Williams v. Anderson,* 562 F2d 1081 (8th Cir 1977) (routine practice of engaging in racially discriminatory practices); *Envirex, Inc. v. Ecological Recovery Associates,* 454 F Supp 1329 (MD Pa 1978), aff'd 601 F2d 574 (3rd Cir 1979) (evidence of routine practice of business to send complete proposal, including page 18, to all general contractors was sufficient to support admission of page 18).

See generally ANNOT., *Admissibility of Evidence of Habit or Routine Practice Under Rule 406, Federal Rules of Evidence,* 53 ALR Fed 703 (1981); ANNOT., *Habit or Routine Practice Evidence Under Uniform Evidence Rule 406,* 64 ALR4th 567 (1988); ANNOT., *Proof of Mailing by Evidence of Business or Office Custom,* 45 ALR4th 476 (1986).

For a discussion of the related concepts of custom and usage, see Text under Rule 401.

RULE 407. ORS 40.185. SUBSEQUENT REMEDIAL MEASURES

When, after an event, measures are taken which, if taken previously, would have made the event less likely to occur, evidence of the subsequent measures is not admissible to prove negligence or culpable conduct in connection with the event. This section does not require the exclusion of evidence of subsequent measures when offered for another purpose,

such as proving ownership, control, or feasibility of precautionary measures, if controverted, or impeachment.

LEGISLATIVE COMMENTARY

Oregon Rule of Evidence 407 indicates the circumstances under which evidence of subsequent remedial measures is admissible. The rule is identical to Rule 407 of the Federal Rules of Evidence.

The first sentence of the rule incorporates conventional doctrine excluding evidence of subsequent remedial measures as proof of fault. The doctrine rests on two grounds. The first is that a subsequent remedial measure is not in fact an admission, because such conduct is also consistent with injury by mere accident or by operation of contributory negligence. However, under a liberal theory of relevancy this ground alone would not support exclusion, as the inference of culpable conduct is still possible. The second and stronger ground for exclusion is a social policy of encouraging people to take, or at least not discouraging them from taking, steps in furtherance of added safety. Courts have applied this principle to exclude evidence of subsequent repairs, installation of safety devices, changes in company rules, and discharge of employees; the language of the rule is broad enough to encompass all such measures. See Falknor, "Extrinsic Policies Affecting Admissibility," in 10 Rutgers L Rev 574, 590 (1956); McCormick *Evidence* § 275 at 666 (2d ed 1972). The rule merely restates decisional law in Oregon. *Rich v. Tite-Knot Pine Mill,* 245 Or 185, 421 P2d 370 (1960); *Phipps v. Air King Manufacturing Corp.,* 263 Or 141, 501 P2d 790 (1972).

The second sentence of the rule directs attention to its limits. Rule 407 only calls for exclusion when evidence of subsequent remedial measures is offered as proof of negligence or culpable conduct. The evidence may be allowable for other purposes such as to impeach, or, if they are controverted, to prove ownership, control, existence of duty of feasibility of precautionary measures. 2 Wigmore, *Evidence* § 283 (3d ed 1940); Annot., 64 ALR 2d 1296; *Parson v. Leavitt,* 249 Or 283, 437 P2d 843 (1968) (control); *Fields v. Fields,* 213 Or 522, 307 P2d 528, 326 P2d 451 (1958) (feasibility of precautionary measures). The requirement that the other purpose be controverted calls for automatic exclusion of the evidence if a genuine issue is not present, and allows the opposing party to lay the groundwork for exclusion by taking an admission. Absent an admission, the factors of undue prejudice, confusion of issues, and misleading the jury still remain for consideration under Rule 403.

The Legislative Assembly takes no position whether ORE 407 applies to exclude evidence of subsequent remedial measures in an action based on strict liability in tort. It leaves the resolution of this issue to decisional law.

TEXT

Subsequent Remedial Measures

Rule 407 declares that evidence of subsequent remedial measures is inadmissible to prove negligence or culpable conduct, both because of its low probative value and the public policy of encouraging such measures to be undertaken.

A wide range of remedial measures fall under the exclusionary principle of Rule 407. Under FRE 407, the following have been held to be subsequent remedial measures: the elimination of provisions in distributorship contracts challenged as violating the anti-trust laws, *Noble v. McClatchy Newspapers*, 533 F2d 1081 (9th Cir 1975), cert denied 433 US 908 (1977); a change in prison regulations that were challenged as unconstitutional, *Ford v. Schmidt*, 577 F2d 408 (7th Cir), cert denied 439 US 870 (1978); new warning labels on drugs regarding potential side effects, *Werner v. Upjohn Co.*, 628 F2d 848 (4th Cir 1980), cert denied 499 US 1080 (1981); changes in credit policies, *Vander Missen v. Kellogg—Citizens National Bank*, 481 F Supp 742 (ED Wis 1979); design changes, *Bauman v. Volkswagenwerk Aktiengesellschaft*, 621 F2d 230 (6th Cir 1980); placing of warning device in accident location, *Bouchard Transportation Co. v. Moran Towing & Transportation Co.*, 428 F Supp 153 (SD NY), aff'd 573 F2d 1291 (2nd Cir 1977); installation of protective devices in accident location, *Knight v. Otis Elevator Co.*, 596 F2d 84 (3rd Cir 1979); disciplinary action against an employee, *Maddox v. City of Los Angeles*, 792 F2d 1408 (9th Cir 1986). See ANNOT., *Admissibility of Repairs, Change of Conditions, or Precautions Taken After Accident—Modern State Cases*, 15 ALR5th 119 (1993).

Presumably other actions, such as changes in operating procedures, changes in operating instructions, and discharge of an employee alleged to have caused an injury, might also be viewed as subsequent remedial measures. However, the measure must be remedial of the "event" that is the basis of the plaintiff's claim, not remedial of some other danger. See *Van Gordon v. Portland General Electric Co.*, 298 Or 497, 693 P2d 1285 (1985) (Rule 407 does not apply to exclude evidence of new warning signs installed in a location that would not have prevented this accident).

A remedial measure will not be viewed as subsequent unless it was implemented subsequent to the event that is the basis for the claim. In *Hackett v. Alco Standard Corp.*, 71 Or App 24, 691 P2d 142 (1984), rev denied 298 Or 822, 698 P2d 963 (1985), the court held that in products liability litigation the "event" referred to by the rule is the resulting injury, not the manufacture of the product. Therefore, a change made prior to the injury is not subject to exclusion by the rule. See also *Arceneaux v. Texaco, Inc.*, 623 F2d 924 (5th Cir 1980), cert denied 450 US 928 (1981) (a design change implemented in 1971 to a 1966 GM pickup would not be excluded under FRE 407 with regard to an accident that occurred in 1974).

Evidence of a remedial measure also will not be viewed as excluded by the rule unless it was undertaken in response to the event, or at least with knowledge of the event. In *Van Gordon v. Portland General Electric Co.,* 298 Or 497, 693 P2d 1285 (1985), the plaintiff was burned in a hot springs at a park owned and operated by the defendant. The plaintiff introduced evidence that after the accident defendant installed new signs warning users of the park of the danger of the hot water. The court found Rule 407 inapplicable, in part because there was no evidence that the new signs were erected because of the injury to the plaintiff. The court held:

> [A] defendant must know of the prior event in order to fashion a safety meas-
> ure to remedy any hazard that caused the event. The evidence is uncontro-
> verted that new signs were not safety measures designed to remedy conditions
> that caused [plaintiff's] injury. The "event" referred to in the rule is the incident
> which caused the harm to the plaintiff. The rule does not apply in this case
> because the new signs were not an aftermath of the accident.

298 Or at 504, 693 P2d at 1289.

It has also been held that the rule is inapplicable to plans or preparation made prior to plaintiff's injury to undertake a remedial measure. *Rozier v. Ford Motor Co.,* 573 F2d 1332 (5th Cir 1978).

The federal courts are divided about the application of FRE 407 to govern-ment mandated remedial measures, such as recall notices. Compare *Kociemba v. G.D. Searle & Co.,* 683 F Supp 1579 (D Minn 1988) (FRE 407 does not apply to subsequent safety measures required by government) with *Chase v. General Motors Corp.,* 856 F2d 17 (4th Cir 1988) (FRE 407 bars evidence of a recall of an automobile made at the request of the National Highway Traffic Safety Admini-stration). It would seem that the rationale of the rule—to encourage potential defendants to act on their own to improve safety—should limit its application to subsequent remedial measures that were undertaken voluntarily. See Note, *The "Superior Authority Exception" to Federal Rule of Evidence 407: The "Remedial Measure" Required to Clarify a Confused State of Evidence,* 1991 U Ill L Rev 843.

Evidence of independent remedial actions undertaken by third parties, al-though not excluded by Rule 407, is generally irrelevant to prove a defendant's culpability. See *McPike v. Encisco's Cocina Mejicana, Inc.,* 93 Or App 269, 762 P2d 315 (1988) (action for death resulting from sulfite in food; evidence properly excluded of subsequent actions by Oregon Legislature and governmental agen-cies to ban or restrict sulfites in food).

Recent Cases

In *Ensign v. Marion County,* 140 Or App 114, 118–120, 914 P2d 5 (1996), the report of a Sheriff's board of review finding a deputy sheriff at fault in an automobile accident was not a "subsequent remedial measure" because "[o]ne cannnot investigate an accident before it occurs"; thus the postaccident investiga-tory report was not excluded by Rule 407; the court found it unnecessary to de-cide whether the reprimand of the deputy sheriff was a subsequent remedial measure that should have been excluded, because the error in admitting it, if any, was harmless.

In *Rush v. Troutman Investment Company*, 121 Or App 355, 854 P2d 968 (1993), where plaintiff was injured by a clothing rack that fell on her, an order by the manager to a sales clerk to take the rack down was held to be a subsequent remedial measure excluded by Rule 407.

Other Purposes

Rule 407 applies only when the evidence is offered to prove negligence or other culpable conduct. It does not exclude evidence offered for impeachment or for some other purpose, such as proving ownership, control, or feasibility of precautionary measures. It is clear from the legislative Commentary that the "other purpose" must be controverted before evidence of subsequent remedial measures may be introduced. The "if controverted" requirement of the rule is intended to apply to all permissible purposes, not just the purpose of proving the feasibility of precautionary measures.

If a party stipulates to an issue that the proponent is attempting to establish, the evidence of subsequent remedial measures should generally be excluded. However, a formal stipulation should not be required. In *Friedman v. National Presto Industries, Inc.*, 566 F Supp 762 (EDNY 1983), the court held that a stipulation of feasibility was not necessary to make an issue not "controverted," provided the defendant agreed not to argue the issue of feasibility.

A defendant may open the door to evidence of subsequent remedial measures by offering evidence that no remedial measures were necessary. In *Rimkus v. Northwest Colorado Ski Corp.*, 706 F2d 1060 (10th Cir 1983), the plaintiff sued defendant for negligence because of failure to mark a rocky outcropping on one of its slopes. Defendant presented evidence that the outcropping was clearly visible on the day in question. The court affirmed the admission of evidence that the outcropping was marked as a hazard on the morning following plaintiff's accident. Because defendant's evidence that the hazard was obvious raised the inference that no warning was necessary, plaintiff was entitled to refute that inference by showing the subsequent placing of the warning. See also *Anderson v. Malloy*, 700 F2d 1208, 1214 (8th Cir 1983), where defendant had testified that installation of peepholes and chain locks on the doors of a motel room where plaintiff had been raped would provide only a false sense of security. Plaintiff's evidence that subsequent remedial measures were later taken was held to be admissible both to show feasibility and to impeach defendant's testimony that such measures would not have been effective.

The Commentary recognizes that Rule 403 may require exclusion of the evidence, even if the evidence is offered for a permissible purpose, in cases where the prejudicial effect of the evidence outweighs its probative value. If the evidence is admitted for a permissible purpose, a limiting instruction under Rule 105 should be available upon request.

Federal Decisions

Evidence of subsequent remedial measures was allowed to prove the feasibility of precautionary measures under FRE 407 in the following cases: *Kenny v. Southeastern Pennsylvania Transp. Auth.*, 581 F2d 351 (3rd Cir 1978), cert denied 439 US 1073 (1979); *Doyle v. United States,* 441 F Supp 701 (DSC 1977); *Brown v. Link Belt Corp.*, 565 F2d 1107 (9th Cir 1977).

In *Dollar v. Long Mfg., N. C., Inc.*, 561 F2d 613, 618 (5th Cir 1977), cert denied 435 US 996 (1978), the court held that a letter from defendant's design engineer warning dealers of certain hazards in a backhoe was admissible under FRE 407 to impeach the trial testimony of the engineer that the backhoe was safe. See also *Polk v. Ford Motor Co.*, 529 F2d 259 (8th Cir), cert denied 426 US 907 (1976).

In *Benitez-Allende v. Alcan Aluminio do Brazil, Inc. S.A.*, 857 F2d 26 (1st Cir 1988), the court held that FRE 407 does not apply to bar internal investigatory reports, even if those investigatory reports may later lead to remedial measures.

An example of a decision excluding evidence of subsequent remedial repairs, which was offered to show the feasibility of such repairs, is *Knight v. Otis Elevator Co.*, 596 F2d 84 (3rd Cir 1979). The court noted: "[T]here was already testimony that such repairs could be made simply, easily and inexpensively. Thus, additional evidence on this issue would have been cumulative at best and prejudicial at worst." 596 F2d at 91. See generally ANNOT., *Admissibility of Evidence of Subsequent Remedial Measures Under Rule 407 of Federal Rules of Evidence,* 50 ALR Fed 935 (1980).

Strict Liability Claims

The legislature intentionally left unanswered the question of whether Rule 407 applies to claims based upon strict liability. Because the rule applies only where evidence of subsequent remedial measures is offered to prove "negligence or culpable conduct," it can be argued that it is not applicable to a strict liability claim.

The issue was finally resolved in *Krause v. American Aerolights, Inc.*, 307 Or 52, 762 P2d 1011 (1988), where the Supreme Court held that Rule 407 applies to products liability cases based upon strict liability. Although the court questioned the legislative rationale for the rule, it held that the stated rationale applied to strict liability claims as well as negligence claims. The court stated:

> [T]he rationale underlying OEC 407 is a legislative rationale, not necessarily a logical nor indeed a realistic rationale. But we do not change legislative policy. We perceive no compelling reason to distinguish between strict liability claims and negligence claims. We therefore apply the exclusionary rule of OEC 407 to strict liability claims as well as to negligence claims. If the legislature does not like this decision, it knows how to correct it. Several states have enacted statutes removing products liability claims from the subsequent remedial repair rule.

307 Or at 61, 762 P2d at 1016.

In applying Rule 407 to strict liability cases, the Oregon Supreme Court adopts the view taken by a majority of federal circuits considering the issue under FRE 407. However, the decision is contrary to the majority view taken by other state appellate courts under their state counterparts to FRE 407. For a listing of state and federal authorities on the issue, see *Krause,* 307 Or at 59, 762 P2d at 1015.

For commentaries on this issue, see ANNOT., *Admissibility of Evidence of Subsequent Repairs or Other Remedial Measures in Products Liability Cases,* 74 ALR 3d 1001 (1976); Henderson, *Product Liability and Admissibility of Subsequent Remedial Measures: Resolving the Conflict by Recognizing the Difference Between Negligence and Strict Tort Liability,* 64 Neb L Rev 1 (1985); NOTE, *Subsequent Remedial Measures in Strict Liability: Later Opinions as Evidence of Defects in Earlier Reasoning,* 32 Cath U L Rev 895 (1983); NOTE, *The Admissibility of Subsequent Remedial Measures in Strict Liability Actions: Some Suggestions Regarding Federal Rule of Evidence 407,* 39 Wash & Lee L Rev 1415 (1982); COMMENT, *Federal Rule of Evidence 407 and its State Variations: The Courts Perform Some Subsequent Remedial Measures Of Their Own in Products Liability Cases,* 49 UMKC L Rev 338 (1981).

Employers' Liability Act Claim

It appears that Rule 407 will be inapplicable to claims arising under the Employers' Liability Act. In *Rich v. Tite-Knot Pine Mill,* 245 Or 185, 199, 421 P2d 370, 377 (1966), the court stated:

> It is the rule that common law negligence may not be proved by the introduction of evidence that subsequent to the accident in question defendant made improvements or repairs to the instrumentality that caused the injury. This rule is inapplicable to a claim under the Employer's Liability Act because of the provisions of ORS 654.305.

ORS 654.305 provides:

> Protection and safety of persons in hazardous employment generally. Generally, all owners, contractors or subcontractors and other persons having charge of, or responsible for, any work involving a risk or danger to the employees or the public, shall use every device, care and precaution which it is practicable to use for the protection and safety of life and limb, limited only by the necessity for preserving the efficiency of the structure, machine or other apparatus or device, and without regard to the additional cost of suitable material or safety appliance and devices.

RULE 408. ORS 40.190. COMPROMISE AND OFFERS TO COMPROMISE

(1) (a) Evidence of furnishing or offering or promising to furnish, or accepting or offering or promising to accept, a valuable consideration in compromising or attempting to compromise a claim which was disputed as to either validity or amount, is not admissible to prove liability for or invalidity of the claim or its amount.

(b) Evidence of conduct or statements made in compromise negotiations is likewise not admissible.

(2) (a) Subsection (1) of this section does not require the exclusion of any evidence otherwise discoverable merely because it is presented in the course of compromise negotiations.

(b) Subsection (1) of this section also does not require exclusion when the evidence is offered for another purpose, such as proving bias or prejudice of a witness, negating a contention of undue delay, or proving an effort to obstruct a criminal investigation or prosecution.

LEGISLATIVE COMMENTARY

Oregon Rule of Evidence 408 indicates the circumstances under which evidence of compromise and offers to compromise may be admitted. The rule is based on Rule 408 of the Federal Rules of Evidence. The language of the federal rule has been divided into subsections and paragraphs for the sake of clarity.

Subsection (1). Paragraph (a). This paragraph states the general rule followed in Oregon, that evidence of an offer to compromise a claim is not receivable in evidence as an admission of either the validity or the invalidity of the claim. McCormick, *Evidence* § 274 (2d ed 1972); ORS 41.810; *Dalk v. Lachmund,* 157 Or 152, 70 P2d 558 (1939). As with evidence of subsequent remedial measures, discussed in Rule 407, exclusion may be based on either relevancy or policy considerations. The evidence can be considered irrelevant on the ground that an offer of compromise may stem as much from a desire for peace as from a sense of weakness. However, the validity of this position depends on the relative amounts of the offer and claim, a small offer to settle a large claim being more easily construed as a desire for peace. A more consistent and weightier ground for exclusion is the promotion of the public policy favoring compromise and settlement of disputes. McCormick §§ 74, 274. While the rule is ordinarily phrased in terms of offers of compromise, it is apparent that a similar attitude must be taken with respect to completed compromises when offered against a party thereto. *Zahumensky v. Fanrich,* 200 Or 588, 267 P2d 664 (1954).

The policy considerations that underlie ORE 408 do not come into play when the effort is to induce a creditor to settle an admittedly due amount for a lesser sum. McCormick § 274 at 663. Therefore, paragraph (a) requires that the claim be disputed as to either validity or amount.

Paragraph (b). This paragraph changes Oregon law by making evidence of conduct or statements made in compromise negotiations inadmissible at trial. Until now, Oregon has followed the common law rule under which an admission of fact made in the course of compromise negotiations is not protected unless it is hypothetical or is expressly stated to be "without prejudice," or is so inseparably connected with the offer that it cannot be correctly understood without reading the two together. ORS 41.180; *Sims v. Sowle,* 238 Or 329, 395 P2d 133 (1964); *Broadway Finance, Inc. v. Tadorovich,* 216 Or 475, 339 P2d 436 (1939). See McCormick § 274 at 663, 664. An inevitable effect of that rule is to inhibit freedom of communication with respect to compromise, even among lawyers. Another effect is to generate controversy whether a negotiating statement is protected or not. The Legislative Assembly was persuaded by these considerations in rejecting the common law rule. Henceforth, evidence of conduct or any statement made in compromise negotiations, as well as the offer or completed compromise itself, is not admissible. The broad purpose of this rule is to insure that frank and open negotiations will take place without fear that what is said during negotiations will be used against the parties at trial.

The policy of favoring compromises and settlement of disputes which ORE 408 is intended to promote also finds expression in ORS 135.435(1)(c). This provides that admissions made by a criminal defendant during plea negotiations are not admissible. However, an effort to "buy off" prosecution or a prosecuting witness in a criminal case is not within the policy of this paragraph, and is not privileged. McCormick § 274 at 665.

Subsection (2). Subsection (2) of Rule 408 limits the application of subsection (1).

Paragraph (a). This paragraph is designed to prevent abuse of underlying policy favoring settlement of disputes. To prevent a party from immunizing evidence by presenting it during negotiations, the rule provides that the other party may discover the evidence by other means, and present it at trial, so long as no reference is made to the compromise negotiations.

Paragraph (b). This paragraph allows admission of evidence of compromise when that evidence is offered for some purpose other than to prove the validity or invalidity of a claim or its amount. The illustrations mentioned in the paragraph are supported by the authorities. McCormick § 274 at 664 (to negate claim of lack of due diligence); Annot., 161 ALR 995 (to show bias or prejudice of witness); contra, *Fenberg v. Rosenthal,* 348 Ill App 510, 109 NE 2d 402 (1952).

TEXT

Offers to Compromise

Rule 408 provides that evidence of a compromise agreement or offer of compromise is generally inadmissible to prove either the validity or invalidity of a claim. It also excludes factual admissions made in the course of compromise negotiations. See *Bourrie v. US. Fidelity and Guaranty Insurance Co.,* 75 Or App 241, 244, 707 P2d 60 (1985) (affirming exclusion of exhibit on ground that it contained statements regarding loss that were made during negotiations to compromise a disputed claim).

Rule 408 contains important qualifications. It does not exclude evidence of furnishing or offering to furnish, or accepting or offering to accept, a valuable consideration unless made "in compromising or attempting to compromise a claim which was disputed as to either validity or amount." The purpose of this language is to restrict the rule to attempts to compromise a genuinely disputed claim.

A billing statement for a specified amount or an acknowledgment of debt for a specified amount is not excluded by the rule, unless a dispute had arisen and the parties were attempting to compromise that dispute. See *Big O Tire Dealers, Inc. v. Goodyear Tire & Rubber Co.,* 561 F2d 1365 (10th Cir 1977), cert dismissed 434 US 1052 (1978) (evidence found to be of "business communications" rather than compromise negotiations). Cf. *Delaney v. Georgia-Pacific Corp.,* 42 Or App 439, 450–1, 601 P2d 475 (1979) (offer to buy the shares of a joint venture was not intended as a compromise or settlement and thus evidence of it was admissible in subsequent litigation). See generally ANNOT., *Evidence Involving Compromise or Offer of Compromise as Inadmissible Under Rule 408 of Federal Rules of Evidence,* 72 ALR Fed 592 (1985).

According to the Commentary, Rule 408 also will not exclude an offer of compromise for a lesser amount when the offeror admits liability for the whole amount, because in this case the claim is not "disputed as to either validity or amount."

The rule is not limited to settlement offers or agreements between the parties. It is improper to use a settlement made with a third person as bearing on the validity or amount of the plaintiff's claim. For example, in a malpractice action against a doctor, it is generally improper to inform the jury about a settlement between the plaintiff and the hospital. *Holger v. Irish,* 316 Or 402, 414, 851 P2d 1122 (1993); *Pounds v. Holy Rosary Medical Center,* 127 Or App 221, 224, 872 P2d 437, 439 (1994), rev denied 320 Or 109, 881 P2d 141 (1994).

Under FRE 408, which is essentially identical, courts have also excluded settlement offers and agreements between a party and a nonparty, when offered "to prove liability for or invalidity of the claim or its amount." *Saf-Gard Products, Inc. v. Service Parts, Inc.,* 491 F Supp 996 (D Ariz 1980); *Scaramuzzo v. Glenmore Distilleries,* 501 F Supp 727 (ND Ill. 1980); *Magnavox Co. v. APF Electronics, Inc.,* 496 F Supp 29 (ND Ill. 1980).

However, if the person with whom the settlement was made is called as a witness, the settlement offer or agreement may be admissible to impeach that witness for bias. *Sharp v. Hall,* 482 F Supp 1 (ED Okla 1978); *John McShain, Inc. v. Cessna Aircraft Co.,* 563 F2d 632 (3rd Cir 1977); *Dongo v. Banks,* 448 A2d 885, 890–1 (Maine 1982). Courts are reluctant to allow settlement agreements with third persons to be used to impeach a party witness. See *Reichenbach v. Smith,* 528 F2d 1072 (5th Cir 1976); 2 McCormick, *Evidence* (4th ed 1992) § 266 at 177.

Any settlement with third persons may not be considered by the jury on the question of damages. In *Yardley v. Rucker Brothers Trucking Inc.,* 42 Or App 239, 243, 600 P2d 485 (1979) the court held that:

> *either:* (1) evidence is not admissible about the existence or amount of the settlement [with a third person]; or (2) in appropriate circumstances evidence of the existence of the settlement can be admitted—for example, to explain why likely defendants are not in the case—provided that the court then instructs the jury in unequivocal language to disregard the settlement and return the verdict for the full amount of the plaintiff's damages.

Other Purposes

Rule 408(2)(b) provides that evidence of a compromise agreement or compromise offer may be admissible for other purposes, such as proving bias or prejudice of a witness, negating a contention of undue delay, or proving an effort to obstruct a criminal investigation or prosecution. The list of permissible purposes set forth in Rule 408(2)(b) does not purport to be exclusive. Perhaps the most significant unresolved issue under this subsection is whether statements made in the course of settlement negotiations can be used at trial to impeach the person who made the statement if that person appears as a witness. The Commentary does not address this issue. The commentators are divided. Compare C. Mueller & L. Kirkpatrick, MODERN EVIDENCE (1995) § 4.29 (admissible to impeach only in "egregious circumstances where the interests of justice compel their introduction") with M. Graham, HANDBOOK OF FEDERAL EVIDENCE (4th ed 1996) § 408.1 (inadmissible to impeach). See 23 C. Wright & K. Graham, FEDERAL PRACTICE AND PROCEDURE (1980) § 5314 at 283–7 (admissible to impeach, but jury should not be told statement made during settlement negotiations). See also Hjelmeset, *Impeachment of Party by Prior Inconsistent Statement in Compromise Negotiations: Admissibility Under Federal Rule of Evidence 408,* 43 Clev. St. L. Rev. 75 (1995).

The rule has been held inapplicable to an offer being introduced to show a failure to mitigate damages. In *Thomas v. Resort Health Related Facility,* 539 F Supp 630 (EDNY 1982), the plaintiff sought damages, reinstatement, and back pay under Title VII. The defendant had made an offer of reinstatement to plaintiff and moved for a partial summary judgment limiting any back pay recovery to the period between the suspension and the time of the offer of reinstatement. The trial court held that evidence of the offer was admissible under FRE 408 because it was not being offered to prove the validity or invalidity of the claim, but only to show that any lost pay subsequent to the time of the offer of reinstatement was not attributable to the defendant.

If a settlement agreement is breached, and a party sues to enforce the agreement, Rule 408 presumably would not exclude evidence of the agreement, because it is not being offered to prove liability on the underlying claim, but only to prove the terms of the agreement. If the party sues on the underlying claim, however, Rule 408 is arguably applicable.

Rule 408 is consistent with ORCP 54E, which provides that a rejected offer of compromise under the procedure provided in ORCP 54E "shall not be given in evidence on the trial." It is also consistent with ORS 41.815, which prohibits evidence of an attempt by a defendant to comply with ORCP 32I in settling a class action.

RULE 409. ORS 40.195. PAYMENT OF MEDICAL AND SIMILAR EXPENSES

Evidence of furnishing or offering or promising to pay medical, hospital or similar expenses occasioned by an injury is not admissible to prove liability for the injury. Evidence of payment for damages arising from injury or destruction of property is not admissible to prove liability for the injury or destruction.

LEGISLATIVE COMMENTARY

Oregon Rule of Evidence 409 is based on Rule 409 of the Federal Rules of Evidence. The first sentence is identical to the federal rule. The second sentence covering payments for property damage was added for consistency with section 79.

The considerations that underlie Rule 409 parallel those behind Rules 407 and 408, dealing respectively with subsequent remedial measures and offers of compromise. As stated in Annot., 20 ALR 2d 291, 293:

> "[G]enerally, evidence of payment of medical hospital or similar expenses of an injured party by the opposing party is not admissible, the reason often given being that such payment or offer is usually made from humane impulses and not from an admission of liability, and that to hold otherwise would tend to discourage assistance to the injured person."

Contrary to Rule 408, Rule 409 does not extend protection to conduct or statements not a party of the act of furnishing or offering or promising to pay. This difference in treatment arises from a fundamental difference in the nature of the transactions. Extensive communication is essential if compromises are to be effected, and consequently broad protection of statements is needed. This is not so in the case of furnishing or offers or promises to pay medical expenses, where factual statements may be expected to be incidental in nature.

The rule does not alter Oregon law. In Oregon, evidence of payment of the expenses of an injured party by the opposing party is not admissible to prove liability. ORS 41.950 to 41.980; *Briggs v. John Yeon Co.*, 168 Or 239, 122 P2d 444 (1942). Statements made in conjunction with the payment of an injured party's expenses, however, are admissible. Id.: *Dunning v. Northwestern Electric Co.*, 186 Or 379, 199 P2d 648 (1949); *Sims v. Sowle*, 238 Or 329, 395 P2d 133 (1964). An advance payment is also admissible as an admission of liability, if the parties so agree in writing. ORS 41.960(1), 41.970.

TEXT

Payment of Medical and Similar Expenses

Rule 409 excludes evidence of furnishing or offering to pay medical, hospital, or similar expenses resulting from an injury, and evidence of payment for damages arising out of injury to property, for purpose of proving liability for such injury.

Although the rule is based on policy considerations similar to those underlying Rule 408, there are significant differences. Rule 409, unlike Rule 408, applies whether or not a controversy has arisen and whether or not the claim is disputed. Also, it does not require exclusion of collateral factual statements, such as admissions of fault, made by the person making the offer, promise, or payment.

Rule 409 would not exclude statements of remorse, such as "I am sorry you were injured," because such a statement is not an offer to pay medical, hospital, or similar expenses. A mere statement of remorse is likely to be excluded as irrelevant under Rule 401, however, because a party may understandably regret injury to another even in a situation where the party is not responsible for such injury. If the statement is an apology for the declarant's conduct or an admission of fault, it may be admissible. See *Sims v. Sowle,* 238 Or 329, 365 P2d 133 (1964).

Evidence of an offer to pay medical, hospital, or similar expenses or property damage offered for a purpose other than "to prove liability for the injury" is not restricted by Rule 409. The admissibility of such evidence would be determined by Rules 401 and 403. If such an offer mentions insurance, Rule 411 must also be considered.

RULE 410.   ORS 40.200. WITHDRAWN PLEA OR STATEMENT NOT ADMISSIBLE

(1) **A plea of guilty or no contest which is not accepted or has been withdrawn shall not be received against the defendant in any criminal proceeding.**

(2) **No statement or admission made by a defendant or a defendant's attorney during any proceeding relating to a plea of guilty or no contest which is not accepted or has been withdrawn shall be received against the defendant in any criminal proceeding.**

LEGISLATIVE COMMENTARY

Oregon Rule of Evidence 410 is a restatement of ORS 135.445. Believing that the current Oregon statute relating to the admissibility of withdrawn or rejected pleas of guilty or no contest is satisfactory, the Legislative Assembly did not adopt Federal Rule 410. The last sentence of that rule would have changed Oregon law by allowing a defendant's statement made in connection with a plea of guilty or no contest to be admitted as evidence under certain conditions, in a subsequent criminal proceeding for perjury or false statement. See *State v. Aldridge*, 33 Or App 37, 575 P2d 675 (1978).

TEXT

Withdrawn Plea; Plea Negotiations

Rule 410 prohibits evidence of a withdrawn or rejected plea of guilty or no contest, as well as evidence of any statements made by defense counsel or a defendant at a hearing on such a plea, from being received against the defendant in any criminal proceeding. Such statements may not be received even for impeachment. The purpose of the rule is to facilitate plea negotiations and to make effective any withdrawal of a guilty plea, when such withdrawal is allowed.

Rule 410, unlike FRE 410, does not exclude statements made in the course of plea negotiations, only statements made at a proceeding relating to a plea of guilty or no contest that is not accepted or has been withdrawn. However, statements made during plea negotiations are excluded by ORS 135.435, which provides:

> (1) Except as provided in subsection (2) of this section, none of the following shall be received in evidence for or against a defendant in any criminal or civil action or administrative proceeding:
> (a) The fact that the defendant or his counsel and the district attorney engaged in plea discussions.
> (b) The fact that the defendant or his attorney made a plea agreement with the district attorney.
> (c) Any statement or admission made by the defendant or his attorney to the district attorney and as part of the plea discussion or agreement.
> (2) The provisions of subsection (1) of this section shall not apply if, subsequent to the plea discussions or plea agreement, the defendant enters a plea of guilty or no contest which is not withdrawn.

Rule 410 does not restrict the use of guilty pleas or no contest pleas that are not withdrawn, nor does it restrict the use of convictions based upon such pleas. See Rule 609; Rule 803(22). A plea of guilty will normally constitute an admission, which may be received in evidence against a party if relevant and not otherwise excluded by rule or statute. See Rule 801(4)(b)(A). See also Rule 804(3)(c) (declaration against interest).

ORS 41.905(2) provides: "A plea of guilty by a person to a traffic offense may be admitted as evidence in the trial of a subsequent civil action arising out of the same accident or occurrence as an admission of the person entering the plea, and for no other purpose."

In the case of traffic infractions, however, ORS 153.585(2) provides: "Notwithstanding ORS 43.130 and 43.160, no plea, finding or proceeding upon any traffic infraction shall be used for the purpose of res judicata or collateral estoppel nor shall any plea, finding or proceeding upon any traffic infraction be admissible as evidence, in any civil proceeding."

The literal language of ORS 135.435 excludes only plea bargaining statements made to the prosecutor. What if the statements are made to a police officer who has or claims to have authority from the district attorney to conduct plea bargain discussions? Federal courts have sometimes excluded a defendant's statements in this circumstance. See Mueller & Kirkpatrick, MODERN EVIDENCE (1995) § 4.31.

If a police officer induces a defendant to make an incriminating statement under a promise of leniency, the admissibility of the statement is subject to the law pertaining to the voluntariness of admissions. In *State v. Aguilar*, 133 Or App 304, 891 P2d 668 (1995), a police officer questioned the defendant about two robberies and promised him that if he confessed he would be charged with only one robbery. The defendant confessed to both robberies and was charged with both. The appellate court held that his confession to the second robbery was properly suppressed as involuntary because it was given in response to an offer of immunity. The court remanded for a further hearing on whether the confession to the first robbery was also involuntary.

In *State v. Pollard*, 132 Or App 538, 543, 888 P2d 1054, rev denied 321 Or 138, 894 P2d 469 (1995), the court reaffirmed that "admissions obtained by an express or implied promise of immunity or leniency are involuntary as a matter of law under the Oregon Constitution, Article I, section 12." There, the court held that the defendant's incriminating statement that he caused the injury that led to the death of his infant son was improperly admitted because the interrogating officer impliedly suggested that by confessing the defendant would receive treatment in lieu of prosecution.

See generally Dahlin, *Will Plea Bargaining Survive United States v. Mezzanatto?*, 74 Or L Rev 1365 (1995).

RULE 411.   ORS 40.205. LIABILITY INSURANCE

(1) **Except where lack of liability insurance is an element of an offense, evidence that a person was or was not insured against liability is not admissible upon the issue whether the person acted negligently or otherwise wrongfully.**

(2) **Subsection (1) of this section does not require the exclusion of evidence of insurance against liability when offered for another pur-**

pose, such as proving agency, ownership or control, or bias, prejudice or motive of a witness.

LEGISLATIVE COMMENTARY

Oregon Rule of Evidence 411 is nearly identical to Rule 411 of the Federal Rules of Evidence. The language of the federal rule has been divided into subsections to provide clearer organization.

Subsection (1). The courts have generally rejected evidence of liability insurance as proof of fault and absence of liability insurance as proof of lack of fault. McCormick, *Evidence* § 201 (2d ed 1972). Oregon is among the jurisdictions taking this position. *Sherrick v. Landstrom,* 229 Or 415, 267 P2d 452 (1961). The inference of fault from the fact of insurance coverage is at best tenuous, and its converse equally so. More important, no doubt, is the feeling that knowledge of the presence or absence of insurance may induce juries to decide cases on improper grounds. McCormick § 201 at 481; Annot., 4 ALR 2d 761. Subsection (1) is drafted in broad terms to include contributory negligence or other fault of a plaintiff, as well as fault of a defendant. It does allow evidence of lack of liability insurance to be admitted to prove fault in the unique case where this is an element of an offense charged. ORS 486.075, 486.991.

Subsection (2). Subsection (2) limits the application of subsection (1). It provides that evidence of insurance is admissible for purposes other than proving fault, such as proving control or prejudice of a witness. *Blake v. Roy Webster Orchards,* 249 Or 348, 437 P2d 757 (1968) (control); *Rigelman v. Gilligan,* 265 Or 109, 506 P2d 710 (1973) (prejudice of witness). Like subsection (3) of Rule 404, however, subsection (2) of Rule 411 does not guarantee the admission of evidence offered for a non-forbidden purpose. See *Fairbrother v. Rinker,* 274 Or 525, 547 P2d 605 (1976) (evidence of insurance coverage, offered to show bias, excluded when there was sufficient other evidence available that could be offered without prejudice).

The procedure that a court must follow when the fact of insurance has been injected into proceedings varies according to the nature of the disclosure. Where the disclosure was inadvertent, the trial judge has discretion to grant a mistrial or instruct the jury to disregard the evidence of insurance. *Blake v. Roy Webster Orchards,* supra; *DeSpain v. Bohlke,* 259 Or 320, 486 P2d 545 (1971), discussed in Note, "DeSpain v. Bohlke and Exclusion of Evidence of Insurance in Oregon," in 8 Will LJ 294 (1972). In this regard, it should be noted that there is a trend against the rule that any reference to insurance is necessarily prejudicial to the litigants. McCormick § 201 at 482. When the reference to insurance is advertent, however, the judge must grant a mistrial. Id.

TEXT

Liability Insurance

Rule 411 adopts the long-established rule that evidence of liability insurance coverage or lack thereof is inadmissible upon the issue of whether a person acted negligently or otherwise wrongfully, except where lack of insurance is an element of the offense. Under Rule 411(2) evidence of liability insurance coverage may be admissible for other purposes, such as proving agency, ownership or control or bias, prejudice or motive of a witness. The rule is applicable to both defendants and plaintiffs, in circumstances where evidence of insurance is being offered to prove negligence or wrongful conduct.

On the issue of whether or not insurance can be mentioned as part of an admission by a party, see *Cameron v. Columbia Builders Inc.,* 212 Or 388, 393–4, 320 P2d 251 (1958) (the reference to insurance should be excluded unless essential to understanding the admission).

Before evidence of insurance is admitted for the purposes specified in Rule 411(2), those issues should be controverted. If the opponent stipulates to the issue, proof of insurance will generally be unnecessary. In some cases, the prejudicial effect of the evidence of insurance will outweigh its probative value, even for a limited purpose, and the evidence may be excluded under Rule 403. The Commentary expressly notes that Rule 411(2) "does not guarantee the admission of evidence offered for a non-forbidden purpose."

Nonetheless, it may be reversible error in some cases for a court to exclude evidence of liability insurance when offered for a purpose other than showing negligence or wrongdoing, particularly if the purpose is to show the bias of a witness. In *Charter v. Chleborad,* 551 F2d 246 (8th Cir), cert denied 434 US 856 (1977), a judgment for defendant was reversed because of the refusal of the trial court to allow the plaintiff to bring out on cross-examination that a witness called by defendant to impeach plaintiff's medical expert was employed by defendant's liability carrier. See also *Rigelman v. Gilligan,* 265 Or 109, 506 P2d 710 (1973) and the Commentary to Rule 609-1.

In *Ouachita Nat'l Bank v. Tosco Corp.,* 686 F2d 1291, 1301 (8th Cir 1982), the court affirmed the admission of evidence of insurance coverage offered by the *defendant,* who was the insured party. The defendant intended to call an insurance adjuster as a witness and wanted to reveal the insurance coverage itself to show the possible bias of the witness, presumably so as not to seem to have been hiding this fact from the jury. The court found that FRE 411 is designed primarily to protect the insured party and that knowledge that the defendant, an oil company, carried insurance would not be prejudicial to the plaintiff.

Rule 411 does not address all issues relating to evidence of insurance that may arise in litigation. It does not cover insurance other than liability insurance. It does not address whether any inquiry relating to insurance can be made of prospective jurors. It does not discuss the appropriate sanctions when improper mention of insurance is made during a trial. See *Washburn v. Holbrook,* 106 Or App 60, 806 P2d 702 (1991) (mention of insurance will result in mandatory mis-

trial only when the subject of insurance is improperly and intentionally introduced); *Broyles v. Estate of Brown,* 295 Or 795, 671 P2d 94 (1983) (if mention of
insurance by witness was inadvertent, whether to grant a mistrial is within the
discretion of the trial court); *Lunski v. Lindemann,* 270 Or 316, 527 P2d 254
(1974) (even intentional mention of insurance does not always compel granting
of mistrial).

Rule 411 also does not address whether the existence of insurance coverage
is a proper matter for discovery. This last question is instead addressed by ORCP
36B(2)(a), which provides:

> A party, upon the request of a adverse party, shall disclose the existence and
> contents of any insurance agreement or policy under which a person transact-
> ing insurance may be liable to satisfy part or all of a judgment which may be
> entered in the action or to indemnity or reimburse for payments made to sat-
> isfy the judgment.

ORCP 36B(2)(c) states:

> Information concerning the insurance agreement or policy is not by reason of
> disclosure admissible in evidence at trial.

Rule 411 is unclear about whether it applies to strict liability claims, because
it excludes only evidence offered to show that the defendant acted "negligently
or otherwise wrongfully." Arguably it should extend to such claims, because the
similar language of Rule 407 has been held applicable to strict liability claims.
See *Krause v. American Aerolights, Inc.,* 307 Or 52, 762 P2d 1011 (1988). See
text after Rule 407, supra.

See generally ANNOT., *Admissibility, After Enactment of Rule 411, Federal
Rules of Evidence, of Evidence of Liability Insurance in Negligence Actions,* 40 ALR
Fed 541 (1978); ANNOT., *Counsel's Argument or Comment Stating or Implying
that Defendant is Not Insured and Will Have to Pay Verdict Himself as Prejudicial
Error,* 68 ALR4th 954 (1989).

RULE 412. ORS 40.210. SEX OFFENSE CASES; RELEVANCE OF VICTIM'S PAST BEHAVIOR

(1) Notwithstanding any other provision of law, in a prosecution for a
crime described in ORS 163.355 to 163.427, or in a prosecution for an
attempt to commit such a crime, reputation or opinion evidence of
the past sexual behavior of an alleged victim of such crime is not admissible.

(2) Notwithstanding any other provision of law, in a prosecution for a
crime described in ORS 163.355 to 163.427, or in a prosecution for an
attempt to commit such a crime, evidence of a victim's past sexual
behavior other than reputation or opinion evidence is also not ad-

missible, unless such evidence other than reputation or opinion evidence is:

(a) Admitted in accordance with subsections 3(a) and (b) of this section; and

(b) Is evidence that:

(A) Relates to the motive or bias of the alleged victim; or

(B) Is necessary to rebut or explain scientific or medical evidence offered by the state; or

(C) Is otherwise constitutionally required to be admitted.

(3) (a) If the person accused of committing rape, sodomy or sexual abuse or attempted rape, sodomy or sexual abuse intends to offer under subsection (2) of this section evidence of specific instances of the alleged victim's past sexual behavior, the accused shall make a written motion to offer such evidence not later than 15 days before the date on which the trial in which such evidence is to be offered is scheduled to begin, except that the court may allow the motion to be made at a later date, including during trial, if the court determines either that the evidence is newly discovered and could not have been obtained earlier through the exercise of due diligence or that the issue to which such evidence relates has newly arisen in the case. Any motion made under this paragraph shall be served on all other parties, and on the alleged victim through the office of the prosecutor.

(b) The motion described in paragraph (a) of this subsection shall be accompanied by a written offer of proof. If the court determines that the offer of proof contains evidence described in subsection (2) of this section, the court shall order a hearing in camera to determine if such evidence is admissible. At such hearing the parties may call witnesses, including the alleged victim, and offer relevant evidence. Notwithstanding subsection (2) of Rule 104 (ORS 40.030(2)), if the relevancy of the evidence which the accused seeks to offer in the trial depends upon the fulfillment of a condition of fact, the court, at the hearing in camera or at a subsequent hearing in camera scheduled for such purpose, shall accept evidence on the issue of whether such condition of fact is fulfilled and shall determine such issue.

(c) If the court determines on the basis of the hearing described in paragraph (b) of this subsection that the evidence which the accused seeks to offer is relevant and that the probative value of such evidence outweighs the danger of unfair prejudice, such evidence shall be admissible in the trial to the extent an order made by the court specifies evidence which may be offered and areas with respect to which the alleged victim may be examined or cross-examined. An order admitting evidence under this subsection may be appealed by the government before trial.

(4) For purposes of this section:

(a) **"In camera" means out of the presence of the public and the jury; and**

(b) **"Past sexual behavior" means sexual behavior other than the sexual behavior with respect to which rape, sodomy or sexual abuse or attempted rape, sodomy or sexual abuse is alleged.**

LEGISLATIVE COMMENTARY

Oregon Rule of Evidence 412, applicable only in prosecutions for crimes of sexual misconduct, specifies the procedure for and conditions under which evidence of the victim's past sexual behavior can be admitted, if the defendant wishes to introduce such evidence.

The rule is based on Rule 412 of the Federal Rules of Evidence, which was enacted by Congress as the Privacy Protection for Rape Victims Act of 1978, PL 95-540 (92 Stat 2046). **[Author's Note: FRE 412 has been significantly amended since adoption of OEC 412.]** Several changes were made. (1) To broaden the scope of the statute in accordance with former ORS 163.475, references to rape were replaced with a reference to rape, sodomy or sexual abuse. (2) To anticipate any problem of the confrontation clause, the situations in which prior behavior evidence may be constitutionally mandated were spelled out. (3) To protect the alleged victim from harassment, language was inserted requiring the defendant to give notice to the victim of intended use of behavior evidence through the office of the prosecutor. (4) To protect the interests of the state and the victim and to ensure uniformity through the development of a body of case law, provision was made for direct appeal of an order admitting evidence under the rule. The preceding amendments required other, internal changes in reference.

The rule replaces ORS 163.475. That statute, in its pre-1977 form, was held unconstitutional as applied because it did not allow the defendant an opportunity to confront witnesses against the defendant. *State v. Jalo,* 27 Or App 845, 851, 557 P2d 1359 (1976), citing *Davis v. Alaska,* 415 US 308, 94 SCt 1105, 39 LEd 2d 347 (1974). Portions of the statute are retained in ORE 412. Those that are not are either suspect or superfluous. The Legislative Assembly did not preserve subsection (3) of that statute because it wanted to avoid the problem of invoking, in a criminal case, a presumption relating to an element of the offense or negating a defense. See commentary to ORE 309, supra. The Legislative Assembly did not preserve subsection (6) as it felt the principle was adequately addressed elsewhere. See ORE 609 and commentary to ORE 403.

The principal purpose of ORE 412 is to protect victims of sexual crimes from the degrading and embarrassing disclosure of intimate details about their private lives. It does so by narrowly circumscribing when such evidence may be admitted. It does not do so, however, by sacrificing any constitutional right possessed by the defendant. The rule balances the interests involved: the interest of the victim of a sexual crime in protecting a private life from unwarranted public exposure, and the defendant's interest in being able to present adequately a defense by offering relevant and probative evidence.

Subsection (1). Reputation or opinion evidence about a victim's prior sexual behavior is not admissible regardless of the party seeking to introduce the evidence. This is in accord with current Oregon law. ORS 163.475; *State v. Workman,* 47 Or App 1055, 615 P2d 1140 (1980).

Subsection (2). Specific instances of a victim's prior sexual conduct are not admissible except in three circumstances.

The first circumstance is where the evidence relates to the motive or bias of the victim. *State v. Jalo,* supra.

The second circumstance in which a court can admit evidence of specific instances of a victim's prior sexual behavior is where the evidence is necessary to rebut or explain scientific or medical evidence offered by the state. This is an expansion of the federal rule. It would allow admission of a hair analysis test, for example, which would not be admissible under current Oregon law unless constitutionally required.

The third circumstance in which the defendant can offer evidence of specific instances of a victim's prior sexual behavior is where the federal or state constitution requires that the evidence be admitted. This general exception is intended to cover those infrequent instances where, because of an unusual chain of circumstances, following the general rule of inadmissibility would deny the defendant a constitutional right.

Subsection (3). Before evidence is admitted at the defendant's request under any of the exceptions listed in paragraph (b) of subsection (2), there must be an *in camera* hearing. At this hearing, the defendant presents the evidence sought to be admitted and the reasons for admission. The prosecution is allowed at that time to argue against admission of the evidence.

The purpose of the *in camera* hearing is twofold. It gives the defendant an opportunity to demonstrate to the court why certain evidence is admissible and ought to be presented to the jury. At the same time, it protects the privacy of the victim in those instances where the court finds that evidence is inadmissible.

In determining the admissibility of evidence, the court should consider all of the facts and circumstances surrounding the evidence, such as the amount of time that has elapsed between the alleged prior act and the act charged in the prosecution. The greater the lapse of time, the less likely it is that the evidence will be admitted. *State v. Lantz,* 44 Or App 695, 607 P2d 197 (1980).

If found to be admissible, the evidence may be presented to the jury in open court. Prior to that however, the state may have an interlocutory appeal on the ruling of the judge.

TEXT

Sex Offense Cases

Rule 412 is in effect a limitation upon Rule 404(2)(b), which allows a criminal defendant to offer evidence of a pertinent character trait of a crime victim to prove that the victim acted in accordance with that character. Under Rule 404(2)(b), a defendant might attempt to offer evidence of the past sexual behavior of a sex crime victim to prove that the victim was likely to have consented on the occasion in question. Rule 412 generally prohibits such evidence.

The purpose of Rule 412 is to protect the victim of a sex crime from embarrassment and to encourage reporting of sex offenses. These interests are deemed to override whatever marginal relevance the sexual history of the victim might have, except in the situations specified in Rule 412(2)(b).

Rule 412 imposes an absolute prohibition against use of reputation or opinion evidence regarding the victim's past sexual behavior. This prohibition applies to both the prosecution and the defense. Specific instances of prior conduct will be allowed only where they (1) relate to the motive or bias of the alleged victim; (2) are necessary to rebut or explain scientific or medical evidence offered by the state; or (3) are otherwise constitutionally required to be admitted. These categories are not mutually exclusive. Evidence admissible under the first two provisions may also be constitutionally required to be admitted.

In *State v. Wright*, 97 Or App 401, 405, 776 P2d 1294, rev denied 308 Or 593, 784 P2d 1100 (1989), the court held that a trial judge must follow a three-step analysis under OEC 412:

> First, it must determine whether the evidence concerns a victim's "past sexual behavior." If it does not, it is not appropriate for it to make further inquiry under OEC 412. Second, if the evidence does concern past sexual behavior and is offered in the form of opinion or reputation, the court must deny its admission under OEC 412(1). If it is offered in some other form, then the court must determine whether the purpose of the offer fits within one of the exceptions in OEC 412(2)(b)(A), (B) or (C). If it does not, then the court may not admit the evidence. Third, if it does fit within an exception, the court must balance the probative value of the evidence against its prejudicial effect.

In *State v. Gilliland*, 136 Or App 580, 587, 902 P2d 616 (1995), the court held that even if sexual history evidence tended to impeach the complaint's credibility (by contradicting certain aspects of her testimony), this does not make it admissible under Rule 412 unless it fits one of the exceptions to the rule.

Past Sexual Behavior

In *State v. Wright*, 97 Or App 401, 406, 776 P2d 1294, rev denied 308 Or 593, 784 P2d 1100 (1989), the court held that "past sexual behavior" means "a volitional or non-volitional physical act that the victim has performed for the purpose of the sexual stimulation or gratification of either the victim or another person or an act that is sexual intercourse, deviate sexual intercourse, or sexual contact, or an attempt to engage in such an act, between the victim and another person." Thus evidence relating to other molestations of the victim by other persons is governed by Rule 412.

The following conduct does not meet this definition and therefore is not regulated by Rule 412: writing a sexually explicit note, receiving special sex counseling, watching pornographic films, describing oral copulation, or speaking freely about sex. 97 Or App at 406. See also *State v. Weeks*, 99 Or App 287, 782 P2d 430 (1989), rev denied 309 Or 334, 787 P2d 889 (1990) (evidence that the victim allegedly asked two neighbor boys to engage in sexual behavior was not "past sexual behavior" of the victim and therefore OEC 412 was inapplicable).

"Past sexual behavior of an alleged victim" under Rule 412(4) has been interpreted to include behavior prior to trial even though subsequent to the charged offense. See *State v. Wattenbarger,* 97 Or App 414, 419, 776 P2d 1292, rev denied 308 Or 331, 780 P2d 222 (1989) (term "includes evidence of sexual behavior occurring subsequent to the crime, but before trial"). See also *United States v. Torres,* 937 F2d 1469, 1472–1773 (9th Cir. 1991) ("past sexual behavior" embraces all sexual behavior by complainant that "precedes the date of the trial").

To Prove Motive or Bias

Evidence tending to show motive or bias of the alleged victim under subparagraph (2)(b)(A) may include situations where the victim had a motive to make a false accusation against the defendant in order to cover up consensual sexual activity with the defendant or some other person or to retaliate against the defendant for revealing or threatening to reveal such activity. See *State v. Jalo,* 27 Or App 845, 557 P2d 1359 (1976) (defendant entitled to offer evidence that 10-year-old complainant in statutory rape prosecution made false accusation against him because he had threatened to report her sexual activities with others to her parents). But see *State v. Bennett,* 55 Or App 92, 637 P2d 208 (1981) (voluntary sexual relations between the victim and the defendant nine years prior to the alleged rape not admissible on issue of motive or bias).

In *State v. Bass,* 69 Or App 166, 683 P2d 1040, rev denied 298 Or 238, 691 P2d 482 (1984), the defendant contended that the alleged victim falsely accused him of rape because he threatened to interfere in a pecuniary sexual relationship the victim was having with another man. The court held that evidence of the sexual relationship between the victim and the third party was admissible, but that the details of the relationship (bondage and discipline) were not.

In *State v. Morgan,* 66 Or App 675, 675 P2d 513 (1984), the court found reversible error in the trial court's refusal to allow the defendant to introduce evidence of prior consensual sexual intercourse between the victim and the defendant. The defendant claimed the victim had consented and was making a false charge against him out of anger over his involvement with another woman. The court held the evidence admissible under Rule 412, because it related to the motive or bias of the alleged victim.

In *State v. Wright,* 97 Or App 401, 406, 776 P2d 1294, rev denied 308 Or 593, 784 P2d 1100 (1989), the court held that evidence that child victim had been molested by others was not admissible under Rule 412. Although defendant argued that such evidence suggested that the victim had a motive to accuse him falsely, because of the attention she receives from reporting sexual molestations, the appellate court stated that "[a]lthough the proffered evidence might show a generalized bias or motive, it does not address any particularized motive or bias that would lead the victim to fabricate the charge made against the defendant."

In *State v. Niles,* 108 Or App 735, 739, 817 P2d 293, 295–6 (1991), rev denied 312 Or 589, 825 P2d 417 (1992), the court held that a rape victim's prior consensual sexual activity with other tavern patrons was irrelevant in developing the defense theory that the victim falsely accused the defendant of rape out of fear of her boyfriend's reaction to her late return home on the night of the incident.

In *State v. Gilliland,* 136 Or App 580, 588–9, 902 P2d 616 (1995), defendant sought to introduce evidence that complainant had sex with two other men after they complimented her appearance as evidence that she was biased against defendant, because he allegedly did same thing. The court held that even if complainant believed "men used compliments as a subterfuge to induce her to have intercourse," this does not demonstrate a motive to falsely accuse defendant of rape. The court remanded on the separate issue of whether an allegedly false allegation of rape against a third person was sufficient to show bias against defendant.

To Rebut Scientific or Medical Evidence

Evidence necessary to rebut or explain scientific or medical evidence offered by the state under Rule 412(2)(b)(B) would presumably include evidence tending to show that some person other than the defendant was the source of any semen or injury found upon medical examination of the victim. Such evidence is expressly allowed by FRE 412. See also *State v. Nab,* 245 Or 454, 421 P2d 388 (1966).

In *State v. Cervantes,* 130 Or App 147, 150, 881 P2d 151 (1994), the court found no error in excluding evidence under OEC 412 that a witness had seen the victim "hanging all over" another man prior to the alleged rape and that the victim had admitted to having had sexual relations with that man. This evidence was offered as an alternative explanation for the semen that had been found in the victim after the alleged rape. However, the state introduced unrefuted medical evidence that semen remains in the cervix for a maximum period of fourteen hours after intercourse, and the defendant's offer of proof could not establish that the claimed intercourse with another man occurred within even twenty-four hours of the alleged rape. Therefore, the evidence was deemed irrelevant.

Evidence Constitutionally Required to Be Admitted

The scope of a criminal defendant's constitutional right to offer evidence of the prior sexual history of the victim, recognized by Rule 412(2)(b)(C), is not clearly defined. The drafters of the FRE deliberately left this category open-ended in order to incorporate continuing constitutional developments under both the state and federal constitutions. For discussion of the scope of the defendant's constitutional right to offer sexual history evidence, see Fishman, *Consent, Credibility, and the Constitution: Evidence Relating to a Sex Offense Complainant's Past Sexual Behavior,* 44 Cath U L Rev 709 (1995). See generally C. Mueller & L. Kirkpatrick, MODERN EVIDENCE (1995) § 4.16.

See also Galvin, *Shielding Rape Victims in the State and Federal Courts: A Proposal for the Second Decade,* 70 Minn L Rev 763 (1986); Tanford and Bocchino, *Rape Victim Shield Laws and the Sixth Amendment,* 128 U Pa L Rev 544 (1980); Ordover, *Admissibility of Patterns of Similar Sexual Conduct: The Unlamented Death of Character for Chastity,* 63 Cornell L Rev 90 (1977); Berger, *Man's Trial, Woman's Tribulation: Rape Cases in the Courtroom,* 77 Colum L Rev 1. (1977); Caulfield, *The New Oregon Sexual Offenses Evidence Law: An Evaluation,* 55 Or L Rev 493 (1976); NOTE, *Indiana's Rape Shield Law: Conflict with the Confrontation Clause?,* 9 Ind L Rev 418 (1976); COMMENT, *Rape Shield Statutes: Constitutional Despite Unconstitutional Exclusions of Evidence,* 1985 Wis L Rev 1219; ANNOT., *Constitutionality of "Rape Shield" Statute Restricting Use of Evidence of Victim's Sexual Experiences,* 1 ALR4th 283 (1980).

The primary constitutional provisions that may provide a defendant a right to offer evidence under Rule 412(2)(b)(C) are (1) the Sixth Amendment to the United States Constitution, which provides: "In all criminal prosecutions, the accused shall enjoy the right ... to be confronted with the witnesses against him; [and] to have compulsory process for obtaining witnesses in his favor ...."; (2) the due process clause of the Fourteenth Amendment, which has been interpreted to allow a defendant the right to present exculpatory evidence, see *Chambers v. Mississippi,* 410 US 284, 93 SCt 1038, 35 LEd2d 297 (1973); and (3) article I, section 11 of the Oregon Constitution, which provides: "In all criminal prosecutions, the accused shall have the right ... to meet the witnesses face to face, and to have compulsory process for obtaining witnesses in his favor."

The right of confrontation is intended *inter alia* to enable a criminal defendant to challenge the credibility of prosecution witnesses and to expose their bias or possible motives to fabricate testimony. Therefore, evidence relating to the motive or bias of the alleged victim offered under Rule 412(2)(b)(A) is also likely to be constitutionally required and hence admissible under Rule 412(2)(b)(C). See *Olden v. Kentucky,* 448 US 227, 109 SCt 480, 102 LEd2d 513 (1988) (error not to allow defendant in kidnapping, rape, and sodomy prosecution to cross-examine complainant regarding her cohabitation with boyfriend, who was defendant's half-brother; evidence relevant to issue of consent and to victim's motive to lie to protect her relationship with her boyfriend); *State v. Jalo,* 27 Or App 845, 557 P2d 1359 (1976).

Admission of evidence of prior sexual behavior by the victim may be constitutionally required when the prior behavior was with the defendant, was not remote in time, and the defendant claims consent as a defense to the charge. FRE 412 (b)(2)(B) expressly allows a court to admit evidence of "past sexual behavior with the accused [that] is offered by the accused upon the issue of whether the alleged victim consented to the sexual behavior with respect to which rape or assault is alleged." Such evidence is also allowed under most other state rape shield statutes. See *State v. Morgan,* 66 Or App 675, 675 P2d 513 (1984) (reversible error to exclude evidence of prior sexual intercourse between victim and defendant, in case where defendant claimed consent and contended that victim was making a false charge out of anger over his involvement with another woman; constitutional issue not addressed); *State v. Reiter,* 65 Or App

304, 672 P2d 56 (1983) (reversible error to exclude evidence offered by the defendant that the alleged rape victim had voluntarily engaged in sexual intercourse with defendant one week prior to the alleged rape; constitutional issue not addressed).

If a prosecuting witness misrepresents a fact, and evidence regarding the victim's prior sexual history is necessary to correct the misimpression created, a defendant may have a constitutional right to offer such evidence. See *State v. Reiter*, supra (victim stated on direct examination that she had known defendant as a "friend"; defendant entitled to offer evidence that victim and defendant had consensual sexual intercourse one week prior to the alleged rape; court stated that if Rule 412 were interpreted to unduly restrict cross-examination it would violate defendant's right of confrontation); *State v. Hill*, 129 Or App 180, 188, 887 P2d 1230, 1235 (1994) (possible error, but harmless, to exclude defense evidence that a child sexual abuse victim had "acted out" sexual behavior even before she began visiting the defendant offered to rebut state's evidence of such "acting out" *after* visiting the defendant; defendant argued that the evidence of her earlier behavior was necessary to rebut or explain the state's evidence or, in the alternative, to impeach the child's statements).

A defendant may have a constitutional right to prove other sexual experience of a complainant to rebut a suggestion by the prosecutor that the alleged victim's sexual experience or sophistication could only have come from sexual contact with defendant. See ANNOT., *Admissibility of Evidence that Juvenile Prosecuting Witness in Sex Offense Case Had Prior Sexual Experience for Purposes of Showing Alternative Source of Child's Ability to Describe Sex Acts*, 83 ALR4th 685 (1991).

Under former ORS 163.475(2) (repealed 1981), the Oregon Court of Appeals found evidence of a victim's prior sexual behavior admissible to rebut her explanation of why she delayed reporting the offense. Because her explanation of the delay was that she was degraded and humiliated by the nature of the assault, the court held that the defendant was entitled to offer evidence of admissions by the victim that she was a prostitute in order to rebut the victim's explanation. *State v. Lantz*, 44 Or App 695, 607 P2d 197 (1980).

However, a defendant does not have a right to prove sexual conduct between the victim and a third person if it is irrelevant to the charge against the defendant. In *State v. Bender*, 91 Or App 420, 755 P2d 151 (1988), the court held that a defendant charged with raping his estranged wife was not entitled to question the wife regarding the truth of a statement she made to him that she had not had an affair with a third person. The court also ruled that defendant could not offer evidence challenging the truth of this statement, because "[t]he truth of the victim's out of court statement to her husband regarding her sexual conduct is not relevant to the disputed issue of consent."

A difficult constitutional question may arise if a defendant attempts to offer evidence of a victim's reputation, claiming reliance upon that reputation in assuming consent would be given. Such a claim is particularly likely to arise when the defendant is charged with an attempted sexual offense and wishes to explain why advances were made. See Caulfield, *The New Oregon Sexual Offenses Evi-*

dence Law: An Evaluation, 55 Or L Rev 493, 514 (1976). Rule 412 imposes an absolute bar against evidence of the reputation of the victim. One commentator has questioned the constitutionality of the identical prohibition under FRE 412. See 1 S. Saltzburg, M. Martin, and D. Capra, FEDERAL RULES OF EVIDENCE MANUAL (6th ed 1994) 562–5. *Doe v. United States,* 666 F2d 43, 48 (4th Cir 1981), which resolved the potential constitutional problem by statutory construction, holding that Congress intended that evidence of reputation be excluded when offered to prove the victim's consent or veracity, but not "when offered solely to show the accused's state of mind." But see *State v. Anderson,* 137 Or App 36, 40–1, 902 P2d 1206 (1995) (victim's reputation for having sex with others irrelevant to whether defendant knew she lacked capacity to consent because of her mental retardation).

Some authorities take the view that a defendant may have a constitutional right to prove a pattern of distinctive, voluntary sexual behavior by the alleged victim that is strongly similar to the facts of the incident being charged. See Berger, *Man's Trial, Woman's Tribulation: Rape Cases in the Courtroom,* 77 Colum L Rev 1 (1977); Ordover, *Admissibility of Patterns of Similar Sexual Conduct: The Unlamented Death of Character for Chastity,* 63 Cornell L Rev 90 (1977). But see *State v. Thompson,* 131 Or App 230, 233–4, 881 P2d 574, 575–6 (1994), rev denied 320 Or 508, 888 P2d 569 (1995) (kidnapping and rape prosecution where defendant claimed that the alleged victim consented and had agreed to trade sex for drugs; defendant sought to introduce evidence of prior instances where the complainant had offered to trade sex for drugs; court held such evidence was properly excluded because of insufficient similarity to the present circumstances and also because the "sex for drugs" evidence did not prove a pattern of distinctive sexual behavior).

Prior False Accusations

Evidence that the victim made prior false accusations is not excluded by the rule. In *State v. LeClair,* 83 Or App 121, 126–7, 730 P2d 609 (1986), rev denied 303 Or 74, 734 P2d 354 (1987), the court held: "Evidence of previous false accusations by an alleged victim is not evidence of *past sexual behavior* within the meaning of the Rape Shield Law and, therefore, is not inadmissible under OEC 412." (Emphasis in original.) Nonetheless, impeachment of witnesses by evidence of prior bad acts is generally prohibited by Rule 608(2).

However, the court in *LeClair* held that a defendant's constitutional right to confront witnesses and to impeach their credibility may override the restrictions of Rule 608(2):

> We conclude that, regardless of the prohibitions of OEC 608, the Confrontation Clause of Article I, § 11, requires that the court permit a defendant to cross-examine the complaining witness in front of the jury concerning other accusations she has made if 1) she has recanted them; 2) the defendant demonstrates to the court that those accusations were false; or 3) there is some evidence that the victim has made prior accusations that were false, unless the probative value of the evidence which the defendant seeks to elicit on

cross-examination (including the probability that false accusations were in fact made) is substantially outweighed by the risk of prejudice, confusion, embarrassment or delay.

83 Or App at 130, 730 P2d at 615.

In *LeClair*, the court found some evidence that prior false accusations were made, but sustained the trial judge's exclusion of the evidence on grounds of delay and likely jury confusion.

In *State v. Wonderling*, 104 Or App 204, 799 P2d 1135 (1990), the court affirmed the exclusion of evidence allegedly showing that the victim had made false accusations of sexual misconduct against another man. Although the earlier statements were somewhat inconsistent, the court concluded that they did not amount either to recantation or falsehood.

In *State v. Hendricks*, 101 Or App 469, 791 P2d 139, rev denied 310 Or 133, 794 P2d 794 (1990), the defendant sought to introduce evidence of a prior false accusation by a sex crime victim. The court held that such evidence did not involve "past sexual behavior" and hence was not regulated by OEC 412. Instead, such evidence was a prior instance of dishonesty, and OEC 608(2) forbids cross-examination regarding specific instances of conduct for impeachment purposes. Under the constitutional right of confrontation, a defendant may be allowed to cross-examine an accuser regarding prior false accusations. However, in this case, the defendant proposed to prove the prior false accusation by testimony of other witnesses rather than by cross-examination of the victim and made no offer of proof with respect to what the victim would have said on cross-examination. Therefore, there was no error in excluding such evidence.

In *State v. Gilliland*, 136 Or App 580, 586–7, 902 P2d 616 (1995), the court reaffirmed that evidence of prior false accusations of rape shold be limited to inquiry on cross-examination.

See generally ANNOT., *Impeachment on Cross-examination of Prosecuting Witness in Sexual Offenses Trial by Showing that Similar Charges were made Against Other Persons*, 75 ALR2d 508 (1961).

Notice 15 Days Prior to Trial

If a defendant intends to offer evidence of a victim's past sexual behavior, notice normally must be given at least 15 days prior to trial by motion accompanied by written offer of proof. The trial judge may allow the motion to be made at a later date, including during trial, "if the court determines either that the evidence is newly discovered and could not have been obtained earlier through the exercise of due diligence or that the issue to which such evidence relates has newly arisen in the case."

In *State v. Lajoie*, 316 Or 63, 65, 849 P2d 479 (1993), the court held exclusion for failure to give the 15-day advance notice required by the rule that is mandatory unless the evidence is newly discovered or relates to a newly arisen issue. The sanction of preclusion for failure to comply with the notice requirement does not violate a defendant's right of confrontation or compulsory process. The remedy of preclusion is neither arbitrary nor disproportionate to the purposes that OEC 412 is intended to serve. A dissenting opinion by three justices took the position that OEC 412 should not be interpreted to require a *per se* rule of preclusion for violation of the 15-day notice requirement. The dissenters would allow trial judges' discretion to decide whether preclusion is an appropriate sanction on the facts of a given case.

Exclusion as a sanction for failure to give notice has also been held constitutional by the United States Supreme Court. See *Michigan v. Lucas*, 111 S Ct 1743 (1991) (exclusion for defendant's failure to give notice under the Michigan rape shield statute of his intention to offer evidence of an alleged rape victim's past sexual conduct did not violate his sixth amendment rights).

The notice requirement applies to evidence that the defendant intends to elicit by cross-examination as well as to extrinsic evidence. *State v. Lajoie*, supra.

However, if defendant could not reasonably anticipate the need to inquire into past sexual conduct on cross-examination and does so only to correct a misimpression created by the complainant's direct testimony, barring such examination because of failure to give pretrial notice could raise constitutional concerns. *State v. Reiter*, 65 Or App 304, 307–8 n2, 672 P2d 56 (1983) (when alleged rape victim described her relationship with defendant as "a friend," it was error to bar defendant from offering evidence that the victim had voluntarily engaged in sexual intercourse with the defendant one week prior to the incident for which he was being prosecuted on grounds of failure to give pretrial notice).

Balancing Test

If the court finds the defense offer of proof to contain evidence meeting the requirements of Rule 412(2), the court must order a hearing in camera to determine the admissibility of the evidence. After a hearing, the court must determine whether the evidence is relevant and whether its probative value outweighs the danger of unfair prejudice. After making this determination, the court is required to enter an order specifying what evidence if any may be introduced, and in what areas the alleged victim may be examined or cross-examined. Rule 412(3)(c) expressly authorizes the prosecutor to appeal in advance of trial an order allowing evidence to be offered of the victim's prior sexual behavior. Cf. *Doe v. United States*, 666 F2d 43 (4th Cir 1981) (complainant also found to have implied right of appeal under FRE 412).

The balancing test under Rule 412 is different from the balancing test under Rule 403. Under Rule 403, if the prejudicial effect and probative value of evidence are equally balanced, it will be admitted. Under Rule 412, the opposite is true. Although Rule 412 lists "unfair prejudice" as the only consideration to be balanced, presumably some of the other factors listed in Rule 403, such as the danger of confusion of the issues or misleading the jury, may be considered by the court to be components of "unfair prejudice" under Rule 412.

If the court determines that the evidence is constitutionally required to be admitted, the balancing test is of course inapplicable because the court would lack authority to exclude the evidence.

In Camera

Rule 412(3)(b) specifies that the hearing on the admissibility of evidence offered under the rule shall be conducted "in camera." The 1993 legislature added an amendment to the rule defining "in camera" as meaning "out of the presence of the public and the jury." OEC 412(4)(a). See Abrams, *The Paper Shield of Oregon Evidence Code 412 After State ex rel. Davey v. Frankel,* 71 Or L Rev 497 (1992).

In *State ex rel Davey v. Frankel,* 312 Or 286, 294, 823 P2d 394, 398 (1991), the court interpreted "in chambers" (the language in the earlier version of the rule) as meaning only that the hearing must take place in the judge's office, but not as categorically excluding the public from attending.

The Oregon Court of Appeals has held that the hearing under the statutory predecessor to Rule 412 may be closed to the public. *State v. Blake,* 53 Or App 906, 633 P2d 831 (1981). The Supreme Court avoided addressing the issue in *State v. Blake,* 292 Or 486, 640 P2d 605 (1982). Cf. *State ex rel Oregonian Publishing Co. v. Deiz,* 289 Or 277, 613 P2d 23 (1980) (order excluding press from juvenile proceeding found to violate state constitution); *Oregonian Publishing Co. v. O'Leary,* 303 Or 297, 736 P2d 173 (1987) (holding unconstitutional ORS 136.617, which provides for closed hearings to determine claims of self-incrimination asserted by witnesses in criminal trials; Article I, § 10 of the Oregon Constitution interpreted to require open hearings in adjudications involving the administration of justice, unless an historical exception is established.)

Recent decisions of the United States Supreme Court have required greater public and press access to judicial proceedings. See *Richmond Newspapers, Inc. v. Virginia,* 448 US 555, 100 SCt 2814, 65 LEd2d 973 (1980) (First Amendment implies a right of access by the press and public to criminal proceedings); *Globe Newspaper Co. v. Superior Court for the County of Norfolk,* 457 US 596, 102 SCt 2613, 73 LEd2d 248 (1982) (rule requiring exclusion of the public from trial of sex offense cases involving minor victims is unconstitutional; balancing on case-by-case basis required); *Press-Enterprise Co. v. Superior Court of California,* 464 US 501, 104 SCt 819, 78 LEd2d 629 (1984) (right of access during voir dire examination); *Waller v. Georgia,* 467 US 39, 104 SCt 2210, 81 LEd2d 31 (1984) (closure orders may violate defendant's Sixth Amendment right to a public trial).

Other Authorities

See generally ANNOT., *Admissibility in Rape Case, Under Rule 412 of Federal Rules of Evidence, of Evidence of Victim's Past Sexual Behavior,* 65 ALR Fed 519 (1983).

ARTICLE V
PRIVILEGES

RULE 503.　ORS 40.225. LAWYER-CLIENT PRIVILEGE

(1) [Definitions.] As used in this section, unless the context requires otherwise:

(a) "Client" means a person, public officer, corporation, association or other organization or entity, either public or private, who is rendered professional legal services by a lawyer, or who consults a lawyer with a view to obtaining professional legal services from the lawyer.

(b) "Confidential communication" means a communication not intended to be disclosed to third persons other than those to

205

whom disclosure is in furtherance of the rendition of professional legal services to the client or those reasonably necessary
for the transmission of the communication.

(c) "Lawyer" means a person authorized, or reasonably believed by
the client to be authorized, to practice law in any state or nation.

(d) "Representative of the client" means a principal, an employee, an
officer or a director of the client:

   (A) Who provides the client's lawyer with information that was
   acquired during the course of, or as a result of, such person's relationship with the client as principal, employee, officer or director, and is provided to the lawyer for the
   purpose of obtaining for the client the legal advice or other
   legal services of the lawyer; or

   (B) Who, as part of such person's relationship with the client as
   principal, employee, officer or director, seeks, receives or
   applies legal advice from the client's lawyer.

(e) "Representative of the lawyer" means one employed to assist the
lawyer in the rendition of professional legal services, but does
not include a physician making a physical or mental examination under ORCP 44.

(2) [General rule of privilege.] A client has a privilege to refuse to disclose
and to prevent any other person from disclosing confidential communications made for the purpose of facilitating the rendition of professional legal services to the client:

(a) Between the client or the client's representative and the client's
lawyer or a representative of the lawyer;

(b) Between the client's lawyer and the lawyer's representative;

(c) By the client or the client's lawyer to a lawyer representing another in a matter of common interest;

(d) Between representatives of the client or between the client and a
representative of the client; or

(e) Between lawyers representing the client.

(3) [Who may claim the privilege.] The privilege created by this section
may be claimed by the client, a guardian or conservator of the client,
the personal representative of a deceased client, or the successor,
trustee, or similar representative of a corporation, association, or
other organization, whether or not in existence. The person who was
the lawyer or the lawyer's representative at the time of the communication is presumed to have authority to claim the privilege but only
on behalf of the client.

(4) [Exceptions.] There is no privilege under this section:

(a) If the services of the lawyer were sought or obtained to enable or
aid anyone to commit or plan to commit what the client knew or reasonably should have known to be a crime or fraud;

(b) As to a communication relevant to an issue between parties who
claim through the same deceased client, regardless of whether the

claims are by testate or intestate succession or by inter vivos transaction;

(c) As to a communication relevant to an issue of breach of duty by the lawyer to the client or by the client to the lawyer,

(d) As to a communication relevant to an issue concerning an attested document to which the lawyer is an attesting witness; or

(e) As to a communication relevant to a matter of common interest between two or more clients if the communication was made by any of them to a lawyer retained or consulted in common, when offered in an action between any of the clients.

LEGISLATIVE COMMENTARY

Oregon Rule of Evidence 503 states the rule of privilege for confidential communications between lawyer and client. The rule is based on proposed Rule 503 of the Federal Rules of Evidence, which was prescribed by the United States Supreme Court and submitted to Congress but not enacted. Aside from minor changes made to conform this rule to the form and style of Oregon statutes, there are two major differences between it and proposed Federal Rule 503. The Oregon rule contains a definition of "representative of the client," which the federal rule does not, and it specifically excludes a physician making a physical or mental examination under ORCP 44 from the definition of "representative of the lawyer."

The rule arguably does not change Oregon law, but its coverage extends to areas in which current law is silent or unclear. See ORS 44.040(1)(b), which is repealed.

Subsection (1). Paragraph (a). The definition of "client" includes governmental bodies and corporations—issues on which existing Oregon law is silent. The definition also extends the status of client to one consulting a lawyer with a view to retaining the lawyer, even though actual employment does not result. McCormick, *Evidence* § 88 (2d ed 1972); *McNamee v. First National Bank,* 88 Or 636, 72 P 801 (1918). The client need not be involved in litigation; the rendition of legal service or advice under any circumstances suffices. 8 Wigmore, *Evidence* § 2294 (McNaughton rev 1961); *Bryant v. Dukehart,* 106 Or 359, 210 P 454 (1922). The services must be professional legal services. Purely business or personal matters do not qualify. McCormick § 88; *Sitton v. Peyree,* 117 Or 107, 241 P 62, 242 P 1112 (1926); *Booher v. Brown,* 173 Or 464, 146 P2d 71 (1944).

Paragraph (b). A confidential communication is defined in terms of intent. Intent is to be inferred from the circumstances, *e.g.,* taking or failing to take precautions. A communication made in public or meant to be relayed to outsiders or which is divulged to third persons by the client or by the lawyer at the direction of the client can scarcely be considered confidential. McCormick § 91; *Leathers v. United States,* 250 F2d 159 (9th Cir 1957) (no privilege for communication knowingly made by client in presence and hearing of third person); *Baum v. Denn,* 187 Or 401, 211 P2d 478 (1949) (no privilege for attorney's negotiation with third party made at client's direction). Unless an intent to disclose is apparent, however, the attorney-client communication is confidential. *Bryant v. Dukehart,* supra (letter from client to attorney offered by opposing party, held privileged regardless of how communication came into possession of party seeking to use it).

The rule allows some disclosure beyond the immediate circle of lawyer and client and their representatives without impairing confidentiality, as a practical matter. It permits disclosure to persons "to whom disclosure is in furtherance of the rendition of professional legal services to the client," contemplating that these, will include a "spouse, parent, business associate, or joint client." Comment, California Evidence Code § 952. It also allows disclosure to persons "reasonably necessary for the transmission of the communication" without loss of confidentiality.

Paragraph (c). A "lawyer" is a person licensed to practice law in any state or nation. There is no requirement that the attorney be in private practice. *State v. Ayer,* 122 Or 537, 259 P 427 (1927). There is also no requirement that the licensing state or nation recognize the attorney-client privilege, thus avoiding an excursion into conflict of laws. "Lawyer" also includes a person reasonably believed to be a lawyer—an issue that has not confronted the Oregon appellate courts. For similar provisions, see California Evidence Code § 950.

Author's Note: Paragraph (d) of the Legislative Commentary has been superseded as a result of the 1987 legislative change adopting a new definition of "representative of the client."

Paragraph (d). Unlike proposed Federal Rule 503, this rule contains a definition of "representative of the client." The Legislative Assembly agrees here with the comment to Rule 503(a)(2) of the Alaska Rules of Evidence (May 1979):

> The Proposed Federal Rules of Evidence as submitted to Congress by the United States Supreme Court did not contain a definition of "representative of the client." Because of uncertainty about the extent of the privilege to be granted to corporate clients, the Advisory Committee came out in favor of a case-by-case analysis. This approach is rejected here. "An ad hoc approach to privilege pursuant to a vague standard achieves the worst of possible worlds: harm in the particular case because information may be concealed; and a lack of compensating long-range benefit because persisting uncertainty about the availability of the privilege will discourage some communications." Note, "Attorney-Client Privilege for Corporate Clients: The Control Group Test," in 84 Harv L Rev 424, 426 (1970).

In determining whether an individual in the corporate context is a representative of the client, the Legislative Assembly specifically adopts the "control group" test, which limits the category to persons with authority to seek out and act upon legal advice for the client. See, e.g., *City of Philadelphia v. Westinghouse Electric Corp.,* 210 F Supp 483 (ED Pa 1962), mandamus and prohibition denied sub nom, *General Electric Co. v. Kirkpatrick,* 312 F2d 742 (3d Cir 1962), cert denied, 372 US 943, 83 SCt 937 (1963); *Garrison v. General Motors Corp.,* 213 F Supp 515 (SD Cal 1963).

Under the control group test, the attorney-client privilege attaches only when the corporate employee is in a position to control or have substantial effect on a decision about any action which the corporation may take upon the advice of an attorney. This group includes, and may be limited to, the director and executive officers of the corporation. Recent case law elsewhere would extend the privilege to a broader range of personnel. *Upjohn Co. v. United States,* 49 US Law Week 4093 (January 13, 1981) (responses of foreign managers to questionnaire sent out as part of internal investigation conducted by general counsel of corporation, concerning matters within scope of employees' duties and for purpose of giving legal advice to upper-echelon management, held privileged under federal common law). However, the Legislative Assembly concurs with the further commentary to the Alaska Rules of Evidence:

"No definition of 'representative of the client' will be perfect, but the best approach to corporate privilege developed to date is the 'control group' test as adopted in Alaska Rule 503(a)(2). See *City of Philadelphia v. Westinghouse Electric Corp.,* 210 F Supp 483, 485 (ED Pa 1962). The 'control group' test is admittedly restrictive and has been criticized by some courts. See, e.g., *Harper & Row Publisher, Inc. v. Decker,* 423 F2d 487, 491–492 (7th Cir 1970), aff'd by an equally divided court per curiam, 400 US 348, 91 SCt 479, 27 LEd2d 433 (1971). However, the restrictive view brings the corporate privilege more in line with the privilege available to unincorporated business concerns. Business organizations should not receive different treatment on evidence questions in courts of law merely because of differences in financial structure.

"If, for example, A runs a taxi service as a sole proprietorship with several employees, and one employee driver is involved in an accident for which A is sued, the employee's statements to A's attorney are not within the attorney-client privilege, even though A may order his employee to talk with the lawyer. [A's report to the attorney, based on information from the driver, would be privileged.] If A incorporates, the ruling should not change. It should be sufficient that A and other corporate officers having the capacity to seek legal advice and to act on it can claim the benefits of the privilege for private communications with counsel. A more permissive privilege would result in suppression of information conveyed to attorneys by employees who are more like witnesses than clients and who have no personal desire for confidentiality."

It is unclear how far Oregon courts would have gone in recognizing the lawyer-client privilege in the case of communications between an attorney and a client's representative. The privilege was applied to communications between an appraiser hired by a client and the client's attorney. *Brink v. Multnomah County,* 224 Or 507, 356 P2d 536 (1960). In that case, the court declared that "a communication by any form of agency employed or set in motion by the client is within the privilege." 224 Or at 516. As for a corporate client, Oregon courts would probably recognize as privileged communications between an attorney and the corporation's officers, board members or registered agent.

Paragraph (e). The definition of "representative of the lawyer" is consistent with present Oregon law. It recognizes that in rendering legal service, a lawyer may use advisors and assistants in addition to those employed in the process of communicating. The definition includes an expert who is hired to assist in rendering legal advice or to help in the planning and conduct of litigation, but not one employed to testify as a witness. A physician making a physical or mental examination under ORCP 44 is also expressly excluded. The definition does not limit a "representative of the lawyer" to an expert. Whether the representative is compensated by the lawyer or by the client is immaterial.

Subsection (2). This subsection sets forth the lawyer-client privilege, using previously defined terms.

The lawyer-client privilege extends to communications (a) between the client or the client's representative and the lawyer or the lawyer's representative; (b) between the lawyer and the lawyer's representative; (c) by the client or the lawyer to a lawyer representing another person in a matter of common interest; (d) between representatives of the client or between the client and a representative of the client; and (e) between lawyers representing the client. All these communications must be specifically for the purpose of obtaining legal services for the client; otherwise the privilege does not attach.

In a case in which lawyers represent different clients who have a common interest, Rule 503 allows each client a privilege as to the client's own statements. Thus, in "joint defense" or "pooled information" situations, if all clients resist disclosure, none will occur. However, if for some reason one client wishes to disclose the client's own statements made at a joint conference, the person is permitted to do so. No privilege applies where there is no common interest to be promoted by joint consultation, and the parties, therefore, meet on a purely adversary basis.

In the past, substantial authority has allowed an eavesdropper to testify to overheard privileged conversations and has admitted intercepted privileged letters. The evolution of ever more sophisticated techniques of recording and interception calls for the abandonment of that position. Accordingly, ORE 503 allows the client to prevent "any other person" from disclosing a privileged communication.

The privilege stated in this subsection agrees with the privilege in ORS 44.040(1)(b), which is repealed, although the latter statute did not set forth specific types of communications to be protected. Rule 503 is also consistent with Oregon case law, which has tended to set the boundaries of the lawyer-client privilege by implication—excluding certain communications from the privilege—rather than by express declaration. See *Baum v. Denn,* supra (communications made to attorney for purpose of dealing with third persons not privileged because they are not confidential); *Minard v. Stillman,* 31 Or 164, 49 P 476 (1897) (when all parties are represented by one attorney, communications made during settlement negotiations for the information of all are not privileged in dispute between parties themselves).

Subsection (3). This subsection does not change existing Oregon law. The lawyer-client privilege belongs, of course, to the client, to be claimed by the client or the client's guardian or conservator or personal representative. *Bergsvik v. Bergsvik,* 205 Or 670, 291 P2d 724 (1956) (privilege intended to benefit only client, and not available to others); *Booher v. Brown,* supra (implying that privilege survives death of client and may be asserted by personal representative). Because the privilege is for the protection of the client, it is not limited merely to the protection of parties, but will also protect a client who is called as a witness. *Bergsvik v. Bergsvik,* supra; *Bryant v. Dukehart,* supra. The successor of a dissolved corporate client may claim the privilege. California Evidence Code § 953; New Jersey Evidence Rule 26(1).

The lawyer may not claim the privilege on the lawyer's own behalf. However, the lawyer may claim it on behalf of the client—indeed, it is assumed that the lawyer will do so except under the most unusual circumstances. An Oregon attorney is prohibited by the ethics of the profession from divulging a client's secrets or confidences. The attorney would therefore be bound to claim the privilege on behalf of the attorney's client if called to testify. See DR 4-101(2) and 7-102(B) of the American Bar Association Code of Professional Responsibility; Canon 37 of the American Bar Association Canons of Professional Ethics.

Subsection (4). The exceptions to the lawyer-client privilege are well established.

Paragraph (a). The privilege does not extend to advice in aid of future wrongdoing. 8 Wigmore § 2298; *State v. Phelps,* 24 Or App 329, 545 P2d 901 (1976). The wrongdoing need not be that of the client. However, the client must know or have reason to know of the criminal or fraudulent nature of the act. This requirement is designed to protect a client who is erroneously advised that a proposed action is within the law.

The law does not require a preliminary finding that there is sufficient evidence apart from the lawyer-client communication to warrant a finding that the legal services were sought to enable the commission of a wrong. See *Clark v. United States,* 289 US 1, 53 SCt 465, 77 LEd 993 (1933). While any general exploration of what transpired between attorney and client would of course be inappropriate, it is feasible, either at the discovery stage or during trial to focus the inquiry by specific questions to avoid any broad intrusion upon the attorney-client relation. Numerous cases reflect this approach.

Paragraph (b). Normally the lawyer-client privilege survives the death of the client and may be asserted by the client's representative under subsection (3) of this rule. When there is a will contest, however, the identity of the person entitled to claim the privilege remains undetermined until the conclusion of the litigation. The choice is between allowing both sides or neither to assert the privilege, with authority and reason favoring the latter view. McCormick § 94; California Evidence Code A 957; Kansas Code of Civil Procedure § 60-426(b)(2); New Jersey Evidence Rule 26(2)(b); *Tanner v. Farmer,* 243 Or 431, 414 P2d 340 (1960) (attorney not prohibited from testifying about execution of will in litigation between parties claiming under will of client).

Paragraph (c). The breach of duty exception is required by considerations of fairness and policy. It will generally arise when there is a controversy over the attorney's fees, a claim of inadequate representation, or charges of professional misconduct. McCormick § 91; California Evidence Code § 958; New Jersey Evidence Rule 26(2)(c). There is no reported decision on the existence of this exception in Oregon.

Paragraph (d). When a lawyer acts as an attesting witness, the approval of the client to the lawyer's doing so may safely be assumed, and the waiver of the privilege as to any relevant lawyer-client communication is a proper result. California Evidence Code § 959. There is no current authority supporting the existence of this exception in Oregon.

Paragraph (e). Communications for the mutual information of joint clients are not confidential and hence not privilege in a subsequent dispute between the clients. McCormick § 91; California Evidence Code § 962; Kansas Code of Civil Procedure § 60-426(b)(4); New Jersey Evidence Rule 26(2); *Minard v. Stillman,* supra. The situation with which this provision deals is to be distinguished from the case of clients with a common interest who retain different lawyers, which is covered under paragraph (2)(c) of this rule.

Oregon law recognizes two other exceptions to the lawyer-client privilege—an exception for assets left with the attorney, *State ex rel Hardy v. Gleason,* 19 Or 159, 23 P 817 (1890), and an exception for the fact of employment and name and address of the client, *Cole v. Johnson,* 103 Or 319, 205 P 282 (1922); *In re Illidge,* 162 Or 393, 91 P2d 1100 (1939). By the adoption of Rule 503 the Legislative Assembly does not intend to affect these latter exceptions.

TEXT

Introduction

The attorney-client privilege is the oldest of all evidentiary privileges and is recognized in every American jurisdiction. It is not, however, immune from criticism. According to Wigmore:

> Its benefits are all indirect and speculative; its obstruction is plain and concrete. It is worth preserving for the sake of a general policy, but it is nonetheless an obstacle to the investigation of the truth. It ought to be strictly confined within the narrowest possible limits consistent with the logic of its principle. (8 J. Wigmore, *Evidence,* § 2291 at 554 (McNaughton rev 1961 (footnote omitted))

See also *United States v. Osborn,* 561 F2d 1334, 1339 (9th Cir 1977) ("Since the effect of the assertion of the attorney-client privilege is to withhold relevant information from the finder of fact, the privilege is to be applied only when necessary to achieve its purpose of encouraging clients to make full disclosure to their attorneys" (citations omitted)).

In addition to the evidentiary privilege created by this rule, there is also a professional duty, subject to limited exceptions, not to "reveal a confidence or secret of the lawyer's client." See Oregon State Bar Disciplinary Rule 4-101(B)(1). As a practical matter, this ethical duty of confidentiality may provide more protection for the confidences or secrets of a client than the evidentiary privilege, because the privilege can generally be asserted only in a judicial, legislative, or administrative proceeding whereas the ethical obligation applies in all settings.

Moreover, the ethical obligation of nondisclosure frequently extends to matters outside the scope of an evidentiary privilege, such as secrets that are not communications and communications that are not confidential. As an example, a client's communication to an attorney in the presence of a third person is generally beyond the reach of the attorney-client privilege, but the attorney may still have an ethical duty not to discuss the communication publicly.

Nonetheless, the scope of the evidentiary privilege is of fundamental importance. In the absence of the privilege, an attorney called as a witness may be judicially compelled to disclose confidential communications from a client, regardless of the ethical standards of confidentiality adopted by the profession and regardless of what assurance of confidentiality was given to the client. The Code of Professional Responsibility specifically creates an exception to the ethical duty of confidentiality when disclosure is "required by law or court order." DR 4-101(C)(2). Well-advised practitioners are careful not to give a confidentiality commitment to clients beyond that allowed by privilege law.

Statutory Protection for Client's Secrets

In addition to the attorney-client privilege and the ethical duty of confidentiality, there is a third source of potential legal protection for a client's secrets. ORS 9.460(3) provides: "An attorney shall: ... (3) Maintain the confidence and secrets of the attorney's clients consistent with the rules of professional conduct. ..."

An earlier version of the statute could have been read as creating an even broader duty of confidentiality than the rules of professional conduct. See *State v. Kennan/Waller,* 307 Or 515, 771 P2d 244 (1989) (discussing differences). The current version is intended to make the scope of the statutory duty "consistent" with the ethical duty.

RULE 503(1)(a)
"Client" Defined; "Professional Legal Services"

Client is defined by Rule 503(1)(a) to include not only individuals but corporations, associations, organizations, and other public and private entities. Whenever the client is other than an individual, it is necessary to determine whether the person making the communication meets the definition of a "representative of the client" under Rule 503(1)(d). If not, the communication may not be privileged.

To be a client, the relationship with the attorney must be for the purpose of obtaining "professional legal services." If the client consults with the lawyer as a friend, counselor, business advisor, executor, investigator, tax preparer, attesting witness, or scrivener, the privilege will not arise. McCormick, *Evidence* (3d ed 1984) § 88 at 209. See *United States v. Davis,* 636 F2d 1028 (5th Cir), cert denied 102 SCt 320 (1981) and *In re Grand Jury Investigation (Schroeder),* 842 F2d 1223 (11th Cir 1987) (attorney acting as tax preparer; no privilege); *United States v. Huberts,* 637 F2d 630 (9th Cir 1980), cert denied 451 US 975 (1981) (attorney acting as business agent to oversee consignment sale of printing press; no privilege); *Diamond v. City of Mobile,* 86 FRD 324 (SD Ala 1978) (attorney acting as investigator; no privilege). Cases where an attorney was consulted in more than one capacity can be best resolved by determining whether the primary purpose of the communication in question was to obtain professional legal services.

Communications to an attorney are privileged if made "for the purpose" of obtaining legal services even if the attorney ultimately decides not to represent the client. Rule 503(2).

Whether the attorney-client relationship exists does not depend on whether a fee was paid to the attorney. *Sitton v. Peyree,* 117 Or 107, 241 P 62 (1925). Communications made to an attorney after the attorney-client relationship terminates are not privileged. *In re Young's Estate,* 59 Or 348, 116 P 95 (1911).

If an expert is hired as a nontestifying consultant, communications with the expert (as the "representative of the lawyer") are normally privileged, and the privilege for those initial communications continues even though the expert is later asked to testify. See *Dyer v. R.E. Christiansen Trucking Co., Inc.,* 118 Or App 320, 329, 848 P2d 104 (1993), rev'd on other grounds 318 Or 391, 868 P2d 1325 (1994) (correspondence between the defendants' attorney and an expert who ultimately became a witness was within the attorney-client privilege, where the correspondence took place before the expert was asked to testify for defendants).

RULE 503(1)(b)
"Confidential Communication"

"Confidential"

Whether the communication is confidential depends upon the intent of the client. If the client intends that the attorney publicly reveal the communication, the privilege does not apply. If unnecessary third parties are present when the communication is made it will not be a confidential communication. The intent of the client to keep the communication confidential can be inferred from the precautions taken and the surrounding circumstances.

Permissible Disclosures: The communication may be disclosed to the following persons without destroying the privilege: (1) Persons to whom disclosure is in furtherance of the rendition of professional legal services to the client; (2) Persons reasonably necessary for the transmission of the communication, such as stenographers and interpreters; (3) Representatives of the client as defined in Rule 503(1)(d); (4) Representatives of the lawyer as defined in Rule 503(1)(e).

It is unclear precisely what the legislature intended by the first category listed above, "those to whom disclosure is in furtherance of the rendition of professional legal services to the client." The Commentary states that this phrase contemplates persons such as a "spouse, parent, business associate, or joint client." This phrase should be construed narrowly. Otherwise, every letter written by an attorney to a third party on behalf of a client could be found to be "in furtherance of the rendition of professional legal services to the client," and hence privileged. This would be a significant departure from prior Oregon law, a result that apparently was not intended. See *Baum v. Denn,* 187 Or 401, 406–407, 211 P2d 478 (1949). ("The client cannot authorize his lawyer to speak for him in dealing with third persons, and then undertake to seal his lips as to what transpired.")

In *Smith v. Alyeska Pipeline Service Co.*, 538 F Supp 977 (D Del 1982), aff'd without opinion 758 F2d 668 (1st Cir 1984), cert denied 471 US 1066 (1985), the court held that the sending of a copy of a letter from an attorney to his client to the opposing attorney was a waiver of the attorney-client privilege with respect to the letter. See generally ANNOT., *Applicability of Attorney-Client Privilege to Communications Made in Presence of or Solely to or by Third Person,* 14 ALR4th 594 (1982).

It has been held by a circuit court judge that a request for a legal opinion from the Attorney General, in circumstances where the opinion would be available to the public, was not a confidential communication. *Bohemia, Inc. v. State,* Coos Co. Case No. 82-1200 (1983) (Barron, J.).

Eavesdroppers: A communication may remain privileged even though overheard by an eavesdropper. If the client intended the communication to be confidential and took reasonable precautions against being overheard, the communication should qualify as confidential under Rule 503(1)(b). Rule 503(2) allows the client to prevent "any other person" from disclosing a privileged communication. See also Rule 512(2), which provides that a communication does not lose its privileged nature if it is disclosed to a third person, arguably including an eavesdropper, "without opportunity to claim the privilege." See Note, *Application of Attorney-Client Privilege to Communications Intercepted by a Third Party,* 69 Iowa L Rev 263 (1983).

Identity of Client and Related Information: Generally, information regarding the fact of representation, the name and address of the client, and even the fee arrangement are not considered to be protected by the privilege. See discussion under Rule 503(4) "Other Exceptions," infra.

Informing Client Regarding Court Appearance Date: In several cases, the issue has been raised whether a communication between an attorney and a client regarding the time and date of a court appearance is within the privilege. If a criminal defendant released on bond or agreement fails to appear, and the prosecutor brings criminal charges for that failure to appear, it is necessary to establish that the defendant was informed of the court date. Because notice of court dates is usually given to defendants through their attorneys, it has often been necessary to ask defense attorneys whether they conveyed that information to their client. Occasionally, defense attorneys have asserted the attorney-client privilege in response to such inquiry.

In *State v. Bilton,* 36 Or App 513, 516, 585 P2d 50 (1978), the court held that communications between the attorney and client in a criminal case as to the time and place of trial are "not within the attorney-client privilege, since they are nonlegal in nature with counsel simply performing a notice function. Clearly, the date set for trial is a matter of public record and cannot conceivably be considered confidential." This result was affirmed by the Oregon Supreme Court in *State v. Ogle,* 297 Or 84, 682 P2d 267 (1984) (communication regarding court appearance date is not for the purpose of facilitating the rendition of professional legal services). See also *State ex rel Schrunk v. Jones,* 63 Or App 132, 662 P2d 788, rev denied 295 Or 631, 670 P2d 1034 (1983).

However, before an attorney can be held in contempt for failure to respond to a question before a grand jury there must be an adjudication by a court of the claimed privilege, a court order to answer, and a subsequent refusal by the witness. *State ex rel Grand Jury v. Bernier,* 64 Or App 378, 668 P2d 455 (1983). The demand for an answer must come from the grand jury, not the prosecutor. *State ex rel Frohnmayer v. Sams,* 293 Or 385, 648 P2d 364 (1982).

Dates of Consultation with Client: In *State v. Keenan/Waller,* 307 Or 515, 771 P2d 244 (1989), an attorney was held in contempt for failing to answer questions regarding the dates when she consulted with her client. The dates were relevant to the issue of whether the defendant was being represented by the attorney when he made a confession to the police. The court affirmed the judgment of contempt, holding: "[W]hen the client relies on the fact that he was represented by an attorney and calls the attorney as a witness, and the fact is disputed, the witness may be examined so far as necessary to decide the issue." 307 Or at 523. The court also found that the information sought by the state did not violate the client's attorney-client privilege, because it did not appear in this case that the disclosure of dates of consultation would not have revealed the substance of a confidential communication. However, the court noted: "One can imagine situations in which it would be improper to probe the frequency and dates of a client's contacts with an attorney ...." 307 Or at 523.

See generally Sobel, *The Confidential Communication Element of the Attorney-Client Privilege,* 4 Cardozo L Rev 649 (1983).

"Communication"

The term *communication* is not itself defined. Nonverbal conduct intended as a substitute for verbal communication, such as nodding of the head or sign language, would seem clearly within the privilege. It is uncertain whether any other observations of nonverbal conduct of the client by an attorney can be within the attorney-client privilege. McCormick states: "A confidential communication may be made by acts as well as by words, as if the client rolled up his sleeve to show the lawyer a hidden scar, or opened the drawer of his desk to show a revolver there." McCormick, *Evidence* (3d ed 1984) § 89 at 213. However, behavior of a client that would be apparent to any observer, such as a staggering walk or slurred speech, should not be within the privilege. Such behavior is neither confidential nor a communication. See generally Saltzburg, *Communications Falling Within the Attorney-Client Privilege,* 66 Iowa L Rev 811 (1981).

A client cannot make unprivileged, preexisting writings subject to the attorney-client privilege by turning them over to an attorney. If the writings were made prior to the attorney-client relationship for business purposes or to communicate with a third person, they do not become privileged by being transferred to an attorney. However, a written communication to an attorney is as much subject to the privilege as is an oral communication. If the document is privileged when in the client's possession, the document will be protected by the attorney-client privilege upon transfer to an attorney for the purpose of obtaining legal advice. *Fisher v. United States,* 425 US 391, 96 SCt 1569, 48 LEd2d 39 (1976).

Tangible objects left with the attorney are not communications and are outside the privilege. The attorney may in fact have an affirmative obligation to turn the items over to proper authorities, at least if they are contraband or constitute evidence of a crime. NOTE, *Ethics Law and Loyalty: The Attorney's Duty to Turn Over Incriminating Physical Evidence,* 32 Stan L Rev 977 (1980); Comment, *Disclosure of Incriminating Physical Evidence Received From a Client: The Defense Attorney's Dilemma,* 52 U Col L Rev 419 (1981). The client may nonetheless have a privilege to prevent the attorney from stating the source of the object on the theory that any statement of ownership or possession would be testimonial in nature and therefore subject to the privilege. See, e.g., *State v. Olwell,* 64 Wash 2d 828, 394 P2d 681 (1964). Not all commentators agree. See, e.g., 2 J. Weinstein and M. Berger, *Weinstein's Evidence* (1988) ¶ 503(b)[03] at 503–55 (footnote omitted): "The client, by giving something to the lawyer, should not, in effect, be permitted to destroy evidence—the nexus between himself and the thing."

Under prior Oregon law it has been held that the existence of assets left with an attorney is not a confidential communication. See *State ex rel Hardy v. Gleason,* 19 Or 159, 23 P 817 (1890).

The privilege may extend to subjects other than "communications" in cases where disclosure of those subjects would reveal confidential communications. In *State v. Keenan/Waller,* 307 Or 515, 522, 771 P2d 244 (1989), the court stated: "We assume that the privilege could shield information beyond communications, such as the identity of the client, if disclosure would have [the effect of revealing the substance of confidential communications]."

RULE 503(1)(c)
"Lawyer" Defined

The definition of *lawyer* contained in Rule 503(1)(c) includes an attorney authorized to practice law anywhere in the world, or reasonably believed by the client to be so authorized. Even communications with a person engaged in the unauthorized practice of law would be privileged if the client reasonably believed that the person was a lawyer. Communications with a law student not acting as a representative of an attorney, and not believed by the client to be so acting, are not subject to the privilege. *Dabney v. Inv. Corp. of Am.,* 82 FRD 464 (ED Pa 1979).

RULE 503(1)(d)
"Representative of the Client"

Definition

The definition of *representative of the client* contained in Rule 503(1)(d) is important because it determines the scope of the attorney-client privilege for corporations, unincorporated associations, and other organizations or entities that can communicate only through a representative. In the original Oregon Evidence Code enacted in 1981, the legislature adopted what is known as the "control group" test, which limited the attorney-client privilege for a corporate client to communications between the corporate attorney and persons who have "authority to obtain professional legal services and to act on advice rendered pursuant thereto, on behalf of the client."

The "control group" test was part of Rule 502(a)(2) of the 1974 Uniform Rules of Evidence and was adopted by a number of other states. See 2 J. Weinstein and M. Berger, *Weinstein's Evidence* (1988) § 503[03]. However, a trend developed toward recognizing a broader standard of lawyer-client privilege in the corporate setting. In 1981, the United States Supreme Court decided the case of *Upjohn v. United States*, 449 US 383, 101 SCt 677, 66 LEd2d 584 (1981), which rejected the "control group" test and broadened the scope of the attorney-corporate client privilege in federal proceedings.

In response to these developments, the 1987 Oregon Legislature adopted a new and extremely broad definition of "representative of the client," which is set forth in Rule 503(1)(d). Under this definition, a "representative of a client" must be a principal, an employee, an officer, or a director of the client. One of two additional conditions must apply: either (1) the individual must have provided "the client's lawyer with information that was acquired during the course of, or as a result of, such person's relationship with the client as principal, employee, officer or director," and "for the purpose of obtaining for the client the legal advice or other legal services of the lawyer"; or (2) "as part of such person's relationship with the client as principal, employee, officer or director," the person must have sought, received, or applied legal advice from the client's lawyer.

Thus the new definition covers both (1) the transmission of information to the client's lawyer by a principal, employee, officer, or director for the purpose of obtaining legal services for the client and (2) the receiving, seeking, or applying of legal advice from the client's lawyer by such an individual, provided the other requirements of the rule are satisfied. See generally Developments in the Law, *Oregon Expands the Protections of the Attorney-Client Privilege for Corporations and Other Business Entities*, 24 Willamette L Rev 157 (1988).

Upjohn *Criteria*

The new Oregon standard goes beyond *Upjohn*. In *Upjohn* the communications to the corporation's attorney were made at the direction of corporate superiors. No such requirement is contained in the Oregon rule.

Whether Rule 503(1)(d) expands the Oregon attorney-corporate client privilege beyond the scope of *Upjohn* in other ways depends upon interpretation of its provisions. In *Upjohn,* the communications to corporate counsel concerned matters within the scope of the employees' corporate duties. Rule 503(1)(d)(A) requires that the information that is the basis of the communication be "acquired during the course of, or as a result of, such person's relationship with the client as principal, employee, officer or director." Does this language mean that a statement to a company lawyer by a file clerk who coincidentally happens to observe a company truck in an accident as she leaves work is now privileged? Is her observation being made "during the course of her employment?" A narrower interpretation is to be preferred. The policies underlying the privilege will be adequately protected if the language "during the course of, or as a result of" is linked to the corporate duties of the employee. An overly broad interpretation of this language could unfairly restrict discovery and raise other policy concerns.

Although Rule 503(l)(d)(A) in defining "representative of the client" makes reference to "providing the client's lawyer with information that was acquired during the course of, or as a result of, such person's relationship with the client," this should not be interpreted as suggesting that the information itself is necessarily privileged, unless it qualifies as a "confidential communication." Rule 503(2) limits the scope of the privilege to "confidential communications." A corporate employee might provide the corporate attorney with preexisting financial records or reports, but they do not become privileged merely by being transferred to the attorney. However, confidential communications by a representative of the client regarding such records or reports may be privileged.

A factor relied upon in *Upjohn* for recognizing the privilege was that the communications from the corporate employees to corporate counsel were considered highly confidential when made and were kept confidential by the company. Rule 503(l)(d) contains no confidentiality requirement. However, Rule 503(2) provides that the privilege is applicable only to communications that are confidential. Therefore, if the communications are disclosed to unnecessary third parties or even to persons within the corporation who do not qualify as "representatives of the client," the privilege may be lost, on grounds of either waiver or a failure to preserve the required confidentiality. It is likely that the broad definition of "representative of the client" in the amended rule will be limited to some extent by more frequent application of the doctrine of waiver.

It is also likely that courts will scrutinize the motive of the employee or agent in making the communication that is given to the corporate lawyer. Rule 503(l)(d)(A) requires that the information be provided to the client's lawyer "for the purpose of obtaining for the client the legal advice or other services of the lawyer." Therefore, a report or other communication by a corporate employee or agent that is made to the corporation primarily for business purposes and is later passed along to the corporate lawyer for legal purposes would not qualify. If obtaining legal services for the client is only a secondary or incidental purpose of the communication courts are likely to find that the requirements of the rule are not satisfied.

Ethical Issues

The expanded definition of "representative of the client" raises ethical issues for parties litigating against a corporation who seek to interview a corporate employee. If the employee qualifies as a "representative of the client," the opposing attorney should refrain from making inquiries of the employee regarding communications with the corporate attorney that are within the corporation's attorney-client privilege. The question has also been raised whether permission must be obtained from corporate counsel before interviewing such an employee in cases where the employee has previously consulted with corporate counsel. See Tomlinson, "Problems for lawyers who contact adverse corporate employees directly," 49 Oregon State Bar Bulletin 18 (November, 1988).

Nature of Advice

Rule 503(1)(d)(B) presents several difficulties of interpretation. It appears to make a principal, employee, officer, or director of the client a "representative of the client" even when obtaining personal legal advice from the client's lawyer rather than obtaining legal advice or services for the client. But see Rule 503(2) (communication must be for purposes of facilitating the rendition of professional legal services *to the client*). The agent must seek, receive, or apply such advice "as part of such person's relationship with the client." Presumably this latter qualification is intended to mean that the advice must relate in some way to the agent's corporate duties. Purely personal, nonbusiness related advice to a corporate employee should not qualify, even though the employee met corporate counsel and was able to obtain such advice because of his employment.

Rule 503(1)(d)(B) applies only to legal advice whereas Rule 503(1)(d)(A) applies to both legal advice and legal services. Therefore, in interpreting Rule 503(1)(d)(B), courts will have to draw a distinction between the two concepts. Such line-drawing may be difficult, because often in the performance of a legal service, such as drafting a legal document, legal advice is given implicitly if not explicitly.

Even though a communication by a corporate employee who does not meet the definition of "representative of the client" is not within the attorney-client privilege of the corporation, it may nonetheless constitute work product of the attorney if the statement was taken in anticipation or preparation of litigation. See *Hickman v. Taylor*, 329 US 495, 67 SCt 385, 91 L Ed 451 (1947); ORCP 36B(3). See discussion of the work product doctrine, infra.

Advice to Corporate Employees

Corporate counsel will need to be cautious in giving legal advice to corporate employees, officers or directors pursuant to this rule, because of possible conflict between the interests of such individuals and those of the corporation and possible confusion regarding who is the holder of the privilege. If the corporation is the holder of the privilege, as this rule appears to contemplate, then the corporation could seek to waive the privilege, despite possible adverse legal consequences to the employee, officer, or director, and despite the fact that the individual receiving the legal advice seeks to assert the privilege.

If the corporation is the sole holder of the privilege, arguably corporate counsel have an obligation to inform employees, officers, or directors of this fact before interviewing them or giving them individual legal advice. Otherwise, employees, officers, or directors may be misled into thinking their communications with corporate counsel are protected by the privilege when in fact the protection may exist only to the extent that the corporation as holder decides to assert the privilege.

To avoid unfairness to individuals receiving personal legal advice under Rule 503(l)(d)(B), courts may decide that both the individual and the client are holders of the privilege and that the privilege may be asserted by either. See *Diversified Industries v. Meredith,* 572 F2d 596, 611 n5 (8th Cir 1977) ("an employee's confidential communications to the corporation's counsel may reveal potential liability of the employee," so the employee "may have a privilege" where he seeks "legal advice from the corporation's counsel for himself" or where counsel acts as "joint attorney.") If the law develops so that there are dual holders of the privilege, corporate counsel may be reluctant to give legal advice to employees, officers, or directors under Rule 503(l)(d)(B) to avoid being placed in a situation where they could receive conflicting instructions from their corporate client and from the employee, officer, or director regarding whether to waive or assert the privilege.

"Representatives" of Individual Clients

It is clear that the legislature contemplated that Rule 503(l)(d) be used to define the scope of the attorney-client privilege for corporations and similar entities who can communicate only through representatives. It is less clear that the legislature intended that individual clients can never have a "representative" when communicating with an attorney.

In *State v. Jancsek,* 302 Or 270, 730 P2d 14 (1986), the defendant wrote his former employer stating that he planned to murder his wife and asking him to obtain legal assistance for defendant. The defendant claimed that the former employer was a "representative of the client" and therefore the letter from the defendant to the former employer was privileged. The court held that "representative of the client" was intended to apply only in cases involving corporations and similar entities. Although this case was decided under the original version of the rule, presumably the holding would be the same under the amended version.

In *Little v. Dep't. of Justice,* 130 Or App 668, 674, 883 P2d 272, 276, rev denied 320 Or 492, 887 P2d 793 (1994), the court held that statements made by clients to a third person and then passed on to clients' attorney were not privileged. The court noted that the third person could not qualify as a "representative of the client" for purposes of the privilege, because only a person acting on behalf of a business entity can be a "representative of a client" and here the clients were individuals.

Shareholder Derivative Litigation

In shareholder derivative litigation, the corporation holds only a qualified privilege, which can be overcome by the shareholders upon a showing of good cause. *Garner v. Wolfinbarger,* 430 F2d 1093 (5th Cir 1970), cert denied 401 US 974 (1971); *Ward v. Succession of Freeman,* 854 F2d 780 (5th Cir 1988), cert denied 109 SCt 2064 (1989).

Other Authorities

See generally, Saltzburg, *Corporate and Related Attorney-Client Privilege Claims: A Suggested Approach,* 12 Hofstra L Rev 279 (1984); Saltzburg, *Corporate Attorney-Client Privilege in Shareholder Litigation and Similar Cases: Garner Revisited,* 12 Hofstra L Rev 817 (1984); Taylor, *Attorney-Client Privilege: A Guide for Corporations,* 7 U Ark L J 115 (1984); Sexton, *A Post-Upjohn Consideration of the Corporate Attorney-Client Privilege,* 57 NYU L Rev 443 (1982); ANNOT., *Attorney-Client Privilege in Federal Courts: Under What Circumstances Can Corporation Claim Privilege for Communications from Its Employees and Agents to Corporation's Attorney,* 9 ALR Fed 685 (1971); Simon, *The Attorney-Client Privilege As Applied to Corporations,* 65 Yale L J 953 (1956); NOTE, *Attorney-Client Privilege for Corporate Clients: The Control Group Test,* 84 Harv L Rev 424 (1970); NOTE, *Applicability of the Attorney-Client Privilege to Corporate Communications,* 48 U of Cin L Rev 819 (1979); ANNOT., *Communications by Corporation as Privileged in Stockholders' Action,* 34 ALR3d 1106 (1970); ANNOT., *Attorney-Client Privilege: Who is "Representative of the Client" Within State Statute or Rule Privileging Communications Between an Attorney and the Representative of the Client,* 66 ALR4th 1227 (1988); COMMENT, *Attorney-Client Privilege for the Government Entity,* 97 Yale L J 1725 (1988).

RULE 503(1)(e)
"Representative of the Lawyer"

A *representative of the lawyer* means one employed to assist the lawyer in the rendition of professional legal services. Such persons are often experts. In some cases, a communication by a client to an expert hired by an attorney will already be within a privilege, such as the physician-patient privilege. By this rule, the communication will be subject to the attorney-client privilege as well, if the expert is acting as the agent of the attorney. See *State v. Corgain,* 63 Or App 26, 663 P2d 773 (1983) (psychiatrist who examined defendant at request of defense counsel was "representative of the lawyer").

In other cases, communication with an expert, such as a certified public accountant, will be nonprivileged, unless that expert is working for an attorney, in which case the communication will be brought within the attorney-client privilege. The Commentary states that the privilege does not apply to an expert employed to testify as a witness.

The rationale is sound for bringing within the privilege communications to an expert who is merely acting as an intermediary between the client and the attorney. Communications to a psychotherapist who examines the client and then reports to the attorney should certainly be as privileged as communications by the client directly to the attorney. The rationale is more questionable for extending the attorney-client privilege to experts who do not act as intermediaries and who never communicate with the client. For example, an appraiser may evaluate property, or an engineer the condition of a wrecked vehicle, without ever consulting the client. Arguably, the work product doctrine is sufficient protection for the reports and communications of such experts. Rule 503(2)(b) provides, however, that communications to the lawyer by such representatives of the lawyer are privileged. This rule is consistent with prior Oregon case law. See *Brink v. Multnomah County,* 224 Or 507, 356 P2d 536 (1960) (report of an appraiser to the client's lawyer is within the attorney-client privilege).

The fact that communications by the expert to the attorney may be privileged does not necessarily mean that the facts learned by the expert are within the privilege or the work product doctrine. In appropriate cases, the expert's knowledge, as distinguished from the communications to the attorney, may be subject to discovery.

A physician making an examination under ORCP 44 is expressly excluded from the definition of a representative of the lawyer. One purpose of ORCP 44 is to override the physician-patient privilege that might otherwise prevent discovery of medical reports in personal injury litigation. That purpose would be defeated if the patient could claim the attorney-client privilege instead.

RULE 503(2)
General Rule of Privilege

The attorney-client privilege as defined by Rule 503(2) protects more than communications by the client or the client's representative to the attorney. Consistent with prior law, it also protects communications by the attorney to the client. See *State v. Muller,* 34 Or App 759, 579 P2d 883 (1978). Subject to the standard qualification that the communication be confidential and made for the purpose of facilitating the rendition of professional legal services to the client, Rule 503(2) protects communications:

(a) Between the client or the client's representative and the client's lawyer or a representative of the lawyer;

(b) Between the client's lawyer and the lawyer's representative;

(c) By the client or the client's lawyer to a lawyer representing another in a matter of common interest;

(d) Between representatives of the client or between the client and a representative of the client;

(e) Between lawyers representing the same client.

See ANNOT., *Attorney-Client Privilege as Affected by Communications Between Several Attorneys,* 9 ALR3d 1420 (1966).

The burden of establishing the existence of the attorney-client privilege and the privileged nature of the communication is on the party seeking to exclude the evidence. *United States v. Osborn,* 561 F2d 1334 (9th Cir 1977); *State v. Moore,* 45 Or App 837, 609 P2d 866 (1980). The determination of facts necessary to establish the existence of the privilege is a preliminary matter for the court under Rule 104(1).

RULE 503(3)
Who May Claim the Privilege

The client is the holder of the privilege. However, the privilege may be claimed not only by the client but also by the client's guardian or conservator or by the successor, trustee, or similar representative of a corporation, association, or organization. The lawyer or lawyer's representative may claim the privilege on behalf of the client, and under the Code of Professional Responsibility normally has an obligation to do so. See DR 4-101(B)(1).

The privilege survives the death of the client and may be claimed by the personal representative. Frankel, *The Attorney-Client Privilege After the Death of the Client*, 6 Geo J Legal Ethics 45 (1992); COMMENT, Evidence—*Attorney-Client Privilege Survives Client's Death*, 25 Suffolk U L Rev 1260 (1991). However, there is an exception to the privilege under Rule 503(4)(b) for communications relevant to an issue between parties who claim through the same deceased client.

A client's spouse normally does not have standing to claim the privilege of the client. In *State v. Wolfs*, 119 Or App 262, 267, 850 P2d 1139, rev denied 317 Or 163, 856 P2d 318 (1993), the defendant claimed that the trial court erred by requiring his wife's attorney to testify that the wife gave the attorney the pistol used by defendant and that the attorney gave it to a police officer. Defendant argued that the testimony was protected by the client-attorney privilege. However, the appellete court held that even if the testimony was privileged, defendant cannot appeal an erroneous privilege ruling by the trial court where he is not the client protected by the privilege.

✋ QUERY:

When an attorney makes a claim of privilege on behalf of a client and the claim is overruled, should the attorney then disclose the communication or refuse to do so, be held in contempt, and raise the issue on appeal? McCormick responds: "It seems clear that, unless in a case of flagrant disregard of the law by the judge, the lawyer's duty is merely to present his view that the testimony is privileged, and if the judge rules otherwise, to submit to his decision." 1 McCormick, *Evidence* (4th ed 1992) § 92 at 341 (footnote omitted). Under Rule 512(1), there is no permanent waiver of the privilege if the disclosure is compelled erroneously. See also DR 4-101(C)(2).

See generally ANNOT., *Appealability by Client of Denial to Quash Subpoena Directed to Attorney or Order Compelling Attorney to Testify or Produce Documents—Federal Criminal Cases*, 109 ALR Fed 564 (1992).

RULE 503(4)
Exceptions to the Privilege

Future Crimes or Frauds

Although reports by a client to an attorney of past crimes or frauds are within the privilege, there is no privilege if the services of the attorney were sought or obtained to enable or aid anyone to commit or plan to commit what the client knew or reasonably should have known to be future crimes or frauds. Rule 503(4)(a). The focus of this exception is on the knowledge of the client, which is a question of fact for the trial judge to determine. *State v. Ray,* 36 Or App 367, 584 P2d 362 (1978). The party seeking disclosure must make a prima facie showing that the legal advice was obtained in furtherance of illegal or fraudulent activity. *In the Matter of Feldberg,* 862 F2d 622 (7th Cir 1988); *In re Berkley and Co.,* 629 F2d 548 (8th Cir 1980).

In *State ex rel N. Pacific Lumber Co. v. Unis.,* 282 Or 457, 464, 579 P2d 1291 (1978), a pre-Code case, the court announced the following standard for application of the future crime or fraud exception:

> [T]he proponent of the evidence must show that the client, when consulting the attorney, knew or should have known that the intended conduct was un-lawful. Good-faith consultations with attorneys by clients who are uncertain about the legal implications of a proposed course of action are entitled to the protection of the privilege, even if that action should later be held improper.

A communication by the client revealing an intent to commit perjury is not protected by the attorney-client privilege, and the attorney may be required to reveal the communication in a subsequent proceeding. *State v. Phelps,* 24 Or App 329, 545 P2d 901 (1976). See generally ANNOT., *Rights and Duties of Attorney in a Criminal Prosecution Where Client Informs Him of Intention to Present Perjured Testimony,* 64 ALR3d 385 (1975).

In *State v. Adams,* 296 Or 185, 674 P2d 593 (1983), the defendant moved for a pretrial ruling excluding testimony sought by the prosecutor from the defendant's prior attorney. The prosecutor contended that the attorney-client privilege was inapplicable because the evidence would fit the exception for future crimes. According to the prosecutor, the evidence would show that the defendant tried to enlist the help of the prior attorney to put on a fabricated defense. Based on this representation, the court indicated that it would be inclined to overrule the privilege claim. On appeal, the defendant contended that this "ruling" was erroneous and caused him not to take the stand in order to avoid having his prior attorney called to impeach him. The Supreme Court refused to decide the privilege question, holding that the trial court had not made a definitive ruling on the issue and that the record was inadequate for review, because it did not show precisely what his former attorney would have said.

In *United States v. Zolin,* 491 US 554 (1989), the United States Supreme Court held that the allegedly privileged communications themselves may be considered by the court in camera in ruling upon whether the future crime or fraud exception is applicable. The Court rejected the view that the existence of the future crime or fraud exception must necessarily be established by evidence independent of the communications claimed to be privileged. However, before an in camera hearing may be held, the party contesting the claim of privilege must show "a factual basis adequate to support a good faith belief by a reasonable person" that such review may reveal evidence establishing the future crime-fraud exception. Even upon such a showing, the trial judge retains discretion whether to conduct an in camera review.

The Court concluded that the Federal Rules of Evidence do not preclude consideration of allegedly privileged communications in deciding the existence of a privilege, and therefore based its decision upon the "developing federal common law of evidentiary privileges." FRE 104(a), which governs the determination of preliminary questions regarding the admissibility of evidence, including the existence of a privilege, was construed as not prohibiting the Court from reviewing communications that have not yet been adjudicated to be privileged. Moreover, the Court refused to treat the allegedly lawyer-client communications as presumptively privileged while the future crime-fraud question is still open. The claim of an exception must be considered as part of the overall determination regarding the existence of the privilege.

The Court held that FRE 104(a) does not apply to the threshold showing in support of an in camera hearing. As part of such showing, the party opposing the privilege may offer any lawfully obtained relevant evidence, but cannot introduce communications adjudicated as privileged. The Court did not address the quantum of proof required to establish the applicability of the future crime-fraud exception, but limited its holding to the type of evidence that may be used in making that determination.

See generally Fried, *Too High a Price for Truth: The Exception to the Attorney-Client Privilege for Contemplated Crimes and Frauds,* 64 N C L Rev 443 (1986); Rieger, *Client Perjury: A Proposed Resolution of the Constitutional and Ethical Issues,* 70 Minn L Rev 121 (1985); ANNOT., *Attorney-Client Privilege as Extending the Communications Relating to Contemplated Civil Fraud,* 31 ALR 4th 458 (1984); ANNOT., *Applicability of Attorney-Client Privilege to Communications With Respect to Contemplated Tortious Acts,* 2 ALR3d 861 (1965).

Claimants Through Same Deceased Client

Rule 503(4)(b) recognizes a privilege for communications relevant to an issue between parties who claim through the same deceased client. The theory for this exception is that, even though the privilege normally survives the death of a client and passes to the client's representative, the identity of that representative may not be known until the conclusion of the litigation. The determination of the proper representative is facilitated by removing the privilege rather than allowing either claimant to assert it.

Breach of Duty

Rule 503(4)(c) states an exception to the privilege in cases where a malpractice or ethical complaint is made by the client against the attorney, or where there is a breach of duty to the lawyer by the client, such as nonpayment of a fee. This exception should be construed narrowly to avoid disclosing any more of the client's confidences than are necessary for the lawyer to defend against the client's claim or obtain redress for breach of duty by the client. See NOTE, *Eliminating "Backdoor" Access to Client Confidences: Restricting the Self-Defense Exception to the Attorney-Client Privilege*, 65 NYU L Rev 992 (1990). Cf. McMonigle and Mallen, *The Attorney's Dilemma in Defending Third Party Lawsuits: Disclosure of the Client's Confidences or Personal Liability?*, 14 Willamette L J 355 (1978).

In re Robeson, 293 Or 610, 652 P2d 336 (1982), presented the question of whether the attorney-client privilege could be breached by an attorney in order to defend himself in a bar disciplinary proceeding against an accusation of wrongdoing filed by a third person rather than the client, under circumstances where the client had not waived the privilege. The court held that the attorney could testify as to attorney-client communications in order to defend himself, but that the Oregon State Bar could not require him to reveal privileged information.

Attested Documents

An exception to the privilege is recognized for communications relevant to an issue concerning an attested document to which the attorney is an attesting witness. It is thought that an attorney who acts as an attesting witness normally does so with the consent of the client and with an understanding of the role of an attesting witness to furnish information relevant to the execution of the document.

Joint Consultation

Rule 503(4)(e) creates an exception where clients jointly consult an attorney but later have a dispute between themselves. This exception can be justified on the ground that no confidentiality was intended between the disputants regarding what the lawyer was told. The rationale for this exception is stated by McCormick:

> In the first place the policy of encouraging disclosure by holding out the promise of protection seems inapposite, since as between themselves neither would know whether he would be more helped or handicapped, if in any dispute between them, both could invoke the shield of secrecy. And secondly, it is said that they had obviously no intention of keeping these secrets from each other, and hence as between themselves it was not intended to be confidential.

1 McCormick, *Evidence* (4th ed 1992) § 91 at 336 . *See generally* ANNOT., *Applicability of Attorney-Client Privilege to Evidence or Testimony in Subsequent Action*

Between Parties Originally Represented Contemporaneously by Same Attorney, with Reference to Communication to or from One Party, 4 ALR4th 765 (1981).

Identity of Client

Under pre-Code law, the fact of employment and the name and address of a client were not considered to be protected by the privilege. See *Cole v. Johnson*, 103 Or 319, 205 P 282 (1922); *In re Illidge*, 162 Or 393, 406, 91 P2d 1100 (1939) ("Where the privilege is claimed, an attorney must name an actual client in order to prove the existence of the relationship; otherwise, no lawyer could ever be questioned as to any fact, since he might always claim that he had learned it from a client whose very existence he need not show.").

The Commentary states that the legislature did not intend to modify the law of these cases, which the Commentary describes as an exception to the privilege. See also *Little v. Dep't of Justice*, 130 Or App 668, 674, 883 P2d 272, 276, rev denied 320 Or 492, 887 P2d 793 (1994) (attorney-client privilege does not shield the identity of an attorney's clients).

Whether the fact of representation is within the privilege was addressed in *State v. Keenan/Waller*, 91 Or App 481, 485, 756 P2d 51 (1988), aff'd 307 Or 515, 771 P2d 244 (1989), where the Court of Appeals stated: "It is difficult to see how [the fact of representation] might be privileged when it is clear that a client who hires or discharges an attorney necessarily anticipates that the attorney will tell others who need to know whether the attorney represents the client." But the Oregon Supreme Court opinion in the same case stated:

> The main dispute concerns whether the dates of communications between Waller and Keenan were privileged information because their disclosure would amount to disclosure of their substance. *We assume that the privilege could shield information beyond communications, such as the identity of the client, if disclosure would have that effect* (emphasis added).

State v. Keenan/Waller, 307 Or 515, 522, 771 P2d 244 (1989)

In narrow circumstances, where disclosure of the client's identity would impair the attorney-client relationship, courts have allowed the claim of privilege. The situation where courts have been most inclined to recognize a privilege for a client's identity is where disclosure of the client's identity would be tantamount to disclosing an otherwise protected confidential communication. See *Tornay v. United States*, 840 F2d 1424, 1428 (9th Cir 1988) (privilege applies only in "exceptional circumstances" where disclosure of the client's identity or the existence of a fee arrangement "would reveal information that is tantamount to a confidential professional communication"); *In re Grand Jury Investigation 83-2-35 (Durant)*, 723 F2d 447 (6th Cir 1983); *Baird v. Koerner*, 279 F2d 623 (9th Cir 1960). For a discussion of recent federal and state cases on this issue, see C. Mueller & L. Kirkpatrick, MODERN EVIDENCE (1995) § 5.19.

See generally ANNOT., *Attorney's Disclosure in Federal Proceedings of Identity of Client as Violating Attorney-Client Privilege*, 84 ALR Fed 852 (1987);

ANNOT., *Disclosure of Name, Identity, Address, Occupation, or Business of Client as Violation of Attorney-Client Privilege,* 16 ALR3d 1047 (1967).

Fee Arrangements

Under federal case law, the exception to the privilege allowing the identity of the client to be revealed has been extended to include the fee arrangement between the client and the lawyer. See *United States v. Sherman,* 627 F2d 189 (9th Cir 1980) (fee arrangement); *United States v. Hodge and Zweig,* 548 F2d 1347 (9th Cir 1977) (identity of client and fee arrangement); *United States v. Strahl,* 590 F2d 10 (1st Cir 1978), cert denied 440 US 918 (1979) (identity of client; payment of legal fee with stolen treasury note). But this exception does not apply where disclosing fee arrangements or a detailed listing of the legal services provided would reveal confidential attorney-client communications. *Ralls v. United States,* 52 F3d 223, 226 (9th Cir 1995) (revealing identity and fee arrangements would be tantamount to revealing privileged communications because so intertwined in this case). See Goode, *Identity, Fees, and the Attorney-Client Privilege,* 59 Geo Wash L Rev 307 (1991).

Assets Left with Attorney

In *State ex rel Hardy v. Gleason,* 19 Or 159, 23 P 817 (1890), the court recognized an exception to the lawyer-client privilege for assets left with the attorney. The Legislative Commentary states that the legislature does not intend to affect this exception.

Waiver—Generally

The attorney-client privilege can be waived by the client expressly or impliedly. Waiver occurs under Rule 511 when the client voluntarily discloses, or consents to disclosure of, any significant part of the matter or communication. See *Weil v. Inv/Indicators, Research and Management Inc.,* 647 F2d 18 (9th Cir 1981) (disclosure by officer-director on deposition waived privilege); *Stark St. Properties Inc. v. Teufel,* 277 Or 649, 562 F2d 531 (1977) (where client concedes he may have given letter from attorney to third person, privilege is waived). Also under Rule 511, the privilege is waived when a psychiatrist has examined the mental condition of a criminal defendant at the request of defendant's lawyer, and at trial the defendant calls any witness who testifies regarding that mental condition. *State v. Corgain,* 63 Or App 26, 663 P2d 773 (1983).

Disclosure of a confidential communication by the attorney without the consent or authorization of the client will not waive the privilege. See Rule 512(2); *State v. McGrew,* 46 Or App 123, 127, 610 P2d 1245 (1980). But see *Goldsborough v. Eagle Crest Partners, Ltd.,* 105 Or App 499, 503–4, 805 P2d 723 (1991), aff'd 314 Or 336, 838 P2d 1069 (1992) (disclosure by attorney of privileged material during discovery presumed to be authorized by client, even though disclosure resulted in waiver of privilege; presumption of attorney's authority to waive privilege can be rebutted but was not in this case).

If a privileged writing is furnished to a witness outside the privilege in order to refresh her recollection for purposes of testifying, the privilege will normally be waived. On the question of whether use of a privileged writing by the client to refresh memory for purpose of testifying will result in compelled disclosure, see discussion under Rule 612.

Inadvertent Waiver

Sometimes a privileged communication will be disclosed inadvertently, such as when a document is mistakenly transmitted to an opposing party during discovery. In *Goldsborough v. Eagle Crest Partners, Ltd.*, 105 Or App 499, 503–4, 805 P2d 723 (1991), aff'd 314 Or 336, 838 P2d 1069 (1992), the court held that the attorney-client privilege was waived with respect to a letter that was voluntarily produced by the defendant's attorney during discovery. The court held that voluntary disclosure waives the privilege and there need not be an "intentional relinquishment" of a known right.

In *GPL Treatment, Ltd v. Louisiana-Pacific Corporation*, 133 Or App 633, 639, 894 P2d 470 (1995), a privileged note had been inadvertently attached to other documents sent to the defendant. Plaintiff's counsel was unaware that the note had been sent until defendant attempted to offer it at trial. Here the court undertook a more refined analysis of the waiver issue and considered the following factors: "[W]hether the disclosure was inadvertent, whether any attempt was made to remedy any error promptly and whether preservation of the privilege will occasion unfairness to the proponent." The court upheld the trial court's finding that there had been no "voluntary" disclosure and hence no waiver of the privilege.

Whether disclosure during discovery results in loss of privilege protection should depend very much on the circumstances, and the issue should be resolved by looking mostly to three factors: First is the degree of care apparently exercised by the claimant. See *In re Grand Jury Proceedings*, 727 F.2d 1352, 1355–7 (4th Cir 1984) (discussing precautions necessary to preserve privilege); *In re Grand Jury Investigation of Ocean Transp.*, 604 F.2d 672, 674–5 (DC Cir 1979) (after producing documents for the government, counsel was asked whether documents marked "P" were privileged, and then failed to assert privilege), cert. denied 444 US 915; *Hartford Fire Insurance Co. v. Garvey*, 109 FRD 323, 330 (ND Cal 1985) (major factor in determining whether inadvertent disclosure has destroyed privilege "is the degree of care used to protect the documents"); *Eigenheim Bank v. Halpern*, 598 F Supp 988, 991 (SDNY 1984) (waiver by inadvertence found where procedures used to maintain confidentiality were "lax, careless, inadequate or indifferent to consequences").

Second is the presence of extenuating circumstances, the most obvious being the press of massive discovery going forward under the pressure of deadlines, where even caution in producing documents is likely to generate occasional mistakes. See *Permian Corp. v. United States*, 665 F2d 1214, 1221 n14

(DC Cir 1981) (inadvertent disclosure during expedited discovery); *Transamerica Computer Co. v. International Business Mach. Corp.*, 573 F2d 646, 648 (9th Cir 1978) (no waiver where IBM had been ordered to produce 17 million pages of material in 90 days; court found that IBM had made a "herculean effort" to cull out privileged items); *Kansas-Nebraska Natural Gas Co. v. Marathon Oil Co.*, 109 FRD 12, 21 (D Neb 1985) (inadvertent disclosure during production of more than 75,000 documents); *Los Sportswear, USA, Inc. v. Levi Strauss & Co.*, 104 FRD 103, 104–5 (SDNY 1985) (inadvertent disclosure during accelerated discovery).

Third is the behavior of the privilege claimant in taking remedial steps after disclosing material. Promptness in discovering the fact of disclosure or seeking return or suppression of material helps the case for continued protection, if only because it supports the notion that disclosure was truly accidental and because it lessens the likelihood that other parties will rely on the disclosed material. See, e.g., *United States v. De La Jara*, 973 F2d 746, 749–50 (9th Cir 1992) (privilege waived where holder failed to reclaim privileged letter seized during government search); *Permian Corp. v. United States*, 665 F2d 1214, 1219–20 & n11 (DC Cir 1981) (privilege waived where attorney did not take reasonable steps to preserve privilege after inadvertent disclosure); *In re Grand Jury Investigation of Ocean Transp.*, 604 F2d 672, 675 (DC Cir 1979) (privilege waived where attorney allowed disclosure of certain documents that appeared to be privileged but a year later sought return on ground that they were privileged and disclosure was inadvertent), cert. denied 444 US 915.

Other factors bear on the calculus as well, including the volume, nature, and importance of disclosed material, and the obviousness of privilege issues. With greater volume, disclosure is more likely to seem careless and perhaps even purposeful, and the notion of waiver more clearly applies and loss of protection seems more justified. Much the same applies if the material is central to issues that are well defined, if the privilege claim seems obvious, and if the claimant grants wide access or discloses more than once.

Finally, loss of protection should be more readily found if the other side has relied on disclosed material in developing its litigation strategy, and upholding protection is easier if no such reliance occurs. See *Weil v. Investment/Indicators, Research & Management, Inc.*, 647 F2d 18, 25 (9th Cir 1981) (court considers fact that disclosure was made to opposing counsel rather than to court, came early in the case, and no prejudice resulted). See generally Marcus, *The Perils of Privilege: Waiver and the Litigator*, 84 Mich. L. Rev. 1605, 1654–5 (1986) (waivers "should be based on fairness, which is the emerging trend," and main concern is that litigant "may affirmatively use privileged material to garble the truth, while invoking the privilege to deny his opponent access to related privileged material that would put the proffered evidence in perspective"); NOTE, *Inadvertent Disclosure of Documents Subject to the Attorney-Client Privilege*, 82 Mich L Rev 598, 623 (1983) (reliance by opposing party should "not be undermined" when objection could have been made earlier). Cf. *Mendenhall v. Barber-Greene Co.*, 531 F Supp 951, 952 n2, 955 (ND Ill. 1982) (unfair reliance is less likely where opponent has seen the privileged documents but has not obtained copies).

An unresolved issue is whether waiver, if found, applies only to the matter disclosed or to other related privileged communications. In other contexts, partial disclosure of privileged matter can lead to a general waiver of the privilege for related communications on the same subject. See *Duplan Corp. v. Deering Milliken, Inc.*, 397 F Supp 1146, 1161 (DSC 1974) (when client "voluntarily waives the privilege as to some documents that the client considers not damaging and asserts the privilege as to other documents the client considers damaging, the rule compelling production of all documents becomes applicable").

The purpose of recognizing a general waiver from partial disclosure is to prevent a party from obtaining unfair advantage by disclosing a portion of privileged matter that may be unrepresentative or misleading. This danger is generally nonexistent in cases where the disclosure was inadvertent. Therefore, the better view is to limit the scope of waiver by inadvertent disclosure to the material already disclosed. See *Parkway Gallery Furniture, Inc. v. Kittinger/Pennsylvania House Group*, 116 FRD 46, 50–2 (MDNC 1987) (inadvertent disclosure was not waiver with respect to other documents on same subject when disclosing party was not seeking unfair advantage from disclosure); *Standard Chartered Bank PLC v. Ayala Intl. Holdings (U.S.) Inc.*, 111 FRD 76, 85 (SDNY 1986) (inadvertent disclosure of "one isolated document among many produced" does not automatically effect general waiver); *Champion Intl. Corp. v. International Paper Co.*, 486 F Supp 1328, 1333 (ND Ga 1980) (inadvertent disclosure of privileged material during discovery in "spirit of openness, cooperation and reason" does not constitute waiver "as to other privileged material"). See generally NOTE, *Fairness and the Doctrine of Subject Matter Waiver of the Attorney-Client Privilege in Extrajudicial Disclosure Situations*, 1988 U. Ill. L. Rev. 999, 1017 (court should find general waiver only where inadvertent disclosure "unfairly and actually prejudices an adversary").

A broader scope of waiver is justified in cases where the disclosing party has obtained unfair advantage by the disclosure or refuses to stipulate that the disclosed material will not be used at trial, thereby creating a need for the opposing party to discover related communications on the same subject. See *Hercules, Inc. v. Exxon Corp.*, 434 F Supp 136, 156 (D Del 1977) (general waiver occurs only where "facts relevant to a particular, narrow subject matter have been disclosed in circumstances in which it would be unfair to deny the other party an opportunity to discover other relevant facts with respect to that subject matter").

See generally Hundley, *"Inadvertent Waiver" of Evidentiary Privileges: Can Reformulating the Issue Lead to More Sensible Decisions?*, 19 S Ill U L J 263 (1995); Davidson & Voth, *Waiver of the Attorney-Client Privilege*, 64 Or L Rev 637 (1986) (urging that courts not find waiver in cases where the attorney who inadvertently releases a document takes prompt steps to recover it prior to reliance by the opposing side); Grippando, *Attorney-Client Privilege: Implied Waiver Through Inadvertent Disclosure of Documents*, 39 U Miami L Rev 511 (1985); Thornburg, *Attorney-Client Privilege: Issue-Related Waivers*, 50 J Air Law & Commerce 1039 (1985); COMMENT, *The Necessity of Intent to Waive the Privilege in*

Inadvertent Disclosure Cases, 18 Pac L J 59 (1986); COMMENT, *Inadvertent Disclosure of Documents Subject to the Attorney-Client Privilege,* 82 Mich L Rev 598 (1983); COMMENT, *When Does a Limited Waiver of the Attorney-Client Privilege Occur?,* 24 B C L Rev 1283 (1983).

Waiver by Claim Assertion

Substantial authority holds the attorney-client privilege to be impliedly waived where the client asserts a claim or defense that places at issue the nature of the privileged material. For example, if the client asserts that he acted pursuant to the advice of counsel, the privilege may be waived with respect to the specific advice given. See *Hearn v. Rhay,* 68 FRD 574, 582–3 (ED Wash 1975) (in civil rights action against prison officials, defendants asserted that they acted pursuant to advice of counsel; assertion of such a defense waives the attorney-client privilege with respect to the advice given).

Similarly, the privilege may be waived where the client alleges malpractice, incompetence, or breach of ethics by the attorney and use of privileged matter is necessary to defend against such charges. *United States v. Moody,* 923 F2d 341, 352–3 (5th Cir 1991) (privilege may be waived concerning discussions with bankruptcy attorney when during opening statement defendant blamed attorney for improperly listing assets in bankruptcy petition), cert. denied 112 SCt 80; *United States v. Woodall,* 438 F2d 1317, 1324 (5th Cir 1970) (challenge to guilty plea on the ground that defense attorney failed to advise client of maximum possible sentence), cert. denied 403 US 933.

It is generally agreed, however, that a client does not waive the privilege merely by denying the allegations of an indictment or complaint. *Lorenz v. Valley Forge Ins. Co.,* 815 F2d 1095, 1098 (7th Cir 1987) (denial of allegations in complaint is not same as affirmatively injecting issues into litigation).

A variety of justifications have been advanced to support the doctrine of waiver by claim assertion. Sometimes the allegation itself, such as that the client acted pursuant to advice of counsel, is viewed as a partial disclosure of the privileged communication. A finding of waiver may be necessary to allow the adversary to verify or explore the actual advice given. Sometimes the assertion of a claim or defense is viewed as an "anticipatory waiver," at least where it is clear that privileged evidence will be necessary to support the claim or defense.

Finally, courts sometimes find implied waiver where the holder asserts a claim the effective rebuttal of which requires disclosure of privileged matter. See, e.g., *United States v. Bilzerian,* 926 F2d 1285, 1292 (2d Cir 1991) (privilege may "implicitly be waived when defendant asserts a claim that in fairness requires examination of protected communications"), cert. denied 112 SCt 63; *Byers v. Burleson,* 100 FRD 436, 440 (DDC 1983) (plaintiff's claim that statute of limitations was tolled by his lack of knowledge that he had a cause of action waived attorney-client privilege with respect to communications bearing on such knowledge). Under this latter view, even if the claim asserted by the holder does not require disclosure of privileged communications, the privilege is waived to the extent the opposing party needs to draw on privileged matter to make a fair response. *Greater Newburyport Clamshell Alliance v. Public Serv. Co.*, 838 F2d 13, 20 (1st Cir 1988) (filing of action for improper interception of attorney-client communications waived privilege as to issues essential to defense; "privilege ends at the point where the defendant can show that the plaintiff's civil claim, and the probable defenses thereto, are enmeshed in important evidence that will be unavailable to the defendant if the privilege prevails").

In all these settings, the attorney-client privilege should not be overridden merely because access to privileged evidence would be useful to an adverse party in responding to a claim or assertion made by a client. The purpose of the privilege is to preserve values external to the litigation process even at the cost of excluding probative evidence. Therefore, in applying the doctrine of waiver by claim assertion, courts must be careful to target only the "type of unfairness that is distinguishable from the unavoidable unfairness generated by every assertion of privilege." *Developments in the Law—Privileged Communications*, 98 Harv L Rev 1450, 1642 (1985).

Work Product Doctrine

Although not within the scope of Rule 503, the work product doctrine should be considered in relation to the attorney-client privilege. The work product doctrine protects from discovery documents and other tangible things prepared by a party, a party's attorney, or other representatives of a party in anticipation of litigation. The immunity is qualified because, unlike the attorney-client privilege, it can be overcome and production required upon a showing of *substantial need and hardship.* ORCP 36B(3) provides:

> Subject to the provisions of Rule 44 ..., a party may obtain discovery of documents and tangible things otherwise discoverable under subsection B(1) of this rule and prepared in anticipation of litigation or for trial by or for another party or by or for that other party's representative (including an attorney, consultant, surety, indemnitor, insurer, or agent) only upon a showing that the party seeking discovery has substantial need of the materials in the preparation of such party's case and is unable without undue hardship to obtain the substantial equivalent of the materials by other means. In ordering discovery of such materials when the required showing has been made, the court shall protect against disclosure of the mental impressions, conclusions, opinions, or legal theories of an attorney or other representative of a party concerning the litigation.

The above rule is merely a partial codification of the work product doctrine, because it protects only "documents and tangible things" whereas the doctrine itself also protects opinions and impressions of a lawyer or a representative of a lawyer that have not been reduced to writing. Cf. *State v. Bockorny*, 125 Or App 479, 486, 866 P2d 1230, 1235 (1993), rev denied 319 Or 150, 877 P2d 87 (1994) (defendant argued that his work product protection was violated because the prosecutor was allowed to elicit an opinion from a defense expert that the "Christmas tree stain method" was an effective scientific method of detecting the presence of sperm; because defense had hired the expert to testify about a different matter, there was no invasion of work product; but court appeared to recognize that work product claim could be made for nonwritten impressions of an expert).

For Oregon cases discussing the work product doctrine, see *Brink v. Multnomah County*, 224 Or 507, 356 P2d 536 (1960); *Nielsen v. Brown*, 232 Or 426, 374 P2d 896 (1962); *Pacific NW Bell Tel Co. v. Century Home Components, Inc.*, 261 Or 333, 491 P2d 1023 (1971), modified on other grounds 494 P2d 884 (1972). There is no work product immunity for a document prepared in the regular course of business without reference to an existing or threatened lawsuit. *City of Portland v. Nudelman*, 45 Or App 425, 608 P2d 1190 (1980). The work product doctrine applies in criminal cases as well as civil cases. See ORS 135.855(1)(a) (exempting work product from criminal discovery process); *United States v. Nobles*, 422 US 225, 95 SCt 2160,45 LEd2d 141 (1975) (recognizing work product doctrine in criminal case).

See generally Waits, *Opinion Work Product: A Critical Analysis of Current Law and a New Analytical Framework*, 73 Or L Rev 385 (1994); Floyd, *A "Delicate and Difficult Task": Balancing the Competing Interests of Federal Rule of Evidence 612, the Work Product Doctrine, and the Attorney-Client Privilege*, 44 Buff L Rev 101 (1996).

Witness Interview Notes

In *Upjohn Co. v. United States*, 449 US 383, 399, 101 SCt 677, 66 LEd2d 584 (1981), the court commented that "[f]orcing an attorney to disclose notes and memoranda of witnesses' oral statements is particularly disfavored because it tends to reveal the attorney's mental processes." The Court held that more than the usual showing of "substantial need" and inability to obtain such information by other means "without undue hardship" would be required to obtain an attorney's interview notes and memoranda.

Some courts have held that no showing of necessity is sufficient to compel disclosure of an attorney's notes based on oral statements from witnesses. See, e.g., *In re Grand Jury Proceedings*, 473 F2d 840, 848 (8th Cir 1973). Another court has held that "special considerations must shape any ruling on the discoverability of interview memoranda ...; such documents will be discoverable only in a 'rare situation.'" *In re Grand Jury Investigation*, 599 F2d 1224, 1231 (3rd Cir 1979).

However, in *State v. Gallup*, 108 Or App 508, 511, 816 P2d 669, 670 (1991), the court held that interview notes of a district attorney were not work product exempt from discovery under ORS 135.855(l)(a). The court held that the interview notes "contain no opinions, theories or conclusions that could be characterized as work product."

Using Writings to Refresh Memory

If a writing protected by the work product doctrine is shown to a witness to refresh their recollection for purposes of testifying, the work product immunity may be waived. *Pac NW Bell Tel Co. v. Century Home Components, Inc.,* 261 Or 333, 491 P2d 1023, modified on other grounds 494 P2d 884 (1972) (right to see prior statement referred to by witness overrides work product immunity). See further discussion under Rule 612.

Other Authorities

See generally Waits, *Work Product Protection for Witness Statements: Time for Abolition,* 1985 Wis L Rev 305; Cohn, *The Work-Product Doctrine: Protection, Not Privilege,* 7 Geo L J 917 (1983); ANNOT., *Development, Since Hickman v. Taylor, of Attorney's "Work Product" Doctrine,* 35 ALR3d 412 (1971).

RULE 504.   ORS 40.230. PSYCHOTHERAPIST-PATIENT PRIVILEGE

(1) **[Definitions.] As used in this section, unless the context requires otherwise:**
   (a) **"Confidential communication" means a communication not intended to be disclosed to third persons except:**
      (A) **Persons present to further the interest of the patient in the consultation, examination or interview;**
      (B) **Persons reasonably necessary for the transmission of the communication; or**
      (C) **Persons who are participating in the diagnosis and treatment under the direction of the psychotherapist, including members of the patient's family.**
   (b) **"Patient" means a person who consults or is examined or interviewed by a psychotherapist.**
   (c) **"Psychotherapist" means a person who is:**
      (A) **Licensed, registered, certified or otherwise authorized under the laws of any state to engage in the diagnosis or treatment of a mental or emotional condition; or**
      (B) **Reasonably believed by the patient so to be, while so engaged.**
(2) **[General rule of privilege.] A patient has a privilege to refuse to disclose and to prevent any other person from disclosing confidential communications made for the purposes of diagnosis or treatment of the patient's mental or emotional condition among the patient, the patient's psychotherapist or persons who are participating in the diagnosis or treatment under the direction of the psychotherapist, including members of the patient's family.**
(3) **[Who may claim the privilege.] The privilege created by this section may be claimed by:**
   (a) **The patient.**
   (b) **A guardian or conservator of the patient.**

(c) The personal representative of a deceased patient.

(d) The person who was the psychotherapist, but only on behalf of the patient. The psychotherapist's authority so to do is presumed in the absence of evidence to the contrary.

(4) [General exceptions.] The following is a nonexclusive list of limits on the privilege granted by this section.

(a) If the judge orders an examination of the mental, physical or emotional condition of the patient, communications made in the course thereof are not privileged under this section with respect to the particular purpose for which the examination is ordered unless the judge orders otherwise.

(b) There is no privilege under this rule as to communications relevant to an issue of the mental or emotional condition of the patient:

(A) In any proceeding in which the patient relies upon the condition as an element of the patient's claim or defense; or

(B) After the patient's death, in any proceeding in which any party relies upon the condition as an element of the party's claim or defense.

(c) Except as provided in ORCP 44, there is no privilege under this section for communications made in the course of mental examination performed under ORCP 44.

(d) There is no privilege under this section with regard to any confidential communication or record of such confidential communication that would otherwise be privileged under this section when the use of the communication or record is allowed specifically under ORS 426.070, 426.074, 426.075, 426.095, 426.120, or 426.307. This paragraph only applies to the use of the communication or record to the extent and for the purposes set forth in the described statute sections.

LEGISLATIVE COMMENTARY

Oregon Rule of Evidence 504 is based on proposed Rule 504 of the Federal Rules of Evidence, which was prescribed by the United States Supreme Court and submitted to Congress, but not enacted. Aside from minor changes made to conform the rule to the form and style of Oregon statutes, the only differences between this and proposed Federal Rule 504 lie in the exceptions.

Subsection (1). Paragraph (a). "Confidential communication" is defined in terms conformable to those of the lawyer-client privilege, with appropriate changes for the different circumstances. Oregon follows the general rule that the burden of establishing the conditions that give rise to a privilege against disclosure is on the party asserting the privilege. *Groff v. S.I.A.C.,* 246 Or 557, 426 P2d 738 (1967).

Paragraph (b). Oregon courts have not yet given a definition of "patient" for purposes of the psychotherapist-patient and physician-patient privilege, but there should be little controversy surrounding the definition except for persons who are subjects of medical research. The definition of "patient" in Rule 504 and 504-1 does not include a person submitting to examination for scientific purposes. This limitation agrees with the current Oregon requirement that a physician be consulted for treatment in order that the physician-patient privilege attach. *State v. O'Neill,* 274 Or 59, 545 P2d 97 (1976).

Paragraph (c). The rule defines "psychotherapist" as a person authorized or thought to be authorized by the patient to engage in, while in fact engaged in, the diagnosis or treatment of a mental or emotional condition. The definition is broad enough to include not only psychiatrists and psychologists but other professionals who treat mental and emotional conditions. In appropriate circumstances such persons may be medical doctors, nurses or clinical social workers. The definition seeks to avoid needless refined distinctions concerning what is and what is not the practice of psychiatry. The Legislative Assembly intends to exclude, from the definition of "psychotherapist," a person who is specifically consulted for a problem of drug or alcohol dependency.

With regard to psychiatrists, the scope of this definition does not change existing Oregon law (although the scope of the privilege is most assuredly changed, see infra). Psychiatrists are included within the term "regular physician or surgeon" under ORS 44.040(1)(d). *Hampton v. Hampton,* 241 Or 277, 405 P2d 549 (1965). However, the implied definition of psychologist is more expansive than the one in ORS 44.040(1)(h), in that it extends the privilege to a psychologist licensed under the laws of any state rather than a person licensed to practice psychology under the provisions of ORS chapter 675. Because of the continuing requirement under chapter 675 that any person practicing psychology in this state must be licensed under the chapter, however, the difference in definition should have little practical effect.

No Oregon court has decided whether the psychotherapist-patient privilege would apply when a patient reasonably but falsely believes the person consulted is a psychotherapist.

Subsection (2). The general rule of privilege is that a patient may refuse to disclose, and prevent anyone else from disclosing, any confidential communication to a psychotherapist made for the purposes of diagnosis or treatment. This applies to any proceeding except in the circumstances listed in subsections (4) and (5) of this rule.

Subsection (2) changes Oregon law in two ways. First, it limits the psychotherapist-patient privilege to communications made for the purpose of diagnosis or treatment, i.e., consultation which is not a part of diagnosis or treatment is not privileged. This represents a narrowing of the current psychologist-patient privilege, which applies to "any communication made ... in the course of professional employment." ORS 44.040(1)(h). It represents a broadening of the current psychiatrist-patient privilege that courts have read into the physician-patient privilege; the latter applies only to "information acquired [by the physician] ... which was necessary to enable the physician ... to prescribe or act for the patient." ORS 44.040(1)(d); *Hampton v. Hampton,* supra. Second, subsection (2) establishes the psychotherapist-patient privilege in all proceedings. This is the extent of the present psychologist-patient privilege. However, the psychiatrist-patient relation has been subject to the physician-patient rule that the privilege does not apply in a criminal case. *State v. Betts,* 235 Or 127, 384 P2d 193 (1963).

Subsection (3). Subsection (3), like subsection (2), draws upon the lawyer-client privilege for its phrasing. See ORE 503(2), (3). This subsection does not change Oregon law. The physician (psychiatrist) patient privilege is not terminated by the death of the patient. *Woosley v. Dunning,* 268 Or 233, 520 P2d 340 (1974). Although there is no rebuttable presumption in Oregon that the physician or psychologist may claim the privilege on behalf of the patient, the courts have declared that the privilege is intended to benefit the patient and normally cannot be invoked by another person. *Hampton v. Hampton ,* supra. There are good policy reasons for allowing a psychotherapist to claim the privilege on behalf of the patient.

Subsection (4). The exceptions to the psychotherapist-patient privilege differ substantially from those to the attorney-client privilege, reflecting the basic differences in the relationships. While it has been argued convincingly that the nature of the psychotherapist-patient relationship demands complete security against legally coerced disclosure, the Legislative Assembly finds that there are some instances in which the incorporated for disclosure is sufficiently great to justify the risk of impairing the relationship. These exceptions are incorporated in subsection (4) of this rule.

Paragraph (a). The relationship between psychotherapist and patient in a court-ordered examination is likely to be at arm's length, although not necessarily so. An exception is needed, in any event, if this important procedure is to be used effectively. It will be observed that the exception deals with a court-ordered examination, not with a court-appointed psychotherapist or physician, and is only effective to the extent of the purpose for which the examination is ordered. This exception changes Oregon law insofar as it erases the distinction between communications made to psychologists and communications made to physicians and psychiatrists during such examinations. See Commentary to subsection (2) of this rule, supra. This paragraph is a rule of privilege and should not be construed as an independent grant of authority to a judge to order an examination.

Paragraph (b). An exception applies whenever the mental or emotional condition of the patient is put in issue. In a criminal proceeding this means that there is no privilege if a defendant raises the defense of not responsible by reason of mental disease or defect, or the mitigating defense of extreme emotional disturbance. In a civil action, it means there is no privilege in a will contest in which the soundness of the testator's mind is challenged. See Rule 511.

Author's Note: The following paragraph beginning with "Note" was included as part of the original Legislative Commentary. However, it has been made obsolete by changes in the mental commitment procedures, which largely abrogate the privilege in such proceedings. See ORS 426.070, 426.074, 426.075, 426.095, 426.120, 426.307. See also Rule 504(4)(d) which was added by the 1987 Legislature.

Note: This subsection also originally provided that there is no privilege in a civil commitment hearing as to communications and observations made during the prehearing detention period. The Governor's Task Force on Mental Health, which recommended this provision, pointed out that the relationship between an allegedly mentally ill person and hospital medical staff during a period of involuntary prehearing detention is more likely to be adversarial than therapeutic, and, therefore, that the policy reasons for the privilege are not as compelling as in an ongoing treatment relationship. Notwithstanding the argument, the Legislative Assembly wished to preserve present Oregon law, which does not exempt communications at any phase of a commitment proceeding from a claim of privilege.

Subsection (5). This subsection retains the exception for communications made in the course of a physical or mental examination performed under ORCP 44.

A number of other statutes currently affect the operation of the physician-patient and psychologist-patient privilege. Except as noted below these statutes remain in force:

Under ORS 44.040(1)(j), a licensed physician or local health official shall not be examined as to the existence or contents of any records of a person examined or treated for an infectious venereal disease without the consent of the person unless the public interest clearly requires disclosure. This provision is repealed by § 98 of this Act as unnecessary. With regard to the local health authority officer or employee, it duplicates the privilege created under ORS 434.055. With respect to the physician, it is unneeded in civil actions because of the existence of the physician-patient privilege. The only unique feature is its application of the physician-patient privilege to criminal cases in which treatment for venereal disease is a relevant issue. The Legislative Assembly does not believe there is sufficient justification for extending the physician-patient privilege to a very limited number of criminal cases.

Under ORS 107.600(2), all communications between spouses and from spouses to counselors, the court, attorneys, doctors or others engaged in conciliation proceedings, made during the proceedings, are confidential within the meaning of ORS 44.040(1)(e). This section is amended by § 88 of this Act.

Under ORS 146.750(1), except as required in subsection (3) of Rule 504 (relating to child abuse), any physician having reasonable cause to suspect that a person brought for examination or treatment has been injured with a deadly weapon by other than accidental means shall report the fact to the appropriate medical examiner as soon as possible.

Under ORS 161.735, a court may order a psychiatric examination of a person convicted of a felony to determine whether the person is suffering from a severe personality disorder indicating a propensity toward criminal activity. Subsection (4) of ORS 161.735 declares that no statement made by a defendant under the section shall be used against the defendant in any civil proceeding or in any other criminal proceeding.

Under ORS 418.750, all public or private officials have a duty to report possible cases of child abuse, except that psychiatrists, psychologists, clergymen and attorneys are not required to report the privileged communications of adults. ORS 418.775 also provides that the physician-patient privilege is not a ground for excluding evidence in court proceedings on child abuse. Thus, even though the psychologist and psychiatrist have similar duties with regard to reporting possible child abuse, the psychiatrist (whose privilege is founded upon the physician-patient privilege) may be compelled to testify at trial. The psychologist, in contrast, may not be required to testify in a child abuse proceeding as there is no mention of the psychologist-patient privilege in ORS 418.775 which abolishes certain privileges in those proceedings. Section 95 of this Act amends ORS 418.775 and thereby abolishes this distinction.

Under ORS 434.055, no local health official shall be examined as to the existence or contents of records of a person examined or treated for an infectious venereal disease without the consent of the person. This is the same privilege as the one described in ORS 44.040(1)(j), without the exception for public interest. It is noteworthy that it extends the physician-patient privilege to criminal cases in the context of venereal disease communications.

TEXT

Psychotherapist-Patient Privilege

Rule 504 merges the privileges for psychologists and psychiatrists, recognized separately under prior law, into a psychotherapist-patient privilege. This privilege applies in both civil and criminal cases. Under prior law, the psychiatrist-patient privilege, unlike the psychologist-patient privilege, did not apply in criminal cases.

Psychotherapist is defined broadly to reach persons other than psychiatrists or psychologists. As the Commentary notes, in some circumstances psychotherapist may include medical doctors, nurses, or clinical social workers who treat mental and emotional conditions. The definition would not reach counselors who treat mental or emotional conditions, unless they are licensed, registered or certified by the state, or reasonably believed by the patient to be so.

There is an ambiguity in the definition of "psychotherapist" regarding whether psychotherapists who are unlicensed are entitled to the privilege. The definition of psychotherapist includes persons licensed or "otherwise authorized under the laws of any state" to practice psychotherapy. "Otherwise authorized" should be construed to mean something equivalent to a licensing procedure rather than merely not prohibited. Otherwise, the persons entitled to a psychotherapist-patient privilege would be greatly expanded, a result that would seem inconsistent with the legislative intent expressed in the Commentary. An unlicensed psychotherapist, such as a psychology resident or intern, may, however, be able to obtain the privilege derivatively. See Rule 504(1)(a).

The Commentary states that a *patient* does not include "a person submitting to examination for scientific purposes." The Commentary also states that the Legislative Assembly "intends to exclude, from the definition of 'psychotherapist,' a person who is specifically consulted for a problem of drug or alcohol dependency." In *State ex rel Juvenile Department v. Ashley*, 312 Or 169, 180, 818 P2d 1270, 1276 (1991), the court held that the psychotherapist-patient privilege does not apply to communications made "during the diagnosis or treatment of drug dependency when that is the specific purpose of the diagnosis or treatment." Confidential communications about drug dependency made during the course of diagnosis or treatment for a mental or emotional condition covered by Rule 504 are within the privilege.

Rule 504(2) changes prior law by providing that the privilege protects confidential communications made to a psychotherapist for purposes of diagnosis as well as treatment. See *Triplet v. Bd. of Social Protection,* 19 Or App 408, 528 P2d 563 (1974).

The privilege extends to confidential writings prepared by the patient in the course of his treatment. *State v. Langley,* 314 Or 247, 262, 839 P2d 692 (1992), adhered to 318 Or 28, 861 P2d 1012 (1993) (written assignments that defendant had prepared as part of a prison treatment program for mentally and emotionally disturbed inmates were subject to the psychotherapist-patient privilege).

In *State v. Miller,* 300 Or 203, 709 P2d 225 (1985), cert denied 475 US 1141 (1986), the court held that "the psychotherapist-patient privilege protects communications made in an initial conference for the purpose of establishing a psychotherapist-patient relationship, even if such a relationship is never actually formed." 300 Or at 212, 709 P2d at 234. In this case, the court held that inculpatory statements made by a defendant talking over the telephone to a receptionist and a psychiatrist at Dammasch State Hospital were privileged, even though the psychiatrist testified that she was not engaged in therapy and was interrogating the defendant over the telephone to hold him until police could arrive at the pay phone where he placed the call. The court held that the relevant issue is the intent of the patient to form a psychotherapist-patient relationship, although there must also be "some indication from the psychotherapist that he or she is willing to embark upon such a relationship. An indication of this intent may be inferred from the circumstances." 300 Or at 212, 709 P2d at 234.

In *Miller,* the court also held that the defendant's statements to the receptionist at the hospital were within the privilege. Because the receptionist asked defendant to describe his problem before she would refer him to a doctor, the court found her to be an assistant employed in the process of communication and thus a person reasonably necessary for the transmission of the communication under Rule 504(1)(a). If an unnecessary third party were present during the communication between patient and psychotherapist, confidentiality would not exist.

Court-Ordered Examinations

The privilege does not apply to communications made in the course of a court ordered examination, unless the judge orders otherwise. But see ORS 161.735(4) (statements made by defendant during court-ordered examination, to determine whether defendant is dangerous offender, are privileged). In *State v. Mains,* 295 Or 640, 669 P2d 1112 (1983), the court held that a psychotherapist about to examine a criminal defendant on behalf of the state must give the following warnings:

If counsel is not present at the examination ... the defendant should be asked by the examiner whether he understands that counsel is entitled to be present and has consented to be examined in the absence of counsel. The defendant should be further informed that the examination is conducted on behalf of the prosecution and its results will be available for use against the defendant without the confidentiality of the doctor-patient relationship.

295 Or at 645, 669 P2d at 1116.

At a court-ordered examination a criminal defendant can be required to answer questions asked by the state psychiatrist, except questions concerning his conduct at or immediately near the time of the commission of the offense. He cannot be required to incriminate himself. *Shepard v. Bowe,* 250 Or 288, 442 P2d 238 (1968); *State ex rel Johnson v. Woodrich,* 279 Or 31, 566 P2d 859 (1977); *State ex rel Ott v. Cushing,* 291 Or 355, 630 P2d 861 (1981). Cf. *State v. Loyer,* 55 Or App 854, 640 P2d 631 (1982) (not reversible error for state psychiatrist to fail to inform defendant of right against self-incrimination prior to interview when defendant is already represented by counsel who can give such advice); *Estelle v. Smith,* 451 US 454, 101 SCt 1866, 68 LEd2d 359 (1981) (criminal defendant has constitutional right not to answer questions at court-ordered examination where answers may be used against defendant at sentencing hearing). See generally COMMENT, *The Privilege Against Self-Incrimination in Pre-Trial Psychiatric Examinations: Oregon's Compromise,* 14 Willamette L J 313 (1978).

A distinction must be drawn between a court-ordered examination and a court-appointed examiner. A communication to a psychotherapist appointed by the court at the request of the defendant is not necessarily outside the scope of the privilege. However, the privilege may not apply if the mental condition of the patient becomes an issue in the litigation. See Rule 504(4)(b); Rule 511. In providing that the psychotherapist-patient privilege may be waived by the assertion of an insanity defense, Rule 504(4)(b) overrules prior case law. See *State v. Moore,* 45 Or App 837, 609 P2d 866 (1980).

As the Commentary notes, the original version of this rule applied the privilege to communications between an allegedly mentally ill person and a psychotherapist during a period of involuntary detention prior to a mental commitment hearing. However, the 1987 legislature amended the rule by adding subsection (4)(d) and largely eliminating the privilege in mental commitment proceedings.

Other Statutes

The psychotherapist-patient privilege is supplemented by ORS 107.600. This statute recognizes an absolute privilege for communications made in the course of marital conciliation proceedings, and the exceptions set forth in Rule 504(4) are not recognized.

The psychotherapist-patient privilege is qualified by ORS 419B.040, which provides that the privilege does not apply in certain judicial proceedings relating to child abuse. In *State v. Hansen,* 304 Or 169, 743 P2d 157 (1987), the trial court had excluded exculpatory communications between a child abuse victim and her psychologist on the ground that the exception applied only in cases where the otherwise privileged information supported the allegation of abuse. The Supreme Court held that the exception also applies in cases where otherwise privileged communications are exculpatory.

See generally Shuman & Weiner, *The Privilege Study: An Empirical Examination of the Psychotherapist-Patient Privilege*, 60 N C L Rev 893 (1982); COMMENT, *The Psychotherapist-Client Testimonial Privilege: Defining the Professional Involved*, 34 Emory L J 777 (1985); COMMENT, *Evidence: The Psychotherapist-Patient Privilege Under Federal Rule of Evidence 501*, 23 Washburn L J 706 (1984); COMMENT, *Psychotherapist-Patient Privilege Under Federal Rule of Evidence 501*, 75 J Crim L & Criminology 388 (1984); ANNOT., *Psychotherapist-Patient Privilege Under Federal Common Law*, 72 ALR Fed 395 (1985).

RULE 504-1.   ORS 40.235. PHYSICIAN-PATIENT PRIVILEGE

(1) [Definitions.] As used in this section, unless the context requires otherwise:

    (a) "Confidential communication" means a communication not intended to be disclosed to third persons except:

        (A) Persons present to further the interest of the patient in the consultation, examination or interview;

        (B) Persons reasonably necessary for the transmission of the communication; or

        (C) Persons who are participating in the diagnosis and treatment under the direction of the physician, including members of the patient's family.

    (b) "Patient" means a person who consults or is examined or interviewed by a physician.

    (c) "Physician" means a person authorized and licensed or certified to practice medicine in any state or nation, or reasonably believed by the patient so to be, while engaged in the diagnosis or treatment of a physical condition. "Physician" includes licensed or certified naturopathic and chiropractic physicians.

(2) [General rule of privilege.] A patient has a privilege to refuse to disclose and to prevent any other person from disclosing confidential communications in a civil action, suit or proceeding, made for the purposes of diagnosis or treatment of the patient's physical condition, among the patient, the patient's physician or persons who are participating in the diagnosis or treatment under the direction of the physician, including members of the patient's family.

(3) [Who may claim the privilege.] The privilege created by this section may be claimed by:

(a) The patient;

(b) A guardian or conservator of the patient;

(c) The personal representative of a deceased patient; or

(d) The person who was the physician, but only on behalf of the patient. Such person's authority so to do is presumed in the absence of evidence to the contrary.

(4) [General exceptions.] The following is a nonexclusive list of limits on the privilege granted by this section:

(a) If the judge orders an examination of the physical condition of the patient, communications made in the course thereof are not privileged under this section with respect to the particular purpose for which the examination is ordered unless the judge orders otherwise.

(b) Except as provided in ORCP 44, there is no privilege under this section for communications made in the course of a physical examination performed under ORCP 44.

(c) There is no privilege under this section with regard to any confidential communication or record of such confidential communication that would otherwise be privileged under this section when the use of the communication or record is specifically allowed under ORS 426.070, 426.074, 426.075, 426.095, 426.120 or 426.307. This paragraph only applies to the use of the communication or record to the extent and for the purposes set forth in the described statute sections.

LEGISLATIVE COMMENTARY

Oregon Rule of Evidence 504-1 provides for a physician-patient privilege. It is styled after Rule 504 of the Federal Rules of Evidence, relating to psychotherapists, which was proposed by the Supreme Court but never adopted. The federal Advisory Committee recommended against enactment of a physician-patient privilege rule in light of the many exceptions that have been carved from it to obtain information required by the public interest or to avoid fraud. The Legislative Assembly considered that the exceptions on Oregon are not so many as to rob the privilege of meaning. It therefore continued, in greater detail, the privilege which was expressly recognized under ORS 44.040(1)(d).

Rule 504-1 closely parallels Rule 504; the Advisory Committee on Evidence Law Revision recommended in fact that the two concepts be merged in a single rule. The Legislative Assembly retained the statutory distinction between communications relating to a physical condition and communications relating to a mental or emotional condition in light of the historical differences in the scope of the applicable privilege. Except where noted below, however, the Commentary to Rule 504 shall be taken to apply to rule 504-1.

Subsection (1). Paragraph (a). The definition of "confidential communication" in paragraph (1)(a) of the rule does not change Oregon law. Currently, the physician-patient privilege in Oregon includes a physician's examination as well as laboratory tests and X-ray pictures. Also covered are oral and written communications intended to convey information as well as the physician's records. *Nielson v. Bryson,* 257 Or 179, 477 P2d 714 (1970).

Paragraph (b). See Commentary to paragraph (1)(b) of ORE 504.

Paragraph (c). The term "physician" includes persons who hold M.D. degrees and are licensed or certified to practice medicine. ORS 677.100 et seq.; *Hampton v. Hampton,* 241 Or 277, 405 P2d 549 (1965). The definition also includes faith healers, chiropractors and naturopaths. ORS 44.040 was amended in 1979 to provide a testimonial privilege in civil actions for a "naturopathic physician licensed under ORS chapter 685 ... as to any information acquired in attending the patient, which was necessary to enable [the physician] to act for the patient." The definition of physician is not limited, as is the definition of psychotherapist, to a person authorized to practice a medical profession under the laws of one of the United States. A physician duly authorized under foreign law is within the privilege.

Subsection (2). Under the privilege between psychotherapist and patient, the physician-patient privilege may only be invoked in civil proceedings. It does not apply in criminal cases. ORS 44.040(1)(d); *State v. Betts,* 235 Or 127, 384 P2d 193 (1963).

Subsection (3). See Commentary to subsection (3) of ORE 504.

Subsection (4). See Commentary to paragraph (4)(b) of ORE 504.

Subsection (5). See Commentary to subsection (5) of ORE 504.

TEXT

Physician-Patient Privilege

The physician-patient privilege, unlike the psychotherapist-patient privilege, applies only in civil cases. Therefore, a physician in a criminal proceeding may lawfully disclose a patient's confession of a crime. See 27 Op Or Att'y Gen 24 (1954). Contrary to prior law, the privilege applies to physicians who are consulted for the purpose of diagnosis as well as treatment.

Physician is defined broadly under this rule to include persons licensed or certified to practice medicine under the law of any state or nation, as well as persons reasonably believed by the patient to be so licensed or certified. The definition also includes licensed or certified naturopathic and chiropractic physicians. See ORS Chapters 684 and 685. Contrary to the statement in the Commentary, this definition does not include faith healers. They are expressly excluded from the legislative definition of naturopath. See ORS 685.030.

Although the rule states that it protects only *communications,* the Commentary suggests that this term should be given a broad interpretation to include a physician's observations in the course of examination as well as laboratory tests and X-rays. It also is intended to include the physician's notations regarding the examination and other records pertaining to the patient.

The rule protects only confidential communications to a physician. Rule 504-1(1)(a) provides that confidentiality will still be found even though third persons are present at the time of the communication, provided that such persons are (1) present to further the interests of the patient in the consultation, examination, or interview; (2) reasonably necessary for the transmission of the communication; or (3) participating in the diagnosis and treatment under the direction of the physician. See *State v. Miller,* 300 Or 203, 709 P2d 225 (1985), cert denied 475 US 1141 (1986).

Other rules and statutes significantly qualify the physician-patient privilege established by Rule 504-1. Rule 511 provides that the privilege is waived in litigation by voluntary disclosure or consent to disclosure of any significant part of the privileged matter, or, in the case of litigation relating to a physical condition, whenever the patient offers any person as a witness to testify regarding the condition. ORCP 44C provides that a party against whom a personal injury claim is filed may generally obtain the medical reports from the claimant's doctor and if such reports are not furnished, may be able to take a deposition of the physician. ORCP 44E provides that a party against whom a personal injury claim is asserted may examine and copy hospital records of the injured person. ORCP 44A and B provide that a party against whom a personal injury claim is asserted may require the claimant to submit to a physical examination. Rule 504-1(5) provides that communications made in the course of such an examination are not privileged.

In *State ex rel Grimm v. Ashmanskas,* 298 Or 206, 690 P2d 1063 (1984), the court held that when a plaintiff in a medical malpractice action takes a deposition of the defendant's doctor, the doctor-patient privilege is waived with respect to other physicians consulted by plaintiff and their depositions can be taken by defendant's attorney. However, the court commented that the fact that the plaintiff submits to a pretrial discovery deposition by the defendant does not constitute a waiver of the physician-patient privilege.

A number of Oregon statutes limit physician-patient confidentiality by requiring physicians to report certain types of information to public authorities. See, e.g., ORS 146.750 (injuries caused by deadly weapons when there is reasonable suspicion that injury was caused by other than accidental means); ORS 146.100 and ORS 432.307(4) (obligation to file report of death under certain circumstances); ORS 419B.010 (obligation to report child abuse); ORS 419B.040 (privilege inapplicable in certain child abuse proceedings); ORS 434.020 (obligation to report cases of venereal disease); ORS 437.010 (obligation to report cases of tuberculosis).

In addition to the evidentiary privilege, physicians may have a duty of confidentiality imposed by statute, professional ethics, or by express or implied contract with the patient. In *Humphers v. First Interstate Bank of Oregon,* 298 Or 706, 696 P2d 527 (1985), the court recognized a cause of action for damages against a physician for breach of the duty of confidentiality. See ANNOT., *Physician's Tort Liability for Unauthorized Disclosure of Confidential Information About Patient,* 48 ALR4th 668 (1986).

The holder of the privilege is the patient, and the privilege cannot be claimed by members of the patient's family unless they are serving as the patient's guardian, conservator, or personal representative. *Doe v. Portland Health*

Centers, Inc., 99 Or App 423, 782 P2d 446 (1989), petition for rev dismissed 310 Or 476, 799 P2d 150 (1990).

See generally Goldberg, *The Physician-Patient Privilege—An Impediment to Public Health,* 16 Pac L J 787 (1985); Shuman, *The Origins of the Physician-Patient Privilege and Professional Secret,* 39 Sw L J 661 (1985); ANNOT., *Physician-Patient Privilege As Applied to Physician's Testimony Concerning Wound Required to be Reported to Public Authority,* 85 ALR3d 1196 (1978); COMMENT, *Medical Privilege in Oregon,* 55 Or L Rev 459 (1976).

RULE 504-2.   ORS 40.240. NURSE-PATIENT PRIVILEGE

A licensed professional nurse shall not, without the consent of a patient who was cared for by such nurse, be examined in a civil action or proceeding, as to any information acquired in caring for the patient, which was necessary to enable the nurse to care for the patient.

LEGISLATIVE COMMENTARY

Oregon Rule of Evidence 504-2 retains the privilege against disclosure in a civil action of necessary information acquired by a nurse in caring for a patient. This was formerly codified in ORS 44.040(l)(g).

TEXT

Nurse-Patient Privilege

The nurse-patient privilege is particularly broad because it is not limited to communications received by the nurse from the patient. The privilege presumably covers observations as well as communications and includes information received from third persons as well as from the patient. However, the privilege applies only if the information was (1) acquired in caring for the patient and (2) was necessary to enable the nurse to care for the patient. Therefore, information received by a nontreating nurse or collateral information not necessary for treatment purposes would be outside the privilege. See *State ex rel Juvenile Dept. of Multnomah Cty. v. Banker,* 47 Or App 1125, 615 P2d 1168 (1980) (nurse-patient privilege inapplicable because nurse not engaged in furnishing nursing care).

Like the physician-patient privilege, the nurse-patient privilege is limited to civil cases, and the patient is the holder. In some cases, the nurse-patient privilege may be superfluous, because communications to the nurse will be encompassed by the physician-patient privilege. Rule 504-1(2) includes "persons who are participating in the diagnosis or treatment under the direction of the physician ...."

The nurse-patient privilege differs from the physician-patient privilege, however, in that under Rule 511 the physician-patient privilege is waived when the physical condition is in issue and the holder offers any person as a witness to testify about the condition. Rule 511 does not provide for waiver of the nurse-patient privilege in this circumstance. Waiver under Rule 511 would occur if the patient voluntarily discloses, or consents to disclosure of, any significant part of the matter or communication protected by the nurse-patient privilege.

The nurse-patient privilege is subject to a number of statutes that may require disclosure of otherwise confidential information in certain circumstances. See ORS 419B.010–.040 (reporting of child abuse; privilege inapplicable in certain judicial proceedings relating to child abuse); and ORS 437.010 (reporting cases of tuberculosis).

RULE 504-3.   ORS 40.245. SCHOOL EMPLOYEE-STUDENT PRIVILEGE

(1) **A certificated staff member of an elementary or secondary school shall not be examined in any civil action or proceeding, as to any conversation between the certificated staff member and a student which relates to the personal affairs of the student or family of the student, and which if disclosed would tend to damage or incriminate the student or family. Any violation of the privilege provided by this subsection may result in the suspension of certification of the professional staff member as provided in ORS 342.175, 342.177 and 342.180.**

(2) **A certificated school counselor regularly employed and designated in such capacity by a public school shall not, without the consent of the student, be examined as to any communication made by the student to the counselor in the official capacity of the counselor in any civil action or proceeding or a criminal action or proceeding in which such student is a party concerning the past use, abuse or sale of drugs, controlled substances or alcoholic liquor. Any violation of the privilege provided by this subsection may result in the suspension of certification of the professional school counselor as provided in ORS 342.175, 342.177 and 342.180. However, in the event that the student's condition presents a clear and imminent danger to the student or to others, the counselor shall report this fact to an appropriate responsible authority or take such other emergency measures as the situation demands.**

LEGISLATIVE COMMENTARY

Oregon Rule of Evidence 504-3 preserves two evidential rules regarding communications made by an elementary or secondary school student to school staff. These were formerly codified in ORS 44.040(1)(i) and (k).

Subsection (1). Subsection (1) prohibits any school staff member from disclosing, in a civil action, information learned from a student that would tend to damage or incriminate the student or the student's family. The rule is more in the nature of a prohibition than a privilege. A true privilege can be waived. The rule does not designate a holder with that power.

Subsection (2). Subsection (2) prohibits the disclosure in either a criminal or a civil proceeding of information concerning past use of controlled substances or alcoholic liquor communicated by a student to a school counselor. This privilege may be waived by the student and is also subject to an exception in the event of clear and imminent danger to the student or to others.

TEXT

Certificated School Staff Member-Student Privilege

Rule 504-3(1) prohibits disclosure in civil cases by a certificated staff member of an elementary or secondary school of conversations between the staff member and a student (1) which relate to the personal affairs of the student or family of the student, and (2) which, if disclosed, would tend to damage or incriminate the student or family. Although the prohibition is described as a "privilege," unlike most privileges there is no express provision for waiver by the student. Arguably the possibility of waiver should be implied in a situation where the student seeks to offer the testimony having concluded its value outweighs the harm. The rule provides for suspension of the certificated staff member for violation of this privilege, although presumably the sanction would not apply if the staff member made the disclosures only pursuant to court order. Because the privilege applies only in civil cases, it may have limited effect in encouraging open communication between students and certificated school staff members.

The rule is qualified by ORS 419B.010, which requires school employees to report cases of suspected child abuse, and by ORS 419B.040, which provides that the privilege is inapplicable in certain judicial proceedings relating to child abuse.

Certificated School Counselor-Student Privilege

Rule 504-3(2) creates a privilege for communications by students to certificated school counselors acting in their official capacity. The privilege applies in any civil proceeding or a criminal proceeding where the student is a party, concerning the past use, abuse, or sale of drugs, controlled substances, or alcoholic liquor.

The privilege is narrower than the psychotherapist-patient privilege provided in Rule 504, although a student might obtain the benefit of the broader privilege if the school counselor qualifies as a "psychotherapist" and the other requirements of Rule 504 are satisfied. The Rule 504-3(2) privilege does not apply in criminal cases (except for the cases specified), and therefore will not provide as broad a protection for disclosures regarding past conduct as Rule 504.

The student is the holder of the privilege and may waive it. If disclosure is made by the school counselor without the student's consent, the counselor is subject to suspension of certification. However, if the student's condition presents a clear and imminent danger to the student or to others, the counselor is authorized to report this fact to an appropriate responsible authority or to take such other emergency measures as the situation demands. Presumably this qualification authorizes disclosure of communications immediately relevant to the emergency condition, but not of all confidential communications by the student to the counselor. Also, disclosure by the counselor under the emergency circumstances specified should not necessarily be viewed as precluding assertion of the privilege by the student at a judicial proceeding where the privilege is applicable.

This privilege is qualified by ORS 419B.010, which requires reporting of child abuse, and ORS 419B.040, which provides that the privilege is inapplicable in certain judicial proceedings relating to child abuse.

RULE 504-4.   ORS 40.250. CLINICAL SOCIAL WORKER-CLIENT PRIVILEGE

A clinical social worker licensed by the State Board of Clinical Social Workers shall not be examined in a civil or criminal court proceeding as to any communication given the clinical social worker by a client in the course of noninvestigatory professional activity when such communication was given to enable the licensed clinical social worker to aid the client, except:

(1) When the client or those persons legally responsible for the client's affairs give consent to the disclosure;

(2) When the client initiates legal action or makes a complaint against the licensed clinical social worker to the board;

(3) When the communication reveals a clear intent to commit a crime which reasonably is expected to result in physical injury to a person;

(4) When the information reveals that a minor was the victim of a crime, abuse or neglect; or

(5) When the licensed clinical social worker is a public employee and the public employer has determined that examination in a civil or criminal court proceeding is necessary in the performance of the duty of the social worker as a public employee.

LEGISLATIVE COMMENTARY

Oregon Rule of Evidence 504-4 retains the privilege against disclosure of any information given by a client to a clinical social worker in the course of noninvestigatory professional activity. This was formerly codified in ORS 44.040(1)(L).

TEXT

Clinical Social Worker-Client Privilege

The clinical social worker-client privilege applies in both civil and criminal proceedings. The client is the holder of the privilege, although persons legally responsible for the client's affairs may waive the privilege. Also, if the registered clinical social worker is a public employee, the employer may authorize disclosure.

The privilege applies only to communications given to a clinical social worker by a client. Information received from third parties is not privileged. Moreover, the privilege applies only to communications made in the course of noninvestigatory professional activity to enable the registered clinical social worker to aid the client. If the information is furnished in the course of an investigation, such as one to determine appropriate custody for a child, it is not privileged.

The privilege would appear to protect against disclosure of past crimes, except where the information reveals that a minor was the victim of a crime, abuse, or neglect. See also ORS 419B.010 (duty to report suspected child abuse); ORS 419B.040 (privilege inapplicable in certain judicial proceedings relating to child abuse). The privilege does not protect communications revealing the intent to commit a future crime that is expected to result in physical injury to a person. The privilege is also inapplicable when the client initiates legal action or makes a complaint against the registered clinical social worker to the State Board of Clinical Social Workers.

Rule 504-4 should be considered in conjunction with ORS 675.580, which provides:

> *Confidentiality of communication by client; exceptions.*
> (1) A licensed clinical social worker, a certified clinical social worker associate or any employees of the licensed clinical social worker shall not disclose any communication given him by a client in the course of noninvestigatory professional activity when such communication was given to enable the registered clinical social worker to aid the client, except:
> (a) When the client or those persons legally responsible for the client's affairs give consent to the disclosure;
> (b) When the client initiates legal action or makes a complaint against the registered clinical social worker to the board;
> (c) When the communication reveals a clear intent to commit a crime which reasonably is expected to result in physical injury to a person;
> (d) When the communication reveals that a minor was the victim of a crime, abuse or neglect; or
> (e) When disclosure of the communication is necessary to obtain further professional assistance for the client.

(2) Nothing in this section is intended to prevent a licensed clinical social worker who is a public employee from disclosing communications from a client when such a disclosure is made in the performance of the licensed clinical social worker's duty as a public employee and the public employer has determined that such disclosure is necessary in the performance of the duty of the licensed clinical social worker as a public employee.

See generally COMMENT, *The Social Worker-Client Privilege Statutes: Underlying Justifications and Practical Operations,* 6 Prob L J 242 (1985).

RULE 505.   ORS 40.255. HUSBAND-WIFE PRIVILEGE

(1) **[Definitions.] As used in this section, unless the context requires otherwise:**
    (a) **"Confidential communication" means a communication by a spouse to the other spouse and not intended to be disclosed to any other person.**
    (b) **"Marriage" means a marital relationship between husband and wife, legally recognized under the laws of this state.**
(2) **[Privilege as to confidential communications.] In any civil or criminal action, a spouse has a privilege to refuse to disclose and to prevent the other spouse from disclosing any confidential communication made by one spouse to the other during the marriage. The privilege created by this subsection may be claimed by either spouse. The authority of the spouse to claim the privilege and the claiming of the privilege is presumed in the absence of evidence to the contrary.**
(3) **[Privilege as to testimony.] In any criminal proceeding, neither spouse, during the marriage, shall be examined adversely against the other as to any other matter occurring during the marriage unless the spouse called as a witness consents to testify.**
(4) **[Exceptions.] There is no privilege under this section:**
    (a) **In all criminal actions in which one spouse is charged with bigamy or with an offense or attempted offense against the person or property of the other spouse or of a child of either, or with an offense against the person or property of a third person committed in the course of committing or attempting to commit an offense against the other spouse;**

    (b) **As to matters occurring prior to the marriage; or**
    (c) **In any civil action where the spouses are adverse parties.**

LEGISLATIVE COMMENTARY

Oregon Rule of Evidence 505 establishes two privileges in connection with the marital state: a privilege as to confidential communications and a privilege as to adverse testimony. The rule is original. It is very different from proposed Rule 505 of the Federal Rules of Evidence, which only recognizes a privilege in criminal cases and there makes the accused the holder. The Legislative Assembly did not adopt the federal rule because it believes that the privilege against disclosure of confidential communications is an aspect of the marital privilege that merits continuation.

Four common law rules of evidence have evolved around the marriage relationship: (1) the incompetency of one spouse to testify for the other; (2) the privilege of one spouse not to testify against the other; (3) the privilege of one spouse not to have the other testify adversely; and (4) the privilege against disclosure of confidential communications between spouses. With the end of disqualification of parties and other persons for interest, the rule of spousal incompetency has virtually disappeared from both civil and criminal actions. McCormick, *Evidence* § 66 (2d ed 1972). ORE 505 gives it no recognition. However, this rule does preserve the elements of the other three aspects of the marital privilege.

The previous Oregon statutes relating to the marital privilege were ORS 44.040(1)(a) and ORS 136.655. It was not clear whether the privilege set forth in ORS 44.040 applied to criminal prosecutions. *State v. Suttles,* 287 Or 3, 597 P2d 786 (1979). Rule 505 replaces ORS 44.040(1)(a), and clearly governs both civil and criminal actions. ORS 136.655 allows a spouse who is charged with a crime to prevent the other spouse from testifying as to any matter with certain exceptions. Section 89 of this Act amends that statute to conform with Rule 505 thereby eliminating the privilege to prevent spousal testimony except as to confidential communications. Other changes are detailed below.

Subsection (1). Paragraph (a). "Confidential communication" is defined in terms of intent. Intent may be inferred from the circumstances, e.g., the taking or failing to take of precautions. A communication made in public or meant to be relayed to outsiders can scarcely be considered confidential. Unless intent to disclose is apparent, a communication between husband and wife is confidential.

By defining "confidential communication" and allowing the privilege only as to such a communication, this paragraph changes Oregon law. Until now, a privilege apparently has applied to all marital communications, whether or not considered confidential. *Pugsley v. Smyth,* 98 Or 448, 194 P 686 (1921).

Paragraph (b). The privilege as to confidential communications and the privilege as to adverse testimony may only be claimed by persons whose marriage is recognized under the laws of this state. This category includes persons who are validly married in Oregon according to the appropriate statutes, and persons whose marriage is recognized by the courts of Oregon although the marriage would not have been valid had it been solemnized in this state. Examples of the latter are a marriage between first cousins and a common law marriage. *Huard v. McTeigh,* 113 Or 279, 291, 232 P 658 (1925); *Wadsworth v. Brigham,* 125 Or 428, 444, 259 P 299, 266 P 875 (1928); *Boykin v. S.I.A.C.,* 224 Or 76, 81–82, 355 P2d 724 (1960). A proxy marriage solemnized in this state is also a marriage for the purposes of this rule. *State v. Anderson,* 239 Or 200, 396 P2d 558 (1964). There is no "marriage," under this paragraph, if the marriage was a sham or if the parties have been divorced.

Subsection (2). Subsection (2) states the marital "communications" privilege. It allows a holder to invoke the privilege in both civil and criminal actions but restricts its scope to confidential communications made during the marriage. This subsection is the only relic of the common law rule that allowed one spouse to prevent the other spouse from testifying in an adverse manner.

Either spouse may claim the "communications" privilege. The last sentence of the subsection presumes that both spouses in fact will do so. This provision prevents the taking of testimony of one spouse when the other is absent and does not know that a situation appropriate for a claim of privilege is presented, e.g., in a proceeding before a grand jury. If the privilege is not claimed by the testifying spouse, the protection of Rule 512 is available.

Subsection (3). This subsection deals with the testimony of a spouse concerning nonconfidential observations and communications with the other spouse during their marriage. In criminal cases one spouse may not prevent the other from testifying, but the spouse called as a witness must consent to testify and may not be compelled. *Trammel v. United States,* 100 S Ct 906 (1980).

The traditional justification for a double privilege—not to testify and not to be testified against by one's spouse—has been the prevention of marital discord and the preservation of the marital union. However, the Legislative Assembly believes that the testifying spouse should determine whether the marriage can or should be preserved. It leaves the decision to testify as to matters other than confidential communications, therefore, to the witness. This is a change in the law. Previously under ORS 136.655, with certain exceptions, the consent of both spouses was required before a spouse could testify in a criminal case in which the other spouse was the party accused.

It should be noted that the privilege not to testify regarding "other matters" ceases upon termination of the marriage. In contrast, the privilege as to confidential communications made during the marriage applies to any action or proceeding either during or after the marriage.

Subsection (4). Subsection (4) contains two exceptions to the privilege against spousal testimony. The need to avoid grave injustice in the case of an offense against the other spouse or a child of either can scarcely be denied. The first exception therefore disallows any privilege against spousal testimony in these situations. The provision eliminates the possibility of suppressing testimony by marrying a witness. The second exception declares that there is no marital privilege for matters occurring before the marriage. In this respect Rule 505 differs from the result in *State v. Anderson,* supra, which held that the defendant's wife could not testify even though the crime for which he was tried had occurred and the defendant had been imprisoned before the marriage.

TEXT

Husband-Wife Privileges

Rule 505 combines two distinct marital privileges: the privilege for confidential marital communications and the privilege of a spouse not to testify against the other spouse in a criminal proceeding.

There are significant differences between the two privileges. The first applies only to communications; the second covers all testimony, whether relating to communications, observations, or independent knowledge. Both spouses are holders of the marital communication privilege, whereas only the spouse called to be a witness is the holder of the spousal testimonial privilege. The privilege for confidential marital communications survives the marriage, whereas the privilege of a spouse not to testify does not.

Confidential Marital Communications

Generally, a marital communication will not be confidential if it was made in the presence of third parties. Courts may still find confidentiality if the only persons present were children too young to understand what was said. See 1 McCormick, *Evidence* (4th ed 1992) § 80 at 300; C. Mueller & L. Kirkpatrick, MODERN EVIDENCE (1995) § 5.34.

By limiting the privilege to confidential marital communications, Rule 505 rejects the common-law decisions, which extended the privilege to confidential marital observations as well. See 1 McCormick, *Evidence* (4th ed 1992) § 79 at 297–8. The new rule is consistent with *United States v. Bolzer,* 556 F2d 948 (9th Cir 1977), which held that the marital communications privilege did not bar testimony of a former wife of the defendant identifying pants as belonging to the defendant, because this testimony pertained to an observation, not a communication. However, confidential conduct of a spouse intended as a substitute for verbal communication, such as pointing to the location of a hidden object, may be found to be a privileged communication under this rule.

The statement in Rule 505(2) that "[t]he authority of the spouse to claim the privilege ... is presumed in the absence of evidence to the contrary" would seem unnecessary in most cases. Because both spouses hold the privilege, either spouse could claim the privilege without needing to show authority from the other.

The statement in Rule 505(2) that "the claiming of the privilege is presumed in the absence of evidence to the contrary" will require interpretation. If the spouse remains silent when evidence of the confidential communication is offered, will assertion of the privilege be "presumed" under this rule or "consent to disclosure" found under Rule 511? Under former law, affirmative consent of the spouse was required to waive the marital communications privilege. See *McKinnon v. Chenoweth,* 176 Or 74, 92, 155 P2d 944, 951 (1945) ("mere silence on her part did not amount to a waiver").

The fact that one spouse revealed the confidential communication without the consent of the other spouse would not constitute a waiver of the privilege. See Rule 512(2); *State v. Suttles,* 37 Or App 695, 588 P2d 635 (1978), rev'd on other grounds 287 Or 15, 597 P2d 786 (1979) (no waiver of marital communications privilege when wife gave incriminating letters from husband to prosecutor without husband's consent); ANNOT., *Applicability of Marital Privilege to Written Communications Between Spouses Inadvertently Obtained by Third Person,* 32 ALR4th 1177 (1984); ANNOT., *Spouse's Betrayal or Connivance as Extending Marital Communications Privilege to Testimony of Third Person,* 3 ALR4th 1104 (1981); Glick, *Is Your Spouse Taping Your Telephone Calls?: Title III and Interspousal Electronic Surveillance,* 41 Cath U L Rev 845 (1992).

If reasonable precautions were taken to prevent overhearing of the communication, arguably the privilege should apply even against testimony by an eavesdropper. However, unlike Rule 503(2), which allows the holder to block testimony by "any other person," Rule 505(2) only allows the holder "to prevent the other spouse from disclosing" the confidential communication.

Testimony by one spouse disclosing any significant part of the communication would constitute a waiver of the privilege by that spouse. See Rule 511; *State v. Schier,* 47 Or App 1075, 615 P2d 1147 (1980).

Spousal Testimonial Privilege

Rule 505 changes Oregon law with regard to the spousal privilege in criminal cases. Under former law, neither spouse could be called to testify against the other in a criminal case without the consent of both. See former ORS 136.655 (amended 1981); former ORS 44.040(1)(a) (repealed 1981). Under the new rule, the privilege rests only with the spouse called as a witness. A criminal defendant may no longer prevent a spouse from testifying against the defendant regarding any matter except confidential communications.

The traditional justification for allowing a criminal defendant the privilege to block adverse testimony by his or her spouse has been to protect the marital relationship. When the witness spouse is willing to testify against the defendant spouse, however, this justification has little persuasive force. The privilege is retained for the witness spouse because that spouse's refusal to testify against the other may indicate a surviving marital relationship that should not be destroyed by the subpoena and contempt power of the state.

Rule 505 is consistent with federal common law. See *Trammel v. United States,* 445 US 40, 100 SCt 906, 63 LEd2d 186 (1980). In *Trammel,* the Supreme Court overturned prior federal law, which allowed a criminal defendant to prevent his or her spouse from testifying on behalf of the prosecution. A privilege not to testify was retained for the witness spouse. Over half of the states have either abolished the testimonial privilege in criminal cases or limited it to the witness spouse. See *Trammel v. United States,* 445 US at 48 n9 (1980).

Rule 505 provides a narrower privilege to the witness spouse than does *Trammel* or the law of most other jurisdictions. The privilege not to testify against a spouse in a criminal proceeding does not apply to matters occurring prior to the marriage. See Rule 505(4)(b). This exception eliminates the problem of criminal defendants avoiding prosecution by marrying the victim of a crime or a key prosecution witness. See ANNOT., *Existence of Spousal Privilege Where Marriage was Entered Into for Purpose of Barring Testimony,* 13 ALR4th 1305 (1982). However, the narrowness of the Oregon privilege means that a spouse could be compelled against his or her will to provide testimony relating to matters occurring prior to the marriage that could be the basis of a criminal conviction of the other spouse. Thus, even though the Commentary indicates that the new rule was not intended to threaten the marital relationship when the witness spouse believes it can be preserved, the rule may in fact do so.

Also, under Rule 505 there may be greater incentive for spouses who are both potentially subject to criminal prosecution to agree to testify against the other spouse. Such arrangements were generally not feasible under prior law, because the defendant spouse could block the testimony. Rule 505 may thus encourage more plea bargaining or grants of immunity to one spouse when both spouses are jointly involved in criminal activity.

The privilege given to a witness spouse not to testify under Rule 505(3) would not bar a criminal defendant from compelling the spouse to testify. The privilege protects the witness spouse only from being "examined adversely against the other" and does not preclude examination by the defendant spouse.

Exceptions

Rule 505(4)(a) provides that no privilege exists in criminal actions in which one spouse is charged with an offense against the other spouse, or a child of either, or against a third person in the course of committing or attempting to commit an offense against the spouse. See also ORS 136.655 (stating same exception); ORS 419B.040 (marital privilege inapplicable in certain child abuse proceedings); *State v. Suttles,* 287 Or 15, 597 P2d 786, rev'd on other grounds 287 Or 15, 597 P2d 786 (1979). This exception modifies prior Oregon law. See *State v. LeFils,* 209 Or 666, 307 P2d 1048 (1957) (privilege of wife not to testify against her husband found applicable, even where the wife filed the criminal complaint against the defendant for attempted assault upon minor daughter).

The rule does not recognize an exception for situations where the husband and wife are joint participants in crime. Such an exception is sometimes recognized in cases under federal common law. See *United States v. Sims,* 755 F2d 1239 (6th Cir 1985), cert denied 108 SCt 1118 (1988) (joint participants exception to communications privilege); *United States v. Clark,* 712 F2d 299, 300–1 (7th Cir 1983) (joint participants exception to testimonial privilege); NOTE, *Partners in Crime: The Joint Participants Exception to the Privilege Against Adverse Spousal Testimony,* 53 Fordham L Rev 1019 (1985).

The exception created by Rule 505(4)(b) for matters occurring prior to the marriage is consistent with prior Oregon law insofar as the marital communications privilege is concerned. Former ORS 44.040(1)(a) (repealed 1981) provided: "A spouse shall not ... during the marriage or afterwards, be, without the consent of the other, examined as to any communication made by one to the other *during the marriage.*" (Emphasis added.) This exception changes prior law regarding the testimonial privilege of a spouse. The former statute recognized no exception for matters occurring before the marriage, and provided simply that "a spouse shall not be examined for or against the other spouse without consent of the other spouse ...." Former ORS 44.040(l)(a) (repealed 1981); see also former ORS 136.655 (amended 1981).

The original version of this rule neglected to recognize an exception to the communications and testimonial privilege in the case of civil litigation between the spouses. This omission was corrected by the 1983 legislature that amended the rule and created an additional exception to the privilege "in any civil action where the spouses are adverse parties." See Rule 505(4)(c).

See generally ANNOT., *Marital Privilege Under Rule 501 of Federal Rules of Evidence*, 46 ALR Fed 735 (1980); Medine, *The Adverse Testimony Privilege: Time to Dispose of a "Sentimental Relic,"* 67 Or L Rev 519 (1988); ANNOT., *Crimes Against Spouse Within Exception Permitting Testimony by One Spouse Against Other in Criminal Prosecution—Modern State Cases*, 74 ALR4th 223 (1989); ANNOT., *Competency of One Spouse to Testify Against Other in Prosecution for Offense Against Third Party as Affected by Fact that Offense Against Spouse Was Involved in Same Transaction*, 74 ALR4th 277 (1989). See generally Creighton, *Spouse Competence and Compellability*, 1990 Crim L Rev 34.

RULE 506.   ORS 40.260. MEMBER OF CLERGY-PENITENT PRIVILEGE

(1) **[Definitions.] As used in this section, unless the context requires otherwise:**
    (a) **"Confidential communication" means a communication made privately and not intended for further disclosure except to other persons present in furtherance of the purpose of the communication.**
    (b) **"Member of the clergy" means a minister of any church, religious denomination or organization or accredited Christian Science practitioner who in the course of the discipline or practice of that church, denomination or organization is authorized or accustomed to hearing confidential communications and, under the discipline or tenets of that church, denomination or organization, has a duty to keep such communications secret.**

(2) **[General rule of privilege.] A member of the clergy shall not, without the consent of the person making the communication, be examined as to any confidential communication made to the member of the clergy in the member's professional character.**

LEGISLATIVE COMMENTARY

Oregon Rule of Evidence 506 states the privilege for confidential communications between a clergyman and penitent. The privilege allows and encourages individuals to fulfill their religious, emotional or other needs by protecting confidential disclosures to religious practitioners.

Rule 506 is intended to restate existing Oregon law. Except for the definition of "confidential communication" and a reorganization for clarity into subsections and paragraphs, the language of the rule is identical to former ORS 44.040(1)(c). The clergyman-penitent privilege has not been construed by an appellate court in this state. *State v. Forsyth,* 20 App 624, 533 P2d 176 (1975).

TEXT

Clergy-Penitent Privilege

Rule 506 retains the clergy-penitent privilege formerly recognized under ORS 44.040(1)(c). The person making the communication is the holder of the privilege, and the clergy member may not be examined regarding confidential communications "made to the member of the clergy in the member's professional character" without that person's consent.

The rule contains a broad definition of "member of the clergy," including a minister of "any church, religious denomination or organization." It would seem that courts should be able to require some minimal evidence of legitimacy to screen out organizations making spurious claims of a religious orientation or affiliation from the application of this rule. See ANNOT., *Who Is "Clergyman" or the Like Entitled to Assert Privilege Attaching to Communications to Clergyman or Spiritual Advisors,* 49 ALR3d 1205 (1973).

With the exception of Christian Science practitioners, the definition of *member of the clergy* seems to require that the person be a *minister.* However, such a title presumably need not be used by the religious organization to qualify under the rule. It would seem sufficient if the person has a leadership role, including responsibility under the tenets of the church, denomination, or organization to hear confidential communications from members and to keep them secret. The use of the word *minister* may place some restrictions on the scope of the privilege with respect to religious organizations where every member is said to be the spiritual counselor of every other member.

The rule allows third persons to be present when the communication is made without destroying its confidentiality, provided that they are "present in furtherance of the purpose of the communication." Presumably such persons could include assistants to the minister as well as persons needed to assist or support the individual making the communication. When a member of the clergy is providing marriage, family, or group counseling, the rule should be interpreted to protect communications to the clergy member by a participant even though other participants are present.

In *State v. Cox*, 87 Or App 443, 742 P2d 694 (1987), a prosecution of defendant for rape of his stepdaughter, the trial court admitted evidence that the defendant had confessed to his clergyman that he had intercourse with the victim. The appellate court found a violation of Rule 506 and reversed the conviction.

See generally Yellin, *The History and Current Status of the Clergy-Penitent Privilege*, 23 Santa Clara L Rev 95 (1983); COMMENT, *Striking Down the Clergyman-Communicant Privilege Statutes: Let Free Exercise of Religion Govern*, 62 Ind L J 397 (1987); NOTE, *Sacred Secrets: A Call for the Expansive Application and Interpretation of the Clergy-Communicant Privilege*, 36 N Y L Sch L Rev 455 (1991).

RULE 507. ORS 40.262. COUNSELOR-CLIENT PRIVILEGE

A professional counselor or a marriage and family therapist licensed by the Oregon Board of Licensed Professional Counselors and Therapists under ORS 675.715 shall not be examined in a civil or criminal court proceeding as to any communications given the counselor or therapist by a client in the course of a noninvestigatory professional activity when such communication was given to enable the counselor or the therapist to aid the client, except:

(1) When the client or those legally responsible for the affairs of the client give consent to the disclosure. If both parties to a marriage have obtained marital and family therapy by a licensed marital and family therapist or a licensed counselor, the therapist or counselor shall not be competent to testify in a domestic relations action other than child custody action concerning information acquired in the course of the therapeutic relationship unless both parties consent;

(2) When the client initiates legal action or makes a complaint against the licensed professional counselor or licensed marriage and family therapist to the board;

(3) When the communication reveals the intent to commit a crime or harmful act; or

(4) When the communication reveals that a minor is or is suspected to be the victim of crime, abuse or neglect.

LEGISLATIVE COMMENTARY

[There is no Legislative Commentary for this Rule. The privilege for professional counselors and licensed marriage and family therapists was enacted by the 1989 Oregon Legislature. See 1989 Or. Laws ch. 721, sec. 20. It was not part of the original Evidence Code.]

NOTE: The Legislative Assembly did not enact a counterpart privilege to Federal Rule 507, on political votes. See Commentary to ORE 514.

TEXT

Counselor-Client Privilege

Rule 507 creates a privilege for licensed counselors and family therapists that applies in both civil and criminal cases. Only communications obtained in the course of noninvestigatory activities are privileged. The communication must have been made by the client to enable the counselor or therapist to aid the client.

The privilege does not apply when the client initiates legal action against the counselor or therapist or makes a complaint to the board. However, the privilege should be considered waived only to the extent necessary for the counselor or therapist to defend against the charges.

An exception to the privilege is recognized where the communication reveals the intent of the client to commit a crime or harmful act. By way of comparison, no such "future crimes" exception is listed for the psychotherapist-patient privilege under Rule 504.

The privilege does not apply where the communication reveals that a minor may be the victim of a crime, abuse, or neglect. See also ORS 419B.010 (requiring the reporting of suspected child abuse).

The privilege may be waived by the client or by those persons legally responsible for the affairs of the client, such as a guardian or parents of a minor child. Where both parties to a marriage have obtained marital or family therapy from a licensed therapist or counselor, that person is not competent to testify in a domestic relations action concerning information acquired in the course of the therapeutic relationship without the consent of both spouses. This limitation does not apply in child custody actions.

Counselors who are part of the Conciliation Services of a Circuit Court have an even broader privilege, one that does not recognize the exceptions contained in this rule. See ORS 107.600(2):

> All communications, verbal or written, between spouses and from spouses to counselors, the court, attorneys, doctors or others engaged in the conciliation proceedings, made in conciliation conferences, hearings and other proceedings pursuant to the exercise of the court's conciliation jurisdiction shall be confidential. A spouse or any other individual engaged in conciliation proceedings shall not be examined in any civil or criminal action as to such communications. Exceptions to testimonial privilege otherwise applicable under ORS 40.225 to 40.295 do not apply to communications made confidential under this section.

RULE 508a.   ORS 40.265. STENOGRAPHER-EMPLOYER PRIVILEGE

A stenographer shall not, without the consent of the stenographer's employer, be examined as to any communication or dictation made by the employer to the stenographer in the course of professional employment.

LEGISLATIVE COMMENTARY

Oregon Rule of Evidence 508a states the privilege for communications of an employer to a stenographer in the course of professional employment. It is designated 508a to distinguish it from proposed Federal Rule of Evidence 508, concerning trade secrets.

This rule is identical to former ORS 44.040(1)(f), and by adopting it the Legislative Assembly intends to retain the stenographer-employer privilege as it has been interpreted by the courts of this state. As under current law, the privilege applies only to a person's stenographic duties and not to other professional duties handled by the person. *State v. Bengston,* 230 Or 19, 367 P2d 366 (1961). Furthermore, the privilege applies only to communications received from the employer rather than those received in the employer's course of business. Thus, communications received from persons with whom the employer deals are not privileged under this rule.

TEXT

Stenographer-Employer Privilege

Rule 508a retains the privilege recognized under prior Oregon law for communications by an employer to a stenographer. The rule covers only communications from the employer, not other communications that may be received by a stenographer in the course of his or her professional duties.

Often an employee with stenographic responsibilities will have many other responsibilities as well. According to the Commentary, the rule is intended to protect only communications pertaining to the stenographic duties, not to the other professional duties handled by the employee. See *State v. Bengtson,* 230 Or 19, 367 P2d 363 (1961).

In the law office setting, the stenographer-employer privilege created by this rule is to some extent duplicative of the privilege already created for employees of an attorney under Rule 503. Rule 503(1)(e) defines "representative of the lawyer" as "one employed to assist the lawyer in the rendition of professional legal services." Rule 503(2)(b) creates a privilege for confidential communications made for the purpose of facilitating the rendition of professional legal services to a client "between the client's lawyer and the lawyer's representative." The significant difference is that the client is the holder of the privilege under Rule 503, whereas the attorney is the holder of the privilege under Rule 508a.

Similarly, stenographers for a psychotherapist or physician may be within a privilege already under Rules 504 and 504-1. A communication remains confidential under both of these rules even though a third person is present provided that person is "reasonably necessary for the transmission of the communication." Presumably, communications to a stenographer for transmission to a patient would be protected under both of these rules. See also Rule 506 (clergy member-penitent privilege).

Rule 508a is particularly significant with respect to privileges that would otherwise not allow a stenographer to receive a confidential communication without destroying the privilege. For example, under the terms of Rule 505, a communication between a husband and wife, which is intentionally disclosed to a third person, including a stenographer, would normally lose its privileged character. However, if a stenographer employed by the wife types a letter from the wife to the husband, Rule 508a would have the effect of preserving the marital communication privilege despite the disclosure. Under Rule 511, a privilege is not waived if the disclosure to a third person is also a privileged communication.

The employer-stenographer privilege is generally disfavored, and almost all other states reject it. It is questionable why a stenographer should be singled out for such a privilege when other business associates, including partners, are denied a privilege. Dean Wigmore commented regarding the adoption of this privilege by the Oregon Legislature in 1929:

> [T]his new privilege is a departure which not only violates a longstanding fundamental principle of the law of evidence, but is not founded on any public necessity.
>
> It is difficult to see what situation could have given rise to a claim for such a privilege. This new section deserves the reprobation of all who wish well to the law of evidence and the administration of justice.

12 Or L Rev 216, 217 (1933) (quoting letter from John H. Wigmore to the *Oregon Law Review*).

It should be noted that the stenographer-employer privilege will be recognized only in Oregon state courts, not in federal courts, except in diversity cases or other cases where state law controls. See FRE 501; *United States v. Schoenheinz*, 548 F2d 1389 (9th Cir 1977) (IRS summons to stenographer to testify and produce records concerning tax affairs of her employer upheld against claim of state employer-stenographer privilege recognized under Oregon law). Therefore, despite Rule 508a, clients cannot be assured that their communications with a stenographer in the course of professional employment will necessarily be protected by the privilege.

RULE 509.   ORS 40.270. PUBLIC OFFICER PRIVILEGE

A public officer shall not be examined as to public records determined to be exempt from disclosure under ORS 192.501 to 192.505.

LEGISLATIVE COMMENTARY

Oregon Rule of Evidence 509 states the privilege of a public officer not to be examined as to the existence or contents of exempt public records. The rule is identical to and replaces ORS 44.040(l)(e). It protects against compelled disclosure in the courtroom of information which is exempt from disclosure in an administrative setting. When privilege is invoked, the subject records are examined in camera and the court determines whether the exemption is valid. *Papadopoulos v. State Board of Higher Education,* 8 Or App 445, 492 P2d 260 (1972). A similar rule exists in a number of other states. 8 Wigmore, *Evidence* § 2378 (McNaughton rev 1961).

The public officer privilege has existed in some form in Oregon since 1862. *General Laws of Oregon* § 702 at 325 (Deady 1845–1862). Originally it extended to communications made to a public officer in official confidence whose disclosure would harm the public interest and was applied to both oral and written communications. *State v. Morrow,* 158 Or 412, 75 P2d 737, 76 P2d 971 (1938); *State v. Ayer,* 122 Or 532, 259 P 427 (1927); *State v. Yee Guck,* 99 Or 231, 195 P 363 (1921). In time, inconsistencies in the scope of privilege developed between ORS 44.040 and ORS 192.300, the precursor of ORS 192.500. See *Papadopolous v. State Board,* supra. Legislation in 1973 replaced ORS 192.030 and other statutes which preserved the confidentiality of records with ORS 192.410 to 192.500, and resolved the statutory conflict by amending ORS 44.040 to refer directly to exempt documents under ORS 192.500. 1973 Or Laws ch 794. There have been no cases interpreting the privilege since.

ORS 192.500(1) is a list of public records that are exempt from disclosure unless the public interest requires disclosure in the particular instance. ORS 192.500(2) is a list of records that are exempt in every instance. The privilege in Rule 509 applies to both sets of records. In the latter case, however, it will only be sustained if the "public interest," a term undefined by the statute, does not require disclosure.

The courts employ a balancing test to determine the public interest in disclosure of a record. As stated in *Papadopoulos v. State Board,* supra, citing *MacEwan v. Holm,* 226 Or 27, 359 P2d 413 (1961):

> [T]he scales must reflect the fundamental right of a citizen to have access to the public records as contrasted with the incidental right of the agency to be free from unreasonable interference. The citizen's predominant interest may be expressed in the terms of the burden of proof which is applicable in this class of cases; the burden is cast upon the agency to explain why the records sought should not be furnished.
>
> Ultimately, of course, it is for the court to decide whether the explanation is reasonable and to weigh the benefits accruing to the agency from nondisclosure against the harm which may result to the public if such records are not made available for inspection 8 Or App at 458.

Accord, *Turner v. Reed,* 22 Or App 177, 538 P2d 373 (1975); see also ORS 192.490(1).

Oregon's public records law spells out the procedure by which a citizen can seek administrative disclosure of exempt documents. ORS 192.450

to 192.490. It does not deal with admissibility of evidence, however, and thus would not clearly operate in litigation either as a privilege or as a rule of exclusion. Without the present rule, there is no privilege a public officer can invoke to parry questions as to exempt documents on the witness stand or in discovery. It would seem that if the contents of a written record were in issue, the officer would not have to testify unless the document was disclosed and introduced as evidence. ORE 1002. However, exceptions to the best evidence rule might still compel the officer's testimony as permissible secondary evidence, on the ground that a writing is in the custody of an adverse party who has failed to produce it after reasonable notice, ORE 1004(3), or that an original document cannot be obtained by any available judicial process, ORE 1004(2). The public officer might still seek a protective order. This would require a case-by-case determination of what "justice requires" under ORCP 36C however, and possibly lead to judicial frustration of legislative intent against disclosure.

For the above reasons, the Legislative Assembly believes it is advisable to retain the privilege formerly codified in ORS 44.040(l)(e). It is significant that the privilege has been kept, despite numerous and substantial revisions of Oregon public records law, for 119 years. While it has rarely been applied or interpreted by the courts, on those occasions when it has been exercised it has proved a workable tool for the protection and determination of the public interest. Its codification as Rule 509 provides the public officer with a clear indication of the officer's own role in disclosing information in the context of litigation.

TEXT

Public Officer Privilege

Rule 509 provides that public officers shall not be examined regarding public records that are determined to be exempt from disclosure under ORS 192.501 to 192.505, the current version of the Oregon public records law. When the Evidence Code was originally adopted, the rule applied to records "exempt from disclosure under ORS 192.500." However, the 1987 legislature repealed ORS 192.500 and enacted ORS 192.501 to ORS 192.505 "in lieu thereof." Therefore, Legislative Counsel changed the reference in Rule 509 to these successor statutes.

The rationale for Rule 509 is that the public records law would be undermined if litigants could learn the contents of confidential public records by inquiry of public officers at depositions or judicial proceedings. Although public officers may also be able to refuse to testify about other records protected from public disclosure, such a privilege would not be based on this rule, which is limited to records protected from disclosure by ORS 192.500 or its successor statutes.

The scope of Rule 509 depends upon how expansively courts construe the public records law. For appellate decisions interpreting former ORS 192.500, see *Sadler v. Oregon State Bar,* 275 Or 279, 550 P2d 1218 (1976); *Jensen v. Schiffman,* 24 Or App 11, 544 P2d 1048 (1976); *Eola Concrete Tile & Products Co. v.*

State, 288 Or 241, 603 P2d 1181 (1979); *Morrison v. School Dist. No. 48,* 53 Or App 148, 631 P2d 784 (1981), rev denied 291 Or 893, 642 P2d 309 (1981); *Lane Co. School Dist. No. 4J v. Parks,* 55 Or App 416, 637 P2d 1383 (1981); *Kotulski v. Mt. Hood Community College,* 62 Or App 452, 660 P2d 1083 (1983); *AFSCME v. City of Albany,* 81 Or App 231, 725 P2d 381 (1986); *Coos County v. Oregon Dept. of Fish and Wildlife,* 86 Or App 168, 739 P2d 47 (1987). See generally COMMENT, *The Right to Inspect Public Records in Oregon,* 53 Or L Rev 354 (1974).

It is unclear whether the privilege set forth in Rule 509 can be waived, and, if so, by whom and under what circumstances. It is also unclear to what extent the rule prohibits examining a public official about independent knowledge of that official about matters that are also contained in a confidential public record. Absent special circumstances, such independent knowledge would seem beyond the protection of this privilege rule.

The scope of the privilege is likely to be more restrictive in cases where the state is a party to the litigation. See *State v. Fleischman,* 10 Or App 22, 32, 495 P2d 277, 282 (1972) ("When the state chooses to prosecute an individual for crime, it is not free to deny him access to evidence that is relevant to guilt or innocence, even when otherwise such evidence is or might be privileged against disclosure."); *State ex rel Juvenile Dept. of Multnomah Cty. v. Lamar,* 7 Or App 132, 490 P2d 191 (1971) (termination of parental rights; state cannot deny parent access to relevant portions of welfare record).

Reliance on Rule 509 may be unnecessary in cases where a litigant is attempting to prove the contents of a public writing through the testimony of a public official. Such evidence will generally be barred by Rule 1002, which requires that the writing itself be offered when its contents are being proven. But see Rule 1004 (allowing secondary evidence, including testimony, to prove contents when writing is unavailable or collateral).

Recent Cases

In *Guard Publishing Co. v. Lane County School District,* 310 Or 32, 40, 791 P2d 854, 858 (1990), the court held that the names and addresses of replacement coaches used during a teachers' strike were not exempt from disclosure, absent a particularized showing of how such disclosure would unreasonably invade the privacy of a particular individual.

In *Jordan v. MVD,* 308 Or 433, 435, 781 P2d 1203 (1989), the court held that the exemption to the public records statutes applied to an individual's residence address contained in the records of the Motor Vehicle Division since the residence address was "information of a personal nature" and "public disclosure would constitute an unreasonable invasion of privacy."

RULE 509-1. ORS 40.272. DISABLED PERSON-SIGN LANGUAGE INTERPRETER PRIVILEGE

(1) As used in this section:

(a) "Disabled person" means a person who cannot readily understand or communicate the spoken English language, or cannot understand proceedings in which the person is involved, because of deafness or because of a physical hearing impairment or cannot communicate in the proceedings because of a physical speaking impairment.

(b) "Sign language interpreter" or "interpreter" means a person who translates conversations or other communications for a disabled person or translates the statements of a disabled person.

(2) A disabled person has a privilege to refuse to disclose and to prevent a sign language interpreter from disclosing any communications to which the disabled person was a party that were made while the interpreter was providing interpretation services from the disabled person. The privilege created by this section extends only to those communications between a disabled person and another, and translated by the interpreter, that would otherwise be privileged under Rule 503 to 514 (ORS 40.225 to 40.295).

LEGISLATIVE COMMENTARY

[There is no Legislative Commentary for this Rule. This is a new privilege adopted by the 1993 Legislature.]

TEXT

Disabled Person-Sign Language Interpreter Privilege

Rule 509-1 creates a privilege for communications from or to a disabled person through a sign language interpreter, provided those communications would otherwise be privileged under Rules 503 to 514 (ORS 40.225 to 40.295).

The privilege applies to confidential communications by the disabled person relating to court proceedings where the disabled person is a party, a witness, or otherwise "involved." But the privilege also applies outside the litigation context in any situation where the communication would be privileged, such as where a disabled person communicates in confidence with a lawyer, psychotherapist, or member of the clergy.

In many cases this privilege is duplicative of a privilege that already exists. In the case of attorneys, for example, Rule 503(1)(b) extends the attorney-client privilege to "persons reasonably necessary to the transmission of the communication." Rule 504(1)(a)(B) also extends the psychotherapist-patient privilege to "persons reasonably necessary for the transmission of the communication." Rule

506(1)(a) extends the clergy-penitent privilege to "persons present in furtherance of the purpose of the communication."

If the communication is made to a privileged person with the intent that it then be disclosed publicly (or at least to a nonprivileged person), the communication would not be considered confidential and no privilege would arise. Also, if the communication of the disabled person to a privileged person is made in a nonconfidential setting (such as where third parties are present), no privilege would arise because of the absence of confidentiality. The privilege would not apply to courtroom testimony by the disabled person because testimony is not a confidential form of communication.

The privilege applies only to communications to which the disabled person "was a party" and to which the interpreter "was providing interpretation services for the disabled person." The disabled person may refuse to disclose the protected communications and can also prevent the sign language interpreter from disclosing them.

RULE 509-2.   ORS 40.273. NON-ENGLISH SPEAKING PERSON-INTERPRETER PRIVILEGE

(1) **As used in this section:**
    (a) **"Interpreter" means a person who translates conversations or other communications for a non-English speaking person or translates the statements of a non-English speaking person.**
    (b) **"Non-English speaking person" means a person who, by reason of place of birth or culture, speaks a language other than English and does not speak English with adequate ability to communicate in the proceedings.**

(2) **A non-English speaking person has a privilege to refuse to disclose and to prevent an interpreter from disclosing any communications to which the non-English speaking person was a party that were made while the interpreter was providing interpretation services for the non-English speaking person. The privilege created by this section extends only to those communications between a non-English speaking person and another, and translated by the interpreter, that would otherwise be privileged under Rule 503 to 514 (ORS 40.225 to 40.295).**

LEGISLATIVE COMMENTARY

[There is no Legislative Commentary for this Rule. This is a new privilege adopted by the 1993 Legislature.]

TEXT

Non-English Speaking Person-Interpreter Privilege

Rule 509-2 creates a privilege for communications from or to a non-English speaking person through an interpreter, provided those communications would otherwise be privileged under Rules 503 to 514 (ORS 40.225 to 40.295).

The privilege applies to confidential communications by the non-English speaking person in any situation where the communication would be privileged, such as where the non-English speaking person communicates in confidence with a lawyer, psychotherapist, or member of the clergy.

In many cases this privilege is duplicative of a privilege that already exists. In the case of attorneys, for example, Rule 503(1)(b) extends the attorney-client privilege to "persons reasonably necessary to the transmission of the communication." Rule 504(1)(a)(B) also extends the psychotherapist-patient privilege to "persons reasonably necessary for the transmission of the communication." Rule 506(1)(a) extends the clergy-penitent privilege to "persons present in furtherance of the purpose of the communication."

If the communication is made to a privileged person with the intent that it then be disclosed publicly (or at least to a nonprivileged person), the communication would not be considered confidential and no privilege would arise. Also if the communication of the non-English speaking person to a privileged person is made in a nonconfidential setting (such as where third parties are present), no privilege would arise because of the absence of confidentiality. The privilege would not apply to courtroom testimony by the non-English speaking person because testimony is not a confidential form of communication.

The privilege applies only to communications to which the non-English speaking person "was a party" and to which the interpreter "was providing interpretation services for the non-English speaking person." The non-English speaking person may refuse to disclose the protected communications and can also prevent the interpreter from disclosing them.

RULE 510. ORS 40.275. IDENTITY OF INFORMER

(1) As used in this section, "unit of government" means the Federal Government or any state or political subdivision thereof.

(2) A unit of government has a privilege to refuse to disclose the identity of a person who has furnished information relating to or assisting in an investigation of a possible violation of law to a law enforcement officer or member of a legislative committee or its staff conducting an investigation.

(3) The privilege created by this section may be claimed by an appropriate representative of the unit of government if the information was furnished to an officer thereof.

(4) No privilege exists under this section:

(a) If the identity of the informer or the informer's interest in the subject matter of the communication has been disclosed to those who would have cause to resent the communication by a holder of the privilege or by the informer's own action, or if the informer appears as a witness for the unit of government.

(b) If it appears from the evidence in the case or from other showing by a party that an informer may be able to give testimony necessary to a fair determination of the issue of guilt or innocence in a criminal case or of a material issue on the merits in a civil case to which the unit of government is a party, and the unit of government invokes the privilege, and the judge gives the unit of government an opportunity to show in camera facts relevant to determining whether the informer can, in fact, supply that testimony. The showing will ordinarily be in the form of affidavits, but the judge may direct that testimony be taken if the judge finds that the matter cannot be resolved satisfactorily upon affidavit. If the judge rules that there is a reasonable probability that the informer can give the testimony, and the unit of government elects not to disclose identity of the informer, the judge on motion of the defendant in a criminal case shall dismiss the charges to which the testimony would relate, and the judge may do so on the judge's own motion. In civil cases, the judge may make any order that justice requires. Evidence submitted to the judge shall be sealed and preserved to be made available to the appellate court in the event of an appeal, and the contents shall not otherwise be revealed without consent of the unit of government. All counsel and parties shall be permitted to be present at every stage of proceedings under this paragraph except a showing in camera, at which no counsel or party shall be permitted to be present.

(c) If information from an informer is relied upon to establish the legality of the means by which evidence was obtained and the judge is not satisfied that the information was received from an informer reasonably believed to be reliable or credible. The judge may require the identity of the informer to be disclosed. The judge shall, on request of the unit of government, direct that the disclosure be made in camera. All counsel and parties concerned with the issue of legality shall be permitted to be present at every stage of proceedings under this paragraph except a disclosure in camera, at which no counsel or party shall be permitted to be present. If disclosure of the identity of the informer is made in camera, the record thereof shall be sealed and preserved to be made available to the appellate court in the event of an appeal, and the contents shall not otherwise be revealed without consent of the unit of government.

LEGISLATIVE COMMENTARY

Oregon Rule of Evidence 510 states the privilege of any unit of government to refuse to disclose the identity of an informer who has furnished information, relating to a possible violation of law. The rule is modeled on proposed Rule 510 of the Federal Rules of Evidence. Any changes in text are to conform the rule to the style of Oregon statutes or to reflect that the rule will be used in state court proceedings.

The Legislative Assembly believes that the adoption of Rule 510 will not change the law in Oregon relating to an informer's privilege. See ORS 135.855; *State v. Evans,* 1 Or App 489, 463 P2d 370 (1970); *State ex rel Kerns v. Read,* 266 Or 382, 514 P2d 1160 (1973).

Subsection (1). This subsection defines "unit of government" for purposes of the rule. It was inserted to make the substantive text less cumbersome. The definition includes the federal government as well as any state or political subdivision thereof, in view of the fact that the United States may be a party in state proceedings and there is frequently federal-state or interstate cooperation in criminal investigations.

The Legislative Assembly adopts the commentary of the federal advisory committee for the remainder of Rule 510.

"The rule recognizes the use of informers as an important aspect of law enforcement, whether the informer is a citizen who steps forward with information or a paid undercover agent. In either event, the basic importance of anonymity in the effective use of informers is apparent, *Bocchicchio v. Curtis Publishing Co.,* 203 F Supp 403 (ED Pa 1962), and the privilege of withholding their identity was well established at common law. *Roviaro v. United States,* 353 US 53, 59, 77 SCt 623, 1 LEd 2d 639 (1957); McCormick, *Evidence* § 111 (2d ed 1972); 8 Wigmore, *Evidence* § 2374 (McNaughton rev 1961).

"[*Subsection (2).*] The public interest in law enforcement requires that the privilege be that of the government, state, or political subdivision, rather than that of the witness. The rule blankets in as an informer anyone who tells a law enforcement officer about a violation of law without regard to whether the officer is one charged with enforcing the particular law. The rule also applies to disclosures to legislative investigating committees and their staffs, and is sufficiently broad to include continuing investigations.

"Although the tradition of protecting the identity of informers has evolved in an essentially criminal setting, noncriminal law enforcement situations involving possibilities of reprisal against informers fall within the purview of the considerations out of which the privilege originated. In *Mitchell v. Roma,* 265 F2d 633 (3rd Cir 1959), the privilege was given effect with respect to persons informing as to Violations of the Fair Labor Standards Act, and in *Wirtz v. Continental Finance & Loan Co.,* 326 F2d 561 (5th Cir 1964), a similar case, the privilege was recognized, although the basis of decision was lack of relevancy to the issues in the case.

"Only identity is privileged; communications are not included except to the extent that disclosure would operate also to disclose the informer's identity. The common law was to the same effect. 8 Wigmore § 2374 at 765. See also *Roviaro v. United States,* supra, 353

US at 60; *Bowman Dairy Co. v. United States,* 341 US 214, 221, 71 SCt 675, 95 LEd 879 (1951).

"[*Subsection (3).*] Normally the 'appropriate representative' to make the claim will be counsel. However, it is possible that disclosure of the informer's identity will be sought in proceedings to which the government, state, or subdivision, as the case may be, is not a party. Under these circumstances effective implementation of the privilege requires that other representatives be considered 'appropriate.' See, for example, *Bocchicchio v. Curtis Publishing Co.,* supra, a civil action for libel, in which a local police officer not represented by counsel successfully claimed the informer privilege.

"[*Subsection (4)*] deals with situations in which the informer privilege either does not apply or is curtailed.

"[Paragraph (a).] If the identity of the informer is disclosed nothing further is to be gained from efforts to suppress it. Disclosure may be direct, or the same practical effect may result from action revealing the informer's interest in the subject matter. See, for example, *Westinghouse Electric Corp. v. City of Burlington,* 351 F2d 762 (DC Cir 1965), on remand *City of Burlington v. Westinghouse Electric Corp.,* 246 F Supp 839 (DDC 1965), which held that the filing of civil antitrust actions destroyed as to plaintiffs the informer privilege claimed by the Attorney General with respect to complaints of criminal antitrust violations. While allowing the privilege in effect to be waived by one not its holder, i.e., the informer ..., is something of a novelty in the law of privilege, if the informer chooses to reveal [the informer's] identity further efforts to suppress it are scarcely feasible.

"The exception is limited to disclosure to 'those who would have cause to resent the communication,' in the language of *Roviaro v. United States,* supra, 353 US at 60, since disclosure otherwise, e.g., to another law enforcing agency, is not calculated to undercut the objects of the privilege.

"If the informer becomes a witness for the [unit of] government, the interests of justice in disclosing [the informer's] status as a source of bias or possible support are believed to outweigh any remnant of interest in nondisclosure which then remains. See *Harris v. United States,* 371 F2d 365 (9th Cir 1967), in which the trial judge permitted detailed inquiry into the relationship between the witness and the government. Cf. *Attorney General v. Briant,* 15 M & W 169, 153 Eng Rep 808 (Exch 1846). The purpose of the limitation to witnesses for the [unit of] government is to avoid the possibility of calling persons as witnesses as a means of discovering whether they are informers.

"[Paragraph (b).] The informer privilege, it was held by the leading case, may not be used in a criminal prosecution to suppress the identity of a witness when the public interest in protecting the flow of information is outweighed by the individual's right to prepare [a] defense. *Roviaro v. United States,* supra. The rule extends this balancing to include civil as well as criminal cases and phrases it in terms of 'a reasonable probability that the informer may be able to give testimony necessary to a fair determination of the issue of guilt or innocence in a criminal case or of a material issue on the merits of a civil case.' Once the privilege is invoked a procedure is provided for determining whether the informer can in fact supply testimony of such nature as to require disclosure of [the informer's] identity, thus avoiding a 'judicial guessing game' in the question. *United States v. Day*, 384 F2d 464, 470 (3rd Cir 1967). An investigation in camera is calculated to accommodate the conflicting interests involved. The rule also spells out specifically the consequences of a successful claim of privilege in a criminal case; the wider range of possibilities in civil cases demands more flexibility in treatment.

"[Paragraph (c).] One of the acute conflicts between the interest of the public in nondisclosure and the avoidance of unfairness to the accused as a result of nondisclosure arises when information from an informer is relied upon to legitimate a search and seizure by furnishing probable cause for an arrest without a warrant or for the issuance of a warrant for arrest and search. *McCray v. Illinois*, 386 US 300, 87 SCt 1056, 18 LEd 2d 62 (1967), rehearing denied, 386 US 1042. A hearing in camera provides an accommodation of these conflicting interests. *United States v. Jackson*, 384 F2d 825 (3rd Cir 1967). The limited disclosure to the judge avoids any significant impairment of secrecy, while affording the accused a substantial measure of protection against arbitrary police action. The procedure is consistent with *McCray* and the decisions there discussed."

TEXT

Identity of Informer

The privilege not to reveal the identity of an informer provided by Rule 510 differs from most of the other privileges in Article V because it is a qualified privilege. It can be overcome in a criminal case by a showing that the informer "may be able to give testimony necessary to a fair determination of the issue of guilt or innocence." In a civil case where the unit of government holding the privilege is a party, the privilege can be overcome if the informer may be able to give testimony regarding "a material issue on the merits." In a hearing challenging the seizure of evidence, the privilege can be overcome if "the judge is not satisfied that the information was received from an informer reasonably believed to be reliable or credible."

The governmental unit rather than the informer is the holder of the privilege. The privilege is inapplicable if the informer's identity or the informer's interest in the subject matter of the communication is disclosed by the holder or by the informer to those who would have cause to resent the communication. Also, the privilege is inapplicable if the government calls the informer as a witness. But see *State v. Goodwin*, 136 Or App 356, 361–2, 902 P2d 131 (1995) (even though informers did not testify, defendant argued their identity should have been disclosed because informers were "in effect witnesses against defendant" because statements by them were introduced; the error, if any, was harmless).

The procedures for determining whether the identity of an informer must be disclosed are set forth in Rule 510(4)(b) and (c). Affidavits may be submitted and an *in camera* hearing at which no counsel or party shall be permitted to be present may be scheduled. The record is to be sealed and preserved to be made available to the appellate court in the event of an appeal.

Disclosure of the informer's identity may be necessary to protect the constitutional rights of the defendant. The United States Supreme Court has stated:

> Where the disclosure of an informer's identity ... is relevant and helpful to the defense of an accused, or is essential to a fair determination of a cause, the privilege must give way ....
>
> ...
>
> We believe that no fixed rule with respect to disclosure is justifiable. The problem is one that calls for balancing the public interest in protecting the flow of information against the individual's right to prepare his defense. Whether a proper balance renders nondisclosure erroneous must depend on the particular circumstances of each case, taking into consideration the crime charged, the possible defenses, the possible significance of the informer's testimony, and other relevant factors. (*Roviaro v. United States,* 353 US 53, 60–62, 77 SCt 623, 628–29, 1 LEd 2d 639, 645–46 (1957) (footnote omitted)).

Courts are likely to require disclosure of the identity of the informer when the informer is the only eyewitness to the crime other than the defendant and government agents. See *Roviaro v. United States,* 353 US at 64. Other relevant factors are the informer's level of involvement with the criminal activity, the relationship between an asserted defense and the informer's likely testimony, and the government's interest in nondisclosure. *United States v. Ayala,* 643 F2d 244 (5th Cir 1981).

A defendant's mere claim that disclosure of the informer's identity is necessary to his defense is insufficient. In *State v. Cortman,* 251 Or 566, 446 P2d 681 (1968), cert denied 394 US 951 (1969), the court stated:

> We hold that in order to predicate error upon the refusal of a court to order the state to produce an informer, the party seeking such an order should make some preliminary showing that the informer's testimony would have some bearing upon the issue of guilt or innocence. The argument that the informer in the case at bar may have "planted" the narcotics is an argument that the defendant is free to make before the jury, whether or not the informer takes the witness stand. The likelihood that an informer would take the stand and admit that he "planted" the state's evidence in order "to frame" the defendant is not, however, so great that we can say that the state had the duty to sacrifice the informer in this case. (251 Or at 575, 446 P2d at 685 (citation omitted)).

See also *State v. Vatland,* 123 Or App 577, 581, 860 P2d 820, 821 (1993), rev denied 318 Or 853, 873 P2d 322 (1994) (correct standard for ordering disclosure of informants' identity is not that they had information that would be "relevant to the issues of knowledge and participation in the charged offense," but rather whether informant could provide evidence "useful to the defense").

Even if the government does disclose the informer's identity, this does not ensure the informer's presence at trial. Although the prosecution may have an obligation to produce an informer at trial or at least to assist the defendant in locating the informer, failure to produce the informer at trial does not necessarily require dismissal of the charges. *State v. Elliott,* 276 Or 99, 553 P2d 1058 (1976) (applying same analysis to failure of production as to failure to disclose identity).

Recent Cases

In *State v. Ritter,* 71 Or App 282, 692 P2d 158 (1984), the court affirmed a trial court ruling sustaining objections to nine defense questions on the ground that the answers would tend to disclose the identity of a confidential informant.

In *State v. Martinez,* 97 Or App 170, 776 P2d 3 (1989), the court held that the order of the trial judge requiring disclosure of the informer's identity is subject to review on appeal from an order of dismissal entered after refusal by the state to disclose. The court also rejected an argument by the state that the defendant must make a showing that the informer is a necessary witness to the "fair determination of the issue of guilt or innocence" before the trial judge could properly take testimony from the arresting officer on the question. The court noted that the rule provides that the appearance of the need to disclose can be established either by "the evidence in the case" or by "other showing by a party." After reviewing the merits of the order requiring disclosure pursuant to an abuse of discretion standard, the appellate court held that the trial judge properly dismissed the charges after the state elected not to disclose the informer's identity.

RULE 510(4)(c)
Informer Furnishing Probable Cause for Search

Rule 510(4)(c) is intended to ensure that a judge is able to make the ultimate determination of whether probable cause for a search existed rather than relying entirely upon the testimony of law enforcement officers that there was a reliable informer. In *McCray v. Illinois,* 386 US 300, 87 SCt 1056, 18 LEd2d 62 (1967), the Supreme Court held that a defendant is not constitutionally entitled to disclosure of an informer's identity in a hearing where probable cause for a search is challenged. However:

> If the magistrate doubts the credibility of the affiant, he may require that the informant be identified or even produced. It seems to us that the same approach is equally sufficient where the search was without a warrant, that is to say, that it should rest entirely with the judge who hears the motion to suppress to decide whether he needs such disclosure as to the informant in order to decide whether the officer is a believable witness. (386 US at 307–308, quoting from *State v. Burnett,* 42 NJ 377, 388, 201 A2d 39, 45 (1964)).

The need for disclosure of the informer's identity will generally be greater in cases where the search was conducted on probable cause alone than in cases where a warrant was obtained in advance. In the former case, there is greater danger of fabrication of the informer's existence to justify the search.

Disclosure of an informer's identity is more likely to be required under Rule 510(4)(c) than under Rule 510(4)(b), because the government can request that the disclosure be made *in camera*. The court will be able to determine whether a reliable informer existed in any case where there is reasonable doubt about the matter, without revealing the informer's identity to the defendant.

Rule 510 should be considered in conjunction with ORS 135.855, which makes the identity of an informer generally immune from discovery. This statute provides:

> (1) The following material and information shall not be subject to discovery under ORS 135.805–135.873:
>
> ...
>
> (b) The identity of a confidential informant where his identity is a prosecution secret and a failure to disclose will not infringe the constitutional rights of the defendant. Except as provided in ORS 135.873, disclosure shall not be denied hereunder of the identity of witnesses to be produced at trial.

RULE 511.   ORS 40.280. WAIVER OF PRIVILEGE BY VOLUNTARY DISCLOSURE

A person upon whom Rules 503 to 514 (ORS 40.225 to 40.295) confer a privilege against disclosure of the confidential matter or communication waives the privilege if the person or the person's predecessor while holder of the privilege voluntarily discloses or consents to disclosure of any significant part of the matter or communication. This section does not apply if the disclosure is itself a privileged communication. Voluntary disclosure does not occur with the mere commencement of litigation or, in the case of a deposition taken for the purpose of perpetuating testimony, until the offering of the deposition as evidence. Voluntary disclosure does occur, as to psychotherapists in the case of a mental or emotional condition and physicians in the case of a physical condition upon the holder's offering of any person as a witness who testifies as to the condition.

LEGISLATIVE COMMENTARY

Oregon Rule of Evidence 511 states the conditions under which a privilege conferred by Article V of the Oregon Evidence Code is waived. Briefly, a privilege is lost when the reason for it ceases to apply. As the Commentary to Federal Rule 511 explains:

> "The central purpose of most privileges is the promotion of some interest or relationship by endowing it with a supporting secrecy or confidentiality. It is evident that the privilege should terminate when the holder by [the holder's] own act destroys this confidentiality. McCormick, *Evidence* §§ 93, 103 (2d ed 1972); 8 Wigmore, *Evidence* §§ 2242, 2327–2329, 2374, 2389–2390 (McNaughton rev 1961).

"...

"By traditional doctrine, waiver is the intentional relinquishment of a known right. *Johnson v. Zerbst,* 304 US 458, 464, 58 SCt 1019, 82 LEd 1461 (1938). However, in the confidential privilege situations, once confidentiality is destroyed through voluntary disclosure, no subsequent claim of privilege can restore it, and knowledge or lack of knowledge of the existence of the privilege appears to be irrelevant. California Evidence Code § 912; 8 Wigmore § 2327."

Disclosure of the substance of a confidential communication. The first two sentences of the rule are identical to proposed Rule 511 of the Federal Rules of Evidence. They state a waiver rule of general application. If the holder has voluntarily disclosed or consented to the disclosure of any significant part of a privileged communication, then the entire communication may be inquired into. Furthermore, the privilege in question is waived as to other communications on the same subject with the same person, and communications on the same subject with other persons. 8 Wigmore § 2327; *State ex rel Calley v. Olsen,* 271 Or 369, 532 P2d 230 (1975); *Triplett v. Bd. of Social Protection,* 19 Or App 408, 528 P2d 563 (1974). The rule indicates that waiver occurs as soon as a "significant" part of a communication is disclosed. It is not necessary that the holder or other person testify to every detail for waiver to be effective. *Bryant v. Dukehart,* 106 Or 359, 210 P 454 (1922); *Gerlinger v. Frank,* 74 Or 517, 145 P 1069 (1915).

Waiver by disclosure of part or all of a privileged communication can occur in any situation, within or without the context of a lawsuit. The rule makes clear that the mere commencement of litigation does not constitute disclosure. *Neilson v. Bryson,* 257 Or 179, 477 P2d 714 (1970) (physician-patient privilege not waived by filing personal injury action). Thereafter, however, waiver can occur during discovery or at trial, either on direct or cross examination. McCormick § 93.

The one exception to the foregoing principle involves a deposition taken for the purpose of perpetuating testimony. Under the rule, the effect of any waiver of privilege that occurs in such a deposition is delayed until the deposition is offered as evidence by a party at trial. The Legislative Assembly added this provision to address the frequent problem where a party, which does not wish to disclose ahead of time the testimony of its expert and waive the privilege as to other experts consulted, must nevertheless do so because the expert whose testimony it wishes to use will not be available for trial. Counsel should be guided by professional responsibility, reinforced if necessary by the courts, in using this exception for its intended purpose.

Testimony on the subject of a confidential communication. ORE 511 replaces the waiver provisions of ORS 44.040(2). That statute indicated that when the holder of a privilege voluntarily testifies on a subject, any communications the holder may have had with any other person on the subject cease to be privileged. See *Patterson v. Skoglund,* 181 Or 167, 276 P 248 (1947); *Fowler v. Phoenix Insurance Co.,* 35 Or 559, 57 P 421 (1899). Taken literally, this would allow the prosecution to call defense counsel as a witness as soon as the accused has finished taking the stand. The rule is obviously phrased too broadly, and for this reason there is inconsistency among Oregon cases whether testimony on the same subject will waive a privilege, or whether it is necessary that there be testimony as to a particular privileged communication. *Stark Street Properties, Inc. v. Teufel,* 277 Or 649, 658 n 12, 562 P2d 531 (1977), citing *Bryant v. Dukehart,* supra, and *McNamee v. First Nat. Bank of Roseburg,* 88 Or 636, 172 P 801 (1918).

Rule 511 resolves the present uncertainty by adopting a restrictive view of waiver. A person, merely by disclosing a subject which the person has discussed with an attorney or spouse or doctor, does not waive the applicable privilege; the person must disclose part of the communication itself in order to effect a waiver. As McCormick points out:

> "By the prevailing view, which seems correct, the mere voluntary taking the stand and testifying to facts which were the subject of consultation with counsel is no waiver of the privilege for secrecy of the communications to [one's] lawyer. It is the communication which is privileged, not the facts." McCormick § 93.

The one exception to the foregoing principle is contained in the final sentence of the rule. Where the holder of a privilege offers any person as a witness who testifies on the subject of the holder's physical, mental, or emotional condition, *all* privileges that might protect communications on that subject between the holder and a physician or psychotherapist, as the case may be, are waived. A simple example of this would be a case in which a party indicates that on a certain day the party was absent from work because of illness. This testimony waives the physician-patient privilege, allowing the opposing party to inquire of the person's doctor as to the person's medical condition. Another example would be a criminal case in which defense counsel considers the use of a mental defense or partial defense. The defendant, at the request of the attorney, may see a number of psychiatrists before finding one who will testify that the defendant was suffering from a mental disease or defect at the time of the crime. If the latter testifies at trial that the defendant was not responsible, under ORE 504 there is no psychotherapist-patient privilege as to any psychotherapist because the mental condition of the defendant is in issue. The non-testifying psychiatrists are still protected by the attorney-client privilege, however, as they are the "representatives of the lawyer" under ORE 503. The last sentence of ORE 511 would waive this (and any other) privilege to the extent of permitting the state to inquire of all medical personnel whom the defendant has seen regarding their findings.

TEXT

Waiver by Voluntary Disclosure

Rule 511 defines when and how the privileges created by Article V are waived. It significantly changes prior Oregon law regarding the waiver of a privilege. Former ORS 44.040(2) (repealed 1981) stated:

If a party to the action or proceeding voluntarily offers testimony as a witness, it is deemed a consent to the examination also of a spouse, attorney, clergyman, physician or surgeon, stenographer, licensed professional nurse, licensed psychologist, licensed naturopath, a registered clinical social worker, a certificated staff member, local health authority officer employee, or a certificated school counselor on the same subject.

The new rule provides that waiver does not occur merely when the holder takes the witness stand and testifies on the same subject as the privileged communication, but only when the holder discloses a significant part of the privileged communication, or consents to such disclosure by another person. Waiver by testimony of the holder is less likely under the new rule than under the former statute.

Rule 511 provides for broader waiver outside of trial than the former statute, although it is consistent with prior case law. The rule states that disclosure of a significant part of the privileged matter or communication to any person will waive the privilege, unless the disclosure is itself a privileged communication. Thus, a person who tells a friend about a communication made to his lawyer, physician, or clergy member may waive the privilege as to that communication. See *Stark St. Properties, Inc. v. Teufel*, 277 Or 649, 657, 562 P2d 531 (1977) ("Where a client concedes, as here, that he might have given to another a letter from his attorney, such a concession dispels the notion that the communication was regarded as secret.").

A distinction must be drawn between disclosure of information pertaining to the subject of the privileged communication and disclosure of the communication itself. Only the communication is privileged, not the holder's knowledge of the facts. Therefore, the holder may disclose the facts to third persons without waiving the privilege. For example, a client may speak freely to nonprivileged persons about the facts of an automobile accident without waiving the right to prevent the attorney from being questioned regarding specific communications from the client about that accident.

Voluntary Disclosure; Consent to Disclosure

The two key concepts in Rule 511 are *voluntary disclosure* and *consent to disclosure*. Unfortunately, these terms are not defined. The rule provides that voluntary disclosure does not occur with the mere commencement of litigation or, in the case of a deposition to perpetuate testimony, until the deposition is offered as evidence. The Commentary indicates that voluntary disclosure can occur by response of a witness on cross-examination as well as direct examination. In this respect the rule appears contrary to prior Oregon case law. See *State v. Schier*, 47 Or App 1075, 615 P2d 1147 (1980) (a party does not waive the marital communications privilege when the privileged subject is opened for the first time on cross-examination); *Bryant v. Dukehart*, 106 Or 359, 210 P 454 (1922).

Neither the rule nor the Commentary directly addresses the issue of whether voluntary disclosure occurs when the holder is involuntarily called as a witness at a deposition or at trial and responds to questions seeking disclosure of a privileged matter without objection. Under prior law, a witness called by the opponent was not viewed as "offering" herself or himself as a witness within the meaning of the former privilege statute, and therefore no waiver occurred. *Nielson v. Bryson,* 257 Or 179, 183, 477 P2d 714, 716 (1970); *Reynolds Metals Co. v. Yturbide,* 258 F2d 321, 334 (9th Cir), cert denied 358 US 840 (1958). However, these precedents have limited value given the change in focus from whether a witness "offers" herself as a witness to whether the witness "voluntarily discloses or consents to disclosure of any significant part of the matter or communication."

In any situation where the holder could reasonably have claimed the privilege but fails to do so and instead voluntarily discloses privileged information, the privilege should be viewed as waived. However, consideration must be given to whether the disclosure was truly "voluntary" and whether the holder was aware of the right to refuse disclosure and had adequate opportunity to claim the privilege.

In *State ex rel Grimm v. Ashmanskas,* 298 Or 206, 213 n3, 690 P2d 1063 (1984), the court held: "We do not believe the legislature intended waiver [of the privilege] to occur when a plaintiff in a personal injury or malpractice case is required by the opponent to submit to a pretrial discovery deposition, because in that situation the holder of the privilege is not voluntarily offering his or her confidential communications or personal condition to the public." However, if the plaintiff in such a deposition goes beyond testimony regarding his or her medical condition and voluntarily discloses privileged communications with the doctor, a stronger argument exists for finding waiver of the privilege.

See generally ANNOT., *Pretrial Testimony or Disclosure on Discovery by Party to Personal Injury Action As to Nature of Injuries or Treatment As Waiver of Physician-Patient Privilege,* 25 ALR3d 1401 (1969); 1 McCormick, *Evidence* (4th ed 1992) § 103 at 387 (disclosure of matter within physician-patient privilege on cross-examination usually held not to be voluntary; no waiver).

Use of Privileged Material to Refresh Witness' Recollection

On the issue of whether using privileged material to refresh a witness' recollection under Rule 612 waives the privilege, see textual discussion after Rules 612 and 503.

Assertion of Claim or Defense

Although the rule provides that commencement of litigation is not sufficient to constitute a waiver of the privilege, this statement may be qualified in the case of the attorney client privilege by Rule 503(4), which provides: "There is no privilege under this section: ... (c) As to a communication relevant to an issue of breach of duty by the lawyer to the client or by the client to the lawyer." Arguably, under this subsection, the filing of a malpractice action by a client against an attorney might in some cases constitute a limited waiver of the attorney-client privilege to the extent privileged matter is necessary to defend against the charge.

Similarly, Rule 504(4)(b), which defines the psychotherapist-patient privilege, provides:

> There is no privilege under this rule as to communications relevant to an issue of the mental or emotional condition of the patient in any proceeding in which the patient relies upon the condition as an element of the patient's claim or defense, or, after the patient's death, in any proceeding in which any party relies upon the condition as an element of the party's claim or defense.

Under this subsection, assertion of a claim or defense by the patient relating to the patient's mental or emotional condition may constitute a waiver of the privilege.

For further discussion of waiver by claim assertion in the context of the attorney-client privilege, see textual discussion after Rule 503, supra.

Waiver as to Other Communications

The Commentary states that if a significant part of the privileged communication is voluntarily disclosed, then "the privilege in question is waived as to other communications on the same subject with the same person, and communications on the same subject with other persons." While such a statement may go beyond the language of the rule, it appears to be consistent with prior Oregon case law. In *State ex rel Calley v. Olsen,* 271 Or 369, 532 P2d 230 (1975), the court held that "once a patient has waived the privilege as to one doctor for the purpose of offering testimony favorable to his claim, he has terminated the doctor-patient privilege and cannot then properly exclude the testimony of another doctor which might not be favorable to his claim." 271 Or at 380, 532 P2d at 235. The court also held that "once a patient has intentionally offered or taken the testimony of one doctor, either on trial or by deposition, the privilege is then terminated for all purposes relating to the injury or illness which was the subject of the testimony of that doctor." 271 Or at 381, 532 P2d at 236 (footnote omitted). Under this view, waiver extends to the entire subject matter of the privileged communication rather than to merely one specific communication. See generally ANNOT., *Waiver of Privilege As Regards One Physician As a Waiver As to Other Physicians,* 5 ALR3d 1244 (1966).

However, when the privilege is waived by inadvertent disclosure, the scope of waiver should ordinarily be limited to the subject matter disclosed. See textual discussion of waiver of the attorney-client privilege by inadvertent disclosure after Rule 503, supra.

The broadest waiver provision in the rule is stated in the last sentence. It provides that the psychotherapist-patient privilege and the physician-patient privilege are waived with respect to a particular mental, emotional, or physical condition when any person, including the patient, is called by the patient as a witness and testifies about that condition. In a personal injury case, offering testimony regarding the condition will waive the privilege with respect to any physician who treated the condition. In a criminal case where the defendant asserts an insanity defense, the privilege will be waived as to any psychotherapist who previously treated the defendant with regard to the claimed mental condition. See *State v. Corgain,* 63 Or App 26, 663 P2d 773 (1983) (defendant offers evidence regarding his mental condition; state allowed to call psychiatrist who had earlier examined defendant at request of defendant's attorney). This new rule is contrary to prior Oregon law. See *State v. Moore,* 45 Or App 837, 843, 609 P2d 866, 869 (1980) (rejecting a rule of waiver and suggesting that such a rule could have serious constitutional implications).

The rule should be construed to limit the waiver to physicians treating the physical condition in question and to psychotherapists treating the mental condition in question, or one reasonably related thereto. The last sentence of the Commentary, stating that Rule 511 would allow the "state to inquire of all medical personnel whom the defendant has seen," would seem to go beyond the rule.

With respect to the physician-patient privilege, the Oregon Supreme Court has approved the following statement:

> [I]t would seem apparent that the privilege is waived only to those matters causally and historically related to the condition put in issue and which have a direct medical relevance to the claim, counterclaim or defense made. If it be shown that there is nothing more than some casual link having no direct medical bearing on the legitimacy of the claim or defense tendered between the condition in issue and the condition on which discovery is sought, the trial court should properly issue a protective order. (*State ex rel Calley v. Olsen,* 271 Or 369, 382, 532 P2d 230, 236 (1975), quoting *Collins v. Bair,* 256 Ind 230, 268 NE2d 95, 101 (1971)).

Scope of Rule

It is unclear whether Rule 511 applies to privileges arising outside the Evidence Code. Rule 514 recognizes the continuing existence of such privileges, and Rule 511 specifically refers to Rule 514. Ambiguity is created by the fact that Rule 511 states that it applies to privileges conferred by Rules 503 to 514 but Rule 514 does not confer a privilege. In *John Deere Co. v. Epstein,* 307 Or 348, 354, 769 P2d 766 (1989), the Supreme Court held that "the unqualified term 'privilege' in OEC 513 must be interpreted to encompass all privileges, including privileges not enumerated within the code." The court would likely reach the same conclusion with respect to OEC 511, at least for privileges not having their own special rules of waiver.

Recent Cases

In *State v. Langley,* 314 Or 247, 262, 839 P2d 692 (1992), adhered to 318 Or 28, 861 P2d 1012 (1993), the court held that written assignments that defendant had prepared as part of a prison treatment program for mentally and emotionally disturbed inmates were subject to the psychotherapist-patient privilege. However, the court found the privilege to have been waived under OEC 511, because two of the documents had been received without objection at the trial of another defendant, and those documents disclosed a "significant part" of the privileged matter.

In *Boon v. Boon*, 100 Or App 354, 357–8, 786 P2d 215, 217 (1990), the court held that a husband waived the psychotherapist-patient privilege with respect to a psychological evaluation of him by showing the report to another psychologist, and then calling the second psychologist as a witness. Therefore, the wife was entitled to discovery of the report.

In *State ex rel Adult and Family Services v. Blacker*, 75 Or App 332, 706 P2d 181 (1985), a filiation proceeding, the defendant sought to offer obstetrical records of the mother to support the defendant's contention regarding the date of conception. The trial court sustained an objection to defendant's offer of the records, apparently under the physician-patient privilege. On appeal defendant argued that under Rule 511 the mother waived the privilege by offering herself as a witness regarding her physical condition, including the conception and birth of the child. The court did not decide the waiver issue, finding that any error in refusal to admit the records was harmless under Rule 103.

RULE 512.   ORS 40.285. PRIVILEGED MATTER DISCLOSED UNDER COMPULSION OR WITHOUT OPPORTUNITY TO CLAIM PRIVILEGE

Evidence of a statement or other disclosure of privileged matter is not admissible against the holder of the privilege if the disclosure was:
(1) Compelled erroneously; or
(2) Made without opportunity to claim the privilege.

LEGISLATIVE COMMENTARY

Oregon Rule of Evidence 512, regarding compelled or otherwise involuntary disclosure of privileged matter, is identical to proposed Rule 512 of the Federal Rules of Evidence.

The Legislative Assembly adopts the commentary of the federal advisory committee:

"Ordinarily a privilege is invoked in order to forestall disclosure. However, under some circumstances consideration must be given to the status and effect of a disclosure already made. Rule 511 immediately preceding, gives voluntary disclosure the effect of a waiver, while the present rule covers the effect of disclosure made under compulsion or without opportunity to claim the privilege.

"Confidentiality, once destroyed, is not susceptible of restoration, yet some measure of repair may be accomplished by preventing use of the evidence against the holder of the privilege. The remedy of exclusion is therefore made available when the earlier disclosure was compelled erroneously or without opportunity to claim the privilege.

"With respect to erroneously compelled disclosure, the argument may be made that the holder should be required in the first instance to assert the privilege, stand [the holder's] ground, refuse to answer, perhaps incur a judgment of contempt, and exhaust all legal resources in order to sustain [the] privilege. [Citations omitted.] However, this exacts of the holder greater fortitude in the face of authority than ordinary individuals are likely to possess, and assumes unrealistically that a judicial remedy is always available.

"In self-incrimination cases, the writers agree that erroneously compelled disclosures are inadmissible in a subsequent criminal prosecution of the holder, Maguire, *Evidence of Guilt* 66 (1959); 8 Wigmore § 2270 (McNaughton rev 1961), and the principle is equally sound when applied to other privileges. The modest departure from usual principles of res judicata which occurs when the compulsion is judicial is justified by the advantage of having one simple rule, assuring at least one opportunity for judicial supervision in every case.

"The second circumstance stated as a basis for exclusion is disclosure made without opportunity to the holder to assert [the holder's] privilege. Illustrative possibilities are disclosure by an eavesdropper, by a person used in the transmission of a privileged communication, by a family member participating in psychotherapy, or privileged data unproperly made available from a computer bank."

There is no prior judicial or legislative authority in Oregon for the principles set forth in this rule. However, there is no reason to believe that the courts in Oregon would not follow them.

TEXT

Disclosure Under Compulsion; No Opportunity to Claim Privilege

Even though a third person may become aware of a privileged communication, Rule 512 provides that it is still not admissible against the holder of the privilege if the disclosure was compelled erroneously or made without opportunity to claim the privilege.

Rule 512(1) to some extent modifies the doctrine of res judicata. It provides that even though a judge at a prior proceeding ruled the privilege not to be applicable and compelled disclosure, a judge at a subsequent proceeding may find that ruling to be in error. Under this rule, the disclosure made in response to the first judge's order will not constitute a waiver of the privilege. Under traditional principles of res judicata, the first ruling on the privilege would control unless reversed on appeal.

Rule 512(2) preserves the privilege when a communication is disclosed without an opportunity to claim the privilege, such as when an eavesdropper overhears the communication. To the extent that Rule 512(2) prevents in-court disclosure of confidential communications overheard by an eavesdropper, it overlaps with protections already contained in some of the other rules in Article

V. These rules define a communication as confidential subject to specified exceptions, if it is "not intended to be disclosed to third persons," even though in fact it may have been overheard. See, e.g., Rules 503(l)(b); 504(l)(a); 504-1(1)(a). These rules allow the holder to prevent "any other person from disclosing" the confidential communication. See Rules 503(2); 504(2); 504-1(2). If the person making the communication took reasonable precautions against being overheard, the court would likely find that the person intended the communication to be confidential and that therefore it is privileged. Thus, it may be possible to prevent testimony by an eavesdropper both under the rule creating the privilege and under Rule 512(2). For other privileges, Rule 512(2) may add a protection not contained within the rule defining the privilege.

Rule 512(2) also preserves the privilege in cases where the nonholder party to the privileged communication discloses the communication without authorization where there was no opportunity for the holder to assert the privilege. For example, unauthorized disclosure by an attorney of a client's confidential communications would not waive the right of the client to prevent the attorney from being questioned in a judicial proceeding about such communications. See *State v. McGrew*, 46 Or App 123, 127, 610 P2d 1245 (1980) (no waiver of attorney-client privilege when attorney not authorized to disclose); *State v. Suttles*, 37 Or App 695, 588 P2d 635 (1978), rev'd on other grounds 287 Or 15, 597 P2d 786 (1979) (no waiver of marital communication privilege when wife gave incriminating letter from husband to prosecutor without husband's consent). Cf. *State v. Wilkins*, 72 Or 77, 142 P 589 (1914) (marital communication privilege not applicable to letters to and from spouse seized from defendant).

RULE 513.   ORS 40.290. COMMENT UPON OR INFERENCE FROM CLAIM OF PRIVILEGE

(1) **The claim of a privilege, whether in the present proceeding or upon a prior occasion, is not a proper subject of comment by judge or counsel. No inference may be drawn from a claim of privilege.**

(2) **In jury cases, proceedings shall be conducted, to the extent practicable, so as to facilitate the making of claims of privilege without the knowledge of the jury.**

(3) **Upon request, any party against whom the jury might draw an adverse inference from a claim of privilege is entitled to an instruction that no inference may be drawn therefrom.**

LEGISLATIVE COMMENTARY

Oregon Rule of Evidence 513 prohibits any comment upon a claim of privilege, and mandates procedures to avoid any inference by a jury based on such a claim. The rule is identical to proposed Rule 513 of the Federal Rules of Evidence.

The Legislative Assembly approves the following note of the federal advisory committee:

"*[Subsection (1).]* In *Griffin v. California,* 380 US 609, 614, 85 SCt 1229, 14 LEd 2d 106 (1965), the Court pointed out that allowing comment upon the claim of a privilege "cuts down on the privilege by making its assertion costly." Consequently it was held that that comment upon the election of the accused not to take the stand infringed upon [the accused's] privilege against self-incrimination so substantially as to constitute a constitutional violation. While the privileges governed by these rules are not constitutionally based they are nevertheless founded upon important policies and are entitled to maximum effect. Hence, [this subsection] forbids comment upon the exercise of a privilege, in accord with the weight of authority. 8 Wigmore, *Evidence* §§ 2243, 2322, 2386 (McNaughton rev 1961); McCormick, *Evidence* § 76 at 156 (2d ed 1972) [citations omitted].

"*[Subsection (2).]* The value of a privilege may be greatly depreciated by means other than expressly commenting to a jury that it was exercised. Thus, the calling of a witness in the presence of the jury and subsequently excusing [the witness] after a sidebar conference may effectively convey to the jury the fact that a privilege has been claimed, even though the actual claim has not been made in their hearing. Whether a privilege will be claimed is usually ascertainable in advance and the handling of the entire matter outside the presence of the jury is feasible. Destruction of the privilege by innuendo can and should be avoided. [Citations omitted.] 6 Wigmore § 1808 at 275–276. This position is in accord with the general agreement of the authorities that an accused cannot be forced to make [the] election not to testify in the presence of the jury. 8 Wigmore § 2268 at 407.

"Unanticipated situations are, of course, bound to arise, and much must be left to the discretion of the jury and the professional responsibility of counsel.

"*[Subsection (3).]* Opinions will differ as to the effectiveness of a jury instruction not to draw an adverse inference from the making of a claim of privilege. See *Bruton v. United States,* 389 US 818, 88 SCt 126, 19 LEd 2d 70 (1968). Whether an instruction shall be given is left to the sound judgment of counsel for the party against whom the adverse inference may be drawn. The instruction is a matter of right, if requested ....

"The right to the instruction is not impaired by the fact that the claim of privilege is by a witness, rather than by a party, provided an adverse inference against the party may result."

This rule changes Oregon law relating to comments upon and inferences from a claim of privilege that is not constitutionally guaranteed. Nearly all the cases involve the husband-wife privilege in a criminal trial.

In Oregon, the prosecution has been able to call the spouse of the defendant as a witness and thus require the defendant to assert the marital privilege in the presence of the jury. After the privilege is claimed, the court has not been required to instruct the jury not to drawn any inference, and the prosecution has been allowed to comment upon the privilege claim. *State v. Inman,* 8 Or App 180, 492 P2d 804 (1972); *State v. Hixon,* 237 Or 402, 291 P2d 388 (1964).

Citing *State v. Johnson,* 243 Or 532, 431 P2d 383 (1966), the Inman court did imply that if the prosecution is aware that a spouse intends to refuse to testify based on the Fifth Amendment privilege against self-incrimination, it cannot call the spouse as a witness. Early case law also suggested that it is improper for an attorney to comment upon an examining physician's refusal to testify. *Kelley v. Highfield,* 15 Or 277, 14 P 744 (1887).

TEXT

Comment on Claim of Privilege

Under the Fifth Amendment, it is established that a defendant in a criminal case cannot be compelled to assert the privilege against self-incrimination in front of a jury, that no comment may be made upon the exercise of the privilege, that no adverse inference may be drawn from the exercise of the privilege, and that the defendant is entitled to an instruction that no adverse inference may be drawn therefrom. *Griffin v. California,* 380 US 609, 85 SCt 1229, 14 LEd2d 106 (1965); *Carter v. Kentucky,* 450 US 288, 101 SCt 1112, 67 LEd2d 241 (1981); *State v. Halford,* 101 Or App 660, 792 P2d 467 (1990) (reversible error for prosecutor to comment on defendant's failure to testify). See ANNOT., *Violation of Federal Constitutional Rule (Griffin v. California) Prohibiting Adverse Comment by Prosecutor or Court upon Accused's Failure to Testify, As Constituting Reversible or Harmless Error,* 24 ALR3d 1093 (1969). Rule 513 extends these procedural protections to nonconstitutional privileges as well.

In *John Deere Co. v. Epstein,* 307 Or 348, 354, 769 P2d 766 (1989), the Supreme Court held that "the unqualified term 'privilege' in OEC 513 must be interpreted to encompass all privileges, including privileges not enumerated within the code." Therefore, the court held that the rule prohibits an adverse inference from being drawn from the assertion of the Fifth Amendment privilege in a civil case.

The purpose of the rule is to protect the practical availability of the privilege and to prevent a party from being prejudiced by the assertion of a legal right. Also, because there are many reasons why a witness may choose to assert a privilege, it is not necessarily warranted for juries to draw an adverse inference from the assertion of a privilege. See *State v.Quintero,* 110 Or App 247, 256, 823 P2d 981, 986 (1991), rev denied 314 Or 392, 840 P2d 710 (1992) (court found reversible error where defendant's wife was required to invoke the spousal privilege in front of the jury on numerous occasions in violation of Rule 513(2); court concluded that "[e]ach time that she invoked the privilege, the jury could have inferred that she was trying to keep damaging testimony about [her husband] from them, and that impression was very likely to have intensified each time that she refused to answer").

Rule 513(1) bars comment by both the judge and counsel. Presumably, the rule is not intended to prevent the attorney representing the party asserting the privilege from arguing that no adverse inference should be drawn.

Rule 513(2) requires the court, to the extent practicable, to allow the claim of privilege to be made without the knowledge of the jury. This requirement is consistent with Rules 103(3) and 104(3). The rule arguably imposes a duty on the party calling the witness or offering the evidence to cooperate in allowing the privilege to be claimed without the jury's knowledge. It would be wise for a party intending to assert a privilege at trial to notify the opponent in advance. The witness may still need to be called to obtain a court ruling on the existence of the privilege, but such a hearing can take place outside of the jury's presence.

Rule 513(3) provides that upon request a party is entitled to an instruction that no adverse inference may be drawn from the assertion of a privilege. Such an instruction should generally be given only at the request of a party. A party may not want such an instruction in order to avoid emphasizing the improper inference to the jury. Cf. *Lakeside v. Oregon*, 435 US 333, 98 SCt 1091, 55 LEd2d 319 (1978) (no constitutional error in the giving of a *no inference* instruction over defense objection where the defendant failed to testify).

See generally O'Brien, *Judicial Responses When a Civil Litigant Exercises a Privilege: Seeking the Least Costly Remedy*, 31 St Louis L J 323 (1987); ANNOT., *Propriety and Prejudicial Effect of Prosecution's Calling as a Witness, to Extract Claim of Self-Incrimination Privilege, One Involved in Offense Charged Against Accused*, 19 ALR4th 368 (1983); ANNOT., *Propriety and Prejudicial Effect of Prosecutor's Argument Commenting on Failure of Defendant's Spouse to Testify*, 26 ALR4th 9 (1983).

RULE 514. ORS 40.295. EFFECT ON EXISTING PRIVILEGES

Unless expressly repealed by section 98, chapter 892, Oregon Laws 1981, all existing privileges either created under the Constitution or statutes of the State of Oregon or developed by the courts of Oregon are recognized and shall continue to exist until changed or repealed according to law.

LEGISLATIVE COMMENTARY

Oregon Rule of Evidence 514 is a new provision adopted to retain all privileges currently recognized under the constitution, statutes or case law of Oregon.

The Legislative Assembly recognizes that the eleven privileges adopted under Rules 503 to 510 are not, and should not be, the only testimonial privileges granted in Oregon. There are others in effect as a result of statute or judicial decision. The adoption of Rules 503 to 510 is not intended to affect any of those privileges with the exception of the privileges repealed by § 98 of this Act. Similarly, the Legislative Assembly does not intend that Article V affect the discovery statutes of Oregon or decisional law relating to the work product of attorneys.

A partial list of testimonial privileges currently recognized in Oregon, and not repealed by the 1981 enactment of the Oregon Evidence Code, includes:

(1)   Records and testimony before a hospital or professional medical committee charged with the training, supervision or discipline of physicians. ORS 41.675.

(2)   Unpublished information, and the source of any information, obtained by a media person in the course of gathering, receiving or processing information for any medium of communication to the public. ORS 44.510 to 44.540.

(3)   Information designated confidential by a person as to a matter before the Legislative Counsel Committee. ORS 173.230.

(4)   Income tax returns. ORS 314.835.

(5)   Juvenile court records and proceedings. ORS 419.567.

(6)   Venereal disease records. ORS 434.055.

(7)   Nervous disorder reports filed with the Motor Vehicles Division. ORS 482.141.

(8)   A voter's choice at an election. *State ex rel Heath v. Kraft*, 20 Or 28, 23 P 663 (1890).

TEXT

Preservation of Other Privileges

Rule 514 preserves all other existing privileges, whether created by the constitution, statute, or case law, unless they are expressly repealed. Rule 514 thus establishes that Article V is intended to be only a partial codification of Oregon privilege law.

Because of Rule 514, common-law privileges, such as the privilege not to reveal a political vote, will continue to be recognized under Oregon law. See *State ex rel Heath v. Kraft*, 18 Or 550, 20 Or 28, 23 P 663 (1890). See also proposed but not adopted FRE 507 ("Every person has a privilege to refuse to disclose the tenor of his vote at a political election conducted by secret ballot unless the vote was cast illegally.").

Mediation Privilege

An important statutory privilege not codified in the Evidence Code is the privilege for mediators. ORS 36.205 provides as follows:

Confidentiality; disclosure of materials and communications.

(1)   Unless there is a written agreement otherwise, mediation communications will be confidential. All memoranda, work products and other materials contained in the case files of a mediator or mediation program are confidential. Communications made in or in connection with such mediation which relates to the controversy being mediated, whether made to the

mediator or a party, or to any other person if made at a mediation session, is confidential. However, a mediated settlement shall not be confidential unless the parties otherwise agree in writing. This section does not apply to any dispute resolution service or mediation proceeding conducted by a public body. Nothing in this section relieves an agency using alternative means of dispute resolution from complying with ORS 192.410 to 192.505 and 192.610 to 192.690.

(2) Confidential materials and communications are not subject to disclosure in any judicial or administrative proceeding except:

    (a) When all parties to the mediation agree, in writing, to waive the confidentiality;

    (b) In a subsequent action between the mediator and a party to the mediation for damages arising out of the mediation; or

    (c) Statements, memoranda, materials and other tangible evidence, otherwise subject to discovery, that were not prepared specifically for use in and actually used in the mediation.

(3) The mediator may not be compelled to testify in any proceeding unless all parties to the mediation and the mediator agree in writing.

(4) When a mediation is conducted on a case that has been filed in a court, nothing in this sectin limits any of the following:

    (a) The ability of the mediator to report to the court the outcome of the mediation at the conclusion of the mediation proceding so long as nothing in the report discloses specific communications in the mediation itself.

    (b) The ability of the court to do any of the following with respect to such case:

        (A) Disclose records reflecting which cases have been referred for mediation.

        (B) Disclose the mediator's report made to the court under paragraph (a) of this subsection.

        (C) Compile and disclose general statistical information concerning cases that have gone to mediation so long as the information does not identify specific cases.

Privilege for Media Representatives

Another important statutory privilege not codified in the Evidence Code is the privilege for media representatives. This privilege is set forth in ORS 44.510–.540:

ORS 44.510. Definitions for ORS 44.510 to 44.540. As used in ORS 44.510 to 44.540, unless the context requires otherwise:

    (1) "Information" has its ordinary meaning and includes, but is not limited to, any written, oral, pictorial or electronically recorded news or other data.

    (2) "Medium of communication" has its ordinary meaning and includes, but is not limited to, any newspaper, magazine or other periodical, book, pamphlet, news service, wire service, news or feature syndicate, broadcast station or network, or cable television system. Any information which is a portion of a governmental utterance made

by an official or employee of government within the scope of his or her governmental function, or any political publication subject to ORS 260.512, 260.522 and 260.532, is not included within the meaning of "medium of communication."

(3) "Processing" has its ordinary meaning and includes, but is not limited to, the compiling, storing and editing of information.

(4) "Published information" means any information disseminated to the public.

(5) "Unpublished information" means any information not disseminated to the public, whether or not related information has been disseminated. "Unpublished information" includes, but is not limited to, all notes, outtakes, photographs, tapes or other data of whatever sort not themselves disseminated to the public through a medium of communication, whether or not published information based upon or related to such material has been disseminated.

44.520. Limitation on compellable testimony from media persons; search of media persons' papers, effects or work premises prohibited: exception. (1) No person connected with, employed by or engaged in any medium of communication to the public shall be required by a legislative, executive or judicial officer or body, or any other authority having power to compel testimony or the production of evidence, to disclose, by subpoena or otherwise:

(a) The source of any published or unpublished information obtained by the person in the course of gathering, receiving or processing information for any medium of communication to the public; or

(b) Any unpublished information obtained or prepared by the person in the course of gathering, receiving or processing information for any medium of communication to the public.

(2) No papers, effects or work premises of a person connected with, employed by or engaged in any medium of communication to the public shall be subject to a search by a legislative, executive or judicial officer or body, or any other authority having power to compel the production of evidence, by search warrant or otherwise. The provisions of this subsection, however, shall not apply where probable cause exists to believe that the person has committed, is committing or is about to commit a crime.

44.530. Application of ORS 44.520. (1) ORS 44.520 applies regardless of whether a person has disclosed elsewhere any of the information or source thereof, or any of the related information.

(2) ORS 44.520 continues to apply in relation to any of the information, or source thereof, or any related information, even in the event of subsequent termination of a person's connection with employment by or engagement in any medium of communication to the public.

(3) The provisions of subsection (1) of ORS 44.520 do not apply with respect to the content or source of allegedly defamatory information, in civil action for defamation wherein the defendant asserts a defense based on the content or source of such information.

44.540 Effect of informant as witness. If the informant offers himself as a witness, it is deemed a consent to the examination also of a person described in ORS 44.520 on the same subject.

The media privilege does not cover the **personal** observations of the newsgatherer, to the extent that those observations were of events that took place in public, were made with the naked eye, and did not relate to work product, informants, or confidential sources. *State v. Pelham*, 136 Or App 336, 344, 901 P2d 972 (1995). See also *Haas v. Port of Portland*, 112 Or App 308, 315, 829 P2d 1008, rev denied 314 Or 391 (1992) (media witness testified from "personal knowledge" about what he remembered).

But the material need not be published to be protected by the privilege. *McNabb v. Oregonian Publishing Co.*, 69 Or App 136, 143, 685 P2d 485, rev denied 297 Or 824 (1984), cert denied 469 US 1216 (1985) (refusing production of reporter's notes, the names of persons interviewed but not named in a newspaper article, and other unpublished information about the reporter's sources).

The media privilege can be required to yield when it impinges on a criminal defendant's right to compulsory process. *State ex rel Meyers v. Howell*, 86 Or App 570, 740 P2d 792 (1987) ("withholding of evidence that is material and favorable to a criminal defendant gives rise to a claim of violation of the Compulsory Process Clauses"). However, defendants are required to show that the material sought is "both material and favorable to their defense." Id. at 578. In *Meyers*, the defendant asserted only that the material sought would clear up "possible inconsistencies between the criminal defendant's and the prosecution's evidence," which was insufficient to trigger an inquiry into the issue of whether the shielded materials had to be disclosed in order to protect defendant's right of compulsory process. Id. at 579. See also *State v. Pelham*, 136 Or App 336, 344, 901 P2d 972 (1995) (insufficient showing that videotape sought was material or exculpatory).

See generally COMMENT, *Shielding Editorial Conversations from Discovery: The Relationship Between Herbert v. Lando and Oregon's Shield Law*, 59 Or L Rev 477 (1981).

Other Statutory Privileges

A number of other Oregon statutes make certain communications or records immune from judicially compelled disclosure. Also, many statutes designate certain information as confidential and in some cases provide penalties for unauthorized release, without stating that such information is immune from judicially compelled disclosure.

The following is a partial listing of the Oregon statutes that create a privilege, provide for some degree of confidentiality, or penalize unauthorized disclosure of specified records, communications, or information:

ORS 1.440 (records of Commission on Judicial Fitness)
ORS 7.211 (adoption proceeding records)
ORS 7.215 (filiation proceeding records)

ORS 41.675 (proceedings before medical committees charged with training, supervision or discipline of physicians)

ORS 41.685 (data submitted by emergency medical service provider and data of medical review committees and governing bodies)

ORS 41.910 (certain intercepted jail communications)

ORS 107.600 (communications in conciliation proceedings)

ORS 109.235 (names of petitioners in adoption proceedings)

ORS 132.210 (grand juror communications or vote)

ORS 132.420 (disclosures by grand juror)

ORS 133.723 (records pertaining to interception of communications)

ORS 135.155 (preliminary hearings reports)

ORS 135.855 (limitations on discovery in criminal cases; protecting work product, identity of informants, and witnesses' statements before the grand jury from discovery in criminal cases)

ORS 137.079 (presentence reports)

ORS 146.780 (reports to medical examiner regarding injuries caused by a deadly weapon)

ORS 147.115 (crime victim compensation application)

ORS 161.735 (psychiatric examination of potentially dangerous offender)

ORS 173.230 (confidential communication to legislative counsel)

ORS 176.765 (energy resource information)

ORS 179.505 (health care service providers' records)

ORS 181.540 (crime records)

ORS 297.060 (tax records)

ORS 308.290 (returns of taxable property)

ORS 314.835 (tax returns)

ORS 336.195 (student records)

ORS 341.290(17) (community college faculty and student records)

ORS 342.850 (teacher personnel records)

ORS 344.600 (information regarding persons applying for or receiving vocational rehabilitation)

ORS 351.065 (faculty personnel files)

ORS 411.320 (public assistance records—adults)

ORS 418.130 (public assistance records—children)

ORS 418.135 (child support records)

ORS 418.770 (child abuse reports)

ORS 419.567 (juvenile records)

ORS 419.584 (fingerprints and photographs of juveniles)

ORS 423.430, .440 (communications to prison ombudsman)

ORS 426.460 (intoxication treatment facility patient records)

ORS 430.475 (communications and evaluations relating to diversion programs)

ORS 432.060 (identity of patient in mortality and morbidity studies)

ORS 432.120 (birth and death certificates)

ORS 432.430 (registration of foundlings)

ORS 441.671 (nursing home patient abuse records)

ORS 468.963(2) (environmental audits—see Gish, *The Self-Critical Analysis Privilege and Environmental Audit Reports*, 25 Envtl L 73 (1995))

ORS 469.090 (energy resource information)

ORS 469.560 (energy department investigations, inspections)

ORS 476.090 (State Fire Marshal records)

ORS 517.900 (surface mining reclamation information)

ORS 646.836 (antitrust investigations)

ORS 654.720 (accident reports to Public Utility Commission)

ORS 657.665 (Employment Division records)

ORS 671.550 (landscape contractors investigations)

ORS 673.415 (names of persons preparing tax returns)

ORS 675.580 (communications to clinical social worker)

ORS 677.425 (information submitted to Board of Medical Examiners)

ORS 679.280 (reports to dental committees or consultants)

ORS 684.185 (information supplied to State Board of Chiropractic Examiners)

ORS 706.720 (reports required by the Bank Act)

ORS 706.730 (names of depositors of a financial institution)

ORS 722.419 (savings and loans company reports)

ORS 731.264 (complaints to Insurance Commissioner)

ORS 744.017 (insurance agents compensation agreements)

ORS 761.380 (notice of movement of hazardous materials)

See also ORCP 36B(3) (limitation on discovery in civil cases of documents prepared in anticipation of litigation).

Constitutional Privileges

Constitutionally-based privileges will, of course, be unaffected by the Evidence Code. The primary constitutional privilege is the privilege against self-incrimination recognized by the Fifth Amendment of the United States Constitution and Article I, section 12 of the Oregon Constitution. The speech and debate clause of the federal constitution has been interpreted to provide members of congress with an evidentiary privilege as well as a substantive immunity. See *United States v. Brewster,* 408 US 501, 92 SCt 2531, 33 LEd2d 507 (1972). A constitutionally based executive privilege is also recognized. See *United States v. Nixon,* 418 US 683, 94 SCt 3090, 41 LEd2d 1039 (1974); COMMENT, *Executive Privileges: What Are the Limits?,* 54 Or L Rev 81 (1975).

Parent-Child Privilege

A number of commentators have advocated or discussed recognition of a parent-child testimonial or communications privilege. See Kraft, *The Parent-Child Testimonial Privilege: Who's Minding the Kids?,* 18 Fam L Q 505 (1985); Watts, *The Parent-Child Privileges: Hardly a New or Revolutionary Concept,* 28 W & M L Rev 583 (1987); NOTE, *Parent-Child Loyalty and Testimonial Privilege,* 100 Harv L

Rev 910 (1986); COMMENT, *Parent-Child Testimonial Privilege: Preserving and Protecting the Fundamental Right to Family Privacy,* 52 U Cin L Rev 901 (1983); COMMENT, *Underprivileged Communications: The Rationale for a Parent-Child Testimonial Privilege,* 36 Sw L J 1175 (1983); COMMENT, *A Parent-Child Testimonial Privilege, Its Present Existence, Whether It Should Exist, and to What Extent,* 13 Cap U L Rev 555 (1984); COMMENT, *The Parent-Child Privilege,* 1984 BYU L Rev 599.

See generally ANNOT., *Testimonial Privilege for Confidential Communications Between Relatives Other Than Husband and Wife—State Cases,* 6 ALR4th 544 (1981); ANNOT., *Testimony Before or Communications to Private Professional Societies, Judicial Commission, Ethics Committee, or the Like, as Privileged,* 9 ALR4th 807 (1981); ANNOT., *"Scholars Privilege" Under Rule 501 of Federal Rules of Evidence,* 81 ALR Fed 904 (1987).

ARTICLE VI

WITNESSES

RULE 601.   ORS 40.310. GENERAL RULE OF COMPETENCY

Except as provided in Rules 601 to 606 (ORS 40.310 to 40.335), any person who, having organs of sense can perceive, and perceiving can make known the perception to others, may be a witness.

LEGISLATIVE COMMENTARY

Oregon Rule of Evidence 601 states the general principle of competency of witnesses.

At common law, a person might be disqualified from testifying because of criminal conviction, interest in the outcome, marital relationship, sex, race or religion. For over a century these common law rules of incompetency have been revised piecemeal by statute, so that today most of the former grounds for excluding a witness from testifying have been converted into mere grounds for impeachment of credibility. McCormick, *Evidence* § 4 at 5 (2d ed 1972). Oregon Rule of Evidence 601 confirms this trend.

Rule 601—and Rules 602 to 606-1 which it incorporates by reference—effectively remove all the old common law disqualifications. Under these rules, any person called upon to testify need only recognize the necessity of telling the truth; have knowledge of the matter from personal observation; have some recollection of that knowledge at the time of testimony; be able to communicate that knowledge; and be free of any disqualification that would render the person's testimony presumably inaccurate or prejudicial, to testify.

Oregon Revised Statutes previously addressed the issue of competency in two sections: ORS 44.020 (persons capable of being witnesses) and ORS 44.030 (common law disqualifications for mental incompetency and infancy). Rule 601, with its exception, restates the first sentence of ORS 44.020. The adoption of Rules 602 to 612 makes the remainder of that statute unnecessary. The Legislative Assembly repealed ORS 44.030. Whether any person has sufficient ability to perceive, recollect and communicate so it is worthwhile for the person to testify is a question for the trial court to decide in the exercise of sound discretion. This is clearly recognized in the case of mental capacity. *State v. Pace,* 187 Or 498, 212 P2d 755 (1949). It appears to be the case as well with infancy. *State v. Jackson,* 9 Or 457 (1881); *State v. Jensen,* 70 Or 156, 140 P 740 (1914) (child witness must have sufficient intelligence to observe and narrate and possess due sense of nature and obligation of oath); see also *State v. Stich,* 5 Or App 511, 484 P2d 861 (1971) (competency of child a preliminary question of fact to be decided by trial judge).

In light of the cases just discussed, the Legislative Assembly believes that the adoption of Rule 601 works no change in Oregon law with regard to competency, except in the case of a witness less than 10 years of age. Although no longer required by ORS 44.030 to examine separately a child who is under 10 years of age for competency, a trial court still may do so to determine whether the child is a competent witness under this Article.

TEXT

Competency of Witnesses

Rule 601 establishes a liberal standard for competency of witnesses. Under Rule 601 and the other rules in Article VI incorporated by it, any witness is deemed competent who is able to satisfy the following four requirements. The witness must: (1) be able to perceive (Rule 601), (2) be able to communicate the perception to others (Rule 601), alone or with the assistance of an interpreter (Rule 604), (3) have personal knowledge of the matter (Rule 602), and (4) have taken an oath or affirmation to testify truthfully (Rule 603). There must be a showing that these four grounds of competency are satisfied before the witness may testify. A witness may be impeached with respect to these four factors, even in cases where the attack is not sufficient to render the witness incompetent. See discussion of impeachment under Rule 607.

Qualifications

Rule 601 is subject to Rule 605, which declares judges incompetent to testify in cases in which they are presiding, and Rule 606, which declares jurors incompetent to testify before a jury of which they are a member. Rule 601 is also qualified by Rule 403, which provides that evidence may be excluded if its probative value is substantially outweighed by the dangers of unfair prejudice, confusion of the issues, or misleading the jury. In a criminal case, the defendant is competent to be a witness only when testifying at his own request. ORS 136.643.

Competency Issue for Court

Whether or not a witness' abilities to perceive and communicate are sufficient to make the witness competent under Rule 601 is an issue for the court to determine under Rule 104(1). However, the issue of whether the witness has personal knowledge is a matter of conditional relevancy that is ultimately decided by the jury under Rule 602 and Rule 104(2).

When a witness' competency to testify is questioned, *voir dire* examination of the witness is appropriate. *State v. Lantz,* 44 Or App 695, 607 P2d 197 (1980). In conducting a competency hearing, the court is not bound by the rules of evidence, except those with respect to privileges. Rule 104(1). Often such hearings should be conducted out of the hearing of the jury. Rule 104(3). Only counsel or the court should be allowed to ask questions at the competency hearing. *State v. Doud,* 190 Or 218, 225 P2d 400 (1950).

There is no authority under the Oregon Evidence Code for a trial judge to order pretrial competency examinations of prospective witnesses by outside experts. In *State v. Hiatt,* 303 Or 60, 733 P2d 1373 (1987), the court found no error in the refusal by the trial judge to order the alleged rape victim to undergo a pretrial psychological examination to determine her competency. The court stated: "The OEC provisions that authorize a trial judge to admit expert testimony *in court* and to exclude incompetent witnesses does not imply a right to call on experts to evaluate the credibility or competency of witnesses in an *out-of-court* proceeding." 303 Or at 66. Some federal cases take a contrary position. See, e.g., *United States v. Gutman,* 725 F2d 417 (7th Cir), cert denied 469 US 880 (1984) (trial court has discretion to order psychiatric examination of a prosecution witness with a history of mental illness). See generally ANNOT., *Necessity or Permissibility of Mental Examination to Determine Competency or Credibility of Complainant in Sexual Offense Prosecution,* 45 ALR4th 310 (1986).

Refusal to Allow Witness to Testify

Although appellate courts generally grant considerable discretion to trial judges in the determination of competency, they occasionally will find reversible error in the refusal to allow a witness to testify. Several cases have found error in the refusal to allow testimony by an apparently competent child in a divorce or child custody proceeding. See *Nichols and Fleischman,* 67 Or App 256, 677 P2d 731 (1984); *Schafer v. Schafer,* 243 Or 242, 412 P2d 793 (1966); *Gonyea v. Gonyea,* 232 Or 367, 375 P2d 808 (1962).

Mental Incapacity

Under Rule 601, as under prior case law, limited mental capacity does not in itself render a witness incompetent. See *State v. Longoria,* 17 Or App 1, 520 P2d 912 (1974). The Advisory Committee's Note to FRE 601, upon which the Oregon rule is based, states:

> No mental or moral qualifications for testifying as a witness are specified. Standards of mental capacity have proved elusive in actual application. A leading commentator observes that few witnesses are disqualified on that ground. Weihofen, Testimonial Competence and Credibility, 34 Geo. Wash. L. Rev. 53 (1965). Discretion is regularly exercised in favor of allowing the testimony. A witness wholly without capacity is difficult to imagine. The question is one particularly suited to the jury as one of weight and credibility, subject to judicial authority to review the sufficiency of the evidence. (2 Wigmore, §§ 501, 509)

In *State v. Milbradt,* 305 Or 621, 625, 756 P2d 620 (1988), the court rejected the defendant's argument that two mentally retarded sex abuse victims should have been ruled incompetent to testify against him, stating: "So long as the witnesses possessed capacity to perceive and communicate factual matters and understand that they were under an obligation to tell the truth, they were sufficiently competent to testify."

Child Witnesses

At the time the Evidence Code was adopted, former ORS 44.030 was repealed, which required a competency examination for children under ten who were called as witnesses. The competency of child witnesses is now determined under Rule 601.

Courts have continuing discretion to conduct competency examinations of children, and when competency of a child witness is challenged such an examination will usually be required. The ruling of the trial court regarding competency will normally be upheld on appeal, provided an adequate record is made supporting the ruling. See *State v. Bauman,* 98 Or App 316, 779 P2d 185 (1985) (affirming finding that four-year-old child sex abuse victim was a competent witness); *State v.Stevens,* 311 Or 119, 138–42, 806 P2d 92 (1991) (an eight-year-old victim and her four-year-old sister were incompetent to be witnesses because they were traumatized by the presence of the defendant and were unable to communicate their perceptions).

Under the federal constitution, a criminal defendant has no right to be personally present at the competency hearing, at least in cases where defense counsel is present and all questions put to the child could be asked again at trial in the defendant's presence. *Kentucky v. Stincer,* 482 US 730, 107 SCt 2658, 96 LEd2d 631 (1987).

See generally Myers, *The Testimonial Competence of Children,* 25 J Fam L 287 (1986–87); Myers, *The Child Witness: Techniques for Direct Examination, Cross-Examination, and Impeachment,* 18 Pac L J 801 (1987); Perry & Teply, *Interviewing, Counseling, and In Court Examination of Children: Practical Approaches for Attorneys,* 18 Creighton L Rev 1369 (1984); COMMENT, *The Young Victim as Witness for the Prosecution: Another Form of Abuse?,* 89 Dick L Rev 721 (1985); Ceci & Bruck, *Suggestibility of the Child Witness: A Historical Review and Synthesis,* 113 Psych Bull 403 (1993).

Accommodations for Child Witnesses or Developmentally Disabled

A new statute adopted by the 1995 Legislature requires attorneys to notify the court at least seven days prior to the trial or proceeding of any special accommodations required by a child witness or developmentally disabled witness. ORS 44.545 provides:

(1) In any case in which a child under 12 years of age or a person with a developmental disability described in subsection (2) of this section is called to give testimony, the attorney or party who plans to call the witness must notify the court at least seven days before the trial or proceeding of any special accommodations needed by the witness. Upon receiving the notice, the court shall order such accommodations as are appropriate under the circumstances considering the age or disability of the witness. Accommodations ordered by the court may include:
  (a) Break periods during the proceedings for the benefit of the witness.
  (b) Designation of a waiting area appropriate for the special needs of the witness.
  (c) Conducting proceedings in clothing other than judicial robes.
  (d) Relaxing the formalities of the proceedings.
  (e) Adjusting the layout of the courtroom for the comfort of the witness.
  (f) Conducting the proceedings outside of the normal courtroom.

(2) For the purposes of this section, "developmental disability" means a disability attributable to mental retardation, autism, cerebral palsy, epilepsy or other disabling neurological condition that requires training or support similar to that required by persons with mental retardation, if either of the following apply:
  (a) The disability originates before the person attains 22 years of age, or if the disability is attributable to mental retardation the condition is manifested before the person attains 18 years of age, the disability can be expected to continue indefinitely, and the disability constitutes a substantial handicap to the ability of the person to function in society.
  (b) The disability results in a significant subaverage general intellectual function with concurrent deficits in adaptive behavior that are manifested during the developmental period.

Alcohol, Drug Use

Alcohol or drug use at the time of the event in question will not automatically render the witness incompetent, but may be used as a basis for impeachment. *State v. Batchelor,* 34 Or App 47, 578 P2d 409 (1978); *State v. Goodin,* 8 Or App 15, 492 P2d 287 (1971); *State v. McKiel,* 122 Or 504, 259 P 917 (1927). ANNOT., *Impeachment of Federal Trial Witness with Respect to Intoxication,* 106 ALR Fed 371 (1992).

Prior False Statements

The fact that the witness has demonstrably lied on a number of occasions and given conflicting accounts of the particular event is not a basis for disqualification. *State v. Lantz,* 44 Or App 695, 607 P2d 197 (1980).

Hypnotized Witnesses

A witness who has been hypnotized is generally rendered incompetent to testify in a criminal case unless statutory procedures have been followed. See ORS 136.675–.695. An attorney would be well advised to follow these statutory procedures or similar procedures in civil cases as well.

In *State v. King,* 84 Or App 165, 733 P2d 472, rev denied 303. Or 455, 737 P2d 1248 (1987), defendant challenged the admission of testimony of a prosecution witness who had been hypnotized. The court stated:

> Oregon law specifies the procedures to be used in offering such testimony. See ORS 136.675 et seq. Defendant does not argue that those provisions were not followed. We have previously held that the testimony of a witness who has been hypnotized is admissible; the issue is the weight to be given the testimony, not its admissibility.

84 Or App at 176.

In addition to proving compliance with the statutory procedures, an attorney calling a witness who has been hypnotized should be prepared to lay the foundation for an expert to discuss the scientific basis and effect of hypnosis, applying the standards of *State v. Brown,* 297 Or 404, 687 P2d 751 (1984). See discussion under Rule 702.

In *Rock v. Arkansas,* 483 US 44 (1987), the Court held that an evidentiary rule rendering a defendant incompetent to testify because her memory had been hypnotically refreshed violated her constitutional right to testify on her own behalf.

On the issue of hypnotized witnesses, see generally Shaw, *The Admissibility of Hypnotically Enhanced Testimony in Criminal Trials,* 75 Marq L Rev 1 (1991); ANNOT., *Admissibility of Hypnotically Refreshed or Enhanced Testimony,* 77 ALR4th 927 (1990); ANNOT., *Admissibility of Hypnotic Evidence at Criminal Trial,* 92 ALR3d 442 (1979); ANNOT., *Fact That Witness Undergoes Hypnosis Examination as Affecting Admissibility of Testimony in Civil Case,* 31 ALR4th 1239 (1984);

COMMENT, *Hypnosis—Its Role and Current Admissibility in the Criminal Law*, 17 Willamette L J 665 (1981); Haward and Ashworth, *Some Problems of Evidence Obtained by Hypnosis*, 1980 Crim L Rev 469; Falk, *Post-Hypnotic Testimony—Witness Competency and the Fulcrum of Procedural Safeguards*, 57 St John's L Rev 30 (1982); Beaver, *Memory Restored or Confabulated by Hypnosis—Is It Competent?*, 6 U Puget Sound L Rev 155 (1983); Mickenberg, *Mesmerizing Justice: The Use of Hypnotically Induced Testimony in Criminal Trials*, 34 Syracuse L Rev 927 (1983); Diamond, *Inherent Problems in the Use of Pretrial Hypnosis on a Prospective Witness*, 68 Calif L Rev 313 (1980); Perry, *The Trend Toward Exclusion of Hypnotically Refreshed Testimony—Has the Right Question Been Asked?*, 31 U Kan L Rev 579 (1983); Fox and Fox, *Reciprocal Hypnosis: A New Standard for the Admission of Post Hypnotic Testimony*, 20 Pac L J 815 (1989).

Lawyers as Witnesses

The original version of the Oregon Evidence Code contained a rule making lawyers generally incompetent to be a witness in a case in which they were acting as counsel for a party. Rule 606-1 provided:

> An attorney representing a party litigant at trial shall not offer to be a witness or offer a member of the attorney's firm as a witness at that trial unless:
> (1)   The testimony of the attorney or member will relate solely to an uncontested matter;
> (2)   The testimony of the attorney or member will relate solely to a matter of formality and there is no reason to believe that substantial evidence will be offered in opposition to the testimony;
> (3)   The testimony of the attorney or member will relate solely to the nature and value of legal services rendered in the case by the lawyer or the lawyer's firm to the client;
> (4)   As to any matter, refusal would work a substantial hardship on the client because of the distinctive value of the lawyer or the lawyer's firm as counsel in the particular case; or
> (5)   The court finds that the interests of justice require the testimony.

However, this Rule was repealed by the 1987 Oregon Legislature. See 1987 Or Laws, ch 352, § 1.

The purpose of Rule 606-1 was to enforce the strictures of the Code of Professional Responsibility regarding testimony by lawyers in proceedings where they were acting as advocates. The rule was based upon DR 5-101(B) of the American Bar Association Code of Professional Responsibility (1969) and incorporated the exceptions recognized in that provision. At that time, DR 5-101(B) was also part of the Oregon Code of Professional Responsibility.

However, the Oregon Code of Professional Responsibility was subsequently revised and a new ethical provision regulating testimony by lawyers was adopted. See DR 5-102, Revised Oregon Code of Professional Responsibility. Rather than amend Rule 606-1 to conform with the new DR 5-102, the legislature chose to repeal the evidence rule.

DR 5-102 provides:

    (A) A lawyer shall not act as an advocate at a trial in which the lawyer is likely to be a witness on behalf of the lawyer's client except where:

        (1) The testimony relates to an uncontested issue.

        (2) The testimony relates to the nature and value of legal services rendered in the case.

        (3) Disqualification of the lawyer would work a substantial hardship on the client.

        (4) The lawyer is appearing pro se.

    (B) A lawyer may act as an advocate in a trial in which another lawyer in the lawyer's firm is likely to be called as a witness on behalf of the lawyer's client.

    (C) If, after undertaking employment in contemplated or pending litigation, a lawyer learns or it is obvious that the lawyer or a member of the lawyer's firm may be called as a witness other than on behalf of the lawyer's client, the lawyer may continue the representation until it is apparent that the lawyer's or firm member's testimony is or may be prejudicial to the lawyer's client.

The primary change made by this new provision is to allow a lawyer to continue representation even though a member of his firm may be called as a witness on behalf of the lawyer's client. Also the revised rule is more liberal in allowing continued representation where a lawyer or a firm member may be called as a witness other than on behalf of the client until it is apparent that the testimony may be prejudicial to the client. An additional exception was added for cases where the lawyer is appearing *pro se.*

Despite the fact that Rule 606-1 was repealed rather than amended to conform with DR 5-102, a trial judge should have authority to refuse to allow a lawyer to testify in circumstances that would violate the revised ethical rule. See *United States v. Brown,* 417 F2d 1068 (5th Cir), cert denied 397 US 998 (1969); *Bronson v. Dept. of Revenue,* 265 Or 211, 508 P2d 423 (1973) (no "substantial hardship" found; lawyer should not have served as both counsel and witness); *Newman v. Stover,* 187 Or 641, 213 P2d 137 (1950). But in criminal proceedings, see ORS 9.490(2) ("A court of this state may not order that evidence be suppressed or excluded in any criminal trial, grand jury proceeding or other criminal proceeding, or order that any criminal prosecution be dismissed, solely as a sanction or remedy for violation of a rule of professional conduct adopted by the Supreme Court.").

The rationale underlying the rule against a lawyer appearing as a witness is stated in Ethical Consideration 5-9, ABA Model Code of Professional Responsibility:

> Occasionally a lawyer is called upon to decide in a particular case whether he will be a witness or an advocate. If a lawyer is both counsel and witness, he becomes more easily impeachable for interest and thus may be a less effective witness. Conversely, the opposing counsel may be handicapped in challenging the credibility of the lawyer when the lawyer also appears as an advocate in the case. An advocate who becomes a witness is in the unseemly and ineffective position of arguing his own credibility. The roles of an advocate and of a

witness are inconsistent; the function of an advocate is to advance or argue the cause of another, while that of a witness is to state facts objectively.

See also Enker, *The Rationale of the Rule That Forbids a Lawyer to be Advocate and Witness in the Same Case,* 1977 Am Bar Found Research J 455.

With respect to the scope of the "substantial hardship" exception of DR 5-102, see Ethical Consideration 5-10, ABA Model Code of Professional Responsibility, which provides:

> In the exceptional situation where it will be manifestly unfair to the client for the lawyer to refuse employment or to withdraw when he will likely be a witness on a contested issue, he may serve as advocate even though he may be a witness. In making such decision, he should determine the personal or financial sacrifice of the client that may result from his refusal of employment or withdrawal therefrom, the materiality of his testimony, and the effectiveness of his representation in view of his personal involvement. In weighing these factors, it should be clear that refusal or withdrawal will impose an unreasonable hardship upon the client before the lawyer accepts or continues the employment. Where the question arises, doubts should be resolved in favor of the lawyer testifying and against his becoming or continuing as an advocate.

See also *Supreme Beef Processors, Inc. v. Am Consumer Indus. Inc.,* 441 F Supp 1064, 1068–9 (ND Tex 1977), where the court stated:

> I turn next to the provisions of DR 5-101(B)(4) which provide that an attorney may testify as to any matter if refusal would work a substantial hardship on the client because of the distinctive value of the lawyer or his firm as counsel in the particular case. This exception generally contemplates only an attorney who has some expertise in a specialized area of the law such as patents and the burden is on the firm seeking to continue representation to prove distinctiveness. ... In addition, the distinctive value must be apparent before the decision to accept or refuse employment is made. Accordingly, the rule is to be very narrowly construed. (citation omitted)

See generally Formal Opinion 339, ABA Committee on Ethics and Professional Responsibility 1974); ANNOT., *Attorney Witness for Client in Federal Case,* 9 ALR Fed 500 (1971); ANNOT., *Defense Attorney as Witness for his Client in State Criminal Case,* 52 ALR3d 887 (1973); Wydick, *Trial Counsel as Witness: The Code and Model Rules,* 15 UCD L Rev 651 (1982); Lewis, *The Ethical Dilemma of the Testifying Advocate: Fact or Fancy?,* 19 Houston L Rev 75 (1981).

Dead Man's Statutes

Oregon does not have a Dead Man's Statute like that of many other states that would render a witness incompetent to testify regarding transactions with a deceased person. The rationale of such statutes is to protect the estates of deceased persons from fraudulent claims. However, ORS 115.195 requires proof by "competent, satisfactory evidence other than the testimony of the claimant" to recover upon a claim that has been disallowed by the personal representative of the estate.

RULE 602.   ORS 40.315. LACK OF PERSONAL KNOWLEDGE

Subject to the provisions of Rule 703 (ORS 40.415), a witness may not testify to a matter unless evidence is introduced sufficient to support a finding that the witness has personal knowledge of the matter. Evidence to prove personal knowledge may, but need not, consist of the testimony of the witness.

LEGISLATIVE COMMENTARY

Oregon Rule of Evidence 602 indicates that a witness may only testify on matters as to which the witness has personal knowledge. It replaces ORS 44.060, which was to the same effect. The rule is a slightly modified version of Rule 602 of the Federal Rules of Evidence. The exception involving Rule 703 which appears as the final sentence of the federal rule, is inserted as an introductory clause in the Oregon rule.

The "rule requiring that witness who testifies to a fact which can be perceived by the senses must have had an opportunity to observe, and must have actually observed the fact" is "one of the most pervasive manifestations" of the common law's "insistence upon the most reliable sources of information." McCormick, *Evidence* § 10 at 20 (2d ed 1972). ORE 602 simply codifies that common law requirement.

A party that offers testimony has the burden of establishing that the witness had an opportunity to observe the fact. According to the rule the testimony of the witness may be sufficient to lay this foundation. Absolute personal knowledge is not a requisite; however, it is necessary that the witness sincerely believe that the witness has such knowledge.

This rule does not govern the situation in which a witness testifies to a hearsay statement having personal knowledge of the making of the statement. Rules 801 and 805 apply in that case. This rule would, however, prevent a witness from testifying to the subject matter of the hearsay statement, as the witness has no personal knowledge of it.

The reference to Rule 703 is designed to avoid any question of conflict between the present rule and Rule 703. The provisions of the latter allow an expert to express opinions based on facts of which the expert does not have personal knowledge.

TEXT

Personal Knowledge Requirement

Rule 602 requires that before a witness may testify, evidence must be introduced sufficient to support a finding that the witness has personal knowledge of the matter. In most cases, the evidence will be testimony of the witness indicating that such personal knowledge exists. Personal knowledge may also be shown by testimony of other witnesses or by other evidence. The personal knowledge requirement does not apply to opinion testimony by experts. See Rule 703.

The determination of the personal knowledge of a witness is ultimately a question for the trier of fact under Rule 104(2). Before allowing a witness to testify, the trial judge need only make a preliminary determination that there is evidence sufficient to support a finding that the witness has personal knowledge of the matter. If it is shown upon cross-examination or otherwise that the jury could not reasonably find that the witness has personal knowledge, the witness' testimony may be stricken.

An objection based on lack of personal knowledge may overlap with an objection that the testimony is hearsay. The determination of which objection is most appropriate depends primarily on the form of the testimony. If the witness is merely quoting the out-of-court declaration of another for the truth of the matter asserted, the usual objection is hearsay. If the witness testifies as though the witness had perceived the event, but it is shown that the knowledge was obtained by other means, such as from statements made by others, the appropriate objection is lack of personal knowledge. See *United States v. Mandel,* 591 F2d 1347, 1369 (4th Cir 1979), cert denied 445 US 961 (1980) ("While the distinction between [lack of personal knowledge] and hearsay is sometimes formal, and the line between the rules often is blurred in practice, the rules do demonstrate that testimony based on hearsay is equally inadmissible as direct hearsay testimony.").

The personal knowledge requirement of Rule 602 applies to a witness reporting the out-of-court declaration of another when such declaration is admissible only to the extent of requiring personal perception of that declaration. The out-of-court declarant, however, is generally required by Rule 602 to have personal knowledge of the matter about which the declaration was made. The Commentary to Rule 803, which lists numerous hearsay exceptions, provides: "Even with hearsay the declarant is still a witness, of course, and neither this rule nor Rule 804 dispenses with the requirement of first-hand knowledge. See ORE 602. Such knowledge may appear from the statement or be inferred from circumstances." But not all hearsay exceptions contain a personal knowledge requirement. See, e.g., Rule 804(3)(d)(A), creating a hearsay exception for a statement of personal or family history, "even though the declarant had no means of acquiring personal knowledge of the matter stated."

See generally Raitt, *Personal Knowledge Under the Federal Rules of Evidence: A Three Legged Stool,* 18 Rutgers L J 591 (1988).

Recent Cases

In *State v. Harris,* 126 Or App 516, 521, 869 P2d 868, 871 (1994), modified 127 Or App 613, 872 P2d 445 (1994), rev denied 319 Or 281, 879 P2d 1284 (1994), a wife's testimony interpreting letters from her husband was properly allowed where nothing in the record suggested her interpretation was based on other than her own personal knowledge of phrases and abbreviations used by him.

RULE 603.   ORS 40.320. OATH OR AFFIRMATION

(1) Before testifying, every witness shall be required to declare that the witness will testify truthfully, by oath or affirmation administered in a form calculated to awaken the conscience of the witness and impress the mind of the witness with the duty to do so.

(2) An oath may be administered as follows: The person who swears holds up one hand while the person administering the oath asks: "Under penalty of perjury, do you solemnly swear that the evidence you shall give in the issue (or matter) now pending between ___ and ___ shall be the truth, the whole truth and nothing but the truth, so help you God?" If the oath is administered to any other than a witness, the same form and manner may be used. The person swearing must answer in an affirmative manner.

(3) An affirmation may be administered as follows: The person who affirms holds up one hand while the person administering the affirmation asks: "Under penalty of perjury, do you promise that the evidence you shall give in the issue (or matter) now pending between ___ and ___ shall be the truth, the whole truth and nothing but the truth?" If the affirmation is administered to any other than a witness, the same form and manner may be used. The person affirming must answer in an affirmative manner.

LEGISLATIVE COMMENTARY

Oregon Rule of Evidence 603 governs the form and administration of oaths and affirmations. It replaces the entirety of ORS 44.310 to 44.360, which are repealed.

Subsection (1). Subsection (1) is identical in substance to Rule 603 of the Federal Rules of Evidence. As a means of discovering the truth, this subsection requires that every witness make an oath or affirmation before testifying. This is important in two respects. First, the making of a promise in a ceremonial setting may induce in the witness a feeling of special obligation to speak the truth. Second, the reference to divine and positive legal sanctions may impress upon the witness the possibility of punishment for perjury, to which the oath or affirmation is a prerequisite.

The requirement of an oath "or" affirmation in this subsection, and the permissive language as to form in subsections (2) and (3), are designed to afford flexibility in dealing with religious adults, atheists, conscientious objectors, mental defectives and children. Although the rule sets forth suggested forms of an oath and affirmation, it does not require any particular verbal formula. Indeed, § 7 of Article I of the Oregon Constitution would prohibit such a device. Any mode of administering an oath or affirmation which is binding upon the conscience of the person to whom the oath or affirmation is administered is allowable.

A flexible approach is particularly relevant in the case of a witness under 10 years of age. ORS 44.310 distinguished between child witnesses and all other witnesses with regard to the necessity for an oath or affirmation. That section allowed testimony of a child under 10 to be given all a promise in open court to tell the truth, if the court determines that the child can safely be admitted to testify in accordance with ORS 44.030. Rule 603 makes no such distinction but requires that every witness make an oath or affirmation. The Legislative Assembly considers this change to be more one of form than substance. An "affirmation" under the rule would include a child's promise to tell the truth, once it has been established to the satisfaction of the court that the child understands the nature and obligation of that promise. Where, by virtue of the child's background, reference to the Deity is appropriate, an oath to the same effect would also satisfy the rule.

Except for the above change, there are no measurable differences between subsection (1) and current Oregon law concerning the form and administration of an oath or affirmation. An oath or affirmation may be administered by any person authorized by law to administer oaths.

Subsection (2). Subsection (2) sets out a suggested form of oath. At a time when witnesses were viewed with more suspicion, the oath was regarded as "a summoning of Divine vengeance upon false swearing. If the witness remained untouched by the hand of God, then the witness was telling the truth." 6 Wigmore, *Evidence* § 1816 (3d ed 1940). Under modern common law theory, the witness is reminded of ultimate Divine punishment for failing to speak truthfully and so must have belief in "superhuman ... retribution to follow false swearing." Id.

The Legislative Assembly felt that some witnesses would be more impressed with their duty to tell the truth if they swore an oath which invokes the Deity, while others may be more impressed with the "under penalty of perjury" language. It therefore included both elements in the suggested form.

Subsection (2), like subsection (3), expressly requires an affirmative response from the witness upon the administration of the oath or affirmation.

Subsection (3). This subsection sets out a suggested form of affirmation. Because atheists and non-believers may be unwilling or incapable of taking an oath, the affirmation, a solemn undertaking to tell the truth, has been devised to impress upon the witness the legal consequences of perjury.

TEXT

Oath or Affirmation

Rule 603 requires that before testifying, a witness must swear or affirm to testify truthfully. The oath or affirmation requirement of Rule 603 is one element of competency. A witness who refuses to declare to testify truthfully, including a defendant in a criminal proceeding, may be barred from testifying. *United States v. Fowler,* 605 F2d 181 (5th Cir 1979), cert denied 445 US 950 (1980) (affirming trial court refusal to allow defendant to testify where defendant refused to take an oath or affirmation).

Rule 603(2) provides a suggested form of oath that warns the witness of the possibility of both criminal and divine punishment, by including both the phrases "under penalty of perjury" and "so help me God." Rule 603(3) provides a suggested form of affirmation that eliminates the reference to the Deity. Neither form can be required, because Article I, section 7 of the Oregon Constitution provides: "The mode of administering an oath, or affirmation shall be such as may be most consistent with, and binding upon the conscience of the person to whom such oath or affirmation may be administered." Thus, any form of oath or affirmation satisfying this constitutional standard is permissible. The precise verbal formulation of the oath or affirmation may be less important than the solemnity with which it is administered.

Any colloquy between the witness and the judge regarding an acceptable form of oath or affirmation should normally be heard outside the presence of the jury to avoid prejudice based on the witness' religious beliefs. See Rules 610, 103(3), and 104(3).

Under prior Oregon law, it has been held that failure to object at the time to the fact that a witness was not sworn waives the objection. *Thomas v. Dad's Root Beer & Canada Dry Bottling Co.,* 225 Or 166, 356 P2d 418, modified on other grounds 357 P2d 418 (1960). It has also been held that no constitutional provision is violated by the receipt of unsworn testimony. *State v. Doud,* 190 Or 218, 225 P2d 400 (1950).

Although technically Rule 603 does not apply to the proceedings listed in Rule 101(4), a court is likely to require an oath or affirmation at any hearing where testimony of a witness is received.

The persons authorized to administer an oath are listed in ORS 44.320, which provides as follows:

> Every court, judge, clerk of a court, justice of the peace, certified shorthand reporter or notary public is authorized to take testimony in any action or proceeding, as are other persons in particular cases authorized by statute or the Oregon Rules of Civil Procedure and is authorized to administer oaths or affirmations generally, and every such other person in the particular case authorized.

RULE 604.   ORS 40.325. INTERPRETERS

An interpreter is subject to the provisions of the Oregon Evidence Code relating to qualification as an expert and the administration of an oath or affirmation that the interpreter will make a true translation.

LEGISLATIVE COMMENTARY

Oregon Rule of Evidence 604 governs the use of interpreters.

Subsection (1). This subsection is identical in substance to Rule 604 of the Federal Rules of Evidence. It requires an individual, before serving as an interpreter, to demonstrate such proficiency in communicating with a handicapped witness and in translating statements of the witness as would qualify the individual as an expert under Rule 702. It also requires that the interpreter promise by oath or affirmation to make a true translation of all proceedings and statements.

With the adoption of this subsection, ORS 45.520 became superfluous and was repealed. ORS 44.095 (itself repealed in light of subsections (2) to (4) infra) repeated the requirement of ORS 45.520 that an interpreter be appointed for any witness who does not understand or speak English. This subsection repeated the requirement of ORS 45.520 that the interpreter be under oath. Subsection (1) of this rule is superior to ORS 45.520 because it affirmatively stresses the broad discretionary power of the trial court to determine the fitness and qualifications of interpreters.

Subsections (2)–(4). [**Author's Note: Subsections (2)–(4) of the original rule have been deleted.**] Subsections (2) to (4) set forth procedures to be followed in the use of a qualified interpreter for a handicapped person. Except for the absence of the masculine pronoun, these subsections are identical to ORS 44.095, which was repealed.

ORS 44.095 was adopted by the 1973 Legislative Assembly as part of legislation to make interpreters available to the handicapped. The statute was never challenged or construed in an Oregon court. However, the Court of Appeals for the Ninth Circuit held, in *United States v. Barrios*, 457 F2d 680 (1972), that a trial judge has broad discretion in appointing and determining the fitness and qualifications of interpreters, and exercise thereof will not be disturbed on review in the absence of prejudice. There is nothing to indicate that Oregon courts would not follow this general rule of law.

Two sections similar to ORS 44.095 were enacted in 1973 and codified as ORS 133.515 (interpreters for handicapped persons in criminal proceedings) and ORS 183.418 (interpreters for handicapped persons in contested case hearings). It is the opinion of the Legislative Assembly that the adoption of Rule 604 in lieu of ORS 44.095 and 45.520, together with the retention of ORS 133.515 and 183.418, preserves Oregon practice with regard to the appointment and use of interpreters in legal proceedings.

TEXT

Interpreters

Rule 604 provides for the appointment of interpreters and requires a special form of oath. It incorporates the requirements of Rule 702 that the interpreter be qualified as an expert by knowledge, skill, experience, training, or education. It also expands on the requirement of Rule 603 by requiring the interpreter to take an oath or affirmation to make a true translation. The rule applies in both civil and criminal cases and to both witnesses and parties. The trial court has broad discretion in determining the fitness and qualifications of interpreters. *Chee v. United States*, 449 F2d 747 (9th Cir 1971).

In *United States v. Armijo*, 5 F3d 1229, 1235 (9th Cir 1993), the court interpreted the special oath of FRE 604 as applying only to interpreters who translate the testimony of witnesses on the stand. When a translator translates a tape recording or writing, the standard witness oath set forth in FRE 603 applies.

The qualifications of interpreters and their appointment procedures are regulated by ORS 45.273–.297. Interpreters may be appointed not only in cases where the witness or party speaks only a foreign language, but also where the person has a hearing or speaking impairment. Often it may be desirable to have one interpreter for the defendant and his counsel and another appointed to translate the testimony of witnesses. See *State v. Dam,* 111 Or App 15, 18 n1, 825 P2d 286, 288, rev denied 313 Or 300, 832 P2d 456 (1992) ("The better practice would be to have one interpreter to work with the defendant and his counsel and a different one to translate for witnesses.").

Sign language interpreters have a privilege under Rule 509-1 and interpreters for non-English speaking persons have a privilege under Rule 509-2 when providing interpretative services for communications that are otherwise privileged under the Evidence Code.

Although Rule 604 does not apply to the hearings or proceedings listed in Rule 101(4), the court is likely to apply its provisions to any hearing where testimony is being taken from a witness or where the substantial rights of a party present at the hearing would be affected. The statute upon which Rule 604(2) is based was not subject to the limitations of Rule 101(4), and there is no indication in the Commentary that the legislature intended to cut back the scope of the former statute.

With respect to the appointment of an interpreter for criminal defendants, see COMMENT, *Trying Non-English Conversant Defendants: The Use of an Interpreter,* 57 Or L Rev 549 (1978); ANNOT., *Disqualification for Bias of One Offered as Interpreter of Testimony,* 6 ALR4th 158 (1983).

RULE 605.   ORS 40.330. COMPETENCY OF JUDGE AS WITNESS

The judge presiding at the trial may not testify in that trial as a witness. No objection need be made in order to preserve the point.

LEGISLATIVE COMMENTARY

Oregon Rule of Evidence 605 addresses the question of the competency of the trial judge to be a witness. The rule is identical to Rule 605 of the Federal Rules of Evidence.

Three views exist concerning testimony by a judicial officer in a case the officer is trying. Under the oldest view the judge is a competent witness with discretion to decline to testify. Under the second view, the judge is disqualified from testifying only as to material facts in dispute. Under the third view, the judge is incompetent to testify on any matter. 6 Wigmore, *Evidence* (3d ed 1940) § 1909 n 1. McCormick, *Evidence* (2d ed 1972) § 68 at 147.

Oregon previously took the first position discussed above, allowing the presiding officer to be a witness. ORS 44.050. Thus, in *State v. Hough-*

ton, 45 Or 110, 75 P 887 (1908), the trial judge was held competent to testify that there was no inconsistency between testimony of the prosecuting witness at the trial in question and testimony at an earlier trial. The opinion gives the impression, however, that the Oregon Supreme Court would have chosen a different policy had the issue not been foreclosed by legislative mandate.

> The position and influence of the trial judge, the weight [the judge's] testimony would necessarily have with the jury in case of a conflict with some other witnesses, and many other reasons which readily suggest themselves to the legal mind point to the conclusion that [the judge's] testimony would, as said by Mr. Justice Dunbar in *Maitland v. Zanga,* 14 Wash 82, 44 P 117, "lead to embarrassment and would have a tendency to lower the standard of courts and bring them into contempt." 45 Or at 112.

The Legislative Assembly believes that the role of a judge as a witness even as to formal matters, is manifestly inconsistent with the essential role of the judge as arbiter in the adversary system of trial. It therefore repealed ORS 44.050 and, in ORE 605, adopts a broad rule of incompetency illustrated by the third view.

Under the rule, an objection is automatic and need not be made to preserve the point. This saves the opponent of judicial testimony from a choice of evils—either not objecting, with the result that the testimony is allowed, or objecting, "with the probable result [that the] testimony [is excluded] but at the price of continuing the trial before a judge likely to feel that [the judge's] integrity has been attacked by the objector." Fed R Evid 605, Comment at 51.

This rule does not prevent a judge from testifying as a witness when the judge has taken a disqualification from presiding.

TEXT

Competency of Judge as Witness

Rule 605, contrary to former ORS 44.050 (repealed 1981), prohibits a judge from testifying as a witness in a trial in which the judge is presiding. The rule provides that no objection need be made to preserve the point, thereby creating an exception to the usual requirements of Rule 103(1)(a).

Nothing in the rule prohibits a judge from being called as a witness at a proceeding in which the judge is not presiding. See *Larson v. Naslund,* 73 Or App 699, 700 P2d 276 (1985) (Rule 605 does not preclude testimony by a judge in a separate proceeding); *United States v. Frankenthal,* 582 F2d 1102 (7th Cir 1978) (approving the calling of a federal judge as a witness in a trial to which he had been originally assigned but from which he had disqualified himself). See generally ANNOT., *Judge As Witness In Cause Not On Trial Before Him,* 86 ALR3d 633 (1978).

The judge's law clerk also normally should not be allowed to testify. In *Kennedy v. Great Atlantic & Pacific Tea Co.,* 551 F2d 593 (5th Cir 1977), error was found in failing to grant defendant's motion to disqualify the law clerk of the trial judge from testifying or in the alternative to disqualify the judge from continuing to try the case.

Rule 605 does not address the question of when a judge may be disqualified from presiding at a trial. See ORS 14.210 (disqualification of judge for cause); ORS 14.250 (disqualification of judge for prejudice); ORS 244.120 (disqualification of judge for conflict of interest).

RULE 606.   ORS 40.335. COMPETENCY OF JUROR AS WITNESS

A member of the jury may not testify as a witness before that jury in the trial of the case in which the member has been sworn to sit as a juror. If the juror is called so to testify, the opposing party shall be afforded an opportunity to object out of the presence of the jury.

LEGISLATIVE COMMENTARY

Oregon Rule of Evidence 606 governs the competency of a juror to be a witness in the same proceeding. Except for pronominal changes, the rule is identical to subdivision (a) of Rule 606 of the Federal Rules of Evidence.

The traditional common law and practice in many jurisdictions, including Oregon, held a juror competent to testify. McCormick, *Evidence* § 70 at 148 (2d ed 1972); ORS 44.050; ORCP 59C(6). This rule changes the law in Oregon, for reasons similar to those that favor exclusion of judicial officers as witnesses. See ORE 605. When a juror is also a witness, opposing counsel may be prevented from adequately cross-examining or impeaching the juror/witness for fear of giving offense. Furthermore, the juror may be disposed to give excessive weight to the juror's testimony and to other testimony of the side whose partisan the juror has been.

Rule 606 imposes upon counsel the responsibility to ensure that a prospective juror is not a potential witness who will be kept from the stand if counsel does not challenge the person during voir dire. Because Oregon law has allowed jurors to testify, this responsibility has not weighed as heavily as it will under the rule. There has been foreshadowing, however. In *State v. Nagel,* 185 Or 486, 202 P2d 640 (1944), the court indicated that opposing counsel, whenever possible, should determine whether a prospective juror will be called as a witness in voir dire, and if so should challenge the person's empanelment. While the court was bound by statute to allow a juror to testify, it clearly did not favor the dual role.

The rule addresses only the competency of a juror to be a witness at trial. It does not purport to describe the circumstances in which a juror may present evidence, by testimony or affidavit, touching the validity of a verdict or indictment. Federal Rule 606 addresses the latter situation in a second subdivision. The Legislative Assembly did not adopt that, or any other statute, believing that Oregon case law adequately states the circumstances under which a court may inquire into the validity of a jury's verdict.

The familiar rule that a juror may not impeach the juror's own verdict stems from a doctrine nurtured by Lord Mansfield in the 18th century. 8 Wigmore, *Evidence* §§ 2352, 2353 (McNaughton rev 1961). It is a simplication of several policies: (1) to prevent an invasion of the privacy of the jury room by litigants or the public; (2) to promote finality of jury verdicts; and (3) to protect jurors from annoyance, embarrassment and harassment. While these are important policies, simply putting verdicts beyond reach can only promote irregularity and injustice.

In the most recent case of *Blanton v. Union Pacific Railroad Co.,* 289 Or 617, 616 P2d 477 (1980), the Supreme Court repeated its position that "... a verdict is impeachable if justice demands that it be set aside ..." and explained:

> "... While jurors' affidavits are receivable in evidence in the sense that the trial court should permit them to be filed, affidavits which disclose nothing more than oral misconduct during the jury's deliberation cannot impeach a verdict ... The kind if misconduct ... that will be considered in an attack upon a verdict by a juror's affidavit ... is misconduct that amounts to fraud, bribery, forcible coercion or any other obstruction of justice that would subject the offender to a criminal prosecution therefor. We do not necessarily use the words "fraud," "bribery," "forcible coercion," and "obstruction of justice" in a purely technical sense, but as words that denote such serious breach of the juror's duties that the trial judge would be justified in citing [the juror] for nothing less than a contempt of court. ...'" 289 Or at 631, quoting *Carson v. Brauer,* 234 Or 333, 345–346, 382 P2d 79 (1963).

The decision cited *State v. Gardner,* 230 Or 569, 371 P2d 558 (1962), which confessed that "there is no way of stating the principle in more definite form" than to indicate that a "verdict will stand unless the evidence clearly establishes ... a serious violation of [a] juror's duty [which deprived the] complainant of a fair trial." 230 Or at 575. The Legislative Assembly takes this to mean, not only that a juror may testify that another juror made an unauthorized inspection of the premises in the action, *Sanders v. Curry County,* 456 P2d 493, 253 Or 578 (1969), but also that a fellow juror was so drunk as to be incapable of participating in the deliberations, or manifested extreme racial prejudice towards one of the parties, or refused to follow the instructions of the trial judge.

The Legislative Assembly intends to discourage the practice of questioning jurors after a trial concerning their deliberations or the methods by which they reached a verdict. Questioning regarding "quotient verdicts," for example, should be prohibited. *Fuller v. Blanc,* 160 Or 50, 58–59, 77 P2d 440, 83 P2d 434 (1938); *Hendricks v. P.E.P. Co.,* 134 Or 366, 372, 289 P 369, 292 P 1094 (1930).

For the effect of constitutional considerations in this area, see *Parker v. Gladden,* 385 US 363, 87 SCt 468, 17 LEd 2d 420 (1966) and the discussion of the case in 2 *Litigation* 31 (1975). In that case, the court held that a bailiff's remarks to a jury constituted a violation of the Sixth Amendment's confrontation requirement.

TEXT

Competency of Juror as Witness

Rule 606, contrary to former ORS 44.050 (repealed 1981), prohibits a juror from testifying as a witness before the jury in the trial of a case in which the member has been sworn to sit as a juror. Any potential witnesses should therefore be challenged during the jury selection process. If a juror is called to testify, the opposing party must be afforded an opportunity to object out of the jury's presence. Rule 606 is identical to FRE 606(a).

Rule 606 does not bar a juror from testifying to the court during the trial or in any posttrial or ancillary proceeding. *United States v. Robinson,* 645 F2d 616 (8th Cir), cert denied 454 US 875 (1981) (juror can be questioned during trial outside the presence of the other jurors regarding seeing defendant in custody of United States Marshals outside courtroom).

Juror Testimony to Impeach Verdict

The legislature did not adopt FRE 606(b), which provides:

Upon an inquiry into the validity of a verdict or indictment, a juror may not testify as to any matter or statement occurring during the course of the jury's deliberations or to the effect of anything upon his or any other juror's mind or emotions as influencing him to assent or to dissent from the verdict or indictment or concerning his mental processes in connection therewith, except that a juror may testify on the question whether extraneous prejudicial information was improperly brought to the jury's attention or whether any outside influence was improperly brought to bear upon any juror. Nor may his affidavit or evidence of any statement by him concerning a matter about which he would be precluded from testifying be received for these purposes.

Because FRE 606(b) was not adopted, the extent to which the testimony or affidavit of a juror may be received to impeach a verdict is controlled by case law. On the extent of privilege and immunity of grand jurors, see ORS 132.210 and ORS 132.220.

In *State v. Gardner,* 230 Or 569, 371 P2d 558, 561 (1962), the Oregon Supreme Court adopted Rule 41 of the Uniform Rules of Evidence (1953), which provides:

Upon an inquiry as to the validity of a verdict or an indictment no evidence shall be received to show the effect of any statement, conduct, event or condition upon the mind of a juror as influencing him to assent to or dissent from the verdict or indictment or concerning the mental processes by which it was determined.

See also *Carson v. Brauer,* 234 Or 333, 382 P2d 79 (1963) (reaffirming adoption of Uniform Rule of Evidence 41).

Under Uniform Rule 41, the testimony or affidavit of a juror can be received only to show jury misconduct that does not relate to the "mental processes by which [the verdict] was determined." The effect of Uniform Rule 41 is to make certain types of jury misconduct immune from challenge by rendering incompetent the very evidence that must be used to raise the issue.

The rationale for limiting juror testimony to impeach verdicts is to protect the sanctity of the jury process. If inquiry into jury verdicts were permitted without limitation, "there would be an open invitation to disappointed litigants and their counsel to contest the verdict. The invitation would carry in its wake the temptation to tamper with jurors and it would open the way for pressures and fraudulent practices to induce members of the jury to repudiate their decisions." *State v. Gardner,* 230 Or 569, 574–5, 371 P2d 558 (1962).

Uniform Rule 41 represents a sound compromise between unlimited impeachment of jury verdicts and allowing virtually no challenge at all. It generally permits objective misconduct to be brought to the attention of the trial court while protecting the privacy of jurors with regard to their reasoning process in reaching a verdict.

Evidence Admissible to Impeach Verdict

Oregon case law generally allows evidence of extraneous information or outside influences upon the jury deliberations. In this respect, it is similar to FRE 606(b), which expressly allows juror testimony "on the question whether extraneous prejudicial information was improperly brought to the jury's attention or whether any outside influence was improperly brought to bear upon any juror."

Evidence of an unauthorized view by jurors may be received. See *Thomas v. Dad's Root Beer & Canada Dry Bottling Co.,* 225 Or 166, 356 P2d 418, modified on other grounds 357 P2d 418 (1960).

In *State v. Dickson,* 63 Or App 458, 665 P2d 352, rev denied 295 Or 541, 668 P2d 384 (1983), habeas corpus granted sub nom *Dickson v. Sullivan,* 849 F.2d 403 (9th Cir 1988), the court received evidence that a deputy sheriff made a statement to two jurors that the defendant "has done something like this before." In a criminal case, communication by outsiders to members of the jury may constitute a violation of the defendant's right of confrontation. See *Parker v. Gladden,* 385 US 363, 87 SCt 468, 17 LEd2d 420 (1966).

In the case of *In re Beverly Hills Fire Litigation,* 695 F2d 207, 214–5 (6th Cir 1982), cert denied 461 US 929 (1983), the court held that an unauthorized experiment by a juror at his home, the results of which were subsequently reported to other jurors, was "extraneous prejudicial information" within the meaning of FRE 606(b).

Evidence should also be admissible of unauthorized use of books or other reference sources by jurors. See ANNOT., *Prejudicial Effect of Jury's Procurement or Use of Book During Deliberations in Civil Cases,* 31 ALR4th 623 (1984); ANNOT., *Prejudicial Effect of Jury's Procurement or Use of Book During Deliberations in Criminal Cases,* 35 ALR4th 626 (1985).

The Legislative Commentary indicates that evidence may be received "that a fellow juror was so drunk as to be incapable of participating in the deliberations." But see *Tanner v. United States,* 483 US 107, 107 SCt 2739, 97 LEd2d 90

(1987) (finding juror testimony on intoxication of fellow jurors inadmissible under FRE 606(b)).

The Legislative Commentary also indicates that evidence may be received that a juror "manifested extreme racial prejudice towards one of the parties."

Evidence Inadmissible to Impeach Verdict

In *Faverty v. McDonald's Restaurants*, 133 Or App 514, 520, 529–30, 892 P2d 703, 706, 711–2, rev allowed 321 Or 512, 900 P2d 509 (1995), the defendant sought a new trial on the basis that a magazine article had quoted one of the jurors as saying that the jury increased its award by $100,000 after speculating that the plaintiff would have to pay a lawyer one-third of his damages for a contingent fee. The court held that this evidence was insufficient to impeach the verdict because it suggested only "oral misconduct" by the jury in how they deliberated and calculated damages, and did not amount to fraud, bribery, forcible coercion, or any other criminal obstruction of justice.

In *State v. Jones*, 126 Or App 224, 227–8, 868 P2d 18, 20 (1994), rev denied 318 Or 583, 873 P2d 322, the posttrial affidavits of two jurors went only to the alleged motives of individual jurors for their votes. Therefore, trial court did not err in denying a new trial and in refusing to allow defense counsel to interview other jurors about how they reached their verdict.

In *Blanton v. Union Pac RR*, 289 Or 617, 616 P2d 477 (1980), the court affirmed the refusal of the trial judge to receive affidavits or testimony from jurors regarding whether they reached what was contended to be a quotient verdict, because such evidence involved the mental processes of the jurors in reaching their verdict.

In *D.C. Thompson and Co. v. Hague*, 300 Or 651, 717 P2d 1169 (1986), the court held that juror affidavits or testimony seeking to impeach a jury's verdict based upon allegations that the jurors misunderstood the effect of their verdict were inadmissible. The jurors in their affidavits and subsequent testimony indicated that they intended their answers on the special verdict form to be in the tenants' favor, whereas the verdict they actually rendered was in favor of the landlord. The court characterized this as a case involving "irregularity" in the jury proceedings rather than jury misconduct. The court held that evidence regarding a jury's mental processes in reaching a verdict is inadmissible in cases involving irregularity in the jury proceedings as well as in cases involving jury misconduct.

The Legislative Commentary to Rule 606 suggests that evidence that a juror "refused to follow the instructions of the trial judge" would be admissible. However, refusal to follow the instructions of the trial judge relates to the mental processes of the jury in reaching its verdict and would not seem admissible under Uniform Rule 41 or prior Oregon case law. See *Winters v. Bisaillon*, 152 Or 578, 580–1, 54 P2d 1169 (1936) (affidavit will not be received to impeach verdict by showing that jury failed to follow court's instructions); *Schmitz v. United States Bakery*, 41 Or App 749, 599 P2d 471 (1979) (jury should not be questioned by judge regarding possible misunderstanding of jury instructions in reaching verdict).

Effect of Misconduct or Prejudicial Information

Under Uniform Rule 41, no inquiry can be made of a juror regarding "the effect of any statement, conduct, event or condition upon the mind of [the juror] as influencing him to assent to or dissent from the verdict or indictment." Therefore, even though the court may receive a juror's testimony or affidavit regarding misconduct that is not a type relating to the mental processes of the jury, it may not receive evidence regarding the **effect** of such misconduct upon any juror. In determining whether the misconduct was sufficiently prejudicial to warrant setting aside the verdict the court must assess the impact of the misconduct without requiring jurors to disclose their own thoughts or mental processes. For an illustration of this distinction, see *United States v. Duncan*, 598 F2d 839 (4th Cir), cert denied 444 US 871 (1979) (juror may testify that she had consulted a dictionary but may not testify as to the effect this extraneous influence had on her own deliberations or those of the other jurors). See also *United States v. Bruscino*, 687 F2d 938 (7th Cir 1982), cert denied 459 US 1228 (1983).

Failure to Disclose on Voir Dire

Rather than attempting to impeach a jury verdict by evidence of juror misconduct during deliberations, another approach is to move for a new trial on grounds of juror misconduct on voir dire in failing to disclose bias or knowledge about the case or making a false statement.

In *State v. Holcomb*, 131 Or App 453, 455–7, 886 P2d 14, 15–7 (1994), the court ordered a new trial based on juror misconduct in lying on voir dire. One of the jurors was shown to have lied in refusing to admit he had been convicted of a crime or to admit that he was a victim of a burglary himself, when the trial was a prosecution for burglary.

Evidence has also been received that a juror had significant knowledge about the case or the parties that was not disclosed upon voire dire and shared that knowledge with other jurors. In *State v. Salas*, 68 Or App 68, 680 P2d 706, rev denied 297 Or 601, 687 P2d 795 (1984), a juror informed a deputy district attorney that during deliberations one juror had told another that she had known defendant when he was in high school, that he had been in trouble with firearms before and that he could not be believed. The appellate court reversed, finding that the failure of the juror to disclose her bias against the defendant stemming from out-of-court knowledge was misconduct justifying a new trial.

In *Ertsgaard v. Beard*, 310 Or 486, 496, 800 P2d 759 (1990), the court held that affidavits of jurors were admissible to impeach a verdict by showing that one juror had discussed private knowledge regarding a party with other jurors. In this case, a juror revealed that the defendant doctor had successfully treated other patients, including a relative of the juror. The court held that such affidavits were admissible on the issue of whether there was juror misconduct during the deliberation process, as well as on whether the juror was untruthful during voir dire. However, the court concluded that: (1) the juror had not given a false answer on voir dire, and (2) the misconduct by the juror in sharing the private knowledge with other jurors was not sufficient to justify a new trial.

Courts in other jurisdictions have also allowed evidence of personal knowledge by a juror that may have affected the verdict to be received in support of a motion for a new trial. See *Hard v. Burlington Northern Railroad,* 812 F2d 482 (9th Cir 1987) (juror told other jurors that defendant paid all medical expenses of injured employees); *State v. Poh,* 116 Wis2d 510, 343 NW2d 108 (1984) (juror discussed defendant's accident and arrest record which had not been revealed at trial).

Grounds for New Trial

In cases where competent evidence is available to impeach a jury verdict, such evidence must be measured against the applicable substantive law standard for determining whether it is sufficient to warrant setting aside the verdict. In *Carson v. Brauer,* 234 Or 333, 345–6, 382 P2d 79 (1963), the Supreme Court articulated the standard as follows:

> The kind of misconduct of a juror that will be considered ... is misconduct that amounts to fraud, bribery, forcible coercion or any other obstruction of justice that would subject the offender to a criminal prosecution therefor. We do not necessarily use the words "fraud," "bribery," "forcible coercion," and "obstruction of justice" in a purely technical sense, but as words that denote such serious breach of a juror's duties that the trial judge would be justified in citing him for nothing less than a contempt of court.

See *Blanton v. Union Pac RR,* 289 Or 617, 616 P2d 477 (1980) (reaffirming approval of this standard).

The Commentary cites the rule of *State v. Gardner,* 230 Or 569, 371 P2d 558 (1962), that a "verdict will stand unless the evidence clearly establishes a serious violation of [a] juror's duty [which deprived the] complainant of a fair trial."

Not all cases where affidavits or testimony of jurors is offered to impeach a verdict involve misconduct by jurors. For example, an outsider may have improperly communicated with the juror or the jury may have had a good faith misunderstanding of the judge's instructions or some aspect of the proceeding. See, e.g., *D.C. Thompson and Co. v. Hauge,* 300 Or 651, 717 P2d 1169 (1986) (jurors misunderstood verdict form). Such cases should be treated as involving an "irregularity in the proceedings of the jury," but not jury misconduct. See ORCP 64B(1).

A clear distinction should be made between what evidence may be received to show misconduct or irregularity in the jury deliberations and what misconduct or irregularity is sufficient under the substantive law to warrant setting aside the verdict and granting a new trial. These issues are often merged or confused. Sometimes a court will avoid the question of whether affidavits or testimony by jurors offered to impeach a verdict are admissible by holding that the evidence, even if true, is insufficient to constitute grounds for granting a new trial. For example, in *Gerke v. Burton Enterprises, Inc.,* 80 Or App 714, 723 P2d

1061, rev denied 302 Or 299, 728 P2d 532 (1986), defendants filed a motion for a new trial based upon affidavits of three jurors stating that an attorney member of the panel "totally dominated" the proceedings, told the jurors that "all doubts were to be resolved against" the defendants, and "thoroughly reprimanded" jurors who embraced opposing opinions. The court avoided the question of whether the affidavits were properly received, holding that the affidavits did not disclose misconduct sufficient to set aside the verdict.

Contacting Jurors

It should be noted that contacting jurors after a trial to determine whether misconduct may have occurred is restricted by court rule. See UTCR 3.120, which provides:

(1) Except as necessary during trial, and except as provided in subsection (2), parties, witnesses or court employees shall not initiate contact with any juror concerning any case which that juror was sworn to try.

(2) After a sufficient showing to the court and on order of the court, a party may have contact with a juror in the presence of the court and opposing parties when:

    (a) there is a reasonable ground to believe that there has been a mistake in the announcing or recording of a verdict;

    (b) there is a reasonable ground to believe that a juror or jury has been guilty of fraud or misconduct sufficient to justify setting aside or modifying the verdict or judgment.

See also DR 7-108(D), (E), (F), and (G) of the Code of Professional Responsibility; Opinion No. 142, Oregon State Bar Legal Ethics Opinions, PROFESSIONAL RESPONSIBILITY MANUAL (1981). In *Niemela v. Collings*, 267 Or 369, 517 P2d 268 (1973), the court held that a juror's affidavit taken in violation of local court rule will not be considered in ruling upon a motion for a new trial. See generally ANNOT., *Propriety of Attorney's Communication With Jurors After Trial*, 19 ALR4th 1209 (1983).

Other Authorities

For a listing of the matters that will and will not be received under FRE 606(b), see Mueller, *Jurors' Impeachment of Verdicts and Indictments in Federal Court Under Rule 606(b)*, 57 Neb L Rev 920 (1978). See generally ANNOT., *Competency of Juror as Witness, Under Rule 606(b) of Federal Rules of Evidence, Upon Inquiry Into Validity of Verdict or Indictment*, 65 ALR Fed 835 (1983); Crump, *Jury Misconduct, Jury Interviews and the Federal Rules of Evidence: Is the Broad Exclusionary Principle of Rule 606(b) Justified?*, 66 N C L Rev 509 (1988); Thompson, *Challenge to the Decision-Making Process—Federal Rule of Evidence 606(b) and the Constitutional Right to a Fair Trial*, 38 Sw L J 1187 (1985); ANNOT., *Criminal Law—Propriety of Reassembling Jury to Change Defective Verdict*, 14 ALR5th 89 (1993); ANNOT., *Propriety of Jurors' Tests or Experiments in Jury Room*, 31 ALR4th 566 (1984); ANNOT., *Propriety and Effect of Jurors' Discussion of*

Evidence Among Themselves Before Final Submission of Criminal Case, 21 ALR4th 444 (1983); NOTE, *Public Disclosures of Jury Deliberations,* 96 Harv L Rev 886 (1983); ANNOT., *Admissibility, in Civil Case, of Juror's Affidavit or Testimony Relating to Juror's Misconduct Outside Jury Room,* 32 ALR3d 1356 (1970); ANNOT., *Disclosure in Criminal Case of Juror's Political, Racial, Religious, or National Origin Prejudice Against Accused or Witnesses As Ground for New Trial or Reversal,* 91 ALR2d 1120 (1963); ANNOT., *Admissibility and Effect, in Criminal Case, of Evidence as to Juror's Statements, During Deliberations, as to Facts Not Introduced into Evidence,* 58 ALR2d 556 (1958); ANNOT., *Admissibility, in Civil Case, of Juror's Affidavit or Testimony to Show Bias, Prejudice, or Disqualification of a Juror Not Disclosed on Voir Dire Examination,* 48 ALR2d 971 (1956); ANNOT., *Testimony or Affidavit by One Other than a Juror, Who Overheard Jury's Deliberations, as Receivable to Impeach Verdict,* 129 ALR 803 (1940).

RULE 607.   ORS 40.345. WHO MAY IMPEACH

The credibility of a witness may be attacked by any party, including the party calling the witness.

LEGISLATIVE COMMENTARY

Oregon Rule of Evidence 607 indicates who may impeach a witness and upon what conditions. The rule is identical in substance to Rule 607 of the Federal Rules of Evidence. Prior versions, proposed by the Advisory Committee on Evidence Law Revision and the Interim Judiciary Committee, treated impeachment of one's own witness by prior inconsistent statements differently from other methods of impeachment. This rule, like Federal Rule 607, does not.

Impeachment of adverse witness. Rule 607 does not place any restrictions on the ability of a party to impeach a witness who is called by another party. In this respect the, rule does not differ from ORS 45.600, the former Oregon statute on impeachment of adverse witnesses. ORS 45.600 was declaratory of the common law. *Sheppard v. Yocum,* 10 Or 402 410 (1882); *State v. Hunsaker,* 16 Or 497, 499, 19 P 605 (1888); *State v. Edwards,* 106 Or 58, 210 P 1079 (1922); *State v. Motley,* 127 Or 415, 272 P 561 (1928); *State v. Gilbert,* 138 Or 291, 4 P2d 923 (1932). The distinctions between Article VI and the common law with regard to adverse witnesses lie not in the right but in the manner of impeachment. See Rules 608, 609, 609-1, 613, infra.

Impeachment of own witness. Rule 607 works a significant change with respect to impeachment of a party's own witness.

At common law, a party was prohibited from impeaching its own witness. This policy was based on the doctrine that a party vouches for the credibility of its witnesses, and the assumption that a party can wrongly coerce its witnesses if allowed to impeach them. These are false premises.

"... [A] party does not vouch for [the party's] witnesses because, except for expert and character witnesses, ... witnesses are
not chosen but [are] those persons who happen to be present and
see the event which is the basis of the case. The second policy
concerned with the situation where a party's witness decides to
change [the witness's] story [and] testify unfavorably ... falsely assumes that whenever a witness changes ... testimony, it will be
from falsehood to truth, that the party coerces the witnesses by
threatening impeachment, and that the truth is thereby suppressed.
Certainly witnesses could be changing their testimony from truth to
falsehood and so the coercion, if there is any, could be supporting,
not suppressing, the truth." Montana Rules of Evidence, Rule 607,
Comment at 44 (1977).

Accord, *Chambers v. Mississippi,* 410 US 284, 296 n 8, 935 SCt 1038,
35 L Ed 2d 297 (1973), acknowledging criticism of the voucher rule as
"archaic, irrational, and potentially destructive of the truth-gathering process" and indicating that application of the rule in criminal cases may raise
constitutional problems. See also, cases collected in 3 Wigmore, *Evidence,*
§ 905 (3d ed 1940).

Denial of any right to impeach one's own witness leaves a party at
the mercy of the witness and the opposing party, and for this reason Oregon has not followed the common law for nearly a century. *Leverich v.
Frank,* 6 Or 212 (1896); *State v. Hunsaker,* supra. Over the years, the law
relating to impeachment of one's own witness evolved into ORS 45.590.
That statute provided that the party producing a witness may not impeach
the witness' credibility by evidence of bad character, but the party may (1)
contradict the witness by other evidence, or (2) show upon proper foundation that the witness made other statements inconsistent with present
testimony (a foundation was not required for an adverse party or its
agent). The statute was interpreted to require that the testimony of a witness be material and prejudicial before the calling party may impeach.
Langford v. Jones, 18 Or 307, 326, 22 P 1064 (1890); *State v. Steever,* 29 Or
85, 104, 43 P 947 (1896); *State v. Yee Gueng,* 57 Or 509, 112 P 424 (1910);
State v. Merlo, 92 Or 678, 173 P 317, 182 P 153 (1919); *Tauscher v. Doern-
becher Mfg. Co.,* 153 Or 152, 56 P2d 318 (1936); *State v. Gardner,* 2 Or
App 265, 467 P2d 125, SCt review denied (1970); *Rhodes v. Harwood,* 273
Or 903, 544 P2d 147 (1975); but see *State v. Estlick,* 269 Or 75, 523 P2d
1029 (1974) (any witness may be impeached to show bias or interest).

The Legislative Assembly found the restrictions in ORS 45.590 against
impeaching one's own witness to be in conflict with the persuasive reasoning of recognized authorities. 3 Wigmore §§ 896–899; McCormick, *Evidence* § 50 at 107 (2d ed 1972). An unqualified rule is more consistent with
the view of trial as a search for truth. The principle of impeachment is
wholesome in this regard, because it treats the witness as a "channel
through which to get at the truth" rather than a partisan of the party calling
the witness. Uniform Rules of Evidence, Rule 20, Comment (1953).

Special mention should be made of impeachment by means of prior
inconsistent statements. If it is feared that the trier of fact will accept prior
statements as substantive evidence, then it is not illogical to place limitations upon their use. The Advisory Committee recommended, for example,
that prior inconsistent statements be allowed for impeachment only if (1)

the testimony at trial is actually injurious to the calling party's case, see cases cited, supra, and (2) the testimony is contrary to what the calling party anticipates, see *State v. Cain,* 230 Or 286, 369 P2d 769 (1962); *State v. Briggs,* 245 Or 503, 420 P2d 71 (1967); *State v. Gardner,* supra; *Rhodes v. Harwood,* supra. Prior inconsistent statements come in as substantive evidence under Rule 801(4)(a)(A), however. There is no need for the requirements of surprise and injury, and the Legislative Assembly rejected both.

TEXT

Who May Impeach

Rule 607 provides that a witness may be impeached by any party, including the party calling the witness. Impeachment means "to attack or discredit the witness and to attack the jury's belief in his or her testimony." *State v. Gilbert,* 282 Or 309, 311, 577 P2d 939 (1978). Five types of impeachment are recognized explicitly or implicitly by the code. They are:

(1) Defect in capacity to perceive, recall, or recount. See Rules 601 (perception, communication) and 602 (personal knowledge).
(2) Character for untruthfulness. See Rule 608(l)(a).
(3) Prior criminal convictions. See Rule 609.
(4) Bias or interest. See Rule 609-1.
(5) Prior inconsistent statements. See Rule 613.

Two additional types of impeachment are recognized by prior case law and continue to be available under the Evidence Code: impeachment by contradiction and impeachment of expert witnesses by use of treatises.

Two types of impeachment are expressly prohibited by the Oregon Evidence Code. Rule 608(2) bars proof, whether by examination of the witness or by extrinsic evidence, of prior bad acts of the witness even though probative of untruthfulness. Rule 610 bars impeachment of witnesses based upon their religious beliefs or opinions.

Evidence received solely for impeachment can be used only to attack the credibility of a witness and not to prove a substantive issue in the case. See *State v. Gill,* 3 Or App 488, 474 P2d 23 (1970) (approving instruction that "I instruct you that impeaching evidence in and of itself is not sufficient to prove any material element or issue in the case."). However, occasionally evidence will be received both for impeachment and substantive purposes. See Rule 801(4)(a)(A) (prior inconsistent statement "given under oath subject to the penalty of perjury at a trial, hearing or other proceeding, or in a deposition" is not hearsay and therefore can be used substantively as well as for impeachment).

Defect in Capacity to Perceive, Recall, or Recount

The general rule regarding impeaching a witness by evidence of use of or dependency on intoxicants is stated in *State v. Batchelor,* 34 Or App 47, 50, 578 P2d 409 (1978):

[T]he rule supported by the majority of cases seems to be that for the purpose of discrediting a witness, evidence is not admissible to show that he is a user of opium, morphine, or similar drugs, or to show the effect of such drugs, unless it is proven that the witness was under their influence at the time of the occurrences as to which he testifies, or at the time of the trial, or that his mind or memory or powers of observation were affected by the habit.

See also *State v. Goodin,* 8 Or App 15, 492 P2d 287 (1971) (witness may be impeached by drug use affecting recollection); *State v. McKiel,* 122 Or 504, 259 P 917 (1927) (witness may be impeached by drunkenness affecting recollection); *State v. Longoria,* 17 Or App 1, 520 P2d 912 (1974) (witness may be impeached by defect of memory); *United States v. Lindstrom,* 698 F2d 1154 (11th Cir 1983) (error to restrict defendant from cross-examining the government's key witness regarding her mental illness that may have influenced her testimony).

See generally ANNOT., *Impeachment of Federal Trial Witness with Respect to Intoxication,* 106 ALR Fed 371 (1992); ANNOT., *Cross-Examination of Witness As To His Mental State or Condition, To Impeach Competency or Credibility,* 44 ALR3d 1203 (1972); ANNOT., *Impeachment of Witness With Respect to Intoxication,* 8 ALR3d 749 (1966).

Impeachment by Contradictory Evidence

A witness may be impeached by evidence contradictkng the witness's testimony. See *State v. Burdge,* 295 Or 1, 6, 664 P2d 1076, 1079–80 (1983) (approving impeachment by contradiction); *State v. Schober,* 67 Or App 385, 678 P2d 746 (1984) (approving evidence of prior instances of drinking by the defendant to rebut the defendant's testimony on direct examination that "for all practical purposes I do not drink.").

This method of impeachment is subject to two qualifications. First, a witness cannot be impeached on a collateral matter. If the matter is found to be collateral the testimony of the witness will stand even though it could be disproven. The rule is sometimes expressed by saying that the examiner must "take the answer" of the witness. 1 McCormick, *Evidence* (4th ed 1996) § 45 at 169-170. *State v. Thompson,* 28 Or App 409, 559 P2d 1294 (1977). See generally ANNOT., *Propriety, in Federal Court Action, of Attack on Witnesses' Credibility by Rebuttal Evidence Pertaining to Cross-Examination Testimony on Collateral Matters,* 60 ALR Fed 8 (1982); Marek, *Limitations on Impeachment by Contradiction: The Collateral Facts Rule and FRE 403,* 33 Drake L Rev 663 (1983–84).

Wigmore states that for evidence to be noncollateral it must be independently admissible for a reason other than to show a contradiction in the testimony of a witness. 3A Wigmore, *Evidence* (Chadbourn Rev 1970) § 1003. This standard has been approved by prior case law. See *State v. Johnson,* 277 Or 45, 48, 559 P2d 496 (1977). Under this traditional approach, evidence is not collateral and can be used to contradict the testimony of a witness only if it is relevant to a substantive issue in the case or admissible as part of some other recognized mode of impeachment. In other words, it must have "dual" relevancy and serve some other permissible purpose rather than merely contradicting the witness.

However, many modern courts adopt the more expansive approach of McCormick that impeachment by contradiction should be allowed of any part of the witness' account of the background and circumstances of a material transaction, which as a matter of human experience he would not have been mistaken about if his story were true. 2 McCormick, *Evidence* (4th ed 1992) § 49 at 184 (footnote omitted). In other words, evidence can be offered that serves only to contradict if the contradiction relates to a sufficiently important point casting a broader shadow on the witness' entire testimony.

Courts sometimes allow impeachment by contradiction of sweeping claims by a witness on direct examination (even on a matter that would otherwise be considered collateral), if the claim has sufficient importance that it could unfairly prejudice a party or mislead the jury if left unchallenged. See Moss, *The Sweeping Claims Exception and the Federal Rules of Evidence,* 1982 Duke L J 61. In such cases, the party offering the evidence is sometimes viewed as having opened the door to the otherwise inadmissible counterproof. See discussion of "Curative Admissibility" under Rule 402, supra.

Testimony can only be impeached by contradiction when it is sufficiently precise to constitute a clear statement of fact that can be rebutted. *State v. Hayes,* 117 Or App 202, 205, 843 P2d 948 (1992), rev denied 316 Or 528, 854 P2d 940 (1993) (in prosecution for sodomy involving his grandchildren, defendant denied on cross-examination being "mean" to his grandchildren; to rebut this statement, the prosecutor introduced testimony from two of defendant's daughters and two other granddaughters who testified about his sexual molestation of them; court held that admission of this testimony was reversible error because defendant's statement that it was intended to contradict was not a sufficiently precise statement of fact, commenting that "if a statement is ambiguous or imprecise, there is a danger that the evidence will seem to contradict something that was not intended").

Evidence offered to contradict also must be sufficiently precise. See *State v. Rood,* 118 Or App 480, 484, 848 P2d 128, rev denied 317 Or 272, 858 P2d 1314 (1993) (excluding a "home study report" by a caseworker containing findings that defendant was qualified to adopt a child offered to impeach allegations of child abuse; to be used for impeachment, a contradictory statement must be "reasonably precise" and not merely a "recitation of opinion and character").

Courts apply the collateral matter bar less strictly when the contradictory evidence can be brought out on cross-examination without the need to prove it with extrinsic evidence. In *State v. Rood,* 118 Or App 480, 484, 848 P2d 128, rev denied 317 Or 272, 858 P2d 1314 (1993), a prosecution of defendant for sexually abusing two boys, the defendant was asked if he had ever taken the boys to a "clothing optional" resort. He argued that the question was objectionable because it amounted to impeachment on a collateral matter. The appellate court found no error because the defendant was impeached by his own testimony on cross-examination rather than by extrinsic evidence.

A second limitation upon impeachment by contradiction is that the opposing party is not allowed to contradict the witness' testimony when the point being contradicted was raised for the first time on cross-examination and goes beyond the scope of the direct testimony. See *State v. Johnson,* 277 Or 45, 49, 559 P2d 496, 498 (1977) (prosecutor asked defendant on cross-examination whether he was a drug dealer in order to impeach with prior conversation admitting he was a drug dealer. Held: reversible error. "It is obvious that the questions were asked on cross-examination for the sole purpose of making a hook on which to hang the legally irrelevant evidence of the police officer's conversation with defendant. Such trial tactics upon the part of the state are to be discouraged"). See also *United States v. Pantone,* 609 F2d 675, 681 (3rd Cir 1979) ("[W]e disapprove of the practice of using cross-examination beyond the scope of the direct testimony for the purpose of laying a foundation for the introduction, as rebuttal, of otherwise inadmissible evidence"); *United States v. Trejo,* 501 F2d 138 (9th Cir 1974). See generally Annot., *Propriety, in Federal Court Action, of Attack on Witnesses' Credibility by Rebuttal Evidence Pertaining to Cross-Examination Testimony on Collateral Matters,* 60 ALR Fed 8 (1982).

Cases Finding Impeachment to Be Collateral

In *State v. Hite,* 131 Or App 59, 66, 883 P2d 890 (1994), rev denied 320 Or 508, 888 P2d 569 (1995), a rape and sodomy prosecution, the defendant denied taking nude photographs of the victim. On cross-examination, the prosecution questioned the defendant about his interest in nude photography and got him to say he "was not interested" in it. Then the state sought to impeach him with nude photographs found in his possession that were not related to the victim. The court held that the photographs were not admissible for impeachment purposes because the issue was a collateral matter and was raised for the first time on cross-examination.

In *Sheagren v. Albrecht,* 123 Or App 553, 556, 860 P2d 868, 870 (1993), the court reaffirmed the rule that a witness cannot be impeached with extrinsic evidence on a collateral matter. Here a doctor sued an attorney for failure to pay an expert witness fee, and the attorney claimed breach of contract for failure to testify in accordance with the opinion letter rendered prior to trial. On cross examination, defendant attorney denied receiving money from his client to pay the plaintiff expert. Plaintiff called the client as a rebuttal witness who testified that he had given the attorney money to pay the expert. The attorney again took the stand to say client was mistaken and that the money was for other expenses. The court held that this evidence of a dispute between client and attorney amounted to improper impeachment on a collateral matter, because the only issue the jury was asked to decide was whether the expert breached his contract with the attorney.

In *State v. Peaslee,* 59 Or App 519, 651 P2d 182, rev denied 294 Or 212, 656 P2d 943 (1982), the defendant asked the robbery victim if she had sold drugs to Schultz on the day of the crime. Upon obtaining a denial from the victim, the defendant attempted to offer Schultz' testimony that he had purchased drugs from the victim at her home on that day, arguing that such evidence was admissible to show that the victim had testified falsely. The court affirmed the trial judge's ruling that the attempted impeachment was improper because it involved a collateral matter and was extrinsic evidence of a prior bad act.

Cases Finding Impeachment Not to Be Collateral

Impeachment by contradiction was allowed in *State v. Smith,* 86 Or App 239, 739 P2d 577 (1987). The defendant was convicted for driving on September 25, while his driver's license was suspended. He called his son as a witness, who testified that the father did not drive on September 25, and that the defendant's car had not moved from the side of the house since that date. In rebuttal, the prosecutor called the arresting officer who testified that he saw the defendant driving the car on September 26. The court found this to be proper impeachment and not prohibited by Rule 404(3).

In *State v.Clark,* 98 Or App 478, 779 P2d 215 (1989), the court held that evidence that a codefendant had been convicted for the same transaction, although not admissible as substantive evidence of defendant's guilt, was admissible to contradict the defendant's testimony, when the defendant opened the door to such evidence.

Impeachment with Illegally Seized Evidence

It has been held not to violate the Federal Constitution to contradict a witness by illegally seized evidence that would not be admissible as substantive evidence. *United States v. Havens,* 446 US 620, 100 SCt 1912, 64 LEd2d 559 (1980) (allowing impeachment of defendant's answer during cross-examination that was clearly within scope of his direct testimony); *Walder v. United States,* 347 US 62, 74 SCt 354, 98 LEd2d 503 (1954).

Impeachment of Experts by Statements in Learned Treatises

Expert witnesses may be impeached by statements in learned treatises that contradict their testimony upon direct examination, provided the expert relied upon the treatise or acknowledges it as a recognized authority in the field. *Devine v. S Pac Co.,* 207 Or 261, 275, 295 P2d 201, 207 (1956); *Kern v. Pullen,* 138 Or 222, 231, 6 P2d 224, 227 (1931). See textual discussion of Rule 702. This foundation requirement should be reconsidered, because it allows the witness to avoid impeachment simply by denying reliance on a treatise or that it is an authority. A number of other jurisdictions have abandoned this rule and allow the impeaching attorney to establish authoritativeness through other witnesses or through judicial notice. See 2 McCormick, *Evidence* (4th ed 1992) § 321 at 350.

In *State v. Smith,* 66 Or App 703, 675 P2d 510 (1984), the court refused to allow an arresting officer to be impeached from a police training manual when it was not shown that the officer had ever read or been taught the section the defendant was attempting to use to impeach.

Because statements in treatises are hearsay they can be used for impeachment only, not as substantive evidence. *Eckleberry v. Kaiser Found N Hosp.,* 226 Or 616, 359 P2d 1090 (1961). A limiting instruction under Rule 105 should be available upon request. The Oregon Legislature did not adopt FRE 803(18), which creates a hearsay exception for statements in learned treatises. See textual discussion under Rule 803, infra.

Impeachment of Party's Own Witness

Both at common law and under former Oregon law, a party could not impeach its own witnesses because a party was deemed to vouch for them. 1 McCormick, *Evidence* (4th ed 1992) § 38 at 126. Former ORS 45.590 (repealed 1981). Rule 607 removes all limitations against a party's impeachment of its own witness. As a matter of strategy, a party may want to impeach its own witnesses, for example, by showing bias or prior criminal convictions, to "take the sting out" of cross-examination and avoid a perception of hiding important information from the jury. Also a party may be genuinely surprised by a "turncoat" witness and need to impeach him to remedy the damage caused by his testimony. See generally Tornquist, *Article VI: Competence, Credibility and Examination of Witnesses,* 19 Will L Rev 395 (1983).

Potential Abuse of Rule 607

The freedom of a litigant to impeach its own witnesses is susceptible to abuse, at least when the impeachment is by evidence of prior inconsistent statements that would not be admissible as substantive evidence. In such circumstances, Rule 607 might be misused as providing an opportunity to parade otherwise inadmissible hearsay before the jury under the guise of impeachment.

The problem arises in cases where the true purpose of a party's "impeachment" of its own witness is not to attack her direct testimony (she may have testified only that "I don't remember" or "I didn't see it"), but to bring out prior statements of the witness that would otherwise be inadmissible as substantive evidence. Even though the jury is instructed to consider impeaching statements only in evaluating the credibility of the witness, such instructions are often disregarded. Thus there is a significant danger that the jury will consider the "impeaching" statements for the truth of what they assert, thus undercutting the hearsay rule.

Rule 607 is essentially identical to FRE 607. At the time FRE 607 was drafted the danger of abuse described above did not exist because under FRE 801(d)(1)(A), as proposed by the Advisory Committee, all prior inconsistent statements of a witness were admissible as not hearsay. Congress amended FRE 801(d)(1)(A) to allow as not hearsay only inconsistent statements made "under oath subject to the penalty of perjury at a trial hearing, or other proceeding, or in a deposition." FRE 607 was not amended. FRE 607 can therefore be used to undermine the policy choice made by Congress in FRE 801(d)(1)(A).

The same problem exists in Oregon; ORE 801(4)(a)(A) is identical to FRE 801(d)(1)(A). The Commentary is in error in stating that "[p]rior inconsistent statements come in as substantive evidence under Rule 801(4)(a)(A)." Only a small percentage of prior inconsistent statements—those made "under oath subject to the penalty of perjury at a trial, hearing or other proceeding, or in a deposition" —are classified as nonhearsay, provided the declarant testifies and is subject to cross-examination. Therefore, another statement in the Commentary becomes pertinent: "If it is feared that the trier of fact will accept prior statements as substantive evidence, then it is not illogical to place limitations upon their use."

A number of courts interpreting FRE 607 have placed limitations on the extent to which a party may impeach its own witness with prior inconsistent statements. See *United States v. Miller,* 664 F2d 94, 97 (5th Cir 1981) ("[T]he prosecutor may not use such a statement under the guise of impeachment for the primary purpose of placing before the jury substantive evidence which is not otherwise admissible"); *United States v. Fay,* 668 F2d 375, 379 (8th Cir 1981) ("[C]ourts must be watchful that impeachment is not used as a subterfuge to place otherwise inadmissible hearsay before the jury") (quoting *United States v. Rogers,* 549 F2d 497 (8th Cir 1976), cert denied 431 US 918 (1977)); *Whitehurst v. Wright,* 592 F2d 834, 840 (5th Cir 1979) ("To use a prior inconsistent statement in that manner ... is an attempt to use hearsay evidence for substantive purposes. We do not believe that the rules of evidence espouse such a revolutionary approach to circumvent the traditional principles of hearsay"); *United States v. Long Soldier,* 562 F2d 601, 605 (8th Cir 1977) (cautioning against allowing the prosecutor to call a witness "solely for the purpose of introducing otherwise inadmissible evidence under the guise of impeachment"); *United States v. Shoupe,* 548 F2d 636, 638 (6th Cir 1977) (finding reversible error in allowing the prosecutor to cross-examine a prosecution witness who had disavowed an earlier confession with "a litany of leading questions which incorporated the entire substance of his unsworn, oral statements ....").

One leading federal case, *United States v. Webster,* 734 F2d 1191 (7th Cir 1984) adopted a "good faith" standard for determining whether a party will be allowed to impeach the party's own witness with an earlier statement that would be hearsay if offered as substantive evidence. If the party can establish a good faith basis for calling the witness in the first place, and the impeachment relates to the testimony elicited, no error will be found. But under a good faith test the court would explore why the witness was called if the attorney knew in advance (or had reason to know) that the witness would not give helpful testimony.

Professor Graham has advocated that a "surprise" and "damage" requirement be read into FRE 607 before allowing a party to impeach its own witness by a prior inconsistent statement:

> If the witness does not give affirmatively damaging testimony, i.e., testimony of positive aid to the adversary, the party simply does not need to attack his credibility. If the witness' testimony does not surprise the party, the litigant should not be permitted to impeach his testimony by placing before the jury the witness' prior statement because he could have refrained from eliciting the statement he seeks to impeach. (1 M. Graham, HANDBOOK OF FEDERAL EVIDENCE, § 607.3 at 682 (4th ed 1996) (footnote omitted))

See also Graham, *Examination of a Party's Own Witness Under the Federal Rules of Evidence: A Promise Unfulfilled,* 54 Tex L Rev 917 (1976); Graham, *The Relationship Among Federal Rules of Evidence 607, 801(d)(1)(A), and 403: A Reply to Weinstein's Evidence,* 55 Tex L Rev 573 (1977); Graham, *Employing Inconsistent Statements For Impeachment and as Substantive Evidence: A Critical Review and Proposed Amendments of Federal Rules of Evidence 801(d)(1)(A), 613, and 607,* 75 Mich L Rev 1565 (1977).

Judge Weinstein suggests excluding under Rule 403 where prior statements offered to impeach are likely to be considered by the jury for their truth:

> Instead of placing so much emphasis on the motive of the profferor, an approach more consistent with the underlying policy of the federal rules of evidence would be to analyze the problem in terms of Rule 403—is the probative value of the impeaching evidence outweighed by its prejudicial impact? (3 J. Weinstein and M. Berger, *Weinstein's Evidence* § 607[01] at 607–20 (1988) (footnote omitted))

Judge Weinstein comments, however, that "[i]n most cases, of course, the Rule 403 analysis and the surprise-damage requirement will lead to the same result …" Id. at 607–21 (footnote omitted).

3 D. Louisell and C. Mueller, FEDERAL EVIDENCE (1979) § 299 at 195 (1979) takes the following position regarding this issue:

> It does not follow that the calling party is entitled under the Rule to impeach his witness by a prior inconsistent statement … where (i) the testimony of the witness has conveyed no data of significance in the case, but (ii) the prior statement does assert important data, and (iii) the statement would violate the hearsay rule if received for its truth. Here, the impeachment effort should be viewed as highly suspect, particularly where it seems to have been the main purpose of the calling party to get the prior statement before the trier of fact. Here, the relevance of the prior statement in undermining credibility seems to be substantially outweighed by the risk of unfair prejudice to the opponent of the calling party, and the trial judge should invoke Rules 403 and 611 to cut short or block altogether the impeaching effort.

See generally Ordover, *Surprise! That Damaging Turncoat Witness is Still With Us: An Analysis of Federal Rules of Evidence 607 801(d)(1)(A) and 403,* 5 Hofstra L Rev 65 (1976); Fenner, *Handling the Turncoat Witness Under the Federal Rules of Evidence,* 55 Notre Dame Law 536 (1980); Gamble, Howard & McElroy, *The Turncoat or Chameleonic Witness: Use of His Prior Inconsistent Statement,* 34 Ala L Rev 1 (1983); ANNOT., *Propriety, Under Federal Rules of Evidence, of Impeachment of Party's Own Witness,* 89 ALR Fed 13 (1988).

Recent Cases

In *State v. Arnold*, 133 Or App 647, 650, 893 P2d 1050 (1995), a young sex crime victim, when called to the stand by the state, testified that she did not know or could not remember earlier events or statements. The state offered her earlier statements to impeach her and first argued that they were "not hearsay" under OEC 801(4)(a)(A). Because the earlier statements were not made under oath at a proceeding, they were held inadmissible under OEC 801(4)(a)(A). The state then argued that the statements were admissible at least for impeachment. The defendant argued that the jury was likely to consider the statements for their truth and, therefore, a limiting instruction should have been given. Although the defendant had not requested a limiting instruction, the court found that the defendant had no basis for requesting such an instruction because the trial judge had ruled the statement admissible for substantive purposes. The court held the admission of the victim's earlier statements to be reversible error.

Author's Note: Even if a limiting instruction had been given it would not necessarily have avoided the danger of the jury considering the earlier hearsay statements for the truth of what they assert, which is the problem discussed above.

In *State v. Warren*, 88 Or App 462, 745 P2d 822 (1987), rev denied 305 Or 45, 749 P2d 1182 (1988), the defendant was convicted of robbery. At trial a witness named Fields was called to testify against the defendant. Fields had previously confessed that he committed the robberies and that the defendant was with him. At trial, Fields denied that he was with the defendant on the night of the crime and denied making a previous statement to the police. The statement was admitted in evidence over the defendant's objection. On appeal, the defendant argued that the prosecutor had called Fields solely to impeach him with his earlier confession, thereby evading the hearsay rule. The appellate court found no violation of Rule 607. Although the court noted that "[t]he use of impeachment evidence against one's own witness is not without limitations," the court found no violation of Rule 607 in this case. The court stated that "the record indicates that the prosecutor was surprised by the testimony. We therefore cannot say that the State put Fields on the stand for the purpose of impeaching his testimony .... The impeachment testimony was permissible to undo the damage that Fields had done to the State's case. The trial court gave the jury an instruction limiting the use of the confession to its impeachment purpose." 88 Or App at 467.

Rehabilitation of Witnesses

A witness can be rehabilitated after being impeached. However, the credibility of witnesses cannot be "bolstered" before they have been impeached. Moreover, one witness may not comment on the credibility of another witness' trial testimony. For a discussion of the cases addressing the impropriety of commenting on the credibility of another witness, see discussion under Rule 702, infra.

Several rules in the code address rehabilitation of witnesses. Rule 613(2) provides that a witness impeached by extrinsic evidence of a prior inconsistent statement must be "afforded an opportunity to explain or deny the same." Rule 609-1(3) provides that: "Evidence to support or rehabilitate a witness whose credibility has been attacked by evidence of bias or interest shall be limited to evidence showing a lack of bias or interest."

Two primary methods of rehabilitation recognized by the code are evidence of truthful character and prior consistent statements. Rule 608(1) authorizes rehabilitation of a witness by reputation or opinion evidence concerning the witness' truthful character "after the character of the witness for truthfulness has been attacked by opinion or reputation evidence or otherwise." The Commentary to Rule 608 states that this method of rehabilitation is available not only when the witness has been impeached by reputation or opinion evidence of untruthful character, but also when the witness has been impeached by evidence of corruption or misconduct, including conviction of a crime. The Commentary states that evidence of bias or interest is not a sufficient attack on the character of the witness for truthfulness to allow this method of rehabilitation. See also Rule 609-1(3), supra.

Rehabilitation by evidence of prior consistent statements is indirectly addressed by Rule 801(4)(a)(B), which defines a prior statement as not hearsay if it is "consistent with the testimony of the witness and is offered to rebut an inconsistent statement or an express or implied charge against the witness of recent fabrication or improper influence or motive," provided the witness is subject to cross-examination regarding the statement. Under former law, a witness' prior consistent statements were admissible to rebut an opponent's suggestion that the testimony was a recent fabrication or the result of failing memory, or to bolster a denial that the prior inconsistent statement was made. *Cook v. Safeway Stores Inc.*, 266 Or 77, 511 P2d 375 (1973); *State v. Newberry*, 39 Or App 119, 591 P2d 404 (1979); *Hale v. Smith*, 254 Or 300, 460 P2d 351 (1969). The consistent statement must have been made prior to the alleged motive to fabricate. *Maeder Steel Products Co. v. Zanello*, 109 Or 562, 220 P 155 (1923). See also *Tome v. United States*, 115 SCt 696 (1995) (interpreting FRE 801(d)(1)(B) as requiring that a prior consistent statement offered to rehabilitate be made prior to the motive to fabricate). See generally ANNOT., *Admissibility, for Purpose of Supporting Impeached Witness, of Prior Statements By Him Consistent With His Testimony*, 75 ALR2d 909 (1961).

The Commentary to Rule 801(4)(a)(B) indicates that the legislature intended to preserve this prior case law, but also to make the prior consistent statement now admissible as substantive evidence as well as for rehabilitation. The legislature appears to have inadvertently changed prior law, however, by encompassing within Rule 801(4)(a)(B) prior consistent statements offered merely "to rebut an inconsistent statement." Prior case law did not go this far. See *Hale v. Smith*, 254 Or 300, 460 P2d 351 (1969). According to McCormick, many courts hold that mere impeachment by prior inconsistent statements does not open the door to proof of prior consistent statements, "since the inconsistency remains despite all consistent statements." 1 McCormick, *Evidence* (4th ed 1992) § 47 at 178.

Rule 801(4)(a)(B) does not require admission of prior consistent statements offered to rebut inconsistent statements; it only provides that under certain circumstances they are not hearsay. Therefore, courts could continue to apply the restrictions on the use of prior consistent statements recognized by prior law.

Other rules in the evidence code may also allow admission of prior consistent statements to rehabilitate a witness. See Rule 106 ("when part of an act, declaration, conversation or writing is given in evidence by one party, the whole on the same subject, where otherwise admissible, may at that time be inquired into by the other ..."); Rule 801(4)(a)(C) (statement of prior identification of a person made after perceiving the person); Rule 803(18a) ("A complaint of sexual misconduct made by the prosecuting witness after the commission of the alleged offense").

No Bolstering of Witness Rule

It is generally not permissible to attempt to enhance or bolster the credibility of a witness by evidence otherwise admissible for rehabilitation until the witness has been impeached. The Commentary to Rule 609-1 states: "It is settled case law that no 'supporting' evidence of lack of bias or interest is admissible unless evidence of bias or interest has been offered. *State v. Van Hooser,* 11 Or App 642, 501 P2d 78 (1972); *State v. Estlick,* [269 Or 75, 523 P2d 1029 (1974)]." Rule 608(1)(b) provides: "Evidence of truthful character is admissible only after the character of the witness for truthfulness has been attacked by opinion or reputation evidence or otherwise." See also *State v. Herrera,* 236 Or 1, 386 P2d 448 (1963) (prior consistent statements not admissible until witness has been impeached); *State v. Zybach,* 93 Or App 218, 223, 761 P2d 1334 (1988), rev'd on other grounds 308 Or 96 (1989) ("[I]t was not proper to approve rehabilitative testimony before there had been any impeachment.")

RULE 608.   ORS 40.350. EVIDENCE OF CHARACTER AND CONDUCT OF WITNESS

(1) The credibility of a witness may be attacked or supported by evidence in the form of opinion or reputation, but:
   (a) The evidence may refer only to character for truthfulness or untruthfulness; and
   (b) Evidence of truthful character is admissible only after the character of the witness for truthfulness has been attacked by opinion or reputation evidence or otherwise.
(2) Specific instances of the conduct of a witness, for the purpose of attacking or supporting the credibility of the witness, other than conviction of crime as provided in Rule 609 (ORS 40.355), may not be

proved by extrinsic evidence. Further, such specific instances of conduct may not, even if probative of truthfulness or untruthfulness, be inquired into on cross-examination of the witness.

LEGISLATIVE COMMENTARY

Oregon Rule of Evidence 608 indicates under what circumstances various types of character evidence regarding credibility may be admitted. The rule is a modified version of Rule 608 of the Federal Rules of Evidence. It replaces ORS 45.590, 45.600 and 45.620, which are repealed.

ORE 404 prohibits the admission of character evidence to prove that a person acted in conformity therewith, subject to several exceptions. One such exception is the admission of character evidence touching a witness' credibility. This rule develops that exception.

Subsection (1). While modern practice has purported to exclude opinion evidence, witnesses who testify to reputation are often offering opinion disguised as reputation. See McCormick, *Evidence* § 44 (2d ed 1972). This subsection recognizes that reality. Consistent with Rule 405, it allows a witness to testify both as to the reputation for veracity of another witness and as to the witness' opinion of another's veracity based upon personal knowledge. The allowance of reputation evidence to impeach or bolster credibility restates Oregon law. ORS 45.600; *McIntosh v. McNair,* 53 Or 87, 99 P 74 (1909); *Lucas v. Kaylor,* 136 Or 541, 299 P2d 197 (1931). The use of opinion evidence, however, is a departure from current practice.

Paragraph (a). In accordance with the bulk of judicial authority, inquiry is limited to character for veracity rather than character generally. The result is to sharpen relevancy and reduce surprise, waste of time and confusion. McCormick § 44 at 91.

Paragraph (b). Character evidence in support of credibility is admissible under this rule only after the witness' character has first been attacked. This limitation is found in Oregon law, ORS 45.620; *State v. Smith,* 4 Or App 261, 478 P2d 417 (1970), and in the common law as well, McCormick § 49 at 105; 4 Wigmore, *Evidence* § 1104 (3d ed 1940). Opinion or reputation that a witness is untruthful specifically qualifies as an "attack." Evidence of corruption or misconduct, including conviction of crime, also qualifies. Evidence of bias or interest does not. McCormick § 49; 4 Wigmore §§ 1106, 1107.

Subsection (2). In conformity with Rule 405, which forecloses the use of evidence of specific incidents to prove character unless character is an issue in the case, ORE 608 bars extrinsic evidence of specific instances of conduct for the purpose of attacking or supporting credibility. The rule carries one exception. A witness may be impeached, through another witness if necessary, by evidence of conviction of a crime of dishonesty or false statement. See Rule 609. Also note that under Rule 405(1) a witness may be indirectly impeached (or rehabilitated) during the cross-examination of witnesses who testify to the witness' character, by inquiry into specific instances of conduct. Both principles are now part of Oregon law.

The Legislative Assembly amended Federal Rule 608 in one respect. ORE 608 does not allow the credibility of a witness to be attacked directly by evidence of prior bad acts that did not result in conviction for a crime. Oregon courts have consistently prohibited such evidence. *Mannix v. Portland Telegram,* 144 Or 172, 23 P2d 138 (1933); *State v. White,* 48 Or 416, 87 P 137 (1906). The Legislative Assembly emphasizes its intention not to disturb this practice.

TEXT

RULE 608(1)
Impeachment by Evidence of Character for Untruthfulness

Rule 608(1) is an exception to Rule 404(2), which generally prohibits use of evidence of a person's character to prove that the person acted in conformity therewith on a particular occasion. Rule 608(1) allows evidence of a witness' character for untruthfulness or truthfulness as circumstantial evidence that the witness was untruthful or truthful during testimony.

This method of impeachment may be used against any person who takes the witness stand, including a criminal defendant. A distinction should be drawn between character evidence offered by a prosecutor under Rule 608(1) and under Rule 404(2)(a). Under Rule 608(1), the prosecutor can offer evidence only concerning the defendant's character for untruthfulness and only if the defendant takes the witness stand. Under Rule 404(2)(a), the prosecutor can offer evidence of a pertinent character trait of the defendant to rebut character evidence offered by the defendant, regardless of whether or not the defendant has taken the witness stand.

Rule 608(1), consistent with Rule 405(1), provides that the character of the witness may be proved by reputation evidence or opinion evidence. The authorization for proof of character by opinion evidence is a change from prior Oregon law. See textual discussion of Rule 405(1). Because opinion evidence is allowed, some courts have held that a character witness may be asked, "Would you believe this person under oath?" See *United States v. Lollar,* 606 F2d 587, 588–9 (5th Cir 1979). Proof of character by specific instances of conduct is not allowed.

A character witness, whether testifying in the form of reputation or opinion, will not be allowed to testify until a foundation has been laid showing that the witness has sufficient acquaintance with the reputation of the person in the relevant community or sufficient personal contact with the individual to have formed a personal opinion. The contact must have been sufficiently recent so that there will be a current basis for the testimony. *State v. Caffee,* 116 Or App 23, 27, 840 P2d 720 (1992), rev denied 315 Or 312, 846 P2d 1161 (1993) (character witness "did not have recent contacts with the victim sufficient to make her able to offer an opinion regarding [the victim's] truthfulness").

1 McCormick, *Evidence* (4th ed 1992) § 43 at 159 states:

[I]t is generally agreed that proof may be made not only of the reputation of the witness where he lives, but also of his repute, as long as it is "general" and established, in any substantial community of people among whom he is well known, such as the group with whom he works, does business or goes to school. (footnotes omitted)

Compare *United States v. Oliver,* 492 F2d 943, 946 (8th Cir 1974), cert denied 424 US 973 (1976) ("[T]hose persons who have had daily contact with the complaining witness, even though it was for a short period of two months, are competent to testify …") with *United States v. Salazar,* 425 F2d 1284, 1286 (9th Cir 1970) ("two months of occasional business dealings" insufficient basis for character testimony). The case of *State v. Miller,* 52 Or App 335, 628 P2d 444 (1981) would appear to stretch the outer limits of the rule. Miller allowed the prosecution to offer testimony by jail guards of defendant's reputation for truth and veracity in the jail "community" where defendant had been incarcerated for four and one-half months prior to his trial. Id. at 343.

To be admissible under this rule, the evidence must pertain to the witness' character for truthfulness or untruthfulness. Evidence regarding the witness' integrity or reliability would not qualify. See *McIntosh v. McNair,* 53 Or 87, 92, 99 P 74 (1909); *State v. Cameron,* 165 Or 176, 106 P2d 563 (1940).

See generally ANNOT., *Attacking or Supporting Credibility of Witness by Evidence in Form of Opinion or Reputation, Under Rule 608(a) of Federal Rules of Evidence,* 52 ALR Fed 440 (1981).

Rehabilitation by Evidence of Character for Truthfulness

Rule 608(1) allows not only impeachment of a witness by evidence of untruthful character, but also rehabilitation of the witness by showing character for truthfulness. Evidence of truthful character will not be allowed, however, until "the character of the witness for truthfulness has been attacked by opinion or reputation evidence or otherwise." See *State v. Neal,* 73 Or App 816, 699 P2d 1171, rev denied 299 Or 663, 704 P2d 514 (1985) (trial court was correct in excluding reputation evidence for truthfulness of witnesses when their character for truthfulness had not been attacked). In other words, it is generally improper to bolster the credibility of a witness before the witness has been attacked.

According to the Commentary, impeachment by evidence of corruption or misconduct, including conviction of a crime under Rule 609, constitutes a sufficient attack to justify this method of rehabilitation. Impeachment by evidence of bias or interest does not. See Rule 609-1(3): "Evidence to support or rehabilitate a witness whose credibility has been attacked by evidence of bias or interest shall be limited to evidence showing a lack of bias or interest."

The mere fact that a witness's testimony is contradicted by opposing testimony has been held not to warrant the introduction of evidence supporting the witness' character for truth and veracity. *State v. Allen,* 276 Or 527, 531, 555 P2d 443 (1976) (admission of reputation testimony to support a witness improper where "a witness's testimony is merely contradicted and no affirmative attack has been waged against his character").

In *State v. Carr,* 302 Or 20, 725 P2d 1287 (1986), a sex offense prosecution, the prosecutor attempted to rehabilitate the victim by calling her aunt as a character witness, who testified that the victim was honest and truthful. The issue on appeal was whether the character of the victim had been sufficiently attacked to justify receipt of such rehabilitation testimony. The state claimed that the character of the victim had been attacked in two ways. First, the victim's mother had testified that the victim was "rebelling right now," referring to the victim's trial testimony. Second, the defendant father had testified that the victim's testimony was not true. The Supreme Court held that neither the testimony of the mother nor the testimony of the father constituted an attack on the character of the victim, and therefore found that it was error to receive the aunt's testimony regarding the victim's truthfulness. Such evidence constituted impermissible bolstering of the victim's testimony. The court held that an attack on the character of a witness within the meaning of this rule does not include testimony by one witness suggesting that another witness is lying. 302 Or at 26.

Whether cross-examination will ever be a sufficient attack on a witness' character depends upon the circumstances.

> Moreover, a slashing cross-examination may carry strong accusations of misconduct and bad character, which the witness's denial will not remove from the jury's mind. If the judge considers that fairness requires it, he may permit evidence of good character, a mild palliative for the rankle of insinuation by such cross-examination. McCormick, EVIDENCE § 49 at 117 (3d ed 1984) (footnote omitted)

Compare *United States v. Lechoco,* 542 F2d 84, 89 n6 (DC Cir 1976) ("The prosecutor's vigorous cross-examination represents the type of attack on credibility contemplated by the term 'otherwise' as contained in Rule 608(a)") with *United States v. Jackson,* 588 F2d 1046 (5th Cir), cert denied 442 US 941 (1979) (close cross-examination not sufficient attack on character of witness to justify rehabilitation by character evidence for truthfulness).

RULE 608(2)
Prior Specific Instances of Conduct

Rule 608(2) bars impeachment of witnesses by inquiry or extrinsic evidence regarding prior specific instances of conduct not resulting in conviction of a crime. The prohibition applies even where the prior specific instances of conduct are probative of the witness' truthfulness or untruthfulness. This rule prevents a freewheeling and possibly prejudicial inquiry into accusations against a witness that have never been proved and that may not even involve violations of law.

Rule 608(2) is consistent with prior Oregon law. See ORS 45.600 (repealed 1981); *State v. Thayer,* 32 Or App 193, 573 P2d 758 (1978). It differs from FRE 608(b), which allows a witness to be cross-examined regarding prior specific instances of conduct not resulting in conviction of a crime that are probative of truthfulness or untruthfulness. See ANNOT., *Construction and Application of Rule*

608(b) of Federal Rules of Evidence, Dealing With Use of Specific Instances of Conduct to Attack or Support Credibility, 36 ALR Fed 564 (1978).

The prohibition against impeachment of a witness by prior specific instances of conduct other than conviction of a crime does not bar impeachment of a witness' direct testimony by contradictory evidence. In *State v. Schober,* 67 Or App 385, 678 P2d 746 (1984), the court held that Rule 608(2) was not violated by the admission of evidence of two prior instances where defendant had been drinking and driving, offered to contradict defendant's testimony on direct examination that "for all practical purposes I do not drink." However, evidence of prior bad acts normally cannot be used to contradict testimony elicited on cross-examination. See *State v. Peaslee,* 59 Or App 519, 651 P2d 182, *rev denied* 294 Or 212, 656 P2d 943 (1982).

There is a fine line between impeachment by prior bad acts and impeachment by contradiction. Impeachment by contradictory evidence involving prior bad acts may sometimes be allowed to rebut sweeping claims made on direct examination, at least in cases where the claim is significant and could unfairly prejudice a party or mislead the jury. See Moss, *The Sweeping Claims Exception in the Federal Rules of Evidence,* 1982 Duke L J 61.

In criminal cases, the prohibition in Rule 608(2) against impeachment of a witness by prior specific instances of conduct may sometimes be overridden by a defendant's right of confrontation. In *State v. LeClair,* 83 Or App 121, 730 P2d 609 (1986), rev denied 303 Or 74, 734 P2d 354 (1987), defendant was convicted of attempted rape and sexual abuse. He sought to impeach the child victim by evidence of prior instances where she had allegedly made false accusations against others. The court held:

> We conclude that, regardless of the prohibitions of OEC 608, the Confrontation Clause of Article 1, § 11, requires that the court permit a defendant to cross-examine the complaining witness in front of the jury concerning other accusations she has made if (1) she has recanted them; (2) the defendant demonstrates to the court that those accusations were false; or (3) there is some evidence that the victim has made prior accusations that were false, unless the probative value of the evidence which the defendant seeks to elicit on the cross-examination (including the probability that false accusations were in fact made) is substantially outweighed by the risk of prejudice, confusion, embarrassment or delay.

83 Or App at 130.

Recent Cases

In *Mulvahill v. Huddleston,* 110 Or App 405, 408, 822 P2d 754, 756 (1991), the court held that a prior pleading and prior statement by defendant that were allegedly false were properly excluded as impeachment evidence by Rule 608(2). The court held that such evidence was "not admissible simply to show that he putatively had a tendency to be untruthful."

In *State v. Moore*, 103 Or App 440, 797 P2d 1073 (1990), rev denied 311 Or 151, 806 P2d 128 (1991), the court held that it was improper to impeach a criminal defendant who had testified by introducing evidence that he may have been having an extramarital relationship with another woman.

In *State v. Hendricks*, 101 Or App 469, 791 P2d 139, rev denied 310 Or 133, 794 P2d 795 (1990), the defendant sought to introduce evidence of prior false accusation by a sex crime victim. The court held that such evidence did not involve "past sexual behavior" and hence was not regulated by OEC 412. Instead, such evidence was a prior instance of dishonesty, and OEC 608(2) forbids cross-examination regarding specific instances of conduct for impeachment purposes. Under the constitutional right of confrontation, a defendant may be allowed to cross-examine an accuser regarding prior false accusations. However, in this case, the defendant proposed to prove the prior false accusation by testimony of other witnesses rather than by cross-examination of the victim, and made no offer of proof with respect to what the victim would have said on cross-examination. Therefore, there was no error in excluding such evidence.

In *State v. Thompson*, 131 Or App 230, 238, 884 P2d 574, 578 (1994), rev denied 320 Or 508, 888 P2d 569 (1995), the court held that evidence that a complainant in a rape prosecution had previously traded sex for drugs was not a proper basis for impeaching her credibility under OEC 608(2).

Cross-Examination of Character Witness

The Commentary makes clear that Rule 608(2) is not intended to restrict the right of a party to cross-examine a character witness regarding prior specific instances of conduct of the person about whose character the witness is testifying. Cross-examination of a character witness by inquiry into relevant specific instances of conduct is expressly authorized by Rule 405(1). Because the only character trait about which a character witness may testify under Rule 608 is truthfulness or untruthfulness, the inquiry on cross-examination into specific instances of conduct must also be limited to incidents that are probative of truthfulness or untruthfulness. The examiner must "take the witness's answer" and may not prove the prior specific instances of conduct by extrinsic evidence. *United States v. Herzberg*, 558 F2d 1219, 1223 (5th Cir), cert denied 434 US 930 (1977).

The examiner must have a good faith factual basis for believing that the prior specific instances actually occurred. *United States v. Crippen*, 570 F2d 535, 538–9 (5th Cir 1978), cert denied 439 US 1069 (1979). The court may require a showing of the basis for the belief outside the presence of the jury. *United States v. Reese*, 568 F2d 1246, 1249 (6th Cir 1977). In *Michelson v. United States*, 335 US 469, 480–1, 69 SCt 213, 221, 93 LEd2d 168, 176 (1948), the court stated:

> Wide discretion is accompanied by heavy responsibility on trial courts to protect the practice from any misuse. The trial judge was scrupulous to so guard it in the case before us. He took pains to ascertain, out of presence of the jury, that the target of the question was an actual event. He satisfied himself that

counsel was not merely taking a random shot … or asking a groundless question to wait an unwarranted innuendo into the jury box. (footnote omitted)

The character witness may be questioned regarding not only prior convictions of the person being testified about, but also regarding prior arrests. *United States v. Watson,* 587 F2d 365 (7th Cir 1978), cert denied 439 US 1132 (1979); *United States v. Edwards,* 549 F2d 362 (5th Cir), cert denied 434 US 828 (1977).

Courts have discretion under Rule 403 to restrict the scope of cross-examination where the questions may be unfairly prejudicial, confuse the issues, or mislead the jury. Courts are likely to restrict questioning about specific instances of conduct that are too remote in time. *State v. Williams,* 44 Or App 387, 605 P2d 1361 (1980); 2 J. Weinstein and M. Berger, *Weinstein's Evidence* (1988) § 405[02]. A limiting instruction should generally be given under Rule 105 that explains the purpose of such evidence.

RULE 609. ORS 40.355. IMPEACHMENT BY EVIDENCE OF CONVICTION OF CRIME; EXCEPTIONS

(1) **For the purpose of attacking the credibility of a witness, evidence that the witness has been convicted of a crime shall be admitted if elicited from the witness or established by public record, but only if the crime (a) was punishable by death or imprisonment in excess of one year under the law under which the witness was convicted, or (b) involved false statement or dishonesty.**

(2) **Evidence of a conviction under this section is not admissible if:**

　　(a) **A period of more than 15 years has elapsed since the date of the conviction or of the release of the witness from the confinement imposed for that conviction, whichever is the later date; or**

　　(b) **The conviction has been expunged by pardon, reversed, set aside or otherwise rendered nugatory.**

(3) **When the credibility of a witness is attacked by evidence that the witness has been convicted of a crime, the witness shall be allowed to explain briefly the circumstances of the crime or former conviction; once the witness explains the circumstances, the opposing side shall have the opportunity to rebut the explanation.**

(4) **The pendency of an appeal therefrom does not render evidence of a conviction inadmissible. Evidence of the pendency of an appeal is admissible.**

(5) **An adjudication by a juvenile court that a child is within its jurisdiction is not a conviction of a crime.**

(6) **A conviction before, on or after November 4, 1993, of any of the statutory counterparts of offenses designated as violations as defined in ORS 161.565, may not be used to impeach the character of a witness in any criminal or civil action or proceeding.**

LEGISLATIVE COMMENTARY

Oregon Rule of Evidence 609 indicates the circumstances in which a witness may be impeached by evidence of a prior conviction. The rule is based on Rule 609 of the Federal Rules of Evidence. However, there are significant differences between the Oregon rule and both Federal Rule 609 and Oregon practice to date.

Subsection (1). The introductory phrase of the subsection states its purpose. The legitimate end of impeachment is not to show that a person who takes the stand is a "bad" person, but to show that the person cannot be believed. *Gordon v. United States,* 383 F2d 936, 940 (DC Cir 1967) (Burger, J.). Not all crimes are equally relevant to this purpose, as Bentham demonstrated more than a century ago:

> "Two men quarrel; one of them calls the other a liar. So highly does he prize the reputation of veracity, that, rather than suffer a stain to remain upon it, he determines to rid his life, challenges his adversary to fight, and kills him. Jurisprudence, in its sapience, knowing no difference between homicide by consent, by which no other human being is put in fear—and homicide in pursuit of a scheme of highway robbery or nocturnal housebreaking, by which every man who has a life is put in fear of it—has made the one and the other murder, and consequently felony. The man prefers death to the imputation of a lie—and the inference of the law is, that he cannot open his mouth but lies will issue from it. Such are the inconsistencies which are unavoidable in the applications of any rule which takes improbity for a ground of exclusion." 7 Bentham, *Rationale of Judicial Evidence* 406 (Brownings ed 1827).

Aside from the low probative value of some convictions, the divulgence of a criminal past often exposes a witness to jury prejudice. In one recent survey 98% of the attorneys, and 43% of the judges, indicated their belief that a jury is unable to follow an instruction to consider prior conviction evidence only for the purpose of evaluating credibility. "To Take the Stand or Not to Take the Stand: The Dilemma of the Defendant with a Criminal Record," in 4 Colum J Law and Soc Prob 213 (1968). To inform the jury in a rape case that the defendant has a prior rate conviction, and then to instruct the jury to consider the conviction only in evaluating the defendant's credibility, is to recommend "a mental gymnastic which is beyond not only their power, but anybody else." *Nash v. United States,* 54 F2d 1006, 1007 (2nd Cir 1932) (L. Hand, J.).

For the reasons just expressed, the Legislative Assembly abandoned Oregon's practice of allowing a witness to be impeached by evidence of any crime. ORS 45.600. Although there has been authority for the view that violation of a city ordinance cannot be used to impeach, *State v. Crawford,* 58 Or 116, 113 P 440 (1911); *Redsecker v. Wade,* 69 Or 153, 164, 134 P 5, 138 P 485 (1914), apparently even such a noncriminal offense has been admissible if it is punishable by incarceration. *State v. Bunse,* 27 Or App 299, 555 P2d 1269 (1977).

As proposed to the Legislative Assembly, this subsection did not allow a witness to be impeached by evidence of former conviction except during cross-examination. Such a rule would prevent the proponent of a witness from presenting this damaging evidence, making it appear that the party or the witness had attempted to hide the conviction from the trier of fact, or at least had not been open about it. In fairness, either side should be allowed to elicit such evidence. The Legislative Assembly therefore deleted the limitation of impeachment by crime to "cross-examination."

Convictions in an Oregon justice or municipal court, or in similar courts of other states, however designated, may not be used for impeachment. The offenses triable in these courts do not involve serious moral depravity. Furthermore, the proceedings are relatively informal and often stray from the standards of a criminal trial in a court of record.

As for proceedings in a court of record, the Legislative Assembly intends that a prior conviction be admitted for the purpose of impeaching a witness' credibility if—and only if—the conviction was for one of two sorts of crime. The categories are described in paragraphs (a) and (b) of this subsection.

An offense is impeachable if its elements place it within one of the two described categories. The Legislative Assembly specifically rejects any further inquiry into the facts behind a judgment to determine its suitability for the purpose of impeachment. Although analyzing the facts of a prior conviction may well be helpful in some cases, it is very time-consuming and leads to uncertainty. A conviction of arson, for example, may not be used to impeach under Rule 609(1)(b), because arson is not a crime of false statement, even if the evidence showed that the particular arson was committed with intent to defraud an insurance company. If the same act were charged and proved as attempt to commit fraud, however, the judgment could be used. By the same reasoning, an arson conviction may not be used to impeach even if the defendant in the earlier trial took the stand and was disbelieved by the jury. If the person were charged and convicted of perjury as a result of that testimony, however, the perjury conviction would be admissible.

Author's Note: The following section of the Legislative Commentary regarding the balancing test in former Rule 609(1)(a) has been superseded by the 1986 amendment to Rule 609 that eliminated the balancing requirement.

Paragraph (a). This paragraph is identical to paragraph (1) of subdivision (a) of Federal Rule 609. The federal commentary makes it clear that the balancing of probative value against prejudice only applies in a criminal case and then only on behalf of the defendant. A felony conviction is otherwise automatically admissible to impeach a witness:

"With regard to the discretionary standard established by paragraph (1) of rule 609(a), the Conference determined that the prejudicial effect to be weighed against the probative value of the conviction is specifically the prejudicial effect *to the defendant*. The danger of prejudice to a witness other than the defendant (such as injury to the witness' reputation in [the] community) was considered and rejected by the Conference as an element to be weighed in determining admissibility. It was the judgment of the Conference that the danger of prejudice to a nondefendant witness is outweighed by the need for the trier of fact to have as much relevant evidence on the issue of credibility as possible. Such evidence should only be excluded where it presents a danger of improperly influencing the outcome of the trial by persuading the trier of fact to convict the defendant on the base of [the defendant's] prior criminal record." (Original emphasis.)

The federal commentary is silent on how to determine admissibility of a prior felony conviction, when balancing is required. Prior to the adoption of the Federal Rules of Evidence, the Circuit Court for the District of Columbia developed a four-factor test. *Gordon v. United States,* supra, 383 F2d at 940–941.

The Legislative Assembly approves this test for use under Rule 609. The factors are:

The nature of the crime. This factor requires the court to analyze the prior crime in terms of relevance to credibility. For example, a smuggling conviction is more probative than an assault. If the prior crime ranks high on a veracity scale, then this factor favors admissibility.

Date of conviction and subsequent criminal history. This factor requires the court to analyze the history of crime in terms of a present disposition to adhere to any norm, including that of telling the truth. For example, a conviction six months before trial is more probative than one that occurred six years before trial. However, a conviction six years earlier gains in relevance if the witness' subsequent record shows a pattern of continuing criminal activity.

Similarity to crime charged. This factor relates to prejudicial impact on the accused. If the elements of the prior conviction are similar to those of the crime charged, then analysis under this factor favors exclusion of the prior conviction. Where multiple convictions of various kinds can be shown, strong reasons arise for excluding those that are for the same or a similar crime. Inevitably there is pressure on lay jurors to use these as substantive evidence of guilt even though they are not admissible as such under ORE 404(3). As a general guide, these convictions should be used sparingly. See, e.g., *United States v. Bailey,* 426 F2d 1236 (DC Cir 1970) (excluding evidence of prior conviction for receiving stolen goods in trial for robbery).

The importance of the defendant's testimony. If the testimony of the accused is crucial to a fair determination of the issues, as it would be in an assault/self-defense case without independent witnesses, then this factor tends to favor exclusion. The more central the issue of credibility is to a fair determination of guilt, the more desirable it is to encourage the accused to testify. The court need not take defendant's testimony to decide its importance. In the interest of judicial efficiency, the court may make this determination based upon a summary of the accused's testimony as presented by defense counsel. Additionally, the court may take into consideration other remarks made by respective counsel about the nature of the case, and evidence already introduced, if any.

With respect to balancing the probative value of evidence against its capacity to prejudice a particular party, the Legislative Assembly does not anticipate any difference between the results of this paragraph and Rule 403.

Paragraph (b). The federal rule allows impeachment by evidence of any crime of "dishonesty or false statement." However, the federal courts have generally concluded that "dishonesty" adds nothing of substance to "false statement" for the purpose of impeachment, and therefore tend to give the terms the same meaning. See, e.g., *United States v. Ortega,* 561 F2d 803 (9th Cir 1977); *United States v. Seamster,* 568 F2d 188 (9th Cir 1978). The Legislative Assembly adopted that conclusion and deleted the reference to "dishonesty."

Author's Note: The 1986 amendment to Rule 609 restored the word "dishonesty."

Crimes of false statement involve some element of untruthfulness, falsification or deceit bearing on the witness' propensity to testify truthfully. The deceit involved is more than the mere effort of the criminal actor to hide the fact of crime or the identity of the actor from the authorities: by this reasoning all crimes would be crimes of deceit. Rather, the operative deceit must be of the crime victim. Depending on the crime, that may be a trier of fact, in the case of perjury; a storekeeper, in the case of negotiating a bad check; a family member, in the case of bigamy; a correspondent, in the case of alteration of a telegraphic message; or the general public, in the case of bribery. Deceit can be said to exist if the victim of the crime is not aware, at the time of its commission, either of its existence, or of its criminality, or of its full range of consequences to the victim. The deception may be affirmative, or it may take the form of allowing a person who is deceived to remain so.

Certain crimes involve false statement by their very nature. The Legislative Assembly has compiled a partial list of such crimes in Oregon. It intends that these, and their inchoate forms, see ORS 161.405 et seq., be admissible for impeachment purposes in every case. A trial court does not have discretion to exclude them.

Offenses Against State & Public Justice

162.015 - Bribe giving
162.025 - Bribe receiving
162.065 - Perjury
162.075 - False swearing
162.085 - Unsworn falsification
162.195 - Failure to appear II
162.205 - Failure to appear I
162.265 - Bribing a witness
162.275 - Bribe receiving by witness
162.285 - Tampering with witness
162.295 - Tampering with physical evidence
162.305 - Tampering with public records
162.325 - Hindering prosecution
162.355 - Simulating legal process
162.365 - Criminal impersonation
162.375 - Initiating a false report
162.425 - Misuse of confidential information
162.465 - Unlawful legislative lobbying

Offenses Against Persons

163.515 - Bigamy
163.605[1] - Criminal defamation—"false" matter

Offenses Against Property

164.015(2) - Theft—by failure to restore known lost property
164.015(4) - Theft—by deception
164.015(5) - Theft—by receiving stolen goods
164.125(1)(a)[3] - Theft of services—by deception
164.125(1)(b) -Theft of services—by exercising control to divert labor/materials
164.135(1)(b) - Unauthorized use of vehicle—diversion while being
            repaired/used

Offenses Involving Fraud or Deception

165.007 - Forgery II
165.013 - Forgery I
165.017 - Criminal possession of forged instrument II
165.022 - Criminal possession of forged instrument I
165.032 - Criminal possession of forgery device
165.037 - Criminal simulation
165.042 - Fraudulently obtaining a signature
165.047 - Unlawfully using slugs
165.055 - Fraudulent use of credit card
165.065 - Negotiating bad check
165.070 - Possession of fraudulent communication device
165.080 - Falsifying business records
165.085 - Sports bribery
165.090 - Sports bribe receiving
165.095 - Misapplication of entrusted property
165.100 - Issuing false financial statement
165.102 - Obtaining execution of documents by deception
165.485 - Wrongful alteration of telegraphic message
165.490 - Use of information contained in message
165.805 - Misrepresentation of age
165.825 - Sale of drugged horse

Offenses Against Public Order; Firearms

166.065(1)(c) - Harassment—false report of death/injury
166.450 - Obliteration/change of mark on firearm

Offenses Against Public Health & Decency

167.212 - Tampering with drug records
167.820 - Concealing birth of infant

Income Taxation Generally

314.075 - Income tax evasion

Higher Education Generally

351.___ - Sale of assignments (HB 2513)

Alcoholic Liquors Generally

471.135 - False age statement for identification card

Controlled Substances

475.992(3) - Creation/delivery of counterfeit substance

The above list is offered by way of illustration, not limitation. There are other crimes, under Oregon law and the law of other jurisdictions, whose elements are substantially equivalent to those listed. Counsel may use such unlisted crimes to impeach a witness upon proper showing. Normally the issue should be raised by motion *in limine,* as the court's ruling may have important tactical consequences at trial. The burden of persuasion rests upon the movant to show, by a preponderance of the evidence, that the elements of a given crime are substantially equivalent to those of a listed crime. The Legislative Assembly intends that the trial court have full discretion in passing on any such motion.

An argument can be made that any offense purporting to be consensual but which is committed against a person who is incapable of giving consent by reason of age or mental capacity, involves an element of deception and should qualify as impeachment material. Other rationales have been suggested for crimes that involve an invasion of privacy, destruction of privilege, trespass or theft. Although the facts of a prior conviction in the latter categories may often involve an element of deceit or untruthfulness, the Legislative Assembly rejected their inclusion on this basis because the elements of the crimes themselves do not involve false statement.

Subsection (2). Oregon statutes and case law have not recognized a time limit on impeachment by evidence of conviction. The Legislative Assembly believes that considerations of fairness and relevancy demand that some time limit be recognized. Subsection (2) provides that upon the expiration of ten years from the later of the date of conviction of a witness or the witness' release from confinement for the offense, the conviction may no longer be used for impeachment.

Subsection (3). This subsection allows a witness impeached by evidence of a prior conviction to explain briefly the circumstances of the crime or former conviction. It is in accord with current Oregon law. *State v. Washington,* 36 Or App 547, 585 P2d 24 (1978); *State v. Gilbert,* 282 Or 309, 577 P2d 939 (1978).

Subsection (4). A presumption of correctness attends all judicial proceedings. It follows that pendency of an appeal does not preclude the use of a conviction for impeachment. *State v. Forsythe,* 20 Or App 624, 533 P2d

176, SCt review denied (1975). However, the pendency of an appeal is a qualifying circumstance which the trier of fact may properly consider.

Subsection (5). An adjudication by a juvenile court that a child is within its jurisdiction is not a "conviction of a crime." Problems of administration, as well as policy, would be raised by the provision in ORS chapter 419 that records of juvenile court proceedings be kept confidential. ORS 419.543. Accord, *State v. Gustafson,* 248 Or 1, 432 P2d 323 (1967).

TEXT

Impeachment by Criminal Convictions

Rule 609 establishes that a witness may be impeached by evidence of a prior criminal conviction, provided that (1) the crime was punishable by death or imprisonment in excess of one year, or (2) the crime, regardless of penalty, involved false statement or dishonesty.

The following additional qualifications apply:

(1)   No more than 15 years can have elapsed from the date of conviction or the date of release of the witness from confinement imposed for that conviction, whichever is the later date.

(2)   The conviction must not have been expunged by pardon, reversed, set aside, or otherwise rendered nugatory.

(3)   A conviction that is being appealed may still be used, but evidence of the pendency of the appeal is admissible.

(4)   The witness shall be allowed to explain briefly the circumstances of the crime or former conviction, and the opposing side shall have an opportunity to rebut the explanation.

(5)   An adjudication by a juvenile court that a child is within its jurisdiction is not a conviction under this rule.

(6)   Offenses designated as violations may not be used to impeach.

Rule 609 does not allow impeachment, in either civil or criminal cases, by misdemeanor convictions not involving false statement or dishonesty. ORS 153.590 prohibits impeachment based on convictions for traffic infractions.

A party may bring out prior criminal convictions of his own witness in order to weaken the impact of prior crime impeachment by the opposing party. See Rule 607; *State v. Gilbert,* 282 Or 309, 577 P2d 939 (1978).

Rule 609 represents a significant modification of previous Oregon law. Prior to the adoption of the Evidence Code, a witness, including a criminal defendant, could be impeached by conviction of any crime, even if the crime was unrelated to veracity, remote in time, or prejudicial. ORS 45.600 (repealed 1981); *Marshall v. Martinson,* 268 Or 46, 518 P2d 1312 (1974). The danger of allowing a criminal defendant to be impeached by evidence of a prior criminal conviction is that the jury may conclude that because of the previous crime, the defendant is more likely to have committed the charged offense. Use of the evidence for such a purpose is expressly prohibited by Rule 404(2), which provides: "Evidence of a person's character is not admissible for the purpose of proving that the person acted in conformity therewith on a particular occasion ....”

The rationale for excluding this evidence has been explained by the United States Supreme Court as follows: “[T]he inquiry is not rejected because character is irrelevant; on the contrary, it is said to weigh too much with the jury and to so over persuade them as to prejudge one with a bad general record and deny him a fair opportunity to defend against a particular charge.” (footnote omitted) *Michelson v. United States*, 335 US 469, 475–6, 69 SCt 213, 218, 93 LEd2d 168, 174 (1948).

RULE 609(1)(a)
Felony Convictions

Although Rule 609(1)(a) does not use the term “felony,” it allows impeachment by any criminal conviction “punishable by death or imprisonment in excess of one year under the law under which the witness was convicted.” In most jurisdictions, this definition encompasses only felony crimes. However, in a few states this definition may include criminal convictions that are not felonies. The determination of whether a conviction fits this definition is made on the basis of the potential punishment, not the punishment actually imposed. In *State v. Smith*, 298 Or 173, 691 P2d 89 (1984), the court held that a witness may be impeached by a showing that he was found guilty of a Class C felony, even though the ultimate judgment entered by the court was for a Class A misdemeanor. The court noted that Rule 609 focuses on whether the crime is “punishable” by imprisonment for more than one year rather than on the actual conviction or punishment imposed.

The original version of Rule 609 required that before prior felony convictions not involving false statement could be admitted against a criminal defendant, the court must first make a finding that “the probative value of admitting this evidence outweighs its prejudicial effect to the defendant.” However, Ballot Measure No. 10, approved by the voters on November 4, 1986, amended the rule to delete this balancing requirement. A balancing requirement continues to exist under FRE 609. See ANNOT., *Construction and Application of Rule 609(a) of the Federal Rules of Evidence Permitting Impeachment of Witness By Evidence of Prior Conviction of Crime*, 39 ALR Fed 570 (1978).

Under Rule 609 as amended, any felony conviction within the applicable time period may be used for impeachment of any witness in either a civil or criminal case. In *State v. King*, 307 Or 332, 768 P2d 391 (1989), the Oregon Supreme Court held that the trial judge had no discretion under Rule 403 to exclude a felony conviction admissible under Rule 609 to impeach a defendant in a criminal case. Similarly, in *Boger v. Norris & Stevens, Inc.*, 109 Or App 90, 95–6, 818 P2d 947, 949–50 (1991), rev denied 312 Or 588, 824 P2d 417 (1992), the court held that prior felony convictions are admissible to attack the credibility of a witness even in civil cases without any balancing of probative value against unfair prejudice. However, trial judges retain discretion to exclude such evidence on grounds that relate to the administration of the proceedings, such as where it is cumulative. See *State v. Pratt*, 316 Or 561, 570–3, 853 P2d 827, cert denied 114 SCt 452 (1993) (where witness admits the prior convictions on cross-examination, court retains discretion to exclude the actual records of conviction as "cumulative").

In *State v. Minnieweather*, 99 Or App 166, 781 P2d 401 (1989), the court rejected the arguments that elimination of the balancing test from OEC 609 with respect to prior crime impeachment violated the defendant's right to be heard in his own defense or the right to an impartial jury. See COMMENT, *Sword and Shield: An Analysis of Criminal Defendant's Right to Be Heard Under Article I, Section 11 of the Oregon Constitution*, 28 Willamette L Rev 127 (1991).

FRE 609 has been amended to require balancing under FRE 403 before prior convictions not involving dishonesty or false statment can be admitted to impeach witnesses other than a criminal defendant. For criminal defendants, FRE 609 allows impeachment by prior convictions only if the probative value of such evidence outweighs its prejudicial effect to the accused.

RULE 609(1)(b)
Crimes Involving False Statement

In both civil and criminal cases, subject to the limitations of Rule 609(2), a witness may be impeached by evidence of a conviction of any crime involving false statement or dishonesty, whether punishable as a felony or misdemeanor. The determination of whether the crime involved false statement or dishonesty will always be necessary for misdemeanors. If the crime was a felony, it will automatically be admissible under Rule 609(1)(a) even though not involving false statement or dishonesty.

The original version of Rule 609(1)(b) referred only to crimes involving "false statement." Ballot Measure No. 10, approved by the voters on November 4, 1986, amended the rule to refer also to crimes involving "dishonesty."

In *State v. Gallant*, 307 Or 152, 764 P2d 920 (1988), the court held that a conviction of second degree theft for shoplifting was admissible as a crime involving dishonesty. In an earlier case under the former version of Rule 609, the Court of Appeals held that shoplifting was not a crime involving "false statement." The *Gallant* decision stated that "Nothing in our decision today is to be construed as a determination of whether shoplifting constitutes a false statement." 307 Or at 157 n6.

Whether a particular crime involves false statement is to be determined by an examination of its statutory elements. The Commentary states:

> The Legislative Assembly specifically rejects any further inquiry into the facts behind a judgment to determine its suitability for the purpose of impeachment. ... A conviction for arson, for example, may not be used to impeach under Rule 609(1)(b), because arson is not a crime of false statement, even if the evidence showed that the particular arson was committed with intent to defraud an insurance company.

A listing of Oregon statutes legislatively determined to involve false statement is included in the Commentary. This listing will be useful not only in determining the admissibility of Oregon convictions, but also as a guideline for determining the admissibility of convictions from other jurisdictions.

The Commentary states that for crimes not on this list the issue can be raised as to whether they involve false statement by the filing of a motion *in limine*. According to the Commentary, the "burden of persuasion rests upon the movant to show ... that the elements of a given crime are substantially equivalent to those of a listed crime." The difficulty with this statement is that either party could be the "movant." The burden should be on the party seeking to use a conviction for impeachment purposes under Rule 609(1)(b) to show that the crime involves false statement or dishonesty and that the requirements of Rule 609 are otherwise satisfied.

Revealing Only Fact of Conviction, Not Crime of Conviction

At one time the appellate courts held that in appropriate cases impeachment of a criminal defendant should be limited to a showing of the fact of prior conviction without disclosing the nature of the conviction. In *State v. McClure,* 298 Or 336, 353, 692 P2d 579 (1984), the court stated that "for future 'similar crimes' cases ... the prosecutor should be limited to merely asking the defendant if he has been convicted of a felony without specifying the type of crime so as to reduce the chances of the jury interpreting the cross-examination as an attack on character as opposed to its proper limits as an attack on credibility."

However, in the more recent case of *State v. Venegas*, 124 Or App 253, 256, 862 P2d 529, 531 (1993), rev denied 318 Or 351, 870 P2d 220 (1994), the court held that a trial judge should not limit OEC 609 impeachment by allowing the prosecutor to prove only the existence of a prior conviction but not the name of the crime for which the witness was convicted.

As a matter of policy, trial courts should have discretion under Rule 403 to limit impeachment to the fact of conviction in any case where there is significant danger that revealing the crime of conviction will cause unfair prejudice to the defendant and be interpreted as an attack on character rather than credibility.

The doctrine of limiting prior crime impeachment to the fact of conviction is recognized in the federal courts. See 1 M. Graham, HANDBOOK OF FEDERAL EVIDENCE (4th ed 1996) § 609.6; *United States v. Fields,* 500 F2d 69, 71–2 (6th Cir), cert denied 419 US 1071 (1974) (McCree, J., concurring in part, dissenting in part) ("Because prejudice arises from informing a jury of an accused's previous convictions in the manner permitted by the district court in this case, I would prohibit such disclosure when an accused is willing, as was Fields, to stipulate to the existence of his prior felony convictions"). Such a suggestion was adopted in *United States v. Wilson,* 556 F2d 1177 (4th Cir), cert denied 434 US 986 (1977), where the court, in a rape prosecution, allowed the prosecution to impeach the defendant only by disclosing that he had been previously convicted of a felony without revealing that the earlier conviction was also for rape. See also *United*

States v. Fay, 668 F2d 375 (8th Cir 1981) (nature of conviction not allowed to be revealed).

Prior to the adoption of the Evidence Code, the Supreme Court commented with approval on the approach of limiting disclosure to the fact of conviction without revealing the nature of the offense. In *Smith v. Durant,* 271 Or 643, 662 n10, 534 P2d 955, 964 n10 (1975), Justice Tongue stated:

> Another alternative would be the adoption of a rule to the effect that upon the impeachment of a witness for the prior conviction of a crime (however that term may be defined or limited) the nature of the crime could not be revealed to the jury by the party impeaching the witness unless the witness denies having been previously convicted of a crime. Thus, except in the event of such a denial, the impeachment would be limited to the more neutral fact of the commission of "a crime." This would minimize the danger of prejudice from the fact that the previous crime involved conduct of the same nature as that for which the party is charged in the subsequent trial and would leave it to the party calling the witness to decide whether on re-examination, to reveal the nature of that crime in the course of explaining any mitigating circumstances relating to the prior conviction.

See generally Gold, *Sanitizing Prior Conviction Impeachment Evidence to Reduce Its Prejudicial Effects,* 27 Ariz L Rev 691 (1985).

Disclosure of Sentence, Punishment Imposed

Apart from the issue of limiting disclosure of the crime of conviction, there is the separate issue of whether the sentence imposed for the prior crime may be disclosed to the jury. The rule does not specifically allow disclosure of the sentence imposed. Disclosing the sentence imposed can raise irrelevant and possibly prejudicial issues. See *State v. Gallant,* 307 Or 152, 764 P2d 920 (1988) (state concedes error in prosecutor's inquiry regarding the fact that sentence of probation was imposed for prior crime used for impeachment and fact that probation was revoked, although court finds error harmless in this case).

See generally ANNOT., *Propriety, On Impeaching Credibility of Witness In Civil Case By Showing Former Conviction, Of Questions Relating to Nature and Extent of Punishment,* 67 ALR3d 761 (1975); ANNOT., *Propriety, On Impeaching Credibility of Witness In Criminal Case By Showing Former Conviction, Of Questions Relating to Nature and Extent of Punishment,* 67 ALR3d 775 (1975).

The Meaning of "Conviction" Under Rule 609

Rule 609 is silent on the admissibility of convictions in foreign jurisdictions or court-martial convictions. Courts interpreting FRE 609 have allowed impeachment on the basis of convictions in foreign jurisdictions, providing the procedural protections were adequate to insure reliability. See *United States v. Wilson,* 556 F2d 1177 (4th Cir), cert denied 434 US 986 (1977) (rape conviction in Germany); *United States v. Manafzadeh,* 592 F2d 81 (2nd Cir 1979) (fraud conviction in Iran). Some courts allow impeachment based on court-martial convictions. See

ANNOT., *Conviction by Court-Martial As Proper Subject of Cross-Examination For Impeachment Purposes,* 7 ALR4th 468 (1981).

Under prior Oregon law, a witness could not be impeached on the basis of a jury verdict of guilty upon which a judgment of conviction had not yet been entered. *State v. Bouthillier,* 4 Or App 145, 476 P2d 209 (1970). However, such use seems appropriate. An apparent majority of courts considering this issue under FRE 609 have allowed witnesses to be impeached on the basis of a guilty verdict upon which a judgment of conviction has not yet been entered. See *United States v. Smith,* 623 F2d 627 (9th Cir 1980); *United States v. Duncan,* 598 F2d 839 (4th Cir), cert denied 444 US 871 (1979); *United States v. Klein,* 560 F2d 1236 (5th Cir 1977), cert denied 434 US 1073 (1978). See generally ANNOT., *Permissibility of Impeaching Credibility of Witness by Showing Verdict of Guilty Without Judgment of Sentence Thereon,* 14 ALR3d 1272 (1967); ANNOT., *Permissibility of Impeaching Credibility of Witness by Showing Verdict of Guilty Without Judgment of Sentence Thereon,* 28 ALR4th 647 (1984).

In criminal cases where guilt or innocence rests on the defendant's credibility, the defendant may not be impeached by prior convictions obtained in violation of the constitutional right to counsel. *Loper v. Beto,* 405 US 473, 92 SCt 1014, 31 LEd2d 374 (1972); *Spiegel v. Sandstrom,* 637 F2d 405 (5th Cir 1981). The Oregon Supreme Court has refused to extend this rule to civil cases. See *Reinsch v. Quines,* 274 Or 97, 546 P2d 135 (1976).

Convictions in Justice Court or Municipal Court

The original version of Rule 609(1) provided: "For the purpose of attacking the credibility of a witness, evidence that the witness had been convicted of a crime *in other than a justice's court or a municipal court* shall be admitted. ..." The Legislative Commentary explained that this limitation was imposed because "offenses triable in these courts do not involve serious moral depravity" and "the proceedings are relatively informal, and often stray from the standards of a criminal trial in a court of record."

As the Oregon Supreme Court explained in *State v. Gallant,* 307 Or 152, 154 n2, 764 P2d 920 (1988):

> For unknown reasons, the drafters of the "Crime Victims' Bill of Rights" omitted the exception for convictions in justice's courts and municipal courts from the text of OEC 609. Compare former OEC 609(1) with Official 1986 General Voters' Pamphlet 50. The ballot measure did not bracket and italicize the deletion, as it did with other deletions of statutory text to show voters what changes were proposed. Nothing in the text of the initiative or its explanation in the voters' pamphlet informed the voters that the enactment would delete this text.

Because the passage of the ballot measure indicates no intention to reverse the 1981 Legislature's decision to prohibit use of justice court or municipal court convictions for impeachment under Rule 609(1), a strong argument can be made that this prohibition should continue to be respected. But this view was rejected in *State v. Linn,* 131 Or App 487, 489–90, 885 P2d 721 (1994) (because this limitation is no longer in current version of rule, prior convictions in municipal court can be used for impeachment purposes under OEC 609).

Evidence of Prior Crimes Admissible for Purposes Other than Rule 609 Impeachment

Rule 609 states when a witness can be impeached by evidence of prior criminal convictions. It does not limit evidence of prior crimes when offered for some other purpose. See Rule 404(3) (evidence of other crimes may be admissible to prove motive, opportunity, intent, etc.); Rule 405(1) (character witness may be cross-examined regarding pertinent instances of conduct, including crimes, of persons about whose character the witness testified); Rule 609-1 (witness may be impeached by evidence of bias, e.g., pending charges against prosecution witness).

In some circumstances, evidence of prior criminal convictions may be allowed to rebut false statements made by the defendant on direct examination or volunteered upon cross-examination. The Report of the Senate Judiciary Committee regarding FRE 609 addressed this issue:

> [T]he committee intends that notwithstanding this rule, a defendant's misrepresentations regarding the existence or nature of prior convictions may be met by rebuttal evidence, including the record of such prior convictions. Similarly, such records may be offered to rebut representations made by the defendant regarding his attitude toward or willingness to commit a general category of offense, although denials or other representations by the defendant regarding the specific conduct which forms the basis of the charge against him shall not make prior convictions admissible to rebut such statement.
>
> In regard to either type of representation, of course, prior convictions may be offered in rebuttal only if the defendant's statement is made in response to defense counsel's questions or is made gratuitously in the course of cross-examination. Prior convictions may not be offered as rebuttal evidence if the prosecution has sought to circumvent the purpose of this rule by asking questions which elicit such representations from the defendant. (5 Rep No. 1277, 93d Cong, 2d Sess 14 (1974))

Such a use of prior convictions has been recognized under prior Oregon law. See *State v. Miles*, 8 Or App 189, 492 P2d 497 (1972) (cross-examination regarding prior traffic convictions allowed where defendant testified on direct examination that he had not been convicted of any traffic violations during previous three years).

Some courts granting motions *in limine* to exclude evidence of prior convictions have conditioned the order on the requirement that the defendant not volunteer testimony suggesting a pristine criminal record. See *United States v. Jackson*, 405 F Supp 938 (EDNY 1975) (excluding prior convictions unless defendant testifies he has never been in trouble with the law).

Motions In Limine

The Commentary expressly sanctions the use of motions *in limine* as a means of determining the admissibility of prior criminal convictions for the purpose of impeachment under Rule 609. Appellate courts interpreting Rule 609 have encouraged trial judges to make a pretrial ruling, when feasible, so that the defendant can make an informed decision on whether or not to testify. See *State v. Busby*, 315 Or 292, 300, 844 P2d 897 (1993) (reaffirming approval of ruling on admissibility of prior crime impeachment as soon as possible after issue is raised, because "a defendant's decision whether to testify has a significant impact on what questions to ask jurors during voir dire, what to say in opening statements, and the questioning of witnesses"). *State v. McClure*, 298 Or 336, 340, 692 P2d 579, 583 (1984).

Although a pretrial ruling is clearly preferable, in some cases it may not be feasible to make the ruling until trial. It has been held that Rule 609 does not entitle a defendant to a pretrial ruling. *State v. Foster*, 296 Or 174, 674 P2d 587 (1983). See also *United States v. Jackson*, 627 F2d 1198 (DC Cir 1980); *United States v. Johnston*, 543 F2d 55 (8th Cir 1976).

A criminal defendant, by not testifying, does not waive the right to challenge on appeal the trial court's ruling allowing impeachment by prior convictions. *State v. McClure*, 298 Or 336, 692 P2d 579 (1984) (defendant may challenge pretrial ruling of a court admitting a prior conviction to impeach the defendant if he testifies, even though the defendant does not take the stand at trial). The rule in federal courts is to the contrary. *Luce v. United States*, 469 US 38, 105 SCt 460, 83 LEd2d 443 (1984) (defendant must take stand at trial in order to challenge FRE 609 ruling).

However, counsel should be certain that any pretrial ruling regarding Rule 609 issues is sufficiently definitive to make a record for appeal. In *State v. Johnson*, 64 Or App 658, 669 P2d 1151 (1983), rev denied 296 Or 638, 678 P2d 739 (1984), the trial judge gave a tentative indication that impeachment by prior convictions would be allowed and the defendant did not take the stand. The appellate court refused to review the Rule 609 issue, stating: "There is no indication in the record as to why defendant chose not to take the stand. The court was not presented with the necessity to rule finally on the admissibility of the prior convictions and there is no final ruling for us to review." 64 Or App at 660, 669 P2d at 1152–3.

Although a pretrial ruling that certain convictions will be admissible to impeach a witness should be sufficient to preserve the issue for appeal, counsel opposing such impeachment may wish to object for the record at trial as well. Once a court has made a ruling allowing prior convictions to impeach a witness, the party calling the witness should be entitled to bring out those convictions on direct examination of the witness without waiving the right to challenge the ruling upon appeal.

See generally ANNOT., *Review On Appeal, Where Accused Does Not Testify, Of Trial Court's Preliminary Ruling That Evidence of Prior Convictions Will Be Admissible Under Rule 609 of the Federal Rules of Evidence If Accused Does Testify,*

54 ALR Fed 694 (1981); ANNOT., *Adequacy of Defense Counsel's Representation of Criminal Client Regarding Prior Convictions,* 14 ALR4th 227 (1982).

Proof of Prior Convictions at Trial

Rule 609(1) provides that the evidence of prior convictions admissible under the rule may either be elicited from the witness or established by public record. If proof is made by public record, usually a duly certified copy of the judgment of conviction will be offered as a self-authenticating document under Rule 902. It has been held to be error to ask a witness about a prior criminal conviction unless the attorney is prepared to prove the conviction by the public record in case of a denial. See *State v. Gustafson,* 248 Or 1, 5, 432 P2d 323, 325 (1967) ("This method of impeaching a witness must be used in good faith. The right to impeach a witness by proving prior convictions may not be used as a subterfuge to blacken the character of the witness by insinuating criminal convictions that cannot be proved" (citation omitted)). See generally ANNOT., *Effect of Prosecuting Attorney Asking Defense Witness Other Than Accused As To Offer Convictions Where He Is Not Prepared to Offer Documentary Proof in Event of Denial,* 3 ALR3d 965 (1965).

In *State v. Jenkins,* 63 Or App 858, 666 P2d 869 (1983), the court held that the trial judge should have granted a mistrial on his own motion in a case where the prosecutor, on cross-examination, asked the defendant about two prior crimes, neither of which were felonies or otherwise admissible under Rule 609. The prosecutor asked about a "strongarm rape" conviction, which turned out to be only a misdemeanor offense of contributing to the delinquency of a minor, and a felony assault conviction involving "aggressive behavior," which turned out to be a misdemeanor conviction in municipal court. The court disapproved of the editorializing comments by the prosecutor, noting that a crime of "strongarm rape" does not even exist. The court stated that a criminal defendant "shall not be tried by innuendo" and held: "The tactics of this prosecutor and their impact on the subsequent course of defendant's trial made the trial *fundamentally* unfair, without regard to how strong evidence of guilt may have been." 63 Or App at 863, 666 P2d at 872.

Under FRE 609, it has been held to be error for an attorney to ask a general question of a witness regarding conviction of other crimes. The question must be focused on crimes admissible under Rule 609. See *United States v. Wolf,* 561 F2d 1376 (10th Cir 1977); *United States v. Cunningham,* 638 F2d 696, 698 (4th Cir 1981).

Generally, the only details that may be elicited by the impeaching party are the fact of conviction, the nature of the offense, and the date of conviction. *United States v. Tumblin,* 551 F2d 1001 (5th Cir 1977). It has been held to be error to allow the examiner to bring out additional details regarding the offense when they would prejudice the defendant. See *United States v. Harding,* 525 F2d 84 (7th Cir 1975); *United States v. Phillips,* 488 F Supp 508 (WD Mo 1980).

Whenever a witness is impeached by a prior criminal conviction under Rule 609, the party calling that witness is entitled to a limiting instruction under Rule

105. The limiting instruction may be given when the evidence of prior conviction is received as well as at the conclusion of the case. Failure to give a limiting instruction, even where one was not requested by the defendant, may be plain error, at least where the prior crime is similar to the offense charged. See *United States v. Diaz,* 585 F2d 116, 118 (5th Cir 1978); *United States v. Larsen,* 596 F2d 347 (9th Cir 1979).

RULE 609(2)(a)
Fifteen-Year Time Limit

Rule 609(2)(a) provides that evidence of a conviction is not admissible to impeach if a period of more than fifteen years has elapsed since the date of the conviction or of the release of the witness from the confinement imposed for that conviction, whichever is the later date. In the original version of the Evidence Code, a ten-year limit was established. However, Ballot Measure No. 10, approved by the voters on November 4, 1986, extended the period to fifteen years.

This provision differs from the corresponding subpart of FRE 609 which gives discretion to trial courts to allow impeachment by convictions more than ten years old. See ANNOT., *Construction and Application of Rule 609(b) of Federal Rules of Evidence, Setting Time Limit on Admissibility of Evidence of Conviction of Crime To Attack Credibility of Witness,* 43 ALR Fed 398 (1979).

Although the beginning date for the calculation of the fifteen-year period is clearly specified by the rule, the ending date is uncertain. The fifteen-year period could be calculated to the date of testimony, the date of commencement of trial, or the date the indictment or complaint was filed. The preferable construction would be to measure the time from the date of commencing the litigation, to avoid any advantage to a party by delay of the trial. This was the position adopted in *United States v. Mullens,* 562 F2d 999 (5th Cir 1977), cert denied 435 US 906 (1978) (time period is measured back from time of indictment).

RULE 609(2)(b)
Convictions that Have Been Reversed, Set Aside, or Expunged by Pardon

Rule 609(2)(b) provides that a witness may not be impeached by a conviction that has been expunged by pardon, reversed, set aside, or otherwise rendered nugatory. This rule differs from the comparable subpart of FRE 609 by eliminating any requirement that the pardon or other procedure has been "based on a finding of rehabilitation or innocence." See ANNOT., *Construction and Application of Rule 609(c) of The Federal Rules of Evidence, Providing That Evidence of Conviction Is Not Admissible to Attack Credibility of Witness If Conviction Has Been Subject of Pardon, Annulment, or Other Procedure Based on Finding of Rehabilitation or Innocence,* 42 ALR Fed 942 (1979).

Although the expungement statutes now adopted by various jurisdictions are not expressly mentioned in the rule, presumably they are included as a procedure that "expunges" a conviction and renders it "nugatory." Oregon convictions set aside pursuant to ORS 137.225 presumably cannot be used for impeachment under this rule. See Hearings on H.B. 2030 Before the House Comm. on Judiciary, 61st Oregon Legislative Assembly (April 2, 1981) Minutes at 9-10.

RULE 609(3)
Right of Witness Briefly to Explain
Circumstances of Conviction

Rule 609(3) entitles a witness impeached by evidence of a prior criminal conviction to explain briefly the circumstances of the crime or former conviction. The extent of explanation may be limited by Rule 403.

Although Rule 609(3) expressly allows an explanation of the circumstances of a prior conviction only when the credibility of the witness is "attacked" by use of the conviction, a brief explanation should also be permitted when a party brings out the prior convictions on direct examination. This apparently was the intent of the legislature, because the Legislative Commentary cites *State v. Gilbert,* 282 Or 309, 577 P2d 939 (1978), a case that involved bringing out prior convictions on direct examination.

A 1986 amendment to the rule added the language "once the witness explains the circumstances, the opposing side shall have an opportunity to rebut the explanation." This amendment allows the opposing party to bring out additional details to correct the record if the witness makes false or misleading statements regarding the circumstances of the prior conviction. See *United States v. Wolf,* 561 F2d 1376 (10th Cir 1977); *State v. Poole,* 11 Or App 55, 56, 500 P2d 726, 729 (1972).

Just as the trial judge has discretion to establish reasonable boundaries upon a witness' explanation of a conviction, appropriate limits may also be placed upon any rebuttal by the opposing party to avoid having the trial diverted to collateral issues.

The fact that the prosecutor is allowed to rebut the witness' explanation of the conviction does not mean that the prosecutor may independently bring out irrelevant and prejudicial matters regarding the prior crime. In *State v. Schwab,* 95 Or App 593, 771 P2d 277 (1989), the defendant testified on direct examination that he had previously been convicted of robbery in the third degree and provided a brief description of the incident. On cross-examination, the prosecutor brought out that the victim of the previous robbery was a 73-year-old woman. The court found this to be error, but held that the trial judge was within his discretion in denying a mistrial.

In *French v. Barrett,* 84 Or App 52, 733 P2d 89 (1987), the defendant testified that he pled guilty to a prior burglary due to a "guilty conscience." The appellate court held that "when a witness attempts to minimize the effect of a prior conviction by showing a guilty plea, he may properly be questioned regarding the factors, other than his guilty conscience, which entered into his decision to plead guilty." 84 Or App at 56. However, the court affirmed the trial judge's refusal to allow the plaintiff to call a police officer, who would testify that the reason that defendant pleaded guilty was that he expected soon to be apprehended. The court stated: "Contrary to plaintiff's assertion, the cited cases do not hold that factors motivating a guilty plea may be established through introduction of extrinsic evidence. Accordingly, the officer's testimony was properly excluded." Id.

RULE 609(4)
Impeachment by Conviction on Appeal

Rule 609(4) provides that a conviction may be used for impeachment even though it is currently on appeal. The opponent is entitled to introduce evidence of the pendency of the appeal. A party takes some risk in impeaching with a conviction that is pending appeal. If the conviction is ultimately reversed, the opponent may move for a new trial in the proceeding where the conviction was used to impeach.

It is by no means certain that such an attack would be successful however. Use of the conviction to impeach, even though the conviction is subsequently reversed, is arguably not error because such impeachment is expressly authorized by Rule 609(4), and the jury can be informed that the conviction is not final. Moreover, even if it were error, it would not necessarily be prejudicial error. See Rule 103(1).

RULE 609(5)
Juvenile Offenses

Rule 609(5) provides that an adjudication by a juvenile court that a child is within its jurisdiction is not a conviction of a crime under this rule. This subpart is intended to prevent juvenile adjudications from being used for impeachment purposes. It differs from FRE 609(d), which provides:

> The court may, however, in a criminal case allow evidence of a juvenile adjudication of a witness other than the accused if conviction of the offense would be admissible to attack the credibility of an adult and the court is satisfied that admission in evidence is necessary for a fair determination of the issue of guilt or innocence.

Although impeachment based upon juvenile adjudications is not allowed under Rule 609, it may be allowed under Rule 609-1 in circumstances where such adjudication would be evidence of bias. *Davis v. Alaska,* 415 US 308, 94 SCt 1105, 39 LEd2d 347 (1974) holds that a criminal defendant is constitutionally entitled to impeach a prosecution witness by a showing of bias, even if this requires disclosure of otherwise confidential facts regarding the juvenile record of the witness. See also *Burr v. Sullivan,* 618 F2d 583 (9th Cir 1980) (constitutional right of defendant to cross-examine prosecution witness outweighed need of the state to maintain confidentiality of its juvenile court records).

RULE 609-1.   ORS 40.360. IMPEACHMENT FOR BIAS OR INTEREST

(1) The credibility of a witness may be attacked by evidence that the witness engaged in conduct or made statements showing bias or interest. However, before this can be done, the statements must be related to the witness and the conduct described, with the circumstances of times, places and persons present, and the witness shall be asked whether the witness made the statements or engaged in such conduct, and, if so, allowed to explain. If the statements are in writing, they shall be shown to the witness.

(2) If a witness fully admits the facts claimed to show the bias or interest of the witness, additional evidence of that bias or interest shall not be admitted. If the witness denies or does not fully admit the facts claimed to show bias or interest, the party attacking the credibility of the witness may then offer evidence to prove those facts.

(3) Evidence to support or rehabilitate a witness whose credibility has been attacked by evidence of bias or interest shall be limited to evidence showing a lack of bias or interest.

LEGISLATIVE COMMENTARY

Oregon Rule of Evidence 609-1 allows any party to impeach a witness by evidence of bias or interest. This is a new rule, based on Oregon case law.

Oregon courts have long recognized that the feelings of a witness toward the parties or the interest of a witness in the outcome of a case will slant the witness' testimony. Acts, relationships or motives that are likely to produce bias or interest therefore have been examinable for the purpose of impeaching credibility.

Bias may take the form of friendly feeling toward a party. It may be evidenced by a family or business relationship, or by particular conduct or statements of the witness. Bias may also take the form of hostility to a party as shown by a history of conflict, or a lawsuit against the party.

Self-interest commonly takes the form of having a stake in the outcome of litigation. Interest is suggested, for example, if a witness testifies for the prosecution when the witness is an accomplice in the same crime, or is the subject of another indictment. In its extreme form, self-interest is manifest in corrupt activity such as taking a bribe to testify falsely, or writing a letter to intimidate another witness into giving perjured testimony. *State v. Moore*, 180 Or 502, 176 P2d 631 (1947).

The principles controlling impeachment of witnesses for bias or interest in Oregon have generally not been established by statute, but by judicial decision. The Legislative Assembly intends that ORE 609-1 codify the case law, with the one exception noted below of admissibility of evidence of a continuing relationship between an expert witness and the party employing the expert.

The rule on impeachment for bias or interest should be compared with ORE 613, the rule on impeachment by means of prior inconsistent statements. Both rules require a foundation to be laid when an inconsistent statement showing bias or interest is used, but the requirements are different. Compare Rule 609-1(1) with 613(1) (basis for line of inquiry), and Rule 609-1(2) (extrinsic evidence). In the event of a conflict, the Legislative Assembly intends that ORE 609-1, the stricter rule, control. See commentary to subsection (1), infra.

Subsection (1). In *State v. Estlick,* 269 Or 75, 523 P2d 1029 (1974), the court declared that ORS 45.590 replaced the common law on impeachment of a party's own witness. As ORS 45.590 did not prohibit a party from impeaching its own witness by showing bias or interest, the majority refused to adopt such a prohibition by judicial decision. As a result, the trial court may allow a party to introduce, on direct examination, evidence of bias or interest of the party's own witness. There has never been doubt that a party may impeach the credibility of an opposing witness by showing bias or interest.

Matters that would otherwise be irrelevant may be offered to show the bias or interest of a witness. Matters that are relevant but prejudicial may likewise be elicited. In *State v. Guerrero,* 11 Or App 284, 501 P2d 988 (1972), questions about the witness' acquaintance with the defendant, used to show bias, were allowed even though the inquiry revealed that the persons had been together in the penitentiary. The trial court has a continuing responsibility in such a case to instruct the jury regarding the purpose for which testimony may be considered.

Before a witness can be impeached by calling other witnesses to prove declarations or conduct showing bias or interest, the witness must be asked about these facts. In *State v. Dowell,* 274 Or 547, 547 P2d 619 (1976), the court noted its previous holdings that ORS 45.610 (the predecessor to ORE 613) required a foundation for evidence of bias or interest if the evidence is a prior inconsistent statement. *State v. Stewart,* 11 Or 52, 4 P 128 (1883); *State v. Holbrook,* 98 Or 43, 188 P 947 (1920). The court noted that it had not considered whether a similar foundation is required before a witness can be impeached by evidence of prior conduct. Quoting McCormick, *Evidence* § 40 at 80–81 (2d ed 1972), the court observed:

> "Some courts, adhering to the analogy of inconsistent statements, make a difference between declarations and conduct evidencing bias, requiring the preliminary question as to the former and not as to the latter. But as suggested in a leading English case, words and conduct are usually intermingled in proof of bias, and 'nice and subtle distinctions' should be avoided in shaping this rule of trial practice. Better require a 'foundation' as to both or neither." 274 Or at 553.

In line with that view, the Supreme Court required that a preliminary foundation be laid for both declarations and conduct evidencing bias.

To evaluate the credibility of a witness fairly, the jury should hear all the facts relating to possible bias and self-interest. *State v. Ellsworth,* 30 Or 145, 47 P 199 (1896); *Clevenger v. Shallhorn,* 205 Or 209, 296 P2d 651 (1955). For example, it is reversible error not to allow a criminal defendant to cross examine the victim whether the latter's testimony is prompted by fear of being charged with an offense. *State v. Sheeler,* 15 Or App 96, 514 P2d 1370 (1973). However, the trial judge retains discretion to control the extent to which proof of bias or interest may go. *McCarty v. Hedges,* 212 Or 497, 309 P2d 186 (1958); *Schrock v. Goodell,* 270 Or 504, 528 P2d 1048 (1974). Relevancy is a question of degree, and the judge may and should draw a fine to exclude that which is of little value. *O'Harra v. Pundt,* 210 Or 533, 310 P2d 1110 (1957). Prejudice is also a consideration.

The trial judge is most often required to exercise discretion, weighing the above interests, when there is testimony by an expert witness or testimony that might inject the element of insurance into the case.

Expert fees. Generally, the pecuniary interest of an expert witness and any bias of the expert in favor of the calling party can always be shown, with inquiry limited only by the sound discretion of the trial judge. An expert may be examined as to fees, compensation, previous relationships with the parties or the attorneys, and frequency of testimony in behalf of a plaintiff or defendant. *State v. Sack,* 210 Or 522, 300 P2d 427 (1957); *State Highway Commission v. Superbilt Manufacturing Co., Inc.,* 204 Or 393, 281 P2d 707 (1955); *Hahn v. Dewey,* 157 Or 433, 72 P2d 593 (1937). In Oregon, however, a party has not been able to question an expert on the amount of fees received for testimony in unrelated trials. *State Highway Commission v. Superbilt Manufacturing,* supra. The Legislative Assembly intends that Rule 609-1 be construed to overrule this last principle. The limitation has been criticized. See Graham *"Impeaching the Professional Expert Witness by a Showing of Financial Interest,"* in 53 Indiana L J 35. The better reasoning is that of the Illinois Supreme Court in *City of Chicago v. Van Schaak Bros. Chemical Works,* 330 Ill 264, 161 NE 486 (1928):

> "… [I]t would manifestly be important, where witnesses had repeatedly testified for [a party], to know whether they were receiving only fair and ordinary compensation for their time, or whether the employment was of such a character and the compensation such as to make it desirable that the employment should continue and that the [party] should be fully satisfied with the opinions given. Undoubtedly it was necessary for the [party] to employ the witnesses, but we think the defendants were entitled to have the jury know what the arrangement was under which the opinions were formed and testified to." 161 NE at 489, citing *Kerfoot v. City of Chicago,* 195 Ill 229, 63 NE 101 (1902).

Insurance. The trial judge and attorneys must exercise particular caution when evidence relating to bias or interest touches upon the existence of liability insurance. Compare *Smith v. Pacific Truck Express,* 164 Or 318, 100 P2d 474 (1940) (claims adjuster who takes stand for defense may be examined as to connection with company that has insured defendant and is conducting defense); *Quigley v. Roath,* 227 Or 336, 362 P2d 328 (1961); *Null v. Siegrist,* 262 Or 264, 497 P2d 664 (1972); with *Fairbrother v. Rinker,* 274 Or 525, 547 P2d 605 (1976) (where private investigator testifying for defense states profession and fact of employment on behalf of defendant and fee, identification of insurance company as employer adds nothing to inference of bias and is properly excludable); *Standholm v. General Construction Company,* 235 Or 145, 382 P2d 843 (1963).

Subsection (2). Some jurisdictions take the position that if a witness fully admits facts claimed to show bias or interest, the impeaching questioner cannot repeat the attack by calling other witnesses to the same facts. If the witness denies or does not fully admit the facts claimed to show bias or interest on the other hand, the attacking party may prove those facts by extrinsic evidence. This is the rule in Oregon. *State v. Hing,* 77 Or 462, 151 P 706 (1915). It is retained to prevent needless delay and the injection of collateral issues.

Subsection (3). This subsection is informed by the same policies that underlie subsection (2). It is settled case law that no "supporting" evidence of lack of bias or interest is admissible unless evidence of bias or interest has been offered. *State v. Van Hooser,* 10 Or App 642, 501 P2d 78 (1972); *State v. Estlick,* supra. Thus, if the state calls a witness who is in jail on another charge, on direct examination it may show both this fact and the fact that no promise of leniency has been made. But the two facts must be shown in that order.

Evidence of the truthfulness of the witness cannot be shown regardless of whether evidence of bias or interest is introduced. See ORE 608(1)(b). Under this subsection, evidence that is used to rehabilitate a witness must address itself to the nature of the impeaching evidence, i.e., it must only show lack of bias or interest. *Sheppard v. Yocum and DeLashtmutt,* 10 Or 402 (1882); *State v. Estlick,* supra.

TEXT

Impeachment for Bias or Interest

Rule 609-1 allows the credibility of a witness to be impeached by evidence that the witness engaged in conduct or made statements indicating bias or interest. The Federal Rules of Evidence do not address this mode of impeachment. See Schmertz & Czapanskiy, *Bias Impeachment and the Proposed Federal Rules of Evidence,* 61 Geo LJ 257 (1972). However, impeachment by bias is allowed by federal case law. *United States v. Abel,* 469 US 45, 105 SCt 465, 83 LEd2d 450 (1984).

Courts have traditionally allowed wide leeway to counsel attempting to show bias or interest on the part of a witness. See *State v. Weinstein,* 108 Or App 486, 487, 814 P2d 565 (1991) (error for the trial court to refuse to allow the defendant to impeach an assault victim by showing that the victim was currently on probation and therefore had a motive to lie about the fight to avoid having his probation revoked); *State v. Sheeler,* 15 Or App 96, 514 P2d 1370 (1973). It has often been stated that bias of a witness is never a collateral matter and matters that would otherwise be irrelevant are allowed to impeach a witness for bias. *United States v. Robinson,* 530 F2d 1076, 1079 (DC Cir 1976). In criminal cases, failure to allow a defendant to impeach prosecution witnesses by evidence of bias or interest has been held to violate the constitutionally guaranteed right of confrontation and cross-examination. *Davis v. Alaska,* 415 US 308, 94 SCt 1105, 39 LEd2d 347 (1974).

Examples of Bias

Bias may be evidenced by personal, family, romantic, sexual, or business relationships; by employment or termination of employment by a party; by statements or conduct indicating positive or negative feelings of the witness towards a party; by claims, litigation, or settlements between the witness and a party; by prior fights or quarrels; by a party offering to give or a witness offering to receive a bribe; by payment of compensation of any nature by the party to the witness; by granting or promising to grant special advantage or favoritism; by a showing of a motive to curry favor with a party, such as showing that a prosecution witness is in custody or facing criminal charges; or by an agreement to grant immunity, recommend leniency, drop another charge, or any other concession by a prosecutor or other law enforcement officer to a witness. See 1 McCormick, *Evidence* (4th ed 1992) § 39 at 130–4.

The Oregon appellate courts have held impeachment for bias or interest to be proper under the following circumstances:

> Where there is evidence that child witness had been told by her father that "she had to say bad things about [defendant] in court." *State v. Philips*, 314 Or 460, 470, 840 P2d 460 (1992).

> Where witness had received funds from Crime Victim's Assistance Fund in exchange for agreeing to cooperate in prosecution of defendant. *State v. Van Norsdall*, 127 Or App 300, 303, 873 P2d 345, 347 (1994), rev denied 320 Or 131, 881 P2d 815 (1994).

> Where witness was a police informant with prior arrests that were relevant to show bias. *State v. Rodriguez*, 115 Or App 281, 285, 840 P2d 711 (1992).

> Where immunity had been granted to a prosecution witness. *State v. Cox*, 87 Or App 443, 742 P2d 694 (1987).

> Where a prosecution witness was facing a pending theft charge and had previously served as a government informant. *State v. Presley*, 84 Or App 1, 733 P2d 452 (1987).

> Where plaintiff's supervisor, who testified that the accident was plaintiff's fault, had made a statement indicating concern that the employer was angry at the supervisor for failing to take precautions to prevent the accident. *Ledbetter v. Complete Abrasive Blasting Systems*, 76 Or App 10, 707 P2d 1292 (1985).

> Where the witness was a party to another legal action, the outcome of which would be influenced directly by the outcome of the present case. *Clevenger v. Schallhorn*, 205 Or 209, 286 P2d 651 (1955).

> Where the witness had a motive to curry favor with the prosecution to avoid his own prosecution. *State v. Bailey*, 208 Or 321, 300 P2d 975 (1956).

> Where defendant sought to cross-examine the arresting officer regarding his knowledge of internal police department procedures and potential sanctions against officers who use unnecessary force, even

though no complaint against the officer had been filed. *State v. Hubbard,* 297 Or 789, 801, 688 P2d 1311, 1320 (1984) ("We agree that a testifying officer's knowledge of departmental procedures for handling suspects and potential sanctions for violation of the procedures tends to show that the officer has an interest in testifying that he followed such procedures, whether in fact he did so.").

Where a witness had accepted a bribe to refrain from testifying. *State v. Dowell,* 274 Or 547, 547 P2d 619 (1976).

Where the defense witness was personally hostile to the plaintiff. *Rhodes v. Harwood,* 280 Or 399, 571 P2d 492 (1977).

Where the defense witness had been an acquaintance of the defendant while both were in the penitentiary. *State v. Guerrero,* 11 Or App 284, 501 P2d 998 (1972). But see *State v. Jones,* 141 Or App 41, 48, 917 P2d 515 (1996) (evidence that prosecution witness had been in prison irrelevant without more to show bias against defendant).

Where the victim was contemplating a civil action against the defendant. *State v. Delucia,* 40 Or App 711, 596 P2d 585 (1979).

Where the victim was potentially subject to criminal prosecution himself. *State v. Sheeler,* 15 Or App 96, 514 P2d 1370 (1973).

In *State v. Brown,* 299 Or 143, 699 P2d 1122 (1985), the court held it was error to admit evidence that the defendant was on probation for an earlier crime to show interest on the part of the defendant in avoiding conviction. The court stated: "In criminal cases, the defendant's interest in avoiding conviction is sufficiently obvious that it does not justify additional demonstration by evidence that he is on probation for another conviction." However, evidence that a prosecution witness is on probation for earlier crimes, thereby causing an interest to testify favorably for the prosecution, is admissible. See *Davis v. Alaska,* 415 US 308, 94 SCt 1105, 39 LEd2d 347 (1974) (defendant's sixth amendment right to confront witnesses violated when he was not allowed to bring out probation status of prosecution witness).

An expert may be examined regarding her compensation, her previous relationship with the attorneys or parties, the frequency of her testimony on behalf of one side in similar cases and any other circumstances that might suggest interest or bias on the part of the expert. The Commentary states that "[t]he Legislative Assembly intends that Rule 609-1 be construed to overrule," *State Highway Comm'n v. Superbilt Mfg. Co.,* 204 Or 393, 281 P2d 707 (1955), insofar as it holds that an expert witness may not be questioned regarding the amount of fees received for testimony in unrelated trials on behalf of the same party. See generally ANNOT., *Propriety of Cross-Examining Expert Witness Regarding His Status as Professional Witness,"* 39 ALR4th 742 (1985); ANNOT., *Cross-Examination of Expert Witnesses as to Fees, Compensation and the Like,* 33 ALR2d 1170 (1954).

On the issue of employment by an insurance company as evidence of bias, see Rule 411(2), which states that Rule 411(1) "does not require the exclusion of evidence of insurance against liability when offered [to prove] bias, prejudice or motive of a witness." A distinction should probably be drawn between impeachment of a regular employee of an insurance company and impeachment of an independent, private investigator retained by the insurance company to investigate a particular case. In the latter case, the court may not necessarily allow disclosure of the identity of the employer as an insurance company. See *Fairbrother v. Rinker,* 274 Or 525, 547 P2d 605 (1976) (witness testified he was employed by law firm, not by insurance company).

The Commentary indicates that Rule 609-1 reaches corruption of a witness by taking or offering to take a bribe. See *State v. Dowell,* 274 Or 547, 547 P2d 619 (1976) (witness may be impeached by evidence that he or she accepted a bribe).

Although Rule 609-1 authorizes proof of bias or interest only by evidence "that the witness engaged in conduct or made statements showing bias or interest," the courts have quite appropriately given the rule a broader construction. In *State v. Brown,* 299 Or 143, 699 P2d 1122 (1985), the court confirmed that "OEC 609-1 was never intended to restrict other forms of impeachment for bias or interest," even though by its terms it is limited to evidence that the witness "engaged in conduct or made statements" showing either bias or interest. The court stated: "[B]ias due to friendship, family relationship, etc., and interest in the form of amount of expert fees, etc., continue to be viable forms of impeachment even though no conduct or statement is involved."

Courts' Discretion to Limit Inquiry

Courts retain discretion to define the outer limits of impeachment by bias and interest. See Rule 611(1), which authorizes the court to "protect witnesses from harassment or undue embarrassment." See also Rule 403.

In *State v. Hubbard,* 297 Or 789, 798, 688 P2d 1311 (1984), the court held that even though the bias or interest of a witness may always be shown, the trial judge has discretion to limit the extent of inquiry into bias or interest.

> The discretion of the trial judge to exclude evidence relevant to bias or interest only obtains once sufficient facts have been established from which the jury may infer that bias or interest. Typically, this would require wide latitude be given to the cross-examiner to ask and receive answers to questions sufficient to demonstrate to the jury the nature of the bias or interest of the witness. ... [except in those cases where the bias or interest has been made apparent by the circumstances or by the direct examination of the witness.]

See also *Morrow v. First Interstate Bank,* 118 Or App 164, 168, 847 P2d 411, rev dismissed as improvidently allowed 317 Or 580, 858 P2d 448 (1993) (although evidence of possible bias by a defense witness against the plaintiff was relevant, it was properly excluded under Rule 403 as cumulative).

But it is error to exclude evidence of bias where it has not been sufficiently established by other evidence. *MacDonald v. Cottle,* 133 Or App 35, 889 P2d 1320, rev denied 321 Or 268, 895 P2d 1362 (1995) ("when questions relating to a witness' bias or interest are curtailed by a trial court without giving the party the opportunity to establish bias or interest, the court does not have the discretion to exclude the evidence.").

In *State v. Davis,* 65 Or App 83, 670 P2d 192 (1983), the trial court refused to allow the defense attorney to cross-examine an alleged victim regarding his refusal to talk with the defendant's investigator, which the defendant argued would show bias of the witness against the defendant. The appellate court refused to find an abuse of discretion, because the relationship between the witness and the defendant had already been made sufficiently apparent to the jury.

In *State v. Barfield,* 79 Or App 688, 692, 720 P2d 394 (1986), a sex abuse prosecution, the court affirmed the refusal of the trial judge to allow the defendant to impeach a prosecution witness by showing that she had an "unusual sensitivity to sexual abuse and sexual matters in general." The court stated that "[e]vidence that the witness was hostile toward sexual abusers generally could not ... show that the witness was hostile toward defendant in any way which would have affected her testimony."

Foundation Requirement

Rule 609-1(1) sets forth much more stringent foundation requirements for impeachment of a witness for bias or interest than does Rule 613(1) for impeachment by prior inconsistent statements. Before extrinsic evidence of bias or interest may be shown, the statements or conduct showing bias or interest must be related to the witness; the times, places, and persons present must be described; and the witness must be asked whether the witness made the statements or engaged in such conduct, and, if so, be allowed to explain. If the statements are in writing, they must be shown to the witness.

The rationale for the foundation requirement is that if the witness admits the bias or interest, it would be a waste of time to entertain further evidence on the issue. Therefore, Rule 609-1(2) prohibits extrinsic evidence of the bias or interest if the witness "fully admits the facts claimed to show the bias or interest." If the witness denies or does not fully admit the facts claimed to show bias or interest, then extrinsic evidence of those facts may be received.

In *Ledbetter v. Complete Abrasive Blasting Systems,* 76 Or App 10, 707 P2d 1292 (1985), the court affirmed the ruling of the trial court excluding a statement evidencing bias of a witness, because the plaintiff did not first attempt to elicit admission of the statement from the witness on cross-examination.

The foundation requirement does not apply to evidence of bias other than prior statements or conduct. In *James v. General Motors of Canada, Ltd.,* 101 Or App 138, 790 P2d 8, rev denied 310 Or 243, 796 P2d 360 (1990), the court held that the foundation requirement of OEC 609-1 does not apply to evidence of bias that is manifested other than through conduct or statements. Therefore, it was error for the trial court not to allow the plaintiff to impeach a defense witness by showing that he was a part-time employee of the defendant, even though the plaintiff had failed to bring out this evidence of bias on cross-examination.

In some cases Rule 609-1 and Rule 613 will overlap, such as where bias or interest is being proven by prior inconsistent statements. In such cases, the Commentary specifies that the foundation requirements of Rule 609-1 control.

Rehabilitation

Rule 609-1(3) provides that the only evidence allowed to rehabilitate a witness who has been impeached for bias or interest is other evidence showing a lack of bias or interest. Rehabilitation by character evidence of truthfulness is not authorized. When a witness is being impeached by alleged corruption rather than mere bias, rehabilitation by evidence of truthful character under Rule 608(1) should be allowed in the discretion of the court. See Commentary to Rule 608(1). On rehabilitation of witnesses, see textual discussion of Rules 607 and 608. This rule does not allow a party to attempt to bolster the credibility of a witness by showing absence of bias until that witness has been impeached for bias.

Impeachment and Rehabilitation by Use
of Plea Bargain Agreements

In *State v. Middleton,* 295 Or 485, 668 P2d 371 (1983), the court held that a prosecution witness who had been impeached by showing that he entered a plea bargain in exchange for his testimony could not be rehabilitated by the prosecutor with a showing that one condition of the plea agreement was that the witness "take a polygraph and pass it." The court rested its holding both upon the ground that polygraph evidence is generally inadmissible and upon the ground that under Rule 609-1 evidence to rehabilitate a witness who has been attacked by evidence of bias is limited to evidence "showing a lack of bias or interest." Accord *State v. Snider,* 296 Or 168, 674 P2d 585 (1983); *State v. Eby,* 296 Or 63, 673 P2d 522 (1983); *United States v. Brown,* 720 F2d 1059 (9th Cir 1983). See generally ANNOT., *Propriety and Prejudicial Effect of Informing Jury that Witness in Criminal Prosecution Has Taken Polygraph Test,* 15 ALR4th 824 (1982).

In *State v. Charboneau,* 323 Or 38, 42-51, 913 P2d 308 (1996), after a prosecution witness had been impeached by evidence of entering a plea bargain in exchange for his testimony, the prosecutor attempted to rehabilitate him by introducing portions of the plea agreement that included statements such as this: the state "believes" that the reduced charge "accurately reflects" the role the witness played in the murder and "has reason to believe" that the murder was primarily committed by others. The court held it was reversible error to admit such statements, because they amounted to an expression of belief by the proscuting attorneys and were analogous to commenting on the credibility of a witness.

In *State v. Corgain,* 63 Or App 26, 663 P2d 773 (1983), a prosecution witness had been impeached by evidence that his testimony had been given in exchange for a plea bargain. The court held that it was error for the state to rehabilitate the witness by reading provisions of the plea agreement into evidence that the witness "would honestly disclose to the police and the district attorney all information regarding his accomplice's criminal activities and that, if he were not truthful in court, any statements he made could be used against him." The court held that such evidence violated Rule 609-1, because it did not show lack of bias or interest, but rather was designed "to show truthfulness *despite* interest." 63 Or App at 30. See also *State v. Eby*, 296 Or 63, 71 n4, 673 P2d 522 (1983) (a condition in a plea agreement that the witness will testify truthfully does not tend to prove a witness' credibility and should be excluded on relevancy grounds).

RULE 610.   ORS 40.365. RELIGIOUS BELIEFS OR OPINIONS

Evidence of the beliefs or opinions of a witness on matters of religion is not admissible for the purpose of showing that by reason of their nature the credibility of the witness is impaired or enhanced.

LEGISLATIVE COMMENTARY

Oregon Rule of Evidence 610 prohibits the use of evidence of religious beliefs or opinions to impair or enhance the credibility of a witness. The substance of the rule is identical to Rule 610 of the Federal Rules of Evidence. It is also consistent with § 6 or Article I of the Oregon Constitution, relating to religious tests for witnesses and jurors.

The Legislative Assembly adopts the following commentary by the federal advisory committee:

"While the rule forecloses inquiry into the religious beliefs or opinions of a witness for the purpose of showing that [the witness'] character for truthfulness is affected by their nature, an inquiry for the purpose of showing interest or bias because of them is not within the prohibition. Thus disclosure of affiliation with a church which is a party to the litigation would be allowable under the rule. Cf. *Tucker v. Reil*, 51 Ariz 357, 77 P2d 203 (1938). To the same effect though less specifically worded, is California Evidence Code § 789. See 3 Wigmore, *Evidence* § 936 (3d ed 1940)."

TEXT

Impeachment on Basis of Religious Belief

Under early common law, witnesses were considered incompetent to testify if they did not believe in a god who would punish untruth. In more recent times, some common-law jurisdictions transformed lack of religious belief from a ground of incompetency into a form of impeachment. See 1 McCormick, *Evi-*

dence (4th ed 1992) § 46. Rule 610 rejects religious belief or absence thereof as a basis for impeachment of witnesses.

Rule 610 also prohibits any attempt to enhance the credibility of a witness by showing that the witness is exceptionally devout or adheres to noble religious beliefs. See *Gov't of the Virgin Islands v. Petersen,* 553 F2d 324 (3rd Cir 1977) (evidence that witness belonged to religious sect espousing nonviolence properly excluded). It is unlikely, however, that this prohibition will be interpreted to preclude questions regarding the occupation of a witness merely because the answer will reveal that the witness is a minister or employee of a religious organization. See generally ANNOT., *Propriety and Prejudicial Effect of Questions or Comments as to Witness' Religious Beliefs or Standards Designed to Enhance Credibility,* 27 ALR4th 1167 (1984); Ariens, *Evidence of Religion and the Religion of Evidence,* 40 Buff L Rev 65 (1992).

Rule 610 does not prohibit use of religious belief to show bias of a witness. In litigation against a church, a witness' membership in that church would be admissible under Rule 609-1 as evidence of bias, and such impeachment would not be prohibited by Rule 610.

Rule 610 is consistent with Article I, section 6 of the Oregon Constitution which provides: "No person shall be rendered incompetent as a witness, or juror in consequence of his opinions on matters of religion (*sic*); nor be questioned in any Court of Justice touching his religious (*sic*) belief to affect the weight of his testimony." Cf. *State v. Barnett,* 251 Or 234, 235, 445 P2d 124 (1968) ("The Oregon Constitution [Art I § 6] does not prohibit a prospective juror from being asked his religious belief.").

In *State v. Duncan,* 131 Or App 1, 3–5, 883 P2d 913 (1994), rev denied 320 Or 508, 888 P2d 569 (1995), the court held it to be a violation of OEC 610 for the prosecutor to ask a child victim about (1) his belief in God; (2) his belief that God would send him to hell if he lied; and (3) that he went to church every weekend.

RULE 611.   ORS 40.370. MODE AND ORDER OF INTERROGATION AND PRESENTATION

(1) **[Control by court.] The court shall exercise reasonable control over the mode and order of interrogating witnesses and presenting evidence so as to make the interrogation and presentation effective for the ascertainment of the truth, avoid needless consumption of time and protect witnesses from harassment or undue embarrassment.**

(2) **[Scope of cross-examination.] Cross-examination should be limited to the subject matter of the direct examination and matters affecting the credibility of the witness. The court may, in the exercise of discretion, permit inquiry into additional matters as if on direct examination.**

(3) **[Leading questions.]** **Leading questions should not be used on the direct examination of a witness except as may be necessary to develop the witness' testimony. Ordinarily leading questions should be permitted on cross-examination. When a party calls a hostile witness, an adverse party, or a witness identified with an adverse party, interrogation may be by leading questions.**

LEGISLATIVE COMMENTARY

Oregon Rule of Evidence 611 contains several guidelines on the manner of asking questions and presenting evidence. The trial court is to follow and enforce these in its discretion. The trial is that of Rule 611 of the Federal Rules of Evidence. It replaces ORS 45.530 to 45.570, which are repealed. Adoption of the federal rule will give Oregon courts and attorneys the benefit of decisional law from other jurisdictions which have also adopted the rule. Particularly where state law is not changed, the benefit of these decisions outweighs whatever benefit there may be in the current statutory wording. The Legislative Assembly believes that with one possible exception, discussed below, this rule does not change Oregon law.

Subsection (1). Detailed rules to govern the mode and order of interrogating witnesses and presenting evidence are neither desirable nor feasible. The ultimate responsibility for the effective working of the adversary system rests with the trial judge. This subsection sets forth the objectives which the judge should seek to attain.

Subsection (2). The practice of limiting cross-examination to the scope of direct and matters affecting credibility promotes the orderly presentation of a case. Thus viewed, the rule is an aspect of the judge's general control over the mode and order of interrogating witnesses and presenting evidence, and is to be administered as such. The matter is not one in which involvement at the appellate level is likely to prove fruitful. The rule is therefore phrased in terms of a suggestion rather than a mandate to the trial judge.

The qualification "as if on direct examination," applicable when inquiry into additional matters is allowed, is designed to terminate at that point the asking of leading questions as a matter of right and to bring into operation subsection (3) of the rule.

Subsection (3). A leading question is one that suggests to the witness the answer that the examining party desires. ORS 45.560. This subsection continues the traditional view that the suggestive powers of the leading question are undesirable. The same tradition recognizes exceptions, however, for the witness who is hostile, unwilling, or biased, the witness with communication problems; the child witness; the witness whose recollection is exhausted; and undisputed preliminary matters. 3 Wigmore, *Evidence* §§ 774–778 (3d ed 1940).

The use of leading questions on cross-examination is phrased as a matter of right. The purpose of the qualification "ordinarily" is to furnish a basis for denying the use of leading questions when the cross-examination is cross-examination in form only and not in fact, as, for example, the "cross-examination" of a party by the party's own counsel after being called by the opponent (savoring more of re-direct), or of an insured defendant who proves to be friendly to the plaintiff.

The one respect in which adoption of Rule 611 may change current law is the use of leading questions to interrogate adverse parties or witnesses on direct examination. In *Sinclair v. Barker*, 236 Or 599, 390 P2d 391 (1964), the court said: "The trial court took the position that when an adverse party is called as a witness [the party] may be examined by leading questions as in cross-examination. The privilege is not quite that broad. Leading questions may be allowed upon the direct examination of an adverse party if [the party] appears to be hostile to the examiner." 236 Or at 607. The rule in Oregon thus appears to have been that a witness must be both adverse and hostile before leading questions may be used on direct examination. Subsection (3) of Rule 611 permits leading questions to any adverse party or witness identified with an adverse party, regardless of hostility. To this extent, it overrules *Sinclair v. Barker* and changes Oregon law.

TEXT

RULE 611(1)
Mode and Order of Interrogation and Presentation

Broad Discretion

Rule 611(1) grants broad discretion to the trial judge with respect to the mode of interrogating witnesses and the order of presentation at trial. The decision of the trial judge will not be reversed unless the substantial rights of a party have been affected. Rule 103(1). Rule 611(1) directs that the discretion be exercised so as to further the ascertainment of truth, avoid needless consumption of time, and protect witnesses from harassment or undue embarrassment. With respect to the discretion of the trial judge, see generally Langum, *Uncodified Federal Evidence Rules Applicable to Civil Trials*, 19 Will L Rev 513 (1983).

Related Statutes and Rules

Rule 611(1) should be considered in conjunction with ORS 44.080, which provides: "It is the right of a witness to be protected from irrelevant, insulting or improper questions, and from harsh or insulting demeanor. The witness is to be detained only so long as the interests of justice require."

Additional authority to regulate the questioning of witnesses is provided by Rule 403, and certain inquiries are expressly prohibited by Rule 608(2) (witness cannot be cross-examined regarding prior bad acts not resulting in conviction of a crime, even if probative of truthfulness of the witness) and Rule 610 (witness cannot be impeached by evidence of religious belief). The usual order of trial proceedings, and judicial authority to alter the usual order, is set forth in ORCP 58.

Statutory authority to regulate judicial proceedings is also given by ORS 1.010, which provides:

Every court of justice has power:

    (1)   To preserve and enforce order in its immediate presence.

    (2)   To enforce order in the proceedings before it, or before a person or body empowered to conduct a judicial investigation under its authority.

    (3)   To provide for the orderly conduct of proceedings before it or its officers.

    (4)   To compel obedience to its judgments, decrees, orders and process, and to the orders of a judge out of court, in an action, suit or proceeding pending therein.

    (5)   To control in furtherance of justice, the conduct of its ministerial officers, and of all other persons in any manner connected with a judicial proceeding before it, in every matter appertaining thereto.

    (6)   To compel the attendance of persons to testify in an action, suit or proceeding pending therein, in the cases and manner provided by statute.

    (7)   To administer oaths in an action, suit or proceeding pending therein, and in all other cases where it may be necessary in the exercise of its powers or the performance of its duties.

Issues Subject to Trial Court Discretion

Under Rule 611(1), courts have broad discretion in determining the following issues:

    (1)   The order of witnesses. See *Peterson v. Schlottman,* 237 Or 484, 487, 392 P2d 262 (1964).

    (2)   The number of witnesses a party may call. *See* ANNOT., *Limiting Number of Noncharacter Witnesses in Civil Case,* 5 ALR3d 169 (1966); ANNOT., *Limiting Number of Noncharacter Witnesses in Criminal Case,* 5 ALR3d 238 (1966); *United States v. Zane,* 495 F2d 683, 698 (2nd Cir 1974) (court acted within discretion in limiting number of character witnesses).

    (3)   The manner of inquiry, including whether narrative testimony will be allowed.

    (4)   The form of questions.

    (5)   Length of examination of any witness.

    (6)   Whether to allow *voir dire* of witness to determine competency or qualifications of an expert.

    (7)   Whether to allow a party to ask questions of a witness in aid of an objection.

    (8)   Whether the court will examine a witness. See *Frangos v. Edmunds,* 179 Or 577, 610, 173 P2d 596 (1946); ANNOT., *Manner or Extent of Trial Judge's Examination of Witnesses in Civil Cases,* 6 ALR4th 951 (1981). But see ORCP 59E (court may not comment on the evidence); *State v. Mains,* 295 Or 640, 658, 669 P2d 1112, 1123 (1983) ("[J]udicial questioning of witnesses or admonition of counsel in the presence of a

jury should be a rare occurrence. Almost any question the judge may pose is fraught with the danger of giving the impression to the jury that the judge is an advocate for one of the parties."). Oregon does not have a counterpart of FRE 614, which expressly authorizes the judge to call and question witnesses. However, the Legislative Commentary provides: "By not adopting Federal Rule 614, the Legislative Assembly does not intend to deny or limit the inherent power of a trial court to call and examine witnesses." See Note immediately preceding Rule 615.

(9) Whether the court will order production of evidence not offered by a party. See *State v. Spicer,* 3 Or App 120, 473 P2d 147 (1970).

(10) Whether recross or redirect examination will be allowed.

(11) Whether a witness may be recalled.

(12) Whether new evidence will be allowed in rebuttal.

(13) Whether jurors will be allowed to ask questions. See ANNOT., *Propriety of Jurors Asking Questions in Open Court During Course of Trial,* 31 ALR3d 872 (1970).

(14) Whether a party may reopen its case. See *Kosmos v. Bergquist,* 51 Or App 451, 625 P2d 1374 (1981).

(15) Use of demonstrative evidence. See ORS 41.660 ("The exhibition of the object [admitted as an exhibit] to the jury shall be regulated by the sound discretion of the court"); ANNOT., *Propriety, at Federal Criminal Trial of Allowing Material, Object or Model of Object Allegedly Used in Criminal Act to be Taken into Jury Room During Deliberations,* 62 ALR Fed 950 (1983).

(16) The timing of jury instructions. See COMMENT, *Memory, Magic, and Myth: The Timing of Jury Instructions,* 59 Or L Rev 451 (1981).

(17) Whether parent may accompany child witness to witness stand. See *State v. Dompier,* 94 Or App 258, 764 P2d 979, rev denied 307 Or 514, 770 P2d 595 (1988) (trial court did not abuse its discretion in allowing a seven-year-old sex crime victim to sit on her foster mother's lap while giving her testimony).

(18) Whether to close the hearing. The trial court's authority to close the trial or hearing to the public is limited by statutory and constitutional provisions. In *State v. Bowers,* 58 Or App 1, 646 P2d 1354 (1982), the court held that it was reversible error for the trial judge at the request of the prosecutor to exclude the public from the courtroom during the testimony of an eleven-year-old sex crime victim. The court held that "[a] defendant has an overriding right to have the state's case against him presented publicly, unless the state makes a substantial showing of a need to limit that right." See also textual discussion under Rule 412.

Parties Have Right to Cross-Examination

The discretion of trial judges is more limited with respect to cross-examination, because parties have an absolute right to cross-examine opposing witnesss. If a witness fails to respond to questions on cross-examination or is otherwise unavailable for cross-examination, the court may in its discretion strike the direct testimony. See *State v. Quintero,* 110 Or App 247, 255, 823 P2d 981, 986 (1991), rev denied 314 Or 392, 840 P2d 710 (1992) (whether to strike direct testimony because of a witness' claim to failure to remember is within the discretion of the trial court); *Best v. Tavenner,* 189 Or 46, 218 P2d 471 (1950); ANNOT., *Propriety of Court's Failure or Refusal to Strike Direct Testimony of Government Witness Who Refuses, On Grounds of Self Incrimination, to Answer Questions on Cross-Examination,* 55 ALR Fed 742 (1981). If a party refuses to be sworn or to answer as a witness, such party's complaint, answer, or reply may be stricken. ORCP 55G.

In *State v.Halsey,* 116 Or App 225, 226, 840 P2d 730 (1992), a speeding prosecution, the court held it was reversible error to refuse to allow the pro se defendant to cross-examine the arresting police officer. The court held that a trial judge "has some power to regulate cross-examination...but it does not have the power wholly to deny the right to cross-examine."

In *Howell-Hooyman & Hooyman,* 113 Or App 548, 833 P2d 328 (1992), the court held that a trial judge has discretion "reasonably to control the presentation of evidence in the examination of witnesses.... The exercise of that authority is reasonable only if it is fundamentally fair and allows opportunities for a reasonably complete presentation of evidence and argument."

A party is entitled to use cross-examination to bring out bias or interest on the part of an adverse witness. In *State v. Hubbard,* 297 Or 789, 799, 688 P2d 1311 (1984), the court stated: "The discretion of the trial judge to control the scope of cross-examination pursuant to OEC 611(2) does not allow the exclusion of evidence offered to impeach a witness for bias or interest."

In criminal cases, the right of cross-examination is guaranteed by the Sixth Amendment right of confrontation. *Davis v. Alaska,* 415 US 308, 94 SCt 1105, 39 LEd2d 347 (1974); *Smith v. Illinois,* 390 US 129, 88 SCt 748, 19 LEd2d 956 (1968). Too severe a restriction on cross-examination may violate the constitutional rights of the defendant. See *United States v. Mayer,* 556 F2d 245, 250 (5th Cir 1977) (the trial court's "discretionary authority to limit cross-examination comes into play only after there has been permitted as a matter of right sufficient cross-examination to satisfy the Sixth Amendment"). Cf. *Alford v. United States,* 282 US 687, 51 SCt 218, 75 LEd2d 624 (1931) (error not to allow defendant to examine prosecution witness regarding place of residence); ANNOT., *Right to Cross-Examine Witness as to His Place of Residence,* 85 ALR3d 541 (1978).

Impeachment of Statements on Cross-Examination

If the matter was raised for the first time on cross-examination, it has been held that a defendant may not be impeached by evidence that is otherwise inadmissible. In *United States v. Pantone,* 609 F2d 675, 683 (3rd Cir 1979), the court stated:

> If we were to construe Rule 611(b) as permitting cross-examination with re-spect to other crimes solely for the purpose of creating credibility issues we would present a defendant who takes the stand with the Hobson's choice of admitting prior uncharged acts of misconduct or of opening the door to pres-entation of evidence of such acts in rebuttal.

But where the cross-examination was "reasonably suggested" by the defen-dant's direct testimony, it has been held to be proper to impeach the defendant with contradictory evidence, including illegally seized evidence. *United States v. Havens,* 446 US 620, 627, 100 SCt 1912, 64 LEd2d 559 (1980).

See further discussion under Rule 607, *supra.*

Offer of Proof Relating to Excluded Cross-Examination

In order to preserve the record for appeal when cross-examination is re-stricted, an offer of proof is required. In *State v. Affeld,* 307 Or 125, 128–9, 764 P2d 220 (1988), the court overturned prior authority and held that an offer of proof is required on cross-examination as well as direct examination. The court stated:

> A record can be adequate [for appellate review] in situations in which the scope of testimony is restricted by the trial court only if an offer of proof is made. There is no reason not to require an offer of proof on cross-examination. The only situations in which an offer of proof is not re-quired are those situations in which an offer of proof is impossible because of a trial court's refusal to allow the offer to be made.

A trial judge should have discretion to bar an offer of proof in question and answer format when it is clear that the "offer" is merely an improper attempt to harass the witness.

RULE 611(2)
Scope of Cross-Examination

Under the majority common-law view, cross-examination is limited to the scope of direct examination. A number of states allow what is referred to as *wide open* cross-examination without such a limitation. 1 McCormick, *Evidence* (4th ed 1992) § 21 at 83. Rule 611(2) largely follows the majority view, but gives discre-tion to the trial judge to allow inquiry into additional matters. Such inquiry must be conducted "as if on direct examination," which means that leading questions generally cannot be asked except as allowed under Rule 611(3).

The Oregon Supreme Court has held that cross-examination "should not be limited to the exact facts stated on the direct examination, but may extend to other matters which tend to limit, explain, or qualify them, or to rebut or modify any inference resulting therefrom, provided they are directly connected with the matter stated in the direct examination." *Ritchie v. Pittman,* 144 Or 228, 231, 24 P2d 328, 329 (1933). The same standard is likely to be applied under Rule 611(2). See ANNOT., *Construction And Application of Provision of Rule 611(b) of Federal Rules of Evidence that Cross-Examination Should be Limited to Subject Matter of Direct Examination,* 45 ALR Fed 639 (1979); 1 McCormick, *Evidence* (4th ed 1992) § 21 at 83–4. In determining the scope of allowable cross-examination, consideration must be given to Rule 106, which provides: "When part of an act, declaration, conversation or writing is given in evidence by one party, the whole on the same subject, where otherwise admissible, may at that time be inquired into by the other."

Rule 611(2) does not address the extent to which a witness, including a criminal defendant, waives the Fifth Amendment privilege against self-incrimination by testifying. In *McGautha v. California,* 402 US 183, 215, 91 SCt 1454, 28 LEd2d 711 (1971), the court stated that a defendant "who takes the stand in his own behalf cannot then claim the privilege against cross-examination on matters reasonably related to the subject matter of his direct examination." ORS 136.643 provides in relevant part: "The defendant or accused, when offering his testimony as a witness in his own behalf, gives the prosecutor a right to cross-examination upon all facts to which he has testified and which tend to his conviction or acquittal." At the same time, Rule 611(2) would not authorize a court to permit cross-examination regarding new matters not covered on direct examination to which the privilege is applicable. See *State v. Tippie,* 15 Or App 660, 668, 517 P2d 1063 (1973), rev'd on other grounds 269 Or 661, 525 P2d 1315 (1974) ("The questions asked of defendant by the prosecuting attorney were in no way related to defendant's testimony on direct examination. They were not permissible under [ORS 136.643] and it was error ... to deny defendant's claim of self-incrimination"). See generally Abramson, *Witness Waiver of the Fifth Amendment Privilege: A New Look at an Old Problem,* 41 Okla L Rev 235 (1988).

Recent Cases

In *Schacher v. Dunne,* 109 Or App 607, 611, 820 P2d 865, 868 (1991), rev denied 313 Or 74, 828 P2d 457 (1992), the appellate court affirmed the granting of a new trial on the ground that the trial court had erred by denying plaintiff the opportunity to cross-examine defendant's expert witness, a medical doctor, about whether plaintiff's symptoms could be explained by psychological factors.

In *State v. Moore,* 103 Or App 440, 445, 797 P2d 1073 (1990), rev denied 311 Or 151, 806 P2d 128 (1991), the court held that it was error to allow the defendant to be cross-examined regarding an alleged affair when such cross-examination was beyond the scope of defendant's direct testimony.

RULE 611(3)
Leading Questions

Rule 611(3) regulates when leading questions may be allowed. A leading question is one which suggests the desired answer, whether by manner of phrasing, the extent of detail, tone of voice, emphasis on particular words, non-verbal conduct, or otherwise. Merely because a question calls for a yes or no response does not make it leading. *Coates v. Slusher,* 109 Or 612, 621, 222 P 311 (1924). Prefacing a question with "state whether or not" does not prevent it from being leading, if the question is so detailed that the desired response is suggested.

A court has considerable discretion with regard to the extent of leading allowed. The Advisory Committee's Note to FRE 611(c) observes that "[a]n almost total unwillingness to reverse for infractions [of the rule against leading questions] has been manifested by appellate courts." A trial court is likely to be most strict in enforcing the rule against leading questions when the testimony is directed to the central issues in the case.

Once a leading question has been asked, the error often cannot be corrected even if an objection is sustained. The answer will already have been suggested to the witness. For this reason, counsel often accompany the objection with a request that the examiner be instructed to refrain from asking further leading questions.

The rule provides that leading questions "ordinarily" should be permitted on cross-examination. The qualification is necessary to allow courts to require that the cross-examination of a party, or witnesses who are identified with the party, called by the opponent be conducted in a nonleading manner. For example, the plaintiffs lawyer ordinarily should not be allowed to put leading questions to the plaintiff when cross-examining the plaintiff after the plaintiff has been called to the stand by the defendant. See *Morvant v. Constr. Aggregates Corp.,* 570 F2d 626, 635 n12 (6th Cir), cert dismissed 439 US 801 (1978).

The rule allows the use of leading questions on direct examination when "necessary to develop the witness' testimony." Courts are likely to allow leading questions when the testimony relates only to undisputed preliminary or background matters; when the witness is reluctant, reticent, confused, forgetful, hostile, biased, infirm, unresponsive, ignorant, frightened, timid, embarrassed, or young; when the witness is called to dispute the testimony of an earlier party; or when the witness is being impeached. See *State v. Williams,* 313 Or 19, 32, 828 P2d 1006, 1015, cert denied *Williams v. Oregon,* 113 SCt 171 (1992) (leading questions allowed where witness was showing hostility and being evasive); *Mace v. Timberman,* 120 Or 144, 251 P 763 (1926) (leading questions allowed to refresh a witness' memory); *State v. Caver,* 222 Or 270, 352 P2d 549 (1960) (leading questions allowed with respect to preliminary matters); *State v. Chase,* 106 Or 263, 211 P 920 (1922) (leading questions of child witness allowed); *Sinclair v. Barker,* 236 Or 599, 390 P2d 321 (1964) (leading questions of hostile witness allowed). On impeaching a party's own witness, see Rule 607.

The rule expressly authorizes leading questions to be asked of a hostile witness, an adverse party, or a witness identified with an adverse party. In allowing leading questions to be asked of an adverse party or of a witness identified with an adverse party who has not shown hostility, the rule may change prior law. See *Sinclair v. Barker,* 236 Or 599, 390 P2d 321 (1964). Ordinarily, an employee, officer, director, or managing agent of a party, or a relative, partner, or close associate, should be considered a witness identified with the adverse party and thus subject to leading questions. See 1 M. Graham, HANDBOOK OF FEDERAL EVIDENCE (4th ed 1996) § 611.8 at 833–4.

RULE 612. ORS 40.375. WRITING USED TO REFRESH MEMORY

If a witness uses a writing to refresh memory for the purpose of testifying, either while testifying or before testifying if the court in its discretion determines it is necessary in the interests of justice, an adverse party is entitled to have the writing produced at the hearing, to inspect it, to cross-examine the witness thereon, and to introduce into evidence those portions which relate to the testimony of the witness. If it is claimed that the writing contains matters not related to the subject matter of the testimony, the court shall examine the writing in camera, excise any portions not so related, and order delivery of the remainder to the party entitled thereto. Any portion withheld over objections shall be preserved and made available to the appellate court in the event of an appeal. If a writing is not produced or delivered pursuant to order under this section, the court shall make any order justice requires, except that in criminal cases when the prosecution elects not to comply the order shall be one striking the testimony or, if the court in its discretion determines that the interests of justice so require, declaring a mistrial.

LEGISLATIVE COMMENTARY

Oregon Rule of Evidence 612 provides the opposing party with access to any writing used by a witness to refresh the witness' memory for the purpose of testifying. Except for its preamble, the rule is identical to Rule 612 of the Federal Rules of Evidence. It makes substantial changes in Oregon law as expressed in ORS 45.580 and 45.630. These statutes are repealed.

Use of writing. It is established trial procedure that during questioning, counsel may hand the witness a written memorandum to inspect which revives the memory and allows the witness to continue speaking. McCormick, *Evidence,* § 9 at 15 (2d ed 1972). Until now, Oregon law has required that the memorandum have the same qualities as a record of past recollection, i.e., it must be written by the witness, or at witness' direction, at or near the time of the event when the facts were still fresh in the witness' memory. ORS 45.580; see ORE 803(5). Rule 612 changes this. It makes no distinction as to the character of the writing used. In accordance with Wigmore and most present day courts, it allows any memorandum to be used without regard to authorship, time of recordation or accuracy, when the purpose is to revive memory.

The above change follows from the difference between a writing used to refresh memory and a record of past recollection. Unlike records of past recollection, writings used to refresh memory are not evidence, but merely aids in the giving of evidence. *State v. Sutton,* 253 Or 24, 450 P2d 748 (1969); *Hall v. Brown,* 102 Or 389, 202 P 719 (1921). The trier of fact does not see them. There is therefore no reason why they should meet the standards of reliability that are imposed on records of past recollection, as Oregon courts have tacitly recognized. In recent years, ORS 45.580 has been more honored in the breach than in the observance. Compare *Manchester Assur. Co. v. Oregon Ry. & Nav. Co.,* 46 Or 162, 79 P 60 (1905) (only writing made by witness can be used); *Walling v. Van Pelt,* 132 Or 243, 285 P 262 (1930) (map not a memorandum for purposes of statute); with *Banks v. Community Church,* 178 Or 1, 7, 165 P2d 65 (1946) (minute entries made by non-witness appropriate to refresh memory); *Waterway Terminals Co. v. P.S. Lord Mechanical Contractors,* 242 Or 1, 57, 406 P2d 556 13 A.L.R. 3d 1 (1965) (suggesting ORS 45.580 applies only to memorandum used as record of past recollection, as "anything which will refresh the memory of a witness may be resorted to"); *State v. Liston,* 18 Or App 26, 523 P2d 609, SCt review denied (1974) (uncertified transcript of tape recording allowed to refresh memory).

Although the rule speaks of a "writing," the Legislative Assembly intends that its policies of permitted use and required disclosure apply to any material that refreshes the memory of a witness. The refreshing material may be a photograph, a recording or any other object. This expansion is only possible as a result of the rule's abandonment of the criteria in ORS 45.580.

A writing is "used" when counsel reads part of it to refresh the witness' memory, even if the witness does not see it. *Waterway Terminals v. P.S. Lord,* supra, 242 Or at 61.

Access by opposing counsel. It is settled law that a writing which is used during testimony to refresh the witness' memory must be made available to opposing counsel at the hearing. ORS 45.580. Dispute exists whether the rule should extend to writings that are used prior to testifying to refresh the memory. ORS 45.580 did not allow this. Rule 612 would, if the court determines that access is necessary in the interests of justice. The change is appropriate, because a writing reviewed immediately before taking the stand can influence a witness as much as one used on the stand. The procedure provides a check on the improper coaching of witnesses and on testimony that is derived entirely from a writing rather than from the witness' independent recollection. Kirkpatrick, "Reforming Evidence Law in Oregon," in 59 Or L Rev 43, 95 (1980). Although ORCP 36 provides for court-ordered discovery in the interests of justice prior to trial access at the hearing or trial, to writings used prior to trial, is not addressed and has been unavailable under ORS 45.580.

Any time a writing is produced, the opposing counsel may inspect it, cross-examine the witness upon it, and read it to the jury.

Protection. This rule makes accessible only writings that are used to refresh memory for the purpose of testifying. The phrase "for the purpose of testifying" provides a safeguard against wholesale exploration of an opponent's files, including the attorney's work product. Fed R Evid 612, Comment at 73. A party required to produce a writing may submit it to the court for examination in camera. The court will then excise the portions unrelated to the witness' testimony. If the adverse party objects to the withholding of any portion, that segment is to be preserved for appellate review. See generally, ORCP 36C and ORS 135.873, the latter providing for in camera review of disclosures in criminal cases subject to a protective order of the court.

Sanctions. The rule directs that if the prosecution in a criminal case does not produce a writing that is used to refresh a witness' memory and is ordered to be produced, the witness testimony is to be stricken or a mistrial declared. The choice lies in the court's discretion. Cf. ORS 135.865 (sanctions for failing to comply with criminal discovery). In civil cases, when a party fails to produce a writing the court has available such remedies as contempt, dismissal and finding issues against the offender. Fed R Evid 612, Comment at 74. The Legislative Assembly intends that the trial court have full discretion in determining the sanction appropriate to the case.

TEXT

Writing Used to Refresh Memory

Rule 612 provides that if a witness refreshes his or her memory from a writing, either while testifying or before testifying, the court may order the writing produced and the adverse party is entitled to inspect it, cross-examine the witness thereon, and introduce into evidence those portions that relate to the testimony of the witness.

The right to production established by Rule 612 should be distinguished from two related doctrines: (1) the right to pretrial discovery of prior statements of witnesses, subject to certain qualifications. See ORCP 43 (request for production); ORCP 36B(3) (qualified privilege for work product); ORS 135.815(1) and ORS 135.835(1) (discovery of witness statements in criminal cases). (2) The right of the adverse party to have prior statements of a witness produced at trial to aid in cross-examination of a witness. See *Pac NW Bell Tel Co v. Century Home Components Inc.,* 261 Or 333, 491 P2d 1023 (1971), modified on other grounds 494 P2d 884 (1972) (civil cases); *State v. Foster,* 242 Or 101, 407 P2d 901 (1965) (criminal cases). See also *State v. Hartfield,* 290 Or 583, 624 P2d 588 (1981) (defendant entitled to examine recording of prosecution witness' testimony to grand jury). If the item used to refresh recollection was a prior statement of the witness, Rule 612 and this latter doctrine overlap.

The Commentary to Rule 612 indicates that if the writing was used to refresh recollection at trial, the adverse party has an absolute right to see it. This was the rule under prior law (see former ORS 45.580 (repealed 1981)), and the majority rule at common law. See 1 McCormick, *Evidence* (4th ed 1992) § 9. If the writing was used to refresh recollection prior to testifying, production is discretionary with the court. The rule itself is less clear on this point, because the legislature deleted the comma after "while testifying" in the first sentence. This permits the argument that the phrase "if the court in its discretion determines it is in the interest of justice" modifies writings used to refresh recollection at trial as well as before. The Commentary states that, except for the preamble, the rule is identical to FRE 612. Under FRE 612, the discretion of the court to require or not require production applies only to writings used before testifying. A similar construction should be given to the Oregon rule.

Rule 612 allows production only of those writings that were used "to refresh memory for the purpose of testifying," not to all writings a witness may have reviewed at some point prior to trial. According to the Advisory Committee's Note to FRE 612:

> The purpose of the phrase "for the purpose of testifying" is to safeguard against using the rule as a pretext for wholesale exploration of an opposing party's files and to insure that access is limited only to those writings which may fairly be said in fact to have an impact upon the testimony of the witness.

The court may exercise its discretion against requiring production of a writing used to refresh recollection prior to trial when the testimony relates to an unimportant matter, the writing is voluminous, or where an order of production would result in excessive expense, inconvenience, or delay.

Items that May Be Used to Refresh Recollection

Although the rule mentions only writings, the Commentary expresses the intent of the legislature that the rule apply to any matter used to refresh the recollection of a witness, including a photograph, record, or other object. "It has been said that anything which will refresh the memory of a witness may be resorted to. ..." *Waterway Terminals Co. v. P. S. Lord Mechanical Contractors,* 242 Or 1, 58, 406 P2d 556 (1965). One court has held that memory may be revived by "a song, a scent, a photograph, an allusion, even a past statement known to be false." *United States v. Rappy,* 157 F2d 964, 967 (2nd Cir 1946), cert denied 329 US 806 (1947).

Whatever is used to refresh the recollection of the witness does not itself constitute evidence and may not be shown or read to the jury, except at the request of the adverse party, unless some other basis is established for its admissibility. Because it is not evidence it need not be authenticated, nor must its reliability be established. If a writing is used, it need not have been prepared contemporaneously and need not have been prepared by the witness. See *Banks v. Community Church,* 178 Or 1, 7, 165 P2d 65 (1946) (writing prepared by person other than witness allowed to refresh recollection). As the Commentary notes, the rule allows "any memorandum to be used without regard to authorship, time of recordation or accuracy, when the purpose is to revive memory." A writing used to refresh recollection may be a copy rather than an original, and Rule 1002 is inapplicable.

Scope of Production Required

Although the first sentence of the rule speaks of production of "the writing," the entire writing will not necessarily be given to the opposing party. The second sentence provides: "If it is claimed that the writing contains matters not related to the subject matter of the testimony, the court shall examine the writing in camera, excise any portions not so related, and order delivery of the remainder to the party entitled thereto."

In *Banister Continental Corp. v. Northwest Pipeline Corp.,* 76 Or App 282, 709 P2d 1103 (1985), decision vacated 301 Or 763, 724 P2d 822 (1986), the court held that the trial judge did not abuse his discretion under Rule 612 in requiring production of only parts of a diary that a witness acknowledged he had reviewed before testifying. The court noted that "broad discretion is necessary [under the rule] because of the myriad situations which face a trial court." 76 Or App at 291, 709 P2d at 1109.

In *United States v. Costner,* 684 F2d 370 (6th Cir 1982), where a witness used a report to refresh memory, the court held that it was error to receive the entire report into evidence when offered by the prosecutor, when it included prejudicial evidence that was not related to the witness's testimony.

Foundation for Refreshing Recollection

Rule 612 does not address whether any showing of loss of memory is necessary before a witness' recollection may be refreshed. Some cases have suggested that such a showing is necessary. See *Waterway Terminals Co. v. P.S. Lord Mechanical Contractors,* 242 Or 1, 60–1, 406 P2d 556 (1965); ANNOT., *Refreshment of Recollection by Use of Memoranda or Other Writings,* 82 ALR2d 473, 493–6 (1962). The better view is that no such foundation is required. As McCormick states: "The witness may believe that he remembers completely but on looking at the memorandum she would be caused to recall additional facts." McCormick, *Evidence* (4th ed 1992) § 9 at 34.

The witness' recollection must be refreshed before the witness will be allowed to testify on the issue. The witness may not simply read from the writing. To test whether the witness is truly testifying from independent recollection, the court may require the witness to surrender the writing. When expert witnesses are testifying or when the matter is so lengthy that the witness could not reasonably be expected to testify without referring to the writing, courts will usually allow the witness to consult the writing during testimony. *United States v. Boyd,* 606 F2d 792, 794 (8th Cir 1979); *Goings v. United States,* 377 F2d 753, 763 n11 (8th Cir 1967), cert denied 393 US 883 (1960). If the writing has already been admitted into evidence, e.g., as a business record under Rule 803(6), the court is likely to allow the witness to consult it without restriction.

If the witness' memory is not refreshed, a foundation may then be laid for introduction of the writing under the past recollection recorded exception to the hearsay rule. To admit the writing under Rule 803(5), a showing must be made that: (1) the witness has insufficient recollection to testify fully and accurately,

(2) the writing was made or adopted by the witness when the matter was fresh in the witness' memory, and (3) the writing correctly reflects the knowledge of the witness at that time. The writing may be read into evidence but may not it-self be received as an exhibit unless offered by an adverse party. See textual discussion of Rule 803(5).

Refreshing Witness' Recollection by Leading Questions

A witness' recollection may sometimes be refreshed by leading questions rather than by showing a writing to the witness. *Waterway Terminals Co. v. P. S. Lord Mechanical Contractors,* 242 Or 1, 57, 406 P2d 556 (1965). Rule 611(3) regulates the use of leading questions to refresh a witness' recollection. It pro-vides: "Leading questions should not be used on the direct examination of a witness except as may be necessary to develop the witness's testimony."

The court has discretion to refuse to allow refreshing of a witness' recollec-tion by leading questions, because this technique may expose the jury to inad-missible evidence. Rule 103(3) provides: "In jury cases, proceedings shall be conducted, to the extent practicable, so as to prevent inadmissible evidence from being suggested to the jury by any means, such as ... asking questions in the hearing of the jury."

The use of leading questions to refresh a witness' recollection was sharply criticized in *United States v. Shoupe,* 548 F2d 636, 641 (6th Cir 1977). The court stated:

> [W]e find no precedent sanctioning the recitation in the presence of the jury of extended unsworn remarks, attributed to a Government witness, which were allegedly recorded in an unverified document and which inculpate the defen-dant. Courts have condemned this practice as ... increasing the probability that the jury will consider the statements as substantive evidence despite any limit-ing instruction to the contrary as placing before the jury the content of patently inadmissible past recollection recorded and as bypassing, to the prejudice of the defendant, reasonable alternative measures to accomplish the same legiti-mate result. (citations omitted)

The court may require that an attempt to refresh a witness' recollection with leading questions take place outside the presence of the jury. If the leading question pertains to a prior inconsistent statement and is being used not to re-fresh the witness' recollection but to impeach the testimony, it may be allowed under Rules 607 and 613.

Applicability of Rule 612 to Privileged Writings

It is unclear whether the right of an adverse party to production of a writing used to refresh the recollection of a witness can override the privileges set forth in Article V or the work product doctrine. Some courts have held under FRE 612 that a privilege or work product immunity with respect to a writing is waived when the writing is used to refresh the recollection of a witness. See *James Jul-*

ian, Inc. v. Raytheon Co., 93 FRD 138 (D Del 1982) (right under FRE 612 to see statement used to refresh memory for purposes of testifying overrides work product immunity); *Wheeling-Pittsburgh Steel Corp v. Underwriters Laboratories Inc.,* 81 FRD 8 (ND Ill 1978); *United States v. Nobles,* 422 US 225, 95 SCt 2160, 45 LEd2d 141 (1975). But see *Berkey Photo Inc. v. Eastman Kodak Co.,* 74 FRD 613 (SDNY 1977). See also *Pac. N. W. Bell Tel. Co. v. Century Home Components Inc.,* 261 Or 333, 491 P2d 1023, modified on other grounds 494 P2d 884 (1972) (right to see prior statement referred to by witness overrides work product immunity).

In *Ramsey v. County of Fresno,* 7 Fed Evid Rptr 954 (ED Cal 1980), the court stated: "Even if a document should qualify as an attorney's work product, counsel cannot have it both ways. If it is to be protected as work product, it must be used solely for the attorney in the preparation and prosecution of the case. On the other hand, if a witness or series of witnesses are allowed to read the product for the purpose of refreshing their recollection, it loses whatever immunity it may have."

Other courts have held that the privileged nature of a writing is a factor for the trial court to consider in deciding whether or not to exercise its discretion to order production of the writing. *Joseph Schlitz Brewing Co. v. Muller & Phipps Ltd.,* 85 FRD 118 (WD Mo 1980). In light of the uncertainty regarding this issue, it would be advisable for attorneys to exercise discretion with regard to what documents are shown to a witness for the purpose of refreshing recollection.

If the witness is shown a privileged communication, and the witness is outside the scope of the privilege, the privilege may be waived regardless of the applicability of Rule 612. Rule 511 provides that voluntary disclosure of a privileged communication to a third person with the consent of the holder generally waives the privilege.

See generally ANNOT., *Use of Writing to Refresh Witness' Memory as Governed by Rule 612 of Federal Rules of Evidence,* 73 ALR Fed 423 (1985); COMMENT, *Federal Rule of Evidence 612 and the Work Product Doctrine—Conflict or Congruity?,* 1986 Ariz St L J 543; NOTE, *Discovery of Attorney Work Product Reviewed by an Expert Witness,* 85 Colum L Rev 812 (1985); NOTE, *Discovery Under the Federal Rules of Civil Procedure of Attorney Work Product Provided to an Expert Witness,* 53 Fordham L Rev 1159 (1985); NOTE, *Resolving the Conflict Between Federal Rule of Evidence 612 and the Work Product Doctrine: A Proposed Solution,* 38 U Kan L Rev 1039 (1990).

Sanctions

If a writing is not produced pursuant to an order under this rule, the court shall make any order justice requires, including striking the testimony, dismissing the case, finding issues against the offending party, or holding a party or witness in contempt. In a criminal case, where the prosecution elects not to comply with the order, the court is required to either strike the testimony, or, if the court determines that the interests of justice so require, declare a mistrial.

The rule does not address the situation where a party acting in good faith is unable to comply with the order because the writing is unavailable not through the fault of the party. A court is likely to adjust its sanctions accordingly or to withhold them. Nonproduction by a prosecutor under these circumstances is unlikely to be found to be an election not to comply with the court's order.

RULE 613. ORS 40.380. PRIOR STATEMENTS OF WITNESSES

(1) **[Examining witness concerning prior statement.] In examining a witness concerning a prior statement made by the witness, whether written or not, the statement need not be shown nor its contents disclosed to the witness at that time, but on request the same shall be shown or disclosed to opposing counsel.**

(2) **[Extrinsic evidence of prior inconsistent statement of witness.] Extrinsic evidence of a prior inconsistent statement by a witness is not admissible unless the witness is afforded an opportunity to explain or deny the same and the opposite party is afforded an opportunity to interrogate the witness thereon, or the interests of justice otherwise require. This provision does not apply to admissions of a party-opponent as defined in Rule 801 (ORS 40.450).**

LEGISLATIVE COMMENTARY

Oregon Rule of Evidence 613 sets forth the proper procedure for examining a witness in connection with a prior inconsistent statement, and the foundation to be laid before extrinsic evidence of such a statement may be introduced. The rule is identical to Federal Rule 613. It substantially changes the practice under ORS 45.610, which is repealed.

The rule markedly relaxes the foundational requirements for use of a prior inconsistent statement at trial. In doing so, it shows the influence of Rule 801(4)(a)(A), which allows any prior inconsistent statement to be received as substantive evidence. In the case of extrinsic evidence a foundation is not dispensed with altogether. The trier of fact is clearly better informed, and fairness better served, if a witness has the opportunity to explain the circumstances and meaning of a prior statement.

To this extent an application of their provisions may conflict, this rule is subject to the stricter foundational requirements of Rule 609-1, relating to impeachment for bias or interest.

Subsection (1). The Queen's Case, 2 Br. & B. 284, 129 Eng Rep 976 (1820), laid down the requirement that a cross-examiner, prior to questioning a witness about the witness' prior statement in writing, must show it to the witness. Abolished by statute in the country of its origin, the requirement nevertheless gained currency in the United States and was faithfully preserved in ORS 45.610. The Oregon statute required not only display of a written statement, but, for any statement, an account of the circumstances including time, place and persons present. This subsection abolishes this useless impediment to cross-examination. Ladd, "Some Observations on Credibility: Impeachment of Witnesses," in 52 Cornell L Q

239, 246–247 (1967); McCormick, *Evidence* § 28 (2d ed 1972); 4 Wigmore, *Evidence* §§ 1259–1260 (3d ed 1940). Both oral and written statements are included.

The provision for disclosure to counsel is designed to protect against unwarranted insinuations that a statement has been made, when the fact is to the contrary.

The rule does not defeat the application of ORE 1002, relating to production of the original when the contents of a writing are sought to be proved.

Subsection (2). This subsection preserves the familiar foundation requirement that an impeaching statement must be shown to the witness before it can be proved by extrinsic evidence, with some modification. See Ladd, supra at 247. The traditional insistence that the witness' attention be directed to the statement on cross-examination is relaxed in favor of simply providing the witness an opportunity to explain the statement and the opposite party an opportunity to examine on the basis of it. No particular time or sequence is specified. Under this procedure, several collusive witnesses can be examined before their prior inconsistent statement is disclosed. See Comment to California Evidence Code § 770. The rule also reduces the dangers of oversight. See McCormick § 37 at 68.

A witness may become unavailable by a time the statement is discovered. For such an event, the rule confers a measure of discretion upon the judge to allow the statement into evidence without satisfying the full requirements of this subsection. Similar provisions are found in California Evidence Code § 770 and New Jersey Evidence Rule 22(b).

Under the principle of *expressio unius,* the rule does not apply to impeachment by evidence of prior inconsistent conduct. The use of inconsistent statements to impeach a hearsay declarant is treated in Rule 806.

TEXT

RULE 613(1)

Examining Witness Concerning Prior Statement

There are two ways to prove a prior statement to impeach a witness: by cross-examination, assuming the witness is willing to admit making the prior inconsistent statement; or by extrinsic evidence. Rule 613(1) addresses the first method of proof, and Rule 613(2) the second.

Rule 613(1) eliminates the requirement of former ORS 45.610 (repealed 1981) that a writing must be shown to a witness before the witness can be examined regarding it. Although this requirement is recognized in many jurisdictions, McCormick comments: "It is believed that its actual invocation in trials is relatively infrequent in most states, and that the generality of judges and practitioners are unaware of this possible hidden rock in the path of the cross-examiner." 1 McCormick, *Evidence* (4th ed 1992) § 28 at 97. It has been stated that the rule is "more honored in the breach than in the observance." *United States v. Dillard,* 101 F2d 829, 837 (2nd Cir 1938), cert denied 306 US 635 (1939). The requirement has been viewed as time-consuming and as an impediment to effective cross-examination. 4 Wigmore, *Evidence* (Chadbourn Rev 1972) § 1259.

Although the new rule does not require that the writing be shown to the witness, Rule 613(1) requires that the statement, whether written or oral, be disclosed to opposing counsel as a check against unfounded implications that a prior inconsistent statement was made. Because of Rules 612 and 613, it does not matter whether a writing is being used to refresh the recollection of a witness or for impeachment. In either case the writing must be produced at the opponent's request.

Although Rule 613(1) dispenses with any obligation to show a witness a prior statement during examination of that witness, ORCP 36B(3) establishes in civil cases the right of a person, including a party, to obtain copies of earlier statements made by that person that are in the possession of a party.

The fact that a witness gives inconsistent testimony goes only to its credibility and does not affect the **sufficiency** of the testimony to support a jury verdict or destroy its probative force as a matter of law. *Hunter v. Farmers Ins. Co.*, 135 Or App 125, 898 P2d 201 (1995).

RULE 613(2)
Extrinsic Evidence of Prior Inconsistent Statement of Witness

Rule 613(2) eliminates the requirement of prior law that a foundation be laid before extrinsic evidence of a prior inconsistent statement could be offered. See former ORS 45.610 (repealed 1981), which provided:

> A witness may be impeached by evidence that he has made, at other times, statements inconsistent with his present testimony; but before this can be done, the statements must be related to him, with the circumstances of times, places and persons present, and he shall be asked whether he made the statements, and if so, allowed to explain them. If the statements be in writing, they shall be shown to the witness before any question is put to him concerning them.

Rule 613(2) requires only that the witness be sufficiently alerted to the statement's existence so that the witness has "an opportunity to explain or deny the same."

To afford the witness an opportunity to explain or deny the prior inconsistent statement it will be necessary to describe the statement to the witness. As a practical matter, this will require disclosure of some of the circumstances surrounding the making of the statement that were required to be disclosed under the former statute. The primary change from former law is that under the new rule extrinsic evidence of the prior inconsistent statement may be admitted *before* the witness is given an opportunity to explain or deny the statement. The rule does not require that the opportunity necessarily come prior to introduction of extrinsic evidence. As the Commentary observes, "no particular time or sequence is specified." It will be sufficient, unless the court orders otherwise, to allow the witness an opportunity to explain or deny the statement and to allow the opposing party an opportunity to interrogate the witness thereon after the introduction of the extrinsic evidence.

Although the rule is not entirely clear on the point, it does not appear to place any burden on the impeaching party to recall a witness who has been impeached by extrinsic evidence of a prior inconsistent statement but who has not yet been afforded an opportunity to explain or deny the statement. See 1 M. Graham, HANDBOOK OF FEDERAL EVIDENCE (4th ed 1996) § 613.3 at 891 ("[T]he foundation requirement is satisfied if the witness remains available for recall by the calling party later in the course of the trial even if that party chooses not to recall the witness."). Compliance with the rule should at least require that the impeaching party alert the opponent and the court that the witness may need to be recalled and should remain under subpoena. The decision whether or not to recall the witness should rest with the opponent.

However, there is authority that a court may prohibit an opponent from offering extrinsic evidence of prior inconsistent statements in circumstances where it would be an undue hardship upon the proponent of the witness to bring back the witness to deny or explain the statements and there was no justification for the failure to confront the witness with the prior inconsistent statements during cross-examination. In *United States v. Lynch,* 800 F2d 765 (8th Cir 1986), cert denied 481 US 1022 (1987), defendant was convicted of murder of a fellow prison inmate. After the government's inmate witnesses had left the stand, defendant sought to impeach them with their prior statements that they saw nothing of the killing. The appellate court held that it was not an abuse of discretion for the trial judge to exclude this impeachment and to refuse to call the witnesses back, in light of the substantial logistical difficulties in producing inmate witnesses.

Exceptions to Rule 613(2)

There are several exceptions to the rule's requirement that the witness be "afforded an opportunity to explain or deny" the prior inconsistent statement and that the opposite party be "afforded an opportunity to interrogate the witness thereon." First, this requirement is not applicable to the admissions of a party opponent as defined in Rule 801(4)(b). Such statements may be received not only for impeachment but also as substantive evidence. Parties will presumably have an adequate opportunity to explain or deny any such statements in their own case-in-chief or rebuttal.

Second, the judge has discretion to dispense with the requirement in the interests of justice and to allow the extrinsic evidence of the prior inconsistent statement in unusual circumstances, such as where the examiner does not learn of the prior inconsistent statement until the witness is beyond the court's jurisdiction.

Third, according to the Commentary the requirement is inapplicable to proof of prior inconsistent conduct.

Finally, the requirement is inapplicable to impeachment of a hearsay declarant by a prior inconsistent statement. See Rule 806.

If the prior inconsistent statement is being used to prove bias or interest rather than merely inconsistency, the stricter foundation requirements of Rule 609-1 apply. See the Commentary to Rule 609-1: "In the event of a conflict, the Legislative Assembly intends that ORE 609-1, the stricter rule, control."

Extrinsic Evidence of Prior Inconsistent Statement When Witness Admits Making Statement

Whether extrinsic evidence of a prior inconsistent statement may be received after the witness fully admits the prior statement is a subject of dispute among commentators. Compare 3 D. Louisell and C. Mueller, FEDERAL EVIDENCE (1979) 548 ("[T]he better view is that such proof may be received even if the witness admits making the statement") (footnote omitted), with 1 McCormick, *Evidence* (4th ed 1992) § 37 at 120 ("[T]he prevailing view is to the contrary."). It has been argued that there is a greater danger that the jury will consider the prior inconsistent statement as substantive evidence, despite an instruction not to do so, when the prior statement is proven by extrinsic evidence than when it is brought out by cross-examination of the witness. See Graham, *Employing Inconsistent Statements for Impeachment and as Substantive Evidence: A Critical Review and Proposed Amendments of Federal Rules of Evidence 801(d)(i)(A), 613, and 607,* 75 Mich L Rev 1565 (1977).

It would seem that extrinsic evidence of prior inconsistent statements should generally not be allowed if the witness unequivocally admits making them. See *United States v. Jones,* 578 F2d 1332, 1340 (10th Cir), cert denied 439 US 913 (1978) (no error to exclude tape recording of prior inconsistent statement admitted by prosecution witness during cross-examination). A court should perhaps be more willing to allow extrinsic evidence of an admitted prior inconsistent statement when it can be proven by a writing rather than testimony of other witnesses. See *Gordon v. United States,* 344 US 414, 420–1, 73 SCt 369, 374, 97 LEd 447, 454 (1953) ("[A]n admission that a contradiction is contained in a writing should not bar admission of the document itself in evidence").

Extrinsic proof of a prior inconsistent statement admitted by a witness should generally be allowed when the statement may be received not only for impeachment, but also as substantive evidence under Rule 801(4)(a)(A) or Rule 803 or 804. The Commentary is in error in stating that Rule 801(4)(a)(A) "allows any prior inconsistent statement to be received as substantive evidence." Under Rule 801(4)(a)(A), a prior inconsistent statement is not hearsay only if it was "given under oath subject to the penalty of perjury at a trial hearing or other proceeding, or in a deposition" provided declarant testifies and is subject to cross-examination regarding the statement.

Impeachment by Statements in Deposition

Statements in depositions probably constitute the largest category of statements that can be used both for impeachment and as substantive evidence under Rule 801(4)(a)(A). (On the use of depositions at trial, see ORS 45.250.) If extrinsic evidence of the statements made in the deposition is necessary, the deposition transcript can be offered as an exhibit. A transcript certified in accordance with ORCP 39G(1) should satisfy the authentication requirements of Rule 901. The transcript may also be authenticated by testimony of the court reporter or other person present at the deposition or by stipulation. A deposition transcript will usually qualify as an exception to the hearsay rule under the public records exception (see Rule 803(8)), or the exception for past recollection recorded (see Rule 803(5)). Reliance on the latter exception will normally require testimony of the court reporter.

Introduction of the transcript is not required in order to impeach a witness based on statements made at a deposition. The court reporter or any witness present at the deposition may be called to testify to the prior inconsistent statement, and, if necessary, that witness' recollection can be refreshed by examining the transcript. On impeachment procedures generally, see Graham, *Impeachment of Witness—Prior Inconsistent Statements,* 21 Am Jur *Proof of Facts* 2d 101 (1980); ANNOT., *Use of Prior Inconsistent Statements for Impeachment of Testimony of Witnesses Under Rule 613, Federal Rules of Evidence,* 40 ALR Fed 629 (1978).

Definition of "Inconsistent"

Rule 613 does not define *prior inconsistent statement.* The Oregon Supreme Court has held that a statement is inconsistent if there is "any material variance" between the statement and the direct testimony. *Rigelman v. Gilligan,* 265 Or 109, 506 P2d 710 (1973). The court further stated: "[T]hat in applying the criterion of material inconsistency a fair range of discretion should be accorded the trial judge, and that the courts should 'lean toward receiving such statements in case of doubt to aid evaluating the testimony.'" (citation omitted). See 1 McCormick, *Evidence* (4th ed 1992) § 34 at 114 ("[U]nder the more widely accepted view any material variance between the testimony and the previous statement will suffice") (footnote omitted); 3A Wigmore, *Evidence* (Chadbourn Rev 1970) § 1040 at 1048 (defining the standard to be whether the witness' expressions "appear to have been produced by inconsistent beliefs"). Inconsistent statements have been held to include omission of material facts from earlier statements, earlier statements that the witness lacked knowledge of the subject, and silence under circumstances where the witness would reasonably have been expected to speak if the facts were as he or she has now testified. See 1 McCormick, *Evidence* (4th ed 1992) § 34 at 114–6.

The Oregon Court of Appeals has held that "when a witness testifies that he is unsure of or does not remember having made a particular statement, the witness may be impeached by evidence that he made the alleged statements." *State v. Van Gorder,* 56 Or App 83, 89, 641 P2d 584, rev denied 293 Or 146, 651 P2d 143 (1982). See also *State v. Bruce,* 31 Or App 1184, 1189, 572 P2d 351 (1977) ("[t]he 'I don't remember' answers ... in response to questions asked concerning the prior inconsistent statements ... were the equivalent of 'No, I did not say that'"). The Commentary to Rule 801(4)(a)(A) states: "The Legislative Assembly intends that 'inconsistent' includes situations where a witness denies making a prior statement or does not remember the content of the statement." See generally ANNOT., *Denial of Recollection As Inconsistent With Prior Statements So As to Render Statement Admissible,* 99 ALR3d 934 (1980).

Inconsistent Statement Must Be that of Witness

The prior inconsistent statement must be made by or reasonably attributable to the witness being impeached. In *Wohlers v. Ruegger,* 58 Or App 537, 649 P2d 602 (1982), the court stated that it is generally improper to impeach a witness with a complaint containing allegations inconsistent with the witness' testimony if the complaint was prepared by the witness' insurance company and the witness had no knowledge of the allegations in it.

Impeachment by Prior Inconsistent Statement Pertaining to Collateral Matter

The proof permitted of prior inconsistent statements by extrinsic evidence is not as broad as the inquiry allowed into prior inconsistent statements by cross-examination. Some prior inconsistent statements must be brought out on cross-examination or not at all. If the inconsistency relates to a collateral matter, extrinsic evidence of the prior inconsistent statement will not be allowed. See *Coles v. Harsch,* 129 Or 11, 18, 276 P 248 (1929); *State v. Deal,* 41 Or 437, 70 P 532 (1902). If the matter is collateral, the examiner is required to "take the answer" of the witness and cannot prove the inconsistency by extrinsic evidence. McCormick, *Evidence* (4th ed 1992) § 36 at 117–8.

Impeachment of Statements Made upon Cross-Examination

Courts generally will not allow evidence otherwise inadmissible to be used to contradict the testimony of a witness when the issue being contradicted was raised on cross-examination going beyond the scope of direct examination. See *State v. Johnson,* 277 Or 45, 49, 559 P2d 496, 497 (1977) (prosecutor asked defendant on cross-examination whether he was a drug dealer in order to impeach defendant with a prior statement admitting he was a drug dealer. Held: reversible error. "It is obvious that the questions were asked on cross-examination for the sole purpose of making a hook on which to hang the legally irrelevant evidence of the police officer's conversation with defendant. Such trial tactics upon the part of the state are to be discouraged."). See also *United States v. Pantone,* 609 F2d 675, 681 (3rd Cir 1979) ("[W]e disapprove of the practice of using cross-examination beyond the scope of the direct testimony for the purpose of laying a foundation for the introduction, as rebuttal, of otherwise inadmissible evidence."); *United States v. Trejo,* 501 F2d 138 (9th Cir 1974).

Good Faith Requirement

It has been stated that:

A good faith basis for inquiring regarding a prior inconsistent statement is required: innuendos or insinuations of a nonexistent statement are improper. [T]he court in its discretion may demand prior to any cross-examination an on the record assurance of counsel that if required to do so he can support the foundation question as to whether the witness had made a prior statement with evidence of the alleged statement. (1 M. Graham, HANDBOOK OF FEDERAL EVIDENCE, § 613.3 at 891-892 (4th ed 1996) (footnotes omitted))

Rule 613 combined with Rule 607 provides a party with an opportunity to impeach its own witness by evidence of prior inconsistent statements. Such a procedure presents the danger that a party may bring out prior inconsistent statements of its own witness with the hope that the jury will ignore a limiting instruction and give substantive effect to such statements. For a discussion of this issue, see textual discussion of Rule 607.

Unconstitutionally-Obtained Prior Statements

It has been held not to violate the Federal Constitution to impeach a defendant with statements or other contradictory evidence that is not admissible as substantive evidence because obtained in violation of defendant's federal constitutional rights. See *Harris v. New York,* 401 US 222, 91 SCt 643, 28 LEd2d 1 (1971); *United States v. Havens,* 446 US 620, 100 SCt 1912, 64 LEd2d 559 (1980); *Walder v. United States,* 347 US 62, 74 SCt 354, 98 LEd503 (1954).

However, in *State v. Isom,* 306 Or 587, 761 P2d 524 (1988), the Oregon Supreme Court held that Article 1, section 12, of the Oregon Constitution precludes the state from impeaching defendant's trial testimony with prior inconsistent statements elicited by police officers after defendant had told the officers that he did not wish to talk to them and that he wanted a lawyer. The court noted: "We are not confronted here with a situation ... [where] no warnings were given and no request for a lawyer was ever made. We do not now decide the admissibility of such uncounseled out-of-court statements offered for impeachment purposes under Oregon law. That issue remains an open question." 306 Or at 594.

The Court of Appeals has held that a defendant who does not take the stand at trial may challenge on appeal a pretrial ruling that statements he made, although inadmissible in the prosecution's case-in-chief, would be allowed for purposes of impeachment, where the defendant claims the ruling deterred him from taking the stand. *State v. Mills,* 76 Or App 301, 710 P2d 148 (1985), rev denied 300 Or 546, 715 P2d 93 (1986).

NOTE REGARDING OMISSION OF FRE 614

LEGISLATIVE COMMENTARY

The Legislative Assembly did not enact Federal Rule 614, which authorizes the trial judge to call and question witnesses. Although that rule is consistent with Oregon law, the Legislative Assembly was reluctant to appear to provide the court with an expanded role in the development of evidence. By not adopting Federal Rule 614, the Legislative Assembly does not intend to deny or limit the inherent power of a trial court to call and examine witnesses. *Frangos v. Edmunds,* 179 Or 577, 610, 173 P2d 596 (1946).

[Author's Note: See discussion of judicial authority to call and examine witnesses in Text after Rule 611(1), supra.]

RULE 615.   ORS 40.385. EXCLUSION OF WITNESSES

At the request of a party the court may order witnesses excluded until the time of final argument, and it may make the order of its own motion. This rule does not authorize exclusion of (1) a party who is a natural person, or (2) an officer or employee of a party which is not a natural person designated as its representative by its attorney, or (3) a person whose presence is shown by a party to be essential to the presentation of the party's cause, or (4) the victim in a criminal case.

LEGISLATIVE COMMENTARY

Oregon Rule of Evidence 615 provides guidelines for the exercise of the court's discretion in excluding witnesses.

The rule is a modified version of Federal Rule 615. Rather than provide that witnesses shall be excluded "... so that they cannot hear the testimony of other witnesses ...," the rule indicates that witnesses may be excluded "... until the time of final argument ...." The Legislative Assembly believes that the purpose of the rule is better served if witnesses who are excluded are kept from all phases of the trial at which testimony might be discussed. Potentially, this includes voir dire, opening statements and offers of proof.

The rule is consistent with the holding of the Court of Appeals in *State v. Bishop,* 7 Or App 558, 492 P2d 509 (1972). Under that decision, when one party moves to exclude witnesses and the other party voices no objection, the motion should always be granted. When the motion is opposed the trial court must exercise its discretion, balancing the good cause shown by the objecting party against the policy favoring exclusion.

State v. Bishop, supra, was a criminal case. It is not clear whether Oregon courts would apply the rule of automatic exclusion of witnesses to an unopposed motion in a civil trial. While recognizing that there is little reason for a distinction, the Legislative Assembly left the language of Rule 615 permissive on this question.

TEXT

Exclusion of Witnesses

Rule 615 authorizes the court at the request of a party or upon its own initiative to exclude the witnesses until final argument. The rule does not authorize exclusion of (1) a party who is a natural person, or (2) an officer or employee of a party who is not a natural person designated as its representative by its attorney, or (3) a person whose presence is shown by a party to be essential to the presentation of the party's cause, or (4) the victim in a criminal case. The last provision was not part of the original rule, but was added by amendment as part of Ballot Measure No. 10, approved by the voters on November 4, 1986.

The rule differs from FRE 615 in not providing an absolute right to have the witnesses excluded. See ANNOT., *Exclusion of Witnesses Under Rule 615 of Federal Rules of Evidence,* 48 ALR Fed 484 (1980). From the Commentary, however, it appears that the legislature intends to preserve the rule in criminal cases that requires exclusion at the request of a party, unless the opposing party objects. *State v. Bishop,* 7 Or App 558, 492 P2d 509 (1972). In *State v. Cetto,* 66 Or App 337, 674 P2d 66, rev denied 296 Or 712, 678 P2d 740 (1984), the court held that Rule 615 requires the exclusion of witnesses upon proper motion, "absent a showing of good cause for not excluding them." 66 Or App at 339, 674 P2d at 67. Failure to request exclusion until after the testimony has begun is not good cause for refusing to grant the motion. *State v. Larson,* 139 Or App 294, 298–300, 911 P2d 953 (1996) (but no presumption of prejudice from erroneous denial of motion).

If the opposing party objects, the court must weigh the reasons offered by the objecting party against the policy favoring exclusion. It is likely that the policy favoring exclusion will generally prevail. The court in *Bishop* stated:

> Thus, if the record contains some showing of good cause for not excluding the witnesses, and if the trial court made a reasonable choice between the good cause shown and the policy favoring exclusion, its decision will not be disturbed on appeal. But if the record contains no reason for not excluding witnesses, or an insufficient reason, then the trial court has abused its discretion. (7 Or App at 564, 492 P2d at 512)

Rationale for the Rule

The rule serves several purposes. When witnesses are excluded who are testifying on behalf of one side regarding the same or related matters, they will be less able to tailor their testimony to avoid inconsistencies. In addition, they will not be able to receive a preview of the questions that are likely to be asked by the opposing attorney on cross-examination. When a witness is excluded who is testifying on behalf of the opposing side, the witness will be less able to "ascertain the precise points of difference between their testimonies, and ... shape his own testimony to better advantage his cause." 6 Wigmore, *Evidence* (1976) § 838 at 461–2.

Constitutionality

The constitutionality of Rule 615 was upheld in *State v. Vosika,* 83 Or App 298, 731 P2d 449, on reconsideration 85 Or App 148, 735 P2d 1273 (1987), where defendant argued that exclusion of witnesses violated Article I, section 10 of the Oregon Constitution. The court stated: "[Rule 615] is consistent with the policy of permitting exclusion of persons who might interfere in, or otherwise obstruct, the proceedings. It was enacted to prevent the witness from being influenced by hearing the testimony of a prior witness. That is sufficient reason for exclusion without violating the Oregon Constitution. We find no error."

However, additional constitutional issues arise when a party is ordered not to confer with counsel or when a court excludes the testimony of a witness as a sanction for violation of the rule. See discussion, infra.

Period of Exclusion

The Legislative Commentary to Rule 615 states that "the purpose of the rule is better served if witnesses who are excluded are kept from all phases of the trial at which testimony might be discussed. Potentially, this includes voir dire, opening statements and offers of proof."

Although the rule only authorizes exclusion up to the time of final argument, it has been held under FRE 615 that a trial judge also has discretion to exclude witnesses during closing argument. *United States v. Juarez,* 573 F2d 267, 281 (5th Cir), cert denied 439 US 915 (1978) ("Because closing arguments of counsel often restate witness testimony, the trial court could justifiably fear that the witnesses present at such arguments might learn the testimony of other witnesses, thus jeopardizing the fairness of a second trial should one be necessary").

In *United States v. Ell,* 718 F2d 291 (9th Cir 1983), the court held that the right to have witnesses excluded under FRE 615 extends to witnesses who have already testified but who might be called again in rebuttal.

Persons Exempted from Exclusion

The rule exempts from an exclusionary order (1) a party who is a natural person, (2) an officer or employee of a party who is not a natural person designated as its representative by its attorney, (3) a person whose presence is shown by a party to be essential to the presentation of the party's cause, and (4) the victim in a criminal case. A request for exemption should be made at the same time as the request for an exclusionary order.

A law enforcement officer responsible for the preparation of the case has been held to be an officer or employee who may be designated by the prosecutor as a representative of a party that is not a natural person. *United States v. Boyer,* 574 F2d 951 (8th Cir), cert denied 439 US 967 (1978); *United States v. Auten,* 570 F2d 1284 (5th Cir), cert denied 439 US 899 (1978). Some courts indicate that the trial judge has discretion to require the government to call the designated officer early in its case. See *In re United States,* 584 F2d 666 (5th Cir 1978).

Counsel should be certain to designate the officer for the record at the beginning of trial to avoid a later contention that the exclusion order was violated if the officer is called as a witness. See *United States v. Nix,* 601 F2d 214 (5th Cir), cert denied 444 US 937 (1979). It is likely that a court will limit counsel for a party not a natural person to designation of only one representative of such party.

The witnesses most frequently falling into the category of persons "whose presence is shown by a party to be essential to the presentation of the party's cause" will likely be experts who are assisting the attorney with the trial of the case. One court has stated: "[W]here a fair showing has been made that the expert witness is in fact required for the management of the case, and this is made clear to the trial court, we believe that the trial court is bound to accept any reasonable, substantiated representation to this effect by counsel." *Morvant v. Construction Aggregates Corp.,* 570 F2d 626, 630 (6th Cir), cert dismissed 439 US 801 (1978).

This category may also include experts who will be testifying later who will be asked a hypothetical question based on testimony of earlier witnesses. Whether such experts will be allowed to remain has been held to be within the discretion of the trial court. *Morvant v. Construction Aggregates Corp.,* supra. Other types of witnesses may also qualify as persons whose presence is essential under the circumstances of the case. See *Gov't of the Virgin Islands v. Edinborough,* 625 F2d 472 (3rd Cir 1980) (affirming trial court refusal to exclude mother of young sex crime victim; if error, not prejudicial).

Recent Cases

In *State v. Stookey,* 119 Or App 487, 490, 850 P2d 1167, rev denied 318 Or 26, 862 P2d 1306 (1993), the court found error in the trial judge's ruling that the fiancee of a murder victim was himself a "victim" within the meaning of OEC 615 who could not be excluded from the court during trial. ORS 131.007 defines "victim" for purposes of OEC 615 as "the person or persons who have suffered financial, social, psychological, or physical harm as a result of a crime and includes, in the case of a homicide, a member of the immediate family of the decedent." The fiancee was not a member of the victim's family, and the bare assertion that he had been living with the victim before she was killed was insufficient to qualify him under the statute. However, the error of allowing him to remain in the courtroom prior to his testimony was harmless on the facts of the case.

In *Bremner v. Charles,* 312 Or 274, 284, 821 P2d 1080, 1086 (1991), cert denied 113 SCt 467 (1992), modified 315 Or 291, 844 P2d 204 (1993), rev denied 318 Or 381, 870 P2d 221 (1994), the court held that the trial judge did not abuse his discretion in excluding a brain-damaged child plaintiff from the courtroom during the liability phase of the trial. "We adopt the standard that a plaintiff who is unable to comprehend, meaningfully participate in the proceedings, or assist his or her lawyer in the presentation of the case may be excluded from the liability portion of a bifurcated trial if the trial court, in the exercise of informed discretion, determines that the party's presence would be unfairly prejudicial."

In *State v. Alexander,* 105 Or App 566, 805 P2d 743 (1991), the court found no violation of Rule 615 in allowing the former Lake County Sheriff to sit with and assist the prosecution during trial. The former sheriff had been the chief investigator in the case and had interviewed most of the witnesses, including defense alibi witnesses. Even though the former sheriff was also called as a prosecution witness, the court held that the refusal to exclude him did not unduly impair defendant's right of cross-examination.

Exclusion Distinguished from Sequestration

Rule 615 refers to exclusion of witnesses rather than "sequestration." In *State v. Burdge,* 295 Or 1, 9 n 6, 664 P2d 1076 (1983), the court stated: "'sequestration' generally applies to a rule requiring no contact of any nature with other witnesses while 'exclusion' generally means excluded from the courtroom."

It may be advisable for an attorney to request more than an order of exclusion. It is generally agreed that the trial judge has authority to "take further measures of sequestration designed to prevent communication between witnesses, such as ordering them to remain physically apart, ordering them not to discuss the case with one another or with an attorney, and ordering them not to read a transcript of the trial testimony of another witness." 1 M. Graham, HANDBOOK OF FEDERAL EVIDENCE (4th ed 1996) § 615.1. The trial court may undertake such measures even without the specific request of counsel. A restriction upon communication between witnesses regarding their testimony may be implied from an order of exclusion, but witnesses may not be aware of the restriction without instruction from the court.

The effect of an exclusionary order will be undermined if the witnesses confer among themselves after their testimony or if counsel or any other person relates trial testimony to an excluded witness. *United States v. Johnston,* 578 F2d 1352 (10th Cir), cert denied 439 US 931 (1978), suggests that when an exclusionary order is granted the court should instruct counsel and the witnesses that "witnesses are not only excluded from the courtroom but also that they are not to relate to other witnesses what their testimony has been and what occurred in the courtroom." 578 F2d at 1355 (footnote omitted).

The granting of an order excluding witnesses should be viewed as prohibiting conduct that would undermine the effect of the order, even in the absence of an explicit list of restrictions by the court. In *Miller v. Universal City Studios Inc.,* 650 F2d 1365 (5th Cir 1981), the court affirmed the refusal of the trial judge to allow an expert to testify after learning that despite the existence of an order excluding witnesses the defendant had provided the expert with daily transcripts of the trial testimony. See also *United States v. Whiteside,* 404 F Supp 261 (D Del 1975) (prosecutor improperly discussed trial testimony with law enforcement officer who had not yet testified).

Right to Consult with Counsel

A court may not, however, interfere with the right of a criminal defendant to discuss the case with the defense attorney. See *Geders v. United States,* 425 US 80, 96 SCt 1330, 47 LEd2d 592 (1976) (order found unconstitutional that prevented a criminal defendant from conferring with his attorney during an overnight recess that intervened between his direct testimony and cross-examination); *United States v. Allen,* 542 F2d 630 (4th Cir 1976), cert denied 430 US 908 (1977). A civil litigant also has a right to discuss testimony with counsel. See *Potashnick v. Port City Constr. Co.,* 609 F2d 1101, 1119 (5th Cir), cert denied 449 US 820 (1980).

In *Perry v. Leeke,* 109 SCt 594, 102 LEd2d 624 (1989), the defendant challenged a state trial court ruling precluding him from conferring with his counsel during a fifteen-minute recess at the conclusion of his direct testimony. The Supreme Court, distinguishing *Geders v. United States,* supra, found no denial of defendant's sixth amendment rights. The Court stated:

> Our conclusion does not mean that trial judges must forbid consultation between a defendant and his counsel during such brief recesses. As a matter of discretion in individual cases, or of practice for individual trial judges, or indeed, as a matter of law in some States, it may well be appropriate to permit such consultation. We merely hold that the Federal Constitution does not compel every trial judge to allow the defendant to consult with his lawyer while his testimony is in progress if the judge decides there is good reason to interrupt the trial for a few minutes.

109 SCt at 602.

Sanctions for Violation of Exclusionary Order

Rule 615 does not address the sanctions available for violation of an exclusionary order. The appropriate remedies are within the discretion of the trial court, with consideration to be given to whether the witness or parties acted in bad faith and the extent of resulting prejudice, if any. Possible sanctions include refusing to allow the witness to testify, declaring a mistrial, allowing the violation to be brought out on cross-examination of the witness, instructing the jury to weigh the credibility of the witness in light of the witness' knowledge of earlier trial testimony, or holding the witness in contempt. See 3 J. Weinstein and M. Berger, *Weinstein's Evidence* (1988) § 615[01]. A witness who violates a sequestration order is not automatically disqualified. *Holder v. United States,* 150 US 91, 92, 14 SCt 10, 37 LEd 1010 (1893). See also *Taylor v. United States,* 388 F2d 786 (9th Cir 1967) (abuse of discretion to refuse to allow witness to testify where no showing that party calling her had a part in the violation or sought to profit from it).

In *Siegfried v. Pacific Northwest Development Corp.*, 102 Or App 57, 60, 793 P2d 330 (1990), plaintiff appealed the trial court's refusal to strike the testimony of the defendant's experts as a sanction for defense counsel's providing the experts with daily transcripts of the testimony, in violation of the court's order excluding witnesses. The trial court had invited the plaintiff to move for a mistrial rather than striking the expert's testimony, but the plaintiff rejected the invitation. The court held that "the refusal of the specific sanction that plaintiff sought was within the court's discretion."

In *State v. Burdge*, 295 Or 1, 664 P2d 1076 (1983), the court held "that a violation of an exclusion order is not, of itself, sufficient to disqualify a defense witness in a criminal case, and that the trial court cannot exclude the testimony based upon this ground alone." 295 Or at 14. The court stated "that exclusion of a witness in a criminal case is too grave a sanction where the violation of the order was not intentional and not procured by connivance of counsel or for some improper motive ... Refusal to allow defense witnesses to testify for violation of an exclusion order should be imposed only when necessary to preserve 'the integrity of the fact-finding process' and requires that the competing interests be closely examined." 295 Or at 14. The opinion indicated that there must be a showing that violation of the exclusion order was undertaken with the "knowledge procurement, or consent" of the defendant or his counsel. The court further stated that in cases where there is violation of a court order issued under Rule 615: "We believe that the trial court is obligated to review its sanction options in an escalating manner, first considering whether contempt is a sufficient sanction, or proceeding by instructing the jury as to the witness's violation of the order or, ultimately, the preclusion sanction." 295 Or at 15, n11. Although a constitutional challenge was not made in this case, the court noted that exclusion of defense witnesses in a criminal case might "raise an issue under the compulsory process provisions of the state and federal constitutions." 295 Or at 10 n8.

See generally ANNOT., *Prejudicial Effect of Improper Failure to Exclude from Courtroom or to Sequester or Separate State's Witnesses in Criminal Case*, 74 ALR4th 705 (1989).

ARTICLE VII

OPINIONS AND EXPERT TESTIMONY

RULE 701.   OPINION TESTIMONY BY LAY WITNESSES
RULE 702.   TESTIMONY BY EXPERTS
RULE 703.   BASES OF OPINION TESTIMONY BY EXPERTS
RULE 704.   OPINION ON ULTIMATE ISSUE
RULE 705.   DISCLOSURE OF FACT OR DATA UNDERLYING
            EXPERT OPINION

RULE 701.   ORS 40.405. OPINION TESTIMONY BY LAY WITNESSES

If the witness is not testifying as an expert, testimony of the witness in the form of opinions or inferences is limited to those opinions or inferences which are:
(1) Rationally based on the perception of the witness; and
(2) Helpful to a clear understanding of testimony of the witness or the determination of a fact in issue.

LEGISLATIVE COMMENTARY

Oregon Rule of Evidence 701 is identical in substance to Rule 701 of the Federal Rules of Evidence. Its objective is to put the trier of fact in possession of an accurate reproduction of the event in question. To this end it allows some, but not all, opinion testimony by lay witnesses.

In adopting this rule, the Legislative Assembly does not intend to make inadmissible an opinion that is presently admissible under Oregon law, even though the requirements of subsections (1) and (2) may not be satisfied. For example, the rule should not disturb the case law permitting a lay witness to evaluate property the witness owns, and other, similar practices established by the courts.

Subsection (1). This subsection restates the familiar requirement of first hand knowledge or observation. See ORE 602.

Subsection (2). This subsection requires that lay opinion testimony be "helpful" before it is admitted. The Legislative Assembly intends that this limitation exclude non-percipient lay opinion on questions such as point of impact, estimated speed based upon observation of skid marks, and certainly opinions as to fault. On the other hand, it may allow a witness to communicate in shorthand what the witness has perceived—things such as the speed of an automobile, the identity of a person, the appearance of another person, the sound of footsteps, footprints, distance, uncomplicated illness or injury, apparent age, and so forth.

Witnesses often find difficulty in expressing themselves in language which is not an opinion or conclusion. While the courts have made concessions in certain recurring situations, to permit opinions and conclusions only if they are "necessary" establishes a standard that is too elusive and too rigid for satisfactory judicial administration. Moreover, the practical impossibility of determining by rule what a "fact" is, demonstrated by a century of litigating the question for purposes of pleading under the Field Code, extends into evidence also. 7 Wigmore, *Evidence* § 1919 (3d ed 1940). The rule assumes that the operation of the adversary system will generally lead to an acceptable result. A detailed account carries more conviction than a broad assertion, and a lawyer can be expected to display the witness to best advantage. If the lawyer fails to do so, cross-examination and argument will point up any weakness. See Ladd, "Expert Testimony," in 5 V and L Rev 414, 415–417 (1952). Similar provisions are found in California Evidence Code § 60-456(a), New Jersey Evidence Rule 56(1) and Uniform Rule 56(1).

This subsection clarifies Oregon law. Older Oregon cases suggest that an opinion by a lay witness is only admissible if it is necessary rather than merely helpful. *Everart v. Fischer*, 75 Or 316, 145 P 33 (1915). However, the Supreme Court has more recently suggested an approach to nonexpert opinions that allows the trial judge more leeway, corresponding to the standard of "helpfulness" adopted by this subsection. See *State v. Garver*, 190 Or 291, 316, 225 P2d 771 (1950); cf. *Youngbluth v. Peoples*, 50 Or App 289, 624 P2d 1100 (1981).

TEXT

Lay Opinion Testimony

Rule 701 adopts a liberal standard of admissibility for lay opinions. A lay witness may testify in the form of an opinion when two requirements are satisfied: (1) The opinion is "rationally based on the perception of the witness"; (2) the opinion is "helpful to a clear understanding of testimony of the witness or the determination of a fact in issue."

The first requirement that the opinion be "rationally based on the perception of the witness" is similar to the personal knowledge requirement of Rule 602. It requires that the opinion be based on the personal or firsthand observation or perception of the witness. In addition, the "rationally based" requirement means that the opinion must be one that a person could reasonably deduce from the perceived facts.

The determination of whether a witness has personal knowledge is a question of conditional relevancy under Rule 104(2). See textual discussion of Rules 104(2) and 602. The judge plays a screening function and must determine whether there is evidence sufficient to support a jury finding that the witness has the requisite personal knowledge. A foundation showing personal knowledge by the witness is necessary before a lay opinion may be expressed. The ultimate determination of whether the witness has personal knowledge is made by the jury.

However, the question of whether the opinion is "rationally based" on that knowledge is a matter for the court. A witness may have personal knowledge that is inadequate to support the opinion being offered. For example, a witness called by a criminal defendant to give an opinion regarding the defendant's peaceable character may be found to have insufficient familiarity with the defendant to provide a rational basis for such an opinion.

With respect to the second requirement, Rule 701 vests a great deal of discretion in the trial judge to determine when lay testimony in the form of an opinion will be "helpful" to the jury. The determination of whether an opinion will be "helpful" is an issue for the court under Rule 104(1).

Opinions are especially likely to be allowed when the observations or knowledge of the witness cannot conveniently be presented or described in a more detailed form or when a mere listing of details would not convey accurately the full impression of the witness. Courts are likely to scrutinize more carefully lay opinions which are directed to a critical issue in the case. Rule 704 provides, however, that merely because an opinion embraces an ultimate issue in the case does not make it inadmissible. Nonetheless, if an attempt is made "to introduce meaningless assertions which amount to little more than choosing up sides, exclusion for lack of helpfulness is called for by the rule." Advisory Committee Note, FRE 701. See also textual discussion under Rule 704.

Rationale for Rule

Rule 701 recognizes that lay opinions often have significant evidentiary value and that, in any case, they are difficult to avoid without frequent interruption of the witness. See *Central R Co. of New Jersey v. Monohan,* 11 F2d 212, 214 (2nd Cir 1926) (Hand, J.) (strict enforcement of opinion rule results in "nagging and checking" the witness and the effect is "often to choke him altogether, which is, indeed, usually its purpose."). This rule should allow the witness

> to speak his ordinary language, unbewildered by admonitions from the judge to testify to facts, when all the while the witness is sure in his own mind that he is testifying to facts. The jury understands what the witness means, and the right of cross-examination removes the likelihood of harm to the other side. (*State v. Garver,* 190 Or 291, 316, 225 P2d 771, 782 (1950))

Although facts remain the preferred form of testimony, the rule recognizes that the distinction between facts and opinions is often one of degree. McCormick states:

It seems fair to observe that the prevailing practice in respect to the admission of the opinions of non-expert witnesses may well be described, not as a rule excluding opinions, but as a rule of preference. The more concrete description is preferred to the more abstract.

McCormick, *Evidence* § 11 at 44 (4th ed 1992).

Speculation, Conjecture, Uncertainty

Rule 701 would preclude opinions based upon conjecture or speculation, as did prior Oregon law. See *Brown v. Spokane, Portland and Seattle Ry,* 248 Or 110, 431 P2d 817 (1967); *South Seattle Auto Auction Inc. v. Ladd,* 230 Or 350, 370 P2d 630 (1962). Such opinions would violate the requirement of Rule 701 that the opinion be rationally based upon the perception of the witness and would also violate the personal knowledge requirement of Rule 602. See *United States v. Cox,* 633 F2d 871 (9th Cir 1980), cert denied 454 US 844 (1981) (defendant told witness that he had "friend" who would blow up car for fifty dollars; error to admit opinion of witness that defendant was himself the "friend").

However, a witness qualifying an opinion by stating "I think" or "I believe" does not render the testimony or opinion inadmissible. As Dean Ladd has stated:

Closely associated with expression of facts in terms of inference is the statement of the facts as the impression of the witness. Illustrative of these expressions are, "I think," "I believe," "my impression is," "I cannot be positive, but I think," "to the best of my recollection," or "it is my understanding." The admissibility of testimony accompanied by such limitations involves the same fundamental issue to be considered when permitting the witness to testify in terms of inference, namely, is the witness speaking from his personal knowledge or is his testimony only a mental speculation. Not infrequently such precautionary statements may strengthen the testimony because they indicate that the witness does not want to overstate the facts. On the other hand, such statements may indicate that his recollection is poor which would weaken the testimony but not exclude it. Only when it appears that the witness has not personally perceived the matter about which he testifies will the testimony be excluded. (Ladd, *Expert and Other Opinion Testimony,* 40 Minn L Rev 437, 440 (1956) (footnote omitted)).

Even if a witness uses qualifying language, the opinion should be allowed if it is clear that the testimony is based on personal knowledge. See *Juckeland v. Miles & Sons Trucking Serv.,* 254 Or 514, 462 P2d 668 (1969) (use of word "guess" by witness does not bar opinion where other testimony by witness indicates opinion is founded on facts).

Intent, Motives, or Emotions of Another

The requirement that the opinion be rationally based on the perception of the witness presents difficulty with respect to testimony describing the intent, motives, or emotions of another, because such matters cannot be directly perceived. Some decisions under FRE 701 have allowed such testimony. See *United States v. Smith,* 550 F2d 277 (5th Cir), cert denied 434 US 841 (1977) (testimony admissible that defendant "knew and understood" requirements of federal program); *United States v. McClintic,* 570 F2d 685 (8th Cir 1978) (defendant knew goods were obtained by fraud); *Bohannon v. Pegelow,* 652 F2d 729 (7th Cir 1981) (not abuse of discretion to admit testimony by lay witness that arrest motivated by racial prejudice); *John Hancock Mutual Life Ins. Co. v. Dutton,* 585 F2d 1289, 1294 (5th Cir 1978) ("When, as here, the witness observes first hand the altercation in question, her opinions on the feelings of the parties are based on her personal knowledge and rational perceptions and are helpful to the jury. The Rules require nothing more for admission of the testimony"). Other decisions exclude such testimony. See *United States v. Jackson,* 569 F2d 1003, 1011 n 17 (7th Cir), cert denied 437 US 907 (1978) (wife not allowed to testify why defendant was depressed); *United States v. Popejoy,* 578 F2d 1346 (10th Cir), cert denied 439 US 896 (1978) (error to admit testimony that defendant knew of robbery).

If the state of mind or emotion of another is manifested by external appearance of the person or other circumstances, including statements of the person, the evidence is likely to be allowed. See *State v. Broadhurst,* 184 Or 178, 249, 196 P2d 407, 436, cert denied 337 US 906 (1948) (opinion admissible that another was upset, worried, and heartbroken; "It is generally held that a witness may testify as to emotions manifested by another and observed by him," quoting from F. Wharton, WHARTON'S CRIMINAL EVIDENCE (11th ed 1935) § 1013; *State v. Pickett,* 37 Or App 239, 586 P2d 824 (1978) (lay opinion admissible that a person is calm or excited).

In *Ensley v. Fitzwater,* 59 Or App 411, 414, 651 P2d 734 (1982), the court stated: "In general, although a party may testify as to his own intent in doing an act or making a declaration, he may not testify to the intent of the other party when intent is the issue." The court reversed the granting of a summary judgment in favor of defendant where *defendant's* affidavit stated that "plaintiff intended this check to be in full accord and satisfaction of any and all claims, demands or judgments." The court did comment, however, that "a witness who is in a position to know may testify about the intention of the parties to an agreement." 59 Or App at 415 n1.

In *State v. Benson,* 63 Or App 467, 471, 664 P2d 1127, 1129–30, rev denied 295 Or 730, 670 P2d 1035 (1983), the court held that testimony by an alleged rape victim about her realization that "if he could get me off my bike and pull me into the bushes that were nearby that he could rape me" did not violate Rule 701. The court viewed this testimony as relating to the state of mind of the victim rather than the intention of the defendant.

Value of Property

The Commentary expresses approval of the rule allowing certain lay opinion testimony on the value of property. See *Weigel v. Ron Tonkin Chevrolet Co.,* 66 Or App 232, 235, 673 P2d 574 (1983), aff'd as modified 298 Or 127, 690 P2d

448 (1984) (allowing an owner of a vehicle to give an opinion about its value). Under prior Oregon law, it has been held that an owner of real or personal property may give an opinion on its fair market value. *Lunda v. Matthews,* 46 Or App 701, 613 P2d 63 (1980); *Jones v. Northside Ford Truck Sales, Inc.,* 276 Or 685, 556 P2d 117 (1976); *Lewis v. Worldwide Imports, Inc.,* 238 Or 580, 395 P2d 922 (1964).

However, a corporate officer who is not shown to have special qualifications may not testify on the value of corporate property. *State Highway Comm'n v. Assembly of God,* 230 Or 167, 368 P2d 937 (1962). Without a showing of special qualifications, a lessee may not give an opinion on the value of the lease. *State Board of Education v. Stewart,* 236 Or 386, 388 P2d 113 (1963). A husband not qualified as an expert has been barred from testifying to the reasonable value of his wife's property. *Davis v. Georgia-Pacific,* 251 Or 239, 445 P2d 481 (1968).

Belief in Truthfulness of Another Witness

In *State v. McQuisten,* 97 Or App 517, 776 P2d 1304 (1989), the court found error in admitting a tape-recorded statement by the investigating officer indicating his belief in the truthfulness of the rape complainant's accusations and his disbelief in the defendant's version of the facts. The court held that a witness, whether or not an expert, is not allowed to comment on the credibility of another witness.

In *State v. Odoms,* 313 Or 76, 80, 829 P2d 690, 691 (1992), *rev* denied 316 Or 529, 854 P2d 940 (1993), a kidnapping and rape prosecution, the court found no error in the admission of a statement by a detective that defendant claimed was a comment on the credibility of the alleged victim. The detective had stated that "he did not believe someone just inadvertently picks on someone and makes allegations about them if there isn't something to it." The court noted that the testimony did not involve testimony by a trial witness about whether another trial witness was telling the truth, and reaffirmed that an opinion of that type would generally be prohibited.

Recent Cases Approving Lay Opinion Testimony

In *State v. Wright,* 315 Or 124, 132, 843 P2d 436 (1992), the court held that a lay witness is capable of offering an opinion as to whether a person is intoxicated and that "ultimate facts about a state of intoxication are admissible, even if expressed in the form of conclusions."

In *United States National Bank of Oregon v. Zellner,* 101 Or App 98, 102, 789 P2d 670, rev denied 310 Or 122, 794 P2d 794 (1990), the court held that testimony by witnesses called by the landlord that the landlord had no obligation to repair the premises did not violate the rule against legal opinions by lay witnesses. The court stated that "[c]ounsel's comments made clear that he was seeking factual information about the content of the parties' agreement about who would be responsible for repairs," not an opinion about the meaning of a legal agreement or standard.

In *State v. Lerch,* 296 Or 377, 677 P2d 678 (1985), the court affirmed the ruling of the trial judge that a police officer could give an opinion that a stain observed on the defendant's kitchen floor was fecal matter. The evidence was relevant because the victim was allegedly strangled in defendant's kitchen and according to the officer some victims defecate when being strangled. The court also found no error in allowing a lay witness to testify that an odor detected in a garbage dumpster where the body was allegedly placed seemed to be the odor of decaying flesh. The court found the opinions admissible because they concerned data difficult to reproduce for a jury, they were rationally based on the witness' own experience and were helpful in the determination of a fact in issue.

The Court of Appeals decision in the same case, *State v. Lerch,* 63 Or App 707, 717, 666 P2d 840, 847 (1983), quoted with approval the following statement from *United States v. Skeet,* 665 F2d 983, 985 (9th Cir 1982):

> Because it is sometimes difficult to describe the mental or physical condition of a person; his character or reputation; the emotions manifest by his acts; speed of a moving object or other things that arise in a day to day observation of lay witnesses; things that are of common occurrence and observation, such as size, heights, odors, flavors, color, heat, and so on; witnesses may relate their opinions or conclusions of what they observed.

In *State v. Cochran,* 72 Or App 499, 696 P2d 11 14 (1985), the court held that it would be proper to allow a police officer who was present when a murder weapon was found in a grass pile to give his opinion that "[t]he hatchet appeared to have been there for quite awhile." 72 Or App at 516, 696 P2d at 1124.

Recent Cases Disapproving Lay Opinion Testimony

In *State v. Hite,* 131 Or App 59, 61–2, 883 P2d 890, 892 (1994), rev denied 320 Or 508, 888 P2d 569 (1995), the court held that the defendant was properly precluded from testifying that his ability to communicate was impaired by the medication he was taking because such testimony about the cause, rather than the nature, of his problem would require the testimony of an expert.

In *State v. Parks,* 71 Or App 630, 693 P2d 657 (1984), the defendant was convicted of assault for a shooting that he claimed was accidental. The court held that the trial judge did not err in striking the testimony of the defendant's wife, a witness to the shooting, that it was "an accident." The court found this evidence properly excluded under Rule 701 as not being helpful to the trier of fact.

Opinions Approved in Commentary

The following are expressly approved in the Commentary as being appropriate subjects for lay opinion testimony by a percipient witness: the speed of an automobile, the identity of a person, the appearance of another person, the sound of footsteps, footprints, distance, uncomplicated illness or injury, and apparent age. In addition, certain lay opinions are expressly authorized by other rules in the Evidence Code. Rules 405 and 608 sanction lay opinions concerning character under certain circumstances. Rule 901(2)(a) authorizes lay opinion that identifies objects. Rule 901(2)(b) authorizes lay opinion regarding the genuineness of handwriting. Rule 901(2)(e) authorizes voice identification by lay opinion.

Prior Oregon Law

The Commentary also states that the legislature did not intend by adopting Rule 701 to make inadmissible any opinion previously admissible under Oregon law. For examples of lay opinions held to be proper under prior Oregon law, see *Brown v. Bryant,* 244 Or 321, 417 P2d 1002 (1966) (intoxication); *Brookes v. Tri-County Metropolitan Transp. Dist.,* 18 Or App 614, 526 P2d 590 (1974) (public attitudes concerning neatness of bus drivers); *Miller v. Liles,* 230 Or 475, 370 P2d 217 (1962) (voice identification); *State v. Welch,* 33 Or 33, 54 P 213 (1898) (visual identification of person); *State v. Garver,* 190 Or 291, 225 P2d 771 (1950) (sanity or mental state); *Thomas v. Dad's Root Beer & Canada Dry Bottling Co.,* 225 Or 166, 356 P2d 418 (1960) (speed of vehicle); *Crosby v. Portland Ry. Co.,* 53 Or 496, 100 P 300 (1909) (general physical condition and appearance of a person); *State v. Broadhurst,* 184 Or 178, 196 P2d 407 (1948), cert denied 337 US 906 (1949) (that another is upset, worried, and heartbroken); *Western Feed Co. v. Heidloff,* 230 Or 324, 370 P2d 612 (1962) (that a particular feed was the cause of disease in pigs); *State v. Pickett,* 37 Or App 239, 586 P2d 824 (1978) (that a person is calm or excited); *Youngbluth v. Peoples,* 50 Or App 289, 622 P2d 1144 (1981) (beer bottles were "fresh empties"); *Smith v. Cram,* 113 Or 313, 230 P 812 (1924) (intent of another revealed to witness); *Banta v. Letter,* 204 Or 538, 284 P2d 348 (1955) (ability of testator to comprehend nature of act).

Examples of cases holding lay opinion to be improper under prior Oregon law include the following: *Meyer v. Harvey Aluminum,* 263 Or 487, 501 P2d 795 (1972) (cause of crop damage); *Marshall v. Mullin,* 212 Or 421, 320 P2d 258 (1958) (opinion as to speed from sound of motor vehicle); *Brannon v. Wood,* 251 Or 349, 444 P2d 558 (1968) (cause of paralysis); *McCarty v. Hedges,* 212 Or 497, 309 P2d 186, 321 P2d 285 (1958) (that an emergency existed prior to the accident); *Vancil v. Poulson,* 236 Or 314, 388 P2d 444 (1964) (point of impact of motor vehicle collision by a nonpercipient witness); *State v. Watson,* 243 Or 454, 414 P2d 337 (1966) (that a crime has been committed); *State v. Gastelum,* 41 Or App 491, 599 P2d 1169 (1979) (opinion that persons not involved in shooting).

Federal Decisions

For examples of lay opinions allowed under FRE 701, see *Verzosa v. Merrill Lynch, Pierce, Fenner & Smith, Inc.,* 589 F2d 974 (9th Cir 1978) (lay opinion admitted that person claiming discrimination was qualified for job); *Martin v. Arkansas Arts Center,* 627 F2d 876 (8th Cir 1980) (testimony admitted that person claiming discrimination not qualified for job); *Farner v. Paccar, Inc.,* 562 F2d 518 (8th Cir 1977) (lay opinion admitted regarding safety of design of product); *United States v. Arrasmith,* 557 F2d 1093, 1094 (5th Cir 1977) (lay opinion admitted identifying odor); *United States v. Borrelli,* 621 F2d 1092 (10th Cir), cert denied 449 US 956 (1980) (admitted testimony of defendant's stepfather that person in bank surveillance photograph was defendant); *Lang v. Texas & Pac. Ry.,* 624 F2d 1275, 1280 (5th Cir 1980) (decedent's foreman allowed to testify as to possible causes of accident).

Other Authorities

See generally ANNOT., *Construction and Application of Rule 701 of Federal Rules of Evidence, Providing for Opinion Testimony by Lay Witnesses Under Certain Circumstances,* 44 ALR Fed 919 (1979); ANNOT., *Ability to See, Hear, Smell, or Otherwise Sense, as Proper Subject of Opinion by Lay Witness,* 10 ALR3d 258 (1966); ANNOT., *Expert or Opinion Testimony as to Speed of Vehicle by One Who Had No View, or Only Momentary View of Vehicle at Time of Accident,* 156 ALR 382 (1945); ANNOT., *Admissibility of Opinion Evidence as to Point of Impact or Collision in Motor Vehicle Accident Case,* 66 ALR2d 1048 (1959); ANNOT., *Competency of Nonexpert's Testimony, Based on Sound Alone, as to Speed of Motor Vehicle Involved in Accident,* 33 ALR3d 1405 (1970); ANNOT., *Opinion Testimony as to Speed of Motor Vehicle Based on Skid Marks and Other Facts,* 29 ALR3d 248 (1970); ANNOT., *Competency of Nonexpert Witness to Testify, in Criminal Case, Based Upon Personal Observation, as to Whether Person Was Under Influence of Drugs,* 21 ALR4th 905 (1983).

RULE 702.   ORS 40.410. TESTIMONY BY EXPERTS

If scientific, technical or other specialized knowledge will assist the trier of fact to understand the evidence or to determine a fact in issue, a witness qualified as an expert by knowledge, skill, experience, training or education may testify thereto in the form of an opinion or otherwise.

LEGISLATIVE COMMENTARY

Oregon Rule of Evidence 702 provides the rationale and authority for the use of expert witnesses. The rule is identical to Rule 702 of the Federal Rules of Evidence, and the Legislative Assembly adopts the commentary of the federal advisory committee:

"An intelligent evaluation of facts is often difficult or impossible without the application of some scientific, technical, or other specialized knowledge. The most common source of this knowledge is the expert witness, although there are other techniques for supplying it.

"Most of the literature assumes that experts testify only in the form of opinions. The assumption is logically unfounded. The rule accordingly recognizes that an expert on the stand may give a dissertation or exposition of scientific or other principles relevant to the case, leaving the trier of fact to apply them to the facts. Since much of the criticism of expert testimony has centered upon the hypothetical question, it seems wise to recognize that opinions are not indispensable and to encourage the use of expert testimony in nonopinion form when counsel believes the trier can itself draw the requisite inference. The use of opinions is not abolished by the rule, however. It will continue to be permissible for the expert to take the further step of suggesting the inference which should be drawn from applying the specialized knowledge to the facts. See Rules 703 to 705.

"Whether the situation is a proper one for the use of expert testimony is to be determined on the basis of assisting the trier. 'There is no more certain test for determining when experts may be used than the common sense inquiry whether the untrained layman would be qualified to determine intelligently and to the best possible degree the particular issue without enlightenment from those having a specialized understanding of the subject involved in the dispute.' Ladd, *Expert Testimony*, in 5 V and L Rev 414, 418 (1952). When opinions are excluded, it is because they are unhelpful and therefore superfluous and a waste of time. 7 Wigmore, *Evidence* § 1918 (3d ed 1940).

"The rule is broadly phrased. The fields of knowledge which may be drawn upon are not limited merely to the 'scientific' and 'technical' but extend to all 'specialized' knowledge. Similarly the expert is viewed, not in a narrow sense, but as a person qualified by 'knowledge, skill, experience, training or education.' Thus within the scope of the rule are not only experts in the strictest sense of the word, e.g., physicians, physicists and architects, but also the large group sometimes caged 'skilled' witnesses, such as bankers or landowners testifying to land values."

Oregon courts have long held that when a question is such that a person of ordinary intelligence and experience is incapable of drawing correct conclusions from the facts in evidence without the assistance of someone who has special skill or knowledge on the subject, the opinion of the expert is desirable and competent evidence. *Fisher v. Oregon Short Line Ry. Co.*, 22 Or 533, 30 P 425 (1892). Therefore, ORE 702 does not change existing law.

The Legislative Assembly leaves for judicial decision the standard to be used in determining the admissibility of novel scientific evidence. The Oregon Court of Appeals recently adopted a reasonable reliability test in *State v. Kersting*, 50 Or App 461 (1981), and the Oregon Supreme Court has accepted review. Other jurisdictions have different standards.

TEXT

Expert Testimony

Rule 702 liberalizes Oregon law regarding testimony by expert witnesses. Under Rule 702, expert testimony may be allowed not only on matters beyond the knowledge of the jury, but also where the knowledge of an expert would help the jury better understand matters about which they already have knowledge. Under prior Oregon law, before allowing expert testimony courts sometimes required that the jury be "incapable" of drawing correct conclusions without an expert's assistance. *Fisher v. Oregon Short Line & Utah N. Ry. Co.,* 22 Or 533, 30 P 425 (1892). Rule 702 provides that a qualified expert may testify when "scientific, technical or other specialized knowledge will *assist the trier of fact* to understand the evidence or to determine a fact in issue." (Emphasis added.) Rule 702 thus adopts the view advocated by Wigmore:

> The true test of the admissibility of such testimony is not whether the subject matter is common or uncommon, or whether many persons or few have some knowledge of the matter, but it is whether the witnesses offered as experts have any peculiar knowledge or experience, not common to the world, which renders their opinions founded on such knowledge or experience *any aid to the Court or the jury* in determining the questions at issue. (Emphasis added.)
> (7 Wigmore, *Evidence* § 1923 at 31–32 (J. Chadbourn rev 1978))

In cases where it is uncertain whether expert testimony would assist the jury, the trial court has "a certain latitude of decision" in excluding or receiving opinion testimony of a qualified expert. *Butler v. Dept. of Corrections,* 138 Or App 190, 204–5, 909 P2d 163 (1995) (no abuse of discretion to exclude where helpfulness of expert opinion "reasonably could be decided either way"); *Yundt v. D & D Bowl, Inc.,* 259 Or 247, 259, 486 P2d 553 (1971). If it is clear that the opinion of an expert would assist the jury, it may be reversible error to exclude the evidence. See *State v. Stringer,* 292 Or 388, 394, 634 P2d 1264 (1982) (reversible error to exclude opinion by qualified expert regarding point of impact when reliable foundation established). See generally ANNOT., *When Will Expert Testimony "Assist Trier of Fact" so as to be Admissible at Federal Trial Under Rule 702 of Federal Rules of Evidence,* 75 ALR Fed 461 (1985); Deatherage, *Article VII: Oregon Follows the Federal Rules on Opinions and Expert Testimony,* 19 Will L Rev 421 (1983).

Unlike Rule 701, Rule 702 is not limited to defining when testimony may be given in the form of an opinion. Rule 702 regulates any testimony by an expert, whether or not in the form of an opinion. Experts may and often do testify in nonopinion form, particularly when they are describing treatments, tests, principles, procedures, or methods.

On the issue of whether an unwilling expert can be compelled to testify, see Maurer, *Compelling the Expert Witness: Fairness and Utility Under the Federal Rules of Civil Procedure,* 19 Ga L Rev 71 (1984); ANNOT., *Right of Independent Expert to Refuse to Testify as to Expert Opinion,* 50 ALR 4th 680 (1986); ANNOT., *Compelling Testimony of Opponent's Expert in State Court,* 66 ALR4th 213 (1988).

When Expert Testimony Is Required

Rule 702 defines when expert testimony is admissible, not when it is required. To determine when expert testimony is essential to recovery on a particular claim, reference must be made to the substantive law.

In *McKee Electric Co. v. Carson Oil Co.,* 70 Or App 1, 5, 688 P2d 1360, 1364, aff'd 301 Or 339, 723 P2d 288 (1986), the court stated that "Expert testimony is an indispensable part of a prima facie negligence case only if the average juror could not be expected to understand the issues involved." The court found expert testimony unnecessary in the case, commenting: "A juror can understand, without expert testimony, that a reasonably prudent person would not park a delivery truck with the engine running where it is reasonably foreseeable that gasoline vapors will be present and that the truck would be affected by, or ignite, those vapors." The court further held that it was not necessary that the plaintiff produce expert testimony in order to obtain a res ipsa loquitur instruction that the type of fire caused here does not ordinarily occur in the absence of negligence. See also *Peery v. Hanley,* 135 Or App 162, 165, 897 P2d 1189 (1995) (expert testimony on causation not required to recover for intentional infliction of emotional distress).

Professional malpractice actions are the category of cases where expert testimony is most likely to be required. See *Jeffries v. Murdock,* 74 Or App 38, 701 P2d 451, rev denied 299 Or 584, 704 P2d 513 (1985) (in the great majority of medical malpractice cases, expert testimony is required to establish what the reasonable practice is in the community); *Tiedemann v. Radiation Therapy Consultants,* 299 Or 238, 249, 701 P2d 440 (1985) (expert medical testimony necessary to establish breach of duty to obtain "informed consent"); *Wales v. Marlatt,* 103 Or App 605, 798 P2d 713 (1990) (expert testimony required in action for professional malpractice against an investment counselor); *Docken v. Ciba-Geigy,* 101 Or App 252, 256, 790 P2d 45, rev denied 310 Or 195, 795 P2d 554 (1990) (expert testimony in action against pharmacist for failure to warn of dangers of prescription drug); *Halverson v. Sooy,* 99 Or App 255, 260, 782 P2d 161 (1989) (expert testimony necessary in malpractice action against accountant).

In *Childers v. Spindor,* 91 Or App 119, 754 P2d 599 (1988), the court reversed a legal malpractice judgment in favor of the plaintiff, finding the expert testimony on the standard of care to be inadequate. The court stated:

> In most negligence actions against professionals, expert testimony is necessary to inform the jury of the applicable standard of care. *Getchell v. Mansfield,* 260 Or 174, 489 P2d 953 (1971). A jury generally is not able to determine what is reasonable professional conduct without such testimony. There are some instances when the breach of a standard of care is within the ordinary knowledge and experience of lay persons; in such cases, a jury can determine the reasonableness of professional conduct without expert testimony. An example of a situation in which expert testimony is usually not required is when an attorney allows the Statute of Limitations to run.... This case involves what an attorney is supposed to do in preparing for trial, presenting evidence and communicating with a client or the court. Generally, that is not within the

knowledge or experience of a lay juror and, in most instances, at least some expert testimony concerning the expert's knowledge of the customary and proper method of handling such legal matters is required.

91 Or App at 122.

See also *Fisher v. Consol. Freightways, Inc.*, 12 Or App 417, 507 P2d 53 (1973) (expert testimony required to show causal connection between symptoms and original injury in workers' compensation claim); *Austin v. Sisters of Charity of Providence*, 256 Or 179, 186, 470 P2d 939 (1970) (expert testimony required to establish causal connection in medical malpractice claim).

See generally ANNOT., *Necessity of Expert Testimony to Show Standard of Care in Negligence Action Against Insurance Agent or Broker*, 52 ALR4th 1232 (1987); ANNOT., *Admissibility and Necessity of Expert Evidence as to Standards of Practice and Negligence in Malpractice Action Against Attorney*, 14 ALR4th 170 (1982); ANNOT., *Necessity of Expert Evidence to Support Action Against Hospital for Injury to or Death of Patient*, 40 ALR3d 515 (1971); ANNOT., *Admissibility and Necessity of Expert Evidence as to Standards of Practice and Negligence in Malpractice Action Against Attorney*, 17 ALR3d 1442 (1968); Oregon State Bar CLE, DAMAGES (1980); Ambrosio and McLaughlin, *The Use of Expert Witnesses in Establishing Liability in Legal Malpractice Cases*, 61 Temple L Rev 1351 (1988).

Qualifications of an Expert—Generally

The determination of an expert's qualifications is a preliminary question of fact for the trial judge under Rule 104(1). Appellate courts apply an "abuse of discretion" standard in reviewing challenges to the qualifications of an expert. See, e.g., *Myers v. Cessna Aircraft Corp.*, 275 Or 501, 553 P2d 355 (1976). In *State v. Caulder*, 75 Or App 457, 460, 706 P2d 1007, rev denied 300 Or 451, 712 P2d 110 (1985), the court held that "whether a witness is qualified to testify as an expert is within the discretion of the trial court and [the trial court's ruling] will not be overturned except for an abuse of discretion."

The expert may be qualified by knowledge, skill, or experience, as well as by training or education. See *United States v. Johnson*, 575 F2d 1347 (5th Cir 1978), cert denied 440 US 907 (1979) (witness qualified by extensive prior use of marijuana as sufficient expert to identify marijuana as coming from Colombia); *State v. Briner*, 198 Neb 766, 255 NW 2d 422 (1977) ("retired" burglar, with five burglary convictions, qualified as an expert to identify burglary tools under Nebraska Evidence Rule 702); *United States v. Andersson*, 813 F2d 1450 (9th Cir 1987) (experienced drug dealer qualified as an expert concerning techniques and methods used during unlawful drug transactions).

An expert qualified to express an opinion on one subject may not be qualified to express an opinion on another subject, even if it is related. See, e.g., *State Dept. of Transportation v. Montgomery Ward Dev.*, 79 Or App 457, 465, 719 P2d 507, rev denied 301 Or 667, 725 P2d 1294 (1986) (witness qualified as real estate appraiser not qualified to express opinion on probability of street being vacated).

Refusal to allow a qualified expert to testify may constitute reversible error. *State Highway Comm'n v. Arnold,* 218 Or 43, 64, 341 P2d 1089, modified on other grounds 343 P2d 11 13 (1959). See ANNOT., *Review on Appeal of Decision of Trial Court as to Qualification or Competency of Expert Witnesses,* 166 ALR 1067 (1947).

Although an opponent may offer to stipulate to qualifications of an expert, it is usually held that the proponent has a right to allow experts to make their qualifications known to the jury. If a court curtails an expert's testimony regarding his or her qualifications, it has been held error to instruct the jury that it may disregard that expert's opinion for lack of education or experience. *Murphy v. Nat'l RR Passenger Corp.,* 547 F2d 816 (4th Cir 1977).

In cases where the opponent wishes to challenge the qualifications of an expert, the opponent may request the court for leave to ask questions in aid of an objection. It is within the discretion of the trial court whether to allow such questions before an opinion is given or to delay the challenge to the expert's qualifications until cross-examination. *Krause v. Eugene Dodge, Inc.,* 265 Or 486, 509 P2d 1199 (1973). If upon cross-examination the expert is shown to be unqualified, the opinion should be stricken and the jury instructed to disregard it. Id. Cf. ANNOT., *Testing Qualifications of Expert Witness, Other than Handwriting Expert, by Objective Tests or Experiments,* 78 ALR2d 1281 (1961).

Qualifications of an Expert—Professional Malpractice Suits

In cases involving professional malpractice, appellate decisions often specify the requisite qualifications of the experts testifying to breach of duty. Medical practitioners are generally entitled to have their treatment of a patient tested by the principles of the school of medicine to which they belong. *Sheppard v. Firth,* 215 Or 268, 334 P2d 190 (1959) (an orthopedic surgeon may not be qualified to render an expert opinion on the quality of treatment by a chiropractor). In *Creasey v. Hogan,* 292 Or 154, 156, 637 P2d 114 (1981), the Oregon Supreme Court stated:

> Where the principles, techniques, methods, practices or procedures of one branch of the healing arts concur or are generally the same as those of another branch of the healing arts, in a malpractice case against a practitioner in one branch, opinion evidence on a point concerning such matters from a practitioner in another branch is admissible.

In *Barrett v. Coast Range Plywood,* 294 Or 641, 649, 661 P2d 926 (1983), the court held that "[T]he diagnosis of functional overlay is within the competence of medical doctors.... The fact that they are not psychotherapists may go to the weight to be accorded their testimony but that fact cannot serve as the reason to disregard the testimony entirely." The court further commented that "[A] witness who is qualified to give expert testimony in a general field need not demonstrate expertise in a specialized aspect of that field." 294 Or at 647, 661 P2d at 929.

In *Bremner v. Charles,* 123 Or App 95, 98–9, 859 P2d 1148, 1151–2 (1993), rev denied 318 Or 381, 870 P2d 221 (1994), a medical malpractice action, the court affirmed the exclusion of testimony by a public-health nurse about the standard care of physicians working in the field of prenatal care. The court stated that "[a]lthough there may be an appropriate case for allowing non-physician witnesses to testify about the standard of care applicable to physicians, this is not that case."

In *Burton v. Rogue Valley Medical Center*, 122 Or App 22, 26, 856 P2d 639, 641 (1993), rev denied 318 Or 24, 862 P2d 1304, the court held that it was error to grant a summary judgment for defendant in a medical malpractice case where plaintiff had filed an affidavit by a doctor finding defendant's conduct to violate the applicable standard of care. There was no basis for holding the affidavit to be insufficient where it stated that the affiant was "very familiar" with the illness in question, its required treatment, and the standard of care in the medical community. The court noted that defendant failed to explain why those statements "which must be accepted as true" do not qualify the doctor as "someone with the necessary skill and knowledge to arrive at an intelligent conclusion about the proper treatment" for a person afflicted with the disease in question.

See generally ANNOT., *Competency of General Practitioner To Testify as Expert Witness in Action Against Specialist for Medical Malpractice*, 31 ALR3d 1163 (1970); ANNOT., *Medical Malpractice: Necessity and Sufficiency of Showing of Medical Witnesses' Familiarity with Particular Medical or Surgical Technique Involved in Suit*, 46 ALR3d 275 (1972); ANNOT., *Malpractice Testimony: Competency of Physician or Surgeon from One Locality to Testify, in Malpractice Case, as to Standard of Care Required of Defendant Practicing in Another Locality*, 37 ALR3d 420 (1971); ANNOT., *Competency of Physician or Surgeon of School of Practice Other than that to which Defendant Belongs to Testify in Malpractice Case*, 85 ALR2d 1022 (1962); ANNOT., *Locality Rule as Governing Hospital's Standard of Care to Patient and Expert's Competency to Testify Thereto*, 36 ALR3d 440 (1971); ANNOT., *Modern Status of "Locality Rule" in Malpractice Action Against Physician who is not a Specialist*, 99 ALR3d 1133 (1980).

Expert Found Qualified

In the following recent cases, the trial court was held to be within its discretion in finding the expert qualified: *State v. Park*, 140 Or App 507, 514, 916 P2d 334 (1996) (Forest Service officer qualified to testify as an expert based on his training and experience that the majority of marijuana plants found in garden were "clones" that were derived from the same mother plant); *MacLean & Associates v. American Guaranty Life Insurance Co.*, 85 Or App 284, 736 P2d 586 (1987) (witness with an education in business economics and management, experience in an engineering firm, and three years of experience at a resort found qualified to testify as an expert about lost profits in a business venture).

Expert Found Not Qualified

In the following recent cases, the trial court was found to be within its discretion in finding the expert *not* qualified: *Hays v. Huard*, 108 Or App 289, 292–

3, 814 P2d 559, 560–1, rev denied 312 Or 234, 829 P2d 730 (1991) (police officer not shown to be qualified to give expert opinion about speed of vehicle when he did not see accident); *State v. Moore,* 72 Or App 454, 695 P2d 985, rev denied 299 Or 154, 700 P2d 251 (1985) (affirming trial court ruling that expert called by defendant did not have the requisite qualifications to testify regarding battered woman syndrome or to give an opinion on the self-defense issue); *State v. Baker,* 87 Or App 285, 742 P2d 633, rev denied 304 Or 405, 745 P2d 1225 (1987) (trial court properly excluded testimony of forensic engineer as to speed of defendant's motorcycle at time of the collision when witness relied solely on police reports and photos); *State v. Robinson,* 64 Or App 770, 669 P2d 1175 (1983) (no error in trial court's refusal to allow two witnesses to testify as experts on brakes, when there was an insufficient showing of their qualifications).

Requisite Certainty of Expert's Opinion

Whether an expert's testimony is certain enough to be received into evidence is an issue that needs to be distinguished from whether the evidence is sufficient under the substantive law to allow the case to be submitted to the jury. See *Feist v. Sears, Roebuck & Co.,* 267 Or 402, 407, 517 P2d 675 (1973); *Henderson v. Union Pac RR Co.,* 189 Or 145, 160, 219 P2d 170 (1950) ("The question here, however, is not one of the admissibility, but of the sufficiency, of evidence; and medical testimony in terms of mere possibility will not lift the case out of the area of uncertainty if the other evidence leaves the question speculative"). See generally ANNOT., *Admissibility of Expert Medical Testimony as to Future Consequences of Injury or Pain as Affected by Expression in Terms of Probability or Possibility,* 75 ALR3d 9 (1977); ANNOT., *Admissibility of Opinion Evidence as to Cause of Death, Disease, or Injury,* 66 ALR2d 1082, § 7 at 1118 (1959); ANNOT., *Sufficiency Of Expert Evidence to Establish Causal Relation Between Accident and Physical Condition or Death,* 135 ALR 516 (1941).

The Oregon Supreme Court has stated:

> It is, of course, an established rule of substantive law that, in order to establish the necessary causal relationship to support recovery in a personal injury case, the evidence must be sufficient to establish that such a causal relationship is reasonably probable and that for this purpose testimony that an injurious consequence is "possible," rather than "probable," is not sufficient.

Fiest v. Sears, Roebuck & Co., 267 Or 402, 407, 517 P2d 675 (1973) (citation omitted). To meet the sufficiency requirement, testimony regarding the causal connection between an accident and an injury is usually solicited from medical experts in terms of "a reasonable medical probability." *Birkes v. Wade,* 266 Or 598, 609, 511 P2d 831 (1973); *McEwen v. Ortho Pharmaceutical Corp.,* 270 Or 375, 415 n36, 528 P2d 522 (1974).

The Oregon Supreme Court has stated: "For medical opinion testimony to have any probative value, it must at least advise the jury that the inference drawn by the doctor is more probably correct than incorrect. If the probabilities are in balance, the matter is left to speculation." *Crawford v. Seufert,* 236 Or 369,

375, 388 P2d 456 (1964). See also *Howerton v. Pfaff,* 246 Or 341, 346, 425 P2d 533 (1967) ("Possibilities are not enough"). But see *Lemons v. State Compensation Dept.,* 2 Or App 128, 131, 467 P2d 128 (1970) (in workers' compensation case, use of phrase "within a reasonable degree of medical probability" held not to be required). Cf. *Gregg v. Oregon Racing Comm'n,* 38 Or App 19, 22, 588 P2d 1290 (1979) ("There is little authority as to the question of where the line is to be drawn on a scale between 50/50 probability and complete conclusiveness").

To be admissible evidence, as distinguished from sufficient evidence, medical testimony does not always have to be based on reasonable medical probability. For example, evidence of the possibility that the plaintiff may suffer certain complications as a result of an injury may be admissible on the question of damages. In *Feist v. Sears Roebuck & Co.,* 267 Or 402, 412, 517 P2d 675 (1973), the court stated:

> We agree that medical testimony to the effect that as the result of a serious physical injury, there will be a "predisposition" to the contracting of some disease, i.e., a possibility, is not sufficient evidence to support an award of damages for permanent injury and cannot be properly considered by a jury for that purpose.
> We hold, however, that such testimony is sufficient as the basis for a finding by the jury of some disability.

Weight of Expert Testimony

The testimony of an expert witness is not binding on the jury. *Marshall v. Martinson,* 264 Or 470, 506 P2d 172 (1973). The jury may disregard the experts' opinions even if uncontradicted. *Cutsforth v. Kinzua Corp.,* 267 Or 423, 517 P2d 640 (1973); *City of Portland v. Ruggero,* 231 Or 624, 373 P2d 970 (1962).

A plaintiff is not necessarily entitled to a directed verdict based on the uncontradicted testimony of an expert, because the weight of the testimony is for the jury to determine. *W.R. Chamberlin & Co. v. Northwestern Agencies, Inc.,* 289 Or 201, 611 P2d 652 (1980). However, it has been held to be error to instruct that opinion evidence by experts is to be viewed with caution. *Kennedy v. State Indus. Accident Common,* 218 Or 432, 345 P2d 801 (1959).

In *Bales v. SAIF,* 294 Or 224, 656 P2d 300 (1982), the court held that the opinion testimony of an expert should not be given less weight as a matter of law simply because the witness holds the view of a particular school of medical thought. In this case, the expert belonged to a school of medical thought that believed that stress does not cause heart attacks and was testifying on the question of whether a claimant's heart attack was caused by his job activity.

Impeachment of Expert Witnesses

Expert witnesses may be impeached to the same extent and by the same methods as lay witnesses. See textual discussion under Rule 607. Impeachment methods include character for untruthfulness (see Rule 608), conviction of prior crime (see Rule 609), evidence of bias or interest (see Rule 609-1), or prior inconsistent statements (see Rule 613). In addition, an expert may be impeached by statements in a treatise, relied upon or acknowledged by the expert to be authoritative, which contradict his or her testimony. *Kern v. Pullen,* 138 Or 222, 6 P2d 224 (1931); *Eckleberry v. Kaieser Foundation Northern Hospitals,* 226 Or 616, 359 P2d 1090 (1961); *Scott v. Astoria RR,* 43 Or 26, 72 P 594 (1903) (dictum).

The foundation required by current Oregon case law for impeachment of an expert witness by use of a treatise is arguably too stringent. The expert must have relied upon the treatise or at least acknowledge that the treatise is recognized by members of the profession as an authority. An expert witness may attempt to avoid impeachment by denying reliance and refusing to concede that the treatise is an authority. In such cases, courts should allow the authoritativeness of the treatise to be established by extrinsic evidence, or, in appropriate cases, by judicial notice. See FRE 803(18).

The statements in the treatise may be read to the jury and the expert cross-examined regarding them. The statements in a recognized treatise are receivable only for purposes of impeachment, not as substantive evidence. The Oregon legislature did not adopt FRE 803(18), which admits statements in treatises used in examining an expert witness, as an exception to the hearsay rule. When statements from a treatise are used in the cross-examination of an expert witness, a limiting instruction should be available upon request under Rule 105.

Under former law it has been held that an expert may state the names of authorities who agree with the expert but may not quote statements from such treatises. *Scott v. Astoria RR,* 43 Or 26, 40, 72 P 594 (1903). However, this seems an even more dangerous form of hearsay to allow the witness to decide what authorities "agree" with him.

Expert Testimony Regarding Value of Property

The admission of opinions by owners regarding the value of their property is expressly approved in the Legislative Commentary to both Rules 701 and 702. Therefore, opinions of value by property owners may be allowed in appropriate cases under either rule. The significance of admitting a property owner's opinion under the more liberal standard of Rule 702 is that the owner may be allowed to rely on inadmissible evidence as the basis for the opinion. See Rule 703. See also *La Combe v. A-T-O, Inc.,* 679 F2d 431 (5th Cir 1982), where the court held that a property owner is entitled to testify as an expert witness under FRE 702 with regard to the value of the property. As an expert, the owner's testimony was subject to FRE 703 and was admissible "despite the fact that he may have been relying to some extent on hearsay."

Expert Testimony Regarding Legal Issues

In general, questions of law are for the court and are not a proper subject for expert testimony to the jury. See *Owen v. Kerr-McGee Corp.,* 698 F2d 236, 239–40 (5th Cir 1983) (no error to exclude expert opinion testimony as to "legal" as opposed to "factual" cause of accident); *United States v. Zipkin,* 729 F2d 384

(6th Cir 1984). But see *Hoke v. The May Department Stores Co.*, 133 Or App 410, 418 n4, 891 P2d 686, 691 (1995) (expert testimony proper on question of whether a store had reasonably investigated a prior complaint against a store employee—dictum); *United States v. Gold*, 743 F2d 800, 817 (11th Cir 1984), cert denied 469 US 1217 (approving receipt of expert testimony that particular claims were reimbursable under Medicare).

In *Olson v. Coats,* 78 Or App 368, 717 P2d 176 (1986), the court held it was error to allow a witness to answer the following question over an objection: "[A]nd did the signs that you had up [at the construction site] comply with whatever the requirements were?" The court stated: "To answer the question, [the witness] had to draw a mixed legal and factual conclusion as to whether the signs complied with statutory requirements. Such a question may not be asked. Rather, the trial court should instruct the jury as to the law; the jury should determine the facts from the evidence and draw its own conclusion."

The federal courts are divided regarding the extent to which expert opinion testimony may be allowed in determining whether a legal obligation or contractual agreement was violated. Compare *Bowen v. United States Postal Service,* 642 F2d 79 (4th Cir 1981), reversed on other grounds 459 US 212 (1983) (allowing expert testimony as to whether union breached duty of fair representation) with *Marx & Co., Inc. v. Diner's Club, Inc.,* 550 F2d 505 (2nd Cir), cert denied 434 US 861 (1977) (error to allow expert to give opinion as to legal obligations of parties under a contract). See also *Energy Oils Inc. v. Montana Power Co.,* 626 F2d 731 (9th Cir 1980) (expert opinion regarding custom and usage admissible, but opinion regarding legal effect of agreement is not).

In *Specht v. Jensen,* 853 F2d 805 (10th Cir 1988), the court held that it was error in a civil rights action to allow an attorney to testify as expert for plaintiff that defendant's action constituted a "search" and that plaintiffs had not "consented" to the search. The court holds that this was legal opinion testimony which was inadmissible and could confuse the jury as to the applicable law.

See generally Ehrhardt, *The Conflict Concerning Expert Witnesses and Legal Conclusions,* 92 W Va L Rev 645 (1990); Baker, *The Impropriety of Expert Witness Testimony on the Law,* 40 U Kan L Rev 325 (1992); Friedland, *Expert Testimony on the Law: Excludable or Justifiable?,* 37 U Miami L Rev 451 (1983).

Expert Testimony Regarding Fallibility of Eyewitness Identification

Trial courts in their discretion may admit expert testimony regarding the fallibility of eyewitness identification. See Westling, *The Case for Expert Assistance to the Jury in Eyewitness Identification Cases,* 71 Or L Rev 93 (1992) (describing increased judicial acceptance of expert testimony on eyewitness identification).

However, appellate courts continue to hold that it is not error for the trial judge to disallow such testimony. *State v. Fox,* 98 Or App 356, 779 P2d 197, rev denied 308 Or 608, 784 P2d 1101 (1989) (no abuse of discretion for trial court to conclude that expert testimony about the fallibility of eyewitness identification would not be helpful to the jury); *State v. Schroeder,* 62 Or App 331, 661 P2d 111, rev denied 295 Or 161, 668 P2d 380 (1983); *State v. Smith,* 66 Or App 374, 675 P2d 1060, rev denied 297 Or 339, 683 P2d 1370 (1984) (no error in the refusal of the trial judge to appoint an expert to testify on the reliability of eyewitness identification).

There have been significant advances in psychological research in recent years indicating the fallibility of eyewitness testimony. See E. Loftus, *Eyewitness Testimony* (1979); P. Wall, *Eyewitness Identification in Criminal Cases* (2d ed 1982); L. Taylor, *Eyewitness Identification* (1982). It is unlikely that most jurors are aware of the extent to which eyewitness identification is unreliable or the conditions which can make it unreliable. In cases where the accuracy of eyewitness identification is a central issue, expert testimony that focuses on the precise circumstances of the eyewitness observations in the case being tried may clearly satisfy the requirement of Rule 702 that it "assist the trier of fact to understand the evidence or to determine a fact in issue."

In any case, an instruction regarding the unreliability of eyewitness identification may and sometimes should be given. In *State v. Calla,* 15 Or App 110, 514 P2d 1354 (1973), cert denied 417 US 917 (1974), the Court of Appeals held that the giving of such an instruction is within the discretion of the trial court. See also *State v. Peterson,* 66 Or App 477, 675 P2d 1055 (1984) (refusal to give defendant's requested instruction on eyewitness identification not error); *State v. Rovles,* 41 Or App 653, 658–9, 598 P2d 1249 (1979); *State v. Schroeder,* 55 Or App 932, 938, 640 P2d 688, rev denied 293 Or 373, 648 P2d 854 (1982).

See generally ANNOT., *Necessity and Prejudicial Effect of Omitting Cautionary Instruction to Jury as to Reliability of, or Factors to be Considered in Evaluating, Eyewitness Identification Testimony—State Cases,* 23 ALR4th 1089 (1983); ANNOT., *Admissibility, at Criminal Prosecution, of Expert Testimony on Reliability of Eyewitness Testimony,* 46 ALR4th 1047 (1986); Wade, *Do the Eyes Have It? Psychological Testimony Regarding Eyewitness Accuracy,* 38 Baylor L Rev 169 (1985); Camper and Loftus, *The Role of Psychologists as Expert Witnesses in the Courtroom: No More Daniels in the Lion's Den,* 9 Law & Psychology Rev 1 (1985); Landsman, *Reforming Adversary Procedure: A Proposal Concerning the Psychology of Memory and the Testimony of Disinterested Witnesses,* 45 U Pitt L Rev 547 (1984); COMMENT, *Expert Testimony on Eyewitness Identification: Invading the Province of the Jury?,* 26 Ariz L Rev 399 (1984); COMMENT, *Eyewitness Identification: Should Psychologists be Permitted to Address the Jury?,* 75 J Crim L & Criminology 1321 (1984); COMMENT, *Admission of Expert Testimony on Eyewitness Identifications,* 73 Calif L Rev 1402 (1985).

Expert Testimony Regarding Psychological "Syndromes"

Expert testimony about battered woman syndrome, rape trauma syndrome, and other psychological syndromes will only be admissible if the criteria for scientific evidence set forth in *State v. Brown,* 297 Or 404, 687 P2d 751 (1984) are satisfied. [The *Brown* case is discussed under scientific evidence, infra.] The admissibility of syndrome evidence must be assessed under Rules 401, 403, and 702.

In *State v. Lawson*, 127 Or App 392, 872 P2d 986 (1994), rev denied 320 Or 110, 881 P2d 141 (1994), defendant daycare provider was charged with assault and criminal mistreatment of children in her care. In her defense, she offered testimony and reports from two psychologists that she lacked the character traits typically seen in child abusers. Although evidence of pertinent character traits of a criminal defendant is normally admissible under OEC 404(2)(a), the appellate court affirmed the exclusion of the evidence, because such "profile" evidence was a form of scientific evidence and there was not a sufficient foundation laid for it under the Brown standard.

See generally McCord, *Syndromes, Profiles and Other Mental Exotica: A New Approach to the Admissibility of Non-traditional Psychological Evidence in Criminal Cases*, 66 Or L Rev 19 (1987); Crowley, O'Callaghan, and Ball, *The Juridical Impact of Psychological Expert Testimony in a Simulated Child Abuse Trial*, 18 Law & Human Behavior 89 (1994); NOTE, *Assisting the Jury in Understanding Victimization: Expert Psychological Testimony on Battered Woman Syndrome and Rape Trauma Syndrome*, 25 Colum J L & Soc Probs 277 (1992); NOTE, *Evaluating and Admitting Expert Opinion Testimony in Child Sexual Abuse Prosecutions*, 41 Duke L J 691 (1991); Schopp, Sturgis & Sullivan, *Battered Woman Syndrome, Expert Testimony, and the Distinction Between Justification and Excuse*, 1994 U Ill L Rev 45; COMMENT, *Criminal Law: Marshaling the Defense—Indigent Defendants Guaranteed Psychiatric Assistance at Trial to Explain Battered Woman Syndrome*, 32 Washburn L J 260 (1993); Comment, *Battered Women in Florida: Will Justice be Served? 20 Fla St U L Rev 679 (1993)*; COMMENT, *Constitutional Law: Battered Child Syndrome Evidence: Balancing an Accused's Right to Due Process with the Evidentiary Problems Inherent in Child Abuse Cases*, 32 Washburn L J 118 (1992); NOTE, *Fourteenth Amendment—Admitting Evidence of Battered Child Syndrome to Prove Intent*, 83 J Crim L & Criminology 894 (1993); Massaro, *Experts, Psychology, Credibility and Rape: The Rape Trauma Syndrome Issue and Its Implications for Expert Psychological Testimony*, 69 Minn L Rev 395 (1985); Buchele & Buchele, *Legal and Psychological Issues in the Use of Expert Testimony on Rape Trauma Syndrome*, 25 Washburn L J 26 (1985); COMMENT, *The Admissibility of Evidence on Battered Wife Syndrome in Support of a Claim of Self-Defense*, 15 Conn L Rev 121 (1982); COMMENT, *The Admissibility of Testimony on Battered Wife Syndrome: An Evidentiary Analysis*, 77 Nw U L Rev 348 (1982); ANNOT., *Admissibility of Expert or Opinion Testimony on Battered Wife or Battered Woman Syndrome*, 18 ALR4th 1153 (1982); ANNOT., *Admissibility, at Criminal Prosecution, of Expert Testimony on Rape Trauma Syndrome*, 42 ALR4th 879 (1985).

Expert Testimony Regarding Characteristics
of Sex Crime Victims

In *State v. Middleton*, 294 Or 427, 657 P2d 1215 (1983), the court held that it was proper to allow expert testimony that a sex crime victim acted similarly to other children who had been sexually abused by family members. The court stated:

> We hold that if a witness is accepted as an expert by the trial court, it is not error to allow testimony describing the reaction of the typical child victim of familial sexual abuse and whether a testifying victim impeached by her prior inconsistent statement reacted in a typical manner when she made that inconsistent statement.

294 Or at 438, 657 P2d at 1221.

The *Middleton* holding was qualified in *State v. Milbradt,* 305 Or 621, 756 P2d 620 (1988), where the court held that a foundation for such evidence must be established that meets the requirements of *State v. Brown,* 297 Or 404, 687 P2d 751 (1984). [See discussion of *State v. Brown* under discussion of scientific evidence, infra.] In *Milbradt,* the court stated: "We suggest that in future cases involving 'syndrome' testimony full foundations be established, if indeed it can be shown that the so-called 'typical' reactions can be demonstrated to be either typical or reliable." 305 Or at 631. The court noted that the expert's testimony regarding normal children's reactions to sexual abuse would likely be irrelevant on retrial in a case involving severely retarded young adults.

In *State v. St. Hilaire,* 97 Or App 108, 775 P2d 876 (1989), the court affirmed the admission of testimony that victims of sexual abuse rarely report the crime immediately, often minimize the activity, and often are imprecise about the dates of occurrences. The court found the testimony to satisfy the applicable criteria of *State v. Brown* (discussed infra). The court commented that these factors "are guidelines, not a checklist." The court noted that "the state might have offered evidence on the existence of specialized literature in the field of the behavior of child abuse victims," but found that it was not essential given the expert's first-hand experience in observing such victims. The court held that the expert may have gone beyond his expertise in testifying why abused children behave as they do, but found that the defendant failed to preserve the error.

In *State v. Dale,* 75 Or App 453, 706 P2d 1009, rev denied 300 Or 451, 712 P2d 110 (1985), the court approved expert testimony that a typical five-to-seven-year-old victim of sexual abuse (1) "acts out" sexually with others and is highly curious about sexual anatomy, (2) delays reporting an incident of sexual abuse, and (3) does not fabricate or fantasize about sexual acts with adults as a result of exposure to sexually explicit materials.

In *State v. Padilla,* 74 Or App 676, 704 P2d 524 (1985), the court held that expert testimony regarding a crime victim's ability to perceive and describe a sexual contact was admissible.

In *State v. Pettit,* 66 Or App 575, 675 P2d 183, rev denied 297 Or 227, 683 P2d 91 (1984), the court held that it was not error to allow an expert to testify whether victims of sexual abuse (1) recall dates, (2) can relate details, (3) tell consistent stories, and (4) report such incidents promptly.

See generally Askowitz & Graham, *The Reliability of Expert Psychological Testimony in Child Sexual Abuse Prosecutions,* 15 Cardozo L Rev 2027 (1994); NOTE, *The Unreliability of Expert Testimony on the Typical Characteristics of Sexual Abuse Victims,* 74 Geo L J 429 (1985).

Expert Testimony Regarding Credibility of Another Witness

In *State v. Middleton,* 294 Or 427, 438, 657 P2d 1215, 1221 (1983), the Oregon Supreme Court held as follows: "We expressly hold that in Oregon a witness, expert or otherwise, may not give an opinion on whether he believes a witness is telling the truth. We reject testimony from a witness about the credibility of another witness, although we recognize that some jurisdictions accept it." But see Rule 608(1), which allows character witnesses to give opinion testimony about the truthful or untruthful **character** of other witnesses (as distinguished from an opinion about whether they are being truthful in their testimony).

In *State v. Milbradt,* 305 Or 621, 756 P2d 620 (1988), the court found reversible error in a psychologist testifying regarding the credibility of mentally retarded victims of sexual abuse. The court stated: "We have said before, and we will say it again, but this time with emphasis—we really mean it—*no psychotherapist may render an opinion on whether a witness is credible in any trial conducted in this state.* The assessment of credibility is for the trier of fact and not for psychotherapists." 305 Or at 629. See also *State v. Isom,* 306 Or 587, 590, 761 P2d 524, 526 (1988) ("[A] basic rule of evidence [is that] no witness may pass upon the credibility of another witness unless authorized by the Oregon Evidence Code.").

The court in *State v. Munro,* 68 Or App 63, 680 P2d 708, rev denied 297 Or 459, 683 P2d 1372 (1984) affirmed the exclusion of expert testimony offered by the defendant on the effect of the alleged victim's emotional state on her truth-telling ability. The court held:

> Although *Middleton* does not make clear the line between permissible and impermissible expert testimony that implicates the veracity of another witness, we conclude that such testimony is improper when it can be fairly characterized as an opinion on the veracity of a *particular* witness, rather than a general opinion on how the conduct of a witness compares with similarly situated members of an identifiable group.

68 Or App at 66, 680 P2d at 710.

However, the fact that a witness affirms a fact or makes a diagnosis that is consistent with testimony of an earlier witness does not mean that the second witness is commenting on the credibility of the first witness. In *State v. Wilson,* 121 Or App 460, 462–7, 855 P2d 657, 658–61 (1993), rev denied 318 Or 61, 865 P2d 1297, a sodomy and sexual abuse prosecution, the court held that testimony by the state's expert that the child had been sexually abused was not an improper comment on the credibility of the complainant. Defendant argued that because there was no physical evidence of abuse the expert necessarily was relying on the truthfulness of the child in making the diagnosis. Because the expert did not directly express an opinion on the truth of the victim's testimony, the court found no error. The court commented: "A medical doctor is not precluded from testifying as to her medical diagnosis simply because the jury may infer from that testimony that another witness is or is not telling the truth." See also *State v. Butterfield*, 128 Or App 1, 10–2, 874 P2d 1339, 1345–46 (1994), rev denied 319 Or 625, 879 P2d 1287 (1994) (trial court allowed testimony from an expert that "a caretaker's changing explanations of the causes of a child's injuries is a textbook symptom of battered child syndrome"; appellate court found this not to be an improper comment on the truthfulness of the defendant or another witness because it was not a "direct" comment about their credibility).

Recent Cases

In *State v. Charboneau*, 323 Or 38, 42–51, 913 P2d 308 (1996), after a prosecution witness had been impeached by evidence of entering a plea bargain in exchange for his testimony, the prosecutor attempted to rehabilitate him by intoducing portions of the plea agreement which included statements such as the following: the state "believes" that the reduced charge "accurately reflects" the role the witness played in the murder and "has reason to believe" that the murder was primarily committed by others. The court held it was reversible error to admit such statements, because they amounted to an expression of belief by the prosecuting attorneys and were analogous to commenting on the credibility of a witness. The court announced the following rule: "A witness's testimony or an exhibit may not, explicitly and directly, contain an opinion as to a trial witness's credibility." 323 Or at 48.

In *State v. Walker*, 140 Or App 472, 475, 915 P2d 1039 (1996), a police officer after describing the training of an undercover informant stated that "none of the information that Ms. Kelley ever told me was untrue." The court reversed defendant's conviction, finding this to be an improper comment on the credbility of another witness."

In *State v. Keller*, 315 Or 273, 285, 844 P2d 195 (1993), the court held that it was reversible error in a sexual abuse prosecution for an examining physician to testify that "[t]here was no evidence of leading or coaching or fantasizing" during the child's interview and that the child was "obviously telling you about what happened to her body." Each of those statements was found to violate the often repeated rule that a witness, expert, or otherwise, may not give an opinion on whether he believes another witness is telling the truth.

In *State v. Bockorny*, 124 Or App 585, 592, 863 P2d 1296, 1300 (1993), rev denied 318 Or 351, 870 P2d 220 (1994), a defense expert testified that defendant suffered from battered woman's syndrome and post-traumatic stress disorder. On cross-examination, the expert admitted that his conclusion depended in part on the truthfulness of the defendant in talking with him and conceded that defendants are generally more truthful when interviewed shortly after arrest than at a later time when their stories may change. Because the expert made no "direct comments" about the credibility of the defendant, the court found no error in admitting his testimony.

In *State v. White*, 119 Or App 424, 428, 850 P2d 1158, rev denied 317 Or 486, 858 P2d 876 (1993), the prosecutor asked the police officer to describe the victim's demeanor when she was being interviewed. He stated that she seemed very "forthright." The trial judge sustained an objection on the ground that the answer was an impermissible comment on the credibility of the victim and instructed the jury to disregard the statement. The appellate court affirmed the trial judge's refusal to deny a mistrial, holding that "we do not believe that the statement was of such magnitude that the jury could not follow the instruction and disregard the statement."

In *State v. Burks*, 107 Or App 588, 813 P2d 1071, rev denied 312 Or 151, 817 P2d 758 (1991), the investigating officer testified that the reason he took the defendant from her father's home to question her was that, in his experience, juveniles are less likely to admit criminal activity in front of their parents. The defendant argued that this testimony was tantamount to an expression of opinion that the defendant, after being separated from her father, told the truth during interrogation. The court held that admission of the testimony was not error, finding it unlikely that the jury would view the statement as a comment on the juvenile's credibility.

In *James v. General Motors of Canada, Ltd.*, 101 Or App 138, 146 n4, 790 P2d 8, rev denied 310 Or 243, 796 P2d 360 (1990), the court rejected a plaintiff's claim that two of the defendant's experts improperly testified regarding her credibility. Instead, the court found that the testimony addressed the effect of her injury on her memory and ability to make reliable statements after the accident. In cross-examination, plaintiff's counsel asked one of the experts if he was commenting on the plaintiff's credibility and the expert said that he was. However, the appellate court stated: "Insofar as that exchange resulted in a characterization of the testimony, it was a legal conclusion that is not binding on us. Insofar as plaintiff's counsel may have elicited testimony about his own client's credibility, any error was invited."

In *State v. Caulder*, 75 Or App 457, 706 P2d 1007 (1985), a sex abuse prosecution, the CSD worker was asked by defense counsel on cross-examination whether she agreed that not all ten-year-olds tell the truth all the time. The witness agreed. On redirect examination, the prosecutor elicited testimony that ten-year-olds are "highly likely to be telling the truth when they report sexual conduct with an adult." The court found no error in such redirect examination, because defense counsel was found to have "opened the door" to such testimony by the cross-examination of the witness regarding the veracity of ten-year-olds. The court stated: "Having opened the door, defendant cannot be heard to complain because the prosecution stepped through." 75 Or App at 461, 706 P2d at 1009.

Expert Testimony Regarding Accident Reconstruction

A witness who is properly qualified may testify as an expert on accident reconstruction. If a proper foundation is established, complying with Rules 702 and 703, the witness may be allowed to render an opinion regarding the "point of impact." *State v. Stringer*, 292 Or 388, 639 P2d 1264 (1982); *Dyer v. R.E. Christiansen Trucking, Inc*, 318 Or 391, 868 P2d 1325, 1329 (1994) (approving admission of testimony by a defense traffic engineer that the collision occurred in defendant's lane of travel). See also *Straight v. Conroy*, 279 Or 289, 566 P2d 1198 (1977) (expert allowed to testify that impact minor was unlikely to injure spine based on photographs of vehicles). But see *Kingsbury v. Hickey*, 56 Or App 492, 642 P2d 339 (1982) (excluding accident reconstruction testimony as speculative).

See generally Schoone & Schapiro, *Reconstruction of Automobile Accidents Through Lay and Scientific Testimony*, 47 Marq L Rev 491 (1964).

But opinions about the point of impact by investigating police officers who are not shown to have special training or experience in accident reconstruction may be excluded. *Madrid v. Robinson*, 138 Or App 130, 133–4, 906 P2d 855 (1995) (error to allow opinions of two investigating police officers that jogger was in traffic portion of roadway when he was struck and killed); *French v. Barrett*, 84 Or App 52, 733 P2d 89 (1987) (error to admit opinion of investigating police officer who did not witness accident that cause of accident was plaintiff's stepping into roadway "did nothing more than tell the jury that he thought defendant should prevail").

In *DeFries v. Post*, 108 Or App 298, 301, 815 P2d 224, 225 (1991), the court found no error in the admission of testimony by a police officer who was not a witness to an accident regarding his opinion as to the speed at which plaintiff was driving prior to the accident.

Recent Cases Allowing Expert Opinion Testimony

Boger v. Norris Stevens, Inc., 109 Or App 90, 818 P2d 947 (1991), rev denied 312 Or 588, 824 P2d 417 (1992). The court approved the admission of expert testimony that plaintiff's brain damage and other serious conditions were caused by concentration of aluminum and other toxic metals in the hot water heater and water supplied by defendants. The court held that assuming the *Brown* test for the admissibility of scientific evidence applied to testimony regarding medical causation, it did not require that the testimony rest on an indisputably correct scientific position. The court held that "whether the proposition is correct is a question of fact, and it relates to weight rather than admissibility."

Faber v. Asplundh Tree Expert Co., 106 Or App 601, 608, 810 P2d 384, rev denied 312 Or 80, 816 P2d 610 (1991). The court admitted testimony by two plaintiff's experts that the defendant's spraying operations fell below the standard of care for the industry. The court found that this testimony regarding "the appropriate methods to be followed under various conditions could have assisted the jury in understanding the other evidence."

State v. Lerch, 296 Or 377, 677 P2d 678 (1984). The court affirmed the admission of expert testimony regarding hair comparison evidence even though the evidence tended to prove no more than that there was a possibility that the hair found in the defendant's apartment was from the victim. The court found the evidence relevant even though not conclusive, and hence the expert opinion was proper.

AMFAC Foods, Inc. v. International Systems & Controls Corp., 294 Or 94, 116, 654 P2d 1092 (1982). The court held that an expert in an industry should be allowed to testify regarding the meaning of a term used in a letter, even though the expert was not the sender or recipient of the letter. The term, "pick it green," was said to have a "specific, somewhat unique meaning in the industry, with which the average juror would not be familiar."

Recent Cases Not Allowing Expert Opinion Testimony

Madrid v. Robinson, 138 Or App 130, 133–4, 906 P2d 855 (1995) (error to allow opinions of two investigating police officers that jogger was in traffic portion of roadway when he was struck and killed).

Butler v. Dept. of Corrections, 138 Or App 190, 204–5, 909 P2d 163 (1995) (no abuse of discretion to exclude expert testimony about types of harm generally suffered by "whistleblowers," although reasonable for trial court to decide either way on issue).

Paragano v. Gray, 126 Or App 670, 680, 870 P2d 837, 843 (1994). The court found no abuse of discretion by the trial judge in excluding expert testimony that normally "attorneys and real estate investors do not review documents after closing." The court announced a general rule that the trial judge "should admit expert testimony when it is clear that the jury needs the help of an expert to find the truth and should exclude it when it does not." But "between these extremes," as in this case, the decision whether to admit the testimony is within the discretion of the court.

State v. Isom, 313 Or 391, 404, 837 P2d 491 (1992). Defendant sought to introduce testimony of an outreach worker that it was common in downtown Portland for middle-aged and older men to carry weapons for self-defense. Defendant wanted to negate any inference that the fact that defendant carried a knife indicated that he was likely to be aggressive and commit assault. The court held that if exclusion of this testimony was error, it was harmless.

State v. Jacobs, 109 Or App 444, 446, 819 P2d 766 (1991). The court held it was error to allow a police officer to predict what a blood alcohol reading would have been if defendant had agreed to take a breathalyzer test. The court found the testimony to be mere speculation.

DeRosa v. Kolb, 90 Or App 548, 752 P2d 1282, rev denied 306 Or 101, 757 P2d 1362 (1988). The court held it was error to allow an expert to testify that: "The sign creates a substantial visibility obstruction that was a substantial factor in causing the accident." The court held that the expert's conclusion did not assist the jury and instead told the jury what result to reach on a contested causation question.

State v. Hansen, 304 Or 169, 743 P2d 157 (1987). The court held that it was error in a child sex abuse case to allow an expert to testify regarding the techniques used by a child abuser to "get close to the victim." The court held: "[T]he danger of unfair prejudice to defendant from the unwarranted inference that, because defendant engaged in acts that sexual child abusers engage in, she, too, is a sexual child abuser is simply too great."

Mission Insurance Co. v. Wallace Security Agency, Inc., 84 Or App 525, 734 P2d 405 (1987). The court found no error in the trial court's refusal (1) to permit testimony from an expert on professional security service regarding industry standards for hiring and training personnel or (2) to permit testimony from psychiatrists about the personality traits of sociopaths and fire-setters.

Tiedemann v. Radiation Therapy Consultants, 299 Or 238, 701 P2d 440 (1985). The court held that a statement in a summary judgment affidavit that "the treatment of [the plaintiff] was not negligent" was improper under Rules 702 and 704. The court commented that the statement was "pure opinion which merely tells the jury which result to reach," noting that "such testimony is directly condemned by the commentary to OEC 704." 299 Or at 243.

Phomvongsa v. Phounsaveth, 72 Or App 518, 696 P2d 567, rev denied 299 Or 203, 700 P2d 251 (1985). The court found reversible error in the admission of testimony by a police officer who did not see the accident that the accident was "unavoidable" and that the defendant did not cause the accident. The court held that the officer was not competent to give his opinion as to whether the defendants were negligent and found that his testimony did not assist the jury.

State v. Brown, 64 Or App 747, 749, 669 P2d 1190 (1983), aff'd 297 Or 404, 687 P2d 751 (1984). The court affirmed the refusal of the trial judge to admit testimony of a psychologist regarding "unconscious transference." The court stated that "[a]dmission of such testimony, without evidence that the victim actually had prior contact with defendant, is at most 'doubtful or reasonably could be decided either way.' Accordingly, excluding the evidence was within the trial court's discretion."

Carlson v. Piper Aircraft Corp., 57 Or App 695, 646 P2d 43, 48–9, rev denied 293 Or 801, 653 P2d 999 (1982). The court affirmed the exclusion by the trial court of a deposition of an aircraft accident investigator for the National Transportation Safety Board on the ground that the testimony amounted to an opinion regarding the cause of the crash, when such an opinion was prohibited by a federal regulation.

Expert Opinions Allowed Under Former Oregon Law

The following are examples of cases where expert opinion was held to be proper under prior Oregon law: *Fulton v. B.F. Goodrich Co.,* 260 Or 245, 490 P2d 178 (1971) (cause of tire blowout); *Plourd v. S. Pac. Transp. Co.,* 266 Or 666, 513 P2d 1140 (1973) (present value of lost future earnings); *Ritter v. Beals,* 225 Or 504, 358 P2d 1080 (1961) (wheelchair ramp dangerous); *Sandow v. Weyerhaeuser Co.,* 252 Or 377, 449 P2d 426 (1969) (testimony of psychologist that emotional distress caused by injury to head); *Chance v. Ringling Bros. Barnum &*

Bailey, Combined Shows, Inc., 257 Or 319, 478 P2d 613 (1970) (propensity of boxer dogs to jump at persons); *St. Paul Fire and Marine Ins. Co. v. Watkins,* 261 Or 473, 495 P2d 265 (1972) (accidents of kind in question do not usually occur without negligence); *Mayor v. Dowsett,* 240 Or 196, 400 P2d 234 (1965) (same); *Welch v. U.S. Bancorp Realty and Mortgage Trust,* 286 Or 673, 596 P2d 947 (1979) (zoning change would probably have been granted); *Carter v. Moberly,* 263 Or 193, 501 P2d 1276 (1972) (point of impact cannot be accurately determined from location of debris); *Groce v. Fidelity Gen. Ins. Co.,* 252 Or 296, 448 P2d 554 (1968) (whether insurance company acted in good faith in failing to settle claim); *Naney v. Lane,* 247 Or 367, 428 P2d 722 (1967) (safety of structural designs); *First Natl Bank v. Fire Ass'n,* 33 Or 172, 53 P 8 (1898) (whether inflammable substance had been placed around the premises where a fire occurred); *State v. Krause,* 251 Or 318, 445 P2d 500 (1968) (opinion of engineer as to location of defendant and victim at time of shooting); *City of Portland v. Nudelman,* 45 Or App 425, 608 P2d 1190 (1980) (value of real property); *Moreland v. Moreland,* 232 Or 309, 374 P2d 741 (1962) (value of legal services); *Timber Structures, Inc. v. C. W. S. Grinding & Machine Works,* 191 Or 231, 229 P2d 623 (1951) (value of labor and materials); *Ashcraft v. Saunders,* 251 Or 139, 444 P2d 924 (1968) (market value of logs); *Simpson v. Sisters of Charity of Providence,* 284 Or 547, 588 P2d 4 (1978) (testimony of economist regarding damages); *State v. Harwood,* 45 Or App 931, 609 P2d 1312 (1980) (opinion of expert that it was not uncommon for children to perceive and remember sexual acts that occurred during sleep); *Horger v. Flagg,* 185 Or 109, 201 P2d 515 (1948) (expert testimony regarding meaning of technical words and phrases); *Wilson v. B.F. Goodrich,* 292 Or 626, 642 P2d 644 (1982) (testimony of economist regarding present value of future earning losses, including opinions regarding future inflation, wage levels, and interest rates). But see *Hall v. State,* 43 Or App 325, 602 P2d 1104 (1979), aff'd 290 Or 19, 619 P2d 256 (1980) (not error to exclude opinion regarding whether sand on highway caused accident); *Yundt v. D&D Bowl, Inc.,* 259 Or 247, 486 P2d 553 (1971) (not error to exclude opinion that adjacent flooring of different heights is dangerous); *Koch v. S. Pac. Co.,* 266 Or 335, 513 P2d 770 (1973) (error to admit opinion that crossing was "extra-hazardous").

Federal Decisions

The following are examples of opinions that have been allowed under the Federal Rules of Evidence: *Frazier v. Continental Oil Co.,* 568 F2d 378 (5th Cir 1978) (improper design); *United States v. Golden,* 532 F2d 1244 (9th Cir), cert denied 429 US 842 (1976) (price of narcotics in several cities); *United States v. Barletta,* 565 F2d 985 (8th Cir 1977) (that defendant was high-ranking member of gambling ring based upon his knowledge of bookmaker jargon heard over telephone); *United States v. Hearst,* 563 F2d 1331 (9th Cir 1977), cert denied 435 US 1000 (1978) (defendant's conduct in robbing bank was "voluntary"); *American Universal Ins. Co. v. Falzone,* 644 F2d 65 (1st Cir 1981) (fire of "human origin"); *Bowen v. United States Postal Service,* 642 F2d 79 (4th Cir 1981), reversed on other grounds 459 US 212 (1983) (defendant union breached duty of fair representation); *United States v. Logan,* 641 F2d 860 (10th Cir 1981) (embezzlement prosecution; opinion that money "improperly taken"); *United States v. Collins,* 559 F2d 561 (9th Cir), cert denied 434 US 907 (1977) (FBI expert may give opinion that shoes and briefcase found in search were most probably same as those depicted in the bank surveillance photograph); *United States v. Sellers,* 566 F2d 884, 886 (4th Cir 1977) (expert opinion regarding identity of person in bank photograph); *United States v. Garvin,* 565 F2d 519, 523 (8th Cir 1977) (expert opinion should have been allowed regarding meaning of the language of insurance policies and forms); *United States v. Pino,* 606 F2d 908, 917–8 (10th Cir 1979) (expert opinion that appearance of defendant in state of shock after accident similar to appearance of being drunk); *Murphy v. Nat'l RR Passenger Corp.,* 547 F2d 816 (4th Cir 1977) (present value of future lost earnings).

In *United States v. Dicker,* 853 F2d 1103 (3rd Cir 1988), the court held that although a witness may be allowed to interpret coded or "code-like" conversations, the interpretation of clear conversations on a tape is not helpful to the jury. In this case the court reversed the conviction because a prosecution witness was allowed to interpret a transcript of a conversation with defendant to state that he understood from the discussion that the defendant wanted him to obtain "phoney paperwork" for a license to export military equipment.

Other Authorities

See generally Weinstein, *Improving Expert Testimony,* 20 U Rich L Rev 473 (1986); Graham, *Expert Witness Testimony and the Federal Rules of Evidence: Insuring Adequate Assurance of Trustworthiness,* 1986 U Ill Rev 43; Younger, *A Practical Approach to the Use of Expert Testimony,* 31 Clev St L Rev 1 (1982); Steinbock, Richman and Ray, *Expert Testimony on Proximate Cause,* 41 Vand L Rev 261 (1988).

See also the following ALR annotations: ANNOT., *Admissibility of Expert Testimony as to Whether Accused had Specific Intent Necessary for Conviction,* 16 ALR4th 666 (1982); ANNOT., *Admissibility of Expert Testimony as to Criminal Defendant's Propensity Toward Sexual Deviation,* 42 ALR4th 937 (1985); ANNOT., *Admissibility of Expert Testimony as to Modus Operandi of Crime-Modern Cases,* 31 ALR4th 798 (1984); ANNOT., *Necessity and Admissibility of Expert Testimony as to Credibility of Witness,* 20 ALR3d 684 (1968); ANNOT., *Products Liability: Admissibility of Expert Opinion Evidence That Product Is or Is Not Defective, Dangerous, or Unreasonably Dangerous,* 4 ALR4th 651 (1981); ANNOT., *Admissibility of Expert Evidence to Decipher Illegible Document,* 11 ALR3d 1015 (1967); ANNOT., *Admissibility, in Civil Case, of Expert Evidence as to Existence or Nonexistence, or Severity, of Pain,* 11 ALR3d 1249 (1967); ANNOT., *Admissibility, In Civil Case, of Expert or Opinion Evidence as to Proposed Witness' Inability to Testify,* 11 ALR3d 1360 (1967); ANNOT., *Necessity and Admissibility, in Federal Trial, of Expert or Opinion Testimony Regarding Use or Reliability of Hypnotically Refreshed Recollections,* 50 ALR Fed 602 (1980); ANNOT., *Admissibility in Wrongful Death Action of Testimony of Actuary Or Mathematician For Purpose of Establishing Present Worth of Pecuniary Loss,* 79 ALR2d 259 (1961); ANNOT., *Admissibility of Testimony of Actuary or Mathematician as to Present Value of Loss or Impairment of Insured Person's General Earning Capacity,* 79 ALR2d 275 (1961); ANNOT., *Expert Testimony as to Modus Operandi of Criminals with Respect to Particular Types of Crimes,* 100 ALR2d 1433 (1965); ANNOT., *Expert or Opinion Evidence as to Speed Based On Appearance Or Condition of Motor Vehicle After Accident,* 93 ALR2d 287 (1964); ANNOT., *Right to Elicit Expert Testimony from Adverse Party Called as Witness,* 88 ALR2d 1186 (1963); ANNOT., *Expert and Opinion Evidence as to Cause or Origin of Fire,* 88 ALR2d 230 (1963); ANNOT., *Compelling Expert to Testify,* 77 ALR2d 1182 (1961); ANNOT., *Safety of Condition, Place, or Appliance as Proper Subject of Expert or Opinion Evidence in Tort Actions,* 62 ALR2d 1426 (1958); ANNOT., *Admissibility of Evidence as to Experiments or Tests in Civil Action for Death, Injury, or Property Damage Against Electric Power Company or the Like,* 54 ALR2d 922 (1957).

Scientific Evidence
State v. Brown *Standard*

Neither Rule 702 nor any other rule specifically addresses the admissibility of scientific tests or procedures. The Legislative Commentary states: "The legislative assembly leaves for judicial decision the standard to be used in determining the admissibility of novel scientific evidence."

In *State v. Brown,* 297 Or 404, 687 P2d 751 (1984), the Supreme Court adopted a new standard for the admissibility of scientific evidence. The court held that the admissibility of scientific evidence should be determined by application of Rule 401 (relevancy), Rule 702 (expert testimony), and Rule 403 (exclusion for unfair prejudice, confusion of the issues, or misleading the jury). In applying Rules 401, 702, and 403, the trial court "must identify and evaluate the probative value of the evidence, consider how it might impair rather than help the factfinder, and decide whether truth-finding is better served by exclusion or admission." 297 Or at 409, 687 P2d at 755.

The court suggested that the following seven factors should be considered by the trial court in ruling on the admissibility of scientific evidence:

1. The technique's general acceptance in the field;
2. The expert's qualifications and stature;
3. The use which has been made of the technique;
4. The potential rate of error;
5. The existence of specialized literature;
6. The novelty of the invention; and
7. The extent to which the technique relies on the subjective interpretation of the expert.

297 Or at 417, 687 P2d at 759.

In a footnote, *Brown* set forth somewhat overlapping additional factors to consider:

1. The potential error rate in using the technique;
2. The existence and maintainance of standards governing its use;
3. Presence of safeguards in the characteristics of the technique;
4. Analogy to other scientific techniques whose results are admissible;
5. The extent to which the technique has been accepted by scientists in the field involved;
6. The nature and breadth of the inference adduced;
7. The clarity and simplicity with which the technique can be described and its results explained;
8. The extent to which the basic data are verifiable by the court and jury;
9. The availability of other experts to test and evaluate the technique;
10. The probative significance of the evidence in the circumstances of the case; and
11. The care with which the technique was employed in this case.

In *Brown,* the Supreme Court rejected the *Frye* standard that prior to the admission of expert testimony based upon the application of a scientific technique, a foundation must be laid showing general acceptance of the technique within the relevant scientific community. See *Frye v. United States,* 293 F 1013 (DC Cir 1923). A number of other state courts have also found the *Frye* standard unnecessarily restrictive to the admissibility of relevant scientific evidence under their state counterpart of FRE 702. See, e.g., *State v. Williams,* 4 Ohio St 3d 53, 446 NE2d 444 (1983); *Barmeyer v. Montana Power Co.,* 657 P2d 594 (Mont 1983); *State v. Williams,* 388 A2d 500 (Maine 1978).

State v. O'Key *Reformulation*

In *State v. O'Key,* 321 Or 285, ___ P2d ___ (1995), the Court reaffirmed the *Brown* standard and extended it by incorporating the analysis of the United States Supreme Court in *Daubert v. Merrell Dow Pharmaceuticals,* 509 US ___, 113 SCt 2786 (1993). In *Daubert,* the Supreme Court rejected *Frye* as the controlling test for admissibility of scientific evidence in federal courts and adopted a new approach based primarily on FRE 702, 401, 402, and 403. *Daubert* established a two-prong approach to the admissibility of scientific evidence. First, the evidence must have scientific validity, i.e., be reliable. The Court derived this requirement from FRE 702's reference to "science" and concluded that this meant valid science, not junk science. Second, the proffered scientific evidence must "fit," i.e., be pertinent to, an issue in the case. The Court derived this requirement from the requirement that the evidence be "helpful" to the trier of fact as well as from the general relevancy requirement of FRE 401.

These two prerequisites—scientific validity and pertinency—are to be determined by the court before the evidence is admitted. Scientific validity is a preliminary question for the court under Rule 104(1) rather than a question for the jury under Rule 104(2). Thus a trial judge may require a hearing outside the presence of the jury where the proponent of the scientific evidence will be required to demonstrate its reliability. In a hearing under Rule 104(1), the court "is not bound by the rules of evidence except those relating to privilege."

A determination of reliability by the trial judge is unnecessary in cases where the admissibility of the particular type of scientific evidence has been approved by appellate precedent, where its validity is so clear that it is subject to judicial notice, and possibly where the evidence is made admissible by statute. See *State v. O'Key*, 321 Or at 293.

The Daubert *Criteria Adopted in* O'Key

When trial judges perform their "gatekeeping" role of determining the reliability of scientific evidence, the Court in *Daubert* suggested that they consider the following four factors (although none is decisive and the list is not exhaustive). In *O'Key* the Oregon Supreme Court "adopted" these factors for consideration by trial judges in determining the admissibility of scientic evidence in state courts. 321 Or at 306.

1. *Whether the theory or technique in question "can be (and has been) tested."* The Court in *Daubert* commented that "[s]cientific methodology today is basd on generating hypothesis and testing them to see if they can be falsified; indeed, this methodology is what distinguishes science from other fields of human inquiry."

2. *Whether the theory or technique has been subject to peer review and publication.* As the *O'Key* opinion noted:

Peer review and publication provide the opportunity for others in the field to examine and critique the reasoning or methodology behind scientific theory. Publication, however, is no longer a *sine qua non* of admissibility. ... In some cases, valid but innovative theories or propositions will not have been published, either because they are too particular, too new, or of limited interest. 321 Or at 304.

3. *The "known or potential rate of error" and the existence of operational standards controlling the technique's operation.* For example, the existence of governmental standards regulating the technique or the experience of regulatory agencies monitoring the technique may provide the court with important information bearing on scientific validity.

4. *The degree of acceptance in the relevant scientific community.* This fourth factor is similar to the old *Frye* "general acceptance" test that was rejected in both *Brown* and *Daubert*. The difference is that this factor is no longer conclusive as it was in *Frye*.

Additional Criteria

The *O'Key* opinion (321 Or at n28) also approved additional criteria for assessing the reliability and admissibility of scientific evidence. These criteria are derived from *United States v. Downing*, 753 F.2d 1224, 1238–41 (3d Cir 1985), an opinion on which *Daubert* draws in part. These criteria are "the non-judicial uses and experience with the process or technique and the extent to which other courts have permitted expert testimony based on the process or technique."

Definition of Scientific Evidence

In *Brown*, the court stated that the term "scientific" refers to "evidence that draws its convincing force from some principle of science, mathematics and the like." 297 Or at 407. In *State v. Milbradt*, 305 Or 621, 631, 756 P2d 620 (1988), the court held that psychological syndrome evidence is a form of "scientific" evidence that will be admitted into evidence only if it satisfies the *Brown* foundational requirements.

An important aspect of the *O'Key* opinion is that it extends the definition of scientific evidence to "proffered expert scientific testimony that a court finds possesses significantly increased potential to influence the trier of fact as 'scientific' assertions." 321 Or at 293. In other words, the Court apparently intends the standard to be not whether scientists would categorize the evidence as "scientific" but whether jurors would perceive it as such. Evidence that is likely to influence (and hence possibly mislead) jurors as conveying the imprimatur of science must satisfy the *Brown/O'Key* foundational requirements. The Court notes that concern about scientific validity is heightened "where the proffered expert testimony is innovative, nontraditional, unconventional, controversial, or close to the frontier of understanding." Id.

Daubert is less specific about what is meant by "scientific" evidence under FRE 702. In *Daubert*, the Court made clear that it was addressing only the foundation for "scientific" evidence and not evidence admissible under FRE 702 as "technical or other specialized knowledge." The line between "scientific" evidence and "technical or other specialized knowledge" will also require further judicial development under OEC 702.

Rationale for Reliability Requirement

Reliability is a central requirement of the *Brown/O'Key* test. The reason why careful scrutiny of scientific evidence is required has been explained as follows:

> There are good reasons why not every ostensibly scientific technique should be recognized as the basis for expert testimony. Because of its apparent objectivity, an opinion that claims a scientific basis is apt to carry undue weight with the trier of fact. In addition, it is difficult to rebut such an opinion except by other experts or by cross-examination based on a thorough acquaintance with the underlying principles. In order to prevent deception or mistake and to allow the possibility of effective response, there must be a demonstrable, objective procedure for reaching the opinion and qualified persons who can either duplicate the result or criticize the means by which it was reached, drawing their own conclusions from the underlying facts. (*United States v. Baller*, 519 F2d 463, 466 (4th Cir), *cert denied* 423 US 1019 (1975) (citations omitted))

Impact of New Standard on Criminal Defendants

A more relaxed standard for the admissibility of scientific evidence is likely to have the greatest impact upon criminal defendants. One court has stated:

> A courtroom is not a research laboratory. The fate of a defendant in a criminal prosecution should not hang on his ability to successfully rebut scientific evidence which bears an "aura of special reliability and trustworthiness," although, in reality the witness is testifying on the basis of an unproved hypothesis in an isolated experiment which has yet to gain general acceptance in its field. (*United States v. Brown,* 557 F2d 541, 556 (6th Cir 1977) (citations omitted))

See also *United States v. Amaral,* 488 F2d 1148, 1152–3 (9th Cir 1973). See generally M. Graham, HANDBOOK OF FEDERAL EVIDENCE (4th ed 1996) § 703.2; Diehm, *Protecting Criminal Defendant's Rights When the Government Adduces Scientific Evidence: The Confrontation Clause and Other Alternatives—A Response to Professor Giannelli,* 22 Cap U L Rev 85 (1993); Harris, *Ake Revisited: Expert Psychiatric Witnesses Remain Beyond Reach for the Indigent,* 68 N C L Rev 763 (1990).

A more liberal standard of admissibility of scientific evidence is likely to lead to requests by indigent criminal defendants for court appointed experts to assist them in challenging the reliability of such scientific evidence. See *United States v. Stifel,* 433 F2d 431, 441 (6th Cir 1970), cert denied 401 US 994 (1971) ("[I]f the government sees fit to use this time consuming, expensive means of fact-finding, it must both allow time for a defendant to make similar tests, and in the instance of an indigent defendant, a means to provide for payment for same"). See ANNOT., *Right of Indigent Defendant in State Criminal Case to Assistance of Chemist Toxicologist, Technician, Narcotics Expert, or Similar Nonmedical Specialist in Substance Analysis,* 74 ALR4th 388 (1989).

Burden on Proponent to Satisfy Brown/O'Key Standard

Unless the particular type of scientific evidence has been approved by statute or a prior appellate decision, the burden is on the proponent of scientific evidence to make a sufficient showing that the test meets the standards for admissibility set forth in *State v. Brown,* supra. Although a court may be willing to take judicial notice of foundation facts that are "not subject to reasonable dispute" and meet the other requirements of Rule 201, judicial notice will not otherwise be available as a substitute for the necessary showing by the proponent of the scientific evidence.

Other Authorities

COMMENT, *Weird Science: Problems with the U.S. Supreme Court's New Evidentiary Standard of Expert Scientific Testimony and Oregon Case Law as a Possible Solution,* 73 Or L Rev 691 (1994); Symposium, *Scientific Evidence After the Death of Frye,* 15 Cardozo L Rev 1745 (1994); Berger, *Procedural Paradigms for*

Applying the Daubert Test, 78 Minn L Rev 1345 (1994); Sanders, *Scientific Validity, Admissibility, and Mass Torts After Daubert,* 78 Minn L Rev 1387 (1994); Eggen, *Toxic Torts, Causation, and Scientific Evidence After Daubert,* 55 U Pitt L Rev 889 (1994); Strong, *Language and Logic in Expert Testimony: Limiting Expert Testimony by Restrictions of Function, Reliability, and Form,* 71 Or L Rev 349 (1992); Symposium, *Expert Evidence,* 16 Law & Hum Behav 253; ANNOT., *Admissibility of Expert Evidence Concerning Meaning of Narcotics Code Language in Federal Prosecution for Narcotics Dealing—Modern Cases,* 104 ALR Fed 230 (1991); Imwinkelried, *The "Bases" of Expert Testimony: The Syllogistic Structure of Scientific Testimony,* 67 N C L Rev 1 (1988).

Approved Scientific Evidence

The following are examples of types of scientific evidence that have been approved in Oregon:

Horizontal Gaze Nystagmus (HGN) evidence is admissible in a DUII proceeding to establish that a defendant was under the influence of intoxicating liquor, subject to a foundational showing that the officer who administered the test was properly qualified, the test was administered properly, and the test results were recorded accurately. HGN evidence is not admissible under ORS 813.010(1)(a) to prove that a defendant had a blood alcohol content of .08 or more. *State v. O'Key,* 321 Or 285, 322–3, ___ P2d ___ (1995).

DNA evidence using the RFLP method. *State v. Herzog,* 324 Or 294, ___ P2d ___ (1996).

DNA evidence using the polymerase chain reaction (PCR) method. *State v. Lyons,* 324 Or 256, ___ P2d ___ (1996).

Chemical analysis for alcohol of a person's breath, blood, urine, or saliva. See ORS 813.300.

Ballistics tests, see *State v. Henderson,* 182 Or 147, 187, 184 P2d 392 (1947).

Radar, see *State v. Ringle,* 40 Or App 393, 595 P2d 824 (1979); see also ANNOT., *Proof, By Radar Or Other Mechanical or Electronic Devices, of Violation of Speed Regulations,* 47 ALR3d 822 (1973).

Fingerprints, see *State v. Smith,* 128 Or 515, 526, 273 P 323 (1929); see also former ORS 43.330(9) (repealed 1981).

Blood tests to determine paternity, see ORS 109.250–.262.

Blood enzyme tests, see *State v. Mower,* 50 Or App 63, 622 P2d 745 (1981).

Bloodhound tracking evidence, see *State v. Harris,* 25 Or App 71, 547 P2d 1394 (1976).

Neutron activation analysis, *State v. Krummacher,* 269 Or 125, 523 P2d 1009 (1974). See ANNOT., *Admissibility of Evidence of Neutron Activation Analysis,* 50 ALR3d 117 (1973).

Blood spatter analysis, *State v. Proctor,* 94 Or App 720, 767 P2d 453 (1988), rev denied 308 Or 33, 774 P2d 1108 (1989) (use of nontraditional collection method goes to weight of evidence, not to admissibility). See ANNOT., *Admissibility, in Criminal Prosecution, of Expert Opinion Evidence as to "Blood Spatter" Interpretation,* 9 ALR5th 369 (1993).

Hair Analysis

Microscopic hair analysis was approved as a scientific technique in *State v. Kersting,* 50 Or App 461, 623 P2d 1095 (1981), aff'd 292 Or 350, 638 P2d 1145 (1982).

With respect to hair analysis, see generally ANNOT., *Admissibility and Weight, in Criminal Case, of Expert or Scientific Evidence Respecting Characteristics and Identification of Human Hair,* 23 ALR4th 1199 (1983); Imwinkelried, *Forensic Hair Analysis: The Case Against the Underemployment of Scientific Evidence,* 39 Wash & Lee L Rev 41 (1982); COMMENT, *Splitting Hairs in Criminal Trials: Admissibility of Hair Comparison Probability Estimates,* 1984 Ariz St L J 521.

Polygraph Evidence Generally

In *State v. Lyon,* 304 Or 221, 744 P2d 231 (1987), the Oregon Supreme Court held that polygraph evidence is inadmissible for any purpose in any legal proceeding subject to the rules of evidence under the Oregon Evidence Code, even when admissibility has been stipulated by the parties. This decision overturns the previous rule that allowed polygraph results by stipulation of the parties. *State v. Green,* 271 Or 153, 531 P2d 245 (1975); *State v. Clifton,* 271 Or 177, 531 P2d 256 (1975).

The holding of *Lyon* is partially qualified by *Fromdahl v. Fromdahl,* 314 Or 496, 508, 840 P2d 683 (1992), a dissolution case, where the court held that evidence that the husband may have failed a polygraph test, and the mother's knowledge of those results, was erroneously excluded where the mother sought to introduce those results to show the reasonableness of her belief that the father had sexually abused the children. The evidence was offered to show its effect on her state of mind and to explain why she fled the state with the children, not to prove that the abuse actually occurred.

References to the **taking** of a polygraph test must generally be redacted from evidence of admissions made by a defendant before or during the taking of the test. See *State v. Harberts,* 315 Or 408, 419, 848 P2d 1187 (1993) (remanding for determination of whether references to polygraph could be redacted from incriminating statements made by defendant without distorting meaning of statements).

However, the fact that a state's witness referred to a polygraph test during defense cross-examination is not necessarily grounds for a mistrial. In *State v. Farrar,* 309 Or 132, 162–4, 786 P2d 161, cert denied *Oregon v. Wagner,* 498 US 879 (1990), and denial of post-conviction relief aff'd *Farrar v. State,* 946 F2d 898 (9th Cir. 1991), the court found no error in denying the defendant's motion for a mistrial after a state's witness mentioned that he had taken a polygraph examination. Although evidence that a material witness submitted to a polygraph examination can be reversible error if "offered to undermine, buttress or rehabilitate that person's credibility," the court found that in this case "the state did not offer the results of a polygraph examination; rather, a witness mentioned a 'lie detector test' in response to a question asked by defense counsel on cross-examination." The court found that no mistrial was warranted because the reference was "made only in passing, the results of the test were not disclosed, and the state never argued that the test had any significance to the witness's credibility or to any other issue in the case."

The prosecutor cannot question defendant in a manner designed to open the door to impeachment about whether he took a polygraph test. See *State v. LaStair*, 81 Or App 558, 726 P2d 1193 (1986), rev denied 302 Or 614, 733 P2d 449 (1987) (improper to introduce evidence that defendant came to the police station for a polygraph examination to rebut defendant's explanation of why he came to the police station, because defendant did not open the door to such evidence by voluntarily testifying about his reasons for coming to the police interview; if the door was opened, it was done by the prosecutor, not by defendant).

However, the fact that admissions were made by defendant during a prepolygraph test interview does not mean they must be suppressed. See *State v. Hart*, 309 Or 646, 653, 791 P2d 125 (1990) (rejecting defendant's claim that use of statements made in prepolygraph test interview would force him to offer an explanation that would make the jury aware of the polygraph test).

It is not permissible to rehabilitate a prosecution witness who has been impeached by evidence that he entered a plea bargain in exchange for his testimony by showing that one condition of the plea agreement was that the witness "take a polygraph and pass it." *State v. Middleton*, 295 Or 485, 668 P2d 371 (1983). See also *State v. Snider*, 296 Or 168, 674 P2d 585 (1983) (same result when condition in agreement was that witness pass polygraph examination in future).

Polygraph evidence may be considered in determining the reliability of an informant, because search warrant proceedings are not subject to the Oregon Evidence Code. *State v. Coffey*, 309 Or 342, 348, 788 P2d 424 (1990); *State v. Fink*, 79 Or App 590, 720 P2d 372, rev denied 302 Or 36, 726 P2d 935 (1986).

See generally ANNOT., *Modern Status of Rule Relating to Admission of Results of Lie Detector (Polygraph) Test in Federal Criminal Trials*, 43 ALR Fed 68 (1979); Wygant, *The Lie Detector in Court: A Review of Oregon Cases*, 40 Or St Bar Bull 10 (October, 1979); Brasch, *The Polygraph Confession*, 9 Will L Rev 54 (1973); COMMENT, *Oregon's Approach to the Admissibility of Polygraph Evidence: State v. Brown*, 21 Will L Rev 167 (1985); Katz, *Dilemmas of Polygraph Stipulations*, 14 Seton Hall L Rev 285 (1984); Raskin, *The Polygraph in 1986. Scientific, Professional and Legal Issues Surrounding Application and Acceptance of Polygraph Evidence*, 1986 Utah L Rev 29; Wygant, *... And Nothing But The Truth: The Current Status of Polygraph*, 49 Or St Bar Bull 27 (November, 1988).

Polygraph Evidence in Prison Disciplinary Hearings

The results of a polygraph test can be considered by a hearings officer in evaluating the credibility of a confidential informant in a prison disciplinary case, although not as the sole basis for deciding that the informant was credible. *Wiggett v. Oregon State Penitentiary,* 85 Or App 635, 738 P2d 580, rev denied 304 Or 186, 743 P2d 736 (1987). See also *Branton v. Oregon State Penitentiary,* 89 Or App 597, 750 P2d 183, aff'd 307 Or 244, 765 P2d 207 (1988); *Nelson v. Oregon State Correctional Institution,* 89 Or App 671, 750 P2d 184, aff'd 307 Or 243, 765 P2d 207 (1988).

Polygraph results may also be used to impeach a witness' testimony at a prison disciplinary proceeding, but they are not to be received as affirmative evidence that the petitioner acted as charged. *Parker v. Oregon State Correctional Institution,* 87 Or App 354, 742 P2d 617 (1987). They may be used to evaluate the credibility of the inmate as well as the credibility of the testimony against him.

An inmate may be entitled to take a polygraph to attempt to obtain evidence bolstering his own credibility, at least in a case where the hearings officer is relying on evidence that the primary adverse witness has passed a polygraph test. *Caron v. OSP,* 141 Or App 347, 353, 918 P2d 120 (1996).

In *Snow v. OSP,* 308 Or 259, 265, 780 P2d 215 (1989), the court held that polygraph evidence was admissible at a prison disciplinary proceeding in a case where the petitioner requested the polygraph examination and did not object to consideration of the results at the hearing. Such proceedings are not subject to the Oregon Evidence Code, and the court noted its prior rulings that polygraph evidence is inadmissible at proceedings governed by the OEC. The applicable administrative rule [OAR 291-46-030(5)] required only that "[t]he evidence considered by the hearings officer will be of such reliability as would be considered by reasonable persons in the conduct of their affairs." The court held that polygraph evidence satisfied this standard under the facts of the case.

Voiceprint Evidence

Courts are divided about the admissibility of voiceprint evidence. See ANNOT., *Admissibility and Weight of Voiceprint Evidence,* 97 ALR3d 294 (1980). Courts favoring admission include: *United States v. Smith,* 869 F.2d 348, 351 (7th Cir. 1989); *United States v. Williams,* 583 F2d 1194 (2nd Cir 1978), cert denied 439 US 1117 (1979); *United States v. Baller,* 519 F2d 463 (4th Cir), cert denied 423 US 1019 (1975). Courts opposing admission include: *United States v. McDaniel,* 538 F2d 408 (DC Cir 1976); *People v. Jeter,* 587 N Y S 583, 80 NY2d 818, 600 NE2d 214 (1992); *Cornett v. State,* 450 NE2d 498 (Ind. 1983). See textual discussion under Rule 901(2)(e). See generally NOTE, *Voice Spectography— Reliability of Voice-Prints Not Established, Therefore Inadmissible,* 18 Seton Hall L Rev 405 (1988); Gregory, *Voice Spectrography Evidence: Approaches to Admissibility,* 20 U Rich L Rev 357 (1986).

Predictions of Future Dangerousness

In *State v. Wagner,* 305 Or 115, 752 P2d 1136 (1988), a forensic psychologist testified that it was more likely than not that the defendant would in the future commit criminal acts of violence. On appeal, the defendant argued that according to a large number of studies and the views of many mental health practitioners such a prediction of future dangerousness cannot reliably be made, and if made, that psychiatrists and psychologists are not better able to make it than a lay person. The court refused to consider this objection, because the testimony was not challenged in the trial court on this ground.

See generally Slobogin, *Dangerousness and Expertise,* 133 U Pa L Rev 97 (1984).

Paternity Index

In *Plemel v. Walter,* 303 Or 262, 278–9, 735 P2d 1209 (1987), the court considered the admissibility of statistics derived from blood test results to establish paternity. The court held that the putative father's paternity index is admissible, but only subject to certain conditions:

> First, the paternity index is admissible so long as the expert explains that the index is not the probability that the defendant is the father, but measures only the chance that the defendant is the father compared to the chance that a randomly selected man is the father. The expert should also not be allowed to use misleading formulations of the paternity index such as "the chance of paternity" and "the chance of nonpaternity" without making this qualification....
>
> Second, the expert, whether testifying in person or by affidavit, ... should never be allowed to present over objection a *single* figure as "the" probability of paternity....
>
> Finally, if the expert testifies to the defendant's paternity index or a substantially equivalent statistic, the expert must, if requested, calculate the probability that the defendant is the father by using more than a single assumption about the strength of the other evidence in the case.

See generally ANNOT., *Admissibility, Weight, and Sufficiency of Human Leukocyte Antigen (HLA) Tissue Typing Tests in Paternity Cases,* 37 ALR4th 167 (1985).

Scientific Evidence Taken in Violation of Statute

In *State v. Milstead,* 57 Or App 658, 646 P2d 63, rev denied 293 Or 483, 650 P2d 928 (1982), the defendant attempted to offer a breathalyzer test result showing a low blood alcohol level. Because the test had been taken in violation of statute, the trial judge excluded it. The appellate court found error, stating: "Clearly, the purpose of preventing conviction on unreliable evidence does not justify excluding the results of tests performed by the state sought to be introduced by a defendant when the test result has an exculpatory tendency. If the state, in fact, believes the test was unreliable, it may offer evidence to that effect in rebuttal." 57 Or App at 622, 646 P2d at 666.

In *State v. Knepper,* 62 Or App 623, 661 P2d 560 (1983), the court held that when a blood alcohol test was taken in violation of statute, not only must it be excluded as substantive evidence, it may not be revealed to the jury at trial to show that it served as a basis under Rule 703 for the prosecution expert's opinion regarding intoxication.

Public Opinion Polls

On the admissibility of public opinion polls or surveys, see textual discussion under Rule 703. See also Becker, *Public Opinion Polls and Surveys as Evidence: Suggestions for Resolving Confusing and Conflicting Standards Governing Weight and Admissibility,* 70 Or L Rev 463 (1991).

Other Authorities

See generally Matthias, *The Admissibility of Novel Scientific Evidence in the Ninth Circuit,* 19 Will L Rev 533 (1983); Braun, *Quantitative Analysis and the Law: Probability Theory as a Tool of Evidence in Criminal Trials,* 1982 Utah L Rev 41; ANNOT., *Admissibility of Bare Footprint Evidence,* 45 ALR4th 1178 (1986); ANNOT., *Admissibility of Expert or Opinion Testimony Concerning Identification of Skeletal Remains,* 18 ALR4th 1294 (1982); ANNOT., *Admissibility of Results of Computer Analysis of Defendant's Mental State,* 37 ALR4th 510 (1985); ANNOT., *Admissibility, in Criminal Cases, of Evidence of Electrophoresis of Dried Evidentiary Bloodstains,* 66 ALR4th 588 (1988); Imwinkelried, *The "Bases" of Expert Testimony: The Syllogistic Structure of Scientific Testimony,* 67 N C L Rev 1 (1988).

RULE 703. ORS 40.415. BASES OF OPINION TESTIMONY BY EXPERTS

The facts or data in the particular case upon which an expert bases an opinion or inference may be those perceived by or made known to the expert at or before the hearing. If of a type reasonably relied upon by experts in the particular field in forming opinions or inferences upon the subject, the facts or data need not be admissible in evidence.

LEGISLATIVE COMMENTARY

Oregon Rule of Evidence 703 indicates what information expert witnesses may rely on for their opinion testimony. The language of the rule is identical to Rule 703 of the Federal Rules of Evidence. The Legislative Assembly adopted the rule in preference to the slowly emerging case law on this subject.

The rule indicates that an expert may base an opinion on data from three sources.

The first source is the expert's personal observation. The most common examples of this are the observations of treating physicians. Expert opinion based upon personal observation has been allowed traditionally in every jurisdiction. Even without Rule 703, it would be admissible under Rule 701.

The second source is the testimony of other witnesses at trial. This basis is recognized in Oregon. The expert learns what the other witnesses say in one of two ways. Counsel may pose a hypothetical question which contains the essential facts drawn from other testimony. Alternatively, the expert may attend and listen to the other witnesses. In the latter case, it is evident that the direct examination of the expert may not alert the trier of fact to potential weaknesses in the expert's testimony, e.g., that the basis has not been established, or that the basis which has been established is not credible. Opposing counsel should use Rule 705 to draw out such information.

The third source consists of data that have been made known to the expert outside of court and other than by the expert's own perception. Many jurisdictions, including Oregon, have not allowed this as basis for expert testimony. The change, however, will bring judicial practice into line with the practice of experts themselves when not in court. A physician bases a diagnosis on information gathered from a number of sources including statements by patients and relatives, opinions from nurses, technicians and other doctors, reports, hospital records and X-rays. Most of these are admissible into evidence, but only by the expenditure of substantial time in producing and examining authenticating witnesses. The physician makes life and death decisions in reliance upon these sources. That validation, expertly performed and subject to cross-examination, ought to suffice for judicial purposes. As McCormick notes, "If the statements are attested by the expert as the basis for a judgment upon which [the physician] would act in the practice of [the] profession, it seems that they should ordinarily be a sufficient basis even standing alone for [the physician's] direct expression of professional opinion on the stand.... McCormick, *Evidence* § 15 at 36 (2d ed 1972). A similar provision is incorporated in California Evidence Code § 801(b). In effect, it represents another exception to the hearsay rule. See Blakey, "An Introduction to the Oklahoma Evidence Code: The 34th Hearsay Exception," in 16 Tulsa L Rev 1 (1980).

Rule 703 anticipates the result of a trend in case law. Although Oregon courts declared that the facts relied upon by a witness in the formation of the witness' opinion must be facts in evidence, recent cases made inroads into this exception. In condemnation cases, for example, an expert may base an opinion in part upon hearsay evidence as to the "going" price in the community for comparable land. *State Highway Commission v. Oswalt,* 1 Or App 449, 463 P2d 602 (1970). Likewise, expert medical witnesses may base their opinions at trial upon medical charts and records to the same extent they would rely upon such documents in treating their patients. *Lewis v. Baker, Richardson-Merrill, Inc.,* 243 Or 317, 326, 413 P2d 400 (1966); *State v. Norton,* 7 Or App 233, 490 P2d 194 (1971).

The fear is expressed that an enlargement of the permissible data basis for expert opinion may erode the rules of exclusion. It should be pointed out that Rule 703 requires that the facts or data in question be of "a type reasonably relied upon by experts in the particular field." Whether data are of such a quality is a preliminary question to be decided by the court under ORE 104(1).

TEXT

Bases of Expert Opinion

Rule 703 specifies the permissible bases for an expert's opinion. The facts or data upon which the expert may rely are the following: (1) those derived from personal perception before or at the trial; (2) those made known to the expert by means of a hypothetical question; (3) those made known to the expert by the testimony of other witnesses at the trial; and (4) those reasonably relied upon by experts in the particular field in forming opinions on the subject. In addition to these four bases, which are directed towards acquainting the expert with the facts of a particular case, prior education, training, and experience may also be relied upon.

The first three of these bases for an expert's opinion have long been recognized under Oregon law. The fourth has been recognized for medical experts and appraisers. See *Lewis v. Baker,* 243 Or 317, 326, 413 P2d 400 (1966) (medical expert may rely on hospital charts and records); *State v. Notion,* 7 Or App 122, 128, 490 P2d 194 (1971) (psychiatrist may rely on test reports of psychologist that are not in evidence); *State Highway Comm'n v. Arnold,* 218 Or 43, 68–9, 341 P2d 1089, modified on other grounds 343 P2d 1113 (1959) (appraiser's opinion of value may be based in part on hearsay). See generally ANNOT., *Admissibility on Issue of Sanity of Expert Opinion Based Partly on Medical, Psychological, or Hospital Reports,* 55 ALR3d 551 (1974); ANNOT., *Admissibility of Hearsay Evidence as to Comparable Sales of Other Land as Basis for Expert's Opinion as to Land Value,* 12 ALR3d 1064 (1967). Rule 703 changes prior law by allowing any expert to rely on facts of a type reasonably relied upon by experts in that particular field in forming opinions upon the subject.

Rule 703 provides with regard to this last category that the facts or data upon which the expert relies need not have been admitted or even be admissible into evidence. Thus, it clearly rejects the "facts in evidence" requirement for expert opinion, which was stated in some earlier Oregon cases. See, e.g., *McEwen v. Ortho Pharmaceutical Corporation,* 270 Or 375, 528 P2d 522 (1974); *Harpole v. Paeschke Farms, Inc.,* 267 Or 592, 595, 518 P2d 1023 (1974).

However, Rule 703 does not change the traditional rule that if an expert is asked a hypothetical question, the elements of the hypothetical question must be consistent with the actual evidence in the case. In *State v. Ollila,* 82 Or App 491, 728 P2d 900 (1986), the court held that it was error to allow the prosecutor to pose the following hypothetical question to the state's expert on the Intoxilyzer test: "Assuming someone weighs 165 pounds ... and he's 5'9", how many beers would he have to drink [in a 2-3 hour period] ... to reach say, a .10?" Such a question was found to be error because there was no evidence in the record indicating defendant's height and weight and the evidence indicated defendant's blood alcohol content at the time of his arrest was .08% rather than .10%. The court held that Rule 703 "does not authorize the introduction of an expert opinion which is based on facts that may or may not be perceived by the jury or the expert."

"Reasonable" Reliance by Expert

When an expert opinion is based on facts not admitted in evidence, it may be necessary to present testimony from other experts in the particular field on whether it is "reasonable" to rely on such facts or data in forming opinions on the subject. The ultimate determination of whether the reliance is reasonable is for the court under Rule 104(1). See *United States v. Sims,* 514 F2d 147 (9th Cir), cert denied 423 US 845 (1975) (psychiatrist rendering opinion on defendant's sanity may reasonably rely upon interviews with government agents); *Higgins v. Kinnebrew Motors, Inc.,* 547 F2d 1223 (5th Cir 1977) (economist may rely on figures from the Bureau of Labor Statistics to determine future damages for loss of spouse); *Bauman v. Centex Corp.,* 611 F2d 1115 (5th Cir 1980) (accountant may reasonably rely upon financial records of corporation not admitted into evidence); *American Universal Ins. Co. v. Falzone,* 644 F2d 65 (1st Cir 1981) (state fire marshal testifying regarding cause of fire may reasonably rely on reports of co-investigators).

The Advisory Committee's Note to FRE 703, which is identical to Oregon Rule 703, provides that the rule "would not warrant admitting in evidence the opinion of an 'accidentologist' as to the point of impact in an automobile collision based on statements of bystanders. ..." See *Dallas & Mavis Forwarding Co., Inc. v. Stegall,* 659 F2d 721 (6th Cir 1981) (opinion of state highway trooper on exact location of automobile accident was not admissible where trooper's opinion based on no physical evidence and was derived primarily from story of eyewitness). See generally ANNOT., *What Information is of Type "Reasonably Relied Upon by Experts" Within Rule 703, Federal Rules of Evidence, Permitting Expert Opinion Based on Information Not Admissible in Evidence,* 49 ALR Fed 363 (1980); *Zenith Radio Corp. v. Matsushita Elec. Indus. Co.,* 505 F Supp 1313 (ED Pa 1981) (containing guidelines for application of FRE 703).

Opinions Based upon Other Opinions

Although Rule 703 refers only to "facts or data" as a basis for an expert opinion, the Commentary makes clear that an expert opinion may also be based upon the opinions of other experts. See *Myers v. Cessna Aircraft Corp.,* 275 Or 501, 553 P2d 355 (1976) (expert opinion may be based on opinions of other experts admitted into evidence). Under Rule 703, the opinion of the other expert need not have been admitted into evidence or even be admissible if it is of a type reasonably relied upon by experts in that particular field in forming opinions on the subject. The Commentary cites the example of a physician basing expert testimony upon "opinions from nurses, technicians and other doctors."

Disclosure to Jury of Data upon Which Opinion Based

Although Rule 703 now allows experts in some circumstances to rely on facts that have not been admitted in evidence, it does not require that such facts be disclosed to the jury. The rule should not be interpreted as establishing the right to bring inadmissible evidence before the jury whenever such evidence qualifies as the basis for expert opinion under Rule 703. 3 D. Louisell & C. Mueller, FEDERAL EVIDENCE (1979) § 389 at 663 states:

> While Rule 703 permits an expert witness to take into account matters which are unadmitted and inadmissible, it does not follow that such a witness may simply report such matters to the trier of fact: The Rule was not designed to enable a witness to summarize and reiterate all manner of inadmissible evidence.

See *Bryan v. John Bean Div. of FMC Corp.*, 566 F2d 541 (5th Cir 1978) (reversible error under circumstances of this case for trial court to allow disclosure of inadmissible hearsay underlying opinion of expert witness). Whether disclosure of the underlying facts should be allowed depends on whether the probative value of the facts as an aid to evaluation of the expert's opinion is substantially outweighed by the danger of unfair prejudice, confusion of the issues, or misleading the jury. See Rule 403.

The primary danger from disclosure of inadmissible facts underlying an expert's opinion is that the jury will consider such facts for their truth rather than as a means of evaluating the soundness of the expert's opinion. In cases where the facts are disclosed to the jury, the opponent should be entitled upon request to a limiting instruction under Rule 105.

In *Mission Insurance Company v. Wallace Security Agency, Inc.*, 84 Or App 525, 734 P2d 405 (1987), the appellate court sustained the trial court's refusal to allow expert witnesses who were fire investigators to testify about specific statements made to them by eyewitnesses. The court held that even though Rule 703 allows an expert to base an opinion on inadmissible evidence, it does not authorize the witness to present that inadmissible evidence to the jury.

In *State v. Knepper*, 62 Or App 623, 661 P2d 560 (1983), the trial court allowed a physician to testify to the results of a blood alcohol test that had been excluded as substantive evidence because taken in violation of statute. The trial court admitted the test result under Rule 703, because it formed the basis of the expert's opinion. The appellate court held this to be reversible error, stating:

> OEC 703 does not authorize an expert witness to tell the jury the inadmissible details of the basis of his opinion. The rule merely provides that the expert may give an opinion based on information that, although not admissible, is reliable. ... If OEC 703 were construed to permit an expert both to rely on a blood test subject to exclusion *and* to reveal the results of the test to the jury, then it would indeed be a "drastic" change in the law. That was not within the contemplation of the legislature.

661 P2d at 561–2.

In *Jefferis v. Marzano,* 298 Or 782, 696 P2d 1087 (1985), the court held that the hearsay rule was not violated by allowing the defendant doctor to relate to the jury that numerous other named doctors in the community had procedures similar to his own. Unfortunately, the opinion failed to clearly distinguish between allowing the expert to rely on out-of-court information as a basis for the expert's opinion, which Rule 703 clearly authorizes, and allowing the expert to relate that out-of-court information to the jury on direct examination, which neither Rule 703 nor any other rule authorizes.

See generally Carlson, *Collision Course in Expert Testimony: Limitations on Affirmative Introduction of Underlying Data,* 36 U Fla L Rev 234 (1984); Rice, *Inadmissible Evidence as a Basis for Expert Opinion Testimony: A Response to Professor Carlson,* 40 Vand L Rev 583 (1987); ANNOT., *Admissibility of Testimony of Expert, as to Basis of His Opinion, to Matters Otherwise Exludible as Hearsay— State Cases,* 89 ALR4th 456 (1991).

Rule 703 Not Exception to Hearsay Rule

The statement in the Commentary that Rule 703 "in effect ... represents another exception to the hearsay rule" is unsound. When an out-of-court statement relied on by an expert is admitted under Rule 703, it is not technically hearsay because it is not being admitted for the truth of the matter asserted, but only to explain the basis for the expert's opinion. See Rule 801(3) (definition of "hearsay"). Although this issue has caused confusion, the clear prevailing view in federal courts and jurisdictions with rules identical to OEC 703 is that it does **not** create a hearsay exception. See M. Graham, HANDBOOK OF FEDERAL EVIDENCE (4th ed 1996) § 703.1 at 109–13 (citation omitted):

> While for most practical purposes admissibility to form the bases of an expert's opinion is equivalent to having the evidence admitted for its truth under a hearsay exception, differences remain. For one, what is proper argument to the trier of fact as to the existence of the fact reasonably relied will differ. More importantly, evidence admitted solely under Rule 703 will *not* support a *prima facie* case.... The simplest way to recognize that evidence reasonably relied upon under Rule 703 is admitted solely as forming the bases of the expert's opinion and not as substantive evidence in the case is to realize that Rule 703 bears a 700 number and not an 803 or 804 number which accompanies hearsay exceptions recognized by the Federal Rules of Evidence.

In *Rose Hall Ltd v. Chase Manhattan Overseas Banking Corp.,* 576 F Supp 107, 158 n70 (D Del 1983), aff'd 740 F2d 958 (3rd Cir 1984), the court held that an expert may given his opinion on the value of land based upon a surveyor's report, but noted: "While an expert witness may base his opinion on such evidence, this does not magically render the hearsay evidence admissible." See also *Department of Corrections v. Williams,* 549 So 2d 1071 (Fla App 1989) ("We reject the notion that the expert may be used as a conduit for the admission of otherwise inadmissible evidence... . [W]hile it was perfectly proper for the expert to consider the affidavit in formulating his opinion, the affidavit itself was hearsay and inadmissible.").

See generally 2 S. Saltzburg, M. Martin, and D. Capra, FEDERAL RULES OF EVIDENCE MANUAL (6th ed 1994) 1138 ("Evidence … is not admitted under this Rule for its truth."); McElhaney, *Expert Witnesses and the Federal Rules of Evidence,* 28 Mercer L Rev 463 (1977).

Evidence should not be admitted for its truth merely because it was reasonably relied upon as a basis for an expert's opinion under Rule 703 when it does not otherwise satisfy evidentiary requirements. To view Rule 703 as creating a hearsay exception might encourage courts to allow disclosure to the jury of inadmissible evidence, even though neither Rule 703 nor Rule 705 requires such disclosure. Moreover, admission of statements relied upon by an expert for the truth of the matter asserted might violate the right of confrontation in criminal cases. See 3 C. Mueller & L. Kirkpatrick, FEDERAL EVIDENCE (2d ed 1994) § 359 at 698; *United States v. Lawson,* 653 F2d 299 (7th Cir 1981), cert denied 454 US 1150 (1982) (admission of expert testimony based entirely on hearsay evidence, while it might satisfy FRE 703, would violate the right of confrontation). See also Carlson, *Experts as Hearsay Conduits: Confrontation Abuses in Opinion Testimony,* 76 Minn L Rev 859 (1992).

Public Opinion or Survey Evidence

Expert testimony based on public opinion polls or surveys is admissible under Rules 702 and 703, when the poll or survey is shown to be conducted in such manner as to be "reasonably relied upon by experts in the particular field in forming opinions or inferences on the subject." See *In Re Sugar Indus. Antitrust Litig.,* 73 FRD 322, 352–3 (ED Pa 1976); *Pittsburgh Press Club v. United States,* 579 F2d 751 (3rd Cir 1978) (survey rejected; inadequate foundation).

Evidence from public opinion polls and surveys has been admitted under prior Oregon law when the survey was shown to be properly conducted and reliable. See *Lift Truck Parts & Service, Inc. v. Bourne,* 235 Or 446, 385 P2d 735 (1963); *W. Bank & W. Bancorp,* 47 Or App 191, 617 P2d 258 (1980); *Baldasarre v. W. Oregon Lumber Co.,* 193 Or 556, 239 P2d 839 (1952) (error to admit unreliable survey of workers regarding safety issue).

Whether a public opinion poll constitutes hearsay depends on the precise response to the question posed and what the survey is being offered to prove. If a person polled when shown product A says "That is product B," the response is arguably not hearsay, because it is not being offered to prove that the product shown was product B but rather that the respondent confused product A with product B. However, if the response is "I think it is product B," the hearsay issue becomes more difficult, because the statement is being offered to prove the truth of the assertion "*I think* it is product B." However, even if the response to a public opinion poll is viewed as hearsay, it is often admissible under Rule 803(3) or 803(26).

Rule 703 provides a way to avoid the problem of whether or not a public opinion poll or survey evidence constitutes hearsay and whether it satisfies an exception to the hearsay rule. See *Zippo Mfg. Co. v. Rogers Imports, Inc.,* 216 F Supp 670 (SDNY 1963). If the survey or poll evidence is being used only as a basis for an expert's opinion under Rule 703, it makes no difference whether it is hearsay or satisfies a hearsay exception. As the Advisory Committee's Note to FRE 703 states: "The rule also offers a more satisfactory basis for ruling upon the admissibility of public opinion poll evidence. Attention is directed to the validity of the techniques employed rather than to relatively fruitless inquiries whether hearsay is involved." See generally Blum and Kalven, *The Art of Opinion Research: A Lawyer's Appraisal of an Emerging Science,* 24 U Chi L Rev 1 (1956); Bonynge, *Trademark Surveys and Techniques and Their Use in Litigation,* 48 ABA J 329 (1962); Zeisel, *The Uniqueness of Survey Evidence,* 45 Cornell LQ 322 (1960); ANNOT., *Admissibility and Weight of Surveys or Polls of Public or Consumers' Opinion, Recognition, Preference, or the Like,* 76 ALR2d 619 (1961).

On the foundation to authenticate a public opinion poll or survey, see Rule 901(2)(i). See also *Pittsburgh Press Club v. United States,* 579 F2d 751 (3rd Cir 1978).

In *State v. Osborne,* 82 Or App 229, 728 P2d 551 (1986), the court held that a public opinion poll that did not purport to provide a random sampling of the public, in which the questions were not neutrally phrased, and from which no useful responses were elicited, was entitled to no weight in the court's decision regarding a change of venue.

RULE 704.   ORS 40.420. OPINION ON ULTIMATE ISSUE

Testimony in the form of an opinion or inference otherwise admissible is not objectionable because it embraces an ultimate issue to be decided by the trier of fact.

LEGISLATIVE COMMENTARY

Oregon Rule of Evidence 704 provides that opinion evidence is not objectionable merely because it embraces an ultimate issue. The rule is identical to Rule 704 of the Federal Rules of Evidence, and the Legislative Assembly adopts the following federal commentary:

"The basic approach to opinions, lay and expert, in these rules is to admit them when helpful to the trier of fact. In order to render this approach fully effective and to allay any doubt on the subject, the so-called 'ultimate issue' rule is specifically abolished by the instant rule.

"The older cases often contained strictures against allowing witnesses to express opinions upon ultimate issues, as a particular aspect of the rule against opinions. The rule was unduly restrictive, difficult of application, and generally served only to deprive the trier of fact of useful information. 7 Wigmore, *Evidence* §§ 1920,1921 (3d ed 1940); McCormick, *Evidence* § 12 (2d ed 1972). The basis usually assigned for the rule, to prevent the witness from 'usurping the province of the jury,' is aptly characterized as 'empty rhetoric.' 7 Wigmore § 1920 at 17. Efforts to meet the felt needs of particular situations led to odd verbal circumlocutions which were said not to violate the rule. Thus a witness could express [the witness'] estimate of the criminal responsibility of an accused in terms of sanity or insanity, but not in terms of ability to tell right from wrong or other more modern standards. And in cases of medical causation, witnesses were sometimes required to couch their opinions in cautious phrases of 'might' or 'could,' rather than 'did,' though the result was to deprive many opinions of the positiveness to which they were entitled, accompanied by the hazard of a ruling of insufficiency to support a verdict. In other instances the rule was simply disregarded, and, as concessions to need, opinions were allowed upon such matters as intoxication, speed, handwriting, and value, although more precise coincidence with an ultimate issue would scarcely be possible.

"Many modern decisions illustrate the trend to abandon the rule completely. *People v. Wilson*, 25 Cal 2d 341,153 P2d 720 (1944) (whether abortion necessary to save life of patient); *Clifford-Jacobs Forging Co. v. Industrial Comm.*, 19 Ill 2d 235, 166 NW 2d 582 (1960) (medical causation); *Dowling v. L.H. Shattuck, Inc.*, 91 NH 234, 17 A2d 529 (1941) (proper method of shoring ditch); *Schweiger v. Solbeck*, 191 Or 454, 230 P2d 195 (1951) (cause of landslide). In each instance the opinion was allowed.

"The abolition of the ultimate issue rule does not lower the bars so as to admit all opinions. Under Rule 701 and 702, opinions must be helpful to the trier of fact, and [under Rule 403 they must not unfairly prejudice, confuse or delay the proceedings]. These provisions afford ample assurances against the admission of opinions which would merely tell the jury what result to reach, somewhat in the matter of the oath-helpers of an earlier day. They also stand ready to exclude opinions phrased in terms of inadequately explored legal criteria. Thus the question, 'Did T have capacity to make a will?' would be excluded, while the question, 'Did T have sufficient mental capacity to know the nature and extent of his property and the natural objects of his bounty and to formulate a rational scheme of distribution?' would be allowed. McCormick § 12.

"For similar provisions see Uniform Rule 56(4); California Evidence Code § 805; Kansas Code of Civil Procedure § 60-456(d); New Jersey Evidence Rule 56(3)."

Opinion testimony has been admissible in Oregon even though it concerns an ultimate issue to be found by the jury. See, e.g., *Shields v. Campbell*, 277 Or 71, 78–9, 559 P2d 1275 (1977); *Rader v. Gibbons and Reed Company*, 261 Or 354, 365, 494 P2d 412 (1972); *Ritter v. Beals*, 225 Or 504, 524–5, 358 P2d 1080 (1961). Rule 704 thus generally codifies the decisional law of this state.

TEXT

Opinion on Ultimate Issue

Rule 704 eliminates any objection to opinion testimony based upon the allegation that the testimony "embraces an ultimate issue to be decided by the trier of fact." Because a jury is not required to accept the opinion of a witness, the province of the jury is not invaded by the rendering of such opinions. See *State v. Middleton,* 294 Or 427, 435, 657 P2d 1215, 1219 (1983) ("[I]t is impossible to usurp the jury's function. Even if there is uncontradicted expert testimony, the jury is not bound by it, for the jury alone must make the ultimate decision.").

Wigmore described the common-law rule excluding opinions on the ultimate issue as "a mere bit of empty rhetoric." 7 Wigmore, *Evidence* (Chadbourn rev 1978) § 1920 at 18. As the Commentary notes, such an objection was generally not recognized under prior Oregon law. Nonetheless, the adoption of Rule 704 may tend to liberalize the types of opinions received under Oregon law. For example, in *Becker v. Port Dock Four, Inc.,* 90 Or App 384, 752 P2d 1235 (1988), the court held that an expert may now testify directly regarding diminution in property value resulting from defendant's tortious conduct rather than being limited to testimony regarding the fair market value before and after the loss and having the jury determine the difference.

Lay opinions can still be excluded under Rule 701 if the opinion is not "(1) Rationally based on the perception of the witness, and (2) Helpful to a clear understanding of testimony of the witness or the determination of a fact in issue." Expert opinions can still be excluded if (1) the witness is not sufficiently qualified as an expert on the subject in question; (2) there is shown to be an inadequate factual basis for the opinion; or (3) the opinion will not "assist the trier of fact to understand the evidence or to determine a fact in issue. ..." See Rules 702 and 703. Opinions can also be excluded under Rule 403 if their probative value is substantially outweighed by the danger of unfair prejudice, confusion of the issues, or misleading the jury.

The adoption of Rule 704 does not make admissible all opinions of a highly generalized nature that do little more than indicate which party to litigation should prevail. In *DeRosa v. Kolb,* 90 Or App 548, 752 P2d 1282, rev denied 306 Or 101, 757 P2d 1362 (1988), the court found error in testimony by the plaintiff's expert that: "The sign creates a substantial visibility obstruction that was a substantial factor in causing the accident." The court found that this testimony did little more than tell the jury what result to reach on the contested causation question. See also *French v. Barrett,* 84 Or App 52, 733 P2d 89 (1987) (error to allow investigating police officer, who did not witness accident, to give his opinion as to cause of accident); *Phomvongsa v. Phounsaveth,* 72 Or App 518, 696 P2d 567, rev denied 299 Or 203, 700 P2d 251 (1985) (error to allow testimony by police officer, who did not witness accident, that the accident was "unavoidable" and that defendant did not cause accident); *State v. Parks,* 71 Or App 630, 693 P2d 657 (1985) (no error to strike testimony of defendant's wife, a witness to the shooting, that it was an "accident"); *Tiedemann v. Radiation Ther-*

apy Consultants, 299 Or 238, 243, 701 P2d 440 (1985) (statement in summary judgment affidavit that "the treatment of [plaintiff] was not negligent" was improper and was "pure opinion which merely tells the jury what result to reach;" "such testimony is directly condemned by the commentary to OEC 704."). See NOTE, *The Admissibility of Ultimate Issue Expert Testimony by Law Enforcement Officers in Criminal Trials,* 93 Colum L Rev 231 (1993).

Opinions Regarding Matters of Legal Interpretation

Generally, a witness should not be allowed to interpret statutory language. The case of *United States v. McCauley,* 601 F2d 336, 339 (8th Cir 1979), which allowed a government expert to testify that the defendant's weapon was "a machine gun required to be registered under the Act," would seem a questionable ruling. While an opinion on whether a weapon is a machine gun is proper, a witness should not be allowed to define statutory language for the jury.

The federal courts are divided regarding the extent to which expert opinion testimony may be allowed in determining whether a legal obligation or contractual agreement was violated. Compare *Bowen v. United States Postal Service,* 642 F2d 79 (4th Cir 1981), reversed on other grounds 459 US 212 (1983) (allowing expert testimony as to whether union breached duty of fair representation) with *Marx & Co., Inc. v. Diner's Club, Inc.,* 550 F2d 505 (2nd Cir), cert denied 434 US 861 (1977) (error to allow expert to give opinion as to legal obligations of parties under a contract). See also *Energy Oils Inc. v. Montana Power Co.,* 626 F2d 731 (9th Cir 1980) (expert opinion regarding custom and usage admissible, but opinion regarding legal effect of agreement is not).

Appropriate Legal Criteria

Even though Rule 704 allows a witness to be questioned regarding opinions on an ultimate issue in the case, the question must be correctly phrased so that it uses the appropriate legal criteria. In a criminal case where the defendant asserts an insanity defense, it would not be proper even under Rule 704 to ask a psychiatrist's opinion of whether the defendant was "legally insane" at the time of the crime. The question would have to be phrased in terms of the definition of legal insanity under Oregon law. See ORS 161.295.

In *State v. Wille,* 317 Or 487, 500, 858 P2d 128, 136 (1993), the court held that a defense expert's conclusions as to whether defendant killed his wife "intentionally" and whether he acted under the influence of "extreme emotional disturbance" were properly excluded. Such testimony went to issues of law rather than fact and were phrased "in terms of inadequately explored legal criteria," thereby justifying exclusion under OEC 704.

In *Angus v. Joseph,* 60 Or App 546, 655 P2d 208, 212 n11 (1982), rev denied 294 Or 569, 660 P2d 683, cert denied 464 US 830 (1983), defendants objected to testimony by a witness that "she was familiar with the enrollment requirements of the tribe, that the natural father is a member of the tribe and that a child of the father would be eligible for membership," on the ground that it was "phrased in terms of inadequately explored legal criteria" under Rule 704. The court held: "We find no basis on which to reverse the trial court's determination that the witness's opinions were 'helpful to a ... determination of a fact in issue.'"

Recent Cases

In *Mark v. Hutchinson*, 132 Or App 613, 617, 889 P2d 361, 364, rev denied 321 Or 94, 893 P2d 540 (1995), the trial judge refused to allow the plaintiff's expert to testify that the walkway where the injury occurred was in an "unreasonably dangerous condition." The court refused to consider whether the ruling was correct under OEC 704, finding that any error was harmless.

In *Zacher v. Petty*, 103 Or App 8, 22, 797 P2d 1042 (1990), rev'd on other grounds 312 Or 590, 826 P2d 619 (1992), the court held that testimony by experts regarding why the defendant performed a surgery did not violate Rule 704. The court found that "the testimony did not tell the jury that defendant was lying or that plaintiff should prevail on the negligence issue."

Federal Decisions

Examples of opinions held to be proper under FRE 704 include the following: *United States v. Hearst*, 563 F2d 1331 (9th Cir 1977), cert denied 435 US 1000 (1978) (defendant committed bank robbery "voluntarily"); *United States v. Miller*, 600 F2d 498 (5th Cir), cert denied 444 US 955 (1979) (securities were obtained by fraud); *United States v. Logan*, 641 F2d 860 (10th Cir 1981) (funds were improperly taken); *United States v. Kelley*, 615 F2d 378 (5th Cir 1980) (allegedly fraudulent loan application had "capacity to influence" lending decision of bank). Courts interpreting FRE 704 have found some opinions to cross the line of permissibility. See, e.g., *United States v. Baskes*, 7 Fed Evid Rep 975, 631 F2d 733 (7th Cir 1980) (improper to cross-examine coconspirator of defendant as to whether witness and defendant did "unlawfully, knowingly, and willfully conspire to defraud the United States."); *United States v. Pino*, 606 F2d 908, 918 n11 (10th Cir 1979) (opinion not allowed that reckless driving inconsistent with defendant's personality); *United States v. Ness*, 665 F2d 248, 250 (8th Cir 1981) (no error in refusing to allow defendant bank employee to call four coworkers who would testify that the defendant did not intend to defraud the bank.)

Effective October 12, 1984, Congress amended FRE 704 to add the italicized new language:

Rule 704

(a) *Except as provided in subdivision (b)*, testimony in the form of an opinion or inference otherwise admissible is not objectionable because it embraces an ultimate issue to be decided by the trier of fact.

(b) *No expert witness testifying with respect to the mental state or condition of a defendant in a criminal case may state an opinion or inference as to whether the defendant did or did not have the mental state or condition consti-*

tuting an element of the crime charged or of a defense thereto. Such ultimate issues are matters for the trier of fact alone.

RULE 705.   ORS 40.425. DISCLOSURE OF FACT OR DATA UNDERLYING EXPERT OPINION

An expert may testify in terms of opinion or inference and give reasons therefor without prior disclosure of the underlying facts or data, unless the court requires otherwise. The expert may in any event be required to disclose the underlying facts or data on cross-examination.

LEGISLATIVE COMMENTARY

Oregon Rule of Evidence 705 relieves the proponent of an expert witness of the general requirement that the facts or data underlying the expert's opinion be disclosed prior to the expert's opinion testimony. The text of the rule is identical to Rule 705 of the Federal Rules of Evidence. Its adoption, and the rejection of Rule 705 as proposed by the Advisory Committee (requiring prior disclosure), leaves present Oregon law intact.

In *Wulff v. Sprouse-Reitz,* 262 Or 293, 498 P2d 766 (1972), the Oregon Supreme Court adopted Uniform Rule 58, a rule similar to Federal Rule 705. The court held that "questions calling for the opinion of an expert witness need not be hypothetical in form unless the judge in [the judge's] discretion so requires, but the witness may state [an] opinion and reasons therefor without first specifying data on which it is based as a hypothesis or otherwise; but upon cross-examination [the witness] may be required to specify such data." 262 Or at 307–308. The opinion marked the end to any rigid insistence on the use of hypothetical questions, a practice in effect at least since *Lehmen v. Knott,* 100 Or 59, 70, 196 P 476 (1921).

Requiring the underlying facts to be disclosed every time an expert offers opinion raises a number of problems. It invites disputes over whether all the facts have been disclosed. In certain cases it requires the expert to divulge facts relied upon that are not themselves admissible evidence. See commentary to ORE 703. Finally, it mandates the use of hypothetical questions, a procedure that consumes time, encourages partisan bias, and affords an opportunity for summation in the middle of a case. The hypothetical question has been abused by counsel on numerous occasions.

The rule adopted is not without its own problems. The Legislative Assembly recognizes that Federal Rule 705 was promulgated against the backdrop of broader pretrial discovery rules than exist in state practice. Rule 26(b)(4) of the Federal Rules of Civil Procedure, as a matter of course, permits pre-trial inquiry into the identity of experts and the data underlying their findings. Without such discovery opposing counsel may not know when the proponent of an expert witness has failed to establish the basis for testimony, or when the testimony rests on an impermissible basis. Despite these dangers, the Legislative Assembly believes that the current law is working well and has not increased the number of mistrials.

The rule indicates that in appropriate situations the trial court can require advance disclosure of the underlying facts—by hypothetical question or otherwise, as the court directs. Thus, the court may permit an adverse party to determine by voir dire whether the requirements of Rule 703 are satisfied before an expert offers an opinion. If the party establishes that they are not, then the opinions and inferences of the expert will be inadmissible until the proponent of the testimony establishes the underlying facts.

In short, prior disclosure should not be mandatory in all cases, nor should it be eliminated. The rule allows counsel to disclose the underlying facts or data as a preliminary to the giving of an expert opinion, if counsel chooses, but it reduces the instances in which counsel is required to do so. This is true whether the expert opinion is based on data furnished to the expert secondhand or observed by the expert firsthand.

In any event, an adverse party may require an expert to state the facts supporting the expert's opinion on cross-examination.

TEXT

Disclosure of Data Underlying Expert Opinion

Rule 705 retains and codifies the holding of *Wulff v. Sprouse-Reitz Co. Inc.,* 262 Or 293, 498 P2d 766 (1972) that an expert may give an opinion without disclosing in advance the facts or data underlying the opinion, unless the court requires otherwise. Disclosure of the underlying facts or data can be required, however, on cross-examination. See generally COMMENT, *Opinion Testimony of Expert Witnesses: Oregon's New Rule,* 52 Or L Rev 443 (1973).

Under Rule 705, the opinion of an expert may be presented in the following ways: (1) underlying facts and data included within a hypothetical question followed by the response of the expert in the form of an opinion; (2) underlying facts and data stated by the expert followed by an opinion; (3) statement of the opinion followed by presentation of the underlying facts and data; (4) statement of opinion alone.

The effect of Rule 705 is to make hypothetical questions generally unnecessary, but permissible. In cases where the expert has no independent knowledge of the facts about which the opinion is requested, hypothetical questions may still be needed.

If a hypothetical question is used, it must be based on facts within the personal knowledge of the expert, facts in evidence, or facts reasonably relied upon by experts in the particular field in forming opinions on the matter. See Rule 703. See also *Peterson v. Schlottman,* 237 Or 484, 392 P2d 262 (1964) (error to allow hypothetical question regarding whether doctor's opinion concerning plaintiff's injuries in automobile accident would be different if evidence showed that plaintiff had attempted to push the car after the collision, when there was no evidence in the record to support this assumption).

The hypothetical question need not include all the facts in evidence but may be based on any fair combination of facts supported by the evidence. *Sam-*

uel v. Vanderheiden, 277 Or 239, 244, 560 P2d 636 (1977). If a hypothetical question is unfair or confusing, objection may be made to it on that ground, and the court may require the question to be reframed. See 1 McCormick, *Evidence* (4th ed 1992) § 14 at 59–60. In order to preserve a challenge to a defective hypothetical question, the objecting party must inform the court of the precise facts misstated or unfairly omitted. *Cobb v. Spokane, Portland & Seattle Ry.,* 150 Or 226, 44 P2d 731 (1935). Hypothetical questions can be used on cross-examination as well as direct examination. *Samuel v. Vanderheiden,* 277 Or 239, 560 P2d 636 (1977).

One danger of the procedure allowed by Rule 705 is that an opinion may be expressed for which there is no adequate foundation under Rule 703. If on cross-examination it appears that the opinion lacks a sufficient basis (for example, it rests on facts not in evidence that are not reasonably relied upon by experts in the particular field), the opinion may be stricken, or, in extreme cases, a mistrial declared. See *Fletcher v. State Department of Roads,* 216 Neb 342, 344 NW2d 899 (1984) (judgment for plaintiff reversed because cross-examination of plaintiff's expert showed an insufficient basis for his opinion that guardrail would have prevented accident.) To avoid such a result, the Commentary indicates that the court may allow the expert to be examined by the opponent prior to expressing the opinion to determine whether the foundation requirements of Rule 703 are satisfied.

If a party calling an expert witness exercises the option generally available under Rule 705 not to disclose the facts or data underlying the opinion in advance, this will make cross-examination of the expert considerably more difficult and dangerous. The Oregon Supreme Court has held that great latitude should be given on the cross-examination of an expert witness whose opinion has been elicited without advance disclosure of the facts or data underlying that opinion. *Samuel v. Vanderheiden,* 277 Or 239, 245–7, 560 P2d 636 (1977).

Attorneys cross-examining experts are under a significant disadvantage in Oregon courts as compared to federal courts, because there is no Oregon procedure comparable to Fed R Civ Pro 26, which allows discovery of the facts and opinions to which the expert is expected to testify and a summary of the grounds for each opinion. It is more likely that Oregon trial courts will exercise their discretion under Rule 705 to require advance disclosure of the facts or data underlying an expert's opinion to compensate for this disadvantage.

Limited discovery of expert medical testimony is available in the following situations: (1) where a doctor refuses to provide required reports and a deposition of the doctor can be taken under ORCP 44D(2), (2) where the plaintiff has been examined by defendant's doctor pursuant to ORCP 44B; and (3) where a plaintiff has waived the physician-patient privilege under Rule 511 by taking a discovery deposition of a treating physician. See *State ex rel Grimm v. Ashmanskas,* 298 Or 206, 213, 690 P2d 1063 (1984) (plaintiff deposed defendant doctor in malpractice action, thereby allowing defendant discovery as to all other doctors who treated plaintiff for the same or related conditions).

On cross-examination, counsel should be cautious about inviting disclosure to the jury of underlying facts or data that constitute inadmissible evidence, yet are a proper basis for expert opinion under Rule 703. The probative value of such information to the jury may be substantially outweighed by the danger of unfair prejudice, confusion of the issues, or misleading the jury. See Rule 403. See textual discussion of this issue under Rule 703.

Rule 705 does not give a party a right to cross-examine an expert who does not give testimony against that party. In *State v. McCormack,* 92 Or App 84, 756 P2d 1281 (1988), the court held that defendant had no right under Rule 705 to cross-examine the Intoxilizer operator who administered the test, when the operator did not testify. In this case, another qualified operator who observed the administration of the test provided the foundation for admission of the test results, and that witness was available for cross-examination.

In *State v. Bigej,* 77 Or App 18, 711 P2d 189 (1985), rev denied 302 Or 36, 726 P2d 935 (1986), the court held that the admission of a certificate attesting to the accuracy of an Intoxilizer machine did not violate the right of the defendant to cross-examine expert witnesses under Rule 705. The court held that the certificate did not constitute expert testimony. Moreover, even if it did, the court held that expert opinions are admissible as part of business or official records.

NOTE REGARDING COURT-APPOINTED EXPERTS

LEGISLATIVE COMMENTARY

NOTE: The Legislative Assembly did not adopt Rule 706 of the Federal Rules of Evidence, relating to court appointment of experts, because it believes that the practice should be discouraged. Court-appointed experts are often an unnecessary expense, and their opinion may wrongly carry special weight in the minds of jurors. By not adopting Federal Rule 706 the Legislative Assembly does not intend to limit the inherent power of a trial court to appoint experts. *State v. Beaver Portland Cement Co.,* 169 Or 1, 124 P2d 524 (1942), only to discourage the practice.

ARTICLE VIII

HEARSAY

RULE 801.   ORS 40.450. DEFINITIONS

As used in Rules 801 to 806 (ORS 40.450 to 40.475), unless the context requires otherwise:
(1) [Statement.] A "statement" is:
   (a) An oral or written assertion; or
   (b) Nonverbal conduct of a person, if intended as an assertion.
(2) [Declarant.] A "declarant" is a person who makes a statement.
(3) [Hearsay.] "Hearsay" is a statement, other than one made by the declarant while testifying at the trial or hearing, offered in evidence to prove the truth of the matter asserted.

LEGISLATIVE COMMENTARY

Oregon Rule of Evidence 801 defines the key terms that are used in Article VIII of the Evidence Code, on hearsay. The rule is identical in substance to Rule 801 of the Federal Rules of Evidence with two exceptions: (1) use of prior consistent statements as substantive evidence to rebut the similar use of prior inconsistent statements, and (2) removal of statements of identification from the category of hearsay.

Subsection (1). The definition of "statement" set forth in subsection (1) is important because the term is used in the definition of "hearsay" in subsection (3). The effect of the definition of "statement" is to exclude from the operation of the hearsay rule all evidence of conduct, verbal or nonverbal, not intended as an assertion. The key to the definition is that nothing is an assertion unless intended to be one.

This subsection is similar to Uniform Rule 62(1), California Evidence Code §§ 225 and 1200, Kansas Code of Civil Procedure § 60-459(1) and

New Jersey Evidence Rule 62(1). Oregon courts did not have occasion to define a "statement" for hearsay purposes.

Paragraph (a). It can scarcely be doubted that an assertion made in words is intended by the declarant to be an assertion. Hence verbal assertions fall into the category of "statement."

Paragraph (b). Whether nonverbal conduct should be regarded as a "statement" requires further consideration. Some nonverbal conduct, such as the act of pointing to identify a suspect in a lineup, is clearly the equivalent of a verbal assertion and should be regarded as a statement. Other nonverbal conduct, however, may be offered as evidence merely of a person's belief in the existence of a condition, from which belief the existence of the condition may be inferred. It can be argued that the conduct still asserts the existence of the condition, and is therefore a "statement." See Morgan, *Hearsay Dangers and the Application of the Hearsay Concept,* in 62 Harv L Rev 177, 214, 217 (1948); and Finman, *Implied Assertions as Hearsay: Some Criticisms of the Uniform Rules of Evidence,* in 14 Stan L Rev 682 (1962). The declarant's perception and narration are also untested. Nevertheless, the Legislative Assembly is of the view that the risks that are posed are minimal in the absence of an intent to assert, and do not justify the loss of evidence on hearsay grounds.

The Legislative Assembly specifically rejects the concept of nonassertive conduct as hearsay put forth in the celebrated case of *Wright v. Tatham,* 7 Adolph & E 313, 386, 112 Eng Rep 488 (Exch Ch 1837), and 5CI & F670, 739, 47 Rev Rep 136 (HL 1838). The case excluded, on the issue of mental capacity, evidence of letters written to the testator offered by the proponent of a will. The opinion indicated that it would also exclude, on the issue of seaworthiness, evidence that a deceased captain examined every part of a vessel before embarking with his family. Nowadays it would exclude, on the issue of weather, evidence that pedestrians carried open umbrellas. Such evidence is not hearsay under Rule 801. It is admissible, if otherwise relevant, as circumstantial evidence of the fact to be proved. No class of evidence is free of the risk of fabrication, but the risk is considerably more remote with nonverbal conduct than with assertive verbal conduct. In the above situations prompting nonverbal conduct, there is virtually no question of sincerity. Motivation, the nature of the conduct and the presence or absence of reliance will bear heavily upon the weight to be given the evidence. Falknor, *The 'Hear-say' Rule as a 'See-do' Rule: Evidence of Conduct,* in 33 Rocky Mt L Rev 133 (1961). Similar considerations govern nonassertive verbal conduct and verbal conduct which is assertive but offered as the basis for inferring something other than the matter asserted. This kind of verbal conduct is excluded from the definition of hearsay by subsection (3) of this rule.

When a party offers evidence of conduct on the theory that it is not a statement, and hence not hearsay, a preliminary question of intent is raised.

Rule 801 is worded so that the opponent of the evidence has the burden of proving that the conduct was intended as an assertion. If a reasonable juror could find to the contrary, the evidence is admitted. Ambiguous and doubtful cases should be resolved in favor of admissibility. The determination of intent involves no greater difficulty than with many other preliminary questions of fact. Maguire, *The Hearsay System: Around and Through the Thicket,* in 14 Vand L Rev 741, 765–767 (1961).

Subsection (2). This subsection defines "declarant." The term appears in Rules 801, 803, 804 and 806.

Subsection (3). The definition of "hearsay" is in accord with the Oregon approach, which relies on McCormick, EVIDENCE § 246 (2d ed 1972). *Timber Access Industries Co. v. U.S. Plywood-Champion Papers, Inc.,* 263 Or 509, 503 P2d 482 (1972). The definition must be read together with the definition of "statement" in subsection (1).

"Hearsay" includes statements offered to prove the truth of the matter asserted. McCormick § 246; 5 Wigmore, EVIDENCE § 1361 (3d ed 1940); 6 Wigmore § 1766. If the significance of an offered statement lies solely in the fact that it was made, no issue is raised as to the intention of the declarant or the truth of anything asserted, and the statement is not hearsay. See *Sheedy v. Stall,* 255 Or 594, 468 P2d 529 (1970); *State v. Dixon,* 5 Or App 113, 481 P2d 629 (1971). The statement is rather an "operative fact," or "verbal act," or "verbal part of an act." In the formation of a contract, for example, the statement "I accept" is admissible regardless of the truth of the matter asserted. Similar rules apply to words of gift, libel, slander, bribery or extortion.

The definition of "hearsay" excludes testimony given by a witness in the course of the instant proceeding, as such testimony complies with all the ideal conditions for truth-finding.

TEXT

Definitions

Article VIII governs the admissibility of hearsay evidence. *Statement* is defined in Rule 801(1), *declarant* in Rule 801(2) and *hearsay* in Rule 801(3). A number of statements that might otherwise fit within the definition of hearsay under Rule 801(3) are defined as not hearsay by Rule 801(4). Rule 802 states the basic rule against hearsay evidence. Rule 803 sets forth the exceptions to the hearsay rule that apply regardless of whether the declarant is unavailable. Rule 804 sets forth the exceptions that apply only when the declarant is unavailable. Rule 805 addresses the admissibility of hearsay within hearsay. Rule 806 provides for impeachment of hearsay declarants.

In criminal cases, hearsay issues must be considered in conjunction with a defendant's constitutional right of confrontation. The right of confrontation is discussed under Rule 802.

RULE 801(1)
"Statement"

Rule 801(1) defines a *statement* for the purpose of the rules governing hearsay as "(a) an oral or written assertion; or (b) nonverbal conduct of a person, if intended as an assertion." Many oral or written communications are therefore not hearsay statements because they are not assertions. A communication may be found to be an assertion, however, even though phrased as a question, request, command, or warning if it contains—expressly or impliedly—an assertion.

Tags, Markers

Tags, labels, inscriptions, and written markings of identification are often found not to be hearsay. See *United States v. Vinson,* 606 F2d 149 (6th Cir 1979), cert denied 444 US 1074 (1980) (envelope with defendant's name on it not hearsay; words on envelope not offered as an assertion, only as circumstantial evidence of identity); *United States v. Snow,* 517 F2d 441 (9th Cir 1975) (tag on briefcase containing firearm bearing the name of defendant is not a hearsay assertion; admissible as circumstantial evidence of ownership). For an argument that such markings are hearsay assertions, see 2 M. Graham, HANDBOOK OF FEDERAL EVIDENCE (4th ed 1996) § 801.6 at 227–9. See generally C. Mueller & L. Kirkpatrick, MODERN EVIDENCE (1995) § 8.19.

In *United States v. Hensel,* 699 F2d 18 (1st Cir), cert denied 461 US 958, 103 SCt 2431, 77 LEd2d 1317 (1983), the court rejected the argument that the following evidence against the defendant constituted hearsay: A glass with defendant's nickname on it found at the alleged location of smuggling and a payroll list of duties, both of which included defendant's name. The court found that these items of evidence were not intended to be assertions, but were merely circumstantial evidence of defendant's involvement.

In *United States v. Singer,* 687 F2d 1135 (8th Cir 1982), modified 710 F2d 431 (8th Cir 1983), the court held that the following evidence was not hearsay: An envelope addressed and mailed to defendant and C, containing a notice from their landlord to terminate their tenancy, offered to prove that defendant was living with C at the address shown. The court found that the envelope did not constitute a hearsay assertion.

Assertive Conduct

Nonverbal conduct intended as an assertion, such as pointing, nodding of the head, or use of sign language, is clearly a statement for purposes of the hearsay rule. See *United States v. Caro,* 569 F2d 411 (5th Cir 1978) (pointing is assertive conduct). In *State v. Mayfield,* 302 Or 631, 733 P2d 438 (1987), the court held that the manipulation of an anatomical doll by a child sex abuse victim was equivalent to a verbal assertion of how she had been abused and constituted a hearsay statement.

A staged demonstration of plaintiff's disability recorded on videotape has also been held to be a hearsay statement. See *Grimes v. Employers Mut. Liab. Ins. Co.,* 73 FRD 607, 611 (D Alaska 1977). However, in *Arnold v. Burlington Northern Railroad,* 89 Or App 245, 748 P2d 174, rev denied 305 Or 576, 753 P2d 1382 (1988), the court held that a videotape without a soundtrack of plaintiff performing activities was not hearsay, where plaintiff testified and explained the videotape, attested to its accuracy and was subject to cross-examination. The court arguably gave insufficient attention to the argument that demonstrative conduct can constitute an out-of-court assertion and that prior assertions even by a testifying witness can be hearsay.

Nonassertive Conduct

Nonverbal conduct not intended as an assertion is not hearsay. Rule 801(1) clearly rejects the view of some older common law cases holding that evidence of a person's nonverbal conduct indicating a belief of that person was hearsay when offered to prove the truth of that belief. See 2 McCormick, EVIDENCE (4th ed 1992) § 250. Under this view, evidence that a driver had started up at an intersection, offered to prove that the traffic light had at that time turned green, would arguably be hearsay because it would reflect a belief or implied assertion on the part of the driver regarding the color of the light. The concern of the common law cases was that this implied assertion should be subject to cross-examination. Under Rule 801(1)(b), this evidence would not constitute hearsay because the nonverbal conduct of starting the car at the intersection was not intended as an assertion. The evidence would be admissible, despite lack of cross-examination of the driver, as circumstantial evidence of the color of the light. Cross-examination is not deemed necessary under the rule when no assertion is intended. C. Mueller & L. Kirkpatrick, MODERN EVIDENCE (1995) § 8.9.

Under Rule 801(1)(b), no hearsay obstacle exists to the admission of nonverbal conduct indicating consciousness of guilt, such as flight, escape, use of a false name, use of a disguise, or other similar evidence. Whereas at common law such conduct was frequently analyzed as hearsay admissible under the admissions exception to the hearsay rule (see 2 McCormick, EVIDENCE (4th ed 1992) § 263) under Rule 801(1)(b) it would usually not even qualify as a hearsay statement because it was not intended as an assertion. Admissibility would be governed by the relevancy standard of Rule 401. See textual discussion under Rule 401.

Whether silence can be assertive conduct constituting a hearsay statement depends upon the circumstances. If the silence is in response to a statement by another that the person intends to adopt, it will be deemed an adoptive admission and received as not hearsay under Rule 801(4)(b)(B). If the silence was not intended to be an assertion, such as absence of complaints by other passengers or customers, it will not be found to be a hearsay statement. See *DeMarines v. KLM Royal Dutch Airlines,* 580 F2d 1193 (3rd Cir 1978) (plaintiff alleged injury caused by loss of cabin pressure; absence of complaints by other passengers admissible to show no pressure loss).

The determination of whether a person intends nonverbal conduct to be an assertion is made by the court under Rule 104(1). The Commentary to Rule 801 states:

> [T]he opponent of the evidence has the burden of proving that the conduct was intended as an assertion. If a reasonable juror could find to the contrary, the evidence is admitted. Ambiguous and doubtful cases should be resolved in favor of admissibility. The determination of intent involves no greater difficulty than many other preliminary questions of fact.

RULE 801(2)
"Declarant"

Rule 801(2) defines *declarant* as a person who makes a statement. This definition makes clear that "statements" by an animal, such as a bloodhound identifying the scent of a person, or a machine, such as a watch stating time, are not subject to the hearsay rule. There has been occasional uncertainty about this issue. See, e.g., *State v. Harris,* 25 Or App 71, 76, 547 P2d 1394 (1976) (citing but rejecting minority rule that bloodhound tracking evidence is hearsay).

In *State v. McCormack,* 92 Or App 84, 756 P2d 1281, rev denied 306 Or 661, 763 P2d 152 (1988), the court held that it was not hearsay for a qualified Intoxilyzer operator who observed the administration of the test to provide the foundation for admission of the test results. The test results were not hearsay, and the court concluded that the operator was testifying about his own observations, not conveying hearsay statements of the operator who actually administered the test.

RULE 801(3)
"Hearsay"

Rule 801(3) adopts the traditional definition of hearsay. Hearsay is defined as "a statement, other than one made by the declarant while testifying at the trial or hearing, offered in evidence to prove the truth of the matter asserted." This definition incorporates the common law view that out-of-court statements, even by the witness who is now testifying, are hearsay if offered for their truth. Rule 801(3) is qualified by Rule 801(4), which declares that certain prior statements by the witness and the admissions of a party-opponent are not hearsay, even though such statements might otherwise meet the definition of hearsay under Rule 801(3).

Offered for Truth

A statement is hearsay only if offered for its truth. If it is offered for some other purpose, it is not hearsay. However, if it is admitted for a narrower purpose, a limiting instruction should be given confining the jury's consideration to the nonhearsay use. *State v. Taylor,* 137 Or App 286, 290, ___ P2d ___ (1995) (error to admit out-of-court statement on nonhearsay argument where no limiting instruction given).

In *State v. Reece,* 56 Or App 169, 641 P2d 1141 (1982), the court held that statements in a letter sent prior to trial by the defendant to a witness for the prosecution that contained veiled threats regarding consequences if the witness testified were hearsay but properly received as an admission. Arguably the letter would not constitute hearsay at all, because presumably it was not being offered to prove the truth of the threats made, but merely the defendant's consciousness of guilt reflected by the fact that he sent such a letter. See also *State v. Lutz,* 90 Or App 247, 752 P2d 845, modified 306 Or 499, 760 P2d 249 (1988) (no error to receive testimony regarding contents of telephone conversation; offered not for truth but to explain actions of the victim's mother).

In *Ledbetter v. Complete Abrasive Blasting Systems,* 76 Or App 10, 707 P2d 1292 (1985), a products liability case, plaintiff was injured by a fall from the top of a sandblasting machine. Plaintiff's job supervisor testified as a witness for the defendant that the accident was the plaintiff's fault. To impeach this witness, plaintiff sought to offer a statement the supervisor had made to plaintiff's wife that their employer was angry at the supervisor for not having built a platform on the sandblaster. The appellate court held, contrary to the trial court, that the statement was not hearsay, because it was not being offered to prove the truth of the matter asserted. Rather, it was being offered to impeach the supervisor's credibility by showing he was biased against plaintiff's case.

Recent Cases Excluding Hearsay

In *Quinn v. Walters,* 320 Or 233, 240–3, 881 P2d 795, 799–801 (1994), the court held that the affidavit of the Registrar of the Cherokee Nation, offered to prove that the mother was a member of the Cherokee Nation of Oklahoma, was inadmissible hearsay.

In *State v. Taylor,* 133 Or App 503, 510–2, 892 P2d 697, 701–3 (1995), modified 134 Or App 501, 895 P2d 357 (1995), it was held prejudicial error to admit the hearsay statements of a shooting victim that he had only one bullet left and that he was not going to bring his gun into the house. Because such statements were offered to prove the truth of what they asserted, they were hearsay and did not satisfy any exception.

In *State v. Hillier,* 132 Or App 40, 42–3, 887 P2d 845, 846–7 (1994), it was held error for the state to introduce an exhibit containing certified copies of Administrative Rules pertaining to breathalyzers, along with memoranda, letters, and other documents pertaining to such equipment. The appended documentation was ruled to be inadmissible hearsay and also prejudicial and misleading under OEC 403.

Purposes Other than Truth

Many out-of-court statements may be received in evidence because they are not being offered for the truth of the matter asserted. The following are examples of purposes other than truth for which out-of-court statements may be offered:

1. *Impeachment.* Prior inconsistent statements of a witness are admissible for the purpose of impeachment, even when not admissible as substantive evidence. See *State v. Derryberry,* 270 Or 482, 528 P2d 1034 (1974). Under the new code some prior inconsistent statements may be admitted both to impeach the witness and to prove the truth of the matter asserted. See Rules 801(4)(a)(A) and 801(4)(b).

In *State v. Philips*, 314 Or 460, 470, 840 P2d 666 (1992), the defendant sought to impeach an alleged child sex abuse victim by offering evidence of her out-of-court statement saying that "her daddy told her she had to say bad things about [defendant] in court." The court held that because this statement was offered only for impeachment under OEC 609-1, it was not hearsay.

However, out-of-court statements of parties **other than the witness** may be hearsay if offered to impeach the witness. In *State v. Reid*, 107 Or App 352, 811 P2d 1380 (1991), the prosecutor offered the statement of an out-of-court declarant that he had "done business with [defendant] before." The state argued that this statement was not hearsay because it was offered to impeach the defendant's trial testimony that he had never sold drugs. The appellate court correctly held that the statement was being offered for its truth and hence was hearsay, because it would not contradict the defendant's testimony unless the jury believed the out-of-court statement to be true.

2. *To prove an operative fact by use of a statement having independent legal significance apart from its truth.* See, e.g., *NLRB v. H. Koch & Sons*, 578 F2d 1287 (9th Cir 1978) (acceptance of a contract); *Sheedy v. Stall*, 255 Or 594, 468 P2d 529 (1970) (satisfaction of condition precedent of contract); *United States v. Herrera*, 600 F2d 502 (5th Cir 1979) (threats); *United States v. Krohn*, 573 F2d 1382 (10th Cir), cert denied 436 US 949 (1978) (misrepresentations); *Snyder v. Rhoads*, 47 Or App 545, 615 P2d 1058 (1980) (misrepresentations); *United States v. Jackson*, 588 F2d 1046 (5th Cir), cert denied 442 US 941 (1979) (oral statement accompanying delivery of instrument to prove nature of transfer). Additional examples stated in the Commentary are out-of-court statements offered to prove "gift, libel, slander, bribery or extortion."

Although out-of-court statements that are **terms** of a contract are not hearsay, a person's out-of-court statement offered to prove that an oral contract was **made** are hearsay. *Holmes v. Morgan*, 135 Or App 617, 626, 899 P2d 738 (1995) (witness testifying to contract was "neither a party to the agreement nor one who heard the parties make the agreement"; instead she was relying on out-of-court statement of another which is hearsay).

3. *To prove the motive, knowledge, good faith, or other relevant attitude of the declarant.* See, e.g., *State v. Harmon*, 77 Or App 705, 714 P2d 271, rev denied 301 Or 240, 720 P2d 1279, cert denied 479 US 867 (1986) (witness' testimony that victim had discussed a "John Harmon" not hearsay because not being offered for truth but to show victim knew defendant); *Utley v. City of Independence*, 240 Or 384, 402 P2d 91 (1965) (statement of plaintiff's employer admitted to show that arrest of plaintiff was reason for laying off plaintiff; evidence relevant to damages in action for false arrest); *Hryciuk v. Robinson*, 213 Or 542, 326 P2d 424 (1958) (statement of hostility by another toward plaintiff admitted as evidence of damage in malicious prosecution action); *Marr v. Putnam*, 213 Or 17, 321 P2d 1061 (1958) ("Hi, Racketeer" as greeting

to plaintiff after publication of alleged libel not hearsay; relevant to damages); *State v. Kincaide,* 43 Or App 73, 602 P2d 307 (1979) (out-of-court statements by victim of theft and forgery indicating distrust of defendant admitted to prove victim was unlikely to have authorized defendant to handle her money); *State v. Harris,* 126 Or App 516, 521, 869 P2d 868, 871 (1994), modified 127 Or App 613, 872 P2d 445; rev denied 319 Or 281, 879 P2d 1284 (1994) (letters from a third party to defendant were not hearsay when they were offered to prove only the contact and relationship between the two parties and not to prove the truth of the matter asserted in the letters); *State v. Booth,* 124 Or App 282, 291, 862 P2d 518, 523 (1993), cert denied 115 SCt 372 (1994) (in sex abuse prosecution, three-year-old victim told her grandmother and aunt: "Mommie said I can't talk about my daddy"; statement not hearsay, because it was not being offered to prove its truth but merely as circumstantial evidence of the child's state of mind at the competency hearing).

4. *To prove effect of statement on another, to show motive, knowledge, good faith, or other relevant attitude of listener.* See, e.g., *Shipman v. City of Portland,* 8 Or App 420, 494 P2d 896 (1972) (statements by city attorney to police officer admitted to show good faith of officer); *State v. Dixon,* 5 Or App 113, 481 P2d 629 (1971), cert denied 404 US 1024 (1972) (statements of dispatcher to police officer admitted to show reasonableness of officer's conduct in light of that information); *United States v. McLennan,* 563 F2d 943 (9th Cir 1977), cert denied 435 US 969 (1978) (statements of lawyer to defendant that planned conduct was illegal admitted to prove defendant's knowledge of illegality); *United States v. Cline,* 570 F2d 731 (8th Cir 1978) (threats made by victim to defendant admitted to show defendant had motive to kill victim); *Oberg v. Honda Motor Co.,* 316 Or 263, 269, 851 P2d 1084 (1993), rev'd on other grounds 114 SCt 2331 (1994) (documents of the Consumer Products Safety Commission about other accidents admissible to prove defendants had notice of the dangerousness of the all terrain vehicle (ATV) that allegedly caused plaintiff's injury); *Fromdahl v. Fromdahl,* 314 Or 496, 508, 840 P2d 683 (1992) (in a child custody proceeding, what mother heard about husband failing polygraph test and report of CSD worker about husband committing sexual abuse on children admissible to show impact on mother in causing her to take children and flee state); *State v. Coleman,* 130 Or App 656, 666, 883 P2d 266, 272 (1994), rev denied 320 Or 569, 889 P2d 1300 (1995) (police "wanted" bulletin stating that defendant was a pimp was properly admitted to show notice on the part of the owner of the house where the bulletin was found); *State v. Beaty,* 127 Or App 448, 451, 873 P2d 385, 387 (1994), rev denied 319 Or 406, 879 P2d 1285 (1994) (in child sexual abuse prosecution, error to exclude statement alleged victim's mother made to her that it was defendant who abused her, because such evi-

dence was offered to show it caused victim to be biased against defendant).

In *State v. Powell,* 82 Or App 13, 727 P2d 136 (1986), rev denied 302 Or 571, 731 P2d 1046 (1987), an unlawful racketeering prosecution, the evidence of numerous civil complaints and claims against defendant's employer was admitted to show the nature of defendant's business practices. Even though these complaints were out-of-court statements, the court held that they were not hearsay, because they were not offered to prove the truth of the matter asserted, but to prove knowledge and state of mind of the defendant.

In *Garcia v. Motor Vehicles Division,* 77 Or App 172, 711 P2d 219 (1985), the issue on appeal was whether at the time that the officer requested petitioner to take a breath test he had reasonable grounds to believe that petitioner had been driving under the influence of intoxicants. The court found reasonable grounds upon the totality of the circumstances. Therefore, the court did not resolve the hearsay issue presented by the case, which was whether a bicyclist's statement that the defendant was driving was inadmissible hearsay. The bicyclist made the statement to a deputy sheriff, who in turn related it to the officer who requested the breath test. It would appear that the statement was not hearsay, because it was not being offered to prove the truth of the matter asserted, but only to show its effect upon the officer in forming probable cause.

Exclusion Under Rule 403

Even if out-of-court statements are not being offered for truth and are not excluded as hearsay, they still may be excluded under Rule 403 or another rule of evidence. In *State v. Mayfield,* 302 Or 631, 733 P2d 438 (1987), the court considered a statement in a treatise that if out-of-court statements are offered for a nonhearsay purpose, e.g., to prove knowledge, and those statements report "complaints of a particular crime by the accused, this is so likely to be misused by the jury as evidence of the fact asserted that it should be excluded as hearsay." McCormick, EVIDENCE (2d ed 1972) § 248 at 587. The court took issue with this view, stating: "That may be one approach, but we believe that when the nonhearsay statements reach this level they should not be converted from nonhearsay to hearsay, but should be excluded under the relevancy balancing test set forth in OEC 403."

Multiple Hearsay

Sometimes testimony will be offered in which the witness quotes one out-of-court declarant who in turn quotes another out-of-court declarant. There can be an entire chain of out-of-court statements. In order for such multilevel statements to be admissible, each level must satisfy a hearsay exception or be categorized as "not hearsay" by Rule 801(4). See Rule 805.

In *State v. Lyon,* 83 Or App 592, 733 P2d 41, aff'd 304 Or 221, 744 P2d 231 (1987), a murder prosecution, the state offered evidence of statements made by the defendant to his father, which were in turn related to a detective. Neither the defendant nor the father took the stand, and the statements came in through the testimony of the detective. Even though the defendant's statements would consti- tute an admission, the court held the evidence inadmissible because the father's statements did not fit an exception. The court held that "the value of the evi- dence was dependent on the truth or falsity of the father's out-of-court assertion that defendant had made the statements to him."

In *Hickey v. Settlemier*, 318 Or 196, 204–6, 864 P2d 372, 376–7 (1993), a defamation action, the plaintiff offered a videotape in which the reporter stated: "[Defendant] says there's no doubt in her mind that [plaintiff] is mistreating ani- mals and dealing in stolen pets." Although the alleged statement by the defen- dant would be admissible as a nonhearsay verbal act, the reporter's statement that defendant made such a defamatory comment was inadmissible hearsay.

Other Authorities

See generally Weissenberger, *Unintended Implications of Speech and the Definition of Hearsay*, 65 Temp L Rev 857 (1992); Park, *"I Didn't Tell Them About You": Implied Assertions as Hearsay Under the Federal Rules of Evidence*, 73 Minn L Rev 783 (1990); Wellborn, *The Definition of Hearsay in the Federal Rules of Evidence*, 61 Tex L Rev 49 (1982); Graham, *"Stickperson Hearsay": A Simplified Approach to Understanding the Rule Against Hearsay*, 1982 U M L Rev 887; Friedman, *Route Analysis of Credibility and Hearsay*, 96 Yale L J 667 (1987); Bacigal, *Implied Hearsay: Defusing the Battle Line Between Pragmatism and The- ory*, 11 So M L J 1127 (1987); Bergman, *Ambiguity: The Hidden Hearsay Danger Almost Nobody Talks About*, 75 Ky L J 841 (1987).

RULE 801(4)(a).

(4) **[Statements which are not hearsay.] A statement is not hearsay if:**
    (a) **[Prior statement by witness.] The declarant testifies at the trial or hearing and is subject to cross-examination concerning the statement, and the statement is:**
        (A) **Inconsistent with the testimony of the witness and was given under oath subject to the penalty of perjury at a trial, hearing or other proceeding, or in a deposition;**
        (B) **Consistent with the testimony of the witness and is offered to rebut an inconsistent statement or an express or implied charge against the witness of recent fabrication or improper influence or motive; or**
        (C) **One of identification of a person made after perceiving the person.**

LEGISLATIVE COMMENTARY

Subsection (4). Several types of statements that would otherwise fall within the definition of "hearsay" are expressly excluded from it:

Paragraph (a). Paragraph (a) focuses upon the admissibility of prior statements of a witness. Much controversy has attended the question whether a prior out-of-court statement by an individual should be considered hearsay when the individual is presently available for cross-examination under oath in the presence of the trier of fact. If the witness admits on the stand that the witness made the statement, and that it was true, then the witness adopts the statement and there is no hearsay problem. The hearsay problem arises when the witness denies having made the statement, or admits having made it but denies its truth, or cannot repeat it.

The argument for treating a prior statement as hearsay rests on the fact that the conditions of oath, cross-examination and demeanor observation did not prevail at the time the statement was made, and cannot adequately be supplied by later examination. Each of these grounds is troubling.

The mere presence of an oath has never been regarded as sufficient to remove a statement from the hearsay category, and oaths receive much less credit than cross-examination as a truth-compelling device. While strong expressions are found to the effect that no conviction can be had or important right taken away on the basis of statements not made under fear of prosecution for perjury, *Bridges v. Wixon,* 326 US 135, 65 S Ct 1443, 89 L Ed 2103 (1945), the fact is that of the many common law exceptions to the hearsay rule, only the exception for reported testimony has required the statement to have been made under oath.

It has never been satisfactorily explained why cross-examination cannot be conducted subsequently with success. The decisions that most contend for its inadequacy, in fact, explore the weaknesses and doubts attending the earlier statement quite thoroughly. *State v. Saporen,* 205 Minn 358, 285 HW 898 (1939); *Ruhala v. Rohy,* 379 Mich 102, 150 HW 2d 146 (1967); *People v. Johnson,* 68 Cal 2d 646, 68 Cal Rptr 599, 441 P2d 111 (1968).

With respect to demeanor, as Judge Learned Hand observed in *Di Carlo v. United States,* 6 F2d 364 (2nd Cir 1925), when the jury decides that the truth is not what the witness says now, but what the witness said before, they are still deciding from what they see and hear in court.

Despite the above criticisms, the bulk of the case law has been against the general use of prior statements of witnesses as substantive evidence. Most commentators and the drafter of Uniform Rule 63(1) take the opposite position.

The Legislative Assembly was unwilling to countenance the general use of prior prepared statements as substantive evidence, but it recognized that particular circumstances justify a contrary result. Rule 801 requires in each instance, as a general safeguard, that the declarant testify as a witness. It then enumerates three situations in which the statement is excepted from the category of hearsay. Compare Uniform Rule 63(1), which allows any out-of-court statement of a declarant who is present at the trial and available for cross-examination.

Subparagraph (a)(A). This subparagraph changes Oregon law, which has admitted prior inconsistent statements as impeachment material but not as substantive evidence. *State v. Derryberry,* 270 Or 482, 528 P2d 1034 (1974); *Madron v. Thompson,* 245 Or 513, 419 P2d 611 (1966); *State v. Watchman,* 20 Or App 709, 533 P2d 361 (1975). Provided the general conditions of paragraph (a) are met, under this rule a prior inconsistent statement is admissible as substantive evidence if it was made under oath and subject to the penalty of perjury at a trial, hearing or other proceeding, or in a deposition. The purpose of these further conditions is to remove any dispute that the statement was made and to provide some assurance as to the reliability of the prior statement. Under these criteria, an inconsistent statement before a grand jury is admissible.

The requirement that the prior statement be inconsistent with the testimony given assures a thorough exploration of both versions while the witness is on the stand and bars any general and indiscriminate use of previously prepared statements. The Legislative Assembly intends that "inconsistent" include situations where a witness denies making a prior statement or does not remember the content of the statement. In such a case, evidence of the prior statement is not hearsay and may be admitted as substantive evidence. When the prior inconsistent statement is made by a party litigant, it constitutes an admission under paragraph (a) of subsection (4) of this rule.

Prior inconsistent statements may, of course, be used to impeach the credibility of a witness under Rule 607, provided the foundation requirements of Rule 613 (and Rule 609-1, where applicable) are met.

Subparagraph (a)(B). Prior consistent statements traditionally have been admissible to rebut charges of recent fabrication or improper influence or motive, but not as substantive evidence. *Cook v. Safeway Stores, Inc.,* 266 Or 77, 511 P2d 375 (1973); *Hale v. Smith,* 254 Or 300, 460 P2d 351 (1969); *Maeder Steel Products Co. v. Zanello,* 109 Or 561, 220 P 155 (1923). Prior statements admissible under subparagraph (a)(B), however, are admitted as substantive evidence. The prior statement reinforces the testimony given on the stand. If the opposite party wishes to open the door for its admission into evidence by attacking the witness, either through the substantive use of prior inconsistent statements or by impugning the witness' motive, no sound reason is apparent why it should not be received generally.

The Legislative Assembly does not intend, in adopting Rule 801(4)(a)(B), to overrule either *Cook v. Safeway Stores* or *Hale v. Smith,* supra. The Legislative Assembly recognizes that in both of those cases the court may have expressed a willingness to allow prior consistent statements for purposes other than to rebut a charge of recent fabrication or improper influence or motive, e.g., to rebut an imputation of inaccurate memory.

Subparagraph (a)(C). The admission of evidence of identification as nonhearsay finds substantial support, although the evidence is beyond a doubt an out-of-court statement. See California Evidence Code § 1238; New Jersey Evidence Rule 63(1)(c); NY Code of Criminal Procedure § 393-b. The basis for the rule is the generally unsatisfactory and inconclusive nature of courtroom identifications compared with those made at an earlier time under less suggestive conditions.

The United States Supreme Court considered the admissibility of prior identification evidence in *Gilbert v. California*, 388 US 263, 87 S Ct 1951, 18 L Ed 2d 1178 (1967). The Court held that a lineup identification must be excluded if the accused did not have assistance of counsel at that time. Significantly, however, the Court refrained from placing its decision on the ground that testimony as to the making of a prior out-of-court identification violates either the hearsay rule or the right of confrontation because the identification was not made under oath, subject to immediate cross-examination, and in the presence of the trier. The Court merely noted "... a split among the States concerning the admissibility of prior extra-judicial identifications, [and] ... [t]he recent trend to admit the prior identification under the exception that admits as substantive evidence a prior communication by a witness who is available for cross-examination at the trial." 388 US at 272 n 3. See also *United States v. De Sisto*, 329 F2d 929 (2nd Cir 1964) and *People v. Gould*, 54 Cal 2d 621 354 P2d 865 (1960), allowing evidence of extrajudicial identifications to be admitted as independent, substantive evidence of identity.

The subparagraph should not be read literally. It is aimed at situations where the declarant is shown a person or photograph of a person and makes an identification as a result of that showing ('that is the person who did it'). It is not aimed at situations where, after an event, the declarant simply makes a statement which identifies the person involved ('X did it').

Oregon law considered extrajudicial identifications to be hearsay evidence admissible under certain circumstances. This subparagraph reclassifies them as nonhearsay evidence. Oregon law did not clearly indicate what the circumstances of admission were. Compare *State v. Nunes*, 251 Or 49, 444 P2d 542 (1968) (victim may testify at trial that victim had previously identified defendant in lineup or from picture), with *State v. Evans*, 98 Or 214, 192 P 1062 193 P 927 (1920); *State v. Thompson*, 228 Or 496, 364 P2d 783 (1961) (police officer's testimony concerning victim's prior identification inadmissible). According to the most recent decision, *State v. Fennell*, 7 Or App 256, 489 P2d 964 (1971), when witnesses have previously identified the defendant from a picture but cannot identify the person at trial, testimony of police officers concerning the witnesses' previous identification is admissible over hearsay objection. Subparagraph (a)(C) appears to be consistent with Oregon practice after *Fennell*.

The Legislative Assembly deleted language that would have required a prior identification to be corroborated before it was admissible as nonhearsay. The deletion does not necessarily mean that an uncorroborated prior identification is sufficient evidence to sustain a conviction. See *People v. Gould*, supra, cited in *State v. Fennell*, supra, 7 Or App at 260.

TEXT

RULE 801(4)(a)
Prior Statements by Witness

Under the definition of Rule 801(3), any prior out-of-court statement by a witness is hearsay if offered to prove the truth of the matter asserted. Rule

801(4)(a) qualifies Rule 801(3) by defining as not hearsay certain prior statements that would otherwise meet the definition of hearsay, provided the declarant testifies at the trial or hearing and is subject to cross-examination concerning the statement.

This rule represents a significant change from prior law, which did not allow prior statements of a witness other than admissions of a party opponent, or statements satisfying an independent hearsay exception to be received as substantive evidence. Under the new rule, not only admissions but also certain prior inconsistent statements, prior consistent statements, and statements of identification can be received as substantive evidence.

Other prior statements of a witness will, of course, continue to be admissible for impeachment and purposes other than proving the truth of the matter asserted. Prior statements of a witness may also qualify as substantive evidence if they satisfy an exception to the hearsay rule. See Rules 803 and 804.

RULE 801(4)(a)(A)
Prior Inconsistent Statements

Rule 801(4)(a)(A) provides that prior inconsistent statements of a witness are not hearsay if (1) the declarant is subject to cross-examination concerning the statement; and (2) the prior inconsistent statement was given under oath subject to the penalty of perjury at a trial hearing or other proceeding, or in a deposition. This rule is identical to FRE 801(d)(1)(A).

Under former law, prior inconsistent statements of a witness were admissible only for the purpose of impeachment and not for the truth of the matter asserted, unless they were admissions of a party opponent or satisfied some other exception to the hearsay rule. Under the new rule, prior inconsistent statements made by a witness at a grand jury proceeding, preliminary hearing, deposition, prior trial, or any other hearing or proceeding where the witness was under oath subject to the penalties of perjury are now admissible as substantive evidence. See ANNOT., *What is "Other Proceeding" Under Rule 801 (d) (1) (A) of Federal Rules of Evidence, Excepting From Hearsay Rule Prior Inconsistent Statement Given "At a Trial, Hearing, or Other Proceeding,"* 37 ALR Fed 855 (1978).

Rationale

The rationale for allowing prior inconsistent statements to be received as substantive evidence has been described as follows:

Section 1235 [California Evidence Code] admits inconsistent statements of witnesses because the dangers against which the hearsay rule is designed to protect are largely nonexistent. The declarant is in court and may be examined and cross-examined in regard to his statements and their subject matter. In many cases, the inconsistent statement is more likely to be true than the testimony of the witness at the trial because it was made nearer in time to the matter to which it relates and is less likely to be influenced by the controversy that gave rise to the litigation. The trier of fact has the declarant before it and

471

can observe his demeanor and the nature of his testimony as he denies or tries to explain away the inconsistency. Hence, it is in as good a position to determine the truth or falsity of the prior statement as it is to determine the truth or falsity of the inconsistent testimony given in court. Moreover, § 1235 will provide a party with desirable protection against the "turn-coat" witness who changes his story on the stand and deprives the party calling him of evidence essential to his case. (Comment of Law Revision Commission, Cal Evid Code § 1235)

It should be noted that this rationale was only partly accepted by the Oregon Legislature. Oregon Rule 801(4)(a) is not as broad as California Evidence Code section 1235, which admits all prior inconsistent statements of a witness as substantive evidence.

In *State v. Arnold,* 133 Or App 647, 650, 893 P2d 1050, 1052 (1995), a young sex crime victim, when called to the stand by the state, testified that she did not know or could not remember earlier events or statements. The state introduced her earlier statements to impeach her and first argued that they were "not hearsay" under OEC 801(4)(a)(A). Because the earlier statements were not made under oath at a proceeding, they were held inadmissible under OEC 801(4)(a)(A).

No Cross-Examination Required at Prior Proceeding

The rule does not require that the witness have been subject to cross-examination at the prior hearing or proceeding. Therefore, evidence of a witness' uncross-examined testimony to a grand jury that is inconsistent with the witness' trial testimony may be received as substantive evidence. *State v. Dickerson,* 112 Or App 51, 54–5, 827 P2d 1354, 1356, rev denied 313 Or 627, 835 P2d 916 (1992) (grand jury proceedings are "other proceedings" within the meaning of Rule 801(4)(a)(A); moreover, when grand jury statements are offered to impeach, the inconsistent grand jury testimony may be proven by a witness other than a grand juror). Cf. *United States v. Coran,* 589 F2d 238 (9th Cir 1977) ("unduly suggestive or conclusory" interrogation of a witness before the grand jury may be grounds for excluding the prior statement for purposes of either substantive evidence or impeachment).

"Inconsistent" Defined

The term "inconsistent" is not defined by the rule. The Commentary states: "The Legislative Assembly intends that 'inconsistent' include situations where a witness denies making a prior statement or does not remember the content of the statement." See textual discussion of Rule 613.

In *United States v. Williams,* 737 F2d 594 (7th Cir 1984), cert denied 470 US 1003 (1985), the court held that evasive answers or purported loss of memory concerning facts that the witness previously testified to in detail may be found to be inconsistent. However, if the prior inconsistent statement was elicited in an "unduly suggestive or conclusory" manner, the court has discretion to exclude it. *United States v. Morgan,* 555 F2d 238, 241 (9th Cir 1977).

Sufficiency of Evidence

The rule does not resolve the question of whether a criminal defendant can be convicted based solely upon the prior inconsistent statement of a prosecution witness made at a prior trial, hearing, or proceeding. The report of the Senate Judiciary Committee regarding FRE 801(d)(1)(A) stated:

> It would appear that some of the opposition to this rule is based on a concern that a person could be convicted solely upon evidence admissible under this Rule. The Rule, however, is not addressed to the question of the sufficiency of evidence to send a case to the jury, but merely as to its admissibility. Factual circumstances could well arise where, if this were the sole evidence, dismissal would be appropriate. (5 Rep No 1277, 93d Cong, 2d Sess 16 n 21, reprinted in 1974 US Code Cong & Admin News, pp 7051, 7063 n 21)

Judge Weinstein comments: "It is doubtful, however, that in any but the most unusual case, a prior inconsistent statement alone will suffice to support a conviction since it is unlikely that a reasonable juror could be convinced beyond a reasonable doubt by such evidence alone." See 4 J. Weinstein and M. Berger, WEINSTEIN'S EVIDENCE (1988) § 801(d)(1)(A)[01] at 801-107.

In *United States v. Orrico,* 599 F2d 113, 118 (6th Cir 1979), the court stated with regard to this question:

> But when such evidence [of prior inconsistent statements admissible as substantive evidence under FRE 801(d)(1)(A)] is the only source of support for the central allegations of the charge, especially when the statements barely, if at all, meet the minimal requirements of admissibility, we do not believe that a substantial factual basis as to each element of the crime providing support for a conclusion of guilt beyond reasonable doubt has been offered by the Government.

See generally Goldman, *Guilt by Intuition: The Insufficiency of Prior Inconsistent Statements to Convict,* 65 N C L Rev 1 (1986); COMMENT, *Due Process and the Sufficiency of Prior Inconsistent Statements as Evidence for Criminal Convictions,* 15 U C D L Rev 1093 (1982).

RULE 801(4)(a)(B)
Prior Consistent Statements

Rule 801(4)(a)(B) defines as not hearsay prior consistent statements of a witness provided (1) the declarant is subject to cross-examination regarding the statement; and (2) the prior consistent statement is offered to rebut an inconsistent statement or an express or implied charge against the witness of recent fabrication or improper influence or motive. Under former law, prior consistent statements were admissible only to rehabilitate a witness, not for the truth of the matter asserted.

Implied Charge

An implied charge of recent fabrication or improper motive or influence is not made in cases where the testimony of a witness is simply impeached by contradictory evidence. See *Powers v. Officer Cheeley,* 307 Or 585, 593, 771 P2d 622, 626 (1989) ("The historical meaning of 'implied charge' and its present meaning do not include cases of simple contradiction concerning the facts of the case among or between witnesses.") In *Powers,* the court also held that it is not proper to attempt to create an implied charge of fabrication by asking an opposing witness to say that any subsequent evidence contrary to that witness' version of the facts would be a "fabrication." Such an approach is objectionable because a witness may not comment on the credibility of another witness, a witness should not be impeached before even testifying, and the question of whether there is a charge of recent fabrication is for the court. Id.

An implied charge of recent fabrication can sometimes be found from vigorous cross-examination that attacks the veracity of the witness. In *Bremner v. Charles,* 123 Or App 95, 99–101, 859 P2d 1148, 1152–3 (1993), rev denied 318 Or 381, 870 P2d 221 (1994), a medical malpractice action, a central issue was whether the mother had notified the physician during the pregnancy about lack of fetal movement. The mother testified that she expressed such concerns, and the physician denied any memory of such statements and did not record any such statements in her notes. On cross-examination, the defense lawyer vigorously challenged the mother's testimony that she mentioned her concerns to the doctor. Under these facts, it was error to exclude evidence of prior consistent statements by the mother to rebut the implied charge of recent fabrication. The evidence that should have been allowed was (1) testimony by a friend that the mother had stated to her during her pregnancy that she had told her doctor about her concerns that something might be wrong with the fetus; and (2) testimony by the grandmother that the mother had expressed her concerns about reduced fetal movement. Taken together, such testimony was relevant because it "made it more probable that mother had been concerned about fetal movement during her pregnancy and had expressed that concern to her physician."

Recent Fabrication

A suggestion of recent fabrication may sometimes be made by showing that the witness failed to report a particular fact previously. For example, in *Keys v. Nadel,* 140 Or App 611, 613–7, 915 P2d 1030 (1996), a medical malpractice action, plaintiff testified that she had notified defendant doctor of her vomiting and bloody stools, and the doctor testified that she had not. Moreover, a defense witness had expressed a belief that plaintiff was not an honest person. On this record it was error to exclude testimony of two acquaintances of plaintiff that plaintiff had told them that she had reported her symptoms to defendant. Plaintiff's earlier statements were properly admissible as prior consistent statements to rebut the attack on her trial testimony.

In *State v. Resendez,* 82 Or App 259, 728 P2d 562 (1986), rev denied 302 Or 614, 733 P2d 449 (1987), a six-year-old sex abuse victim testified that the defendant had sexual intercourse with her. Defendant impeached the victim by showing that on the night of the incident, she had not told her babysitter or the investigating police officer that any penetration had occurred. At trial, a Children's Services Division worker was allowed to testify that four days after the incident the victim said that defendant had sexual intercourse with her. The testimony of the CSD worker was held to be properly received to rebut the implied charge of recent fabrication.

Improper Motive

The improper motive or influence can be of various types, and can include such things as bribery, threats, promises of leniency, vengeance, or personal animosity. See, e.g., *State v. Middleton,* 294 Or 427, 657 P2d 1215 (1983).

Statement Must Be Made Prior to Motive to Fabricate

The consistent statements have been made prior to the time when the alleged motive to fabricate arose. See *Powers v. Officer Cheeley,* 307 Or 585, 591, 771 P2d 622, 626 (1989) ("[T]he prior consistent statement which may be admitted is one made before the alleged motive to fabricate arose."); *State v. Middleton,* 294 Or 427, 657 P2d 1215 (1983). In *Tome v. United States,* 115 SCt 696 (1995), the Supreme Court interpreted FRE 801(d)(1)(B) as requiring that a prior consistent statement offered to rehabilitate a witness be made *prior* to the event alleged to have caused a motive on the part of the witness to fabricate her testimony.

However, it is not always easy to determine the time when the motive or influence to fabricate began. See, e.g., *Powers v. Officer Cheeley,* 307 Or 585, 592, 771 P2d 622 (1989) ("There is no reference point for use in determining when a claimed motive or influence to falsify may have arisen here.") The best trial courts can do is to insure that the prior consistent statement was made at a sufficiently prior point in time so that it has relevance in rebutting the claim of recent fabrication or improper motive or influence rather than just providing a reiteration of trial testimony.

Rehabilitation After Impeachment
by Prior Inconsistent Statement

There is a significant difference between Rule 801(4)(a)(B) and FRE 801(d)(1)(B). The Oregon rule allows prior consistent statements as not hearsay to rebut a prior inconsistent statement whereas the federal rule does not. See ANNOT., *Effect of Rule 801(d)(1)(B) of the Federal Rules of Evidence Upon the Admissibility of a Witness' Prior Consistent Statement,* 47 ALR Fed 639 (1980). If the rule is intended to mean that prior consistent statements are admissible whenever a witness has been impeached by a prior inconsistent statement, the rule changes prior Oregon case law. Previous decisions have generally limited the use of consistent statements to situations where the witness has been impeached by suggestions of recent fabrication, or failing memory (see *Cook v. Safeway Stores, Inc.,* 266 Or 77, 88, 511 P2d 375 (1973)), or impeached by prior inconsistent statements that the witness denies making (see *Hale v. Smith,* 254 Or 300, 460 P2d 351 (1969)).

According to McCormick, many courts do not allow rehabilitation by use of prior consistent statements every time a witness is impeached by a prior inconsistent statement, because "inconsistency remains despite all consistent statements." 1 McCormick, EVIDENCE (4th ed 1992) § 47 at 178–9. The Commentary does not reveal an intent to expand the circumstances under which prior consistent statements may be received; instead, it only intends to allow them now to be received as substantive evidence as well as for rehabilitation. Courts may therefore interpret Rule 801(4)(a)(B) as not authorizing unlimited use of prior consistent statements to rebut prior inconsistent statements. However, even if courts continue to impose the requirement that there be an express or implied charge of recent fabrication or failing memory, such a charge often seems easily found. See, e.g., *Roach v. Hockey,* 53 Or App 710, 634 P2d 249 (1981), rev denied 292 Or 108, 642 P2d 310 (1981). See further discussion of this issue and rehabilitation of witnesses generally under Rule 607, supra. *See also* Rule 403 and Rule 61 1(1).

Evidence of Prior Consistent Statement

Typically, the evidence that a prior statement consistent with trial testimony was made will come from the witness giving the trial testimony. However, the prior consistent statement could be offered by another witness who heard the prior consistent statement. In *Powers v. Officer Cheeley,* 307 Or 585, 589 n1, 771 P2d 622 (1989), the court noted:

> There is a split of authority under FRE 801(d), which is similar to OEC 801(4), on the question of whether the declarant must be the witness through whom the out-of-court statement is introduced. Compare *United States v. Gonzalez,* 700 F2d 196, 202 (5th Cir 1983) (declarant need not be the witness through whom the prior inconsistent statement is introduced at trial) with *United States v. West,* 670 F2d 675, 686–87 (7th Cir 1982) (declarant must be the witness through whom the prior consistent statement is elicited). The majority rule appears to be that the declarant need not be the witness through whom the statement is elicited at trial. *See id.* at 687. We need not decide whether Oregon follows one view or the other since no objection was offered on that ground.

Admissible Only After Witness Has Testified

Prior consistent statements of a witness should not be admissible until the witness has testified. In *Livestock Transportation, Inc. v. Ashbaugh,* 64 Or App 7, 666 P2d 1356, rev denied 295 Or 773, 670 P2d 1036 (1983), the plaintiff called the investigating officer who related statements made by the plaintiff regarding the accident prior to any testimony by the plaintiff. The statements were consistent with the later trial testimony of the plaintiff, and plaintiff argued the prior consistent statements were admissible because defendant had made an implied charge of recent fabrication against plaintiff. The defendant claimed error, because the "rehabilitation" of the plaintiff by prior consistent statements occurred before the plaintiff had even testified. The majority held that if there was error, it was harmless. The dissenting judge stated: "Defendant's hearsay objection should have been sustained. It may be infrequent that taking a witness out of order constitutes reversible error; however, it does in this case: with an aura of official authority, he set the stage for plaintiff's case, based on what was hearsay at the time it was offered." 64 Or App at 12, 666 P2d at 1360.

Prior Consistent Statements Admissible Under Other Rules

Certain prior consistent statements may qualify for admission under other rules. See, e.g., Rule 106 ("When part of an act, declaration, conversation or writing is given in evidence by one party, the whole on the same subject, where otherwise admissible, may at that time be inquired into by the other"); Rule 801(4)(a)(C) (prior statements of identification); Rule 803(2) (excited utterance); Rule 803(18a) (prior complaint of sexual misconduct).

RULE 801(4)(a)(C)
Prior Identification

Rule 801(4)(a)(C) defines as not hearsay a statement of identification of a person made after perceiving the person, provided that the declarant testifies at the trial or hearing and is subject to cross-examination regarding the statement. This rule allows evidence of an earlier identification by a witness when the witness is unable or unwilling to make the same identification at trial. See *United States v. Watts,* 532 F2d 1215 (8th Cir), cert denied 429 US 847 (1976); ANNOT., *Admissibility and Weight of Extrajudicial or Pretrial Identification Where Witness Was Unable or Failed to Make In-Court Identification,* 29 ALR4th 104 (1984). The earlier statement of identification may also be used to corroborate the in-court identification. *United States v. Fosher,* 568 F2d 207, 210 n9 (1st Cir 1978). An identification made at an earlier point in time may have greater probative value than a later in-court identification.

The statement of identification may have been made in person—such as at a lineup—or it may have been made of a photograph or sketch of the person. See *United States v. Marchand,* 564 F2d 983, 996 (2nd Cir 1977), cert denied 434 US 1015 (1978) (photographs and sketch); *United States v. Hudson,* 564 F2d 1377 (9th Cir 1977) (photograph). Cf. ANNOT., *Admissibility in Evidence of Composite Picture or Sketch Produced by Police to Identify Offender,* 42 ALR3d 1217 (1972). Constitutional requirements governing lineups, showups, and photograph displays must, of course, be satisfied. See *Gilbert v. California,* 388 US 263, 87 SCt 1951, 18 LEd2d 1178 (1967); *Stovall v. Denno,* 388 US 293, 87 SCt 1967, 18 LEd2d

1199 (1967); *Simmons v. United States,* 390 US 377, 88 SCt 967, 19 LEd2d 1247 (1968); *State v. Classen,* 285 Or 221, 590 P2d 1198 (1979). See generally COMMENT, *Evidence—Pretrial Photographic Identification of Criminal Suspects: State v. Classen,* 60 Or L Rev 443 (1981).

Evidence of the earlier statement of identification may be offered by the declarant or by a third person who witnessed the identification being made, provided the declarant testifies and is subject to cross-examination regarding the statement. *United States v. Elemy,* 656 F2d 507 (9th Cir 1981); *United States v. Cueto,* 611 F2d 1056 (5th Cir 1980). The United States Supreme Court has held that a statement of identification made by a witness who is unable, because of a memory loss, to testify concerning the basis for the identification is nonetheless admissible under the federal counterpart of this rule and does not violate the federal Confrontation Clause. *United States v. Owens,* 484 US 554, 108 SCt 838, 98 LEd2d 951 (1988).

The Commentary states:

> The subparagraph should not be read literally. It is aimed at situations where the declarant is shown a picture or photograph of a person and makes an identification as a result of that showing ("that is the person that did it"). It is not aimed at situations where after an event, the declarant simply makes a statement which identifies the person involved ("X did it").

Presumably, evidence of the prior identification may be received even though the witness now repudiates that identification or denies it was made. It has been held that evidence of the earlier statement of identification is admissible even when the witness has made a misidentification in court. *United States v. Lewis,* 565 F2d 1248 (2nd Cir 1977), cert denied 435 US 973 (1978).

This rule is not the only means by which prior statements of identification may be admitted. In some cases they may qualify for admission under some other rule, for example, as prior inconsistent statements under Rule 801(4)(a)(A), prior consistent statements under Rule 801(4)(a)(B), or admissions of a party-opponent under Rule 801(4)(b). In some circumstances a statement of prior identification may also satisfy one of the hearsay exceptions, such as the excited utterance exception (see Rule 803(2)), the past recollection recorded exception (see Rule 803(5)), or one of the residual hearsay exceptions (see Rules 803(24) and 804(3)(f)). A hearsay issue arises only if the statement of identification was made out of court. If a witness testifies at trial, "I saw the defendant shoot the victim," this is not hearsay.

This rule does not address the question of the form in which photographs may be submitted to the jury. Mug shots or any photograph suggesting a prior conviction or arrest of the defendant are generally prohibited. See *United States v. Fosher,* 568 F2d 207, 213–4 (1st Cir 1978); *State v. Thorne,* 41 Or App 583, 588–9, 599 P2d 1206 (1979); ANNOT., *Admissibility, and Prejudicial Effect of Admission, of "Mug shot," "Rogue's Gallery" Photograph, or Photograph Taken in Prison, of Defendant in Criminal Trial,* 30 ALR3d 908 (1970).

RULE 801(4)(b).

(4) [Statements which are not hearsay.] A statement is not hearsay if:

(b) [Admission by party-opponent.] The statement is offered against a party and is:

(A) That party's own statement, in either an individual or a representative capacity;

(B) A statement of which the party has manifested the party's adoption or belief in its truth;

(C) A statement by a person authorized by the party to make a statement concerning the subject;

(D) A statement by the party's agent or servant concerning a matter within the scope of the agency or employment, made during the existence of the relationship; or

(E) A statement by a coconspirator of a party during the course and in furtherance of the conspiracy.

LEGISLATIVE COMMENTARY

Paragraph (b). Paragraph (b) changes Oregon law with regard to admissions by a party opponent. An admission is presently considered to be hearsay, but is admissible under an exception to the hearsay rule. Under paragraph (b) an admission is not hearsay. The practical result is the same.

Admissions are excluded from the category of hearsay on the theory that their admissibility is the result of the adversary system rather than satisfaction of the conditions of the hearsay rule. Strahorn, *A Reconsideration of the Hearsay Rule and Admissions,* in 85 U Pa L Rev 484, 564 (1937); Morgan, *Basic Problems of Evidence* 265 (1962); 4 Wigmore § 1048. No guaranty of trustworthiness is required. The technical demands of the opinion rule and the rule requiring personal knowledge are suspended. The apparent widespread satisfaction with the results calls for a generous construction of this paragraph.

The responsibility of a party for five categories of statements is considered enough to justify their reception in evidence against the party:

Subparagraph (b)(A). A party's own statement is the classic example of an admission. See former ORS 41.900(2) (repealed). Under Rule 801, if a statement is offered against a party in a representative capacity, there is no requirement that the party have been acting in that capacity at the time of the statement; the statement need only be relevant to representative affairs Accord, California Evidence Code § 1220. This is a departure from Oregon case law, holding that the declarations of an executor or administrator of an estate made before appointment may not be used against the executor or administrator in the person's representative capacity. *Johnson v. Underwood,* 102 Or 680, 203 P 879 (1922); *Williams v. Culver,* 39 Or 337, 64 P 763 (1901). See also Uniform Rule 63(7).

Subparagraph (b)(B). An admission may be made by adopting or acquiescing in the statement of another. See former ORS 41.900(3) (repealed); *Oxley v. Linnton Plywood Ass'n,* 205 Or 78, 284 P2d 766 (1955). While knowledge of the contents of the other statement would ordinarily be essential, it is not inevitable. "X is a reliable person and knows what she is talking about" is the foundation for a proper admission. See *McCormick* § 270 at 651 n 72. Adoption or acquiescence may be manifested in any appropriate manner. The greatest issues surround silence, where the theory is that the person would have protested an untrue statement. This calls for an evaluation of probable human behavior under the circumstances. In civil cases the results have been generally satisfactory. In criminal cases, troublesome questions are raised. The inference involved is fairly weak to begin with. Silence may be motivated by advice of counsel or a realization that "anything you say may be used against you." Unusual opportunity is afforded to manufacture evidence. Encroachment upon the privilege against self-incrimination seems inescapable. Not surprisingly, in *Doyle v. Ohio,* 426 US 610, 96 S Ct 2240, 49 L Ed 2d 91 (1976) and *United States v. Hale,* 422 US 171, 95 S Ct 2133, 45 L Ed 2d 99 (1975), the United States Supreme Court held that evidence of silence during police interrogation is inadmissible at the defendant's subsequent trial for the purpose of impeaching the defendant's credibility. Such evidence was declared to be insolubly ambiguous, fundamentally unfair and possessed of an intolerably prejudicial impact. The Legislative Assembly agrees. This subparagraph should not be construed to follow the admission, for any purpose in a criminal case, of evidence of silence during police interrogation after the defendant has been informed of the right to remain silent as provided in *Miranda v. Arizona,* 384 US 436, 86 S Ct 1602, 16 L Ed 2d 694 (1966). In light of the *Doyle* and *Hale* decisions, Rule 801 contains no special provisions concerning failure to deny in criminal cases.

Subparagraph (b)(C). It is evident that a statement which is authorized by a party should have the status of an admission by the party. *Hildebrand v. United Artisans,* 50 Or 159, 91 P 542 (1907). However, the question arises whether only statements to third persons should be so regarded, or also statements by the agent to the principal. Oregon courts have not decided the question. This subparagraph is phrased broadly to encompass both. While it may be argued that an agent authorized to make statements to a principal does not speak for the principal, Morgan, *Basic Problems of Evidence* 273 (1962), generally communication to an outsider has not been thought an essential characteristic of an admission. Thus, a party's books or records are usable against the party without regard to any intent to disclose to third persons. 5 Wigmore § 1557; McCormick § 267 at 639–647. Compare New Jersey Evidence Rule 63(8)(a) (stating the within rule) with Uniform Rule 63(8)(a) and California Evidence Code § 1222 (limiting admissions to statements authorized by a party to be made "for" the party, a perhaps ambiguous reference to statements to third persons). See also Falknor, *Vicarious Admissions and the Uniform Rules,* in 14 Vand L Rev 855, 860–1 (1961).

Subparagraph (b)(D). The traditional test in Oregon for the admissibility of statements by agents, as admissions, has been the test of agency. Was the statement made by the agent acting in the scope of employment? *Timber Access Industries v. U.S. Plywood-Champion Papers,* supra, citing

Hansen v. Oregon-Washington R. & N. Co., 97 Or 190, 188 P 963 (1920); *Madron v. Thompson, supra.* Because few principals employ agents for the purpose of making damaging statements, the usual result was exclusion of the statement. Dissatisfaction with this loss of valuable and helpful evidence has been increasing. A substantial trend favors the adopted ride, which admits statements related to any matter within the scope of an agency or employment if the statements are made during the relationship. *Grayson v. Williams,* 256 F2d 61 (10th Cir 1958); *Koninklijke Luchtvaart Maatschappij N. V. KLM Royal Dutch Airlines v. Tuller,* 292 F2d 774 (DC Cir 1961); *Martin v. Savage Truck Lines, Inc.,* 121 F Supp 417 (DDC 1954); and state court decisions collected in 4 Wigmore, 1964 Supp at 66–73, with the editor's comment that the statements should have been excluded as not within the scope of agency. Similar provisions are found in Uniform Rule 63(9)(a), Kansas Code of Civil Procedure § 60-460(i)(1) and New Jersey Evidence Rule 63(9)(a).

Subparagraph (b)(E). This subparagraph admits the statements of a coconspirator if they were made during the course and in furtherance of the conspiracy. See former ORS 41.900(6) (repealed); *State v. Garrison,* 16 Or App 588, 519 P2d 1295 (1974); *State v. Keller,* 143 Or 589, 21 P2d 807 (1933). While the view of agency taken in subparagraph (b)(D) above suggests a wider admissibility of coconspirators' statements, the agency theory of conspiracy is a fiction at best and ought not serve as a basis for admissibility beyond that already established. See Levie, *Hearsay and Conspiracy,* in 52 Mich L Rev 1159 (1954); Comment; 25 U Chi L Rev 530 (1958). Subparagraph (b)(E) is consistent with the position of the United States and Oregon Supreme Courts in denying admission to statements made after the objectives of a conspiracy have either failed or been achieved. *Krulewitch v. United States,* 336 US 440, 69 S Ct 716, 93 L Ed 790 (1949); *Wong Sun v. United States,* 371 US 471, 490, 83 S Ct 407, 9 L Ed 2d 441 (1963); *State v. Gardner,* 225 Or 376, 358 P2d 557 (1961); *State v. Weitzel,* 157 Or 334, 69 P2d 958 (1937).

TEXT

RULE 801(4)(b)
Admissions Generally

Rule 801(4)(b) defines admissions of a party-opponent as not hearsay. Under prior law admissions were hearsay but admissible as an exception to the hearsay rule. *Oxley v. Linnton Plywood Ass'n,* 205 Or 78, 98, 284 P2d 766 (1955). Under the new code admissions are distinguished from hearsay exceptions because they have a different rationale. They are admissible not because they are necessarily reliable, but because they are statements of a party-opponent. Even if they are unreliable, the party will have an opportunity to explain why he or she made the statements. The primary concern of the hearsay rule is lack of cross-examination. This concern is eliminated when the party making the statement and the party who would be conducting the cross-examination are the same. See Park, *The Rationale of Personal Admissions,* 21 Ind L Rev 509 (1988).

According to the Commentary "the technical demands of the opinion rule and the rule requiring personal knowledge are suspended" with respect to admissions. See Rule 701; Rule 602. Allowing admissions in the form of opinions is consistent with prior law. See *Kraxberger v. Rogers*, 231 Or 440, 373 P2d 647 (1962). In *Washington v. Taseca Homes, Inc.*, 310 Or 783, 802 P2d 70 (1990), the court held it was error to exclude a statement by the defendant during a deposition responding "no" to the question, "Is there anything that [plaintiff] did in your opinion which was careless that caused this car wreck?" The plaintiff argued that exclusion of this statement was proper because it was an opinion on a legal issue. The court held that admissions in the form of opinions are nonetheless admissible against a party-opponent.

On the applicability of competency requirements to admissions, see AN-NOT., *Admissibility as Evidence in Civil Cases of Admissions by Infants*, 12 ALR3d 1051 (1967).

Rule 801(4)(b) recognizes five categories of admissions: party admissions, adoptive admissions, authorized admissions, vicarious admissions, and admissions by a coconspirator. Some admissions existing under former law are not expressly recognized by the new Oregon Evidence Code. ORS 41.830 (repealed 1981) provided:

> Where one derives title to real property from another, the declaration, act, or omission of the latter, while holding the title, in relation to the property, is evidence against the former.

ORS 41.890 (repealed 1981) provided:

> When the question in dispute between the parties is the obligation or duty of a third person, whatever would be evidence for or against that third person is primary evidence between the parties.

Admissions by a person in privily or a predecessor in interest receivable under these prior statutes may in some circumstances qualify for admission under Rule 801(4)(b)(C) (authorized admission), Rule 801(4)(b)(D)(vicarious admission), Rule 804(3)(c) (statement against interest); or Rule 803(24) or 804(3)(f) (residual hearsay exceptions). See *Huff v. White Motor Corp.*, 609 F2d 286 (7th Cir 1979) (admission by plaintiff's decedent in wrongful death case admissible against plaintiff under residual hearsay exception established by FRE 803(24) and FRE 804(b)(5), provided decedent was mentally competent at time the statement was made).

RULE 801(4)(b)(A)
Party's Admissions

Under Rule 801(4)(b)(A), a party's own prior out-of-court statements may be received against that party, even though they would be hearsay under Rule 801(3) if offered by that party. See ANNOT., *Admissibility of Party's Own Statement Under Rule 801(d)(2)(A) of the Federal Rules of Evidence*, 48 ALR Fed 922 (1980). Consistent with prior law, there is no requirement that the admissions have been against interest at the time they were made. See *Kraxberger v. Rogers,* 231 Or 440, 451–2, 373 P2d 647, 652 (1962). For this reason, the phrase "admission against interest" is not used in the new code and should be avoided. Such terminology invites confusion with the hearsay exception for statements against interest. See Rule 804(3)(c).

For an example of a party admission, see *State v. Wright,* 323 Or 8, 12, ___ P2d ___ (1996) (prosecution properly offered out-of-court statement by defendant to friend affirming that everything was going okay "except for the guns").

Prior Testimony

Statements by a party in an earlier proceeding are admissible against that party in a later proceeding. See *State v. Yock,* 49 Or App 749, 621 P2d 592 (1980). Statements of a party in a deposition, so far as otherwise admissible under the rules of evidence, may be received against the party for any purpose.

> At the trial or upon the hearing of a motion or an interlocutory proceeding, any part or all of a deposition, so far as admissible under the rules of evidence, may be used against any party who was present or represented at the taking of the deposition or who had due notice thereof, in accordance with any of the following provisions of this subsection:
>
> ...
>
> (b) The deposition of a party, or of anyone who at the time of taking the deposition was an officer, director or managing agent of a public or private corporation, partnership or association which is a party, may be used by an adverse party for any purpose. (ORS 45.250(1))

Judicial Admissions

A judicial admission "is a formal concession in pleadings or stipulations that withdraws a fact from issue." *State v. Anderson,* 137 Or App 36, 42, 902 P2d 1206 (1995) (prosecutor's statements in a colloquy with the court are not a judicial admission).

Testimony of a party in the current proceeding may be binding on the party as a judicial admission, but only if it is testimony as to a concrete fact and not as to a matter of opinion, estimate, appearance, inference or uncertain memory, or a matter outside the special knowledge of that party. *Pope v. Benefit Trust Life Ins. Co.,* 261 Or 397, 494 P2d 420 (1972); *Krause v. Eugene Dodge Inc.,* 265 Or 486, 503, 509 P2d 1199, 1207 (1973); *Morey v. Redifer,* 204 Or 194, 214, 282 P2d 1062, 1070 (1955).

In *Celli v. Santos,* 132 Or App 516, 519, 888 P2d 1067 (1995), the defendant mother appealed a judgment obtained by the plaintiff daughter for injuries suffered in an automobile accident. Because the plaintiff had testified at trial that her mother was not negligent, the defendant argued that this was a "judicial admission" entitling the defendant to a directed verdict. The court held that the plaintiff's testimony was not a judicial admission because it consisted more of opinion than a direct assertion of fact. The court found other sufficient evidence in the record to support a judgment for plaintiff.

In *Smith v. Williams*, 98 Or App 258, 261, 779 P2d 1057 (1989), the court affirmed that an opening statement is only evidence, not a binding "judicial admission," citing *Stone v. Stone*, 268 Or 446, 450, 521 P2d 534 (1974). Therefore, the defendant could offer evidence contradicting his attorney's opening statement.

Prior Pleadings

Admissions by a party in a pleading in another case, or in an earlier pleading in the same case which has been amended or otherwise superseded, are admissible against the party as evidentiary admissions. *Moudy v. Boylan*, 219 Or 448, 347 P2d 983 (1959); *Smith v. State Accident Ins. Fund*, 12 Or App 12, 504 P2d 1062 (1973). Unlike pleadings presently before the court, withdrawn or superseded pleadings are not judicial admissions binding on a party. See *Beck v. Gen. Ins. Co. of America*, 141 Or 446, 18 P2d 570 (1933).

In *MacDonald v. Cottle*, 133 Or App 35, 889 P2d 1320, rev denied 321 Or 268, 895 P2d 1362 (1995), a dental malpractice action, the defendant before trial amended a response previously given to a request for admission under ORCP 45. The defendant originally admitted giving the plaintiff no preoperative antibiotics, but prior to trial amended this response to state that antibiotics were given before the tooth extraction. The court held that despite the amendment, the original response was admissible at trial, not as a judicial admission but as an evidentiary admission.

Prior pleadings are not necessarily admissible against a party. In *Garman v. Griffin*, 666 F2d 1156 (8th Cir 1981), a wrongful death action on behalf of a boy killed by a school bus, the trial court had allowed the defendant driver to introduce an earlier complaint, later dismissed, filed by the same plaintiff against the manufacturer of the bus. The complaint alleged that the mirror of the bus contained a blind spot, which prevented the driver from seeing the boy. The Court of Appeals reversed a judgment for the defendant, holding that it was error to admit the earlier pleading because it involved the conduct of a party who was no longer in the case. To allow such a pleading would undermine the policy of the procedural rules allowing multiple theories of liability against multiple parties.

In *Schneider v. Lockheed Aircraft Corp.*, 658 F2d 835 (DC Cir 1981), cert denied 455 US 994 (1982), the court held that statements and allegations in a pleading made by the defendant in a hearing on a claim against a third party could not be offered against the defendant in a later proceeding as an admission. The statement hypothetically conceded plaintiff's damages for purposes of maintaining the third-party claim. The court stated that "the goals of efficient federal procedure would be frustrated if hypothetical pleadings from third party proceedings could be introduced into evidence." 658 F2d at 843.

In *Hardy v. Johns-Mansville Sales Corp.*, 851 F2d 742 (5th Cir 1988), the court held that even though statements in trial pleadings are admissible, statements in appellate briefs do not qualify as admissions under FRE 801.

Guilty Pleas

A plea of guilty to a crime may be received as an admission in subsequent litigation involving that party, provided the plea is not rejected or withdrawn and is relevant. See Rule 401; Rule 410. A plea of guilty to a traffic *offense* may also be received, although evidence of a bail forfeiture may not. ORS 41.905 states:

(2) A plea of guilty by a person to a traffic offense may be admitted as evidence in the trial of a subsequent civil action arising out of the same accident or occurrence as an admission of the person entering the plea, and for no other purpose.

(3) Evidence of forfeiture of bail posted by a person as a result of a charge of a traffic offense shall not be admitted as evidence in the trial of a subsequent civil action arising out of the same accident or occurrence.

Evidence of a plea of guilty to a traffic *infraction* may not be received in evidence. See ORS 153.585(2). See generally, *Ryan v. Ohm*, 39 Or App 947, 593 P2d 1296 (1979).

Admissions by Codefendants

Admissions offered under this subsection must be made by the party against whom they are offered. Admissions made by codefendants are generally admissible against a party only if they qualify under the subsequent subsections of Rule 801(4)(b), such as the exceptions for authorized admissions or coconspirator admissions. In *State v. Damofle/Quintana*, 89 Or App 620, 750 P2d 518, rev denied 305 Or 671, 757 P2d 421 (1988), the defendants were convicted of criminal mistreatment based upon providing dangerous and inadequate conditions for their children. The defendant father objected to the admission of a tape-recorded statement by the mother in which she stated that the parents were aware of a particularly hazardous condition. The court ruled that the tape-recorded statement was properly received as the admission of a party under this rule. The ruling appears erroneous, because the statement was that of the mother, but it was received against both defendants.

Evidence of guilty pleas by codefendants may not be received against defendants. See ANNOT., *Prejudicial Effect of Prosecuting Attorney's Argument or Disclosure During Trial That Another Defendant Has Been Convicted or Has Pleaded Guilty*, 48 ALR2nd 10 16 (1956).

Unlawfully Obtained Admissions

In *State v. Marple*, 98 Or App 662, 780 P2d 772 (1989), after defendant was asked by a police officer whether controlled substances found in his coat pockets were his, the defendant replied "I'd rather not say." The court held that this evidence was improper because the prosecutor used defendant's exercise of the right to remain silent under article I, section 12 of the Oregon Constitution as evidence of guilt. The court held that this constitutional provision does not permit the state in its case-in-chief to draw the jury's attention to a defendant's exercise of the right to remain silent, citing *State v. White*, 303 Or 333, 340, 736 P2d 552 (1987).The court found that a defendant can assert the constitutional right to remain silent even though he is not in custody and even though *Miranda* warnings have not yet been given. 98 Or at 666 n.2. Defendant took the stand and testified that the coat was not his. On cross-examination, the prosecutor asked, "So you never told [the officer] that night that you had on somebody else's coat, did you?" 98 Or App at 665. The court found it unnecessary to decide whether such evidence of silence by the defendant at the time of questioning by a police officer could be used to impeach his testimony at trial.

In *State v. Aguilar*, 133 Or App 304, 891 P2d 668 (1995), a police officer questioned the defendant about two robberies and promised him that if he confessed he would be charged only with one robbery. The defendant confessed to both robberies and was charged with both. The appellate court held that his confession to the second robbery was properly suppressed as involuntary because it was given in response to an offer of immunity. The court remanded for a further hearing on whether the confession to the first robbery was also involuntary.

In *State v. Pollard*, 132 Or App 538, 543, 888 P2d 1054, 1058, rev denied 321 Or 138, 894 P2d 469 (1995), the court reaffirmed that "admissions obtained by an express or implied promise of immunity or leniency are involuntary as a matter of law under the Oregon Constitution, Article I, section 12." Here, the court held that the defendant's incriminating statement that he caused the injury that led to the death of his infant son was improperly admitted because the interrogating officer impliedly suggested that by confessing the defendant would receive treatment in lieu of prosecution.

In *Wainwright v. Greenfield*, 474 US 284, 106 SCt 634, 88 LEd2d 623 (1986), the Supreme Court held that a defendant's refusal to answer questions before speaking with counsel after being advised of his *Miranda* rights could not be used to rebut a defense of mental disease or defect. The court held that use of such refusal was fundamentally unfair and violated the implicit assurance contained in the *Miranda* warnings that silence would carry no penalty.

In *State v. Wall*, 78 Or App 81, 715 P2d 96, rev denied 301 Or 241, 720 P2d 1280 (1986), the defendant's conviction was reversed because of violation of the new *Greenfield* rule. However, in *Wall,* the court held that only evidence of the defendant's silence and desire to consult an attorney are excludable. Other statements or actions by the defendant, such as his refusal to be photographed before consulting an attorney, may be admissible, because they are beyond the scope of the defendant's constitutional rights.

See generally ANNOT., *Impeachment of Defendant in Criminal Case by Showing Defendant's Prearrest Silence—State Cases,* 35 ALR4th 731 (1985); COMMENT, *The Admissibility of Prior Silence to Impeach the Testimony of Criminal*

Defendants, 18 U Mich J L Ref 741 (1985); COMMENT, *The Use of Post-Arrest, Pre-Warning Silence is Permissible to Impeach Defendant's Exculpatory Trial Testimony: Fletcher v. Weir,* 102 S Ct 1309, 61 Wash U L Q 861 (1983).

On the admissibility of suppressed confessions in subsequent civil litigation, see ANNOT., *Admissibility, in Civil Action, of Confession or Admission Which Could Not Be Used Against Party in Criminal Prosecution Because Obtained by Improper Police Methods,* 43 ALR3d 1375 (1972).

Recall Notices

To be received against a party an admission usually must be voluntary. For this reason, federal courts are divided regarding the admissibility of recall letters sent under compulsion of law. Compare *Farner v. Paccar Inc.,* 562 F2d 518 (8th Cir 1977) (admitting recall letter) with *Vockie v. General Motors Corp.,* 66 FRD 57 (ED Penn 1975), aff'd 523 F2d 1052 (3rd Cir 1975) (excluding recall letter).

Instructions to the Jury

ORS 10.095(4) provides that the jury is to be instructed "on all proper occasions" that the oral admissions of a party are to be viewed with caution. It has been held that "the failure to give [this] statutory instruction in a proper case, i.e., where there is evidence to support it, is error." *State v. Swee,* 51 Or App 249, 253, 624 P2d 1108, 1109 (1981).

RULE 801(4)(b)(B)
Adoptive Admissions

Rule 801(4)(b)(B) defines as not hearsay a statement offered against a party which the party has manifested adoption of or belief in. Application of this rule is clear in cases where a party expressly adopts the statement of another. For example, statements in a pleading drafted by an attorney but signed by a client may constitute adoptive admissions of the client.

Implied Adoption

Greater difficulty is presented in cases where the adoption of another's statement is by implication. See *State v. Osborne,* 82 Or App 229, 728 P2d 551 (1986) (statements by hired murderer made in defendant's presence were properly received as adoptive admissions, because defendant manifested his belief in the statements by his own conduct and statements). But see *State v. Severson,* 298 Or 652, 658, 696 P2d 521 (1985) (no adoptive admission of psychiatrist's report merely because defendant quoted portion of report in an affidavit challenging qualifications of the expert; circumstances must indicate that "party used the statement or document in such a way as to indicate approval of or agreement with the statement" before it will be considered an adoptive admission).

Adoption by implication may be found when a party remains silent in response to a statement where a reasonable person, under the circumstances, would deny, correct, or otherwise answer the statement if false. See *United States v. Flecha*, 539 F2d 874 (2nd Cir 1976); *United States v. Hoosier*, 542 F2d 687 (6th Cir 1976); ANNOT., *Admissibility of Statement Under Rule 801(d)(2)(B) of Federal Rules of Evidence, Providing That Statement Is Not Hearsay If Party-Opponent Has Manifested His Adoption or Belief In Its Truth*, 48 ALR Fed 721 (1980); ANNOT., *Admissibility of Evidence of Party's Silence, As Implied or Tacit Admission, When a Statement is Made By Another In His Presence Regarding Circumstances of An Accident*, 70 ALR2d 1099 (1960); ANNOT., *Silence Upon Hearing Statement By Spouse As Evidence of Admission in Civil Case*, 158 ALR 465 (1945). Cf. ANNOT., *Nonverbal Reaction to Accusation, Other Than Silence Alone, As Constituting Adoptive Admission Under Hearsay Rule*, 87 ALR3d 706 (1978).

The burden is on the proponent of the evidence to establish that the statement was an adoptive admission. *State v. Severson*, 298 Or 652, 696 P2d 521 (1985).

The leading Oregon case on adoptive admissions is *State v. Carlson*, 311 Or 201, 808 P2d 1002 (1991), where defendant was charged and convicted of unlawful possession of methamphetamine. While being questioned by police about needle marks on his arm, the defendant stated that the marks were injuries he had received from working on a car. His wife broke into the questioning, stating: "You liar, you got them from shooting up in the bedroom with all your stupid friends." Defendant "hung his head and shook his head back and forth," saying nothing. The court held that this response was too ambiguous to be an adoptive admission of the wife's accusatory statement.

The doctrine of adoptive admissions implied from a party's silence has been recognized under prior Oregon law. See *Walls v. Clark*, 252 Or 414, 449 P2d 141 (1969) (plaintiff acquiesced in her husband's statement to police officer regarding facts of accident).

Under precode law, adoption has been found when a party responded to portions of a letter but did not respond to or challenge other statements in the letter. *Wieder v. Lorenz*, 164 Or 10, 99 P2d 38 (1940).

Adoption—A Question for the Court

In *State v. Carlson*, 311 Or 201, 808 P2d 1002 (1991), the Oregon Supreme Court held that the issue of whether a third person's statement has been adopted by a party is a question for the court under Rule 104(1) rather than an issue of conditional relevancy for the jury under Rule 104(2). The reason for this approach is to prevent the prejudice that would result if the jury were allowed to hear the third person's hearsay statement before there has been a determination that it was adopted by a party. Even if the jury were to conclude that the statement had not been adopted, it might be difficult for the jury to avoid being influenced by the statement.

Compare the approach in federal court followed in *United States v. Moore*, 522 F2d 1068, 1075–6 (9th Cir 1975), cert denied 423 US 1049 (1976):

Before admitting the proffered admission by silence, the trial court must determine, as a preliminary question [*see* FRE 104(a); ORE 104(1)], whether the statement was such that under the circumstances an innocent defendant would normally be induced to respond .... Ordinarily, the jury then decides, with proper instructions from the court, whether in the light of all the surrounding facts, the defendant actually heard, understood, and acquiesced in the statement ....

But even as to the questions ultimately left to the jury, i.e., whether the defendant heard, understood, and acquiesced in the statement, the trial judge must exercise a preliminary measure of control. Specifically, he should not submit the proffered admission by silence to the jury unless he first finds that sufficient foundational facts [*see* FRE 104(b); ORE 104(2)] have been introduced for the jury reasonably to infer that the defendant did hear and understand the statement.

Likewise, the judge should not admit the statement unless he determines that the evidence would sustain a finding by the jury that the defendant did accede to the accusatory statement. To submit a proffered admission by silence to the jury when there is insufficient foundational evidence to support reasonable inferences that the accused heard, understood, and acquiesced in the accusatory statement would expose the jurors to testimony that they legally could not consider but that might seem, nevertheless, to be extremely prejudicial to the defendant. (Citations omitted)

See also *United States v. Giese,* 597 F2d 1170 (9th Cir), cert denied 444 US 979 (1979); 4 J. Weinstein and M. Berger, WEINSTEIN'S EVIDENCE (1988) § 801-197. For factors to be considered in determining whether silence indicates adoption of a statement, see 2 McCormick, EVIDENCE (4th ed 1992) § 262 at 17-178, which lists the following:

(1) The statement must have been heard by the party claimed to have acquiesced. (2) It must have been understood by the party. (3) The subject matter must have been within the party's knowledge .... (4) Physical or emotional impediments to responding must not be present. (5) The personal makeup of the speaker, e.g., young child, or the person's relationship to the party of the event, e.g., bystander, may be such as to make it unreasonable to expect a denial. (6) Probably most important of all, the statement itself must be such as would, if untrue, call for a denial under the circumstances ....

Criminal Cases

As the Commentary indicates, adoption by silence should rarely be found in a criminal case where the defendant has failed to respond to an accusation made by or in the presence of a law enforcement officer. A defendant may have sound reasons other than guilt for silence in such circumstances. Constitutional restrictions exist against offering evidence of the defendant's silence after the defendant has been advised of the right to remain silent pursuant to *Miranda* warnings. *Doyle v. Ohio,* 426 US 610, 96 SCt 2240, 49 LEd2d 91 (1976). But see *Fletcher v. Weir,* 455 US 603, 102 SCt 1309, 71 LEd2d 490 (1982) (no constitutional bar to cross-examination of defendant who takes stand, regarding postarrest silence between time of defendant's arrest and defendant's receipt of *Miranda* warnings; impeachment by such postarrest silence is a matter of state evidence law); *Jenkins v. Anderson,* 447 US 231, 100 SCt 2124, 65 LEd2d 86 (1980) (prearrest silence may be used without violating Federal Constitution when no governmental action induced the defendant to remain silent before arrest).

Silence in the face of accusations by persons other than law enforcement officers may be admissible against the defendant in a criminal case. See *State v. Pickett,* 37 Or App 239, 586 P2d 824 (1978) (failure to explain behavior to store detective as defendant explained it at trial is admissible). Also, if the defendant did not exercise the right to remain silent but gave a different story to the police than was given at trial, there is no constitutional impediment to use of the earlier statement for purposes of impeachment. Id.

It has been held that statements in an affidavit of an informer presented to the court by the government to obtain a search warrant are admissible against the government as an adoptive admission. *United States v. Morgan,* 581 F2d 933, 938 (DC Cir 1978).

RULE 801(4)(b)(C)
Authorized Admissions

Rule 801(4)(b)(C) defines as not hearsay a "statement by a person authorized by the party to make a statement concerning the subject." The person authorized to speak for the party may be an attorney, partner, associate, employee, spouse, parent, guardian, or friend. The agent's statement is admissible under this rule only if the authority of the agent extends to the making of the statement. A statement of an agent, not admissible under this rule because not authorized, should be analyzed for admissibility as a vicarious admission under Rule 801(4)(b)(D). The Commentary states that even if the agent's authority is limited to making statements to the principal and not to third persons, such statements are nonetheless admissible against the principal under this rule. Courts construing FRE 801(d)(2)(C) have held that authorized admissions include internal memoranda, intraorganizational communications, and other statements authorized to be made only to the principal. See, e.g., *Kingsley v. Baker/Beech-Nut Corp.,* 546 F2d 1136, 1141 (5th Cir 1977).

The authority of an agent to speak on behalf of a principal must be proved by independent evidence apart from the statement itself. 2 McCormick, EVIDENCE (4th ed 1996) § 259; 4 J. Weinstein and M. Berger, WEINSTEIN'S EVIDENCE (1988) § 801(d)(2)(C)[01] at 801-209. See *Wicks v. O'Connell,* 89 Or App 236, 748 P2d 551 (1988) (defendant claimed error on appeal because plaintiff did not lay a foundation that the declarant was the defendant's agent with evidence independent of declarant's testimony; the court refused to consider the point because it was not challenged at the trial level).

If an officer of a corporation is designated by that corporation as its representative at a deposition of a corporate party, the deposition to the extent otherwise admissible under the rules of evidence may be admitted against the corporation for any purpose. See ORCP 39(c)(6); ORS 45.250.

Authorized admissions may include statements by a party's attorney, including statements made in pleadings, written stipulations, and responses to requests for admission. See *Yates v. Large,* 284 Or 217, 585 P2d 697 (1978) (pleadings). But see *United States v. Martin,* 773 F2d 579 (4th Cir 1985) (direct admission of defendant's criminal liability by defendant's attorney may not be admissible; but here court finds admissible statement by attorney to IRS auditor that defendant had unreported income but did not know it should have been reported). See generally Humble, *Evidentiary Admissions of Defense Counsel in Federal Criminal Cases,* 24 Amer Crim L Rev 93 (1986).

Allegations in a pleading currently before the court are binding upon a party as a judicial admission. *Albino v. Albino,* 279 Or 537, 568 P2d 1344 (1977). Statements in an amended or superseded pleading are not binding against a party but may be received as an evidentiary admission. *Moore v. Drennan,* 269 Or 189, 523 P2d 1250 (1974); *Ralston v. Spoor,* 39 Or App 883, 593 P2d 1285 (1979). See generally ANNOT., *Admissibility in Evidence of Withdrawn, Superseded, Amended, or Abandoned Pleading As Containing Admissions Against Interest,* 52 ALR2d 516 (1957).

With respect to admissions by partners, ORS 68.230 provides: "An admission or representation made by any partner concerning partnership affairs within the scope of his authority as conferred by this chapter is evidence against the partnership."

RULE 801(4)(b)(D)
Vicarious Admissions

Rule 801(4)(b)(D) defines as not hearsay "a statement by the party's agent or servant concerning a matter within the scope of the agency or employment, made during the existence of the relationship." Under former law an admission by an agent was generally not admissible against the principal unless the agent was authorized to make the statement and it was made during the existence of the relationship. *Timber Access Industries, Inc. v. U.S. Plywood-Champion Papers, Inc.,* 263 Or 509, 515-8, 503 P2d 482, 485-6 (1972). But see *Kashmir Corp. v. Patterson,* 43 Or App 45, 602 P2d 294 (1979), aff'd 289 Or 589, 616 P2d 468 (1980). If the agent was named as a defendant, the agent's admission was receivable against the agent and could thereby indirectly be used against the principal under the doctrine of respondeat superior. See *Madron v. Thomson,* 245 Or 513, 419 P2d 611 (1966), modified on other grounds 245 Or 513, 423 P2d 496 (1967).

Rule 801(4)(b)(D) extends admissions by agents beyond authorized admissions. Under this rule admissions by an agent may be received against the principal, even though the agent was not authorized to make the statement, provided that (1) the statement concerned a matter within the scope of the agency or employment and (2) the statement was made during the existence of the relationship. For example, an admission of fault by an employee after an accident will now generally be admissible against the employer. See *Rush v. Troutman Investment Company,* 121 Or App 355, 854 P2d 968 (1993) (in case where plaintiff was injured by a clothing rack that fell on her, court held that a statement by the manager that the rack "wasn't safe" was properly admitted as a vicarious admission); *Kaiser Aluminum & Chemical Corp. v. Illinois Cent. Gulf R.R.*, 615 F2d 470, 476 (8th Cir), cert denied 449 US 890 (1980) (admission by director of freight claims that it is likely that contamination originated in rail car admissible against railroad under FRE 801(d)(2)(D)); *Miles v. M.N.C. Corp.*, 750 F2d 867 (11th Cir 1985) (racial slur by defendant's assistant superintendent admissible even though he did not have direct authority to hire and fire, because statement about a matter within the scope of his employment).

Admissions by an employee have been allowed under FRE 801(d)(2)(D) even where the employee lacked personal knowledge. See *Mahlandt v. Wild Canid Survival & Research Center Inc.*, 588 F2d 626 (8th Cir 1978) (admission of employee that employer's wolf bit a child admissible even though based on interviews with witnesses rather than personal knowledge). Judge Weinstein argues that personal knowledge should be required under this rule. See 4 J. Weinstein and M. Berger, WEINSTEIN'S EVIDENCE (1988) § 801(d)(2)(D)[01] at 801-218. The second paragraph of the Commentary to Rule 801(4)(b) states that, with respect to admissions, "the rule requiring personal knowledge [is] suspended." However, it is not clear that this statement is intended to apply to all types of admissions under Rule 801(4)(b).

It has been held that statements by government employees may not be received against the government in criminal cases under this rule. See *United States v. Kampiles,* 609 F2d 1233, 1246 (7th Cir 1979), cert denied 446 US 954 (1980). See generally Imwinkelried, *Of Evidence and Equal Protection: The Unconstitutionality of Excluding Government Agents' Statements Offered as Vicarious Admissions Against the Prosecution,* 71 Minn L Rev 269 (1987). But statements by an employee that are adopted by a government agency may constitute adoptive admissions. See textual discussion of Rule 801(4)(b)(B). In civil cases vicarious admissions by government employees have been received. See *Hoptowit v. Ray,* 682 F2d 1237, 1262 (9th Cir 1982); *United States v. Am. Tel. & Tel. Co.,* 498 F Supp 353, 358 (DDC 1980).

RULE 801(4)(b)(E)
Admissions of Coconspirators

Rule 801(4)(b)(E) defines as not hearsay "a statement by a coconspirator of a party during the course and in furtherance of the conspiracy." In *State v. Cornell*, 314 Or 673, 677, 842 P2d 394 (1992), the court held that admission of a coconspirator's statement requires "(1) That there was a conspiracy in which both the accused and declarant were members; (2) that the declarant made his or her statement during the course of the conspiracy; and (3) that the statement was made in furtherance of the conspiracy." Whether the foundation requirements are met is a preliminary question of fact to be determined by the trial court under OEC 104(1), and each element must be established by a preponderance of the evidence.

Statements are admissible under this rule with respect to the prosecution of crimes involving joint participants, even though conspiracy is not charged. *United States v. Trowery*, 542 F2d 623 (3rd Cir 1976), cert denied 429 US 1104 (1977). The report of the Senate Judiciary Committee regarding FRE 801(d)(2)(E), which is identical to Oregon Rule 801(4)(b)(E), states:

> While the rule refers to a coconspirator, it is this committee's understanding that the rule is meant to carry forward the universally accepted doctrine that a joint venturer is considered as a coconspirator for purposes of this rule even though no conspiracy has been charged. *United States v. Rinaldi*, 393 US 97, 99 (2nd Cir), *cert denied* 393 US 913 (1968); *United States v. Spencer*, 415 F2d 1301, 1304 (7th Cir 1969). (5 Rep No 1277, 93d Cong, 2d Sess 26-27 (1974)).

See COMMENT, *Federal Rule of Evidence 801(d)(2)(E): Admissibility of Statements From an Uncharged Conspiracy That Does Not Underlie the Substantive Charge,* 52 Fordham L Rev 933 (1984).

It is unnecessary to rely on this rule to admit a statement of a coconspirator when the statement made is an operative act of the conspiracy. See *United States v. Wolfson*, 634 F2d 1217, 1219 (9th Cir 1980). For example, the threats or demands of a bank robber made to a bank teller are not hearsay under Rule 801(3), because they are not being offered for the truth of the matter asserted, but rather to show the steps taken toward commission of the criminal offense. Statements of a coconspirator may also be admissible for other nonhearsay purposes. See *State v. Hattersley*, 56 Or App 265, 641 P2d 634 (1982), aff'd 294 Or 592, 660 P2d 674 (1983) (incriminating statements in note by coconspirator admissible prior to establishment of conspiracy to explain personal admissions made by defendant when confronted with note).

Determination that Conspiracy Existed

Before an admission by a coconspirator may be received, there must be evidence establishing both the conspiracy and the defendant's participation in it. See *State v. Osborne*, 82 Or App 229, 728 P2d 551 (1986). The determination of whether a conspiracy existed is a matter for the court under Rule 104(1) rather than for the jury under Rule 104(2). *State v. Cornell*, 314 Or 673, 677, 842 P2d 394 (1992); *Bourjaily v. United States*, 483 US 171, 107 SCt 2775, 97 LEd2d 144 (1987). Judge Weinstein has stated:

> To ask the jurors to consider highly prejudicial statements of coconspirators only if they first find the existence of the conspiracy and the defendant's participation in it, is to present them with too tricky a task. In cases where the conspiracy is charged it creates the absurdity of asking the jury in effect to decide the issue of guilt before it may consider evidence which is probative of guilt. Giving these preliminary questions to the jury violates the spirit of Rule 104, which calls for preliminary determinations by the judge in all cases involving a high potential for prejudice. (footnote omitted) 1 J. Weinstein and M. Berger, WEINSTEIN'S EVIDENCE § 104 [05] at 104–40 (1988).

When the court makes its preliminary determination under Rule 104(1), the existence of the conspiracy and the defendant's participation in it must be proven by a preponderance of the evidence. *State v. Cornell*, 314 Or 673, 677, 842 P2d 394 (1992); *Bourjaily v. United States*, 483 US 171, 107 SCt 2775, 97 LEd2d 144 (1987). The Evidence Code should be viewed as changing prior Oregon law which required only a *prima facie* showing that a conspiracy existed. See *State v. Pottle*, 62 Or App 545, 550, 662 P2d 351, 354 (1983), aff'd on other grounds 296 Or 274, 677 P2d 1 (1984) (interpreting former statute).

Under the coconspirator exception, the hearsay statement itself may be considered in making the determination of whether a conspiracy existed and defendant's participation in it. See *State v. O'Brien*, 96 Or App 498, 774 P2d 1109, rev denied 308 Or 446, 781 P2d 1214 (1989); *Bourjaily v. United States*, supra ("We think that there is little doubt that a co-conspirator's statements could themselves be probative of the existence of a conspiracy and the participation of both the defendant and the declarant in the conspiracy."). However, it is doubtful that the statement alone could be sufficient to establish the existence of the conspiracy. In *Bourjaily*, the Court stated: "We need not decide in this case whether the courts below could have relied solely upon [the coconspirator's] hearsay statements to determine that the conspiracy had been established by a preponderance of the evidence." See ANNOT., *Necessity and Sufficiency of Independent Evidence of Conspiracy To Allow Admission of Extrajudicial Statements of Coconspirators*, 46 ALR3d 1148 (1972).

It may not always be necessary to identify which coconspirator made the statement. In *United States v. Helmel*, 769 F2d 1306 (8th Cir 1985), the court held that a ledger containing records of an illegal gambling business was admissible under this exception even though the author of the records was unidentified. The ledger was found in the home of one of the coconspirators and bore the fingerprints of two other coconspirators.

During Course of Conspiracy

Federal courts interpreting FRE 801(b)(2)(E) tend to strictly construe the "during the course of" and "in furtherance of" requirements of the rule. Courts generally hold that a conspiracy terminates after its objectives have either failed or have been achieved. See ANNOT., *Admissibility of Statement by Coconspirator Under Rule 801(d)(2)(E) of Federal Rules of Evidence*, 44 ALR Fed 627 (1979). Most courts hold that a statement by a conspirator after arrest does not qualify. See *United States v. Flecha*, 539 F2d 874 (2nd Cir 1976); *United States v. Blackshire*, 538 F2d 569 (4th Cir), cert denied 429 US 840 (1976). But there may be a continuing conspiracy even after the arrest of one conspirator. *United States v. Smith*, 578 F2d 1227 (8th Cir 1978). A conspiracy does not always terminate immediately after commission of the crime. In *United States v. Knuckles*, 581 F2d 305, 313 (2nd Cir), cert denied 439 US 986 (1978), the court suggested that a conspiracy may sometimes continue until "the spoils are divided among the miscreants." A conspiracy may extend into a concealment phase in some circumstances. See *United States v. Mackey*, 571 F2d 376, 384 (7th Cir 1978).

In *United States v. Guerro,* 693 F2d 10 (1st Cir 1982), the court admitted a statement made by a coconspirator in a conspiracy involving narcotics shortly after his arrest on another charge. The court held that because the arrest was for an unrelated charge and the defendant might have been released on bail, the narcotics conspiracy was still continuing at the time of the statement.

It has been held that a coconspirator's statement may be offered against a defendant who joins the conspiracy at a later date. *United States v. Tombrello,* 666 F2d 485, 491 (11th Cir), cert denied 456 US 994 (1982); *United States v. Heater,* 689 F2d 783, 788 (8th Cir 1982).

In Furtherance of Conspiracy

To be admissible under this rule, the statements of the coconspirator must be in furtherance of the conspiracy. This requirement changes former law, which required only that the statements "relate" to the conspiracy. See *State v. Pottle,* 62 Or App 545, 662 P2d 351 (1983), aff'd on other grounds 296 Or 274, 677 P2d 1 (1984).

In *State v. Cornell,* 314 Or 673, 677, 842 P2d 394 (1992), the court held that "conduct before or after the commission of the elements of the underlying crime are part of a conspiracy, if the conduct is either in planning, preparing for, or committing the crime, or in eluding detection for, disposing of, or protecting the fruits of the crime." In this robbery prosecution, the court found the conspiracy to continue "until the articles stolen are removed from the scene of the crime or are disposed of in some manner." A statement made in the presence of a coconspirator may be in furtherance of the conspiracy "if the statement demonstrates the desire to encourage a co-conspirator to carry out the conspiracy or to develop comraderie in order to ensure the success of the continuing conspiracy." In this case, the coconspirator statement was made just after the alleged crime had been completed and the defendant and a coconspirator were fleeing from the scene with stolen articles. In these circumstances, a trier of fact would be entitled to infer that the coconspirator statements were made to encourage the defendant to carry out the conspiracy or to develop comraderie with the defendant in order to ensure the success of the continuing conspiracy.

Casual admissions of culpability by the conspirators to each other or to third persons have been held not to be in furtherance of the conspiracy and not admissible under this rule. See *United States v. Eubanks,* 591 F2d 513 (9th Cir 1979); *United States v. Fielding,* 645 F2d 719 (9th Cir 1981); *United States v. James,* 510 F2d 546 (5th Cir), cert denied 423 US 855 (1975). Statements by a conspirator to recruit other persons into the conspiracy have been held to be in furtherance of the conspiracy and admissible under this rule. *United States v. Mangan,* 575 F2d 32 (2nd Cir), cert denied 439 US 931 (1978). Statements made to assure a potential customer that there existed a steady source of drug supply were also held to be in furtherance of the conspiracy. *United States v. Cambindo Valencia,* 609 F2d 603 (2nd Cir 1979), cert denied 496 US 940 (1980).

In *State v. Harris,* 126 Or App 516, 519–21, 869 P2d 868, 871 (1994), modified 127 Or App 613, 872 P2d 445, rev denied 319 Or 281, 879 P2d 1284 (1994), where defendant was charged as a participant in a murder, the court approved the admission of testimony by S that her husband R told her that defendant and a coparticipant were going to post $10,000 bail for him and that in return he was to kill the victim. The testimony was found admissible as relating the declaration of a coconspirator. There was sufficient evidence of a conspiracy, in light of defendant's own testimony that he helped post R's bail. There was sufficient evidence that R's statement to his wife was in furtherance of the conspiracy, because it could have been made "in order to further commit himself to the plan, or to obtain her reassurance or assent, or to attempt to draw her into the conspiracy."

See generally Alarcon, *Suspect Evidence: Admissibility of Co-Conspirator Statements and Uncorroborated Accomplice Testimony*, 25 Loy L A L Rev 953 (1992).

Right of Confrontation

In *State v. Cornell*, 109 Or App 396, 401–2, 820 P2d 11, 15 (1991), aff'd, 314 Or 673, 842 P2d 394 (1992), the court held that the hearsay exception for coconspirator admissions is "firmly rooted" and therefore satisfies the requirements of the federal and state confrontation clauses, provided the declarant is shown to be unavailable.

Cornell modifies the earlier decision of *State v. Farber,* 295 Or 199, 210, 666 P2d 821, appeal dismissed 464 US 987 (1983), where the court applied the following criteria in determining whether the statements were sufficiently reliable to be admissible under the Confrontation Clause:

> (1) [W]hether the declaration contained assertions of past fact; (2) whether the declarant had personal knowledge of the identity and role of the participants in the crime; (3) whether it was possible that the declarant was relying upon faulty recollection; ... (4) whether the circumstances under which the statements were made provided reason to believe that the declarant had misrepresented the defendant's involvement in the crime.

In construing the federal coconspirator rule, the United States Supreme Court has held that an individualized assessment of reliability is not necessary. *Bourjaily v. United States,* 483 US 171, 107 SCt 2775, 97 LEd2d 144 (1987) ("We think that the co-conspirator exception to the hearsay rule is firmly enough rooted in our jurisprudence that ... a court need not independently inquire into the reliability of such statements.").

In *United States v. Inadi,* 475 US 387, 106 SCt 1121, 89 LEd2d 390 (1986), the Court held that no showing of the unavailability of the declarant is required under the federal Confrontation Clause before the statement of a coconspirator may be admitted in a criminal trial.

See generally Mueller, *The Federal Coconspirator Exception: Action, Assertion, and Hearsay,* 12 Hofstra L Rev 323 (1984).

RULE 801(4)(c).

(4) [Statements which are not hearsay.] A statement is not hearsay if:
   (c) The statement is made in a deposition taken in the same pro-
       ceeding pursuant to ORCP 39I.

LEGISLATIVE COMMENTARY

[There is no Legislative Commentary for this rule. This rule was not part of
the original Evidence Code but instead was added by the 1987 Legislature. See
1987 Or Laws, ch. 275, § 3.]

TEXT

Deposition Statements

The purpose of this rule is to make admissible statements made in perpetuation depositions taken pursuant to ORCP 39I, without requiring a showing
of unavailability of the declarant at trial as would otherwise be required by Rule
804(1) if the deposition were offered under the former testimony exception to
the hearsay rule (see Rule 804(3)(a)). Given that ORS 45.250(2)(f) now authorizes use of depositions at trial that were taken pursuant to ORCP 39I, it can be
argued that this rule is unnecessary.

However, there is an ambiguity in ORS 45.250(2), which allows use of
depositions at trial "so far as admissible under the rules of evidence." Also ORCP
39I(3) speaks of admitting the deposition "subject to the Oregon Evidence
Code." This rule, by classifying ORCP 39I depositions as "not hearsay" under the
Evidence Code, eliminates hearsay as a basis for objecting to the admissibility of
such depositions.

ORCP 39I provides as follows:

I. Perpetuation of testimony after commencement of action.

   I.(1) After commencement of any action, any party wishing to perpetuate
the testimony of a witness for the purpose of trial or hearing may do so by
serving a perpetuation deposition notice.

   I.(2) The notice is subject to subsections C(1) through (7) of this rule and
shall additionally state:

   I.(2)(a) A brief description of the subject areas of testimony of the witness; and

   I.(2)(b) The manner of recording the deposition.

   I.(3) Prior to the time set for deposition, any other party may object to
the perpetuation deposition. Such objection sham be governed by the standards of Rule 36 C. At any hearing on such an objection, the burden shall be
on the party seeking perpetuation to show that: (a) the witness may be unavailable as defined in ORS 40.465(1)(d) or (e) or 45.250(2)(a) through (d); or
(b) it would be an undue hardship on the witness to appear at the trial or
hearing; or (c) other good cause exists for allowing the perpetuation. If no

objection is filed, or if perpetuation is allowed, the testimony taken shall be admissible at any subsequent trial or hearing in the action, subject to the Oregon Evidence Code.

I.(4) Any perpetuation deposition shall be taken not less than seven days before the trial or hearing on not less than 14 days' notice, unless the court in which the action is pending allows a shorter period upon a showing of good cause.

I.(5) To the extent that a discovery deposition is allowed by law, any party may conduct a discovery deposition of the witness prior to the perpetuation deposition.

I.(6) The perpetuation examination shall proceed as set forth in subsection D of this rule. All objections to any testimony or evidence taken at the deposition shall be made at the time and noted upon the record. The court before which the testimony is offered shall rule on any objections before the testimony is offered. Any objections not made at the deposition shall be deemed waived.

The Oregon State Bar Procedure and Practice Committee, which sponsored this legislation, submitted the following proposed commentary to ORCP 39I:

Section 39I allows perpetuation of testimony after commencement of an action. It supplements the allowable deposition uses outlined in ORS 45.250. This section is new and not drawn from any existing federal or state rule.

The use of a deposition which has not been noticed for perpetuation purposes under this Section remains governed by ORS 45.250.

Under this Section, the party seeking perpetuation is not required to show unavailability as defined in ORS 45.250(2)(a)–(e). Unavailability in a "practical sense," primarily relates to inconvenience of the witness due to vacation, conflicting business schedules and the like. [Author's note: The phrase "unavailability in a 'practical sense'" was eliminated from the final form of the rule.] The expense of bringing a witness to trial versus perpetuating his testimony may also be a factor in practical unavailability.

Under §§ I(3), the testimony which is admissible at any subsequent trial or hearing is subject to the evidentiary objections discussed in §§ I(7). Once a perpetuation deposition is taken, the party offering the deposition does not need to show the witness is unavailable at the time of trial. If the trial is rescheduled to a different date other than the one set at the time the deposition is taken, the party offering the testimony need not show unavailability of the witness for the new date.

No expansion of the scope of discovery deposition is intended by allowing a discovery deposition under §§ I(5). For example, this subsection does not govern whether a discovery deposition is available for expert testimony. A discovery deposition of an expert under §§ I(5) is allowed only in those circumstances where these rules or case law so provide. The expense of any perpetuation deposition is governed by other rules within ORCP, *see* ORCP 46 and 68.

Exhibit to HB 2298, House Judiciary Committee, 1987 Oregon Legislative Assembly.

RULE 802. ORS 40.455. HEARSAY RULE

Hearsay is not admissible except as provided in Rules 801 to 806 (ORS 40.450 to 40.475) or as otherwise provided by law.

LEGISLATIVE COMMENTARY

Oregon Rule of Evidence 802 is the rule against admission of hearsay. It is a modified version of Rule 802 of the Federal Rules of Evidence. Like the federal rule, it considers Rules 801 through 806 to contain the primary list of hearsay exceptions, but recognizes that the admission of hearsay evidence may be allowed by specific sections of Oregon Revised Statutes outside the Evidence Code. In any event, the Legislative Assembly intends that hearsay only be admitted pursuant to some statutory or constitutional authority. This practice will encourage the development of a suitable framework of analysis for both the trial and appellate courts.

The rule is in complete accord with Oregon law, which embraces the traditional rule against hearsay. However, it is only effective when invoked: hearsay which is offered, and not objected to, will be received into evidence.

TEXT

Hearsay Inadmissible Except as Otherwise Provided

Rule 802 provides that hearsay as defined in Rule 801(3) is not admissible except as otherwise provided by Article VIII or by other law. The hearsay exceptions are listed in Rules 803 and 804. Various statements, which otherwise meet the definition of hearsay contained in Rule 801(3), are defined as not hearsay by Rule 801(4).

Although the reference to hearsay exceptions "provided by law" could include case law exceptions, the Commentary states that "the Legislative Assembly intends that hearsay only be admitted pursuant to some statutory or constitutional authority." Court-created exceptions should be developed only within the framework of the residual hearsay exceptions. See Rules 803(24) and 804(3)(f).

For examples of statutes outside the Evidence Code authorizing the admission of hearsay, see ORS 41.930 (affidavit of custodian of hospital records admissible); ORS 43.450 (official records of United States Armed Forces admissible); ORS 135.105 (statement of defendant at preliminary hearing admissible before grand jury and at trial). See also ORCP 47 (affidavits admissible to support or oppose motion for summary judgment). Cf. Westling, *The Ghost of Christmas Past: A Revival of the Unsworn Statement in Oregon,* 13 Willamette L J 23 (1976).

If no objection is made to hearsay evidence, it may be received. Hearsay evidence received without objection is "competent evidence sufficient to support a verdict." *Laubach v. Indus. Indem. Co.,* 286 Or 217, 222, 593 P2d 1146, 1150 (1979).

The fact that evidence satisfies an exception to the hearsay rule does not guarantee its admissibility. It must also comply with the other rules of evidence, such as relevancy (Rule 402), authentication (Rule 901), and the best evidence rule (Rule 1002). In criminal cases and all other proceedings where the Sixth Amendment is applicable, evidence may still be excluded as violating the defendant's right of confrontation even though Rule 802 is satisfied.

Hearsay and the Confrontation Clause

The hearsay rule and the Confrontation Clause are not coextensive. Evidence may be admissible under the Confrontation Clause, yet be inadmissible under the hearsay rule. Conversely, evidence may be admissible as an exception to the hearsay rule under state evidence law, yet be inadmissible under the Confrontation Clause. See *Pointer v. Texas,* 380 US 400, 85 SCt 1065, 13 LEd2d 923 (1965). If the hearsay declarant testifies at trial and is subject to cross-examination, the confrontation requirement is satisfied. *California v. Green,* 399 US 149, 90 SCt 1930, 26 LEd2d 489 (1970). If the hearsay declarant does not testify at trial and the out-of-court statement is admitted as a hearsay exception, whether or not the Confrontation Clause is violated depends on whether there is a satisfactory basis for the trier of fact to evaluate the truth of the prior statement and whether the statement possesses sufficient "indicia of reliability." *Dutton v. Evans,* 400 US 74, 91 SCt 210, 27 LEd2d 213 (1970).

As the Supreme Court stated in *Ohio v. Roberts,* 448 US 56, 66, 100 SCt 2531, 65 LEd2d 597 (1980):

> The Court has applied this "indicia of reliability" requirement principally by concluding that certain hearsay exceptions rest upon such solid foundations that admission of virtually any evidence within them comports with the "substance of the constitutional protection." ... This reflects the truism that "hearsay rules and the Confrontation Clause are generally designed to protect similar values," *California v. Green,* 399 U.S. at 155, and "stem from the same roots," *Dutton v. Evans,* 400 U.S. 74, 86 (1970). It also responds to the need for certainty in the workaday world of conducting criminal trials.
>
> In sum, when a hearsay declarant is not present for cross-examination at trial, the Confrontation Clause normally requires a showing that he is unavailable. Even then, his statement is admissible only if it bears adequate "indicia of reliability." Reliability can be inferred without more in a case where the evidence falls within a firmly rooted hearsay exception. In other cases the evidence must be excluded, at least absent a showing of particularized guarantees of trustworthiness.

As this quoted statement indicates, if the declarant is shown to be unavailable and the statement satisfies a "firmly rooted" exception to the hearsay rule, compliance with the Confrontation Clause is almost certain to be found. If no showing is made of the unavailability of the declarant (and no such showing is required for Rule 803 hearsay exceptions), or if the hearsay exception is not "firmly rooted," there is greater uncertainty regarding whether the Confrontation Clause is satisfied.

See generally Jonakait, *Restating the Confrontation Clause to the Sixth Amendment,* 35 UCLA L Rev 557 (1988); Graham, *The Confrontation Clause, the Hearsay Rule, and Child Sexual Abuse Prosecutions: The State of the Relationship,* 72 Minn L Rev 523 (1988); Kirst, *The Procedural Dimensions of Confrontation Doctrine,* 66 Neb L Rev 485 (1987); Kirkpatrick, *Confrontation and Hearsay: Exemptions from the Constitutional Unavailability Requirement,* 70 Minn L Rev 665 (1986); Lilly, *Notes on the Confrontation Clause and Ohio v. Roberts,* 36 U Fla L Rev 207 (1984); Westen, *The Future of Confrontation,* 77 Mich L Rev 1185 (1979); Younger, *Confrontation and Hearsay: A Look Backward, A Peek Forward,* 1 Hofstra L Rev 32 (1973); Seidelson, *Hearsay Exceptions and the Sixth Amendment,* 40 Geo Wash L Rev 76 (1971); Massaro, *The Dignity Value of Face-to-Face Confrontations,* 40 U Fla L Rev 863 (1988); Apps, *Passing the Confrontation Clause Stop Sign: Is All Hearsay Constitutionally Admissible?,* 77 Ky L J 7 (1988-89); Garcia, *The Winding Path of Bruton v. United States: A Case of Doctrinal Inconsistency,* 26 Am Crim L Rev 401 (1988).

State and Federal Confrontation Provisions Compared

The Sixth Amendment of the United States Constitution provides: "In all criminal prosecutions, the accused shall enjoy the right ... to be confronted with the witnesses against him." Article I, section 11 of the Oregon Constitution provides: "In all criminal prosecutions, the accused shall have the right ... to meet witnesses face-to-face."

To date, the Oregon Supreme Court has tended to adopt the precedents of the United States Supreme Court "in determining what constitutes unavailability of a hearsay declarant and what constitutes adequate indicia of reliability of hearsay declarations to satisfy our state constitutional confrontation clause." *State v. Campbell,* 299 Or 633, 648, 705 P2d 694, 703 (1985).

It remains to be seen whether the "face-to-face" language in the state constitution will result in any differences in interpretation with respect to issues such as the admissibility of videotaped testimony, the use of closed-circuit television, or the use of a screen between the defendant and a prosecution witness.

In *Coy v. Iowa,* 487 US 1012 (1988), the Supreme Court held that it was unconstitutional to erect a screen between a child witness and the defendant. However, in *Maryland v. Craig,* 497 US 836 (1990), the Court upheld testimony by a child sex crime victim via one-way closed-circuit television, provided there is a showing that the child would be seriously traumatized by testifying in the defendant's presence.

In *State v. Barkley,* 108 Or App 756, 760, 817 P2d 1328, 1330 (1991), aff'd and remanded 315 Or 420, 846 P2d 390, cert denied 114 SCt 116 (1993), the court found no violation of the right of confrontation in the admission of videotaped statements by a child accusing her father of sexual abuse. Because the child testified and was subject to cross-examination, defendant's right of confrontation was not violated.

See generally Nesson & Benkler, *Constitutional Hearsay: Requiring Foundational Testing and Corroboration Under the Confrontation Clause,* 81 Va L Rev

149 (1995); Mosteller, *Remaking Confrontation Clause and Hearsay Doctrine Under the Challenge of Child Sexual Abuse Prosecutions*, 1993 U Ill L Rev 691; Wendel, *A Law and Economics Analysis of the Right to Face-to-Face Confrontation Post Maryland v. Craig: Distinguishing the Forest from the Trees*, 22 Hofstra L Rev 405 (1993); Bartels, *The Hearsay Rule, the Confrontation Clause, and Reversible Error in Criminal Cases*, 26 Ariz St L J 967 (1994); ANNOT., *Closed-Circuit Television Witness Examination*, 61 ALR4th 1155 (1988); Graham, *Indicia of Reliability and Face to Face Confrontation: Emerging Issues in Child Sexual Abuse Prosecutions*, 40 U Miami L Rev 19 (1985); Thompson, *The Use of Modern Technology to Present Evidence in Child Sex Abuse Prosecutions: A Sixth Amendment Analysis and Perspective*, 18 U W LA L Rev 1 (1986); Feher, *The Alleged Molestation Victim, the Rules of Evidence, and the Constitution: Should Children Really be Seen and Not Heard?*, 14 Am J Crim L 227 (1987); COMMENT, *Closed Circuit Television Testimony for Sexually Abused Children: The Right to Avoid Confrontation?*, 27 Santa Clara L Rev 117 (1987).

Unavailability

In *State v. Campbell*, 299 Or 633, 652, 705 P2d 694 (1985), the court stated: "We hold … that before any out-of-court declaration of any available living witness may be offered against a defendant in a criminal trial, the witness must be produced and declared incompetent by the court to satisfy either Article I, § 11 of the Oregon Constitution or the Sixth Amendment to the United States Constitution." It is unlikely that the court intended its holding to be quite so broad, because under a literal reading of this holding prosecutors could not use any Rule 803 hearsay exceptions except in cases where the declarant was shown to be unavailable.

In *State v. Nielsen*, 316 Or 611, 618, 853 P2d 256 (1993), the court held unavailability to be a preliminary question of fact for the trial court to decide under OEC 104(1), and the proponent of the hearsay statement has the burden of proving it by a preponderance of evidence.

In *State v. Campbell*, supra, the court held that the question of the unavailability of a hearsay declarant in a criminal trial should not be resolved by stipulation of the parties. Instead, the prosecution has the burden to produce the potential witness for a competency hearing.

In *State v. Vosika*, 83 Or App 298, 731 P2d 449, modified 85 Or App 148, 735 P2d 1273 (1987), the trial judge admitted the hearsay statement of a three-year-old sex crime victim after ruling that the child was not competent to testify based upon observing a videotape of the child being interviewed by a doctor. The appellate court reversed the conviction, holding that "to satisfy a defendant's constitutional confrontation rights, the trial court must personally observe a child and conduct a competency hearing," at least in the absence of a stipulation allowing another procedure.

In *State v. Stevens*, 311 Or 119, 138–42, 806 P2d 92 (1991), the court found that an eight-year-old abuse victim and her four-year-old sister were unavailable as witnesses and, therefore, their hearsay statements were admissible under

Rules 803(4) and 803(18a) without violating state and federal rights of confrontation. Unavailability was shown by the fact that the eight-year-old became hysterical upon seeing the defendant, and expert testimony established that the children would be too traumatized to communicate their perceptions.

In *United States v. Inadi*, 475 US 387, 106 SCt 1121, 89 LEd2d 390 (1986), the court held that a coconspirator statement admissible under FRE 801(d)(2)(E) is not subject to a constitutional requirement of unavailability.

In *White v. Illinois*, 112 SCt 736 (1992), the Supreme Court held that the unavailability requirement does not apply where the proffered out-of-court statements fall within the federal hearsay exceptions for excited utterances or for statements made for the purpose of medical diagnosis or treatment.

It is unclear whether *White* will be followed under the state constitution. See *State v. Jensen*, 313 Or 587, 598, 837 P2d 525 (1992) (refusing to reach question of whether the Confrontation Clause requires a showing of unavailability of the child-witness before hearsay may be admitted under medical diagnosis exception, because the defendant failed to make an objection on this ground at trial). See generally COMMENT, *Sixth Amendment's Confrontation Clause—Is a Showing of Unavailability Required?* 75 S Ill U L J 573 (1993).

"Firmly Rooted" Exceptions

If a hearsay statement qualifies for admission under a "firmly rooted" exception to the hearsay rule, it is presumed to be sufficiently reliable to justify admission under the state and federal confrontation clauses. In the following cases, the courts have held various hearsay exceptions to be firmly rooted and have therefore admitted hearsay statements satisfying those exceptions.

State v. Moen, 309 Or 45, 786 P2d 111 (1990). The court held that the OEC 803(4) hearsay exception for statements for purposes of treatment and diagnosis is "firmly rooted." Therefore, statements qualifying for admission under this exception are sufficiently reliable to satisfy the requirements of the confrontation clause without an independent inquiry into reliability. The court also held the excited utterance exception of OEC 803(2) to be a firmly rooted hearsay exception. 309 Or at 65. In addition, the court held that transcripts of testimony properly admitted under the former testimony exception do not violate the state or federal confrontation clause. 309 Or at 86.

State v. Cornell, 109 Or App 396, 401–2, 820 P2d 11, 15, 314 Or 673, 842 P2d 394 (1992). The court held that the hearsay exception for coconspirator admissions is "firmly rooted" and therefore "the reliability of such statements can be inferred without more."

State v. Campbell, 299 Or 633, 705 P2d 694 (1985). The court held that Rule 803(18a) constitutes a "firmly rooted" hearsay exception, thereby satisfying the state and federal confrontation clauses without any further analysis of reliability.

Cf. State v. Hill, 129 Or App 180, 183–4, 877 P2d 1230 (1994). The court held that a child's statements about sexual abuse that meet the reliability standard of OEC 803(18a)(b) are inherently trustworthy and can be admitted without violating a defendant's confrontation rights. See also *State v. Booth*, 124 Or App

282, 291, 862 P2d 518, 523 (1993), *Booth v. Oregon*, cert. denied 115 S Ct 372 (1994).

Exceptions Not "Firmly Rooted"

Although *State v. Tucker*, 109 Or App 519, 525, 820 P2d 834, 837–8 (1001), rev denied 317 Or 188, 855 P2d 150 (1993), suggested that the exception for statements against interest is a "firmly rooted" hearsay exception, the Supreme Court has disagreed. In *State v. Nielsen*, 316 Or 611, 853 P2d 256 (1993), the court held that a statement against penal interest is not a "firmly rooted" exception to the hearsay rule, and an individualized showing of reliability is constitutionally required. The court found such "a showing of particularized guarantees of trustworthiness" in this case.

In *State v. Wilson*, 323 Or 498, 513–8, 918 P2d 826 (1996), the court analyzed statements against penal interest for reliability in deciding their admissibility under the state and federal confrontation clauses. The court noted that the statements were made in the declarant's own home to a friend (rather than to the police while in custody), declarant was sober and made the statements without protracted questioning, the statements were quite detailed and were made on the day of the murder, and they admitted declarant's equally culpable involvement in the murder rather than attempting to shift the blame to defendant. Thus, they had sufficient "indicia of reliability" to survive a confrontation challenge.

See generally Goldman, *Not So "Firmly Rooted": Exceptions to the Confrontation Clause*, 66 N C L Rev 1 (1987); NOTE, *Of Confrontation: The Right Not to Be Convicted on the Hearsay Declarations of an Accomplice*, 1990 Utah L Rev 855.

State v. Lissy, 85 Or App 484, 737 P2d 617, aff'd 304 Or 455, 747 P2d 345 (1987). The defendant was convicted of aggravated murder and challenged the admission of tape-recorded statements of Wilson, the person defendant allegedly hired to commit the murder. Wilson claimed the privilege against self-incrimination and refused to testify at trial. The prosecution introduced tape-recorded statements Wilson had made in a telephone conversation with an informant. The court held that the admission of these statements did not violate defendant's right of confrontation under the state or federal constitution, because the declarant was shown to be unavailable and the statements had sufficient indicia of reliability.

The Court of Appeals has held that certificates attesting to the accuracy of an Intoxilyzer are admissible as either public records or business records without violating a criminal defendant's right of confrontation. See *State v. Conway*, 70 Or App 721, 690 P2d 1128 (1984), rev denied 298 Or 704, 695 P2d 1371 (1985) (admitted under business records exception); *State v. Smith*, 66 Or App 703, 675 P2d 510 (1984) (admitted under public records exception); *State v. Sparks*, 66 Or App 974, 675 P2d 191, rev denied 297 Or 339 (1984); *State v. Bigej*, 77 Or App 18, 711 P2d 189 (1985), rev denied 302 Or 36, 726 P2d 935 (1986).

In *Idaho v. Wright*, 497 US 805 (1990), the Court held admission of hearsay statements pursuant to Idaho's residual hearsay exception to violate the confrontation clause of the United States Constitution. Although the declarant was shown to be unavailable, the residual hearsay exception was not a "firmly rooted hearsay exception," and the totality of the circumstances did not provide the necessary "particularized guarantees of trustworthiness."

In *United States v. Regner*, 677 F2d 754 (9th Cir), cert denied 459 US 911 (1982), the court found that the admission of a certificate showing the absence of a public record under FRE 803(10) did not violate defendant's confrontation rights.

Cross-Examination

The right of confrontation includes the right to cross-examine prosecution witnesses. Sometimes restrictions on a criminal defendant's cross-examination will violate the Confrontation Clause. See textual discussion under Rule 611(2).

In *State v. LeClair*, 83 Or App 121, 730 P2d 609 (1986), rev denied 303 Or 74, 734 P2d 354 (1987), defendant was convicted of attempted rape and sexual abuse. He sought to impeach the child victim by evidence of prior instances where she had allegedly made false accusations against others. The court held that Rule 608(2) forbids any inquiry or cross-examination into specific instances of conduct for impeachment purposes, including prior false statements. However, the court held that the restrictions of the rule will in some instances be overridden by the defendant's right of confrontation under the state and federal constitutions. The court held:

> We conclude that, regardless of the prohibitions of OEC 608, the Confrontation Clause of Article I, § 11, requires that the court permit a defendant to cross-examine the complaining witness in front of the jury concerning other accusations she has made if (1) she has recanted them; (2) the defendant demonstrates to the court that those accusations were false; or (3) there is some evidence that the victim has made prior accusations that were false, unless the probative value of the evidence which the defendant seeks to elicit on the cross-examination (including the probability that false accusations were in fact made) is substantially outweighed by the risk of prejudice, confusion, embarrassment or delay.

In *State v. Hendricks*, 101 Or App 469, 791 P2d 139, rev denied 310 Or 133, 794 P2d 795 (1990), the court found no error in excluding proof of a prior false accusation by a sex crime victim by testimony of other witnesses rather than by cross-examination of the alleged victim.

In *State v. Bonner*, 77 Or App 572, 582, 714 P2d 245, 251 (1986), defendant alleged that his right of confrontation was violated by the refusal of the trial court to allow him to cross-examine a police detective concerning the location of the confidential vehicle identification numbers on the car defendant allegedly stole. The court found no error, stating: "Defendant has not demonstrated that whether the confidential VINs were in one place versus another would have been of any value whatsoever in impeaching [the prosecution witness]."

A difficult issue arises if the ability to cross-examine a witness is limited by the witness' loss of memory. In *United States v. Owens*, 484 US 554, 108 SCt 838, 98 LEd2d 951 (1988), the Supreme Court held that there is no violation of the federal right of confrontation for a crime victim to testify under FRE 801(d)(1)(C) that he had identified the defendant as his assailant earlier, but that he has no present recollection of the incident or whether the defendant was the assailant. The earlier statement of identification may be received as substantive evidence, despite the victim's loss of memory. The court held that for purposes of the right of confrontation, "It is sufficient that the defendant has the opportunity to bring out such matters as the witness's bias, his lack of care and attentiveness, his poor eyesight, and even (what is often a prime objective of cross-examination) the very fact that he has a bad memory." 108 SCt at 842. See generally Graham, *The Confrontation Clause, the Hearsay Rule, and the Forgetful Witness*, 56 Tex L Rev 151 (1978).

In *State v. Quintero*, 110 Or App 247, 254–5, 823 P2d 981, 985–6 (1991), rev denied 314 Or 392, 840 P2d 710 (1992), defendants moved to strike a witness' direct testimony, arguing that her forgetfulness on cross-examination constituted a refusal to testify in violation of defendants' rights. The court held that the question of whether to strike testimony because of a witness' claimed failure to remember is within the discretion of the trial court. The court held that defendants' confrontation rights were not violated because defendants were given a full and fair opportunity for cross-examination and were free to question and impeach the witness.

In *State v. Tucker*, 109 Or App 519, 522, 820 P2d 834, 836 (1991), rev denied 317 Or 188, 855 P2d 150 (1993), the court held that defendant's confrontation rights were not violated by a state law prohibiting the use of wiretap evidence to impeach a prosecution witness.

In *State v. Verley*, 106 Or App 751, 809 P2d 723, rev denied 311 Or 644, 815 P2d 1273 (1991), the court found no violation of the defendant's right of cross-examination by the fact that he was not present when a videotape was made of the child victim's statement for purposes of medical diagnosis. The court noted that the child testified at trial and was available for cross-examination.

Police Laboratory Reports

In *State v. Hancock*, 317 Or 5, 854 P2d 926 (1993), the court upheld the constitutionality of ORS 475.235, which allows police laboratory reports to be offered into evidence without requiring the criminalist who prepared the report to be called as a witness at trial. Because the defendant may subpoena the criminalist to testify, the court viewed the statute as not denying the right of confrontation, but merely establishing "reasonable procedures" that must be followed in order for a defendant to exercise that right. Three dissenting justices viewed the statute as fundamentally and unconstitutionally altering established trial burdens in a way that "deprives a criminal defendant of the benefit of the adversary process."

Admissions of Codefendants

On the constitutionality of admitting statements under the coconspirator exception, see textual discussion under Rule 801(4)(b)(E), supra. See also *United States v. Inadi,* 475 US 387 (1986).

The United States Supreme Court has held that if a defendant and a co-defendant are tried together, the Sixth Amendment right of confrontation is violated if the confession of a nontestifying codefendant that implicates both defendants is admitted in a joint trial, even if the jury is instructed to consider the confession only against the codefendant who made it. The danger is too great that the jury will disregard the limiting instruction and consider the confession against the defendant, who is denied the opportunity to confront and cross-examine the codefendant who made the statement. *Bruton v. United States,* 391 US 123, 88 SCt 1620, 20 LEd2d 476 (1968). See *State v. Flores-Ortiz,* 133 Or App 62, 889 P2d 266 (1995) (affirming a trial court ruling that admitting a codefendant's confession in a joint trial would violate the *Bruton* doctrine).

In *Cruz v. New York,* 481 US 186, 107 SCt 1714, 95 LEd2d 162 (1987), the Supreme Court held that where a nontestifying codefendant's confession facially incriminating the defendant is not directly admissible against the defendant, the Confrontation Clause bars its admission at their joint trial, even if the jury is instructed not to consider it against the defendant, and even if the defendant's own confession is admitted against him. The Court rejects the plurality opinion in *Parker v. Randolph,* 442 US 62, 99 SCt 2132, 60 LEd2d 713 (1979), which held that the *Bruton* rule did not apply when the defendant had himself confessed and his confession "interlocked" with the incriminating confession of a codefendant. But see *State v. Graham,* 129 Or App 111, 877 P2d 1225, rev denied 320 Or 131, 881 P2d 815 (1994) (finding harmless error where court admitted in a joint trial a codefendant's confession that also implicated defendant; court held any error to be harmless because the defendant's own confession was introduced, which stated essentially the same facts).

In *Richardson v. Marsh,* 481 US 200, 107 SCt 1702, 95 LEd2d 176 (1987), the Court held that the rule of *Bruton* is not violated when the confession of a co-defendant is offered in redacted form to omit any reference to the defendant and the jury is instructed not to consider the confession against the defendant, even though the defendant might nonetheless be linked to the confession by evidence properly admitted against him at trial.

Confrontation and Privileges

In some cases, the constitutional rights of confrontation and compulsory process may prevail over evidentiary privileges. For a listing of cases from other jurisdictions, see Mueller & Kirkpatrick, MODERN EVIDENCE § 5.5 (1995).

In *State v. Quintero*, 110 Or App 247, 253–4, 823 P2d 981, 984–5 (1991), rev denied 314 Or 392, 840 P2d 710 (1992), the appellate court approved a holding of the trial court that the defendants' confrontation rights were superior to the spousal privilege of a codefendant's wife. Therefore, in order to protect the confrontation right, the court overrode the wife's claim of statutory privilege and required her to give testimony supporting the theory of the codefendants that her husband played a leading role in the conduct giving rise to the assault and attempted murder charges. However, the court instructed the jury that her testimony not be considered as evidence against her own husband.

Discovery

The constitutional right of criminal defendants to confront and cross-examine witnesses does not necessarily create an expanded right to discovery. In *Pennsylvania v. Ritchie*, 480 US 39, 107 SCt 989, 94 LEd2d 40 (1987), the Court held that the fact that the defendant was not allowed pretrial discovery of the records of the Youth Services Agency for purposes of examining a prosecution witness did not violate his Sixth Amendment right of confrontation.

In *State v. Rood*, 118 Or App 480, 483, 848 P2d 128, rev denied 317 Or 272, 858 P2d 1314 (1993), the court held that the right of confrontation does not guarantee a right to call an alleged sex crime victim as a witness prior to trial to detemine if the victim would recant earlier accusations made against another person.

RULE 803. ORS 40.460. HEARSAY EXCEPTION; AVAILABILITY OF DECLARANT IMMATERIAL

The following are not excluded by Rule 802 (ORS 40.455), even though the declarant is available as a witness:
(1) [Reserved.]

LEGISLATIVE COMMENTARY

Oregon Rule of Evidence 803 is a list of 23 specific exceptions and one general exception to the hearsay rule, which apply whether or not the declarant is available as a witness. The hearsay rule is stated in ORE 802. "Declarant" is defined in ORE 801(2). Rule 803 is identical to Rule 803 of the Federal Rules of Evidence, except that subsections (1) and (18), relating to present sense impressions and learned treatises, have been omitted; subsection (22), relating to judgments of previous conviction, has been amended; and a new subsection (18a) has been added, relating to complaints of sexual misconduct.

The exceptions to the rule against admissibility of hearsay evidence set forth in this rule are phrased in negative terms of nonapplication of the hearsay rule, rather than in positive terms of admissibility. This is done to repel any implication that other grounds for excluding the evidence are eliminated from consideration.

Rule 803 proceeds upon the theory that a hearsay statement may possess such circumstantial guaranties of trustworthiness that the declarant need not be produced at the trial even though the declarant may be available. The theory finds vast support in the many exceptions to the hearsay rule developed by the common law in which unavailability was not a relevant factor. This rule is a synthesis of those exceptions, revised where modern developments have made that course appropriate.

Even with hearsay the declarant is still a witness, of course, and neither this rule nor Rule 804 dispense with the requirement of firsthand knowledge. See ORE 602. Such knowledge may appear from the statement or be inferred from circumstances.

Subsection (1). Certain of the federal hearsay exceptions were not adopted by the Legislative Assembly. One of these is the "present sense impression" exception. Fed R Evid 803(1). This exception allows the admission of a statement describing an event or condition if the statement was made while the declarant was perceiving the event or condition, or immediately thereafter.

Although similar to the "excited utterance" exception to the hearsay rule, which the Legislative Assembly did adopt, the exception for "present sense impression" does not require the statement in question to have been made under a condition of emotional excitement; nor, as stated in Federal Rule 803 does it require strict contemporaneity of statement and event. In permitting use of a statement made after the event, albeit soon after, the federal rule expands the scope of this exception beyond that given by the few jurisdictions which recognize it.

An example of the operation of the "present sense impression" exception to the hearsay rule is found in *Houston Oxygen Co., Inc. v. Davis,* 139 Tex 1, 161 SW2d 474 (1942). Defendant offered testimony of a Mrs. Cooper that when plaintiff's car passed her about four miles before the accident, she said "they must have been drunk, [and] we would find them somewhere on the road wrecked if they kept that rate of speed up." Objection to the testimony concerning the remark was sustained. The Texas Supreme Court reversed. The statement was held to be "sufficiently spontaneous to save it from the suspicion of being manufactured evidence. There was no time for a calculated statement." 161 SW2d at 476.

Although strong arguments have been made in support of this exception, McCormick *Evidence* § 298 (2d ed 1972), the Legislative Assembly believes that the exception is so broad as to allow the admission of practically every unexcited declaration made at or near the scene and time of an event, and that those declarations lack whatever assurance of reliability there is in the effect of an exciting event.

Although the Oregon Supreme Court has approved, under the cover of *res gestae,* the admission into evidence of a statement made contemporaneously with an unexciting event, *Hornschuch v. Southern Pacific Co.,* 101 Or 280, 203 P 886 (1921), it cannot be said that Oregon recognizes a "present sense impression" exception to the hearsay rule. Therefore, the rejection of that exception by the Legislative Assembly marks no change in Oregon law.

TEXT

Introduction

Rule 803 sets forth 23 exceptions to the hearsay rule that are applicable even though the declarant is available as a witness. Rule 804 sets forth six additional exceptions that may be used only when the declarant is unavailable. Rule 803 is carefully phrased to state only that the statement is not excluded by the hearsay rule if it fits one of the 23 listed exceptions. The rule does not guarantee admissibility, because the evidence may nonetheless be excluded by some other rule, law, or constitutional provision. Rule 403 would appear applicable to evidence falling within a hearsay exception. Thus, a court may exclude evidence within a hearsay exception if its probative value is substantially outweighed by the dangers of unfair prejudice, confusion of the issues or misleading the jury, or by considerations of undue delay or needless presentation of cumulative evidence.

There are some statutory exceptions to the hearsay rule outside Rules 803 and 804. See, e.g., ORS 167.027(1) ("On the issue of whether a place is a place of prostitution as defined in ORS 167.002, its general repute and repute of persons who reside in or frequent the place shall be competent evidence.").

Most of Rule 803 is identical to FRE 803. Subsections (1) and (18)—the exceptions for present sense impressions and learned treatises—were omitted. FRE 803(1) creates a hearsay exception for:

> A statement describing or explaining an event or condition made while the declarant was perceiving the event or condition or immediately thereafter.

FRE 803(18) creates a hearsay exception for:

> To the extent called to the attention of an expert witness upon cross-examination or relied upon by him in direct examination, statements contained in published treatises, periodicals, or pamphlets on a subject of history, medicine, or other science or art, established as a reliable authority by the testimony or admission of the witness or by other expert testimony or by judicial notice. If admitted the statements may be read into evidence but may not be received as exhibits.

In addition, subsection (18a) was modified by adding (18a)(a) and (18a)(b), relating to complaints of sexual misconduct.

Learned Treatises

In a note following the Commentary to Rule 18a, the reason for not adopting FRE 803(18) is explained as follows:

> NOTE: The Legislative Assembly did not adopt the federal hearsay exception for learned treatises which appears as subsection (18) of Fed R Evid 803. It wishes to retain the Oregon practice of using treatises in the cross-examination of expert witnesses. Learned treatises should not be admitted as substantive

evidence as they are likely to be misunderstood and misapplied in the absence of expert assistance and supervision.

This explanation is somewhat puzzling, because FRE 803(18) expressly requires that an expert witness be on the stand subject to examination before a statement in a learned treatise may be introduced.

Although the omission of FRE 803(18) means that statements in treatises cannot be received for their truth, they still may be used to impeach the testimony of an expert witness. For a discussion of the use of treatises as a mode of impeachment of expert witnesses, see the textual discussion under Rules 607 and 702.

In *Travis v. Unruh,* 66 Or App 562, 674 P2d 1192, rev denied 297 Or 82, 679 P2d 1367 (1984), the court held it was error for the trial court to allow the plaintiff's expert to summarize a study in a medical journal. The court held that treatises or authoritative articles can be used for impeachment only.

See generally ANNOT., *Treatises, Periodicals or Pamphlets as Exception to Hearsay Rule Under Rule 803(18) of the Federal Rules of Evidence,* 64 ALR Fed 971 (1983); Heckert, *Use of Learned Treatises at Trial,* 28 Trial Law Guide 165 (1984).

Res Gestae Doctrine Abolished

There is an unfortunate reference in the Commentary to an earlier Oregon case, *Hornschuch v. Pac. Co.,* 101 Or 280, 203 P 886 (1921), where the court allowed into evidence a statement made contemporaneously with an unexciting event under the doctrine of res gestae. This reference should not be construed to indicate legislative approval of the discredited doctrine of res gestae. The term res gestae is carefully avoided in the Oregon Evidence Code. It is a common-law doctrine that created considerable confusion because it encompassed multiple concepts. The doctrine overlapped with several independent exceptions to the hearsay rule and even included statements which were not hearsay. See Morgan, *A Suggested Classification of Utterances Admissible As Res Gestae,* 31 Yale L J 229 (1922); 2 McCormick, EVIDENCE (4th ed 1992) § 268; Oregon State Bar Continuing Legal Education, EVIDENCE (1986) § 42.16. Reference to the doctrine of res gestae is improper and should not be used with respect to cases tried under the Oregon Evidence Code. See Legislative Commentary to Rule 802 ("[T]he Legislative Assembly intends that hearsay only be admitted pursuant to some statutory or constitutional authority").

RULE 803. ORS 40.460. HEARSAY EXCEPTION; AVAILABILITY OF DECLARANT IMMATERIAL

The following are not excluded by Rule 802 (ORS 40.455), even though the declarant is available as a witness:

(2) **[Excited Utterance]. A statement relating to a startling event or condition made while the declarant was under the stress of excitement caused by the event or condition.**

LEGISLATIVE COMMENTARY

Subsection (2). Hearsay exclusion policies do not apply if there is a condition of excitement which temporarily stills the capacity for reflection and produces utterances free of conscious fabrication. 6 Wigmore, *Evidence* § 1747 at 135 (3d ed 1940). This is the theoretical basis for the "excited utterance" exception to the hearsay rule set forth in subsection (2). Oregon law recognizes the exception, and bases it on the same conditions as Rule 803(2). The key factor in determining whether an utterance is "excited," and therefore qualifies under the exception, is the degree to which it is spontaneous.

While the theory of this subsection has been criticized on the ground that excitement impairs accuracy of observation even as it eliminates fabrication, Hutchins and Slesinger, *Some Observations on the Law of Evidence: Spontaneous Exclamations,* in 28 Colum L Rev 432 (1928), the exception finds support in numerous cases. See cases in 6 Wigmore § 1750; ANNOT., *Statements as to Cause of or Responsibility for Motor Vehicle Accident,* 53 ALR 2d 1245; ANNOT., *"Accusatory Statements by Homicide Victims,"* 4 ALR 3d 149.

With respect to contemporaneity of event and utterance, the standard of measurement under this exception is the duration of the state of excitement. "How long can excitement prevail? Obviously there are no pat answers and the character of the transaction or event will largely determine the significance of the time factor." Slough, *Spontaneous Statements and State of Mind,* in 46 Iowa L Rev 224, 243 (1961); McCormick § 297 at 706. Recent Oregon case law indicates that the time interval is one of the most important factors in determining spontaneity, particularly if there is evidence that the declarant engaged in reflective thought during the interval. *Zeller v. Dahl,* 262 Or 515, 499 P2d 1316 (1972).

Participation in the event by the declarant is not required. An onlooker may be moved to describe the object of perception. One may be startled by an event even though not an actor in it. Slough, supra; McCormick § 297 at 706; 6 Wigmore § 1755; ANNOT., 78 ALR 2d 300; *Wright v. Swann,* 261 Or 440, 493 P2d 148, 50 ALR 3d 706 (1972); *State v. Wilson,* 20 Or App 553, 532 P2d 825 (1975). A bystander need not be identified for the bystander's statements to be admissible. *Wright v. Swann,* supra.

Whether proof of the starting event may be made by the statement itself is largely an academic question, as usually there is at least circumstantial evidence that something of a startling nature must have occurred. For cases in which the evidence consists of the condition of the declarant, e.g., injuries or state of shock, see *Insurance Co. v. Mosely,* 75 US (8 Wall) 397, 19 L Ed 437 (1869); *Wheeler v. United States,* 211 F2d 19 (DC Cir 1953), *cert denied,* 347 US 1019, 74 S Ct 876, 98 L Ed 1140 (1954); *Wetherbee v. Safety Casualty Co.,* 219 F2d 274 (5th Cir 1955); *Lampe v. United States,* 229 F2d 43 (DC Cir 1956). Nevertheless, on occasion the only evidence may be the content of the statement itself. Rulings that it may be sufficient are described as "increasing," Slough, supra at 246, and as "the prevailing practice," McCormick § 297 at 705. Illustrative are *Armour & Co. v. Industrial Commission,* 78 Colo 569, 243 P 546 (1926) and *Young v. Stewart,* 191 NC 297, 131 SE 735 (1926). Note that under Rule 104 the trial judge is not limited by the hearsay rule in passing upon preliminary questions of fact.

Under the "excited utterance" exception, the declarant's statement need only "relate" to the startling event or condition, thus affording a broad scope of subject matter. 6 Wigmore §§ 1750, 1754; Quick, *Hearsay, Excitement, Necessity and the Uniform Rules. A Reappraisal of Rule 63(4),* in 6 Wayne L Rev 204, 206–9 (1960).

TEXT

Excited Utterance

Rule 803(2) establishes a hearsay exception for "a statement relating to a startling event or condition made while the declarant was under the stress of excitement caused by the event or condition." Three requirements must be satisfied: (1) a startling event or condition must have occurred, (2) a statement must have been made while the declarant was under the stress of excitement caused by the event or condition, and (3) the statement must relate to the startling event or condition. The determination of whether these requirements are satisfied is an issue for the court under Rule 104(1). It has been held that the trial court is given considerable discretion in determining whether a hearsay statement is admissible as an excited utterance. *Vander Veer v. Toyota Motor Distrib., Inc.,* 282 Or 135, 577 P2d 1343 (1978).

The rationale underlying the excited utterance exception is that

[t]he utterance is really an effusion. Being spontaneous in nature the declaration is free from the elements of design, contrivance and self-service which at times color testimony given from the witness stand. The credibility of a declaration of that kind is not dependent solely upon the veracity of the declarant. The pain, excitement or horror of the event had stilled the powers of reflection and had enabled the event itself to speak through the tongue of the declarant. It is the startling event rather than the will of the declarant that propelled his tongue. If one who sought the truth were required to make a choice between the spontaneous declaration and the testimony under oath of the declarant he possibly would choose the former. The circumstances under which the spontaneous declaration was made commend it as a reliable index to the truth. (*State v. Hutchison,* 222 Or 533, 537, 353 P2d 1047,1049 (1960).)

In determining whether or not a statement was an excited utterance, the court should consider not only the lapse of time between the event and the statement, but also the nature of the event, the condition of the declarant, and the spontaneity of the statement. A statement is not admissible as an excited utterance if it was the result of reflective thought. *Zeller v. Dahl,* 262 Or 515, 519, 499 P2d 1316, 1318 (1972).

An excited utterance is admissible even if made by a bystander rather than a party, and even if the declarant is unidentified. *Wright v. Swann*, 261 Or 440, 493 P2d 148 (1972). A statement made in response to a question may be admissible, although this fact should be considered in determining whether the response was the result of reflective thought. *Bosin v. Oak Lodge Sanitary Dist. No. 1*, 251 Or 554, 564, 447 P2d 285, 290 (1968); *State v. Crawley*, 242 Or 601, 410 P2d 1012 (1966). An excited utterance is admissible even though self-serving and offered by the testimony of a party. *Wright v. Swann*, supra.

The permissible lapse of time between the event and the statement for the statement to qualify as an excited utterance must be determined on a case-by-case basis considering all relevant circumstances surrounding the making of the statement. The existence of shock, pain, or temporary unconsciousness on the part of the declarant may all bear on the length of time allowed between the event and the statement. See *United States v. Knife*, 592 F2d 472 (8th Cir 1979) (statements several days after shooting not excited utterance); *United States v. Moss*, 544 F2d 954 (8th Cir 1976), cert denied 429 US 1077 (1977) (statements several hours after bank robbery not excited utterance); *Vander Veer v. Toyota Motor Distrib., Inc.*, 282 Or 135, 577 P2d 1343 (1978) (statements one hour after accident held not to be excited utterance); *United States v. Iron Shell*, 633 F2d 77 (8th Cir 1980), cert denied 450 US 1001 (1981) (statements to police regarding assault 45 to 75 minutes after event held to be excited utterance); *State v. Hawkins*, 49 Or App 1065, 621 P2d 660 (1980) (statements 20 minutes after sexual assault held to be excited utterance); *Garcia v. Watkins*, 604 F2d 1297 (10th Cir 1979) (statement more than one hour after event may be excited utterance; question remanded); *State v. Mahoney*, 33 Or App 73, 575 P2d 681 (1978) (statement made over an hour after assault not admissible as excited utterance); *State v. Jones*, 27 Or App 767, 557 P2d 264 (1976) (telephone call to police 20 minutes to 1½ hours after rape admissible as excited utterance). See generally, ANNOT., *When Is Hearsay Statement An "Excited Utterance" Admissible Under Rule 803(2) of the Federal Rules of Evidence*, 48 ALR Fed 451 (1980).

The Commentary adopts the view of McCormick that the "prevailing practice" is to allow the existence of the startling event to be proven by the statement itself. McCormick, EVIDENCE (3d ed 1984) § 297 at 854–5. In *State v. Jones*, 27 Or App 767, 557 P2d 264 (1976), the court allowed the statement itself to be used to prove that it was made in a state of excitement.

The hearsay statement must "relate" to this startling event. The following cases from the Advisory Committee's Note to FRE 803(2) indicate what was contemplated by the term "relate":

> See *Sanitary Grocery Co. v. Snead*, 67 App. D.C. 129, 90 F.2d 374 (1937), slip-and-fall case sustaining admissibility of clerk's statement, "That has been on the floor for a couple of hours," and *Murphy Auto Parts Co., Inc. v. Ball*, 101 U.S. App. D.C. 416, 249 F.2d 508 (1957), upholding admission, on issue of driver's agency, of his statement that he had to call on a customer and was in a hurry to get home.

Most courts hold that an excited utterance of a declarant is admissible even in circumstances where the declarant is incompetent to testify as a witness in court. See ANNOT., *Admissibility of Testimony Regarding Spontaneous Declarations Made by One Incompetent to Testify at Trial,* 15 ALR 4th 1043 (1982).

Recent Cases

State v. Moen, 309 Or 45, 59–60, 786 P2d 111 (1990). The the court commented in dicta that a statement by a mother-in-law to a doctor treating her for depression that she feared her son-in-law might kill both her and her daughter was admissible under Rule 803(2) (after previously ruling the statement was admissible under Rule 803(4)). The mother-in-law was in a state of agitation and anxiety at the time the statement was made. The opinion is unclear regarding the precise lapse of time between the events causing the stress and the statement to the doctor.

State v. Wolfs, 119 Or App 262, 266, 850 P2d 1139, rev denied 317 Or 163, 856 P2d 318 (1993). The court held that statements by the defendant's wife to police dispatchers and a responding officer that the defendant had a gun pointed at his head and had fired one shot were admissible as excited utterances. The court found that the statements were made while the wife was still under the excitement of the event and in fear for her husband's safety.

State v. Carlson, 311 Or 201, 215–9, 808 P2d 1002 (1991). The defendant was convicted of unlawful possession of methamphetamine. While being questioned by police regarding needle marks on his arm, he stated that the marks were injuries he received from working on a car. His wife broke into the interrogation, stating, "You liar, you got them from shooting up in the bedroom with all your stupid friends." The court upheld the admission of this statement as an excited utterance. The court held that the husband's falsehood was a sufficiently "startling event" under the circumstances of the case to support admission of the wife's statement as an excited utterance. The court found evidence sufficient to support a finding that the wife's accusatory statement was made while she was under the stress of excitement caused by the event and that her statement related to the event. Therefore, it was admissible under Rule 803(2).

State v. Jensen, 107 Or App 35, 810 P2d 865 (1991), aff'd 313 Or 587, 837 P2d 525 (1993). A statement made by a child to a nurse ninety minutes after his injuries regarding the cause of his injuries was held to qualify as an excited utterance.

State v. Maco, 67 Or App 753, 681 P2d 140, rev denied 297 Or 339, 683 P2d 1370 (1984). The court held that statements made by a four-year-old girl to her mother accusing the defendant of sexual abuse were admissible as excited utterances. The statements were made shortly after the mother returned home where she had left the defendant babysitting with the child. The court found that "[l]ess than two hours had elapsed between the event and the statement, and it was the first opportunity for the child to complain. There is no indication that she had had an opportunity, reason or ability to fabricate." 670 Or App at 758. The court further found that the evidence did not violate the defendant's right of confron-

515

tation, because the evidence was trustworthy and fit a well-recognized exception to the hearsay rule.

State v. Hollywood, 67 Or App 546, 680 P2d 655 (1984), rev denied 298 Or 553, 695 P2d 49 (1985). The court found that statements by a four-year-old girl to her grandmother, accusing the defendant of rape, were not shown to have been made sufficiently contemporaneously with the event to qualify for admission as excited utterances.

State v. Tucker, 86 Or App 413, 740 P2d 182 (1987), vacated on other grounds 305 Or 43, 749 P2d 576, on remand 90 Or App 506, 753 P2d 427 (1988), aff'd 307 Or 386, 768 P2d 397 (1989), the court held that hearsay statements of a murder victim identifying a car as belonging to persons who had previously threatened him were not admissible under Rule 803(2), because the event that precipitated the statements was not startling.

RULE 803. ORS 40.460. HEARSAY EXCEPTION; AVAILABILITY OF DECLARANT IMMATERIAL

The following are not excluded by Rule 802 (ORS 40.455), even though the declarant is available as a witness:

(3) [Then existing mental, emotional or physical condition.] A statement of the declarant's then existing state of mind, emotion, sensation or physical condition, such as intent, plan, motive, design, mental feeling, pain or bodily health, but not including a statement of memory or belief to prove the fact remembered or believed unless it relates to the execution, revocation, identification, or terms of the declarant's will.

LEGISLATIVE COMMENTARY

Subsection (3). Related to the present sense impression, but having a different emphasis on the mental or physical condition of the declarant, the hearsay exceptions or statements of state of mind or body is well established in Oregon law. *State v. Wright,* 12 Or App 73, 504 P2d 1065 (1973); *State v. McCauley,* 8 Or App 571, 494 P2d 438 (1972); *State v. Shirley,* 7 Or App 166, 488 P2d 1401 (1971).

The subsection excludes statements of memory or belief, to prove the fact remembered or believed. This exclusion from the exception is necessary to avoid the virtual destruction of the hearsay rule. Otherwise, state of mind provable by a hearsay statement, could serve as the basis for an inference of the happening of the event which produced the state of mind. Maguire, *The Hillmon Case—Thirty-three Years After,* in 38 Harv L Rev 709, 719–731 (1925); Hinton, *State of Mind and the Hearsay Rule,* 1 U Chi L Rev 394, 421–3 (1934). The exclusion is consistent with current Oregon law.

Timber Access Indus. v. U.S. Plywood-Champion Papers, Inc., 263 Or 509, 503 P2d 482 (1972); *In re Bond,* 172 Or 509, 143 P2d 244 (1943).

The carving out, from the exclusion for statements of memory or belief, of statements relating to the declarant's will represents an ad hoc judgment appealing to expediency rather than logic. McCormick § 296 at 702–3. There is ample recognition in statute and case law of the need for and practical value of this kind of evidence. California Evidence Code § 1260; Annot., 34 ALR 2d 588, ANNOT., 62 ALR 2d 855.

With regard to the use, under subsection (3), of a declaration to prove an act on the part of a person other than the declarant when that act is itself an important issue in the case, the Legislative Assembly adopts the reasoning of the dissenting opinion by Justice Traynor in *People v. Alcalde,* 24 Cal 2d 177, 148 P2d 627, 633 (1944):

> "It is my opinion that the trial court erred in admitting the testimony that the deceased said ... that she was going out with 'Frank' [the evening of her murder] ... A declaration of intention is admissible to show that the declarant did the intended act .... A declaration as to what one person intended to do, however, cannot safely be accepted as evidence of what another probably did .... The declaration of the deceased in this case that she was going out with Frank is also a declaration that he was going out with her, and it could not be admitted for the limited purpose of showing that she went out with him at the time in question without necessarily showing that he went out with her."

In approving this, the Legislative Assembly intends to limit the doctrine of *Mutual Life Insurance Co. v. Hillmon,* 145 US 285, 295–300, 12 S Ct 909, 36 L Ed 706 (1892), so as to render statements of intent by a declarant admissible only to prove the declarant's future conduct, not the future conduct of another person. *State v. Farnam,* 82 Or 211, 161 P 417 (1916), which accepted the *Hillmon* doctrine, is overruled to this extent.

TEXT

Then Existing Mental, Emotional, or Physical Condition

Rule 803(3) allows as exceptions to the hearsay rule the following types of statements: (1) statements of an existing physical condition to prove the declarant's physical condition at the time the statements were made; (2) statements of existing mental or emotional condition to prove the mental or emotional condition of the declarant at the time the statements were made; (3) statements of mental or emotional condition or state of mind, including intent, plan, motive, or design, to prove subsequent conduct in accordance with that state of mind or mental or emotional condition; and (4) statements of memory or belief to prove the fact remembered or believed when it relates to the execution, revocation, identification, or terms of the declarant's will.

Statements reflecting the declarant's state of mind often will be admissible apart from this exception because they do not constitute hearsay under Rule 801(3). For example, a statement by an allegedly mentally ill person that "I am

Napoleon" may be admitted as not hearsay by many courts because it is not being offered to prove the truth of the statement, only to prove that the declarant is suffering from an insane delusion. It is admitted as circumstantial evidence of the declarant's state of mind. A direct statement of belief, such as "I believe I am Napoleon," is more likely to be viewed as hearsay because it is offered to prove the truth of the declarant's belief. See C. Mueller & L. Kirkpatrick, MODERN EVIDENCE (1995) § 8.20. It would be admissible, however, under Rule 803(3).

Commentators disagree about whether statements that constitute circumstantial evidence rather than direct evidence of the declarant's state of mind are hearsay. See 2 M. Graham HANDBOOK OF FEDERAL EVIDENCE (4th ed 1969) § 801.6 at 234–8; 2 McCormick, EVIDENCE (4th ed 1992) § 249 at 101; 4 J. Weinstein and M. Berger, WEINSTEIN'S EVIDENCE (1988) 803(3) [02]. The issue has little practical significance. If hearsay, the statements will nonetheless be admissible under the state-of-mind exception.

An important qualification to this hearsay exception is that the exception does not authorize admission of a statement of memory or belief to prove the fact remembered or believed, except in the relatively limited circumstance where it relates to the execution, revocation, identification, or terms of the declarant's will. As Justice Cardozo stated in *Shepard v. United States*, 290 US 96, 105–6, 54 SCt 22, 26, 78 LEd2d 196, 202 (1933), "[d]eclarations of intention, casting light upon the future, have been sharply distinguished from declarations of memory, pointing backwards to the past. There would be an end, or nearly that to the rule against hearsay if the distinction were ignored."

If a statement about the declarant's state of mind is offered to prove the past events that caused that state of mind, the statement is not admissible under this exception. For example, evidence that a murder victim made a statement expressing fear of the defendant is inadmissible if it is being offered merely to prove the occurrence of prior acts by the defendant causing that fear. See, e.g., *State v. Charo*, 754 P2d 288 (Ariz 1988); *State v. Blanchard*, 315 NW2d 427, 432 (Minn 1982). See also *Prather v. Prather*, 650 F2d 88 (5th Cir 1981) (statement by plaintiff to others that plaintiff was working for defendant for $1000 per month was hearsay and improperly admitted to show plaintiff's "state of mind"; the real purpose of such evidence was to prove the matter asserted); *United States v. Cohen*, 631 F2d 1223 (5th Cir 1980) (declarant's statements of fear admissible, but not a description of the past acts causing the fear); *State v. Parr*, 93 Wash 2d 95, 606 P2d 263 (1980) (improper to admit evidence of threats made to murder victim as part of proof of her fearful state of mind).

The problem with admitting a victim's statement that the victim is fearful of the defendant or a third person is that the victim's state of mind is not a relevant issue in a murder prosecution. The statement generally has relevance only to show that the person feared was the assailant or that the person did something to make the victim fearful. Thus, the purpose for which the statement has relevance is not the usage allowed by Rule 803(3), which expressly excludes a "statement of memory or belief to prove the fact remembered or believed."

In *State v. Mendez*, 308 Or 9, 774 P2d 1087 (1989), the defendant claimed error in the exclusion of a statement by the murder victim two weeks prior to his death that he feared a third person, Moen, would kill him. The evidence was offered to show that someone other than the defendant had an equal motive to kill the victim, which tended to undercut the prosecution's theory that defendant was the murderer. The court held that to the extent the statement was offered to prove the truth of the matter asserted, i.e., that Moen wanted to kill the victim, the statement was relevant, but the court also held that such usage of the statement was hearsay and did not qualify for admission under Rule 803(3) or any other exception. But see *State v. Brown*, 310 Or 347, 800 P2d 259 (1990) (admitting victim's statement of fear).

A statement admitted to show the declarant's state of mind, emotion, sensation, or physical condition may also contain an assertion regarding other facts. A limiting instruction under Rule 105 may be necessary to prevent the jury from considering the statement for the truth of the factual assertion contained within it. In some cases the factual assertion contained within an otherwise admissible statement offered to show the declarant's state of mind may be so prejudicial or likely to confuse the issues or mislead the jury that exclusion will be required under Rule 403. See *United States v. Brown*, 490 F2d 758, 773, 774 (DC Cir 1973); *State v. Parr*, 93 Wash2d 95, 606 P2d 263 (1980).

Intent to Prove Future Conduct

Evidence of intent is admissible under this hearsay exception for two purposes. The state of mind or intent of the declarant may itself be a relevant issue. For example, in a civil case involving domicile, or a criminal case where specific intent must be shown, the declarant's state of mind or intent will be relevant. Evidence of intent may also be offered to prove future conduct in accordance with that intent. The leading case is *Mutual Life Ins. Co. v. Hillmon*, 145 US 285, 12 SCt 909, 36 LEd 706 (1892), which involved claims against a life insurance policy of Hillmon by the beneficiary. The beneficiary contended that a body found at Crooked Creek, Kansas, in 1879 was Hillmon's. The insurance company claimed that the body was that of a man named Walters, who was allegedly accompanying Hillmon at the time. The trial court excluded letters offered by the insurance company from Walters to his sister and fiancee indicating an intent to take a trip with Hillmon. The Supreme Court reversed, holding that

> [t]he letters in question were competent, not as narratives of facts communicated to the writer by others, nor yet as proof that he actually went away from Wichita, but as evidence that, shortly before the time when other evidence tended to show that he went away, he had the intention of going, and of going with Hillmon, which made it more probable both that he did go and that he went with Hillmon, than if there had been no proof of such intention. (*Hillmon*, 145 US at 295–6, 12 SCt at 912–13, 36 LEd at 710)

Walters' statement of intent to take the trip was admitted not only to show that he did go, but also to show "that he went with Hillmon." The Commentary to Rule 803(3) states that the legislature intends to limit *Hillmon* "so as to render statements of intent by a declarant admissible only to prove the declarant's future conduct, not the future conduct of another person." See *Holmes v. Morgan*, 135 Or App 617, 626, 899 P2d 738 (1995) (decedent's statements that he was going to commit suicide and that he was going to change the beneficiary on his insurance were admissible, but statements that he was doing so because defendant had agreed to help him were not).

Some other states have allowed a statement of intent to prove the conduct of a third person. See, e.g., *State v. Via*, 146 Ariz 108, 704 P2d 238 (1985), cert denied 475 US 1048 (1986) (note from murder victim indicating time and place he agreed to meet with defendant admissible to prove defendant was person he met); *State v. Terrovona*, 105 Wash 2d 632, 716 P2d 295 (1986) (declarant's statement of intent to do a future act, which necessarily involves the future conduct of another person, is sufficiently trustworthy proof of the future conduct of both the declarant and the third person). See generally Weissenberger, *Hearsay Puzzles: An Essay on Federal Evidence Rule 803(3)*, 64 Temple L Rev 145 (1991); McFarland, *Dead Men Tell Tale:. Thirty Times Three Years of the Judicial Process After Hillmon*, 30 Vill L Rev 1 (1985); NOTE, *Federal Rule of Evidence 803(3) and the Criminal Defendant: The Limits of the Hillmon Doctrine*, 35 Vand L Rev 659 (1982); COMMENT, *One Person's Thoughts, Another Person's Acts: How the Federal Circuit Courts Interpret the Hillmon Doctrine*, 33 Cath U L Rev 699 (1984).

Evidence of state of mind to prove likely future conduct of the declarant was admitted in *State v. Engwiler*, 118 Or App 132, 135, 846 P2d 1163, rev denied 317 Or 486, 858 P2d 876 (1993). The defendant was charged with murder, rape, and sodomy. The state offered evidence that the victim had made statements prior to her death that she did not like the defendant anymore and "didn't want to have anything to do with him." Such evidence was offered to show lack of consent by the victim. The court held such evidence admissible under OEC 803(3) to prove the victim's likely future conduct, i.e., that she did not consent to sexual contact with the defendant. Although the defendant argued that such evidence of the victim's mental state was inadmissible to infer his future conduct, the court held that statements of future intent "are not rendered inadmissible merely because they also tend to suggest something about defendant's conduct."

For an example of a case allowing evidence of intent to prove future conduct under the Federal Rules of Evidence, see *United States v. Calvert*, 523 F2d 895, 910 (8th Cir 1975), cert denied 424 US 911 (1976) (a murder victim's statement that he intended to speak to the defendant about ending their partnership was admissible under Rule 803(3) as evidence that he probably carried out his intent and therefore provided the defendant with the motive for the murder). See also ANNOT., *Exception to Hearsay Rule, Under Rule 803(3) of Federal Rules of Evidence, With Respect to Statement of Declarant's Mental, Emotional, or Physical Condition*, 75 ALR Fed 170 (1985).

Evidence of threats, even though not communicated to the intended victim, may be admissible under this exception to prove future conduct in accordance with the hostile state of mind. See ANNOT., *Admissibility of Evidence of Uncommunicated Threats on Issue of Self-Defense in Prosecution for Homicide*, 98 ALR2d 6 (1964); ANNOT., *Admissibility of Evidence of Uncommunicated Threats on Issue of Self-Defense in Prosecution for Assault*, 98 ALR2d 195 (1964).

Other Uses

The state-of-mind exception has sometimes been cited as a basis for the admission of public opinion surveys or polls. See *Randy's Studebaker Sales, Inc. v. Nissan Motor Corp.,* 533 F2d 510 (10th Cir 1976). For a discussion of the admissibility of evidence of surveys or polls, see textual discussion of Rule 703.

The last phrase in Rule 803(3), allowing statements of memory or belief to prove the fact remembered or believed when it relates to the execution, revocation, identification, or terms of the declarant's will has been justified by McCormick as follows:

> Impetus to recognize such an exception is furnished by the unavailability of the person who best knew the facts and often was the only person with that knowledge, viz. the testator. Special reliability is suggested by the undeniable firsthand knowledge and lack of motive to deceive, though the possibility may exist that the testator wished to deceive his relatives. 2 McCormick, EVIDENCE (4th ed 1992) § 276 at 241.

On the rationale for admitting hearsay statements of memory or belief in will cases, see also *Timber Access Industries Co. v. U.S. Plywood/Champion Papers, Inc.,* 263 Or 509, 518, 503 P2d 482 (1972).

Recent Cases

In *State v. Batty,* 109 Or App 62, 69, 819 P2d 732, 736 (1991), rev denied 312 Or 588, 824 P2d 417 (1992), a murder prosecution, the defendant offered the testimony of his mother that defendant said in a telephone conversation that "he loved the victim and that he was going to try to protect her." Even though this statement was hearsay when offered by the defendant, it was properly admitted to show the defendant's state of mind under Rule 803(3). However, other statements by the defendant to his mother describing a murder plot were not admissible under the state of mind exception. Out-of-court statements by the defendant suggesting fear were held not admissible, because fear was not a fact of consequence to the determination of the action under Rule 401.

In *State v. Beaty,* 127 Or App 448, 454, 873 P2d 385, 387 (1994), rev denied 319 Or 406, 879 P2d 1285 (1994), a child sexual abuse prosecution, the trial court properly excluded evidence that a CSD worker would testify that G told him about statements that G heard the mother and child victim make about hearing voices that no one else could hear. Even if the child's statements themselves would qualify under the state of mind exception, there was no hearsay exception for G's reporting of the statements to the CSD worker. When multiple hearsay is involved, each level must satisfy a hearsay exception. Moreover, statements by the mother about her state of mind were not admissible to establish the child's state of mind.

Rule 803(3) was cited as a basis for admission of evidence in *State v. Wood,* 67 Or App 218, 678 P2d 1238, rev denied 297 Or 124, 681 P2d 134 (1984); *State v. Benson,* 63 Or App 467, 471, 664 P2d 1127, 1129–30, rev denied 295 Or 730, 670 P2d 1035 (1983).

RULE 803. ORS 40.460. HEARSAY EXCEPTION; AVAILABILITY OF DECLARANT IMMATERIAL

The following are not excluded by Rule 802 (ORS 40.455), even though the declarant is available as a witness:

(4) [Statements for purposes of medical diagnosis or treatment.] Statements made for purposes of medical diagnosis or treatment and describing medical history, or past or present symptoms, pain or sensations, or the inception or general character of the cause of [*sic*] external source thereof insofar as reasonably pertinent to diagnosis or treatment.

LEGISLATIVE COMMENTARY

Subsection (4). In this subsection, an exception to the hearsay rule is created for statements made for the purposes of medical diagnosis or treatment. Several changes to Oregon law result.

Even those few jurisdictions which have shied away from admitting statements of present condition generally, see ORE 803(3), supra, have allowed them if made to a person for the purpose of diagnosis or treatment in view of the declarant's strong motivation to be truthful. McCormick § 292 at 690. The guaranty of trustworthiness extends to statements of past condition made for the purpose of diagnosis or treatment, i.e., medical history, although until now Oregon courts have not accepted this. See *Reid v. Yellow Cab Co.,* 131 Or 27, 279 P 635 (1929). The guaranty also extends to statements regarding causation of a condition, if reasonably pertinent, in accord with the current trend. *Shell Oil Co. v. Industrial Commission,* 2 Ill 2d 590, 119 NE 2d 224 (1954); McCormick § 292 at 691, 692; New Jersey Evidence Rule 63(12)(c).

Statements as to fault ordinarily would not qualify under the language of this subsection. Thus, a statement that the declarant was struck by an automobile would not be excluded, as touching causation; a statement that the car was driven through a red light would, as touching fault.

This subsection does not require that statements be made to a physician to be admissible. Statements to hospital attendants, ambulance drivers or even members of the family or friends may be within the scope of the exception. No Oregon case has indicated that the scope of the Oregon exception for is this broad.

Oregon has been among the jurisdictions which exclude from the exception, as not within its guaranty of truthfulness, statements to a physician consulted only for the purpose of enabling the physician to testify. See *Henderson v. Union Pac. R.R.,* 189 Or 145, 219 P2d 170 (1950); *Reid v. Yellow Cab Co.,* supra. While these statements were not admissible as substantive evidence, the expert usually was allowed to state the basis of the expert's opinion and so reveal them. Juries were most unlikely to make the distinction. For this reason the Legislative Assembly abolished the limitation. Its position is consistent with ORE 703, providing that facts on which expert testimony is based need not be admissible in evidence if of a kind ordinarily relied upon by experts in the field.

This exception is not intended to affect adversely either present or future privilege rules.

TEXT

Statements for Purposes of Medical Diagnosis or Treatment

Rule 803(4) creates a hearsay exception for "[s]tatements made for purposes of medical diagnosis or treatment and describing medical history, or past or present symptoms, pain or sensations, or the inception or general character of the cause of [sic] external source thereof in so far as reasonably pertinent to diagnosis or treatment." The rationale underlying this exception is that the patient's desire for proper treatment or diagnosis outweighs any motive to falsify.

This exception broadens prior Oregon law. It allows statements made to physicians for purposes of medical diagnosis as well as medical treatment. It allows statements of past as well as present medical condition. It allows statements for the purpose of treatment or diagnosis even though made to a person other than a physician, such as a nurse, family member, or ambulance driver. It allows statements by persons other than the person who is the subject of the diagnosis or treatment. Finally, it authorizes receipt of statements concerning the general character or the cause of the injury "in so far as reasonably pertinent to diagnosis or treatment." See generally, ANNOT., *Admissibility of Statements Made for Purposes of Medical Diagnosis or Treatment as Hearsay Exception Under Rule 803(4) of the Federal Rules of Evidence,* 55 ALR Fed 689 (1981).

Some statements that may be received under this subsection may also be received under Rule 803(3). Statements of present mental, emotional, or physical condition made for purposes of treatment would be admissible under either rule.

One court has cautioned against use of this rule "to permit a doctor to testify to his patient's version of other doctors' opinions." See *O'Gee v. Dobbs Houses Inc.,* 570 F2d 1084, 1089 (2nd Cir 1978).

Requirements of Rule

To qualify for admissibility under this rule, it is not enough that the declarant made the statement with an intent to facilitate medical diagnosis or treatment. The statement must in fact be reasonably pertinent to diagnosis or treatment.

In *State v. Moen,* 309 Or 45, 54–65, 786 P2d 111 (1990), the court held that there are three requirements under Rule 803(4): (1) the statement must be made for the purpose of medical diagnosis or treatment; (2) it must describe medical history, current symptoms, or the cause or external source of the injury; and (3) the statement must be "reasonably pertinent" to treatment.

The leading federal case, *United States v. Iron Shell,* 633 F2d 77 (8th Cir 1980), cert denied 450 US 1001 (1981), establishes a two-part test for admissibility under FRE 803(4): (1) the patient's motive must be to seek medical treatment; and (2) the statement made to the physician must be of a type reasonably relied upon by doctors in treating such injuries.

Only statements made for purposes of obtaining medical treatment or diagnosis are admissible. The doctor's own statements and personal conclusions about the patient do not fit the rule, unless the doctor is attempting to obtain further medical treatment or diagnosis for the patient. See *Holmes v. Morgan,* 135 Or App 617, 630, 899 P2d 738 (1995) (doctor's "conclusion" that patient had a suicide pact with a third person does not fit OEC 803(4), because patient did not tell him that).

The rule has been held to cover statements to mental health professionals even if they are not licensed by the state. See *State ex rel Juvenile Department v. Cornett,* 121 Or App 264, 855 P2d 171 (1993), rev dismissed as improvidently allowed 318 Or 323, 865 P2d 1295 (1994) (approving admission of statements made to a graduate student who was a "Qualified Mental Health Professional," but who was not a doctor or psychologist or licensed by the state).

Purpose of Making Statements

The rule requires that the statements be made for purposes of medical diagnosis or treatment. When the patient is a child, sometimes a question is raised whether the child is too young to understand that she is undergoing a medical examination and to intend or know that her statements are being used for the purpose of treatment or diagnosis. In *State v. Booth,* 124 Or App 282, 287, 862 P2d 518, 521 (1993), *Booth v. Oregon,* cert. denied 115 S Ct 372 (1994), the court held that statements made by a three-year-old child to a doctor examining her for sexual abuse were properly admitted under OEC 803(4). The court found sufficient evidence to infer "that the child understood she was undergoing a medical examination and that her answers to the doctor's specific questions were a part of the examination."

Sometimes a question is also raised whether the statements are being obtained from a crime victim not for the purpose of diagnosis or treatment but for the primary purpose of investigating and prosecuting the crime. In *State v. Logan,* 105 Or App 556, 806 P2d 137, rev dismissed 312 Or 16, 815 P2d 703 (1991), the dissenting judge questioned whether Rule 803(4) is properly applicable in cases where a suspected sex crime victim is taken, not to a regular treating physician, but to a program designed to assist law enforcement agencies in the investigation of child sex abuse. The dissent stated that the record in the case was "absolutely clear that the child was taken to [the doctor], not for medical treatment, but only for the purpose of obtaining a diagnosis that she was a sexually abused child and obtaining evidence that defendant was the one who abused her."

Videotaped Statements

A properly authenticated videotape of a patient's statements to a doctor is admissible to the same extent as the statement itself. *State ex rel Juvenile Department v. Cornett*, 121 Or App 264, 855 P2d 171 (1993), rev dismissed as improvidently allowed 318 Or 323, 865 P2d 1295 (1994) (approving admission of hearsay statements, a videotape, and drawings by a sex abuse victim identifying her father and stepfather as the abusers); *State v. Logan*, 105 Or App 556, 561–2, 806 P2d 137, rev allowed 312 Or 16, 815 P2d 703, rev dismissed 312 Or 16, 815 P2d 703 (1991); *State v. Verley*, 106 Or App 751, 753, 809 P2d 723, rev denied 311 Or 644, 815 P2d 1273 (1991).

A child's demonstration on a videotape of the nature of the sexual abuse by using anatomically correct dolls is hearsay (because it is assertive conduct), but it can also be admitted under Rule 803(4) if it is for the purpose of medical diagnosis or treatment. *State v. Barkley*, 315 Or 420, 423, 846 P2d 390, cert denied 114 SCt 116 (1993).

But a statement by a child on the videotape describing what she had previously told a teacher is hearsay within hearsay that does not fit an exception. *State v. Barkley*, supra.

Causation, Fault

Facts about an accident or incident causing injury that do not relate to diagnosis or treatment are inadmissible under this exception. Information about the general cause of an injury usually is reasonably pertinent to diagnosis or treatment ("I was hit by a car"), but specific details, particularly when involving the issue of fault, usually are not ("The other driver ran a red light."). The court may have overlooked this distinction in *O'Donnell v. Floan*, 82 Or App 656, 728 P2d 956 (1986), where the court admitted hearsay statements from plaintiffs medical history under this exception to establish that the cause of plaintiff's fall was that she tripped on defendant's stairwell. Which stairwell caused the fall would not seem reasonably pertinent to diagnosis or treatment.

Sometimes parties fail to object to testimony regarding statements to a doctor that go beyond information relevant to diagnosis or treatment. See, e.g., *Powers v. Officer Cheeley*, 307 Or 585, 596, 771 P2d 622 (1989) ("The evidence was received without objection even though the specifics as to defendant's conduct may not have been germaine [sic] to treatment.").

Psychiatric History

This rule, consistent with prior law, will generally allow a psychiatrist to relate the history relied upon in making a diagnosis of the mental condition of a patient in cases where such condition is at issue. See *State v. Larsen*, 44 Or App 643, 606 P2d 1159 (1980). In criminal cases, the trial court must weigh the probative value of such evidence against the possibility of prejudice to the defendant in determining admissibility. *State v. Olds,* 35 Or App 305, 581 P2d 118 (1978). See Rule 403. Statements of psychiatric history often present greater danger of prejudice than do statements of medical history.

Statements Describing Physical Abuse and/or Sexual Abuse

This exception is frequently used in prosecutions for physical or sexual abuse to admit statements by the victim describing the nature of the injury and, when pertinent to treatment, the identity of the perpetrator. In *State v. Jensen,* 313 Or 587, 590–8, 837 P2d 525 (1992), the defendant in appealing his first-degree assault conviction assigned as error the admission of testimony of a nurse who had treated the three-year-old victim about the child's description of how he was scalded in the bathtub. When asked how he got hurt, the child had responded, "Daddy dunked me." The court held this statement to the nurse admissible under OEC 803(4) as made for purposes of medical diagnosis or treatment. The court noted that identification of the abuser may be "reasonably pertinent" to treatment in cases where the abuser is a member of the household and the course of treatment may include removing the child from the home. See also *State v. Stevens,* 311 Or 119, 138–42, 806 P2d 92 (1991).

In *State v. Moen,* 309 Or 45, 54–65, 786 P2d 111 (1990), the defendant was convicted of aggravated murder of his wife and mother-in-law. He claimed error in the admission of testimony that the mother-in-law told her doctor, who was treating her for depression, that she feared defendant might kill both her and her daughter. The court found the evidence properly admitted under Rule 803(4), because it was made for the purpose of medical diagnosis or treatment, described current symptoms and the "general character of the cause [or] external source thereof," and was "reasonably pertinent to diagnosis or treatment." The court held this exception to be "firmly rooted" for purposes of confrontation analysis, but did not distinguish between statements for purposes of treatment and statements for purposes of diagnosis, which at common law were not within the exception. See Mosteller, *Child Sexual Abuse and Statements for the Purpose of Medical Diagnosis or Treatment,* 67 N C L Rev 257 (1989).

Child victim's statements identifying the abuser were admitted in the following cases: *State v. Wilson,* 121 Or App 460, 467–70, 855 P2d 657, 661–2 (1993), rev denied 318 Or 61, 865 P2d 1297; *State v. Alvarez,* 110 Or App 230, 234–5, 822 P2d 1207, 1209–10 (1991), rev denied 314 Or 176, 836 P2d 1345 (1992); *State v. Logan,* 105 Or App 556, 806 P2d 137, rev dismissed 312 Or 16, 815 P2d 703 (1991); *State v. Bauman,* 98 Or App 316, 779 P2d 185 (1989); *State v. Newby,* 97 Or App 598, 777 P2d 994, rev denied 308 Or 660, 784 P2d 1102 (1989).

In *State v. Roberts,* 97 Or App 217, 775 P2d 342 (1989), a woman who was badly beaten went to a hospital emergency room for treatment. She was initially unwilling to state what happened to her, wishing merely to be treated and allowed to leave the hospital. The doctor persuaded her to identify her assailant, and she identified the defendant, who was her boyfriend. At trial the doctor testified that he sought the identity of the assailant, because of concern that the victim was involved in an abusive relationship. He testified that he sometimes advises such patients to leave the relationship for their own self-protection and to seek psychological counseling. The issue on appeal was whether it was error to admit the statement of the victim to the doctor identifying defendant as her assailant. The court reaffirmed its adoption of the two-part test of *United States v. Iron Shell,* 633 F2d 77, 84 (8th Cir 1980), cert denied 450 US 1001 (1981) that: (1) the declarant's motive in making the statement must be to promote treatment or diagnosis; and (2) the content of the statement is such that a physician would reasonably rely upon in treatment or diagnosis. Although the defendant argued that the state made an insufficient showing that the victim's motive in making the statement was to promote her diagnosis or treatment, the appellate court stated "[w]e presume that the trial court found to the contrary." Because the presumed finding was supported by the evidence, the court affirmed the admission of the statement.

A number of federal courts also have held that the identity of the perpetrator is pertinent to treatment, at least in those cases where the perpetrator may be a family member or a related person likely to have future access to the victim. See *United States v. Renville,* 779 F2d 430 (8th Cir 1985) (sexual abuse by stepfather; treating physician has obligation to address psychological injury); *Goldade v. State,* 674 P2d 721 (Wyo 1983), cert denied 467 US 1253 (1984) (statement to emergency room nurse and physician that "Mommy" caused the bruises on her body).

RULE 803. ORS 40.460. HEARSAY EXCEPTION; AVAILABILITY OF DECLARANT IMMATERIAL

The following are not excluded by Rule 802 (ORS 40.455), even though the declarant is available as a witness:

(5) [Recorded recollection.] A memorandum or record concerning a matter about which a witness once had knowledge but now has insufficient recollection to enable the witness to testify fully and accurately, shown to have been made or adopted by the witness when the matter was fresh in the memory of the witness and to reflect that knowledge correctly. If admitted, the memorandum or record may be read into evidence but may not itself be received as an exhibit unless offered by an adverse party.

LEGISLATIVE COMMENTARY

Subsection (5). Subsection (5) sets forth the hearsay exception for a record of past recollection. This exception is generally recognized and has "long been favored by the federal and practically all the state courts that have had occasion to decide the question." *United States v. Kelly,* 349 F2d 720, 770 (2nd Cir 1965), citing numerous cases and sustaining the exception against a claimed denial of the right of confrontation. Many additional cases are cited in Annot 82 ALR 2d 473, 520. The guaranty of trustworthiness is found in the inherent reliability of a record made while events were stiff fresh in mind and intended accurately to reflect them.

The principal controversy attending the exception has centered, not on its propriety, but on the question whether a preliminary requirement of impaired memory on the part of the witness should be imposed. The authorities are divided. If the only concern is accuracy of the evidence, impairment of the memory of the witness adds nothing to it and should not be required. McCormick § 303 at 715; 3 Wigmore § 738 at 76; *Jordan v. People,* 151 Colo 133, 376 P2d 699 (1962), *cert denied* 373 US 944, 83 S Ct 1553, 10 L Ed 2d 699 (1963); *Hall v. State,* 223 Md 158, 162 A2d 751 (1960); *State v. Bindhammer,* 44 NJ 372, 209 A2d 124 (1965). However, the Legislative Assembly believes that the absence of the requirement would encourage the use of statements carefully prepared for purposes of litigation under the supervision of attorneys' investigators or claims adjusters. The subsection therefore includes a requirement that the witness not have "sufficient recollection to enable the witness to testify fully and accurately." Accord, *Elam v. Soares,* 282 Or 93, 577 P2d 1336 (1978); California Evidence Code § 1237; New Jersey Evidence Rule 63(1)(b).

As a further safeguard against abuse of the recorded recollection, this subsection provides that the record may be read into evidence by the witness but may not be admitted as an exhibit unless offered by the adverse party. This clarifies Oregon law. In *Elam v. Soares,* supra, as the memorandum was not admissible the Oregon Supreme Court did not decide whether to adopt the federal rule requirement that "the memorandum may not be received as an exhibit unless offered by the adverse party." 282 Or at 99 n 2. Likewise, in *State v. Harvey,* 49 Or App 123, 126 n 1, 619 P2d 288 (1980), the same issue was not resolved because defendant did not argue it on appeal. Under Oregon decisions prior to *Elam* and *Harvey,* the writing itself could be admitted as evidence or handed or shown to the jury by the party offering it if it was verified and adopted by the witness. *Simms v. School District No. 1,* 13 Or App 119, 508 P2d 236 (1973).

The rule does not require any particular method of establishing the initial knowledge of the declarant or the contemporaneity and accuracy of the record. These are left to be dealt with as the circumstances of the case may indicate.

The involvement of several persons in the process of observing and recording is entirely consistent with the exception, e.g., an employer dictating to a secretary, a secretary making a memorandum at direction of an employer, or information being passed along a chain of persons. See *Curtis v. Bradley,* 65 Conn 99, 31 A 591 (1894); *Rathbun v. Brancatella,* 93 NJL 222, 107 A 279 (1919). When the verifying witness has not prepared the record but merely examined it and found it accurate, the witness has still adopted the record and it is admissible.

TEXT

Recorded Recollection

Under Rule 803(5), a memorandum or record concerning a matter about which a witness once had knowledge is admissible as an exception to the hearsay rule upon a showing of the following: (1) the witness now has insufficient recollection to testify fully and accurately; (2) the memorandum or record was made or adopted by the witness; (3) the making or adoption occurred at a time when the matter was fresh in the memory of the witness; and (4) the memorandum or record correctly reflects that knowledge. The determination of whether this foundation has been established is for the trial court under Rule 104(1).

If admitted, the memorandum or record may be read into evidence but may not itself be received as an exhibit, unless offered by an adverse party. The purpose of this restriction is to prevent writings received under this exception from receiving greater emphasis in the jury room than testimony given on the witness stand.

Attesting to Accuracy

A possibly troublesome aspect of the foundation is the requirement that the witness state that the writing accurately reflects his or her prior knowledge. The problem presented is how a witness can verify the accuracy of a writing regarding an event that the witness no longer recalls. Courts are usually willing to accept testimony that the witness would not have made or signed the writing if not accurate, or a showing of the procedures followed in making the record or memorandum that suggest the writing's reliability is high. If the witness is unwilling to endorse the accuracy of the writing, the writing must be excluded. See *State v. Watkins*, 228 NW 2d 635 (SD 1975).

Record Prepared by More than One Maker

Rule 803(5) also presents a problem in cases where one person observing an event makes a statement about the event and another person records that statement, such as an observer reporting to another person the license number of a getaway vehicle. The rule does not appear to address this issue in cases where the oral statement (e.g., license number) has been forgotten and the written notation has neither been "made" nor "adopted" by the person who observed the license number. However, the Legislative Commentary states that "the involvement of several persons in the process of observing and recording is entirely consistent with the rule." A sufficient foundation should be found if both persons who participated in the making of the statement properly testify, e.g., A testifies that he saw the license number but can no longer remember it but that he accurately reported it to B, and B can testify that he accurately transcribed the oral report that was made. See *United States v. Booz*, 451 F2d 719, 724–5 (3rd Cir 1971). Cf. *United States v. Patterson*, 678 F2d 774 (9th Cir), cert denied 459 US

911 (1982) (court admitted grand jury testimony under the past recollection recorded exception to the hearsay rule after a witness was unable to recall the event at trial, but acknowledged that the matter was fresh in his memory at the time of his grand jury testimony and that the grand jury transcript was accurate).

Time Lapse

The rule sets no limit on the amount of time that may lapse between the occurrence of the event and the preparation of the writing. The rule requires only that the preparation occur at a time when the event is fresh in the declarant's memory. Some courts construing the federal rule have allowed records made more than a year after the event described. See *United States v. Orrico,* 599 F2d 113 (6th Cir 1979); *United States v. Senak,* 527 F2d 129 (7th Cir 1975), cert denied 425 US 907 (1976).

First-Hand Knowledge Requirement

The declarant must have had first-hand knowledge about the recorded event. The introductory section of the Legislative Commentary regarding Rule 803 states: "Neither this rule nor Rule 804 dispenses with the requirement of firsthand knowledge. See ORE 602." See also *Simms v. School Dist. No. 1,* 13 Or App 119, 508 P2d 236 (1973). The original writing requirement of Rule 1002 is also applicable, but a duplicate is generally allowed in lieu of the original by Rule 1003.

Police Reports as Past Recollection Recorded

In *State v. Scally,* 92 Or App 149, 758 P2d 365 (1988), a DUII prosecution, the court allowed the arresting officer to read from his police report after he had testified that he had no present recollection. The court held that the police report may be read aloud as recorded recollection under this rule, even though police reports are not admissible against criminal defendants under Rule 803(8)(b). The court found no violation of defendant's right of confrontation, stating: "When the officer testifies, the danger of unreliability is minimized, because the trier of fact has the opportunity to weigh credibility and to consider the circumstances surrounding the preparation of the report." 92 Or App at 152.

Federal courts are divided regarding whether police reports expressly excluded by FRE 803(8)(b) may be received under FRE 803(5). In *United States v. Oates,* 560 F2d 45, 72 (2nd Cir 1977), the Second Circuit found "clear congressional intent that reports not qualifying under FRE 803(8)(B) or (C) should, and would, be inadmissible against defendants in criminal cases." But see *United States v. Sawyer,* 607 F2d 1190 (7th Cir 1979), cert denied 445 US 943 (1980) (admitting reports under FRE 803(5) that were inadmissible under FRE 803(8)). In contrast to Rule 803(8), Rule 803(5) will normally require the police officer to be present to lay the foundation for the writing. See *United States v. Riley,* 657 F2d 1377 (8th Cir 1981) cert denied 459 US 1111 (1983) (no confrontation violation where signed statement of prosecution witness read to jury under FRE 803(5) after showing witness had no refreshable memory of matters recorded but that she had knowledge at time she signed the recorded statement). See generally, ANNOT., *Admissibility, Over Hearsay Objection, of Police Observations and Investigative Findings Offered by Government In Criminal Prosecution, Excluded From Public Records Exception to Hearsay Rule Under Rule 803(8)(B) or (C), Federal Rules of Evidence,* 56 ALR Fed 168 (1982).

Other Authorities

For federal interpretations of this rule, see ANNOT., *Admissibility of Statement Under Rule 803(5) of Federal Rules of Evidence, Providing for Recorded-Recollection Exception to Hearsay Rule,* 35 ALR Fed 605 (1977).

RULE 803.   ORS 40.460. HEARSAY EXCEPTION; AVAILABILITY OF DECLARANT IMMATERIAL

The following are not excluded by Rule 802 (ORS 40.455), even though the declarant is available as a witness:

(6) [Records of regularly conducted activity.] A memorandum, report, record, or data compilation, in any form, of acts, events, conditions, opinions, or diagnoses, made at or near the time by, or from information transmitted by, a person with knowledge, if kept in the course of a regularly conducted business activity, and if it was the regular practice of that business activity to make the memorandum, report, record, or data compilation, all as shown by the testimony of the custodian or other qualified witness, unless the source of information or the method of [sic] circumstances of preparation indicate lack of trustworthiness. The term "business" as used in this subsection includes business, institution, association, profession, occupation, and calling of every kind, whether or not conducted for profit.

LEGISLATIVE COMMENTARY

Subsection (6). Subsection (6) provides an exception to the hearsay rule for business records. The exception is an established feature of Oregon law. See former ORS 41.680 to 41.710 (repealed); *Mayor v. Dowsett,* 240 Or 196, 400 P2d 234 (1965); *Sullivan v. Carpenter,* 184 Or 485, 199 P2d 655 (1948); *Gallagher v. Portland Traction Co.,* 181 Or 385, 182 P2d 354 (1947). The unusual reliability of business records, which makes them admissible, is variously ascribed to the regular entries and systematic checking which produce habits of precision, to actual reliance of the business upon them, and to the duty of the record keeper to make an accurate record. McCormick §§ 306, 308, 310; Laughin, "Business Entries and the Like," in 46 Iowa L Rev 276 (1961).

The definition of "business" is very broad and includes institutions and associations such as schools, churches and hospitals. ORS 41.680 similarly defined a business as "every kind of business, profession, occupation, calling or operating of institutions, whether carried on for profit or not." See also *State v. Roisland,* 1 Or App 68, 459 P2d 555 (1969) (interpreting "business" to include jail).

The amplification of the kinds of activities that may produce admissible records has led to problems that conventional business records by nature avoid. These problems relate to the source of the recorded information, entries in opinion form, motivation, and the involvement of the declarant as a participant in the matters recorded.

Source. Source of information presents no substantial problem with records of a conventional business. All participants including the declarant are acting routinely, under a duty of accuracy, and with employer reliance on the result—in short, "in the regular course of business." If the supplier of the information does not act in the regular course of business, however, an essential link is broken: the assurance of accuracy does not extend to the information itself, and the fact that it may be recorded with scrupulous accuracy is of no avail. An illustration is the police report incorporating information obtained from a bystander. The officer qualifies as acting in the regular course of business, but the informant does not. The leading case, *Johnson v. Lutz,* 253 NY 124, 170 NW 517 (1930), held that a report thus prepared was inadmissible. Most of the authorities have agreed with the decision. *Gencarella v. Fyfe,* 171 F2d 419 (1st Cir 1948); *Gordon v. Robinson,* 210 F2d 192 (3rd Cir 1954); *Standard Oil Co. of California v. Moore,* 251 F2d 188, 214 (9th Cir 1957), *cert denied* 356 US 975, 78 S Ct 1139, 2 L Ed 2d 1148 (1958); *Yates v. Bair Transport, Inc.,* 249 F Supp 681 (SDNY 1965); Annot., 69 ALR 2d 1148. Cf. *Hawkins v. Gorea Motor Express, Inc.,* 360 F2d 933 (2nd Cir 1966). Contra, 5 Wigmore § 1530a at 391–392 n 1. Under this subsection, a court may refuse to admit a record otherwise admissible when "the source of information or the method or circumstances of preparation indicate lack of trustworthiness." Similar language appeared in ORS 41.690, and was interpreted to vest the trial court with wide discretion in admitting or refusing to admit business records as evidence. *State v. White,* 4 Or App 151, 477 P2d 917 (1970).

Opinion. Entries in opinion form were not encountered in traditional business records because of the factual nature of the item recorded, but they now commonly appear as medical diagnoses, prognoses and test results among other things. This subsection specifically includes diagnoses and opinions as proper subjects of admissible entries. However, with regard to opinions in hospital records, the subsection should be read in light of *Streight v. Conroy,* 279 Or 289, 566 P2d 1198 (1977). That case sustained a trial court's refusal to allow a medical witness to read another doctor's report into the record verbatim:

"When an expert opinion is offered by a witness personally testifying, the expert is available for cross-examination on that opinion. If the opinion is offered by means of a hospital record, no cross-examination is possible. Consequently, there is a tendency somewhat to limit those opinions which can be introduced by this method. The admissibility of ordinary diagnostic findings customarily based on objective data and not usually presenting more than average difficulty of interpretation is usually conceded. On the other end of the continuum, diagnostic opinions which on their face are speculative are reasonably excluded. In the absence of the availability of the declarant for explanation and cross-examination, the probative value of this evidence is outweighed by the danger that it will be abused or mislead the jury. 279 Or at 295, citing McCormick § 313 at 732."

The Legislative Assembly does not intend, by its adoption of ORE 803(6), automatically to allow into evidence all business records containing opinions or diagnoses. A trial judge retains discretion under this rule to exclude an opinion or diagnosis on the ground that the record does not exhibit the necessary degree of trustworthiness.

Motivation. The motivation of the declarant has been a source of difficulty and disagreement. See Fed R Evid 803(6), Comment at 115–116. This subsection proceeds on the basis that records made in the course of a regularly conducted business activity are admissible—subject, again, to the trial court's authority to exclude them if "the source of information or the method or circumstances of preparation indicate lack of trustworthiness."

Involvement. Occasionally, decisions have reached for more accurate business records by requiring that the declarant participate in matters reported. *Clainos v. United States,* 163 F2d 593 (DC Cir 1947) (error to admit police records of convictions); *Standard Oil Co. of California v. Moore,* 251 F2d 188 (9th Cir 1957), *cert denied* 356 US 975, 78 S Ct 1139, 2 L Ed 2d 1148 (1958) (error to admit employees' records of observed business practices of others). Subsection (6) makes no such requirement. Records that are wholly acceptable may involve matters merely observed, e.g., the weather.

Under this subsection, the hearsay statement may be a "memorandum report, record or data compilation, in any form." Similar latitude was provided in ORS 41.720. See *State v. White,* supra (photocopy). "Data compilation" is used to describe any means of storing information other than conventional words and figures in written or documentary form. The expression includes but is not limited to, electronic computer storage. The term is borrowed from revised Rule 34(a) of the Federal Rules of Civil Procedure.

This subsection is consistent with Oregon law in requiring that the record be made by, or from information transmitted by, a person with knowledge. In the latter case, the Oregon Supreme Court has held, the person making the entry must be under a duty to ascertain the truth of the facts recorded. *Wynn v. Sundquist,* 259 Or 125, 485 P2d 1085 (1971). The use of the phrase "person with knowledge" should not imply that the proponent of a business record must be able to produce, or even identify, the specific individual upon whose firsthand knowledge the record is based. A sufficient foundation is laid if the proponent shows that it was the regular practice of the activity to base such a record upon a transmission from a person with knowledge. Thus, in the case of contents of a shipment of goods, it is sufficient to produce a report from the company's computer programmer or a person having knowledge of the particular record system. In short, the phrase "person with knowledge" is meant to be coterminous with the custodian of the evidence or other qualified witness. The Legislative Assembly believes this represents the desired rule in light of the complexity of modern business organizations.

TEXT

Records of Regularly Conducted Activity

Rule 803(6) authorizes the admission of records of regularly conducted activity, provided that the following foundation is established by the custodian of the record or another qualified witness: (1) the record was made at or near the time of the event; (2) the record was made by or from information transmitted by a person with knowledge and a duty to report; (3) it was the regular practice of the business activity to make such a record; and (4) the record is kept in the course of a regularly conducted business activity. The record will be excluded if the source of the information or the method or circumstances of preparation indicate lack of trustworthiness. The term business is defined to include "business, institution, association, profession, occupation, and calling of every kind, whether or not conducted for profit."

A proper foundation must be laid or the record will be excluded. See *Appel v. Standex International Corp.*, 62 Or App 208, 212–3, 660 P2d 686, rev denied 295 Or 446, 668 P2d 382 (1983) (nursing home records properly excluded where witness "did not testify as to the mode of preparation of the incident reports, when they were prepared or whether they were made in the regular course of business."); *Northstar Broadcasting v. Tacher Co.*, 60 Or App 579, 655 P2d 200 (1982).

On the procedures for obtaining and admitting hospital records, see ORCP 55H and ORCP 44E.

Authenticating Witness

Unlike the hearsay exception for public records, which does not require an authenticating witness (see Rule 803(8)), the foundation for this hearsay exception must be established by the custodian of the records or another qualified witness. See *State v. Cappleman*, 10 Or App 176, 180, 499 P2d 1372, 1374 (1972) (foundation satisfied by testimony of sales manager even though he was not custodian of records). The witness need not be the person who made the record or had supervision over its preparation. *United States v. Flom*, 558 F2d 1179, 1182 (5th Cir 1977). The witness need not have personal knowledge of the contents of the document, nor be familiar with all the circumstances surrounding its preparation. *United States v. Sand*, 541 F2d 1370, 1377 (9th Cir 1976), cert denied 429 US 1103 (1977); *United States v. Page*, 544 F2d 982 (8th Cir 1976). It is not necessary that the witness have been employed by the business at the time the record was made. *United States v. Evans*, 572 F2d 455, 490 (5th Cir), cert denied 439 US 870 (1978). The current custodian may testify that the procedures employed at the time the record was made are the same as those employed by the business at the time of trial. *United States v. Rose,* 562 F2d 409, 410 (7th Cir 1977).

Contemporaneity

To qualify under this rule, the record must have been made at or near the time of the event. See *Thomas v. Howser,* 262 Or 351, 497 P2d 1163 (1972) (possible error to admit office diary for billing purposes when relevant entries were not made contemporaneously, but not basis for reversal in light of other evidence); *Allan v. Oceanside Lumber Co.,* 214 Or 27, 328 P2d 327 (1958) (record prepared a year after event held not admissible as business record); *Hansen v. Bussman,* 274 Or 757, 786, 549 P2d 1265, 1281 (1976) (letter written 17 months after incident not admissible as business record).

Regularity

If a record is not routine, or if it is not made with sufficient regularity to assure reliability, it is unlikely to qualify under the business records exception. In *Osborne v. International Harvester Co.,* 69 Or App 629, 688 P2d 390, petition for review dismissed 298 Or 334, 691 P2d 483 (1984), the court held that an investigative report of an accident prepared by a county employee based upon his interview with the driver did not qualify for admission as a business record. The court noted that there was no showing that the reports were made routinely, and they lacked the indicia of reliability of a regularly prepared business record. See also *State v. Echeverria,* 51 Or App 513, 516, 626 P2d 897, rev denied 291 Or 118, 631 P2d 341 (1981) (list of stolen property prepared by burglary victim who died prior to trial not admissible as business record).

Correspondence, at least if it is not of a routine nature such as a billing statement, is generally inadmissible as a business record. See *Scanlon v. Hartman,* 282 Or 505, 579 P2d 851 (1978) (letter from physician inadmissible as business record; isolated memoranda such as correspondence are not made with sufficient regularity to qualify as business records); see also *Hansen v. Bussman,* 274 Or 757, 549 P2d 1265 (1976) (letter from physician excluded).

Some federal courts have held business diaries to be a record of regularly conducted business activity admissible under FRE 803(6). *In Re Japanese Electronic Products Antitrust Litigation,* 723 F2d 238 (3rd Cir 1983); *Keogh v. Commissioner of Internal Revenue,* 713 F2d 496 (9th Cir 1983). But see *Clark v. City of Los Angeles,* 650 F2d 1033 (9th Cir 1981), cert denied 456 US 927 (1982) (diary inadmissible as business record).

Business Duty

The person making or recording the statements in a business record must have been acting under a duty to the business or organization for which the record was made. Although the duty to report requirement is not clearly stated in the rule itself, it is a traditional requirement of the business records exception and is expressly adopted by the Commentary:

> If the supplier of the information does not act in the regular course of business, however, an essential link is broken: the assurance of accuracy does not extend to the information itself, and the fact that it may be recorded with scrupulous accuracy is of no avail. An illustration is the police report incorporating information obtained from a bystander. The officer qualifies as acting in the regular course of business, but the informant does not. The leading case, *Johnson v. Lutz*, 253 NY 124, 179 NW 517 (1930), held that a report thus prepared was inadmissible. Most of the authorities have agreed with the decision.

The duty to report requirement was recognized under prior Oregon law. See *Miller v. Lillard*, 228 Or 202, 212, 364 P2d 766 (1961). The duty to report requirement is also recognized by courts interpreting FRE 803(6). See *United States v. Plum*, 558 F2d 568 (10th Cir 1977); *United States v. Robertson*, 588 F2d 575 (8th Cir 1978), cert denied 441 US 945 (1979); *United States v. Yates*, 553 F2d 518 (6th Cir 1977); *Meder v. Everest & Jennings Inc.*, 637 F2d 1182 (8th Cir 1981).

Multilevel Statements

A record is admissible under this exception, even though it contains multilevel statements involving a number of different employees of the business organization, if these employees were all acting within the course of their business duties in making, transmitting, or recording the statements. For example, the statement of a night nurse to a day nurse transmitted to a treating physician and recorded in the patient's hospital chart is admissible as part of a business record, if the other requirements of the rule are satisfied.

However, a statement in a business record from a person not acting under a duty to report is not admissible, unless the statement satisfies an independent exception to the hearsay rule or is exempted from the definition of hearsay by Rule 801(4). For example, a statement from a hospital visitor regarding the patient that is recorded in the patient's hospital chart is not admissible, unless it independently satisfies a hearsay exception. See Rule 805 (providing for the admissibility of multiple hearsay if each level of statement satisfies an independent hearsay exception).

Untrustworthy Business Records

Rule 803(6) does not directly adopt the rule of *Palmer v. Hoffman*, 318 US 109, 63 SCt 477, 87 LEd2d 645 (1943), which upheld the exclusion of an accident report made by a since-deceased engineer, offered by the defendant railroad trustees in a grade-crossing collision case. The court held that the report was not made "in the regular course of business" because it was prepared for use in litigating, not railroading. The difficulty with this analysis is that it suggests that business records might be excluded on the basis of being self-serving. As Judge Clark said in his dissent when the case was before the Court of Appeals, "I submit that there is hardly a grocer's account book which could not be excluded on that basis." *Hoffman v. Palmer,* 129 F2d 976, 1002 (2nd Cir 1942), aff'd 318 US 109 (1943).

The approach taken by Rule 803(6) is to omit any requirement directly pertaining to the motivation of the preparer of the records, but to provide that the court may exclude the records if "the source of information or the method or circumstances of preparation indicate lack of trustworthiness." See *Lepire v. Motor Vehicles Div.,* 47 Or App 67, 613 P2d 1084 (1980) (police report prepared in anticipation of litigation by a police officer who died prior to trial held inadmissible because it lacked indicia of trustworthiness central to the rationale of the business records exception); *Forward Communications Corp. v. United States,* 608 F2d 485 (Ct Cl 1979) (appraiser's report prepared for purposes of giving opinion inadmissible as business record); ANNOT., *Accident Reports By Employees of Litigant As Admissible Under the Federal Business Records Act (28 USC § 1732),* 10 ALR Fed 858 (1972).

In *Hansen v. Abrasive Engineering and Manufacturing, Inc.,* 317 Or 378, 388–9, 856 P2d 625, 630, 631 (1993), the court held that a doctor's report prepared by plaintiff's employer's insurer as part of insurer's defense of plaintiff's workers' compensation claim was admissible as a business record under OEC 803(6), even though it was prepared in contemplation of possible future litigation.

In *Steiner v. Beaver State Scaffolding Equipment Co.,* 97 Or App 453, 459, 777 P2d 965, 968 (1989), the court excluded a portion of an accident report because the defendant failed to establish "the source of the information and the knowledge of the persons from whom it might have come."

Opinions or Diagnoses

Rule 803(6) expressly authorizes the receipt of opinions and diagnoses contained in business records. The Commentary makes clear, however, that the legislature did not intend "automatically to allow into evidence all business records containing opinions or diagnoses. A trial judge retains discretion under this rule to exclude an opinion or diagnosis on the ground that the record does not exhibit the necessary degree of trustworthiness." Routine opinions formed in the course of professional activity, e.g., "Plaintiff has a broken leg," are likely to be admitted. However, more speculative, controversial, or complicated opinions, particularly when they directly relate to a central, contested issue in the case, e.g., "Plaintiff is permanently and totally disabled," are more likely to be excluded. See *Streight v. Conroy,* 279 Or 289, 294–5, 566 P2d 1198, 1201 (1977).

It has been held that the qualifications of the expert whose opinion is contained in the business record do not necessarily have to be established before the record may be received. See *United States v. Licavoli,* 604 F2d 613 (9th Cir 1979), cert denied 446 US 935 (1980).

Police Reports

Records expressly excluded by Rule 803(8), such as police reports offered against a defendant in a criminal case, are generally inadmissible under Rule 803(6). In *United States v. Oates,* 560 F2d 45 (2nd Cir 1977), the court held that reports by law enforcement agents inadmissible under FRE 803(8) could not be received under any other hearsay exception. See also *United States v. Cain,* 615 F2d 380 (5th Cir 1980). But see *United States v. King,* 613 F2d 670 (7th Cir 1980) (admitting government reports inadmissible under FRE 803(8) as business records). Compare 2 M. Graham, HANDBOOK OF FEDERAL EVIDENCE (4th ed 1996) § 803.6 at 472–3 (favoring *Oates* rule) with 4 J. Weinstein and M. Berger, WEINSTEIN'S EVIDENCE § 803(6)[07] (criticizing *Oates* rule). See generally ANNOT., *Admissibility, Over Hearsay Objection, of Police Observations and Investigative Findings Offered by Government In Criminal Prosecution, Excluded From Public Records Exception to Hearsay Rule Under Rule 803(8)(B) or (C), Federal Rules of Evidence,* 56 ALR Fed 168 (1982); ANNOT., *Admissibility in State Court Proceedings of Police Reports as Business Records,* 77 ALR3d 115 (1977).

Computer Records

In *Brown v. J.C. Penney Co.,* 297 Or 695, 688 P2d 811 (1984), the court held that a computer printout of police records regarding crime reports in a particular shopping center was admissible under former ORS 41.690, the business records statute. The court also noted that the printout would be admissible under Rule 803(6). The court held that even though the computer printout was not made "at or near the time" of the events, the making of a computer record is determined by the date of the entries into the computer, not the date of the printout.

See generally Horning, *Electronically Stored Evidence,* 71 Wash & Lee L Rev 1335 (1985); COMMENT, *Admitting Computer Generated Records: A Presumption of Reliability,* 18 John Marshall L Rev 115 (1984); ANNOT., *Proof of Business Records Kept or Stored On Electronic Computing Equipment,* 11 ALR 3rd 1377 (1967).

Federal Cases

For examples of records that have been held to be admissible as business records under FRE 803(6), see *United States v. Licavoli,* 604 F2d 613 (9th Cir 1979), cert denied 446 US 935 (1980) (insurance company appraisal of allegedly stolen goods); *United States v. McPartlin,* 595 F2d 1321 (7th Cir), cert denied 444 US 833 (1979) (desk calendar appointment diaries of coconspirator); *United States v. Beecroft,* 608 F2d 753 (9th Cir 1979) (Dun & Bradstreet credit reports); *United States v. Grossman,* 614 F2d 295 (1st Cir 1980) (sales catalog). But see *United States v. Hitsman,* 604 F2d 443 (5th Cir 1979) (copy of college transcript inadmissible as business record in absence of qualified witness to testify how such records are kept); *United States v. Reese,* 561 F2d 894 (DC Cir 1977) (copy of car rental agreement not admissible as business record without foundation being established by qualified witness).

Prior Oregon Law

Under prior Oregon law, the following are examples of records that have been held to be admissible as business records: *Lepire v. Motor Vehicles Division,* 47 Or App 67, 613 P2d 1084 (1980) (police reports); *Stanfield v. Laccoarce,* 284 Or 651, 588 P2d 1271 (1978) (psychological tests, records, and results); *State v. Scott,* 48 Or App 623, 617 P2d 681 (1980) (records of U.S. executive department (i.e., Social Security Administration and computer printouts of the Public Welfare Division); *Mayor v. Dowsett,* 240 Or 196, 400 P2d 234 (1965) (hospital records); *Babbitt v. Pacco Investors Corp.,* 246 Or 261, 425 P2d 489 (1967) (corporate minutes). On the procedures for admitting hospital records see ORCP 55H; ORS 41.930; ORS 41.945.

Other Authorities

See generally Egan & Cunningham, *Admission of Business Records into Evidence: Using the Business Records Exception and Other Techniques,* 30 Duq L Rev 205 (1992); Weissenberger, *Hearsay: Business Records and Public Records,* 51 U Cin L Rev 42 (1982); ANNOT., *Admissibility of Records Other than Police Reports, Under Rule 803(6), Federal Rules of Evidence, Providing for Business Records Exception to Hearsay Rule,* 61 ALR Fed 359 (1983); ANNOT., *Business Records: Authentication and Verification of Bills and Invoices Under Rule 803(6) of the Uniform Rules of Evidence,* 1 ALR4th 316 (1980); ANNOT., *Admissibility Under Uniform Business Records as Evidence Act or Similar Statute of Medical Report Made by Consulting Physician to Treating Physician,* 69 ALR3d 104 (1976); ANNOT., *Admissibility Under Business Entry Statutes of Hospital Records in Criminal Case,* 69 ALR3d 22 (1976); RECENT DEVELOPMENT, *Evidence Another Complication in Oregon's Business Records Exception to the Hearsay Rule: State v. Harvey,* 59 Or L Rev 143 (1980); ANNOT., *Admissibility of Credit Reports Under Federal Business Records Act (28 USCS § 1732(a)),* 19 ALR Fed 988 (1974); ANNOT., *Personal Checkbook or Account as Business Record Under Federal Business Records Act (28 USC § 1732),* 8 ALR Fed 919 (1971).

RULE 803. ORS 40.460, HEARSAY EXCEPTION; AVAILABILITY OF DECLARANT IMMATERIAL

The following are not excluded by Rule 802 (ORS 40.455), even though the declarant is available as a witness:

(7) [Absence of entry in records kept in accordance with the provisions of subsection (6) of this section.] Evidence that a matter is not included in the memoranda, reports, records, or data compilations, and in any form, kept in accordance with the provisions of subsection (6) of this section, to prove the nonoccurrence or nonexistence of the

matter, if the matter was of a kind of which a memorandum, report, record, or data compilation was regularly made and preserved, unless the sources of information or other circumstances indicate lack of trustworthiness.

LEGISLATIVE COMMENTARY

Subsection (7). In this subsection, failure of a record to mention a matter that would ordinarily be mentioned is made satisfactory evidence of the nonexistence of the matter. While such evidence is probably not hearsay as defined in ORE 801(3), decisions may be found which classify it not only as hearsay but also as not within any exception. To set the question at rest in favor of admissibility, it is specifically treated here. McCormick § 307 at 722; Morgan, *Basic Problems of Evidence* 314 (1962); 5 Wigmore § 1531; Uniform Rule 63(14); California Evidence Code § 1272; Kansas Code of Civil Procedure § 60-460(n); New Jersey Evidence Rule 63(14).

Under Oregon law, there has been no general hearsay exception for the absence of an entry in business records to prove the nonoccurrence or nonexistence of some matter. However, certain specialized statutes give effect to the principle. See, e.g., ORS 57.781 (certificate as to nonexistence of facts relating to corporations, which would appear from absence of documents filed in office of Corporation Commissioner, shall be taken as prima facie evidence thereof).

TEXT

Absence of Entry in Records of Regularly Conducted Activity

Rule 803(7) creates a hearsay exception for evidence that a matter is not included in records of regularly conducted activity as defined in Rule 803(6) "to prove the nonoccurrence or nonexistence of the matter, if the matter was of a kind of which a memorandum, report, record, or data compilation was regularly made and preserved, unless the sources of information or other circumstances indicate lack of trustworthiness."

Absence of an entry or record is probably not a hearsay "statement" as the term is defined by Rule 801(1), because not making an entry or record is usually not "intended as an assertion." The Commentary indicates that this exception is included to eliminate any doubt about the matter.

Presumably the custodian of the records or other qualified witness must be called to prove that the records were "kept in accordance with the provisions of subsection (6) of this section." See *United States v. Rich,* 580 F2d 929 (9th Cir), cert denied 439 US 935 (1978) (assumes without deciding that the custodian or other qualified witness must be called as a necessary predicate to the admission of the evidence); *United States v. Lanier,* 578 F2d 1246 (8th Cir), cert denied 439 US 856 (1978) (testimony may be received from auditor that computer records contained no entries of specified deposits).

The witness must testify that in the normal course of events an entry would have been made, or that the record would exist if the event in question had occurred. The witness should testify to the procedures that would have brought the event to the attention of the person regularly making the records so that the matter would have been recorded contemporaneously with the event if it had occurred.

Rule 1002 does not apply to proof of absence of an entry in a writing. See the Commentary to Rule 1002, which states:

> Nor does this section apply to testimony that books or records have been examined and found not to contain any reference to a designated matter. (*State v. Nano,* 273 Or. 366, 543 P.2d 660 (1975)). Under the holding of the case, such testimony is not proof of the contents or terms of a document, and, therefore, the "best evidence rule" has no application.

Therefore, oral testimony regarding the absence of an entry in a writing is not excluded by the so-called "best evidence" rule, and production of the writing itself is not required.

RULE 803.   ORS 40.460. HEARSAY EXCEPTION; AVAILABILITY OF DECLARANT IMMATERIAL

The following are not excluded by rule 802 (ORS 40.455), even though the declarant is available as a witness:

(8) **[Public records and reports.] Records, reports, statements, or data compilations, in any form, of public offices or agencies, setting forth:**

(a) **The activities of the office or agency;**

(b) **Matters observed pursuant to duty imposed by law as to which matters there was a duty to report, excluding however, in criminal cases matters observed by police officers and other law enforcement personnel; or**

(c) **In civil actions and proceedings and against the government in criminal cases, factual findings, resulting from an investigation made pursuant to authority granted by law, unless the sources of information or other circumstances indicate lack of trustworthiness.**

LEGISLATIVE COMMENTARY

Subsection (8). Embodied in this subsection is the public records exception to the hearsay rule. Public records are a recognized exception at common law and have been the subject of numerous statutes. McCormick § 315; ORS 43.370 (repealed by this Act).

This exception is justified by the assumption that a public official will perform the official's duty, and by the unlikelihood that a person will remember details independently of the record.

Paragraphs (a) and (b). These paragraphs involve records of regularly conducted activities. They draw combined support from the reliability factors mentioned above and in subsection (6).

Paragraph (c). The most controversial area of public records is that of the so-called "evaluative" report, addressed in this paragraph. Disagreement among the decisions has been partly due, no doubt, to the variety of situations encountered as well as to differences in principle. Cases sustaining admissibility include *United States v. Dumas*, 149 US 278, 13 S Ct 872, 37 L Ed 734 (1893) (statement of account certified by Postmaster General in action against postmaster); *McCarty v. United States*, 185 F2d 520 (5th Cir 1950), *reh denied* 187 F2d 234 (1951) (Certificate of Settlement of General Accounting Office showing indebtedness and letter from army official stating government had performed, in action on contract to purchase and remove waste food from army camp); *Moran v. Pittsburgh-Des Moines Steel Co.*, 183 F2d 467 (3rd Cir 1950) (report of Bureau of Mines as to cause of gas tank explosion); Petition of W, 164 F Supp 659 (Ed Pa 1958) (report by Immigration and Naturalization Service investigator that petitioner was known in community as wife of man to whom she was not married). To the opposite effect and denying admissibility are *Franklin v. Skelly Oil Co.*, 141 F2d 568 (10th Cir 1944) (State Fire Marshal's report of cause of gas explosion); *Lomax Transp. Co. v. United States*, 183 F2d 331 (9th Cir 1950) (Certificate of Settlement from General Accounting Office in action for naval supplies lost in warehouse fire); *Yung Jin Teung v. Dulles*, 229 F2d 244 (2nd Cir 1956) ("Status Reports" offered to justify delay in processing passport application).

The Legislative Assembly intends that this paragraph not provide a sweeping exception for public records containing evaluations or opinions. "Factual findings" is to be strictly construed to allow as evidence only those reports, otherwise in accord with the rule, which are based on firsthand observation by the public official making the report. See, e.g., *Finchcum v. Lyons*, 247 Or 255, 428 P2d 980 (1967) (admitting findings of pathologist that potatoes were infected with ring rot because evidence did not suggest that investigation involved exercise of discretion); *Davis v. Georgia Pacific*, 251 Or 239, 445 P2d 481 (1968) (admitting results of investigation by State Sanitary Authority on amount of fallout from mill because statements in documents were fact and not opinion). Where there are still factors present that cast doubt upon the trustworthiness of a record, this subsection authorizes the trial judge to exclude it.

The hearsay exception for evaluative reports is very specific in one respect. Such reports are only admissible in civil cases and against the government in criminal cases. Any other employment in criminal cases almost certainly would collide with the confrontation rights of the accused.

Notwithstanding this subsection, it should be noted that a number of Oregon statutes declare certain public writings inadmissible for policy reasons unrelated to their hearsay status. See ORS 41.675 (data related to committees for professional training, supervision or discipline of hospital medical staff); ORS 179.045 (crime conviction reports made to Corrections Division); ORS 483.610 (accident reports made to Department of Motor

Vehicles); ORS 486.061 (records of action taken by Department of Motor Vehicles under financial responsibility law); ORS 654.720 (accident reports made to Public Utility Commissioner); ORS 657.665 (unemployment compensation records, except where assistant director or state is a party).

TEXT

Public Records and Reports

Rule 803(8) creates a hearsay exception for certain records reports, statements, or data compilations, in any form, of public offices or agencies. The records or reports are within the exception to the extent that they set forth: (a) the activities of the office or agencies; (b) matters observed pursuant to duty imposed by law as to which matters there was a duty to report; (c) factual findings resulting from an investigation made pursuant to authority granted by law, unless the sources of information or other circumstances indicate lack of trustworthiness. Expressly excluded from category (b) in criminal cases are reports of "matters observed by police officers and other law enforcement personnel." Excluded from category (c) are factual findings resulting from investigations made pursuant to authority granted by law offered against a defendant in a criminal case.

There is an overlap between Rule 803(8) and Rule 803(9), which creates a hearsay exception for records of vital statistics. There is also an overlap between Rule 803(8) and Rule 803(6). Records of public offices admissible under Rule 803(8) will often also qualify as records of regularly conducted activity under Rule 803(6). Rule 803(8), unlike Rule 803(6), does not require that the agency have a "regular practice" of making such a record or that the record have been made contemporaneously.

Rule 803(8), unlike Rule 803(6), also does not require that a witness be called to establish the foundation for admissibility. Most public records admissible under Rule 803(8) can be self-authenticated under Rule 902. However, the certificate must be limited to authentication of the public document and cannot extend to interpretation of it. *United States v. Stone,* 604 F2d 922 (5th Cir 1979).

Record or Report

The rule does not define public "record" or "report." Records and reports of public offices at all levels of government—municipal, state, and federal—are admissible under this exception, providing its requirements are otherwise satisfied. See *Campbell v. Board of Medical Examiners,* 16 Or App 381, 518 P2d 1042 (1974) (public records of sister state admitted); *United States v. Hansen,* 583 F2d 325 (7th Cir), cert denied 439 US 912 (1978) (city building inspector's report). Public records from foreign jurisdictions are also admissible. See *United States v. Grady,* 544 F2d 598 (2nd Cir 1976) (records of government agency in Northern Ireland admitted under FRE 803(8)). Copies of public reports are generally admissible in lieu of originals under Rules 1003 and 1005. See also ORS 192.050.

Public records or reports will not be allowed under this rule if they are privileged or otherwise declared by law to be inadmissible. For a listing of statutes protecting the confidentiality of various public records or reports, see textual discussion of Rule 514.

RULE 803(8)(a)
Agency Activities

The dividing lines among the three categories of records described in the rule are not entirely clear, and classification may sometimes be difficult. Subsection (a) appears to contemplate records such as police or fire department records of calls received, returns of process, and transcripts of judicial proceedings. See *United States v. Arias,* 575 F2d 253 (9th Cir), cert denied 439 US 868 (1978) (transcript admissible as public record). The Advisory Committee's Note to FRE 803(8), which is identical to Oregon Rule 803(8), lists the following examples of records admissible under this subpart:

> Cases illustrating the admissibility of records of the office's or agency's own activities are numerous. *Chesapeake & Delaware Canal Co. v. United States,* 250 U.S. 123, 39 S. Ct. 407, 63 L. Ed. 889 (1919), Treasury records of miscellaneous receipts and disbursements; *Howard v. Perrin,* 200 U.S. 71, 26 S. Ct. 195, 50 L. Ed. 374 (1906), General Land Office records; *Ballew v. United States,* 160 U.S. 187, 16 S. Ct. 263 40 L. Ed. 388 (1895), Pension Office records.

RULE 803(8)(b)

Subsection (b) includes reports of police, public investigators, social workers, welfare caseworkers, and other public employees regarding matters observed pursuant to duty. This subsection requires not only that the observations have been pursuant to duty, but that the making of the report was pursuant to duty as well. Therefore, statements or reports by persons outside the public agency are inadmissible under this exception. But see Rule 805 (hearsay within hearsay admissible if each level independently satisfies a hearsay exception).

The Advisory Committee's Note to FRE 803(8) sets forth the following examples of records admissible under this subsection:

> Cases sustaining admissibility of records of matters observed are also numerous. *United States v. Van Hook,* 284 F.2d 489 (7th Cir. 1960), *remanded for re-sentencing* 365 U.S. 609, 81 S. Ct. 823, 5 L. Ed. 2d 821, letter from induction officer to District Attorney, pursuant to army regulations, stating fact and circumstances of refusal to be inducted; *T'Kach v. United States,* 242 F.2d 937 (5th Cir. 1957), affidavit of White House personnel officer that search of records showed no employment of accused, charged with fraudulently representing himself as an envoy of the President; *Minnehaha County v. Kelley,* 150 F.2d 356 (8th Cir. 1945); Weather Bureau records of rainfall; *United States v. Meyer,* 113 F.2d 387 (7th Cir. 1940), *cert denied* 311 U.S. 706, 61 S. Ct. 174, 85 L. Ed. 459, map prepared by government engineer from information furnished by men working under his supervision.

In order to protect the defendant's right to confrontation, subsection (b) excludes reports by law enforcement personnel in criminal cases. It has been held that this exclusion applies only to police reports offered against the defendant, not to those offered by the defendant. See *United States v. Smith,* 521 F2d 957 (DC Cir 1975). But see *United States v. MacDonald,* 688 F2d 224, 229–30 (4th Cir 1982), cert denied 459 US 1103 (1983) (even though government investigative reports may qualify for admission against the government under FRE 803(8), they may be excluded under FRE 401 and 403).

It has been held that the exclusion of law enforcement reports in criminal cases does not apply to reports of "routine, nonadversarial matters" or purely "ministerial observations." See *State v. Smith,* 66 Or App 703, 706–7, 675 P2d 510, 512 (1984) (document certifying that breathalyzer equipment was in proper operating order admissible as a public record); *State v. Conway,* 70 Or App 721, 690 P2d 1128 (1984), rev denied 298 Or 704, 695 P2d 1371 (1985) (admission of public record certifying breathalyzer equipment does not violate defendant's constitutional right of confrontation). In *Smith,* the court limited its holding to "nonadversarial" documents not related to the prosecution of a specific defendant in a specific case. However, in *State v. Spencer,* 82 Or App 358, 728 P2d 566 (1986), reversed on other grounds 305 Or 59, 750 P2d 147 (1988), the court held that a police officer's "Intoxilyzer Operator's Checklist" made in a specific case was admissible as a public record because it dealt with purely ministerial observations.

Federal decisions also tend to allow routine, nonadversarial law enforcement reports. See *United States v. Orozco,* 590 F2d 789 (9th Cir), cert denied 439 US 1049 (1978) (record of border crossings on particular date); *United States v. Gilbert,* 774 F2d 962 (9th Cir 1985) (fingerprint card); *United States v. Hernandez-Rojas,* 617 F2d 533 (9th Cir), cert denied 449 US 864 (1980) (warrant showing record of previous deportation).

On the issue of who are "other law enforcement personnel" whose reports are excluded under this rule, see *United States v. Oates,* 560 F2d 45 (2nd Cir 1977) (chemist for U.S. Customs Service was "law enforcement personnel"); *United States v. Ruffin,* 575 F2d 346 (2nd Cir 1978) (IRS employees who make records regularly used in criminal prosecution are "law enforcement personnel"); *United States v. Hansen,* 583 F2d 325 (7th Cir), cert denied 439 US 912 (1978) (city building inspector not "law enforcement personnel").

In *State v. Scally,* 92 Or App 149, 758 P2d 365 (1988), the court held that police reports not admissible under Rule 803(8)(b) may be read aloud as recorded recollection under Rule 803(5). The court stated: "When the officer testifies, the danger of unreliability is minimized, because the trier of fact has the opportunity to weigh credibility and to consider the circumstances surrounding the preparation of the report." 92 Or App at 152. The court also found no violation of the defendant's right of confrontation, because the officer was available for cross-examination.

In federal courts, there has been a split of authority regarding whether a public record prohibited from being offered against a criminal defendant under subsection (b) may be received under any other hearsay exception. Compare

United States v. Oates, 560 F2d 45 (2nd Cir 1977) (not admissible under other exceptions) with *United States v. Sawyer,* 607 F2d 1190 (7th Cir 1979), cert denied 445 US 943 (1980) (allowing memorandum of law enforcement agent under FRE 803(5), even though it would not have been admissible under FRE 803(8)) and *United States v. Yakobov,* 712 F2d 20 (2nd Cir 1983) (certificate showing absence of entry in public record admissible against criminal defendant). See ANNOT., *Admissibility, Over Hearsay Objection, of Police Observations and Investigative Findings Offered by Government In Criminal Prosecution, Excluded From Public Records Exception to Hearsay Rule Under 803(8)(B) or (C), Federal Rules of Evidence,* 56 ALR Fed 168 (1982).

It is uncertain whether the last phrase of the rule authorizing exclusion if "the sources of information or other circumstances indicate lack of trustworthiness" applies only to subsection (c) or to subsections (a) and (b) as well. Even if this phrase is construed to apply only to records offered under subsection (c), Rule 403 would authorize exclusion of untrustworthy reports offered under subsection (a) or (b) when their probative value is substantially outweighed by the danger of unfair prejudice, confusion of the issues, or misleading the jury.

See generally Imwinkelried, *The Constitutionality of Introducing Evaluative Laboratory Reports Against Criminal Defendants,* 30 Hastings L J 621 (1979); Alexander, *The Hearsay Exception for Public Records in Federal Criminal Trials,* 47 Alb L Rev 699 (1983); ANNOT., *Admissibility in State Court Proceedings of Police Reports Under Official Record Exception to Hearsay Rule,* 31 ALR4th 913 (1984).

Laboratory Analysis of Controlled Substances

The 1989 Legislature adopted legislation allowing a certified copy of an analytical report by the state police crime law to be accepted as prima facie evidence of the result of any analytical findings. ORS 475.235 provides as follows:

> (3) In all prosecutions under ORS 475.005 to 475.285 and 475.805 to 475.999 involving the analysis of a controlled substance or sample thereof, a certified copy of the analytical report signed by the director of the state police crime detection laboratory or the criminalist conducting the analysis shall be accepted as prima facie evidence of the result of the analytical findings. (4) Notwithstanding any statute or rule to the contrary, the defendant may subpoena the criminalist to testify at the preliminary hearing and trial of the issue at no cost to the defendant.

This statute is intended to provide an expanded hearsay exception for public reports without requiring the presence of the preparer. The statute instead authorizes the opposing side to subpoena the preparer to testify at a preliminary hearing or at trial of the issue.

The constitutionality of this statute was upheld in *State v. Hancock,* 317 Or 5, 854 P2d 926 (1993). Because the defendant may subpoena the criminalist to testify, the court viewed the statute as not denying the right of confrontation, but merely establishing "reasonable procedures" that must be followed in order for a defendant to exercise that right. Three dissenting justices viewed the statute as fundamentally and unconstitutionally altering established trial burdens in a way that "deprives a criminal defendant of the benefit of the adversary process."

Other Authorities

See generally ANNOT., *Construction and Application of Provision of Rule 803(8)(B), Federal Rules of Evidence, Excluding From Exception to Hearsay Rule in Criminal Cases Matters Observed By Law Enforcement Officers,* 37 ALR Fed 831 (1978); ANNOT. *Admissibility of Police Reports Under Federal Business Records Act (Federal Rules of Evidence, Rule 803, and Predecessor Amendments),* 31 ALR Fed 457 (1977); ANNOT., *Admissibility of Report of Police or Other Public Officer or Employee, or Portions of Report, As to Cause of or Responsibility for Accident, Injury to Person, or Damage to Property,* 69 ALR2d 1148 (1960).

RULE 803(8)(c)
Investigative Findings

Subsection (c) authorizes factual findings resulting from government investigations to be received in civil actions and against the government in criminal cases, unless the sources of information or other circumstances indicate lack of trustworthiness. See NOTE, *The Trustworthiness of Government Evaluative Reports Under Federal Rule of Evidence 803(8)(C),* 96 Harv L Rev 492 (1982). The line between admissible "factual findings" and more questionable opinions and conclusions is often difficult to draw.

As a guide to interpretation of FRE 803(8)(C), the Advisory Committee's Note to the rule contains the following statement:

> Factors which may be of assistance in passing upon the admissibility of evaluative reports include: (1) the timeliness of the investigation, McCormick, *Can the Courts Make Wider Use of Reports of Official Investigations?* 42 Iowa L. Rev. 363 (1957); (2) the special skill or experience of the official, *id.,* (3) whether a hearing was held and the level at which conducted, *Franklin v. Skelley Oil Co.,* 141 F.2d 568 (10th Cir. 1944); (4) possible motivation problems suggested by *Palmer v. Hoffman,* 318 U.S. 109, 63 S. Ct. 477, 87 L. Ed. 645 (1943). Others no doubt could be added.

Examples of additional factors bearing on trustworthiness would be: (1) the opportunity of others, including the opposing party, to review, analyze, test, and verify the information; (2) the importance of the information to the work of the public agency; (3) the extent to which such information is reasonably relied upon by others; (4) the finality of the information contained in the report.

Under FRE 803(8)(C), a wide range of findings have been admitted. See *Lloyd v. Am. Export Lines Inc.,* 580 F2d 1179 (3rd Cir), cert denied 439 US 969 (1978) (findings of Coast Guard hearing examiner); *Garcia v. Gloor,* 618 F2d 264 (5th Cir 1980), cert denied 449 US 1113 (1981) (findings of Equal Employment Opportunity Commission); *Hodge v. Seiler,* 558 F2d 284 (5th Cir 1977) (HUD report); *King v. Horizon Corp.,* 701 F2d 1313 (10th Cir 1983) (findings of FTC administrative law judge). But see *Denny v. Hutchinson Sales Corp.,* 649 F2d 816 (10th Cir 1981) (excluding report of Colorado Civil Rights Commission in civil rights case as outside FRE 803(8)(C), on the ground that findings in the report were not based on the preparer's personal knowledge and lacked trustworthiness because they were based upon ex parte investigation).

In *Beech Aircraft Corp. v. Rainey,* 488 US 153, 109 SCt 439, 103 LEd2d 445 (1988), the United States Supreme Court gave a broad construction to FRE 803(8)(C), holding that statements contained in a public record that are in the form of opinions or conclusions are not necessarily excluded from the exception, provided that the other requirements of the rule are satisfied. However, cases interpreting FRE 803(8)(C) may have limited value in construing the Oregon rule, because the Commentary expresses the intent of the legislature that Rule 803(8)(c) be given a narrow construction:

> [T]his paragraph [should] not provide a sweeping exception for public records containing evaluations or opinions. 'Factual findings' is to be strictly construed to allow as evidence only those reports, otherwise in accord with the rule, which are based on *first hand observation* by the public official making the report. (emphasis added)

The first-hand knowledge requirement would clearly require rejection of federal authorities such as *Baker v. Elcona Homes Corp.,* 588 F2d 551 (6th Cir 1978), cert denied 441 US 933 (1979), where the court allowed a police report to be received under FRE 803(8)(C) containing a factual finding by the police officer regarding the color of the traffic light at the time of the collision, based on interviews with witnesses at the scene. Oregon courts are more likely to follow federal decisions taking a narrower view of FRE 803(8)(C), such as *Miller v. Caterpillar Tractor Co.,* 697 F2d 141, 142–4 (6th Cir 1983) (evaluative reports of government employees regarding cause of accident not admissible, because largely based on hearsay statements of third persons).

Nonetheless, the interpretation of the rule suggested by the Commentary seems unduly restrictive. The "first-hand observation" criterion could require exclusion of reports where the actual observations or measurements were made by subordinates of the officer signing the report. Such a result seems not to have been intended. The Commentary cites with approval the case of *Davis v.. Georgia-Pacific Corp.,* 251 Or 239, 445 P2d 481 (1968). In *Davis,* the actual measurements in the records held to be admissible were made by subordinates. The opinion states: "If the head of the Air Quality Control Section of the Authority, whose documents were in question, had been called as a witness he could have testified to the results of the measurements made by the employees of the Authority under his supervision." 251 Or at 248, 445 P2d at 485.

Under prior law, "[a] prerequisite to the use of any given entry in an official record as evidence in a court of this state is that the official making the entry must have had either personal knowledge of the facts noted *or a duty to ascertain the truth of those facts." State ex rel Juvenile Dept. v. Thomas T.,* 30 Or App 385, 388, 567 P2d 135, 137 (1977) (emphasis added). See also *Wynn v. Sundquist,* 259 Or 125, 133–4, 485 P2d 1085 (1971).

The prior law standard should provide reasonable protection against admission of official records that merely compile or repeat hearsay statements of others. In addition, the court can regulate the quality of factual or evaluative findings received under this exception by excluding public records whenever "the sources of information or other circumstances indicate lack of trustworthiness." Therefore, reliable findings based upon a factual investigation should not necessarily be excluded merely because they have an evaluative component.

Even though Rule 803(8)(c), unlike Rule 803(8)(b), may allow an official report that is based in part on information supplied by outsiders, the actual statements of the outsiders are not admissible under this exception to prove the truth of matters asserted in those statements. See *John McShain, Inc. v. Cessna Aircraft Co.*, 563 F2d 632 (3rd Cir 1977) (accident reports submitted to government agency by third parties not admissible).

Recent Cases

In *McCuller v. Gaudry*, 59 Or App 13, 650 P2d 148 (1982), the court held that a finding of racial discrimination by the Civil Rights Division of the Oregon Department of Labor was admissible in a civil suit for discrimination. Although the hearsay issue was not discussed, the Civil Rights Division finding constituted hearsay, because it was apparently offered to prove that an act of discrimination had occurred. Whether the finding would have been admissible under Rule 803(8)(C) over proper objection would depend on the extent to which the finding was one of fact rather than opinion, and the extent to which the finding was based on personal knowledge rather than hearsay information.

Prior Oregon Law

Examples of prior Oregon cases admitting documents under the public records exception include: *State v. Caswell*, 53 Or App 693, 633 P2d 24, rev denied 292 Or 108, 642 P2d 310 (1981) (entries in printout of defendant's driving record from the Motor Vehicles Division); *Snyder v. Rhoads*, 47 Or App 545, 615 P2d 1058 (1980) (tax records); *Miller v. Lillard*, 228 Or 202, 364 P2d 766 (1961) (certificate of registration of a party's cattle brand); *Campbell v. Bd of Medical Examiners*, 16 Or App 381, 518 P2d 1042 (1974) (certified copies of application for license as physician in another state, minutes of such state's medical board denying application and document entitled "Notification of Personnel Action" from a federal agency in another state).

Other Authorities

See generally Grossman & Shapiro, *The Admission of Government Fact Findings Under Federal Rule of Evidence 803(8)(C): Limiting the Dangers of Unreliable Hearsay*, 38 U Kan L Rev 767 (1990); ANNOT., *Admissibility, Under Rule 803(8)(C) of Federal Rules of Evidence, Of "Factual Findings Resulting From Investigation Made Pursuant to Authority Granted By Law,"* 47 ALR Fed 321 (1980);

ANNOT., *Official Death Certificate As Evidence of Cause of Death in Civil or Criminal Action,* 21 ALR3d 418 (1968); Sapir & King, *Cross-Examination of Breath Alcohol Machine Operators,* 13 S Ill U L J 83 (1988); Giannelli, *The Admissibility of Laboratory Reports in Criminal Trials: The Reliability of Scientific Proof,* 49 Ohio St L J 671 (1988).

RULE 803. ORS 40.460. HEARSAY EXCEPTION; AVAILABILITY OF DECLARANT IMMATERIAL

The following are not excluded by Rule 802 (ORS 40.455), even though the declarant is available as a witness:

(9) [Records of vital statistics.] Records or data compilations, in any form, of births, fetal deaths, deaths or marriages, if the report thereof was made to a public office pursuant to requirements of law.

LEGISLATIVE COMMENTARY

Subsection (9). Due to their personal importance, records of vital statistics are painstakingly accurate and often the subject of particular statutes making them admissible in evidence. Uniform Vital Statistics Act, 9C ULA 350 (1957). In Oregon, ORS 43.380 provides that each certificate provided for in ORS chapter 432, relating to vital statistics, when filed within six months after the time prescribed for its filing, shall be prima facie evidence of the facts stated therein.

This subsection is patterned on California Evidence Code § 1281. In principle it is narrower than Uniform Rule 63(16), which includes the reports that are required of persons performing functions authorized by statute. In practical effect, however, the two rules are substantially the same. Uniform Rule 63(16), Comment.

TEXT

Records of Vital Statistics

Rule 803(9) creates a hearsay exception for records or data compilations, in any form, of births, fetal records, deaths, or marriages, if the report thereof was made to a public office pursuant to requirements of law. Whereas Rule 803(8) covers reports *of* a public office, Rule 803(9) covers reports *to* a public office. Under this rule the person preparing the report is not required to be a public officer. The declarant may be a family member, doctor, minister, or undertaker. See also ORS 432.120(1)(b) (a certified copy of a vital record "shall be prima facie evidence of the facts stated therein.").

No witness need be called to lay the foundation for admission of a record under this exception. Usually a copy of the public record certified pursuant to Rule 902(4) will be offered.

It is uncertain whether opinions and conclusions contained in records of vital statistics, such as the conclusion of a coroner regarding the cause of death, are always admissible under this exception. To allow such a conclusion against a defendant in a criminal case would raise a substantial right of confrontation issue.

In *Seater v. Penn Mut. Life Ins. Co.,* 176 Or 542, 156 P2d 386, 159 P2d 826 (1945), the court held that statements regarding the cause of death in a death certificate were inadmissible. The Commentary to Rule 803(12) states that *Seater* is modified by that rule. This statement in the Commentary should not be viewed as indicating a legislative intent that all opinions and conclusions in records of vital statistics admissible under Rule 803(9) or certificates admissible under Rule 803(12) are allowed, no matter how ill-founded or unreliable. Such an interpretation would be inconsistent with the clearly expressed legislative intent to narrowly confine the admissibility of "factual findings" in public records in Rule 803(8)(c).

A better approach would be for courts, pursuant to Rule 403, to apply a standard similar to that of Rule 803(6) and Rule 803(8)(c), and exclude the opinion or conclusion if "the sources of information or other circumstances indicate lack of trustworthiness."

RULE 803.   ORS 40.460. HEARSAY EXCEPTION; AVAILABILITY OF DECLARANT IMMATERIAL

The following are not excluded by Rule 802 (ORS 40.455), even though the declarant is available as a witness:

(10) [Absence of public record or entry.] To prove the absence of a record, report, statement, or data compilation, in any form, or the nonoccurrence or nonexistence of a matter of which a record, report, statement, or data compilation, in any form, was regularly made and preserved by a public office or agency, evidence in the form of a certification in accordance with Rule 902 (ORS 40.510), or testimony, that diligent search failed to disclose the record, report, statement, or data compilation, or entry.

LEGISLATIVE COMMENTARY

Subsection (10). In this subsection, the principle that allows proof of the nonoccurrence of an event by evidence of the absence of a record, developed in subsection (7) with respect to business activities, is extended to public records of the kind mentioned in subsections (8) and (9). 5 Wigmore § 1633(6) at 519. Some harmless duplication of subsection (7) no doubt exists.

The subsection applies where the absence of a public record is the very point of inquiry, e.g., *People v. Love,* 310 Ill 558, 142 NE 204 (1923) (certificate of Secretary of State admitted to show failure to file documents required by securities law), as well as where the absence of a record is offered to prove the non-occurrence of an event ordinarily recorded.

The common law refused to allow proof by certificates of lack of record or entry. There is no apparent justification for this position. 5 Wigmore § 1678(7) at 752. Subsection (10) abandons it. Accord, Uniform Rule 63(17); California Evidence Code § 1284; Kansas Code of Civil Procedure § 60-460(c); New Jersey Evidence Rule 63(17).

Oregon has no statute or case law providing a general hearsay exception for the absence of a public record or an entry in a public record. However, there are specialized statutes that give effect to the underlying principle. See, e.g., ORS 57.781, 319.740(2). See also Swearingen, *How the Adoption of the Uniform Rules of Evidence Would Affect the Law of Evidence in Oregon, Rules 62-66,* in 42 Or L Rev 200, 232 (1963).

TEXT

Absence of Public Record or Entry

Rule 803(10) creates a hearsay exception for evidence in the form of testimony or a certificate pursuant to Rule 902 that diligent search failed to disclose a record, report, statement, data compilation, or entry to prove (1) the absence of that record, report, statement, or data compilation; or (2) the nonoccurrence or nonexistence of a matter of which a record, report, statement, or data compilation was regularly made and preserved by a public office or agency.

The public records referred to in Rule 803(10) are those specified in Rules 803(8) and 803(9). Unlike Rule 803(7), Rule 803(10) does not require testimony of a witness. A certificate complying with Rule 902 that a diligent search failed to disclose the record, report, statement, data compilation, or entry is expressly authorized. *State v. Wrisley,* 138 Or App 344, 350, 909 P2d 877 (1995) (ATF certification that search of its records could not find registration of firearm admissible under this exception).

Courts are likely to require a factual showing of the nature of the search and the specific efforts undertaken rather than merely a conclusory statement that a diligent search was conducted. The words "diligent search" should be used in the certificate, although failure to do so should not be found to be error if the certificate otherwise complies with the rule. See *United States v. Harris,* 551 F2d 621, 622 (5th Cir), cert denied 434 US 836 (1977). Cf. *United States v. Robinson,* 544 F2d 110, 115 (2nd Cir 1976), cert denied 434 US 1050 (1978) ("[A] casual or partial search cannot justify the conclusion that there was no record"); *United States v. Yakobov,* 712 F2d 20 (2nd Cir 1983) (certificate inadequate when search shown to have been based upon a misspelling of defendant's name).

The certification is only valid if it pertains to the nonexistence of records or entries in records regularly made and preserved by a particular public office or agency. *United States v. Stout,* 667 F2d 1347, 1352–3 (11th Cir 1982) (certification improper because it extended to records not regularly made and preserved by office).

Apart from particularized statutory provisions (see, e.g., ORS 57.781), such a hearsay exception was not recognized under prior Oregon law. See *State v. Harris,* 288 Or 703, 609 P2d 798 (1980); RECENT DEVELOPMENT, *Evidence—New Confusion Under the Hearsay Rule: State v. Harris,* 59 Or L Rev 497 (1981).

Evidence offered under FRE 803(10), which is identical to Oregon Rule 803(10), has been held to be properly admissible against defendants in criminal cases. See *United States v. Johnson,* 577 F2d 1304 (5th Cir 1978) (certificate admitted to prove that no record existed of tax returns filed by defendant); *United States v. Cepeda Penes,* 577 F2d 754 (1st Cir 1978) (certificate admitted to show failure to file tax returns); *United States v. Lee,* 589 F2d 980 (9th Cir), cert denied 444 US 969 (1979) (certificate admitted to show that defendant had not been employed by CIA).

RULE 803.   ORS 40.460. HEARSAY EXCEPTION; AVAILABILITY OF DECLARANT IMMATERIAL

The following are not excluded by Rule 802 (ORS 40.455), even though the declarant is available as a witness:

(11) [Records of religious organizations.] Statements of births, marriages, divorces, deaths, legitimacy, ancestry, relationship by blood or marriage, or other similar facts of personal or family history, contained in a regularly kept record of a religious organization.

LEGISLATIVE COMMENTARY

Subsection (11). Currently, records of activities of religious organizations are not excluded as hearsay at least to the extent of the business records exception to the hearsay rule. 5 Wigmore § 1523 at 371. However, the business records doctrine requires that the person furnishing the information be one in the business or activity. The result is such decisions as *Daily v. Grand Lodge,* 311 Ill 184, 142 NE 478 (1924), holding a church record admissible to prove the fact, date and place of a baptism, but not the age of a child except that the information would be furnished on occasions of this kind, this subsection contains no requirement that the declarant be regularly engaged in the activity of the religious organization. See California Evidence Code § 1315 and Comment thereto. Until this subsection, Oregon's position on a hearsay exception for records of religious organizations has been unclear.

TEXT

Records of Religious Organizations

Rule 803(11) creates a hearsay exception for statements of births, marriages, divorces, deaths, legitimacy, ancestry, relationship by blood or marriage, or other similar facts of personal or family history contained in a regularly kept record of a religious organization. In most cases such records will be admissible as records of regularly conducted activity under Rule 803(6). Rule 803(6), however, contains a "duty to report" requirement for all declarants. A statement included in a business record not made by a person having a "duty to report" is inadmissible unless it satisfies an independent hearsay exception. See discussion of Rule 803(6). Rule 803(11) eliminates the "duty to report" requirement for records of religious organizations. In cases where the record appears highly untrustworthy and the danger of unfair prejudice or of misleading the jury substantially outweighs its probative value, Rule 403 authorizes exclusion.

See generally ANNOT., *Exception to Hearsay Rule, Under Rule 803(11) or Rule 803(12) of Federal Rules of Evidence, With Respect to Information Contained in Records of Religious Organization*, 78 ALR Fed 361 (1986).

RULE 803. ORS 40.460. HEARSAY EXCEPTION; AVAILABILITY OF DECLARANT IMMATERIAL

The following are not excluded by Rule 802 (ORS 40.455), even though the declarant is available as a witness:

(12) [Marriage, baptismal and similar certificates.] A statement of fact contained in a certificate that the maker performed a marriage or other ceremony or administered a sacrament, made by a clergyman, public official, or other person authorized by the rules or practices of a religious organization or by law to perform the act certified, and purporting to have been issued at the time of the act or within a reasonable time thereafter.

LEGISLATIVE COMMENTARY

Subsection (12). Keeping with the principle of proof by certification, recognized as to public officials in subsections (8) and (10), this subsection creates a hearsay exception for marriage, baptismal and similar certificates. It duplicates the other subsections to the extent the person performing the ceremony and signing the certificate is a public official, such as a judge. However, it extends the exception to the certificates of non-public officials who are authorized to perform ceremonies. Certificates of clergy regarding marriage, baptism or confirmation are thus included. See 5 Wigmore § 1645 (marriage certificates). For similar rules, some limited to certificates of marriage and with variations in foundation requirements, see Uniform Rule 63(18); California Evidence Code § 1316; Kansas Code of Civil Procedure § 60-460(p); New Jersey Evidence Rule 63(18).

When a certificate is executed by a person who is not a public official it lacks the self-authenticating character of a document purporting to emanate from a public official. See ORE 902. In that case, proof is required that the declarant was authorized and did make the certificate. Once authority and authenticity are established, the court may safely take the date and time from the certificate, particularly in view of the presumption that a document is executed on the date it bears.

The Oregon decisions have not agreed on a hearsay exception for marriage, baptismal and similar certificates. Although it was not technically a hearsay ruling, a marriage certificate has been allowed into evidence as part of the res gestae to prove the identity of parties to a marriage. *State v. Isenhart*, 32 Or 170, 52 P 569 (1898). A death certificate has also been held competent evidence of the facts therein, although these were not within the personal knowledge of the declarant. *State v. McDonald*, 55 Or 419, 104 P 967 (1909), *aff'd on rehearing*, 59 Or 520, 117 P 281 (1911), *appeal dismissed*, 63 Or 467, 128 P 835 (1912). More recently, however, statements in a death certificate that death was due to an accident and that a fall was the means of injury were held inadmissible. *Seater v. Penn Mutual Life Ins. Co.*, 176 Or 542, 156 P2d 386 (1945). Insofar as Seater is declarative of the law in Oregon, subsection (12) changes that law.

TEXT

Marriage, Baptismal, and Similar Certificates

Rule 803(12) creates a hearsay exception for marriage, baptismal, and similar certificates. The certificate may be made by any person, specifically including a clergy member or public official, authorized by the rules or practices of a religious organization or by law to perform the act certified. The certificate must have been issued at the time of the act or within a reasonable time thereafter.

Where the maker of the certificate is a public official, this exception overlaps with Rule 803(8), which creates a hearsay exception for public records. According to the Commentary, the purpose of this rule is to extend "the exception to the certificates of non-public officials who are authorized to perform ceremonies." Rule 803(12) also overlaps with Rule 803(9), which admits marriage certificates and other certificates filed with a public office, and with Rule 803(11), which admits records of religious organizations.

Although the Commentary refers to death certificates, the admissibility of death certificates is more appropriately analyzed under Rule 803(9). Rule 803(12) is directed towards certificates proving performance of ceremonial acts.

See generally ANNOT., *Exception to Hearsay Rule, Under Rule 803(11) or Rule 803(12) of Federal Rules of Evidence, With Respect to Information Contained in Records of Religious Organization*, 78 ALR Fed 361 (1986).

RULE 803.   ORS 40.460. HEARSAY EXCEPTION; AVAILABILITY OF DECLARANT IMMATERIAL

The following are not excluded by Rule 802 (ORS 40.455), even though the declarant is available as a witness:

(13) [Family records.] Statements of facts concerning personal or family history contained in family bibles, genealogies, charts, engravings on rings, inscriptions on family portraits, engravings on urns, crypts, or tombstones, or the like.

LEGISLATIVE COMMENTARY

Subsection (13). Evidence that is otherwise hearsay may be admissible if its source is certain family records. Subsection (13) describes these records. The coverage is substantially identical to California Evidence Code § 1312.

Oregon had no developed law on this issue. However, there is a long tradition elsewhere of receiving records of family history kept in family bibles. 5 Wigmore §§ 1495, 1496, citing numerous statutes and decisions. The opinions also admit inscriptions on tombstones, publicly displayed pedigrees and engravings on rings. *Id.*

The Legislative Assembly intends that "statements of facts concerning personal or family history" be read to include the specific types of such statements enumerated in subsection (11) of this rule.

TEXT

Family Records

Rule 803(13) creates a hearsay exception for statements of facts concerning personal or family history contained in family Bibles, genealogies, charts, engravings on rings, inscriptions on family portraits, engravings on urns, crypts, or tombstones, or the like. The statements of personal or family history admissible under this exception include statements of births, marriages, divorces, deaths, legitimacy, ancestry, or relationship by blood or marriage.

The rule does not require that the statement has been made by a family member. The rationale of the rule is that an erroneous statement would not be allowed to remain in family records without challenge or correction.

RULE 803. ORS 40.460. HEARSAY EXCEPTION; AVAILABILITY OF DECLARANT IMMATERIAL

The following are not excluded by Rule 802 (ORS 40.455), even though the declarant is available as a witness:

(14) [Records of documents affecting an interest in property.] The record of a document purporting to establish or affect an interest in property, as proof of content of the original recorded document and its execution and delivery by each person by whom it purports to have been executed, if the record is a record of a public office and an applicable statute authorizes the recording of documents of that kind in that office.

LEGISLATIVE COMMENTARY

Subsection (14). Yet another exception to the hearsay rule is that for records of documents affecting an interest in property. The recording of title documents is a purely statutory development, and under any theory of admissibility of public records the records of title documents should be receivable as evidence of the contents of the recorded document. Any other rule would reduce the recording process to a nullity.

When the record is offered for the further purpose of proving execution and delivery, as opposed to contents, a problem of lack of firsthand knowledge by the recorder is presented. This problem is solved, seemingly in all jurisdictions, by qualifying for recording only those documents shown to have been executed and delivered by a specified procedure, either acknowledgment or a form of probate. 5 Wigmore §§ 1647–1651.

This subsection is similar to ORS 93.650, which admits the record or transcript of a conveyance duly recorded and certified by the county clerk in whose office the document is recorded. In addition, ORS 43.340 provides that a public record of a private writing may be proved by the original record or by a copy certified by the legal keeper of the record. Other more specialized statutes give effect to the principle underlying the exception for records of title documents. ORS 43.420 (admitting record or copy of sheriffs deed if original destroyed); ORS 93.670 (admitting land sale contracts); ORS 93.680 (admitting government land grant patents, decrees of equity courts requiring execution of a conveyance, approved lists of lands granted to the state, and conveyance of state lands by any state officer).

TEXT

Records of Documents Affecting an Interest in Property

Rule 803(14) creates a hearsay exception for the record of a document purporting to establish or affect an interest in property, offered to prove (1) the content of the original recorded document, and (2) its execution and delivery by each person by whom it purports to have been executed. This exception requires that the record be a record of a public office and that an applicable statute authorize the recording of documents of that kind in that office. See ORS 93.610–.800.

This exception applies only when a record of the document rather than the document itself is offered. When the original document is offered, Rule 803(15) applies. Rule 803(14) overlaps with Rule 803(8), which creates a hearsay exception for public records.

This rule is consistent with ORS 93.650, which provides:

> The record of a conveyance duly recorded, or a transcript thereof certified by the county clerk in whose office it is recorded may be read in evidence in any court in the state, with the like effect as the original conveyance. However, the effect of such evidence may be rebutted by other competent testimony.

RULE 803. ORS 40.460. HEARSAY EXCEPTION; AVAILABILITY OF DECLARANT IMMATERIAL

The following are not excluded by Rule 802 (ORS 40.455), even though the declarant is available as a witness:

(15) [Statements in documents affecting an interest in property.] A statement contained in a document purporting to establish or affect an interest in property if the matter stated was relevant to the purpose of the document, unless dealings with the property since the document was made have been inconsistent with the truth of the statement or the purport of the document.

LEGISLATIVE COMMENTARY

Subsection (15). Dispositive documents often contain recitals of fact. A deed purporting to have been executed by an attorney in fact may recite the existence of the power of attorney. A land sales contract may recite that the sellers are all the heirs of the last owner of record. Under this subsection, these recitals are exempted from the hearsay rule. Accord, ORS 43.420 (in certain circumstances, record of sheriff's deed is "prima facie evidence of all facts therein recited"); *Sperry v. Wesco,* 26 Or 483, 38 P 623 (1894) (deed description admissible to show location of boundary line); *Altschul v. Casey,* 45 Or 182, 76 P 1083 (1904) (deed recital prima facie evidence of authority to execute deed). The statements may be trusted for several reasons: (1) the circumstances under which the dispositive documents were executed, (2) the requirement that the recital be germane to the purpose of the document, and (3) the provision that the exception does not apply if dealings with the property have been inconsistent with the document. The age of the document is of no significance, although in practice it will most often be an ancient document. See subsection (16), infra; Uniform Rule 63(29), Comment. Similar provisions are contained in California Evidence Code § 1330; Kansas Code of Civil Procedure § 60-460(aa); New Jersey Evidence Rule 63(29).

TEXT

Statements in Documents Affecting an Interest in Property

Rule 803(15) creates a hearsay exception for statements contained in a document purporting to establish or affect an interest in property if the matter stated was relevant to the purpose of the document, unless dealings with the property since the document was made have been inconsistent with the statement's truth or the document's purport. The rule does not require that the document have been recorded for this exception to apply.

This rule should be considered in conjunction with ORS 42.300, which provides: "Except for the recital of a consideration, the truth of the facts recited from the recital in a written instrument shall not be denied by the parties thereto, their representatives or successors in interest by a subsequent title."

In *Star Rentals v. Seeberg Construction Company, Inc.*, 83 Or App 44, 730 P2d 573 (1986), plaintiff attempted to prove posting of the notice of completion of a construction project by an affidavit on the back of the completion notice. The court held that this affidavit was hearsay and did not qualify for admission under Rule 803(15). The court stated: "In order for that exception to apply, the document must establish or affect an interest in property." 83 Or App at 49.

RULE 803.   ORS 40.460. HEARSAY EXCEPTION; AVAILABILITY OF DECLARANT IMMATERIAL

The following are not excluded by Rule 802 (ORS 40.455), even though the declarant is available as a witness:

(16) [Statements in ancient documents.] Statements in a document in existence 20 years or more the authenticity of which is established.

LEGISLATIVE COMMENTARY

Subsection (16). Subsection (16) creates a hearsay exception for authenticated ancient documents. The mere fact that an ancient document has been authenticated, see ORE 901(2)(h), does not decide whether statements that are in it are admissible as against a hearsay objection. 7 Wigmore § 2145a.

As Wigmore points out, however, a variety of ancient documents have been authenticated whose only possible evidential value is as statements—letters, contracts, maps, certificates, and title papers, for example.

The practice reflects a persistent belief that the documents can be trusted. *Id.* § 2145. Danger of mistake is minimized by authentication requirements, and age affords assurance that the writing antedates the present controversy. McCormick § 323. See *Dallas County v. Commercial Union Assurance Co.,* 286 F2d 388 (5th Cir 1961) (upholding admissibility of 58-year-old newspaper story). Cf. Morgan, *Basic Problems of Evidence* § 364 (1962), but see *id.* at 254. Although Oregon law recognized the ancient document rule for purposes of authentication, ORS 41.360(34) and 42.080, there are no reported cases holding that statements in an ancient document are admissible as substantive evidence as an exception to the hearsay rule.

TEXT

Statements in Ancient Documents

Rule 803(16) creates a hearsay exception for statements in a document in existence 20 years or more the authenticity of which is established. Under Rule 901(2)(h), authentication is established by a showing that the document: (1) is in such condition as to create no suspicion concerning its authenticity; (2) was in a place where, if authentic, it would likely be; and (3) has been in existence 20 years or more at the time it is offered.

This rule marks a change in Oregon law. Under prior law the fact that a document was ancient could serve to authenticate the document, but would not render it admissible for the truth of the matter asserted therein. See ORS 41.360(34) (repealed 1981). Documents within the new rule are now admissible as substantive evidence.

For cases construing the identical federal rule, see *Bell v. Combined Registry Co.,* 397 F Supp 1241 (ED Ill 1975), aff'd 536 F2d 164 (7th Cir), cert denied 429 US 1001 (1976) (court admitted letters and newspaper articles from the 1930s and 1940s as ancient documents); *Sekaquaptewa v. MacDonald,* 448 F Supp 1183 (D Ariz 1978), modified on other grounds 619 F2d 801 (9th Cir), cert denied 449 US 1010 (1980) (historical material admitted).

The term "document" in FRE 803(16) "embraces written materials of all kinds, including letters, diaries, newspapers, contracts, receipts, maps, and so forth." 4 C. Mueller & L. Kirkpatrick, FEDERAL EVIDENCE (2d ed 1994) § 466. The offering party can be required to show that the declarant had the requisite knowledge to make the statement, unless such knowledge is evident from the face of the document or other circumstances.

RULE 803. ORS 40.460. HEARSAY EXCEPTION; AVAILABILITY OF DECLARANT IMMATERIAL

The following are not excluded by Rule 802 (ORS 40.455), even though the declarant is available as a witness:

(17) [Market reports and commercial publications.] Market quotations, tabulations, lists, directories, or other published compilations, generally used and relied upon by the public or by persons in particular occupations.

LEGISLATIVE COMMENTARY

Subsection (17). Ample authority at common law supported the admission into evidence of items that fall within the categories listed in this subsection, i.e., market reports and commercial publications. The trier of fact may trust such hearsay, because the public or a particular segment of the public trusts it, and because the compiler is motivated to foster reliance by being accurate. While Wigmore's text is narrowly oriented to lists that are prepared for the use of a trade or profession, 6 Wigmore § 1702, it cites authorities that exempt other kinds of publications such as newspaper market reports, telephone directories and city directories. *Id.* §§ 1702-1706. For similar provisions, see Uniform Rule 63(30); California Evidence Code § 1340; Kansas Code of Civil Procedure § 60-460(bb); New Jersey Evidence Rule 63(30).

This subsection is consistent with present Oregon law. Although there are no reported cases in which market reports or commercial publications have been admitted as exceptions to the hearsay rule, ORS 72.7240 provides for the admission of market reports in official publications, trade journals and newspapers of general circulation to prove the prevailing price of goods. Standard mortality tables have been admitted as evidence in several cases. *Snyder v. Portland Tractor Co.,* 182 Or 344, 185 P2d 563 (1947); *Frangos v. Edmunds,* 179 Or 577, 173 P2d 596 (1946).

TEXT

Market Reports and Commercial Publications

Rule 803(17) creates a hearsay exception for market quotations, tabulations, lists, directories, or other published compilations, generally used and relied upon by the public or by persons in particular occupations. This rule supplements ORS 72.7240, which admits "reports in official publications or trade journals or in newspapers or periodicals of general circulation published as the reports of such [established commodity) market" to prove the prevailing price of goods.

For cases interpreting FRE 803(17), see *United States v. Anderson,* 532 F2d 1218, 1225 (9th Cir), cert denied 429 US 839 (1976) (Wall Street Journal admitted to prove stock price); *United States v. Johnson,* 515 F2d 730, 732 (7th Cir 1975)

("Red Book" published by National Market Report admissible to show wholesale and retail price of automobile); *United States v. Grossman,* 614 F2d 295, 297 (1st Cir 1980) (catalog of manufacturer would be admissible to show retail value of stolen property). See also ANNOT., *Admissibility in Evidence of Professional Directories,* 7 ALR4th 638 (1981).

It is questionable whether credit reports are admissible under this subsection, at least to the extent that they contain evaluations and conclusions as distinguished from objective facts. See 4 J. Weinstein and M. Berger, WEINSTEIN'S EVIDENCE (1988) § 803(17)[01].

AUTHOR'S NOTE REGARDING FRE 803(18)

FRE 803(18) creates a hearsay exception for:

> To the extent called to the attention of an expert witness upon cross-examination or relied upon by him in direct examination, statements contained in published treatises, periodicals, or pamphlets on a subject of history, medicine, or other science or art, established as a reliable authority by the testimony or admission of the witness or by other expert testimony or by judicial notice. If admitted the statements may be read into evidence but may not be received as exhibits.

In a note following the Commentary to Rule 18a, the reason for not adopting FRE 803(18) is explained as follows:

> NOTE: The Legislative Assembly did not adopt the federal hearsay exception for learned treatises which appears as subsection (18) of Fed R Evid 803. It wishes to retain the Oregon practice of using treatises in the cross-examination of expert witnesses. Learned treatises should not be admitted as substantive evidence as they are likely to be misunderstood and misapplied in the absence of expert assistance and supervision.

This explanation is somewhat puzzling, because FRE 803(18) expressly requires that an expert witness be on the stand subject to examination before a statement in a learned treatise may be introduced.

Although the omission of FRE 803(18) means that statements in treatises cannot be received for their truth, they still may be used to impeach the testimony of an expert witness. For a discussion of the use of treatises as a mode of impeachment of expert witnesses, see the textual discussion under Rules 607 and 702. With an appropriate foundation, it may also sometimes be possible to introduce a statement from a treatise as a basis for expert testimony under Rule 703, but not to establish the truth of the matter asserted.

In *Travis v. Unruh,* 66 Or App 562, 674 P2d 1192, rev denied 297 Or 82, 679 P2d 1367 (1984), the court held it was error for the trial court to allow the plaintiff's expert to summarize a study in a medical journal.

See generally ANNOT., *Treatises, Periodicals or Pamphlets as Exception to Hearsay Rule Under Rule 803(18) of the Federal Rules of Evidence,* 64 ALR Fed

971 (1983); Heckert, *Use of Learned Treatises at Trial,* 28 Trial Law Guide 165 (1984).

RULE 803.   ORS 40.460. HEARSAY EXCEPTION; AVAILABILITY OF DECLARANT IMMATERIAL

The following are not excluded by Rule 802 (ORS 40.455), even though the declarant is available as a witness:

> **(18a)(a) [Complaint of sexual misconduct.] A complaint of sexual misconduct or complaint of abuse as defined in ORS 419B.005 made by the witness after the commission of the alleged misconduct or abuse at issue. Except as provided in paragraph (b) of this subsection, such evidence must be confined to the fact that the complaint was made.**

LEGISLATIVE COMMENTARY

Subsection (18a)(a). Although the Federal Rules of Evidence do not mention this exception, the Legislative Assembly exempted a complaint of sexual misconduct from the hearsay rule. This subsection recognizes the holding in *State v. Waites,* 7 Or App 137 470 P2d 188 (1971) and the trend in other jurisdictions

> "In rape cases, and increasingly in cases of sex offenses generally, evidence is admissible that the victim made complaint. The only time requirement is that the complaint have been made without a delay which is unexplained or inconsistent with the occurrence of the offense—in general, a much less demanding time aspect than with the typical excited utterance situation. In its origin, the theory of admissibility was to repel any inference that because the victim did not complain, no outrage in fact transpired. Accordingly, if the victim did not testify, evidence of complaint was not admissible ..." McCormick § 297 at 709.

The Oregon rule provides that a person to whom a complaint of sexual misconduct is made by the prosecuting witness can testify that a complaint was made, but cannot testify as to the details of the complaint. *State v. Waites,* supra, 7 Or App at 140; *State of Oregon v. Tom,* 8 Or 177 (1879); *State v. Sargent,* 32 Or 110, 49 P 889 (1897); *State v. Ogden,* 39 Or 195, 65 P 449 (1901); *State v. Whitman,* 72 Or 415, 143 P 1121 (1914); *State v. Matson,* 120 Or 666, 253 P 527 (1927); *State v. Haworth,* 143 Or 495, 21 P2d 172 (1964); *State v. Emery,* 4 Or App 527 at 530 n 1, 480 P2d 445 (1971); *State v. Wilson,* 20 Or App 553, 532 P2d 825 (1975). Accordingly, it has been held that testimony as to prior assaults and as to the location of the assault in question, *State v. Waites,* supra, and testimony as to the identity of the assailant, *State v. Wilson,* supra, is beyond the scope of the exception and inadmissible.

The Legislative Assembly intends to retain in full the present Oregon law relating to this exception.

> NOTE: The Legislative Assembly did not adopt the federal hearsay exception for learned treatises which appears as subsection (18) of Fed R Evid 803. It wishes to retain the Oregon practice of using treatises in the cross-examination of expert witnesses. Learned treatises should not be admitted as substantive evidence as they are likely to be misunderstood and misapplied in the absence of expert assistance and supervision.

TEXT

RULE 803(18a)(a)
Prior Complaint of Sexual Misconduct

Rule 803(18a) creates a hearsay exception for a complaint of sexual misconduct made by the prosecuting witness after the commission of the alleged offense. The exception only allows receipt of the fact that the complaint was made, not the identity of the alleged perpetrator or other facts surrounding the alleged offense, except as provided in Rule 803(18a)(b). The term "prosecuting witness" has been interpreted to mean the victim of sexual assault or abuse regardless of whether the victim testifies at trial. *State v. Campbell,* 299 Or 633, 641, 705 P2d 694 (1985).

The need to offer evidence under this exception usually arises in cases where the victim delayed reporting a sexual offense to authorities. To rebut the inference that no crime occurred, that the victim consented, or that the accusation was recently fabricated, this exception allows evidence of earlier complaints made to friends, family members, or other persons. The complaint may have been made in response to questioning. *State v. Robertson,* 55 Or App 1000, 640 P2d 701 (1982).

According to the Legislative Commentary, "testimony as to prior assaults and as to the location of the assault in question ... and testimony as to the identity of the assailant ... is beyond the scope of the exception and inadmissible." The exception is intended to allow for evidence of the fact that a prior complaint was made, but not for a verbatim account or listing of all the details of that complaint. However, it would be difficult for the jury to understand what kind of earlier complaint had been made if no details at all were allowed. Therefore, in *State v. Campbell,* 299 Or 633, 646, 705 P2d 694, 702 (1985), the court held that the rule "allows in enough of the hearsay declaration to show the nature of the complaint, even though it involves to some extent the particulars thereof."

There can be overlap between this exception and Rule 801(4)(a)(B), which provides for the admission of prior consistent statements under certain circumstances. It can be argued that a prior complaint of sexual misconduct does not even constitute hearsay, in cases where it is being offered not for the truth of what it asserts but merely as circumstantial evidence that the alleged victim behaved in a manner consistent with that of a person who had been sexually abused.

This exception is not recognized in the Federal Rules of Evidence. It is included to preserve prior Oregon case law. In addition to the cases cited in the Commentary, see *State v. Baker,* 46 Or App 79, 610 P2d 840 (1980); *State v. Hackett,* 49 Or App 857, 621 P2d 609 (1980); *State v. Robertson,* 55 Or App 1000, 640 P2d 701 (1982); *State v. Wolfe,* 56 Or App 795, 643 P2d 404 (1982). Reliance upon this exception is unnecessary in cases where the statement qualifies as an excited utterance under Rule 803(2) or a prior consistent statement under Rule 801(4)(a)(B). See *State v. Middleton,* 294 Or 427, 657 P2d 1215 (1983). See generally Graham, *The Cry of Rape: The Prompt Complaint Doctrine and the Federal Rules of Evidence,* 19 Will L Rev 489 (1983).

Recent Cases

State v. Arnold, 133 Or App 647, 650, 893 P2d 1050 (1995). The court held that out-of-court statements by a young sex crime victim went beyond OEC 803(18a)(a) because they proved more than a complaint had been made. They provided an elaborate description of the alleged abuse and identified the defendant as the perpetrator.

State v.Stevens, 311 Or 119, 138–42, 806 P2d 92 (1991). Statements of child sex abuse victims were admitted under Rule 803(18a).

State v. Vosika, 83 Or App 298, 731 P2d 449, on reconsideration 85 Or App 148, 735 P2d 1273 (1987). In this prosecution of a mother for sexual abuse of her three-year-old daughter, the court held that the testimony of the foster mother, an examining physician, and a police officer who had interviewed the child was admissible under this rule to establish that the child had made a prior complaint that she had been abused, but only the testimony of the physician was admissible under Rule 803(4) to establish the identity of the abuser.

State ex rel Juvenile Department v. Karabetsis, 77 Or App 583, 713 P2d 1075 (1986). The thirteen-year-old appellant appealed from an order finding him to be within the jurisdiction of the juvenile court for having engaged in sexual intercourse with his nine-year-old sister. The court ruled that testimony by a CSD worker and a police officer that the victim had made a prior report of sexual abuse was admissible under Rule 803(18a) and was sufficient to corroborate defendant's confession to the misconduct. However, the court found that additional details reported by the victim regarding the sexual activity were not admissible under either this exception or Rule 803(24).

State v. Campbell, 299 Or 633, 705 P2d 694 (1985). The court held the mother of a three-year-old sex crime victim would be allowed under this rule to relate the fact that the statement of sexual abuse was made by her daughter, without identifying the person accused of the offense. The court found that the statement regarding the abuse, even though not identifying the defendant, would be sufficient to corroborate the confession of the defendant. The court held that admission of a hearsay statement under this exception would not violate a defendant's right of confrontation, provided that either (1) the declarant testifies at trial and is subject to cross-examination, or (2) the unavailability of the declarant is established. In this case, the parties had stipulated that the declarant was incompetent to testify. However, the court held that the issue of competency should not be resolved by stipulation of counsel and remanded the case for a judicial determination of competency. On the right of confrontation, see textual discussion under Rule 802.

RULE 803. ORS 40.460. HEARSAY EXCEPTION; AVAILABILITY OF DECLARANT IMMATERIAL

The following are not excluded by Rule 802 (ORS 40.455), even though the declarant is available as a witness:

(18a)(b) A statement made by a child victim or person with developmental disabilities as described in paragraph (d) of this subsection, which statement concerns an act of abuse, as defined in ORS 419B.005, or sexual conduct performed with or on the child or person with developmental disabilities by another, is not excluded by Rule 802 (ORS 40.455) if the child or person with developmental disabilities either testifies at the proceeding and is subject to cross-examination or is chronologically or mentally under 12 years of age and is unavailable as a witness. However, when a witness under 12 years of age or a person with developmental disabilities is unavailable as a witness, the statement may be admitted in evidence only if the proponent establishes that the time, content and circumstances of the statement provide indicia of reliability, and in a criminal trial that there is corroborative evidence of the act of abuse or sexual conduct and of the alleged perpetrator's opportunity to participate in the conduct and that the statement possesses indicia of reliability as is constitutionally required to be admitted. No statement may be admitted under this paragraph unless the proponent of the statement makes known to the adverse party the proponent's intention to offer the statement and the particulars of the statement no later than 15 days before trial, except for good cause shown. For purposes of this paragraph, in addition to those situations described in Rule 804(1) (ORS 40.465(1)), the child or person with developmental disabilities shall be considered "unavailable" if the child or person with developmental disabilities has a substantial lack of memory of the subject matter of the statement, is presently incompetent to testify, is unable to communicate about the abuse or sexual conduct because of fear or other similar reason or is substantially likely, as established by expert testimony, to suffer lasting severe emotional trauma from testifying. Unless

566

otherwise agreed by the parties, the court shall examine the child or person with developmental disabilities in chambers and on the record or outside the presence of the jury and on the record. The examination shall be conducted immediately prior to the commencement of the trial in the presence of the attorney and the legal guardian or other suitable adult as designated by the court. If the child or person with developmental disabilities is found to be unavailable, the court shall then determine the admissibility of the evidence. The determinations shall be appealable under ORS 138.060(3). The purpose of the examination shall be to aid the court in making its findings regarding the availability of the child or person with developmental disabilities as a witness and the reliability of the statement of the child or person with developmental disabilities. In determining whether a statement possesses indicia of reliability under this paragraph, the court may consider, but is not limited to, the following factors:

(A) The personal knowledge of the child or person with developmental disabilities of the event;

(B) The age and maturity of the child or extent of disability of the person with developmental disabilities;

(C) Certainty that the statement was made, including the credibility of the person testifying about the statement and any motive the person may have to falsify or distort the statement;

(D) Any apparent motive the child or person with developmental disabilities may have to falsify or distort the event, including bias, corruption or coercion;

(E) The timing of the statement of the child or person with developmental disabilities;

(F) Whether more than one person heard the statement;

(G) Whether the child or person with developmental disabilities was suffering pain or distress when making the statement;

(H) Whether the child's young age makes it unlikely that the child fabricated a statement that represents a graphic, detailed account beyond the child's knowledge and experience;

(I) Whether the statement has internal consistency or coherence and uses terminology appropriate to the child's age or to the extent of disability of the person with developmental disabilities;

(J) Whether the statement is spontaneous or directly responsive to questions; and

(K) Whether the statement was elicited by leading questions.

(c) This subsection applies to all civil, criminal and juvenile proceedings.

(d) For the purposes of this subsection, "developmental disabilities" means any disability attributable to mental retardation, autism, cerebral palsy, epilepsy or other disabling neurological condition that requires training or support similar to that required by persons with mental retardation, if either of the following apply:

   (A) The disability originates before the person attains 22 years of age, or if the disability is attributable to mental retardation the condition is manifested before the person attains 18 years of age, the disability can be expected to continue indefinitely, and the disability constitutes a substantial handicap to the ability of the person to function in society.

   (B) The disability results in a significant subaverage general intellectual functioning with concurrent deficits in adaptive behavior that are manifested during the developmental period.

LEGISLATIVE COMMENTARY

[There is no Legislative Commentary to OEC 803(18a)(b). It was not part of the original Evidence Code. It was enacted by the 1989 Legislature and further amended in 1991 and 1995.]

TEXT

Statements of Child Sex Abuse Victims; Developmentally Disabled

Rule 803(18a)(b) creates a hearsay exception for statements of child sex abuse victims under twelve years of age and persons with developmental disabilities. The exception applies in civil, criminal, and juvenile court proceedings.

If the child or person with developmental disabilities testifies at the proceeding and is subject to cross-examination, the exception presents relatively few difficulties. The proponent of the statement must give fifteen days' notice of the intent to offer such a statement.

The real utility of the exception is likely to arise in cases where the child or person with developmental disabilities is unavailable to testify at trial. In such cases, the rule makes it possible, under carefully defined circumstances, to offer the child's or person's hearsay statement at trial. The proponent must establish to the satisfaction of the court outside the presence of the jury that the time, content, and circumstances of the statement provide indicia of reliability. In a criminal case, if the child or person with developmental disabilities is unavailable as a witness, the statement may be admitted only if there is corroborative evidence of the act of sexual conduct and of the defendant's opportunity to participate in the conduct. Constitutional requirements of reliability must also be satisfied.

Unavailability

The Rule specifies four grounds of unavailability: (1) the child has a substantial lack of memory of the subject matter of the statement; (2) the child is presently incompetent to testify, usually because of immaturity; (3) the child is unable to communicate about the offense because of fear or other similar reason; or (4) the child is substantially likely, as established by expert testimony, to suffer lasting severe emotional trauma from testifying. The rule also incorporates the grounds of unavailability specified in Rule 804(1).

In *State v. Higgins*, 136 Or App 590, 595–6, 902 P2d 612 (1995), the court found an insufficient showing of unavailability where the children were able to communicate about the allegations of sexual abuse at the pretrial hearing but recanted prior to trial. Even though there was evidence that the recantation might have resulted from threats or inducements, the court held that "[t]here is nothing in the statutory language that equates a recantation of prior testimony with the inabililty to communicate or testify in court."

Hearing on Unavailability

In determining availability, the judge is authorized to conduct an examination of the child or developmentally disabled person in chambers or otherwise outside the presence of the jury, provided the examination is conducted on the record. The examination is to be conducted in the presence of the attorney and the child's legal guardian or other suitable adult as designated by the court.

The rule is silent on whether the defendant is entitled to be present at the pretrial hearing. However, in *State v. Kitzman*, 323 Or 589, 920 P2d 134 (1996), the court held that the defendant has a constitutional right under Article I, section 11 of the Oregon Constitution to be present at a pretrial availability hearing while a child who allegedly is a victim of sexual abuse is testifying and to have defense counsel examine the child at such hearing. In order to OEC 803(18a)(b) to be constitutional, the court interpreted the rule as guaranteeing these rights. The court applied the maxim that when there are two plausible interpretations of a statute, the court will assume that the legislature intended the constitutional meaning.

See generally Montoya, *Something Not So Funny Happened on the Way to Conviction: The Pretrial Interrogation of Child Witnesses*, 35 Ariz L Rev 927 (1993).

Reliability and Corroboration

In addition to determining whether the child is unavailable, the trial judge must also determine whether the statement possesses indicia of reliability. The rule provides eleven factors to be considered by the court in making this determination.

In *State v. Hill*, 129 Or App 180, 184–6, 877 P2d 1230 (1994), the court held that a four-year-old child's statements that she had been sexually abused by the defendant were sufficiently reliable to satisfy this exception. Moreover, the court found that the hearsay statements were sufficiently corroborated by medical evidence and evidence of the child "acting out" sexual activity. However, the court interpreted the exception as applying only to abuse of the declarant and held that the declarant's statements about similar sexual abuse of her two-year-old sister were inadmissible.

In *State v. Renly*, 111 Or App 453, 462–6, 827 P2d 1345, 1350 (1992), the court held that the child's hearsay statement alleging sexual misconduct was improperly admitted because the corroboration of the statute was not properly satisfied. The court noted that there was no "independent corroborating evidence... showing that the accused had access to the purported victim." The court found that "the legislature clearly intended that a defendant not be convicted on hearsay alone."

In *State ex rel Juvenile Department v. Hill*, 116 Or App 379, 841 P2d 2 (1992), the court noted that corroboration is not a constitutional mandate, but is required to "insure that an accused not be convicted solely on the basis of hearsay." The court found sufficient corroboration based on an admission made by the accused.

In *State v. Booth*, 124 Or App 282, 291, 862 P2d 518, 523 (1993), *Booth v. Oregon*, cert denied, 115 SCt 372 (1994), the court held that the statements by a three-year-old girl alleging sexual abuse by her father were sufficiently reliable on the facts of the case to satisfy the requirements of the rule.

In *State v. Kitzman*, 323 Or 589, 920 P2d 134 (1996), the court held that noncompliance with ORS 418.747 (1991), which regulates the interrogation of child abuse victims, does not require suppression of statements taken in violation of the statute. Nonetheless, the procedures used to obtain the statements may bear on their admissibility under OEC 803(18a)(b).

See generally Amer Psych Ass'n, *The Suggestibility of Children's Recollections* (John Davis ed., 1991); Patton, *Evolution in Child Abuse Litigation: The Theoretical Void Where Evidentiary and Procedural Worlds Collide*, 25 Loy L A L Rev 1009 (1992).

Right of Confrontation

In cases where the child testifies, the rule would appear to satisfy the right of confrontation, provided a careful assessment is made of the reliability of the hearsay statement. In cases where the child does not testify, the rule must be applied in such a way so as to satisfy both the reliability and the unavailability standards required by the confrontation guarantees of the federal and state constitutions.

In *State v. Kitzman*, 323 Or 589, 920 P2d 134 (1996), the court held that it is a violation of Article I, section 11 of the Oregon Constitution (1) to exclude a defendant from a pretrial availability hearing while a child who allegedly is a victim of sexual abuse is testifying and (2) to preclude a defendant's lawyer from examining the child at such hearing.

In *Idaho v. Wright*, 497 US 805 (1990), the United States Supreme Court found constitutional error in the admission of hearsay statements of child sex abuse victims under the Idaho residual hearsay exception. The Court held that the residual exception was not a "firmly rooted" hearsay exception and, therefore, the prosecution had to demonstrate particularized guarantees of trustworthiness. Such guarantees must be found from the totality of relevant circumstances surrounding the making of the statement and must be at least as reliable as evidence admitted under a "firmly rooted" hearsay exception. Subsequent corroboration of the criminal act is not to be considered in determining the statement's trustworthiness. The court identified four factors for the trial court to consider, in addition to other factors, in assessing reliability: (1) spontaneity and consistent repetition; (2) mental state of the declarant; (3) use of terminology unexpected of a child of such an age; and (4) lack of motive to fabricate. These factors are already included among the factors listed in Rule 803(18a)(b). The rule appears to be more strict than the *Wright* standard, in that even after the determination of unavailability and reliability is made the rule requires corroboration of the act of sexual conduct and of the defendant's participation in it. Thus, the rule does not allow a conviction to be based upon the hearsay statement alone.

In *State v. Booth*, 124 Or App 282, 291, 862 P2d 518, 523 (1993), *Booth v. Oregon*, cert denied, 115 S Ct 372 (1994), the court held that statements qualifying for admission under this rule do not violate a defendant's right of confrontation under the state and federal constitutions. See also *State ex rel Juvenile Department v. Hill*, 116 Or App 379, 841 P2d 2 (1992) (upholding constitutionality of rule); *State v. Renly*, 111 Or App 453, 462, 827 P2d 1345, 1350 (1992) (same).

RULE 803. ORS 40.460. HEARSAY EXCEPTION; AVAILABILITY OF DECLARANT IMMATERIAL

The following are not excluded by Rule 802 (ORS 40.455), even though the declarant is available as a witness:

(19) **[Reputation concerning personal or family history.] Reputation among members of a person's family by blood, adoption or marriage, or among a person's associates, or in the community, concerning a person's birth, adoption, marriage, divorce, death, legitimacy, relationship by blood or adoption or marriage, ancestry, or other similar fact of a person's personal or family history.**

LEGISLATIVE COMMENTARY

Subsections (19), (20) and (21). These three subsections involve reputation as an exception to the rule against hearsay. Reputation evidence can be trusted "when the topic is such that the facts are likely to have been inquired about and that persons having personal knowledge have disclosed facts which have thus been discussed in the community; and thus the community's conclusion, if any has been formed, is likely to be a trustworthy one." 5 Wigmore § 1580. On this common foundation, courts have admitted reputation as to land boundaries, customs, general history, character and marriage. The breadth of the underlying principle suggests an equally broad exception, but tradition has in fact been much narrower and more particularized, and this is the pattern of these exceptions in the rule.

Subsection (19). This subsection is concerned with matters of personal and family history. Marriage is universally conceded to be a proper subject of proof by evidence of reputation. 5 Wigmore § 1602. The decisions are divided on other topics such as legitimacy, relationship, adoption, birth and death. *Id.* § 1605. In principle, all of these items appear to be susceptible of well-founded repute. *Lipp v. Mutual Life Ins. Co.,* 125 Or 522, 267 P 519 (1928); CRS 41.900(11) (repealed by this Act) (admitting reputation of pedigree before controversy arose). The relevant "world" in which reputation may exist may be a person's family, associates or community. The boundaries have expanded with changing times from the single neighborhood, in which all activities take place, to the multiple and unrelated worlds of work, religious affiliation and social activity, in each of which a reputation may form. *People v. Reeves,* 360 Ill 55, 195 NE 443 (1935); *State v. Axilrod,* 248 Minn 204, 79 NW 2d 677 (1956); 5 Wigmore § 1616. The family, however, has often served as the beginning point for allowing community reputation. 5 Wigmore § 1488; ORS 41.840 (declaration of deceased or unavailable family member admissible as evidence of common reputation). This subsection is generally consistent with Oregon law. For comparable provisions see Uniform Rules 63(26), (27)(c); California Evidence Code §§ 1313, 1314.

TEXT

Reputation Concerning Personal or Family History

Rule 803(19) provides a hearsay exception for evidence of reputation concerning a person's birth, adoption, marriage, divorce, death, legitimacy, relationship by blood or adoption or marriage, ancestry, or other similar fact of a person's personal or family history. The reputation must be among (1) the person's family by blood, adoption, or marriage; (2) the person's associates, including those connected with the person's work, religious affiliation, and social activities; or (3) the community at large.

Reputation evidence is trustworthy

when the topic is such that the facts are likely to have been generally inquired about and that persons having personal knowledge have disclosed facts which have thus been discussed in the community; and thus the community's conclusion, if any has been formed, is likely to be a trustworthy one. (5 J. Wigmore, EVIDENCE § 1580 at 545 (Chadbourn Rev 1974)

The witness called to testify about the person's reputation must be shown to be familiar with that reputation among members of the person's family, associates, or in the community. See *Cooper v. Harris,* 499 F Supp 266, 268 (ND Ill 1980) ("All the testimony and statements by plaintiff, her relatives and Nelson Bluitt's relatives unequivocally establish that Bluitt was Donna Cooper's natural father. They were clearly admissible and reliable.") (citing, inter alia, FRE 803(19)).

This rule should be considered in conjunction with Rule 804(3)(d), which creates a hearsay exception for statements of personal or family history when the declarant is unavailable.

RULE 803. ORS 40.460. HEARSAY EXCEPTION; AVAILABILITY OF DECLARANT IMMATERIAL

The following are not excluded by Rule 802 (ORS 40.455), even though the declarant is available as a witness:

(20) [Reputation concerning boundaries or general history.] Reputation in a community, arising before the controversy, as to boundaries of or customs affecting lands in the community, and reputation as to events of general history important to the community or state or nation in which located.

LEGISLATIVE COMMENTARY

Subsection (20). The first portion of this subsection admits evidence of reputation concerning land customs and public and private land boundaries. McCormick § 324 at 749 n 54; ORS 41.900(11) (repealed by this Act). See also ORS 41.360(12) (ownership of property presumed from reputation) (repealed by this Act). The reputation is required to antedate the controversy, though not necessarily to be ancient. The second portion is designed to facilitate proof of events of general history when judicial notice is not available. It is likewise supported by authority. McCormick § 324; ORS 41.900(11) (reputation of facts of public or general interest more than 30 years old); ORS 41.670 (facts of general notoriety and interest in historical works, books and published maps by disinterested persons). The historical nature of the subject matter dispenses with any need that the reputation antedate the controversy in which the evidence is offered. This subsection does not change Oregon law. For similar provisions see Uniform Rule 63(27)(a), (b); California Evidence Code §§ 1320, 1322; Kansas Code of Civil Procedure § 60-460(y)(1), (2); New Jersey Evidence Rule 63(27)(a), (b).

TEXT

Reputation Concerning Boundaries or General History

Rule 802(20) creates a hearsay exception for (1) reputation in a community, arising before the controversy, as to boundaries of or customs affecting lands in the community; and (2) reputation as to events of general history important to the community or state or nation in which located. The Commentary states that this rule is intended to be consistent with prior Oregon law. See former ORS 41.900 (repealed 1981), which provided: "Evidence may be given to the following facts: ... (11) Common reputation, existing previous to the controversy, respecting facts of a public or general interest, more than 30 years old, and in cases of pedigree and boundary."

It is unclear whether the legislature contemplated that the thirty-year provision of the former statute would be the standard for determining whether an event was a matter of "history" under the new rule. While reputation as to boundaries or customs must have arisen prior to the controversy, the Commentary states that for events of "general history" the historical nature of the subject matter dispenses with any need that the reputation antedate the controversy in which the evidence is offered.

The rationale underlying this exception is that a reputation in the community regarding boundaries, customs affecting lands or events of general history, suggests reliability. The assumption is presumably that community discussions over time would tend to sift out falsehoods, misunderstandings, or error. See 4 J. Weinstein and M. Berger, WEINSTEIN'S EVIDENCE (1988) § 803(20)[01]. For a federal case construing this rule, see *Ute Indian Tribe v. State of Utah,* 521 F Supp 1072 (D Utah 1981), modified 716 F2d 1298 (10th Cir. 1983).

See generally ANNOT., *Admissibility of Evidence of Reputation as to Land Boundaries or Customs Affecting Land Under Rule 803(20) of Uniform Rules of Evidence and Similar Formulations,* 79 ALR4th 1044 (1990).

RULE 803. ORS 40.460. HEARSAY EXCEPTION; AVAILABILITY OF DECLARANT IMMATERIAL

The following are not excluded by Rule 802 (ORS 40.455), even though the declarant is available as a witness:

(21) [Reputation as to character.] Reputation of a person's character among associates of the person or in the community.

LEGISLATIVE COMMENTARY

Subsection (21). This subsection recognizes the traditional acceptance of reputation evidence as a means of proving human character. See ORE

405(1). It may broaden Oregon practice in admitting evidence of a person's reputation among associates as well as in the community. Otherwise it is consistent with the statute and case law. ORS 45.600 (adverse party may impeach witness by evidence of bad reputation for veracity); *Brooks v. Bergholm,* 256 Or 1, 470 P2d 154 (1970) (evidence of defendant's reputation for pugnacity admitted in action for assault); *Rich v. Cooper,* 234 Or 300, 380 P2d 613 (1963) (evidence of reputation admitted following plea of self-defense in action for assault and battery); *State v. Holbrook,* 98 Or 43, 192 P 640 (1920) (evidence of deceased's reputation for peacefulness admitted to refute assertion he was about to commit lawless act in prosecution for homicide). The exception deals only with the hearsay aspect of this kind of evidence. Limitations upon admissibility based on other grounds are found in ORE 404 (relevancy of character evidence) and ORE 608 (character of witness). The exception is in effect a reiteration, in the context of hearsay, of ORE 405. Similar provisions are contained in Uniform Rule 63(28); California Evidence Code § 1324; Kansas Code of Civil Procedure 60-460(z).

TEXT

Reputation as to Character

Rule 803(21) creates a hearsay exception for reputation of a person's character among associates of the person or in the community. Reputation is an authorized method of proving character under Rules 405(1) and 608(1). Proof of character is allowed, however, only in very limited circumstances. See Rule 404.

When evidence of reputation is offered to prove character, it constitutes a hearsay assertion under Rule 801(3) because it is being offered for the truth of the matter asserted. This exception is needed for such hearsay evidence to be received.

Rule 412(1) expressly prohibits the use of reputation evidence regarding the past sexual behavior of an alleged victim of a sexual offense.

RULE 803.   ORS 40.460. HEARSAY EXCEPTION; AVAILABILITY OF DECLARANT IMMATERIAL

The following are not excluded by Rule 802 (ORS 40.455), even though the declarant is available as a witness:

(22) [Judgment of previous conviction.] Evidence of a final judgment, entered after a trial or upon a plea of guilty, but not upon a plea of no contest, adjudging a person guilty of a crime other than a traffic offense, to prove any fact essential to sustain the judgment, but not including, when offered by the government in a criminal prosecution for purposes other than impeachment, judgments against persons

other than the accused. The pendency of an appeal may be shown but does not affect admissibility.

LEGISLATIVE COMMENTARY

Subsection (22). This subsection admits a judgment of conviction from an earlier trial as hearsay evidence of any fact whose proof was essential to the judgment, in a later trial. The earlier judgment, it will be noted, could have any of three evidential consequences: (1) it could conclude the particular question under the doctrine of res judicata, either as a bar or by collateral estoppel; (2) it could be received as evidence of a fact in issue; or (3) it could be assigned no evidential weight at all.

This subsection does not deal with the operation of a judgment as a bar or collateral estoppel. The principles of res judicata generally are left to the courts to develop and apply, subject to legislative modification. Compare *Meyers v. Burwell,* 271 Or 84, 530 P2d 833 (1975) (using traffic offense conviction to collaterally estop) with ORS 41.905, 484.395, and *Reinsch v. Quines,* 274 Or 97 547 P2d 135 (1976) (overruling Meyers on use of traffic convictions for any purpose statute and case law the Legislative Assembly affirms). When the doctrine of res judicata does not apply to make the judgment either a bar or an estoppel, however, a choice is presented between the second and third alternatives.

Subsection (22) adopts the second alternative for a conviction of a criminal offense. Although there are no Oregon cases admitting a prior judgment as evidence of a fact in issue (and in this respect the subsection changes Oregon law), this is the clear direction of the decisions. Annot., 18 ALR 2d 1287, 1299. The Legislative Assembly was reluctant to reject entirely the results of earlier fact-finding processes outside the confines of res judicata. While this may leave a jury with evidence of conviction without the means of evaluating it, it is safe to assume that the jury will give substantial weight to a judgment unless the defendant satisfactorily explains it—a possibility that is not foreclosed. See *North River Ins. Co. v. Militello,* 104 Colo 28, 88 P2d 567 (1939) (jury verdict for plaintiff on fire policy despite evidence of plaintiff's conviction for arson). For supporting federal decisions see *New York & Cuba Mail 5.5. Co. v. Continental Cas. Co.,* 117 F2d 404, 411 (2nd Cir 1941) (Clark, J.); *Connecticut Fire Ins. Co. v. Farrara,* 277 F2d 388 (8th Cir 1960).

Subsection (22) adopts the third alternative for a conviction of a non-criminal offense, i.e., a violation or traffic infraction. See ORS 161.505. These offenses should not be given evidential weight, not because the administration of justice in the lower echelons is unsound, but because the motivation to defend at this level is often minimal or nonexistent. *Cope v. Gobie,* 39 Cal Ap 2d 448, 103 P2d 598 (1940); *Jones v. Talbot,* 87 Idaho 498, 394 P2d 316 (1964); *Warren v. Marsh,* 215 Minn 615, 11 NW 2d 528 (1943); Annot., 18 ALR 2d 1287 1295–1297; 16 Brooklyn L Rev 286 (1950); 50 Colum L Rev 529 (1950); 35 Cornell L Q 872 (1950).

Judgments of conviction based upon a plea of no contest are expressly excluded. So is a judgment of conviction of a third party when offered against a criminal defendant. While the Oregon Evidence Code does not purport to give constitutional answers, it attempts to avoid collision with constitutional principles. To admit a third party conviction against an accused would probably run a foul of the right of confrontation. See *Kirby v. United States,* 174 US 47, 19 S Ct 574, 43 L Ed 890 (1899) (error to convict of possessing stolen postage stamps when only evidence of theft is record of conviction). The situation is to be distinguished, however, from (1) cases in which the conviction of another person is an element of the crime, e.g., interstate shipment of fire arms to a felon, and (2) as specifically provided, cases in which a conviction is used as evidence tending to impeach a defense witness.

For comparable provisions see Uniform Rule 63(20); California Evidence Code § 1300; Kansas Code of Civil Procedure § 60-460(r).

TEXT

Judgment of Previous Conviction

Rule 803(22) creates a hearsay exception for evidence of criminal convictions to prove any fact essential to sustain the judgment of conviction, but not including convictions of persons other than the accused when offered by the government in a criminal prosecution for purposes other than impeachment. This exception admits only a judgment of a criminal conviction. It does not authorize admission of civil judgments or convictions of violations or traffic offenses. The criminal conviction may be based on a jury verdict after trial or on a guilty plea, but not on a plea of no-contest. The pendency of an appeal may be shown but does not affect admissibility. There would appear to be significant danger in introducing convictions pending appeal, however. If the conviction is reversed, its introduction as evidence in any other litigation to prove a fact underlying that conviction would likely be found to be reversible error.

The exclusion of convictions of traffic offenses from this rule is consistent with ORS 41.905(1) and ORS 153.585(2):

A judgment of conviction or acquittal of a person charged with a traffic offense is not admissible in trial of a subsequent civil action arising out of the same accident or occurrence to prove or negate the facts upon which such judgment was rendered. ORS 41.905(1).

Notwithstanding ORS 43.130 and 43.160, no plea, finding or proceeding upon any traffic infraction shall be used for the purpose of res judicata or collateral estoppel, nor shall any plea, finding or proceeding upon any traffic infraction be admissible as evidence, in any civil proceeding. ORS 153.585(2).

See generally ANNOT., *Admissibility of Traffic Conviction in Later Civil Trial,* 15 ALR4th 691 (1989).

Rule 803(22) is broader than FRE 803(22), which is limited to convictions of crimes "punishable by death or imprisonment in excess of one year." This rule encompasses convictions for misdemeanors as well as felonies.

Prior convictions are not admissible under this exception when they are irrelevant, or when their probative value is substantially outweighed by the considerations set forth in Rule 403. *Rozier v. Ford Motor Co.,* 573 F2d 1332, 1346–7

(5th Cir 1978). A judgment of acquittal is not admissible under this exception to prove the defendant's noninvolvement in the matters previously charged. *United States v. Viserto*, 596 F2d 531, 536–7 (2nd Cir), cert denied 444 US 841 (1979). It will sometimes be difficult to determine what facts are "essential to sustain the [earlier] judgment" of conviction. See *United States v. First Nat'l State Bank*, 469 F Supp 612, 619 n 6 (D NJ 1979), modified on other grounds 616 F2d 668 (3rd Cir), cert denied 447 US 905 (1980) (specific amount stated in indictment for tax evasion is probably not a fact essential to the judgment).

When a judgment of conviction is introduced under this exception, the trial court should allow the opponent to offer rebutting or explanatory evidence. See *Lloyd v. Am. Export Lines Inc.*, 580 F2d 1179, 1190 (3rd Cir), cert denied 439 US 969 (1978) ("Alvarez is free to offer such explanation or mitigating circumstances with respect to the proceedings or judgment as may be deemed admissible by the district court in this connection").

How frequently this exception will be used is uncertain, in light of the broad scope of collateral estoppel adopted by the Oregon Supreme Court in *Casey v. N.W. Sec. Ins. Co.*, 260 Or 485, 491 P2d 208 (1971) and *Meyers v. Burwell*, 271 Or 84, 530 P2d 833 (1975). Under these decisions it appears that both felony and misdemeanor convictions will generally have the effect of collateral estoppel with regard to any factual issues determined therein and hence will be binding on the defendant in subsequent civil litigation. To the extent that the issue is resolved by collateral estoppel, it will be unnecessary to offer the earlier conviction to prove an underlying fact under this exception.

See generally Motomura, *Using Judgments as Evidence*, 70 Minn L Rev 979 (1986).

RULE 803. ORS 40.460. HEARSAY EXCEPTION; AVAILABILITY OF DECLARANT IMMATERIAL

The following are not excluded by Rule 802 (ORS 40.455), even though the declarant is available as a witness:

(23) [Judgment as to personal, family or general history, or boundaries.] Judgments as proof of matters of personal, family or general history, or boundaries, essential to the judgment, if the same would be provable by evidence of reputation.

LEGISLATIVE COMMENTARY

Subsection (23). This subsection admits judgments on family, boundary and general historical issues, if evidence of reputation of the same would be admissible. See subsections (19) and (20), supra. The hearsay exception was originally justified on the ground that a verdict is evidence of reputation. As trial by jury graduated from a mere neighborhood inquest, however, this theory lost its validity. It never was valid as to chancery decrees. The rule persisted nonetheless, and judges and writers shifted ground and began saying that a judgment or decree is evidence as good as reputation. See *City of London v. Clerke,* Carth 181, 93 Eng Rep 710 (KB 1691); *Neill v. Duke of Devonshire,* 8 App Cas 135 (1882). The shift appears to be sound, for the process of inquiry and scrutiny that makes reputation reliable is present in perhaps greater measure in litigation. While this last suggests a broader area of application, the affinity of judgments to reputation remains strong, and subsection (21) goes no further, not even to include character. The leading case in this country is *Patterson v. Gaines,* 47 US (6 How) 550, 599, 12 L Ed 553 (1847). In the pattern of the English decisions, it mentions, as matters provable: manorial rights, public rights of way, disputed boundaries, immemorial custom and pedigree. More recent decisions on point include *Grant Bros. Construction Co. v. United States,* 232 US 647, 34 S Ct 452, 58 L Ed 776 (1914) (Immigration Service board decision admissible to prove alienage of laborers, in action for penalties under Alien Contract Labor Law); *United States v. Mid-Continent Petroleum Corp.,* 67 F2d 37 (10th Cir 1933) (records of commission enrolling Indians admissible on pedigree); *Jung Yen Loy v. Cahill,* 81 F2d 809 (9th Cir 1936) (board decision as to citizenship of plaintiffs father admissible in proceeding for declaration of citizenship). Oregon case law apparently has been to the contrary. *Routledge v. Githens,* 118 Or 70, 245 P 1072 (1926) (divorce decree not admissible in suit to declare marriage void). This subsection may therefore mark a change in Oregon practice.

TEXT

Judgment as to Personal, Family or General History, or Boundaries

Rule 803(23) creates a hearsay exception for judgments as proof of matters of personal, family or general history, or boundaries, essential to the judgment, if the same would be provable by evidence of reputation. This rule supplements Rule 803(19) and Rule 803(20) by allowing the matters specified in those rules to be proven by judgment as well as reputation.

Personal or family history would presumably include a person's birth, adoption, marriage, divorce, death, legitimacy, relationship by blood or adoption or marriage, ancestry, or other similar facts.

Introduction of a prior judgment under this exception to prove a fact essential to the judgment is unnecessary in cases where the judgment has the effect of res judicata or collateral estoppel.

RULE 803. ORS 40.460. HEARSAY EXCEPTION: AVAILABILITY OF DECLARANT IMMATERIAL

The following are not excluded by Rule 802 (ORS 40.455), even though the declarant is available as a witness:

(24) Notwithstanding the limits contained in subsection (18a) of this section, in any proceeding in which a child under 12 years of age at the time of trial, or a person with developmental disabilities as described in subsection (18a)(d) of this section, may be called as a witness to testify concerning an act of abuse, as defined in ORS 419B.005, or sexual conduct performed with or on the child or person with developmental disabilities by another, the testimony of the child or person with developmental disabilities taken by contemporaneous examination and cross-examination in another place under the supervision of the trial judge and communicated to the courtroom by closed circuit television or other audiovisual means. Testimony will be allowed as provided in this subsection only if the court finds that there is a substantial likelihood, established by expert testimony, that the child or person with developmental disabilities will suffer severe emotional or psychological harm if required to testify in open court. If the court makes such a finding, the court, on motion of a party, the child, the person with developmental disabilities or the court in a civil proceeding, or on motion of the district attorney, the child, or the person with developmental disabilities in a criminal or juvenile proceeding, may order that the testimony of the child of the person with developmental disabilities be taken as described in this subsection. Only the judge, the attorneys for the parties, the parties, individuals necessary to operate the equipment and any individual the court finds would contribute to the welfare and well-being of the child or person with developmental disabilities may be present during the testimony of the child or person with developmental disabilities.

LEGISLATIVE COMMENTARY

[There is no Legislative Commentary to this Rule. It is not part of the original Evidence Code. It was enacted by the 1989 Legislature and further amended in 1991 and 1995.]

TEXT

Televised Testimony

This new rule authorizes testimony by means of closed circuit television for children under 12 years of age or persons with developmental disabilities who are testifying regarding an act of sexual conduct involving the child. The rule provides that the examination and cross-examination of the child or person with developmental disabilities must be "contemporaneous," which would preclude videotaped depositions taken at an earlier time. The purpose of the rule is to protect young children and persons with developmental disabilities from the trauma of in-court testimony and to allow the testimony contemporaneously "in another place" that would then be "communicated to the court room by closed circuit television or other audio visual means."

A hearsay exception is necessary to allow such testimony, because the statement is being given out of court even though it is contemporaneous. Rule 801(3) defines hearsay as "a statement, *other than one made by the declarant while testifying at the trial or hearing,* offered in evidence to prove the truth of the matter asserted." (emphasis added).

Testimony under this exception is allowed only after the court has made a finding "that there is a substantial likelihood ... that the child or person with developmental disabilities will suffer severe emotional or psychological harm if required to testify in open court." Such a finding must be supported by expert testimony.

This exception applies to civil proceedings generally, as well as to juvenile proceedings and criminal proceedings. In civil proceedings, the motion to have the testimony of the child or person with developmental disabilities may be made by any party, the child, the person with developmental disabilities, or the court. However, in criminal or juvenile proceedings, only the district attorney, the child, or person with developmental disabilities, but not the defendant or the court, may move to have testimony taken under this rule.

The defendant, and the attorney for the defendant, are allowed to be present at the location where the testimony is given. Therefore, this exception will have its greatest utility in cases where the trauma to the child comes from testifying in open court, in the presence of a jury or spectators, rather than from testifying in the defendant's presence. On the issue of closing judicial proceedings where testimony is received, see discussion under Rule 412, supra.

Given that the witness is subject to cross-examination, this new exception should raise relatively few hearsay concerns. There is a partial loss of the jury's opportunity to view the demeanor of the witness during direct and cross-examination, but the extent of that loss can be minimized by providing for a high quality audiovisual transmission of the child's testimony.

See generally Mitchell, *What Would Happen if Videotaped Depositions of Sexually Abused Children Were Routinely Admitted in Civil Trials? A Journey Through the Legal Process and Beyond,* 15 U Puget Sound L Rev 261 (1992).

RULE 803. ORS 40.460. HEARSAY EXCEPTION; AVAILABILITY OF DECLARANT IMMATERIAL

The following are not excluded by Rule 802 (ORS 40.455), even though the declarant is available as a witness:

(25) Any document containing data prepared or recorded by the Oregon State Police pursuant to ORS 813.160(1)(b)(C) or (E), or pursuant to ORS 475.235(3), if the document is produced by data retrieval from the Law Enforcement Data System or other computer system maintained and operated by the Oregon State Police, and the person retrieving the data attests that the information was retrieved directly from the system and that the document accurately reflects the data retrieved.

LEGISLATIVE COMMENTARY

[There is no Legislative Commentary to this Rule. It was not part of the original Evidence Code. It was enacted by the 1995 Legislature.]

TEXT

State Police Data Retrieval

Rule 803(25) creates a hearsay exception for certain documents containing data prepared or recorded by the Oregon State Police, provided the document is produced by data retrieval from the Law Enforcement Data System (LEDS) or other computer system maintained and operated by the Oregon State Police. The person retrieving the data must attest (1) that it was retrieved directly from the system and (2) that the document accurately reflects the data retrieved.

The data must be prepared or reported pursuant to ORS 813.160(1)(b)(C) or (E) or pursuant to ORS 475.235(3). ORS 813.160(1)(b)(C) provides for testing and certifying the accuracy of equipment used by police officers for chemical analyses of a person's breath. ORS 813.160(1)(b)(E) provides for issuance of permits to police officers who have completed prescribed training to use the testing equipment. ORS 475.235(3) provides that in certain prosecutions relating to controlled substances "a certified copy of the analytical report signed by the director of the state police crime detection laboratory or the criminalist conducting the analysis shall be accepted as prima facie evidence of the results of the analytical findings."

RULE 803. ORS 40.460. HEARSAY EXCEPTION; AVAILABILITY OF DECLARANT IMMATERIAL

The following are not excluded by Rule 802 (ORS 40.455), even though the declarant is available as a witness:

(26) [Other exceptions.]

   (a) A statement not specifically covered by any of the foregoing exceptions but having equivalent circumstantial guarantees of trustworthiness, if the court determines that:

   (A) The statement is relevant;

   (B) The statement is more probative on the point for which it is offered than any other evidence which the proponent can procure through reasonable efforts; and

   (C) The general purposes of the Oregon Evidence Code and the interests of justice will best be served by admission of the statement into evidence.

   (b) A statement may not be admitted under this subsection unless the proponent of it makes known to the adverse party the intention to offer the statement and the particulars of it, including the name and address of the declarant, sufficiently in advance of the trial or hearing, or as soon as practicable after it becomes apparent that such statement is probative of the issues at hand, to provide the adverse party with a fair opportunity to prepare to meet it.

LEGISLATIVE COMMENTARY

Subsection (26). This subsection allows evidence to be admitted which could not be admitted under any other hearsay exception, if a court finds that it has guaranties of trustworthiness equivalent to or exceeding the guaranties found in the other exceptions, and that it is highly probative and necessary.

The above features were present in an example cited by the drafters of Federal Rule 803(24), *Dallas County v. Commercial Union Assurance Co., Ltd.,* 286 F2d 388 (5th Cir 1961). The issue in that case was whether the tower of the Dallas County Courthouse had collapsed because it was struck by lightning, in which case the loss was insured, or because the tower had become structurally unsound, in which case it was not. Investigation revealed that certain of the timbers were charred. To show that lightning may not have been the cause of the charring, the insurer offered a copy of a local newspaper published over 50 years earlier containing an unsigned article describing a fire in the courthouse while it was under construction. The newspaper did not qualify for admission as a business record or as an ancient document, nor did it fit within any other recognized hearsay exception. Nevertheless, the court concluded, the article was trustworthy because it is inconceivable that a journalist in a small town would report a fire in the courthouse if none had occurred. See also *United States v. Barbati*, 284 F Supp 409 (EDNY 1968).

Oregon cases suggest a similar common sense attitude in favor of the admission of data that would reasonably be relied upon in serious affairs outside the courtroom. See *Lewis v. Baker, Richardson, Merrell, Inc.,* 243 Or 317, 413 P2d 400 (1966); *State Highway Commission v. Fisch-Or Inc.,* 241 Or 412, 399 P2d 1011, 406 P2d 539 (1965); *State Highway Commission v. Arnold,* 218 Or 43, 341 P2d 1089 (1959); *State Highway Commission v. Oswalt,* 1 Or App 449, 463 P2d 602 (1970). Only one decision, discussed below, would not qualify under this exception.

In *Timber Access Industries Co. v. U.S. Plywood-Champion Paper, Inc.,* 263 Or 509, 503 P2d 482 (1972), plaintiff contracted to sell "peeler logs" to U.S. Plywood. At issue was whether U.S. Plywood had unconditionally agreed to the purchase, or had agreed conditional upon delivery by a specific date. Timber Access, by its president, offered a statement by Girard, the buying agent for U.S. Plywood at the time of the contract, that it was Girard's intention to purchase the logs unconditionally. Girard had taken another position by the time the contract expired, and died prior to the time of trial. The trial court admitted his statement over defendant's hearsay objection. On appeal, the Supreme Court recognized that the statement did not qualify as an admission, and fell into none of the traditional categories of hearsay exception, e.g., statement of mental condition or statement against pecuniary interest. Yet the court ruled the evidence admissible, finding that the declaration was trustworthy because Girard was in a position to have knowledge of the facts and normally would not make a statement against his interest (pecuniary or otherwise) unless it was truthful.

The Legislative Assembly feels that the court in Timber Access went too far in admitting Girard's statement under a general exception to the hearsay rule, and, to this extent only, intends to change Oregon law. The criticism rests on several observations. First, the statement simply does not have the same aura of exceptional trustworthiness as the newspaper article in *Dallas County v. Commercial Union Assurance,* supra. Second, the statement should only have been admitted if it was more probative than other evidence on point that could reasonably have been procured, and the opinion does not indicate that plaintiff attempted to procure such other evidence. Third, the Legislative Assembly questions the determination that the statement was not against Girard's interest or the interest of Girard's employer, as he remained with U.S. Plywood at all times; it is unrealistic to conclude that Girard was not acting within the course and scope of his employment when he made the statement. In short, the ruling in Timber Access is a better example of the expanded declaration against interest exception, found in Rule 804(2)(c), than it is of the general hearsay exception under Rule 803(24) [now 803(26)]. Recently the Supreme Court indicated that Timber Access may mark the outer limits of admissibility under a general hearsay exception. *Reynoldson v. Jackson,* 275 Or 641, 644, 552 P2d 236 (1976). If so, current Oregon law is not very dissimilar from this subsection.

Because exceptional cases like Dallas County may arise in the future, the Legislative Assembly adopted this residual hearsay exception in Rule 803 and a similar one in Rule 804(2)(d). It intends that these provisions be used very rarely, and only in situations where application of the hearsay rule and its other exceptions would result in injustice. These rules are not a broad grant of authority to trial judges to admit hearsay statements.

Despite the format of this subsection, which is borrowed from the federal rule, it is worth noting that there are in fact six prerequisites to admission of a hearsay statement under this exception: (1) the evidence is not admissible under any other exception; (2) the evidence carries equivalent circumstantial guaranties of trustworthiness; (3) the evidence is relevant; (4) the evidence is more probative of the point in question than any other evidence the proponent can introduce; (5) admission of the evidence would serve the general purposes of justice and the Evidence Code; and 6) the proponent of the evidence has given reasonable advance notice of the intent to offer it. The Legislative Assembly relaxed the last requirement from the federal standard, to accommodate an unforeseeable discovery of important hearsay in the course of a proceeding.

TEXT

Residual Exception

Rule 803(26) creates an exception for hearsay statements not satisfying any of the foregoing exceptions.

This rule is variously referred to as the residual, catch-all, or open-ended hearsay exception. Before a hearsay statement is admissible under this exception, the following six requirements must be satisfied:

(1) The statement must not be admissible under any of the other exceptions in Rule 803;
(2) It must have circumstantial guarantees of trustworthiness equivalent to those of the other hearsay exceptions in Rule 803;
(3) It must be relevant;
(4) It must be "more probative on the point for which it is offered than any other evidence which the proponent can procure through reasonable efforts";
(5) Admission of the statement into evidence must best serve "[t]he general purposes of the Oregon Evidence Code and the interests of justice" (with respect to this requirement, see Rule 102); and
(6) The proponent must notify the adverse party of "the intention to offer the statement and the particulars of it, including the name and address of the declarant, sufficiently in advance of the trial or hearing, or as soon as practicable after it becomes apparent that such statement is probative of the issues at hand, to provide the adverse party with a fair opportunity to prepare to meet it."

Advance Notice Requirement

Rule 803(26) is essentially identical to FRE 803(24). The only significant difference is that the Oregon rule contains a qualification to the requirement that advance notice be given in all cases of the intention to offer a hearsay statement under this exception. Under the Oregon rule, it is sufficient if notice is given "as soon as practicable after it becomes apparent that such statement is probative of the issues at hand." This qualification is intended to provide for situations where a party was unaware of the statement, or its relevance to the issues in the case, until just before or even during trial. Where hearsay statements are allowed under this exception without advance notice to the adverse party, the court can minimize the danger of error by allowing the adverse party a continuance, if requested, to prepare to meet or respond to the hearsay statement.

Comparison with Rule 804(3)(f)

Rule 803(26) is also essentially identical to Rule 804(3)(f), except that the latter rule requires the witness to be unavailable. Arguably, this rule also contains an unavailability requirement, because a showing must be made that the hearsay statement is more probative on the point for that it is offered than any other evidence which the proponent can procure through reasonable efforts. See *United States v. Mathis,* 559 F2d 294 (5th Cir 1977). While availability of a witness will often prevent this requirement from being satisfied, it will not do so in all cases. The court may find that requiring production of the witness is not reasonable under the circumstances, or the court may find that the hearsay statement, particularly if it is in writing and involves a matter not easily remembered, is likely to be more probative on the point than the testimony of the declarant.

Guarantees of Trustworthiness

In determining whether the statement has guarantees of trustworthiness equivalent to the other hearsay exceptions, one court has held

> the trustworthiness of a statement should be analyzed by evaluating not only the facts corroborating the veracity of the statement but also the circumstances in which the declarant made the statement and the incentive he had to speak truthfully or falsely. Further, consideration should be given to factors bearing on the reliability of the reporting of the hearsay by the witness. (*United States v. Bailey,* 581 F2d 341, 349 (3rd Cir 1978))

It should be noted that the trustworthiness of the other Rule 803 hearsay exceptions would seem to vary considerably.

Rule to Be Narrowly Construed

The Commentary makes clear the intent of the legislature that this exception be construed narrowly. It states that the Legislative Assembly

> intends that these provisions be used very rarely, and only in situations where application of the hearsay rule and its other exceptions would result in injustice. These rules are not a broad grant of authority to trial judges to admit hearsay statements.

The report of the United States Senate Committee on the Judiciary considering the federal counterpart to this rule (FRE 803(24)) states:

> The residual exceptions are not meant to authorize major judicial revisions of the hearsay rule, including its present exceptions. Such major revisions are best accomplished by legislative action. It is intended that in any case in which evidence is sought to be admitted under these subsections, the trial judge will exercise no less care, reflection and caution than the courts did under the common law in establishing the now-recognized exceptions to the hearsay rule.
>
> In order to establish a well-defined jurisprudence, the special facts and circumstances which, in the court's judgment, indicate that the statement has a sufficiently high degree of trustworthiness and necessity to justify its admission should be stated on the record. It is expected that the court will give the opposing party a full and adequate opportunity to contest the admission of any statement sought to be introduced under these subsections (5 Rep No 1277, 93rd Cong, 2d Sess 20 (1974))

In *State v. Campbell*, 299 Or 633, 705 P2d 694 (1985), the court stated, citing McCormick, EVIDENCE (3d ed 1984) § 324.1, that the attitude of Congress toward FRE 803(24) "'was clearly one of conservativism resorting to the exception and the courts have generally announced respect for that position.' The same could be said of the attitude of the legislative assembly in Oregon." 299 Or at 639–640 n4, 705 P2d at 698 n4.

This exception should not be used as a means of avoiding difficult questions regarding whether or not a hearsay statement fits within another exception in Rule 803. The court must clearly find that no other exception will authorize the statement's receipt before admission under this rule is allowed. Also the exception should not be used as a means of avoiding express restrictions contained in other hearsay exceptions. See COMMENT, *Admitting "Near Misses" Under the Residual Hearsay Exceptions,* 66 Or L Rev 599 (1987).

Right of Confrontation

Courts are likely to be particularly conservative in allowing use of this exception against defendants in criminal cases because of the danger of infringement upon the defendant's right of confrontation. See *Idaho v. Wright,* 497 US 805 (1990) (hearsay admitted pursuant to Idaho's residual hearsay exception held to violate defendant's sixth amendment confrontation rights; residual hearsay exception was not a "firmly rooted hearsay exception," and the totality of circumstances did not provide the necessary "particularized guarantees of trustworthiness").

Although the precise scope of the right to confrontation has not yet been clearly defined in court decisions, the chance of a confrontation violation is significantly reduced if any hearsay statement admitted against a criminal defendant satisfies a well established hearsay exception. See *Ohio v. Roberts,* 448 US 56, 100 S Ct 2531, 65 L Ed 2d 597 (1980). *See* textual discussion of hearsay and the Confrontation Clause following Rule 802.

See generally NOTE, *Evidence—Constitutional Law—The Confrontation Clause and the Catch-All Exception to the Hearsay Doctrine,* 17 Land & Water L Rev 703 (1982).

Prior Oregon Law

Rule 803(26) may narrow, rather than expand, prior Oregon law. Oregon first recognized a general hearsay exception in *Timber Access Indus. Co. v. U.S. Plywood-Champion Papers Inc.,* 263 Or 509, 503 P2d 482 (1972). A variety of hearsay statements not satisfying established hearsay exceptions have been admitted under the rule of *Timber Access.* See *State v. Echeverria,* 51 Or App 513, 626 P2d 897, rev denied 291 Or 118, 631 P2d 341 (1981) (admitting list of stolen property that a deceased burglary victim had prepared for the police shortly after the event); *State v. Letterman,* 47 Or App 1145, 616 P2d 505 (1980), aff'd by equally divided court 291 Or 3, 627 P2d 484 (1981) (testimony by police officer concerning extrajudicial statements made to officer through an interpreter). The Commentary indicates the view of the legislature that the precise statement admitted in *Timber Access* would not be properly admissible under this rule. Moreover, this rule adds prerequisites to admissibility, such as the advance notice requirement, that were not clearly required under prior law.

Hearsay Statements of Sex Crime Victims

In *State v. Campbell,* 299 Or 633, 705 P2d 694 (1985), the court held that the residual hearsay exception cannot be used as a means of introducing hearsay statements by sex crime victims, because the admissibility of such hearsay is governed and explicitly restricted by Rule 803(18a). This decision overrules earlier decisions, such as *State v. Hollywood,* 67 Or App 546, 680 P2d 655 (1984), rev denied 298 Or 553, 695 P2d 49 (1985), which allowed the hearsay statement of a child sex crime victim to be received under Rule 803(25) [now 803(26)], even though it went beyond the scope of Rule 803(18a). Based upon the *Campbell* holding, error was found in admitting evidence under the residual exception in the following cases: *State ex rel Juvenile Department v. Karabetsis,* 77 Or App 583, 713 P2d 1075 (1986); *State v. Scripture,* 75 Or App 320, 705 P2d 1162, rev denied 300 Or 451, 712 P2d 110 (1985); *State v. Harris,* 78 Or App 490, 717 P2d 242 (1986).

See generally McGrath & Clemens, *The Child Victim as a Witness in Sexual Abuse Cases,* 46 Mont L Rev 229 (1985); McNeil, *The Admissibility of Child Victim Hearsay in Kansas: A Defense Perspective,* 23 Washburn L J 265 (1984); Skoler, *New Hearsay Exceptions for a Child's Statement of Sexual Abuse,* 18 John Marshall L Rev 1 (1984); COMMENT, *Sexual Abuse of Children—Washington's New Hearsay Exception,* 58 Wash L Rev 813 (1983); COMMENT, *Confronting Child Victims of Sex Abuse: The Unconstitutionality of the Sexual Abuse Hearsay Exception,* 7 U Puget Sound L Rev 387 (1984); COMMENT, *A Comprehensive Approach to Child Hearsay Statements in Sex Abuse Cases,* 83 Colum L Rev 1745 (1983); COMMENT, *Legislative Responses to Child Sexual Abuse Case: The Hearsay Exception and the Videotape*

Deposition, 34 Cath U L Rev 1021 (1985); COMMENT, *Child Witnesses in Sexual Abuse Criminal Proceedings: Their Capabilities, Special Problems and Proposals for Reform,* 13 Pepperdine L Rev 157 (1985); Tueukheimer, *Convictions Through Hearsay in Child Sexual Abuse Cases: A Logical Progression Back to Square One,* 72 Marq L Rev 47 (1988).

Recent Oregon Cases

Koennecke v. State of Oregon, 122 Or App 100, 104, 857 P2d 148, 151 (1993), rev denied 318 Or 26, 862 P2d 1306 (1993). The court found no error in the exclusion of a tape-recorded statement of a coworker repeating what a juror told him. The recording was hearsay and did not contain sufficient circumstantial guarantees of trustworthiness to justify its admission under the residual exception.

State v. Carter, 105 Or App 483, 487, 805 P2d 721, rev denied 312 Or 81, 816 P2d 610 (1991). The trial court admitted an exhibit prepared by an officer listing the value of stolen property. The trial court found it to have a "circumstantial guarantee" of trustworthiness. The appellate court did not rule on whether the evidence was properly admitted, instead finding any error to be harmless given the existence of other testimony on the value of the stolen items.

State v. Mendez, 308 Or 9, 774 P2d 1082 (1989). The defendant claimed error in the exclusion of a statement by the murder victim two weeks prior to his murder that he feared a third party would kill him. The statement was offered to prove that the third party rather than the defendant may have been the assailant. The court held that this statement did not qualify for admission under Rule 803(24) (now Rule 803(26)), because it did not have equivalent circumstantial guarantees of trustworthiness as other recognized hearsay exceptions.

State v. Carskadon, 86 Or App 421, 739 P2d 1054 (1987). The court held that it was error to admit the testimony of a witness that the defendant's ex-wife had told him that defendant had caused injuries to her. The State conceded that the testimony was hearsay and was only admissible under Rule 803(24) (now Rule 803(26)). The court stated: "We decline to apply the catch-all provision to this case, because we see nothing about the statement indicating that it has circumstantial guarantees of trustworthiness equivalent to the specific exceptions found in OEC 803."

Hodge and Hodge, 84 Or App 62, 733 P2d 458, rev denied 303 Or 370, 738 P2d 199 (1987). The court held that it was error to admit a blood test report under the residual exception, when the report was not accompanied by an affidavit or expert testimony, as required by statute.

Star Rentals v. Seeberg Construction Company, 83 Or App 44, 730 P2d 573 (1986). The plaintiff attempted to prove posting of the notice of completion by offering into evidence the notice of completion with an affidavit on the back stating that the notice had been posted. Even though the affidavit was hearsay, plaintiff argued that it qualified for admission under Rule 803(24) (now Rule 803(26)). The court affirmed the trial court's exclusion of the affidavit, stating: "The exception embodied in OEC 803(24) [now OEC 803(26)] is to be used rarely and only in situations where the interests of justice require. Here the declaration was of a material fact in the case which could have been proven by the testimony of the declarant. The record shows that Lamar was available as a witness but was not called by plaintiff. There was no reason to admit the statement under the residual exception."

Federal Cases

For examples of the types of evidence admitted under FRE 803(24), see *United States v. Friedman*, 593 F2d 109 (9th Cir 1979) (letter by Chilean official confirming presence of defendant in Chile on specified dates); *United States v. White*, 611 F2d 531 (5th Cir), cert denied 446 US 992 (1980) (statement of government check payee that he did not receive check or endorse it); *United States v. Williams*, 573 F2d 284 (5th Cir 1978) (prior affidavit of witness); *United States v. Pfeiffer*, 539 F2d 668 (8th Cir 1976) (delivery receipts prepared by person not under business duty to transmit); *United States v. McPartlin*, 595 F2d 1321 (7th Cir), cert denied 444 US 833 (1979) (desk calendar appointment diary); *United States v. Hitsman*, 604 F2d 443 (5th Cir 1979) (college transcript); *Games v. Employers Mut. Ins. Co.*, 73 FRD 607 (D Alaska 1977) (day-in-the-life film of plaintiff); *Huff v. White Motor Corp.*, 609 F2d 286 (7th Cir 1979) (admission of plaintiff's decedent in wrongful death action).

Other Authorities

See generally Rand, *The Residual Exceptions to the Federal Hearsay Rule: The Futile and Misguided Attempt to Restrain Judicial Discretion*, 80 Geo L J 873 (1992); Beaver, *The Residual Hearsay Exception Reconsidered*, 20 Fla St U L Rev 787 (1993); Raeder, *The Effect of the Catchalls on Criminal Defendants: Little Red Riding Hood Meets the Hearsay Wolf and Is Devoured*, 25 Loy L A L Rev 925 (1992); ANNOT., *Uniform Evidence Rule 803(24): The Residual Hearsay Exception*, 51 ALR4th 999 (1987); ANNOT., *Admissibility of Statement Under Rule 803(24) of Federal Rules of Evidence, Providing for Admissibility of Hearsay Statement Not Covered by Any Specific Exception But Having Equivalent Circumstantial Guaranties of Trustworthiness*, 36 ALR Fed 742 (1978); Imwinkelried, *The Scope of The Residual Hearsay Exceptions in the Federal Rules of Evidence*, 15 San Diego L Rev 239 (1978); Jonakait, *The Subversion of the Hearsay Rule: The Residual Hearsay Exceptions, Circumstantial Guarantees of Trustworthiness, and Grand Jury Testimony*, 36 Case West Res L Rev 431 (1986); Grant, *The Equivalent Circumstantial Guarantees of Trustworthiness Standard for Federal Rule of Evidence 803(24)*, 90 Dick L Rev 75 (1985); Lewis, *The Residual Exceptions to the Federal Hearsay Rule: Shuffling the Wild Cards*, 15 Rutgers L J 101 (1983); Sonenshein, *The Residual Exceptions to the Federal Hearsay Rule: Two Exceptions in Search of a Rule*, 57 NYU L Rev 867 (1982); Yasser, *Strangulating Hearsay: The Residual Exceptions to the Hearsay Rule*, 11 Tex Tech L Rev 587 (1980); Black, *Federal Rules of Evidence, 803(24) and 804(b)(5)—The Residual Exceptions—An Overview*, 25 Houston L Rev 13 (1988).

RULE 804. ORS 40.465. HEARSAY EXCEPTIONS WHERE THE DECLARANT IS UNAVAILABLE

(1) **[Definition of unavailability.]** "Unavailability as a witness" includes situations in which the declarant:

    (a) Is exempted by ruling of the court on the ground of privilege from testifying concerning the subject matter of a statement;

    (b) Persists in refusing to testify concerning the subject matter of a statement despite an order of the court to do so;

    (c) Testifies to a lack of memory of the subject matter of a statement;

    (d) Is unable to be present or to testify at the hearing because of death or then existing physical or mental illness or infirmity; or

    (e) Is absent from the hearing and the proponent of the declarant's statement has been unable to procure the declarant's attendance (or in the case of an exception under subsection (3)(b), (c) or (d) of this section, the declarant's attendance or testimony) by process or other reasonable means.

(2) **[Exception to unavailability.]** A declarant is not unavailable as a witness if the declarant's exemption, refusal, claim of lack of memory, inability, or absence is due to the procurement or wrongdoing of the proponent of the declarant's statement for the purpose of preventing the witness from attending or testifying.

LEGISLATIVE COMMENTARY

Oregon Rule of Evidence 804 is a list of five specific exceptions and one general exception to the hearsay rule, which apply when the declarant is "unavailable" as a witness as the rule defines that term. The rule is based on Rule 804 of the Federal Rules of Evidence and Oregon case and statute law. Paragraph (b) of subsection (3) has been changed to agree with Oregon case law allowing dying declarations to be admitted in criminal as well as civil cases. Under Federal Rule 804, such declarations are admissible only in civil actions and prosecutions for homicide. A new exception is added in paragraph (e) to preserve a statutory provision that is otherwise repealed.

Subsection (1). The definition of "unavailability" in this subsection implements the division of hearsay exceptions into those that apply generally, ORE 803, and those that apply when the witness is unavailable, ORE 804(3). The definition is much more expansive than the one that has been in use in Oregon. Five instances of unavailability are specified in this rule. Oregon has recognized only three of them until now: claim of privilege, death or illness, and beyond the court's jurisdiction.

With respect to the two last mentioned forms of unavailability, this subsection also clarifies Oregon law by eliminating the ambiguity in ORS 41.900(8). As detected by the court in *Rogers v. Donovan,* 268 Or 24, 518 P2d 1306 (1974), the ambiguity was whether the statute authorized the admission of former testimony of an unavailable party to a present action, or the admission of the former testimony of an unavailable nonparty witness as well. The issue was never resolved. Subsection (1) clearly applies to both parties and nonparty witnesses.

Paragraph (a). There is substantial authority for the position that a claim of privilege by the declarant satisfies the requirement of unavailability. *Wyatt v. State,* 35 Ala App 147, 46 S2d 837 (1950); *State v. Stewart,* 85 Kan 404, 116 P 489 (1911); Annot., 45 ALR2d 1354; Uniform Rule 62(7)(a); California Evidence Code § 240(a)(1). This paragraph requires an affirmative ruling by the court that a privilege exists, which presupposes a claim. The written rule is in accord with Oregon practice. *State v. Rawls,* 252 Or 556, 451 P2d 127 (169); *State v. Bryant,* 20 Or App 562, 532 P2d 815 (1975).

Paragraph (b). A witness is unavailable if the witness refuses to testify about the subject matter of a prior statement despite judicial urging to do so. This rule has not been recognized in Oregon, but it is supported by the same practical considerations that underlie paragraph (a). *Johnson v. People,* 152 Colo 586 384 P2d 454 (1963); *People v. Pickette,* 339 Mich 294, 63 NW 2d 681, 45 ALR 2d 1341 (1954). Contra, *Pleau v. State,* 255 Wis 362, 38 NW 2d 496(1949).

Paragraph (c). Under this paragraph, a witness is unavailable if the witness claims not to remember the subject matter of an earlier statement. This position is new to Oregon practice. It finds support in the cases, though not without dissent. McCormick, *Evidence* § 253 at 611 (2d ed 1972). The practical effect of the claim is to put testimony beyond reach, as in the other instances. However, it will be noted that the lack of memory must be established by the witness' own testimony, which clearly contemplates the production and cross-examination of the person.

Paragraph (d). Death, illness and infirmity find general recognition as grounds for declaring a witness to be unavailable. McCormick §§ 253, 280, 322; Uniform Rule 62(7)(c); California Evidence Code § 240(a)(3); Kansas Code of Civil Procedure § 60-459(g)(3); New Jersey Evidence Rule 62(6)(c). *Laam v. Greene,* 106 Or 311, 211 P 791 (1923); *Hansen-Rynning v. Oregon-Wash. R.R. & Nav. Co.,* 105 Or 67, 209 P 462 (1922) (mental or physical inability to testify). Cf. ORS 41.900(8); *State v. Crawley,* 242 Or 601, 410 P2d 1012 (1966); *State v. Walton,* 53 Or 557, 99 P 431 (1909) (allowing former testimony in the event of death or infirmity).

Paragraph (e). Absence of the declarant from the hearing, coupled with an inability to compel attendance by process or other reasonable means, also amounts to unavailability. McCormick § 253; Uniform Rule 62(7)(d), (e); California Evidence Code § 240(a)(4), (5); Kansas Code of Civil Procedure § 60-459(g)(4), (5); New Jersey rule 62(6)(b), (d). Cf. ORS 41.900(8); *Rogers v. Donovan,* supra (allowing former testimony in the event of absence from state). The effect of the parenthetical expression in this paragraph is to require the proponent of the hearsay to attempt to depose the declarant, as well as to seek the declarant's attendance, before the person will be considered unavailable.

Subsection (2). This subsection provides that if the conditions that would otherwise constitute unavailability result from procurement or wrongdoing of the proponent of the statement, then the requirement of unavailability is not satisfied. This is a rule of fairness.

TEXT

Hearsay Exceptions Where the Declarant Is Unavailable

Rule 804 supplements Rule 803 by listing six additional hearsay exceptions that are applicable when the declarant is shown to be unavailable. Unavailability is defined in Rule 804(1). The six hearsay exceptions are listed in Rule 804(3). The following statement in the Commentary to Rule 803 applies to Rule 804 as well:

> The exceptions to the rule against admissibility of hearsay evidence set forth in this rule are phrased in negative terms of nonapplication of the hearsay rule, rather than in positive terms of admissibility. This is done to repel any implication that other grounds for excluding the evidence are eliminated from consideration.

The Commentary to Rule 803 further states:

> [N]either this rule nor Rule 804 dispenses with the requirement of first hand knowledge. See ORE 602. Such knowledge may appear from the statement or be inferred from circumstances.

The opinion rule should be generally inapplicable to statements offered under Rule 804. The opinion rule is a rule of preference, and if the declarant is unavailable it will not be possible to have the statement rephrased in more specific form. See 2 M. Graham HANDBOOK OF FEDERAL EVIDENCE (4th ed 1992) § 804.0 at 585; 1 McCormick, EVIDENCE (4th ed 1992) § 18 at 75.

RULE 804(1)
Definition of Unavailability

At common law, the definition of unavailability varied depending upon the hearsay exception in question. Rule 804(1) establishes a uniform standard of unavailability for all Rule 804 hearsay exceptions with one exception: The requirement with respect to procurement of testimony of an unavailable declarant under Rule 804(1)(e) is applicable only to the hearsay exceptions listed in Rule 804(3)(b), (c), and (d).

Rule 804(1) lists five circumstances in which a hearsay declarant will be deemed unavailable for purposes of this rule:

1. The declarant is exempted, by ruling of the court on the ground of privilege, from testifying concerning the subject matter of a statement;
2. The declarant persists in refusing to testify concerning the subject matter of a statement despite an order of the court to do so;
3. The declarant testifies to a lack of memory of the subject matter of a statement;
4. The declarant is unable to be present or to testify at the hearing because of death or then existing physical or mental illness or infirmity; or

5. The declarant is absent from the hearing and the proponent of the declarant's statement has been unable to procure the declarant's attendance by process or other reasonable means. In the case of dying declarations, statements against interest, and statements of personal or family history, it must be shown not only that the proponent is unable to procure the declarant's attendance, but also that the proponent is unable to procure the declarant's testimony by other means, such as a deposition.

Rule 804(2) provides that a declarant is not unavailable as a witness if the declarant's exemption, refusal, claim of lack of memory, inability, or absence is due to the procurement or wrongdoing of the proponent of the declarant's statement for the purpose of preventing the witness from attending or testifying. The court determines under Rule 104(1) whether the requirements of unavailability have been satisfied.

The five grounds listed in the rule are not exclusive. In *State v. Bounds*, 71 Or App 744, 749 n 1, 694 P2d 566, 588 n1, rev denied 299 Or 732, 705 P2d 1157 (1985), the court held that "unavailability of a witness" includes situations in which a declarant is incompetent to testify because of age. See also *State v. Swader*, 72 Or App 593, 697 P2d 557, rev'd on other grounds 299 Or 729, 705 P2d 196 (1985) (three-year-old found incompetent and unavailable); *State v. Vosika*, 83 Or App 298, 731 P2d 449, modified 85 Or App 148, 735 P2d 1273 (1987).

In *Hansen v. Abrasive Engineering and Manufacturing, Inc.*, 317 Or 378, 385-7, 856 P2d 625 (1993), the court addressed the apparent conflict between OEC 804(1)(e) and ORS 45.250(2)(c) with respect to the admissibility of a discovery deposition. The statute requires only a showing that the declarant is beyond the reach of subpoena at the time of trial whereas the rule requires "other reasonable means" to obtain a declarant's attendance before prior testimony may be offered. The court concluded that compliance with the statute is sufficient, because nothing suggests that by enacting the rule the legislature "intended to limit the force of ORS 45.250(2)."

Privilege

For a witness to be unavailable because exempted from testifying on the ground of privilege, the court must rule that the proposed testimony is protected by a privilege. *United States v. Pelton*, 578 F2d 701 (8th Cir), cert denied 439 US 964 (1978); *United States v. Mangan*, 575 F2d 32 (2nd Cir), cert denied 439 US 931 (1978). But see *United States v. Thomas*, 571 F2d 285 (5th Cir 1978) (no express assertion of a Fifth Amendment privilege is required when the declarant is a codefendant, because codefendant clearly has right not to testify). Under Rule 513(2), the assertion of the privilege should usually take place outside of the jury's presence. If the court rules against the claim of privilege, but the witness persists in refusing to testify despite a court order, the witness will be found unavailable under Rule 804(1)(b).

In *State v. Ordonez-Villanueva*, 138 Or App 236, 244, ___ P2d ___ (1995), the court held that a unilateral statement by the prosecutor that a witness would assert the Fifth Amendment privilege if called is an insufficient showing of unavailability.

Similarly, in *State v. Thoma*, 313 Or 268, 277, 834 P2d 1020 (1992), the court found the assumption that the declarant would claim lack of memory regarding the statements or invoke the privilege against self-incrimination to be speculative. Therefore, the court found an insufficient showing of unavailability.

In *State v. Farber*, 295 Or 199, 209, 666 P2d 821, 826–7, appeal dismissed 464 US 987 (1983), the defense counsel reported to the court that a particular witness was unavailable to testify, because counsel had heard through that witness' lawyer that the witness was planning to assert the privilege against self-incrimination. Defense counsel did not call the witness and make a record of this claim of privilege out of a belief that it would be unethical to do so in open court. The Supreme Court stated: "Without deciding whether this is a correct assessment of the situation, we suggest that such a claim of privilege should be made part of the record. This could be done outside the presence of the jury to obviate any possible ethical problems. The court also held that a witness claiming the privilege against self-incrimination can be found unavailable even though the prosecutor could have made the witness available by granting immunity.

A sufficient showing of unavailability may be found when a witness claims the privilege against self-incrimination as to part of her testimony, if that part is in any way central or critical. In *State v. Douglas*, 310 Or 438, 444, 800 P2d 288 (1990), the court held that a witness was sufficiently unavailable to permit admission of her former testimony when she asserted the privilege
against self-incrimination only as to questions about controlled substances. The court held that her story "would have lacked coherence if all references to drugs had been excised." The court stated that "[b]ecause she could not testify meaningfully without mentioning drugs, the trial court did not err in concluding that she was unavailable within the meaning of OEC 804(1)(a)."

Lack of Memory

A declarant will be found unavailable under Rule 804(1)(c) if the declarant appears as a witness and testifies to a lack of memory of a statement's subject matter. The Report of the House Committee on the Judiciary of the United States Congress on FRE 804(a)(3), which is identical to Oregon Rule 804(1)(c), stated: "[T]he Committee intends no change in existing federal law under which the court may choose to disbelieve the declarant's testimony as to his lack of memory. See *United States v. Insana*, 423 F.2d 1165, 1169-1170 (2nd Cir), *cert denied*, 400 US 841 (1970)." H R Rep No 650, 93d Cong, 1st Sess 15 (1973), reprinted in 1974 US Code Cong & Ad News, 7075, 7088.

Physical or Mental Illness

The determination of whether a declarant is unavailable under Rule 804(l)(d) because of then existing physical or mental illness is a matter for the court under Rule 104(1). See *Sproul v. Fossi,* 274 Or 749 548 P2d 970 (1976) (testimony of plaintiff's wife that plaintiff was ill with a coronary heart problem and hypertension, supported by a letter from plaintiff's doctor, was sufficient to establish unavailability). If the disability is temporary, the court may choose to grant a continuance until the witness recovers. In *United States v. Amaya,* 533 F2d 188 191 (5th Cir 1976), cert denied 429 US 1101 (1977), the court stated:

> Although the duration of an illness is a proper element of unavailability, the establishment of permanence as to the particular illness is not an absolute requirement. The duration of the illness need only be in probability long enough so that, with proper regard to the importance of the testimony, the trial cannot be postponed. (citation omitted)

To avoid a violation of a defendant's right to confrontation, courts in criminal cases are likely to be particularly reluctant to declare a prosecution witness unavailable because of a temporary disability. See *Barber v. Page,* 390 US 719, 88 SCt 1318, 20 LEd2d 255 (1968); McCormick, EVIDENCE (2d ed 1972) § 253 at 610 ("A mere temporary disability appears not to conform with the standard established by *Barber v. Page*") (footnote omitted); C. Mueller & L. Kirkpatrick, MODERN EVIDENCE (1995) § 8.55.

In *State v. Pinnell,* 311 Or 98, 115, 806 P2d 110 (1991), the court held that there was a sufficient showing of physical and mental infirmities to justify a finding of unavailability of a witness, thereby allowing the former testimony of the witness to be admitted.

Attendance Cannot Be Procured by Process

Under Rule 804(1)(e) a declarant whose attendance cannot be procured by process or other reasonable means is unavailable. A good faith effort to locate the witness is required. See *State v. Montgomery,* 88 Or App 163, 744 P2d 592, rev denied 304 Or 548, 747 P2d 999 (1987) (state found to have made required good faith effort to locate witness and secure her attendance at trial).

The reach of process to secure attendance of witnesses differs in civil and criminal cases. Compare ORCP 55E with ORS 136.632–.637.

In addition to process, the rule requires that the proponent of the declarant's statement use "other reasonable means" before the declarant will be found to be unavailable. It is unclear what this requirement encompasses, and reasonableness may depend on factors such as the amount at stake, the cost of producing the witness, and the importance of the witness' testimony. In most cases, the rule presumably requires at a minimum a request to a witness beyond the court's jurisdiction to return voluntarily to testify.

For dying declarations (Rule 804(3)(b)), statements against interest (Rule 804(3)(c)), and statements of personal or family history (Rule 804(3)(d)), the standard of unavailability set forth in Rule 804(1)(e) requires a showing not only that the declarant's attendance cannot be obtained, but also that a deposition cannot be obtained. According to the Commentary, "the proponent of the hearsay [must] attempt to depose the declarant, as well as to seek the declarant's attendance, before the person will be considered unavailable." This requirement may impose the significant expense of an out-of-state deposition on a party seeking to offer hearsay under Rule 804(3)(b), (c) or (d).

This requirement is adopted verbatim from FRE 804(a)(5). It was not part of FRE 804 as originally promulgated by the United States Supreme Court but was added by House amendment in Congress. The argument against this requirement was well stated by the Report of the Senate Committee on the Judiciary:

> Under the house amendment, before a witness is declared unavailable, a party must try to depose a witness (declarant) with respect to dying declarations, declarations against interest, and declarations of pedigree. None of these situations would seem to warrant this needless, impractical and highly restrictive complication. A good case can be made for eliminating the unavailability requirement entirely for declarations against interest cases.
>
> In dying declaration cases, the declarant will usually, though not necessarily, be deceased at the time of trial. Pedigree statements which are admittedly and necessarily based largely on word of mouth are not greatly fortified by a deposition requirement.
>
> Depositions are expensive and time consuming. In any event, deposition procedures are available to those who wish to resort to them. Moreover, the deposition procedures of the Civil Rules and Criminal Rules are only imperfectly adapted to implementing the amendment. No purpose is served unless the deposition, if taken, may be used in evidence. Under Civil Rule (a)(3) and Criminal Rule 15(e), a deposition, though taken, may not be admissible and under Criminal Rule 15(a) substantial obstacles exist in the way of even taking a deposition (footnote omitted) (5 Rep No 1277, 93d Cong, 2d Sess 20, reprinted in 1974 US Code Cong & Ad News 7051,7067)

For these reasons, the Senate Committee deleted the House amendment to FRE 804(a)(5). The amendment was reinstated, however, in conference committee.

Judge Weinstein comments as follows regarding the deposition requirement;

> Despite this Congressional change to Rule 804(a)(5) it would be a mistake to read the phrase, "unable to procure testimony" by deposition, woodenly. There may be instances where it is impracticable but not legally impossible to obtain a deposition. Where a relatively small claim, for example, would be overbalanced by the cost of a foreign deposition or where the evidence comes to light during the trial and a continuance is not possible, the proponent can be found to be "unable" to procure the deposition. This interpretation is enhanced by reading the phrase "reasonable means" to cover both depositions and physical procurement of the witness—a parsing consistent with the clause's syntax. (4 J. Weinstein and M. Berger, WEINSTEIN'S EVIDENCE § 804(a)[01] at 804–56 (1988)).

Representations by counsel that attendance of a declarant cannot be procured, although permissible, may be insufficient to show unavailability or constitute grounds for reversal if inaccurate. See *Perricone v. Kansas City Ry.*, 630 F2d 317 (5th Cir 1980) (declarant's statement admitted upon representation by plaintiff's counsel that declarant could not be located; after trial, defendant located declarant living one mile from courthouse; judgment for plaintiff reversed). But see *Bailey v. S P Transp. Co.*, 613 F2d 1385 (5th Cir), cert denied 449 US 836 (1980) (not abuse of discretion for trial court to accept counsel's representations regarding unavailability). See generally ANNOT., *Sufficiency of Efforts To Procure Missing Witness' Attendance To Justify Admission of His Former Testimony—State Cases*, 3 ALR4th 87 (1981).

Constitutional Standard of Unavailability

In criminal cases or other proceedings where the Sixth Amendment is applicable, Rule 804(1) must be considered in conjunction with the constitutional standard of unavailability required by the Confrontation Clause. See text under Rule 802 for discussion of the constitutional right of confrontation. In criminal cases, the Confrontation Clause requires a more stringent showing of unavailability by the prosecution than is required by Rule 804(1). See *United States v. Rothbart*, 653 F2d 462, 465–6 (10th Cir 1981).

The Confrontation Clause requires the prosecutor to show a good faith effort to locate and attempt to secure the voluntary attendance of prosecution witnesses. In *Barber v. Page*, 390 US 719, 724–5, 88 SCt 1318, 1322, 20 LEd2d 255, 260 (1968), the United States Supreme Court held:

> In short, a witness is not "unavailable" for purposes of the foregoing exception to the confrontation requirement unless the prosecutorial authorities have made a good-faith effort to obtain his presence at trial.

The court further stated:

> For witnesses not in prison, the Uniform Act to Secure the Attendance of Witnesses From Without a State in Criminal Proceedings provides a means by which prosecuting authorities from one State can obtain an order from a court in the State where the witness is found directing the witness to appear in court in the first State to testify. The State seeking his appearance must pay the witness a specified sum as a travel allowance and compensation for his time. As of 1967 the Uniform Act was in force in 45 States, the District of Columbia, the Canal Zone, Puerto Rico, and the Virgin Islands. See 9 Uniform Laws Ann. 50 (1967 Supp.). For witnesses in prison, quite probably many state courts would utilize the common-law writ of habeas corpus ad testificandum at the request of prosecutorial authorities of a sister State upon a showing that adequate safeguards to keep the prisoner in custody would be maintained. (390 US at 723–24 n 4, 88 S Ct at 1231 n 4, 20 L Ed 2d at 259 n 4)

The requirements of *Barber v. Page* were elaborated on in *Ohio v. Roberts*, 448 US 56, 74–5, 100 SCt 2531, 2543, 65 LEd2d 597, 613 (1980):

But if there is a possibility, albeit remote, that affirmative measures might produce the declarant, the obligation of good faith may demand their effectuation. "The lengths to which the prosecution must go to produce a witness is a question of reasonableness." *California v. Green,* 399 U.S. at 189, n 22 (concurring opinion, citing *Barber v. Page,* supra). The ultimate question is whether the witness is unavailable despite good-faith efforts undertaken prior to trial to locate and present that witness. As with other evidentiary proponents, the prosecution bears the burden of establishing this predicate.

See also *State v. Anderson,* 42 Or App 29, 599 P2d 1225 (1979), cert denied 446 US 920 (1980); Oregon Constitution Article 1, § 11.

Witness in Foreign Nation

If the witness lives in a foreign nation and there are no established procedures for obtaining the cooperation of that government in securing the witness' return, unavailability "presupposes at least a good faith but unsuccessful attempt to notify the witness and to request his attendance." *State v. Smyth,* 286 Or 293, 301, 593 P2d 1166, 1170 (1979). See *Mancusi v. Stubbs,* 408 US 204, 212, 92 SCt 2308, 2313, 33 LEd2d 293 301 (1972); *United States v. Sindona,* 636 F2d 792 (2nd Cir 1980), cert denied 451 US 912 (1981) (witness properly found to be unavailable when prosecutor showed a good faith attempt to obtain the cooperation of Italian authorities to secure the witness' attendance).

Unavailability Procured by Prosecution

The courts are divided on whether a prosecution witness can be found to be unavailable when the witness' absence was caused in part by government action. See *United States v. Mann,* 590 F2d 361, 368 (1st Cir 1978) ("Implicit … in the duty to use reasonable means to procure the presence of an absent witness is the duty to use reasonable means to prevent a present witness from becoming absent"). But see *United States v. Mathis,* 550 F2d 180 (4th Cir 1976), cert denied 429 US 1107 (1977) (prosecution witness found to be unavailable, even though unavailability was due to government negligence in erroneously releasing the witness from prison rather than another prisoner with the same name).

In *State v. Brooks,* 64 Or App 404, 668 P2d 466, rev denied 296 Or 56, 672 P2d 1192 (1983), the court held that the unavailability of a witness was not the fault of the state, even though the state had drafted a plea agreement requiring the witness to testify only at the first trial, not at subsequent trials. The court therefore held that the witness' testimony at the first trial was admissible in the second trial under the former testimony exception to the hearsay rule. But see *State v. Herrera,* 286 Or 349, 594 P2d 823 (1979) (witness not unavailable who asserts privilege against self-incrimination after prosecutor rescinded immunity agreement without explanation).

Depositions

When a witness' deposition is offered in lieu of testimony, the unavailability requirements of Rule 804(1) must be considered in conjunction with ORS 45.250(2), and satisfaction of either provision suffices. ORS 45.250(2) provides:

> At the trial or upon the hearing of a motion or an interlocutory proceeding, any part or all of a deposition, so far as admissible under the rules of evidence, may be used against any party for any purpose, if the party was present or represented at the taking of the deposition or had due notice thereof, and if the court finds that:
>
> (a)   the witness is dead; or
>
> (b)   the witness's residence or present location is such that the witness is not obliged to attend in obedience to a subpena as provided in ORCP 55E.(1), unless it appears that the absence of the witness was procured by the party offering the deposition; or
>
> (c)   the witness is unable to attend or testify because of age, sickness, infirmity or imprisonment; or
>
> (d)   the party offering the deposition has been unable to procure the attendance of the witness by subpena; or
>
> (e)   upon application and notice, such exceptional circumstances exist as to make it desirable, in the interest of justice and with due regard to the importance of presenting the testimony of witnesses orally in open court, to allow the deposition to be used.
>
> (f)   the deposition was taken in the same proceeding pursuant to ORCP 39I.

In *Hansen v. Abrasive Engineering and Manufacturing, Inc.*, 112 Or App 586, 594, 831 P2d 693 (1992), aff'd 317 Or 378, 856 P2d 625 (1993), the court held that telephone depositions could be read into evidence upon a showing that the witnesses were out of state and beyond the reach of process. Even though Rule 804(1)(e) normally requires an additional showing that the attendance of the witness cannot be procured by "other reasonable means" in order to establish unavailability, no such showing is required by ORS 45.250 with respect to depositions.

With respect to depositions taken pursuant to ORCP 39I, see Rule 801(4)(c), which classifies statements made in such depositions as "not hearsay."

Telephone Testimony

Testimony by telephone is authorized by statute for certain nonjury proceedings. ORS 45.400(1) provides as follows:

> Upon motion of any party and for good cause shown, the court may order that the testimony of the party or any witness for the moving party be taken by telephone or by other two-way electronic communication device in any nonjury civil proceeding, juvenile dependency proceeding or termination of parental rights proceeding.

The moving party is required to give written notice to all other parties at least 30 days before the trial or hearing, unless the court allows a shorter time for good cause shown. ORS 45.400(2). The criteria for determining whether telephone testimony will be allowed are set forth in ORS 45.400(3).

RULE 804.   ORS 40.465. HEARSAY EXCEPTIONS WHERE THE DECLARANT IS UNAVAILABLE

(3) [Hearsay exceptions.] The following are not excluded by Rule 802 (ORS 40.455) if the declarant is unavailable as a witness:
(a) [Former testimony.] Testimony given as a witness at another hearing of the same or a different proceeding, or in a deposition taken in compliance with law in the course of the same or another proceeding, if the party against whom the testimony is now offered, or, in a civil action or proceeding a predecessor in interest, had an opportunity and similar motive to develop the testimony by direct, cross, or redirect examination.

LEGISLATIVE COMMENTARY

Subsection (3). Rule 803, supra, rests upon the premise that a hearsay statement within one of its exceptions is of such a quality that the declarant's availability is not a relevant factor in determining admissibility. Rule 804 is based on a different theory: that hearsay which is admittedly not equal in quality to testimony of the declarant on the stand may nevertheless be admitted, if the declarant is unavailable and if the statement meets a specified standard. This rule expresses preferences: testimony given on the stand is preferred over hearsay, and hearsay, if of the specified quality, is preferred over complete loss of the evidence of the declarant. The exceptions listed in this subsection illustrate these preferences, and for the most part were developed by the common law.

Paragraph (a). This paragraph sets forth an exception for former testimony. Former testimony does not rely upon a set of circumstances to substitute for oath and cross-examination: oath and opportunity to cross-examine were present when the former testimony was given. The only ideal condition that is missing is the presence of the trier and of the opponent, i.e., demeanor evidence. As this element is missing in all hearsay exceptions, it could be argued that former testimony is the best hearsay evidence, and should be included under Rule 803. However, it is the very opportunity to observe demeanor that largely confers depth and meaning upon testimony, for the setting is otherwise contrived. The exceptions under Rule 803 do not rely on demeanor for their evidential value nearly as heavily. Tradition, in any event, founded in experience, uniformly favors the production of a witness if the witness is available. This exception continues that policy. Preference for the person is also apparent in rules and statutes on the use of depositions, which deal with substantially the same problem.

Under the exception, prior testimony may be offered (1) against the party against whom it was previously offered, or (2) against the party by whom it was previously offered. In each instance, the important question is whether it is fair to impose the handling of the witness on an earlier occasion on the party against whom the testimony is now offered. (1) If the party against whom now offered is the one against whom the testimony was offered previously, it is generally not unfair to require the party to accept the result of the party's cross-examination or failure to cross-examine. But see, infra. (2) If the party against whom now offered is the one by whom the testimony was offered previously, a satisfactory rationale becomes more difficult. One possibility is to compare the testimony to an adoptive admission, i.e., the proponent adopts the testimony by offering it. However, this savors of discarded concepts of witnesses belonging to a party and litigants being able to choose witnesses and vouching for them. McCormick § 269 at 650, 651; 4 Wigmore, *Evidence* § 1075 (3d ed 1940). A more acceptable approach is simply to treat direct and redirect examination of one's own witness as the equivalent of cross-examination of an opponent's witness. Falknor, *Former Testimony and the Uniform Rules: A Comment,* in 38 NYU L Rev 651 n 1 (1963); McCormick § 255 at 617; *see also* 5 Wigmore § 1383. The techniques allowed for dealing with hostile, double-crossing, forgetful and mentally deficient witnesses leave no substance to a claim that one could not adequately develop one's own witness at a former hearing. Even less appealing is the argument that the failure to develop fully resulted from deliberate choice. But see, *infra.*

The Legislative Assembly recognizes that the foregoing principles may not apply in at least two situations. In a civil deposition, a party may not necessarily have a "similar motive" to examine or cross-examine a potential witness. A deposition taken solely for discovery purposes, for example, will be conducted very differently from one designated to perpetuate testimony. Again, in a preliminary hearing in a criminal case, neither party may have the opportunity or similar motive to develop testimony. Testimony in these two situations is admissible under this paragraph if the proponent can show equivalent opportunity and motive. *California v. Green,* 399 US 149, 90 S Ct 1930, 26 L Ed 2d 489 (1970) (testimony given at preliminary hearing satisfied confrontation requirements). Otherwise, it should be excluded. It should be added that failure to cross-examine a witness at a preliminary hearing does not necessarily waive the right to object to admission of the testimony in a subsequent proceeding.

Common law did not limit the admissibility of former testimony to testimony given in an earlier trial of the same case, but it did require identity of issues as a means of insuring that the former handling of the witness was equivalent to what would presently be done if the opportunity were presented. Modern decisions reduce the requirement to "substantial" identity. McCormick § 257 at 621.

In the further interest of fairness, Oregon and the common law insisted upon identity of parties, deviating only to the extent of allowing the substitution of successors in interest. *Patty v. Salem Flowering Mills Co.,* 53 Or 350, 96 P 1106 (1908). With the demise of the doctrine of mutuality, the requirement of identity of the offering party disappears, except as it might affect the motive of the party-against whom offered to develop testimony.

With respect to the latter the legislative Assembly emphasizes that any predecessor in interest in a civil proceeding must have had an opportunity and similar motive to examine the witness. Falknor, *supra* at 652; McCormick § 256 at 617, 618.

TEXT

Former Testimony

Provided that the declarant is shown to be unavailable as a witness under Rule 804(1), Rule 804(3)(a) creates a hearsay exception for former testimony if the party against whom the testimony is now offered—or in a civil action or proceeding a predecessor in interest—had an opportunity and similar motive to develop the testimony by direct, cross, or redirect examination. This rule replaces ORS 41.900 (repealed 1981), which provided in pertinent part: "Evidence may be given of the following facts: ... (8) The testimony of a witness deceased, or out of the state, or unable to testify, given in a former action, suit, or proceeding, or trial thereof, between the same parties, relating to the same matter." The rule eliminates the "between the same parties" requirement and provides only that the party *against* whom the testimony is now offered (or, in a civil action, a predecessor in interest) was a party to the earlier proceeding where the testimony was given. The rule also eliminates the "relating to the same matter" requirement, substituting a requirement that there must have been "an opportunity and similar motive to develop the testimony by direct, cross, or redirect examination."

The unavailability requirement does not apply to perpetuation depositions taken pursuant to ORCP 39I. Rule 801(4)(c) categorizes statements made in such depositions as "not hearsay."

Similar Motive

The party against whom the testimony is offered may be the party who offered the testimony in the earlier proceeding. Thus, failure to develop the testimony of a witness by direct or redirect examination when there is "an opportunity and similar motive" to do so poses the danger that the incomplete testimony may be offered against the party at a subsequent proceeding if the witness becomes unavailable. The Commentary expressly notes, however, that a party at a discovery deposition and a defendant at a preliminary hearing may not have motives to develop the witness' testimony similar to those motives that would exist at trial. See generally ANNOT., *Admissibility or Use in Criminal Trial of Testimony Given at Preliminary Proceeding by Witness not Available at Trial,* 38 ALR4th 378 (1985); COMMENT, *Confrontation Rights and Preliminary Hearings,* 1986 Utah L Rev 75.

In *State v. Montgomery,* 88 Or App 163, 744 P2d 592, rev denied 304 Or 548, 747 P2d 999 (1987), the defendant argued on appeal that it was error for the prosecutor to have offered the preliminary hearing testimony of his sister who identified the defendant as the perpetrator of the crime. The defendant contended that he did not have a "similar motive" to develop her testimony at the preliminary hearing as he had at trial. The court rejected the argument, finding sufficient similarity of motive at the two proceedings. The defendant also argued that his right of confrontation was violated, because the cross-examination at the preliminary hearing cannot serve as a substitute for cross-examination at trial. Again, the court rejected this argument, noting that the defendant not only was afforded the opportunity to cross-examine at the preliminary hearing, but in fact exercised that right and vigorously cross-examined the witness.

In *State v. Pinnell*, 311 Or 98, 116–7, 806 P2d 110 (1991), the court held that after a showing of unavailability, the former testimony of a witness at a security release hearing was admissible because the defendant had an opportunity to cross-examine the witnesses at the earlier hearing and a similar motive to do so. See also *State v. Douglas*, 310 Or 438, 445, 800 P2d 288 (1990) (same).

In *State v. Moen*, 309 Or 45, 84–86, 786 P2d 111 (1990), the court held that transcripts from preliminary hearings in previous proceedings involving the defendant were properly admitted where the declarants were shown to be deceased and the declarants were subject to cross-examination by defendant's counsel at such proceedings. The court found that the "'opportunity and similar motive' criteria of OEC 804(3)(a) were unquestionably met in this case." The court noted that "[t]his is not a situation where the witness in the preliminary hearing testified to a matter and the defendant did little or no cross-examination for tactical reasons, such as to use the preliminary hearing primarily for discovery."

Opportunity to Cross-Examine

Former testimony is not admissible under this exception if the party against whom the testimony is offered—or in a civil case the predecessor in interest—did not have an opportunity to examine the witness at the earlier proceeding. For this reason grand jury testimony may not be received against a criminal defendant under this rule. On the issue of whether grand jury testimony may be received against the government under this exception, see *United States v. Salerno*, 112 SCt 2503 (1992).

In *State v. Monsebroten*, 106 Or App 761, 809 P2d 1366, rev denied 311 Or 482, 813 P2d 1064 (1991), the court found no error in excluding prior testimony by a defense witness where the prosecutor had never been allowed an opportunity to complete its cross-examination of the witness. At the first trial where the witness testified, cross-examination was not completed because a mistrial was declared after the prosecutor asked a question bringing out that the defense witness had met the defendant in prison. The court held that it would not necessarily be unfair to require the state to accept its limited cross-examination of the witness at the first trial if the prosecutor at the first trial had intentionally asked an improper question with the intent of causing a mistrial. However, the court found no evidence of such intent in this case.

There is no requirement that counsel for the party be the same at the proceeding where the former testimony is offered as at the earlier proceeding where the testimony was given. See *United States v. Amaya,* 533 F2d 188 (5th Cir 1976), cert denied 429 US 1101 (1977) (former testimony admitted even though defendant represented by different counsel at second trial).

Proof of Former Testimony

Former testimony may be proven by the recollection of a participant at the prior proceeding. It is not necessary to call the court reporter, nor is it necessary to offer a transcript of the testimony. *State v. Crawley,* 242 Or 601, 410 P2d 1012 (1966). If a transcript is offered, it must be in proper form. *Nalley v. First National Bank,* 135 Or 409, 296 P 61 (1931) (partial transcript by person other than official court reporter not admissible).

On the question of evidentiary objections to former testimony, see ANNOT., *Former Testimony Used at Subsequent Trial As Subject to Ordinary Objections and Exceptions,* 40 ALR4th 514 (1985).

Predecessor in Interest

The rule recognizes only one circumstance where former testimony may be offered against a party who was not a party to the earlier proceeding where the testimony was given: a civil action where a predecessor in interest of the party was present at the earlier proceeding and had "an opportunity and similar motive to develop the testimony by direct, cross, or redirect examination." Unfortunately, the rule does not define *predecessor in interest,* and the federal cases are not in agreement. A predecessor in interest should be interpreted as a person in privity or having a similar relationship with the party against whom the evidence is now offered. See generally ANNOT., *Who is "Predecessor in Interest" For Purposes of Rule 804(b)(1) of Federal Rules of Evidence,* 47 ALR Fed 895 (1980).

Predecessor in interest should mean something more than a person with "an opportunity and similar motive" to develop the testimony. The decision of *Lloyd v. Am. Export Lines Inc.,* 580 F2d 1179, 1191 (3rd Cir), cert denied 439 US 969 (1978), which appeared to equate these concepts, seems wrongly decided. As the concurring opinion noted: "[T]he majority's analysis which reads 'predecessor in interest' to mean nothing more than person with 'similar motive' eliminates the predecessor in interest requirement entirely." See 4 J. Weinstein and M. Berger, WEINSTEIN'S EVIDENCE (1988) § 804(b)(1)[04] at 804-85-95.

See generally Turner, *Federal Rule of Evidence 804: Will the Real Predecessor in Interest Please Stand Up,* 19 Akron L Rev 215 (1985); COMMENT, *Fairness v. Trustworthiness: The Predecessor in Interest Controversy of Rule 804(b)(1),* 1984 BYU L Rev 79; Weissenberger, *The Former Testimony Hearsay Exception: A Study in Rulemaking, Judicial Revisionism, and the Separation of Powers,* 67 N C L Rev 295 (1989).

Depositions

Depositions taken to perpetuate testimony under ORCP 39I are defined as "not hearsay" by Rule 801(4)(c). Therefore, such depositions are admissible to the extent the testimony therein complies with the other rules of evidence.

The admissibility of other depositions in civil cases is governed by ORS 45.250 as well as Rule 804(3)(a). Although the provisions of the statute and rule are very similar, they differ in some respects. The courts have held that depositions are admissible if they qualify for admission under either ORS 45.250 or Rule 804(3)(a). In *Hansen v. Abrasive Engineering and Manufacturing, Inc.*, 317 Or 378, 389–92, 856 P2d 625, 631–3 (1993), the court addressed the apparent conflict between OEC 804(1)(e) and ORS 45.250(2)(c) with respect to the admissibility of a discovery deposition. The statute requires only a showing that the declarant is beyond the reach of subpoena at the time of trial, whereas the rule requires "other reasonable means" to obtain a declarant's attendance before prior testimony may be offered. The court concluded that compliance with the statute is sufficient, because nothing suggests that by enacting the rule the legislature "intended to limit the force of ORS 45.250(2)."

ORS 45.250(2) provides that a deposition be admitted "so far as admissible under the rules of evidence." This language should not be interpreted to mean that the admissibility of depositions is exclusively controlled by Rule 804(3)(a), but rather that the contents of depositions offered into evidence are still subject to the rules of evidence generally.

Pursuant to statute, a deposition in an earlier proceeding may be received against a successor in interest in a later proceeding involving the same subject matter. ORS 45.270 provides:

> Substitution of parties shall not affect the right to use the depositions previously taken; and when an action, suit or proceeding has been dismissed and another action, suit or proceeding involving the same subject matter is afterward brought between the same parties or their representatives or successors in interest, any deposition lawfully taken and duly filed in the former action, suit or proceeding may be used in the latter as if originally taken therefor, and is then to be deemed the evidence of the party reading it.

See generally ANNOT., *Admissibility of Depositions Under Federal Rule of Evidence 804(b)(1)*, 84 ALR Fed 668 (1987); COMMENT, *Admissibility of Prior Action Depositions and Former Testimony Under Fed R of Civ P 32(a)(4) and Fed R of Evid 804(b)(1): Courts' Differing Interpretations*, 41 Wash & Lee L Rev 155 (1984); Citrin, *Rules and Case Law Governing Videotape Depositions*, 12 Am J Trial Advoc 87 (1988).

Other Bases for Admission of Former Testimony

Former testimony may be admitted apart from this rule. In some cases, former testimony may satisfy another hearsay exception or qualify as not hearsay under Rule 801(4). Former testimony will not constitute hearsay if it is not being offered for the truth of the matter asserted, such as in a perjury prosecution. Former testimony may also be received to impeach the testimony of a witness.

When the former testimony was given at a deposition, it may be admissible under Rule 801(4)(c) (perpetuation depositions), ORS 45.250–.270 (depositions in civil cases), or ORS 136.080–.100 and ORS 136.420 (depositions in criminal cases). There is a statutory provision for use of the transcript of a witness' testimony at the first trial, if that witness is unavailable to testify at a new trial ordered pursuant to a post-conviction relief proceeding. See ORS 138.670.

RULE 804.   ORS 40.465. HEARSAY EXCEPTIONS WHERE THE DECLARANT IS UNAVAILABLE

(3) (b) **[Statement under belief of impending death.] A statement made by a declarant while believing that death was imminent, concerning the cause or circumstances of what the declarant believed to be impending death.**

LEGISLATIVE COMMENTARY

Paragraph (b). This paragraph is the familiar common law hearsay exception for dying declarations, expanded somewhat beyond its traditional limits. While the original religious justification for the exception may have lost its conviction for some persons, it can scarcely be doubted that powerful psychological forces are present when a person believes that death is imminent. See 5 Wigmore § 1443 and the classic statement of Chief Baron Eyre in *Rex v. Woodcock,* 2 Leach 500, 563, 168 Eng Rep 352, 353 (KB 1789).

The common law required that the statement be that of the victim offered in a prosecution for criminal homicide. While no doubt there was exceptional need for the evidence in such cases, the theory of admissibility runs further. Declarations by victims in prosecutions for other crimes, e.g., rape where the victim dies in child birth, and all declarations in civil cases, were beyond the scope of the common law exception. An occasional statute has removed these restrictions or expanded the area of offenses to include rape. 5 Wigmore § 1432 at 224 n 4. As often, however, the change came by judicial action. Kansas courts extended the exception to civil cases in *Thurston v. Fritz,* 91 Kan 468, 138 P625 (1914). Oregon courts did so in *McCarty v. Siriannii,* 132 Or 290, 293, 285P 825 (1930). Furthermore, the Oregon Supreme Court indicated it will admit dying declarations in all criminal cases, id., although the exception has only been used in prosecutions for homicide, *State v. Achziger,* 10 Or App 198, 497 P2d 383 (1972), *State v. Brewton,* 220 Or 266, 344 P2d 744 (1959); *State v. Garver,* 190 Or 291, 225 P2d 771 (1950). Paragraph (b) preserves Oregon law by allowing the admission of dying declarations in all criminal and civil cases. It is thus a broader hearsay exception than Federal Rule 804(b)(2), which allows the use of dying declarations only in civil actions and homicide prosecutions.

The only respect in which Oregon law is changed is the removal of the requirement that the declarant must actually have died before the hearing in which the statement is offered. ORS 41.900(4) implied that this was necessary. No Oregon case suggested otherwise. Under this paragraph, actual death of the declarant is not necessary for a dying declaration to be admissible. The declarant can be "unavailable" for any of the reasons listed in subsection (1) of this rule.

Like Oregon law, the paragraph requires that the declarant make the statement believing death is imminent, and that the declaration relate to the circumstances of the impending death. *Mercep v. State Indus. Accident Comm'n,* 167 Or 460, 118 P2d 1061 (1941); *McCarty v. Sirianni,* supra; *State v. Doris,* 51 Or 136, 94 P 44 (1908). Because of the psychological intensity of the moment, it has been suggested that the law abandon the limitation regarding circumstances of death. However, the Legislative Assembly believes that the influence of a statement dealing with matters other than supposed impending death is sufficiently attenuated to justify the limitation. Any problem as to declarations in opinion form is laid to rest by ORE 701. The requirement of firsthand knowledge in ORE 602 continues.

Comparable provisions are found in Uniform Rule 63(5), California Evidence Code § 1242, Kansas Code of Civil Procedure § 60-460(e), and New Jersey Evidence Rule 63(5).

TEXT

Statement Under Belief of Impending Death

Provided the declarant is shown to be unavailable as a witness under Rule 804(1), Rule 804(3)(b) creates a hearsay exception for a statement—made while the declarant believed that death was imminent—concerning the cause or circumstances of what the declarant believed to be impending death. Unlike FRE 804(b)(2), which applies only to civil actions and homicide cases, this rule applies to civil actions and all types of criminal cases.

Proof of the declarant's belief in the imminence of his or her death may be shown by circumstantial evidence, such as the nature of the declarant's wounds, statements made by the declarant, statements made to the declarant or in the declarant's presence, or opinions of physicians that because of the severity of the injuries or illness the declarant must have been aware of imminent death. See 4 J. Weinstein and M. Berger, WEINSTEIN'S EVIDENCE (1988) § 804(b)(2)[01] at 804–14; ANNOT., *Statements of Declarant as Sufficiently Showing Consciousness of Impending Death to Justify Admission of Dying Declaration,* 53 ALR3d 785 (1973); ANNOT., *Sufficiency of Showing of Consciousness of Impending Death, by Circumstances Other than Statements of Declarant, to Justify Admission of Dying Declaration,* 53 ALR3d 1196 (1973).

In *Shepard v. United States,* 290 US 96, 100, 54 SCt 22, 24, 78 LEd2d 196, 199 (1933), the Court stated:

> [D]eath will not avail itself to make a dying declaration. There must be "a settled hopeless expectation" that death is near at hand and what is said must have been spoken in the hush of its impending presence. The patient must have spoken with the consciousness of a swift and certain doom. (Citations omitted)

The determination of whether the rule's requirements are satisfied is a preliminary matter for the court under Rule 104(1). The rule thus changes prior law that allowed the jury to be instructed not to consider the statement if the jury found it was not made under a sense of impending death. *State v. Garver,* 190 Or 291, 311, 225 P2d 771 (1950). However, evidence that the declarant did not believe death was imminent may be admissible under Rule 104(5) to the extent it is found to bear on the credibility of the declarant or the weight to be accorded the dying declaration.

The rule does not require that the death have been caused by the event that is the subject of litigation, but the dying declaration must concern the cause or circumstances of what the declarant believed to be impending death. The rule does not require that the declarant actually die for the statement to be admissible under this exception, if the declarant is otherwise unavailable at the time of trial. See Rule 804(1).

The Commentary states that the declarant must have first-hand knowledge under Rule 602 for this exception to apply. The personal knowledge requirement is retained because dying declarations based upon speculation or conjecture would be more damaging than helpful to the truth-finding function. Dying declarations in the form of opinions may generally be received if they otherwise satisfy the requirements of this exception. As the Commentary notes: "Any problem as to declarations in opinion form is laid to rest by ORE 701." Because the declarant is unavailable, the court cannot require the statement to be rephrased. See generally ANNOT., *Admissibility in Criminal Trial of Dying Declarations Involving an Asserted Opinion or Conclusion,* 86 ALR2d 905 (1962).

In *State v. Holterman,* 69 Or App 509, 687 P2d 1097, rev denied 298 Or 172, 691 P2d 481 (1984), the court held that a dying murder victim's identification of the defendant through a hand signal system in response to questions from a police officer was properly admissible under the dying declaration exception to the hearsay rule. The court held that the suggestiveness of the questions affects the credibility and weight to be given to the testimony, not its admissibility. The court further held that the trial judge did not err in concluding from the evidence that the victim was competent and was able to comprehend the questions and respond.

RULE 804. ORS 40.465. HEARSAY EXCEPTIONS WHERE THE DECLARANT IS UNAVAILABLE

(3) (c) [Statement against interest.] A statement which was at the time of its making so far contrary to the declarant's pecuniary or pro-

prietary interest, or so far tended to subject the declarant to civil or criminal liability, or to render invalid a claim by the declarant against another, that a reasonable person in the declarant's position would not have made the statement unless the person believed it to be true. A statement tending to expose the declarant to criminal liability and offered to exculpate the accused is not admissible unless corroborating circumstances clearly indicate the trustworthiness of the statement.

LEGISLATIVE COMMENTARY

Paragraph (c). This paragraph embodies the statement against interest exception to the hearsay rule. The principle involved was recognized in numerous Oregon statutes now repealed. ORS 41.830 (declarations of grantor); ORS 41.850 (declarations of deceased person); ORS 41.860 (writings of deceased person); ORS 41.890 (declarations of nonparties); ORS 41.900(4) (declarations of decedent relating to pedigree and real property). A statement against interest carries a circumstantial guaranty of reliability, because people generally do not make statements that are damaging to their interests unless they believe they are true. *Hileman v. Northwest Engineering Co.,* 346 F2d 668 (6th Cir 1965). If the statement is that of a party offered by an opponent, it comes in as an admission under ORE 801(4)(b). There is no occasion to inquire whether the statement is against interest in that case, because this is not a condition precedent to the admissibility of an admission.

The common law required that the interest of the declarant be either pecuniary or proprietary. *Mace v. Timberman,* 120 Or 144, 251 P 763 (1926). However, the common law also showed striking ingenuity in discovering an against-interest aspect that fell within these categories. *Higham v. Ridgway,* 10 East 109, 103 Eng Rep 717 (KB 1808); *Reg. v. Overseers of Birmingham,* 1 B & 5 763, 121 Eng Rep 897 (QB 1861); McCormick § 279 at 675 nn 42, 43.

This paragraph abandons the common law restrictions and expands the exception to its logical limit. This has two notable results. One result is to remove any doubt that declarations tending to establish a tort liability against the declarant, or to extinguish one the declarant might assert, are admissible. This is in accord with the trend of the decisions. McCormick § 671-672.

Another result is to include criminal liability as a qualifying "interest." An increasing amount of decisional law has recognized exposure to criminal punishment as a sufficient stake. *People v. Spriggs,* 60 Cal 2d 868, 36 Cal Rep 841, 389 P2d 377 (1964); *Sutter v. Easterly,* 354 Mo 282, 189 SW 2d 284 (1945); *Band's Refuse Removal, Inc. v. Fairlawn Borough,* 62 NJ Super 522, 163 A2d 465 (1960); *Newberry v. Commonwealth,* 191 Va 445, 61 SW 2d 318 (1950); Annot., 162 ALR 446. Oregon did not, before this rule. *State v. Anderson,* 10 Or App 34, 497 P2d 1216 (1962), citing *State v. Coleman,* 119 Or 430, 249 P 1049 (1928); *State v. Farnam,* 82 Or 211, 161 P 1417 (1916); *State v. Fletcher,* 24 Or 295, 33 P 575 (1893); see also *State v. Morse,* 35 Or 462, 57 P 631 (1899). However, the Supreme Court recently observed that limiting the scope of the exception to declarations that fit neatly within a "pecuniary" or "proprietary" interest has long been questioned. *Timber Access Industries Co. v. U.S. Plywood-Champion Papers, Inc.,* 263 Or 509, 520, 503 P2d 482 (1972), citing 5 Wigmore, *Evidence* § 1455 at 259 (3d ed 1940). Recognition of the penal interest is thus the only change—if it is a change—this paragraph works in Oregon law.

The common law refused to concede the adequacy of penal interest in large part because it distrusted evidence of confessions by third persons offered to exculpate the accused. This reflected a suspicion that either the fact or the contents of the confession were fabricated, enhanced in either case by the required unavailability of the declarant. To meet that concern, ORE 804 requires that a statement against penal interest be corroborated. This requirement must be satisfied prior to admission, see ORE 104(1), as the situation after an accused offers such a statement is not well adapted to control by rulings as to the weight of evidence. The trial court should construe the corroboration requirement in a manner that effectuates its purpose to circumvent fabrication.

Ordinarily, a third-party confession is thought of in terms of exculpating the accused, but this is by no means always the case. The confession may include statements which implicate the accused, and under the general theory of declarations against interest these would be admissible as related statements. *Douglas v. Alabama,* 380 US 415, 85 S Ct 1074, 13 L Ed 2d 934 (1965) and *Bruton v. United States,* 389 US 818, 88 S Ct 126, 19 L Ed 2d 70 (1968) both involved confessions by codefendants that implicated the accused. While the confession in Douglas was not offered into evidence, the conduct of trial effectively put it before the jury and was held to be error. Whether the confession might have been admissible as a declaration against penal interest was not discussed. Bruton assumed the inadmissibility as against the accused of the implicating confession of the codefendant, and focused on the question of the effectiveness of a limiting instruction. Neither decision, therefore, holds that all statements implicating another person must be excluded from the category of declarations against interest.

Whether a statement is in fact against the declarant's interest must be determined from the circumstances of each case. *See* McCormick § 279. A statement admitting guilt and implicating another person, made while in custody, may well spring from a desire to curry favor with the authorities and hence fail to qualify as being against the declarant's interest. See the dissenting opinion of Mr. Justice White in Bruton. On the other hand, the same words spoken under different circumstances, e.g., to an acquaintance, would have no difficulty in qualifying.

Paragraph (c) does not purport to deal with questions of the right of confrontation. Nor does it affect the existing exception to the Bruton principle where the codefendant takes the stand and is subject to cross-examination, as the declarant in that event would not be "unavailable." For comparable provisions see Uniform Rule 63(10), California Evidence Code § 1230, Kansas Code of Civil Procedure § 60-460(j), and New Jersey Evidence Rule 63(10).

TEXT

Statement Against Interest

Provided the declarant is shown to be unavailable as a witness under Rule 804(1), Rule 804(3)(c) provides a hearsay exception for a statement that a reasonable person in the declarant's position would not have made unless the person believed it to be true, because the statement at the time of its making: (1) was contrary to the declarant's pecuniary or proprietary interest; (2) tended to subject the declarant to civil liability; (3) tended to subject the declarant to criminal liability; or (4) tended to render invalid a claim by the declarant against another. A statement tending to expose the declarant to criminal liability and offered to exculpate the accused is not admissible unless corroborating circumstances clearly indicate the trustworthiness of the statement.

This exception is directed toward statements against interest of nonparty witnesses. See, e.g., ANNOT., *Admissibility in Action for Death of Statements Against Interest By Decedent,* 114 ALR 921 (1938). Reliance on this exception is unnecessary when the declarant is a party opponent because admissions of a party opponent are defined as not hearsay by Rule 801(4)(b).

Unlike admissions, statements against interest: (1) must be based on personal knowledge (see Rule 602; *United States v. Lang,* 589 F2d 92 (2nd Cir 1978)); (2) must have been made by a now unavailable declarant; and (3) must have been against the declarant's interest at the time they were made. Presumably, the rule requires that the declarant had been able to appreciate that the statement was against his or her interest when made. Otherwise, the rationale for reliability underlying this exception—namely, that "a reasonable person in the declarant's position would not have made the statement unless the person believed it to be true"—would be inapplicable. See *Reynoldson v. Jackson,* 275 Or 641, 645, 552 P2d 236, 238 (1976) ("[T]here [must] be some evidence, or at least an inference which could be drawn which indicates that the declarant realized that the statements were against his pecuniary interest at the time they were made").

Statements Against Penal Interest

Statements against penal interest may now be admitted as an exception to the hearsay rule. At common law, statements against penal interest were excluded out of "fear of opening a door to a flood of witnesses testifying falsely to confessions that were never made or testifying truthfully to confessions that were false." McCormick, EVIDENCE (3d ed 1984) § 278 at 823. To meet such a concern, the rule requires that before a statement against penal interest may be received to exculpate a criminal defendant, the court must find that "corroborating circumstances clearly indicate the trustworthiness of the statement." If the statement appears untrustworthy or if corroboration is lacking, the statement must be excluded. *United States v. Guillette,* 547 F2d 743 (2nd Cir 1976), cert denied 434 US

839 (1977); *United States v. Bagley,* 537 F2d 162 (5th Cir 1976), cert denied 429 US 1075 (1977).

Statements against penal interest may be offered by the prosecution as well as a criminal defendant. See *State v. Osborne,* 82 Or App 229, 728 P2d 551 (1986) (in murder prosecution where defendant was charged with hiring a third party to kill his wife, inculpatory statements by the third party were held properly admissible as statements against that party's penal interest); *State v. Lissy,* 85 Or App 484, 737 P2d 617, aff'd on other grounds 304 Or 455, 747 P2d 345 (1987) (same). But see discussion below of limitations on the use of statements against interest that inculpate other persons, where accusations against others are not against the declarant's penal interest.

A statement against penal interest may also be offered in a civil case. See *Holmes v. Morgan,* 135 Or App 617, 626, 899 P2d 738 (1995) (in action for interference with economic relations, plaintiff offered evidence of suicide pact between decedent—who was plaintiff's son—and defendant; statements by decedent were not against his penal interest because he was planning to commit suicide himself and not commit the crime of assisting someone else to commit suicide).

A statement may be found to be against penal interest even though it is not a direct confession of guilt. *United States v. Thomas,* 571 F2d 285, 288–9 (5th Cir 1978); *United States v. Barrett,* 539 F2d 244, 251 (1st Cir 1976); *United States v. Lang,* 589 F2d 92, 97 (2nd Cir 1978); *United States v. Bagley,* 537 F2d 162, 165 (5th Cir 1976), cert denied 429 US 1075 (1977). See generally ANNOT., *What Constitutes Statement Against Interest Admissible Under Rule 804(b)(3) of Federal Rules of Evidence,* 34 ALR Fed 412 (1977).

A court is unlikely, however, to find a statement to be against penal interest if the statute of limitations has run, immunity has been granted, the declarant has been convicted or acquitted of the offense, or prosecution is barred by the double jeopardy clause. See *Withan v. Mabry,* 596 F2d 293 (8th Cir 1979) (statement not against penal interest where declarant has already been convicted); *United States v. Love,* 592 F2d 1022 (8th Cir 1979) (statement not against penal interest where charges against declarant have been resolved by bond forfeiture); *United States v. Gonzalez,* 559 F2d 1271 (5th Cir 1977) (statement made after immunity granted not against penal interest); *United States v. Bailey,* 581 F2d 341 (3rd Cir 1978) (statement made after plea bargain not against penal interest).

As the Commentary further notes, "[a] statement admitting guilt and implicating another person, made while in custody, may well spring from a desire to curry favor with the authorities and hence fail to qualify as being against the declarant's interest."

The Admissibility of Statements Not Against Interest that Accompany or Are Part of Statements Against Interest

A controversial issue in this area is whether statements that are not against the declarant's interest, i.e., are neutral or collateral, may be admitted if they are part of a statement that is against the declarant's interest. The argument against admitting such statements has been stated as follows:

> The basis of this exception is not that a declarant is in a general trustworthy frame of mind. The probability of trustworthiness comes from the facts asserted being disserving in character. Once those facts are left behind the probability of trustworthiness for other statements seems highly speculative and conjectural. It would seem, therefore, that the courts are not justified in admitting self-serving statements merely because they accompany disserving statements, and a neutral collateral statement should fare no better. (Jefferson, *Declarations Against Interest: An Exception to the Hearsay Rule,* 58 Harv L Rev 1, 60 (1944)).

See also *United States v. Lilley,* 581 F2d 182, 188 (8th Cir 1978) ("To the extent that a statement is not against the declarant's interest, the guaranty of trustworthiness does not exist and that portion of the statement should be excluded."). Often statements against penal interest that include a statement inculpating a criminal defendant are made by coconspirators. If courts were to liberally allow such inculpatory statements under this exception, it might tend to undercut the requirement of the coconspirator admissions rule that statements by a coconspirator must have been made "during the course and in furtherance of the conspiracy." (See Rule 801(4)(b)(E)).

In *United States v. Williamson,* 114 S Ct 2431 (1994), the Supreme Court held that the federal version of the hearsay exception for declarations against penal interest (FRE 804(b)(3)) requires that **all** parts of the statement be against the penal interest of the declarant. Neither self-serving portions nor collateral or neutral segments qualify for admission. Thus, the Court raised serious questions about the admissibility of statements by a third-party declarant implicating the defendant. The Court noted that such statements often are self-serving and are designed to curry favor with the authorities. In other cases, such statements are merely collateral to self-incriminating declarations and therefore are inadmissible because they are not against interest. Such statements are admissible only in circumstances where implicating another is shown to be against the declarant's interest. By finding collateral statements inadmissible as a matter of evidence law, the Court found it unnecessary to address whether their admission would violate the confrontation clause.

However, the Oregon Supreme Court has refused to follow the *Williamson* decision and had allowed statements by one conspirator implicating another as a statement against penal interest, despite lack of showing that the part of the statement implicating the other was against the declarant's interest.

In *State v. Wilson,* 323 Or 498, ___ P2d ___ (1996), a murder prosecution, after Charboneau claimed the privilege against self-incrimination, the court approved the admission of out-of-court statements by Charboneau implicating both himself and Wilson in the murder of Largo. The court refused to require any showing that the portion of the statement implicating Wilson was against Charboneau's penal interest, noting at 323 Or 513 n9 that state courts are not required to follow the *Williamson* decision. (Interestingly, the Supreme Court rejected the *Williamson* rule without considering the possibility that it might have been satisfied on the facts of this case.)

In *State v. Nielsen*, 316 Or 611, 853 P2d 256 (1993), the court approved the admission of a woman's statement that incriminated both herself and her male companion (the defendant) in forgery. Immediately after arrest, the woman confessed to the forgery and stated that the check used had been obtained by defendant in a burglary. Because the woman was unavailable at trial, the court held that her hearsay statement to the police was properly admitted as a statement against her penal interest. The court found the statement to be sufficiently trustworthy even though it was made in police custody, because there was no indication that it was made to curry favor or shift blame from herself. A dissenting opinion argued that the portion of her statement accusing the defendant was not against the declarant's penal interest and should not have been admitted (taking essentially the same view as the majority in *Williamson*).

Confrontation Issues

To the extent that Oregon courts admit portions of statements that are not against the declarant's interest under this exception, a confrontation challenge can be raised. To admit inculpatory statements under Rule 804(3)(c) merely because they were made as part of a statement against penal interest raises confrontation concerns because such statements often lack sufficient "indicia of reliability." See *Lee v. Illinois*, 476 US 530, 106 SCt 2056, 90 LEd2d 514 (1986) (statement against penal interest of codefendant, made in response to police interrogation, found to be unreliable and violative of defendant's right of confrontation); *Dutton v. Evans*, 400 US 74, 91 SCt 210, 27 LEd 213 (1970); *Bruton v. United States*, 391 US 123, 88 SCt 1620, 20 LEd2d 476 (1968).

In *State v. Wilson*, 323 Or 498, 513–8, 918 P2d 826 (1996), the court found a statement against penal interest that implicated both the declarant and the defendant to be admissible under the state and federal confrontation clauses. The court noted that the statement was made in the declarant's own home to a friend (rather than to police while in custody), declarant was sober and made the statements without protracted questioning, the statements were quite detailed and were made on the day of the murder, and they admitted declarant's equally culpable involvement in the murder rather than attempting to shift the blame to defendant. Thus, they had sufficient "indicia of reliability" to survive a confrontation challenge.

In *State v. Tucker*, 109 Or App 519, 525–6, 820 P2d 834, 837–8 (1991), rev denied 317 Or 188, 855 P2d 150 (1993), the court held that the admission of evidence pursuant to the exception for statements against penal interest does not violate defendant's confrontation rights. However, Justice Fadeley dissented from the denial of the petition for review and would have remanded the case to consider further whether the declaration against penal interest was sufficiently reliable to justify its admission under the confrontation clauses of the state and federal constitutions. Justice Fadeley also noted that neither the Oregon Supreme Court nor the United States Supreme Court have yet held that in all circumstances the hearsay exception for statements against penal interest is "firmly rooted."

See generally textual discussion under Rule 802, supra; COMMENT, *Federal Rule of Evidence 804(b)(3) and Inculpatory Statements Against Penal Interest*, 66 Cal L Rev 1189 (1978); COMMENT, *Inculpatory Statements Against Penal Interest and the Confrontation Clause*, 83 Colum L Rev 159 (1983).

Corroboration Requirement

With respect to the corroboration requirement, the federal courts are divided regarding whether the trustworthiness of the witness' report that the statement was made can be considered, or only the trustworthiness of the declarant. Compare *United States v. Bagley*, 537 F2d 162, 167 (5th Cir 1976), cert denied 429 US 1075 (1977) (trustworthiness of witness can be considered) with *United States v. Atkins*, 558 F2d 133, 135 (3rd Cir 1977), cert denied 434 US 1071 (1978) (rule focuses on trustworthiness of declarant, not witness). See also *United States v. Satterfield*, 572 F2d 687 (9th Cir), cert denied 439 US 840 (1978) (analyzing arguments for both positions, but finding it unnecessary to resolve the issue on the facts of the case). See generally Goodman & Waltuch, *Declarations Against Penal Interest: The Majority Has Emerged*, 28 NY L Rev 51 (1983).

According to the Commentary, the corroboration requirement was intended by the legislature to meet the concern that "either the *fact* or the contents of the confession were fabricated" (emphasis added). The Commentary further states: "The trial court should construe the corroboration requirement in a manner that effectuates its purpose to circumvent fabrication." In light of these expressions of legislative intent, it would seem appropriate for courts to consider the trustworthiness of the witness as well as of the declarant in determining whether the corroboration requirement is satisfied.

Professor Graham argues that certainty that the statement was made is a corroborating factor that can appropriately be considered by the trial court:

> One of the truly beneficial effects of the Federal Rules of Evidence is the recognition that the issue of certainty of making of an out-of-court declaration should not be left in all instances solely to exploration on cross-examination. Cross-examination of a person merely repeating what he says was said is not likely to be effective. Certainty of making should be considered in determining the issue of "corroborating circumstances" under Rule 804(b)(3). (2 M. Graham, HANDBOOK OF Federal EVIDENCE § 804.3 at 656 n 18 (4th ed 1996).

Too strict an application of the corroboration requirement, however, may conflict with the constitutional right of a criminal defendant to offer exculpatory evidence. See *Chambers v. Mississippi*, 410 US 284, 93 SCt 1038, 35 LEd2d 297 (1973). In *United States v. Barrett*, 539 F2d 244, 253 (1st Cir 1976), the court stated that in interpreting FRE 804(b)(3), courts

> should be mindful of the possible relationship between constitutional cases such as *Chambers* and the new federal rule. *Chambers* holds, on facts far more compelling than anything here, that it is a violation of due process to exclude

such exculpatory evidence as a well established confession of another to the crime for which the accused is on trial.

While statements against penal interest are usually offered by defendants as exculpatory evidence, the prosecution sometimes offers statements against the defendant. See, e.g., *United States v. White*, 553 F2d 310 (2nd Cir), cert denied 431 US 972 (1977). Cf. 4 J. Weinstein and M. Berger, WEINSTEIN'S EVIDENCE § 804(b)(3)[03] at 804-113 ("Because of the dangers involved exclusion should almost always result when a statement against penal interest is offered against an accused"). Some courts have held that inculpatory statements must satisfy the same corroboration requirement that the rule imposes on exculpatory statements before they will be admissible. See *United States v. Alvarez*, 584 F2d 694 (5th Cir 1978); *United States v. Riley*, 657 F2d 1377 (8th Cir 1981), cert denied 459 US 1111 (1982). One commentator has argued that it is unconstitutional to require corroboration for statements offered by the defendant but not for statements offered by the prosecution. See Tague, *Perils of the Rulemaking Process: The Development, Application, and Unconstitutionality of Rule 804(b)(3)'s Penal Interest Exception*, 69 Geo L J 851 (1981).

In *State v. Lissy*, 85 Or App 484, 737 P2d 617, aff'd on other grounds 304 Or 455, 747 P2d 345 (1987), the Court of Appeals held that it was unnecessary to decide whether corroborating evidence was required for inculpatory use of statements against interest, because sufficient corroborating evidence was found to exist in this case. In *State v. Tucker*, 109 Or App 519, 525–6, 820 P2d 834, 837–8 (1991), rev denied 317 Or 188, 855 P2d 150 (1993), the court held that the corroboration requirement of Rule 803(3)(c) applies only to statements against penal interest that are exculpatory, not inculpatory. The court did not consider whether it is unconstitutional to require corroboration for exculpatory statements but not inculpatory statements.

Recent Cases

Holmes v. Morgan, 135 Or App 617, 626, 899 P2d 738 (1995). In an action for interference with economic relations, plaintiff offered statements by her son who committed suicide about a suicide pact with defendant whereby she would help him commit suicide in exchange for becoming the beneficiary on his life insurance policy; statements by decedent not against his penal interest because he was planning to commit suicide himself and not commit the crime of assisting someone else to commit suicide; plaintiff argued statements were also against decedent's pecuniary interest because evidence of suicide might void his life insurance policy; court holds that his pecuniary interest not affected because he would not collect the insurance.

State v. Thoma, 313 Or 268, 277, 834 P2d 1020 (1992). In this murder prosecution, the court affirmed the exclusion of evidence that a third party had admitted committing the murder offered by the defense as a statement against penal interest. The trial court had rejected the exculpatory hearsay statement on the ground that it was not sufficiently corroborated, as is required by Rule

804(3)(c).The appellate court disagreed, citing circumstances showing the statement to be trustworthy, but affirmed on the ground that defendant had failed to' show the unavailability of the declarant who made the statement.

State v. Jacob, 125 Or App 643, 647, 866 P2d 507, 509 (1994), rev denied 318 Or 583, 873 P2d 321. The court held that statements by witnesses to a killing were not sufficiently against their interest to qualify for admission as declarations against penal interest. The witnesses had been allowed to claim the privilege against self-incrimination at trial, but the appellate court refused to find this fact conclusive on whether their statements were in fact against their penal interest. The court noted that defendant failed to challenge the propriety of the witnesses' assertion of the privilege against self-incrimination.

State v. Batty, 109 Or App 62, 70, 819 P2d 732, 737 (1991), rev denied 312 Or 588, 824 P2d 417 (1992). The court held that it may have been error to exclude a statement by a murder victim refusing to deny that she was part of a conspiracy to hurt the defendant, because her statement may have qualified as against her penal interest. Any error in refusing to receive the statement was found harmless on the facts of the case.

State v. Lyman, 107 Or App 390, 812 P2d 23 (1991). The defendant's wife made statements to a police officer implicating her husband in driving while intoxicated. At trial the wife asserted the marital privilege and refused to testify. The state offered the wife's hearsay statements on the theory that they were admissible as a declaration against interest, because she would suffer pecuniary loss and be adversely affected by the criminal action against her husband. The court rejected this argument, concluding that "the risk of pecuniary loss to [the wife] was too attenuated to ensure that the statements were reliable." The court stated that "pecuniary loss to defendant from the penal sanctions was only a secondary effect, and pecuniary loss to [the wife] because of her husband's loss was even further removed."

RULE 804.   ORS 40.465. HEARSAY EXCEPTIONS WHERE THE DECLARANT IS UNAVAILABLE

(3) (d) [Statement of personal or family history.]

      (A) A statement concerning the declarant's own birth, adoption, marriage, divorce, legitimacy, relationship by blood or adoption or marriage, ancestry, or other similar fact of personal or family history, even though the declarant had no means of acquiring personal knowledge of the matter stated; or

      (B) A statement concerning the foregoing matters, and death also, of another person, if the declarant was related to the other by blood, adoption, or marriage or was so intimately associated with the other's family as to be likely to have accurate information concerning the matter declared.

LEGISLATIVE COMMENTARY

Paragraph (d). This paragraph exempts statements of personal or family history from the general rule against admission of hearsay evidence. It lists the same topics as to which reputation is admissible under ORE 803(19). The common law requirement that the statement have been made when the declarant had no motive to distort truth, usually before the controversy arose or the action was commenced, has been dropped, as bearing more appropriately on weight than admissibility. See 5 Wigmore § 1483. The paragraph maintains Oregon law as codified in ORS 41.840 and 41.900(4), with two exceptions, noted below. For comparable provisions see Uniform Rule 63(23), (24), (25); California Evidence Code §§ 1310, 1311; Kansas Code of Civil Procedure § 60-460(u), (v), (w); New Jersey Evidence Rule 63(23), (24), (25).

Subparagraph (d)(A). This provision expressly disclaims any need for firsthand knowledge. In some instances the declarant's knowledge is self-evident (marriage); in others it is impossible and traditionally not required (date of birth). The subparagraph is broader than ORS 41.840, which it replaces, which admitted statements of pedigree only when the declarant was unavailable by reason of death or location outside the state.

Subparagraph (d)(B). This provision deals with declarations concerning the history of another person. As at common law, the declarant is qualified if related by blood or marriage. 5 Wigmore § 1489. In addition, and contrary to the common law, a declarant qualifies by virtue of intimate association with the family. Id. § 1487. The quondam requirement that the declarant must qualify in both respects, when the subject of the statement is a relationship between two other persons, is omitted. Knowledge of related or intimate families is presumed to be reciprocal. Id. § 1491. The subparagraph is broader than ORS 41.900(4), which it replaces, which admits only statements of a relative and only when the declarant is unavailable by reason of death. *State v. McDonald,* 55 Or 419, 103 P 512 (1910); *Thompson v. Woolf,* 8 Or 454 (1880).

TEXT

Statement of Personal or Family History

Rule 804(3)(d) contains two hearsay exceptions. First, provided the declarant is shown to be unavailable as a witness under 804(1), a statement concerning the declarant's own personal or family history may be admitted. The statement may concern the declarant's own birth, adoption, marriage, divorce, legitimacy, relationship by blood or adoption or marriage, ancestry, or other similar fact of personal or family history. The rule specifically exempts the statement from the personal knowledge requirement.

Second, provided the declarant is shown to be unavailable as a witness under Rule 804(1), statements regarding the personal or family history of another person may be received, if the declarant was related to that person by blood, adoption, or marriage or was so intimately associated with the other's family as to be likely to have accurate information concerning the matter declared. The matters of personal or family history may include the person's birth, adoption, marriage, divorce, legitimacy, relationship by blood or adoption or marriage, ancestry, or death. Contrary to the common law and former Oregon law, the declarant need not be a member of the other's family. Depending upon the circumstances, the declarant could be a servant, housekeeper, roommate, chaplain, or intimate friend.

This rule replaces ORS 41.900(4) (repealed 1981), which provided in pertinent part: "Evidence may be given of the following facts: (4) The declaration or act, verbal or written, of a deceased person, in respect to the relationship, birth, marriage, or death of any person related by blood or marriage to such deceased person. ..."

This exception is closely related to 803(19), which creates a hearsay exception for reputation concerning personal or family history. It is identical to FRE 804(b)(4). For a case admitting statements of family history under this rule, see *Cooper v. Harris*, 499 F Supp 266 (ND Ill 1980).

In *United States v. Medina-Gasca*, 739 F2d 1451 (9th Cir 1984), the court held that in a prosecution of a defendant for transporting illegal aliens, a prior out-of-court statement by one of the persons transported that his place of birth was Mexico was properly admissible under FRE 804(b)(4). However, because this hearsay went to a central issue, the court stated that the statement should have been excluded on confrontation grounds, although no reversible error was found on the facts of this case.

RULE 804. ORS 40.465. HEARSAY EXCEPTIONS WHERE THE DECLARANT IS UNAVAILABLE

(3) (e) [Statement made in professional capacity.] A statement made at or near the time of the transaction by a person in a position to know the facts stated therein, acting in the person's professional capacity and in the ordinary course of professional conduct.

LEGISLATIVE COMMENTARY

Paragraph (e). This paragraph retains the hearsay exception for statements made in a professional capacity by a person having knowledge of the facts who is unavailable. This was formerly codified in ORS 41.860(2). The exception includes statements of opinion as well as fact. *Williams v. Laurence-David Inc.*, 271 Or 712, 534 P2d 173 (1975).

TEXT

Statement Made in Professional Capacity

Provided the declarant is shown to be unavailable as a witness under Rule 804(1), Rule 804(3)(e) creates a hearsay exception for a statement made at or near the time of the transaction by a person in a position to know the facts stated therein, acting in professional capacity and in the ordinary course of professional conduct. This exception is not included in the Federal Rules of Evidence. However, it could be viewed as a narrower version of FRE 803(1), the exception for present sense impressions, but limited to professional observers who are unavailable to testify at trial. FRE 803(1), which was not adopted as part of the Oregon Evidence Code, creates a hearsay exception for "A statement describing or explaining an event or condition made while the declarant was perceiving the event or condition, or immediately thereafter."

According to the Commentary, Rule 804(3)(e) is intended to retain the exception formerly codified in ORS 41.860(2) (repealed 1981). This statute provided:

> Entries or other writings of like character of a person deceased or without the state, made at or near the time of the transaction and in a position to know the facts stated therein, may be read as primary evidence of those facts when it was made:
>
> ...
>
> (2) In a professional capacity, and in the ordinary course of professional conduct.

The grounds of unavailability under the new rule are broader than those of the former statute. See Rule 804(1). Also, the rule allows oral statements, while the former statute was limited to "entries" or "writings."

Medical records of a deceased doctor regarding the plaintiff were admitted under the former statute. See *Williams v. Laurence-David Inc.*, 271 Or 712, 534 P2d 173 (1975). Entries in a deceased attorney's book of accounts were also admitted. See *O'Day v. Spencer*, 96 Or 73, 189 P 394 (1920).

The leading case under this rule to date is *Persad v. Kaiser Foundation Hospital, Inc.*, 106 Or App 615, 809 P2d 706, rev denied 312 Or 80, 816 P2d 610 (1991). The plaintiff claimed the defendant's agent failed to call an ambulance in response to his first request, thereby causing the death of his wife. The defendant's agent was unavailable because she had no recollection whether she placed a call initially. However, a coworker was allowed to testify that when the plaintiff called a second time, the agent stated, "Where is that ambulance that I dispatched or sent out?" This hearsay statement was admissible as evidence that an earlier call had been placed. The court rejected the plaintiff's contention that the statement should have been excluded as self-serving or untrustworthy.

RULE 804. ORS 40.465. HEARSAY EXCEPTIONS WHERE THE DECLARANT IS UNAVAILABLE

(3) (f) [Other exceptions.] A statement not specifically covered by any of the foregoing exceptions but having equivalent circumstantial guarantees of trustworthiness, if the court determines that
- (A) the statement is offered as evidence of a material fact;
- (B) the statement is more probative on the point for which it is offered than any other evidence which the proponent can procure through reasonable efforts; and
- (C) the general purposes of the Oregon Evidence Code and the interests of justice will best be served by admission of the statement into evidence. However, a statement may not be admitted under this paragraph unless the proponent of it makes known to the adverse party the intention to offer the statement and the particulars of it, including the name and address of the declarant, sufficiently in advance of the trial or hearing, or as soon as practicable after it becomes apparent that the statement is probative of the issues at hand, to provide the adverse party with a fair opportunity to prepare to meet it.

LEGISLATIVE COMMENTARY

Paragraph (f). In language and purpose, paragraph (f) is identical to subsection (24) of Rule 803. See the commentary to that provision.

TEXT

Other Exceptions

Rule 804(3)(f) creates a hearsay exception that is virtually identical to Rule 803(25), except that under this exception the declarant must be unavailable as a witness. See textual discussion of Rule 803(25). Before a hearsay statement is admissible under this exception, the following seven requirements must be satisfied:

(1) The declarant must be shown to be unavailable as a witness under Rule 804(1);

(2) The statement must not be admissible under any of the other exceptions in Rule 804;

(3) The statement must have equivalent circumstantial guarantees of trustworthiness as the other Rule 804 exceptions;

(4) The statement must be offered as evidence of a material fact;

(5) The statement must be "more probative on the point for which it is offered than any other evidence which the proponent can procure through reasonable efforts";

(6) "The general purposes of the Oregon Evidence Code and the interests of justice will best be served by the admission of the statement into evidence"; and

(7) The proponent of the statement must notify the adverse party of "the intention to offer the statement and the particulars of it, including the name and address of the declarant, sufficiently in advance of the trial or hearing, or as soon as practicable after it becomes apparent that the statement is probative of the issues at hand, to provide the adverse party with a fair opportunity to prepare to meet it."

See generally Lewis, *The Residual Exceptions to the Federal Hearsay Rule: Shuffling the Wild Cards,* 15 Rutgers L J 101 (1983); ANNOT., *Admissibility of Statement Made to Government Agent by Unavailable Witness, Under Rule 804(b)(5) of Federal Rules of Evidence, Providing for Admissibility of Hearsay Statement not Covered by Any Specific Exception but Having Equivalent Guaranties of Trustworthiness,* 61 ALR Fed 915 (1983); ANNOT., *Residual Hearsay Exception Where Declarant Unavailable: Uniform Evidence Rule 804(b)(5),* 75 ALR4th 199 (1990).

Recent Oregon Cases

Holmes v. Morgan, 135 Or App 617, 626, ___ P2d ___ (1995). In action for interference with economic relations, plaintiff offered evidence of suicide pact between her son and defendant whereby defendant would assist son to commit suicide in exchange for his changing his life insurance policy to make defendant the beneficiary; evidence consisted of son's statements to plaintiff; error to admit this hearsay under residual exception because plaintifff was "a financially interested party" and had a "motivation for falsehood" that made evidence untrustworthy. Interestingly, the court focused on the trustworthiness of the witness reporting the hearsay rather than the trustworthiness of the declarant.

State ex rel Children's Services Division v. Page, 66 Or App 535, 674 P2d 1196 (1984). The court held that evidence that fails to satisfy the requirements of a specific hearsay exception should not be admissible under the residual hearsay exception. The case involved testimony by a psychologist that an eight-year-old girl had reported that she had been sexually abused by her father. The court concluded that because this hearsay statement of identification was specifically excluded by Rule 803(18a) it was also inadmissible under Rule 803(3)(f).

State v. Bounds, 71 Or App 744, 694 P2d 566, rev denied 299 Or 732, 705 P2d 1157 (1985). The court held that the hearsay statement of a four-year-old daughter that the defendant father had raped her was admissible under the residual hearsay exception to corroborate the defendant's confession of rape. The statement was made to her mother within the first few minutes that she was outside of the defendant's presence after the sexual attack and while she continued to suffer the pain of the assault. The child's statement was corroborated by physical evidence on her person, and her statement was consistent with information the child gave to an examining physician.

State v. Apperson, 85 Or App 429, 736 P2d 1026 (1987). At defendant's trial for assault, the alleged victim, defendant's girlfriend, testified that she could not remember any physical contact between herself and defendant nor specifically what she told the police officer on the night in question. The prosecutor then called the officer to testify about statements that the victim had made to him. The appellate court held that it was error to admit this hearsay under the residual exception to the hearsay rule. The court stated: "We conclude that there is nothing in those facts to give the statements a guarantee of trustworthiness equivalent to that accorded the kinds of statements specified in OEC 804(3), because they lack the motivational basis for truthtelling that the specific exceptions in the rule have." 85 Or App at 433.

Federal Cases

For examples of the types of evidence admitted under FRE 804(b)(5), which is essentially identical to Oregon Rule 804(3)(f), see *Copperweld Steel Co. v.. Demag-Mannesmann-Bohler,* 578 F2d 953 (3rd Cir 1978) (statement by former employee damaging to party employer admitted); *Furtado v. Bishop,* 604 F2d 80 (1st Cir 1979), cert denied 444 US 1035 (1980) (affidavit of deceased attorney admitted); *Huff v. White Motor Corp.,* 609 F2d 286 (7th Cir 1979) (statements of plaintiff decedent made prior to his death from injuries caused in an accident admitted in wrongful death case); *United States v. Lyon,* 567 F2d 777 (8th Cir 1977), cert denied 435 US 918 (1978) (FBI agent allowed to read transcribed statement of a witness when witness claimed lack of memory at trial); *United States v. Medico,* 557 F2d 309 (2nd Cir), cert denied 434 US 986 (1977) (statements of two unidentified bystanders relayed to bank employee regarding license number on bank robbery getaway car admitted).

Hearsay was held not to be admissible under this exception in the following cases: *DeMars v. Equitable Life Assurance Soc'y of the United States,* 610 F2d 55 (1st Cir 1979) (error to admit letter of deceased physician because more probative evidence was available); *United States v. Bailey,* 581 F2d 341 (3rd Cir 1978) (error to admit statement of unavailable accomplice incriminating the defendant in a bank robbery); *United States v. Fredericks,* 599 F2d 262 (8th Cir 1979) (statement by an unavailable witness not admissible because witness had motive to fabricate and other eyewitness testimony was available); *United States v. Gonzalez,* 559 F2d 1271 (5th Cir 1977) (error to admit grand jury testimony of a prosecution witness who refused to testify at trial).

Grand Jury Testimony

A controversial issue arising under this exception is whether grand jury testimony can be admitted when the declarant is unavailable at trial because of death, assertion of privilege, refusal to testify, or otherwise. Some federal courts have allowed grand jury testimony to be received under FRE 804(b)(5). See *United States v. Boulahanis,* 677 F2d 586, 588–9 (7th Cir), cert denied 459 US 1016 (1982); *United States v. Garner,* 574 F2d 1141 (4th Cir), cert denied 439 US 936 (1978); *United States v. West,* 574 F2d 1131 (4th Cir 1978); *United States v. Carlson,* 547 F2d 1346 (8th Cir 1976), cert denied 431 US 914 (1977); *United States v. Balano,* 618 F2d 624 (10th Cir 1979), cert denied 449 US 840 (1980). Contra *United States v. Gonzalez,* 559 F2d 1271 (5th Cir 1977) (grand jury testimony not allowed).

See generally ANNOT., *Admissibility of Testimony Before Grand Jury of Unavailable Witness Under Rule 804(b)(5), Federal Rules of Evidence, Providing For Admission of Hearsay Statement Not Covered By Any Specific Exception But Having Equivalent Circumstantial Guaranties of Trustworthiness,* 50 ALR Fed 848 (1980); Burstein, *Admission of an Unavailable Witness's Grand Jury Testimony: Can It Be Justified?,* 4 Cardozo L Rev 263 (1983); COMMENT, *The Admissibility of Grand Jury Testimony Under 804(b)(5): A Two-Test Proposal,* 74 J Crim L 1446 (1983); COMMENT, *Admissibility of an Unavailable Witness's Grand Jury Testimony: Upholding the Purposes Behind the Confrontation Clause,* 18 Val U L Rev 965 (1984); COMMENT, *Admission of Grand Jury Testimony Under the Residual Hearsay Exception,* 59 Tul L Rev 1033 (1985).

The United States Supreme Court has not yet addressed this issue. The petition for writ of certiorari was denied in *United States v. Garner,* supra. However, Justices Stewart and Marshall stated in dissent:

> Although they are not coextensive, the Confrontation Clause and the hearsay rule "stem from the same roots." *Dutton v. Evans* 400 U.S. 74, 86 (1970). Considered under either the Sixth Amendment or the Federal Rules of Evidence, I have grave doubts about the admissibility of Robinson's grand jury testimony.
>
> That the evidence was first given before a grand jury adds little to its reliability. In grand jury proceedings, the ordinary rules of evidence do not apply. Leading questions and multiple hearsay are permitted and common. Grand jury investigations are not adversary proceedings. No one is present to cross-examine the witnesses, to give the defendant's version of the story, or to expose weaknesses in the witnesses' testimony.
>
> The only factor that generally makes grand jury testimony more trustworthy than other out-of-court statements is the fact that it is given under oath. The witnesses speak under the threat of prosecution for material false statements. But that usual indication of trustworthiness was missing here. Robinson recanted his grand jury testimony at the trial. By disclaiming under oath his earlier sworn statements, he put himself in a position where one of his two sworn statements had to be false. Without further proof, Robinson would appear to have violated federal law, and, after the petitioners' trial, the Government did, indeed, indict Robinson for violation of 18 U.S.C. § 1623 ....
>
> I would grant certiorari to determine the limits placed upon the admissibility of this kind of evidence by either the Federal Rules of Evidence or the Constitution. (439 US at 938-40 (1978))

Some courts that have allowed grand jury testimony to be received are undoubtedly influenced by a desire to prevent defendants from benefitting by the fact that they caused a witness to become unavailable, either through intimidation, threats, or murder. At the same time, the reliability of testimony to a grand jury that has not been subjected to cross-examination is questionable. Courts admitting grand jury testimony under the residual hearsay exception have generally done so only after identifying "strong indicators of reliability." *United States v. Garner,* 574 F2d 1141, 1144 (4th Cir), cert denied 439 US 936 (1978). For example, in *United States v. Carlson,* 547 F2d 1346 (8th Cir 1976), cert denied 431 US 914 (1977), the witness, although refusing to testify at trial, affirmed the grand jury testimony. For a discussion of corroborating circumstances, see *United States v. West,* 574 F2d 1131, 1135 (4th Cir 1978).

Apart from the question of whether grand jury testimony may properly be received under the residual hearsay exception, there is the separate question of whether such testimony will satisfy the confrontation requirements of the federal and state constitutions. See Graham, *The Confrontation Clause, the Hearsay Rule, and the Forgetful Witness,* 56 Tex L Rev 151 (1978). If the defendant is shown to be responsible for the unavailability of the witness, a number of courts have held the right of confrontation to be waived. See *United States v. Balano,* 618 F2d 624 (10th Cir 1979), cert denied 449 US 840 (1980); *United States v. Carlson,* 547 F2d 1346 (8th Cir 1976), cert denied 431 US 914 (1977); *United States v. Thevis,* 665 F2d 616 (5th Cir), cert denied 459 US 825 (1982).

RULE 805. ORS 40.470. HEARSAY WITHIN HEARSAY

Hearsay included within hearsay is not excluded under Rule 802 (ORS 40.455) if each part of the combined statements conforms with an exception set forth in Rule 803 or 804 (ORS 40.460 or ORS 40.465).

LEGISLATIVE COMMENTARY

Oregon Rule of Evidence 805 provides for the non-exclusion of hearsay within hearsay so long as each level of hearsay falls within a recognized exception. The rule is based on Rule 805 of the Federal Rules of Evidence. References in the federal rule to "hearsay rule" and "these rules" have been made more specific.

As a matter of principle, it scarcely seems open to doubt that the hearsay rule should not call for exclusion of a hearsay statement which includes a further hearsay statement when both conform to the requirements of a hearsay exception. A hospital record might contain an entry of a patient's age based on information furnished by the spouse. The record would qualify as a business record except that the person who furnished the information was not acting in the routine of business. However, the statement of the spouse qualifies independently as a statement of pedigree, if the spouse is unavailable, or as a statement made for purposes of diagnosis or treatment in any event. Each link in the chain bears a sufficient mark of trustworthiness. Therefore the whole should be admitted. Another example is a dying declaration which incorporates a declaration against interest by another declarant. Still another is a police accident report that contains an assertion by one driver made immediately after a collision. The driver's statement may be an excited utterance, and the police report a business record. The police report should be admissible as against a hearsay objection to prove the truth of the driver's excited utterance. See McCormick, *Evidence* § 310 at 726, § 313 at 731 (2d ed 1972).

Only "hearsay" within hearsay need qualify under this rule. An exclusion from hearsay, such as an admission, would be exempt in any case under ORE 801(4)(b). See *State v. Waite,* 377 A2d 96 (Maine 1977).

This rule is in accord with current Oregon practice. See the concurring opinion of Justice Denecke in *Mayor v. Dowsett,* 240 Or 196, 440 P2d 234 (1965), commented upon by Lacy, *Oregon Evidence Law in the Sixties: Problems, Patterns and Projections,* in 49 Or L Rev 188 at 198-199, and *Williams v. Laurence-David, Inc.,* 271 Or 712, 534 P2d 173 (1975).

TEXT

Rule 805 provides that multiple hearsay is admissible provided that each level of hearsay satisfies an exception to the hearsay rule. If one level of statement qualifies as "not hearsay" under Rule 801(4), Rule 805 is inapplicable to that level and no hearsay exception need be found.

Not all multiple level statements—where one declarant quotes another who quotes another—constitute multiple hearsay. Business records, for example, often are a report by one employee of statements by or information transmitted from one or more other employees. As long as each employee is acting within the scope of business duty all the statements, even though multiple, qualify as one level of hearsay and are admissible as a business record. See Rule 803(6) and the discussion thereof. If one person in the chain of communication was not under a business duty to report, then a second level of hearsay arises unless the statement made by that person qualifies as not hearsay under Rule 801(4). If it is hearsay, Rule 805 requires that an independent hearsay exception be found for that statement.

If the identity of the declarant at one level of statement cannot be determined, it may be difficult to determine whether the statement satisfies a hearsay exception or qualifies as not hearsay under Rule 801(4). In *Cedeck v. Hamiltonian Fed Sav. and Loan Ass'n,* 551 F2d 1136 (8th Cir 1977), a Title VII action claiming sex discrimination, the court held that the trial judge properly excluded testimony by the plaintiff that her superior told her that someone else in the company remarked to him that plaintiff could not be promoted unless she were a man. This evidence involved double hearsay. The first level statement by the superior was admissible under FRE 801(d)(2)(D) as an admission by an agent. The second level of statement, the remark to the superior, was held not admissible because it was unclear whether the declarant was a person whose remarks would qualify as not hearsay under FRE 801(d)(2).

If a hearsay statement does not fit an exception, any hearsay quoted in that statement is also inadmissible, even though it might otherwise qualify for admission. For example, in *State v. Lyon,* 83 Or App 592, 733 P2d 41, aff'd 304 Or 221,

744 P2d 231 (1987), a murder prosecution, the state offered evidence of statements made by the defendant to his father, which in turn were related to a detective. Neither the defendant nor the father took the stand, and the statements came in through the testimony of the detective. The court held that this evidence of the son's statements was inadmissible (even though they would otherwise qualify as admissions), because "the value of the evidence was dependent on the truth or falsity of the father's out-of-court assertion that defendant had made the statements to him."

Recent Cases

In *Hansen v. Abrasive Engineering and Manufacturing, Inc.*, 317 Or 378, 388–9, 856 P2d 625, 630–1 (1993), the court held that a doctor's report prepared by plaintiff's employer's insurer as part of insurer's defense of plaintiff's workers' compensation claim was admissible as a business record under OEC 803(6), even though it was prepared in contemplation of possible future litigation. Plaintiff's own statements contained in the doctor's report constituted a second level of out-of-court statement, but they qualified as admissions under OEC 801(4)(b)(A). Thus, each level of statement satisfied an independent hearsay exception, making the multiple hearsay admissible under OEC 805. The court stated that "the language of OEC 805 should be read to embrace statements in the chain that qualify as 'not hearsay' under OEC 801(4)."

In *State v. Pinnell*, 311 Or 98, 117 n 29, 806 P2d 110, 122 (1991), the court noted that although a transcript of former testimony may involve multiple hearsay, it is admissible provided each level of hearsay satisfies an independent exception.

In *State v. Beaty*, 127 Or App 448, 454, 873 P2d 385, 387 (1994), rev denied 319 Or 406, 879 P2d 1285 (1994), a child sexual abuse prosecution, the trial court properly excluded evidence that a CSD worker would testify that G told him about statements that G heard the mother and child victim make about hearing voices that no one else could hear. Even if the child's statements themselves would qualify under the state of mind exception (OEC 803(3)), there was no hearsay exception for G's reporting of the statements to the CSD worker. When multiple hearsay is involved, each level must satisfy a hearsay exception.

In *State v. Bauman*, 98 Or App 316, 779 P2d 185 (1989), the court held that it was error to admit a police officer's testimony that the victim's mother told him that victim told her that the babysitter's boyfriend abused her. The court found the officer's testimony to be "hearsay about hearsay," and because not all levels satisfied a hearsay exception, it was inadmissible under Rule 805. However, the error was found harmless in light of the other evidence in the case.

RULE 806.   ORS 40.475. ATTACKING AND SUPPORTING CREDIBILITY OF DECLARANT

When a hearsay statement, or a statement defined in Rule 801(4)(b)(C), (D) or (E) (ORS 40.450(4)(b)(C), (D) or (E)), has been admitted in evidence, the credibility of the declarant may be attacked, and if attacked may be supported, by any evidence which would be admissible for those purposes if the declarant had testified as a witness. Evidence of a statement or conduct by the declarant at any time, inconsistent with the hearsay statement of the declarant, is not subject to any requirement under Rule 613 (ORS 40.380) relating to impeachment by evidence of inconsistent statements. If the party against whom a hearsay statement has been admitted calls the declarant as a witness, the party is entitled to examine the declarant on the statement as if under cross-examination.

LEGISLATIVE COMMENTARY

Oregon Rule of Evidence 806 prescribes the manner and limits of impeaching, rehabilitating and cross-examining a hearsay declarant. The rule is based on Rule 806 of the Federal Rules of Evidence. Its reference to ORE 613 replaces a federal reference to the opportunity to deny or explain, and was made necessary by the specific retention of Oregon practice on inconsistent statements in that rule.

Impeachment of absent hearsay declarant. The declarant of a hearsay statement that is admitted into evidence is in effect a witness. Therefore, in fairness, the declarant's credibility should be subject to impeachment (and to rehabilitation) as if the declarant had in fact testified. See Rules 608 to 609-1. There are problems in doing this, however. These arise from the factual differences between hearsay and live witnesses, and between kinds of hearsay, and principally involve the foundational requirement for impeachment by inconsistent statement.

An inconsistent statement of a live witness is inevitably a prior statement, which may be called to the witness' attention in accordance with ORS 613. A statement that is inconsistent with hearsay may be subsequent to it, and cannot be called to the declarant's attention. If the court insists on the usual rules for impeachment by inconsistent statements in a hearsay situation, it must deny the opponent, who is already barred from cross-examination, any benefit of this important technique. The writers favor allowing the inconsistent statement. McCormick, *Evidence* § 37 at 74 (2d ed 1972); 3 Wigmore, *Evidence* § 1033 (3d ed 1940). The cases, however, are divided. Compare *People v. Collup,* 27 Cal 2d 829, 176 P2d 714 (1946); *People v. Rosoto,* 58 Cal 2d 304, 23 Cal Rptr 770, 373 P2d 867 (1962); *Carver v. United States,* 164 US 694, 17 S Ct 228, 41 L Ed 602 (1897) (allowing impeachment), with *Mattox v. United States,* 156 US 237, 15 S Ct 337, 39 L Ed 409 (1895); *People v. Hines,* 284 NY 93, 29 NE 2d 483 (1940) (disallowing impeachment).

When the inconsistent statement was made after the hearsay statement, the kind of hearsay involved seems unimportant The opponent may not have been totally deprived of cross-examination when the hearsay is former testimony, ORE 804(3)(a), but the opponent still was deprived of cross-examination along lines suggested by the trial.

When the inconsistent statement was made before the hearsay statement, there are differences among kinds of hearsay that arguably call for different treatment. (1) If the hearsay consists of a simple statement, e.g., a dying declaration or a declaration against interest, it is no more possible to give the declarant an opportunity to deny or explain the inconsistent statement than it would be if the statement were subsequent (see above), although here the impossibility stems from the absence of a hearing at which the matter could be put. The courts overwhelmingly favor allowing the statement to be used under these circumstances. McCormick § 37 at 72; 3 Wigmore § 1033. (2) If, however, the hearsay consists of former testimony at a trial or deposition, the possibility of calling the prior statement to the attention of the declarant is not ruled out, as there was opportunity to cross-examine. It might thus be concluded that the conventional foundation should be required with former testimony. Most of the cases involve depositions, and Wigmore describes them as divided. 3 Wigmore § 1031. Deposition procedures are cumbersome at best, and to require the foundation may impose an undue burden. The possibility always exists that knowledge of the inconsistent statement was not acquired until after the time of cross-examination. Finally, the expanded admissibility of former testimony, under ORE 804(3)(a), seems to call for more tolerance in admitting impeachment material. For these reasons, the legislative Assembly dispensed with the foundation requirement in all hearsay situations, leaving a rule which is readily administered and fair.

The reference to subparagraphs (C), (D) and (E) of Rule 801(4)(b) (admission by statement of agent or co-conspirator) was added to allow the credibility of the absent declarant of those statements to be attacked in the same manner as the credibility of a hearsay declarant.

The above matters had not been addressed in Oregon statute or case law. Federal Ninth Circuit law is in accord, however. *McConney v. United States,* 421 F2d 248, 251 (1969); see also *Carver v. United States,* supra.

Cross-examination of hearsay declarant called. The sentence providing for cross-examination of a declarant upon the declarant's hearsay statement is a corollary of the general principles of cross-examination. A similar provision is found in California Evidence Code § 1203.

TEXT

Rule 806 provides that a hearsay declarant or a declarant whose statement is offered as not hearsay pursuant to Rule 801(4)(b)(C), (D) or (E) can be impeached on the same grounds as a witness who testifies in court. Such methods of impeachment can include a showing of (1) deficient capacity to perceive, recall, or recount; (2) character for untruthfulness; (3) prior criminal convictions; (4) bias or interest; or (5) prior inconsistent statements. See textual discussion of Rule 607 discussing impeachment generally.

Personal admissions or adoptive admissions by a party opponent admissible under Rule 801(4)(b)(A) or (B) are beyond the scope of this rule. The rationale for this exclusion, according to the United States Senate Committee that considered essentially identical FRE 806, is that "the party-opponent is always subject to an attack on his credibility." 5 Rep No 1277 93rd Cong 2d Sess (1974).

As an example of impeachment of a hearsay declarant by a prior inconsistent statement, see *United States v. Wuagneux*, 683 F2d 1343, 1357–8 (11th Cir 1982), cert denied 464 US 814 (1983), where the defendant in a tax fraud prosecution had introduced as a declaration against interest a statement of his accountant that the failure to report certain interest was the fault of the accountant or his employees. The court held that it was proper under FRE 806 for the prosecution to impeach the hearsay statement of the accountant with a prior inconsistent statement made by the accountant to an IRS agent.

Rule 806 provides that if a hearsay declarant is impeached by prior inconsistent statements or conduct, the requirement of Rule 613(2) that the witness be given "an opportunity to explain or deny" the statement does not apply. Therefore there is no necessity that the declarant be called or even be available as a witness to respond to the impeachment by prior inconsistent statements.

Unfortunately the rule does not provide that the foundation required for impeachment by evidence of bias is also inapplicable. Compliance with Rule 609-1 would require that the hearsay declarant be called as a witness before he or she could be impeached by evidence of bias. This was clearly not the intent of the legislature. The Commentary states: "[T]he Legislative Assembly dispensed with the foundation requirement in all hearsay situations."

The rule has properly been interpreted by the Oregon Supreme Court as allowing extrinsic evidence of a hearsay declarant's bias despite noncompliance with the foundation requirement of Rule 609-1. In *State v. Philips*, 314 Or 460, 470, 840 P2d 666 (1992), a stepfather was charged with sexual abuse of a four-year-old child. The child's accusatory out-of-court statements were admitted against the defendant under OEC 803(4) and OEC 803(18a)(b). At trial, the defendant attempted to impeach these hearsay accusations by testimony of the victim's mother that the victim had been told by her natural father that "she had to say bad things about [defendant] in court." It was error to exclude this testimony because it was proper impeachment for bias under OEC 609-1. The court further held that the foundation requirements of OEC 609-1(1) do not apply to evidence offered to impeach a hearsay declarant.

Rule 806 creates a potential trap for a defense attorney who introduces out-of-court statements of the defendant in a case where the defendant does not take the stand. By introducing the defendant's earlier statements, the defendant becomes subject to impeachment under Rule 806 and defendant's prior criminal convictions may be received, to the extent they are admissible for impeachment under Rule 609. See *United States v. Lawson*, 608 F2d 1129 (6th Cir 1979), cert denied 444 US 1091 (1980) (defendant on cross-examination of government agent brought out defendant's prior statements denying the crime; held, impeachment of defendant by showing prior criminal convictions permissible under Rules 609 and 806). See also *United States v. Bovain*, 708 F2d 606 (11th Cir 1983) (after codefendant's hearsay statement admitted, defendant allowed to impeach codefendant under Rules 609 and 806 by evidence of his prior criminal convictions); *United States v. Newman*, 849 F2d 156 (5th Cir 1988).

If a hearsay declarant is impeached pursuant to this rule, the party offering the hearsay statement should be allowed to rehabilitate the declarant who has been impeached. See textual discussion of rehabilitation of witnesses under Rule 607.

See generally Glass, *Impeachment of Nontestifying Hearsay Declarants: A Neglected Weapon of Trial Practice*, 43 Ala L Rev 445 (1992).

Article IX
Authentication
and Identification

RULE 901.   ORS 40.505. REQUIREMENT OF AUTHENTICATION OR IDENTIFICATION

(1) **[General provision.] The requirement of authentication or identification as a condition precedent to admissibility is satisfied by evidence sufficient to support a finding that the matter in question is what its proponent claims.**

(2) **[Illustrations.] By way of illustration only, and not by way of limitation, the following are examples of authentication or identification conforming with the requirements of subsection (1) of this section:**

    (a) **[Testimony of witness with knowledge.] Testimony by a witness with knowledge that a matter is what it is claimed to be.**

    (b) **[Nonexpert opinion on handwriting.] Nonexpert opinion as to the genuineness of handwriting, based upon familiarity not acquired for purposes of the litigation.**

    (c) **[Comparison by trier or expert witness.] Comparison by the trier of fact or by expert witnesses with specimens which have been authenticated.**

    (d) **[Distinctive characteristics and the like.] Appearance, contents, substance, internal patterns or other distinctive characteristics, taken in conjunction with circumstances.**

    (e) **[Voice identification.] Identification of a voice, whether heard firsthand or through mechanical or electronic transmission or recording, by opinion based upon hearing the voice at any time under circumstances connecting it with the alleged speaker.**

    (f) **[Telephone conversation.] Telephone conversations, by evidence that a call was made to the number assigned at the time by the telephone company to a particular person or business, if:**

    (A) In the case of a person, circumstances, including self-identification, show the person answering to be the one called; or

    (B) In the case of a business, the call was made to a place of business and the conversation related to business reasonably transacted over the telephone.

(g) [Public records or reports.] Evidence that a writing authorized by law to be recorded or filed and in fact recorded or filed in a public office, or a purported public record, report, statement, or data compilation, in any form, is from the public office where items of this nature are kept.

(h) [Ancient documents or data compilation.] Evidence that a document or data compilation, in any form:

    (A) Is in such condition as to create no suspicion concerning its authenticity;

    (B) Was in a place where it, if authentic, would likely be; and

    (C) Has been in existence 20 years or more at the time it is offered.

(i) [Process or system.] Evidence describing a process or system used to produce a result and showing that the process or system produces an accurate result.

(j) [Methods provided by statute or rule.] Any method of authentication or identification otherwise provided by law or by other rules prescribed by the Supreme Court.

LEGISLATIVE COMMENTARY

(a) This section is a modified version of Rule 901 of the Federal Rules of Evidence. With the exception of paragraph (2)(c) this Rule is consistent with Oregon Law.

Authentication and identification represent a special aspect of relevancy. Michael and Adler, *Real Proof,* 5 V and L Rev 344, 362 (1952); McCormick, *Evidence,* §§ 212 and 218 (2d ed 1972); Morgan, *Basic Problems of Evidence,* 378 (1962). A telephone conversation may be irrelevant as having an unrelated topic, or because the speaker is not identified. The latter aspect is the one here involved. Wigmore describes the need for authentication as "an inherent logical necessity." Wigmore, *Evidence,* § 2129, p 564 (3d ed 1940).

This requirement of showing authenticity or identity falls in the category of relevancy dependent upon fulfillment of a condition of fact and is governed by the procedure set forth in subsection (2) of section 5 (Rule 104) of this Act.

The common law approach to authentication of documents has been criticized as an "attitude of agnosticism," McCormick, *Cases on Evidence,* 388 n 4 (3rd ed 1956), as one which "departs sharply from men's customs in ordinary affairs," and as presenting only a slight obstacle to the introduction of forgeries in comparison to the time and expense devoted to proving genuine writings which correctly show their origin on their face.

McCormick, *Evidence,* § 218, pp 544 and 545 (2d ed 1972). Today, such available procedures as requests to admit and pretrial conferences allow elimination of much of the need for authentication or identification. Also, significant inroads upon the traditional insistence on authentication and identification have been made by accepting as at least prima facie genuine items of the kind treated in § 69 (Rule 902) of this Act, infra. However, the need for suitable methods of proof still remains, since criminal cases pose their own obstacles to the use of preliminary procedures; unforeseen contingencies may arise, and cases of genuine controversy will still occur.

Subsection (1). Subsection (1) sets forth the well-accepted requirement that whenever a piece of evidence is offered there must be certain minimum assurances that the evidence is what it purports to be, what it is offered as being and what its value depends upon.

The treatment of authentication and identification draws largely upon common law and statutes to illustrate the general principle set forth in subsection (1) of this section.

Subsection (2). The examples in subsection (2) of this section are not exclusive allowable methods but are meant to guide and suggest, leaving room for growth and development in this area of the law.

The examples relate for the most part to documents, and some to voice communications and computer print-outs. As Wigmore noted, no special rules have been developed for authenticating chattels. Wigmore, *Code of Evidence,* § 2086 (3rd ed 1942). Compliance with requirements of authentication or identification by no means assures admission of an item into evidence, as other bars such as hearsay may remain.

Paragraph (a). Paragraph (a) of subsection (2) contemplates a broad spectrum of testimony ranging from testimony of a witness who was present at the signing of a document, to testimony establishing narcotics as taken from an accused and accounting for custody through the period until trial, including laboratory analysis. McCormick, *Evidence,* § 219 (2d ed 1972). See *California Evidence Code,* § 1413, eyewitness to signing. The phrase "by a witness with knowledge" has been added to paragraph (a) from the Federal Rules of Evidence to emphasize that a witness must have firsthand knowledge of the subject matter of his testimony.

Paragraph (b). Paragraph (b) of subsection (2) allows conventional lay identification of handwriting, recognizing that a sufficient familiarity with the handwriting of another person may be acquired by seeing the other write by exchanging correspondence, or by other means, to afford a basis for identifying it on subsequent occasions. McCormick, *Evidence,* § 221 (2d ed 1972). See also *California Evidence Code,* § 1416. Testimony based upon familiarity acquired for purposes of the litigation is reserved to the expert.

Paragraph (c). The history of common law restrictions upon the technique of proving and disproving the genuineness of a disputed specimen of handwriting, through comparison with a genuine specimen, by either the testimony of expert witnesses or direct viewing by the triers themselves, is detailed in 7 Wigmore, *Evidence,* §§ 1991 to 1994 (3d ed 1940). In breaking away, the English Common Law Procedure Act of 1854, 17 and 18 Vict, c 125 § 27, cautiously allowed expert or trier to use exemplars proved to the satisfaction of the judge to be genuine for purposes of comparison. The language found its way into numerous statutes in this country, e.g. *California Evidence Code,* §§ 1417 and 1418. While breaking precedent in the handwriting situation, the reservation to the judge of the question of the genuineness of exemplars and the imposition of an unusually high standard of persuasion are at variance with the general treatment of relevancy which depends upon fulfillment of a condition of fact. See § 5 (Rule 104) of this Act. No similar attitude is found in other comparison situations, e.g. ballistics comparison by jury, as in *Evans v. Commonwealth,* 230 Ky 411 19 SW Zd 1091 (1929), or by experts, Annot., 26 A.L.R. 2d 892; and there is no reason for its continued existence in handwriting cases. Consequently, paragraph (c) of subsection (2) sets no higher standard for handwriting specimens, and treats all comparison situations alike, to be governed by subsection (2) of § 5 (Rule 104) of this Act.

Federal precedent supports the acceptance of visual comparison as sufficiently satisfying preliminary authentication requirements for admission in evidence. *Brandon v. Collins,* 267 F2d 731 (2nd Cir 1959); *Wausau Sulphate Fibre Co. v. Commissioner of Internal Revenue,* 61 F2d 879 (7th Cir 1932); *Desimone v. United States,* 227 F2d 864 (9th Cir 1955).

Present Oregon law requires that the exemplar for comparison be admitted as genuine by the party against whom it is offered or be treated as genuine by such party. See *State v. Cahill,* 208 Or 538, 293 P2d 169, 298 P2d 214 (1956), interpreting ORS 42.070. The justification advanced for this rule is that it prevents the raising of collateral issues regarding the genuineness of the writing offered as the standard of comparison. 41 Ore L Rev 154 at 159 (1962). However, the rule has been criticized by legal scholars because it seriously limits the documents which may be used as exemplars and often leaves none at all available. 7 Wigmore, *Evidence,* § 193 (3rd ed 1940).

However, the exemplar may be used for comparison if the foundation evidence for the exemplar is sufficient to support a finding by the trier of fact that the exemplar is "genuine." See subsection (b) of § 5 of this Rule.

Paragraph (d). In paragraph (d) of subsection (2) of this section the characteristics of the offered item itself, considered in the light of circumstances, afford authentication techniques in great variety. The Legislative Assembly recommends the following guidelines for application of this example: (adopted from Weinstein *Evidence: Commentary on Rules of Evidence for the United States Courts and Magistrates.* (M. Bender 1976)).

(i) *Subject Matter.* A document or telephone conversation may be shown to have emanated from a particular person or business by the fact that it would be unlikely for anyone other than the purported author or declarant to be familiar with the subject matter of the document or conversation. McCormick, *Evidence,* § 225 (2d ed 1972); *Globe Automatic Sprinkler Co. v. Braniff,* 89 Okl, 214 P 127 (1923); *California Evidence Code,* § 1421; *State ex rel Kunz v. Woodmansee,* 156 Or 607, 60 P2d 298 (1937).

(ii) *Physical Attributes.* The appearance, physical characteristics, and identifying marks of a writing may sufficiently identify the source of the document.

(iii) *Internal Patterns.* Writings may be authenticated by evidence that the internal word or thought patterns are particularly characteristic of the purported writer. *Magnuson v. State,* 187 Wis 122, 203 NW 749 (1925); Arens and Meadow, *Psycholinguists and the Confession of Dilemma,* 56 Colum L Rev 19 (1956).

(iv) *External Circumstances.* Circumstances preceding, surrounding and following the transmission of a writing may sufficiently authenticate the writing.

(v) *Reply-letter Technique.* A letter or telegram may be authenticated by testimony or other proof that the writing was sent in reply to a duly authenticated writing. McCormick, *Evidence,* § 225 (2d ed 1972); *California Evidence Code,* § 1420.

Paragraph (e). Since aural voice identification is not a subject of expert testimony, the requisite familiarity may be acquired either before or after the particular speaking which is the subject of the identification, in this respect resembling visual identification of a person rather than the identification of handwriting. Cf Paragraph (b) of subsection (2) of this section; McCormick *Evidence,* § 226 (2d ed 1972); see *State v. Miller,* 6 Or App 366, 487 P2d 1387 (1971) (impliedly recognizing aural identifications part of tape recording authentication); *People v. Nichols,* 389 Ill 487, 38 NE 2d 766 (1942); *McGuire v. State,* 200 Md 601, 92 A2d 582 (1952); *State v. McGee,* 336 Mo 1082, 83 SW 2d 98 (1935).

Paragraph (f). The cases are in agreement that a mere assertion of identity by a person talking on the telephone is not sufficient evidence of the authenticity of the conversation and that additional evidence of the person's identity is required. The additional evidence need not fall in any set pattern, and the content of statements or the reply technique, under paragraph (d) of subsection (2) of this section, or voice identification under paragraph (e) of subsection (2) of this section may furnish the necessary foundation. Outgoing calls made by the witness involve additional factors bearing upon authenticity. The calling of a number assigned by the telephone company reasonably supports the assumption that the listing is correct and that the number is the one reached. If the number is that of a place of business, the mass of authority allows an ensuing conversation if it relates to business reasonably transacted over the telephone, on the theory that the maintenance of the telephone connection is an invitation to do business without further identification. *Mattan v. Hoover Co.,* 350 Mo 506, 166 SW 2d 557 (1942); *City of Pawhuska v. Crutchfield,* 147 Okla 4, 293 P 1095 (1932); *Zurich General Acc. & Liability Ins. Co. v. Baum,* 159 Va 404, 165 SE 518 (1932). Otherwise, some additional circumstances of identification of the speaker are required. The authorities divide on the question whether the self-identifying statement of the person answering suffices. Paragraph (f) of subsection (2) of this section answers in the affirmative on the assumption that usual conduct respecting telephone calls furnishes adequate assurances of regularity, bearing in mind that the entire matter is open to exploration before the trier of fact. In general, see McCormick, *Evidence,* § 226 (2d ed 1972); 7 Wigmore, *Evidence,* § 2155 (3d ed 1940) Annot., 71A.L.R.5.

Paragraph (g). Public records are regularly authenticated by proof of custody. McCormick, *Evidence,* § 224 (2d ed 1972); 7 Wigmore, *Evidence,* § 224 (2d ed 1972); 7 Wigmore, *Evidence,* §§ 2158 and 2159 (3d ed 1940). Paragraph (g) of subsection (2) of this section extends the principles to include data stored in computers and similar methods, increasingly used in public records. See *California Evidence Code,* §§ 1532 and 1600.

Paragraph (h). The familiar ancient document rule of the common law is extended to include data stored electronically or by other similar means. Since the importance of appearance diminishes in this situation, the importance of custody or place where found increases correspondingly. This expansion is necessary in view of the widespread use of methods of storing data in forms other than conventional written records.

Any time period selected is bound to be arbitrary. The common law period of 30 years is here reduced to 20 years, with some shift of emphasis from the probable unavailability of witnesses to the unlikeliness of a still viable fraud after the lapse of time. The shorter period is specified in the English Evidence Act of 1938, 1 & 2 Geo 6, c 28. Numerous statutes prescribe periods of less than 30 years in the case of recorded documents. 7 Wigmore, *Evidence,* § 2143 (3d ed 1940).

The applicability of paragraph (h) of subsection (2) of this section is not subject to any limitation to title documents or to any requirement that possession, in the case of a title document, has been consistent with the document. See McCormick, *Evidence,* § 223 (2d ed 1972).

Despite the utility of paragraph (h) of subsection (2) of this section, it is merely a rule of authentication, and its satisfaction does not necessarily guarantee the admission of the writing authenticated. Thus, a writing may be properly authenticated under any of the methods suggested and yet be inadmissible as hearsay or secondary evidence. A partial overlap exists between the requirements of this section and a doctrine that recitals in certain types of ancient instruments may be received as evidence of the facts recited. The latter doctrine, however, constitutes an exception to the rule against hearsay and is quite distinct from the principles of this section concerning authentication. McCormick, *Evidence,* § 223 at p 550 (2d ed 1972).

Paragraph (i). Paragraph (i) of subsection (2) of this section is designed for situations in which the accuracy of a result is dependent upon a process or system which produces it such as X-rays. Recent developments include the computer. [See *Transport Indemnity Co. v. Seib,* 178 Neb 253, 132 NW 2d 871 (1965); *State v. Veres,* 7 Ariz App 117, 436 P2d 629 (1968); *Merrick v. United States Rubber Co.,* 7 Ariz App 443, 440 P2d 314 (1968); Freed, *Computer Print-Outs as Evidence,* 16 Am Jur Proof of Facts 273; Symposium, *Law and Computers in the Mid-Sixties,* ALI-ABA (1966); 37 Albany L Rev 61 (1967).] Paragraph (i) of subsection (2) of this section does not, of course, foreclose taking judicial notice of the accuracy of the process or system.

This example only contemplates authentication of the process or system itself and further foundation may be required to insure that the process or system thereof was properly utilized to obtain the product offered into evidence. McCormick, *Evidence,* § 214 (2d ed 1972).

Paragraph (j). Paragraph (j) of subsection (2) of this section makes clear that other methods of authentication provided by the Legislative Assembly or by the Supreme Court are not intended to be superceded. The phrase "pursuant to statutory authority," which appears in Federal Rule 901(b)(10) is omitted from subsection (2) in order to make the paragraph apply to rules prescribed by the Supreme Court pursuant to its constitutional and supervisory powers as well as those powers granted by statute.

TEXT

RULE 901(1)
Authentication

Rule 901(1) states that the requirement of authentication or identification as a condition precedent to the admissibility of evidence is satisfied by the introduction of evidence sufficient to support a finding that the matter in question is what its proponent claims. The requirement of authentication is a particularized application of the requirements of relevancy. See Rules 401 and 402. For evidence to be found relevant, it must be shown to be what it purports to be, and that what it purports to be satisfies Rule 401.

Rule 901(1) provides only for a preliminary determination of authenticity by the court sufficient to allow the evidence to be received. The opponent may still offer counter-evidence contesting authenticity at trial, and the final determination of authenticity is made by the trier of fact after receipt of all evidence. Authentication is thus a matter of conditional relevancy under Rule 104(2).

At least in civil cases, the time, expense and uncertainty associated with authenticating evidence under Rule 901 can often be avoided by pretrial procedures such as stipulations, requests for admission under ORCP 45, admissions in pleadings, admissions in depositions, or agreements at a pretrial conference.

See generally Westling, *Articles IX and X: Authentication and the Best Evidence Rule,* 19 Will L Rev 427 (1983).

RULE 901(2)
Illustrative Foundations

Rule 901(2) lists ten methods by which the requirements of Rule 901(1) may be satisfied. These illustrate, but do not limit, the permissible methods of authentication. Any other method of authentication that provides evidence "sufficient to support a finding that the matter in question is what its proponent claims" will also satisfy the requirements of Rule 901. The examples of authentication listed in Rule 901(2) sometimes overlap, and a particular method of authentication may satisfy more than one subpart of this rule.

RULE 901(2)(a)
Testimony of Witness with Knowledge

Rule 901(2)(a) provides that evidence may be authenticated by a witness with knowledge who testifies that a matter is what it is claimed to be. This is perhaps the most frequently used method of authentication.

Tangible Objects

A writing, gun, knife, article of clothing, or other tangible object, if otherwise admissible, may be received into evidence upon testimony of a witness with knowledge that the object is what its proponent claims. See *United States v. Fortes,* 619 F2d 108, 122 (1st Cir 1980) (dime wrappings authenticated by testimony of witness and circumstantial evidence). A court will not necessarily require absolute certainty on the part of a witness making the identification. See *United States v. Johnson,* 637 F2d 1224, 1247–8 (9th Cir 1980) (ax received in evidence where victim of assault testified only that he was "pretty sure" it was the ax used against him; court found adequate identification based on victim's testimony that he had seen the ax that was used by the defendant and had personally used the ax in the past).

For exhibits with unique or distinctive characteristics, showing of a chain of custody is usually unnecessary. The object may be identified based on its distinctive features, such as a serial number. It is a common practice for law enforcement officers and private investigators to affix their initials or other identifying marks to a physical object to aid identification at trial.

If the item cannot be easily recognized or distinguished from other substances or objects, or if it is susceptible to deterioration or alteration, proof of the chain of custody may be required. *Vander Veer v. Toyota Motor Distributors Inc.,* 282 Or 135, 577 P2d 1343 (1978). Problems in proving chain of custody do not necessarily require exclusion of the evidence, but may affect the weight to be accorded the evidence by the jury. See *State v. Anderson,* 242 Or 368, 409 P2d 681 (1966) (evidence admitted even though one witness in chain of custody not called); *United States v. White,* 569 F2d 263, 266 (5th Cir), cert denied 439 US 848 (1978) ("[T]he mere possibility of a break in the chain does not render the physical evidence inadmissible ..."). See also *United States v. McKinney,* 631 F2d 569 (8th Cir 1980); *United States v. Glaze,* 643 F2d 549 552 (8th Cir 1981). See generally Giannelli, *Chain of Custody and the Handling of Real Evidence,* 20 Am Crim L Rev 527 (1983); C. Mueller & L. Kirkpatrick, MODERN EVIDENCE (1995) § 9.5.

In *Fox v. Olsen,* 87 Or App 173, 741 P2d 924, rev denied 304 Or 405, 745 P2d 1225 (1987), the court found no error in the exclusion of blood test results when there was no affidavit or testimony from the person at the testing laboratory who had transferred the blood to a tray from which the results were read. The trial court found this to be a "monumental gap in the chain of custody," and the appellate court affirmed this conclusion.

A court has discretion to exclude a material object offered as an exhibit where there has been no showing that the object is in the same condition it was in at the relevant time. See *White v. Keller,* 188 Or 378, 388, 215 P2d 986 (1950) (no abuse of discretion for trial court to exclude spring and axle of car purchased from wrecking yard several months after accident; "It is elementary that before a material object may be admitted in evidence, it must be shown that there has been no substantial change in condition since the time in issue"). Such a requirement has the greatest significance with respect to objects or substances that are susceptible to changes or alterations that would affect their relevancy or mislead the jury.

As to whether a tangible object may be exhibited to the jury, see ORS 41.660:

Whenever an object, cognizable by the senses, has such a relation to the facts in dispute as to afford reasonable grounds of belief respecting it, or to make an item in the sum of the evidence, the object may be exhibited to the jury, or its existence, situation and character may be proved by witnesses. The exhibition of the object to the jury shall be regulated by the sound discretion of the court.

Writings

A writing may be authenticated by the witness who wrote or executed it. *United States v. Gipson,* 609 F2d 893, 894–5 (8th Cir 1979) (order forms authenticated by testimony of person who signed them). A writing may also be authenticated by a witness who personally observed another write or execute of it. See *Ivey v. Transouth Fin Corp (In re Clifford),* 566 F2d 1023, 1025 (5th Cir 1978) (deed authenticated by testimony of notary public as to execution). Other methods of authenticating writings include identification of the handwriting (see Rule 901(2)(b) and (c)), a showing of their contents or distinctive characteristics (see Rule 902(2)(d)), a showing that they are public records or reports (see Rule 901(2)(g)), or a showing that they are ancient documents (see Rule 901(2)(h)). The foundation necessary for a writing to be admitted as an exception to the hearsay rule usually includes identification of the writing and therefore also satisfies the requirements of Rule 901. See, e.g., Rule 803(6) (records of regularly conducted activity).

In *State v. Park,* 140 Or App 507, 513, 916 P2d 334 (1996), the court held that a letter offered as an admission by the defendant may be admitted upon evidence sufficient to support a jury finding that it was written by defendant. Here the letter was sufficiently authenticated by the testimony of handwriting experts, signature specimens obtained from defendant that a reasonable trier of fact could find matched, and other evidence connecting defendant with the letter.

Photographs

A photograph may be authenticated by a witness with knowledge who testifies that the photograph accurately represents the scene depicted at the relevant time. See *United States v. Brannon,* 616 F2d 413, 416–7 (9th Cir), cert denied 447 US 908 (1980); *United States v. Richardson,* 562 F2d 476, 479 (7th Cir 1977), cert denied 434 US 1072 (1978). The authenticating witness need not be the photographer. *United States v. Clayton,* 643 F2d 1071, 1074 (5th Cir 1981); *Harpole v. Paeschke Farms, Inc.,* 267 Or 592, 518 P2d 1023 (1974). Even if the conditions depicted in the photograph have changed, the photograph may still be admitted at the discretion of the court if the changed conditions are explained to the jury and the jury would not be misled. *DeMaris v. Whittier,* 280 Or 25, 569 P2d 605 (1977) (admitting photograph despite changed conditions); *Isom v. River Island Sand & Gravel, Inc.,* 273 Or 867, 543 P2d 1047 (1975) (affirming exclusion of photograph where conditions had changed). Photographs may be excluded if their probative value is substantially outweighed by the danger of unfair prejudice, confusion of the issues, or misleading the jury. See Rule 403.

The above rules also generally apply to motion pictures and videotapes. See *State v. Zimmerman,* 11 Or App 166, 501 P2d 1304 (1972) (error to admit videotape against defendant where prosecution's witness stated in response to questions in aid of an objection that the videotape was not an accurate portrayal of the defendant on the night in question). For the procedures for authenticating X-rays, see Rule 901(2)(i).

See generally C. Mueller & L. Kirkpatrick, MODERN EVIDENCE (1995) § 9.15 (1995); Fagan, *Smile: How Prejudicial Can the Candid Camera Be? The Admission of Photographs in a Criminal Trial,* 9 St Johns J Legal Comment 145 (1993); NOTE, *Jurors at the Movies: Day-in-the-Life Videos as Effective Evidentiary Tool or Unfairly Prejudicial Device?* 27 Suffolk U L Rev 789 (1993); NOTE, *A Picture Is Worth a Thousand Lies: Electronic Imaging and the Future of the Admissibility of Photographs into Evidence,* 18 Rutgers Computer & Tech L J 365 (1992).

Maps, Drawings, Diagrams

A map, drawing or diagram may be admissible upon a showing that it is an accurate portrayal of the matter in question. McCormick, EVIDENCE (3d ed 1984) § 213; *Mansfield v. S. Oregon Stages,* 136 Or 669, 1 P2d 591 (1931); *Jones v. Mitchell Bros. Truck Lines,* 266 Or 513, 511 P2d 347 (1973) (drawing excluded because not shown to be accurate portrayal and not based on first-hand knowledge). The map, drawing, or diagram need not be drawn to scale. *Babcock v. Gray,* 165 Or 398, 107 P2d 846 (1940). A map, drawing, or diagram is usually received only to assist the jury to better understand the testimony, not as substantive evidence. *Walling v. Van Pelt,* 132 Or 243, 285 P 262 (1930); *Austin v. Portland Traction Co.,* 181 Or 470 182 P2d 412 (1947). A drawing showing a proposed use of property is not admissible to show lost profits, but may be admissible "for the specific purpose of showing the adaptability to which ... land could be put and for the highest and best use of this particular piece of property." *State Highway Comm'n v. Compton,* 9 Or App 264, 275, 490 P2d 743 (1971), rev'd on other grounds 265 Or 339, 507 P2d 13 (1973).

Computations

An exhibit setting forth a mathematical computation may be admissible upon a showing that it accurately reflects the evidence in the record. *Hastings v. Top Cut Feedlots Inc.,* 285 Or 261, 590 P2d 1210 (1979).

Computer Animations

The rapid advances in computer technology have made possible a dramatic new type of demonstrative evidence in the form of on-screen simulations and other forms of computer graphics. Such evidence must satisfy the general authentication standards for comuter output. In addition, as a form of scientific evidence, computer animations usually must be authenticated by an expert and satisfy applicable standards for scientific proof. Upon a proper foundation, computer models or animations may be admitted into evidence, although to date there are relatively few reported cases. Courts tend to be more receptive to computer imagery when it is offered to illustrate an expert's theory of an accident than when it is offered as a recreation or simulation of the accident itself. See *Robinson v. Missouri Pac. R. Co.*, 16 F.3d 1083 (10th Cir. 1994) (no abuse of discretion to admit video animation of train-automobile accident, where cautionary instruction given that animation was not a recreation of the accident).

Computer-generated video imagery can have a powerful impact on the jury, perhaps overwhelming its fair consideration of other conflicting evidence. Moreover, unlike experimental evidence, computer-generated imagery gives boundless leeway to its creator and is not restricted by the laws of gravity or other scientific principles. For these reasons, courts retain broad discretion under OEC 403 to exclude computer animations, particularly where they are based on questionable assumptions or project such a slanted or distorted view of the evidence as to be unfairly prejudicial or misleading.

See generally Cerniglia, *Computer-Generated Exhibits—Demonstrative, Substantive or Pedagogical—Their Place in Evidence*, 18 Am J Trial Advoc 1 (1994); Henke, *Admissibility of Computer-Generated Animated Reconstructions and Simulations*, 35 Trial Law Guide 434 (1991); COMMENT, *Admission of Computer Generated Visual Evidence: Should There Be Clear Standards?*, 6 Software L J 325 (1993); COMMENT, *Lights, Camera, Action: Computer-Animated Evidence Gets Its Day in Court*, 34 B C L Rev 1087 (1993).

RULE 901(2)(b)
Nonexpert Opinion on Handwriting

Rule 902(1)(b) states that a writing can be authenticated by the opinion of a lay witness as to the genuineness of the handwriting, provided that the requisite familiarity was not acquired for purposes of the litigation. Because a lay witness is expected to give an opinion based on independent knowledge, such a witness should not be asked at trial to give an opinion based on a comparison of the questioned document with an exemplar. Under Rule 901(2)(c), only an expert witness or the trier of fact may make such a comparison.

The witness' familiarity with the handwriting can be challenged prior to the opinion being given in evidence by questions in aid of an objection. If insufficient familiarity is shown, the opinion will be excluded. *United States v. Pitts*, 569 F2d 343, 348 (5th Cir), cert denied 436 US 959 (1978).

RULE 901(2)(c)
Comparison by Trier or Expert Witness

Rule 901(2)(c) authorizes the trier of fact or expert witnesses to authenticate an exhibit by comparing it to specimens that have themselves been authenticated. For the exhibit to be admissible, it must appear to the court to be sufficiently similar to the authenticated specimens to support a jury finding of genuineness; or a qualified expert must offer testimony sufficient to support such a finding. This rule is applicable to a wide variety of evidence, including handwriting, fingerprints, footprints, shoeprints, tireprints, typewriter comparisons, and ballistics evidence.

If the genuineness of the specimen is not admitted by stipulation or otherwise, it must first be authenticated by any method that would support a finding that it is what it purports to be. This rule changes Oregon law. Previously, specimens of signatures had to be admitted or established to be genuine. See former ORS 42.070 (repealed 1981). Under the new rule, the authenticity of the specimen is determined by the jury, not the court. At trial, the opponent can contest the authenticity not only of the signature or of other comparison evidence, but of the specimen as well.

No specialized education or training is required for a witness to qualify as an expert for purposes of making a comparison under this rule. The necessary expertise can be found from the witness's work experience or demonstrated knowledge, however acquired. See Rule 702.

RULE 901(2)(d)
Distinctive Characteristics and the Like

Rule 901(2)(d) authorizes authentication of documents, communications, or objects by their appearance, contents, substance, internal patterns, or other distinctive characteristics. The court must determine whether these characteristics are sufficiently distinctive to be satisfactory circumstantial evidence of the authenticity of the matter in question.

This rule incorporates the common-law "reply doctrine," which authenticates a communication shown to be in response to an earlier communication. Unusual phrases or the use of slang, code terms or nicknames may also be sufficient to authenticate particular communications under this rule, as will contents of a communication that reveal unique knowledge. See *United States v. Helberg,* 565 F2d 993 (8th Cir 1977) (ledger sufficiently authenticated by circumstances, including fact that defendant's nickname and his mother's telephone number appeared in ledger); *United States v. Mangan,* 575 F2d 32, 41–2 (2nd Cir), cert denied 439 US 931 (1978) ("Wigmore's conclusion that mere contents will not suffice unless only the author would have known the details is contrary to the federal rules and unsound," quoting J. Weinstein and M. Berger, 5 WEINSTEIN'S EVIDENCE § 901(b)(4)[01] at 901–47).

The plaintiff unsuccessfully attempted to authenticate a statement on the basis of unique knowledge in *Irby v. Fred Meyer, Inc.,* 98 Or App 726, 780 P2d 797 (1989). The plaintiff sought to offer evidence that an unidentified bystander to plaintiff's injury from falling mirror tiles stated: "Those mirrors fell again." Because it was assumed that the statement would be inadmissible hearsay unless it could be shown to be the admission of a store employee, the plaintiff argued that the knowledge of previous incidents (indicated in the statement) was sufficient to support a finding that the statement was made by a store employee. The plaintiff argued that the statement was authenticated by the distinctive character of its content (reflecting knowledge of prior incidents), relying on OEC 901(2)(d). The appellate court affirmed the ruling of the trial judge that such a contention was speculative.

The developing field of psycholinguistics attempts to identify verbalizations of different individuals based on their distinctive word patterns. Arens and Meadow, *Psycholinguistics and the Confession Dilemma,* 56 Colum L Rev 19 (1956). Use of an expert in psycholinguistics to aid in authentication is not addressed by this rule. See Rule 702.

Circumstances surrounding the sending of the communication, such as place of making, date of making, or manner of sending, may also be sufficient to authenticate the communication in some circumstances. See *United States v. Gordon,* 634 F2d 639 (1st Cir 1980) (mail fraud prosecution; documents properly admitted against defendant when they purported to come from person having his name, address, and telephone number, were mailed from various states when defendant was in those states, and generated responses containing checks that were deposited in the bank account of defendant by his wife).

The fact that writings or objects were found in the possession or custody of a defendant is a factor the court can consider, in conjunction with other factors, in determining whether evidence is adequately authenticated. In *State v. Millar,* 127 Or App 76, 79, 871 P2d 482, 484 (1994), the court held that a pornographic magazine was sufficiently authenticated as belonging to defendant by testimony that it was found under the couch where defendant regularly slept and in a house where only he and an elderly relative lived. See also *United States v. Luschen,* 614 F2d 1164, 1174 (8th Cir), cert denied 446 US 939 (1980); *Durns v. United States,* 562 F2d 542, 548 (8th Cir), cert denied 434 US 959 (1977).

The fact that a particular person's name is on a writing or object has been held "not to be sufficient in itself" to authenticate the writing or object, but is a factor that may be considered in conjunction with others. *United States v. Gutierrez,* 576 F2d 269, 275–6 (10th Cir), cert denied 439 US 954 (1978). However, a letterhead "should suffice to authenticate a writing as from the indicated source, at least in the absence of something highly suspicious in the appearance or content of the letterhead itself or the accompanying written matter, or of counterproof indicating mistake or fraud." C. Mueller & L. Kirkpatrick, MODERN EVIDENCE (1995) § 9.8.

RULE 901(2)(e)
Voice Identification

Rule 901(2)(e) allows authentication of a conversation by identification of the speaker's voice, whether heard firsthand, over the telephone, or on a tape recording. Rule 602 requires that the witness identifying the voice have personal knowledge. Courts have been liberal with regard to the degree of familiarity required before voice identification may be made. *United States v. Axselle,* 604 F2d 1330, 1338 (10th Cir 1979) (hearing voice one other time sufficient familiarity); *United States v. Vitale,* 549 F2d 71 (8th Cir), cert denied 431 US 907 (1977) (two other occasions sufficient); *United States v. McCartney,* 264 F2d 628 (7th Cir), cert denied 361 US 845 (1959) (three occasions sufficient). The familiarity with the voice can be acquired subsequent to the conversation in question. *United States v. Axselle,* 604 F2d 1330, 1338 (10th Cir 1979). See generally Shmukler, *Voice Identification in Criminal Cases Under Article IX of the Federal Rules of Evidence,* 49 Temple LQ 867 (1976).

Courts sometimes allow voice identification to be made by experts relying on voice prints or a spectrograph. See *United States v. Williams,* 583 F2d 1194 (2nd Cir 1978), cert denied 439 US 1117 (1979); *United States v. Baller,* 519 F2d 463 (4th Cir), cert denied 423 US 1019 (1975); *United States v. Franks,* 511 F2d 25 (6th Cir), cert denied 422 US 1042 (1975). Contra *United States v. McDaniel,* 538 F2d 408 (DC Cir 1976). See generally ANNOT., *Admissibility and Weight of Voice-print Evidence,* 97 ALR3d 294 (1980); Thomas, *Voiceprint—Myth or Miracle (The Eyes Have It),* 3 U San Fran U L Rev 15 (1974); COMMENT, *Expert Testimony and Voice Spectrogram Analysis,* 1975 Wash U L Rev 775; Kamine, *The Voiceprint Technique: Its Structure and Reliability,* 6 San Diego L Rev 213 (1969).

Voice identification is an important part of the requisite foundation for introduction of tape recordings. A witness who was present at a conversation may be able to authenticate a tape recording of that conversation by identifying the speakers and testifying that the tape recording fully, fairly, and accurately reflects the conversation. C. Mueller & L. Kirkpatrick, MODERN EVIDENCE (1995) § 9.14. When the authenticating witness was not present at the conversation, foundation testimony may be required as to: "(1) Capability of the device for recording, (2) competency of the operator, (3) proper operation of the device, (4) preservation of the recording with no changes, additions, or deletions, along with (5) identification of the speakers. ..." Id.

These criteria were approved in *State v. Miller,* 6 Or App 366, 487 P2d 1387 (1971), with the following additional two requirements: (1) "establishment of the authenticity and correctness of the recording," and (2) "a showing that the testimony elicited was voluntarily made without any kind of inducement." Arguably, the first requirement will necessarily be satisfied by fulfillment of the other requirements, and the second requirement has primary significance in criminal cases. On the requisite foundation for tape recordings, see generally *United States v. McKeever,* 169 F Supp 426 (S D N Y 1958), rev'd on other grounds 271 F2d 669 (2nd Cir 1959); *United States v. McMillan,* 508 F2d 101 (8th Cir 1974), cert denied 421 US 916 (1975); *United States v. Biggins,* 551 F2d 64 (5th Cir 1977); *United States v. King,* 587 F2d 956 (9th Cir 1978); Jacobson, *A Primer on the Use of Tape-Recorded Evidence,* 6 Litigation 30 (1980); NOTE, *A Foundational Standard for the Admission of Sound Recordings into Evidence in Criminal Trials,* 52 S Cal L Rev 1273 (1979); ANNOT., *Admissibility of Tape Recording or Transcript of "911" Emergency Telephone Number,* 3 ALR5th 784 (1992).

The fact that portions of the tape are inaudible or unintelligible does not require the court to reject the tape, provided any technical difficulty does not make the tape untrustworthy. *State v. Dills,* 244 Or 188, 416 P2d 651 (1966);

ANNOT., *Omission or Inaudibility of Portions of Sound Recording as Affecting its Admissibility in Evidence,* 57 ALR3d 746 (1974).

In some cases, courts have allowed transcripts of tapes to be prepared and distributed to members of a jury to assist them when listening to a tape recording in court. *United States v. McMillan,* 508 F2d 101 (8th Cir 1974), cert denied 421 US 916 (1975); *United States v. Fontanez,* 628 F2d 687 (1st Cir 1980), cert denied 450 US 935 (1981). The court should instruct the jury that in case of any discrepancy they should rely on what they hear on the tape rather than what they read in the transcript.

See generally ANNOT., *Cautionary Instructions to Jury as to Reliability of, or Factors to be Considered in Evaluating Voice Identification Testimony,* 17 ALR5th 851 (1994).

RULE 901(2)(f)
Telephone Calls

Rule 901(2)(f) specifies one of several methods of authenticating telephone conversations. Telephone calls may also be authenticated by voice identification, by distinctive characteristics, by unique knowledge possessed by the speaker, and by other circumstances that would support a finding that the speaker is the person the proponent claims. See Rules 901(2)(d) and (e).

This rule concerns only identifying the person receiving the call, not the person making the call. A call to a person will be sufficiently authenticated by showing that the call was made to the number assigned by the telephone company, and that the person answering identified himself as the person called. The call may also be authenticated by circumstances other than self-identification that reveal the person to be the one called.

A call to a business will be sufficiently authenticated, even if the person answering does not identify himself, if the call was placed to the number assigned to the business and the conversation related to business that would be reasonably transacted over the telephone.

If evidence of a telephone conversation was obtained by unlawful wiretap or other illegal interception, the evidence is subject to exclusion under either ORS 41.910 or applicable constitutional exclusionary rules.

RULE 901(2)(g)
Public Records and Reports

Rule 901(2)(g) authorizes certain documents to be authenticated by a showing that they are from the public office where items of that nature are normally kept. This rule covers two types of documents: (1) writings authorized by law to be recorded or filed, which in fact are recorded or filed in a public office; and (2) a purported public record, report, statement, or data compilation, in any form. The first category would include documents such as recorded deeds, contracts, security interests, or filed tax returns. The second category would include documents such as licensing records, property tax assessments, weather bureau records, police reports, and court orders or judgments. Presumably the term "public office" encompasses all levels of government—state, county, and local—within and without Oregon, as well as all levels of federal government. See 5 C. Mueller & L. Kirkpatrick, FEDERAL EVIDENCE (2d ed 1994) § 528.

To authenticate a writing under this rule, the proponent must show only that the document is one of the two types indicated above and that it is from the public office where it would normally be kept. It is not necessary to call the custodian or a person from the office where the document is kept. Any person with knowledge can be the authenticating witness. If appropriately certified and affixed with an official seal, the original public document may be self-authenticating under Rule 902(1), (2), or (3). For the requirements for self-authentication of a copy of a public document or record, see Rule 902(4). Cf. Rule 1005.

If the public document or record is being offered for the truth of the matter asserted, it may be admissible under the public records and reports exception to the hearsay rule. See Rule 803(8).

RULE 901(2)(h)
Ancient Documents

Rule 901(2)(h) provides a method for authenticating ancient documents or data compilations. The rule requires evidence that the document or data compilation (1) is in such condition as to create no suspicion concerning its authenticity; (2) was in a place where, if authentic, it would likely be; and (3) has been in existence twenty years or more at the time it is offered.

There is no requirement that the ancient document be a public document or record. The rule also embraces personal correspondence, memoranda, newspapers, diaries, and other private writings. 5 C. Mueller & L. Kirkpatrick, FEDERAL EVIDENCE (2d ed 1994) § 529.

The age of the writing may be proven by various methods, including testimony of attesting witnesses or other witnesses with knowledge, expert testimony, contents, physical appearance, or surrounding circumstances indicating execution at a certain date. The date on the face of the writing generally will not alone be sufficient to qualify the writing as an ancient document. 2 McCormick, EVIDENCE (4th ed 1992) § 223 at 45 n6.

The rule requires that the document be free from suspicion. This means that it should be located in the place where it probably would have been kept; free from deletions, erasures, or discontinuity of writing; and in apparently proper form. There is no requirement, however, that possession in the case of a title document have been consistent with the document.

A document authenticated under this rule as an ancient writing may be admitted to prove the truth of its contents under Rule 803(16), which creates a hearsay exception for "statements in a document in existence twenty years or more the authenticity of which is established."

RULE 901(2)(i)
Process or System

Rule 901(2)(i) authorizes evidence to be authenticated by a showing that a particular process or system was used to produce a result and that the process or system produces accurate results. This method is often used to authenticate computer printouts, X-rays, bank surveillance photographs, polls and surveys, statistical samples, radar speed measurements, electrocardiograms, and other scientific tests. See *United States v. Fendley,* 522 F2d 181, 186–7 (5th Cir 1975) (computer printouts); *United States v. Scholle,* 553 F2d 1109 (8th Cir), cert denied 434 US 940 (1977) (computer analysis); *United States v. Clayton,* 643 F2d 1071 (5th Cir 1981) (bank surveillance photographs); *Union Carbide Corp. v. Ever-Ready Inc.,* 531 F2d 366, 381–8 (7th Cir), cert denied 429 US 830 (1976) (public opinion survey); *Randy's Studebaker Sales, Inc. v. Nissan Motor Corp.,* 533 F2d 510, 519–21 (10th Cir 1976) (customer survey). See also Freed, *Computer Printouts as Evidence,* 16 Am Jur Proof of Facts 273 (1975); ANNOT., *Proof of Public Records Kept or Stored On Electronic Computing Equipment,* 71 ALR3d 232 (1976); ANNOT., *Admissibility of X-Ray Report Made by Physician Taking or Interpreting X-Ray Picture—Admissibility,* 6 ALR2d 406 (1949); ANNOT., *Proof, By Radar or Other Mechanical or Electronic Devices of Violation of Speed Regulations,* 47 ALR3d 822 (1973); ANNOT., *Admissibility in Civil Action of Electroencephalogram, Electrocardiogram, or Other Record Made by Instrument Used in Medical Test, or of Report Based Upon Such Test,* 66 ALR2d 536 (1965). On the admissibility of expert opinion testimony based on scientific evidence, see textual discussion under Rule 702. On the admissibility of expert opinion testimony based on public opinion polls or surveys, see textual discussion under Rule 703.

The reliability of the process may be established by the testimony of a witness who is qualified to testify regarding the process, or in some cases by judicial notice. In addition to showing that the particular process or system produces an accurate result when properly operated, it is necessary to show that the process or system was correctly operated by a qualified person on the occasion in question.

When opinion polls and surveys are presented in conjunction with expert testimony, proof of the validity of the underlying method should include evidence:

> (a) that the "universe" of persons surveyed or polled was properly defined with reference to the underlying subject, (b) that a representative sample of the universe was selected and questioned, (c) that the questions were clear, simple, and nonleading, (d) that sound interview procedures were followed, (e) that the information was carefully gathered and recorded, (f) that the data were properly collated and analyzed, and (g) that the objectivity of the process was adequately protected by keeping the polling or survey separate from the litigation. 5 C. Mueller & L. Kirkpatrick, FEDERAL EVIDENCE §530 (2d ed 1994).

To introduce evidence of computer output, it has been stated that the foundation should include evidence of the following:

(a) competent computer operators were employed,

(b) the computer used is accepted in the field as standard and efficient equipment,

(c) careful procedures were followed in connection with the input and output of information, employing reasonable controls, tests, and checks for accuracy,

(d) the machine was operated and programmed properly, and

(e) the output therefore has the significance which the proponent claims for it. Id.

See generally COMMENT, *Computer Printouts as Evidence: Stricter Foundation or Presumption of Reliability*, 75 Marq L Rev 439 (1992); NOTE, *Lights, Camera, Action: Computer-Animated Evidence Gets Its Day in Court*, 34 BC L Rev 1087 (1993); Rychlak & Rychlak, *Real and Demonstrative Evidence Away from Trial*, 17 Am J Trial Advoc 509 (1993).

RULE 901(2)(j)
Methods Provided by Statute or Rule

Rule 901(2)(j) incorporates by reference as sufficient authentication any other method of authentication or identification provided by law or by other rules prescribed by the supreme court. See, e.g., ORS 432.175 (proof of birth certificate); ORCP 39 G(1) (authentication of depositions); ORS 8.360 (transcript of testimony certified by court reporter "shall be *prima facie* a correct statement thereof").

RULE 902.   ORS 40.510. SELF-AUTHENTICATION

Extrinsic evidence of authenticity as a condition precedent to admissibility is not required with respect to the following:

(1) [Domestic public documents under seal.] A document bearing a seal purporting to be that of the United States, or of any state, district, commonwealth, territory, or insular possession thereof, or the Panama Canal Zone, or the Trust Territory of the Pacific Islands, or of a political subdivision, department, officer, or agency thereof, and a signature purporting to be an attestation or execution.

(2) [Domestic public documents not under seal.] A document purporting to bear the signature, in an official capacity, of an officer or employee of any entity included in subsection (1) of this section, having no seal, if a public officer having a seal and having official duties in the district or political subdivision of the officer or employee certifies under seal that the signer has the official capacity and that the signature is genuine.

(3) [Foreign public documents.] A document purporting to be executed or attested in an official capacity by a person authorized by the laws of a foreign country to make the execution or attestation, and accompanied by a final certification as to the genuineness of the signature and official position of (A) the executing or attesting person, or (B) any foreign official whose certificate of genuineness of signature and official position relates to the execution or attestation or is in a chain of certificates of genuineness of signature and official position relating to the execution or attestation. A final certification may be made by a secretary of embassy or legation, consul general, consul, vice consul, or consular agent of the United States, or a diplomatic or consular official of the foreign country assigned or accredited to the United States. If reasonable opportunity has been given to all parties to investigate the authenticity and accuracy of official documents, the court may, for good cause shown, order that they be treated as presumptively authentic without final certification or permit them to be evidenced by an attested summary with or without final certification.

(4) [Certified copies of public records.] A copy of an official record or report or entry therein, or of a document authorized by law to be recorded or filed and actually recorded or filed in a public office, including data compilations in any form, certified as correct by the custodian or other person authorized to make the certification, by certificate complying with subsection (1), (2) or (3) of this section or otherwise complying with any law or rule prescribed by the Supreme Court.

(5) [Official publications.] Books, pamphlets or other publications purporting to be issued by public authority.

(6) [Newspapers and periodicals.] Printed materials purporting to be newspapers or periodicals.

(7) [Trade inscriptions and the like.] Inscriptions, signs, tags or labels purporting to have been affixed in the course of business and indicating ownership, control or origin.

(8) [Acknowledged documents.] Documents accompanied by a certificate of acknowledgment executed in the manner provided by law by a notary public or other officer authorized by law to take acknowledgments.

(9) [Commercial paper and related documents.] Commercial paper, signatures thereon and documents relating thereto to the extent provided by ORS chapters 71 to 83.

(10) [Presumptions under law.] Any signature, documents or other matter declared by law to be presumptively or prima facie genuine or authentic.

(11) [Document bearing seal of tribal government.]

    (a) A document bearing a seal purporting to be that of a federally recognized Indian tribal government or of a political subdivision, department, officer, or agency thereof, and a signature purporting to be an attestation or execution.

(b) A document purporting to bear the signature, in an official capacity, of an officer or employee of any entity included in paragraph (a) of this subsection, having no seal, if a public officer having a seal and having official duties in the district or political subdivision or the officer or employee certifies under seal that the signer has the official capacity and that the signature is genuine.

(12) [State police data.] Any document containing data prepared or recorded by the Oregon State Police pursuant to ORS 813.160 (1)(b)(C) or (E), or pursuant to ORS 475.235(3), if the document is produced by data retrieval from the Law Enforcement Data System or other computer system maintained and operated by the Oregon State Police, and the person retrieving the data attests that the information was retrieved directly from the system and that the document accurately reflects the data retrieved.

LEGISLATIVE COMMENTARY

This section is a modified version of Rule 902 of the Federal Rules of Evidence. Federal rules 902(4), 902(9) and 902(10) were slightly modified and subsection (11) of this section was added to clarify the authentication procedures for Indian tribal documents. Subsection (11) of this section was derived from Rule 902(1) and Rule 902(2) of the Federal Rules of Evidence.

Case law and statutes have, over the years, developed a substantial body of instances in which authenticity is taken as sufficiently established for purposes of admissibility without extrinsic evidence to that effect. Sometimes this occurs for reasons of policy, but perhaps more often because practical considerations reduce the possibility of fraud and error to a very small dimension. This section collects and incorporates these situations, in some instances expanding them to occupy a larger area which their underlying considerations justify. In no instance is the opposite party foreclosed from disputing authenticity.

This section is basically consistent with existing practices with a few exceptions and sets forth several general principles of authentication while existing Oregon law, in contrast, consists of numerous exacting statutes which pertain to specific types of documents. It is possible, therefore, that many of these principles may be judicially extended beyond the scope of existing authentication procedures.

Subsection (1). The acceptance of documents bearing a public seal and signature, most often encountered in practice in the form of acknowledgments or certificates authenticating copies of public records, is actually of broad application.

Whether theoretically based in whole or in part upon judicial notice, the practical underlying considerations are that forgery is a crime and detection is fairly easy and certain. 7 Wigmore, *Evidence,* § 2161, p 638 (3d ed 1940); *California Evidence Code,* § 1452.

The acceptance of documents bearing a public seal and signature without extrinsic evidence of authenticity is in accord with the following Oregon statutes which include this method as a permissible mode of authentication: ORS 43.110—Authentication of the judicial records of Oregon or of the United States;

ORS 43.410—Authentication of records in the custody of the State Archivist (legislative record or public record of certain writings);

ORS 43.430—Authentication of books, records and documents of the United States executive department or government owned corporation.

However, the broad application of subsection (1) of this section to other states and territories of the United States is contrary to some of the existing authentication practices in this state. For example, under current Oregon law governing authentication of the judicial record of a sister state or of a territory of the United States, the legal keeper of the records must certify a copy of the record and affix the seal of the court, and the chief judge of the court must also certify that the keeper's certificate is in due form and made by the person having legal custody of the records. ORS 43.110.

Subsection (2). While statutes are found which raise a presumption of genuineness of purported official signatures in the absence of an official seal, 7 Wigmore, *Evidence,* § 2167 (3d ed 1940) and *California Evidence Code,* § 1453, the greater ease of effecting a forgery under these circumstances is apparent. Hence, subsection (2) of this section calls for authentication by an officer who has a seal. Other special situations are covered in subsection (10) of this section.

Subsection (2) of this section applies only to officials "having no seal." However, the officer using a seal to authenticate another officer's signature will by inference also be certifying that there is no seal in the other's possession which the other could himself have used. When presented with the document under the seal of the second officer, the courts shall assume that the affixing officer had the authority to affix such seal to the document. Weinstein *Evidence,* § 902(2)[01] at 902-15 (M. Bender 1976).

While the practice of having a public officer use a seal to authenticate another officer's signature is not specifically provided for under existing Oregon law, some authority for the procedure of an officer certifying a purportedly official signature may be gleaned from ORS 43.110, which requires that the chief judge of a foreign court certify the validity of the certification by the legal keeper of the judicial records.

Subsection (3) of this section provides a method for extending the presumption of authenticity to foreign official documents by a procedure of certification. It is derived from Rule 44(a)(2) of the Federal Rules of Civil Procedure but is broader in applying to public documents rather than being limited to public records.

Under current Oregon practice, a judicial record of a foreign country may be proved by a copy of the record certified by the clerk or other person having legal custody of the record, with the seal of the court affixed, together with a certification by the chief judge or presiding magistrate that the certificate is in due form and made by the person having legal custody of the original. ORS 43.110. This section, in contrast, provides a much broader rule in that it allows the copy to be attested or certified by any authorized official instead of restricting it to the custodian or chief judge only. Weinstein *Evidence,* § 902(8)[01] at 902-31 (M. Bender 1976).

The common law and numerous statutes have recognized the procedure of authenticating copies of public records by certificate. The certificate qualifies as a public document, receivable as authentic when in conformity with subsection (1), (2) or (3) of this section. Rule 44(a) of the Federal Rules of Civil Procedures and Rule 27 of the Federal Rules of Criminal Procedure have provided authentication procedures of this nature for both domestic and foreign public records. The certification procedure here provided extends only to public records, reports and recorded documents, all including data compilations, and does not apply to public documents generally. Hence documents provable when presented in original form under subsection (1), (2) or (3) of this section may not be provable by certified copy under subsection (4) of this section.

ORS 43.340 and 43.350 are examples of Oregon law in accord with the principles set forth in subsection (4) of this section.

Subsection (4). In subsection (4) of this section, the words "with any law or rule prescribed by the Supreme Court" were substituted for the federal phrase "with any Act of Congress or rule prescribed by the Supreme Court pursuant to statutory authority" in Federal Rules of Evidence 902(4).

Subsection (5). Dispensing with preliminary proof of the genuineness of purportedly official publications, most commonly encountered in connection with statutes, court reports, rules and regulations, has been greatly enlarged by statutes and decisions. 5 Wigmore, *Evidence,* § 1684 (Chadbourn rev 1974). Subsection (5) of this section, it will be noted, does not confer admissibility upon all official publications; it merely provides a means whereby their authenticity may be taken as established for purposes of admissibility.

Numerous existing Oregon statutes have the same basic effect except that this section requires only that the books or publications purport to be printed by public authority. See subsections (1), (2), (4) and (5) of ORS 43.330 and 43.310. Thus, any reputable private printer's version should be accepted since typically it is such versions upon which the bench and bar rely.

Subsection (6). The likelihood of forgery of newspapers or periodicals is slight indeed. Hence no danger is apparent in receiving them pursuant to (6) of this section. Establishing the authenticity of the publication may, of course, still leave open questions of authority and responsibility for items therein contained. See 7 Wigmore, *Evidence,* § 2150 (3d ed 1940). Cf. 39 USC § 4005(b) (public advertisement prima facie evidence of agency of person names, in postal fraud order proceedings) and Canadian Uniform Evidence Act, Draft of 1936 (printed copy of newspaper prima facie evidence that notices or advertisements were authorized). This section is consistent with current Oregon law.

Subsection (7). Several factors justify dispensing with preliminary proof of genuineness of commercial and mercantile labels and the like. The risk of forgery is minimal. Trademark infringement involves serious penalties. Great efforts are devoted to introducing the public to buy in reliance on brand names and substantial protection is given them. Hence the fairness of this treatment finds recognition in the cases. *Curtiss Candy Co. v. Johnson,* 163 Miss 426, 141 So 762 (1932) (Baby Ruth candy bar); *Doyle v. Continental Baking Co.,* 262 Mass 516, 160 NE 325 (1928) (loaf of bread); *Weiner v. Mager & Throne, Inc.,* 167 Misc 338, 3 NY S2d 981 (1938) (same). And see W Va Code 1966, §§ 3 to 5 (trademark on bottle prima facie evidence of ownership). Contra, *Keegan v. Green Giant Co.,* 150 Me 283, 110 A 2d 599 (1954); *Murphy v. Campbell Soup Co.,* 62 F2d 564 (1st Cir 1933). Cattle brands have received similar acceptance in the western states. Rev Code Mont 1947, § 46-606; *State v. Wolfley,* 75 Kan 406, 89 P 1046 (1908); Annot., 11 LRA (NS) 87. Inscriptions on trains and vehicles are held to be prima facie evidence of ownership or control. *Pittsburgh, Ft. W. & C Ry. v. Callaghan,* 157 Ill 406, 41 NE 909; 9 Wigmore, *Evidence,* § 2510a (3d ed 1940). See also 19 USC § 1615(2) declaring that marks, labels, brands or stamps indicating foreign origins are prima facie evidence of foreign origin of merchandise.

This section is consistent with current Oregon law. See ORS 604.180 which provides that the brand of any animal is prima facie evidence that the animal belongs to the owner of the brand.

Subsection (8). In virtually every state, acknowledge title documents are receivable in evidence without further proof.

Statutes are collected in 5 Wigmore, *Evidence,* § 1676 (Chadbourn rev 1974). If this authentication suffices for documents of the importance of those affecting titles, logic scarcely permits denying this method when other kinds of documents are involved. Instances of broadly inclusive statutes are *California Evidence Code,* § 1451 and NY CPLR 4538, McKinney's Consol. Laws 1963.

> "The theory behind this form of authentication is simple. If a person comes before a notary and is known to the notary so that the notary knows that the name on the document is the same as the name of the person before him and additionally, the person before him says that he did in fact execute the document, it can reasonably be assumed that the document was executed by such person. The notary or other authorized officer preserves this chain of events in the certificate of acknowledge for use at a later time. His seal attached to the certificate attests that the certificate is itself-authentic." Weinstein *Evidence,* § 902(8)701] at 902-31 (M. Bender 1976). This section is consistent with current Oregon law. See ORS 93.380.

Subsection (9). Under subsection (9) of this section, commercial paper and related documents, to the extent provided by ORS chapters 71 to 83, should be admitted in the same way as other self-authenticating documents if on their face they appear to be what the proponent claims them to be.

Four specific provisions of the Oregon Uniform Commercial Code are relevant to the discussion of the method of authentication outlined in subsection (9). ORS 71.1020 makes certain documents required by an existing contract "prima facie" evidence of their own authenticity. ORS 73.3070 and 78.1050 presume the genuineness of signatures on negotiable instruments. ORS 73.5100 provides that a formal certificate of protest, a stamp by the drawee that the payment was refused, or bank records are all admissible in evidence and create a presumption of dishonor.

The words "ORS chapters 71 to 83" were substituted for the federal phrase "general commercial law" in Federal Rules of Evidence 902(9).

Subsection (10). Subsection (10) of this section allows any mode of self-authentication specifically provided for by law in addition to the procedures specified in this section, and is consistent with existing Oregon law.

The words "by law" were substituted for the federal phrase "by Act of Congress" in Federal Rules of Evidence 902(10).

Subsection (11). Subsection (11) of this section was added to clarify the procedures for authentication of Indian tribal documents. It was the intent of the legislation that Indian tribal documents be treated in the same manner as documents from any other political subdivision in the United States but should be specifically set forth in a separate subsection. See subsections (1) and (2) of this section.

This section provides methods for authenticating Indian tribal documents which were not provided for under existing law. In *State v. Gowdy,* 1 Or App 424, 462 P2d 461 (1969), tribal regulations were admitted into evidence after certification under the official seal of the Yakima Indian agency through the U.S. Department of the Interior. That procedure is similar to the one set forth in paragraph (b) of subsection (11) of this section.

TEXT

RULE 902
Self-Authentication

Rule 902 provides that certain types of evidence are self-authenticating. Whereas Rule 901 in most cases requires that a witness be called to make a prima facie showing of authenticity, Rule 902 dispenses with the need for an authenticating witness for the categories of evidence listed. In general, Rule 902 expands the types of evidence deemed to be self-authenticating beyond those recognized by prior law.

Like Rule 901, Rule 902 addresses only whether or not an exhibit is sufficiently authenticated to be admissible. At trial, the opponent may introduce evidence contesting authenticity, and the trier of fact makes the ultimate determination of authenticity. Moreover, even though an exhibit is adequately self-authenticated, it is still subject to exclusion under other rules of evidence.

RULE 902(1)
Domestic Public Documents Under Seal

Rule 902(1) provides that public documents bearing a signature purporting to be an attestation or execution accompanied by the seal of one of the listed governmental entities are self-authenticating. Presumably only authorized persons will have access to an official seal. Also, misuse of a governmental seal is subject to criminal penalties in most jurisdictions.

Execution means that the document was apparently written or adopted by the signer, and *attestation* means that the signer examined it after the fact and found it to be a genuine public document or record. 5 C. Mueller & L. Kirkpatrick, FEDERAL EVIDENCE (2d ed 1994) § 539 at 156. Execution may also require some form of delivery. See ORS 42.020: "The execution of a writing is the subscribing and delivering it, with or without affixing a seal." A facsimile signature and facsimile seal should be sufficient to satisfy the requirements of this rule when they were intended to have the same effect as an original, and in the case of a seal was also sufficiently elaborate to provide a safeguard against falsification. There is no requirement in the rule that the signature or seal themselves be authenticated, such as by the sealed certificate of another officer.

The rule is very broad, reaching records of the legislative, judicial, and administrative branches of federal, state, and territorial governments, as well as political subdivisions, departments, officers, or agencies thereof, including counties and municipalities. A certification of a government agency under seal qualifies under this rule. See *State v. Wrisley*, 138 Or App 344, 350, 909 P2d 877 (1995) (ATF certification that search of its records found no registration of firearm qualifies as self-authenticating document).

This rule applies only to original public documents. For self-authentication of copies of public documents, see Rule 902(4). For documents acknowledged by a notary public, see Rule 902(8). For proof of absence of public records, see Rule 803(10).

RULE 902(2)
Domestic Public Documents Not Under Seal

Rule 902(2) provides for self-authentication of documents purporting to bear the signature, in an official capacity, of an officer or employee of a designated governmental entity who has no seal, provided that another officer with official duties in that jurisdiction and with a seal certifies under seal that the signer has official capacity and that the signature is genuine. The requirement that the signature of an officer without a seal be certified by an officer with a seal differs from the law in some other jurisdictions that presumes the genuineness of purported official signatures even in the absence of a seal. See, e.g., California Evidence Code section 1453. It also modifies prior Oregon law, which accepted an official signature without a seal as sufficient authentication in some circumstances. See, e.g., former ORS 43.330 (repealed 1981).

The rule does not require that the certifying officer be a superior officer or even that the officer be employed by the same governmental entity. Nor does the rule require that the certifying officer state that the signature was made in an official capacity or with lawful authority, only that the signer "has the official capacity."

The necessary contents of the certificate have been described is follows:

> [T]he certificate should (a) indicate in some way the official position of its maker and the name and location of his office or authority, (b) state that the

signature on the document is genuine, or that the certifier knows the signature of the apparent signer and believes the signature to be genuine, and (c) state the signer of the document has the authority to execute documents of the sort in question (if the signature is one of execution) or that the signer is in a position by virtue of his duties to know whether such documents are genuine (if the signature is one of attestation). No particular form of words is required, so long as the certifier supplies information supporting appropriate conclusions on these points. 5 C. Mueller & L. Kirkpatrick, FEDERAL EVIDENCE §540 at 161–162 (2d ed 1994).

This rule applies only to original public documents. For self-authentication of copies of public documents, see Rule 902(4). For documents acknowledged by a notary public, see Rule 902(8). For proof of absence of public records, see Rule 803(10).

RULE 902(3)
Foreign Public Documents

A foreign public document may be self-authenticating provided the following two requirements are satisfied. First, the document must purport to be executed or attested to in an official capacity by a person authorized by the laws of the foreign country to make the execution or attestation. Second, the document must be accompanied by a final certification. The final certification may be as to the genuineness of the signature and official position of the executing or attesting person, or, if the person making the final certification does not have such knowledge, as is likely, the final certification may be as to the genuineness of the signature and official position of any foreign official "whose certificate of genuineness of signature and official position relates to the execution or attestation or is in a chain of certificates of genuineness of signature and official position relating to the execution or attestation." A final certification may be made by a member of the diplomatic or consular staff of the United States or of the foreign country in question, provided the official is "assigned or credited to the United States." The court may dispense with the requirement of final certification upon a showing of good cause, provided reasonable opportunity has been given to all parties to investigate the authenticity and accuracy of the documents. No seal is required on the final certificate or on any intermediate certificates. A seal would add some assurance of genuineness; thus, a sealed certificate should be obtained if possible. For further discussion of this rule see 5 C. Mueller & L. Kirkpatrick, FEDERAL EVIDENCE (2d ed 1994) § 541; NOTE, *A Blow to International Judicial Assistance,* 41 Cath L Rev 545 (1992); Comment, *Five Years After Aerospatiale: Rethinking Discovery Abroad in Civil and Commercial Litigation Under The Hague Evidence Convention and the Federal Rules of Civil Procedure,* 13 U Pa J Int'l Bus L 425 (1992).

In *United States v. Howard-Arias,* 679 F2d 363 (4th Cir), cert denied 459 US 874 (1982), the court affirmed the admission of a certificate from a Colombian Admiral that the defendant's fishing trawler was not registered in Colombia after 1979 as the defendant had claimed. The document was authenticated by a chain of Colombian officials, culminating in the Colombian Consular Chief, whose signature was in turn attested to by a United States Consular Official in Colombia. The court held that the statement was admissible even though it did not include an express statement by the Admiral that he was the official authorized to make such certifications.

RULE 902(4)
Certified Copies of Public Records

Rule 902(4) provides for self-authentication of copies of official records or reports, or documents recorded or filed pursuant to law in a public office. The only requirement for self-authentication is that the custodian or other authorized person certify the copy as correct by a certificate complying with subsections (1), (2) or (3) of Rule 902 or otherwise complying with any law or rule prescribed by the supreme court. The certificate should indicate the official position of its maker, that the maker has compared the copy with the original document on file in the public office and that the copy is true and correct.

The requirement that the certificate comply with subsections (1), (2) or (3) of Rule 902 means that in the case of domestic public documents the certificate must contain a seal or be accompanied by a certificate that contains a seal, unless another mode of certification is allowed by law outside the evidence code. This requirement is more stringent than prior Oregon law. Under former ORS 43.340 (repealed 1981) and former ORS 43.350 (repealed 1981), copies of various public records were self-authenticating by the certificate of the official custodian even in the absence of a seal. Under new Rule 902(4), if the officer certifying a domestic public document does not have a seal, an additional certificate will now have to be obtained from an officer with a seal certifying that the signer of the original certificate "has the official capacity and that the signature is genuine." See Rule 902(2).

The rule requires a discernible seal. In *State v. Mueller,* 96 Or App 185, 188, 772 P2d 433 (1989), the court stated:

> [I]t is clear that there must be some physical manifestation of a "seal" for self-authentication of documents under OEC 902(1). It follows that the impression, imprint or likeness must be sufficiently discernible that the factfinder can say that it purports to be a seal. It is not sufficient that the person signing the certification states that the signature is under seal.

An original signature on the certification is clearly preferable. Under former law, however, a photocopied authentication certificate and signature were held sufficient to authenticate a suspension order of the Department of Motor Vehicles. *State v. Barckley,* 54 Or App 351, 634 P2d 1373 (1981). The court stated: "Our concern is whether the *process* that certification contemplates has actually occurred. If the nature of the certified document suggests that the process *has* occurred, we should not erect artificial barriers to its admission as reliable evidence." 54 Or App at 356 (citation omitted).

The limitation of this subsection to "official" records or reports or lawfully recorded or filed documents is presumably intended to preclude introduction of tentative or preliminary drafts, writings made outside the scope of authority, internal memoranda, or other records or reports that a court finds to be unofficial.

The fact that a certified copy of a public record is self-authenticating under this rule does not establish its admissibility. It must comply with other evidentiary requirements, including the hearsay rule (Rule 802) if the document is offered for the truth of the matter asserted. But see Rule 803(8) (creating hearsay exception for public records and reports). See also *Robbins v. Whelan,* 653 F2d 47 (1st Cir 1980), cert denied 454 US 423 (1981) (error to exclude copy of government report entitled "Performance Data for New 1971 Passenger Cars and Motorcycles"; report was self-authenticating under FRE 902(4) and admissible as a hearsay exception under FRE 803(8)).

Rule 902(4) should be considered in conjunction with Rule 1005, which provides that a copy of an official record or a document authorized to be recorded or filed and actually recorded or filed, and certified as correct in accordance with Rule 902, satisfies the original writing rule (Rule 1002).

For examples of statutes authorizing admission of certified copies of public records or documents filed with a public office, see ORS 56.050(1) (Corporation Division records); ORS 93.650 (conveyances); and ORS 696.430 (Real Estate Commissioner records).

RULE 902(5)
Official Publications

Rule 902(5) provides that books, pamphlets, and other publications purporting to be issued by public authority are self-authenticating. This rule does not establish their admissibility. If a publication is offered to prove the truth of its contents, it will be hearsay (see Rule 801(3)), but will be admissible in some circumstances under an exception to the hearsay rule. See Rules 803 and 804. See also Rule 801(4).

The Commentary expresses legislative intent that law books by private publishers be included within this exception, perhaps because such books are often published pursuant to contract or agreement with courts or other public authority. Other books by private publishers will generally have to be authenticated under Rule 901. In some cases, books may be authenticated by judicial notice under Rule 201.

Authentication concerns arise only if the book or other publication is being offered into evidence. A court is not bound by rules of evidence when informing itself of the law. A court may also review books or other publications in obtaining factual information necessary to resolve preliminary questions concerning the admissibility of evidence without regard to authentication requirements. In making such determinations the court is not bound by the rules of evidence. See Rule 104(1).

RULE 902(6)
Newspapers and Periodicals

Rule 902(6) provides for self-authentication of printed materials purporting to be newspapers or periodicals. The rule does not require that the publication be generally known and it appears to include highly specialized or obscure newspapers and periodicals.

The hearsay rule (Rule 802) will preclude the introduction of newspapers or periodicals to prove the truth of their contents unless they qualify under an exception to the hearsay rule (see Rules 803 and 804) or are defined as not hearsay by Rule 801(4).

As the Commentary notes, authentication of a newspaper or periodical under this rule still leaves open "questions of authority and responsibility for items therein contained."

RULE 902(7)
Trade Inscriptions and the Like

Rule 902(7) provides that inscriptions, signs, tags, or labels purporting to have been affixed in the course of business and indicating ownership, control, or origin are self-authenticating. The criminal and civil penalties for unauthorized use of such inscriptions and labels are deemed to provide sufficient assurance of authenticity.

This rule may authorize self-authentication of a wide range of printed material by businesses to which trademarks or trade names are affixed, such as advertisements, catalogues, price lists, instructions for assembly and use, warranties, and so forth. See 5 C. Mueller & L. Kirkpatrick, FEDERAL EVIDENCE (2d ed 1994) § 545 at 194–5.

RULE 902(8)
Acknowledged Documents

Rule 902(8) provides for self-authentication of documents acknowledged before a notary public or similar official. The rule does not state what the certification must contain. According to Judge Weinstein:

> The certificate should state in some form that the person executing or acknowledging the execution of the particular document in question has (1) come before a public official authorized to take an acknowledgment or a notary public, (2) that his identity was known to the said official or notary, and (3) that he swore under oath to the notary that he executed the document of his own free will. (5 J. Weinstein and M. Berger, WEINSTEIN'S *Evidence* paragraph 902(8)[01] at 902–35 (1988) (footnote omitted))

If the document is in the name of a partnership or corporation, the person should indicate that the document has been acknowledged on behalf of the partnership or corporation.

This rule is not limited to acknowledgments taken within the state of Oregon. Documents acknowledged before a notary public in any other state should also be admissible. But see *Credit Bureau Inc. v. Shafer,* 275 Or 87, 549 P2d 1129 (1976) (reaching a contrary result under prior law). See generally ORS 194.505–.595 (Uniform Law on Notarial Acts).

RULE 902(9)
Commercial Paper and Related Documents

Rule 902(9) provides for self-authentication of commercial paper, signatures thereon, and documents relating thereto to the extent provided by ORS Chapters 71–83. Several provisions of the Uniform Commercial Code appear to be particularly relevant. ORS 71.2020 provides:

> A document in due form purporting to be a bill of lading, policy or certificate of insurance, official weigher's or inspector's certificate consular invoice, or any other document authorized or required by the contract to be issued by a third party shall be *prima facie* evidence of its own authenticity and genuineness and of the facts stated in the document by the third party.

ORS 78.1050(2) provides:

> In any action on a security: ... (b) when the effectiveness of a signature is put in issue the burden of establishing it is on the party claiming under the signature but the signature is presumed to be genuine or authorized.

In *United States v. Carriger,* 592 F2d 312 (6th Cir 1979), the court reversed a conviction for tax evasion, holding that the trial court erred in excluding promissory notes offered by the defendant. The court cited FRE 902(9) and noted that "[u]nder Uniform Commercial Code § 3-307 mere production of a note is prima facie evidence of its validity and of the holder's right to recover on it." Id. at 316. In *United States v. Little,* 567 F2d 346, 349 n 1 (8th Cir 1977), cert denied 435 US 969 (1978), the court held that corporate checks were admissible under 902(9) as self-authenticating commercial paper.

RULE 902(10)
Presumptions Under Law

Rule 902(10) provides that evidence may be made self-authenticating by law creating a presumption of authenticity or providing that a particular matter is prima facie genuine or authentic. See, e.g., ORS 41.930 (presumption of truth of facts stated in affidavit of custodian of hospital records to self-authenticate such records).

It is unclear whether this rule includes presumptions created by federal law as well as state law. See, e.g., 26 USC § 6064 (signature on tax return prima facie genuine); 15 USC § 77f(a) (signature on SEC registration presumed genuine).

RULE 902(11)
Document Bearing Seal of Tribal Government

Rule 902(11) provides for self-authentication of a document bearing the seal of a tribal government. This subsection was added by the Advisory Committee which assisted in drafting the code, and is not included in FRE 902. It is modeled after Rule 902(1) and (2).

RULE 902(12)
State Police Data

Rule 902(12) provides for self-authentication of certain documents containing data prepared or recorded by the Oregon State Police, provided the document is produced by data retrieval from the Law Enforcement Data System (LEDS) or other computer system maintained and operated by the Oregon State Police. The person retrieving the data must attest (1) that it was retrieved directly from the system and (2) that the document accurately reflects the data retrieved.

The data must be prepared or reported pursuant to ORS 813.160 (1)(b)(C) or (E) or pursuant to ORS 475.235(3). ORS 813.160 (1)(b)(C) provides for testing and certifying the accuracy of equipment used by police officers for chemical analyses of a person's breath. ORS 813.160(1)(b)(E) provides for issuance of permits to police officers who have completed prescribed training to use the testing equipment. ORS 475.235(3) provides that in certain prosecutions relating to controlled substances "a certified copy of the analytical report signed by the director of the state police crime detection laboratory or the criminalist conducting the analysis shall be accepted as prima facie evidence of the results of the analytical findings."

RULE 903.   ORS 40.515. SUBSCRIBING WITNESS' TESTIMONY UNNECESSARY

The testimony of a subscribing witness is not necessary to authenticate a writing unless required by the laws of the jurisdiction whose laws govern the validity of the writing.

LEGISLATIVE COMMENTARY

This section is identical to Rule 903 of the Federal Rules of Evidence.

This section is consistent with existing Oregon law even though ORS 113.005, under most circumstances, requires the affidavit or testimony of witnesses attesting to a will. However, this section only eliminates the need for the subscribing witness where the testimony is *not* required "by the laws of the jurisdiction whose laws govern the validity of the writing."

The common law required that attesting witnesses be produced or accounted for. Once the subscribing or attesting witness had been produced or an absence satisfactorily explained, authenticity could be demonstrated in the usual manners, including the testimony of others who saw the document executed or proof of the genuineness of the signature and facts surrounding the execution or circumstantial evidence. Weinstein *Evidence,* § 903[01] at 903-4 (M. Bender 1976). Today the requirement has generally been abolished except with respect to documents which must be attested to be valid, e.g. wills in some states. McCormick, *Evidence,* § 220 (2d ed 1972). Uniform Rule 71; *California Evidence Code,* § 1411; *Kansas Code of Civil Procedure,* § 60-468.

TEXT

Testimony of Subscribing Witness Unnecessary

Rule 903 provides that the testimony of a subscribing witness is not necessary to authenticate a writing, unless required by the laws of the jurisdiction whose laws govern the validity of the writing. ORS 42.030 defines a subscribing witness as follows: "A subscribing witness is one who sees a writing executed or hears it acknowledged, and at the request of the party thereupon signs his name as a witness."

Rule 903 is consistent with ORS 42.040, which provides: "Any attested writing other than a will may be proved in the same manner as though it had not been attested." For wills, ORS 113.055 generally requires either an affidavit or testimony of a subscribing witness.

If the law of a jurisdiction other than Oregon controls, testimony of a subscribing witness could be required by either statute or case law of that jurisdiction. In cases where the applicable law does not require the testimony of a subscribing witness, the writing can be authenticated under Rule 901 or 902.

ARTICLE X

CONTENTS OF WRITINGS, RECORDINGS, AND PHOTOGRAPHS

RULE 1001.   ORS 40.550. DEFINITIONS

As used in Rules 1001 to 1008 (ORS 40.550 to 40.585), unless the context requires otherwise:

(1) **[Duplicate.] "Duplicate" means a counterpart produced by the same impression as the original, or from the same matrix, or by means of photography, including enlargements and miniatures, by mechanical or electronic re-recording, by chemical reproduction, by optical imaging, or by other equivalent techniques that accurately reproduce the original, including reproduction by facsimile machines if the reproduction is identified as a facsimile and printed on nonthermal paper.**

(2) **[Original.] "Original" of a writing or recording is the writing or recording itself or any counterpart intended to have the same effect by a person executing or issuing it. An "original" of a photograph includes the negative or any print therefrom. If data are stored in a computer or similar device, any printout or other output readable by sight, shown to reflect the data accurately, is an "original."**

(3) **[Photographs.] "Photographs" includes still photographs, X-ray films, video tapes and motion pictures.**

(4) [Writings and recordings.] "Writings" and "recordings" mean letters, words or numbers, or their equivalent, set down by handwriting, typewriting, printing, photostating, photographing, magnetic impulse, optical imaging, mechanical or electronic recording or other form of data compilation.

LEGISLATIVE COMMENTARY

This section is based on Rule 1001 of the Federal Rules of Evidence and works a considerable change in existing Oregon law. There are no statutes defining terms used in the application of the "best evidence rule." In the early case of *Heneky v. Smith*, 10 Or 349 (1882), the Oregon Supreme Court limited the application of the "best evidence rule" to "writing." In the almost 100 years since that decision, there have been no cases specifically dealing with the issue of whether recordings or photographs are "writings" for the purpose of the rule. Insofar as they are not, this section broadens Oregon law to include computer printouts, X-rays and motion pictures as "writings" and "originals."

Subsection (1) defines "duplicates" as counterparts produced by the same impression as the original; from the same matrix; by means of photography; by mechanical or electronic re-recording; by chemical reproductions or by other equivalent techniques which accurately reproduce the original. The definition excludes copies subsequently produced manually, whether handwritten or typed, and includes only copies produced by methods possessing an accuracy which virtually eliminates the possibility of error.

Under subsection (1), a "duplicate" means any counterpart produced by any means which accurately reproduce the original. In Oregon, "duplicate" signifies more than a mere copy; the instrument must be identical verbally and in legal import. *Nicholas v. Title & Trust Co.*, 76 Or 226, 154 P 391 (1916). Under subsection (2) of this section, a current Oregon "duplicate" would become an "original."

Subsection (2). An "original" is the writing or recording itself or any counterpart intended to have the same effect by a person executing or issuing it. An "original" of a photograph includes the negative or any print therefrom. If data are stored in a computer, any printout or other output readable by sight, shown to reflect the data accurately, is an "original." Similarly, a carbon copy of a contract executed in duplicate becomes an original, as does a sales ticket carbon copy given to a customer.

Under subsection (2), an "original" is the original or any counterparts intended to the have same effect such as executed copies, computer printouts and copies of sales tickets given to customers. In *First National Bank v. Jamison*, 63 Or 594, 129 P 433 (1913) and *Hall v. Pierce*, 210 Or 98, 307 P2d 998 (1956), carbon copies of documents were held to be "originals."

Subsection (3). "Photographs" include all forms of chemically or magnetically produced pictorial representations.

Subsection (4). Traditionally, the "best evidence rule" was one essentially related to writings. Modern techniques have expanded methods of storing data, yet the essential form which the information ultimately assumes for usable purposes is words and figures. Therefore, the considerations underlying the rule dictate its expansion to include computers, photographic systems and other modern developments.

TEXT

Definitions

Rule 1001 defines the terms used in Article X.

Duplicates

A "duplicate" is defined expansively to include photocopies, carbon copies, rerecordings of tapes or videotapes, and all other modern copying techniques that "accurately reproduce the original." Transcriptions of tape recordings and subsequent handmade copies of writings are not included in the definition.

Original

An "original" of a writing or recording is the writing or recording in issue or any counterpart intended to have the same effect by a person executing or issuing it. A carbon copy or even a photocopy may be an original if that is the intent of the executing party or if that is the copy in issue in the litigation. See *Snyder v. Rhoads*, 47 Or App 545, 552, 615 P2d 1058, 1062 (1980) (photocopy is "original" because it is document defendant claims he saw and relied upon).

If data are stored in a computer or similar device, any printout from the device that accurately reflects the data qualifies as an original. See *State v. Menchaca*, 94 Or App 407, 766 P2d 395 (1988) (in a case where the test results of an Intoxilyzer were printed simultaneously on two onion skin sheets of paper and one cardboard sheet, the court suggested that any of the three copies may qualify as an original).

There may be more than one "original" if multiple copies, e.g., counterparts of a contract, are each intended to have the effect of originals by the executing party. The determination of which writing is the original will depend upon what issue is being proven and upon the applicable substantive law. See 2 McCormick, *Evidence* (4th ed 1992) § 235 at 71; C. Mueller & L. Kirkpatrick, MODERN EVIDENCE (1995) § 10.3. The Advisory Committee's Note to FRE 1001 states: "[W]hat is an original for some purposes may be a duplicate for others. Thus a bank's microfilm record of checks cleared is the original as a record. However, a print offered as a copy of a check whose contents are in controversy is a duplicate."

Because Rule 1002 expands the common law "original writing" rule to include "photographs" and "recordings," these terms are also defined. The definition of "photographs" includes X-rays, videotapes, and motion pictures. Very few photographs offered into evidence will be subject to the requirements of Rule 1002, because normally photographs are not offered to prove their contents, but merely to illustrate and explain the testimony of a witness.

Photographs

Examples of photographs to which Article X may be applicable because they are being offered to prove their contents rather than merely illustrate testimony include: photographs from automatic cameras, such as bank surveillance or check cashing cameras; X-rays; or photographs in obscenity prosecutions. See *United States v. Levine,* 546 F2d 658 (5th Cir 1977) (original motion picture required in obscenity prosecution). Even in those limited circumstances where Rule 1002 is applicable to photographs and the original must be produced, compliance should present little difficulty, because Rule 1001(2) defines the negative of a photograph and any print therefrom as an original. The primary effect of the rule, when applicable, is to bar a testimonial description in lieu of producing the photograph.

Writings; Recordings

Rule 1001(4) defines *writings* and *recordings.* The definition is broad, including letters, words, numbers or their equivalent set down by virtually all known means of writing, recording, or data compilation. It is uncertain to what extent this rule reaches material objects, containing writing or numbering, such as a police badge, license plate, tombstone, flag, or an engagement ring. Compare *United States v. Duffy,* 454 F2d 809 (5th Cir 1972) (best evidence doctrine does not bar testimony regarding laundry mark "DUF" on shirt) with *Davenport v. Ourisman-Mandell Chevrolet, Inc.,* 195 A2d 743 (DC 1963) (best evidence doctrine bars testimony regarding mileage shown on automobile service sticker; sticker should have been produced).

McCormick states:

> In the final analysis, it is perhaps impossible to improve upon Wigmore's suggestion, followed by a number of courts, that the judge shall have discretion to apply the [original writing] rule to inscribed chattels or not in light of such factors as the need for precise information as to the exact inscription, the ease or difficulty of production, and the simplicity or complexity of the inscription. 2 McCormick, *Evidence* § 234 at 69 (4th ed 1992) (footnotes omitted).

A court will be more inclined to admit testimony regarding an inscribed chattel in cases where the precise terms of the inscription are not in issue, are so simple and clear that testimony regarding them is likely to be accurate, where the inscription is of minor importance in the case, or where production of the inscribed chattel is difficult or infeasible. Nonetheless, it would be wise for parties seeking to offer evidence regarding an inscribed chattel to produce the chattel whenever possible, or at least to produce a photograph of it. A photograph could qualify as a "duplicate" under Rule 1001(1). If the original of the inscribed chattel is shown to be unavailable, or if it pertains only to a collateral matter, any secondary evidence of the inscription, including testimony, may be received. See Rule 1004.

On the applicability of the Best Evidence Doctrine to musical scores, see NOTE, La[w]—*A Note to Follow So: Have We Forgotten the Federal Rules of Evidence in Music Plagiarism Cases?*, 65 S Cal L Rev 1583 (1992).

RULE 1002.　ORS 40.555. REQUIREMENT OF ORIGINAL

To prove the content of a writing, recording or photograph, the original writing, recording or photograph is required, except as otherwise provided in Rules 1001 to 1008 (ORS 40.550 to 40.585) or other law.

LEGISLATIVE COMMENTARY

This section is based on Rule 1002 of the Federal Rules of Evidence. The words "sections 71 to 78 of this Act or other law" have replaced the federal phrase "these rules or by Act of Congress." The statement of the rules in this section is to require production of the original of a document to prove its contents, expanded to include writings, recordings and photographs, as defined in section 71 (Rule 1001) of this Act.

Application of this section requires a resolution of the question whether contents are sought to be proved. If the contents of a document are not sought to be proved, this section does not apply. Nor does this section apply to testimony that books or records have been examined and found not to contain any reference to a designated matter. (*State v. Nano*, 273 Or 366, 543 P2d 660 (1975). Under the holding of the case, such testimony is not proof of the contents or terms of a document, and, therefore, the "best evidence rule" has no application.)

However, situations will arise in which contents are sought to be proved. Copyright, defamation and invasion of privacy by photograph fall in this category. Contents must be proved in situations in which a picture is offered as having independent probative value; an automatic photograph of a bank robber, for example.

The most commonly encountered example of the latter situation is the X-ray. Section 59 (Rule 703) of this Act allows an expert to give an opinion based on matters not in evidence and this section must be read as being limited accordingly in its application. Hospital records which may be admitted as business records under subsection (6) of section 64 (Rule 803) of this Act commonly contain reports interpreting X-rays by the staff radiologist, who qualifies as an expert, and these reports need not be excluded from the records under this section.

Except as expanded to include recordings and photographs, the statement of the "best evidence rule" in this section is the same as the current rule in Oregon. ORS 41.610. If the terms or contents of a writing are directly in issue, the original document must be produced and secondary evidence of the contents is excluded unless sufficient reason is given for its nonproduction. ORS 41.610 and 41.640. The "best evidence rule" is not applicable if execution, delivery or existence of a document is at issue. Nor does it apply to issues involving the appearance or condition of physical objects. *Heneky v. Smith,* 10 Or 349 (1882).

The rule only applies when the actual terms or conditions of the document are in issue. *Dockery v. Gardner,* 141 Or 64, 15 P2d 481 (1932); *Lumbermans Mutual Casualty Company v. Jamieson,* 251 Or 608, 447 P2d 384 (1968).

TEXT

Requirement of Original

Rule 1002 sets forth what is commonly referred to as the "original document rule" or, less accurately, as the "best evidence rule." It requires that to prove the content of a writing, recording, or photograph the original must be offered, except as otherwise provided by these rules or other law. Rule 1002 extends prior Oregon law by making this requirement applicable to recordings and photographs as well as writings.

When Rule 1002 is read with its exceptions, it can be seen that the exceptions largely swallow the rule. Rule 1003 allows duplicates in lieu of the original in most circumstances. Rule 1004 allows testimony or other types of evidence to prove the contents when the original is shown to be unavailable or when it relates only to a collateral matter. Rule 1005 allows the use of a certified copy to prove a public record or a document filed or recorded pursuant to law. Rule 1006 allows the use of a chart, summary, or calculation to prove the contents of voluminous writings, recordings, or photographs. Rule 1007 dispenses with the requirement of an original when the opponent has admitted in testimony or writing the contents of the writing, recording or photograph. Various statutes also provide that a duplicate may be received in lieu of an original. See, eg., ORS 192.050.

The primary effect of Rule 1002, when it does apply, is to bar the use of oral testimony to prove the contents of a writing, recording, or photograph. If the contents are in issue, proof must be made by producing the original or, as is generally allowed under Rule 1003, a duplicate.

Offered for Proof of Content

The most difficult task arising under Rule 1002 is determining whether evidence of a writing, recording or photograph is being offered to prove its contents or for some other purpose. As the Advisory Committee's Note to FRE 1002 states:

> Application of the rule requires a resolution of the question whether contents are sought to be proved. Thus an event may be proved by nondocumentary evidence, even though a written record of it was made. If, however, the event is sought to be proved by the written record, the rule applies. For example, payment may be proved without producing the written receipt which was given. Earnings may be proved without producing books of account in which they are entered. *McCormick* § 198; 4 *Wigmore* § 1245. Nor does the

rule apply to testimony that books or records have been examined and found not to contain any reference to a designated matter.

Proof by Other Evidence Where Writing or Recording Exists

Even though a writing, recording or photograph exists that could be used to prove a particular fact, a party is not barred by the best evidence doctrine from using alternative forms of proof.

In *State v. Brungard*, 101 Or App 67, 71, 789 P2d 683, modified 102 Or App 509, 794 P2d 1257 (1990), rev denied 311 Or 427, 812 P2d 827 (1991), the court held that the best evidence rule was not violated by testimony that defendant had been previously mentally committed on two occasions. The defendant argued that the commitment orders should have been produced. The court stated that "[t]he orders may be the most efficient way to prove that he was committed, but nothing in the statute precludes other proof."

In *Angus v. Joseph,* 60 Or App 546, 554, 655 P2d 208, 213 (1982), rev denied 294 Or 569, 660 P2d 683, cert denied 464 U S 830, 104 SCt 107, 78 LEd2d 109 (1983), the defendant objected to introduction of a copy of a membership roll of the Nez Perce Indians kept by the Bureau of Indian Affairs on the ground that the membership roll kept by the tribe was the "best evidence" of tribal membership. The court affirmed the admission of the evidence, stating: "[D]efendant's objection ... reflects a common misunderstanding of the best evidence rule, which applies only when the actual terms or conditions of a document are in issue and are attempted to be proved. ... The contents of the tribal membership roll were not an issue here, only membership itself."

The rule does not require the production of a tape recording to prove a conversation merely because the conversation was taped. If it is what the person said that is in issue, and the statements can be proven by a witness who heard the statements made, the rule is inapplicable. *United States v. Gonzales-Benitez,* 537 F2d 1051, 1053–4 (9th Cir), cert denied 429 US 923 (1976); *United States v. Rose,* 590 F2d 232, 237 (7th Cir 1978), cert denied 442 US 929 (1979). See *Meyers v. United States,* 171 F2d 800, 812–4 (DC Cir 1948), cert denied 336 US 912 (1949) (trial testimony on prior occasion may be proven by witness who heard the testimony instead of by trial transcript). If the witness did not hear the conversation personally, and only gained knowledge of the statements from a recording, the rule applies and the recording must be produced.

If a writing is being used as the basis for an expert's opinion, but not to prove the contents of the writing, the rule is inapplicable. In *Jack Jacobs, Inc. v. Allied Systems Co.,* 68 Or App 554, 559, 683 P2d 1011, 1014, rev denied 298 Or 37, 688 P2d 845 (1984), the court held as follows:

> Defendants also assign error to the trial court's denial of their motions to strike the testimony of one of the plaintiff's principles that, in his opinion, sales in 1980 would have reached five to six million dollars. Defendants objected on the ground that the records upon which that opinion was based were not present in the courtroom. ... Although the projection of future sales was partly based on the witness' examination of various records, it does not follow that

his testimony was evidence of the contents of the records on which the projection was based. The testimony went to identifying the basis for his opinion, not to establishing the existence, content or accuracy of the records identified as its basis.

Photographs

Rule 1002 is rarely applicable to photographs, because they are usually offered to illustrate and explain the testimony of other witnesses rather than to prove their contents. *See* discussion under Rule 1001. As the Advisory Committee's Note to FRE 1002 states:

> The assumption should not be made that the rule will come into operation on every occasion when use is made of a photograph in evidence. On the contrary, the rule will seldom apply to ordinary photographs. Cases in which an offer is made of the testimony of a witness as to what he saw in a photograph or motion picture, without producing the same, are most unusual. The usual course is for a witness on the stand to identify the photograph or motion picture as a correct representation of events which he saw or of a scene with which he is familiar. In fact he adopts the picture as his testimony, or, in common parlance, uses the picture to illustrate his testimony. Under these circumstances, no effort is made to prove the contents of the picture, and the rule is inapplicable. Paradis, *The Celluloid Witness,* 37 U. Colo. L. Rev. 235, 249-251 (1965).
>
> On occasion, however, situations arise in which contents are sought to be proved. Copyright, defamation, and invasion of privacy by photograph or motion picture falls in this category. Similarly as to situations in which the picture is offered as having independent probative value, e.g., automatic photograph of bank robber.

X-Rays

A type of photograph likely to be offered to prove its contents is an X-ray. Generally, no witness is able to say that an X-ray accurately depicts what it portrays. Therefore, the rule would require production of the X-ray if offered as independent proof of its contents. If offered merely to show the basis for an expert's opinion, production would not be required. As the Commentary notes, Rule 703 "allows an expert to give an opinion based on matters not in evidence, and this section must be read as being limited accordingly in its application." Hospital records admissible as business records under Rule 803(6) that contain reports interpreting X-rays also are not excluded by this rule.

Photocopy Can Be "Original"

Confusion sometimes arises in determining which writing is the "original" in applying the general requirement of the rule that the original must be produced if it is available. The original is the writing, recording, or photograph whose contents are at issue in the particular case. An "original" for purposes of the rule can be a carbon copy or even a photocopy, if it is the writing at issue. For example, in a fraud case, the fraudulent statements may have been presented to plaintiff by means of a photocopy, which would make the photocopy the "original" writing for purposes of Rule 1002. See textual discussion under Rule 1001. See also *Brown v. J.C. Penney Co.,* 297 Or 695, 688 P2d 811 (1984) (no best evidence violation in admitting computer printout summary of police reports rather than reports themselves; plaintiff was seeking to prove contents of printout, not of reports themselves, and therefore printout was the original writing); *State v. Menchaca,* 94 Or App 407, 766 P2d 395 (1988).

Harmless Error

Courts may be more inclined to find harmless error for violations of Rule 1002 than other rules. In *State v. Fox,* 57 Or App 533, 535, 645 P2d 588, 589, rev denied 293 Or 456, 650 P2d 928 (1982), a case tried prior to the effective date of the Code, the court made the following statement: "[T]he best evidence rule is not to be applied where the party invoking it does not challenge the accuracy of the secondary evidence offered." This statement would no longer appear to be correct, because under Rule 1002 a party should be able to assert a best evidence objection without challenging the accuracy of the secondary evidence. The question of whether erroneously received secondary evidence was accurate or misleading would seem more properly a question to be considered in determining whether a substantial right of the objecting party was affected under Rule 103(a).

Writing Speaks for Itself

An objection under Rule 1002 should not be confused with the objection, "the writing speaks for itself," which is sometimes made when a witness is asked to read a writing after it has been introduced into evidence. If the writing, recording or photograph has already been admitted to prove its contents, the concerns of Rule 1002 are ended. It is a matter within the discretion of the trial court whether and when the writing may be read, the recording played, or the photograph shown to the jury. See Rule 611.

Illustrative Cases

An illustration of the type of evidence excluded by Rule 1002 is provided by *United States v. Winkle,* 587 F2d 705 (5th Cir), cert denied 444 US 827 (1979). The defendant was charged with submitting false Medicare claims. The prosecution called a doctor who testified to what treatment was actually given based on the patient's medical charts. The court of appeals held that the trial judge "incorrectly overruled an objection to the doctor's testifying with respect to the contents of the charts, notwithstanding the Government's failure to produce the charts themselves, which concededly were available," citing Rule 1002. 587 F2d at 712.

Other Authorities

See generally C. Mueller & L. Kirkpatrick, MODERN EVIDENCE §10.5–10.7 (1995); Nance, *The Best Evidence Principle,* 73 Iowa L Rev 227 (1988); Westling, *Articles IX and X: Authentication and the Best Evidence Rule,* 19 Will L Rev 427 (1983).

RULE 1003. ORS 40.560. ADMISSIBILITY OF DUPLICATES

A duplicate is admissible to the same extent as an original unless:
(1) A genuine question is raised as to the authenticity of the original; or
(2) In the circumstances it would be unfair to admit the duplicate in lieu of the original.

LEGISLATIVE COMMENTARY

This section is identical to Rule 1003 of the Federal Rules of Evidence and is consistent with current Oregon law.

When the only concern is with getting the words or other contents before a court with accuracy and precision, then a counterpart is the product of a method which insures accuracy and genuineness. By definition in subsection (1) of section 71 (Rule 1001) of this Act, a "duplicate" possesses this character.

Under this section, duplicates are given the status of originals if: (1) the method of reproduction assures the accuracy of the copy; (2) a genuine question is not raised as to the authenticity of the original; and (3) it would not be unfair to do so. For example, a photocopy would be admissible to prove the contents of the original document while a handwritten or typed copy would not be admissible.

In *State v. White,* 4 Or App 151, 477 P2d 917 (1970), defendant was convicted of knowingly uttering and publishing a forged money order. A photocopy of a stolen money order inventory was admitted to show the forged order used by the defendant was the same. The court held that when there is no good faith dispute about the accuracy of the document presented, the "mystical ideal" of seeking the original will not be pursued.

Under paragraph (d) of subsection (1) of ORS 41.640 (1979 Replacement Part), a duplicate is admissible when the original is a record or other document of which a certified copy, or of which a photostatic, microphotographic or photographic reproduction, is expressly made evidence by statute. Examples of such statutes are ORS 41.720 (1979 Replacement Part), admissibility of reproductions of business records, and ORS 41.730 (1979 Replacement Part), admissibility of telegraphic copies of certified instruments.

TEXT

Admissibility of Duplicates

Rule 1003 significantly qualifies Rule 1002 by providing that a duplicate, as defined in Rule 1001(1), is admissible in lieu of an original in most instances. The only circumstances in which a duplicate is inadequate and the original must be produced are those in which: (1) a genuine question is raised as to the authenticity of the original; or, (2) it would be "unfair" to admit the duplicate in lieu of the original. See *State v. Menchaca,* 94 Or App 407, 766 P2d 395 (1988).

In large measure, Rule 1003 gives "duplicates" the status of originals. It does so because the definition of "duplicate" contained in Rule 1001(1) virtually eliminates the possibility of error in the making of duplicates. In the vast majority of cases, the original is no longer required. See *United States v. Georgalis,* 631 F2d 1199, 1205 (5th Cir 1980). The focus of evidentiary concern is changed from requiring an original instead of a duplicate to requiring either an original or a duplicate instead of oral testimony when the contents of a writing, recording, or photograph are being proven.

Trial courts will have considerable discretion in determining when it would be "unfair" to offer duplicates in lieu of the original. One such circumstance might be where it is impossible to verify the accuracy of the duplicates because the originals have been lost or destroyed in bad faith by the proponent. See Rule 1004(1).

Rule 1003 is qualified by Rule 1005 in the case of official records or other documents that are filed or recorded in a public office pursuant to law. Rule 1005 requires that copies of such documents be certified pursuant to Rule 902, whereas Rule 1003 contains no certification requirement. Rule 1005, as the more specific provision, should control.

See generally ANNOT., *Admissibility of Duplicates Under Rules 1001 (4) and 1003 of the Federal Rules of Evidence,* 72 ALR Fed 732 (1985); C. Mueller & L. Kirkpatrick, MODERN EVIDENCE (1995) § 10.8.

RULE 1003-1. ORS 40.562. ADMISSIBILITY OF REPRODUCTION

(1) **If any business, institution or member of a profession or calling, in the regular course of business or activity, has kept or recorded any memorandum, writing, entry, print, representation or a combination thereof, of any act, transaction, occurrence or event, and in the regular course of business has caused any or all of the same to be recorded, copied or reproduced by any photographic, photostatic, microfilm, micro-card, miniature photographic, optical imaging or other process that accurately reproduces or forms a durable medium for so reproducing the original, the original may be destroyed in the regular course of business unless held in a custodial or fiduciary ca-**

pacity and the principal or true owner has not authorized destruction or unless its preservation is required by law. Such reproduction, when satisfactorily identified, is as admissible in evidence as the original itself in any judicial or administrative proceeding whether the original is in existence or not and an enlargement or facsimile of such reproduction is likewise admissible in evidence if the original reproduction is in existence and available for inspection under direction of the court. The introduction of a reproduced record, enlargement or facsimile does not preclude admission of the original.

(2) If any department or agency of government, in the regular course of business or activity, has kept or recorded any memorandum, writing, entry, print, representation or combination thereof, of any act, transaction, occurrence or event, and in the regular course of business, and in accordance with ORS 192.040 to 192.060 and 192.105, has caused any or all of the same to be recorded, copied or reproduced by any photographic, photostatic, microfilm, micro-card, miniature photographic, optical imaging or other process that accurately reproduces or forms a durable medium for so reproducing the original, the original may be destroyed in the regular course of business unless held in a custodial or fiduciary capacity and the principal or true owner has not authorized destruction or unless its preservation is required by law. Such reproduction, when satisfactorily identified, is as admissible in evidence as the original itself in any judicial or administrative proceeding whether the original is in existence or not and an enlargement or facsimile of such reproduction is likewise admissible in evidence if the original reproduction is in existence and available for inspection under direction of the court. The introduction of a reproduced record, enlargement or facsimile does not preclude admission of the original.

LEGISLATIVE COMMENTARY

[There is no Legislative Commentary for this Rule. It was enacted by the 1995 Legislature and was not part of the original Evidence Code.]

TEXT

Admissibility of Reproductions

Rule 1003-1 was enacted to allow businesses, institutions, members of a profession, and governmental agencies to store their records by means of microfilm, optical imaging, or similar techniques and to destroy the originals without losing the right to prove the content of the originals at trial if the need should arise.

Arguably this new rule, which was adopted by the 1995 Legislature, is unnecessary. Duplicates are generally admissible under Rule 1003, and duplicates are defined by Rule 1001(1) to include photographic, electronic, or chemical reproduction techniques "which accurately reproduce the original." The storage methods described in Rule 1003-1 would generally satisfy the definition of duplicates.

Moreover, under Rule 1004(1), a party is generally allowed to introduce other evidence to prove the content of originals once they have been shown to be lost or destroyed, "unless the proponent lost or destroyed them in bad faith." If original records are destroyed in the normal course of business and their contents preserved by means of microfilm, optical imaging, or similar techniques, it seems unlikely that the opposing party could prove they were destroyed in "bad faith."

Rule 1003-1 is apparently designed to overcome any possible danger of exclusion of the reproductions on grounds of "unfairness" under Rule 1003 or "bad faith" under Rule 1004.

Rule 1003-1 arguably contains its own "bad faith" limitation because it can be used only where the originals were shown to have been destroyed "in the regular course of business." Moreover, the originals cannot be destroyed if held in a custodial or fiduciary capacity (unless the principal or owner has authorized destruction) or where preservation is required by law.

To be admissible under Rule 1003-1, the reproduction must be "satisfactorily identified," which presumably means complying with the authentication requirements of Rule 901. Moreover, the reproduction is admissible only to the same extent as the original itself. Thus, the original must be shown to qualify for admission under the evidence code. If offered for a hearsay purpose, the document must satisfy an exception to the hearsay rule, such as for business or public records. See Rules 803(6) and 803(8). The reproduction is admissible "whether the original is in existence or not," and introduction of a reproduction does not preclude admission of the original.

An enlargement or facsimile of the reproduction is also admissible in evidence, provided the original reproduction is in existence and available for inspection. Thus the rule in essence authorizes the introduction of a copy of a copy.

Rule 1003-1 is modeled after the Federal Business Records Act, 28 U.S.C. § 1732. Cases construing the federal statute are likely to be persuasive authority in interpreting Rule 1003-1.

RULE 1004.   ORS 40.565. ADMISSIBILITY OF OTHER EVIDENCE OF CONTENTS

The original is not required, and other evidence of the contents of a writing, recording or photograph is admissible when:

(1) **[Originals lost or destroyed.] All originals are lost or have been destroyed, unless the proponent lost or destroyed them in bad faith;**

(2) **[Original not obtainable.] An original cannot be obtained by any available judicial process or procedure;**

(3) **[Original in possession of opponent.] At a time when an original was under the control of the party against whom offered, that party was put on notice, by the pleadings or otherwise, that the contents would be a subject of proof at the hearing, and the party does not produce the original at the hearing; or**

(4) **[Collateral matters.] The writing, recording or photograph is not closely related to a controlling issue.**

LEGISLATIVE COMMENTARY

This section is identical to Rule 1004 for the Federal Rules of Evidence and is generally consistent with current Oregon law.

Basically, the "best evidence rule" is a rule of preference: If failure to produce the original is satisfactorily explained, secondary evidence is admissible. This section specifies the circumstances under which production of the original is excused, and in an effort to avoid unwarranted complexities, recognizes no degrees of secondary evidence. It is believed that the normal motivation of a party to present the most convincing evidence possible makes an extended scheme of preferences unnecessary.

Subsection (1). Loss or destruction of the original, unless due to the bad faith of a proponent, is a satisfactory explanation of nonproduction. Paragraph (b) of ORS 41.640 may be traced to *Wiseman v. Northern Pacific Railroad,* 20 Or 425, 26 P 272 (1891), an early Oregon case. In *Wiseman,* the Oregon Supreme Court set out the general guidelines:

> If the cause of action or defense is founded on the supposed writing, the party offering the evidence will be required to show a greater degree of diligence in the attempt to produce the original than if it is desired to be used as evidence in some collateral matter. The proof of search and proof of loss required is always proportionate to the character and value of the paper supposed to be lost.
>
> ...
>
> No precise rule has been or can be laid down as to what shall be considered a reasonable effort (to produce the original), but the party alleging the loss or destruction of the document is expected to show "that he has in good faith exhausted in a reasonable degree all the sources of information and means of discovery which the nature of the case would naturally suggest and which were accessible to him. ..."

In a more contemporary case, the Supreme Court looked to *Wiseman* and expressed approval of its doctrine, while expanding it to vest the "ultimate determination of the sufficiency of the search" entirely with the discretion of the trial court. *Stipe v. First National Bank,* 208 Or 251, 262, 301 P2d 175 (1956).

Subsection (2). When the original is in the possession of a third party, inability to procure it from him by resort to process or other judicial procedure is a sufficient explanation of nonproduction. Judicial procedure includes subpena duces tecum as an incident to the taking of a deposition in another jurisdiction.

Subsection (3). A party who has an original in his control has no need for the protection of the rule if put on notice that proof of contents will be made. He can prevent the admission of secondary evidence by offering the original.

Paragraph (a) of ORS 41.640 permits use of evidence other than the original document where the adverse party has possession but withholds it after reasonable notice to produce it has been given. ORS 41.610 (1979 Replacement Part) does not require such notice where the writing itself is a notice or where the writing was wrongfully obtained or withheld by the adverse party.

For other cases dealing with the introduction of secondary evidence when the original is in the possession of an opponent, see *Schreyer v. Turner Flouring Co.,* 29 Or 1, 43 P 719 (1896) and *Sugar Pine Door & Lumber Co. v. Garrett,* 28 Or 168, 42 P 129 (1895).

Subsection (4). Situations will arise in which no good purpose is served by production of the original. Numerous cases are collected in McCormick, *Evidence,* § 200, p 412, (2d ed 1972).

The collateral facts exception to the best evidence rule is in a state of uncertainty in Oregon. Under this exception, a writing involved in a case only collaterally may be proved without production of the original. If reference to a writing is merely incidental, the need for perfect exactitude is outweighed by the interest of expedition of the trial. The determination of whether or not a writing is "collateral" is left to the trial court's discretion and should involve a consideration of the centrality of the writing to the principal issues, the existence of a genuine dispute as to the contents of the writing and the complexity of the relevant features of the writing. McCormick, *Evidence,* § 234 (2d ed 1972). This exception has been recognized in Oregon, but the exact holding of the court is in doubt by a reference to a showing of diligence. *Peters v. Queen City Ins. Co.,* 63 Or 382, 126 P 1005 (1912). Subsection (4) of this section eliminates the doubt and clarifies existing law by removing any necessity for a showing of diligence when applying the collateral facts exceptions.

TEXT

Other Evidence of Contents

Rule 1004 provides that an original is not required to prove the contents of a writing, recording, or photograph when it has been lost or destroyed, is not obtainable through judicial process, is in the possession of an opponent who is notified that the contents will be the subject of proof at the hearing, or is pertinent only to a collateral matter. See ANNOT., *Admissibility, Pursuant to Rule 1004(1) of Other Evidence of Contents of Writing, Recording or Photograph, Where Originals Were Allegedly Lost or Destroyed,* 83 ALR Fed 554 (1987).

When a sufficient showing of unavailability is made under this rule, any other evidence of the contents of the writing, recording, or photograph may be offered. Article X does not recognize degrees of secondary evidence, except for the requirement of a certified copy of an official document. See Rule 1005. Once unavailability of the original is shown, oral testimony may be offered even though a copy is available. However, it is unlikely that a party will do so because of the adverse inference that might be drawn by the failure to offer stronger evidence. See ORS 10.095(7), (8). Other forms of secondary proof are also available. See, e.g., *Amoco Production Co. v. United States,* 619 F2d 1383 (10th Cir 1980) (allowing under Rule 406 evidence of routine practice of including a particular clause in a deed to show that the clause was in the deed in question).

Original Lost or Destroyed

Rule 1004(1) win normally require that the proponent show that a diligent search was made in order to establish that the original was lost or destroyed. The extent of search required will depend upon the circumstances, including the nature and ownership of the document and its normal, expected place of deposit. See *Velasquez v. Freeman,* 244 Or 40, 415 P2d 514 (1966). The Oregon Supreme Court has held:

> Ordinarily it is not sufficient that the paper is not found in its usual place of deposit, but all papers in the office or place should be examined. It is true the party need not search every possible place where it might be found, for then the search might be interminable, but he must search every place where there is a reasonable probability that it might be found.

Stipe v. First National Bank, 208 Or 251, 262, 301 P2d 175, 181 (1956), quoting *Wiseman v. N. Pac. R.R.,* 20 Or 425, 428, 26 P 272, 273 (1891).

If the original was lost or destroyed by the proponent in bad faith, secondary evidence of its contents is not admissible. Destruction by a proponent should be interpreted to include soliciting or aiding another to lose or destroy the original.

In *State v. Young,* 560 A2d 1095 (Me 1989), the prosecution offered testimony of a child sex abuse victim regarding the content of letters sent to her by the defendant. The victim had burned the letters soon after she received them. Even though the letters had been voluntarily destroyed, the court found they were not destroyed in bad faith. Therefore, her testimony was admissible over a best evidence objection.

Original Beyond Judicial Process

Rule 1004(2) authorizes the use of secondary evidence to prove the contents of a writing, recording or photograph if the original cannot be obtained by any available judicial process or procedure. Available judicial process would include a subpoena duces tecum. See ORCP 55B; ORCP 55F(1); ORS 136.580.

Even a witness outside the state may be subject to judicial process. See ORCP 38B and C; ORS 136.627.

Original in Possession of Opponent

Rule 1004(3) authorizes proof of contents by secondary evidence when: (1) the original is under the control of the party against whom the evidence is offered; (2) that party was put on notice, by the pleadings or otherwise, that the contents would be the subject of proof at the hearing; and (3) the party does not produce the original at the hearing. No form of notice is specified. A written notice denominated a "notice to produce" should be sufficient, although it should not be confused with a request for production under ORCP 43.

Collateral Matters

Rule 1004(4) essentially provides an escape clause from Rule 1002. It dispenses with the requirement of producing an original when the writing, recording, or photograph is not closely related to a controlling issue. This collateral fact exception gives courts discretion to allow oral testimony or other evidence of contents when the writing, recording, or photograph has only tangential importance in the litigation. Thus incidental references by a witness to road signs, street names, addresses, license plate numbers, billboards, newspaper headlines, names on commercial establishments, brand names, tickets, and similar writings will normally be permitted unless the terms of the writing have particular significance in the litigation.

McCormick states:

> Recognition of an exception exempting "collateral writings" from the operation of the basic rule has followed as a necessary concession to expedition of trials and clearness of narration, interests which outweigh, in the case of merely incidental references to documents, the need for perfect exactitude in the presentation of these documents' contents. McCormick, *Evidence* § 234 at 706 (3d ed 1984).

Although its precise scope is uncertain, the collateral fact exception is a significant qualification upon Rule 1002. Reliance upon the collateral fact exception is not necessary, however, in cases where the evidence of a writing, recording, or photograph is being offered for purposes other than to prove its contents. In such cases, Rule 1002 is by its terms inapplicable. For a discussion of the scope of the collateral fact exception under prior Oregon law, see NOTE AND COMMENT, 41 Or L Rev 138, 148–9(1962).

RULE 1005.   ORS 40.570. PUBLIC RECORDS

The contents of an official record or of a document authorized to be recorded or filed and actually recorded or filed, including data compilations

in any form, if otherwise admissible, may be proved by copy, certified as correct in accordance with Rule 902 (ORS 40.510) or testified to be correct by a witness who has compared it with the original. If such a copy cannot be obtained by the exercise of reasonable diligence, then other evidence of the contents may be given.

LEGISLATIVE COMMENTARY

This section is identical to Rule 1005 of the Federal Rules of Evidence and is consistent with paragraph (c) of subsection (1) of ORS 41.640 (1979 Replacement Part) and ORS 192.050. ORS 41.640 allows introduction of copies or reproductions of an original document in the custody of a public officer. ORS 192.050 provides that a photocopy of any public record in official custody shall be deemed an original. The Legislative Assembly does not believe that this section changes current Oregon law.

Since removing public records from their usual place of storage would cause serious inconvenience to the public and to the records' custodian, this section provides that no explanation need be given for failure to produce the original of a public record. To prevent the introduction of all kinds of secondary evidence of the contents of public records, the section gives preference to certified or compared copies.

By admitting that a writing offered in evidence was a correct copy of a public record, the requirement of producing the original or a certified copy was waived. *First National Bank v. Miller,* 48 Or 587, 87 P 892 (1906).

TEXT

Public Records

Rule 1005 dispenses with any requirement of producing the original of an official record or document filed or recorded pursuant to law and provides that the contents may be proven by a copy certified as correct under Rule 902. Presumably, the certification would be made under Rule 902(4) which requires: (1) certification by the custodian or other authorized person that the copy is correct; and (2) compliance with subsection (1), (2), or (3) of Rule 902, which generally requires that a seal be affixed.

It might seem that Rule 1005 is unnecessary, because Rule 1003 already allows the use of duplicates in lieu of originals in most circumstances. Rule 1005 is apparently intended to qualify Rule 1003 in two ways. First, Rule 1005 requires that an official record or a duly filed or recorded document be proven by a certified copy rather than by an uncertified copy, as would be allowed under Rule 1003, unless "such a copy cannot be obtained by the exercise of reasonable diligence." The requirement of certification would seem mandatory, or else the rule would be deprived of meaning. Second, Rule 1005 appears to establish the adequacy of proof by a certified copy, thus limiting the discretion of a court that would otherwise exist under Rule 1003 to require production of the original.

RULE 1006.   ORS 40.575. SUMMARIES

The contents of voluminous writings, recordings or photographs which cannot conveniently be examined in court may be presented in the form of a chart, summary or calculation. The originals, or duplicates, shall be made available for examination or copying, or both, by other parties at a reasonable time and place. The court may order that they be produced in court.

LEGISLATIVE COMMENTARY

This section is identical to Rule 1006 of the Federal Rules of Evidence, and is consistent with current Oregon practice, and the Legislative Assembly, by the adoption of the section, does not intend to change current Oregon law.

The Legislative Assembly believes that the admission of voluminous books, records or documents offers the only practical way of making their contents available to judge and jury. This section, with appropriate safeguards, provides that the originals of voluminous documents need not be produced.

In *Scott v. Astoria Railroad Co.,* 43 Or 26, 72 P 594 (1903), it was held that [in] a calculation by an expert witness of the average daily rainfall on Astoria, actual records would have unduly burdened the court.

The Oregon Supreme Court, in *Hubble v. Hubble,* 130 Or 177, 279 P 550 (1929), a case in which it was necessary to determine whether a lease had been paid, allowed a bookkeeper to testify that the lease was treated as paid up. The court held that when books are voluminous, intricate or uncertain, resort may be had to the testimony of an expert bookkeeper to explain the entries and true state of accounts.

In *Carrey v. Haun,* 111 Or 586, 227 P 315 (1924), a statement of the affairs of a business firm prepared by an expert accountant was held admissible. However, if the summary is not the general result of the whole, or if there is no showing that the originals consisted of numerous accounts which could not be examined in court without a great loss of time, the summary will not be admissible. *Loggers & Contractors Machinery Co. v. Owen,* 193 Or 9, 238 P2d 309 (1951).

In *State Highway Commission v. DeLong Corporation,* 9 Or App 550, 495 P2d 1215 (1972), a case in which an immense volume of oral and documentary evidence was necessary to properly understand the controversy, the court, in response to defendant's challenge to the admission of summaries of other writings and record, held that summaries taken from other evidence, material or documents available to the parties for examination are admissible. The court did not limit summaries to writings composed of words and figures, but allowed the admission of other types of "graphic representations" such as charts.

See also *Shepherd v. Hub Lumber Co.,* 273 Or 331, 541 P2d 439 (1975), in which it was held that, in order for a summary of accounting records to be admissible, all of the original records which set forth the facts and figures forming the basis for such a summary must be produced in court for inspection by the opposing party for the purpose of verifying the accuracy of the summary.

Other Oregon cases dealing with the voluminous writings exception to the best evidence rule are *Smith v. Abel,* 211 Or 571, 316 P2d 793 (1957) and *City of Hillsboro v. James and Yost,* 240 Or 433, 420 P2d 511 (1965).

TEXT

Summaries

Rule 1006 allows the contents of voluminous writings, recordings, or photographs, which cannot conveniently be examined in court, to be proven by the use of a chart, summary, or calculation. The summary or calculation may presumably be oral as well as written. Whether the writings, recordings, or photographs are sufficiently voluminous is a matter for the discretion of the trial court. See *Javelin Inv., S.A. v. Municipality of Ponce,* 645 F2d 92, 96 (1st Cir 1981) (ten simple, short documents not sufficiently voluminous to justify use of Rule 1006); *United States v. Seelig,* 622 F2d 207 (6th Cir), cert denied 449 US 869 (1980) (165 exhibits sufficiently voluminous to justify use of chart summary; Rule 1006 does not require that it be "impossible" to examine the underlying records before a summary or chart may be used).

In order to authenticate a chart, summary, or calculation, it will usually be necessary first to authenticate the underlying documents and then to offer testimony indicating the accuracy or correctness of the chart, summary, or calculation. Rule 1006 is an exception to the duty of producing voluminous originals under Article X and does not exempt the underlying material from having to satisfy the hearsay rule and other evidentiary requirements. *United States v. Johnson,* 594 F2d 1253 (9th Cir), cert denied 444 US 964 (1979). The chart, summary, or calculation will normally not be admissible if the underlying documents are not. *Needham v. White Laboratories, Inc.,* 639 F2d 394 (7th Cir 1981), cert denied 454 US 927 (1981); *Ford Motor Co. v. Auto Supply Co.,* 661 F2d 1171, 1175 (8th Cir 1981) (a summary, if drawn from data that is inadmissible, must be excluded). Rule 1006 does not provide for the admission of summaries of the testimony of out-of-court witnesses. *United States v. Goss,* 650 F2d 1336, 1344 n 5 (5th Cir 1981). The rule does not require that the underlying documents be offered into evidence, although the judge may order that they be produced in court.

The authenticating witness will usually need to be the person who made the chart, summary, or calculation. However, in some circumstances, another witness may be able to provide sufficient authentication. See *Davison v. Parker,* 50 Or App 129, 622 P2d 11 13, rev denied 642 P2d 307 (1981) (defendant's president, who supervised but did not personally compile the summary of costs of replacing defective pipe, provided sufficient authentication to render the summary admissible by testifying as to its mode of preparation and the accuracy of its contents).

A chart, summary, or calculation may be excluded where the underlying documents were not made available to the opponent for examination. *United States v. Seelig,* 622 F2d 207 (6th Cir), cert denied 449 US 869 (1980). The chart, summary, or calculation should also be made available in advance of trial in order to make the examination of the underlying documents meaningful. If the summary is likely to confuse or mislead the jury or create unfair prejudice, it may be excluded under Rule 403.

The rule does not state whether the chart, summary, or calculation may be considered by the trier of fact as substantive evidence, or only as an illustration of the evidence being summarized. The summary should be considered as evidence, at least in those cases where the underlying documents are not introduced. Even in those cases where the originals are introduced, the summary can properly be considered evidence because the very reason for introducing the summary is that the originals are "voluminous" and "cannot conveniently be examined in court." However, in case of any discrepancy between the summary and the originals, the jury should be instructed to rely on the originals.

On this point, compare 5 J. Weinstein and M. Berger, WEINSTEIN'S EVIDENCE ¶1006[02] at 1006–6 (1988) ("Whether or not the originals are introduced at the trial, the summaries may be relied upon as evidence-in-chief."); *United States v. Smyth,* 556 F2d 1179 (5th Cir), cert denied 434 US 862 (1977) (summary is evidence) with *United States v. Lemire,* 720 F2d 1327 (DC Cir 1983), cert denied 467 US 1226, 104 SCt 2678, 81 LEd2d 874 (1984) (when summary admitted in addition to underlying documents, jury should be instructed that summary is not evidence); *United States v. Radseck,* 718 F2d 233 (7th Cir 1983), cert denied 465 US 1029, 104 SCt 1291, 79 LEd2d 693 (1984) (same).

If the summary is being used only for pedagogical purposes or as demonstrative evidence rather than as a substitute for the originals, then Rule 1006 is inapplicable and the summary should not be considered as evidence. See C. Mueller & L. Kirkpatrick, MODERN EVIDENCE (1995) § 10.15.

See generally ANNOT., *Admissibility of Summaries of Writings, Recordings, or Photographs Under Rule 1006 of the Federal Rules of Evidence,* 50 ALR Fed 319 (1980); ANNOT., *Use and Admissibility in Evidence in Federal Tax Evasion Prosecutions, of Summaries of, or Charts Summarizing, Testimony or Exhibits in Evidence,* 16 ALR Fed 542 (1973); ANNOT., *Requirements of Notice As Condition For Admission In Evidence of Summary of Voluminous Records,* 80 ALR3d 405 (1977); NOTE, *Chart Summaries: Jury Aids or Evidence,* 34 Baylor L Rev 168 (1982); see ANNOT., *Admissibility of Evidence Summaries Under Uniform Evidence Rule 1006,* 59 ALR4th 971 (1988).

RULE 1007.   ORS 40.580. TESTIMONY OR WRITTEN ADMISSION OF PARTY

Contents of writings, recordings or photographs may be proved by the testimony or deposition of the party against whom offered or by the

party's written admission, without accounting for the nonproduction of the original.

LEGISLATIVE COMMENTARY

This section is identical to Rule 1007 of the Federal Rules of Evidence.

The scope of the oral admissions exception to the best evidence rule in Oregon is unclear under existing law.

This section limits the admissions exception to the best evidence rule to admissions made in the course of giving testimony or in writing. The section may be thought by some to be unnecessary because admissions of a party litigant are generally admissible. However, a sworn statement by a party in which the party describes the contents of another document which description is against his interest, can be objected to under both the hearsay and best evidence rules. The document could certainly be introduced as an admission by a party opponent. However, in the absence of this section, that portion of the statement describing the contents of another document would still be inadmissible under the best evidence rule. This section is intended to prevent such exclusion of evidence.

TEXT

Testimony or Written Admission of Party

Rule 1007 dispenses with the requirement of an original when the contents can be proven by the testimony or deposition of the opponent or by the opponent's written admission. Rule 1007 is not conditioned upon a showing of unavailability of the original under Rule 1004. A party may use testimony or written admissions of an opponent in any case where production of the original to prove contents would otherwise be required.

Nontestimonial oral admissions are not included within the rule because of their lesser reliability. However, nontestimonial oral admissions may be received as secondary evidence to prove contents when the unavailability of the original has been shown under Rule 1004.

RULE 1008.   ORS 40.585. FUNCTIONS OF COURT AND JURY

When the admissibility of other evidence of contents of writings, recordings or photographs under Rules 1001 to 1008 (ORS 40.550 to 40.585) depends upon the fulfillment of a condition of fact, the question whether the condition has been fulfilled is ordinarily for the court to determine in accordance with Rule 104 (ORS 40.030). However, the issue is for the trier of fact to determine as in the case of other issues of fact when the issue raised is:

(1) **Whether the asserted writing ever existed;**

(2) **Whether another writing, recording or photograph produced at the trial is the original; or**

(3) **Whether the other evidence of contents correctly reflects the contents.**

LEGISLATIVE COMMENTARY

This section is based on Rule 1008 of the Federal Rules of Evidence. The words "sections 71 to 78 of this Act" are substituted for the federal phrase "these rules."

The legislative Assembly believes that this section is consistent with current Oregon law.

Most preliminary questions of fact in connection with applying the rule preferring the original as evidence of contents are for the judge, under the general principles announced in § 5 (Rule 104) of this Act. Thus, the question whether the loss of the originals has been established, or of the fulfillment of other conditions specified in § 74 (Rule 1004) of this Act, is for the judge. However, questions may arise which go beyond the mere administration of the rule preferring the original and into the merits of the controversy. For example, plaintiff offers secondary evidence of the contents of an alleged contract, after first introducing evidence of loss of the original, and defendant counters with evidence that no such contract was ever executed. If the judge decides that the contract was never executed] and excludes the secondary evidence, the case is at an end without ever going to the jury on a central issue. Levin, *Authentication and Content of Writings,* 10 Rutgers L Rev 632, 644 (1956). The latter portion of this section is designed to insure treatment of these situations as raising jury questions.

In *Rosendorf v. Hirschberg,* 8 Or 240, 17 P 271 (1880), the court declared: "The paper being lost and a pretended copy being produced, this being secondary evidence, it was necessary for the party producing it to show that the original was lost and could not be produced. The question of loss was for the court. This being determined in the affirmative, then it was necessary to prove the copy." The court held that the question whether the writing produced was a copy of an original allegedly signed by the parties was for the jury.

TEXT

Functions of Court and Jury

Rule 1008 allocates the fact-finding function under Article X between the trial court and the jury, and is a more particularized application of Rule 104. Issues relating to the administration of the rules in Article X are for the court. For example, the court determines whether a document qualifies as a duplicate under Rule 1001(4), whether it would be unfair to admit the duplicate in lieu of the original under Rule 1003, whether a document has been lost or destroyed under Rule 1004(1), whether the document is obtainable by available judicial process under Rule 1004(2), whether a document is a public record under Rule 1005, and whether contents of a writing are too voluminous to be examined in court under Rule 1006.

The three issues expressly allocated to the jury for final determination are: "(1) Whether the asserted writing ever existed; (2) Whether another writing, recording or photograph produced at the trial is the original; or (3) Whether the other evidence of contents correctly reflects the contents." If the trial court were to make the final determination regarding these issues, the right to a jury trial might be infringed.

Although the above issues are assigned to the jury for final determination, the trial judge must still determine whether there is sufficient evidence to support a jury finding regarding these issues before they will be submitted to the jury. See Rule 104(2).

APPENDIX A

FEDERAL RULES OF EVIDENCE FOR UNITED STATES COURTS

(As amended through December 1, 1995)

ARTICLE I.
GENERAL PROVISIONS

ARTICLE II.
JUDICIAL NOTICE

ARTICLE VII.
OPINIONS AND EXPERT TESTIMONY

ARTICLE VIII.
HEARSAY

ARTICLE IX.
AUTHENTICATION AND IDENTIFICATION

ARTICLE X.
CONTENTS OF WRITINGS, RECORDS, AND
PHOTOGRAPHS

ARTICLE XI.
MISCELLANEOUS RULES

ARTICLE I.   GENERAL PROVISIONS

Rule 101. Scope. These rules govern proceedings in the courts of the United States and before United States bankruptcy judges and United States magistrate judges, to the extent and with the exceptions stated in rule 1101.

Rule 102. Purpose and Construction. These rules shall be construed to secure fairness in administration, elimination of unjustifiable expense and delay, and promotion of growth and development of the law of evidence to the end that the truth may be ascertained and proceedings justly determined.

Rule 103. Rulings on Evidence

(a) Effect of erroneous ruling. Error may not be predicated upon a ruling which admits or excludes evidence unless a substantial right of the party is affected, and

(1) Objection. In case the ruling is one admitting evidence, a timely objection or motion to strike appears of record, stating the specific ground of objection, if the specific ground was not apparent from the context; or

(2) Offer of proof. In case the ruling is one excluding evidence, the substance of the evidence was made known to the court by offer or was apparent from the context within which questions were asked.

(b) Record of offer and ruling. The court may add any other or further statement which shows the character of the evidence, the form in which it was offered, the objection made, and the ruling thereon. It may direct the making of an offer in question and answer form.

(c) Hearing of jury. In jury cases, proceedings shall be conducted, to the extent practicable, so as to prevent inadmissible evidence from being suggested to the jury by any means, such as making statements or offers of proof or asking questions in the hearing of the jury.

(d) Plain error. Nothing in this rule precludes taking notice of plain errors affecting substantial rights although they were not brought to the attention of the court.

Rule 104. Preliminary Questions

(a) Questions of admissibility generally. Preliminary questions concerning the qualification of a person to be a witness, the existence of a privilege, or the admissibility of evidence shall be determined by the court, subject to the provisions of subdivision (b). In making its determination it is not bound by the rules of evidence except those with respect to privileges.

(b) Relevancy conditioned on fact. When the relevancy of evidence depends upon the fulfillment of a condition of fact, the court shall admit it upon, or subject to, the introduction of evidence sufficient to support a finding of the fulfillment of the condition.

(c) Hearing of jury. Hearings on the admissibility of confessions shall in all cases be conducted out of the hearing of the jury. Hearings on other preliminary matters shall be so conducted when the interests of justice require or, when an accused is a witness and so requests.

(d) Testimony by accused. The accused does not, by testifying upon a preliminary matter, become subject to cross-examination as to other issues in the case.

(e) Weight and Credibility. This rule does not limit the right of a party to introduce before the jury evidence relevant to weight or credibility.

Rule 105. Limited Admissibility. When evidence which is admissible as to one party or for one purpose but not admissible as to another party or for another purpose is admitted, the court, upon request, shall restrict the evidence to its proper scope and instruct the jury accordingly.

Rule 106. Remainder of or Related Writings or Recorded Statements. When a writing or recorded statement or part thereof is introduced by a party, an adverse party may require the introduction at that time of any other part or any other writing or recorded statement which ought in fairness to be considered contemporaneously with it.

ARTICLE II.   JUDICIAL NOTICE

Rule 201. Judicial Notice of Adjudicative Facts.
(a) **Scope of rule.** This rule governs only judicial notice of adjudicative facts.
(b) **Kinds of facts.** A judicially noticed fact must be one not subject to reasonable dispute in that it is either (1) generally known within the territorial jurisdiction of the trial court or (2) capable of accurate and ready determination by resort to sources whose accuracy cannot reasonably be questioned.
(c) **When discretionary.** A court may take judicial notice, whether requested or not.
(d) **When mandatory.** A court shall take judicial notice if requested by a party and supplied with the necessary information.
(e) **Opportunity to be heard.** A party is entitled upon timely request to an opportunity to be heard as to the propriety of taking judicial notice and the tenor of the matter noticed. In the absence of prior notification, the request may be made after judicial notice has been taken.
(f) **Time of taking notice.** Judicial notice may be taken at any stage of the proceeding.
(g) **Instructing jury.** In a civil action or proceeding, the court shall instruct the jury to accept as conclusive any fact judicially noticed. In a criminal case, the court shall instruct the jury that it may, but is not required to, accept as conclusive any fact judicially noticed.

ARTICLE III.   PRESUMPTIONS IN CIVIL ACTIONS AND PROCEEDINGS

Rule 301. Presumptions in General in Civil Actions and Proceedings. In all civil actions and proceedings not otherwise provided for by Act of Congress or by these rules, a presumption imposes on the party against whom it is directed the burden of going forward with evidence to rebut or meet the presumption, but does not shift to such party the burden of proof in the sense of the risk of nonpersuasion, which remains throughout the trial upon the party on whom it was originally cast.

Rule 302. Applicability of State Law in Civil Actions and Proceedings. In civil actions and proceedings, the effect of a presumption respecting a fact which is an element of a claim or defense as to which State law supplies the rule of decision is determined in accordance with State law.

ARTICLE IV.   RELEVANCY AND ITS LIMITS

Rule 401. Definition of "Relevant Evidence". "Relevant evidence" means evidence having any tendency to make the existence of any fact that is of consequence to the determination of the action more probable or less probable than it would be without the evidence.

Rule 402. Relevant Evidence Generally Admissible; Irrelevant Evidence Inadmissible. All relevant evidence is admissible, except as otherwise provided by the Constitution of the United States, by Act of Congress, by these rules, or by other rules prescribed by the Supreme Court pursuant to statutory authority. Evidence which is not relevant is not admissible.

Rule 403. Exclusion of Relevant Evidence on Grounds of Prejudice, Confusion, or Waste of Time. Although relevant, evidence may be excluded if its probative value is substantially outweighed by the danger of unfair prejudice, confusion of the issues, or misleading the jury, or by considerations of undue delay, waste of time, or needless presentation of cumulative evidence.

Rule 404. Character Evidence Not Admissible to Prove Conduct; Exceptions; Other Crimes
(a) **Character evidence generally.** Evidence of a person's character or a trait of character is not admissible for the purpose of proving action in conformity therewith on a particular occasion, except:
    (1) **Character of accused.** Evidence of a pertinent trait of character offered by an accused, or by the prosecution to rebut the same;
    (2) **Character of victim.** Evidence of a pertinent trait of character of the victim of the crime offered by an accused, or by the prosecution to rebut the same, or evidence of a character trait of peacefulness of the victim offered by the prosecution in a homicide case to rebut evidence that the victim was the first aggressor;
    (3) **Character of witness.** Evidence of the character of a witness, as pro vided in rules 607, 608, and 609.
(b) **Other crimes, wrongs, or acts.** Evidence of other crimes, wrongs, or acts is not admissible to prove the character of a person in order to show that action in conformity therewith. It may, however, be admissible for other purposes, such as proof of motive, opportunity, intent, preparation, plan, knowledge, identity, or absence of mistake or accident, provided that upon request by the accused, the prosecution in a criminal case shall provide reasonable notice in advance of trial, or during trial if the court excuses pretrial

697

notice on good cause shown, of the general nature of any such evidence it intends to introduce at trial.

Rule 405. Methods of Proving Character

(a) **Reputation or opinion.** In all cases in which evidence of character or a trait of character of a person is admissible, proof may be made by testimony as to reputation or by testimony in the form of an opinion. On cross-examination, inquiry is allowable into relevant specific instances of conduct.

(b) **Specific instances of conduct.** In cases in which character or a trait of character of a person is an essential element of a charge, claim, or defense, proof may also be made of specific instances of that person's conduct.

Rule 406. Habit; Routine Practice. Evidence of the habit of a person or of the routine practice of an organization, whether corroborated or not and regardless of the presence of eyewitnesses, is relevant to prove that the conduct of the person or organization on a particular occasion was in conformity with the habit or routine practice.

Rule 407. Subsequent Remedial Measures. When, after an event, measures are taken which, if taken previously, would have made the event less likely to occur, evidence of the subsequent measures is not admissible to prove negligence or culpable conduct in connection with the event. This rule does not require the exclusion of evidence of subsequent measures when offered for another purpose, such as proving ownership, control, or feasibility of precautionary measures, if controverted, or impeachment.

Rule 408. Compormise and Offers to Compromise. Evidence of (1) furnishing or offering or promising to furnish, or (2) accepting or offering or promising to accept, a valuable consideration in compromising or attempting to compromise a claim which was disputed as to either validity or amount, is not admissible to prove liability for or invalidity of the claim or its amount. Evidence of conduct or statements made in compromise negotiations is likewise not admissible. This rule does not require the exclusion of any evidence otherwise discoverable merely because it is presented in the course of compromise negotiations. This rule also does not require exclusion when the evidence is offered for another purpose, such as proving bias or prejudice of a witness, negativing a contention of undue delay, or proving an effort to obstruct a criminal investigation or prosecution.

Rule 409. Payment of Medical and Similar Expenses. Evidence of furnishing or offering or promising to pay medical, hospital, or similar expenses occasioned by an injury is not admissible to prove liability for the injury.

Rule 410. Inadmissibility of Pleas, Plea Discussions, and Related Statements. Except as otherwise provided in this rule, evidence of the following is not, in any civil or criminal proceeding, admissible against the defendant who made the plea or was a participant in the plea discussions:

(1) a plea of guilty which was later withdrawn;

(2) a plea of nolo contendere;

(3) any statement made in the course of any proceedings under Rule 11 of the Federal Rules of Criminal Procedure or comparable state procedure regarding either of the foregoing pleas; or

(4) any statement made in the course of plea discussions with an attorney for the prosecuting authority which do not result in a plea of guilty or which result in a plea of guilty later withdrawn.

However, such a statement is admissible (i) in any proceeding wherein another statement made in the course of the same plea or plea discussions has been introduced and the statement ought in fairness be considered contemporaneously with it, or (ii) in a criminal proceeding for perjury or false statement if the statement was made by the defendant under oath, on the record and in the presence of counsel.

Rule 411. Liability Insurance. Evidence that a person was or was not insured against liability is not admissible upon the issue whether the person acted negligently or otherwise wrongfully. This rule does not require the exclusion of evidence of insurance against liability when offered for another purpose, such as proof of agency, ownership, or control, or bias or prejudice of a witness.

Rule 412. Sex Offense Cases; Relevance of Alleged Victim's Past Sexual Behavior or Alleged Sexual Predisposition

(a) **Evidence generally inadmissible.** The following evidence is not admissible in any civil or criminal proceeding involving alleged sexual misconduct except as provided in subdivision (b) and (c):

(1) Evidence offered to prove that any alleged victim engaged in other sexual behavior.

(2) Evidence offered to prove any alleged victim's sexual predisposition.

(b) **Exceptions.**

(1) In a criminal case, the following evidence is admissible, if otherwise admissible under these rules:

(A) evidence of specific instances of sexual behavior by the alleged victim offered to prove that a person other than the accused was the source of semen, injury or other physical evidence;

(B) evidence of specific instances of sexual behavior by the alleged victim with respect to the person accused on the sexual misconduct offered by the accused to prove consent or by the prosecution; and

(C) evidence the exclusion of which would violate the constitutional rights of the defendant.

(2) In a civil case, evidence offered to prove the sexual behavior or sexual predisposition of any alleged victim is admissible if it is otherwise admissible under these rules and its probative substantially outweighs

the danger of harm to any victim and of unfair prejudice to any party. Evidence of an alleged victim's reputation is admissible only if it has been placed in controversy by the alleged victim.

(c) Procedure to determine admissibility.

(a) A party intending to offer evidence under subdivision (b) must—

(A) file a written motion at least 14 days before trial specifically describing the evidence and stating the purpose for which it is offered unless the court, for good cause requires a different time for filing or permits filing during trial; and

(B) serve the motion on all parties and notify the alleged victim or, when appropriate, the alleged victim's guardian or representative.

(2) Before admitting evidence under this rule the court must conduct a hearing in camera and afford the victim and parties a right to attend and be heard. The motion, related papers, and the record of the hearing must be sealed and remain under seal unless the court orders otherwise.

Rule 413. Evidence of Similar Crimes in Sexual Assault Cases

(a) In a criminal case in which the defendant is accused of an offense of sexual assault, evidence of the defendant's commission of another offense or offenses of sexual assault is admissible, and may be considered for its bearing on any matter to which it is relevant.

(b) In a case in which the Government intends to offer evidence under this rule, the attorney for the Government shall disclose the evidence to the defendant, including statements of witnesses or a summary of the substance of any testimony that is expected to be offered, at least fifteen days before the scheduled date of trial or at such later time as the court may allow for good cause.

(c) This rule shall not be construed to limit the admission or consideration of evidence under any other rule.

(d) For purposes of this rule and Rule 415, "offense of sexual assault" means a crime under Federal law or the law of a State (as defined in section 513 of title 18, United States Code) that involved—

(1) any conduct proscribed by chapter 109A of title 18, United States Code;

(2) contact, without consent, between any part of the defendant's body or an object and the genitals or anus of another person;

(3) contact, without consent, between the genitals or anus of the defendant and any part of another person's body;

(4) deriving sexual pleasure or gratification from the infliction of death, bodily injury, or physical pain on another person; or

(5) an attempt or conspiracy to engage in conduct described in paragraphs (1)–(4).

Rule 414. Evidence of Similar Crimes in Child Molestation Cases

(a) In a criminal case in which the defendant is accused of an offense of child molestation, evidence of the defendant's commission of another offense or offenses of child molestation is admissible, and may be considered for its bearing on any matter to which it is relevant.

(b) In a case in which the Government intends to offer evidence under this rule, the attorney for the Government shall disclose the evidence to the defendant, including statements of witnesses or a summary of the substance of any testimony that is expected to be offered, at least fifteen days before the scheduled date of trial or at such later time as the court may allow for good cause.

(c) This rule shall not be construed to limit the admission or consideration of evidence under any other rule.

(d) For purposes of this rule and Rule 415, "child" means a person below the age of fourteen, and "offense of child molestation" means a crime under Federal law or the law of a State (as defined in section 513 of title 18, United States Code) that involved—

    (1) any conduct proscribed by chapter 109A of title 18, United States Code, that was committed in relation to a child;

    (2) any conduct proscribed by chapter 110 of title 18, United States Code;

    (3) contact between any part of the defendant's body or an object and the genitals or anus of a child;

    (4) contact between the genitals or anus of the defendant and any part of the body of a child;

    (5) deriving sexual pleasure or gratification from the infliction of death, bodily injury, or physical pain on a child; or

    (6) an attempt or conspiracy to engage in conduct described in paragraphs (1)–(5).

Rule 415. Evidence of Similar Acts in Civil Cases Concerning Sexual Assault or Child Molestation

(a) In a civil case in which a claim for damages or other relief is predicated on a party's alleged commission of conduct constituting an offense of sexual assault or child molestation, evidence of that party's commission of another offense or offenses of sexual assault or child molestation is admissible and may be considered as provided in Rule 413 and Rule 414 of these rules.

(b) A party who intends to offer evidence under this Rule shall disclose the evidence to the party against whom it will be offered, including statements of witnesses or a summary of the substance of any testimony that is expected to be offered, at least fifteen days before the scheduled date of trial or at such later time as the court may allow for good cause.

(c) This rule shall not be construed to limit the admission or consideration of evidence under any other rule.

ARTICLE V. PRIVILEGES

Rule 501. General Rule. Except as otherwise required by the Constitution of the United States or provided by Act of Congress or in rules prescribed by the Supreme Court pursuant to statutory authority, the privilege of a witness, person, government, State, or political subdivision thereof shall be governed by the principles of the common law as they may be interpreted by the courts of the United States in the light of reason and experience. However, in civil actions and proceedings, with respect to an element of a claim or defense as to which State law supplies the rule of decision, the privilege of a witness, person, government, State, or political subdivision thereof shall be determined in accordance with State law.

ARTICLE VI. WITNESSES

Rule 601. General Rule of Competency. Every person is competent to be a witness except as otherwise provided in these rules. However, in civil actions and proceedings, with respect to an element of a claim or defense as to which State law supplies the rule of decision, the competency of a witness shall be determined in accordance with State law.

Rule 602. Lack of Personal Knowledge. A witness may not testify to a matter unless evidence is introduced sufficient to support a finding that the witness has personal knowledge of the matter. Evidence to prove personal knowledge may, but need not, consist of the witness' own testimony. This rule is subject to the provisions of Rule 703, relating to opinion testimony by expert witnesses.

Rule 603. Oath or Affirmation. Before testifying, every witness shall be required to declare that the witness will testify truthfully, by oath or affirmation administered in a form calculated to awaken the witness' conscience and impress the witness' mind with the duty to do so.

Rule 604. Interpreters. An interpreter is subject to the provisions of these rules relating to qualification as an expert and the administration of an oath or affirmation to make a true translation.

Rule 605. Competency of Judge as Witness. The judge presiding at the trial may not testify in that trial as a witness. No objection need be made in order to preserve the point.

Rule 606. Competency of Juror as Witness
(a) **At the trial.** A member of the jury may not testify as a witness before that jury in the trial of the case in which the juror is sitting. If the juror is called

so to testify, the opposing party shall be afforded an opportunity to object out of the presence of the jury.

(b) **Inquiry into validity of verdict or indictment.** Upon an inquiry into the validity of a verdict or indictment, a juror may not testify as to any matter or statement occurring during the course of the jury's deliberations or to the effect of anything upon that or any other juror's mind or emotions as influencing the juror to assent to or dissent from the verdict or indictment or concerning the juror's mental processes in connection therewith, except that a juror may testify on the question whether extraneous prejudicial information was improperly brought to the jury's attention or whether any outside influence was improperly brought to bear upon any juror. Nor may a juror's affidavit or evidence of any statement by the juror concerning a matter about which the juror would be precluded from testifying be received for these purposes.

Rule 607. Who May Impeach. The credibility of a witness may be attacked by any party, including the party calling the witness.

Rule 608. Evidence of Character and Conduct of Witness

(a) **Opinion and reputation evidence of character.** The credibility of a witness may be attacked or supported by evidence in the form of opinion or reputation, but subject to these limitations: (1) the evidence may refer only to character for truthfulness or untruthfulness, and (2) evidence of truthful character is admissible only after the character of the witness for truthfulness has been attacked by opinion or reputation evidence or otherwise.

(b) **Specific instances of conduct.** Specific instances of the conduct of a witness, for the purpose of attacking or supporting the witness' credibility, other than conviction of crime as provided in rule 609, may not be proved by extrinsic evidence. They may, however, in the discretion of the court, if probative of truthfulness or untruthfulness, be inquired into on cross-examination of the witness (1) concerning the witness' character for truthfulness or untruthfulness, or (2) concerning the character for truthfulness or untruthfulness of another witness as to which character the witness being cross-examined has testified.

The giving of testimony, whether by an accused or by any other witness, does not operate as a waiver of the accused's or the witness' privilege against self-incrimination when examined with respect to matters which relate only to credibility.

Rule 609 Impeachment by Evidence of Conviction of Crime

(a) **General rule.** For the purpose of attacking the credibility of a witness, (1) evidence that a witness other than an accused has been convicted of a crime shall be admitted, subject to Rule 403, if the crime was punishable by death or imprisonment in excess of one year under the law under which the witness was convicted, and evidence that an accused has been convicted of such a crime shall be admitted if the court determines that the probative value of admitting this evidence outweighs its prejudicial effect to the accused; and (2) evidence that any witness has been convicted on a crime shall be admitted it it involved dishonesty or false statement, regardless of the punishment.

(b) **Time limit.** Evidence of a conviction under this rule is not admissible if a period of more than ten years has elapsed since the date of the conviction or of the release of the witness from the confinement imposed for that conviction, whichever is the later date, unless the court determines, in the interests of justice, that the probative value of the conviction supported by specific facts and circumstances substantially outweighs its prejudicial effect. However, evidence of a conviction more than 10 years old as calculated herein, is not admissible unless the proponent gives to the adverse party sufficient advance written notice of intent to use such evidence to provide the adverse party with a fair opportunity to contest the use of such evidence.

(c) **Effect of pardon, annulment, or certificate of rehabilitation.** Evidence of a conviction is not admissible under this rule if (1) the conviction has been the subject of a pardon, annulment, certificate of rehabilitation, or other equivalent procedure based on a finding of the rehabilitation of the person convicted, and that person has not been convicted of a subsequent crime which was punishable by death or imprisonment in excess of one year, or (2) the conviction has been the subject of a pardon, annulment, or other equivalent procedure based on a finding of innocence.

(d) **Juvenile adjudications.** Evidence of juvenile adjudications is generally not admissible under this rule. The \scourt may, however, in a criminal case allow evidence of a juvenile adjudication of a witness other than the accused if conviction of the offense would be admissible to attack the credibility of an adult and the court is satisfied that admission in evidence is necessary for a fair determination of the issue of guilt or innocence.

(e) **Pendency of appeal.** The pendency of an appeal therefrom does not render evidence of a conviction inadmissible. Evidence of the pendency of an appeal is admissible.

Rule 610. Religious Beliefs or Opinions. Evidence of the beliefs or opinions of a witness on matters of religion is not admissible for the purpose of showing that by reason of their nature the witness' credibility is impaired or enhanced.

Rule 611. Mode and Order of Interrogation and Presentation

(a) **Control by court.** The court shall exercise reasonable control over the mode and order of interrogating witnesses and presenting evidence so as to (1) make the interrogation and presentation effective for the ascertainment of the truth, (2) avoid needless consumption of time, and (3) protect witnesses from harassment or undue embarrassment.

(b) **Scope of cross-examination.** Cross-examination should be limited to the subject matter of the direct examination and matters affecting the credibility of the witness. The court may, in the exercise of discretion, permit inquiry into additional matters as if on direct examination.

(c) Leading questions. Leading questions should not be used on the direct examination of a witness except as may be necessary to develop the witness' testimony. Ordinarily leading questions should be permitted on cross-examination. When a party calls a hostile witness, an adverse party, or a witness identified with an adverse party, interrogation may be by leading questions.

Rule 612. Writing Used to Refresh Memory. Except as otherwise provided in criminal proceedings by section 3500 of title 18, United States Code, if a witness uses a writing to refresh memory for the purpose of testifying, either—

(1) while testifying, or

(2) before testifying, if the court in its discretion determines it is necessary in the interests of justice,

an adverse party is entitled to have the writing produced at the hearing, to inspect it, to cross-examine the witness thereon, and to introduce in evidence those portions which relate to the testimony of the witness. If it is claimed that the writing contains matters not related to the subject matter of the testimony the court shall examine the writing in camera, excise any portions not so related, and order delivery of the remainder to the party entitled thereto. Any portion withheld over objections shall be preserved and made available to the appellate court in the event of an appeal. If a writing is not produced or delivered pursuant to order under this rule, the court shall make any order justice requires, except that in criminal cases when the prosecution elects not to comply, the order shall be one striking the testimony or, if the court in its discretion determines that the interests of justice so require, declaring a mistrial.

Rule 613. Prior Statements of Witnesses

(a) Examining witness concerning prior statement. In examining a witness concerning a prior statement made by the witness, whether written or not, the statement need not be shown nor its contents disclosed to the witness at that time, but on request the same shall be shown or disclosed to opposing counsel.

(b) Extrinsic evidence of prior inconsistent statement of witness. Extrinsic evidence of a prior inconsistent statement by a witness is not admissible unless the witness is afforded an opportunity to explain or deny the same and the opposite party is afforded an opportunity to interrogate the witness thereon, or the interests of justice otherwise require. This provision does not apply to admissions of a party-opponent as defined in rule 801(d)(2).

Rule 614. Calling and Interrogation of Witnesses by Court

(a) Calling by court. The court may, on its own motion or at the suggestion of a party, call witnesses, and all parties are entitled to cross-examine witnesses thus called.

(b) Interrogation by court. The court may interrogate witnesses, whether called by itself or by a party.

(c) Objections. Objections to the calling of witnesses by the court or to interrogation by it may be made at the time or at the next available opportunity when the jury is not present.

Rule 615. Exclusion of Witnesses. At the request of a party the court shall order witnesses excluded so that they cannot hear the testimony of other witnesses, and it may make the order of its own motion. This rule does not authorize exclusion of (1) a party who is a natural person, or (2) an officer or employee of a party which is not a natural person designated as its representative by its attorney, or (3) a person whose presence is shown by a party to be essential to the presentation of the party's cause.

ARTICLE VII. OPINIONS AND EXPERT TESTIMONY

Rule 701. Opinion Testimony by Law Witnesses. If the witness is not testifying as an expert, the witness' testimony in the form of opinions or inferences is limited to those opinions or inferences which are (a) rationally based on the perception of the witness and (b) helpful to a clear understanding of the witness' testimony or the determination of a fact in issue.

Rule 702. Testimony by Experts. If scientific, technical, or other specialized knowledge will assist the trier of fact to understand the evidence or to determine a fact in issue, a witness qualified as an expert by knowledge, skill, experience, training, or education, may testify thereto in the form of an opinion or otherwise.

Rule 703. Bases of Opinion Testimony by Experts. The facts or data in the particular case upon which an expert bases an opinion or inference may be those perceived by or made known to the expert at or before the hearing. If of a type reasonably relied upon by experts in the particular field in forming opinions or inferences upon the subject, the facts or data need not be admissible in evidence.

Rule 704. Opinion on Ultimate Issue.
(a) Except as provided in subdivision (b), testimony in the form of an opinion or inference otherwise admissible is not objectionable because it embraces an ultimate issue to be decided by the trier of fact.
(b) No expert witness testifying with respect to the mental state or condition of a defendant in a criminal case may state an opinion or inference as to whether the defendant did or did not have the mental state or condition constituting an element of the crime charged or of a defense thereto. Such ultimate issues are matters for the trier of fact alone.

Rule 705. Disclosure of Facts or Data Underlying Expert Opinion. The expert may testify in terms of opinion or inference and give reasons therefor without first testifying to the underlying facts or data, unless the court requires otherwise. The expert may in any event be required to disclose the underlying facts or data on cross-examination.

Rule 706. Court Appointed Experts

(a) **Appointment.** The court may on its own motion or on the motion of any party enter an order to show cause why expert witnesses should not be appointed, and may request the parties to submit nominations. The court may appoint any expert witnesses agreed upon by the parties, and may appoint expert witnesses of its own selection. An expert witness shall not be appointed by the court unless the witness consents to act. A witness so appointed shall be informed of the witness' duties by the court in writing, a copy of which shall be filed with the clerk, or at a conference in which the parties shall have opportunity to participate. A witness so appointed shall advise the parties of the witness' findings, if any; the witness' deposition may be taken by any party; and the witness may be called to testify by the court or any party. The witness shall be subject to cross-examination by each party, including a party calling the witness.

(b) **Compensation.** Expert witnesses so appointed are entitled to reasonable compensation in whatever sum the court may allow. The compensation thus fixed is payable from funds which may be provided by law in criminal cases and civil actions and proceedings involving just compensation under the fifth amendment. In other civil actions and proceedings the compensation shall be paid by the parties in such proportion and at such time as the court directs, and thereafter charged in like manner as other costs.

(c) **Disclosure of appointment.** In the exercise of its discretion, the court may authorize disclosure to the jury of the fact that the court appointed the expert witness.

(d) **Parties' experts of own selection.** Nothing in this rule limits the parties in calling expert witnesses of their own selection.

ARTICLE VIII. HEARSAY

Rule 801. Definitions. The following definitions apply under this article:

(a) **Statement.** A "statement" is (1) an oral or written assertion or (2) nonverbal conduct of a person, if it is intended by the person as an assertion.

(b) **Declarant.** A "declarant" is a person who makes a statement.

(c) **Hearsay.** "Hearsay' is a statement, other than one made by the declarant while testifying at the trial or hearing, offered in evidence to prove the truth of the matter asserted.

(d) **Statements which are not hearsay.** A statement is not hearsay if—

(1) **Prior statement by witness.** The declarant testifies at the trial or hearing and is subject to cross-examination concerning the statement, and the statement is (A) inconsistent with the declarant's testimony, and was given under oath subject to the penalty of perjury at a trial, hearing or other proceeding, or in a deposition, or (B) consistent with the declarant's testimony and is offered to rebut an express or implied charge against the declarant of recent fabrication or improper influence or motive; or (C) one of identification of a person made after perceiving the person; or

(2) **Admission by party-opponent.** The statement is offered against a party and is (A) the party's own statement, in either an individual or a representative capacity or (B) a statement of which the party has manifested an adoption or belief in its truth, or (C) a statement by a person authorized by the party to make a statement concerning the subject, or (D) a statement by the party's agent or servant concerning a matter within the scope of the party's agency of employment, made during the existence of the relationship, or (E) a statement by a coconspirator of a party during the course and in furtherance of the conspiracy.

Rule 802. Hearsay Rule. Hearsay is not admissible except as provided by these rules or by other rules prescribed by the Supreme Court pursuant to statutory authority or by Act of Congress.

Rule 803. Hearsay Exceptions; Availability of Declarant Immaterial. The following are not excluded by the hearsay rule, even though the declarant is available as a witness:

(1) **Present sense impression.** A statement describing or explaining an event or condition made while the declarant was perceiving the event or condition, or immediately thereafter.

(2) **Excited utterance.** A statement relating to a startling event or condition made while the declarant was under the stress of excitement caused by the event or condition.

(3) **Then existing mental, emotional, or physical condition.** A statement of the declarant's then existing state of mind, emotion, sensation, or physical condition (such as intent, plan, motive, design, mental feeling, pain, and bodily health), but not including a statement of memory or belief to prove the fact remembered or believed unless it relates to the execution, revocation, identification, or terms of declarant's will.

(4) **Statements for purposes of medical diagnosis or treatment.** Statements made for purposes of medical diagnosis or treatment and describing medical history, or past or present symptoms, pain, or sensations, or the inception or general character of the cause or external source thereof insofar as reasonably pertinent to diagnosis or treatment.

(5) **Recorded recollection.** A memorandum or record concerning a matter about which a witness once had knowledge but now has insufficient recol-

lection to enable the witness to testify fully and accurately, shown to have been made or adopted by the witness when the matter was fresh in the witness' memory and to reflect that knowledge correctly. If admitted, the memorandum or record may be read into evidence but may not itself be received as an exhibit unless offered by an adverse party.

(6) Records of regularly conducted activity. A memorandum, report, record, or data compilation, in any form, of acts, events, conditions, opinions, or diagnoses, made at or near the time by, or from information transmitted by, a person with knowledge, if kept in the course of a regularly conducted business activity, and if it was the regular practice of that business activity to make the memorandum, report, record, or data compilation, all as shown by the testimony of the custodian or other qualified witness, unless the source of information or the method or circumstances of preparation indicate lack of trustworthiness. The term "business" as used in this paragraph includes business, institution, association, profession, occupation, and calling of every kind, whether or not conducted for profit.

(7) Absence of entry in records kept in accordance with the provisions of paragraph (6). Evidence that a matter is not included in the memoranda, reports, records, or data compilations in any form, kept in accordance with the provisions of paragraph (6), to prove the nonoccurrence or nonexistence of the matter, if the matter was of a kind of which a memorandum, report, record, or data compilation was regularly made and preserved, unless the sources of information or other circumstances indicate lack of trustworthiness.

(8) Public records and reports. Records, reports, statements, or data compilations, in any form, of public offices or agencies, setting forth (A) the activities of the office or agency, or (B) matters observed pursuant to duty imposed by law as to which matters there was a duty to report, excluding, however, in criminal cases matters observed by police officers and other law enforcement personnel, or (C) in civil actions and proceedings and against the Government in criminal cases, factual findings resulting from an investigation made pursuant to authority granted by law, unless the sources of information or other circumstances indicate lack of trustworthiness.

(9) Records of vital statistics. Records or data compilations, in any form, of births, fetal deaths, deaths, or marriages, if the report thereof was made to a public office pursuant to requirements of law.

(10) Absence of public record or entry. To prove the absence of a record, report, statement, or data compilation, in any form, or the nonoccurrence or nonexistence of a matter of which a record, report, statement, or data compilation, in any form, was regularly made and preserved by a public office or agency, evidence in the form of a certification in accordance with Rule 902, or testimony, that diligent search failed to disclose the record, report, statement, or data compilation, or entry.

(11) Records of religious organizations. Statements of births, marriages, divorces, deaths, legitimacy, ancestry, relationship by blood or marriage, or other similar facts of personal or family history, contained in a regularly kept record of a religious organization.

(12) **Marriage, baptismal, and similar certificates.** Statements of fact contained in a certificate that the maker performed a marriage or other ceremony or administered a sacrament, made by a clergyman, public official, or other person authorized by the rules or practices of a religious organization or by law to perform the act certified, and purporting to have been issued at the time of the act or within a reasonable time thereafter.

(13) **Family records.** Statements of fact concerning personal or family history contained in family Bibles, genealogies, charts, engravings on rings, inscriptions on family portraits, engravings on urns, crypts, or tombstones, or the like.

(14) **Records of documents affecting an interest in property.** The record of a document purporting to establish or affect an interest in property, as proof of the content of the original recorded document and its execution and delivery by each person by whom it purports to have been executed, if the record is a record of a public office and an applicable statute authorizes the recording of documents of that kind in that office.

(15) **Statements in documents affecting an interest in property.** A statement contained in a document purporting to establish or affect an interest in property if the matter stated was relevant to the purpose of the document, unless dealings with the property since the document was made have been inconsistent with the truth of the statement or the purport of the document.

(16) **Statements in ancient documents.** Statements in a document in existence twenty years or more the authenticity of which is established.

(17) **Market reports, commercial publications.** Market quotations, tabulations, lists, directories, or other published compilations, generally used and relied upon by the public or by persons in particular occupations.

(18) **Learned treatises.** To the extent called to the attention of an expert witness upon cross-examination or relied upon by the expert witness in direct examination, statements contained in published treatises, periodicals, or pamphlets on a subject of history, medicine, or other science or art, established as a reliable authority by the testimony or admission of the witness or by other expert testimony or by judicial notice. If admitted, the statements may be read into evidence but may not be received as exhibits.

(19) **Reputation concerning personal or family history.** Reputation among members of a person's family by blood, adoption, or marriage, or among a person's associates, or in the community, concerning a person's birth, adoption, marriage, divorce, death, legitimacy, relationship by blood, adoption, or marriage, ancestry, or other similar fact of personal or family history.

(20) **Reputation concerning boundaries or general history.** Reputation in a community, arising before the controversy, as to boundaries of or customs affecting lands in the community, and reputation as to events of general history important to the community or State or nation in which located.

(21) Reputation as to character. Reputation of a person's character among associates or in the community.

(22) Judgment of previous conviction. Evidence of a final judgment, entered after a trial or upon a plea of guilty (but not upon a plea of nolo contendere), adjudging a person guilty of a crime punishable by death or imprisonment in excess of one year, to prove any fact essential to sustain the judgment, but not including, when offered by the Government in a criminal prosecution for purposes other than impeachment, judgments against persons other than the accused. The pendency of an appeal may be shown but does not effect admissibility.

(23) Judgment as to personal, family, or general history, or boundaries. Judgments as proof of matters of personal family or general history, or boundaries, essential to the judgment, if the same would be provable by evidence of reputation.

(24) Other exceptions. A statement not specifically covered by any of the foregoing exceptions but having equivalent circumstantial guarantees of trustworthiness, if the court determines that (A) the statement is offered as evidence of a material fact; (B) the statement is more probative on the point for which it is offered than any other evidence which the proponent can procure through reasonable efforts; and (C) the general purposes of these rules and the interests of justice will be best served by the admission of the statement into evidence. However, a statement may not be admitted under this exception unless the proponent of it makes known to the adverse party sufficiently in advance of the trial or hearing to provide the adverse party with a fair opportunity to prepare to meet it, the proponent's intention to offer the statement and the particulars of it, including the name and address of the declarant.

Rule 804. Hearsay Exceptions; Declarant Unavailable

(a) Definition of unavailability. "Unavailability as a witness" includes situations in which the declarant—

    (1)   is exempted by ruling of the court on the ground of privilege from testifying concerning the subject matter of the declarant's statement; or

    (2)   persists in refusing to testify concerning the subject matter of the declarant's statement despite an order of the court to do so; or

    (3)   testifies to a lack of memory of the subject matter of the declarant's statement; or

    (4)   is unable to be present or to testify at the hearing because of death or then existing physical or mental illness or infirmity; or

    (5)   is absent from the hearing and the proponent of his statement has been unable to procure the declarant's attendance (or in the case of a hearsay exception under subdivision (b)(2), (3), or (4), the declarant's attendance or testimony) by process or other reasonable means.

A declarant is not unavailable as a witness if exemption, refusal, claim of lack of memory, inability, or absence is due to the procurement or wrongdoing of the proponent of a statement for the purpose of preventing the witness from attending or testifying.

(b) Hearsay exceptions. The following are not excluded by the hearsay rule if the declarant is unavailable as a witness:

(1) Former testimony. Testimony given as a witness at another hearing of the same or a different proceeding, or in a deposition taken in compliance with law in the course of the same or another proceeding, if the party against whom the testimony is now offered, or, in a civil action or proceeding, a predecessor in interest, had an opportunity and similar motive to develop the testimony by direct, cross, or redirect examination.

(2) Statement under belief of impending death. In a prosecution for homicide or in a civil action or proceeding, a statement made by a declarant while believing that the declarant's death was imminent, concerning the cause or circumstances of what the declarant believed to be impending death.

(3) Statement against interest. A statement which was at the time of its making so far contrary to the declarant's pecuniary or proprietary interest, or so far tended to subject the declarant to civil or criminal liability, or to render invalid a claim by the declarant against another, that a reasonable person in the declarant's position would not have made the statement unless believing it to be true. A statement tending to expose the declarant to criminal liability and offered to exculpate the accused is not admissible unless corroborating circumstances clearly indicate the trustworthiness of the statement.

(4) Statement of personal or family history. (A) A statement concerning the declarant's own birth, adoption, marriage, divorce, legitimacy, relationship by blood, adoption, or marriage, ancestry, or other similar fact of personal or family history, even though declarant had no means of acquiring personal knowledge of the matter stated; or (B) a statement concerning the foregoing matters, and death also, of another person, if the declarant was related to the other by blood, adoption, or marriage or was so intimately associated with the other's family as to be likely to have accurate information concerning the matter declared.

(5) Other exceptions. A statement not specifically covered by any of the foregoing exceptions but having equivalent circumstantial guarantees of trustworthiness, if the court determines that (A) the statement is offered as evidence of a material fact; (B) the statement is more probative on the point for which it is offered than any other evidence which the proponent can procure through reasonable efforts; and (C) the general purposes of these rules and the interests of justice will best be served by admission of the statement into evidence. However, a statement may not be admitted under this exception unless the proponent of it makes known to the adverse party sufficiently in advance of the trial or hearing to provide the adverse party with a fair opportunity to prepare to meet it, the proponent's intention to offer the statement and the particulars of it, including the name and address of the declarant.

Rule 805. Hearsay Within Hearsay. Hearsay included within hearsay is not excluded under the hearsay rule if each part of the combined statements conforms with an exception to the hearsay rule provided in these rules.

Rule 806. Attacking and Supporting Credibility of Declarant. When a hearsay statement, or a statement defined in Rule 801(d)(2), (C), (D), or (E), has been admitted in evidence, the credibility of the declarant may be attacked, and if attacked may be supported, by any evidence which would be admissible for those purposes if declarant had testified as a witness. Evidence of a statement or conduct by the declarant at any time, inconsistent with the declarant's hearsay statement, is not subject to any requirement that the declarant may have been afforded an opportunity to deny or explain. If the party against whom a hearsay statement has been admitted calls the declarant as a witness, the party is entitled to examine the declarant on the statement as if under cross-examination.

ARTICLE IX. AUTHENTICATION AND IDENTIFICATION

Rule 901. Requirement of Authentication or Identification
(a) General provision. The requirement of authentication or identification as a condition precedent to admissibility is satisfied by evidence sufficient to support a finding that the matter in question is what its proponent claims.
(b) Illustrations. By way of illustration only, and not by way of limitation, the following are examples of authentication or identification conforming with the requirements of this rule:
  (1) Testimony of witness with knowledge. Testimony that a matter is what it is claimed to be.
  (2) Nonexpert opinion on handwriting. Nonexpert opinion as to the genuineness of handwriting, based upon familiarity not acquired for purposes of the litigation.
  (3) Comparison by trier or expert witness. Comparison by the trier of fact or by expert witnesses with specimens which have been authenticated.
  (4) Distinctive characteristics and the like. Appearance, contents, substance, internal patterns, or other distinctive characteristics, taken in conjunction with circumstances.
  (5) Voice identification. Identification of a voice, whether heard firsthand or through mechanical or electronic transmission or recording, by opinion based upon hearing the voice at any time under circumstances connecting it with the alleged speaker.
  (6) Telephone conversations. Telephone conversations, by evidence that a call was made to the number assigned at the time by the telephone company to a particular person or business, if (A) in the case of

a person, circumstances, including self-identification, show the person answering to be the one called, or (B) in the case of a business, the call was made to a place of business and the conversation related to business reasonably transacted over the telephone.

(7) **Public records or reports.** Evidence that a writing authorized by law to be recorded or filed and in fact recorded or filed in a public office, or a purported public record, report, statement, or data compilation, in any form, is from the public office where items of this nature are kept.

(8) **Ancient documents or data compilation.** Evidence that a document or data compilation, in any form, (A) is in such condition as to create no suspicion concerning its authenticity, (B) was in a place where it, if authentic, would likely be, and (C) has been in existence 20 years or more at the time it is offered.

(9) **Process or system.** Evidence describing a process or system used to produce a result and showing that the process or system produces an accurate result.

(10) **Methods provided by statute or rule.** Any method of authentication or identification provided by Act of Congress or by other rules prescribed by the Supreme Court pursuant to statutory authority.

Rule 902. Self-Authentication. Extrinsic evidence of authenticity as a condition precedent to admissibility is not required with respect to the following:

(1) **Domestic public documents under seal.** A document bearing a seal purporting to be that of the United States, or of any State, district, Commonwealth, territory, or insular possession thereof, or the Panama Canal Zone, or the Trust Territory of the Pacific Islands, or of a political subdivision, department, officer, or agency thereof, and a signature purporting to be an attestation or execution.

(2) **Domestic public documents not under seal.** A document purporting to bear the signature in the official capacity of an officer or employee of any entity included in paragraph (1) hereof, having no seal, if a public officer having a seal and having official duties in the district or political subdivision of the officer or employee certifies under seal that the signer has the official capacity and that the signature is genuine.

(3) **Foreign public documents.** A document purporting to be executed or attested in an official capacity by a person authorized by the laws of a foreign country to make the execution or attestation, and accompanied by a final certification as to the genuineness of the signature and official position (A) of the executing or attesting person, or (B) of any foreign official whose certificate of genuineness of signature and official position relates to the execution or attestation or is in a chain of certificates of genuineness of signature and official position relating to the execution or attestation. A final certification may be made by a secretary of embassy or legation, consul general, consul, vice consul, or consular agent of the United States, or a diplomatic or consular official of the foreign country assigned or accredited to the United States. If reasonable opportunity has been given to all parties

to investigate the authenticity and accuracy of official documents, the court may, for good cause shown, order that they be treated as presumptively authentic without final certification or permit them to be evidenced by an attested summary with or without final certification.

(4) **Certified copies of public records.** A copy of an official record or report or entry therein, or of a document authorized by law to be recorded or filed and actually recorded or filed in a public office, including data compilations in any form, certified as correct by the custodian or other person authorized to make the certification, by certificate complying with paragraph (1), (2), or (3) of this rule or complying with any Act of Congress or rule prescribed by the Supreme Court pursuant to statutory authority.

(5) **Official publications.** Books, pamphlets, or other publications purporting to be issued by public authority.

(6) **Newspapers and periodicals.** Printed materials purporting to be newspapers or periodicals.

(7) **Trade inscriptions and the like.** Inscriptions, signs, tags, or labels purporting to have been affixed in the course of business and indicating ownership, control, or origin.

(8) **Acknowledged documents.** Documents accompanied by a certificate of acknowledgment executed in the manner provided by law by a notary public or other officer authorized by law to take acknowledgments.

(9) **Commercial paper and related documents.** Commercial paper, signatures thereon, and documents relating thereto to the extent provided by general commercial law.

(10) **Presumptions under Acts of Congress.** Any signature, document, or other matter declared by Act of Congress to be presumptively or prima facie genuine or authentic.

Rule 903. Subscribing Witness' Testimony Unnecessary. The testimony of a subscribing witness is not necessary to authenticate a writing unless required by the laws of the jurisdiction whose laws govern the validity of the writing.

ARTICLE X.   CONTENTS OF WRITINGS, RECORDINGS, AND PHOTOGRAPHS

Rule 1001. Definitions. For purposes of this article the following definitions are applicable:

(1) **Writings and recordings.** "Writings" and "recordings" consist of letters, words, or numbers, or their equivalent, set down by handwriting, typewriting, printing, photostating, photographing, magnetic impulse, mechanical or electronic recording, or other form of data compilation.

(2) **Photographs.** "Photographs" include still photographs, X-ray films, video tapes, and motion pictures.

(3) **Original.** An "original" of a writing or recording is the writing or recording itself or any counterpart intended to have the same effect by a person executing or issuing it. An "original" of a photograph includes the negative or any print therefrom. If data are stored in a computer or similar device, any printout or other output readable by sight, shown to reflect the data accurately, is an "original."

(4) **Duplicate.** A "duplicate" is a counterpart produced by the same impression as the original, or from the same matrix, or by means of photography, including enlargements and miniatures, or by mechanical or electronic rerecording, or by chemical reproduction, or by other equivalent techniques which accurately reproduces the original.

Rule 1002. Requirement of Original. To prove the content of a writing, recording, or photograph, the original writing, recording, or photograph is required, except as otherwise provided in these rules or by Act of Congress.

Rule 1003. Admissibility of Duplicates. A duplicate is admissible to the same extent as an original unless (1) a genuine question is raised as to the authenticity of the original or (2) in the circumstances it would be unfair to admit the duplicate in lieu of the original.

Rule 1004.   Admissibility of Other Evidence of Contents. The original is not required, and other evidence of the contents of a writing,
recording, or photograph is admissible if—

(1) **Originals lost or destroyed.** All originals are lost or have been destroyed, unless the proponent lost or destroyed them in bad faith; or

(2) **Original not obtainable.** No original can be obtained by any available judicial process or procedure; or

(3) **Original in possession of opponent.** At a time when an original was under the control of the party against whom offered, that party was put on notice, by the pleadings or otherwise, that the contents would be a subject of proof at the hearing, and that party does not produce the original at the hearing; or

(4) **Collateral matters.** The writing, recording, or photograph is not closely related to a controlling issue.

Rule 1005. Public Records. The contents of an official record, or of a document authorized to be recorded or filed and actually recorded or filed, including data compilations in any form, if otherwise admissible, may be proved by copy, certified as correct in accordance with Rule 902 or testified to be correct by a witness who has compared it with the original. If a copy which complies with the foregoing cannot be obtained by the exercise of reasonable diligence, then other evidence of the contents may be given.

Rule 1006. Summaries. The contents of voluminous writings, recordings, or photographs which cannot conveniently be examined in court may be presented in the form of a chart, summary, or calculation. The originals, or duplicates, shall be made available for examination or copying, or both, by other parties at reasonable time and place. The court may order that they be produced in court.

Rule 1007. Testimony or Written Admission of Party. Contents of writings, recordings, or photographs may be proved by the testimony or deposition of the party against whom offered or by that party's written admission, without accounting for the nonproduction of the original.

Rule 1008. Functions of Court and Jury. When the admissibility of other evidence of contents of writings, recordings, or photographs under these rules depends upon the fulfillment of a condition of fact, the question whether the condition has been fulfilled is ordinarily for the court to determine in accordance with the provisions of Rule 104. However, when an issue is raised (a) whether the asserted writing ever existed, or (b) whether another writing, recording, or photograph produced at the trial is the original, or (c) whether other evidence of contents correctly reflects the contents, the issue is for the trier of fact to determine as in the case of other issues of fact.

ARTICLE XI.   MISCELLANEOUS RULES

Rule 1101. Applicability of Rules
(a) **Courts and magistrates.** These rules apply to the United States district courts, the United States bankruptcy courts, the District Court of Guam, the District Court of the Virgin Islands, the District Court for the Northern Mariana Islands, the United States courts of appeals, the United States Claims Court, and to United States bankruptcy judges and United States magistrate judges, in the actions, cases, and proceedings and to the extent hereinafter set forth. The terms "judge" and "court" in these rules include United States bankruptcy judges and United States magistrate judges.
(b) **Proceedings generally.** These rules apply generally to civil actions and proceedings, including admiralty and maritime cases, to criminal cases and proceedings, to contempt proceedings except those in which the court may act summarily, and to proceedings and cases under title 11, United States Code.
(c) **Rule of privilege.** The rule with respect to privileges applies at all stages of all actions, cases, and proceedings.
(d) **Rules inapplicable.** The rules (other than with respect to privileges) do not apply in the following situations:
   (1) **Preliminary questions of fact.** The determination of questions of fact preliminary to admissibility of evidence when the issue is to be determined by the court under rule 104.
   (2) **Grand jury.** Proceedings before grand juries.
   (3) **Miscellaneous proceedings.** Proceedings for extradition or rendition; preliminary examinations in criminal cases; sentencing, or granting or

revoking probation; issuance of warrants for arrest, criminal summonses, and search warrants; and proceedings with respect to release on bail or otherwise.

(e) Rules applicable in part. In the following proceedings these rules apply to the extent that matters of evidence are not provided for in the statutes which govern procedure therein or in other rules prescribed by the Supreme Court pursuant to statutory authority: the trial of misdemeanors and petty offenses before United States magistrate judges; review of agency actions when the facts are subject to trial de novo under section 706(2)(F) of title 5, United States Code; review of orders of the Secretary of Agriculture under section 2 of the Act entitled "An Act to authorize association of producers of agricultural products" approved February 18, 1922 (7 U.S.C. 292), and under sections 6 and 7(c) of the Perishable Agricultural Commodities Act, 1930 (7 U.S.C. 499f, 499g(c)); naturalization and revocation of naturalization under sections 310-318 of the Immigration and Nationality Act (8 U.S.C. 1421–1429); prize proceedings in admiralty under sections 7651–7681 of title 10, United States Code; review of orders of the Secretary of the Interior under section 2 of the Act entitled "An Act authorizing associations of producers of aquatic products" approved June 25, 1934 (15 U.S.C. 522); review of orders of petroleum control boards under section 5 of the Act entitled "An Act to regulate interstate and foreign commerce in petroleum and its products by prohibiting the shipment in such commerce of petroleum and its products produced in violation of State law, and for other purposes," approved February 22, 1935 (15 U.S.C. 715d); actions for fines, penalties, or forfeitures under part V of title IV of the Tariff Act of 1930 (19 U.S.C. 1581–1624), or under the Anti-Smuggling Act (19 U.S.C. 1701–1711); criminal libel for condemnation, exclusion of imports, or other proceedings under the Federal Food, Drug, and Cosmetic Act (21 U.S.C. 301–392); disputes between seamen under sections 4079, 4080, and 4081 of the Revised Statutes (22 U.S.C. 256–258); habeas corpus under sections 2241–2254 of title 28, United States Code; motions to vacate, set aside or correct sentence under section 2255 of title 28, United States Code; actions for penalties for refusal to transport destitute seamen under section 4578 of the Revised Statutes (46 U.S.C. 679); actions against the United States under the Act entitled "An Act authorizing suits against the United States in admiralty for damage caused by and salvage service rendered to public vessels belonging to the United States, and for other purposes," approved March 3, 1925 (46 U.S.C. 781–790), as implemented by section 7730 of title 10, United States Code.

Rule 1102. Amendments. Amendments to the Federal Rules of Evidence may be made as provided in section 2076 of title 28 of the United States Code.

Rule 1103. Title. These rules may be known and cited as the Federal Rules of Evidence.

APPENDIX B

A BRIEF HISTORY OF THE OREGON EVIDENCE CODE

The formulation of the new evidence code began in 1974 when the Advisory Committee on Evidence Law Revision was appointed by the Law Improvement Committee. The Law Improvement Committee was a legislatively created body charged with examining the "statutes and common law of the state for the purpose of discovering defects and anachronisms ... and recommending needed reforms." *See* former ORS 173.310–173.340 (repealed 1979). The following distinguished attorneys and judges served as members of the Advisory Committee on Evidence Law Revision: Manley B. Strayer, Chairman; James M. Brown; John D. Burns; William V. Deatherage; Chief Justice Arno H. Denecke; Burl L. Green; Wendell E. Gronso; Judge Robert E. Jones; Roy Kilpatrick; Professor Ronald B. Lansing; Asa L. Lewelling; Gordon H. Moore; J. Michael Starr; Roger B. Todd; Judge Richard L. Unis. Professor John Strong, formerly of the University of Oregon Law School assisted the Advisory Committee in its early deliberations.

The Advisory Committee undertook a comprehensive five-year examination of Oregon evidence law. In September, 1979, it submitted a proposed new code accompanied by an extensive commentary to the Interim Joint Committee on the Judiciary of the Oregon Legislature. For a description and analysis of the proposed code along with suggested amendments, *see* Kirkpatrick, *Reforming Evidence Law in Oregon*, 59 Or. L Rev 43–123 (1980). During 1979–80, the Subcommittee on Evidence of the Interim Judiciary Committee considered the proposed code, received testimony from numerous individuals and groups, and in December, 1980, submitted its recommended version of the code to the 1981 Oregon Legislative Assembly. *See Proposed Oregon Evidence Code, Report of the Legislative Interim Committee on the Judiciary* (1980). The report included the Advisory Committee commentary supplemented by the separate commentary of the Interim Judiciary Committee. The members of the Subcommittee on Evidence were: Representative Tom Mason; Senator Walt Brown; Representative Joyce Cohen; Senator Vern Cook, ex officio member; Representative Dave Frohnmayer; Senator Jim Gardner; Representative Bill Rutherford; Representative Norm Smith, Vice Chairperson; Senator Jan Wyers.

The final legislative commentary was prepared by Stephen L. Griffith, Legal Counsel for the House Committee on the Judiciary and Kristena A. LaMar, Legal Counsel for the Senate Justice Committee.

The proposed code was introduced at the 1981 Oregon Legislative Assembly as H.B. 2030. A number of significant modifications and amendments were adopted by the legislature. The House Judiciary Committee and the Senate Justice Committee revised and integrated the commentary of the Advisory Committee and Interim Judiciary Committee and added additional commentary to explain changes made by the legislature. The bill was passed by the legislature on August 2, 1981, and signed by Governor Atiyeh on August 22, 1981. It became Chapter 892, 1981 Oregon Session Laws. The evidence code is now set forth in Chapter 40, Oregon Revised Statutes.

TABLE OF CASES

Page references are **bold**.

A

Table of Cases

C

Table of Cases

D

E

F

G

Table of Cases

H

Table of Cases

I

J

K

L

Table of Cases

M

N

O

P

Q

R

S

Table of Cases

Table of Cases

Table of Cases

Table of Cases

Table of Cases

U

Table of Cases

Table of Cases

Table of Cases

V

W

Y

Z

TABLE OF STATUTES

OREGON REVISED STATUTES

*The following is a list of the Oregon Revised Statutes numbers in this volume. Page references are **bold**.*

Table of Statutes

Table of Statutes

INDEX

A

Absence of Accident
Other acts or conduct to prove, Rules 404, 404(3)

Absence of Complaint
Admissibility as nonhearsay statement, Rule 801(1)

Absence of Record or Entry
Business record, hearsay exception for absence of entry, Rule 803(7)
Public record or entry, hearsay exception for absence of, Rule 803(10)

Accident Reconstruction
Expert testimony regarding, Rule 702

Accountants
Communications with, lawyer-client privilege, Rule 503(1)(e)

Accused
Testimony by, Rule 104(4)

Acknowledged Documents, Rule 902(8)

Acquittal, Rule 404(3)

Adjudicative Facts
Criminal cases, Rule 201(g)
Discretionary and mandatory authority, Rule 201(c)
Instructing jury, Rules 201(a), 201(g)
Kinds of facts to be judicially noticed, Rule 201(b)
Legislative facts distinguished, Rule 201(a)

Administrative Acts and Proceedings
Applicability of OEC, Rule 101
Judicial notice of administrative acts, Rule 202

Admissibility of Evidence
See also more specific headings
In camera, Rule 412
Curative admissibility, Rule 402
Limited admissibility
    bias or interest, use for impeachment, Rule 609-1
    business practices, Rule 401
    character, Rules 105, 404(1), (2), (3)
    codefendant's confession, Rule 105
    company rules, industry standards, construction contracts, Rule 401
    evidence admissible as to one purpose or party generally, Rule 105

Index

Agency

Admissions of party-opponent authorized, Rules 801(4)(b), 801(4)(b)(C)
vicarious, Rule 801(4)(b)(D)
Authority, similar contracts, admitted to show, Rule 401
Insurance admitted to establish, limiting instruction, Rules 105, 411
Preliminary question, conditional relevancy, Rule 104(2)

Agent's and Employee's Admission, Rules 801(4)(b), 801(4)(b)(D)

Authentication of evidence by party's admission, Rule 901(1)
Bias or interest, effect of witness's admission of facts on impeachment
procedure, Rule 609-1
Coconspirator's admission nonhearsay, Rules 801(4)(b), 801(4)(b)(E)
Compromise negotiations, admissions in, Rule 408
Corporate officer's admission in deposition, Rule 801(4)(b)(C)
Depositions
admissions of party-opponent in, Rule 801(4)(b)(A)
authentication of evidence by admissions in, Rule 901(2)(a)
corporate officer's admissions in, Rule 804(4)(b)(C)
proof of contents of writing, recording or photography by admission in,
Rule 901(2)(a)
Handwriting exemplar, genuineness, Rule 901
Judicial admissions, Rule 801(4)(b)(A)
Jury instruction, oral admission of party to be viewed with caution, Rule
801(4)(b)(A)
Party-opponent's admissions as nonhearsay, Rule 801(4)(b)
Payment of medical expenses or property damage, collateral factual
statements, Rule 409
Pleadings, admissions of party in, Rules 801(4)(b)(A), 801(4)(b)(B)
Plea negotiations, admissions in, Rules 408, 410
Plea of guilty as admission of party-opponent, Rule 801(4)(b)(A)
Prior inconsistent statements
extrinsic evidence of, compared to admission of party opponent in hearsay
issue, Rule 613
witness's admission of, effect on procedure for impeachment, Rule 613(2)
Remedial measures subsequently taken as, Rule 407
Statements against interest of nonparty witness
hearsay exception, principle and illustrations, Rule 804(3)(c)
nonhearsay admission of party opponent distinguished, Rule 801(4)(b)(A)
preliminary question of against-interest requirement, Rule 104
Value of property, party's statement of, Rule 401
Vicarious, Rule 801(4)(b)(D)
Voluntariness requirement, Rule 801(4)(b)(A)
Writings, recordings, photographs, proof of contents by, Rule 1008

Index

Alcohol and Drugs
Treatment for, exclusion from privilege rules
psychotherapist, Rule 504
school employee, Rule 504-3
Witnesses, use by
competency, bearing on, Rule 601
impeachment ground, Rules 602, 607

Allegations. *See* Pleadings

Allocation of Burdens, Rules 305, 307

Ancient Documents
Authentication methods and conditions, Rules 803(16), 901, 901(2)(h)
Hearsay exception, Rules 803(16), 901, 901(2)(g)

Appeal
Affirmance notwithstanding error, Rules 103, 103(1)
Applicability of oec to appellate courts, Rule 101(1)
Conviction of crime used to impeach
effect of appeal on admissibility, Rules 609, 609(4), 803, 803(22)
failure to testify, effect on appeal from ruling, Rule 609
reversal of conviction, effect on admissibility, Rules 609, 609(2)(b)
Grounds, statement of, Rule 103(1)
Harmless error, Rule 103(1)
Invited error, Rule 103(4)
Judgment of conviction as hearsay exception, effect of appeal, Rules 803, 803(22)
Judicial notice taken on appeal, Rule 201(f)
Lawyer-client privilege, procedure after claim overruled, Rule 503(3)
Limiting admissibility of evidence, effect of failure to request, Rule 105
Plain error, Rules 103, 105
Record
designating portions, Rule 103(1)
offer of proof and ruling, Rule 103
trial court's responsibility, Rule 103(3)
Rulings on evidence, standards and procedures for assignment as error, Rule 103(1)-(4)
Writing used to refresh memory, preserving portions withheld, Rule 612

Appraisers
Lawyer-client privilege applied to client's appraiser, Rules 503, 503(2)

Argument
Burden of persuasion, commenting on during closing remarks, Rule 306
Inadmissible evidence revealed during, Rule 103(3)

Attorney-Client Privilege
See also Lawyer-Client Privilege

796

Generally, Rule 503

Attorneys
Admissions of party-opponent in stipulation by, Rule 801(4)(b)(C)
Authorized admission of party opponent by, Rule 801(4)(b)(C)
Deceased attorney's records hearsay exception, Rule 804
Harassment of witness by, Rule 103(3)
Inadmissible evidence, revealing to jury, Rule 103(3)
Joint client, Rule 503(4)(e)
Jurors, attorney's contacts with, Rule 606
Lawyer-client privilege
  see also Privileges
  definitions, Rules 503, 503(1)(a)-(e)
  exceptions, Rules 503, 503(4)
  persons who may claim, Rules 503, 503(3)
  rule and applications, Rules 503, 503(2)
Misconduct, exception to privilege rules, Rules 503, 503(4)
Personal knowledge or opinion, asserting to jury, Rule 103(3)
Rules of professional responsibility governing, Rule 503
Statement made in professional capacity, hearsay exception, Rule 804
Witness, attorney as attesting witness, exception to privilege rules, Rule 503
  competence as, Rule 601
Work product doctrine
  corporation employee's communication to corporation's attorney, Rule 503(1)(d)
  expert's communications within, Rule 503(1)(e)
  scope, Rule 503(4)
  waiver by witness's reference to, Rule 511
  writing used for refreshing memory, protecting privileged material, Rule 612

Attorneys' Fees
Disputes on, exception to privilege rules, Rule 503
Identity of client revealed by agreements for, privilege rule, Rules 503(1)(b), 503(4)
Payment of, significance in determining lawyer-client relationship, Rule 503(1)(a)

Authentication and Identification
Admission of party, authentication by, Rule 901(1)
Ancient documents and data compilations, Rules 803, 901, 901(2)(h)
Best evidence rule, authenticity of original in question, Rules 901-1003
Birth certificates, Rule 901(2)(j)
Business records, for admission under hearsay exception, Rules 803, 803(6)
Communication in response to another communication, Rule 901(2)(d)
Comparison with specimens by trier or experts as method, Rules 901, 901(2)(c)

B

Index

Shifting, Rules 306, 307
Witness's opportunity to observe fact, Rule 602

Burden of Proof
See also Burden of persuasion; Burden of producing evidence
Defined and distinguished, Rule 305

Business Practices
Limited admissibility in negligence cases, Rule 401
Routine practice, admissibility rules and examples, Rule 406

Business Records
Authentication, Rule 803(6)
Destruction of, Rule 1003-1
Hearsay exception for absence of entry, Rule 803(7)
Hearsay exception for business records
  definition of business, Rule 803(6)
  duty to report requirement, Rule 803(6)
  examples, Rule 803(6)
  foundation, source, Rule 803(6)
  generally, Rules 803(1)-(7)
  hospital records included within, Rule 803(6)
  motivation, Rule 803(6)
  opinion and diagnosis entries, Rule 803(6)
  police reports as, Rule 803(6)
Hearsay exception for church records, overlap, Rule 803(11)

C

Capacity, of Witnesses, Rule 601

Certified Copies of Public Records, Rules 902(4), 1005

Chain of Custody
Exhibits with distinctive characteristics, Rule 901(2)(a)

Character Evidence
Accused, character traits of, Rules 404, 404(2)
Admissibility generally, Rules 404, 404(2)
Bias and interest, character for truthfulness to refute, Rule 609-1
Character witnesses examination and cross-examination, Rules 405, 608(2)
  foundation, Rules 405, 608
  number, limiting, Rule 405
  opinion testimony by, Rule 608
  religious belief, Rule 105
Circumstantial evidence of, Rule 404
Defined, Rule 404(1)

Index

Index

Index

limitation to direct, Rules 607, 611, 611(2)

Sequestration order violation by witness, referring, Rule 615

Unavailability of witness for generally. *See* Witnesses confrontation right. *See* Confrontation, right of

sanctions, Rule 611(2)

Writing used to refresh memory, right of cross-examination, procedure, Rule 612

Cumulative Evidence

Ground for excluding relevant evidence, Rule 403

Curative Admissibility

Principle illustrated, Rule 403

D

Damages

Settlement with third persons, admissibility, Rule 408

Dangerousness

Admissibility of prior bad acts to prove, Rule 404(3)

Data Compilations

Authentication methods and conditions, Rule 901

Computer printouts, admissibility as originals under best evidence rule, Rule 1001

Dead Man's Statute, Rule 601

Death and Decedents

Hearsay rule and exceptions relating to

death certificates, Rule 803(12)

mortality tables, Rule 803(17)

religious organization's records, Rule 803(11)

reputation concerning personal or family history, Rule 803(19)

statements of memory or belief relating to wills, Rule 803(3)

statements under belief of impending death, Rule 804(3)(b)

vital statistics record exception, Rule 803(9)

Presumption of, from seven-year absence, Rule 311

Privilege rules

lawyer-client privilege, effect of client's death; claim by personal representative, Rules 503, 503(3)

lawyer-client privilege, parties claiming through same deceased client, Rule 503

physician-patient privilege, effect of patient's death, Rule 504

physician's report of death, Rule 504-1

psychotherapist-patient privilege, application after patient's death, Rule 504

Wills. *See* Wills

Declarant
Definition of, for hearsay purposes, Rule 801(2)

Declaration Against Interest. *See* Statement Against Interest

Declaratory Judgment Proceedings
Burden of persuasion, Rule 305

Defamation
Informer privilege, Rule 510
Media representative's privilege, Rule 514

Defects
Prior conduct or events admissible to show, Rule 401
Remedial measures, limited admissibility, instructions, Rules 105, 407

Definitions. *See* Words and Phrases

Delay
Compromise and offers, admissibility to negate contention of delay, Rule 408
Ground for excluding relevant evidence, Rule 403

Demonstrative Evidence, Rule 401
Court's discretion in use of, Rule 611(1)
Display of wounds and injuries, admissibility, Rule 401

Depositions
Admissions in authentication or identification of evidence by, Rule 901(2)(a)
    corporate officer's admission, Rule 801(4)(b)(C)
    proof of contents of writing, recording or photograph, Rule 1007
Authentication of deposition statutory method, Rule 901(2)(j)
    stipulating, Rule 613(2)
Exhibit, deposition offered as, Rule 613(2)
Foreign jurisdiction, taking deposition in, Rule 1004
Former testimony hearsay exception, Rule 804(3)(a)
Offer of proof by, Rule 103(1)
Part, introduced, admissibility of whole, Rule 106
Prior inconsistent statements, use for impeachment or substantive evidence, procedure, Rule 613(2)
Privilege rules
    applicability generally, Rule 101
    examination of public officers or records, Rule 509
    waiver of privilege in deposition, Rules 503(4), 511
Sentencing hearing, witness unable to appear, Rule 101
Statements of party in, purpose for which admissible, Rules 801(4)(b)(A), 801(4)(b)(C)
Transcript, qualification as recorded recollection or public record, Rule 613(2)
Unavailability of witness test in certain hearsay exceptions, Rules 804(1), (3)(a)

Index

E

F

Index

Character witness, Rules 405, 608
Coconspirator's admission, Rule 801(4)(b)(E)
Conditional relevancy, determination of foundation's sufficiency, Rule 104
Dying declaration, Rule 804(3)(b)
Experiments, Rule 401
Expert's opinion
    Bases for opinion, Rules 703, 705
    public opinion poll or survey, Rule 703
    scientific tests or procedures, Rule 702
Impeachment of hearsay declarant, Rule 806
Marriage, baptismal and similar certificates, Rule 803(12)
Personal knowledge of witness requirement, Rule 602
Prior inconsistent statements
    extrinsic evidence of, Rule 613(2)
    impeachment of hearsay declarant by, Rule 806
Public records, Rule 803(8)
Recorded recollection, Rule 803(5)
Tape recordings, Rule 901(2)(e)
Telephone conversation, Rule 901
Vital statistic records, Rule 803(9)
Writings
    handwriting exemplar, Rule 901
    used to refresh recollection, Rule 612

Fraud and Misrepresentation

Prior similar frauds, limited admissibility, Rule 401
Privilege rules, exception to lawyer-client communication, Rule 503(4)

G

Grand Jury Proceedings

Applicability of oec generally, Rule 101
Hearsay issue
    application of hearsay rules to grand jury proceeding, Rule 101
    former testimony, limitation in criminal trial, Rule 804(3)(a)
    inconsistent statements before, Rule 801(4)(a)(A)
    residual exception, when declarant unavailable, Rule 803(3)(f)
    statement of defendant at preliminary hearing, admissibility in, Rule 802
Privilege and immunity of grand jurors, Rule 606
Privilege rules applicable to, Rule 101
Reports of experts, receipt in evidence, Rule 101
Witness unable to appear, affidavit, Rule 101

Guardians and Conservators

Authorized admission against party-opponent by, Rule 801(4)(b)(C)
Lawyer-client privilege, persons who may claim, Rule 503(3)

822

Guilty Plea. *See* Pleas

H

Habit and Routine Practice
Amissibility rules and examples, Rule 406

Handicapped Persons
Iterpreters for, Rule 604

Handwriting
Comparison by trier or expert witness, Rule 901(2)(c)
Exemplar for comparison by expert, foundation, Rule 901
Exemplar for comparison by nonexpert, Rule 901(2)(b)
Nonexpert opinion on, Rule 901(2)(b)

Harassment of Witnesses. *See* Witnesses

Harmless Error
Examples of, Rule 103

Hearings
See also specific types
Closed hearings, constitutional considerations, Rule 412
Interpreters at, Rule 604
Oath or affirmation required at, Rule 603

Hearsay
Absence of complaint as nonhearsay, Rule 801(1)
Absence of entry in business record exception, Rule 803(7)
Absence of public record or entry exception, Rule 803(10)
Admissions of party-opponent as nonhearsay
adoptive admissions, acquiescence or silence, Rule 801(4)(b)(B)
agents' and employees' admissions, Rule 801(4)(b)(D)
authorized admissions, Rule 801(4)(b)(C)
coconspirator's admission, Rule 801(4)(b)(E)
depositions, admissions in, Rule 801(4)(b)(A)
extrinsic evidence of prior inconsistent statement compared, compared,
Rules 613, (2), 613(1)
generally, Rule 801(4)(b)
party's own admission, Rule 801(4)(b)(A)
pleadings, admissions of party in, Rule 801(4)(b)(A)
plea of guilty as, Rule 801(4)(b)(A)
writings, recordings, photographs, proof of contents by, Rule 1008
Agent's statement as admission of party-opponent, Rules 801(4)(b),
801(4)(b)(C)
Ancient documents

Index

Index

Historical Matters

Index

Homicide Victim

Photograph of

relevancy, Rule 401

Hospitals

Payment of hospital expenses, proof of liability for injury, Rule 409

Records

affidavit of custodian, statutory presumption from, Rules 802, 902(10)

business record hearsay exception applied to, Rule 803(6)

privilege exception in personal injury cases, Rule 504-1

Statements to attendant, hearsay, Rule 803(4)

X-ray interpretation by expert in, best evidence rule, Rule 1002

Hostile Witness

Leading questions, Rule 611(1), (3)

Husband and Wife

See also Family Matters

Authorized admissions, Rule 801(4)(b)(C)

Conciliation proceedings, applicability of privilege rules, Rule 504

Lawyer-client privilege, effect of disclosure to spouse, Rule 503(1)(b)

Marriage certificates as exception to hearsay rule, authentication and identification, Rule 803(12)

Presumption of marriage from deportment as, Rule 311

Privilege

asserting in presence of jury, Rule 513

crime against spouse or child, Rule 505(4)(a)

criminal proceedings, applicability to, Rule 505

definitions, Rule 505(1)

exceptions, Rules 505(4)(a), 505(4)(b)

inference from claim of privilege, Rule 513

nonverbal communications, Rule 505

persons who may claim, Rule 505

pre-marital communications, Rule 505

presence of third persons, effect on confidentiality, Rule 505

rules and applications, Rule 505

termination of marriage, effect, Rule 505(3)

waiver and consent, Rules 505, 513

witness, spouse as, Rules 505, 513

Hypnosis

Competence of hypnotized witness, Rule 601

Hypothetical Questions. *See* Experts

I

Identification
Evidence. *See* Authentication and identification
Person's identity
    client's, lawyer-client privilege, Rule 503(1)(d)
    extrajudicial identification of person as nonhearsay, Rule 801(4)(a)
    informant. *See* Informers opinion testimony of lay witness, Rule 701
    other crimes, wrongs or acts, admissibility to prove, Rule 404(3)
    presumption, identity of person from identity of name, Rule 311

Immateriality. *See* Materiality

Immunity
See also Privilege
Congressional and executive, Rule 514
Grand jury witness, Rule 606

Impeachment
Collateral matters, Rules 607, 613(2)
Evidence, relevancy of, Rule 401
Hearsay declarant, Rule 806
Jury verdict, Rule 606
Potential abuses, Rule 607
Witness. *See* Witnesses, impeachment of

Inconsistent Statements. *See* Witnesses

Indian Tribes
Authentication of documents under seal, Rule 902(11)

Indigents
Expert appointed for defendant in criminal case, Rule 702
Interpreters, appointment for, Rule 604

Industry Standards
Admissibility of evidence
    limited admissibility, Rule 401

Inferences
Burden of persuasion, effect of inference on, Rule 311
Burden of producing evidence, effect of inference on, Rule 307
Criminal cases
    judicial notice compared, Rule 201(g)
    presumptions submitted as inferences, Rules 309, 311
Cross-examination to rebut or modify, right of, Rule 611(2)
Examples listed, Rule 311
Opinion testimony. *See* Opinion evidence
Oral testimony, inference from failure to offer stronger evidence, Rule 1004
Presumptions

Index

Invited Error
Effect on appeal, Rule 103(4)

Irrelevant Evidence, Rule 401

J

Judges
See also Courts
Commenting on evidence
determination of relevancy, Rule 401
effect of inference instruction as, Rule 309
prohibition generally, Rule 611(1)
Discretion. *See* Discretion guidelines
Extrajudicial action by, presumption of prejudicial error, Rule 103(1)
Personal knowledge and judicial knowledge compared, Rule 201(b)
Preliminary determination of fact, role in, Rules 104(1), (2)
Witnesses
control by judge, Rule 611
court examination, discretion, Rule 611(1)
judges as, competency and restrictions, Rules 601, 605
preventing harassment or embarrassment, Rules 609-1, 611

Judgments
Affirming notwithstanding erroneous ruling on evidence, Rule 103(1)
Conviction of crime used for impeachment, proof by, Rules 609, 803(22)
Hearsay exceptions
judgment concerning personal, family or general history or boundaries,
Rule 803(23)
judgment of previous conviction, Rule 803(22)

Judicial Admissions
Agent's and employee's admission, Rule 801(4)(b)(A)

Judicial Notice
Adjudicative facts
criminal cases, Rule 201(g)
discretionary and mandatory authority, Rule 201(c)
instructing jury, Rules 201(a), 201(g)
kinds of facts to be judicially noticed, Rule 201(b)
legislative facts distinguished, Rule 201(a)
Authentication and identification of evidence by
basis of self-authentication, Rule 902
books and publications, Rule 902(6)
process or system's reliability, Rule 901(2)(i)
Burden of producing evidence, effect of judicial notice on, shifting, Rule 307

Insurance coverage inadvertently mentioned, instruction to disregard, Rule 411

Judicially noticed facts

civil and criminal cases, form of instruction distinguished, Rule 201(g)

nonevidence facts compared, Rule 201(a)

timing of instruction, Rule 201(f)

withdrawal of instruction, Rule 201(e)

Juror's refusal to follow, impeachment of verdict, Rule 606

Limiting evidence to one party or purpose

bias or interest, matters offered to show, Rule 609-1

expert's opinion, facts forming basis, Rule 703

generally, Rule 105

learned treatises used to impeach expert, Rules 607, 702

other crimes, wrongs or acts to prove character, Rules 404(3), 405, 608(2), 609

out-of-court statement defined as nonhearsay for specific purpose, Rule 105

prior statement of witness used to impeach, Rule 607

state of mind or physical condition admitted under hearsay exception, Rule 803(3)

Opinion evidence

expert found to be unqualified, jury to disregard, Rule 702

expert's opinion evidence to be viewed with caution, Rule 702

limiting instruction on facts forming basis, Rule 703

Oral admission of party to be viewed with caution, Rule 801(4)(b)(A)

Presumptions and inferences

civil cases, Rules 308, 311

criminal cases, Rule 309

privilege, inference from claim of, Rule 513

Privilege claim, no inference to be drawn, Rule 513

Timing, discretion of court, Rule 611(1)

Transcript of tape recording, discrepancies in, Rule 901(2)(e)

Jury View, Rule 401

Juvenile Court Proceedings

Applicability of OEC, Rule 101

Conviction of crime used for impeachment, juvenile adjudication as, Rule 609(5)

K

Knowledge

Evidence of prior bad acts to show, Rule 404

Personal, Rule 602

attorney's assertion of, Rule 103(3)

L

Lawyer-Client Privilege

Index

Learned Treatises
Experts, impeachment, Rule 607
Hearsay, Rules 607, 803, 803(18)

Legislative Facts, Rule 201(a)

Liability Insurance
Relevant evidence, Rule 411

Lie Detector, Rule 702

Limitation of Actions
Effect on admissibility of statements against penal interest, Rule 804(3)(c)

Limited Admissibility
Bias or interest, use for impeachment, Rule 609-1
Business practices, Rule 401
Character, Rules 105, 404(1),(2), (3)
Codefendant's confession, Rule 105
Company rules, industry standards, construction contracts, Rule 401
Evidence admissible as to one purpose or party generally, Rule 105
Expert's opinion, facts forming basis of, Rule 703
Insurance coverage, Rules 105, 411
Learned treatises, Rule 607
Options in procedure, Rule 105
Out-of-court statement defined as hearsay for specific purpose, Rule 105
Prior conduct or events, Rule 401
Prior crimes, Rules 105, 609
Prior similar frauds, Rule 401
Prior specific acts in cross-examination of character witness, Rule 608(2)
Prior statements of witness used to impeach, Rule 607
Remedial measures, Rules 105, 407
Similar contracts, Rule 401
State of mind or physical condition admitted under hearsay exception, Rule 803(3)
Usage, Rule 401

Lineups
Hearsay issue, Rule 801(4)(a)

M

Malpractice
Lawyer-client privilege, Rules 503(4), 511
Physicians
expert testimony requirement, Rule 702
qualification of expert to testify on breach of duty, Rule 702

Maps
Testimony of witness as to accuracy, authentication and identification, Rules 901, 901(2)(a)

Marketing reports
Hearsay exception, Rule 803(17)

Marriage. *See* Husband and Wife

Marriage Certificates, Rule 803(12)

Materiality
See also Relevancy
Defined, Rule 401
Included within relevancy concept, Rule 401

Medical matters
Diagnoses and opinions in business records, hearsay exception, Rule 803(6)
Diagnosis and treatment, hearsay exception for statements concerning, Rule 803(4)
Hospitals. *See* Hospitals
Malpractice
    expert testimony required, Rule 702
    qualification of experts to testify on breach of duty, Rule 702
Nurses. *See* Nurses
Payment of medical and similar expenses, limited admissibility, Rule 409
Physicians. *See* Physicians
Psychiatrists. *See* Psychiatrists
Psychotherapist-patient privilege. *See* Privileges
Reasonable medical probability test for expert testimony, Rule 702
Reports and records. *See also* Specific types, this heading
    business records, medical test results in, hearsay issue, Rule 803(6)
    discovery in personal injury cases, Rule 503(1)(e)
    nurse's reports to public authorities, Rule 504-2
    physician's, hearsay exception, Rule 804(3)(e)
    physician's records on patient, privilege, Rule 504-1
    physician's reports to public authorities, Rule 504-1
Sex offenses, victim's past behavior to rebut state's medical evidence, Rule 412
Statements made in professional capacity, hearsay exception, Rule 804(3)(e)
Statements of present physical condition, hearsay exception, Rule 803(4)
Tuberculosis reports
    nurse's duty, Rule 504-2
    physician's duty, Rule 504-1
Venereal disease records and reports, privilege rules, Rules 504, 504-1
Weapons, reports on injuries from, Rule 504-1
X-rays
    admissibility under best evidence rule, Rules 1001, 1002

Grounds for exclusion of, Rule 403
Statements to doctors, hearsay exception, Rule 803(4)

Motions. *See* more specific headings

Motive
Insurance coverage to show, limited admissibility, Rule 411
Opinion testimony on, by lay witness, Rule 701
Other crimes, acts or wrongs, admissibility to prove, Rules 404(3), 405, 609
Prior consistent statement to refute, Rules 607, 801(4)(a), 801(4)(a)(B)
Sex offenses, victim's past behavior to show, Rule 412
State of mind hearsay exception, Rule 803(3)

Motor Vehicles
Speed, opinion testimony of lay witness, Rule 701

N

Negligence
Business practices, limited admissibility in negligence cases, Rule 401
Evidence of limited admissibility, rules and instructions on, Rules 105, 401, 407
Insurance coverage, Rule 411
Prior conduct or event to prove, Rule 401
Remedial measures, Rules 105, 407

News Media
See also Publications
Privilege rules, definitions and exceptions, Rule 514

Newspapers, Hearsay
Authentication requirements and procedures, Rule 902(6)

New Trial
Grounds for, Rule 606

Nonconviction Misconduct, Rule 404

Nonevidence Facts, Rule 201(a)

Nonparty Declarant
Statement against interest of
hearsay exception, principle and illustrations, Rule 804(3)(c)
nonhearsay admission of party-opponent distinguished, Rule 801(4)(b)(A)
preliminary question of against-interest requirement, Rule 104(1)

Nonverbal Conduct. *See* Hearsay

Index

Notice

Character evidence, advance notice other-crimes evidence to be offered, Rule 404(3)

Hearsay exception for statements not otherwise covered by oec, intent to offer

  declarant not available, Rule 804(3)(f)

  declarant's availability not material, Rule 803(24)

Judicial. *See* Judicial notice

Original evidence in possession of opponent, notice to produce, Rule 1004

Privilege, notice of intent to assert, Rule 513

Sex offenses, motion to introduce victim's past behavior, Rule 412

Usage, advance notice before offering under ucc, Rule 401

Nurses

Nurse-patient privilege, Rule 504-2

Physician-patient privilege applicable to, Rule 504-2

Psychotherapist-patient privilege applicable to, Rule 504

O
_____

Oath or Affirmation

Indigent's inability to obtain interpreter, Rule 604

Interpreter's, Rule 604

Witnesses'

  child's inability to understand nature and obligation, competency test, Rule 601

  child's oath, Rule 603

  competency, bearing on, Rules 602, 603

  forms, Rule 603

  hearsay, significance of oath on, Rule 801(4)(a)

  persons who may administer, Rule 603

  refusal, consequences, Rules 603, 611(2)

  requirement generally, Rule 603

Objections

Bases for objections in OEC rules

  ambiguous, Rule 611(1)

  argumentative, Rule 611(1)

  authentication, lack of, Rule 901

  best evidence rule, Rule 1002

  beyond scope of direct examination, Rule 611(2)

  compound question, Rule 611(1)

  cumulative, Rules 403, 611(1)

  former testimony, Rule 804(3)(a)

    residual exception, Rule 804(3)(f)

    statement against interest, Rule 804(3)(c)

hospital records, interpretation of X-rays in, Rule 1002
hypothetical questions, Rules 703, 705
opinion of other expert as basis, Rule 703
out-of-court knowledge as source of data, Rules 703, 705
out-of-court statement as hearsay, Rule 703
personal knowledge of witness requirement, exception, Rule 602
personal observation as source of data, Rules 703, 705
public opinion poll or survey as basis, Rule 703
reasonable reliability test, Rules 702, 703, 705
scientific tests and procedures, opinion based on, Rule 702
sufficiency and weight, Rule 702
testimony of other witnesses at trial as source of data, Rules 703, 705
types allowed, examples, Rules 702, 704
ultimate issue, opinion on, Rule 704
voice identification, Rule 901(2)(e)
Hearsay
business records, entries in opinion form, Rule 803(6)
declarant's unavailability, effect on opinion rule, Rule 804
hospital records, opinions in, Rule 803(6)
public records containing evaluations or opinions, Rule 803(8)
statement made in professional capacity, Rule 804(3)(e)
statement under belief of impending death, Rule 804(3)(b)
Lay witness's testimony
character or character traits, proof by, Rules 405, 607
handwriting, Rule 901(2)(b)
rules and examples, Rule 701
sex offenses, victim's past behavior, Rule 412
ultimate issue, opinion on, Rule 704
voice identification, Rule 901

Opportunity to be Heard, Rule 201(e)

Optical Imaging, Rule 1001(4)

Order of Proof
Part of transaction proved, contemporaneous admission of whole, Rule 106

Oregon Evidence Code
See also more specific headings
Applicability to impending cases, Rule 100
Applicability to specific courts, Rule 101
Applicability to specific procedures generally, Rule 101(2)
administrative proceedings, Rule 101(1)
contempt hearings, Rule 101(2)
depositions, Rule 101(3)
extradition hearings, Rule 101(4)(c)
grand jury proceedings, Rule 101(4)(b)
judicial notice, determination on, Rules 104(1), 202

P

Parties

Admissibility of evidence as to one party, procedure, options, limiting instructions, Rule 105

Exclusion of witnesses from courtroom, rule as to party, Rule 615

Handicapped, interpreter for, Rule 604

Settlements between parties and non-parties, effect of rule limiting admission, Rule 408

Partnership

Acknowledgment of documents, form, Rule 902(8)

Authorized admission of party opponent by, Rule 801(4)(b)(C)

Presumption of, from persons acting as, Rule 311

Past Recollection Recorded. *See* Recollection

Payment

Medical expenses or property damage, admissibility to prove liability, Rule 409

Presumptions related to, listed, Rule 311

Periodicals, Hearsay

Authentication requirements and procedures, Rule 902(6)

Perjury

Lawyer-client privilege, communication indicating client to commit, Rule 503(4)

Permissive Presumptions, Rule 311

Personal Knowledge

Attorney's assertion of, Rule 103(3)

Authentication and identification, first-hand knowledge requirement, generally, Rule 901

Foundation requirements and procedure, Rule 602

Judge's, judicial notice compared, Rule 201

Prior conduct or events admissible to prove, Rules 104, 404

Requirement for hearsay

business records, Rule 803(6)

dying declarations, Rule 804(3)(b)

generally, Rules 602, 803(1)

public records and reports, Rule 803(8)

recorded recollection, Rule 803(5)

records of documents affecting interest in property, Rule 803(14)

statement against interest, Rule 804

statement of personal or family history, Rule 804(3)(d)

unavailability of witness, effect on, Rule 804

vicarious admissions, Rule 801

Vicarious admissions against party-opponent, Rule 801(4)(b)(D)

Of witness. *See* Witnesses

Index

Photographs
Authentication
- change of condition, Rule 901(2)(a)
- testimony of witness with knowledge, Rule 901(2)(a)

Grounds for exclusion of, Rule 403

Of homicide victim, relevancy of, Rule 401

Mug shots, display to jury, Rule 801(4)(a)(C)

Proof of contents, best evidence rule definition of photograph, Rule 1001
- original, photocopy as, Rule 1005
- original defined, Rule 1001(2)
- purpose of introduction, significance, Rule 1001

Writing used to refresh memory, photograph as, Rule 612

Phrases. *See* Words and Phrases

Physicians
See also Medical Matters

Chiropractors as, Rule 504-1

Confession of crime, disclosure by physician, Rule 504-1

Deceased doctor's records, hearsay issue, Rule 804(3)(e)

Deposition of, when reports not furnished, Rule 504-1(5)

Faith healers as, Rule 504-1

Malpractice
- expert testimony requirement, Rule 702
- qualification of expert to testify on breach of duty, Rule 702

Naturopathic physician as, Rule 504-1

Privileged communications
- *see also* Privileges
- nurses covered by physician-patient privilege, Rule 504-2
- physician as representative of a lawyer in lawyer-client privilege, Rules 503(e), 504
- physician included in psychotherapist-patient privilege, Rule 504
- physician-patient privilege, definitions, rules and exceptions, Rule 504-1
- stenographers covered by physician-patient privilege, Rule 508(a)

Psychiatrist as, Rule 504

Records and reports. *See* Medical matters

Plain Error Doctrine, Rule 103(4)

Plain Error Rule. *See* Error

Pleadings
Admissions of party-opponent in, hearsay issue, Rules 801(4)(b)(A), 801(4)(b)(B), 801(4)(b)(C)

Authentication and identification by admissions in, Rule 901(2)

Burden of persuasion, effect of form of pleadings on allocation of, Rule 305

Striking, party's refusal to be sworn or answer as witness, Rule 611(2)

Pleas

Admission of party-opponent, Rule 801(4)(b)(A)

Impeachment and rehabilitation by use of, Rule 609(1)

Judgment of conviction based on, hearsay exception, Rule 803

Withdrawn guilty or no contest pleas and negotiations, admissibility in criminal case, Rule 410

Police Reports

Data retrieval, hearsay exceptions, Rule 803(25)

Public records and reports, hearsay exception for, Rules 802, 803(8)

Recorded recollection hearsay exception, Rules 803(5), 803(6)

Self-authentication, Rule 902(12)

Polls, Rule 703

Polygraph, Rule 702

Posttrial Proceedings

See also specific procedures

Judicial notice taken at, Rule 201(f)

Privilege rules, applicability to, Rules 101(3), (4)

Prejudice

Character evidence

in camera hearing to avoid prejudice in cross-examination of character witness, Rule 405

discretion of court, Rule 405

justification for admission or exclusion, Rule 404

other crimes, wrongs or acts, Rules 404, 404(3)

specific acts of misconduct, Rule 405

Conviction of crime used for impeachment, balancing test, Rule 609

Exclusion of evidence for

hearsay exceptions generally, Rule 803

in lieu of limiting instruction, Rule 105

relevant evidence excluded on ground of prejudice, Rule 403

Grand jury proceedings, error in, Rule 101

Hearsay exceptions generally, Rule 803

Insurance coverage admitted to show, limiting instruction, Rules 105, 411

Judge's extrajudicial action, presumption of prejudicial error from, Rule 103(1)

Opinion evidence, balancing test, Rules 704, 705

Presumption from erroneous ruling, Rule 103(1)

Psychiatric histories, Rule 803

Religious records, Rules 803(11), (12)

Remedial measures subsequently taken, Rule 407

State of mind hearsay exception, Rule 803(3)

Witness's. *See* Bias and interest

Preliminary Fact Determination

Accused testifying on, cross-examination on other matters, Rule 104(4)

Index

Index

To prove identity
    recent cases admitting, Rule 404(3)
    recent cases excluding, Rule 404(3)
To prove intent
    recent cases admitting, Rule 404(3)
    recent cases excluding, Rule 404(3)
Of violence, admissibility, Rule 404(3)

Prior Conduct and Events
Conviction of crime used for impeachment. *See* Witnesses
Examples of limited admissibility, instruction, Rules 105, 401

Prior Consistent Statements
Charge of recent fabrication, improper influence or motive, refuting, Rules
    607, 801(4)(a)(B)
Hearsay issue, nonhearsay uses, Rules 801(4)(a), 801(4)(a)(B)
Inconsistent statement, consistent statement to refute, Rule 801(4)(a)(B)
Refreshing memory by, Rule 801(4)(a)(B)
Rehabilitation of witness by, Rules 608, 601(1), 801(4)(a)(B)
Substantive evidence, use for, Rule 801(4)(a)

Prior Crimes, Rule 404(3)

Prior Inconsistent Statements
Impeachment, use for
    bias or interest, procedures for impeachment compared, Rule 613(2)
    collateral matter, prior statement relating, Rule 613(2)
    cross-examination, prior statement made on, Rule 613(2)
    depositions, impeachment by statements in, Rule 613(2)
    discovery, Rule 612
    experts, impeachment by, Rule 702
    extrinsic evidence of, conditions, procedure, Rules 613, 613(1), (2)
    generally, Rules 613, 613(1), (2)
    hearsay declarants, Rule 806
    leading questions on, Rule 612
    limiting instruction, Rule 607
    nonhearsay uses, Rule 607
    work-product immunity conflict, Rule 612
    writing used to refresh memory, overlap, Rule 612
Substantive evidence, use for, Rule 801(4)(a)(A)

Prior Litigation
Relevancy of, Rule 401

Privileged Communications
Physicians
    see also Privileges
    nurses covered by physician-patient privilege, Rule 504-2

Index

Public Opinion Polls
Authentication for use by expert, Rule 703
Hearsay issue, Rule 703

Public Records, Reports and Documents
Absence of public record or entry, hearsay, proof, Rule 803(10)
Authentication. *See* Authentication and identification, and specific entries, this
  heading
Best evidence rule applied to, Rules 1004, 1005
Birth certificate, proof of, Rule 901(2)(j)
Certified copies, Rule 1005
Deposition transcript as, Rules 613(2), 804(4)(a)(A)
Filed documents as
  authentication methods, Rule 901(2)(g)
  best evidence rule, Rule 1004
Foreign, authentication, Rule 902(3)
Hearsay exceptions for generally, Rules 613, 801
  absence of public record or entry in, Rule 803(10)
  death certificate, overlap, Rule 803(12)
  deposition, qualification as, Rule 613(2)
  evaluative reports, Rule 803(8)
  examples, Rule 803(8)
  first-hand knowledge requirement, Rule 803(8)
  law-enforcement records, Rule 803(8)
  official publications, Rule 902(5)
  privileged records, exclusion, Rule 803(8)
  records of documents affecting interest in property, overlap, Rule 803(15)
  statutory exclusions, Rule 803(8)
  vital statistics, Rules 803(8), (9)
Indian tribal documents, authentication, Rule 902(11)
Privileged records. *See also* Privileges
  examination of public officer as to, Rule 509
  lists of records confidential in some degree, Rules 509, 514
  student records, Rule 504-3
Recorded documents as authentication and identification, Rules 901(2)(g),
  902(4)
  proof under best evidence rule, Rules 1004, 1005
Scaled documents, authentication, Rule 902
Vital statistics, Rules 803(8), (9)

R

Rape. *See* Sexual Offenses and Misconduct

Real Property. *See* Property

Index

Index

Index

Reports

S

Index

Index

T

Index

U

Utterances, Excited
Accident reports, multiple hearsay example, Rule 805
Hearsay exception, Rule 803(2)
Present sense impression compared, Rule 803(1)

V

Value
Opinion testimony by owner, Rule 701
Prices previously or subsequently paid as evidence of, Rule 401
Similar property as evidence of, Rule 401

Verdict
Directed against accused, effect of presumption, Rule 309
Impeachment by juror, Rules 605, 606

Victims
Child abuse exception from various privileges, Rules 504, 504-1, 504-2, 504-3, 504-4
Cross-examination to show bias, Rule 609-1
Peaceableness, character trait, Rule 404
Sex offenses, past sexual behavior, Rules 404, 412
Sex offenses, victim's complaint of, hearsay exception, Rule 803(18a)
Social worker-client privilege, minor victim exception, Rule 504-4
Statement of victim to physician on cause of injury, Rule 803(4)

Videotapes. *See* Motion Pictures and Videotapes

View
Jury, Rule 401

Violent Behavior
Civil case of assault and battery, character evidence, Rule 404

Vital Statistics
Hearsay exception, Rules 803(8), 803(9)

Voice
Admissibility of voice-print evidence, Rule 702
Identification
experts relying on voice prints, Rule 901(2)(e)
generally, Rule 901
opinion based on previous hearing, Rule 901(2)(e)
personal knowledge requirement, Rule 901(2)(e)
tape recordings, foundation, Rule 901(2)(e)
telephone calls, Rule 901(2)(f)

Voir Dire
Juror, Rule 606

Index

Jury
    attorney's comments on burden of persuasion during, Rule 306
    inadmissible evidence revealed during, Rule 103(3)
Witness
    ability to perceive and communicate, determination on, Rule 601
    expert's competency and qualifications, Rules 611(1), 702
    expert's opinion, basis, Rule 705

W

Waivers
    Confrontation right, defendant responsible for witness's unavailability, Rule
      804(3)(f)
    Interpreter, right to, Rule 604
    Limiting instruction, failure to request as waiver of error, Rule 105
    Privileges
      claim assertion, Rule 503(4)
      disclosure compelled erroneously, Rules 503(3), 512(1)
      disclosure without authority, Rule 512
      husband and wife privilege, Rules 505, 512
      informant as witness, Rule 514
      lawyer-client privilege, Rules 503, 511
      nurse-patient privilege, Rule 504-2
      physician-patient privilege, Rules 504-1, 511
      psychotherapist-patient privilege, Rules 504, 511
      public officer privilege, Rule 509
      school employee-student privilege, Rule 504-3
      social worker-client privilege, Rule 504-4
      voluntary disclosure and consent generally, Rule 511
      work-product, witness's reference to, Rule 511
      writing used to refresh memory, Rule 612
    Public record, requirement of original or certified copy, Rule 1005
    Self-incrimination
      testifying on direct, effect on privilege against cross-examination, Rule
        611(2)
      testifying on preliminary question, Rule 104(4)

Warrants
    Informer's affidavit, statements as adoptive admissions against government,
      Rule 801(4)(b)(B)
    Probable cause, informers, Rule 510
    Procedure for issuance, applicability of OEC, Rule 101
    Search and seizure
      applicability of OEC to procedures for issuance, Rule 101(4)(f)

informer's affidavit for, statements as adoptive admissions of government, Rule 801(4)(b)(B)

probable cause, informers, Rule 510(4)(c)

Weapons

Other-crimes evidence, admissibility as element of firearm charge, Rule 404(3)

Physician's report on injuries caused by, Rule 504(1)

Weight of Evidence

Chain of custody problems, Rule 901(2)(a)

Hearsay evidence in sentencing hearing, Rule 101(4)(b)

Preliminary questions, effect of determination on right to attack weight, Rules 104, 104(5)

Religious belief, effect on weight, Rule 104(5)

Wills

Contests, applicability of psychotherapist-patient privilege, Rule 504

Statements of memory or belief relating to, hearsay exception, Rule 803(3)

Testimony or affidavit of subscribing witness, necessity for, Rule 903

Witnesses

Absence of. *See* Unavailability, this heading

Affirmation. *See* Oath or affirmation, this heading

Alcohol or drug use by

effect on competency, Rule 601

use for impeachment, Rules 601, 607

Attesting or subscribing witness

attorney as, exception to privilege rules, Rule 503

testimony, necessity for, Rule 903

Attorney as

attesting witness, exception to privilege rules, Rule 503

competency generally, Rules 601, 606(1)

ethical considerations, Rule 503

Attorney's conduct toward, Rule 103(3)

Authentication and identification of evidence by testimony of. *See* Authentication and identification

Bias and interest of witness admission by witness of facts claimed to show, Effect, Rule 609-1

adverse or own witness, generally, Rules 607, 609-1

character evidence of truthfulness to refute, Rule 609-1

compromise and offers, admissibility to show, Rule 408

confidential facts revealed by showing, Rule 609(5)

constitutional right to impeach by showing, Rule 609-1

discretion of court as to extent of proof, Rule 609-1

examples of facts constituting, Rule 609-1

expert witness's bias, facts claimed to show, Rules 609-1, 702

foundation, Rule 609-1

harassment or embarrassment of witness in showing, Rule 609-1

continuance for temporary disability, Rule 804(1)

cross-examination, striking direct when witness unavailable for, Rule 611

hearsay declarant's. *See* Hearsay

Voir dire

   competency determination, Rule 601

   competency or qualification of experts, Rules 611(1), 702

   opinion evidence, facts or data underlying, Rule 705

Writings used to refresh memory, Rule 612

Writings used to show bias or interest, procedure, Rule 609-1

Words and Phrases

Adjudicative facts (judicial notice), Rule 201(a)

Admission against interest, Rule 801(4)(b)(A)

Best evidence rule, Rule 1002

Burden of persuasion, Rule 305

Burden of producing evidence, Rule 307

Burden of proof, Rule 305

Business (hearsay exception for business records), Rule 803(6)

Character, Rule 404

Character (contrasted with habit), Rule 406

Character in issue, Rule 404

Clear and convincing evidence, Rule 305

Client (lawyer-client privilege), Rule 503

Collateral matter (impeachment by contradictory evidence), Rule 607

Comprehensive plan (judicial notice), Rule 202

Conclusive presumption, Rule 311

Conditional relevancy, Rule 104(2)

Confidential communication

   husband-wife privilege, Rule 505

   lawyer-client privilege, Rule 503

   physician-patient privilege, Rule 504-1

   psychotherapist-patient privilege, Rule 504

Confidential communication (clergyman-penitent privilege), Rule 506

Conviction (impeachment by conviction of crime), Rule 609

Crime of false statement, Rule 609

Curative admissibility, Rule 402

Data compilation, Rule 803(6)

Declarant (hearsay rule), Rule 801

Diligent search (best evidence rule), Rule 1004

Distinctive (to qualify as habit), Rule 406

Duplicate (best evidence rule), Rules 1001, 1003

Factual findings (public records exception to hearsay rule), Rule 803(8)

Habit, Rule 406

Handicapped person (need for interpreter), Rule 604

Harmless error, Rule 103(1)

Hearsay, Rule 801

Index

X